PHONOLOGICAL
THEORY

PHONOLOGICAL THEORY

Evolution and Current Practice

VALERIE BECKER MAKKAI

University of Illinois at Chicago Circle

HOLT, RINEHART AND WINSTON, INC.

New York   Chicago   San Francisco   Atlanta   Dallas
Montreal   Toronto   London   Sydney

To the Memory
of
BERNARD BLOCH
Professor at Yale University 1943–1965
Rigorous Teacher
and
Scholar of Integrity
He showed us how to listen
to all sides of an argument.

PREFACE

It is the purpose of the present anthology to gather together, in one easily accessible place, those articles which through the years have contributed most to the development of phonological theory in general, and of various specific schools of thought on phonology in particular.

Colleges and universities in the United States and abroad are establishing new programs in linguistics, and the libraries of newer institutions often cannot keep up with the demands of professors and students for holdings in linguistics, particularly the back issues of rarer journals. Some of the most significant articles lie hidden in obscure journals published abroad or long out of print. This volume is intended to make these articles available to the student of phonology, in a form that will reflect the evolution of thought that went into the theories as they stand today.

Thus the articles are presented in more or less chronological order within four major sections, and the sections themselves are arranged chronologically so that the newest theories are presented last. They deal, respectively, with the development of Bloomfieldian phonology, prosodic analysis, distinctive features and transformational-generative phonology, and finally stratificational phonology. Although one may not wish to read the articles in the order in which they occur here, the chronological arrangement was decided upon in order to emphasize the evolutionary nature of the theories. It is all too easy to think of a theory as set and fixed, and to regard all the articles written within a particular theoretical framework as reflecting the same basic assumptions. Nothing could be further from the truth, as I hope to illustrate.

Each major section begins with a brief introductory essay that traces the development of the theory, characterizing each of the articles included in this volume (as well as other important works) in terms of its relation to the scholarship that had gone before and its original contributions to the theory. At the end of each of these discussions is a bibliography of other works which one should read in order to have a full understanding of the theory. The works listed in these bibliographies are arranged under four main headings: Theoretical Discussion, Applications of the Theory, Bibliographies and Bibliographical Studies, and Collections and Anthologies.

In addition, the book contains a number of topical bibliographies dealing with specific problems of phonological analysis that have occasioned much discussion. One or two articles representative of each of these discussions have been reprinted here, followed by the topical bibliographies that refer the reader to other writings on the same subject. For the most part, those items listed in the topical bibliographies deal specifically and primarily with the topic at hand. Other articles and books treating the subject to a lesser degree may be found in the general bibliographies.

Within the articles, all page number references to other articles included in the volume have been left with the original pagination, followed by bracketed references to the page numbers used here. Each article included has also been given a number, and every time an article is mentioned anywhere in the volume, its reference number follows in brackets.

At the end of the book is a comprehensive bibliography of all works referred to in the volume plus a few others (marked with an asterisk *) that did not conveniently fit into any of the specialized bibliographies. In the comprehensive bibliography each citation is followed by the reference numbers of all articles and topical bibliographies in the volume in which that item is mentioned.

It is hoped that this extensive system of cross-referencing will encourage the reader to make continual comparisons among the ideas of various linguists, especially among representatives of different schools of thought. It is often the case that there are identities or similarities of opinion that are ignored through a failure to read sufficiently widely or thoroughly in theories other than one's own.

No changes have been made in any of the articles except for the correction of typographical errors and errors made in the citation of bibliographical references. Citations and punctuation throughout the volume also have been changed to conform to the publisher's uniform standard. Otherwise the original form has been kept, with all editorial material enclosed in square brackets and marked [—VBM].

It has proved impossible to include all the articles I would have liked to include. Many important works have had to be omitted for lack of space. Thus, some longer articles, and some that are readily available elsewhere, do not appear here, although ideally they should. In general I have tried to choose those articles which best reflect the development of ideas, those which exemplify the controversies and dialogues of the era, those which have contributed significantly to the theory of phonology. I have had to omit most articles consisting primarily of applications of the theory in favor of those containing theoretical discussion.

The number of articles in the various sections is rather disproportionate, but intentionally so. It has been my aim to give at least some exposure to many schools of thought, but to concentrate primarily on those which have had some impact on linguistics in America. Thus, in Prague school phonology, which is already admirably represented in other recent works, only contributions to distinctive feature theory are included here. There exist very few theoretical discussions of Firthian prosodies, and thus that section is quite small, although a number of excellent applications of the theory are listed in the bibliographies. The Copenhagen school, and particularly Hjelmslev's glossematics, is generally very poorly known in this country, and thus, no doubt, deserve a volume of their own. I have been forced, however, to limit myself to two articles that are particularly valuable for their comparisons of Hjelmslevian phonematics with other schools of thought. There are few articles in the stratificational phonology section simply because the theory is still so new that very little has yet been written on this aspect of stratificational grammar.

It should be noted that the inclusion of an article in a particular section, or its listing in a particular bibliography, does not necessarily mean that the author is generally of that theoretical persuasion, but only that the article has bearing on the issues at hand and has contributed in some way to thinking on the subject.

No doubt my prejudices show here and there, although I have tried not to let them. I have probably left out someone's favorite article, and included papers that some will consider unimportant. But if I have been able to reflect the excitement and challenge that goes with linguistic inquiry and exploration, and to show the fruitfulness of the heated exchange of ideas, then I will have achieved my goal.

My thanks go to all the authors and publishers who so graciously gave me permission to reprint their material; to Rulon S. Wells III, David G. Lockwood, Sydney M. Lamb, Charles F. Hockett, W. F. Twaddell, Einar Haugen, and Hans Kurath for their many excellent suggestions; to Mrs. Radha Srinivasan for her patient and efficient assistance in gathering material; and especially to my husband, Adam Makkai, for his constant help and encouragement with all aspects of the preparation of this volume.

University of Illinois at Chicago Circle
October 1971

V.B.M.

CONTENTS

PHONOLOGICAL THEORY

I

BLOOMFIELDIAN PHONOLOGY

INTRODUCTION

This section is divided into three parts: the first illustrating the thinking that went into the development of the phonemic principle, especially as it has been used in America; the second showing the early attempts by Bloomfield and others to apply and expand the principle; and the third demonstrating modifications in the principle and its applications that were necessitated as linguists delved more deeply into the problems involved in phonemic description. These later developments have been variously termed neo-Bloomfieldian, structuralist, taxonomic, and so on. I use the term Bloomfieldian to refer to all work that has its theoretical base in Bloomfield's concept of linguistics, since the terms structuralist and taxonomic have been applied to various European schools as well.

The phoneme is not a unique American invention, as most linguists well know. In fact, the first awareness and discussion of a phoneme-type unit began in Europe in the late nineteenth century, long before American linguistics was born. Jan Baudouin de Courtenay and his pupil Kruszewsky (who apparently invented the term *fonema*) in Poland, Henry Sweet in England, and Paul Passy in France were all working with the idea. The topical bibliography on the history and development of the phoneme, following Swadesh's "The Phonemic Principle" [3], suggests further reading on this subject.

It is not clear whether Edward Sapir, at the time of the writing of "Sound Patterns in Language" (1925) [1], was aware of these developments in Europe or not, but it appears that he was at least beginning to think along the same lines. He does not use the term phoneme in the sense in which later linguists used it, but he talks about variations in a sound "dependent on the phonetic conditions" in which it occurs. He says these variations "stand outside of the proper phonetic pattern of the language" and "correspond to nothing significant in the inner structure of the phonetic pattern." In other words, he is dealing here with what today would be called allo-phones of a phoneme. Thus it is with Sapir that we can date the beginnings of American investigations of the phonemic principle.

With the appearance of Bloomfield's *Language* and Sapir's "The Psychological Reality of Phonemes" [2], both in 1933, it becomes apparent that the idea of the phoneme was beginning to catch on in America. Sapir and Bloomfield viewed the phoneme quite differently, however. Sapir's approach was a psychological one, with the phonemes essentially designed to explain the speaker's tacit knowledge of his language. Bloomfield, on the other hand, represents the break from this "mentalistic" approach to language and marks the beginning of "behaviorism" in American linguistics, with its insistence on strictly scientific observation and the elimination of all psychological considerations.

Thus began an era of much lively discussion, starting with Morris Swadesh's careful exposition of "The Phonemic Principle" in 1934 [3]. This article, in which the terms "complementary distribution" and "substitution" were first used in print in their current senses, was the first complete and concise statement of the principles and methods of phonemic analysis as he and others used them. W. F. Twaddell's monograph *On Defining the Phoneme* (1935) found fault both with the mentalistic view of the phoneme and with the view that it is a physical reality. He considered the phoneme to be an abstraction with no basis in reality at all. A rapid exchange then ensued, with Swadesh's critique "Twaddell on Defining the Phoneme" (1935) [4], answered by Twaddell in "On Various Phonemes" (1936) [5], and also M. J. Andrade's "Some Questions of Fact and Policy Concerning Phonemes" (1936) and Twaddell's reply "Answers to Andrade's Questions" (1936).

By this time the existence of the phoneme, however one viewed its precise nature, was an accepted fact in America. Phonemics became the central concern of Bloomfieldian linguists and remained so for at least the next decade. Linguists began to investigate the ramifications of the phoneme theory, one of the earliest of these investigations being Y. R. Chao's "The Non-Uniqueness of Phonemic Solutions of Phonetic Systems" (1934), which brought up the problem of deciding which phonetic entities to put into which phonemes. Chao felt that there was no necessarily "right" way and that alternative analyses were always possible. Morris Swadesh, in "The Phonemic Interpretation of Long Consonants" (1937) [6], argued that there are, nevertheless, objective criteria that one can apply in reaching a decision. He illustrated his point with an analysis of consonant length.

Bloomfield's "Menomini Morphophonemics" (1939) [7] broached another subject that was arousing the concern of linguists—namely, alternation between phonemes among members of the same morpheme, and specifically, in this case, what we would now call phonologically conditioned alternations. Bloomfield talks here of morphophonemes, although he does not specify what he means by the term. In fact, at this time linguists had not yet clearly worked out the relationship of morphophonemics to phonemics and to the rest of linguistic structure. Most Bloomfieldian linguists have not accepted morphophonemes as such, although they do speak of morphophonemic alternations. On the other hand, discussions of morphophonemes or archiphonemes and neutralization occupied an important position in Prague school linguistics. See the bibliography, "Neutralization and Morphophonemics," following Bloomfield's article, for further reading in this area. See also David G. Lockwood's "Neutralization, Biuniqueness, and Stratificational Phonology" [56] in Part IV.

Bernard Bloch, in his "Phonemic Overlapping" (1941) [8], set forth for the first time the principle that a given sound cannot belong unpredictably once to one phoneme and once to another—a principle that subsequently was extended even to predictable cases, and that ultimately came to be accepted by most Bloomfieldian linguists. In addition, Bloch also tacitly took a stand against the use of meaning criteria in determining a phonemic analysis, a position that later was the subject of much controversy, although the majority of American linguists believed as Bloch that meaning should have only a contrastive value at this level. For

further reading on this subject see the bibliography "Grammar and Meaning versus Phonology."

Trager and Bloch's "The Syllabic Phonemes of English" (1941) [9] reflected a continuing concern with how to deal with English vowels and diphthongs. It was a landmark article in several ways: it was the first time that slant lines / / were used to enclose phonemic transcription; the term "allophone" was first used in print here and in Bloch's simultaneously published "Phonemic Overlapping" [8], although it reportedly had been invented by Benjamin Lee Whorf several years before; it was the first attempt to treat juncture on the phonemic level; and it was here that the widely accepted idea of a postvocalic /h/ was first suggested. The authors here analyzed the vowels of English into six phonemes, a view they later abandoned in favor of the nine-vowel system of Trager and Smith's *An Outline of English Structure* (1951). Haugen and Twaddell's "Facts and Phonemics" (1942) [10] was a criticism of Trager and Bloch's analysis. At the time it appeared, Trager and Bloch claimed that their views were still basically the same (see their note appended to Haugen and Twaddell's article), but the eventual revision of their analysis was no doubt due, at least in part, to the comments of Haugen and Twaddell both in their article and in the extensive correspondence among the four of them.

In 1942 appeared two important codifications of Bloomfieldian procedure: Bloch and Trager's *Outline of Linguistic Analysis,* an admirably concise introduction to the methodology of all levels of language analysis as then practiced by American linguists; and Charles F. Hockett's "A System of Descriptive Phonology" [11], which formulated a system of phonological principles reflecting the current practices of descriptive linguists. It stands as evidence of how much the ideas of Bloomfieldian linguists had progressed in the previous decade.

At this point it should be noted that several of the articles so far considered have made reference to the work of the Prague school, especially to the writings of N. S. Trubetzkoy and Roman Jakobson. American linguists then, as now, were probably better aware of what was being done in Prague than in other linguistic centers in Europe. The contributions of the Prague school in the area of neutralization and archiphonemes have already been mentioned. But the development that eventually has had more impact on linguistics in America than any other was the breakdown of sounds into their acoustic distinctive features. Much more will be said on Prague school distinctive features in Part III, but it is important to bring it up here in order to understand the context in which Zellig Harris' "Simultaneous Components in Phonology" (1944) [12] was written. Linguists on both sides of the Atlantic had been concerned with a desire to account for the facts of language as economically as possible. The development of the archiphoneme was an attempt at such economy. But already in the 1930s Prague school linguists were working on the idea that perhaps what was needed was an analysis of the sounds of each language in terms of the features that serve to mark distinctions among sounds. This resulted eventually in breaking each segment of sound into one or more co-occurring acoustic elements. In 1941 Harris had reviewed [27] Trubetzkoy's *Grundzüge der Phonologie* (1939), but Trubetzkoy's features were not acoustic. Roman Jakobson suggested the idea of acoustic features in 1939 (see his "Observations sur le classement phonologique des consonnes" [28]), but by the time of Harris' "Simultaneous Components" this theory had by no means been entirely worked out. So, although Harris was aware of what was going on in Prague, his ideas were largely an independent development along similar lines. But his components were not acoustic features. In fact, they are quite like the idea of prosodies, which was first to be proposed by J. R. Firth in England in 1948 (see Part II). Harris' components, just as prosodies, can extend over several sound segments, and only those components are extracted that simplify the description of the language in question. But he does not do away with phonemes or allophones, rather he merely suggests analysis into simultaneous components as a supplementary device to handle problems that traditional phonemic analysis would not handle as well.

Rulon S. Wells's "The Pitch Phonemes of English" (1945) [13] was the first systematic analysis of phonemes of pitch, showing that these combine into morphemes just as the

segmental phonemes do. Linguists had already been working with stress and juncture phonemes, and there had been discussions of the possibility of extracting other things, such as nasality in certain languages, and treating them as suprasegmental. This latter idea, particularly, harks back to the componential analysis of Harris. For some of the more important contributions to the discussion of suprasegmentals, see the topical bibliography following Wells's article.

In "On the Phonemic Status of English Diphthongs" (1947) [14], Kenneth Pike rejected the previous analyses of the vowels and diphthongs of English as exemplified in Swadesh's "The Vowels of Chicago English" (1935) and Trager and Bloch's "The Syllabic Phonemes of English" [9], and proposed still another type of analysis, in which some of the units that are phonetically diphthongs, namely, the tense vowels, are considered to be single phonemes while others are considered to be sequences of phonemes. Pike suggested that immediate constituent analysis, as applied in syntactic and morphological studies, could be valid in phonological analysis as well and that such analysis applied to the syllables of English justified his interpretation of the English vowels. His proposals did not meet with much acceptance among more rigorously inclined Bloomfieldian linguists. They felt that he was improperly using grammatical information to arrive at a phonemic analysis and that he was violating the principle, by then generally established, of "once a phoneme, always a phoneme."

In his "Grammatical Prerequisites to Phonemic Analysis" (1947) [15], Pike took exception to the widely held view, as stated in Hockett's "A System of Descriptive Phonology," that no grammatical facts should be used in determining a phonemic analysis. He insisted that it is not only desirable but unavoidable to utilize such information. His claim that distribution alone cannot result in an adequate analysis stirred up considerable criticism and debate. Bernard Bloch's "A Set of Postulates for Phonemic Analysis" (1948) [16] was an attempt to establish a systematic approach whereby it would be possible to use distribution as the sole theoretical foundation for phonemic analysis without regard to meaning or grammatical considerations. He did not, however, rule out the use of meaning contrasts as a practical device in working out phonemic analyses. Bloch later revised his specific postulates many times in an effort to close loopholes that had become apparent to him. It was in this article, incidentally, that Bloch first introduced the term "idiolect."

Hockett's "Two Fundamental Problems in Phonemics" (1949) [17] was a critical discussion of Pike's work and an argument against his use of grammar and meaning in phonology, not only in his "Grammatical Prerequisites" but also in his books *Phonemics* (1947) and *Tone Languages* (1948).

Pike replied to the charges of Hockett, Bloch, and others in "More on Grammatical Prerequisites" (1952) [18]. He claimed that not only is the use of meaning a convenient practical procedure but that it is a necessity on the theoretical plane as well and that, in fact, his critics themselves did allow facts other than distribution to influence their phonemic analyses.

Bloch's "Contrast" (1953) [19] represented a revision of his distributional definition of contrast in the face of criticism not only from Pike but also from Eli Fischer-Jørgensen in "Remarques sur les principes de l'analyse phonémique" (1949) and John Lotz in "Speech and Language" (1950). (Note the bibliography on distribution following Miss Fischer-Jørgensen's "On the Definition of Phoneme Categories on a Distributional Basis" [50].)

In the meantime, Trager and Smith's *An Outline of English Structure* had appeared in

1951, with its revision of the vowels of English into a nine-vowel system, but still treating the tense vowels of English as diphthongs consisting of two phonemes, in contrast to what Pike had proposed in his "On the Phonemic Status of English Diphthongs." Trager and Smith's system has been generally accepted by Bloomfieldian linguists, although not without some misgivings (see James Sledd's review in 1955). But some strict Bloomfieldians, such as Hans Kurath in his "The Binary Interpretation of English Vowels: A Critique" (1957) [20], still held to the analysis of all English syllabics as unitary phonemes. Kurath also criticized at some length the postvocalic /h/ of Trager and Bloch. Kurath's remarks were answered by Sledd in "Some Questions of English Phonology" (1958) followed by Kurath's "Some Questions of English Phonology: A Reply" (1958).

By this time interest in phonemic theory had waned in America as Bloomfieldians turned to matters of morphology and syntax and as transformational grammar began to attract more and more interest. In 1962 Archibald A. Hill wrote his "Various Kinds of Phonemes" [21], which sums up the different approaches to phonemic theory that had developed in recent years, including the beginnings of transformational-generative phonology. (See Part III for more on the latter.)

It is appropriate to conclude the section on Bloomfieldian phonology with Hill's "The Current Relevance of Bloch's 'Postulates'" (1967) [22], a tribute to the lasting impact of the groundwork Bloch had so carefully laid.

BIBLIOGRAPHY 1
Bloomfieldian
Phonology

In this and all of the topical bibliographies, the items are arranged in an order that best reflects the development of ideas. For the most part the order is chronological, but whenever one article is an answer to another they are placed together, even if this disrupts the chronological arrangement. Reviews of books are listed immediately after the listing of the book itself. Only the author, date, and title of each item are given here. The full bibliographical citation will be found in the general bibliography, along with the reference numbers of all articles in this volume that mention the item.

The Bloomfieldian bibliography (as well as those on prosodic analysis, distinctive features, transformational-generative phonology, phonematics, and stratificational phonology) is arranged in the following four divisions: a. Theoretical Discussion; b. Applications of the Theory; c. Bibliographies and Bibliographical Studies; and d. Collections and Anthologies. For further references on specialized subjects see the topical bibliographies.

A. THEORETICAL DISCUSSION
SAPIR, E. (1921) *Language*
BLOOMFIELD, L. (1926) "A Set of Postulates for the Science of Language"
—— (1933) *Language*

Reviewed by: BOLLING, G. M. (1934)
KENT, R. G. (1934)
CHAO, Y. R. (1934) "The Non-Uniqueness of Phonemic Solutions of Phonetic Systems"
HEFFNER, R.-M. S. (1934) "Concerning Transcription"
GRAFF, W. L. (1935) "Remarks on the Phoneme"
TWADDELL, W. F. (1935) *On Defining the Phoneme*
ANDRADE, M. J. (1936) "Some Questions of Fact and Policy Concerning Phonemes"

TWADDELL, W. F. (1936) "Answers to Andrade's Questions"
BLOCH, B., and G. L. TRAGER (1942) *Outline of Linguistic Analysis*

Reviewed by: EMENEAU, M. B. (1943)
STURTEVANT, E. H. (1943)
KURATH, H. (1945)
TRAGER, G. L. (1942) "The Phoneme 'T': A Study in Theory and Method"
TWADDELL, W. F. (1942) "Phonemics"
PIKE, K. L. (1943) *Phonetics*

Reviewed by: TRAGER, G. L. (1943)
HOENIGSWALD, H. M. (1944)
STETSON, R. H. (1945) *Bases of Phonology*

Reviewed by: TREVIÑO, S. N. (1946)
TWADDELL, W. F. (1946)
NIDA, E. A. (1947)
PIKE, K. L. (1947) *Phonemics: A Technique for Reducing Languages to Writing*

Reviewed by: THOMAS, C. K. (1948)
ECHOLS, J. M. (1949)
FISCHER-JØRGENSEN, E. (1949)
HAUGEN, E. (1949)
MARTINET, A. (1949)
VOEGELIN, C. F. (1949)
EVANS, E. M. (1950)
TRAGER, G. L. (1950)
PIKE, K. L. (1948) *Tone Languages*
For reviews see bibliography on suprasegmentals.

HOCKETT, C. F. (1948) "Implications of Bloomfield's Algonquian Studies"
FISCHER-JØRGENSEN, E. (1949) "Remarques sur les principes de l'analyse phonémique"
VACHEK, J. (1949) "Yaleská škola a strukturalistická fonologie" (The Yale School and Structuralist Phonology)
FRIES, C. C., and K. L. PIKE (1949) "Coexistent Phonemic Systems"
HAUGEN, E. (1950) "Problems of Bilingualism"

HARRIS, Z. S. (1951) *Methods in Structural Linguistics*

Reviewed by: FOWLER, M. (1952)
  HOCKETT, C. F. (1952)
  HOUSEHOLDER, F. W. (1952)
  MCQUOWN, N. A. (1952)

TWADDELL, W. F. (1952) "Phonemes and Allophones in Speech Analysis"

HOENIGSWALD, H. M. (1952) "The Phonology of Dialect Borrowings"

WEINREICH, U. (1953) *Languages in Contact*

HARRIS, Z. S. (1955) "From Phoneme to Morpheme"

HOCKETT, C. F. (1955) *A Manual of Phonology*

Reviewed by: MARTIN, S. E. (1956)
  CHOMSKY, N. A. (1957)

FERGUSON, C. A. (1957) "A Manual of Phonological Description"

WEINREICH, U. (1957) "On the Description of Phonic Interference"

HOCKETT, C. F. (1958) *A Course in Modern Linguistics*

SLEDD, J. H. (1958) "Some Questions of English Phonology"

KURATH, H. (1958) "Some Questions of English Phonology: A Reply"

FRANCESCATO, G. (1959) "A Case of Coexistence of Phonemic Systems"

HOUSEHOLDER, F. W. (1959) "On Linguistic Primes"

LADEFOGED, P. N. (1960) "The Value of Phonetic Statements"

PERCIVAL, W. K. (1960) "A Problem in Competing Phonemic Solutions"

GLEASON, H. A., JR. (1961) *Introduction to Descriptive Linguistics* (2d ed.)

MALONE, K. (1962) "On Symmetry in Phonemic Analysis"

BEVER, T. G. (1963) "Theoretical Implications of Bloomfield's 'Menomini Morphophonemics'"

MCCAWLEY, J. D. (1967) "Sapir's Phonologic Representation"

PIKE, K. L. (1967) *Language in Relation to a Unified Theory of the Structure of Human Behavior* (2d ed.)

Reviews of first edition: ROBINS, R. H. (1955 and 1956)
  GAUTHIER, M. (1956)
  MCQUOWN, N. A. (1957)

MAKKAI, V. B. (1969) "On the Correlation of Morphemes and Lexemes"

B. APPLICATIONS OF THE THEORY

BLOOMFIELD, L. (1930) "German ç and x"

TRAGER, G. L. (1930) "The Pronunciation of 'Short *a*' in American English"

JOOS, M. (1934) "Regional and Personal Variations in General American"

—— (1934) "Stressed Vowels Plus *r* in General American"

SWADESH, M. (1934) "The Phonetics of Chitimacha"

TRAGER, G. L. (1934) "The Phonemes of Russian"

BLOCH, B. (1935) "Broad Transcription of General American"

BLOOMFIELD, L. (1935) "The Stressed Vowels of American English"

KENYON, J. S. (1935) *American Pronunciation* (6th ed.)

SWADESH, M. (1935) "The Vowels of Chicago English"

TRAGER, G. L. (1935) "The Transcription of English"

VOEGELIN, C. F. (1935) "Shawnee Phonemes"

MALONE, K. (1936) "The Phonemic Structure of English Monosyllables"

TRAGER, G. L. (1939) "The Phonemes of Castillian Spanish"

MALONE, K. (1940) "The Phonemes of Current English"

TRAGER, G. L. (1940) "One Phonemic Entity Becomes Two: The Case of 'Short *a*'"

HARRIS, Z. S. (1942) "The Phonemes of Moroccan Arabic"

HALL, R. A., JR. (1944) "Italian Phonemes and Orthography"

ASCHMANN, H. P. (1946) "Totonaco Phonemes"

HALL, R. A., JR. (1946) "Colloquial French Phonology"

HODGE, C. T. (1946) "Serbo-Croatian Phonemes"

HOCKETT, C. F. (1947) "Peiping Phonology"

—— (1947) "Componential Analysis of Sierra Popoluca"

NEWMAN, S. S. (1947) "Bella Coola I: Phonology"

SWADESH, M. (1947) "On the Analysis of English Syllabics"

LEOPOLD, W. F. (1948) "German ch"

BLOCH, B. (1950) "Studies in Colloquial Japanese IV: Phonemics"

HOCKETT, C. F. (1950) "Peiping Morphophonemics"

MARTIN, S. E. (1951) "Korean Phonemics"

TRAGER, G. L., and H. L. SMITH, JR. (1951) *An Outline of English Structure*

Reviewed by: O'CONNOR, J. D. (1951)
               SLEDD, J. H. (1955)

FRANCIS, W. N. (1958) *The Structure of American English*

HILL. A. A. (1958) *Introduction to Linguistic Structures: From Sound to Sentence in English*

KURATH, H., AND R. I. MCDAVID, JR. (1961) *The Pronunciation of English in the Atlantic States*

GUDSCHINSKY, S. (1964) "Phonetic Similarity and the Phonemes of Maxakalí"

HENDON, R. S. (1966) *The Phonology and Morphology of Ulu Muar Malay*

Reviewed by: MAKKAI, A. (1968)

C. BIBLIOGRAPHIES AND BIBLIOGRAPHICAL STUDIES

HALL, R. A., JR. (1951) "American Linguistics, 1925–1950"

HAUGEN, E. (1951) "Directions in Modern Linguistics"

BLOCH, B. (1952) *A Bibliography of Descriptive Linguistics: American Writings to 1952*

O'CONNOR, J. D. (1957) "Recent Work in English Phonetics"

PIKE, K. L., and E. V. PIKE (1960) *Live Issues in Descriptive Linguistics* (2d ed.)

SEBEOK, T. A. (1963) "Selected Readings in General Phonemics (1925–1964)"

PIKE, K. L. (1967) *Language in Relation to a Unified Theory of the Structure of Human Behavior* (2d ed.), especially pp. 344–63.

D. COLLECTIONS AND ANTHOLOGIES

SPIER, L., A. I. HALLOWELL, and S. S. NEWMAN (eds.) (1941) *Language, Culture, and Personality: Essays in Memory of Edward Sapir*

MANDELBAUM, D. G. (ed.) (1949) *Selected Writings of Edward Sapir in Language, Culture, and Personality*

Reviewed by: HARRIS, Z. S. (1951)

JOOS, M. (ed.) (1957) *Readings in Linguistics*

I.a

*Formation
of the Phonemic
Principle*

1

SOUND PATTERNS
IN LANGUAGE*
EDWARD SAPIR

There used to be and to some extent still is a feeling among linguists that the psychology of a language is more particularly concerned with its grammatical features, but that its sounds and its phonetic processes belong to a grosser physiological substratum. Thus, we sometimes hear it said that such phonetic processes as the palatalizing of a vowel by a following *i* or other front vowel ("umlaut") or the series of shifts in the manner of articulating the old Indo-European stopped consonants which have become celebrated under the name of "Grimm's Law" are merely mechanical processes, consummated by the organs of speech and by the nerves that control them as a set of shifts in relatively simple sensorimotor habits. It is my purpose in this paper, as briefly as may be, to indicate that the sounds and sound processes of speech cannot be properly understood in such simple, mechanical terms.

Perhaps the best way to pose the problem of the psychology of speech sounds is to compare an actual speech sound with an identical or similar one not used in a linguistic context. It will become evident almost at once that it is a great fallacy to think of the articulation of a speech sound as a motor habit that is merely intended to bring about a directly significant result. A good example of superficially similar sounds is the *wh* of such a word as *when,* as generally pronounced in America (i.e., voiceless *w* or, perhaps more accurately analyzed, aspiration plus voiceless *w* plus voiced *w*-glide), and the sound made in blowing out a candle, with which it has often been compared. We are not at the present moment greatly interested in whether these two articulations are really identical or, at the least, very similar. Let us assume that a typically pronounced *wh*

is identical with the sound that results from the expulsion of breath through pursed lips when a candle is blown out. We shall assume identity of both articulation and quality of perception. Does this identity amount to a psychological identity of the two processes? Obviously not. It is worth pointing out, in what may seem pedantic detail, wherein they differ.

1. The candle-blowing sound is a physical by-product of a directly functional act, the extinguishing of the candle by means of a peculiar method of producing a current of air. So far as normal human interest is concerned, this sound serves merely as a sign of the blowing out, or attempted blowing out, itself. We can abbreviate our record of the facts a little and say that the production of the candle-blowing sound is a directly functional act. On the other hand, the articulation of the *wh*-sound in such a word as *when* has no direct functional value; it is merely a link in the construction of a symbol, the articulated or perceived word *when,* which in turn assumes a function, symbolic at that, only when it is experienced in certain linguistic contexts, such as the saying or hearing of a sentence like *When are you coming?* In brief, the candle-blowing *wh* means business; the speech sound *wh* is stored-up play which can eventually fall in line in a game that merely refers to business. Still more briefly, the former is practice; the latter, art.

2. Each act of blowing out a candle is functionally equivalent, more or less, to every other such act; hence the candle-blowing *wh* is, in the first instance, a sign for an act of single function. The speech sound *wh* has no singleness, or rather primary singleness, of reference. It is a counter in a considerable

*Reprinted from *Language* 1. 37–51 (1925) by permission.

variety of functional symbols, e.g., *when, whiskey, wheel.* A series of candle-blowing sounds has a natural functional and contextual coherence. A series of *wh*-sounds as employed in actual speech has no such coherence; e.g., the series *wh(en), wh(iskey), wh(eel)* is non-significant.

3. Every typical human reaction has a certain range of variation and, properly speaking, no such reaction can be understood except as a series of variants distributed about a norm or type. Now the candle-blowing *wh* and the speech sound *wh* are norms or types of entirely distinct series of variants.

First, as to acoustic quality. Owing to the fact that the blowing out of a candle is a purely functional act, its variability is limited by the function alone. But, obviously, it is possible to blow out a candle in a great number of ways. One may purse the lips greatly or only a little; the lower lip, or the upper lip, or neither may protrude; the articulation may be quite impure and accompanied by synchronous articulations, such as a *x*-like (velar spirant) or *sh*-like sound. None of these and other variations reaches over into a class of reactions that differs at all materially from the typical candle-blowing *wh*. The variation of *wh* as speech sound is very much more restricted. A *when* pronounced, for instance, with a *wh* in which the lower lip protruded or with a *wh* that was contaminated with a *sh*-sound would be felt as distinctly "off color." It could be tolerated only as a joke or a personal speech defect. But the variability of *wh* in language is not only less wide than in candle-blowing, it is also different in tendency. The latter sound varies chiefly along the line of exact place (or places) of articulation, the former chiefly along the line of voicing. Psychologically *wh* of *when* and similar words is related to the *w* of *well* and similar words. There is a strong tendency to minimize the aspiration and to voice the labial. The gamut of variations, therefore, runs roughly from *hW* (I use *W* for voiceless *w*) to *w*. Needless to say, there is no tendency to voicing in the candle-blowing *wh,* for such a tendency would contradict the very purpose of the reaction, which is to release a strong and unhampered current of air.

Second, as to intensity. It is clear that in this respect the two series of variations differ markedly. The normal intensity of the candle-blowing sound is greater than that of the linguistic *wh;* this intensity, moreover, is very much more variable, depending as it does on the muscular tone of the blower, the size of the flame to be extinguished, and other factors. All in all, it is clear that the resemblance of the two *wh*-sounds is really due to an inter-crossing of two absolutely independent series, as of two independent lines in space that have one point in common.

4. The speech sound *wh* has a large number of associations with other sounds in symbolically significant sound-groups, e.g., *wh-e-n, wh-i-s-k-ey, wh-ee-l.* The candle-blowing sound has no sound associations with which it habitually coheres.

5. We now come to the most essential point of difference. The speech sound *wh* is one of a definitely limited number of sounds (e.g., *wh, s, t, l, i,* and so on) which, while differing qualitatively from one another rather more than does *wh* from its candle-blowing equivalent, nevertheless belong together in a definite system of symbolically utilizable counters. Each member of this system is not only characterized by a distinctive and slightly variable articulation and a corresponding acoustic image, but also—*and this is crucial*—by a psychological aloofness from all the other members of the system. The relational gaps between the sounds of a language are just as necessary to the psychological definition of these sounds as the articulations and acoustic images which are customarily used to define them. A sound that is not unconsciously felt as "placed"[1] with reference to other sounds is no more a true element of speech than a lifting of the foot is a dance step unless it can be "placed" with reference to other movements that help to define the dance. Needless to say, the candle-blowing sound forms no part of any such system of sounds. It is not spaced off from nor related to other sounds—say the sound of humming and the sound of clearing one's throat—which form with it a set of mutually necessary indices.

It should be sufficiently clear from this one example—and there are of course plenty

[1]This word has, of course, nothing to do here with "place of articulation." One may feel, for instance, that sound A is to sound B as sound X is to sound Y without having the remotest idea how and where any of them is produced.

of analogous ones, such as *m* versus the sound of humming or an indefinite series of timbre-varying groans versus a set of vowels—how little the notion of speech sound is explicable in simple sensorimotor terms and how truly a complex psychology of association and pattern is implicit in the utterance of the simplest consonant or vowel. It follows at once that the psychology of phonetic processes is unintelligible unless the general patterning of speech sounds is recognized. This patterning has two phases. We have been at particular pains to see that the sounds used by a language form a self-contained system which makes it impossible to identify any of them with a non-linguistic sound produced by the "organs of speech," no matter how great is the articulatory and acoustic resemblance between the two. In view of the utterly distinct psychological backgrounds of the two classes of sound production it may even be seriously doubted whether the innervation of speech-sound articulation is ever actually the same type of physiological fact as the innervation of "identical" articulations that have no linguistic context. But it is not enough to pattern off all speech sounds as such against other sounds produced by the "organs of speech." There is a second phase of sound patterning which is more elusive and of correspondingly greater significance for the linguist. This is the inner configuration of the sound system of a language, the intuitive "placing" of the sounds with reference to one another. To this we must now turn.

Mechanical and other detached methods of studying the phonetic elements of speech are, of course, of considerable value, but they have sometimes the undesirable effect of obscuring the essential facts of speech-sound psychology. Too often an undue importance is attached to minute sound discriminations as such; and too often phoneticians do not realize that it is not enough to know that a certain sound occurs in a language, but that one must ascertain if the sound is a typical form or one of the points in its sound pattern, or is merely a variant of such a form. There are two types of variation that tend to obscure the distinctiveness of the different points in the phonetic pattern of a language. One of these is individual variation. It is true that no two individuals have precisely the same pronunciation of a language, but it is equally true that they aim to make the same sound discriminations, so that, if the qualitative differences of the sounds that make up A's pattern from those that make up B's are perceptible to a minute analysis, the relations that obtain between the elements in the two patterns are the same. In other words, the patterns are the same pattern. A's *s*, for instance, may differ quite markedly from B's *s*, but if each individual keeps his *s* equally distinct from such points in the pattern as *th* (of *think*) and *sh* and if there is a one to one correspondence between the distribution of A's *s* and that of B's, then the difference of pronunciation is of little or no interest for the phonetic psychology of the language. We may go a step further. Let us symbolize A's and B's pronunciations of *s*, *th*, and *sh* as follows:

$$\text{A:} \quad th \quad s \quad sh$$
$$\text{B:} \quad th_1 \; s_1 \; sh_1$$

This diagram is intended to convey the fact that B's *s* is a lisped *s* which is not identical with his interdental *th*, but stands nearer objectively to this sound than to A's *s;* similarly, B's *sh* is acoustically somewhat closer to A's *s* than to his *sh*. Obviously we cannot discover B's phonetic pattern by identifying his sounds with their nearest analogues in A's pronunciation, i.e., setting $th_1 = th$, $s_1 = $ variant of *th*, $sh_1 = s$. If we do this, as we are quite likely to do if we are obsessed, like so many linguists, by the desire to apply an absolute and universal phonetic system to all languages, we get the following pattern analysis:

$$\text{A:} \quad th \quad s \quad sh$$
$$\wedge$$
$$\text{B:} \quad th_1 \; s_1 \; sh_1 \quad —$$

which is as psychologically perverse as it is "objectively" accurate. Of course the true pattern analysis is:

$$\text{A:} \quad th \quad s \quad sh$$
$$\text{B:} \quad th_1 \quad s_1 \quad sh_1$$

for the objective relations between sounds are only a first approximation to the psychological relations which constitute the true phonetic pattern. The size of the objective differences $th—s$, $s—sh$, $th_1—s_1$, $s_1—sh_1$, $th—s_1$, $s_1—s$, $s—sh_1$, and $sh_1—sh$ does not correspond to the psychological "spacing" of the phonemes *th, s,* and *sh* in the phonetic pattern which is common to A and B.

The second type of variation is common to all normal speakers of the language and is dependent on the phonetic conditions in which the fundamental sound ("point of the pattern") occurs. In most languages, what is felt by the speakers to be the "same" sound has perceptibly different forms as these conditions vary. Thus, in (American) English there is a perceptible difference in the length of the vowel *a* of *bad* and *bat,* the *a*-vowel illustrated by these words being long or half-long before voiced consonants and all continuants, whether voiced or unvoiced, but short before voiceless stops. In fact, the vocalic alternation of *bad* and *bat* is quantitatively parallel to such alternations as *bead* and *beat, fade* and *fate.* The alternations are governed by mechanical considerations that have only a subsidiary relevance for the phonetic pattern. They take care of themselves, as it were, and it is not always easy to convince natives of their objective reality, however sensitive they may be to violations of the unconscious rule in the speech of foreigners. It is very necessary to understand that it is not because the objective difference is too slight to be readily perceptible that such variations as the quantitative alternations in *bad* and *bat, bead* and *beat, fade* and *fate* stand outside of the proper phonetic pattern of the language (e.g., are not psychologically parallel to such qualitative-quantitative alternations as *bid* and *bead, fed* and *fade,* or to such quantitative alternations as German *Schlaf* and *schlaff,* Latin *āra* and *ārā*), but that the objective difference is felt to be slight precisely because it corresponds to nothing significant in the inner structure of the phonetic pattern. In matters of this kind, objective estimates of similarity or difference, based either on specific linguistic habits or on a generalized phonetic system, are utterly fallacious. As a matter of fact, the mechanical English vocalic relation *bad: bat* would in many languages be quite marked enough to indicate a relation of distinct points of the pattern, while the English pattern relation *-t: -d,* which seems so self-evidently real to us, has in not a few other languages either no reality at all or only a mechanical, conditional one. In Upper Chinook, for instance, *t:d* exists objectively but not psychologically; one says, e.g., *inat* 'across,'

but *inad* before words beginning with a vowel, and the two forms of the final consonant are undoubtedly felt to be the "same" sound in exactly the same sense in which the English vowels of *bad* and *bat* are felt by us to be identical phonetic elements. The Upper Chinook *d* exists only as a mechanical variant of *t;* hence this alternation is not the same psychologically as the Sanskrit sandhi variation *-t: -d.*

Individual variations and such conditional variations as we have discussed once cleared out of the way, we arrive at the genuine pattern of speech sounds. After what we have said, it almost goes without saying that two languages, A and B, may have identical sounds but utterly distinct phonetic patterns; or they may have mutually incompatible phonetic systems, from the articulatory and acoustic standpoint, but identical or similar patterns. The following schematic examples and subjoined comments will make this clear. Sounds which do not properly belong to the pattern or, rather, are variants within points of the pattern are put in parentheses. Long vowels are designated as *a·; ŋ* is *ng* of *sing; θ* and *δ* are voiceless and voiced interdental spirants; *x* and *γ* are voiceless and voiced guttural spirants; ' is glottal stop; ' denotes aspirated release; *ε* and *ɔ* are open *e* and *o.*

A:

a	*(ε)*	*(e)*	*i*	*u*	*(o)*	*(ɔ)*
(a·)	*(ε·)*	*(e·)*	*i·*	*u·*	*(o·)*	*(ɔ·)*
'	*h*	*w*	*y*	*l*	*m*	*n*	*(ŋ)*
p	*t*	*k*				
p'	*t'*	*k'*				
(b)	*(d)*	*(g)*				
f	*θ*	*s*	*x*			
(v)	*(δ)*	*(z)*	*(γ)*			

but B:

a	*ε*	*e*	*i*	*u*	*o*	*ɔ*
(a·)	*(ε·)*	*(e·)*	*(i·)*	*(u·)*	*(o·)*	*(ɔ·)*
(')	*h*	*(w)*	*(y)*	*(l)*	*m*	*n*	*ŋ*
p	*t*	*k*				
(p')	*(t')*	*(k')*				
b	*d*	*g*				
(f)	*(θ)*	*s*	*(x)*			
v	*δ*	*z*	*γ*			

We will assume for A and B certain conditional variants which are all of types that may be abundantly illustrated from actual languages. For A:

1. ε occurs only as palatalized form of *a* when following *y* or *i*. In many Indian languages, e.g., *yε = ya*.
2. *e* is dropped from *i*-position when this vowel is final. Cf. such mechanical alternations as Eskimo *-e: -i-t*.
3. *o* is dropped from *u*-position when this vowel is final. Cf. 2.
4. ɔ occurs only as labialized form of *a* after *w* or *u*. Cf. 1. (In Yahi, e.g., *wɔwi* 'house' is objectively correct, but psychologically wrong. It can easily be shown that this word is really *wawi* and "feels" like a rhyme to such phonetic groups as *lawi* and *bawi;* short ɔ in an open syllable is an anomaly, but ɔ· is typical for all Yana dialects, including Yahi.)
5. ŋ is merely *n* assimilated to following *k*, as in Indo-European.
6. *b, d, g, v, z,* δ, γ are voiced forms of *p, t, k, f, s,* θ, *x* respectively when these consonants occur between vowels before the accent (cf. Upper Chinook *wa'pul* 'night': *wabu'l-max* 'nights'). As the voiced consonants can arise in no other way, they are not felt by the speakers of A as specifically distinct from the voiceless consonants. They feel sharply the difference between *p* and *p'*, as do Chinese, Takelma, Yana, and a host of other languages, but are not aware of the alternation *p: b*.

And for B:

1. Long vowels can arise only when the syllable is open and stressed. Such alternations as *ma·'la: u·'-mala* are not felt as involving any but stress differences. In A, *ma·la* and *mala* are as distinct as Latin "apples" and "bad" (fem.).
2. ' is not an organic consonant, but, as in North German, an attack of initial vowels, hence *'a-* is felt to be merely *a-*. In A, however, as in Semitic, Nootka, Kwakiutl, Haida, and a great many other languages, such initials as *'a-* are felt to be equivalent to such consonant + vowel groups as *ma-* or *sa-*. Here is a type of pattern difference which even experienced linguists do not always succeed in making clear.
3. *w* and *y* are merely semi-vocalic developments of *u* and *i*. Cf. French *oui* and *hier*. In A, *w* and *y* are organically distinct consonants. Here again linguists often blindly follow the phonetic feeling of their own language instead of clearly ascertaining the behavior of the language investigated. The difference, e.g., between *aua* and *awa* is a real one for some languages, a phantom for others.
4. *l* arises merely as dissimilated variant of *n*.
5. *p', t', k'* are merely *p, t, k* with breath release, characteristic of B at the end of a word, e.g., *ap-a: ap'*. This sort of alternation is common in aboriginal America. It is the reverse of the English habit: *tame* with aspirated *t* (*t'e·ᶦm*) but *hate* with unaspirated, or very weakly aspirated, release (*he·ᶦt*).
6. *f,* θ, and *x* similarly arise from the unvoicing of final *v,* δ and γ; e.g., *av-a: af. z* and *s* also alternate in this way, but there is a true *s* besides. From the point of view of B, *s* in such phonemes as *sa* and *asa* is an utterly distinct sound, or rather point in the phonetic pattern, from the objectively identical *as* which alternates with *az-a*.[2]

[2]If B ever develops an orthography, it is likely to fall into the habit of writing *az* for the pronounced *as* in cases of type *az-a: as,* but *as* in cases of type *as-a: as*. Philologists not convinced of the reality of phonetic patterns as here conceived will then be able to "prove" from internal evidence that the change of etymological *v, z,* δ, γ to *-f, -s, -*θ, *-x* did not take place until after the language was reduced to writing, because otherwise it would be "impossible" to explain why *-s* should be written *-z* when there was a sign for *s* ready to hand and why signs should not have come into use for *f,* θ, and *x*. As soon as one realizes, however, that "ideal sounds," which are constructed from one's intuitive feeling of the significant relations between the objective sounds, are more "real" to a naive speaker than the objective sounds themselves, such internal evidence loses much of its force. The example of *s* in B was purposely chosen to illustrate an interesting phenomenon, the crossing in a single objective phoneme of a true element of the phonetic pattern with a secondary form of another such element. In B, e.g., objective *s* is a pool of cases of "true *s*" and "pseudo-*s*." Many interesting and subtle examples could be given of psychological difference where there is objective identity, or similarity so close as to be interpreted by the recorder as identity. In Sarcee, an Athabaskan language with significant pitch differ-

The true or intuitively felt phonetic systems (patterns) of A and B, therefore, are:

```
A:  a                    i      u
    a·                   i·     u·

            ʼ    h    w y    l m n

        p  t  k
        p' t' k'
        f  θ    x s

B:  a    ε    e        i        u    o    ɔ

                 h                    m  n  ŋ

        p    t    k
        b    d    g
                 s
        v  δ  z      γ
```

which show the two languages to be very much more different phonetically than they at first seemed to be.

The converse case is worth plotting too. C and D are languages which have hardly any sounds in common but their patterns show a remarkable one to one correspondence. Thus:

```
C:  a    ε        i        u
    a·   ε·

    h         w   y   l   m   n

    p   t       k   q (velar k)
    b   d       g   g̣ (velar g)
    f   s       x   x̣ (velar x)

D:  ä    e        i        ü
    ä·   e·

    h         v   j[3]   r   m   ŋ
```

```
p'   t'        k'   q'
β[4] δ         γ    γ (velar γ)
f    š         x̣[5] h̦ (laryngeal h)
```

Languages C and D have far less superficial similarity in their sound systems than have A and B, but it is obvious at a glance that their patterns are built on very much more similar lines. If we allowed ourselves to speculate genetically, we might suspect, on general principles, that the phonetic similarities between A and B, which we will suppose to be contiguous languages, are due to historical contact, but that the deeper pattern resemblance between C and D is an index of genetic relationship. It goes without saying that in the complex world of actual linguistic history we do not often find the phonetic facts working out along such neatly schematic lines, but it seemed expedient to schematize here so that the pattern concept might emerge with greater clarity.

An examination of the patterns of C and D shows that there is still a crucial point that we have touched on only by implication. We must now make this clear. We have arranged the sounds of C and D in such a way as to suggest an equivalence of "orientation" of any one sound of one system with some sound of the other. In comparing the systems of A and B we did not commit ourselves to specific equivalences. We did not wish to imply, for instance, that A's *s* was or was not "oriented" in the same way as B's, did or did not occupy the same relative place in A's pattern as in B's. But here we do wish to imply not merely that, e.g., C's *p* corresponds to D's *p'* or C's *h* to D's *h*, which one would be inclined to grant on general phonetic grounds, but also that, e.g., C's *w* corresponds to D's *v* while C's *b* corresponds to D's *β*. On general principles such pattern alignments as the latter are unexpected, to say the least, for bilabial *β* resembles *w* rather more than dentolabial *v* does. Why, then, not allow *β* to occupy the position we have assigned to *v*? Again, why should D's *j* be supposed to correspond to C's *y* when it is merely the voiced form of *š*? Should it not rather be placed under *š* precisely as, in C's system, *b* is placed under *p*? Naturally, there is no reason why the intuitive pattern align-

---

ences, there is a true middle tone and a pseudo-middle tone which results from the lowering of a high tone to the middle position because of certain mechanical rules of tone sandhi. I doubt very much if the intuitive psychology of these two middle tones is the same. There are, of course, analogous traps for the unwary in Chinese. Had not the Chinese kindly formalized for us their intuitive feeling about the essential tone analysis of their language, it is exceedingly doubtful if our Occidental ears and kymographs would have succeeded in discovering the exact patterning of Chinese tone.

[3]As in French *jour*.

[4]Bilabial *v*, as in Spanish.

[5]As in German *ich*.

ment of sounds in a given language should not be identical with their natural phonetic arrangement and, one need hardly say, it is almost universally true that, e.g., the vowels form both a natural and a pattern group as against the consonants, that such stopped sounds as *p, t, k* form both a natural and a pattern group as opposed to the equally coherent group *b, d, g* (provided, of course, the language possesses these two series of stopped consonants). And yet it is most important to emphasize the fact, strange but indubitable, that a pattern alignment does not need to correspond exactly to the more obvious phonetic one. It is most certainly true that, however likely it is that at last analysis patternings of sounds are based on natural classifications, the pattern feeling, once established, may come to have a linguistic reality over and above, though perhaps never entirely at variance with, such classifications. We are not here concerned with the historical reasons for such phonetic vagaries. The fact is that, even from a purely descriptive standpoint, it is not nonsense to say that, e.g., the *s* or *w* of one linguistic pattern is not necessarily the same thing as the *s* or *w* of another.

It is time to escape from a possible charge of phonetic metaphysics and to face the question, "How can a sound be assigned a 'place' in a phonetic pattern over and above its natural classification on organic and acoustic grounds?" The answer is simple. "A 'place' is intuitively found for a sound (which is here thought of as a true 'point in the pattern,' not a mere conditional variant) in such a system because of a general feeling of its phonetic relationship resulting from all the specific phonetic relationships (such as parallelism, contrast, combination, imperviousness to combination, and so on) to all other sounds." These relationships may, or may not, involve morphological processes (e.g., the fact that in English we have morphological alternations like *wife: wives, sheath: to sheathe, breath: to breathe, mouse: to mouse* helps to give the sounds *f, θ, s* an intuitive pattern relation to their voiced correlates *v, δ, z* which is specifically different from the theoretically analogous relation *p, t, k: b, d, g*: in English, *f* is nearer to *v* than *p* is to *b*, but in German this is certainly not true).

An example or two of English sound-patterning will help us to fix our thoughts. *P, t,* and *k* belong together in a coherent set because, among other reasons: 1, they may occur initially, medially, or finally; 2, they may be preceded by *s* in all positions (e.g. *spoon: cusp, star: hoist, scum: ask*); 3. they may be followed by *r* initially and medially; 4, they may be preceded by *s* and followed by *r* initially and medially; 5, each has a voiced correspondent (*b, d, g*); 6, unlike such sounds as *f* and *θ*, they cannot alternate significantly with their voiced correspondents; 7, they have no tendency to be closely associated, either phonetically or morphologically, with corresponding spirants (*p:f* and *t:θ* are not intuitively correct for English; contrast Old Irish and Hebrew *t:θ, k:x*, which were intuitively felt relations—Old Irish and Hebrew *θ* and *x* were absolutely different types of sounds, psychologically, from English *θ* and German *x*). These are merely a few of the relations which help to give *p, t, k* their pattern place in English.

A second example is *η* of *sing*. In spite of what phoneticians tell us about this sound (*b:m* as *d:n* as *g:η*), no naïve English-speaking person can be made to feel in his bones that it belongs to a single series with *m* and *n*. Psychologically it cannot be grouped with them because, unlike them, it is not a freely movable consonant (there are no words beginning with *η*). It still *feels* like *ηg*, however little it sounds like it. The relation *ant:and = sink:sing* is psychologically as well as historically correct. Orthography is by no means solely responsible for the "*ng* feeling" of *η*. Cases like *-ηg-* in *finger* and *anger* do not disprove the reality of this feeling, for there is in English a pattern equivalence of *-ηg-:-η* and *-nd-:-nd*. What cases like *singer* with *-η-* indicate is not so much a pattern difference *-ηg-:-η-*, which is not to be construed as analogous to *-nd-:-n-* (e.g., *window:winnow*), as an analogical treatment of medial elements in terms of their final form (*singer:sing* like *cutter:cut*).[6]

[6]Incidentally, if our theory is correct, such a form as *singer* betrays an unconscious analysis into a word of absolute significance *sing* and a semi-independent agentive element *-er*, which is appended not to a stem, an abstracted radical element, but to a true word. Hence *sing: singer* is not psychologically analogous to such Latin forms as *can-:can-tor*. It would almost seem that the English insistence on the absoluteness of its significant words tended at the same time to give many of its derivative suffixes

To return to our phonetic patterns for C and D, we can now better understand why it is possible to consider a sibilant like *j* as less closely related in pattern to its voiceless form *š* than to such a set of voiced continuants as *v, r, m, ŋ*. We might find, for instance, that *š* never alternates with *j*, but that there are cases of *š:δ* analogous to cases of *f:β* and *x:γ*; that *ava, aja, ara* alternate with *au, ai, ar*; that combinations like *-aβd, -aδg, -aγd* are possible, but that combinations of type *-ajd* and *-avd* are unthinkable; that *v-* and *j-* are possible initials, like *r-, m-,* and *ŋ-,* but that *β-, δ-, γ-, γ-* are not allowed. The product of such and possibly other sound relations would induce a feeling that *j* belongs with *v, r, m, ŋ;* that it is related to *i;* and that it has nothing to do with such spirants as *š* and *δ*. In other words, it "feels" like the *y* of many other languages, and, as *y* itself is absent in D, we can go so far as to say that *j* occupies a "place in the pattern" that belongs to *y* elsewhere.

In this paper I do not wish to go into the complex and tangled problems of the nature and generality of sound changes in language. All that I wish to point out here is that it is obviously not immaterial to understand how a sound patterns if we are to understand its history. Of course, it is true that mechanical sound changes may bring about serious readjustments of phonetic pattern and may even create new configurations within the pattern (in Modern Central Tibetan, e.g., we have *b-, d-, g-: B'-, D'-, G'-*,[7] while in classical Tibetan we have, as correspondents, *mb-, nd-, ŋg-: b-, d-, g-; mb-, nd-, ŋg-* are here to be morphologically analyzed as nasal prefix + *b-, d-, g-*). But it is equally true that the pattern feeling acts as a hindrance of, or stimulus to, certain sound changes and that it is not permissible to look for universally valid sound changes under like articulatory conditions. Certain typical mechanical tendencies there are (e.g., *nb > mb* or

-az > -as or *tya > tša*), but a complete theory of sound change has to take constant account of the orientation of sounds in our sense. Let one example do for many. We do not in English feel that *θ* is to be found in the neighborhood, as it were, of *s*, but that it is very close to *δ*. In Spanish, *θ* is not far from *s*, but is not at all close to *δ*.[8] Is it not therefore more than an accident that nowhere in Germanic does *θ* become *s* or proceed from *s*, while in certain Spanish dialects, as so frequently elsewhere, *θ* passes into *s* (in Athabaskan *θ* often proceeds from *s*)? In English *θ* tends to be vulgarized to *t* as *δ* tends to be vulgarized to *d*, never to *s;* similarly, Old Norse *θ* has become *t* in Swedish and Danish. Such facts are impressive. They cannot be explained on simple mechanical principles.

Phonetic patterning helps also to explain why people find it difficult to pronounce certain foreign sounds which they possess in their own language. Thus, a Nootka Indian in pronouncing English words with *ŋ* or *l* invariably substitutes *n* for each of these sounds. Yet he is able to pronounce both *ŋ* and *l*. He does not use these sounds in prose discourse, but *ŋ* is very common in the chants and *l* is often substituted for *n* in songs. His feeling for the stylistic character of *ŋ* and for the *n-l* equivalence prevents him from "hearing" English *ŋ* and *l* correctly. Here again we see that a speech sound is not merely an articulation or an acoustic image, but material for symbolic expression in an appropriate linguistic context. Very instructive is our attitude towards the English sounds *j, ŋ,* and *ts*. All three of these sounds are familiar to us (e.g., *azure, sing, hats*). None occurs initially. For all that the attempt to pronounce them initially in foreign words is not reacted to in the same way. *ŋa-* and *tsa-* are naïvely felt to be incredible, not so *ja-,* which is easily acquired without replacement by *dja-* or *ša-*. Why is this? *ŋa-* is incredible because there is no *mba-, nda-, ŋ(g)a-* series in English. *tsa-* is incredible because there is no *psa-, tsa-, ksa-,* series in English; *-ts* is always morphologically analyzable into *-t + -s,* hence no feeling develops for *ts* as a simple

---

a secondary, revitalized reality. *-er,* for instance, might almost be construed as a "word" which occurs only as the second element of a compound, cf. *-man* in words like *longshoreman.* As Prof. L. Bloomfield points out to me, the agentive *-er* contrasts with the comparative *-er,* which allows the adjective to keep its radical form in *-ŋg-* (e.g., *long* with *-ŋ: longer* with *-ŋg-*).

[7] *B, D, G* represent intermediate stops, "tonlose Medien." In this series they are followed by aspiration.

[8] The slight objective differences between English and Spanish *θ* and *δ* are of course not great enough to force a different patterning. Such a view would be putting the cart before the horse.

phoneme despite the fact that its phonetic parallel *tš* (*ch* of *church*) is found in all positions.[9] But *ja-* is not difficult, say in learning French, because its articulation and perception have been mastered by implication in the daily use of our phonetic pattern. This is obvious from a glance at the formula:

$$-j-\quad -z-\quad -\delta-\quad -v-$$
$$-\quad\quad z-\quad \delta-\quad v-$$

which is buttressed by:

$$-š-\quad -s-\quad -\theta-\quad -f-$$
$$š-\quad s-\quad \theta-\quad f-$$

Is it not evident that the English speaker's pattern has all but taught him *j-* before he himself has ever used or heard an actual *j-?*

There are those who are so convinced of the adequacy of purely objective methods of studying speech sounds that they do not hesitate to insert phonetic graphs into the body of their descriptive grammars. This is to confuse

linguistic structure with a particular method of studying linguistic phenomena. If it is justifiable in a grammatical work to describe the vocalic system of a language in terms of kymograph records,[10] it is also proper to insert anecdotes into the morphology to show how certain modes or cases happened to come in handy. And a painter might as well be allowed to transfer to his canvas his unrevised palette! The whole aim and spirit of this paper has been to show that phonetic phenomena are not physical phenomena *per se,* however necessary in the preliminary stages of inductive linguistic research it may be to get at the phonetic facts by way of their physical embodiment. The present discussion is really a special illustration of the necessity of getting behind the sense data of any type of expression in order to grasp the intuitively felt and communicated forms which alone give significance to such expression.

---

[9]Obviously we need not expect *-ts* and *-tš* to develop analogously even if *s* and *š* do.

[10]Needless to say, such records are in place in studies explicitly devoted to experimental phonetics.

2

THE PSYCHOLOGICAL REALITY OF PHONEMES*

EDWARD SAPIR

The concept of the "phoneme" (a functionally significant unit in the rigidly defined pattern or configuration of sounds peculiar to a language), as distinct from that of the "sound" or "phonetic element" as such (an objectively definable entity in the articulated and perceived totality of speech), is becoming more and more familiar to linguists. The difficulty that many still seem to feel in distinguishing between the two must eventually disappear as the realization grows that no entity in human experience can be adequately defined as the mechanical sum or product of its physical properties. These physical properties are needed of course to give us the signal, as it were, for the identification of the given entity as a functionally significant point in a complex system of relatednesses; but for any given context it is notorious how many of these physical properties are, or may be, overlooked as irrelevant, how one particular property, possessing for the moment or by social understanding an unusual sign value, may have a determinedness in the definition of the entity that is out of all proportion to its "physical weight."

As soon, however, as we admit that all significant entities in experience are thus revised from the physically given by passing through the filter of the functionally or relatedly meaningful, as soon as we see that we can never set up a scale of added or changed meanings that is simply congruent to the scale of physical increments, we implicitly make a distinction, whether we know it or not, between the phoneme and the sound in that particular framework of experience which is known as language (actualized as speech). To say that a given phoneme is not sufficiently defined in articulatory or acoustic terms but needs to be fitted into the total system of sound relations peculiar to the language is, at bottom, no more mysterious than to say that a club is not defined for us when it is said to be made of wood and to have such and such a shape and such and such dimensions. We must understand why a roughly similar object, not so different to the eye, is no club at all, and why a third object, of very different color and much longer and heavier than the first, is for all that very much of a club.

Some linguists seem to feel that the phoneme is a useful enough concept in an abstract linguistic discussion—in the theoretical presentation of the form of a language or in the comparison of related languages—but that it has small relevance for the actualities of speech. This point of view seems the reverse of realistic to the present writer. Just as it takes a physicist or philosopher to define an object in terms of such abstract concepts as mass, volume, chemical structure, and location, so it takes very much of a linguistic abstractionist, a phonetician pure and simple, to reduce articulate speech to simple physical processes. To the physicist, the three wooden objects are equally distinct from each other,

*Published originally in French under the title "La réalité psychologique des phonèmes," *Journal de Psychologie Normale et Pathologique* 30.247–265 (1933). Reprinted from *Selected Writings of Edward Sapir in Language, Culture, and Personality*, ed. by D. G. Mandelbaum, 46–60. Berkeley and Los Angeles: University of California (1949). Reprinted by permission of The Regents of the University of California.

"clubs" are romantic intrusions into the austere continuities of nature. But the naïve human being is much surer of his clubs and poles than of unnamed objects to be hereinafter defined in physical terms. So, in speech, precise phonetic stations can be abstracted only by patient observation and frequently at the expense of a direct flouting of one's phonetic (one should say "phonemic") intuitions. In the physical world the naïve speaker and hearer actualize and are sensitive to sounds, but what they feel themselves to be pronouncing and hearing are "phonemes." They order the fundamental elements of linguistic experience into functionally and aesthetically determinate shapes, each of which is carved out by its exclusive laws of relationship within the complex total of all possible sound relationships. To the naïve speaker and hearer, sounds (i.e., phonemes) do not differ as five-inch or six-inch entities differ, but as clubs and poles differ. If the phonetician discovers in the flow of actual speech something that is neither "club" nor "pole," he, as phonetician, has the right to set up a "halfway between club and pole" entity. Functionally, however, such an entity is a fiction, and the naïve speaker or hearer is not only driven by its relational behavior to classify it as a "club" or a "pole," but actually hears and feels it to be such.

If the phonemic attitude is more basic, psychologically speaking, than the more strictly phonetic one, it should be possible to detect it in the unguarded speech judgments of naïve speakers who have a complete control of their language in a practical sense but have no rationalized or consciously systematic knowledge of it. "Errors" of analysis, or what the sophisticated onlooker is liable to consider such, may be expected to occur which have the characteristic of being phonetically unsound or inconsistent but which at the same time register a feeling for what is phonemically accurate. Such "errors," generally overlooked by the practical field linguist, may constitute valuable evidence for the dynamic reality of the phonemic structure of the language.

In the course of many years of experience in the recording and analysis of unwritten languages, American Indian and African, I have come to the practical realization that what the naïve speaker hears is not phonetic elements but phonemes. The problem reaches the stage of a practical test when one wishes to teach an intelligent native, say one who can read and write English reasonably well and has some intellectual curiosity besides, how to write his own language. The difficulty of such a task varies, of course, with the intelligence of the native and the intrinsic difficulty of his language, but it varies also with the "phonemic intuitiveness" of the teacher. Many well-meaning linguists have had disappointing experiences in this regard with quite intelligent natives without ever suspecting that the trouble lay, not with the native, but with themselves. It is exceedingly difficult, if not impossible, to teach a native to take account of purely mechanical phonetic variations which have no phonemic reality for him. The teacher who comes prepared with a gamut of absolute phonetic possibilities and who unconsciously, in spite of all his training, tends to project the phonemic valuations of his own language into what he hears and records of the exotic one may easily befuddle a native. The native realizes when what he is taught "clicks" with what his phonological intuitions have already taught him; but he is made uncomfortable when purely phonetic distinctions are pointed out to him which seem real enough when he focuses his attention on them but which are always fading out of his consciousness because their objective reality is not confirmed by these intuitions.

I have selected for brief discussion five examples of phonemic versus phonetic hearing and writing out of many which have come to me in the course of my experience with natives and students. In each of these, it will be observed, we have clear evidence of the unconscious reinterpretation of objective facts because of a disturbing phonological preparedness not precisely adjusted to these facts.

I   When working on the Southern Paiute language of southwestern Utah and northwestern Arizona I spent a little time in trying to teach my native interpreter, a young man of average intelligence, how to write his language phonetically. Southern Paiute is an unusually involved language from the phonological standpoint and, as my point of view at that time stressed phonetic accuracy rather than phonemic adequacy, I doubt if I could have succeeded in teaching him well enough to satisfy my standard even if I had devoted far more time to the effort than I did. As an example of a comparatively simple word I selected *pá·βa‘* "at the water" (voiceless labial stop; stressed long *a;* voiced bilabial spirant; unstressed short *a;* final aspiration). I instructed Tony to divide the word into its syllables and to discover by careful hearing what sounds entered into the composition of each of the syllables, and in what order, then to attempt to write down the proper symbol for each of the discovered phonetic elements. To my astonishment Tony then syllabified: *pa·,* pause, *pa‘.* I say "astonishment" because I at once recognized the paradox that Tony was not "hearing" in terms of the actual sounds (the voiced bilabial *β* was objectively very different from the initial stop) but in terms of an etymological reconstruction: *pa··* "water" plus postposition **-pa‘* "at." The slight pause which intervened after the stem was enough to divert Tony from the phonetically proper form of the postposition to a theoretically real but actually nonexistent form.

To understand Tony's behavior, which was not in the least due to mere carelessness nor to a tendency of the speakers of this language "to confuse sounds," to quote the timeworn shibboleth, we must have recourse to the phonology of Southern Paiute. The treatment of the stopped consonants may be summarized in the following table:

nasalized and geminated stops becoming aspirated (*mp‘, p·‘; nt‘, t·‘; ŋk‘, k·‘; ŋkW, k·W*). It is impossible here to give a systematic idea of the phonologic processes which bring about the sound interchanges within a given articulatory series, but it is important to know that the spirantized, nasalized, and geminated stops can occur only in postvocalic position and that they are largely determined by the nature of the element (stem or suffix) which precedes them and which may be said to have an inherently spirantizing, nasalizing, or geminating force. The stem *pa··* is a spirantizing stem, and the spirantizing of a theoretical **-pa‘* "at" to *-βa‘* is parallel to the spirantizing of *pɔ··*"trail" to *-βɔ··* in such a compound as *pa·-βɔ··,* "water-trail." In other words, the language is so patterned that examples of type *pɔ··: -βɔ··* lead to the proportion **pa‘: -βa‘*[2] and, while **pa‘* "at" does not actually exist as an independent element but must always be actualized in one of the three possible postvocalic forms, its theoretical existence suddenly comes to the light of day when the problem of slowly syllabifying a word is presented to a native speaker for the first time. It then appears that the *-βa‘* of speech behavior, as a self-contained syllabic entity without immediately preceding syllable, is actually felt as a phonologic *pa‘,* from which it differs in two important phonetic respects (voiced, not voiceless, consonant; spirant, not stop).

		POSTVOCALIC			
	INITIAL	1. Spirantized	2. Nasalized	3. Geminated	
				a. After voiced vowel	b. After unvoiced vowel
Labial	*p*	*β*	*mp*	*p·*	*p*
Dental	*t*	*r*	*nt*	*t·*	*t*
Guttural	*k*	*γ*	*ŋk*	*k·*	*k*
Labialized guttural	*kw*	*γw*	*ŋkw*	*k·w*	*kw*

The postvocalic forms of the stops of types 1, 2, and 3*a* are further modified before an unvoiced vowel, the voiced spirants becoming unvoiced spirants (*φ, R, χ, χW*),[1] and the

All this has an important bearing on the construction of a maximally correct orthography of Southern Paiute, if by "maximally cor-

---

[1] *W* represents voiceless *w.*

[2] This theoretical **pa‘,* occurring only as *-βa‘, -mpa‘, -p·a‘* in postvocalic position, is not to be confused with secondary *-pa‘ (type 3b) < -p·a‘ (type 3a).*

rect" we mean, not most adequate phonetically, but most true to the sound patterning of the language. As it happens, there is reason to believe from both internal and comparative evidence that the spirantized form of a consonant is its normal or primary form after a vowel and that the nasalized and geminated forms are due to the emergence of old nasal and other consonants that had disappeared in the obsolete form of the preceding element.[3] It follows that the postvocalic -β- is more closely related functionally to a simple initial p- than is the postvocalic -p- (after unvoiced vowel), which must always be interpreted as a secondary form of -p·-. These relations are summarized in the following table of theoretical nonfinal forms.

PHONETIC ORTHOGRAPHY	PHONOLOGIC ORTHOGRAPHY
1. pa-	pa-
2. paβa-	papa-
3. paϕA-[4]	papa-
4. pap·a-	pap·a-
5. pApa-	pap·a-
6. pap·A-	pap·a-

The phonetic orthography is more complex and, in a sense, more adequate, but it goes against the grain of the language in one important respect, for it identifies the second p in type 5 with the initial p, which is phonologically unsound. The phonologic orthography, on the other hand, is useless for one who has not mastered the phonology of the language, as it leads, or seems to lead, to incorrect pronunciations which would have the cumulative effect of making the language, so read, entirely unintelligible to a native. To a slightly schooled native, however, there can be no serious ambiguity, for the phonetic forms result from the phonologic only by the application of absolutely mechanical phonetic laws of spirantizing, alternating stresses, and unvoicing. It is not necessary to deal with these laws here[5]

[3] The analogy to French liaison and, still more, to the three types of consonantal treatment in Old Irish (spirantized or "aspirated," nasalized or "eclipsed," and geminated) is obvious.

[4] A represents voiceless a.

[5] They are described in detail in E. Sapir, *The Southern Paiute Language*, Proceedings of the American Academy of Arts and Sciences, 65 (1930).

but we can indicate their operation by the following table of theoretical final forms:

PHONETIC ORTHOGRAPHY	PHONOLOGIC ORTHOGRAPHY
1. páϕA	papa
2. paβá‘	papa·
3. pá·ϕA	pa·pa
4. pá·βa‘ "water-at"	pa·pa·
5. páp·A	pap·a
6. pApá‘	pap·a·
7. pá·p·A	pa·p·a
8. pá·p·a‘	pa·p·a·
9. maβáϕA	mapapa
10. maβáβa‘	mapapa·
11. maβá·ϕA	mapa·pa
12. maβá·βa‘	mapa·pa·
13. maβáp·A	mapap·a
14. maβáp·a‘	mapap·a·
15. maβá·p·A	mapa·p·a
16. maβáApa‘	mapa·p·a·
17. MApáϕA[6]	map·apa
18. MApáβa‘	map·apa·
19. MApá·ϕA	map·a·pa
20. MApá·βa‘	map·a·pa·
21. MApáp·A	map·ap·a
22. MApáp·a‘	map·ap·a·
23. MApá·p·A	map·a·p·a
24. MApáApa‘	map·a·p·a·

Obviously, in such a language as this, spirants, whether voiced or voiceless, and voiceless vowels are not phonemes but are merely phonetic reflexes of stopped consonants and voiced vowels under fixed dynamic conditions. Long consonants and long vowels are sub-phonemes. The former are the resultants of simple phonemes (stopped consonants) and the operation of certain phonologic (and morphologic) latencies in given syllables, present or formerly present. The latter are phonologically resolvable into short vowel plus short vowel, i.e., into two syllables of unit length (moras), of which the second begins with a zero consonant.

Southern Paiute, then, is a language in which an unusually simple phonemic structure is actualized by a more than ordinarily complex phonetic one. Tony's "error" unconsciously registered this contrast.

II   When working on Sarcee, an Athabaskan

[6] M is voiceless m.

language of Alberta, Canada, I was concerned with the problem of deciding whether certain words that seemed homonymous were actually so or differed in some subtle phonetic respect that was not immediately obvious. One such homonymous, or apparently homonymous, pair of words was *dìní*[7] "this one" and *dìní* "it makes a sound." In the early stage of our work I asked my interpreter, John Whitney, whether the two words sounded alike to him and he answered without hesitation that they were quite different. This statement, however, did not prove that he was objectively correct, as it is possible for perfectly homonymous words to give the speaker the illusion of phonetic difference because of the different contexts in which they appear or because of the different positions they occupy in their respective form systems.[8] When I asked him what the difference was, he found it difficult to say, and the more often he pronounced the words over to himself the more confused he became as to their phonetic difference. Yet all the time he seemed perfectly sure that there was a difference. At various moments I thought I could catch a slight phonetic difference, for instance, (1) that the *-ní* of "this one" was on a slightly lower tone than the *-ní* of "it makes a sound"; (2) that there was a slight stress on the *dì-* of "this one" (analysis: stem *dì-* "this" plus suffix *-ní* "person") and a similarly slight stress on the *-ní* of "it makes a sound" (analysis: prefix *dì-* plus verb stem *-ní*); (3) that the *-ní* of "this one" ended in a pure vowel with little or no breath release, while the *-ní* of "it makes a

[7]The grave accent represents a low tone, the acute accent a high one. Sarcee is a tone language.
[8]Thus, in English, the word *led* (e.g., "I *led* him away") is felt as having a vowel which has been deflected from the vowel of *lead* (e.g., "I *lead* him away") and is therefore not psychologically homonymous with the word for a metal, *lead,* in which the vowel is felt to be primary, not deflected (cf. further, "the *leading* of the windowpane," "the *leaded* glass," "the different *leads* now recognized by chemists"). The homonymy of *led* and *lead* (metal) is therefore of a different psychological order from the homonymy of *yard* ("He plays in my *yard*") and *yard* ("I want a *yard* of silk"), for the last two words enter into roughly parallel form systems (e.g., "Their *yards* were too small to play in": "I want two *yards* of silk"; *"yard* upon *yard* of railroad tracks": "*yard* upon *yard* of lovely fabrics"). It is probably easier for the naïve speaker, who does not know how to spell either *led* or *lead* (metal), to convince himself that there is a phonetic difference between these two words than between the two words *yard*.

sound" had a more audible breath release, was properly *-ní'*. These suggestions were considered and halfheartedly accepted at various times by John, but it was easy to see that he was not intuitively convinced. The one tangible suggestion that he himself made was obviously incorrect, namely, that the *-ní* of "it makes a sound" ended in a "*t*." John claimed that he "felt a *t*" in the syllable, yet when he tested it over and over to himself, he had to admit that he could neither hear a "*t*" nor feel his tongue articulating one. We had to give up the problem, and I silently concluded that there simply was no phonetic difference between the words and that John was trying to convince himself there was one merely because they were so different in grammatical form and function that he felt there ought to be a difference.

I did not then know enough about Sarcee phonology to understand the mysterious "*t*" theory. Later on it developed that there are phonologically distinct types of final vowels in Sarcee: smooth or simple vowels; and vowels with a consonantal latency, i.e., vowels originally followed by a consonant which disappears in the absolute form of the word but which reappears when the word has a suffix beginning with a vowel or which makes its former presence felt in other sandhi phenomena. One of these disappearing consonants is *-t'*, of which *-'* may be considered a weakened form. Now it happens that all final vowels are pronounced with a breath release in the absolute form of the word and that there is no objective difference between this secondary *-'*, which may be symbolized as *-(')*, phonologically zero, and the etymologically organic *-'*, which may affect certain following consonants of suffixed elements or, in some cases, pass over to one of certain other consonants, such as *t'*. The *-ní* of "this one," phonetically *-ní* in absolute form, is phonologically simple *-ní;* the *-ní* of "it makes a sound," phonetically *-ní'* in absolute form, can be phonologically represented as *-ní' (-nít'-)*. We can best understand the facts if we test the nature of these two syllables by seeing how they behave if immediately followed by suffixed relative *-í* "the one who . . ." and inferential *-la*[9] "it turns out that."

[9]The lack of a tone mark indicates that this syllable is pronounced on the middle tone.

	plus -*i*	plus -*la*
dìní "this one"	*dìná·ᵃ*[10]	*dìníla*
dìní "it makes a sound"	*dìnít'í*	*dìníła*[11]

We see at once that *dìní* "this one" behaves like a word ending in a smooth vowel (witness contraction of *í* + *i* to an over-long vowel and unaffected *l* of -*la*), while *dìní* "it makes a sound" acts as though the final vowel had a voiceless consonantal latency, which registers partly as -' (-'-*la* passing, as always, to -*ła*), partly as -*t'*-.

It is clear that, while John was phonetically amateurish, he was phonologically subtle and accurate. His response amounted to an index of the feeling that *dìní* "this one" = *dìní*, that *dìní* "it makes a sound" = *dìní'*, and that this -*ní'* = -*nít'*. John's certainty of difference in the face of objective identity is quite parallel to the feeling that the average Englishman would have that such words as *sawed* and *soared* are not phonetically identical. It is true that both *sawed* and *soared* can be phonetically represented as *sɔ·d*,[12] but the -*ing* forms of the two verbs (*sawing, soaring*), phonetically *sɔ·iŋ* and *sɔ·riŋ*, and such sentence sandhi forms as "Saw on, my boy!" and "Soar into the sky!" combine to produce the feeling that the *sɔ·d* of *sawed* = *sɔ·-d* but that the *sɔ·d* of *soared* = *sɔ·r-d*. In the one case zero = zero, in the other case zero = *r*. Among educated but linguistically untrained people who discuss such matters differences of orthography are always held responsible for these differences of feeling. This is undoubtedly a fallacy, at least for the great mass of people, and puts the cart before the horse. Were English not a written language, the configuratively determined phonologic difference between such doublets as *sawed* and *soared* would still be "heard," as a collective illusion, as a true phonetic difference.

---

[10]*a·ᵃ* is an over-long *a*, consisting of a long *a·* followed by a weak rearticulated *a*. Syllables of this type result in Sarcee from contraction of old final vowels with following suffixed vowels. The change in quality from -*í* to -*á·ᵃ* is due to historical factors. -*ní* "person" is an old *-*né* (with pepet vowel), relative -*í* is old *-*é*; two pepet vowels contract to long open *-*ɛ·ᵋ*; as Athabaskan *ɛ* becomes Sarcee *a*, this older *-*ɛ·ᵋ* passes into Sarcee -*á·ᵃ*.

[11]*ł* is voiceless spirantal *l*, as in Welsh *ll*.

[12]These remarks apply to British, not to normal American, usage.

III The most successful American Indian pupil that I have had in practical phonetics is Alex Thomas, who writes his native language, Nootka,[13] with the utmost fluency and with admirable accuracy. Alex's orthography, as is natural, is phonologic in spirit throughout and it is largely from a study of his texts that I have learned to estimate at its true value the psychological difference between a sound and a phoneme. Anyone who knows the phonetic mechanics of Nootka can easily actualize his orthography. Thus, *ḥi*,[14] phonologically parallel to *si* or *ni*, is actually pronounced *ḥɛ*, with a vowel which is much nearer to the *e* of English *met* than to that of *sit*. This is due to the peculiar nature of the laryngeal consonants, which favor an *a*-timbre and cause the following vowels *i* and *u* to drop to *ɛ* and *ɔ* respectively. The orthographies *ḥi* and *ḥu* are entirely unambiguous because there can be no phonologically distinct syllables of type *ḥɛ* and *ḥɔ*.

Another mechanical peculiarity of Nootka is the lengthening of consonants after a short vowel when followed by a vowel. This purely mechanical length has no morphological or phonological significance and is ignored in Alex's orthography. His *ḥisi·k* and *ḥisa·* are, then, to be normally pronounced *ḥis·i·k'* and *ḥɛs·a·*. It sometimes happens, however, that a long consonant, particularly *s·* and *š·*, arises from the meeting of two morphologically distinct consonants (e.g., *s* + *s* > *s·* or *š* + *š* > *š·* or, less frequently, *š* + *s* or *s* + *š* > *s·*). In such cases the long consonant is not felt to be a mechanical lengthening of the simple consonant but as a cluster of two identical consonants, and so we find Alex writing, for example, *tsi·-qšit'łassatłni*[15] "we went there only to speak," to be analyzed into *tsi·qšitł-'as-sa-('a)tł-ni*. The *s* of -*'as* "to go in order to" and the *s* of -*sa* "just, only" keep their phonologic independence and the normal intervocalic -*s·*- of -*'as·atł* is interpreted as -*ss*-. Similarly, *kwissiła* "to

---

[13]This is spoken on the west coast of Vancouver Island, B. C.

[14]*ḥ* is a voiceless laryngeal spirant, almost identical with the Arabic *ḥā*.

[15]I have slightly modified Alex's orthography to correspond to my present orthography, but these changes are merely mechanical substitutions, such as *tł* for ʟ, and in no way affect the argument. *q* is velar *k* (Arabic *ḳ*), *tł* is a lateral affricative, *t'ł* its glottalized form.

do differently," to be analyzed into *kwis-siła*. It does not seem, however, that there is an actual phonetic difference between the *-s-* (phonologically *-s-*) of such words as *tłasatł* "the stick takes an upright position on the beach" (= *tła-satł*), pronounced *tłas·atł*, and the *-s·-* of *-'assatł* above. Here again we have objectively identical phonetic phenomena which receive different phonologic interpretations.

IV In the earlier system of orthography, which Alex was taught, the glottalized stops and affricatives were treated differently from the glottalized nasals and semivowels. The former were symbolized as *p!*, *t!*, *k!*, *k!w*, *q!*, *q!w*, *ts!*, *tc!* (= *iš*), and *L!* (= *ił*); the latter as *'m*, *'n*, *'y*, and *'w*. The reason for this was traditional. The glottalized stops and affricatives, as a distinctive type of consonants, had been early recognized by Dr. F. Boas in many American Indian languages and described as "fortes," that is, as stops and affricatives "pronounced with increased stress of articulation." The type *'m*, *'n*, *'l*, *'y*, and *'w* was not recognized by Dr. Boas until much later, first in Kwakiutl, and described as consisting of nasal, voiced lateral, or semivowel immediately preceded by a glottal closure. The orthography for these consonants (later discovered in Tsimshian, Nootka, Haida, and a number of other languages, but not as widely distributed as the so-called "fortes") suggested their manner of formation, but the orthography for the glottalized stops and affricatives was purely conventional and did not in any way analyze their formation except to suggest that more energy was needed for their pronunciation.[16]

As a pure matter of phonetics, while the Nootka glottalized stops and affricatives are roughly parallel in formation with the glottalized sonantic consonants, they are not and cannot be entirely so. In a glottalized *p*, for instance, our present *ṗ* and former *p!*, there is a synchronous closure of lips and glottal cords, a closed air chamber is thus produced between the two, there is a sudden release of the lip closure, a moment of pause, and then the release of the glottal closure. It is the release of the lip (or other oral) closure in advance of the glottal closure that gives consonants of this type their superficial "click-like" character.[17] On the other hand, in a glottalized *m*, our *'m*, while the lip closure and glottal closure are synchronous as before,[18] the glottal closure must be released at the point of initial sonancy of the *m*. Roughly speaking, therefore, *ṗ* may be analyzed into *p + '*, while *'m* may be analyzed into *' + m*. Such an orthographic difference as *p!* versus *'m*, therefore, which I had inherited from the Americanist tradition, was not unjustified on purely phonetic grounds.

We now come to the intuitive phonologic test whether *ṗ* and *'m* are consonants of the same type or not. Alex learned to write consonants of type *ṗ* and *is* very readily (our earlier *p!* and *ts!*), e.g., *ṗapi·* "ear" (earlier *p!ap!i̇*), *isa·ak* "stream" (earlier *ts!a'ak*). To my surprise Alex volunteered *m!* in such words as *'ma·'mi·qsu* "the older [brother or sister]," which he wrote *m!ām!īqsu*. In other words, we had valuable evidence here for the phonologic reality of a glottalized class of consonants which included both type *ṗ* (with prior release of oral closure) and type *'m* (with prior

---

[16]This, incidentally, is not necessarily true. In some languages the glottalized stops and affricatives seem to be somewhat more energetic in articulation than the corresponding unglottalized consonants, in others there is no noticeable difference so far as "stress of articulation" is concerned. In the Athabaskan languages that I have heard (Sarcee, Kutchin, Hupa, Navaho) the aspirated voiceless stops and affricatives (of type *t'*, *k'*, *ts'*) are far more "fortis" in character than the corresponding glottalized consonants (e.g., *i̇*, *k̇*, *is*). There is no necessary correlation between laryngeal type of articulation (voiced, voiceless, glottalized; or any of these with aspiration) and force of articulation (fortis, lenis). So far as Nootka is concerned, it did not seem to me that the glottalized stops and affricatives (Boas' "fortes")

were significantly different in emphasis from the ordinary stops and affricatives. In such languages as recognize a phonological difference of emphatic and nonemphatic and, at the same time, possess glottalized consonants, there is no reason why the glottalized consonants may not appear in both emphatic and nonemphatic form. As Prince Trubetzkoy has shown, some of the North Caucasic languages, as a matter of fact, possess both emphatic and nonemphatic glottalized stops and affricatives.

[17]These consonants are apparently identical with the "ejectives" of Daniel Jones. There is another, apparently less common, type of glottalized stop or affricative in which the oral and glottal releases are synchronous.

[18]The pronunciation of *'m*, *'n*, *'w*, and *'y* as a simple sequence of glottal stop (') plus *m*, *n*, *w*, and *y* is rejected by the Nootka ear as incorrect.

release of glottal closure). A phonologically consistent orthography would require $\dot{p}$ and $\dot{m}$ (or p! and m!). Once more, a naïve native's phonetic "ignorance" proved phonologically more accurate than the scientist's "knowledge." The phonologic justification for Alex's "error" is not difficult. Consonants of type $\dot{p}$ are entirely analogous to consonants of type 'm for the following reasons.

1. Each occurs at the beginning of a syllable and, since no word can begin with a cluster of consonants, both $\dot{p}$ and 'm are felt by Nootka speakers to be unanalyzable phonologic units. In other words, the glottal stop can no more easily be abstracted from 'm than from $\dot{p}$. Similarly, the affricatives and glottalized affricatives are phonologically unanalyzable units.

2. All consonants can occur at the end of a syllable except glottalized stops and affricatives, glottalized sonantic consonants ('m, 'n, 'y, 'w), semivowels (y, w), nasals (m, n),[19] the glottal stop ('), and h. This rule throws consonants of type 'm more definitely together with consonants of type $\dot{p}$.

3. Many suffixes which begin with a vowel have the effect of "hardening"[20] the preceding consonant, in other words, of glottally affecting it. Under the influence of this "hardening" process p, t, $\dot{k}$ become $\dot{p}$, $\dot{t}$, $\dot{k}$, while m and n become 'm and 'n. For example, just as the suffixes '-a'a[21] ('-a·'a) "on the rocks" and '-aḥs "in a receptacle" change the stem wi·ṅap- "to stay, dwell" to wi·naṗ- (e.g., wi·naṗa'a "so stay on the rocks") and wik- "to be not" to wik̇ - (e.g., wikaḥs "to be not in a receptacle, a canoe is empty"), so t'ɫum- (alternating with t'ɫup-) "to be hot" becomes t'ɫu'm- (alternating with t'ɫuṗ-) (e.g., ɫu'ma·'a "to be hot on the rocks" and ɫu'maḥs "to be hot in a receptacle, there is hot water"; compare ɫuṗi·tšḥ "summer, hot season" = parallel ɫup- + '-i·tcḥ "season") and kan- "to kneel"

(e.g., kanɫ "to kneel in the house") becomes ka'n- (e.g., ka'naḥs "to kneel in a canoe"). As there seem to be no stems ending in h or ', the group 'm, 'n, 'w, 'y[22] is left over as functionally related to the group m, n, w, y in the same sense as the group exemplified by $\dot{p}$ is related to the group exemplified by p. Morphology, in other words, convincingly supports the phonologic proportion $p:\dot{p} = m:$'m. It is maintained that it was this underlying phonologic configuration that made Alex hear 'm as sufficiently similar to $\dot{p}$ to justify its being written in an analogous fashion. In other languages, with different phonologic and morphologic understandings, such a parallelism of orthography might not be justified at all and the phonetic differences that actually obtain between 'm and $\dot{p}$ would have a significantly different psychologic weighting.

V In a course in practical phonetics which I have been giving for a number of years I have so often remarked the following illusion of hearing on the part of students that there seems no way of avoiding a general phonologic theory to explain it. I find that, after the students have been taught to recognize the glottal stop as a phonetic unit, many of them tend to hear it after a word ending in an accented short vowel of clear timbre (e.g., a, ε, e, i). This illusion does not seem to apply so often to words ending in a long vowel or an obscure vowel of relatively undefined quality (ə) or an unaccented vowel. Thus, a dictated nonsense word like smε or pilá would occasionally be misheard and written as smε' and pilá' but there seems far less tendency to hear a final glottal stop in words like píla or pilá·. What is the reason for this singular type of "overhearing?" Is it enough to say that students who have learned a new sound like to play with it and that their preparedness for it tends to make them project its usage into the stream of acoustic stimuli to which they are asked to attend? No doubt such a general explanation is a correct dynamic formula so far as it goes but it is not precise enough for a phonologist because it does not take sufficient account of the limitations of the illusion.

---

[19]m and n may be followed by a murmured vowel of i-timbre which is a reduced form of a, u, or i. Syllables or half-syllables of type m^i or n^i are preceded by i, an assimilated product of a, u or i; in^i and im^i result therefore, in part, from sequences of type ama, umi, anu. Simple -am or -an become -ap, -at.

[20]A term borrowed from Boas' equivalent Kwakiutl phenomenon.

[21]The symbol ' indicates the "hardening" effect of a suffix.

[22]The phonologic details involving 'w and 'y and their relation to w and y and other consonants are too intricate for a summary statement in this place.

It must be remembered that the language of my students is English. We may therefore suspect that the illusion of a final glottal stop is due to some feature in the phonologic structure of English. But English has no glottal stop. How, then, can English phonology explain the overhearing of a consonant which is alien to its genius to begin with? Nevertheless, I believe that the students who projected a final glottal stop into the dictated words were handling an exotic phonetic element, the glottal stop, according to a firmly established but quite unconscious phonologic pattern. It requires both the learning process, with its consequent alert preparedness to recognize what has been learned, and English phonology to explain the illusion. If we study the kinds of syllables in English which may normally constitute an accented monosyllabic word or an accented (or secondarily accented) final syllable of a word, we find that they may be classified into three types:

A. Words ending in a long vowel or diphthong, e.g., *sea, flow, shoe, review, apply.*
B. Words ending in a long vowel or diphthong plus one or more consonants, e.g., *ball, cease, dream, alcove, amount.*
C. Words ending in a short vowel plus one or more consonants, e.g., *back, fill, come, remit, object.*

The theoretically possible fourth class:

D. Words ending in a short vowel, e.g., French *fait, ami;* Russian *xărăšɔ'*

does not exist in English. English-speaking people tend to pronounce words of type D in a "drawling" fashion which transfers them to type A (e.g., *amí·* for *ami*). Observe that the apparently inconsistent possibility of a nonfinal accented syllable ending in a short vowel (e.g., *fiddle, butter, double, pheasant*) is justified by the English theory of syllabification, which feels the point of the syllabic division to lie in the following consonant (*d, t, b, z,* in the examples cited), so that the accented syllables of these words really belong phonologically to type C, not to type D. Intervocalic consonants like the *d* of *fiddle* or *z* of *pheasant,* in spite of the fact that they are not phonetically long, are phonologically "flanking" or two-

faced, in that they at one and the same time complete one syllable and begin another. Should the point of syllabic division shift back of the consonant, the preceding vowel at once lengthens in spite of its "short" quality (type. A), and we thus get dialectic American pronunciation of words like *fiddle* and *pheasant* in which the accented vowel keeps its original quality but has been lengthened to the unit length of "long vowels" of type *feeble, reason,* and *ladle.*

We are now prepared to understand the illusion we started with. Such words as *smɛ* and *pilá* are unconsciously tested as possible members of class A or class C. Two illusions are possible, if the hearer is to be a victim of his phonologic system. Inasmuch as a final accented short vowel is an unfamiliar entity, it can be "legitimized" either by projecting length into it (misheard *smɛ·* and *pilá·* fall into class A) or by projecting a final consonant after it (class C). We shall call this imaginary consonant "*x*" and write *smɛx* and *pilάx.* Now the fact that one has added the glottal stop to his kit of consonantal tools leads often to the temptation to solve the phonologic problem symbolized as *smɛx* and *pilάx* in terms of the glottal stop and to hear *smɛ'* and *pilá'.* The glottal stop is the most unreal or zerolike of consonants to an English or American ear and is admirably fitted, once its existence has been discovered, to serve as the projected actualization of a phonologically required final consonant of minimum sonority. The illusion of the final glottal stop is essentially the illusion of a generalized final consonant ("*x*") needed to classify the dictated words into a known category (type C). Or, to speak more analytically, English phonology creates the groundwork (-*x*) of the synthetic illusion, while the learning process colors it to the shape of -'. The error of hearing a glottal stop where there is none, in words of type D, is fundamentally a more sophisticated form of the same error as hearing a dictated final glottal stop as *p* or *t* or *k,* which occurs frequently in an earlier stage of the acquiring of a phonetic technique.

The danger of hearing a glottal stop when the dictated word ends in a long vowel or diphthong is of course rendered very unlikely by the fact that such words conform to a common English pattern (type A). The reason why the error does not so easily occur in hearing dictated words ending in an unaccented short vowel (e.g., *ó·nɛ, sú·li*) is that such words, too, conform to an English pattern, though the range of the qualities allowed a vowel in this position is not as great as when the vowel is covered by a following consonant (e.g., *idea, very, follow*).

3

THE PHONEMIC PRINCIPLE*
MORRIS SWADESH

As basic as the phonemic principle is to linguistic science, it is only quite recently that it has had the serious attention of linguists. In studying the phonemes of Chitimacha (an Indian language of Louisiana) I knew of no single source from which I could learn to understand all the phenomena that I observed. There seemed to be a need for an adequate and complete exposition of the phonemic principle including, especially, an account of how it applies to the more marginal and difficult types of phenomena. I at first intended to include this discussion in my paper on the Chitimacha phonemes, but the wider interest of the general discussion makes it more appropriate that it be published separately. The specific treatment of Chitimacha, which can now appear without theoretical digressions, will serve to illustrate many of the points discussed here. I do not attempt to cite previous authors[1] on all of the points treated in this paper, though I recognize fully my dependence on them. On a few points my treatment attempts to avoid weaknesses in previous treatments, and a point or two are perhaps introduced here for the first time. However, the chief ideals of this paper are theoretical comprehensiveness, consistency of treatment, and brevity.

The phonemic principle is that there are in each language a limited number of elemental types of speech sounds, called phonemes, peculiar to that language; that all sounds produced in the employment of the given language are referable to its set of phonemes; that only its own phonemes are at all significant in the given language.

The phonemes of a language are, in a sense, percepts to the native speakers of the given language who ordinarily hear speech entirely in terms of these percepts. If they hear a foreign tongue spoken, they still tend to hear in terms of their native phonemes. Bi-linguals and phonetically schooled individuals hear speech in a language native to them now in terms of the native phonemic system, now in terms of other percepts. If linguists occasionally have difficulty in discovering the phonemes of a language, it is usually when the language is not native to them, unless, indeed, in dealing with their own language, they be confused by some irrelevant or only partly relevant insight (as, for example, the knowledge of etymology or phonetics). At any rate, it is well to realize that one can learn nothing about the phonemes of one language by knowledge of those of another.

If the phonemes are percepts to the native speakers of the language, they are not necessarily percepts that he experiences in isolation. They occur ordinarily as the elements of words

[1]The principal works consulted were:

Bloomfield, *Language,* Chaps. 5–8. New York: Henry Holt, 1933.

Jones, "On Phonemes," *Travaux du cercle linguistique de Prague* (*TCLP*) 4.74–79.

"Projet de terminologie phonologique standardisé," *TCLP* 4.309–322.

Sapir, "Sound Patterns in Language," *Language* 1.37–51 [1];

"La réalité psychologique des phonèmes," *Journal de psychologie* 30.247–265 [2].

Troubetzkoy, "Zur allgemeinen Theorie der phonologischen Vokalsysteme," *TCLP* 1.39–67; "Die phonologischen Systeme," *TCLP* 4.96–116.

Ułaszyn, "Laut, Phonema, Morphonema," *TCLP* 4.53–61.

I am most directly indebted to Professor Sapir, as my teacher, for my understanding of the phonemic principle. The present paper has benefited by discussion with him and with my colleagues Dr. Stanley Newman, Dr. George Herzog, and Mrs. Mary Haas Swadesh.

*Reprinted from *Language* 10.117–129 (1934) by permission.

or sentences. Phonemes are perceptive units in the sense that the native can recognize as different, words different as to one of the component phonemes, e.g., *bid* and *hid* or *bid* and *bed* or *bid* and *bit*. The phoneme is the smallest potential unit of difference between similar words recognizable as different to the native. Given a correct native word, the replacement of one or more phonemes by other phonemes (capable of occurring in the same position) results in a native word other than that intended, or a native-like nonsense word. Other possible or conceivable differences are either not perceived, or are perceived as distortions of proper phonemes, or are chance oral sounds that are not classed as speech sounds at all.

The word sometimes has regular variant forms; in this event, two forms may differ as to one or more phonemes though they are in a sense the same word. Since variants sometimes confuse the phonemic problem, it may be well to point out some of the types of variants:

I Free variants (either variant is equally correct in any position)
  A Particular (applying to a single word or a limited number of isolated words), e.g., Nootka *ʔapw'inqis, ʔapw'inʔis* 'in the middle of the beach'
  B General (applying to all words of a given class), e.g., Chitimacha words of three or more syllables ending in -vʔv vary with -v as *k'ahtiʔi, k'ahti* 'he bites'.
II Conditional variants (determined by position in the sentence)
  A Particular, e.g., Eng. *a, an*
  B General
    (*a*) Phonetically conditioned, e.g., Sanskrit *punar, punaḥ* 'back, again'
    (*b*) Structurally conditioned, e.g., Tunica disyllabic words of the form cvʔv have that form only when spoken in isolation; in context they become cv as: *riʔi* 'house', context form *ri*.[2]

Conditional variants may be regular, as the examples given, or may be optional, as the Eng. sandhi type of *as you* [az yu, až(y)u],

both of which are sometimes interchangeably employed by the same speakers.

CHARACTERISTICS OF THE PHONEME

A phoneme, as a speech sound type, is defined by the separate instances of the type. If I say "Peter Piper," I have produced three instances of the English phoneme *p* and every time anyone pronounces these words or others like *dip, pit, speed, supply,* further instances of the phoneme are produced. On the basis of the separate occurrences (or a proper sampling of them) it is possible to define the type in terms of a norm and of deviation from the norm. Each individual has his own norm and range of deviation, the social norm being a summation of the individual norms. The description of the phoneme in terms of norm and deviation belongs to the science of phonetics.

The norm of the phoneme may be a multiple one. That is, instead of one norm, there may be two or more. Such variant norms are ordinarily conditional, depending on the phonetic surroundings in which the phoneme occurs. Thus one may distinguish at least three norms for English *p:*

1. Relatively fortis, aspirated: e.g., in initial position, as in *pit*
2. Fortis unaspirated: e.g., medially between vowels, as in *upper*
3. Lenis unaspirated: e.g., after *s*, as in *spill.*

Positional variants may be even more strikingly different, as, for example, the two variants of German *x* (*ch*) in, e.g., *Macht, Licht.* Positional variants are unlike phonemes in that to substitute one positional variant for the other distorts the word, sometimes beyond recognition, but never changes it into another native word.

Occasionally one finds free variants, that is, non-conditional or optional variants. Thus, there are many people in the Connecticut Valley who interchangeably use either an *r* or a mid-mixed vowel with or without retroflexion in words like *board* and *far*.[3] It sometimes happens that one of a pair of free variants coin-

---

[2]Data on Tunica (an Indian language of Louisiana) were supplied by Mary Haas Swadesh.

[3]I have this information from Professor Hans Kurath, director of the Linguistic Atlas of the United States and Canada.

cides with some other phoneme. Thus, Chitimacha *w', y', m', n'* may be pronounced with or without a glottal stricture, coinciding in the latter instance with the phonemes *w, y, m, n.* Another instance of this phenomenon, which may be called phonemic interchange, is the interchange of initial ð with *d* in words like *the* and *they* in Edgecombe County (near Rocky Mount), North Carolina.[4] Optional employment or omission of a phoneme occurs, for example, in the case of postvocalic *r* (e.g., *barn*) in certain sections of New England.[5]

DISTRIBUTION

In a given language, some phonemes are frequent, some are infrequent. Sometimes the disparity in relative frequencies is great indeed, as that between English *s* and ð. Sometimes, a phoneme occurs in only one or a few isolated words; thus *g* occurs in Tunica only in the stem *-gatci* 'mother'.

All phonemes, as a general thing, are limited as to the positions in which they may occur. Two stops may not occur together at the beginning of an English word; yet such clusters do occur in certain other languages, as Sahaptin (e.g., *tkwalwípt* 'evening meal')[6] or ancient Greek. Again, English *l* does not occur after *d* or *t* at the beginning of a word. Every phoneme has its positional limitations, so that range of distribution constitutes a definite characteristic of each phoneme.

If a phoneme is much more limited as to positions of occurrence than other comparable phonemes of the same language, one may refer to it as a defective phoneme. Such a phoneme is ŋ in English, since it occurs only after and between vowels and never at the beginning of a word.

PHONEME CLASSES

English *p, t,* and *k* have common phonetic characteristics, relatively analogous positional variants, and relatively similar ranges of dis-

tribution; they are relatively different in these three respects from all other phonemes of the language. They therefore constitute a special class of English phonemes. English *t, d,* and θ have roughly the same articulating position and have distributional features in common, for example, that they occur initially before *r* but never initially before *l.* They constitute a class intercrossing with the *p, t, k* set. On the basis of similarities, all the sounds of a language may be thus classified, sub-classified, and cross-classified. The principal classes are those whose members have the most significant features in common, the sub-classes those that have less significant features in common. The bases of classification are common phonetic, variational, and distributional features. Classes are significant because of the general tendency of these features to occur in correlation.

But even in the absence of variational and distributional similarities, phonetic analogies are significant when they are recurrent. Whenever the phonetic relation of two sounds like English *b* and *p* is found to be the same as that of another pair like *d* and *t,* it is evident that the relation is not haphazard but systematic. Phonemes tend to occur in more or less consistent patterns.[7]

It is important to distinguish between the phonetic differentiae of phoneme classes and psychologically separable synchronous features. Thus nasalization is the phonetic differentia which in French distinguishes the nasalized vowel phonemes from their non-nasalized parallels; the tone upon which vowels are pronounced in French belongs to the prosody of the sentence and the occurrence of this or that phoneme on this or that pitch does not change its phonemic identity. In addition to patterns of sentence prosody, psychologically separable synchronous phonemes include tonemes in tone languages and tasemes (phonemes of stress) in stress languages, for these features apply to the syllables rather than to any of the phonemes in particular. Syllabic phonemena are necessarily most evident in connection with the vowel, but also apply, where possible, to the consonants. In Navaho *ńs-nè'z* 'I am tall', the tone of the first syllable is actualized

---

[4] Observed by Dr. Lowman for the Linguistic Atlas, and mentioned in his paper "Regional Differences in Virginian Speech," read at the tenth annual meeting of the Linguistic Society of America.

[5] I owe this information to Dr. Lowman. The interchange was observed, for example, in one of his informants at Rockport, Massachusetts.

[6] See Jacobs, "A Sketch of Northwest Sahaptin Grammar," *University of Washington Publications in Anthropology* 4.85–292.

[7] See the papers of Sapir and Troubetzkoy cited above.

in the syllabic consonant *n* and not with the consonant *s,* the tone of the second syllable is carried by the vowel and both consonants.

But prosodic features, often psychologically separable from the sounds with which they occur, do sometimes constitute mere differentiae of phonemes. In Chitimacha *ə* is distinguished from the other vowels by quality, quantity, and force of enunciation. Thus stress constitutes one of its differentiae.

Considerations mentioned above give rise to three fundamental kinds of phonemes, as follows:

1. Sentence phonemes (patterns of sentence prosody)
2. Syllable phonemes (tonemes, tasemes)
3. Self-contained phonemes, phonemes proper.

All languages have phonemes of type 3, but may or may not have phonemes of types 1 and 2. English has all three types; French has 1 and 3; Navaho has 2 and 3; Nitinat has only type 3. Of course, it is impossible to speak without prosody, but unless a prosodic feature has some contrastive significance, it is not phonemic. Thus, Nitinat has a very noticeable melody, but there is generally speaking only one melody which then is a concomitant of the sentence. In Navaho, the succession of syllable tones gives the effect of a sentence melody, but this melody has no significance of its own.

WORD STRUCTURE

Each language has a characteristic word and syllabic structure. Some of the limitations of occurrence of phonemes are best accounted for as connected with principles of word structure. Thus in Chitimacha all words begin in a single consonant followed immediately by a vowel. In Nootka a monosyllabic word may end in a consonant or a long vowel, but never in a short vowel. Any language will be found to have a whole set of such rules.

The limits of the word are often marked in special ways. Phonemes may have a special variant for the beginning or end of words. Thus the aspirate stops of Chitimacha are unaspirated at the end of the word; at the beginning of the word they are more fully aspirated than at the beginning of a medial or final syllable. Again, the limits of the word may be indicated

by some non-phonemic element like the word accent of Latin or Polish, the initial glottal stop in German, or the aspiration that follows a final vowel in Nitinat. Such elements are not phonemes, but mechanical signs of the limits of the word units.

The sentence too may have characterizing phonetic features. A common mark of the sentence is the pause.

METHOD

The phonemes of a language can be discovered only by inductive procedure. This going from particular instances to general conception is as characteristic of the unconscious process of a native acquiring his language as it must be of conscious scientific study. But the scientist studying an alien language will make more rapid progress if he understands the essential details of the inductive process involved. A useful set of criteria, which follow from the nature of the phoneme, is given below. It should be remembered that they apply to any single given language, not to all languages taken together.

1. *The criterion of consistency of words.* Except for word variants (see above, pp. 118–119 [p. 33]) different occurrences of the same word have the same phonemic make-up. If differences are observed in different pronunciations of the same word, these are to be taken as showing the range of deviation of the component phonemes.
2. *The criterion of partial identities.* By a thorough-going comparison of all sets of words having a phonetic resemblance (e.g., *pit—bit, late—latent,* etc.), one arrives at a notion of the significant elemental sound types. But in the application of this criterion one must bear in mind the one given next.
3. *The criterion of constant association.* If a set of phonetic elements only occur together, they constitute a phonemically unitary complex; thus, the stop and the aspiration in English initial *p.* One or both of the phonetic elements may recur in other complexes without affecting the unitary nature of the complexes; in this event, all the phonemes that involve a given phonetic element constitute a phonemic class.
4. *The criterion of complementary distribution.* If it is true of two similar types of

sounds that only one of them normally occurs in certain phonetic surroundings and that only the other normally occurs in certain other phonetic surroundings, the two may be sub-types of the same phoneme. If the distribution of one type of sound is complementary to that of more than one other, it is to be identified with one rather than the other if there is a more definite phonetic similarity in that direction; an example is the *p* of English *speech* whose distribution is complementary to that of the voiced labial *b* as well as to that of the voiceless labial stop sounds of *peak, keep, happen,* but goes with the latter rather than the former because of the phonetic similarity. If a sound in a relation of complementary distribution to two sounds is not particularly similar to either of them, it has to be reckoned as phonemically independent.

5. *The criterion of pattern congruity.* Particular formulations must be congruous with the general phonemic pattern of the given language. Thus, although Navaho *i* (occurring only after consonants) and *y* (occurring only before vowels) are complementary in distribution, they are nevertheless independent phonemes because of the fact that Navaho is generally characterized by a sharp distinction between vowel and consonant. (As a matter of fact, any vowel would be found to be in complementary distribution to almost any consonant.) In another language, non-syllabic and syllabic *i* might be positional variants of the same phoneme.

Throughout the phonemic study of a language, one may frequently employ with profit:

6. *The test of substitution.* This consists in pronouncing a word with some modification in one of the phonemes. If the modification cannot be perceived by a native, it is within the range of normal deviation. If the modification seems to trouble the native, it is an extreme deviation from the norm, a distortion. If the native definitely hears some other word or feels that one has the word wrong, one may conclude that the modification has amounted to the substitution of one phoneme for another.

Since the phonemic facts may be dependent on position in the word and the sentence, it is necessary always to determine the limits of the word and the sentence and the phonetic and phonemic peculiarities of the word and the sentence as units.

Discovering the phonemes is the first step in the phonemic study of a language. The second step consists in defining the nature of each phoneme in terms of (1) its norm and range of deviation for each position in which it may occur; (2) its positional distribution. One may also study its frequency, though this is somewhat less essential. Finally, it is necessary to study the phonemic system in its totality to find the significant classes, sub-classes, and cross-classes into which the phonemes fall.

ORTHOGRAPHY

A phonemic orthography provides the most adequate, economical, and effective method of writing a language. Morphological and grammatical study of a language and the recording of its conclusions looks to orthography as an instrument of fundamental importance. A phonemic alphabet is the only kind that is truly adequate, for it alone represents all the pertinent facts and only the pertinent facts. Each sign in a phonemic alphabet represents one phoneme, and the implicit or explicit definition of each sign is an account of the norms (and deviations) of the phoneme in the various positions in which it may occur. If the writing is entirely in keeping with the phonemics of the language, a mechanical substitution of the values of the signs for the signs will reproduce the recorded forms correctly and completely.

Even in the problem of phonemics itself, orthography is a valuable technique. Indeed, the problem of ascertaining the phonemes of a language may be stated in large part in terms of the devising and defining of a set of symbols that will represent the sounds of the language most adequately and most economically. The test of an adequate phonemic writing is that it be possible for one who does not know the meaning of the words to read them off correctly and without serious distortions (it is assumed in this that the reader has made himself familiar with the key to the system and that he has learned to produce the required sounds). The test of an economical phonemic writing is that it employ as few and as simple signs as possible. However, these tests are insufficient in some details of the choice of signs for sound-types of complementary distribution; this matter is explained above, p. 123 [35-36] (criterion 4).

Where convenient, the phonemic symbols should be made to reflect the phonemic pattern by having some point of resemblance in the signs for the members of each class of phonemes;[8] such a situation is attained in part when some diacritical mark is used to represent a given feature of differentiation, e.g., Hungarian *í, ű, ú, é, ő, ó, á* (long vowels)[9], Chitimacha *p', t', k', č, c, w', y', m', n', ŋ'* (glottalized consonants). Finally, it is important that the symbols be in general accord with those generally in use, except that this consideration is secondary to the two essentials of accuracy and simplicity.

Since the phonemes of different languages are different as to their norms and even more strikingly so as to their positional variants, one might argue that it is necessary to have different symbols for each new language, that the English voiceless labial stop, for example, be written differently from that of French. It is obvious that such a treatment would make linguistic science extremely difficult. It has therefore become conventional to use the same or similar signs in different languages to represent roughly similar phonemes. This method works out perfectly as long as one does not carelessly assume standard or familiar values for given signs wherever they occur.

NORMALIZATION

When two or more forms of a word are both correct, two courses are possible, namely, to record the form employed at each given time, or to always write one of the variants. The latter treatment is called normalization. In the case of particular word-variants, normalization would have to be entirely arbitrary and is therefore to be avoided. In the case of

optional general variants,[10] it is usually possible to normalize without obscuring the fact of variation. This is possible when one can so define one's symbols that the affected phonemes in such a variation are readable in two ways. For example, one may write *äz yu* for English 'as you', and indicate as part of the definition of the symbol *z* that before *y* it may have the value *ž*, the *y* being sometimes then lost; to be complete one may indicate that the variation is usually a function of speed and care of speech, the series being *äz yu, äž yu, äžu* (not to speak of *äžə*). Similarly, in the case of phonemic interchange, one may write the distinctive form and mention the interchange in the definition of the phonemic symbol.

PHONETICS

Phonetics (the science of the study of speech sounds) benefits the student of phonemics in two ways. First, it is valuable in the discovery of the phonemes of a foreign language. Secondly, it provides the technique for study and description of the phonemes once they are known.

At the outset of one's study of a foreign language, it is convenient to make a phonetic record based on aural observation and written in terms of a general phonetic alphabet which provides symbols for selected characteristic points in the total range of possible speech sounds. As one continues to work with a language, one replaces the strict phonetic alphabet with a tentative phonemic alphabet which is then corrected from time to time until one arrives at a final, adequate phonemic orthography. A certain number of linguists feel that a phonetic orthography is in itself sufficient, and some even hold that a phonemic orthography is incorrect. However, as I have shown, a phonemic writing (together with its key giving the value of the signs employed) records all the pertinent phonetic facts. A phonetic writing, on the other hand, is lacking in the following ways:

1. It does not indicate the phonetic units that are significant for the given language.
2. It is overly microscopic, complex, and hard to handle.

---

[8]An ideal working out of this principle would give us a phonemic "visible speech" in which each phonemic sign would be a composite of elements each of which would represent one of the class, subclass, and cross-class differentiae or sets of differentiae of the phoneme. However, such an orthography might prove impractical for other reasons.

[9]*ű* and *ő* represent long *ü* and *ö* respectively.

[10]See pp. 118-119 [p. 33].

3. It does not distinguish errors and distortions from normal forms.

4. It is likely to be phonetically inaccurate.

On the last point, I quote Bloomfield who says (*Language* 84−85):

Practical phoneticians sometimes acquire great virtuosity in discriminating and reproducing all manner of strange sounds. In this, to be sure, there lies some danger for linguistic work. Having learned to discriminate many kinds of sounds, the phonetician may turn to some language, new or familiar, and insist on recording all the distinctions he has learned to discriminate, even when in this language they are nondistinctive and have no bearing whatever. . . . The chief objection to this procedure is its inconsistency. The phonetician's equipment is personal and accidental; he hears those acoustic features which are discriminated in the languages he has observed. Even his most "exact" record is bound to ignore innumerable non-distinctive features of sound; the ones that appear in it are selected by accidental and personal factors. There is no objection to a linguist's describing all the acoustic features that he can hear, provided he does not confuse these with the phonemic features. He should remember that his hearing of non-distinctive features depends upon the accident of his personal equipment, and that his most elaborate account cannot remotely approach the value of a mechanical record.

Furthermore, in the extreme concentration required for minute discrimination of certain features of sound, the phonetician may easily overlook other features that may be of prime importance in the given language.

Some linguists employ a normative phonetic writing in preference to either phonemic or strict phonetic writing. If the interpretation of actual sounds in terms of the norms of the language is correct and if the correction of errors is made without error, a normative phonetic orthography shares some of the advantage of a phonemic orthography. Simplification of the phonetic writing of a given language is also an improvement in the general direction of phonemic writing. As a matter of fact a phonemic orthography is the inevitable result if normalization and simplification are carried out thoroughly, consistently, and correctly.

HISTORICAL PHONOLOGY

In determining the phonemic system of a language, only phonetic data are relevant. Historical phonology is not relevant. To base one's spelling of a word on the form of the word in a known or reconstructed parent language neither benefits historical study of language nor provides a dependable method of accurate phonemic analysis. Historical etymology in a matter of phonemics is an acceptable aid only when one is dealing with an inadequately recorded non-contemporary language. Of course, phonemes are a historical product and a step in a historical development, but to argue from phonetic law to descriptive fact is discovering the arguments from the conclusion when the procedure should always be the opposite.

The fact that a phonemic system is a step in historical development suggests that one way to understand historical change is to understand phonemics more fully.[11] On the basis of facts pointed out in this paper and on the basis of some simple truths about historical phonetic change, one may make the following suggestions. Phonetic change must consist in the change of the norm of a sound or one of its positional variants. Change in a phonemic norm does not affect the actual phonemic pattern unless the phoneme thereby comes to coincide with some other phoneme or splits up into more than one phoneme. The intermediate step in coalescence of phonemes is the condition of phonemic interchange. The intermediate step in the split-up of a phoneme is the presence of markedly different positional variants; in this situation, if, through analogy or borrowing of foreign words one of the variants comes to be employed in positions other than within its original limits, it takes on the character of an independent phoneme. I shall not illustrate these processes, since the matter is only incidental to my subject; instances are

---

[11]This important incidental value of phonemics was called to my attention by Professor Sapir.

to be found everywhere where we have an actual record of a historical change.

MORPHO-PHONOLOGY

Morpho-phonology includes, in addition to the study of the phonemic structure of morphemes, the study of interchange between phonemes as a morphologic process. If a given morphologic interchange is sufficiently regular and characteristic, the interchanging phonemes may be regarded as a morphologically unitary set. Examples are Indo-European *e/o/ē/ō/*zero, English *f/v* (in, e.g., *leaf, leaves*). Whether it is a convenient fiction or a true reflection of linguistic psychology, morphological processes are usually described as having a definite order. *Leaves* is taken to be a secondary formation from *leaf*, and in consequence *v* is the mutation of *f* and not *f* that of *v*. But *f* does not always change to *v* in the morphological process of plural formation; thus, we have *cuff, cuffs*. The *f* of *cuff* is therefore morphologically different from the *f* of *leaf*, though phonemically it is the same entity. Morphologically, we have two *f*'s so that $f_1 : v :: f_2 : f$. Morphologically distinct phonemes are called morpho-phonemes.

A morpho-phoneme is one of a class of like phonemes considered as components of actual morphemes which behave alike morphologically, i.e., have a like place in the same mutation series. The morpho-phoneme is never to be confused with the phoneme as such, even in the event that all instances of a given phoneme are members of the same morpho-phonemic class. One may devise a morphologic writing for use in morphological discussion or in a dictionary, but such a writing is not to be employed in ordinary linguistic records.[12]

The phonemic principle when properly understood provides the only completely consistent and adequate method of understanding the nature of the phonetics of a given language. Phonetics provides the technique of discovering and defining the phonemes. Morphology includes a study of the phonemic structure of morphemes and of morphological interrelations among phonemes as components of morphemes. Historical phonology studies the evolution of phonemes. In these ways phonemics interrelates with other phases of linguistic science, but it does not compete with these other phases. In developing the phonemic principle, its proponents are only bringing into plain view a hitherto imperfectly lighted area in which there has always been a certain amount of stumbling.

[12] Of course there are instances where it is desirable to use non-phonemic diacritical marks as a special aid to non-native students.

BIBLIOGRAPHY 2
History of the Phoneme

SWEET, H. (1877) *A Handbook of Phonetics*

KRUSZEWSKY, M. (1881) *Über die Lautab-wechslung*

BAUDOUIN DE COURTENAY, J. (1894) *Próba teorji alternacyj fonetycznych*

—————— (1895) *Versuch einer Theorie phonetischer Alternationen*

SWEET, H. (1900) *The Practical Study of Languages*

SIEVERS, E. (1901) *Grundzüge der Phonetik*, 5th ed.

ŠČERBA, L. V. (1911) *Court exposé de la prononciation russe*

—————— (1912) *Russkie glasnye v kačestvennom i količestvennom otnošenii*

JESPERSEN, O. (1912) *Lehrbuch der Phonetik*, 2d ed.

PASSY, P. (1912) *Petite phonétique comparée*

AREND, Z. M. (1934) "Baudouin de Courtenay and the Phoneme Idea"

FIRTH, J. R. (1934) "The Word 'Phoneme'"

ABERCROMBIE, D. (1949) "Forgotten Phoneticians"

JONES, D. (1957) *The History and Meaning of the Term "Phoneme"*

JAKOBSON, R. (1966) "Henry Sweet's Paths Toward Phonemics"

4

TWADDELL
ON DEFINING
THE PHONEME
Language Monograph No. 16*
MORRIS SWADESH

Twaddell examines previous definitions of the phoneme, all of which he finds "open to serious if not unanswerable objection" (*Language Monograph* 16.33), and then offers a definition, or rather a procedure of definition, of his own. Of his criticism of particular definitions, much, but far from all, seems apt. His own definition is carefully grounded and explicit, but establishes a concept which is not the phoneme and which, in my estimation, is not likely in its present form to serve any important scientific function.

Twaddell classifies previous definitions of the phoneme into two groups, namely, those that regard it as a mental reality, and those that regard it as a physical reality. He himself considers it preferable to regard it as a convenient "abstractional, fictitious unit" (33). The somewhat round-about procedure which this entails would be justifiable only if there were no simpler, theoretically sound approach. Thus Twaddell must deal with a fictitious unit to which correspond fractions of phonetic events or utterances. These (fractional) phonetic events can just as well be regarded as instances of a type or members of a class (see my paper, "The Phonemic Principle" [3], *Language* 10.117 [32] ff.). We need only to recognize the class of all fractional phonetic events that have certain phonetic and distributional characteristics as contrasted with other classes in the same language. The phoneme *p* of English, for example, is the class of all the recurrent fractional phonetic events in English speech which are characterized by lip-closure

as opposed to other articulations, of voicelessness as contrasted with voicing, of relatively fortis as opposed to relatively lenis articulation, and, in certain definable positions, of aspirated as contrasted with unaspirated release. The phoneme is to be defined as an elemental type of speech sound in a given language (see *Language* 10.118 [32]); and the characteristics of the type are to be described in terms of (1) a norm or a positionally conditioned set of norms and (2) the range of deviation from the norm or norms, as measured in a representative sampling of occurrences of the type. Practical limitation of instruments of observation may restrict the exactness with which the measurements may be carried out; but, even if measurement must depend on aural impression alone, it is always desirable to think of the phonemes in terms of norms and ranges of deviation.

The fact that a class is called a fiction in nominalist-realist philosophy does not bear on our problem, because even those who call classes fictions recognize them to be fictions of a different kind from fictitious entities.

A definition of the phoneme on the basis of its phonetic characteristics must take into account the fact that it sometimes has positionally limited variants which differ from each other. In his chapter on "The Phoneme as a Physical Reality" Twaddell points out two kinds of definitions of the phoneme, which represent two different methods of dealing with the matter of positional variants: (1) as a constant characteristic feature that distin-

*Reprinted from *Language* 11.244–250 (1935) by permission.

guishes the sounds in question from others, (2) as the sum of all the speech-sounds in question. Bloomfield employs the first definition, Jones the second. Bloomfield is criticised mainly for looking to the future development of laboratory phonetics to find the distinctive features of the phoneme. Twaddell contends that the laboratory is already able to record all frequencies within the range in which fall the acoustic elements essential for communication, and that it has not found any characteristics in the sound waves which identify all occurrences of a given phoneme. I am unable to pass judgment on this phase of the argument, but it seems to me that a possible error in methodology (looking to acoustic instead of, or in addition to, articulatory data) does not invalidate the theory as represented in the definition. On the other hand, I believe that Bloomfield's theory is weakened by not recognizing, or seeming not to recognize, all the characteristics of the phoneme including those that occur only in some of the positions in which the phoneme occurs. Let us consider an imaginary case, which is yet not too different from actual quotable cases. Suppose we find in some language:

In open syllables: [i], [e], [ɛ]
In closed syllables: [ɪ], [ɛ], [æ]

If this summarizes all the pertinent data, a correct theory should require the recognition of just three phonemes:

	Norm in open syll.	Norm in closed syll.
(a)	[i]	[ɪ]
(b)	[e]	[ɛ]
(c)	[ɛ]	[æ]

If, as Bloomfield says, a phoneme is a distinctive feature of sound, it might be difficult to find a distinctive feature in [i] and [ɪ] that is not balanced by the similarity of [e] and [ɪ]; and it would be impossible to say that the [ɛ] of phoneme b has a feature of sound in common with [e] that it does not have in common with the [ɛ] of phoneme c. The difficulty is avoided by defining the phoneme as a type which may have more than one norm, provided that no more than one of these norms belongs to any one given position of occurrence (defined, e.g., in terms of place in the word, type of syllable, neighboring phonemes).

Jones' definition, Twaddell finds, has the shortcoming that it is unable to place a sound which has resemblance to two others, with both of which it is in complementary distribution. I have proposed a criterion for dealing with such cases: "If the distribution of a type of sound is complementary to two others, it is to be identified with one rather than the other, if there is a more definite phonetic similarity in that direction. . . . If a sound in a relation of complementary distribution to two sounds is not particularly similar to either of them, it has to be reckoned as phonemically **independent**" (*Language* 10.124 [36]). To illustrate the first part of this rule, I use the example of the *p* of *spill,* which is in complementary distribution to both *p* and *b,* but which is phonetically more similar to the former. Twaddell quotes this example and argues that the *p* of *spill,* being voiceless, lenis, unaspirated, is just as similar to the *b* of *bill* (voiced, lenis, unaspirated) as it is to the *p* of *upper* (voiceless, fortis, unaspirated). This would be true if the degree of articulatory strength were the same in both the *p* of *spill* and the *b* of *bill.* This is doubtless the case in some pronunciations of the two words, but the qualitative and quantitative value of a phonetic type is to be determined only on the basis of a representative sampling of utterances in terms of a norm and range of deviation. Now the strength of articulation of the *p* of *spill* has its norm near but not at the same point as that of *b;* some of the occurrences are certainly the same in the matter of articulatory strength as some of those of *b,* but the range of deviation is clearly in the other direction (especially in careful or emphatic speech). If this were not true and if the question of pattern congruity were not involved, then the sound in question would have to be considered phonemically independent. I may add here that it is my experience that states of perfect balance, where a sound falls phonetically exactly between two others with which it is in complementary distribution, are rare. Twaddell finds a set of such cases in the vowels before *r* in his dialect of English. If in terms of their norms and ranges of deviation, the phonetic resemblance of the given vowels is ambiguous, then they illustrate a rare, but not unknown, phenomenon which should not disturb a soundly formulated phonemic theory.

At this point it is necessary to add some

data (pointed out to me by Dr. S. S. Newman) regarding the *p* and *b* phonemes which I overlooked in writing my paper. This oversight was unfortunate because the facts are actually such as to take the *p* of *spill* entirely out of the realm of difficult cases—unwittingly I have put Twaddell to the trouble of discussing as an instance of arbitrary procedure what is actually as clear-cut a case as say the assignment of the *s* of *spill* to the *s* phoneme. Twaddell's discussion and mine up to this point is on the basis of the assumption that the nearest related proven variety of the *p* phoneme is that illustrated in *upper*. Actually, we have contrasts like *respect* : *asbestos* which show us the same sound as that of *spill* in actual contrast with the same sound as that of *bill*.

Twaddell also criticises my criterion of pattern congruity, saying it involves a circularity. I submit that any scientific procedure that aims at finding the elements of a closed system is valid only if it takes into account the totality of the system. The preferred theory is the simplest theory that takes into accurate account all the pertinent data, and the simplest theory of the phonemic system of a language is necessarily one formulated in terms of the total pattern.

The term phoneme has been used by a few linguists to refer to what I should call the psychological correlate of the phoneme, but this type of definition has been losing ground; thus: "the Cercle linguistique de Prague, which in 1929 defined phonemes as 'images acoustico-motrices,' in 1931 shifts the emphasis to a functional characterization" (Twaddell 16). Twaddell gives several instances of the definition of the phoneme as a psychological entity and criticises them by pointing out (recapitulating Bloomfield) that "such a definition is invalid because (1) we have no right to guess about the working of an inaccessible 'mind', and (2) we can secure no advantage from such guesses."

In the same chapter, called "The Phoneme as a Mental or Psychological Reality," Twaddell mentions functional definitions of the phoneme (e.g., Mathesius: "Laute die in dem analysierten System funktionelle Geltung haben" or Sapir: "unité qui a une signification fonctionelle dans la forme ou le système rigidement déterminés des sons propres à une langue"). These definitions do not represent the phoneme as a mental entity. Twaddell does not offer any specific criticism of them, unless he feels that his remarks on psychological-reality definitions cover them, too. He discusses Sapir's writings, but I gather that his criticism here depends on the misunderstanding that the phoneme is a mental entity for Sapir. But Sapir has never defined the phoneme as something in the mind of the speaker, although he has frequently stressed the psychological importance of the phoneme and has consequently used such expressions as "the intuitively felt," "the mind of the speaker," etc. Certainly, if the phoneme has to do with speech and language, which are part of the life of the individual, then it is to be inferred that there is something in the psychology of the individual that corresponds to the phoneme. It is the purpose of Sapir's paper, "La réalité psychologique des phonèmes" [2], to give evidence derived from his experience (not "experiments" as Twaddell erroneously translates) showing that the behavior of native speakers of a language proves a psychological reality for the phoneme (this is not the same as saying the phoneme is a psychological reality). Sapir's line of argument may be stated thus: (1) if the native reacts similarly in response to objectively different stimuli, then these objectively different stimuli are somehow the same for him (see anecdotes 1, 4, and 5); (2) if a phonetically untrained native reacts differently to stimuli which are not objectively different (anecdote 2), or which are objectively only slightly different (anecdote 3), they are somehow different for him. Aside from anecdote 2, which seems actually to demonstrate a morpho-phonemic rather than a phonemic difference, the argument is completely convincing.

My discussion so far shows that some definitions of the phoneme are not "open to serious if not unanswerable objection." It follows, then, that there is not the absolute need for a new approach to the problem which Twaddell represents. We should still appreciate any improvement in the formulation, even if it involves a radical change; but Twaddell's procedure involves two fundamental weaknesses, both of which detract seriously from its possible value.

Twaddell sets up two entities to replace the phoneme. The *micro-phoneme* is "the term of any minimum phonological difference among forms" (e.g., that which in *pit* is different from the corresponding fraction of *bit*). The *macro-phoneme* is "the sum of all similarly ordered terms (micro-phonemes) of similar minimum phonological differences among forms" (e.g., if *pit* : *bit* :: *sop* : *sob,* then both *p*'s taken together with the *p*'s of all possible similar sets of words constitute a macro-phoneme, and similarly the *b*'s).

The definition of the micro-phoneme seems to lack an explicit principle for determining how large a phonetic fraction is to be considered. Perhaps the reference to "minimum phonological difference" is intended to indicate the unit that is to be taken to arrive at the micro-phoneme, but it seems to me that "minimum phonologic difference" is one thing that a phonemic theory has to define. In the absence of a principle for determining the size of the phonetic fraction to be considered, we are not prevented from making such a comparison as *pit* : *bet* and arriving at the micro-phonemes [pɩ] : [bɛ], or even *apple* : *staple* giving as micro-phonemes [æ] : [ste]. Less obvious difficulties arise even in such examples as Twaddell quotes. He is obviously thinking in terms of the generally accepted phonemic analysis of his forms. If he did not have this analysis in advance and had to use a tentative phonetic analysis, he would find himself facing the difficulty that the micro-phonemic analysis of a word would differ according to the set of minimally different forms in which he considered it. Thus, using a rough phonetic analysis ([h] represents aspiration, [R] and [L] = voiceless *r* and *l*, [k̂] and [ĝ] = fronted *k* and *g*):

kill [k̂hɩ] : *gill* [ĝɩ] : *skill* [sk̂ɩ] : *hill* [hɩ] shows [k̂h] : [ĝ] : [sk̂] : [h]

kill : *pill* [phɩ] : *till* [thɩ] : *hill* shows [k̂] : [p] : [t] : zero

kill : *cool* [khul] shows [k̂hɩ] : [khu] or [k̂ . . ɩ] : [k . . u]

kick [k̂hɩk] : *crick* [kRɩk] : *click* [kLɩk] shows [k̂h] : [kR] : [kL]

pay [pheɩ] : *pray* [pReɩ] : *play* [pLeɩ] shows [h] : [R] : [L]

The phonetic analysis employed above is a rough one, but the difficulties would only be greater if a more exact phonetic analysis were used. Consistent results can be obtained only if there is an explicit and satisfactory method of determining what fractions are to be considered. That method could not well be other than to take as a criterion simplicity of total formulation (the simplest adequate account of all the pertinent phenomena is the preferred one).

The weakness in Twaddell's macro-phoneme is its failure to recognize phonetic similarity as a criterion. It is well to stress the importance of relative rather than absolute phonetics. It is well to insist on the essential nature of systematic gaps of distribution (e.g., that a form like **seeng* does not exist and would not fit into the English phonemic pattern). But any phonemic theory that fails to recognize the similarity between *sing* and *sin,* and the fact that this similarity is greater than that between *sing* and *seen,* loses much and gains nothing. Twaddell's theory would declare as different: the vowels of *sing* and *sin,* of *length* and *Len,* of *long* and *lawn,* of *sung* and *sun,* of *sang* and *man,* the *s*'s of *still* and *sill,* the *t*'s of *gust* and *gut,* the *r*'s of *tray* and *buttress* (the latter contrasts with *l,* as in *butler,* the former cannot contrast with *l*), etc., etc., etc. It is hard to imagine where such a theory would lead one. In emphasizing the importance of systematic gaps of distribution, it fails to recognize the systematic nature of phonetic resemblances.

5

ON VARIOUS PHONEMES*
W. F. TWADDELL

Morris Swadesh, in *Language* 11.244–250 [4], has subjected my monograph, "On Defining the Phoneme," to a thorough and penetrating review. He has quite properly omitted useless repetitions in points upon which we patently agree, and has devoted himself to an exposition of points of disagreement. I hope it will not be interpreted as incorrigible obstinacy if I attempt to stand my ground on many of the points at issue, particularly those in which I believe Swadesh's criticisms might lead to misinterpretations of my true position. The presentation of rebuttals is complicated by the technique which Swadesh occasionally uses: an inadequate presentation of my position, confronted by an authoritarian repetition of his own earlier pronouncements with little or no additional arguments to support them, e.g., on a positive vs. fictional phoneme, on the *p*'s of *speech* and *spill,* and on "pattern congruity."

Swadesh notes (245) [41] that my definition "establishes a concept which is not the phoneme and which, in my estimation, is not likely in its present form to serve any important scientific function." On the first point, I believe I enjoy the distinction of being the only writer on the subject who is not convinced that his own particular phoneme is the phoneme; cf. Monogr. 52. On the second point let us take a specific case: Swadesh (246) [42] sets up a language in which we find "in open syllables: [i, e, ε]; in closed syllables: [ɩ, ε, æ]. If this summarizes all the pertinent data, a correct theory should require the recognition of just three phonemes:

	Norm in open syll.	Norm in closed syll.
(a)	[i]	[ɩ]
(b)	[e]	[ε]
(c)	[ε]	[æ]"

Now it is clear that according to the principles expounded in my monograph (46ff.), this and only this required arrangement must be arrived at, since the differential relations of the two classes of vowels are similar and in a one-to-one relation. Swadesh's own methods, however, cannot possibly lead to this arrangement. He has written (*Language* 10.123 [3.36]): "If the distribution of one type of sound is complementary to that of more than one other, it is to be identified with one rather than the other if there is a more definite phonetic similarity in that direction." The distribution of [ε] in closed syllables is obviously complementary to that of [i] and [e] and [ε] in open syllables. Swadesh must now search for a "definite phonetic similarity." And he will have no choice: he must combine the closed-syllable [ε] of phoneme (b) with the open-syllable [ε] of phoneme (c), on his principle of phonetic similarity. If a phoneme definition is to be judged by its success in this example of Swadesh's, I hint, as unobjectionably as possible, that mine "serves that scientific function," and his does not.

In his general discussion of the phoneme (245) [41], I miss any attempt on Swadesh's part to defend his purely verbal, dictionary type of definition as against a procedural or operational definition. It seems to me beyond question that a useful definition will not merely mark off the phoneme in general from a taxeme or a morpheme, but will identify a given phoneme as such when it has been discovered or determined. A phoneme is not merely different from a morpheme, it is different from another phoneme. Swadesh's definition ("an elemental type of speech sound in a given language") does not specify the nature of that difference; mine, I believe, does.

Swadesh writes at some length (247f.)

*Reprinted from *Language* 12.53–59 (1936) by permission.

[42f.] on the disposal of the stop in *spill* as a variant norm of his *p*-phoneme. I may say that my discussion of this point in the monograph (30f.) was entirely within the frame of the data supplied by Swadesh in his earlier writing. Swadesh now wishes to adduce two further considerations to justify his combining the stops of *pill* and *spill* in a single phoneme: (1) The stop of *spill* isn't after all quite so weakly articulated as a [b], though in some cases it may be. (2) S. S. Newman has discovered that the contrast of *respect/asbestos* indicates that a differentiation of [p]/[b] after [s] does exist in American English. On the first point, I see no importance in this new attitude toward the strength of articulation. Swadesh still admits that, on his principle of phonetic similarity, the stop of *spill* resembles a [b] with respect to strength of articulation. With respect to aspiration, the same is true. His phonetic similarity between the stops of *pill* and *spill* is as before in the single category of voice. The contrast of *respect/asbestos* is not clear to me. Are we to understand Swadesh as asserting that in these words the [p] and the [b] occur in similar phonetic contexts? The radical differences in accentual pattern and syllable division make it inconceivable that the two environments should be regarded as identical. Further, the pronunciation of *asbestos* (as a popular word) with a definitely voiced sibilant, as soon as the pattern approaches that of *respect,* is worth pondering.

In this connection, Swadesh observes (247) [42]: "I may add here that it is my experience that states of perfect balance, where a sound falls phonetically exactly between two others . . . , are rare." The turn of phrase here illustrates, I believe, a basic unstated assumption of Swadesh's: that phonetic similarity is one-dimensional and absolute, that precise degrees of phonetic similarity or difference can be objectively determined and unambiguously indicated by points on a straight line. Only in terms of some such unconscious assumption could one speak of a sound as falling "phonetically exactly between two others." Phonetic similarity is a complex of many factors, not immediately comparable with one another; much depends upon the selection of one particular dimension in which similarity is to be found; and that selection must in some cases be arbitrary. This basic assumption

weakens, I believe, Swadesh's criterion of phonetic similarity as a sovereign solution of problems in phoneme distribution, quite apart from the disastrous results of its application to his hypothetical language above. Further, we are not here concerned with hypothetical cases of "perfect balance," but with certain actual cases in which phonetic similarity is not decisively in the one direction or the other. If one cannot measure precisely, a lack of decisive similarity prevents a solution on Swadesh's principle just as effectively as a "perfect balance."

In Swadesh's defense of his "criterion of pattern congruity" (248) [43], I miss any attempt to justify the assumption that there is an a priori phonemic system or pattern. Until he establishes such a system as existent, and existent apart from the phonemic relations, I must continue to regard his "criterion of pattern congruity" a dangerously circular one to apply in the determination of particular phonemic relations.

Swadesh remarks (248) [43] of certain functional definitions: "Twaddell does not offer any specific criticism of them, unless he feels that his remarks on psychological-reality definitions cover them, too." It may be proper to note that the final paragraph of Monogr. 15 indicates that I do so feel.

Of Swadesh's defense of Sapir, there is little I can say, except to state that I cannot interpret Sapir's recent writings on this and related subjects other than as indicating a conviction that psychological realities are pertinent to the study of linguistics, that phonemes can be demonstrated if not determined on psychological grounds, that phonemes co-exist in mental series, as a "feeling in the bones." If I misinterpret him, it is without malice.

Swadesh's objections (249) [44] to the failure explicitly to justify the term "minimum" are, I believe, well taken. I hoped it would be clear to those interested in the phoneme who might read the discussion that what was there presented as a straight-line development would inevitably, in practical work, be accomplished only at the cost of considerable trial and error. Swadesh properly notes that it would be possible, taking such a series as *apple, staple, grapple, nipple, supple,* etc., to arrive at a class of microphonemes [æ, ste, græ, nɪ, sʌ], etc. Of course, such a series might be useful,

e.g., from a morphological point of view. But I should have made it clear that I was concerned with the totality of American English forms, not merely those ending in [pəl]. The possibility of regarding [pɪ/bɛ] as a minimum difference (between *pit* and *bet*) is of course removed as soon as one discovers the forms *pet* and *bit;* cf. Monogr. 43.

The ingenious table which Swadesh presents (250) [44] is quite another matter. Here Swadesh represents me as advocating starting in the middle of my procedure and working both ways at once. A careful rereading of the monograph reveals to me no justification for ascribing to me any principle which could produce such an assemblage of the irrelevant and misleading. If one restricted one's attention to the series *kill: till: pill: hill,* one could arrive at alternative microphonemic classes [kh], [th], [ph], [h] or [k], [t], [p], zero. But I find it hard to imagine any linguist working with quite so narrow a universe of discourse; and the addition of the form *ill* at once rules out the second alternative. One would, I assumed, record the forms as accurately as possible; then, working with these and a multitude of other forms, one would discover no significant differentiations [l/L], [r/R], [k̂/k], [kh/k], etc. It may be pointed out that the only real difficulty presented by Swadesh's table arises in the group *kill: skill;* and there one must query the a priori assumptions—on the basis, probably, of "phonetic similarity"—(1) that the aspiration of [k] in *kill* is identical with the glottal fricative in *hill,* and (2) that the '[k]' of *skill* is identical with the [k] of *kill,* except for the aspiration.

It is natural that Swadesh should find (250) [44] that "the weakness in Twaddell's macro-phoneme is its failure to recognize phonetic similarity as a criterion." It is also natural, and perhaps pardonable, that I should find the strength in my suggested procedure precisely in its substitution of a principle of differential correspondences for the earlier reliance upon an undefined and indeterminable (and sometimes misleading) entity, "phonetic similarity." All of us are agreed, for example, that from *pin/tin* we may deduce a phonemic differentiation [p-]/[t-]; from *nip/nit* a phonemic differentiation [-p]/[-t]. How can [p-] and [-p], or [t-] and [-t], be brought into relation with each other? The earlier procedure has

been to say that they must be identical, that the intuition of phonetic similarity is overwhelming. That intuition may or may not be "correct"; the fact remains that an intuition has no business in a science, if we can get along without it. Until a positive unit of phonetic similarity emerges from the laboratory, I can see no better criterion for phoneme grouping than that of differential correspondence.

Swadesh summarizes (250) [44]: "Twaddell's theory would declare as different: the vowels of *sing* and *sin,* of *length* and *Len,* of *long* and *lawn,* of *sung* and *sun,* or *sang* and *man,* the *s*'s of *still* and *sill,* the *t*'s of *gust* and *gut,* the *r*'s of *tray* and *buttress* (the latter contrasts with *l* as in *butler,* the former cannot contrast with *l*), etc., etc., etc." I should be interested to know by what processes Swadesh arrived at some of the items in this list; but this is not the place for that discussion. It is not too much to say, however, that it is no "theory" of mine, but commonplace observation, which recognizes as different the vowels of *sing* and *sin.* The question is whether the phonemes involved should be identical, and whether a principle which recognizes the objective difference is necessarily weaker than one which ignores it. Swadesh finds it convenient so to define the phoneme that the difference is ignored; he can thus write a language with relatively few symbols. But for the study of the language, he will have to take into account just those differences which he has earlier chosen to ignore; where I have separate phonemes for *sing* and *sin,* he will later have to recognize two variant norms of his single phoneme, and where I have different phonemes for the stops of *pill* and *spill,* he will have one phoneme, but two variant norms. I cannot see that "simplicity of total formulation" (Swadesh 250 [44]) is overwhelmingly on one side or the other. I maintain that for some purposes it is convenient to regard the phonemes involved as different: *sin* is different from *seen,* a type of relation in which *sing* cannot participate, in the American English language. The example of *tray, buttress,* and *butler* involves again the factor of syllable division; Sapir's article (263 f.) [30] quoted by Swadesh, furnishes the proper clue here. On this basic issue Swadesh and I go separate ways; the reasons for my choice are outlined in the sixth section of my monograph; until Swadesh takes issue with that argument and refutes it, I can offer no further defense.

What Swadesh wants, I believe, is a set of some 30 to 60 units, "elemental types of speech sound," which can be combined in various ways to build up "words," "forms." Those units, those ultimate building-blocks, he wants to call phonemes. For him, they would be the elements of the language, since they are the elements of its forms; the forms would be secondary, derived complexes. The phonemes would be atoms, and the forms molecules. This is a respected approach, and adequately sanctioned, by tradition and wide acceptance. It leads to difficulties, as Chao has pointed out (*Bulletin of the Institute of History and Philology, Academia Sinica* 4.4.363–397); but it does good work, e.g., in establishing sanctions for transcription, providing a theory of phonetic change, etc.

But there is another point of view, explicitly presented by Jespersen almost a half century ago, and an organic development, I believe, of the essential core of truth in the Junggrammatiker doctrine. According to this view the smallest real unit in language is the form, preferably the free form, in Bloomfield's terminology. The free form or "word" stands, potentially autonomous and indivisible, as the object of study. When we dissect it, we find segments that are not linguistic—i.e., communicatory or expressive—units. Now a form is related, from the point of view of the phonetic events to which it corresponds, to many other forms of the language; the study of these relations (which must be differential, except for homonyms) is a study in which the entity I have defined may, I hope, be useful. For that kind of study we cannot operate with a minimum set of elemental constituent phonemes; we must have a specifically relational, abstractional unit, which is explicitly defined as the term of a relation. Only similarities in the relations can be valid; not phonetic similarity of the units themselves. If we are studying, say, the relation of older sister and younger brother, we cannot bring into that study only child John Smith, age 18, height 5′9″, weight

150, eyes brown, etc., merely because William Jones (who has an older sister) is aged 18, height 5′8″, weight 145, eyes brown, etc. The physiological similarity may be valid for statistics on military service, but has no significance in a study of sibling-relationships. Phonetic similarity is a valid criterion for some purposes; but in many fields of linguistics, the differential relation is crucially significant. *Sing* is an only child; *sin* has an older sister *seen*.

Swadesh concludes his review of my study: "In emphasizing the importance of systematic gaps of distribution, it fails to recognize the systematic nature of phonetic resemblances." To this there can be no reply beyond a request to those interested to read my study, with the further note that if the criticism were just, I should be expelled from the LSA.

Penultimately, I record my regret at giving the impression of translating (erroneously or otherwise) anything in Sapir's article as "experiments." That term I used as a not unduly dignified synonym for "incidents," "cases"— what Swadesh calls "anecdotes."

Finally, I recall that in the preparation of my monograph I was at considerable pains to say neither more nor less than I meant, and I hoped that those readers who had a real interest in the problem would by careful reading be able to discern my position. In some important respects I seem to have failed; I record my gratitude to Swadesh for indicating so clearly the points upon which I left my position unclear and open to misinterpretation, and for making it possible for me perhaps to correct some mistaken impressions.*

---

*Since early in October, Swadesh and I have been in correspondence on the issues raised in his review and my attempt at rebuttal above. Swadesh wishes to have two points here mentioned, in connection with the discussion: (1) He proposes not *absolute*, but *relative* phonetic similarity as a phonemic criterion, and now offers a more unambiguous statement: Micro-phonemes that, on the basis of their phonetic nature, occupy a like place in comparable series are equivalent. (2) He accepts "totality of forms" (introduced above) as a satisfactory basis for determining "minimum phonological difference among forms."

I.b

*The Early
Bloomfieldian
Era*

6

THE PHONEMIC INTERPRETATION OF LONG CONSONANTS*

MORRIS SWADESH

Is phonemic procedure arbitrary? It can be, but I submit that it need not be. If one defines a phoneme as "one of an exhaustive list of classes of sounds in a language,"[1] one admits an endless variety of treatments and the choice of one or another treatment is arbitrary. The ideal of exhaustiveness is not in itself sufficient to define a unique scientific procedure. But if we also take the ideals of simplicity and self-consistency, we have the basis for a non-arbitrary method, particularly in view of the essentially systematic nature of phonetic totalities. The aim of a phonemic analysis may then be stated as: the smallest number of elements having the largest number of permutations and the most systematic relationships. To attain this ideal, it is necessary to consider always the totality[2] of phenomena in the given language. A formulation as to any detail must be made on the basis of all pertinent and comparable data anywhere in the totality of the given phonetic system. In the present paper I propose to demonstrate this method in application to a selected type of phenomenon, long consonants, in different phonetic totalities.[3]

A rigorous definition of long consonants is not necessary for the present purpose. I include any consonantal sound involving the maintainance of essentially the same articulating position and mechanism for a relatively protracted time, being long by reference to other sounds in the same language. A phonetic feature which generally has to be considered is syllabic treatment, whether the long consonant goes with one syllable (is unisyllabic) or with two (is ambisyllabic).

---

[1]Y. R. Chao, "The Non-Uniqueness of Phonemic Solutions of Phonetic Systems" 367 (*Bull. of the Inst. of History and Philology, Academia Sinica,* 4.363–397). I do not wish to imply that Chao's definition is not justified; a definition must be broad to include the range of usage of this term, as was Chao's intention.

[2]The criterion of totality is mentioned by Twaddell ("On Various Phonemes") [5], *Language* 12.56 [47]. As I conceive totality, it involves material (sounds), permutations (combinations of sounds), and pattern (phonetic and permutational relationships of sounds).

[3]The material on which this paper is based was taken from my own experience and from that of colleagues, and in a few cases from printed sources. In practically all cases, I have had the opportunity

of checking the data with native informants. Colleagues to whom I am indebted include Prof. Sapir, Prof. Lipari, M. B. Emeneau, M. R. Haas, G. Herzog, J. Kepke, G. L. Trager, C. F. Voegelin. Printed sources which need to be mentioned specifically are: Trubetzkoy, "Die Konsonantensysteme der ostkaukasischen Sprachen," *Caucasica* 8.1 ff.; Voegelin, "Shawnee Phonemes," *Language* 11.23–37; Swadesh, "The Phonetics of Chitimacha," *Language* 10.345–362.

Forms are quoted in phonemic transcription, one symbol for each phoneme. The orthography is thus in terms of my conclusions regarding the phonetic system of each language, but I try to state all the pertinent phonetic and distributional facts in each case, and I trust the reader's judgment will not be influenced by my orthography. In the use of symbols, the aim was to follow general usage, but it was necessary to adapt the symbols to the requirements of the particular languages.

Since this paper was submitted there has appeared Trubetzkoy's "Die phonologischen Grundlagen der sogenannten 'Quantität' in den verschiedenen Sprachen," *Scritti in onore di Alfredo Trombetti* 155–174 (Milano, Ulrico Hoepli, 1936). In the main, the conclusions agree. My emphasis is on the relative nature of all phonemics (see my last paragraph). Trubetzkoy (170) says: "Bei den geminierten Konsonanten setzt die Zuordnung des Einsatzes und des Absatzes an verschiedene Silben (bezw. Moren) die gesonderte Existenz des Anfangs- und des Schlussteils voraus. Bei jenen 'langen' Konsonanten aber, die dieser Bedingung nicht entsprechen,

---

*Reprinted from *Language* 13.1–10 (1937) by permission.

As in other phonemic problems, word division often plays a part. In this connection, the word is considered as a phonetic rather than as a semantic unit. For our purposes, *Antarctic* is two words (say, an unstressed proclitic and a stressed nuclear word) in the speech of everyone who syllabifies *Ant-arc-tic,* in spite of the semantic unity of the whole. Syllable division is one of the most common marks of word division (cp. Eng. *cease taking* : *ceased aching* : *see stakes*), but is of course not universally significant. In Hungarian, word division does not affect syllabification in normal speech (e.g., *dobd el* is syllabified *dob-del*), but the word stress on the first syllable marks the beginning of each new word. In some languages, word division has very limited phonetic significance; in Nootka, for example, the only phonetic difference to be made is that there is more likely to be a pause between words than between syllables within the word.

It is to be expected that long consonants (or any other kind of phonetic complex) will have different phonemic status in different phonetic totalities. I have found the following phonemic types:

I. Phoneme variants
  1. Free variants
  2. Positional variants
II. Phonemically distinct entities
  A. Sequences of like phonemes
    1. Sequences of identical phonemes (geminate clusters)
    2. Sequences of homorganic but not identical clusters
  B. Distinct unit phonemes.

Not uncommonly, the same language has long consonants of different phonemic types; for example, English has long consonants both as

positional variants and as geminate clusters, the two types being, nevertheless, completely distinct as to position and syllabic treatment.

I LONG CONSONANTS
AS PHONEME VARIANTS

It is a usual thing for phonemes to vary in length according to manner and tempo of speech. Free length variation of this type is identifiable by the fact that all the utterances are homonymous to natives. Sometimes such free variation applies more characteristically to consonants in certain positions. For instance, in Navaho, an intervocalic stop consonant after a short vowel, as *g* in *ƚigai* 'it is white', may be quite long, though it is often no longer than stops in other positions. Another interesting case occurs in Finnish, where syllabically final consonants in the initial syllable of the word, e.g., *k* in *üksi* 'one', may be quite long in slow speech. Incidentally, syllabic final consonants in Finnish are more fortis than syllabic initial ones.

Positionally conditioned length variants are illustrated in English liquids and nasals. The long variants occur in final position, e.g., *šə'n* (shun), *wɔ'r* (war), and before final voiced consonants, e.g., *šə'nd* (shunned), *wɔ'rd* (warred, ward), and the short variants occur in other positions, including the position before final voiceless consonants, e.g., *šə'nt* (shunt), *wɔ'rt* (wart). That the long consonants are not distinct phonemic entities, either single phonemes or phoneme combinations, is evident from the fact that there is no position within the word in which more than one type of liquid or nasal has to be recognized. The variation is parallel to and related with the length variation of vowels seen in *ple'* (play), *ple'd* (played), *ple't* (plate).

In Swedish, consonant length is bound up with vowel length. Both phenomena occur only in syllables having primary or secondary stress. Long consonants occur only immediately after short stressed vowels, which are in turn limited to this position. Long stressed vowels occur before short consonants and in final position. Examples[4] with stressed short

___

können Einsatz und Absatz nicht als verschiedene Punkte, sondern nur als ein Ganzes gewertet werden." Such rules, it seems to me, cannot have general validity. There will be phonetic systems in which they are contradicted. I also cannot agree with Trubetzkoy's conclusion (173) that quantity as such plays no part in phonemics. If "das Sprachgebilde ist ja zeitlos," then it cannot have syllabic division or distinction between beginning and end of sounds. And if it has not the phonetic feature of duration, then must it not also lack every other phonetic feature, including intensity, which Trubetzkoy does recognize? That length does not ordinarily occur as the sole phonetic differentia, I recognize.

[4]Raised ¹ indicates primary stress with falling pitch, ² indicates primary stress with rising pitch, · indicates secondary stress. Stress mark after the vowel indicates that the vowel is long, stress mark after the first post-vocalic consonant indicates that the vowel is short and the consonant long.

vowel followed by long consonant: *kat¹* 'cat', *hŭg²a* 'to chop', *fas¹t* 'fast', *bin²da* 'to bind', *ar²m ban·d* 'bracelet'; examples with long stressed vowel in final position or followed by short consonant: *se¹* 'to see', *tvo¹* 'two', *ta¹k* 'roof', *jŭ²ga* 'to prevaricate', *jŭ¹pt* 'depth', *afrika¹nsk* 'African', *ta²vla* 'table'.⁵ It cannot be claimed that either consonant length or vowel length is primary, and so it is necessary to recognize both as manifestations of two rhythmic types applicable to stressed syllables: type (a) with short vowel and long consonant, and type (b) with long vowel and short consonant or no consonant. A third type, with short vowel and short consonant, occurs in unstressed syllables. Different combinations of stress, intonation, and rhythm type define seven different prosodic phonemes in the language.

II A.1. LONG CONSONANTS
AS GEMINATE CLUSTERS

In English, long ambisyllabic consonants occur within the phrase at the juncture of two words, e.g., *šu't tạ'gərz* (shoot tigers), or of a word and certain proclitics and enclitics, e.g., *ə'n no'n* (unknown), *se'n nəs* (saneness), but never within the word proper. Such long consonants contrast with two phonetically different kinds of short consonants in the same position: word final consonant followed by initial vowel of the following word, e.g., *šu't ɛ'ləfənts* (shoot elephants); and word initial consonant preceded by final vowel of the preceding word, e.g., *si' tạ'gərz* (see tigers). Since phonetically different short consonants occur in the same position, it is out of the question to think of the long consonant as a positional variant of the simple consonant. Phonetically, the long consonant sounds essentially like a word-final consonant followed by a word-initial consonant. The conditions of the particular phenomenon and of the phonetics as a whole are met, if we interpret the long consonants as clusters of two identical consonants, in every other respect comparable to non-geminate clusters in the same position, e.g., *-k t-* in *kv'k tạ'gərz* (cook tigers).

⁵Examples like the last three show that long vowels may be followed by more than one consonant, and contradict the rule given in Björkhagen, *Modern Swedish Grammar* 34: "In a stressed syllable the vowel is long if it is followed by one consonant. The vowel is short if it is followed by more than one consonant."

The process followed in coming to this simple conclusion may seem unnecessarily roundabout. It may appear simpler to reason that the long *t* is *-t + t-* because *šu't tạ'gərz* consists of *šu't + tạ'gərz*. While the results are the same in this case, process does not always have this simple relation to resulting form. For instance, there are a few cases in English where *t + t* results in single *t*, e.g., *ga'tə < ga't + tu* (as in "I've got to go"). In many languages, sandhi changes are quite extensive, and there is no means by which one may know in advance where sandhi changes will or will not be found. It follows that consideration of the elements in morphological or syntactic composition cannot serve as a dependable method of inductively determining phonetic pattern. A thorough and careful examination of each detail in terms of the totality remains the only effective method.

Chitimacha ambisyllabic long stops, occurring in word-juncture, e.g., *pu·p pušna* 'rabbit's heart', are phonetically different from geminate stops of medial position, the latter being pronounced with a fully released and heavily aspirated stop preceding the second stop, e.g., *kappa* 'light'. But pre-consonantic stops are always heavily aspirated within the word, e.g., *p* in *wopki* 'he heard me', or *t* in *natma?i* 'he told him', while final stops are regularly not aspirated, e.g., *pu·p te·ti?i* 'the rabbit said'. Thus, *-pp-* is a fully characteristic instance of stop + stop in medial position, and *-p p-* is just as characteristic an instance of stop + stop in word juncture.

Finnish has ambisyllabic long consonants in the juncture of syllables within the word, e.g., *europpa* ('Europe'). Such long consonants are often shorter than some cases of unisyllabic long consonants in syllabic final position (see above), but are always distinctive by their ambisyllabic character. In this they share a regular feature of Finnish consonant clusters. The ambisyllabic consonants conceived as geminate clusters come within regular classes of clusters (e.g., stop + stop, nasal + nasal). The pronunciation is essentially the same as that of other clusters. So all indications point to the interpretation of the ambisyllabic long consonants as geminate clusters. A final corroboration lies in the fact that there are certain consonants, *v d j g*, which do not occur in syllabic final, and it is precisely these which do not occur double.

Geminate clusters pronounced as long consonants are not necessarily medial and ambisyllabic. In Hungarian and modern Arabic, long consonants contrasting with short consonants and comparable to other consonant clusters occur at the end of words; Hungarian example: *jobb* 'better', contrast *žeb* 'pocket', compare *dobd* 'throw it!'. Initial long geminates may be illustrated from Czech, e.g., *k kra·lu* 'to the king', *s silou* 'with strength', or Berber,[6] e.g., *ggɛn* 'to sleep'—habituative.

Sometimes long consonants conceived as geminate clusters involve a phonetic specialization of the first of the pair of phonemes. Thus, Arabic *t k* are ordinarily aspirated when they occur in syllabic final, e.g., *k* in Egyptian Arabic *dakta·b* 'this is a book'. If they retained this characteristic in geminate clusters, there would result two completely separate articulations with aspiration between. In the pronunciation of *tt kk* as long consonants, the first stop is given a special phonetic variant (unreleased fortis stop). But the occurrence of special phonetic variants in given positions is one of the most characteristic phenomena of phonemics, and does not invalidate a fact that is otherwise clearly evident.

In some languages, long consonants conceived as geminate clusters involve types of clusters which do not occur otherwise. Italian has ambisyllabic long consonants occurring between vowels or between a vowel and a liquid, e.g., *fa'tto* 'done', *matti'na* 'morning', *spɛ'ttro* 'spectre'. This phonic type contrasts with unisyllabic syllabic-initial short consonant in the same position, e.g., *fa'to* ('fate'), *mati'ta* 'pencil', *tea'tro* 'theatre'. There is an ambisyllabic long consonant for practically every consonant in the language, but only five consonants, *m n l r s*,[7] occur in syllabic final outside of clusters. Since these also occur initially in the syllable (along with all other single phonemes and a number of clusters including *s* + stop, stop + *r*, etc.) there is no difficulty in establishing that *mm nn ll rr ss* are geminate

clusters. To relate the other long consonants to these cases, one may proceed by comparing such sets of words as *a'nno* 'year' : *kua'nto* 'how much?' : *a'tto* 'act'. All three medial complexes have in common the fact that they are ambisyllabic. The first two are phonetically alike in their first half, the last two are phonetically alike in their last half. The second half of *tt* in *a'tto* is rather clearly *t* and it is clear that some syllabically final consonant precedes it. That consonant is equatable to no other syllabically initial consonant than *t*. There being furthermore no contradictory evidence, *-tt-* is seen to be *t + t,* and *t* has to be defined as a consonant phoneme that occurs freely in syllabic initial position and in syllabic final only in the geminate cluster. The same positional limitation applies to all Italian consonants except *m n l r s*.[8]

It is important to recognize the great difference in pattern between the different languages treated in this section. They are alike in that, within the pattern of each language, the long consonants constitute geminate clusters. But they are different to a remarkable degree even with reference to the very criteria by which their geminate nature is determined. These criteria may be stated in general terms as follows: if long consonants are to be classed as clusters, (1) they must contrast with the corresponding single consonant in at least some positions; (2) they must have some of the characteristic features of other clusters; (3) the treatment must not conflict with the identification of other complexes as geminates.

The third criterion has not been used in the discussion so far, but is necessary because long consonants may be non-geminate clusters, as is shown in the next section. In such a case as Italian *ɔ'ǯǯi* ('today'), two hypotheses are suggested for the syllabic-final first con-

---

[6] Meinhof, *Die Sprachen der Hamiten* 87ff. (Hamburg, L. Friederichsen, 1912). Meinhof does not tell how the geminates are pronounced.

[7] According to Grandgent and Wilkens, *Italian Grammar* 6 (Boston, Heath, 1915), *s* in groups of *s* + consonant goes with the following syllable. That this traditional rule is incorrect was brought to my attention by Prof. A. Lipari.

[8] G. L. Trager informs me that palatalized *nⱼ lⱼ* are always long in medial position. These long medials are then in complementary distribution with the short initial *nⱼ lⱼ*. The situation presents an interesting complication, since complementation is one of the characteristics of positional variants. If the rest of the system supported it, we could consider the long and short sounds as phonemically equivalent. As it is, consistency with the great preponderance of cases requires that long medial *nⱼ lⱼ* be considered geminate clusters: *nⱼ lⱼ* are defective, occurring only initially (in rather few words) and in medial geminate clusters.

sonant: that it is *d*, that it is *ǯ*. Phonetically the long consonant in question has the articulating position of *ǯ*. Moreover, we have seen that syllabic-final consonants in Italian are restricted to *m n l r s* except that any consonant may occur in syllabic final before an identical syllabic-initial consonant; this identifies the first consonant in *ɔ'ǯǯi* as *ǯ*.

II A.2. LONG CONSONANTS
AS NON-GEMINATE CLUSTERS

English -*d ǯ*- in *gu'd ǯa'b* (good job) is pronounced either with a characteristic *d* closure followed by a shift of articulating position to the *ǯ* position, or with a single long closure in the *ǯ* position. The latter pronunciation is similar to that of Italian *ɔ'ǯǯi*, but English pattern differs in a number of ways from that of Italian. First, there is a considerable amount of accomodation of phonemes to surrounding ones in English; a *d* pronounced in the *ǯ* position before a *ǯ* in English is quite in keeping with the normal tendency. Secondly, English clusters are not limited in the way that clusters are limited in Italian. Finally -*d ǯ*- in English contrasts with the doubly released cluster in *nɔ'ǯ ǯa'n* (nudge John); the latter cluster is clearly -*ǯ ǯ*- and so the former can be only -*d ǯ*-.

In Muskogee, *t* and *c* are articulated in virtually the same position, so there is nothing in the articulating position to indicate whether the first part of *tc* in *totci·nin* 'three' is *t* or *c*. Furthermore, there is no contrasting *cc* that I have been able to find. However, it is a general feature of Muskogee consonant clusters, including geminate clusters, that they do not involve special variants for either of the component phonemes. If, then, there were a *cc*, one would expect an affricative pronunciation of the first *c* as is normal in syllabic final position, e.g., *icki* 'mother'. The fact that there is no affrication in the first part of *tc* is therefore a good pattern indication that it is *t* rather than *c*.

Sanskrit -*dd'*- of *budd'a* 'awakened', doubtless pronounced as a long ambisyllabic dental closure with aspirated release, consists of *d* followed by *d'*. The only other likely hypothesis, that this cluster might be *d'd'* with a special variant for the first *d'*, has to be rejected on account of the general rule of

Sanskrit that aspirated stops never occur before other stops.

In Shawnee, long consonants (*tt* and *kk*) occur only in positions where other clusters occur, and in rapid speech there is nothing to prevent their being classed as geminate clusters. But there is a complication in slow speech. Most long consonants of rapid speech are replaced by doubly articulated consonants (with strongly aspirated first consonant) in slow speech, but there are a few exceptions, e.g., *nowiκκato* 'three years', *nooττa* 'I arrive at it'. The doubly articulated sounds are clearly geminate *kk* and *tt,* so the exceptional long stops of slow speech cannot be considered geminates. There are two ways of treating them: (1) to recognize a set of defective long and ambisyllabic consonant phonemes limited to a few words; or (2) to recognize a defective κ and τ characterized by the lack of the normal aspirational release and occurring only in syllabic final before homorganic stops of the next syllable. The second formulation is perhaps the better because it recognizes the fact that the second half of the long consonant is phonetically like the normal syllabic initial stop, and because it is in keeping with the fact that ambisyllabic consonants are not found otherwise in the language.

Another type of non-geminate long consonant is that which results in such a case as *kæ'č ši'p* (catch sheep). The affricative element of *č* with the homorganic fricative *š* gives the effect of an ambisyllabic sibilant, a little longer than *š* alone.

II B. LONG CONSONANTS
AS DISTINCT UNIT PHONEMES

I have found no cases in which length is the only differentiating feature of distinct unit phonemes.[9] The feature of length is often associated with differences of voicing, of force of articulation, of aspiration.[10] For present purposes, it will perhaps be sufficient to take two cases in which length is a prominent differentiating feature.

[9]Trubetzkoy reported this situation in liquids and nasals in some Caucasic languages, but these sounds are geminates rather than unit phonemes, as Trubetzkoy (*op. cit.* 171) now recognizes.

[10]See S. Einarsson, "Parallels to the Stops in Hittite," *Language* 8.177–182.

Tabasaran, along with many other Caucasic languages, differentiates a strong and a weak series of consonants. The stronger consonants are fortis and, especially in intervocalic position, long; the lenis consonants are short. These are the only differences in the case of the spirants, but in the case of stops there is the further differentiation that the weak consonants are also aspirated. The strong consonants occur in many of the positions in which the weak consonants occur, e.g., *x'oj* 'dog', contrast *xoj* 'oath'; *k·um* 'nail, head', contrast *kum* 'smoke'; *jak·* 'ram', contrast *wak* 'light'; *t·at·ar* 'hands', contrast *tatar* 'Tartars'. Consonant clusters do not occur initially and clusters of more than two consonants, except those involving one or two liquids or nasals or semivowels, e.g., *q·arq·linc'a* 'lightning', do not occur anywhere in the word. It is thus impossible to take the strong consonants to be clusters in many cases, e.g., *x·oj, jak·, dust·* 'friend', *ašp·az* 'cook'. Being neither positional variants nor clusters, the Tabasaran strong consonants must be distinct unit phonemes.

In Malayalam,[11] the strong consonants are noticeably longer and very much more fortis than the weak consonants; they are limited in occurrence to medial position between vowels and after lateral and rolled continuants. They are often, but not always, ambisyllabic, depending on the rhythm of the word. There is a tendency to break long words into rhythmic groups of syllables, each consisting of two syllables; within the syllable group the strong consonants tend to be ambisyllabic, at the beginning of a group they go entirely with the following syllable (thus, in the imaginary words *ananap·a, ap·anana, anap·ana, p·* is ambisyllabic in the first two cases but not in the last one). Weak consonants, always short and very lightly articulated,[12] are less restricted in position of occurrence. The two types share the intervocalic and the post-lateral positions, e.g., *pa·kə* 'to plant', *pa·k·ə* 'arrack nut'; *nalkun·u* 'to present', *nu·lk·un·u* 'to spin'. The strong consonants are different from clusters in that clusters are always ambisyllabic and do not occur after continuants (that is, there are no clusters of three consonants). The strong consonants cannot be counted either as positional variants of weak consonants nor as clusters of weak consonants. They are distinct unit phonemes, even though they do not occur initially in the word.

The criteria by which long consonants are to be classed as distinct unit phonemes are: (1) they must contrast with the corresponding short consonants in at least some positions; (2) they must have the general characteristics of single consonants rather than of consonant clusters.

The general criterion of phonemics is relativity within the totality of the given language. Sounds must be classified according to similarities of phonetic and permutational characteristics. If in this procedure we seek to find the maximally simple, self-consistent, and complete total formulation, we reduce the subjective element in phonetics. Trying to be objective is not likely to succeed fully without an intelligent understanding of the nature of phonetic systems and a constant effort to see each detail in its relation to every other detail. There is a real danger that pattern-conscious investigators may distort the facts in order to make the pattern seem more symmetrical, but this danger is small in comparison with the danger of distorting or failing to notice facts because of giving no attention to pattern.

[11]A Dravidian language of southwestern India. The facts are given for common Malayalam. Elegant Malayalam, employing many Sanskrit and English words, has a considerably larger number of phonemes and allows a whole new set of consonant clusters. In consequence, the case of the strong consonants is more complicated, but they have the same status of independent unit phonemes.

[12]In medial position, they tend to be partly voiced and spirantal.

BIBLIOGRAPHY 3
Length

ULDALL, H. J. (1934) "A Note on Vowel Length in American English"

PARMENTER, C. E., and S. N. TREVIÑO (1935) "The Length of the Sounds of a Middle Westerner"

TRUBETZKOY, N. S. (1936) "Die phonologischen Grundlagen der sogenannten 'Quantität' in den verschiedenen Sprachen"

HEFFNER, R.-M. S. (1937) "Notes on the Length of Vowels"

ZWIRNER, E. (1939) "Phonologische und phonometrische Probleme der Quantität"

HEFFNER, R.-M. S. (1941) "Notes on the Length of Vowels"

EDGERTON, W. F. (1947) "Stress, Vowel Quantity, and Syllable Division in Egyptian"

CARNOCHAN, J. (1951) "A Study of Quantity in Hausa"

HOCKETT, C. F. (1953) "Short and Long Syllable Nuclei"

CARNOCHAN, J. (1957) "Gemination in Hausa"

MITCHELL, T. F. (1957) "Long Consonants in Phonology and Phonetics"

PALMER, F. R. (1957) "Gemination in Tigrinya"

SIERTSEMA, B. (1959) "Problems of Phonemic Interpretation II: Long Vowels in a Tone Language"

BOLINGER, D. L. (1963) "Length, Vowel, Juncture"

7

MENOMINI
MORPHOPHONEMICS*
LEONARD BLOOMFIELD

1 The Menomini language is spoken by some 1700 people in Wisconsin; most, but not all, speak English as a first or second language; some, especially among the pagans, have also a speaking knowledge of Ojibwa or Potawatomi. Menomini texts will be found in Publications of the American Ethnological Society, volume 12 (New York, 1928). Menomini belongs to the widespread Algonquian family of languages; see Michelson in the 28th Annual Report of the American Bureau of Ethnology (Washington, 1912).

2 Analysis of Menomini speech-forms by formal-semantic resemblances yields a fairly clean division of forms into phrases, compound words, and simple words. The words in a phrase and the members in a compound word differ but little in different combinations; such variations as occur, constitute the *external* or *syntactic* sandhi of the language and will not be discussed in this paper. Simple words and the members of compounds, in turn, resolve themselves, under analysis, into morphologic elements which vary greatly in different combinations; the present paper describes these variations, the *internal sandhi* or *morphophonemics* of the language.

3 It is necessary to distinguish these morphophonemic alternations from certain others, which we may call *morpholexical* variations. In Menomini, as in other Algonquian languages, different words often contain morphological elements of otherwise identical meaning but differing somewhat in form. Thus, the word tahkīkamiw *it is cold water* contains a suffix -kamy- *water, liquid*, but this form of the suffix occurs only in a few words; the freely

usable form of the suffix is -ākamy-, which may, of course, be described as consisting of -kamy- and a presuffixal element -ā-: menwākamiw *it is good liquid*, apīsākamiw *it is black liquid*, maskāwākamiw *it is strong liquid*, and so on. These morpholexical variations are quite distinct from internal sandhi; we shall deal with them only to the extent that they appear in the necessary preliminary survey of morphology, §§ 6 to 9.

4 The process of description leads us to set up each morphological element in a theoretical *basic* form, and then to state the deviations from this basic form which appear when the element is combined with other elements. If one starts with the basic forms and applies our statements (§§ 10 and following) in the order in which we give them, one will arrive finally at the forms of words as they are actually spoken. Our basic forms are not ancient forms, say of the Proto-Algonquian parent language, and our statements of internal sandhi are not historical but descriptive, and appear in a purely *descriptive order*. However, our basic forms do bear some resemblance to those which would be set up for a description of Proto-Algonquian, some of our statements of alternation (namely, those in §§ 10 to 18) resemble those which would appear in a description of Proto-Algonquian, and the rest (§§ 19 and following), as to content and order, approximate the historical development from Proto-Algonquian to present day Menomini.

In our theoretical forms we shall separate morphologic constituents by hyphens. The symbol ~ means "is replaced in alternation by." The colon (:) means "appearing in the actual Menomini word"; the word cited after

*Reprinted from *Travaux du Cercle Linguistique de Prague* 8.105–115 (1939) by permission.

the colon will generally involve alternations which have not yet been stated at the time of citation, but a reader who has gone through all of our statements will be able, returning to the citation, to account for all of these features.

5   The morphophonemes in our basic forms are:

Syllabics (short and long vowels)

	front		back		
higher	e	ē	o	u	ō
lower	ə	ε	c̄	a	ā

Non-Syllabics
semivowels	y	w								
consonants	p	t	k	č	s	h	?	m	n	N

In actual speech, ə is replaced by e, § 36, and N by n, § 13. On the other hand, the alternations result in two additional phonemes i and ī §§ 20, 35 and a semi-phoneme ū, § 35. The morphophoneme u seems to occur in only one suffix, -uw- forming transitive verbs, as pītuwεw *he brings it to him;* in the actual language, u arises also by the alternation of §35. Hence the actual Menomini phonemes are

Syllabics (short and long vowels)

	front		back	
high	i	ī	u	(ū)
mid	e	ē	o	ō
low	ε	c̄	a	ā

Non-Syllabics
semivowels	y	w						
consonants	p	t	k	č	s	h	?	m	n

The *clusters* in our basic forms are

č	before	p, k
s	before	p, t, k
?	before	p, t, k, č, s, n
h	before	p, t, k, č, s, n
n	before	p, t, k, č, s

In the actual language, the basic clusters of n plus consonant are replaced by those with h plus consonant, § 23. In the basic forms, any consonant or cluster may be followed by one or two semivowels; in the actual language such combinations are greatly restricted by § 16 and § 20.[1]

[1]A few phonetic indications, while not strictly relevant, may be of interest. The high vowels, i, ī, u, ū, are much as in French *mis, mise, doux, blouse;*

6   The morphologic features of Algonquian appear in three layers: inflection, secondary derivation, and primary formation. All three consist chiefly in the use of suffixes. Processes other than suffixation demand some preliminary comment (§§ 7 to 9).

7   In inflection, suffixes are added to stems of nouns, verbs, and a few particles. Four prefixes are used in inflection: kε- *thou,* Nε- *I,* wε *he,* and, occurring only in some dependent nouns (§ 9), mε- *indefinite personal possessor:* kenēh *thy hand or arm,* kenēhkenawan *our (inclusive) hands,* kenēhkowawan *your hands,* nenēh *my hand,* nenēhkenawan *our (exclusive) hands,* onēh *his hand* (§ 17), onēhkowawan *their hands,* menēh *someone's hand, a hand.* Before a vowel, the prefixes (in their basic form, hence by morpholexical variation, §3), add t: ōs *canoe,* ketōs *thy canoe,* otōnowaw *their canoe,* and so on.

There are certain irregularities of prefixation, of which we shall mention only one: before dependent noun stems (§ 9) in ē- and ō-, the prefixes drop their vowel: kēyaw *thy body,* nēyaw *my body,* wēyaw *his body,* kōhnε? *thy*

the long mid vowels ē, ō much as in German *weh, wo;* the short mid vowels e, o somewhat as in English *pit, put,* but ow is somewhat as in English *sowing;* ε, c̄ are even lower than the vowels of American English *bed, bad;* short a ranges from German *hat* to English *hut;* ā from French *pâte* to English *saw.* The semivowels y, w are as in English, but after a non-syllabic, yā, wā are falling diphthongs: payyāt *when he came,* kwāhnεw *he jumps* are phonetically [payi:at, ku:ahnεw]. Of the consonants, only m, n are voiced; ? is a well-marked glottal stop, often with vocalic echo; p, t, k, č, s are lenes with slow opening. Non-syllabics are often strongly palatalized or labiovelarized by the preceding vowel, initial non-syllabics by the following vowel: mīp *early in the morning* (both consonants palatalized); mwāk *loon* (both consonants labiovelarized); nekī?s *my son* (palatal k); okī?san *his son* (labiovelar k). In word, compound, or close-knit phrase, a long vowel in the next-to-last syllable and a long vowel followed in the next syllable by a short vowel, have a strong stress accent: pakāmεw *he struck him* (stress on -kā-); pemātεsew *he lives* (stress on -mā-). This seems to be the only actualized difference between ow and ōw: nēmowak *they dance* (stress on nē-), manētōwak *game animals* (stress on -tō-). Successions of syllables that do not contain such an accent, are varied by less stable ups and downs of stress: pε?tεnamoken *it is said that they touched it by error* will be stressed on the first and third, or on the second and fourth syllables, or in other ways.

father, nōhnɛ^ʔ *my father,* w-ōhn-: ōhnan *his father* (§ 17), cf. owōhnemaw *the father, a father.*

8   Certain inflectional forms of verbs have *initial change:* the first vowel of the stem is altered as follows:

a, ɛ ~ ē: a^ʔtɛw *it is in place,* ē^ʔtɛk *that which is in place;* kɛmew-: kemēwah *if it rains,* kēmew- : kēmewah *when it rained;* wɛn-ɛt- : onēt *it is pretty,* wēn-ɛt-k- : wēnɛh *that which is pretty.*

o ~ ō: koskōset *if he wakes up,* kōskoset *when he woke up.*

y- prefixes a: yāčehtok *if he renews it,* ayāčehtok *when he renewed it.*

Stems beginning with consonant plus y or w prefix ay to the y or w: pyāt *if he comes,* payyāt *when he came;* kwāhnɛt *if he jumps,* kaywāhnɛt *when he jumped.*

Otherwise, long vowel prefixes ay: wāpamak *if I look at him,* wayāpamak *when I looked at him;* āčemit *if he narrates,* ayāčemit *when he narrated;* pōne^ʔtat *if he ceases,* payōne^ʔtat *when he ceased.*

There are some irregularities, which we shall not here describe.

9   Features of inflection are in some cases retained in secondary derivation. Apart from this, secondary derivation consists in the addition of suffixes to the stems of nouns or verbs, as enēniw *man,* enēniwew *he is a man, manly.*

In primary formation suffixes are added to a root: root mat- *bad,* suffix -a^ʔnɛmw- *dog:* matā^ʔnɛm *nasty cur.*

Throughout the morphology, zero suffixes must sometimes be set up. It is a striking feature of Algonquian that in certain cases we must set up the root of a word as zero. In a few verb forms the stem is replaced by zero; thus, the stem ɛn- *say so to* is replaced by zero before the inflectional suffix -ək-: enēw *he says so to him,* ekwāh *the other one says so to him,* netēkwah *he says so to me.* A large class of noun stems and certain particles contain no root and occur only with the prefixes of § 7: these are *dependent* nouns and particles, such as -nɛhk-, -ēyaw-, -ōhn- in § 7, or, say (with two suffixes), -ēt-a^ʔnɛmw- in kēta^ʔnɛm *thy fellow-cur,* wēta^ʔnɛmon *his fellow-cur.* No root begins with a cluster; since every word begins with a root or one of the four prefixes,

no Menomini word begins with a cluster. The vowel e is probably nowhere to be set up in the first syllable of a basic form.

Roots, like suffixes, show morpholexical variation. Reduplication is the commonest form of this. Normally, it consists in prefixing the first non-syllabic followed by ā: pakam- : pakāmēw *he strikes him,* pā-pakam- : pāpakamēw *he beats him.* There are also irregular types of reduplication, as pōhkonam *he breaks it across by hand,* pō^ʔpōhkonam *he repeatedly breaks it.*

10   When an element ending in non-syllabic precedes an element beginning with a consonant, a *connective* -e- is inserted. Thus, root pōN- *cease* with suffix -m- *by speech* gives pōN-e-m- : pōnemɛw *he stops talking to him.* Contrast, on the one hand, pōN-ēNem- : pōnēnemɛw *he stops thinking of him,* and, on the other hand, kēhkā-m- : kēhkamɛw *he berates him.*

11   If an element ending in vowel plus w precedes an element with initial w, the -e- is used: kaw-e-wēp-: kawēwēpɛnɛw *he flings him prostrate;* contrast kaw-ɛN- : kawēnēw *he lays him prostrate,* and sēk-wēp- : sīkwēpɛnam *he flings it scattering.*

Irregularly, -e- is used between consonant and w in a few combinations, as ɛsp-e-wēp- : espēwēpahɛw *he tosses him aloft by tool. or on horns.*

12   Irregularly, certain combinations do not take connective -e-. Root ɛn- *thither, thus* with suffix -pahtā- *run,* gives ɛn-pahtā- : ehpāhtaw *he runs thither;* cf. ɛn-ēNem- : enēnemɛw *he thinks so of him,* and wāk-e-pahtā- : wāke-pāhtaw *he runs a crooked course.* Verb stem kɛmewan-, with initial change (§ 8) kēmewan-, with inflectional suffix -k- gives kēmewan-k- : kēmewāhken *whenever it rains,* kēmewah *when it rained;* cf. kemēwan *it is raining* and ē^ʔtɛken *whenever it is in place,* ē^ʔtɛk *when it was in place.*

In such forms, if the first consonant is other than n, it is replaced by h: sēnak-at-k- : sēnakāhken *whenever it is difficult,* sēnakah *when it was difficult,* cf. sanākat *it is difficult;* atōt-pw- : atūhpwan *table,* cf. atōtapiw *he sits on something,* sakīpwak *if I bite him.*

13 Before e, ē, y, final t ~ č and n ~ s. Thus, pyēt-e-m- ~ pyēčem- : pīčemɛw *he calls him hither;* cf. pyēt-ohnē- : pītohnɛw *he walks hither.* ɛn-yā- ~ ɛsyā- : esyāt *if he goes thither;* cf. ɛn-ohnē- : enōhnɛt *if he walks thither or thus.* -ēn-e- ~ -ēse-: wēs *his head;* cf. wēnowawan *their heads.* ōn-e- ~ ōse-: ōs *canoe;* cf. ōnan *canoes.* pɛ?t-e- ~ pɛ?če- : pē?č *by error;* cf. pɛ?tɛnam *he touches or handles it by error.*

In a few cases, the mutation is made before the suffix -əh- which derives local particles from nouns: wēseh beside wēneh *on his head.*

Certain n's are not subject to this alternation; we designate these in our basic forms by N; in actual speech, then, this theoretical N is replaced by n.

14 Irregularly, in certain forms, t is replaced by s before ɛ and ā. So always before -ɛhk- *by foot or body movement* and -āp- *look:* pyēt-ɛhk- ~ pyēsɛhk- : pīsɛhkaw *it moves hither;* wɛht-āp- : ohsāpomɛw *he looks at him from there,* cf. wɛht-ɛN- : ohtēnam *he takes it from there.* Other suffixes, less often: wɛht-ɛčyē- : ohsēčīnam *he takes it bodily from there.*

15 Successive vowels are in every instance modified.

After long, short other than o drops: asyē-ɛN- : asyēN- : asīnam *he pushes it back, rejects it,* cf. kāhtɛnam *he shoves it.* nakā-ɛN- : nakānam *he stops it by hand,* cf. nakā?taw *he stops, comes to a standstill.*

ā-o ~ ō: kyā?tā-ohnē- : kyā?tōhnɛw *he walks in a circle,* cf. kyā?tā-hsemw- : kyā?tāhsemow *he dances in a circle* and pōN-e--hsemw- : pōnehsemow *he stops dancing.*

ē-o ~ yā: asyē-ohnē- : asyāhnɛw *he walks backwards.*

ā-ā ~ ā: nakā-āpyē- : nakāpīna?sow *he brings his horses to a stop,* cf. mat-āpyē- : matāpīna?sow *he drives badly.*

Between other long vowels, y is inserted. akwā-ē?n- : akwāyē?nɛn *it is blown to shore,* cf. akwā-čemē- : akwāčemɛw *he paddles to shore;* asyē-ē?n- ~ asyēyē?n- : asīyē?nɛmɛw *he blows him back;* wɛNē-āhkw- : onīyāhkwahɛw *he gets him up from bed,* cf. wɛNē- : onēw *he gets up.*

16 After consonant, the first of two semi-

vowels is dropped: ahkɛhkw-yān- : ahkēhkyan *hearth,* cf. ahkēhkoh *in the kettle* (§ 20); a?sɛNy-wēk- ~ a?senwēk- : a?senīkat *it is hard-woven cloth,* cf. a?sɛnyak *stones,* wāpesk-wēk- : wāpeskīkan *white linen,* wāpeskɛsew *he is white;* mɛhkw-wēk- ~ mɛhkwēk- : mɛhkīkan *red flannel,* cf. mɛhkwākom *red blanket,* netākom *my blanket.* In some basic forms, we write twy instead of ty merely to bar § 13; thus, we set up pēnt-ēkon-āhtwy-to give pēhčekonāh *sacred bundle,* plural pēhčekonāhtyan.

17 Initial w-ō- ~ ō-: with kēyaw, nēyaw, wēyaw compare kōhnɛ?, nōhnɛ?, w-ōhn- : ōhnan in § 7.

Initial w-ɛ- ~ o-: with the preceding compare the normal forms of the prefixes: kɛ-, etc., as ketan *thy daughter,* netan *my daughter,* wɛ-tāN- : otānan *his daughter,* otānew *he has a daughter,* but, with initial change, wētānet *the parent of a daughter.*

Initial w does not occur before o; initial y does not occur before short vowels, either in basic forms or in the actual language.

Initial wyē- ~ ī- is set up for a few forms like wyēw-ēw: īwēw *futuit illam.*

18 When an element in vowel plus w precedes an element with initial ɛ or ə, the combination is normally retained, as kaw-ɛN- : nekāwenan *I lay it flat.* Irregularly, however, in certain forms, a replacement is made. This happens always when the w ends a verb stem and the ɛ or ə begins an inflectional ending, but there are also other cases. The following rules hold for ə as well as for ɛ.

awɛ, āwɛ, owɛ ~ ō: kɛt-ɛnaw-ɛne- ~ kɛtenōne- : ketēnōn *I resemble thee,* cf. kɛt-ɛnaw-c-m : ketēnawem *thou resemblest me;* -amow-ɛne- ~ amōne- : kesāka?samōn *I give thee tobacco,* cf. kesāka?samowem *thou givest me tobacco;* Nɛt-ɛhtanaw-ɛm- ~ netɛhtanōm- : netēhtanom *my domestic animal.*

Before k, t, s, however, verb stems in -aw- and -amow- have ā instead of ō: ɛnaw--əkw- : enāk *the other one resembles him;* -amow-əkw- : nesāka?samāk *he gives me tobacco;* ɛnaw-ɛtw- : enātowak *they resemble each other;* -amow-ɛsw- : nātamasow *he helps himself,* cf. nātamowēw *he helps him.*

uwɛ, wāwɛ ~ wā: pyēt-uw-əkw- ~

pyɛ̄twākw- : pītwāk *the other brings it to him,*
cf. pītuwɛw *he brings it to the other;* mam-
wāw-əkw- : mamwāk *the other takes it from
him,* cf. mamwāwɛ̄w *he takes it from the other.*

ewɛ, ēwɛ, ɛ̄wɛ, yāwɛ ~ yā: wēt-yɛ̄w-əkw-
~ wēčyākw- : wīčyāk *the other one accompanies him,* cf. wīčīwɛ̄w *he accompanies the
other;* -nɛNyew-ɛhkwɛ̄w- ~ -nɛnyāhkwɛ̄w- :
maskīhkīwenɛnyāhkiw *medicine woman,* cf.
maskīhkīwenɛniw *medicine man* and pītɛhki-
wɛ̄w *he brings a woman;* omɛ̄ʔnomenɛ̄w-
-ɛhkwɛ̄w- : omɛ̄ʔnomenyāhkiw *Menomini
woman,* cf. omɛ̄ʔnomenɛ̄w *Menomini;* nɛ̄w-
-əkw- : nyāk *the other sees him,* cf. nɛ̄wɛ̄w *he
sees the other;* kyāw-ɛhkom- : kyāhkomɛw *he
is jealous of him,* cf. kyāwɛ̄w *he is jealous.*

In a few forms, however, ēwɛ, ɛ̄wɛ is replaced by īyo : wyɛ̄w-əkw- ~ īw-əkw- : īyok
fututa est ab illo; wyɛ̄w-ɛtw- ~ īw-ɛtw- :
iyotowak *alter alteram futuunt.*

19 Irregularly, in a few forms, vowel plus w
contracts with other vowels, chiefly aw-ā ~
wā : kēsaw-ākamy- ~ kēswākamy- : kīswāka-
miw *it is warm liquid,* cf. kēsawan *it is warm.*

20 After consonant, y, w plus vowel other
than a, ā are replaced by vowels.

yē ~ ē: kōNy-ēwe- : kōnēwew *it is snowy,*
cf. kōNy- : kōn *snow,* plural kōNy-ak : kūnyak
lumps or masses of snow, and awētok-ēwe- :
awētokewew *he, it is of spirit nature,* from
awētok *spirit,* plural awētokak.

wē ~ ō: Nētyānw-ēwe- : nīčyānōwew *he
is childish,* cf. Nētyānw- : nīčyān *child,* plural
Nētyānw-ak : nīčyānok (§ 21) *children.*

ye, we ~ i: Nɛ-mɛnw-e-hsenē- ~ nɛmɛni-
hsenē- : nemēnihsenēm *I am well placed,* cf.
mɛnw-āp-ant- : menwāpahtam *he sees it well.*

yɛ̄, wɛ̄ ~ ī: mɛnw-ɛ̄Nent- : menīnehtam
he likes it, cf. ɛn-ɛ̄Nent- : enēnehtam *he thinks
so of it;* pyɛ̄-w : pīw *he comes,* cf. pyā-t : pyāt
if he comes, and, for the morpholexical variation of ā and ɛ̄, nepɛ̄w *he sleeps,* nepāt *if he
sleeps.* To stems which we set up with wyɛ̄-
(§ 17), the prefixes are added with t and the
replacement is made; kɛt-wyɛ̄w-āw : ketīwāw
futuis eam. Similarly, kɛt-wyɛ̄w-ɛnɛ- : ke-
tīyon (§ 18) *te futuo.* However, wɛ̄ after consonant is kept in -wɛp- *throw* (§ 7) and in a few
words such as mahwɛ̄w *wolf,* moswēn *shawl.*

yɛ, yə ~ e: aʔnapy-ɛhkɛ̄- : aʔnapehkɛw *he
makes nets,* cf. aʔnap *net,* aʔnapyak *nets,* and

wēkewamɛhkɛw *he builds houses,* wēkewam
house, plural wēkewaman; aʔsɛNy-əh :
aʔsɛneh *on the stone,* cf. aʔsɛn *stone,* aʔsɛnyak
stones, and wēkewameh *in the house;* aʔsɛNy-
-ɛns-ak ~ aʔsɛnensak : aʔsɛnēhsak *little
stones,* cf. wēkewām-ɛns-an- : wēkewamēhsan
(§§ 22, 34) *little houses.*

wɛ, wə ~ o: ahkɛhkw-ɛhkɛ̄- : ahkɛ̄hko-
hkɛw *he makes kettles,* cf. ahkɛhkw- : ahkɛ̄h
kettle, ahkɛhkw-ak : ahkɛ̄hkok' (§ 21) *kettles;*
ahkɛhkw-əh : ahkɛ̄hkoh *in the kettle;* ahkɛ-
hkw-ɛns-ak ~ ahkɛ̄hkonsak : ahkɛ̄hkōhsak
little pails; sak-e-pw-ɛnt- ~ sakepont- :
sakɛ̄poh *if he is bitten,* cf. sak-e-pw-ak :
sakīpwak *if I bite him,* and suffix -ɛnt- in
pakam-ɛnt- : pakāmeh *if he is struck;* sak-e-
-pw-əkw- ~ sakepokw- : sakɛ̄pok *the other bit
him,* cf. pakam-əkw- : pakāmek *the other
struck him.* To initial wɛ- the prefixes are
added with t and replacement is made: Nɛt-
-wɛtāNe- ~ nɛtotāne- : netōtānem *I have a
daughter,* cf. wɛtāNe- : otānew *he has a
daughter,* from wɛ-tāN- : otānan *his daughter.*

For yō, yo I can cite no cases.

wō ~ ō: there seems to be no example in
my notes; as I am not a native speaker, I
cannot guarantee words which I form, but
I should not hesitate to say ɛ̄hkw-ōnt- :
ɛ̄hkōhtah *as far as he carried it on his back,*
cf. ɛ̄hkwahah *as far as he went into the water,*
and panōhtam *he dropped it from his back.*

wo ~ o: ɛ̄hkw-ohnē- : ɛ̄hkohnɛt *as far as
he walked,* cf. ɛ̄n-ohnē- : ɛ̄nohnɛt *the way he
walked.*

21 ya, wa, yā, wā are retained: aʔsɛnyak
stones, mɛʔtɛkwak *trees,* pyāt *if he comes,*
mwāk *loon.* In actual sound, yā, wā after non-
syllabic are falling diphthongs [i:a, u:a].

Irregularly, in certain forms, wa after
consonant is replaced by o. This occurs when
the a begins an inflectional ending in the paradigms of most nouns and verbs: ahkɛhkw-ak :
ahkɛ̄hkok *kettles;* contrast, with wa kept,
mɛʔtɛkwak *trees;* mɛhk-amw-ak : mɛhkāmok
they find it, cf. mɛhk-amw- : mɛhkām *he finds
it,* and pītāwak *they bring it,* beside pītāw *he
brings it.* In word-formation less often: wāp-
-osw-akom- : wāposokom beside wāposwakom
rabbit skin, but always apɛhs-osw-akom- :
apɛ̄hsosokom *deerskin,* cf. wāpos *rabbit,*
apɛ̄hsos *deer,* with plurals wāposok, apɛ̄hso-
sok.

22 Before n plus consonant, ε is replaced by e: pakam-εnt ~ pakament- : pakāmeh *if he is struck;* εn-εnt- ~ εnent- : enēh (§ 31) *if he is called so;* kε-set-εns-an ~ kεsetens-an : kesētēhsan (§ 34) *thy toes;* mēt-εnkwāmw- ~ mētenkwāmw- : mītehkwamow *dormiens se concacat.*

23 Clusters of n plus consonant are replaced by h plus consonant; examples in' § 22.

24 Final vowels are dropped: āsetē- : āset *in return,* cf. āsetē-hsem- : āsetēhsemεw *he lays them to overlap,* āsetē-εhkaw- : āsetē-hkawεw *he crosses paths with him;* contrast the treatment of final t before -εhk- in § 14; ōse- : ōs *canoe,* etc., § 13.

25 Final non-syllabics are dropped until only one is left: mε²tεkw- : mε²tεk *tree,* cf. mε²tεkwak *trees;* ahkεhkw- : ahkēh *kettle;* a²napy- : a²nap *net,* cf. a²napyak *nets.*

Excepted are the clusters ²č and ²s: pε²t-e- ~ pε²če- : pē²č *by error;* namē²s- : namē²s *fish.*

26 Irregularly, in certain forms, one of two like consonants together with the intervening vowel, is dropped (haplology): sēhk-ākamy- : sēhkamiw *it is open accessible water,* cf. sēhkehnεn *it lies beached;* kεhk-e-kātē- ~ kεhkātē : nekēhkatεp *my garter,* cf., without haplology, kεhk-e-kātē- : kεhkēkātεp *garter.*

27 Metathesis and distant dissimilation occur in a very few forms: wēskew-εse- ~ wēskyāse- : wyāskεsew *he is good,* cf. wēskew-at-w- : wēskewat *it is good,* and mat-εse- : matēsew *he is bad, ugly;* mε-motwy-ens- : menūtīh *someone's bag, a bag,* cf. kemūtīh *thy bag,* nemūtīh *my bag,* omūtīh *his bag.*

28 Alternation of short and long vowels is complex but very regular. In this alternation, the long vowel corresponding to ə is ē; for basic u I have no example. Certain words are excepted from this alternation; we shall call them *atonics.*[2])

[2]Historically, they are either words which were atonic at a bygone time when the language had a stress accent which produced the present alternations of quantity, or loan words from languages which have not the Menomini alternation. Stress is not distinctive in the present-day language.

29 In monosyllables, short vowels are replaced by long: pε²t-e ~ pε²č- : pē²č *by error;* mw-əkw- ~ mok- : mōk *the other eats him.* Contrast atonics: sew *as it were.*

30 A syllable whose vowel is followed by a cluster is *closed;* any other syllable is *open.* After a closed syllable, a long vowel in an open syllable is replaced by a short vowel: kōhn-ēw : kōhnεw *he swallows him,* cf. mēnēw *he gives it to him;* mεtεhn-ēw : metēhnεw *he tracks him;* nε²n-ēw : nε²nεw *he kills him;* kēhkā-m- : kēhkamεw *he berates him,* cf. kēhkā-nt- : kēhkāhtam *he berates it.* Exceptions, e.g., anohkīw *he works,* maskīhkīwen-εniw *medicine man.*

31 If the first two vowels of a word are short, the second is replaced by a long. Excepted are *glottal* words, whose first syllable contains a short vowel followed by ². Nε-pεmāt-εse- : nepēmātεsem *I live,* cf. pemātεsew *he lives;* pεm-ohnē- : pemōhnεw *he walks along,* cf. pītohnεw *he walks hither,* Nε-pεm-ohnē- : nepēmohnεm *I walk along,* pēm-ohnē- : pēmohnεt *when he walked by;* kan-əkw- : kanēk *the other escaped him,* cf. pakam-əkw- : pakāmek *the other struck him;* εn-εnt- ~ εnent- : enēh *if he is called so,* cf. pakam-εnt- : pakāmeh *if he is struck;* Nεt-ahkow-əkw- ~ nεtahkōkw- : netāhkok *he comes next after me,* cf. ahkow--əkw- : ahkōk *the other comes next after him,* so also in the compound word nenaw-ahkōk *he will come next after me,* for internal sandhi does not carry across the suture of compound words. Further, for instance, mεhk-amw- : mεhkām *he finds it,* Nε-mεhk-ān- : nemēhkan *I find it,* but, in compound, nekēs-mεhkān *I have found it;* contrast pōn-amw- : pōnam *he puts it in the pot,* nepōnān *I put it in the pot.*

Glottal words are excepted: nε²nεw *he kills him;* when a prefix is added, the resulting form is not a glottal word: Nε-nε²n- : nenē²-naw *I killed him;* pε²tεnam *he takes it by error.* Atonic, for example, nekot *one* (but nekōtēs *at one time*); mesek *and, also;* anohkīw *he works* (but netānohkim *I work*).

32 If the even (second, fourth, etc.) syllable after the next preceding long vowel or after the beginning of a glottal word, is open and has a long vowel, this long vowel is replaced by short: nōhtaw-ēw : nōhtawɛw *he hears him,* cf. pakam-ēw : pakāmēw *he strikes him,* pāpakam-ēw : pāpakamēw *he beats him;* pā-pɛm-e-ke-h-ēw : pāpɛmekehɛw *he brings him up;* ačet-e-kāpowe-h-ēw : ačēčekapowehēw *he stands him upside down,* cf. ɛn-e-kāpowe- : esēkāpowew *he stands so;* Nɛ-kɛhken-ān- : nekēhkenan *I know it,* cf. nenaw-kɛhkēnān *I shall know it;* aʔsek-ɛN-ēw : aʔsekɛnɛw *he picks them up,* cf. pɛʔt-ɛN-ēw : pɛʔtɛnēw *he touches him by error.*

33 If the even syllable (as in § 32) is closed and contains a short vowel, this short vowel is replaced by a long: kēhken-ank-wāʔ : kēhkenāhkwaʔ *that which they know,* cf. kēhken--ank- : kēhkenah *that which he knows,* kɛhken-ank-wāʔ : kɛhkīnahkwaʔ *if they know it,* kɛhken-ank- : kɛhkēnah *if he knows it;* kēmew-an-ken- : kēmewāhken *whenever it rains,* cf. kēmew-an-k- : kēmewah *when it rained,* kɛmew-an-k- : kemēwah *if it rains;* māmat-ɛhkā- : māmasēhkaw *it goes poorly,* cf. pōnɛhkaw *it stops going;* koʔt-ank-wāʔ : kuʔtāhkwaʔ *if they fear it,* cf. koʔtah *if he fears it,* and, with initial change (not a glottal word, since the first vowel is long), kōʔt-ank-wāʔ : kūʔtahkwaʔ *that which they fear;* aʔsek-ɛN--ank-wāʔ : aʔsekɛnāhkwaʔ *if they pick it up,* cf. aʔsekɛnah *if he picks it up,* pɛtʔɛnahkwaʔ *if they take it by accident.*

34 Certain forms retain a long vowel against the above habits. So the suffix -wēk- *cloth,* as wāpeskīkan *white linen;* the word onāwanīk *brown squirrel.* The diminutive suffix -ɛns- (together with its variations, such as -ons- § 20) always lengthens its vowel: kesētēhsan *thy toes,* anɛmw-ɛns- ~ anɛmons- : anɛmōhsak *little dogs.* Some alternations of quantity are morpholexical rather than morphophonemic. Thus, when the abstract noun suffix -N is added to verb stems in -kē-, the result is -kaN : kēskɛsekēw *he cuts things through,* kēskɛsekan *scythe.*

35 If postconsonantal y, w, or any one of the high vowels, i, ī, u, ū, follows anywhere in the word, the vowels ē and ō are raised to ī and ū, and the vowel o in the first syllable of a glottal word is raised to u: mayīčekwaʔ *that which they eat,* cf. mayēček *that which he eats;* ātɛʔnūhkuwɛw *he tells him a sacred story,* cf. ātɛʔnōhkɛw *he tells a sacred story;* sɛhk-e-hsen-k-wāʔ ~ sɛhk-ē-hsehkwāʔ : sɛhkīhsehkwaʔ *if they lie down,* cf. sɛhkēhseh *if he lies down;* kuʔnatwāʔ *if they fear him,* cf. koʔnačen *if he fears him.* This alternation sometimes fails to take place in long words: kēwaskɛpīw beside kīwaskɛpīw *he is drunk.* On the other hand, it is often extended to compound words and short phrases: kīs-pīw beside kēs-pīw *he has come.* Since ū occurs only in this alternation, it is not a full phoneme.

36 The morphophoneme ə is replaced by e: pakam-əkw- : pakāmek *the other one struck him;* wēkewam-əh : wēkewameh *in the house.*

37 The vowel ɛ is replaced by e in the first syllable of words except before a cluster of h or ʔ plus consonant: pɛmohnē- : pemōhnɛw *he walks along;* Nɛset- : nesēt *my foot.* Contrast Nɛhsehs- : nɛhsēh *my younger brother or sister;* Nɛʔnɛhs- : nɛʔnɛh *my elder brother;* pɛʔtɛnam *he touches it by error;* kɛhkēnam *he knows it.*

38 The forms now arrived at are *phonemic* forms of the actual Menomini language. Menomini phonetics, however, allows a great deal of latitude to some of its phonemes, and of some overlapping between phonemes. Thus, phonemic ɛ is rather widely replaced by e, except where h, ʔ plus consonant follows; we have used the morphophoneme ə for the cases where this replacement is universal and therefore phonemic. Some speakers partially and some quite constantly replace i by e.

BIBLIOGRAPHY 4
Neutralization
and Morphophonemics

TRUBETZKOY, N. S. (1929) "Sur la 'morphonologie'"

UŁASZYN, H. (1931) "Laut, Phonema, Morphonema"

MARTINET, A. (1936) "Neutralisation et archiphonème"

SWADESH, M., and C. F. VOEGELIN (1939) "A Problem in Phonological Alternation"

TRNKA, B. (1939) "On the Combinatory Variants and Neutralization of Phonemes"

SEBEOK, T. A. (1943) "Vowel Morphophonemics of Hungarian Suffixes"

HALPERN, A. M. (1946) "Yuma II: Morphophonemics"

BAZELL, C. E. (1949) "On the Neutralisation of Syntactic Oppositions"

BERGER, M. D. (1949) "Neutralization in American English Vowels"

WELLS, R. S. (1949) "Automatic Alternation"

HOCKETT, C. F. (1950) "Peiping Morphophonemics"

CHOMSKY, N. A. (1951) *Morphophonemics of Modern Hebrew*

BAZELL, C. E. (1956) "Three Conceptions of Phonological Neutralisation"

HALL, R. A., JR. (1960) "Italian [z] and the Converse of the Archiphoneme"

HALLE, M., and N. A. CHOMSKY (1960) "The Morphophonemics of English"

BEVER, T. G. (1963) "Theoretical Implications of Bloomfield's 'Menomini Morphophonemics'"

AUSTERLITZ, R. P. (1967) "The Distributional Identification of Finnish Morphophonemes"

BEVER, T. G. (1967) *Leonard Bloomfield and the Phonology of the Menomini Language*

SMITH, H. L., JR. (1967) "The Concept of the Morphophone"

STANKIEWICZ, E. (1967) "Opposition and Hierarchy in Morphophonemic Alternations"

CAIRNS, C. E. (1969) "Markedness, Neutralization, and Universal Redundancy Rules"

MAKKAI, A. (1969) "On the Validity and Limitations of Generative Morphophonemics"

See also the following article in this volume:

LOCKWOOD, D. G. (1969) "Neutralization, Biuniqueness, and Stratificational Phonology" [56]

8

PHONEMIC OVERLAPPING*
BERNARD BLOCH

The first step in the phonemic analysis of a language or dialect is to group the infinitely varied sounds which make up the spoken utterances of the speech community into a limited number of classes called phonemes. The principles governing this classification do not concern us here;[1] but it is obvious that each phoneme, defined as a class, will include as many actual and objectively different speech sounds as there are utterances containing a member of the class.

We know that the sounds comprising a single phoneme—the allophones, to give them a convenient name—sometimes differ strikingly among themselves. Most writers on the subject have dwelt on this fact, and all readers are familiar with the stock examples offered as illustrations: the different varieties of [k] in *keep cool,* of [l] in *leaf* and *feel,* or of the velar spirant in German *ich* and *ach.*[2] To offset this diversity among the allophones, some writers postulate a basic resemblance which unifies the entire class, by defining the phoneme, like Daniel Jones,[3] as a "family" of sounds clustering around a norm or, like

Bloomfield,[4] as a constant feature in the sound waves.

But though writers are agreed that allophones of the same phoneme are often very different phonetically, they appear to be uniformly silent on another aspect of the phonemic interrelation of sounds. I do not know of any published work that has even posed the question—important as it is both in practice and in theory—whether phonemes may intersect: whether a given sound, that is, may belong to two or more different phonemes in the same dialect. If the question has ever occurred to writers on phonemic theory, they appear to have treated their answer to it, whatever it may be, as a tacit assumption. It is my purpose here to state explicitly what is usually tacit, and to offer arguments in support of a principle which is usually assumed.

Is the phonemic analysis of a dialect valid if it forces us to assign successive occurrences of the same sound to different phonemes? For the purposes of this discussion, we may define a sound as a recurrent particular combination of sound features (such as labial or alveolar position, stop or spirant or lateral articulation, voicing or voicelessness, aspiration or the lack of it, etc.), of which some are distinctive in the language and some not; and we may agree that two sounds are "the same" if they represent the same particular combination of such features.[5] The intersection or overlapping of phonemes will be called partial if a given sound *x* occurring under one set of phonetic conditions is assigned to phoneme A,

[1]For several divergent statements of these principles see Leonard Bloomfield, *Language* (New York, 1933), Chap. 5; Morris Swadesh, "The Phonemic Principle" [3], *Language* 10.117–129 (1934); W. F. Twaddell, *On Defining the Phoneme* (*Language Monograph* No. 16, 1935); N. S. Trubetzkoy, *Grundzüge der Phonologie* (*Travaux du Cercle Linguistique de Prague* No. 7, 1939).

This paper was read at the 17th annual meeting of the Linguistic Society of America, Dec. 1940. For clarification of my views on phonemic theory I am indebted especially to Professor Bloomfield, Dr. George L. Trager, and Dr. Charles F. Hockett.

[2]See, for example, Daniel Jones, *An Outline of English Phonetics,* 3d ed. (Cambridge, 1932), pp. 48–49; John S. Kenyon, *American Pronunciation,* 6th ed. (Ann Arbor, 1935), pp. 33–35.

[3]*Op. cit.,* p. 48. Cf. also Ida C. Ward, *The Phonetics of English* (Cambridge, 1931), p. 60.

[4]*Language,* pp. 78–81.

[5]This statement does not, of course, solve the difficult question of phonetic identity. Since we know from laboratory evidence that no two sounds are exactly alike (and that even one sound is never uniform throughout its duration), but since on the other hand we know that the best-trained ear can distin-

*Reprinted from *American Speech* 16.278–284 (1941) by permission of Columbia University Press.

while the same *x* under a different set of conditions is assigned to phoneme B; it will be called complete if successive occurrences of *x* under the same conditions are assigned sometimes to A, sometimes to B.

Our question concerning the possibility of intersection is best answered by examining specific examples. These are all taken from varieties of Midwestern American English, since this is the only dialect for which I have worked out the phonemic analysis at first hand. I shall begin with some cases of partial intersection.

In the speech of many Americans, the [t] phoneme includes as one of its constituent sounds or allophones an alveolar flap (something like the *r* of London English *very*), which occurs intervocalically after a stressed vowel, and in this position varies freely with the familiar voiced *t* and with the aspirated voiceless *t*, as in *butter, betting, kitty* (contrast *budded, bedding, kiddy*). In the speech of some of these persons, the [r] phoneme includes as one of its allophones the same alveolar flap, occurring after [θ] in words like *three, throw,* less commonly after [ð] in dissyllabic pronunciations of words like *withering, gathering.* (The flap after [θ] is often partly or wholly voiceless; but the voiced variety also occurs.) In this dialect of English, then, the [t] phoneme and the [r] phoneme appear to intersect in the alveolar flap; but the intersection is only partial and never leads to uncertainty or confusion: every such flap between vowels belongs to the [t] phoneme, every flap after a dental spirant belongs to the [r] phoneme.

It is a well-known fact, emphasized especially by Menzerath,[6] that in the articulation of any sound in the stream of speech, the speaker normally anticipates part or even all of one or more following sounds. The phenomenon is of course familiar to students of his-

torical grammar as the cause of regressive assimilation. In words like *tool, cool,* where the initial stop is followed by a rounded vowel, the articulation of the stop often anticipates the lip-rounding of the next sound (contrast the stops in *tin, keen*). These labialized stops are of course nothing but positionally determined allophones of the [t] and the [k] phoneme, and their labialization is non-distinctive. The same kind of lip-rounding appears before [w] in words like *twin, queen;* but in a rapid and relaxed pronunciation of such words the separate phonetic fraction constituting the [w] may be considerably reduced or even lost altogether, so that this anticipatory lip-rounding of the stops remains as the only trace of its presence. (Forms of *twin, tweezers, twist, queen, quick, quiz,* and the like with a labialized stop immediately followed by a front vowel are not too common, but they are familiar to observers of the spoken language.) In such pronunciations, then, the lip-rounding of the stop is all by itself an allophone of the [w] phoneme, even though it appears simultaneously with the articulation of another sound, and even though in words like *tool, cool* the phonetically identical lip-rounding is non-distinctive, a mere positional feature of the allophones of [t] and [k]. The intersection is obvious, but again it is only partial; for the character of the following vowel always distinguishes the two values of the lip-rounding.

My third example of partial intersection, which I owe to a communication from Dr. Charles F. Hockett of the University of Michigan, is more complicated. In Hockett's dialect, and probably in that of many other Midwestern speakers, *mints, mince, dents, dense* all end either in [-ns] or in [-nts], *warmth* ends either in [-mθ] or in [-mpθ], *length* ends either in [-ŋθ] or in [-ŋkθ], *finds* and *fines* both end either in [-nz] or in [-ndz]. The facts can be formulated by saying that at the end of a stressed syllable after a nasal, there is free variation between a spirant and a cluster of stop plus spirant (the stop being homorganic with the nasal but voiced or voiceless like the spirant). Now, when the nasal is [n] and the spirant is [ʃ] or [ʒ], there is the same free variation between [ʃ] and [tʃ], [ʒ] and [dʒ]: *bench* ends either in [-nʃ] or in [-ntʃ], *hinge* ends either in [-nʒ] or in [-ndʒ]. As Hockett observes, the clusters [ts], [dz] and the unit phonemes [tʃ], [dʒ] are phonetically quite comparable, and [tʃ], [dʒ] differ from [ʃ], [ʒ] very much as [ts], [dz] differ from [s], [z]. That [tʃ], [dʒ] are unit phonemes and not, like [ts], [dz], clusters of two phonemes each, appears from their patterning elsewhere (their distribution, their occurrence before and after other consonants, etc.); yet at the end of a stressed syllable after a nasal, they behave exactly like ordinary clusters of stop plus spirant. The simplest way to describe the facts, it seems to me, is to posit partial intersection: in all positions except the one here defined, the sounds in question are phonemic units; in this one position they are clusters of two phonemes each, [t] + [ʃ] and [d] + [ʒ], and alternate in free variation with the corresponding simple spirants [ʃ] and [ʒ] just as other clusters do.

Similar examples could easily be added, from this and other dialects of English as well as from other languages. Partial intersection, as our illustrations show, can never lead to uncertainty in practice and may therefore be admitted in theory without violating sound phonemic method. The same cannot be said, however, of complete intersection. Examples are rare, and are always the result of an error in the analysis.

The unstressed vowels of English have long been a problem. Some writers, including Jones and Kenyon, treat the unstressed vowel of *about, sofa, condemn* as a separate phoneme, but regard the unstressed vowels of other words (as *adding, city, window,* etc.) as belonging to classes that include also stressed allophones. Other writers, notably Bloomfield, classify all unstressed vowels in terms of the vowel phonemes found in stressed syllables. A special problem is created by words that appear in two distinct forms according to the accentual conditions under which they are uttered; thus the word *at* has the vowel of *cat* in the phrase *where át,* but the second vowel of *sofa* in the phrase *at hóme.* Since the two vowels in this word always appear under different phonetic conditions and are thus in complementary distribution, it is possible to make out a fairly good case for treating both vowels as allophones of the same phoneme. But against this treatment there are two alternative objections, both involving intersection.

If the weak vowel of *at hóme* is a member of the same phoneme as the stressed vowel of *where át* because it alternates with the latter vowel in complementary distribution, what shall we do with the weak vowels of *about, sofa, confess,* and many other words, which never alternate with a stressed vowel? Those who agree with Bloomfield, as I do, that stress in English is phonemic (distinctive) and who are therefore unwilling to posit a separate phoneme to accommodate the unstressed vowel of the words just mentioned, will probably class this vowel, on the basis of phonetic similarity and pattern congruity,[7] with the stressed vowel of *cut, come, rush.* But if the weak vowel of *abóut, atóne* is thus identified with the vowel of *cut,* while the weak vowel of *at hóme* is identified with the vowel of *cat,* then successive occurrences of the same sound under the same phonetic conditions have been assigned to different phonemes.

The alternative objection involves intersection on an even greater scale. The same reasoning by which the weak vowel of *at hóme* is identified with the stressed vowel of *where át* leads us to identify the weak vowels of such phrases as *sée them gó, théy could gó, théy will gó, nót so múch* (all phonetically identical in my speech with the second vowel of *sofa*) with the stressed vowels of the phrases *not thém, they cóuld, they wíll, not só,* etc. In short, the "neutral" vowel which appears at the end of *sofa* would come to function as the unstressed member of nearly all the syllabic phonemes of English; or, to put it differently, all the syllabic phonemes would intersect in their unstressed allophones.

Now it is of course true that such intersection will not seem troublesome if we know in advance which phoneme is represented in a particular occurrence of the ambiguous allophone. Knowing the stressed forms of the words *at* and *them* (as in *where át, not thém*), we are able to assign the identical unstressed vowels of *at hóme* and *sée them gó* unhesitatingly to their respective classes. But what

[7]On pattern congruity, see Swadesh, "The Phonemic Principle" [3], and cf. his article "The Phonemic Interpretation of Long Consonants" [6], *Language* 13.1–10 (1937). For the analysis of the weak vowel in *sofa* on the basis here mentioned, as well as for what I regard as the correct interpretation of the other unstressed vowels, see G. L. Trager and Bernard Bloch, "The Syllabic Phonemes of English" [9], *Language* 17.223–246 (1941).

if we know only the unstressed form, either because we have not heard the stressed alternant or because such an alternant happens not to exist? Suppose that we are studying a new and unfamiliar dialect of English, and that we have succeeded in pairing the stressed and the unstressed vowels of such words as *at, them, could, will, so,* and the like: if we now hear a phrase like *óut of tówn,* with the unstressed vowel of the second word perceptually the same as those which we have already identified with various stressed alternants, how are we to treat this? We must defer the phonemic analysis until we chance to hear a stressed form of the same word, which may not occur at all in the dialect we are studying, or which, if it does occur, we may fail to recognize as "the same word." In the case of English or any other familiar language, such an objection may seem less than academic; but it becomes practically important in working with a new language (especially one that has no written literature), and is theoretically important even for an understanding of the structure of our mother tongue. In short, a system in which successive occurrences of a given sound x under the same conditions must be assigned to different phonemes necessarily breaks down, because there can be nothing in the facts of pronunciation—the only data relevant to phonemic analysis—to tell us which kind of x we are dealing with in any particular utterance.

With this general principle stated, I proceed now to what I regard as my most seductive example of apparent intersection. I observed it first in my own speech, but have noticed it also in the speech of others. Indeed, since my pronunciation agrees rather closely, in its general pattern, with the Chicago dialect described by Bloomfield,[8] the feature may be fairly common in Midwestern English.

 The pairs of words *bit bid, bet bed, bat bad, but bud, bite bide, beat bead,* etc., have respectively the same vowel phoneme, but exhibit a regular and fairly constant difference in the length of the vowel allophones. This

[8]"The Stressed Vowels of American English," *Language* 11.97–116 (1935). The phonemic difference between the vowels of *pot* and *balm,* noted below, is attributed to the Chicago dialect (*ibid.,* pp. 97–98); but my pronunciation of the two phonemes and their distribution in my speech both differ slightly from Bloomfield's.

difference is summarized in the well-known habit of English pronunciation, that vowels and diphthongs (and also liquids and nasals) are longer before a voiced than before a voiceless consonant. The alternation between longer and shorter allophones runs through the whole phonemic system. The vowel of *pot* is affected by the same automatic alternation: in the pairs *pot pod, cop cob, font fond,* the vowel of the first word is regularly shorter than that of the second; and there is nothing, so far, to show that a pair like *pot pod* is not in every way comparable to *bit bid.*

In my speech *bomb* is different from *balm, bother* does not rime with *father,* and *sorry* does not rime with *starry:* the vowel quality is the same in all these words, but in the first word of each pair the vowel is short (just as it is in *pot*), in the second noticeably longer. Since the difference in length cannot be explained as an automatic alternation (like the difference in *bit bid*), we conclude that *bomb* and *balm, bother* and *father, sorry* and *starry* have different vowel phonemes; and we naturally identify the vowel of *bomb, bother, sorry* with the phoneme of *pot.* The vowel of *balm, father, starry* appears also in *alms, palm, pa, star, card.* Again there is nothing, so far, to show that the phonemic organization is in any way abnormal. But now comes a hitch.

In the sentence *Pa'd go* (*if he could*), the utterance fraction *pa'd* must be analyzed, according to what we have just said, as containing the phoneme of *balm.* In the sentence *The pod grows,* the utterance fraction *pod* must be analyzed, again according to what we have said, as containing the phoneme of *pot.* But *pod,* with a vowel distinctly longer than that of *pot* (just as the vowel of *bid* is longer than that of *bit*), is phonetically identical with *pa'd!* Two occurrences of x under the same conditions have been assigned to different phonemes.

Approaching the intersection, as we have done, from different directions, and starting each time from a body of data already systematized, the conclusion seems inevitable. But the intersection here, as elsewhere, is inadmissible; for if we start from the facts of pronunciation as we meet them, there is never any clue in the utterance itself to tell us which kind of x we are dealing with. The apparent intersection of the phonemes of *pot* and *balm* reveals the fact (which otherwise could scarcely have been suspected) that the analysis we have made is faulty, even though we have proceeded on both sides of the intersection according to sound principles and usually valid methods.

If the fraction *pa'd* in *Pa'd go* is identical, under the same conditions, with the fraction *pod* in *The pod grows*, then both contain the same phoneme. We must choose between assigning the vowel of *pa'd* to the phoneme of *pot*, and assigning the vowel of *pod* to the phoneme of *balm*. Our choice will be determined by the validity of the resulting analysis.

If we say that *pa'd* has the phoneme of *pot, bomb, bother, font*, and the like, we must necessarily classify the vowels of *pa, balm, father, alms, card*, and so on, in the same way; that is, we must deny the obvious fact that in the dialect here considered *bomb* and *balm* are different, and the pairs *bother* and *father, sorry* and *starry* do not rime.

We are left, then, with the other alternative. By classifying the vowel of *pod*—and consequently also the vowels of *rob, nod, bog, fond*, and the like—as members of the phoneme of *balm,* we destroy the neat parallelism of the pairs *bit bid, bet bed, bite bide, pot pod:* the words in the last pair, instead of exhibiting shorter and longer allophones of the same phoneme, have totally different phonemes. But by sacrificing this symmetry we are able to account for all the facts of pronunciation, which is surely the more important requirement. The resulting system is lopsided; but the classes it sets up are such that if we start from the actual utterances of the dialect we can never be in doubt of the class to which any particular fraction of utterance must be assigned.

BIBLIOGRAPHY 5
Bilingualism and Coexistent Phonemic Systems

SWADESH, M. (1941) "Observations of Pattern Impact on the Phonetics of Bilinguals"

WONDERLY, W. L. (1946) "Phonemic Acculturation in Zoque"

FRIES, C. C., and K. L. PIKE (1949) "Coexistent Phonemic Systems"

HAUGEN, E. (1950) "Problems of Bilingualism"

HOENIGSWALD, H. M. (1952) "The Phonology of Dialect Borrowings"

WEINREICH, U. (1953) *Languages in Contact*

HAUGEN, E. (1954) "Bilingualism and Mixed Languages: Problems of Bilingual Description"

GRIMES, J. E. (1955) "Style in Huichol Structure"

HAMP, E. P. (1957) "Stylistically Modified Allophones in Huichol"

HAUGEN, E. (1955) "Problems of Bilingual Description"

—— (1956–1957) "The Phoneme in Bilingual Description"

WEINREICH, U. (1957) "On the Description of Phonic Interference"

FERGUSON, C. A. (1959) "Diglossia"

FRANCESCATO, G. (1959) "A Case of Coexistence of Phonemic Systems"

PIKE, K. L. (1960) "Toward a Theory of Change and Bilingualism"

DIEBOLD, A. R., JR. (1961) "Incipient Bilingualism"

SJOBERG, A. F. (1962) "Coexistent Phonemic Systems in Telugu: A Socio-Cultural Perspective"

9

THE SYLLABIC PHONEMES
OF ENGLISH*

GEORGE L. TRAGER and BERNARD BLOCH

[After a brief statement concerning junctures, prosodemes, and consonants, the paper is devoted to a phonemic analysis of the syllabic sounds of English (the vowels and diphthongs) on the basis of their phonetic character, their distribution, and their mutual relations. The results of the analysis are summarized in a table of syllabics and in a concise description of the total pattern.]

1 There are several methods of setting forth the phonemic analysis, partial or complete, of a language.[1] The one followed here in presenting the syllabic phonemes of English proceeds inductively from a statement of the phonetic data (the occurrence of sound-types, their distribution under different conditions, and their relation to each other) to an interpretation in terms of linguistic structure.

Not all the syllabic sounds heard in English occur in all positions; they occur according to selective rules which limit them, or some of them, to certain kinds of context. The procedure involved in grouping these sounds into phonemes is to record the occurrence of each sound-type,[2] with a full statement of the conditions under which it appears; to list the contrasting sound-types in each position; and then to bring together into classes similar sound-types occurring in complementary distribution (i.e., in mutually exclusive positions). These classes are the phonemes.

The sound-types constituting a phoneme must be phonetically similar, complementarily distributed, and congruently patterned; and the class thus composed must be in contrast and mutually exclusive with every other such class in the language. Intersection of phonemes is inadmissible: if a given sound-type x in a given position has been assigned to phoneme A, another occurrence of x in the same position cannot be assigned to phoneme B.[3]

---

[1]We have made use of the following works, among others, bearing on phonemic theory: Leonard Bloomfield, *Language,* Chaps. 5–8 (New York, 1933); id., "A Set of Postulates for the Science of Language," *Language* 2.153–164 (1926); Edward Sapir, "Sound Patterns in Language" [1], *Language* 1.37–51 (1925); Morris Swadesh, "The Phonemic Principle" [3], *Language* 10.117–129 (1934); id., "The Phonemic Interpretation of Long Consonants" [6], *Language* 13.1–10 (1937); id., *Language* 11.244–250 (1935); W. F. Twaddell, *On Defining the Phoneme, Language Monograph* No. 16, 1935; id., "On Various Phonemes" [5], *Language* 12.53–59 (1936); N. S. Trubetzkoy, *Grundzüge der Phonologie, Travaux du Cercle Linguistique de Prague* No. 7, 1939. Our indebtedness to these works, especially to Bloomfield's, will be apparent to the reader.

[2]A sound-type, as we use the term, is a class of the phonetic events called sounds; each sound is a sum of sound-features (as voicing, aspiration, occlusion, labial position, etc.), which may occur in various combinations. The repetition of what is perceptually the same combination constitutes the sound-type, which is thus an abstraction from a series of utterances clustering about a norm.

[3]The reason is that the facts of the utterance give us no clue in any particular instance as to the kind of x we are dealing with; that is, such assignment can be made only on the basis of morphological, lexical, or even more extraneous (e.g., historical) grounds. Apparent instances of complete intersection or overlapping of phonemic classes are therefore always the result of an error in the analysis, though cases of partial intersection (different phonemic interpretations of the same sound-type in different positions) seem to be common enough. See B. Bloch, "Phonemic Overlapping" [8], in *American Speech* 16.3.

---

*Reprinted from *Language* 17.223–246 (1941) by permission. The analysis presented here has been corrected and replaced by the version in G. L. Trager and H. L. Smith, *An Outline of English Structure,* 1951 (7th reprint by A.C.L.S., 1966). See the Introduction to Part I of this book for more details.

Sound-types as members of a phonemic class are called allophones.

2 The sound-types observed in the utterances of a speech community may be of several kinds, forming different orders of phonemes. Those that relate to the way in which utterances begin and end (or secondarily to the way in which elements of an utterance are joined together) we call juncture phonemes; they are defined by factors of rhythm, of the onset and contour of stress, and of the use of pre- and post-pausal allophones (§4). Variations in loudness, tone, and quantity constitute the accentual or prosodic phonemes, the prosodemes (§5). These two kinds of phonemes are usually recognizable only as modifications of other sound-types; they are suprasegmental. Segmental phonemes, following one another in a sequence, are typically the vowels and consonants. In the structure of the syllable vowels are nuclear, consonants marginal.

A logical order of exposition (though not usually the empirical order of investigation) will begin with the juncture phenomena, and proceed to the prosodemes, then to the nuclear segmental phonemes, and finally to the marginal phonemes. The present study, being only a partial presentation of English phonemics, will deal with junctures, stresses, and consonants only in summary, and then devote itself to the syllabic nuclei.

3 Our observations and analyses are based primarily on our individual dialects. These are both varieties of standard American English of the "General American" type (i.e., not belonging either to a New England or to a Southern regional type), though GLT has certain Eastern features lacking in BB's more Midwestern speech. Both of us make a nearly maximum number of distinctions among the syllabic phonemes. After working out the analysis of our own dialects, we examined other varieties of English; our general conclusions are applied to all the varieties known to us. In the discussion and the examples, differences in phonemic structure between dialects are clearly labeled.[4]

[4]The following studies, dealing in whole or in part with the same subject-matter as this paper, have helped us to arrive at our analysis: Henry

4 Juncture phenomena have been too little studied to permit more than a tentative formulation here. The transition from the pause preceding an isolated utterance to the first segmental phoneme, and from the last segmental phoneme to the following pause, we call open juncture. By contrast, the transition from one segmental phoneme to the next within the utterance (whether this is a morphologically simple form like *black, port,* or a morphologically complex one like *blacker, importation, the man*) we call close juncture.

A study of post-pausal and pre-pausal allophones reveals several recurrent differences between these and the corresponding allophones occurring elsewhere than at points of open juncture. Initial vowels may begin smoothly (with the glottis already in the position for voice) or with a glottal stop; the two kinds of onset are in so-called free variation, i.e., they do not contrast significantly, but the precise conditions (of style, emphasis, emotional coloring, or the like) under which each one occurs have never been analyzed and perhaps cannot be. Since the glottal stop is never significant, it is not a separate phoneme but

Sweet, *The Sounds of English*[2], Oxford, 1923; id., *A Primer of Spoken English*[4], Oxford, 1932; Leonard Bloomfield, "The Stressed Vowels of American English," *Language* 11.97–116 (1935); Morris Swadesh, "The Vowels of Chicago English," *Language* 11.148–151 (1935); John S. Kenyon, *American Pronunciation*[6], Ann Arbor, 1935 (and later edd.); Daniel Jones, *An Outline of English Phonetics*[3], Cambridge, 1932; Martin Joos, "Regional and Personal Variations in General American," *Le Maître Phonétique* No. 45, 3–6 (1934); id., "Stressed Vowels Plus *r* in General American," *ibid.* No. 48, 93–97 (1934); Bernard Bloch, "Broad Transcription of General American," *ibid.* No. 49, 7–10 (1935); G. L. Trager, "The Transcription of English," *ibid.* No. 49, 10–13 (1935); A. C. Lawrenson, "On the Broad Transcription of Southern English," *ibid.* No. 50, 22–24 (1935), and many other short articles by various writers in the same journal; Kemp Malone, "The Phonemes of Current English," *Studies for William A. Read* 133–165 (Baton Rouge, 1940).

We are indebted also to several of our colleagues, especially Prof. Leonard Bloomfield, Dr. Charles F. Hockett, and the late Benjamin Whorf, for criticism and for many valuable suggestions on English phonemics. Our statements concerning other dialects than our own are based partly on casual observation, partly on the reports of native speakers, partly on the findings of the Linguistic Atlas of the United States and Canada.

merely an optional feature of vowels in open juncture. Voiceless stops after open juncture are short, and aspirated even before a weak-stressed vowel (§5), whereas internally they are aspirated only at the beginning of a strong-stressed syllable; other consonants after open juncture are also uniformly short in normal speech, though they may be lengthened for emphasis. Pre-pausal syllabics consisting of one of the so-called long vowels and diphthongs (§9) are exceptionally long or "drawled," the drawl extending over the whole syllabic; and the same is true of final nasals and liquids ending a stressed syllable. Final stops are usually unreleased; final voiceless stops are unaspirated; final voiced stops and spirants are partially unvoiced at the end; and final voiceless spirants are longer than at the beginning of an utterance.

A loud stress on the first syllable after a pause sets in simultaneously with the beginning of the first segmental phoneme and rises rapidly in strength; a loud stress on the last syllable before a pause falls off slowly and is accompanied by drawling of the segmental phonemes. A weak stress on the last syllable before a pause is usually still weaker than in other positions, and may decrease in loudness toward the end of the syllable. On the basis of this complex of phenomena—a complex which involves prosodic and segmental phonemes as well as rhythmic factors on the level of sentence intonation—we may set up a tentative definition: Open juncture is the totality of phonetic features which characterize the segmental and suprasegmental phonemes at the beginning and at the end of an isolated utterance.

Further observation shows that the features of open juncture are present not only before and after pause, but also internally in some utterances. These utterances, we know from the morphology of English, are derivatives, compounds, and phrases—never simple words. Compare *syntax* (with close juncture between the two syllables) : *tin-tax* 'a tax on tin' (with open juncture: drawled [n] similar to [n] before pause); *minus, onus* (close) : *slyness, slowness* (open: drawled syllabics); *nitrate* (close) : *night-rate* (open: unaspirated [t] in the first syllable) : *dye-trade* (open: drawled syllabic); *another, a name, a talk* (close) : *an udder, an aim, at auction* (open:

onset of stress coincident with beginning of vowel).[5] These examples show that internal open juncture is phonemically different from close juncture. Is it also different from the open juncture before and after pause? We believe that it is, but we cannot prove our contention;[6] to do so will require a careful study of experimental data, specially prepared, concerning segmental, prosodic, and rhythmic features. Until such data have been assembled by a laboratory phonetician, we shall avoid the risk of obliterating a possible contrast, and distinguish the two kinds of open juncture in our transcription: external open juncture (the kind that occurs before and after pause) will be marked by a space between symbols, internal open juncture by a hyphen; close juncture will then be implied wherever the symbols are not separated by a space or a hyphen.

As in morphology the basic unit is the

[5]On such cases as *a name : an aim, ceasing : seasick*, etc., see Daniel Jones, "The 'Word' as a Phonetic Entity," *Le Maître Phonétique* No. 36, 60–65 (1931); G. Dietrich, "Das Wort als Phonetische Einheit," *ibid.* No. 38, 31–33 (1932). Jones assembles an imposing list of words and phrases differing in juncture, and draws attention to most of the phonetic features that distinguish the two kinds of juncture; but he does not systematize his findings, and of course does not use the terminology here proposed.

The characterizing features of open juncture are in many cases akin to (sometimes identical with) the features which Trubetzkoy calls Grenzsignale; see his *Grundzüge der Phonologie* 241–261. As appears from his discussion (though the English example *we learn : will earn* on 249 is badly chosen), features of open juncture correspond to boundary signals of the kind that he calls "aphonematisch"; but though such features (e.g., the aspiration of voiceless stops in English) do not distinguish segmental phonemes, they serve to characterize one term of a distinctive contrast on the suprasegmental level, and are therefore on that level phonemic.

What Sweet, *Sounds of English*[2] 58–65, calls sound-junction is of course not the same thing as juncture.

[6]Note, however, the contrast between *That horse is running* and *That horse's running (delights me)*. In the former phrase the rhythmic pattern seems to be *that-horse is-running;* in the latter, *that-horse's running*. Both phrases have open juncture before the *r* of *running;* but we hear the final consonant of *is* as weaker than the final consonant of *horse's*. Prof. Charles C. Fries once suggested that the different aspects of the verbal form in *-ing* may be distinguished by a difference in rhythm: cf. *John-is-going to-the-store* (progressive) and *John-is going-to-the-dogs* (descriptive).

word (minimal free form), so in phonemics we may set up as a basic unit an utterance or utterance fraction bounded by external open junctures (spaces) and containing one loud stress (or its surrogate, contrastive stress); and as a word may contain more than one morpheme, so our phonemic unit may contain any number of subordinate stresses in addition to the one loud stress, and any number of internal open junctures (hyphens). As a name for this unit we suggest PHONEMIC PHRASE.

5 We have stated that a phonemic phrase contains only one stress of the loudest kind, either the ordinary main stress or the specially loud contrastive stress, with or without other stresses of subordinate loudness. We must now establish the number of significantly different degrees of stress in English and their relation to each other.

Limiting our examination first to utterances of two or more syllables without internal open juncture, we may compare *lófty* : *alóft*, *cúrrent* : *corréct*, *béllow* : *belów*, *énemy* : *anémic* : *animátion*, etc. The position of the main stress is obviously an essential part of the total complex of distinctive features which constitute and identify the utterance. There are, it is true, other differences than in the degree of stress between the loud and the less loud syllables—notably in the quality of the syllabic; but though it is possible to formulate a description of the facts by regarding stress differences as non-distinctive features of different vowel phonemes, we get a simpler and more compact statement if we regard the degrees of stress as phonemic in themselves. Minimal contrasts are few (e.g., *tránsport* : *transpórt*, *íncrease* : *incréase*, *díscus* : *discúss*), but the non-minimal contrasts involve the entire lexicon. The two stresses illustrated in *lófty* : *alóft*, *cúrrent* : *corréct*, etc., may be called loud and weak; loud will be symbolized by an acute accent over the vowel letter (since the vowel, as the nucleus of the syllable, is the principal bearer of prosodemes), weak by the absence of any special mark.

In words like *cóntents*, *cónduct*, *sýntax*, *rótate*, etc., we find that the first syllable has a loud stress, but that the second syllable is not as weak as the weak syllables of *lófty*, *cúrrent*, *díscus*. The difference is especially noticeable when we compare the final syl-

lables of *áxis* and *áccess*, *óxen* and *áccent*, *málady* and *hóliday*, *éffigy* and *réfugee*. There are clearly two different degrees of stress in addition to the loud; the stronger of these we shall call medial, and mark with a grave accent: *cóntènts*, *sýntàx*, *rótàte*, *áccèss*, *áccènt*, *hólidày*, *réfugèe*. Medial stress is especially common in words of three or more syllables, where it is often distributed in relation to the loud stress in a fairly regular way; but there are many exceptions to this regularity (cf. *exàminátion* : *àlimentátion*). That medial stress is phonemically different from weak stress is shown in such contrasts as *ánimàte* vb. : *ánimate* adj., *cómplimènt* vb. : *compliment* n., *delíberàte* vb. : *delíberate* adj.; cf. also American *nécessàry*, *sécretàry* : British *nécess(a)ry*, *sécret(a)ry*.

A monosyllable pronounced in isolation has a loud stress, phonetically identical (so far as we can judge) with the loud stress of polysyllables, and with exactly the same kind of onset and contour in relation to the segmental phonemes. Further, when a monosyllable has contrastive stress (specially loud stress combined with the intonation characteristics of emphatic utterance), it shows the same prosodic features that are found elsewhere with this kind of stress. This is confirmed by the fact that some speakers occasionally pronounce an inherently weak-stressed monosyllable in isolation with contrastive stress. As we shall see later (§7), the vowels [ʌ] and [ə] are allophones of the same phoneme, the first occurring with loud or medial stress, the second with weak; accordingly, the word *just* in standard English regularly has [ʌ] when it is the loud-stressed adjective, but [ə] when it is the weak-stressed adverb (*I just cán't*, etc.). When the adverb is pronounced with contrastive stress, either in isolation or for special emphasis in context, some speakers retain the [ə] of the weak-stressed form instead of substituting the normal loud-stressed [ʌ]; in this case the word may be said to have inherently weak stress, which can alternate (as in any other weak-stressed syllable) with contrastive stress.[7] Cf. also the substandard *fer*

---

[7]We owe this example to Dr. Morris Swadesh, who cites it from his own speech; but we do not know whether he would now accept this explanation of it. An instance of a dissyllabic word with inherent weak stress is GLT's pronunciation of *twenty*. This

'for', as in *What fer?*, restressed from the weak form with retention of the weak-stressed allophone. Other monosyllables with inherent weak stress are auxiliary verbs, prepositions, conjunctions, articles, and the like; but these are usually in morphophonemic alternation with phonemically different loud-stressed forms.

We proceed now to phonemic phrases with internal open juncture (hyphen). These are numerous, including most compounds: *blackbird, redcap, army-cot, coal-bin, stage-struck, trolley car*, etc. (The presence or absence of a hyphen or a space in the traditional orthography has of course nothing to do with phonemic junctures.) In these examples, the first syllable has a loud stress, the last has a subordinate stress which is louder than the medial stress of words like *cóntènts, réfugèe*. A direct contrast to confirm the phonetic difference is found in *syntax : tin-tax;* but the latter has internal open juncture (§4), and it might be argued that this conditions the slightly louder stress. Evidence for the phonemic difference between this stress and medial stress is ' furnished by compounds involving longer elements. The word *àuditórium* has medial stress on the first syllable, loud stress on the third, weak stress on all the others; according to a well-known habit of English morphology, a loud stress becomes less loud when the word in which it occurs becomes the secondary member of a compound; therefore, in a compound like *movie-auditorium*, the loud stress on the third syllable of *àuditórium* is reduced in loudness. But this reduced stress remains louder than the medial stress on the syllable *àu;*[8] and the difference between them cannot be explained by any phonologically valid rules of position or alternation. We conclude that the stress on *-tor-* in the compound *movie-*

auditorium is phonemically different from both ordinary loud stress and medial stress, though it is obviously in morphophonemic alternation with the former. We shall call it the reduced loud stress, and mark it with a circumflex accent: *bláck-bîrd, réd-câp, ármy-côt, cóal-bîn, stáge-strûck, trólley-câr, tín-tâx, móvie-àuditôrium, élevàtor-ôperàtor, excêss-prófits, êxcèss-prófits-tâx*.

There are then four phonemically different stresses in English, not counting the contrastive stress which may alternate on an intonational level with any one of them. The combinatory patterns of the four stresses are extremely varied and complex even within single words; learned words may have several medial stresses (e.g., *cònstitùtionálity*), while reduced loud stresses occur most frequently in native compounds. The presence of internal open juncture does not always imply a reduced loud stress; cf. *hỳdro-eléctric, slý-ness*.

Syntactic constructions involve the same four stresses, often with the addition of intonational prosodemes irrelevant to English morphology. A syntactic phrase may be a phonemic phrase if it contains only one loud stress; original loud stresses in syntactically subordinate words appear as reduced loud, medial, or even weak, and original external junctures (spaces) appear as internal (hyphens). As a result of such morphophonemic alternations we get a great variety of stress patterns and contrasts; cf. *a black bird* (phonemically stressed *abláck-bírd*) : *a blackbird* (phonemically stressed *ablack-bîrd*).

The loud, reduced loud, and medial stresses are conveniently called strong, in contrast to the weak.

6 The consonant phonemes of English are /p, t, k, b, d, g, č, ǰ, f, θ, s, š, v, ð, z, ž, m, n, ŋ, l, r, w, j, h/.[9] All of them except /ž, ŋ/ can be shown to be in direct contrast with each other initially: *pill, till, kill, bill, dill, gill, chill, Jill, fin, thin, sin, shin, vine, thine, zeal, meal, kneel, lay, ray, way, yard, hard*.[10] All of them

---

has, in isolation, not the vowel of *ten* but the second vowel of *handed* (see §7 for the relation between these two); the latter vowel is normal for the weak-stressed form of the numeral in the compounds *twenty-one*, etc., and appears with contrastive stress (restressed) in the simplex.

[8]In our judgment of stress, more than anywhere else, we feel the lack of relevant experimental data. Although we are fairly sure of the difference between the reduced loud and the medial stress in *movie-auditorium* and similar compounds, we hope to prove this difference by submitting a series of test words or a prepared text to a laboratory phonetician for recording and electrical measurement.

[9]Phonemic symbols are enclosed between diagonals to distinguish them from spellings (cited in italics) and from phonetic symbols (enclosed in square brackets). For the consonant phonemes we use Bloomfield's symbols; see his *Language* 91.

[10]It is esthetically satisfying to find minimally contrasting pairs like *vine : thine*, and especially pleasant to find a whole series like *pill : till : kill*, etc.;

also, except /r, w, j, h/, are clearly found in medial and final position; /w, j, h/ occur medially before a strong-stressed vowel (awáy, beyónd, ahéad), /r/ occurs in any medial position (merry, arouse). The phonemes /ž, ŋ/ occur medially before a weak-stressed vowel and finally: measure, confusion (cf. mesher, Confucian), singer (cf. sinner, finger); rouge (cf. ruche), sing (cf. sin, sink).

Speakers who distinguish wheel and weal, which and witch, whale and wail, etc., have the cluster /hw/ in the first member of each pair. That this is a cluster and not a unit phoneme can be shown by comparison with the clusters /hj/ in huge and /kw, gw, tw, dw/ in queen, Gwen, twice, dwarf.

That /č, ǰ, š, ž/ are unit phonemes appears partly from their distribution with respect to points of open juncture, partly from their behavior in clusters (cf. belch, bulge; shrink). There may be some dialects in which they can be analyzed as /tj, dj, sj, zj/ respectively, but considerations of pattern congruity make this unlikely. Under no circumstances can /č, ǰ/ be analyzed as /tš, dž/.

To examine the distribution of consonants in clusters is beyond the scope of this paper.

7   We are now ready to examine the syllabic sounds of English. We begin our analysis with monosyllabic words pronounced in isolation and bearing a loud stress, ending in a voiceless stop and containing, immediately before this consonant, a vowel which is phonetically short and non-diphthongal. We find that such units reveal six categories of contrasting sound-types, illustrated by pit, pet, pat, pot, putt, put. The vowels of these words may be written phonetically (impressionistically) as [ɪ, ɛ, æ, ɑ, ʌ, ʊ].[11] We look next at words of the same

kind but ending in a voiced stop: bid, bed, bade, cod, cud, could (for GLT's pronunciation of bad and BB's pronunciation of cod see below); here the six sound-types are the same in quality (or nearly so) but noticeably longer, and the distribution of the lengths is complementary. Before spirants, the differences in length may be still greater,[12] but again depend on the character (specifically the voice-term) of the following consonant, and no contrast is possible: miss, mess, mass (BB but not GLT), toss, cuss, puss : Liz, fez, has, Boz, does; [ʊ] does not occur before a voiced spirant except in the dissyllabic word bosom. The same sounds, again with the exception of [ʊ],[13] occur also without a preceding consonant: ill, ell, at, odd, up.

We have here six vowels that are clearly separate phonemes. They occur freely before and after consonants and clusters of all kinds, though [ʊ] is statistically less common (for historical reasons). In GLT's dialect [æ] is rare in monosyllables except before /p, t, k, č/, the [æ] of other dialects being elsewhere replaced by a long tense vowel with a central

---

here the mean-mid-front vowel of pet (not, as in that system, the lower-mid-front vowel of French faire); [a] denotes a low-central vowel (not low-front); [ɑ] denotes a low-back unrounded vowel; [ɚ] denotes a variety of mid-central retroflex vowels, whether actually articulated with inversion of the tongue tip or with retraction and lateral compression of the body of the tongue; [i̯, u̯] and the like denote nonsyllabic vowels or brief glides. Vowel length is marked by a raised dot; a small arrowhead pointing up is used as a diacritic after vowel letters to denote a somewhat higher vowel than the variety written with the unmodified symbol.

It is to be borne in mind that our phonetic transcriptions are intended to be only approximate, and purposely ignore features irrelevant to the discussion. On the principles underlying our practice see Bloch's statement in Hans Kurath and others, Handbook of the Linguistic Geography of New England, Chap. 4, esp. §§1–3, 21–28 (Providence, 1939).

[12]Our judgments of length are admittedly subjective, and lack the precision of mechanical or electrical measurements (cf. fn. 8). Nevertheless we believe that our statements regarding relative length are valid within the limits of this investigation.

[13]Unless the exclamation oops has [ʊ]; but this is not really part of our active vocabulary. Hermann Michaelis and Daniel Jones, A Phonetic Dictionary of the English Language, 426 (Hannover and Berlin, 1913), list only Ulrich, Ulrica, and Uruguay—besides ugh and an occasional weak form of who—as beginning with [ʊ] in the speech of Southern England.

---

but such contrasts are by no means necessary to prove a phonemic difference. Thus, it is not easy to find a pair of words exhibiting a minimal contrast between /ž/ and /ŋ/, but the lack of such a pair is easily supplied by the series singer : sitter, letter : leisure or ring : rim, room : rouge. In languages with a more complex morphological structure, even short series like these are often hard to find.

[11]Symbols enclosed in square brackets are phonetic, not phonemic. In the phonetic transcriptions, we use (except for a few changes imposed by typographical limitations) the system presented in B. Bloch and G. L. Trager, Tables for a System of Phonetic Description (preliminary ed.), New Haven, 1940. Most of the symbols are familiar; [ɛ] denotes

off-glide which we may write [æ·ə]; this sound is often in contrast with short [æ]: thus *bad, can* 'tin container', *adds* with [æ·ə], present a minimal contrast to *bade, can* 'am able', *adze* with [æ]; *have, has, had* have [æ], *halve, jazz, mad* have [æ·ə].[14] In BB's dialect *bomb* has a rather short [ɑ] (though slightly longer than the vowel of *pot*), while *balm* has a much longer vowel of the same quality [ɑ·], which appears also in *rob* and *pod*. The contrast *bomb : balm* shows that [ɑ] and [ɑ·] are phonemically different; the former is rare except before /p, t, k, č/. A similar distinction obtains in several other varieties of English. GLT has a short [ɑ] in *pot, rock*, a longer vowel of the same quality in *pod, bomb*, but a different, more advanced long vowel, which may also be written [ɑ·] for convenience, in *balm, father, pa*. This is the situation described by Bloomfield for the speech of the older generation in Chicago.[15] For the phonemic interpretation of [ɑ·] see §12.

In words of more than one syllable the six phonemes already established are found to occur with all of the three strong stresses: with loud stress in *pítting, pétting, pátting, pótting, cútting, pútting;* with reduced loud in the second members of *háir-pîn, púp-têti, dóor-mât, ármy-côt, téar-dûct, hánd-bôok;* and with medial in *cónvìct, cóntènts, áutomàt, ápricòt, cónduìct, spóonfùl.* It should be noted that in all such words the vowels occur only in syllables ending in a consonant or a consonant cluster. They are never found finally with one of the three strong stresses.

Weak-stressed vowels in comparable syllabic situations differ in quality from the strong-stressed vowels discussed above; but this difference does not justify the postulation of a separate series of phonemes. All the weak-

[14]See G. L. Trager, "The Pronunciation of 'Short *a*' in American English," *American Speech* 5.396–400 (1930); id., "One Phonemic Entity Becomes Two: The Case of 'Short *a*,'" *ibid.* 15.255–258 (1940). Sapir once remarked on a similar distinction in his own speech: he pronounced all words of this class with a rather low [æ], the length of the vowel being regulated by the voice-term of the following consonant; but in the pair *have : halve* he pronounced respectively the normal medium-long [æ] and a distinctly overlong vowel of the same quality. His own explanation of this anomaly was that the word *halve* contained, in his speech, a unique phoneme found nowhere else (cf. fn. 33).

[15]See *Language* 11.97–98.

stressed vowels are of course in complementary distribution with all the strong-stressed ones; their phonetic interrelationship and the phonetic resemblance which each one bears to one of the strong-stressed vowels makes it possible to arrive at a satisfactory phonemic identification of the two series. In general, it will be seen that the weak-stressed member of a phoneme is more centralized (i.e., pronounced with a tongue position less clearly front or back) than the strong-stressed vowel which it most nearly resembles.

Thus the weak-stressed [ɪ] in words like *habit, habitat, candid, helping, incite,* and the weak-stressed [ʊ] in words like *educate, regular, careful* (when this is not pronounced with syllabic [l̩] or with [fəl]) are respectively more centralized than the vowels of *pit* and *put.* The rather uncommon weak-stressed [æ] in the second syllable of *àdvantágeous* or the first syllable of *Calcútta,* and the weak-stressed [ɑ] in *Octóber, postérior,* both of which occur only before a syllable with loud stress, bear the same relation to the vowels of *pat* and *pot.* The obvious phonetic resemblance between these centralized vowels and the corresponding peripheral ones leaves no doubt as to the phonemic groupings.

It will have been noted that the weak-stressed [ɪ, ʊ] occur in free syllables (ending in a vowel, as in *habitat, educate*), as well as in checked syllables (ending in a consonant, as in *habit, careful*); this is an important difference in distribution between weak- and strong-stressed vowels. Further, many American and most British speakers have weak-stressed [ɪ], less commonly also weak-stressed [ʊ], in final position, as in *city, value.* In our own speech, however, and in most other types of "General American" pronunciation, these vowels do not occur finally: *city* ends in [ɪ̯i] (very short, almost [i]), *value* ends in [ʊ̯u] (almost [u]). These higher and more diphthongal sounds must be analyzed differently; see §9.

Words like *about, sofa, condemn, cautious* contain in the weak-stressed syllables a sound-type that may be written [ə]. This vowel varies considerably with different speakers; it is most often mean-mid-central, but may be higher- or lower-mid-central, sometimes even advanced lower-mid-back, almost like [ʌ]. It is an extremely common vowel in all types of English, occurring in both checked and free syllables; in our own speech, as perhaps in most varieties of American English, it is the only weak-stressed vowel that appears in final position (*sofa*). In certain words, speakers and regions differ greatly in the use of [ə] and [ɪ]: thus in *believe, refer*, BB has [ə] while GLT has [ɪ]; but in other words most dialects agree on one vowel or the other: thus *habit, discuss* generally have [ɪ], *sofa, condemn* generally have [ə].

In the weak-stressed syllables of *roses, handed, hardest, exist* we have, like many other American speakers, a vowel different from both [ɪ] and [ə], best described as a slightly advanced higher-mid-central [ə˄]. Note these contrasts: *roses* [ə˄] : *Rosa's* [ə], *handed* [ə˄] : *candid* [ɪ]. The weak-stressed vowels [ə] and [ə˄] are in complementary distribution with [ʌ] and [ɛ] (the other strong-stressed vowels having been already paired with corresponding weak ones); their phonetic resemblance to these and their phonetic relation to each other[16] again settle the question of the phonemic grouping: [ə] belongs with [ʌ], [ə˄] with [ɛ].

There are then in weak-stressed syllables the same six vowel phonemes as in strong-stressed ones. We can accordingly simplify our transcription and write henceforth the six symbols /i/ (*wínning*), /e/ (*pétted*), /a/ (*abstráct*), /o/ (*concóct*), /ə/ (*abóve*), /u/ (*pút, éducàte*).[17]

8 In weak-stressed syllables we find the syllabic consonants [l̩, n̩] and less commonly [m̩], as in *apple, button, rhythm*. These cannot be simply the phonemes /l, n, m/, since we have contrasts like *gamboling* [l̩] : *gambling* [l], *evening* 'making even' [n̩] : *evening* 'early night' [n], *fathoming* [m̩] : *rhythmic* [m].

Moreover, there is often free (stylistically determined) variation between the syllabic consonant and the sequence [ə] + consonant; thus *idol* is pronounced with final [l̩] or [əl], *mountain* with final [n̩] or [ən] (cf. the New England form with [ɪn]). The phonetic similarity of the nucleus of such syllables is greatest to some allophones of the already established phoneme /ə/, and this lateral- or nasal-colored syllabicity is in complementary distribution with the members of that phoneme. We conclude that [l̩, n̩, m̩] are /əl, ən, əm/. The phoneme /ə/ has then a wide range of allophones: [ʌ] in *ùndóne*, [ə] in *sofa*, syllabicity in *apple, button, rhythm*.[18]

The weak-stressed retroflex vowel [ɚ] in *pertáin, fáther* appears to be similarly structured as a combination of /ə/ + consonant. The consonant, here retroflexion of the vowel itself (but in some dialects a segmental fraction of greater retroflexion following a weakly retroflex vowel), is in complementary distribution with prevocalic /r/ and obviously similar to it phonetically. It follows that /ɚ/ is phonemically /ər/. For the treatment of the strong-stressed retroflex vowel of *bird, burr, furry*, see §§11, 13.

9 We turn now to the so-called long vowels and diphthongs. At the outset, a striking difference is to be noted between the distribution of these syllabics and that of the six sound-types already discussed: whereas the latter, when bearing one of the three strong stresses, occur only in checked syllables, the long vowels and diphthongs occur also in free syllables and even in final position (thus *feel, feeling, fee; toil, toiling, toy*). This difference in the freedom of occurrence should be borne in mind throughout the following discussion.

In words like *beat, bait, bite, Hoyt, boot, boat, bout* we pronounce vocalic sounds which in a phonetic (impressionistic) transcription may be approximately written as [ɾi̯, ɛɪ̯, ae̯, ɔɪ, u˄u̯, ʌu̯, aọ]; many other speakers of American English have the same or very similar sound-types. Of these, [ɾi̯] and [u˄u̯] may vary with all speakers to monophthongal [i·] and [u·] respectively; Midwestern speakers often have minimally diphthongal [i·, u·], and even [e·, o·] corresponding to our [ɛɪ̯, ʌu̯]. In all

---

[16]The weak vowel of *handed* is both higher and somewhat farther front than the weak vowel of *sofa*, just as the vowel of *pet* is somewhat higher and of course considerably farther front than the vowel of *cut*. (The greater frontness of the vowel of *handed* does not appear from the makeshift transcription here used.)

[17]Our vowel symbols differ somewhat from the corresponding symbols used by Bloomfield in the works cited above (fnn. 1, 4). The letters /i, e, u/ have the same value in both systems; but our /a/ = Bloomfield's /ɛ/, our /o/ = his /ɑ/, and our /ə/ = his /o/.

[18]See Swadesh, *Language* 11.150.

dialects the syllabics of such words ending in a voiceless stop are rather short in normal speech, though easily lengthened for emphasis or special effect; under such lengthening the diphthongal quality is regularly more noticeable than otherwise, and often appears even in those dialects which normally pronounce monophthongs in *beat, boot, bait, boat.*

In words ending in a voiced stop, as *bead, laid, hide, enjoyed, food, load, loud,* the syllabics are considerably longer and as a rule more clearly diphthongal, though the variations in this respect are comparable to those observed in the shorter varieties. Before final voiceless spirants, as in *peace, pace, dice, choice, loose, dose, house,* the syllabics are pronounced long by some speakers, short by others; before final voiced spirants, as in *peas, pays, pies, joys, lose, pose, cows,* all speakers pronounce them long. The greatest contrast in length appears when we compare these syllabics in final position and before a cluster of voiceless consonants: *bee, bay, buy, boy, boo, beau, bough* : *beasts, pastes, bites, joists, boosts, posts, ousts.* In all these examples, corresponding sound-types of different length are obviously in complementary distribution.

When the syllable containing one of these long vowels and diphthongs is followed by another syllable (with close juncture), the relative lengths remain as described, and are determined by the character of the intersyllabic consonant or cluster, or by the absence of such a consonant. When there is no consonant, the first syllabic is long and in most dialects plainly diphthongal, and its final element usually forms a clear glide between the two syllables: *being, baying, buying, enjoying, booing, going, allowing.* In these cases the intersyllabic glide is ambisyllabic (i.e., forms phonetically the end of the first and the beginning of the second syllable), so that these words exhibit a syllabic structure exactly parallel to that of such words as *bidding, bedding, padding, nodding, budding, pudding,* where one of the six short vowels is followed by an ambisyllabic voiced stop.

In normal English we do not find in final position any sound-types exactly like initial [j] and [w]. But the final elements of the long vowels and diphthongs, usually [i̥, ɪ̥, e̥] on the one hand and [u̥, ʊ̥, o̥] on the other, not only are in complementary distribution with [j] and

[w], but bear them respectively an obvious phonetic resemblance.[19] By the requirements of phonemic theory, we must group these final elements and the two semivowels together, since there is no contrast between them. We can then write the seven diphthongs so far examined as [ɪˇj, ɛj, aj, ɔj, uˇw, ʌw, aw], leaving the phonemic character of the prior element still undecided. In favor of the analysis of these diphthongs not as unit phonemes but as combinations of a vowel phoneme with a following semivowel, two facts of distribution, already referred to, are here again to be emphasized: first, that the six short-vowel phonemes occur with a strong stress only in checked syllables, whereas the long vowels and diphthongs occur also in free syllables; and second, that when one of these long vowels and diphthongs occurs before another vowel with no intervening consonant, its final element appears as an ambisyllabic glide, just as an intersyllabic consonant is ambisyllabic when it follows one of the six short-vowel phonemes.

It may be objected that in words like *attáck, redúce, belíeve,* the consonant following the weak-stressed vowel goes with the second syllable (i.e., the onset of stress coincides with the beginning of the consonant), whereas in words like *bìólogy, còérce, òásis,* the diphthong of the first syllable is not divided into a short vowel and a semivowel beginning the next syllable, but instead remains diphthongal with the semivowel still ambisyllabic. Now, /j/ and /w/ may form a special

---

[19]The articulation of [j] and [w] in normal English may be described as follows. For [j], the tongue moves to the position of a following vowel from any relatively higher and more advanced position, the lips being unrounded at least at the beginning of the glide; for [w], the tongue moves to the position of a following vowel from any relatively higher and more retracted position, the lips being rounded at least at the beginning of the glide. The articulation of the nonsyllabic elements here in question is precisely the reverse of this. For the final elements of the diphthongs in *bee, bay, buy, boy,* the tongue moves from the position of the preceding vowel to a relatively higher and more advanced position, the lips being unrounded at least at the end of the glide; for the final elements of the diphthongs in *beau, boo, bough,* the tongue moves from the position of the preceding vowel to a relatively higher and more retracted position, the lips being rounded at least at the end of the glide.

subclass of consonant phonemes, behaving differently from other consonants in syllabic division. But the real answer to this objection is the difference in stress: the first syllables of *bìólogy, còérce, òásis*, and the like are stronger than those of *attáck, redúce, belíeve*, as a comparison with *a-yéarning, awáy* will show. That the intersyllabic semivowel is in these words ambisyllabic bears out our statement that a strong-stressed short vowel cannot end a syllable. As a confirmation we may cite the behavior, under comparable syllabic conditions, of the weak-stressed diphthongs [ɪʲj, ʊʌw] in words like *reálity, duálity;* here the onset of stress does in fact very commonly coincide with the beginning of the semivowel, resulting in pronunciations of the type of [rɪʌ'jælɪtɪʌi̥, dʊʌ'wælɪtɪʌi̥].

10 Accepting the analysis of the long vowels and diphthongs in *beat, bait, bite, Hoyt, boot, boat, bout*, etc., as consisting of short vowels plus /j/ and /w/, it remains to decide what the prior elements are, and whether all or any of them are allophones of the six vowel phonemes already established. We may clear the ground by noting that all these doubtful elements are in complementary distribution with all of the six short vowels. The problem can be solved, therefore, only on the basis of phonetic similarity and phonetic interrelationship. We must bear in mind also the principle of economy: the analysis to be preferred is the one which accounts adequately and accurately for all the facts with the smallest number of separate phonemic entities.

It is perfectly clear that the prior elements of [ɪʲj, ʊʌw] are by both criteria to be assigned to the phonemes /i/ and /u/ respectively. Accordingly we shall write *beat, bead, peace, peas, bee, being, reality* and *boot, food, loose, lose, do, doing, duality* as /bíjt, bíjd, píjs, píjz, bíj, bíjiŋ, rijálitij/ and /búwt, fúwd, lúws, lúwz, dúw, dúwiŋ, duwálitij/.

Nor does [ɛj] offer any difficulty. It is obviously /ej/, and we therefore write *bait, paid, base, bays, bay, baying, chaotic* as /béjt, péjd, béjs, béjz, béj, béjiŋ, kejótik (kèjótik)/. For the analysis of the Midwestern monophthongal [e·] as /ej/ compare the parallel treatment of [o·] in the next paragraph.

When pronounced [ʌw] (as it is, approximately, in our speech), the diphthong of *boat*

seems to have a prior element phonetically similar to the vowel of *cut*, an allophone of /ə/; the pronunciations [ɔw, ow, o·w] and the like are susceptible of the same analysis, since we have already observed that /ə/ has a rather wide range of allophones and since the lip-rounding of the prior element in such pronunciations can be most satisfactorily explained as conditioned by the following /w/.[20] Even a monophthongal [o·] of Midwestern speakers is to be analyzed, on the basis of pattern congruity, in the same way.[21] We then write *boat,*

---

[20]That the first vowel of *away* is not similarly rounded is due to a difference in syllabification; cf. §9, last paragraph.

[21]In dialects that have monophthongs instead of diphthongs of this type, we encounter four fairly uniform long vowels, [i·, e·, u·, o·], in words like *beat, bait, boot, boat;* in words like *bead, paid, food, load* and *bee, bay, too, go*, the vowels tend to be less uniform; and in words like *being, baying, doing, going* there is often a clear glide, [j] or [w], between the two vowels. The total pattern is best revealed if we state that the long vowels of *beat, bait, boot, boat* are respectively /ij, ej, uw, əw/; in such a dialect the allophones of the two phonemes in each of these four combinations can be described by a statement such as this: /i, e, u, ə/ combine with the homorganic semivowel—/i, e/ with /j/, /u, ə/ with /w/—so that the phonetic result is an approximation of the two elements to each other; that is, /i, e/ are raised while /j/ is lowered (in comparison with the allophones in *pit, pet, yes*), and /u, ə/ are both raised and rounded while /w/ is lowered.

If a language has a pattern for combinations of phonemes such as /Vj/ and /Vw/, and if some of the possible combinations are lacking while at the same time certain phonetically pure long vowels are present which are not paralleled by similar vowels elsewhere in the language, the requirements of phonemic theory (complementary distribution, economy in the total number of units, etc.) force us to analyze these long vowels as the lacking combinations of vowel plus semivowel, the identifications resting on phonetic similarity and pattern congruity. In the present case, [i·] is obviously more similar to /i/ + /j/ than is [e·], and [e·] is more similar to /e/ + /j/ than it is to /i/ + /j/, and [i·] is higher than [e·] just as /i/ is higher than /e/; the relations among the back vowels are parallel.

The principle of pattern analysis here invoked has never been better stated than in the following passage by Swadesh, *Language* 13.10 [56]. "The general criterion of phonemics is relativity within the totality of the given language. Sounds must be classified according to similarities of phonetic and permutational characteristics. If in this procedure we seek to find the maximally simple, self-consistent, and complete total formulation, we reduce the subjective element in phonetics [emphasized by Bloom-

load, dose, doze, go, going, cooperate, polo
as /bə́wt, lə́wd, də́ws, də́wz, gə́w, gə́wiŋ,
kə̀wópərèjt, pə́wləw/.

The syllabic of *bout, loud,* etc., in many
varieties of English begins with a low vowel
rather definitely front, though in other varieties the beginning is more retracted; thus GLT
has a prior element which is sometimes almost
[æ], whereas BB has [a]. Provided that the beginning of the diphthong is more advanced
than the vowel of *pot,* as it is in most varieties
of English,[22] the phonetic relation of this prior
element to the beginnings of the other diphthongs and its phonetic resemblance to the
vowel of *pat* (which is admittedly not always
very close) suggest the analysis of this diphthong into /a/ plus /w/; so that we can write
*bout, loud, house, cows, cow, allowing, how-
ever* as /bə́wt, lə́wd, hə́ws, kə́wz, kə́w, əláwiŋ,
hàwévər/. But many speakers have a prior
element here which is much farther back,
sometimes even raised almost or quite to the
vowel of *cut.* For these speakers, is the syllabic of *bout* perhaps /ow/ or even /əw/? If it is
/əw/, then our analysis of the diphthong in
boat breaks down, except for those dialects
—e.g., Nova Scotian—where *a boat* and *about*
sound alike: both probably /əbə́wt/. In standard dialects which pronounce *a boat* as
[ə'bowt] and *about* as [ə'bʌwt] the relation of
these diphthongs to each other and to the short
vowels makes it probable that *boat* is still
/bə́wt/ and that *about* is /əbówt/; the allophone of /o/ is here a somewhat higher and
more centralized vowel than in *pot, rock,* etc.
The situation is complicated by the fact that
many speakers in our Southern states have
[æw] in *about* and [ɔw] or [ow] in *boat,* but
pronounce *bought* with a diphthong of the type
of [ɒw]. Here we have the three combinations
/aw, ow, əw/ side by side, in *bout, bought,*

and *boat* respectively. But sometimes the
phonemic interpretation is not so easy. Thus,
there are some varieties of Southern speech
that show strikingly different pronunciations
of the diphthong in question before a voiceless
and before a voiced consonant: *house* may
have [ʌw], *houses* [æw].[22a] For the present
we are content to leave such problems unsolved.

To analyze the syllabic in *bite* we proceed
as before. There are, as always, varying pronunciations: most standard speakers have a
low-central vowel as the prior element; some
have a more advanced variety; others, for
example in New York City and Philadelphia,
have a vowel noticeably farther back (cf. also
the comic Irish 'Oi' for *I*). We believe that the
best analysis for standard speakers is /aj/:
as in the diphthong /aw/, the allophone of /a/
is here lower and more retracted than the
vowel of *pat;* and we write *bite, bide, vice,
buys, buy, buying, biology* as /bájt, bájd, vájs,
bájz, báj, bájiŋ, bàjóləjij/. For some speakers,
however, a better analysis will be /oj/, especially in those substandard dialects where
nine rimes with *join.*

This leaves the syllabic of *boy.* In the
speech of those who distinguish the vowel of
bomb, bother from that of *balm, father,* the
allophone of /o/ in the former pair of words is
a low-back or retracted low-central vowel,
with or without lip-rounding (in American
English generally unrounded except in eastern
New England). In *boy, boil, noise,* etc., the
prior element is always a back vowel and
nearly always rounded in standard speech,
but varies in height (and correspondingly in
the degree of rounding) from higher-low to
higher-mid, the lower-mid vowel [ɔ] being
probably the most common variety. We suggest, with some hesitation, that the analysis
which best fits the situation is /oj/, with the
allophone of /o/ defined here as a rounded
vowel. For speakers who distinguish *boy* and

field, *Language* 84]. Trying to be objective is not
likely to succeed fully without an intelligent understanding of the nature of phonetic systems and a
constant effort to see each detail in its relation to
every other detail. There is a real danger that pattern-
conscious investigators may distort the facts in order
to make the pattern seem more symmetrical, but
this danger is small in comparison with the danger
of distorting or failing to notice facts because of
giving no attention to pattern."

[22]And provided that in those dialects where
pot, rod, and the like have a rounded vowel, the beginning of the diphthong in *bout* is unrounded.

[22a]On this diphthong in Virginia speech see
E. F. Shewmake, *MLN* 40.489 ff. (1925); id., *En-
glish Pronunciation in Virginia* 24 (n.p., n.d.);
Argus Tresidder, "Notes on Virginia Speech,"
American Speech 16.113–116 (1941). The findings
of the Linguistic Atlas of the South Atlantic States
were presented in a paper ("The Diphthong *au* in
Virginia") by Guy S. Lowman, Jr., read before the
Practical Phonetics group of the Modern Language
Association at the 52d annual meeting, 1935.

buy, as all standard dialects do, the respective analyses /bój/ and /báj/ are certainly correct in pattern, since *boy* regularly has a more retracted vowel than *buy,* just as *pot* has a more retracted vowel than *pat.* Midwestern speakers who have a short rounded back vowel in *wash, watch,* etc., and Eastern speakers who normally pronounce a rounded back vowel in all words of the type of *pot, pod, bomb,* will have no difficulty in identifying this vowel with the prior element of the diphthong in *boy.* Accordingly we shall write *Hoyt, Boyd, voice, noise, boy, toying* as /hójt, bójd, vójs, nójz, bój, tójiŋ/. But in substandard New York City speech, where *bird* and *Boyd* are identical and where *bide* has a back vowel, the most satisfactory analysis is probably /bə́jd/ for *bird* and *Boyd,* and /bójd/ for *bide.*[23]

11 Syllabics preceding the consonant phoneme /r/ constitute a separate problem. In the variety of English that we both use (which makes, as we have mentioned, a nearly maximum number of distinctions among the syllabic phonemes), all of the six short vowels appear with strong stress before the combination /r/ plus weak-stressed vowel: *mirror, merry, marry, sorry, hurry, jury* /mírər, mérij, márij, sórij, hə́rij, júrij/. GLT usually pronounces *hurry* with a long retroflex vowel, as [ˈhɚ·rɪ̂i],

[23]The analysis made in §10 is essentially the same as that described by Bloomfield in *Language* 11.101, fn. 8, as "the customary alternative statement." Except for Bloomfield's summary, however, we know of no place where such a statement has appeared. Our analysis differs from Bloomfield's in the following respects: in his treatment, the vowels of *balm* and *law* are considered unit phonemes, written /a, ɔ/; then the syllabics of *buy, boy* are analyzed as /aj, ɔj/ respectively, and the syllabic of *cow* as /aw/. As appears from §§11, 12 below, we analyze the syllabics in *balm* and *law* differently, as non-unitary sequences of phonemes; this enables us to deal with the diphthongs in *buy, boy, cow* more simply in relation to the six short vowels. Cf. also Bloomfield, *ibid.* 100, last two sentences and fn. 7.

It may be noted here that we regard /juw/ as a normal sequence of three phonemes, in no way structurally different from the combinations /ruw, wuw, waj/ in *prove, woo, wine;* this analysis is confirmed by such series as *Yale : yowl : yule, yeoman : Yuman,* and the like. In addition to the word *piano* with /pj/ before a syllabic other than /uw/ (Bloomfield, *ibid.* 101, fn. 8), we may cite the local pronunciation of *Pueblo* (Colorado) as /pjéblǝw/, and the Southern pronunciation of *car, garden,* and the like with /kj, gj/.

but also uses the form with [ʌ]; BB says [ˈhʌrɪ̂i]. Note that in our speech, as in that of many others, *Mary* differs from both *merry* and *marry*—[ˈmæ·ǝrɪ̂i] (GLT) or [ˈmɛ·ǝrɪ̂i] (BB) : [ˈmɛrɪ̂i, ˈmærɪ̂i]; *boring* is [ˈbɔ·̂ǝrɪŋ]; and the following pairs do not rime: *dearer* and *mirror* [ˈdɪ ·ǝrɚ : ˈmɪrɚ], *starry* and *sorry* [ˈstɑ·rɪ̂i : ˈsɑrɪ̂i], *furry* and *hurry* [ˈfɚ·rɪ̂i : ˈhʌrɪ̂i], *poorer* and *juror* [ˈpu·̂ǝrɚ : ˈjurɚ]. Compare also the series *fierce, scarce, farce, horse, purse, bourse* [fɪ·̂ɚs, skæ̂ɚs (skɛ̂ɚs), fɑ̂ɚs, hɔ·̂ɚs, pɚ·s, bu·̂ɚs] and *beer, bear, bar, bore, burr, boor* [bɪ·̂ɚ, bæ·̂ɚ (bɛ·̂ɚ), bɑ·ɚ, bɔ·̂ɚ, bɚ·̂, bu·̂ɚ]. It is clear that these two series contain the same syllabic phonemes as the series *dearer, Mary, starry, boring, furry, poorer,* and that these phonemes, while bearing a pattern relation to each other similar to that of the six short vowels, are phonemically different from them.

Before considering these differences, we can point out that in those varieties of English where orthographic final and preconsonantal *r* is pronounced as retroflexion, this is an allophone of the /r/ phoneme (cf. §8), so that words like *beer, bear,* etc., have /r/ as their final phoneme. The distribution of this retroflexion is complementary with the frictionless [r] initially and between vowels, the fricative [r] after [t, d], and the other obvious allophones of this consonant phoneme. The important point here is that *burr* also must contain some kind of rather long vowel followed by /r/; to analyze the syllabic of *burr, cur, purse, worm,* etc., as a special "*r*-vowel" phoneme is theoretically bad, because it fails to give maximum economy in the statement of the number of phonemes and distorts the pattern clearly established by the parallel series just illustrated.

It is of course no accident that the three series *dearer, Mary, starry, boring, furry, poorer; fierce, scarce, farce, horse, purse, bourse; beer, bear, bar, bore, burr, boor* each exhibit the same number of contrasting categories as the short-vowel series of §7. The conclusion is inescapable that the syllabics of these three series consist phonemically of the six short vowels plus a lengthening element, which we may write provisionally with a raised dot. We can decide at once that *dearer, fierce, beer* are /dí·rǝr, fí·rs, bí·r/ and that *poorer, bourse, boor* are /pú·rǝr,.bú·rs, bú·r/. If we compare *dearer* to *mirror* and *poorer* to *juror,* the parallel contrast between *furry* and *hurry* shows that *furry, purse, burr* are /fə́·rij, pə́·rs, bə́·r/. The analysis of the remaining words is clear from the pattern relationship: *Mary, scarce, bear* are /mé·rij, ské·rs, bé·r/; *starry, farce, bar* are /stá·rij, fá·rs, bá·r/; *boring, horse, bore* are /bó·riŋ, hó·rs, bó·r/. We note immediately that the allophone of /a/ before the lengthening element is phonetically very similar to the allophones of the same phoneme before /j/ and /w/ (§10), and that the allophone of /o/ before this element is similar to its allophone before /j/; the phonetics and the pattern analysis therefore agree, as they should. The element /e·/ shows an allophone of /e/ which in the pronunciation of some speakers is close to the /a/ of *pat;* but the analysis is supported by two considerations:[24] many other speakers (including BB) pronounce words like *Mary, scarce, bear* with a syllabic that is much closer to the vowel of *pet;* and in either case, the phonetic relation of /e·/ to the next-higher vowel in the series /i·/ and to the next-lower /a·/ is exactly parallel to the relation of /e/ to /i/ and /a/ respectively in *pet, pit, pat.*

The elements /i·/ and /u·/ do not contrast with /ij/ and /uw/ before /r/, as the latter do not appear in that position. But /e·/ contrasts with /ej/ in several dialects: GLT has /ej/ in *eyrie* (admittedly a book word); BB has it in *pharaoh* (here contrasting with /e·/ in *faro*); and in eastern New England there is normally a sharp distinction between words like *Mary, dairy, Sarah* with [ei̯, ε·i̯] and words like *bearing, fairest* with [εə, æə].[25] Many speakers in all parts of the country distinguish between *nor* and *bore, for* and *four, horse* and *hoarse, morning* and *mourning,*[26] etc., by pronouncing the second word in each pair with a closer vowel of the type of [o·ə]; since this is in complementary distribution with the diphthong /əw/ in *boat* and phonetically very close to it, it seems reasonable to analyze the words with [o·ə] as /bə́wr, fə́wr, hə́wrs, mə́wrniŋ/,

etc. (For a possible different interpretation see §13.)

Other combinations of vowel plus semivowel before /r/ may be illustrated by *Irish* /ájriš/, *Moira* /mójrə/, *cowrie* /káwrij/. In *hire* and *flour* both of us pronounce two syllables, /hájər, fláwər/, just as in *higher* and *flower;* in the dialect of those who distinguish these words, *hire* and *flour* are /hájr, fláwr/. In our speech the combination /awr/ occurs with medial stress in the word *òursélves,* and /ajr/ varies with /ajər/ in *Ireland.*

For many speakers there are no contrasts at all between /i·, u·/ and /ij, uw/, so that /i·/ and /u·/ can be disposed of simply by equating them to /ij/ and /uw/. But even for such speakers we have still to account for /e·, a·, o·, ə·/, which are found in all the "r-pronouncing" dialects of English. From the general pattern it would appear that the element heard as a lengthening of the vowel, often with the addition of a glide in the direction of [ə], may be some kind of semivowel. Before deciding its phonemic interpretation, we must look for evidence of its existence elsewhere than before /r/.

12 Vowels almost identical with the syllabics of *bar* and *bore* appear respectively in words like *balm, pa, father* and in words like *dawn, long, law.* (In the speech of those who distinguish between *for* and *four, horse* and *hoarse,* etc., the vowel of *law* is closer to that of *for, horse.*) The element /i·/ contrasts with /ij/ in BB's pronunciation of *idea* and *bee* [ae̯'dir̯ə : bṛi̯], though it is rare except before /r/; and /u·/ contrasts with /uw/ in his pronunciation of *St. Louis* (the city) and *loose* [luə̯s : luûs]. The common American English word spelled *yeah* or *yeh* has a syllabic almost identical with that of *bear.* We have evidence, then, for the five "long vowels" /i·, e·, a·, o·, u·/ in other positions than before /r/.[27] The two low vowels /a·, o·/ are common in nearly all types of English; /i·, u·/ are rare, at least in American English. The vowel /e·/ is also rare in the

---

[24] In addition to the not irrelevant fact that when we have analyzed the other syllabics, there is no other category left for the syllabic of *bear.*

[25] Cases like *hay-rick, pay-roll* with /ej/ are beside the point here, since these words have open juncture before the /r/. But in New England speech both *dairy* with /ej/ and *bearing* with /e·/ have close juncture.

[26] See Hans Kurath, *"Mourning and Morning," Studies for William A. Read* 166–173.

[27] By manufacturing an example ad hoc, it is possible to adduce evidence also for /ə·/. If the exclamation *huh* may be used, like *hem* and *haw,* as a verb meaning 'to say huh', then its preterit is *huh'd.* This *huh'd,* in our pronunciation of it, does not rime with *cud,* but has a distinctly longer vowel. We conclude that *cud* has /ə/ but that *huh'd* has /ə·/.

standard dialects, but is an important element in those varieties of English (like GLT's) which distinguish between *bad, jazz, can* 'tin container', *halve, adds* with [æ·ə̣] and *bade, has, can* 'am able', *have, adze* with [æ] (cf. §7). In such dialects the [æ·ə̣] of *bad, adds,* etc., is phonetically and thus also phonemically the same as the syllabic of *Mary, scarce, bear, yeah,* that is /e·/. As for /ə·/, this occurs frequently in the mixed dialect of those who have both "*r*-pronouncing" and "*r*-less" forms in their speech—i.e., who pronounce *bird, purse,* and the like sometimes with and sometimes without retroflexion.

What is the phonemic interpretation of the lengthening element which we have been writing with a raised dot? It cannot be any of the vowels, not even /ə/ (in spite of the phonetic resemblance), since there is no example anywhere else in the total pattern for two vowels in succession. It functions like the two semivowels /j/ and /w/, and like these must be reckoned a consonant—either identical with one of the twenty-four consonants listed in §6, or a separate phoneme.

The only consonant with which this element is in complementary distribution is /h/ : /h/ never occurs immediately after one of the six short vowels with strong stress[28] or before another consonant, but the lengthening element occurs precisely here and nowhere else.

Is there any phonetic similarity between this element and [h]? In English pronunciation, [h] is a voiceless sound (occasionally, as between vowels, a murmured sound) whose tongue and lip position anticipates either completely or approximately that of the following voiced sound;[29] when the anticipation is only approximate, the tongue position of [h] tends to be more centralized (more nearly "neutral") than that of the following sound. The lengthening element can be accurately defined as a

voiced continuation of a preceding vocalic sound with either the same or a progressively centralized tongue position. It appears that these two elements, considered in relation to contiguous sounds, are strikingly similar.[30] We therefore group the two together in one phoneme, written /h/,[31] and we write *yeah, pa, law* as /jéh, páh, lóh/. BB's *idea* and *St. Louis* are /àjdíh, sèjnt-lúhs/; GLT's *bad, adds* are /béhd, éhdz/; *balm, father, dawn, caught* are /báhm, fáhðər, dóhn, kóht/; the *r*-less pronunciation of *bird, purse* in the speech of those who use forms both with and without retroflexion is /bə́hd, pə́hs/.

13 We return now to the syllabics before /r/. The words *Mary, scarce, bear; starry, farce, bar; boring, horse, bore; furry, purse, burr* present no further problem: They are to be written /méhrij, skéhrs, béhr; stáhrij, fáhrs, báhr; bóhriŋ, hóhrs, bóhr; fə́hrij, pə́hrs, bə́hr/.

In words like *part, farce; port, horse; pert, purse,* where the postvocalic /r/ is followed by a voiceless consonant, many speakers always or sometimes pronounce retroflex vowels noticeably shorter than the syllabics of *card, cord, bird.* These might perhaps be explained as consisting simply of the short vowels /a, o, ə/ + /r/, with the covering statement that the allophones of these vowels before final and

---

[28]Pronunciations of the Irish names *Flaherty* and *Doherty* with a short stressed vowel plus [h] must be regarded as outside the phonemic system of normal English, like the nasal vowels of such French words as *fiancée* and *lingerie.*

[29]Cf. Kenyon, *American Pronunciation*[6] §§37, 200. Kenyon's description of [h] involves a stress pulse coinciding with the beginning of the sound; but we can see no difference between the stress pulse in *ahéad* and the one in *attáck.* No one has ever considered such a pulse essential to the articulation of [t] or any other consonant.

[30]Cf. the demonstration of the similarity between /j, w/ and the diphthongal glides in §9, fn. 19. The fact that [h] is voiceless while the lengthening element is voiced need not disturb us. Note that /h/ is the only spirant phoneme in English which does not (in Trubetzkoy's terminology) take part in the correlation of voice—in clearer terms, it is the only voiceless spirant which is not phonetically paired with a voiced counterpart.

[31]It is scarcely necessary to point out that in a phonemic transcription the symbols need not in every case have the values traditionally assigned to them in conventional spelling or in phonetic notation. Naturally we do not suppose that words like *pa, law* end in the "puff of breath" with which the letter *h* is usually associated. There is no pressing reason, really, for using *h:* the raised dot would serve just as well, provided that we used it also for the initial phoneme of words like *hat, hill, hay.* It might even be wiser to cut loose from all phonetic association by using a symbol like ¿; in that case *pa, law, hill, hall* would appear as /pá¿, ló¿, ¿íl, ¿ó¿l/. Readers who are disturbed by the looks of our phonemic transcription—and we admit that it looks unfamiliar —should consider Bloomfield's definitive statement on the choice of symbols, *Language* 11.98, fn. 3.

preconsonantal /r/ differ in length but not in quality from the allophones before /hr/. But there is usually no possibility of contrast between the longer and the shorter allophones; and it seems preferable to regard all the syllabics before final and preconsonantal /r/ as consisting of vowel plus semivowel.

We have stated (§11) that there is no contrast between /ih, uh/ and /ij, uw/ before /r/ in words like *beer, boor*. The syllabics in these words might be written /ih, uh/, following the pattern in *bear, bar, bore, burr;* but we have observed that in the latter set of words a following /hr/ noticeably affects the phonetic quality of the vowel allophone, whereas in our pronunciation of *beer, boor* [bɪˆ·ɚ, buˆ·ɚ] the vowel is not strikingly different from the allophones in *pit, put* or in *beat, boot*. There may sometimes, however, be a need for distinguishing between /ih, uh/ and /ij, uw/ even in this position. Speakers who pronounce *poorer, tourist* and the like with [uˆ·ər] before the weak-stressed vowel, but *poor, your* and the like with [oˆ·ɚ], may have /uw/ in the former but /uh/ in the latter; and the syllabic of *bore, four, hoarse, mourning,* in the speech of those who distinguish these words from *nor, for, horse, morning,* may also be /uh/. However, the analysis of this syllabic as /əw/ proposed in §11 seems to be more obvious and is to be preferred. In our own speech, similarly, it seems preferable to use /ih, uh/ only in such rare cases as BB's *idea, St. Louis,* and to write /ijr, uwr/ instead of the possible alternatives /ihr, uhr/ in *fierce, beer* and *bourse, boor*.

In most types of Midwestern speech the situation of the syllabics before /r/ is greatly simplified. Here *mirror* rimes with *dearer, hurry* with *furry,* and *juror* with *poorer; Mary, merry,* and *marry* are the same. The only analysis required for these words is then /mírər, dírər; hə́rij, fə́rij; júrər, púrər; mérij/. *Beer, bear, bar, for, burr, boor,* correspondingly, are /bír, bér, bár, fór, bə́r, búr/ (*bore* is usually /bə́wr/); *starry* is /stárij/, which is unambiguous because *marry,* like *merry,* is /mérij/; and *sorry* is /sórij/, which again is unambiguous because *boring* is /bə́wriŋ/. The simplicity of this pattern is disturbed in the speech of many educated Midwesterners who have adopted at least some of the additional distinctions found in Eastern American En-

glish; by doing so they have changed their phonemic system so as to require all syllabics before /r/ to be analyzed as vowel plus semivowel, even when these differ little or not at all phonetically from the corresponding syllabics of other Midwestern speakers.

14 In those dialects of English where orthographic *r* in final position and before consonants is not pronounced as retroflexion (the "*r*-less" dialects), there are two alternative interpretations of the syllabics in *beer, bear, bar,* etc., and in *dearer, Mary, starry,* etc. Either an original /Vr/ has become /Vh/, probably through the intermediate stage /Vhr/; or else /Vr/ and /Vh/ are still distinct, so that /r/ must be reckoned a fourth semivowel.

The former situation perhaps obtains in the standard pronunciation of Southern England. If the difference between postvocalic /r/ and /h/ has here been eliminated, we must analyze all words with final and preconsonantal orthographic *r* as having /h/, with /r/ restricted to pre- or intervocalic position: *star* is /stáh/, *starry* is /stáhri/; *dear* is /díh/, *dearest* is /díhrist/, and *dear old fellow* is /díhrəwld . . ./.[32]

The second possibility (already suggested in footnote 32 for Southern British English) is illustrated by some of the "*r*-less" dialects of New York City. Here we find again the distinction referred to in §§7, 12, between *had, bade, can* 'am able', *adze* with /a/ and *bad, can* 'tin container', *adds* with /eh/. Since *bared,* though pronounced without retroflexion, is different from *bad* /béhd/, we analyze it as /bérd/, with postvocalic /r/ functioning as a fourth semivowel. Further, educated New

---

[32]The combinations /ih, eh, oh, uh/ are of course the "centring diphthongs" described by Daniel Jones, *An Outline of English Phonetics*[3] 108–114. A point which does not appear from Jones's practical treatment is that the vowels in *palm* and *bird* (described *ibid.* 72–75 and 86–89) are structurally parallel to these diphthongs. The relation of the diphthong in *course* to the long vowel in *cause* needs to be further studied. If the two are different, it may be that *course* has /or/ and *cause* has /oh/; and in that case all the centering diphthongs would be /Vr/, so that *starry, dearest, dear old* would be /stárri, dírrist, dírrəwld/. Jones also mentions a long [æ·] in *bad, sad,* contrasting with short [æ] in *lad, pad* (*ibid.* 218). Since *bad* is different from *bared,* the latter may again have /Vr/ while the former has /Vh/: *lad, bad, bared* would then be /lád, béhd, bérd/).

		A /V/	B /Vj/	C /Vw/	D /Vh/	E /Vr/	F /Vjr/	G /Vwr/	H /Vhr/
1.	/i/	pit	beat	—	idea	mirror	beer	—	—
2.	/e/	pet	bait	—	yeah	merry	eyrie	—	bear
3.	/a/	pat	bite	bout	balm	marry	Irish	cowrie	bar
4.	/o/	pot	Hoyt	—	law	sorry	Moira	—	bore
5.	/ə/	cut	—	boat	huh	hurry	—	—	burr
6.	/u/	put	—	boot	—	jury	—	boor	—

Yorkers of the younger generation commonly pronounce *bird, third, first,* and the like (the words which in substandard New York speech have /əj/, see §10 end) with a retroflex vowel, but *burr, sir, fur* and also *burred, furred, occurred* with a non-retroflex vowel of the same general type as the one used by British speakers. For this dialect *bird* is /bə́rd/ or perhaps even /bə́hrd/; *burred* is /bə́hd/. For the other syllabics before orthographic *r* there is no such contrast: *beer, bar, bore, boor* are probably /bíh, báh, bóh, búh/, but they may be /bír, bár, bór, búr/; further study of the dialect is needed to settle the choice.

15 The pattern of English syllabic phonemes can be summed up as follows. There are six vowels; with weak stress they occur in any kind of syllables, but with strong stress (loud, reduced loud, or medial) only in checked syllables: according to the analysis here presented, every syllable containing a strong-stressed syllabic ends in a consonant phoneme. Among the consonants there are three (in some dialects four) forming a special group which we have called semivowels; they are defined as a group by the fact that they call for special allophones of the vowels which precede them, and that they combine with such vowels to form what are phonetically long vowels and diphthongs. Structurally these compound syllabics are /VC/, so that *buy, bough, bah* /báj, báw, báh/ exhibit the same structure as *bat* /bát/; but they appear more freely than other combinations of vowel plus consonant, being found even before clusters of three and four other consonants, as in *wilds, waltzed* /wájldz, wóhltst/. With weak stress some of these combinations are rare, and their distribution is limited also in other ways.

The table shows the syllabic phonemes and phoneme clusters distinguished in our own

varieties of English (18 not followed by /r/ + 16 followed by /r/). Dashes represent other possible combinations, several of them found in other dialects.[33] The columns are lettered and the rows numbered for reference in the notes that follow.

A1, 2, 3, 5, 6, B1, 2, 3, 4 /i, e, a, ə, u, ij, ej, aj, oj/ hold for all types of standard English known to us. C3, 5, 6, D4 /aw, əw, uw, oh/ probably hold for most types, but see §10 and C1 below.

A4 /o/ is less common than the other simple vowels in Midwestern American. BB has it only before voiceless stops, voiceless spirants, nasals, and liquids (*cop, cot, rock, crotch, doff, possible, josh, bomb, honest, gong, holly, sorry*), replacing the corresponding phoneme of Eastern American before other consonants by /ah/; other speakers[34] have /o/ in only a few words, chiefly after /w/ (*wash, Washington*). In GLT's Eastern dialect, on the other hand, /o/ does not occur after /w/ (so that *wash* is /wáhš/), but is common elsewhere and contrasts with /ah/ in *bother* /bóðər/ : *father* /fáhðər/; §§7, 12. In New England and Southern British English, simple /o/ is phonetically a rounded vowel; in most types of American English it is unrounded.

B5 /əj/ in the typical New York City pronunciation of *bird,* and in the substandard New York City pronunciation of both *bird* and

[33]We do not claim that the compartments of this table will accommodate all the syllabic phonemes of all dialects of English, though we believe that the exceptions will be very few and in each dialect statistically unimportant. Thus, BB pronounces *gonna* (*I'm not gonna do it*) with a short vowel in the first syllable which is phonetically very close to the vowel of German *Sonne.* Though it occurs nowhere else in his pronunciation of English, it must perhaps be reckoned an independent phoneme parallel to the six short vowels of §7. Cf. fn. 14.

[34]Among them Dr. C. F. Hockett, who has given us our information on this point.

Boyd; §10. A similar pronunciation, requiring the same analysis, occurs in parts of southern New England, New Jersey, the South, and elsewhere.

B6 /uj/ in a monosyllabic pronunciation of *ruin* and in a pronunciation of *buoy* different from *boy;* perhaps also in the Scotch pronunciation of *good* as [gy·d] or the like.[35]

C1 /iw/ in *mute, beauty, pew, new, due, tune, cute,* etc., pronounced with [ɪu̯] by many American speakers (but rarely in the South), corresponding to the combination /juw/ of other speakers.[36] A minimal contrast is found in some dialects between *ewe* /íw/ or /jíw/, *yew* /jíw/, and *you* /júw/. This may also be the analysis, instead of /uw/, of the high-central rounded vowel (sometimes slightly diphthongal) used by many Southern speakers, especially in the Virginia Piedmont, in words like *boot, moon, do,* etc.

C2 /ew/ may be the proper analysis, instead of /əw/, for the diphthong in *boat* in the extreme type of Boston and London English, where the prior element is an advanced central or even a front vowel.

C4 /ow/ in Southern American *law, dawn,* etc.; §10.

D1 /ih/ in a dissyllabic pronunciation of *idea* and *theater* (both perhaps more commonly with /ijə/ in American English); §13. Also in the *r*-less pronunciation of *beer, fierce,* etc.; §14.

D2 /eh/ not only in *yeah* but also in *bad, can* 'tin container', *jazz, adds* in those dialects which distinguish these words from *bade, can* 'am able', *has, adze;* §12. Also in London English *bear, scarce;* §14 and fn. 32.

D3 /ah/ probably also in London English *bar, farce;* §14. A few types of American English appear to lack this combination, pronouncing *palm, pa, father,* etc. (and also *bar, starry,* H3), with the syllabic of *law, dawn* (and *for, horse,* H4).

D5 /əh/ in New York City and London English *burr, furred;* §14. In "General Amer-

ican," if *huh* is ruled out as an interjection, this combination appears only before /r/, H5.

D6 /uh/ in a common local pronunciation of the city name *St. Louis;* §12. Further, in the *r*-less pronunciation of *boor, bourse;* §14. The "New England short *o*" is also to be analyzed as /uh/: this is a weakly rounded, centralized higher-mid-back vowel, often followed by a centering off-glide, which occurs in some New England pronunciations of such words as *whole* (but not *hole*), *road* (but not *rode, rowed*), *coat, home, stone.*[37]

E1, 2, 3, 4, 5, 6 /ir, er, ar, or, ər, ur/ also in Midwestern *beer, bear, bar, for* (but not *bore*), *burr, boor;* §13.[38] Speakers who normally have only /VSr/ (where S = any semivowel) may also have a few cases of /Vr/. GLT pronounces the name of Newark (his native city) [nuɚk] and uses [nu^·ɚk] only in imitating the pronunciations of strangers; the former must be /núrk/, while the latter is the expected /núwrk/.

F1 /ijr/ may be always /ihr/, H1; §13.

F2 /ejr/ rare except in New England speech; §11.

F3 /ajr/ rather rare; found in some pronunciations of *hire, higher,* etc.; §11.

F4 /ojr/ very rare. (Is *Moira* the only example?)

F5, 6 /əjr, ujr/ probably nonexistent, unless /ujr/ occurs in Scotch *poor, sure,* and the like; cf. B6 above.

G1 /iwr/ in *pure, bureau, furious,* etc., in those dialects that have /iw/ for the more general /juw/; cf. C1 above.

G2 /ewr/ probably nonexistent.

G3 /awr/ rather rare; found in some pronunciations of *flour, flower,* etc.; §11.

G4 /owr/ possibly in those dialects that have /ow/ in *law,* but probably there only when the /r/ is followed by another vowel, as in *Lawrence;* cf. C4 above.

G5 /əwr/ in *bore, four, hoarse, mourning,* etc., in dialects that distinguish these words from *nor, for, horse, morning;* §§11, 13.

G6 /uwr/ may be always /uhr/, H6; §13.

---

[35]Joseph Wright, *The English Dialect Grammar* 465 (Oxford, 1905), lists the following pronunciations of *good* which may be analyzed as containing /uj/: [gyd] Sh. I. sn. & nm. Sc., [gy·d] wm. Sc. n. Cum. e.Dev., [guɪd] sw. & ms. Yks.
[36]This is the diphthong transcribed [ɪu] and described for his own dialect by Kenyon, *American Pronunciation*[6] §§341–355.

[37]On the "New England short *o*" see *Handbook of the Linguistic Geography of New England* 3 (and Chart 1), 128 (§17).
[38]/ir, er, ar, or, ur/ may also be the correct analyses, instead of /ih, eh, ah, oh, uh/, for the *r*-less pronunciation of *beer, bear, bar, bore, boor;* §14, fn. 32.

H1 /ihr/ perhaps always instead of /ijr/, F1 above.

H2, 3, 4, 5 /ehr, ahr, ohr, əhr/ probably not found in "r-less" dialects. Note that in many varieties of English /ohr/ occurs in *nor, for, horse, morning* but not in *bore, four, hoarse, mourning* (cf. G5 above).

H6 /uhr/ perhaps always instead of /uwr/, G6 above.

16 We can now draw up a final statement of the phonemic functioning of the vowels and semivowels in our own dialects of English. To fit other dialects, parts of this statement will need revision; but it seems significant and convincing that the syllabic phonemes of all English dialects known to us (with such unimportant exceptions as are referred to in footnote 33) can be accommodated without forcing in the general system here set up. To interpret the syllabic phenomena of any dialect in terms of this system, it is only necessary to take account of the phonetic data (including facts of distribution) and of the consequent pattern relationships.

We arrange the simple vowels according to the phonetic description of their chief allophones:

	FRONT	BACK
HIGH	i	u
MID	e	ə
LOW	a	o

Before a semivowel, the vowels undergo certain allophonic changes which can be stated, in terms of this diagram, as follows. Before /j/, the high- and mid-front vowels /i, e/ are slightly raised; the low vowels /a, o/ are shifted counterclockwise. Before /w/, the high- and mid-back vowels /u, ə/ are slightly raised and rounded; the low-front vowel /a/ is retracted. Before /h/, the mid and low vowels /e, a, o, ə/ are shifted counterclockwise.

These facts allow us to establish five overlapping groups which define the occurrence of vowel allophones before a following semivowel:

1. The higher vowels /i, e, ə, u/ are raised before a homorganic semivowel.
2. The higher-front vowels /i, e/ are raised before /j/.
3. The higher-back vowels /u, ə/ are raised and rounded before /w/.
4. The lower vowels /e, a, o, ə/ move counterclockwise before /h/.
5. The low vowels /a, o/ move counterclockwise before /j/ (and /w/).

BIBLIOGRAPHY 6
Diphthongs,
Semivowels,
and Vowels

JOOS, M. (1934) "Stressed Vowels Plus *r* in General American"

BLOOMFIELD, L. (1935) "The Stressed Vowels of American English"

SWADESH, M. (1935) "The Vowels of Chicago English"

HEFFNER, R.-M. S. (1937) "Notes on the Length of Vowels"

ULDALL, H. J. (1939) "On the Structural Interpretation of Diphthongs"

HEFFNER, R.-M. S. (1941) "Notes on the Length of Vowels"

BLOCH, B., and G. L. TRAGER (1942) *Outline of Linguistic Analysis*

TRAGER, G. L. (1942) "The Phonemic Treatment of Semivowels"

SWADESH, M. (1947) "On the Analysis of English Syllabics"

BERGER, M. D. (1949) "Neutralization in American English Vowels"

TRAGER, G. L., and H. L. SMITH, JR. (1951) *An Outline of English Structure*

HOCKETT, C. F. (1953) "Short and Long Syllable Nuclei"

O'CONNOR, J. D., and J. L. M. TRIM (1953) "Vowel, Consonant, and Syllable—A Phonological Definition"

BOWEN, J. D., and R. P. STOCKWELL (1955) "The Phonemic Interpretation of Semivowels in Spanish"

SAPORTA, S. (1956) "A Note on Spanish Semivowels"

BOWEN, J. D., and R. P. STOCKWELL (1956) "A Further Note on Spanish Semivowels"

SLEDD, J. (1958) "Some Questions of English Phonology"

KURATH, H. (1958) "Some Questions of English Phonology: A Reply"

HAUGEN, E. (1962) "On Diagramming Vowel Systems"

BOLINGER, D. L. (1963) "Length, Vowel, Juncture"

VACHEK, J. (1963) "The Phonematic Status of Modern English Long Vowels and Diphthongs"

See also the following articles in this volume:

HAUGEN, E., and W. F. TWADDELL (1942) "Facts and Phonemics" [10]

PIKE, K. L. (1947) "On the Phonemic Status of English Diphthongs" [14]

KURATH, H. (1957) "The Binary Interpretation of English Vowels" [20]

10
FACTS AND PHONEMICS*
EINAR HAUGEN and W. F. TWADDELL

1 "The Syllabic Phonemes of English" [9] by Trager and Bloch (*Language* 17.223–246) is an attempt to set forth a partial phonemic analysis of American English. The analysis, though partial, is ambitious; it displays thoughtful ingenuity and confident independence; and its conclusions are in some particulars spectacular. It is accordingly in order to consider whether the procedures of analysis represent sound and fruitful techniques. If they do, the scope of linguistic investigation has been substantially broadened; if not, they are seductive but dangerous.

The authors declare their intention to proceed "inductively from a statement of the phonetic data . . . to an interpretation in terms of linguistic structure." What is the nature of this statement and of this interpretation? The statement of phonetic data is subjective; the interpretation is determined, eclectically, by the principles of phonetic similarity, complementary distribution, congruent patterning, or economy in the total number of units.

In some crucial respects, these procedures appear to us to be invalid and capricious.[1]

2 As their "basic unit" the authors establish what they call "a phonemic phrase." Its definition involves two elements: (1) external open junctures at beginning and end; (2) one loud stress. The first item means that it must be an isolated utterance, preceded and followed by a pause, since external open juncture by definition occurs only there (225, line 3) [73]. The second item limits it to a rather short isolated utterance, since an utterance of any length will contain several loud stresses. The problem of splitting up any long utterance into "phonemic phrases," either by introducing pauses or by

subordinating the main stresses under one extra loud stress, has not been touched. How is this "phonemic phrase" related to the flow of speech? Until this is made clear, the meaning and value of the various kinds of juncture and of the degrees of stress will remain in question. The length and tempo of the phrase may determine the very existence of, e.g., such internal open junctures as that of *tin-tax;* it is very questionable whether this is distinguished from *syntax* in rapid speech. On this point the authors offer us no positive evidence.

In their discussion of stress they establish four degrees which they are willing to call phonemic: loud, reduced loud, medial, and weak. The loud is the one loudest stress which dominates a "phonemic phrase"; the reduced loud includes both the stress of preceding modifiers (*a blâck bóot*) and of following compounded elements (*a bóotblâck*). The medial includes pre-tonic rhythmically determined stresses within long, classical words (*exàminátion*) and post-tonic vowels which could not get less stress without being exchanged for schwa or [ɪ] (*áccènt, ábstràct, ápricòt, ámbùsh*). The weak includes [ə], [ɪ], [i], [u], and sporadic instances of the other vowels.

It is evident that each of these classes includes disparate phonetic types. The *black* of *a blâck bóot* is not identical in stress or intonation with that of *a bóotblâck*. The stress of the first *a* in *exàminátion* is not that of the second *a* in *ábstràct*. The stress of the last *i* in *wílling* is not identical with that of *a* in *alóft*. In each of these cases it happens that the distributions are mutually exclusive, since they depend on the relationship to the loudest stress, and on the rhythmic and morphological structure of the words. Hence it is possible to use identical symbols without ambiguity, but it is in no way mandatory.

[1]Haugen prepared the first draft of §§2, 5, 7; Twaddell of §§1, 3, 4, 6, 8.

*Reprinted from *Language* 18.228–237 (1942) by permission.

This becomes even more apparent when we discover that in no case is it possible to find a position in which all four stresses may be demonstrated as applicable to substantially identical vowels. In fact, once the position of the chief stress is fixed (by extra-phonemic considerations), the remaining syllables are limited to two possibilities, (comparatively) loud and (comparatively) weak. Thus one may say either *a lông shóre* or *along shóre;* if the main stress is shifted to *long* (giving it the maximum of three possibilities available to any one vowel in English), making it *alóngshòre* (or *alóngshôre?*), the last syllable is as weak as it can possibly be. The type called "weak" (as in *a-*) may be objectively weaker than the last-named, but the two cannot be demonstrated under comparable conditions.

The entire scale of stresses is established by a series of impressionistic comparisons between incommensurable entities. The contrast of weak with medial is exemplified exclusively by comparisons of post-tonic regular vowels (*cóntènts, cóndùct, sýntàx, rótàte*) with the special group of short vowels [ə], [ɪ], and [i] (*cúrrent, áxis, lófty*). The contrast of medial and reduced loud is exemplified (a) by such pairs as *tín-tâx* and *sýntàx*, where the contrast is complicated by internal open juncture (as noted by Trager-Bloch), and (b) by sequential groups like *móvie-àuditôrium*, in which *-tôr-* is given its own level between *mó-* and *aùd-*. With enough semi-stressed syllables, one can of course work out even more steps, e.g., *fóurteen-ninety-twó*, in which *-teen* and *nine-* could by the same reasoning establish two "medial" levels between reduced loud and weak. A comparison of such pairs as *àlternátions* and *âll the nátions,* or *dìscombòoberátion* and *thìs consìderátion,* suggests that the difference between (anticipatory) reduced loud and medial may be one of pitch pattern rather than stress. After the main stress one may compare *ápricòt* and *ármy côt, pólàcks* and *póle-âx, ámbùsh* and *róse bûsh, áspic* and *íce-pìck, réfugèe* and *spélling bêe.* A number of factors are involved in whatever differences exist here, such as the number of syllables, the type of juncture, etc.; and to comprise all of these under the terms here proposed is rather to conceal than to reveal the facts.

In general the patterning here adopted does not seem to fit the facts too well. The classes are either too few or too many. We are painfully confronted with the fact that no direct instrumental check has yet been devised for the factor "stress" in language. Stress may indeed be only a name for various groupings of such measurable factors as vowel quality, pitch, tone pattern, quantity, amplitude, and rhythmic sequence. It is interesting in this connection to note that in a recent study of the relation between quantity and stress, R-M. S. Heffner has shown the existence of two (and only two) sharply differentiated vowel lengths correlated to differences of stress.[2] We need many more such studies of the measurable factors in stress before any general scheme like the present can be established with assurance.

In any such scheme a terminology must also be devised for including the factor of sequence. While Trager-Bloch begin their discussion by referring to "the position of main stress," they proceed to analyze the "degrees of stress" as if they were talking about the same thing. In any such "minimal contrast" as *tránsport* n. and *transpórt* v. the real opposition is not limited to degrees of stress: just as important, perhaps crucial, is the difference between, say, iambic and trochaic sequence.

3   A crucial "statement of the phonetic data" is the setting up on p. 229 [77] of an order of six categories [ɪ, ɛ, æ, ɑ, ʌ, ʊ] on allegedly phonetic grounds ("phonetically short and non-diphthongal"). Apparently it is the shortness which is the determining criterion; for the authors specifically decline to regard monophthongal [iˑ, eˑ, uˑ, oˑ] as categories of the same order as [ɪ, ɛ, æ, ɑ, ʌ, ʊ]. (These "long" vowels are interpreted as assimilated diphthongs, 235 [81].) The issue is accordingly quite clear: [ɪ, ɛ, æ, ɑ, ʌ, ʊ] are unambiguously asserted to be unambiguously short, as a matter of phonetic fact. If this phonetic classification falls, then all the subsequent interpretations of other vowel-sounds in terms of the six-member pattern must also fall. And how do the authors set about proving this crucial phonetic classification of [ɪ, ɛ, æ, ɑ, ʌ, ʊ] as unmistakably short vowels? They write (230) [77]: "Our judgments of length are admittedly subjective, and lack the precision of mechani-

---

[2]*American Speech* 16.204–207 (1941).

cal or electrical measurements. Nevertheless we believe that our statements regarding relative length are valid within the limits of this investigation." On a point of cardinal importance, so cavalier a procedure is simple recklessness. The authors present no measurements of the length of their vowels: techniques for obtaining such measurements exist, and although the task requires diligence, it involves no arcane processes. If the authors were unwilling to measure their own vowels, they could at the least have examined the measurements made by other investigators. Such measurements have been made and the results published in American journals during the past five years.[3] If the phonetic length of vowels is a relevant datum, then a body of available information on the phonetic length of vowels should not have been ignored in favor of "admittedly subjective . . . judgments of length."

The authors do not explain what constitutes short vowel duration (e.g., 0.20 sec. or less). They do say that the vowels of *bid*, etc., are "noticeably longer" than those of *pit*, etc. (230) [77]. According to the data of R-M.S. Heffner and W. P. Lehmann, the figures are, respectively, for Heffner, 0.20 sec. and 0.15 sec., for Lehmann, 0.20 sec. and 0.16 sec. (based on 527 measurements in all). We do not know if Trager's and Bloch's vowels show the same relations, for they have not provided the data; if so, we do not know whether they are capable of noticing a difference of 0.04 or 0.05 sec.

If they can indeed discriminate so carefully, it is remarkable that they are apparently unable to notice such differences as that between [æ] and [ɪ] before [d]: 0.11 sec. for Heffner, 0.09 sec. for Lehmann; before [t], Heffner's [æ] is 0.06 sec. longer than his [ɪ], Lehmann's 0.09 sec. longer. To be sure, these figures may not apply to Trager and Bloch; all the more distressing, then, is our lack of real data on their vowels.

Since the authors present no evidence (aside from their subjective judgment) in support of the crucial statement that [ɪ, ɛ, æ, ɑ, ʌ, ʊ] are *the* phonetically short and non-diphthongal vowels, we must ask whether their judgment is likely to be correct.

The average durational values[4] given by Heffner and Lehmann are based upon nearly 13,000 measurements of vowels in monosyllables, pronounced in isolation and bearing a loud stress, ending in a single consonant— precisely the conditions for which Trager and Bloch make statements 229 [76] ff. Here are their findings for vowel lengths before the stops: [H = Heffner; L = Lehmann; * = no measurements for this vowel before this consonant; the numbers represent duration in one-hundredths of a second, and each number is an average of from 27 to 193 separate measurements].

HEFFNER'S VOWELS BEFORE
[p]: 14 ɪ, ʊ; 16 ʌ, ɛ; 18 u; 19 i; 20 ɑ; 21 æ, ɚ, o; 23 aɪ, e; 25 ɔ; *aʊ.
[b]: 19 ɪ, ʌ; 22 ɛ; 25 ɑ, u, ɚ; 26 æ; 28 ɔ, e; *ʊ, i, o, aɪ, aʊ.
[t]: 15 ɪ, ʊ; 17 ʌ; 18 ɛ, ɑ; 21 æ, i; 22 ɔ; 23 u, ɚ, e; 24 aɪ; 25 o; 27 aʊ.
[d]: 20 ɪ, ʊ, ʌ; 22 ɛ; 26 ɑ; 28 i; 29 u, ɚ; 30 e, o; 31 æ; 32 ɔ, aɪ; 33 aʊ.
[k]: 14 ɪ; 16 ʊ, ʌ; 17 ɛ; 20 i; 21ɚ; 22 ɑ, e; 23 æ, o, u; 25 ɔ, aɪ, aʊ.
[g]: 22 ɪ, ʌ; 24 ɛ; 26 æ; 28 o, ɚ; 29 e; 30 ɔ; *ʊ, ɑ, i, u, aɪ, aʊ.

LEHMANN'S VOWELS BEFORE
[p]: 18 ɪ, ʌ; 20 ɛ, i, u; 23 ɚ; 25 o, aɪ; 26 e; 27 ɑ; 28 æ; 29 ɔ; *ʊ, aʊ.
[b]: 21 ʌ; 23 ɪ; 24 ɛ; 30 u; 33 ɚ; 34 ɑ, æ, ɔ; 35 e; 37 aɪ; *ʊ, i, o, aʊ.
[t]: 16 ɪ; 17 ʊ, ʌ; 18 ɛ; 19 i; 20 u; 21 ɚ; 23 aɪ; 24 ɑ, e, aʊ; 25 æ, o; 26 ɔ.
[d]: 19 ʌ, ʊ; 20 ɪ; 21 ɛ; 27 ɚ; 28 i, u; 29 ɑ, æ, e; 30 o, ɔ; 32 aɪ, aʊ.
[k]: 17 ɪ; 19 ʌ, ʊ, u; 20 ɛ, i; 23 ɚ; 25 aɪ; 26 e, o; 29 ɑ; 30 æ, ɔ; *aʊ.
[g]: 22 ɪ; 25 ʌ, ɛ; 36 æ, ɚ; 37 ɑ, ɔ; *ʊ, e, u, aɪ, aʊ, i, o.

It is no simple matter, on the basis of these real data, to bring oneself to talk about "phonetically short" vowels as a definite group; but at all events, the "phonetic shortness" of [ɪ, ɛ, æ, ɑ, ʌ, ʊ] is something less than certain. The position of [i] and [u] is interesting. Likewise the durational relations of [æ] and [ɚ]:

[3]For example, by Heffner and co-workers, in *American Speech* 12.128–134 (1937).

[4]In part as yet unpublished.

In two of these 12 series, [æ] and [ɚ] are of equal duration; in two (i.e., before [t] and [g]), [ɚ] is 0.02 sec. longer than [æ]; in eight, [æ] is longer than [ɚ]. For H, and even more decisively for L, [ɚ] is a vowel which is phonetically shorter than [æ] and non-diphthongal. Is it otherwise with Trager and Bloch? We do not know. We know only that (229) [77] [æ] is described as "phonetically short" and that (238 [83] the vowel of *burr, cur, purse, worm*, etc., is interpreted as containing "some kind of rather long vowel followed by /r/." Either Trager's and Bloch's varieties of General American differ radically from Heffner's and Lehmann's or their subjective judgment of the length of non-diphthongal [ɚ] is unreliable.

4 In the interpretative steps, Trager and Bloch have made a most desirable tabulation of the various phonetic combinations in which vowels occur. This they call recording the occurrence of sound-types; and the work is valuable.

It is the further steps, the bringing together of the sound-types into "phonemes," that appear to us to be characterized by caprice and violence to the facts. To us, in all sobriety, the processes whereby Trager and Bloch combine sound-types into phonemes appear more akin to artistic composition than to scientific classification; and the pleasure of watching their operations with the material is rather esthetic satisfaction than scholarly conviction.

The notion of "pattern" which underlies this whole discussion needs clarification before it can become a useful term. If it is a set of habits that exist in the neural system of the speakers, then its effect on the functioning of language must be demonstrated. If it is only a working hypothesis, a "fiction," its value for the study of language must be unequivocally stated.

In attempting to justify certain of their procedures, Trager and Bloch invoke "phonemic theory": 234 [80]: "By the requirements of phonemic theory, we must . . ."; 235 [81]: "the requirements of phonemic theory (complementary distribution, economy in the total number of units, etc.) force us . . ."; 238 [83]: "to analyze the syllabic of *burr, cur, purse, worm*, etc., as a special '*r*-vowel' is theoretically bad . . ." Where is this canon of phonemic theory, which requires, which forces,

and according to which an interpretation of [ɚ] in harmony with phonetic fact is theoretically bad? Trager and Bloch adduce "phonetic similarity and phonetic interrelationship" without defining these dangerously loose terms. They justify their interpretation of monophthongs as being really diphthongs by asserting that "the total pattern is best revealed" in this way; and they expound this sovereign "principle of pattern analysis" by quoting, as its classic formulation, an eloquent magnificat to "Pattern," with only the vaguest of indications of the nature or the application of this principle. By its fruits must we judge it; pattern analysis interprets monophthongs as diphthongs on p. 235 [81]; on p. 238 [83], pattern analysis interprets monophthongal [ɚ] (average 0.26 sec.) as "a rather long vowel followed by /r/"; and on p. 238 [84], in another connection, "the phonetics and the pattern analysis therefore agree, as they should."

5 The striving for fewer symbols leads to some curious results. One is struck on perusing the table of vowels (243) [87] by the considerable dissimilarity among the sound-types that are grouped together into unitary phonemes. Here the first vocalic elements of *bite, bout, balm,* and *bar* are classed with the vowels of *pat* and *marry*, while *pot* [pɑt] and *sorry* ['sɑrɪ̯j] have joined hands with *law, bore,* and *Hoyt*. Almost as incongruous seems the collocation of *boat* with *burr* and *cut;* while the weddings of *pit* with *beat* and *put* with *boot* are only a shade less repulsive. These "allophones" which move up and down, or counterclockwise, at the command of the following "semivowel"—what holds them together?

Fundamentally, there is just one fact on which the whole system is constructed: that in stressed syllables there are six vowels which cannot occur in free syllables (the syllabics of *pit, pet, pat, pot, cut, put*). As will be shown later, even this fact is not true of all American speech. In any case, it is not a phonetic, but a distributional fact, and the difficulties of the entire system arise because there is no necessary correlation between these two kinds of facts.

The Trager-Bloch article is essentially an attempt to describe the remaining vowels or vocalic elements in terms of the six so determined. Their goal is a statement that every

syllable contains one of these six vowels, followed by at least one consonant, whenever it
is stressed (243) [87].

The first step is to eliminate the possibility that some stressed syllables may end
in a vowel. The most obvious cases are the
recognized diphthongs, as in *lay* and *cow*.
Their off-glides are grouped with prevocalic
j and *w*, which is not in itself objectionable.
The only question arises when we are categorically told that they *must* be so grouped,
"because there is no contrast between them."
On this criterion, the diphthongs might just
as well be written *ei* and *au,* or *eɪ* and *aʊ.*

The second step is built on the somewhat
shaky first. While it is not phonetically unreasonable to hold that *j* and *w* are consonants,
there are still the vocalic endings of *pa* and
law to explain. These are held to be "long"
and the "lengthening element" cannot possibly
be a vowel, "since there is no example anywhere else in the total pattern for two vowels in
succession" (240) [85]. The only reason there
is no example is that the diphthongs have just
been ruled out in step 1. Otherwise there would
be nothing to prevent one from regarding these
vowels (granting for the sake of argument that
they should be treated as long) as composed of
two short vowels: /aa/ or /oo/ for instance.
Since the final element cannot be a vowel, it
must of course be a consonant; one consonant
is still happily unengaged, to wit *h,* so it is
pressed into service. This rounds out the pattern, and we are presented with three consonants, alias semi-vowels, *j, w,* and *h.* One of
these is postulated at the end of every stressed
syllable which we had previously thought
ended in a vowel. The authors are not disturbed by the rather considerable phonetic
dissimilarity of prevocalic and postvocalic *h;*
they even manage to turn it into a "striking
similarity" by taking the somewhat dubious
position that *h-* is merely a voiceless anticipation of the vowel.

Among the other vowels that do not appear to lend themselves too easily to this treatment are [i] and [u]. The system demands that
even when these are clearly monophthongs,
they shall be described as /ij/ and /uw/. The
arguments are twofold: (1) that they "can be
described" as assimilated diphthongs (but no
reason appears either why they must or should
be described as something they are not; and

historical terms—"phonetic result," "raised,"
etc.—seem out of place in a descriptive statement); (2) that when some combinations in the
pattern are lacking, similar units may be
brought in to fill the missing spaces ("there is
no other category left," footnote 24). This principle clearly demands that the fact be trimmed
to suit the pattern.

Yet it appears again, and more harmfully,
in the handling of the first elements of diphthongs and "long" vowels, especially those
beginning with [ɑ] or [ɔ]. This requires a good
deal of not very convincing argument, since
sounds resembling [ɑ] (e.g., in mid-western
loud) have been forced into the same rubric
as the [æ] of *pat* to make room for elements in
the [ɔ]-range. In the case of *loud,* the authors
admit that the resemblance "is not always
close" (236) [82]. The [ɑɪ] of *buy* is grouped
with [æ] and the [ɔɪ] of *boy* with [ɑ] because
"the first is further front." This appeal to the
two-dimensional chart of the phonetician is
justified by calling it "pattern analysis" (footnote 21), but it really stems from an unwillingness to grant the vowel of *law* unitary status
because it can occur in free syllables. This
leaves only two categories in this range, /a/
and /o/, and all the low vowels must be
squeezed into one or the other.

In the same way are handled the vowels of
bar, bore (and consequently *balm, law*). The
authors find themselves with three vowels and
three spaces in the system. So the vowels [æ·]
in *Mary,* [ɑ·] in *starry,* [ɔ·] in *boring* are arranged along a front-back line of phonetic relationship and fitted into the rubrics which
already contain the similarly arranged but
quite different [ɛ] of *pet,* [æ] of *pat,* and [ɑ] of
pot. The obvious parallels of [æ] with [æ·] and
[ɑ] with [ɑ·] are deliberately neglected. The
authors are pleasantly surprised when they
discover that this group comes out just like
the preceding one. But how could it do otherwise?

The same principle runs through the analysis of the weakly stressed vowels. Here the
basic distinction between free and checked
syllabics does not obtain at all. Yet again [i]
and [u] are denied monophthongal status (e.g.,
in *city* and *value*). These and the other vowels
eliminated from the list of unitary phonemes
by the preceding analysis are pushed aside,
leaving by great good luck a group of six

vowels to identify. By a scheme of "phonetic interrelationship" these are again assigned to their respective spaces.

The weakly stressed syllabic consonants are pressed into the same pattern by the ingenious device of declaring that these syllables (as in *apple, button, rhythm, better*) shall be analyzed as vowel plus consonant, even though the vowel is no more audible than the *h* at the end of *law*. The vowel is called "syllabicity" and grouped with [ə]. This is possible because every non-syllabic vowel has been rigidly identified as a consonant, but it seems like a deus ex machina. If one can thus take a general phonetic feature and call it a phoneme at will, why not abstract e.g., "backness" and reduce the Trager-Bloch list of vowels from six to three (symbol /q/ : /u/ could be written /iq/, /ə/ = /eq/, /o/ = /aq/)? Or one might abstract "voice" and use the symbol /x/ to turn the voiced consonants into consonant clusters (/z/ = /sx/, /b/ = /px/).

The conclusion one inevitably reaches after analyzing the Trager-Bloch analysis is that syllabic distribution is no unfailing criterion for a systematic description of English. Not all the vowels that occur only in checked syllables are shorter than those that occur also in free, and the vowels of free syllables are not necessarily diphthongs. Nor is it inevitable or even probable that all vowels either can or must be identified with the basic six (or five) which are limited to checked syllables. There is no reason to suppose that the system resulting from the application of any one set of criteria (e.g., syllabic distribution) will agree with that resulting from any other (e.g., phonetic similarity). The additional concept of "phonetic interrelationship" or "pattern analysis" (which is not the same as Hockett's pattern congruity and is only referred to in passing by him in his programmatic statement in *Language* 18.3 [99] ff. seems to be little more than a covert appeal to the system that is to be established, and therefore a circular argument.

6 There are dialects in which the vowel of *boot* is, as Trager and Bloch put it (235) [81], "a fairly uniform long vowel." (For its actual length, see above.) But it is still to be interpreted as /uw/, with assimilation, so that /w/, in such circumstances, is lowered, while /u/ is raised, to produce a uniform vowel. This is

the same /w/ which has earlier been linked by "phonetic similarity" to /w/ in *way*. Here, then, is a phoneme which has a greater phonetic similarity to another phoneme's allophone (raised /u/) than to its own allophone (initial /w/). The justification for asserting "phonetic similarity" between initial and postvocalic /w/ is given on p. 234 [80]; it is that in both we find articulatory movements which are related though opposite in direction. Then, under the pressure of a "phonemic principle," a final /w/ is somehow present, even when the movement does not take place.

The most striking innovation is the discovery of a post-vocalic /h/ after the vowels of *bear, bore, balm, law*, etc. In these vowels, Trager and Bloch discern one of their "short, non-diphthongal" vowels plus "a lengthening element." They cannot interpret this lengthening element as a vowel, since there are no other examples of "two vowels in succession." The vowels of *bear, law*, etc., cannot be regarded as unit phonemes, since that would shatter the hard-won six-term "economy." So what to do? Patently, a consonant must be found. And one consonant is as yet unemployed in post-vocalic position. This is [h]. So *bear, bore, balm, law* are interpreted as /behr, bohr, bahm, loh/.

To this interpretation we object, and not because it "looks unfamiliar," nor even because of the "puff of breath with which the letter *h* is usually associated." Our objections are (1) phonemic and (2) pragmatic.

(1) Initial [h] is declared to be subject to draft as an allophone of a voiced post-vocalic lengthening element because "it is the only spirant phoneme in English which does not take part in the correlation of voice" (240) [85]. Whatever a spirant may be, this statement appears dangerously naive. Is there no correlation between the modes of inaugurating the vowel in *hill* and in *ill*? Is there any reason for finding three sounds in *hill* and two in *ill*, except the conventional orthography? Are not [h] and [—] alternative modes of "initial" vowel onset in English? And should not a phonemic analysis take cognizance of this fact by writing the two words, perhaps, as /hɪl/ and /÷ɪl/?[5] The description would be fairly simple:

[5]Cf. Y. R. Chao, "The Non-Uniqueness of Phonemic Solutions of Phonetic Systems," *Bulletin of the Institute of History and Philology (Academia Sinica)* 4.374 (1934).

[h] represents an articulation in which the onset of breath-flow and the onset of glottal vibration are consecutive; [÷], in which they are simultaneous. On these terms, the "lengthening element" might more plausibly be interpreted as [÷] than [h], on the principle of "phonetic similarity" (movements related in kind though opposite in direction). But we hasten to add that we make no such proposal, for we consider it just as useless as that of Trager and Bloch.

(2) Our pragmatic objection to the /behr, bohr, loh/ interpretation is that it is meaningless. We know nothing after such manipulation of symbols that we didn't know before. It is a familiar fact that the sound [h] occurs in American English before stressed vowels; it is a familiar fact that certain vowels are longer than others. That much we knew. What more do we know now? Only that Trager and Bloch prefer a system of notation whereby the first part of the vowel of *law* is represented by the same symbol as the vowel of *pot,* and the latter part of the vowel of *law* by the same symbol as the beginning of *hill.* This is a statement of orthographical preference, not a contribution to linguistic knowledge.

There are other conclusions in the study which mar the excellent work of collection and description. We mention only two more: The assumption (237) [83] that the vowel of *cute* is "a normal sequence of three phonemes" /juw/ fits some but by no means all of the demands of pattern congruity. The ukase that "under no circumstances can /č, ǰ/ be analyzed as /tš, dž/" (229) [77] is without support. There is an oblique allusion to "points of open-juncture." But since Trager and Bloch have already found specific "juncture phonemes" (224) [73], we can hardly admit the validity of such contrasts as *Blotch-eye* and *blot-shy* as establishing *both* a phonemic difference in juncture *and* a phonemic difference between [č] and [tš].[6] The argument that /č, ǰ/ are unit phonemes because of their behavior in clusters is of course circular: Since [č] and [ǰ] are assumed, by Trager and Bloch, they discover these unit phonemes behaving in clusters in a certain way; if [tš] and [dž] had been assumed, then these non-unit phonemes would have behaved in quite the same way.

[6]Cf. Chao 369.

7   So long as the authors adhere to an analysis of their own speech systems, it is venturesome for anyone else to pursue their identifications in detail. But their title as well as their summary in §15 aims at much more: they suggest a desire to "accommodate all the syllabic phonemes of all dialects of English," in spite of modest disclaimers.

In so doing they are attempting a task which there is no reason to believe is possible. There is certainly a marked difference in pattern between British and American English, and among the various types of American English. It is clear from this article that certain differences exist between the speech of the two authors.

While it cannot be denied that by interpreting a sufficient number of vowels as diphthongs or consonants, one can accommodate any type of English to a six-vowel system, one may doubt that such a system would automatically suggest itself to students of many varieties of English. A concrete instance is our mid-western American, not conspicuously different from that of BB. A notable deviation is the fact that it does not distinguish the vowels of *bomb* and *balm, bother* and *father* (for EH, *sorry* and *starry* have different vowel qualities). This means that the vowel of *pot* must be grouped with that of *pa,* and the two are in every way parallel to the vowels of *taught* and *law.* The vowel [ɑ] occurs in free as well as checked syllables. Hence it cannot be one of the six "basic vowels"; if it is included anyway, [ɔ] will have to go with it. This destroys the Trager-Bloch system, or at least an important aspect of it, by taking away its sextet of unitary phonemes. All phonetic considerations would unite in suggesting the inclusion of [i] and [u], perhaps also [o]. In hiatus, EH's pronunciation does not normally include any semi-vocalic glide; he says [ri'ælɪti], not [rɪˈjælɪtɾi]. Without pursuing the analysis any further, it becomes clear that anyone starting with this pronunciation of English would not be likely to arrive at the same groupings as those suggested by Trager and Bloch.

8   To what end, then, is this sort of phonemic analysis directed? We can see only one purpose which is served: It is possible, through the conventions suggested by Trager and Bloch, to contrive a broad transcription with relatively few vowel symbols. Here is indeed

a kind of economy, but the same kind of economy which Basic English offers in the lexical realm: relatively few symbols, but used in so many senses that the saving is only apparent.

[Haugen and Twaddell have pointed out serious weaknesses in our manner of presentation, and some errors of detail; but we do not believe that they have proved our methods of analysis to be incorrect, or the assumptions underlying those methods to be untenable. Although we have modified our views on one or two points, we still regard our classification of the English vowels and diphthongs as fundamentally sound. This, however, is not the place to attempt a refutation of our critics' objections. GLT, BB]

A SYSTEM
OF DESCRIPTIVE PHONOLOGY*
CHARLES F. HOCKETT

[The paper delimits the field of descriptive phonology, formulates a system thereof, and briefly points out some of its implications.]

1 Linguistics is a classificatory science. The starting-point in such a science is to define (1) the universe of discourse and (2) the criteria which are used in making the classifications. Selection and preliminary ordering of data determine the *range* of analysis; the choice of criteria fixes the *level* of analysis. In linguistics there are various ranges, discussed in §2, and two basic levels, *phonological* and *grammatical,* each with subdivisions. The phonological level is the subject of this paper.[1]

2 The universe of discourse of any linguistic study is a set of utterances. It is necessary, therefore, to define the term "utterance" and the limits of the various types of sets.

2.1 An *utterance* is an act of speech. An act of speech is an item of human behavior with certain physiological and sociological characteristics.

2.11 The physiological characteristic of an act of speech is that it occurs in a specific locus of a human body: the respiratory tract and the mouth, rarely (as in esophagal speech) the stomach.

2.12 Not all the events in this tract are utterances. All the behavior of a human organism is *biophysical:* it is subject to physical and biological analysis. Certain acts are, in addition, *biosocial.*[2] A biosocial act is one which (1) is determined ultimately by the life-history of the individual in a given social group, (2) functions directly or indirectly as a stimulus for the behavior of others and of the actor himself, and (3) does this in a manner similarly determined by the life-histories of the individuals involved.

Utterances are biosocial. A sneeze occurs in the same area; it may function as a stimulus for others, and it may do this in a socially determined way, but the source of the sneeze is purely physiological. Therefore a sneeze is not biosocial, and is not a speech act. On the other hand, a cough in our society, where it may be an indication of polite embarrassment, or a belch in some parts of Africa, where it shows appreciation to one's host, fulfills all the requirements of biosocial behavior, takes place in the proper portion of the body, and must therefore be considered an act of speech. This does not mean that such events cannot be proved to have a marginal status (§2.22).

2.2 Range varies from one linguistic investigation to another. A large random sample

---

[1]The present paper derives from the phonemic systems of Bloomfield, Sapir, Trubetzkoy, and their followers. It owes most to Bloomfield, though rather to the methodological rigor of his work than to his phonemic theories. Apart from published material, the writer's chief stimulus has been his correspondence and discussion with George L. Trager and Bernard Bloch. He owes thanks also to Morris Swadesh for many suggestions in the past; to Mary R. Haas for specific criticism of the present paper; and above all to Bloch for advice and active assistance in giving the paper its final shape.

Many of the principles here set forth are illustrated and applied to the problem of English vowels by G. L. Trager and B. Bloch, "The Syllabic Phonemes of English" [9], *Language* 17.223–246 (1941). For a general bibliography on phonemic theory, see fn. 1 of that article.

[2]Albert P. Weiss, *A Theoretical Basis of Human Behavior*[2]; Columbus, 1929.

*Reprinted from *Language* 18.3–21 (1942) by permission.

of the speech-acts of some one individual over a period of a few months will afford a safe basis for the description of the speech behavior of that one individual for that short period. When a number of such specific studies have been made, more or less completely, in a single community, one can generalize therefrom to describe the typical behavior of the whole community. But in any case only statistical sampling is possible, and the resulting description will always be incomplete.

A particular universe of discourse is subject to certain *orderings*. Those orderings which are made before the criteria of classification are applied may be termed *extra-systemic*. Those which result from the analysis itself are *intra-systemic*. Finally, some of the latter have extra-systemic implications and may be termed *mixed*.

2.21 The material may be ordered with respect to time. Thus if one classes together those utterances that were produced in January, and those that were produced in February or a year or ten years or a century later, the result of analysis will be to show the change in speech behavior during that time. Such treatment is termed *historical*. Similarly, if the material is ordered with respect to geography or social status, the resulting analysis is synchronically *comparative,* indicating the difference between the English of Michigan and that of Rhode Island, or between that of carpenters and that of sailors.

But historical and comparative study implies first the completion of *descriptive* analysis of each of the temporally or spatially or socially grouped ranges of material. Descriptive procedure establishes the fiction that the various utterances to be dealt with have no temporal or spatial or social order. This fiction is valid only when the time or space or social span covered by the material is relatively small; it breaks down, for instance, when we take our records of Old English as a single unordered set. If the actual course of change in speech behavior through time be pictured as a curve, then the approximation of descriptive technique to the actual situation can be represented by a tangent to the curve at a given point.

2.22 The English interjection *pst* does not conform to the statistically most frequent phonetic and grammatical habits. These facts, which are only revealed by analysis of the data, show the marginal character of the interjection. It is this type of evidence which puts conventionalized coughs and belches in their proper place, though as a matter of procedure the linguist may choose to predict this result and exclude such items from consideration at the very beginning.

2.23 It may turn out that a randomly selected sample of speech-acts from some individuals includes forms from two (or more) distinct languages or dialects. It is the analysis itself which shows this, since it makes clear a clustering of the material around two (or more) norms. Therefore this ordering might be termed intra-systemic. But careful examination reveals that the social situations in which one set of forms is produced are different from those in which the other set occurs. The ordering is therefore not purely intra-systemic, but mixed. These statements hold likewise for *stylistic* contrasts, involving such things as tempo or the difference between *he arrived prematurely* and *he came too soon.*

2.3 It will be assumed in the rest of this paper that the set of utterances to be handled descriptively is homogeneous enough to require none of the kinds of ordering just described.

3.1 Since speech acts are biophysical, they are subject to biophysical analysis and classification. The technique of doing this will here be called *α-phonetics;*[3] α-phonetic analysis uses physiological and acoustic procedures, with the necessary symbolic devices—charts, diagrams, and α-phonetic transcription.

3.2 An oscillograph record of the stream of speech shows it as a continuum. Articulatory analysis, on the other hand, shows it as segmented.[4] An examination of articulation reveals a concurrent sequence of motions or phases of rest of the various organs of the

[3]The term "phonetics" has two distinct meanings in current usage, unfortunately not always kept clearly apart. To avoid coining one or two completely new terms, this paper uses the expressions α-phonetics and β-phonetics for the two different meanings.

[4]Kenneth L. Pike, *A Reconstruction of Phonetic Theory;* University of Michigan dissertation, 1941. This is the purest treatment of α-phonetics known to the writer; most of the α-phonetic material here presented is taken from Pike's work.

speech area. If a cross section be taken of the stream of speech at a given moment, each of the organs concerned is seen to have at that moment a specific functional status; for example, the lungs are pushing, the vocal cords are drawn apart, the entrance to the nasal passage is closed, the tip of the tongue is just leaving the alveolar ridge, the lips are open. A moment later the situation will be different.

3.3 Obviously, the different organs do not change from one functional status to another always at the same moment; the statuses overlap. A diagram can be made of any articulatory sequence, with horizontal lines showing the functioning of the several organs; the temporal cross section is represented by a vertical line cutting through all the horizontal lines. A *change-point* is any point at which any organ changes from one type of function to another. The segment between two successive change-points is an *α-sound*. In deciding just where to draw the lines representing change-points there is some ambiguity, but it turns out that this does not matter for phonological purposes.

3.4 An *α*-sound is nothing more than the simultaneity of the functionings of the various organs. But for terminological reasons it is convenient to speak of these functionings as qualities, rather than as things or events; the initial sounds in *peat* and *beat*[5] share the quality of having the lips closed. All such qualities may be termed *α-phonetic elements*.

4 The next step is to describe the classification of all the utterances of a descriptive range into *phonological equivalence classes*.

4.11 Two utterances which have approximately the same elements in the same arrangement are said to be *α-phonetically similar*. This is, of course, a matter of degree.

4.12 Two speech acts are *biosocially equivalent* if they are produced under similar conditions and act similarly as biosocial stimuli. This, also, is a matter of degree.

4.2 Phonological equivalence involves, generally, the two factors of *α*-phonetic similarity and biosocial equivalence. The correlation is not absolute, and an examination of

the limiting cases will clarify the general situation.

4.21 *α*-phonetic similarity is not measurable in the isolated case, but only in the light of a careful examination of all the material. Thus the Spanish words *sur* and *sud* both mean 'south'. Furthermore, the *α*-phonetic difference between *sur* and *sud* is slight. Nevertheless the total set of utterances of these words constitutes two phonological equivalence classes, not one; for although in this particular pair of sets the contrast between the final consonants is biosocially irrelevant, in other pairs, say *sed* 'thirst' and *ser* 'to be', the same difference is biosocially important.

4.22 If a number of utterances of the English word *meat* and a number of *meet* be examined,[6] the following facts are revealed: (1) The *α*-phonetic differences between the various cases of *meat* and those between the various cases of *meet* cover the same range. No phonetician, and no native speaker of the language, could tell by listening to successive utterances of the two words which of them was involved in any particular utterance. (2) The biosocial nature of the various cases of *meat* is fairly constant, and so is that of the various cases of *meet;* but (3) the biosocial nature of the cases of *meat* and of *meet* are different. Thus it is seen that biophysical similarity does not necessarily imply biosocial equivalence. In a situation of this kind the forms constitute a single phonological equivalence class.

4.3 An utterance, by definition, begins and ends with a pause. Sometimes a consecutive portion of one utterance is phonologically identical with all of another except for the absence of pause at one or both of its ends. The term *phrase* may be used to subsume both utterances and such portions of utterances. It is convenient to extend the definition of phonological equivalence class so that its members are phrases instead of utterances.

4.4 In further classification on the phonological level, one transcription is used to denote ambiguously any member of a phonological equivalence class. Such an ambiguous name, which denotes an indefinite single member of a specified class, is termed in logic

---

[5]Phrases in the form "the initial sound in *beat*" are to be taken as shorthand for the logically correct but cumbersome "the first sound of an utterance consisting of the word represented in traditional orthography as *beat*."

[6]It is assumed that all the utterances involved have the same prosodic features; *meat?* and *meat!* are of course phonologically different.

a variable. So the transcriptions ['sɪi̯] and /síi̯/ are variables.[7] Phonological analysis is not concerned with anything which differentiates the various members of an equivalence class.

5.1 An α-phonetic element which recurs in a certain position in all the members of some equivalence class is a *distinctive* element. To this there is one exception: an element which is constant in all the members of the *range* is not distinctive. Thus the peculiarities of one person's voice are eliminated, if the range includes only his utterances; if it includes more, the differences of voice quality give rise to an intra-systemic ordering which has extra-systemic significance in that it serves to identify the speaker—a mixed ordering.

A distinctive element is distinctive wherever within the range it is found, even though in some positions it is sometimes present, sometimes absent. For example, in English, aspirate release of stop consonants is a distinctive element, since it occurs always after the first consonant of *put* or *tack* or *keep;* at the end of those same utterances the aspiration is sometimes present, sometimes lacking. Since this variation is subphonemic, even though it involves the presence or absence of a distinctive element, it may be termed *free variation.*

An element which is nowhere distinctive is *non-distinctive.* Non-distinctive elements are always found tangled up with distinctive ones, but are no more significant linguistically than is any other concurrent action of a speaker, such as scratching the nose or gum-chewing; they are simply harder to get rid of.

5.2 By going through all of the equivalence classes of a range it is possible to list all of the distinctive elements that occur. But this is not enough, for it turns out that some things which have been treated α-phonetically as elements, and which prove to be distinctive, are constantly associated in groups of two or more, one appearing wherever the others do.

Where this is true, the two or more elements clearly constitute a single unit, one of the minimum units into which the utterances of the range may be analyzed. These units are termed *features;* like elements, they will be treated terminologically as qualities.

The determination of features and of the positions in which they occur is the business of *β-phonetics.*

5.21 For the determination of features the method of contrastive pairs is useful. It is well known that in many languages minimal pairs in the traditional sense are rare. Let us suppose for a moment that in English pairs like *weave : wife, fought : vat, peach : pine* were plentiful, but that there were very few like *fat : vat, peep : pipe.* Such a situation would not hinder analysis; for it is easy to see that part of the difference between *weave* and *wife* recurs in *fought : vat,* another part in *peach : pine.*

Indeed, in English as it actually is, the α-phonetic elements which make up the contrast between *fat* and *vat* are not bound up exclusively with any other α-phonetic elements found in that pair, any more than the [v] of *weave* is bound up with the [ɪi], or the [f] of *wife* with the [aɪ], in the hypothetical case given above. In *sip : zip* the contrast is made by the same elements which make it in *fat : vat,* but in a different context, while in *fat : sat* one of the elements common to *fat* and *vat* is changed.

For this reason the term "contrastive pair," meaning any pair between which there are differences in a context of similarity, any pair usable for the listing of features, is used here instead of the traditional term "minimal pair."

5.22 In some English dialects stops are either voiced and lenis (*bid*) or voiceless and fortis (*pit*). In others some stops are voiced and lenis (*bid*), others voiceless and fortis (*pit*), still others voiced and fortis (*matter*). In the first case voicelessness and fortisness, two separate α-phonetic distinctive elements, constitute a single feature, as do voice and lenisness; in the second case voicelessness, voice, fortisness, and lenisness are all separate features.[8]

[7]Transcriptions used in this paper are of two kinds, which it will be necessary to keep rigorously distinct. Phonemic transcriptions are enclosed between diagonals; β-phonetic transcriptions are enclosed between square brackets (α-phonetic transcriptions do not occur). This way of distinguishing the two kinds of transcription is adopted from the article by Trager and Bloch (see fn. 1).

[8]Examples from English in the rest of this paper are from the writer's dialect, which is of the second of these two types.

It is perfectly possible that within a specified range, element *a* should be found only in connection with element *b*, but that element *b* should also be found elsewhere. In this case both elements *a* and *b* are features. Constant reciprocal association is necessary before two elements can be termed a single feature.

5.31   When all the features have been determined and listed, they are subject to several classifications. Most of these must wait until later to be introduced (§8), but one is important here.

Features which clearly follow each other in the stream of speech are *segmental*. Those which clearly extend over a series of several segmental groupings are *suprasegmental*. Thus the positions of articulation of the final two consonants in *crypt* are segmental, while the modes of articulation, voiceless and fortis, are suprasegmental.

5.32   A *β-sound* differs from an *α*-sound in the following two particulars: (1) Only distinctive features are concerned in the characterization of *β*-sounds. (2) A suprasegmental feature is treated as a *β*-sound in itself, and the segmental phases which it covers are regarded, without the superimposed feature, as independent *β*-sounds. Thus, like features, *β*-sounds fall into two classes, segmental and suprasegmental. For example, the final two consonants in *crypt* constitute five *β*-sounds. The three segmental ones are characterized respectively by the features of bilabial stop closure, apical stop closure, and aspiration. The stop character of the first two is not continuous from one to the other (as it is in *chapbook*), and so is not a suprasegmental feature. The suprasegmental *β*-sounds are absence of nasality and the fortis-voiceless character of the group. In addition, the entire utterance has the suprasegmental *β*-sound of loud stress, and this characterizes also each of the segments at the end of the utterance.[9]

5.33   Among features which are suprasegmental one can distinguish between those which are always so and those which are sometimes segmental. In *beat* the final consonant consists of two segmental *β*-sounds, [t'], each of which is characterized by several features; the first *β*-sound has apical position, stop closure, voicelessness, fortisness, and lack of nasality. So voicelessness and fortisness are not always suprasegmental, as they are in *crypt*. On the other hand, loud stress never accompanies a single segmental phase in English, and is therefore always suprasegmental.

6   The difference between a *β*-sound and a *phone* is that a phone is a member of a phoneme. Phones are again of two main kinds, segmental and suprasegmental; the latter class is subdivided into *accentual* and *junctural*. Whereas a *β*-sound may be sometimes segmental, sometimes suprasegmental, a phone is always one or the other; what is *β*-phonetically segmental may prove to be phonemically suprasegmental, and conversely, since this classification for phones depends on function as well as on *β*-phonetic character. Nor do the borders between segmental phones necessarily coincide with those between *β*-sounds: a single phone may include two or more adjacent *β*-sounds, and conversely. *Phonemics* is the analysis of *β*-phonetic material into phones, and the classification of the phones into phonemes.

6.1   A *phoneme* is a class of phones determined by six criteria. (1) *Similarity:* if *a* and *b* are members of one phoneme, they share one or more features. (2) *Non-intersection:* any phone which shares this feature or set of features is a member of the phoneme.[10] (3) *Contrastive and complementary distribution:* if *a* and *b* occur in corresponding positions in utterances of different equivalence classes, they are members of different phonemes; if *a* and *b* are in complementary distribution (i.e., if they occur in mutually exclusive positions), they may be—though they are not necessarily —members of the same phoneme. (4) *Completeness:* every feature characterizing each *β*-sound must be considered in making the classification; every *β*-sound must be all of or part of or more than some single phone; and every phone must be a member of a phoneme.

These first four criteria might still permit several alternative classifications. The danger

---

[9]On the phonemic interpretation of English stress see Trager and Bloch, "The Syllabic Phonemes of English," *Language* 17.226–229 [75–76].

[10]On the problem of intersection see Bernard Bloch, "Phonemic Overlapping" [8], *American Speech* 16.278–284 (1941).

of arbitrary procedure is obviated by the two other criteria.

6.11   (5) *Pattern congruity:* two contrasting β-segments (single β-sounds or groups of such sounds) which occur in similar β-phonetic environments are to be analyzed as having similar structures; either they are both unit phones, members of different phonemes belonging to the same functional class, or else they are similar clusters of two or more phones. This statement emphasizes the importance of structural parallelism: like function, like structure. But when such structural parallelism is absent, β-phonetic parallelism between two sets of β-phonetic segments may afford a basis of parallel analysis (see §7.33).

6.12   (6) *Economy:* if several different analyses equally satisfy the other requirements, that which establishes the smallest number of phonemes is the one to be preferred. This is a corollary of the general scientific principle that the simplest description which accounts adequately and accurately for all the facts is to be preferred.

6.2   A *homeophone* is a class of phones such that all members of the class are characterized by all the features that characterize any one member; obviously all the members of a homeophone will belong to the same phoneme. An *allophone* is a class of phones such that all are members of the same phoneme and occur in similar β-phonetic environments (the same position).

7.1   The first two criteria of phonemic analysis may be illustrated by English /p/. Every /p/ is characterized by fortis articulation, voicelessness, lack of nasality, labial position, stop closure, and some other features. /p, b/ share the features of non-nasality, labial position, and stop closure, /p, b, m/ the features of labial position and stop closure, /p, t, k/ the features of fortis articulation, non-nasality, and stop closure; but /p/ does not share *all* of its constant features with the members of any other phoneme.

7.2   It is not necessary to illustrate contrastive and complementary distribution, except to discuss what may be termed *partial complementation.*[11] Of the Spanish[12] phones

/r, r̄/, only the latter occurs initially, only the former in syllable-final;[13] both are found medially between vowels or after /d, b, k, t/. In the contrasting positions the units /r/ and /r̄/ are of course phonemically distinct, and it is impossible to regard the latter as a geminate cluster of the former, since it patterns like a single consonant. In the position where there is no contrast, the type of trill is in each case more similar to [r] or to [r̄] of the contrasting positions, and the phonemic membership is determined accordingly. The simple statement of distribution made above gives the facts without any complications; any talk of neu-

---

On Defining the Phoneme 30–32 (*Language Monograph* No. 16, 1935) and *Language* 12.54–56 (1936) [45–47]; but this problem is not a real one. If a phone *a* in a certain position is in complementary distribution with two other phones *b* and *c,* and is phonetically similar to both, either (1) both *a* and *b* or both *a* and *c* can be unambiguously assigned to the same phoneme, or else (2) *a, b,* and *c* are members of three separate phonemes.

(1) The stop in English *spin* (voiceless, fortis, unaspirated) is in complementary distribution with both the stop in *pin* (voiceless, fortis, aspirated) and the stop in *bin* (voiced, lenis, unaspirated). In §7.1 we have defined /p/ as characterized by fortis articulation, voicelessness, and some other features; this definition unambiguously includes the stop in *spin.*

(2) To illustrate the other possibility we must invent an example, for no real case is known to the writer. In a certain language, /i/ and /e/ are found in contrasting positions everywhere except before /n/; before /n/ there is a vowel phone which is exactly half-way between /i/ and /e/ and which occurs nowhere else. The latter vowel shares with /i/ and /e/ the distinctive feature of palatal articulation, but does not share the feature of intermediate tongue-height with any other phone. If these statements include all the relevant facts, then the cases of the intermediate vowel (in spite of its limited distribution) constitute a separate phoneme. Certain dialects of English in the South, where *pin* and *pen* are homonyms, may require this analysis.

[12]Spanish data are from Navarro-Tomás, *Manual de Pronunciación Española*[4], Madrid, 1932; G. L. Trager, "The Phonemes of Castillian Spanish," *TCLP* 8.217–222 (1939); and the writer's observations.

[13]Variations of sonority may occur α-phonetically; β-phonetically these may be distinctive or not. The terms "syllable," "nucleus," and "non-syllabic" are used here only on the phonemic level, to designate a grouping of phones which is useful in describing the phonemics of a particular language. Where nothing is said to the contrary, it is assumed that points of syllable division are non-distinctive, or that they are definable in terms of the other features involved.

---

[11]Another problem, that of multiple complementation, has been discussed by W. F. Twaddell,

tralization or cancellation or archiphonemes[14] confuses the facts without adding anything.

7.31   In the following two examples, certain single β-sounds, such as [i·], are regarded as constituting two phones.

In Winnebago,[15] long vowels [i·, e·, a·, o·, u·] are found under the same conditions as rising and falling diphthongs such as [i̯e, i̯a, i̯o, ae̯, ai̯]. These are all contrasting units, and there are no further types, such as [ii] different from [i·] or [i̯e] different from [i̯e]. Pattern congruity requires either (1) that all the long nuclei, homogeneous and heterogeneous, be treated as separate unit phones, or (2) that each be regarded as a cluster of two short phones, thus /ii, ee, aa, oo, uu, ie, ia, io, ae, ai/. Economy demands the acceptance of the second analysis, which sets up only five vowel phonemes (plus three nasal ones not considered here), whereas the first demands about thirty.

In Kickapoo[16] there are four vowel phonemes; /i/ includes [i, j, i̯], /o/ includes [o, w, u̯], and the four long nuclei are geminate clusters. Thus [ɛ·hki·ka·powa·towɛ·ki] 'where Kickapoo is spoken' is /eehkiikaapooaatooeeki/. There is no ambiguity in the phonemic orthography: [w] does not occur before /o/, nor [j] before /i/; so that /ooii/, for example, is always [owi·] and never [o·ji].

7.32   In the following example, two successive segmental β-sounds are treated as constituting a single phone: [t'] = /t/.

In English, fortis stop types occur with and without following aspiration. The possibility that the aspiration may be a part of the following phone is eliminated by its occurrence where no phone follows, as finally in *put, tack, keep,* though here it is variable. If this aspiration is a phone in itself, either the cases of it constitute a separate phoneme, or they are members of the same phoneme which includes also the β-phonetically distinct but similar independent aspiration of *hat.* The cases of it cannot constitute a separate phoneme, since the dependent aspiration is in complementary distribution with the independent aspiration and is β-phonetically similar to it. Therefore

such a form as *pin* is either /phín/ or /pín/. But the aspirated stops are, at each point of articulation, in complementary distribution with the unaspirated (except in final position, where there is free variation between the two types); and furthermore, the aspirated stops participate in clusters like other β-sounds that are clearly unit phones, not like β-sounds that are clearly clusters: [p'] behaves (patterns) like [p] and [b], not like [ps, bz, sp]. Therefore *pin* is /pín/, and the other aspirated stops are likewise unit phones, members of the same phonemes that include the unaspirated fortis stops.

7.33   In Old English there were ten syllable-nuclei that were β-phonetically short, ten that were long: *i, e, æ, a, o, u, y, ie, ea, eo; ī, ē, ǣ, ā, ō, ū, ȳ, īe, ēa, ēo.* The members of the two sets can be paired off so that the terms of each pair differ only in length and presumably in some minor qualitative ways. There seems to be no functional difference between the short and the long: both occur in stressed and in unstressed syllables, checked and unchecked, etc. But neither is there any functional classification which goes against the short–long grouping. In the absence of a functional classification to support or deny the β-phonetic grouping, the latter may be taken as a basis for analysis; the longs may be analyzed in one way, the shorts in another. Just what the analysis is in detail is not certain; probably there are ten vowel phonemes and two accentual phonemes, shortness and length, so that every syllable nucleus is a vowel phone plus an accentual phone.

When there are both functional classifications and β-phonetic parallelism, then the former, not the latter, must be taken as the basis for analysis. Modern English [ɑ·, ɔ·] (as in *palm, law*) are monophthongs, like the vowels of *bet, bit, put;* but structurally they are like the diphthongs of *ride, bait, read,* and their analysis must reflect the structural fact rather than the phonetic—provided that this is possible in a manner that satisfies all the other principles of phonemic analysis.[17]

7.4   There are four possible relations between a homeophone and an allophone if some phones are common to both.

---

[14]See N. S. Trubetzkoy, *Grundzüge der Phonologie* 206–218 (Prague, 1939).

[15]Winnebago data are from Amelia Susman.

[16]Kickapoo data are from the writer's notes.

[17]It is possible; see Trager and Bloch, *Language* 17.237–241 [82–85].

7.41   The homeophone and the allophone may be identical: all the members of one are members of the other, and conversely. For example, Dutch [g], a member of the /k/ phoneme, occurs only before a voiced consonant in the next syllable and never varies with any other β-phonetic variety of /k/ in that position.[18]

7.42   The homeophone may include the allophone and also have members which are not in the allophone. An example is English [p'], the only β-phonetic type of the /p/ phoneme found in phrase-initial before a stressed vowel, but also occurring optionally in utterance-final and in some other positions.

7.43   The allophone may include the homeophone, and also have members which are not in the homeophone. In some Spanish dialects /f/ before a voiced consonant in the next syllable varies between [f] and [v]; the latter occurs only in this position.

7.44   In some cases, finally, a homeophone and an allophone may intersect but each may include phones which are not members of the other. The Spanish [f] just mentioned is an example: the allophone includes also [v], and the homeophone includes also [f] in other positions. Further, the final consonant of English *tap* may be aspirated or not, and both varieties occur elsewhere.

These last two paragraphs illustrate free variation, mentioned in §5.1.

7.5   There is sometimes, in some definable position in utterances, a *free alternation* between phones that must be assigned to different phonemes. In some dialects of Spanish, for instance, there is free alternation between /d/ and /r/ before a stressed vowel, as in *pedir* 'ask' and *parar* 'prepare'. This is different, of course, from free variation between phones of different homeophones but the same allophone.

Free alternation is a matter of phonemics because the conditions for the alternation can be given in purely phonological terms. In some other dialects of Spanish such words as *pedir* have either /d/ or /r/, but such as *parar* have always /r/. This is not free alternation, since one cannot predict on phonological grounds alone where the alternation will occur and

where it will not; for this reason it is not part of phonemics, but rather of morphophonemics (a subdivision of grammar; see §10.1).

7.61   In the following example, a segmental β-sound, [h], is treated as a suprasegmental phone.

In early classical Greek,[19] there were two accentual phones which may be termed breath-types; they may be written respectively with /'/ before the vowel and with zero. Syllable nuclei bearing the aspirate breath-type occurred in phrase-initial, after initial and medial /r/, after initial and medial /p, t, k, pt, kt/, and after /m, n, l, r/ when these were preceded by /p, t, k/. The phonetic influence of the aspirate breath-type on the vowel itself is not known. An initial aspirated vowel had an aspiration before it; a preceding /r/ was probably voiceless; preceding voiceless stop had aspirate release, even if /m, n, l, r/ or another voiceless stop intervened. Thus orthographic ὅστις, φῶς, φλέξ, φράζω, θνήσκω, φθάνω, ῥέω, θάρρος were phonemically /'óstis, p'oás, pl'éks, pr'ádsoa, tn'eáiskoa, pt'ánoa, r'éoa, t'árr'os/.[20]

There are two other possible analyses; one does not satisfy the criterion of pattern congruity so well, though it gives fewer phonemes, and the other, though it satisfies pattern congruity, gives several more phonemes. The first is to consider the aspiration as a separate segmental phone (which could be written /h/) wherever it occurs; this would require recognition of such clusters as /phth/, for which there is no pattern at all. The other is to consider aspiration a separate segmental phone except where it accompanies the trill or a voiceless stop, and to set up as separate phonemes the classes of aspirated stops and trill—four additional phonemes. This is feasible because the dependent and the independent aspiration were probably β-phonetically distinct, though similar. The drawbacks to these two analyses lead one to accept instead the treatment first given above.

---

[18]Willem L. Graff, *Language and Languages* 41 (New York and London, 1932).

[19]Greek and Latin data are from E. H. Sturtevant, *The Pronunciation of Greek and Latin*[2]; Linguistic Society of America, 1940. The phonemic analysis of the Greek breath-types is G. L. Trager's.

[20]The transcription of vowels represents the phonemic analysis by G. L. Trager and the writer; its correctness is irrelevant to the validity of these examples. The phonemic nature of zeta is not known.

7.62 In the following examples a β-sound which is generally suprasegmental, or at least on the borderline, is treated as phonemically segmental.

In Winnebago there is a single consonant phoneme in each stop or spirant position, which is represented in different environments by phones with different β-phonetic features. The first member of a cluster of two obstruents (stop or spirant) is voiceless; if it is a stop it is aspirated unless followed by /h/. The second member of such a cluster, unless it is /ʔ/, is slightly voiced, unaspirated, and lenis. Thus /p, pt, h, ʔ, ph/ are [p', p'd, h, ʔ, p].[21] The crucial case is /pʔ/, β-phonetically [p'] (glottalized [p]): here two segmental phones correspond to two overlapping features.

In Takelma[22] there is a single set of stops and spirants, occurring initially, medially, and finally; clusters of two, including those with /h/ or /ʔ/ as first member, occur initially and medially, and those with /ʔ/ as first member occur finally. As first member of a cluster, a stop other than the glottal stop is aspirated (as is the latter in such a cluster in final position); as second member it is unaspirated and lenis. Thus /hp/ is [p], and /p/ is [p']; /ʔp/ is [p'] initially and medially, [ʔ'p'] finally. Here again two overlapping features, glottalization and oral stop closure, are treated phonemically as segmental.

7.7 A suprasegmental phone has a *domain,* defined as the type of sequence of segmental phones which it covers. Thus the domain of English stresses and ancient Greek breath-types is the syllable nucleus. This does not mean that only phones of that particular group are β-phonetically affected, but that the limits of the β-phonetic influence of the suprasegmental phone can be described in each case in terms of the segmental phones involved. When the starting point of the influence, or its end point, is not so determinable,

it may be called *determining,* and there must be some device in the phonemic orthography to record it.

The beginnings and endings of utterances, where there is by definition the β-phonetic feature of leaving a pause or starting one, are also characterized in some languages by special features, such as typical intonations, stresses, quantities, or other features of sonority. These same features are in some cases found within the utterances, accompanied by shorter pause or by none at all. The segmental and other suprasegmental phones adjacent to such points will be accompanied by these differences, and will not sound the same as they do elsewhere within utterances. Under such circumstances, the analytical principles will frequently demand that these accompanying features be extracted from their context and set up as independent suprasegmental phones. In other cases the same principles will lead instead to a greater differentiation of the other phones.

A suprasegmental phoneme is *junctural* if each member phone has a determining starting-point (or a determining end-point), and if either (1) every utterance begins (or ends) with a member of the phoneme, or (2) the phoneme is one of a contrastive set such that every utterance begins (or ends) with a phone which is a member of one of the phonemes of that set.

The fact that a junctural feature may be constant at the beginning or at the end of an utterance does not mean, according to the criterion of §5.1, that it is non-distinctive. For it occurs elsewhere in utterances, at points where it is not common to all the utterances of the range, and must therefore be regarded as distinctive wherever it is found.

7.71 Winnebago syllabic nuclei consist of a single vowel or of a cluster of two vowels. Each nucleus occurs in two types, stressed and unstressed; the preceding consonants are also influenced by the stress, but this influence is determined, not determining. The vowels can be arranged in the order /i, u, e, o, a/; those to the right are "stronger," those to the left "weaker." If a cluster of two phones has identical vowels, the distribution of stress, β-phonetically, is even; if the vowels are different, the stronger vowel—whatever the order of the two—bears the greater part of the stress. The nucleus types are thus /a, á, aa, áa/, as in

---

[21]Our traditional predilection for treating [p] as a unit and [p'] as a cluster can only lead us astray in dealing with Winnebago; for the former here patterns like a cluster, the latter like a unit phone, and the habitual voicing of the second member of clusters explains quite adequately how /pha/ is [pa]. A similar comment applies to the example immediately following.

[22]Edward Sapir, "Takelma" (in Franz Boas, *Handbook of American Indian Languages,* vol. 2; Washington, 1922).

/hapé/ 'he waited for him', /haapé/ 'I waited for him', /hačhá/ 'he sees him', /hačháak/ 'he sees him moving about'; the domain of stress is the syllabic nucleus as a whole.

In classical Greek, on the other hand, where also the nuclei contain either one vowel or certain clusters of two or three, the domain of the accent (which α-phonetically may have been either stress or pitch, though probably it was the latter) was a single vowel. The nucleus types were /a, á, aa, áa, aá/, written α, ά, ᾱ, ᾱ̆, ᾰ.

In some languages (perhaps Japanese) the situation is like that in ancient Greek except that both members of the nucleus may bear the accent, giving the nucleus types /a, á, aa, áa, aá, áá/.

7.72   The domain of an accentual phone is not necessarily nuclear. In Potawatomi[23] there are two contrasting accentual situations, which may be called fortis and lenis strength. The domain of fortis strength is a single obstruent (here /p, t, č, k, s, š/) or a cluster of two or more obstruents. The starting-point of influence is determined: it is the first obstruent of the group, preceded by the beginning of the phrase, by a vowel, or by a non-obstruent consonant. The end-point is determining, for /s·s/ and /ss·/ are different. A syllable beginning with a fortis obstruent or cluster is more strongly accented than one beginning with a lenis obstruent or cluster or with a non-obstruent consonant. In utterance-final there occur fortis non-syllabics, lenis obstruent non-syllabics, and non-obstruent non-syllabics, as well as vowels. Thus, although fortis strength has both nuclear and marginal β-phonetic effects in some positions, the fact that in phrase-final it has only marginal implications means that its domain is marginal. It is an accent, not a juncture, since it is not constant in phrase-final and since it does not belong to a contrastive set of which one member is found in every phrase-final.

7.73   There may be also accentual phones which have the entire syllable as domain; the tones of Chinese and Thai may belong here.

7.74   Junctural phones are not matters of grammatical segmentation, though a junctural situation may define phonological segments which are of grammatical significance. English examples will show the type of corre-

lation that may exist; in the following transcriptions[24] a juncture phone that might be called "drawl release" is indicated by a hyphen: *syntax* /síntàks/ : *tin-tax* /tín-tâks/; *mistake* /mistéjk/ : *Miss Tait* /mîs-téjt/; *psychological* /sàjkəwláhǰikəl, sàjkəláhǰikəl/ : *psycho-logical* /sâjkəw-láhǰikəl/; *minus* /májnəs/ : *slyness* /sláj-nəs/; *conquered* /káhŋkərd/ : *Concord* (place name) /káhŋ-kərd/; *a board, aboard* /əbórd/.

7.75   In Czech there seem to be three independent junctural phones: pause, here written with zero, since it occurs before the beginning of the phrase; loud stress, here written with a raised tick; and point of onset of stress, here written with a space. All three are found at the beginning of an utterance; the second and the third together are found at some points within utterances; and the third alone, without the loud stress, is found infrequently at points within the segment between two loud stresses. Orthographic *nevíme o tom ani vy ani já* 'we do not know that, neither you nor I' may be transcribed as /'ne vjiime 'o tom 'anji 'vi 'anji 'jaa/.[25]

7.76   Our phonetic information for Latin is defective, but it seems quite possible that the stress in early classical Latin was not an accent but part of a junctural phone. It can be located mechanically if certain borders are assumed. Grammatically these borders are clear, but without adequate material it is impossible to tell whether they were also phonological or not. In later times, however, when such words as *vīgintī, trīgintā, audīt, adhūc* no longer followed the penultimate rule, we may be certain that the stress was an accent, as it was in Vulgar Latin and is in those Romance languages which maintain it.

7.8   Sometimes when a β-sound contrasts with the absence of that sound, the absence is phonemically simply zero; in other cases

---

[23]Potawatomi data are from the writer's notes.

[24]The phonemic transcription of English here used, including the marking of stress and juncture, follows the practice described by Trager and Bloch. An acute accent over a vowel symbol denotes the loud stress, a circumflex the reduced loud, a grave the medial; absence of a mark denotes the weak stress.

[25]A. Mazon, *Grammaire de la langue tchèque;* Paris, 1921. The cited phrase occurs in §161; stress is discussed in §6. The transcription given here is certainly erroneous on several points, but the junctural indications are probably correct. The writer has not heard Czech himself.

it also is a phone, of the same structural class as the presence of the β-sound. The interpretation depends on the presence or absence of parallelism in the function of the two. The two features of shortness and length in Old English (§7.33) parallel each other in their function, and so if either is an accent, both are. In ancient Greek (§7.61) aspiration and its absence parallel each other, with differences; both are accents. Winnebago stress does not parallel the absence of stress: every utterance contains a stress, but some do not contain any unstressed nuclei; therefore the stress is an accent, its absence is not. The pitch (or stress) of classical Greek is a similar case. In Potawatomi the fortis strength has a determining end point, but the lenis strength does not; only the former is an accent.

7.9 One of the types of segmental features which it is easy to overlook is hiatus. Hiatus is not α-phonetic zero, nor need it be non-distinctive; if it is distinctive it may be a phone, not simply the absence of a phone.

7.91 In Potawatomi the absence of a consonant in phrase-initial and certain positions within the phrase patterns like the presence of a consonant. This absence of a consonant is describable α-phonetically as consisting sometimes of hiatus, or point of sharp syllable division, sometimes of a glottal stop. Because of its patterning, this must be set up as a consonantal phone.

In German there is a similar "absence of a consonant" which often is α-phonetically a glottal stop, but sometimes just point of onset of stress. But in German this distinctive feature turns out to be part of a junctural phone, not a segmental phone in itself.

In English the same thing exists, with the same analysis as in German; α-phonetically there is the difference that the "absence of a consonant" is much less frequently a glottal stop, more frequently just point of onset of stress.

7.92 A good case of relevant hiatus is found in Delaware.[26] Here there is a consonantal phone which may be written /ʔ/, since there is no contrasting glottal stop, and which

patterns like /h/. These two occur initially before a vowel and medially between vowels, and the latter also occurs in a medial geminate cluster. Both occur as first members of clusters when the second member is a stop. In all these positions /h/ is [h]. Initially and medially /ʔ/ is hiatus; before a stop it is a short phase of closure at the point of articulation of the stop that follows, so that /ʔp/ is [p·]. The preaspirated and long stops occur only medially, and they are the only medial non-syllabics (except /hh/) which cannot be divided into an occurrent final plus an occurrent initial. This suggests that these two sets of non-syllabics have parallel structures. It is not possible to analyze the long stops as geminates, because various real geminates occur initially and medially, doubly released in the case of stops. No other analysis than the one here given conforms to pattern congruity, except by the introduction of many more phonemes. The parallelism between /ʔ/ and /h/ is disturbed only by the presence of the cluster /hh/.

It is also quite possible that hiatus in Sanskrit, between words and within such words as *títaü* 'sieve' and *práüga* 'wagon-pole', was a phone, not the absence of a phone. This would add one consonantal phoneme, but would give only three vowels and clear patterns, instead of a larger number of vowel phonemes and obscure patterns. There are problems which must still be solved; but if Sanskrit hiatus was a phone, we may write /títaʔu, práʔuga, vrīhi-yavāu/ 'rice and barley' /uriihiiauaau/, and the like.[27]

8.1 A feature which characterizes all the members of a phoneme is *determining* for that phoneme; a feature which characterizes all the members of some allophone, but not all the members of the phoneme which includes that allophone, is *determined*. Thus, every English /t/ is fortis, apical, a stop, and non-nasal; these features are determining. In phrase-initial position, /t/ is voiceless and aspirated; these are determined. In phrase-final position it is sometimes aspirated, sometimes

---

[26]Observed by the writer in a class under C. F. Voegelin at the Linguistic Institute of 1939. Voegelin's orthography for Delaware is quite unambiguous and therefore perfectly satisfactory for the collection of texts, though it does not agree with the present analysis.

[27]Whitney, *Sanskrit Grammar*[5] §§125b, 329f, 338e, 353a. Some rule must be establishable, of course, to tell exactly when /u/ or /r/ will be consonantal and when vocalic. If it is impossible to discover such a rule, then the proposed analysis cannot be accepted.

unreleased; these features in this position may be called indeterminate.

8.11 A single feature may be determining for one set of phones, determined or indeterminate for others. In Spanish, for example, nasalization is determining for /m, n, ñ/, since these phones are always nasalized; determined for the /o/ of *conscribir* 'to conscript', since /o/ in that position is always nasalized, but not elsewhere; and indeterminate for the /a/ of *mano* 'hand', since /a/ in that position (between two nasal consonants) is sometimes nasalized, sometimes not.

8.12 In §7.7 the word "determining" was used in connection with the limits of the domain of a suprasegmental phone. It had there the technical meaning here assigned to it. The starting-point of the β-phonetic influence of fortis strength in Potawatomi is not constant. In /nos·/ 'my father' the fortisness begins and ends with the same segmental phone; in /ʔesp·ən/ 'raccoon' it begins with the /s/ and ends with the /n/. But the starting-point can always be predicted in terms of the sequence of segmental phones involved, and is therefore determined. The end-point of the β-phonetic influence cannot be so predicted. But it can be predicted in terms of an assigned end-point of the domain of fortisness; this is constant by definition, and therefore determining.

8.2 The relation between determining and determined features is of one of two kinds; the distinction is a practical one, concerning the method by which the various features can be most simply presented.

8.21 In certain cases a determining feature is a matter of clear-cut alternatives: Spanish /d/ is either a stop, as in phrase-initial *dar* 'give', *condenar* 'condemn', *Aldaba,* or else it is a frictionless spirant, as in *ayudar* 'assist', *sed* 'thirst'. In this case the terms of the contrast must be given, along with the circumstances under which each term is found. The determining feature is that Spanish /d/ is a lenis obstruent; the determined feature is that it is a stop in a particular position, a frictionless spirant in another position.

8.22 In other cases the determining feature is a general area, and the precise point within the area which is hit by a particular phone is determined, but the listing of all the points is difficult or impossible. Thus Spanish /k/ occurs in phrase-initial before all the vowels and before /r, l/; in phrase-medial after

any vowel or certain consonants, and before any vowel or certain other consonants; and in phrase-final at least after /a/. Each of these positions defines an allophone. The members of the different allophones vary over a relatively small area of points of articulation, and the areas of the different allophones intersect. The facts are covered adequately by stating that the general position is dorsal and that the exact position varies within certain extreme limits according to the adjacent phones— more fronted next to front vowels, further back next to back vowels, neutral next to consonants.

But it is essential to include this blanket statement; the variation cannot be taken for granted. In Potawatomi, /k/ varies much like the Spanish phone just discussed, but over a much smaller range; the accommodation of the point of contact to the articulatory positions of adjacent sounds is less than it is in Spanish. In Nootka, where there are two distinct dorsal stop positions, giving /k, q/, the phone which varies is not the consonant but the vowel, very strikingly in the case of /i/.

8.3 Determining features can be classified according to the phones in which they occur. In English, bilabial articulation is a determining feature for three consonants, /p, b, m/; /p/ has fortis quality as another determining feature, which is shared by /t, č, k, f, θ, s, š/; /p/ is a stop, as are /b, t, d, č, ǰ, k, g/. Such an inventory could continue until all the determining features had been considered.

8.31 An ideal diagram of the determining features would have as many dimensions as there are such features; if the total number of dimensions is *n,* then any *n*-minus-one–dimensional cross section of the diagram will include all those phones which share a particular feature. This can be illustrated for sixteen English consonants by setting two such cross sections side by side (with diagonal brackets omitted for convenience):

$$p \quad t \quad č \, k \qquad b \quad\quad d \quad ǰ \, g$$
$$f \, θ \quad s \, š \qquad\quad v \, ð \quad z \, ž$$

Those in the same flat cross section have the same strength (fortis or lenis); those in the same vertical plane have the same point of contact; those in the same horizontal plane have the same manner of articulation (stop or spirant).

8.32 Phones in a single line in a diagram that is so arranged constitute the members of a *minimal contrast*—minimal in that only one determining feature is different in the set. The *context* of the contrast is the complex of determining features that are shared by the set. In a particular context—that is, in any particular straight line in the diagram—there may be any number of members of the contrast: a contrast is bipolar, tripolar, and so on. Position of articulation in English, for stops, constitutes a quadripolar contrast: /p, t, č, k/. Strength, for stops, constitutes a bipolar contrast, e.g. /p, b/.

Non-minimal contrasts are those involving more than a single determining feature. *Direct* contrasts are those between phones which share some determining feature, e.g., /p : f/; *indirect* contrasts those between phones which share no determining feature, e.g., /p/ and loud stress.

8.33 It is the survey of the participation of determining features in phones that classifies those features in the way suggested by such names as "point of articulation," "strength," "manner of articulation," and so on. Sometimes a set of determining features belongs to a single class of this kind when from the α-phonetic point of view they seem to have no relation. This is probably true of lenis strength, fortis-aspirated strength, and glottalization for stops in Navaho.

8.34 The suborganization of phones in different contexts need not be parallel. In the diagram given above, the organization in the fortis plane and that in the lenis plane are parallel, but the organization in the stop plane and in the spirant plane is not: different points of contact are involved. Vowel articulation and consonant articulation are contrasting determining features in English; but the subdivision in the consonant cross section of the total diagram is nothing at all like that in the vocalic cross section.

8.35 If one flattens out the ideal multidimensional diagram of determining features and phones, so that it appears as a series of two-dimensional tables, the result is a phonologically accurate diagram which superficially resembles the more haphazard "tables of sounds" to be found in many of the older treatises on specific languages, in Trubetzkoy's *Grundzüge der Phonologie,* and elsewhere.

9.*1*   When determining features are classified according to their participation in phones, the result is also a classification of phones according to the determining features which characterize them. This classification is a matter of β-phonetics.

9.2   The structural classification of phones and phonemes is based on the principle that two phonemes belong in a single structural class if their member phones occur in similar environments. Every possible environment forms a test.

9.21   Spanish segmental phones may serve as an example. The vowels /i, e, a, o, u/ are distinguished from the consonants in constituting the domain of the stress; /i, u/ are distinguished from the other vowels in being sometimes syllabic, sometimes not, whereas the others are always syllabic; /i/ forms a class by itself in that it does not occur unstressed after /ñ, ʎ, j/ before a vowel. Of the consonants, /r/ forms a class by itself in that it does not occur in utterance-initial; /p, t, k, b, d, g, f/ occur before /r/ in the same syllable, the other consonants do not; /p, k, b, g, f/ occur before /l/ in the same syllable; /t, k, b, d, θ, s, n, r/ occur in utterance-final. And so forth.

9.22   The structural classification of phonemes in Spanish shows very little correlation with the β-phonetic classification of the phones. Thus /p, t, k, b, d, g, f/, which form a structurally defined set, include the voiceless stops except /č/, the lenis obstruents except /j/, and one member only of the fortis spirants. The set of occurrent finals /t, k, b, d, θ, s, n, r/ includes miscellaneous members of several β-phonetic groups.

A similar situation exists in English. The β-phonetic contrast between /f/ and /v/ is minimal, while that between /f/ and /ð/ is not minimal, though direct. But the structural contrast between /f/ and /v/ is entirely comparable to that between /f/ and /ð/: /f/ participates in initial clusters, while the other two do not; /f/ occurs before /t, s/ in final clusters, /v/ and /ð/ only before /d, z/. Other structural facts show the same relation.[28]

In some languages there is a much closer connection between β-phonetic groupings and structural groupings. In Polish and German,

---

[28]See the exhaustive structural classification of English non-syllabics in Bloomfield's *Language* 131–134 (New York, 1933). Bloomfield establishes 38 overlapping sets defined by the occurrence of consonants singly and in clusters.

for instance, the voiceless obstruents occur in final position, the voiced obstruents do not.[29]

10   This completes the presentation of the principles of phonology. There are three comments to be made about phonology as a whole.

10.1   The criteria for grammatical classification are (1) recognition of morpheme, word, and construction, and of the borders between them, (2) the phonemic shape of morphemes, words, and constructions, and (3) biosocial function, or meaning. The third is used in determining the first. The branch of grammar which deals with the phonemic shape of morphemes, words, and constructions, without regard to their meaning, is *morphophonemics*.

It is important to recognize that the criterion of biosocial function used in grammar is not at all the same as the criterion of biosocial equivalence used in phonology. The latter involves only the observation of whether two situations are the same in general outline, whereas the former involves extensive analysis of situations. There is no circularity; no grammatical fact of any kind is used in making phonological analysis.

From these definitions it follows that phonological analysis is necessary, though not sufficient, for the completion of grammatical analysis. Grammatical work is carried on, of course, in cases where phonological information is incomplete, either slightly deficient as it is for Old English, or sadly inadequate as for ancient Egyptian. But many of the gaps and ambiguities in such grammar have their source directly in the lack of complete phonemicization, and the recognition of that fact clarifies the issue as much as it can be clarified.

10.2   It has not been proved that the phonological system presented in this paper is the correct one, or even that there is just one correct phonology. The writer has attempted to

[29]G. L. Trager, "La Systématique des phonèmes du polonais," *Acta Linguistica* 1.179–188 (1939).

satisfy six requirements which seem essential for a correct system, but which no other system that he knows of completely fulfills. (1) Range and criteria must be accurately and unambiguously defined. (2) There must be no mentalism. (3) The terminology must involve no logical contradictions; terms defined as variables, class names, and quality names must be consistently used in those values. (4) No material should be excluded which might prove to be of grammatical importance, and none should be included which cannot be of grammatical importance. (5) There must be no circularity; phonological analysis is assumed for grammatical analysis, and so must not assume any part of the latter. The line of demarcation between the two must be sharp. (6) The way should be left open for the introduction of any criteria whatsoever on the grammatical level, barring mentalism.

10.3   Analytical procedure is a trial-and-error process, in which the analyst makes successive approximations. He gathers phonological and grammatical material at the same time, though he may emphasize now one, now the other. He makes errors of omission and commission, and later corrects them. At certain stages he may work by "feelings," but later he substitutes rigorous criteria. Finally the correct statement of the material emerges. In this, the organization depends on what is most efficient for the particular language concerned; if the source material is a body of written records, the very defects of the record may condition the order of presentation.

Thus neither the process of analysis, nor the presentation of the results of analysis, need resemble the general picture of phonology given in this paper. The system given here is a *frame of reference*. If the analyst operates constantly in terms of such a frame, being careful not to confuse the distinctions made in it, and using terms in logically valid ways, the resulting description is the clear-cut, efficient statement of facts which a classificatory science requires.

I.c

Further Development of Bloomfieldian Phonology

12

SIMULTANEOUS COMPONENTS IN PHONOLOGY*

ZELLIG S. HARRIS

1.0 This paper[1] investigates the results that may be obtained when phonemes, or utterances in general, are broken down into simultaneously occurring components: as when the English phoneme /b/ is said to consist of voicing plus lip position plus stop closure, all occurring simultaneously.[2]

1.1 The analysis presented here rests on the fact that two independent breakdowns of the flow of speech into elements are physically and logically possible. One is the division of the flow of speech into successive segments; this is used throughout phonology and morphology, and gives us the standard elements (allophones or positional variants; phonemes; morphemes; words; phrases) of descriptive linguistics. The other is the division of each segment into simultaneous components, as when the single sound ['á] (high-pitched loud-stressed low mid vowel) is said to be the resultant of three components: high pitch, loud stress, and low-mid vowel articulation. It is this type of breakdown, only little used in phonemics today, that is investigated here.

1.2 This investigation will show that intonations, prosodemes and "secondary phonemes," pitch and stress morphemes and pho-

nemes, and suprasegmental features in general, can all be obtained as a result of the single operation of analyzing the utterances of a language into simultaneous components. It will show that the various limitations of phonemic distribution, including defective distribution of phonemes, can be compactly expressed by means of the same operation. When this operation is carried out for a whole language, it breaks all or most of the phonemes into new sub-elements (components). Each of the old phonemes will be a particular simultaneous combination of one or more of these new elements; and the total number of different components will be much smaller than the previous total number of different phonemes. It will be possible to select and symbolize the components in such a way as to show immediately the limitations of distribution, and in many cases the phonetic composition, of the phonemes in which they occur.

1.3 It will be seen that the linguistic status of these components varies with their length. Components which are precisely the length of a phoneme, i.e. which represent merely the simultaneous breakdown of each phoneme by itself, enable us to eliminate phonemes of defective distribution and to indicate the phonetic composition of each phoneme (§5.3, 4).[2a] We shall also permit some components to have the length of more than one phoneme, i.e., we shall say that such a component stretches over a sequence of phonemes. When phonemes are written with such long components, we shall be able to know the limitations

---

[1] I am glad to express here my thanks to Dr. Henry Hoenigswald and the members of the linguistic seminar at the University of Pennsylvania for valuable criticism and for linguistic material. I am particularly indebted to Dr. Roman Jakobson for an interesting conversation on the phonetic breakdown and grouping of phonemes. I owe an exceptionally heavy debt to Dr. Bernard Bloch, who has helped me state many of the more difficult points.

[2] This example of phonetic components is given here only for introductory simplicity. The analysis presented below is primarily distributional rather than phonetic.

[2a] E.g., it is this technique that enables us, in languages which have a phonemic tone on each vowel (Fanti, Chinese, etc.), to extract the tones as separate phonemic elements.

*Reprinted from *Language* 20.181–205 (1944) by permission.

of distribution of any phoneme by looking at the components of which it is composed (§5.2). Some of these long components will extend over all the phonemes of an utterance or linguistic form. These components will turn out to constitute the intonational or other contours of the language (§5.1).

In the following sections, these three groups of components which differ as to their length will be kept separate.

PRESENT TREATMENT

2.0 We have then a large number of linguistic situations which, it will turn out, can all be described by means of the analysis into simultaneous components. It will be helpful if we briefly note how these situations are usually treated at present.

2.1 Pitch and Stress There is a particular group of phonetic features which has customarily been separated from the rest of the linguistic material even though simultaneous with it. This is pitch and stress. The extraction of these features out of the flow of speech is due to the fact that they constitute morphemes by themselves, independent of the rest of the speech, with which they are simultaneous. In *You. : You? : Yes. : Yes?* we have four different sound-sequences, and four different meanings. These must therefore have four different phonemic compositions. This requirement would be satisfied if we had phonemic /U/ and /E/ as high-pitched vowels contrasting with low-pitched /u/ and /e/. Then we would write /yuw/, /yUw/, /yes/, /yEs/. However, the pitch features which are symbolized by /U, E/ have the specific meaning of interrogation. We therefore wish to consider some part of /yUw/, /yEs/ as the morphemes "you," "yes" and another part as the morpheme "interrogation." This can be done only if we consider /U, E/ to consist of two simultaneous components /u, e/ and /'/. Then the phonemes /u, e/ are part of the morphemes for "you" and "yes"; and the phoneme /'/, or rather the rising pitch which extends over the whole utterance, is the morpheme for interrogation.

In most languages that have been investigated, pitch and stress have been found to constitute the elements of special morphemes (such as phrase and sentence intonation or the English contrastive stress). These elements are pronounced simultaneously with the other morphemes of the language. It would be impossible to isolate the other morphemes without extracting the pitch and stress morphemes that occur simultaneously with them. Perhaps as a result of this, it has been customary to extract pitch and stress features even when they form part of the phonemic make-up of ordinary segmental morphemes (words and parts of words). Thus we do not usually say that a language has ten vowels, five loud and five weak, but rather that it has five vowel phonemes plus two degrees of stress.

2.2 Relations Among Phonemes, and the limitations of distribution of particular phonemes, are not presented in linguistics as an essential part of the individual phonemes. There exists no method which would enable us to say "/b/ is phonemic everywhere except after /s/" or "/t/ is a phoneme except after initial /k/, etc." Instead we say that /b/ and /t/ are phonemes, and then tack on statements which correct the phonemic list by pointing out that /b/ does not occur after /s/, i.e., that there is no allophone occurring after /s/ which is assigned to /b/. If a number of phonemes have identical distributions, a single statement is devoted to them all. We say, for example, that English /ŋ/ occurs before no consonant other than /g, k/, or that morpheme-medial clusters in English hardly ever include both a voiceless consonant and a voiced one which has a voiceless homorganic counterpart: we get /ft/, /ks/ in *after* and *axiom,* but not /vt/, etc.[2b] If a phoneme occurs in few positions as compared with other phonemes in the language, as is the case with English /ŋ/, we say that it is defective in distribution. But the writing system which we create does not reveal all these limitations. Given the phonemes of a language, a person would not know how to avoid making non-extant sequences unless he kept in mind the distribution statements.

The phonologists of the Prague Circle tried to indicate some of these limitations of distribution by saying that a phoneme which does not occur in a given position is "neutralized" by one which does, and that an "archiphoneme" symbol can be written to represent either phoneme in that position. Thus /b/ and

---

[2b]Voiced-voiceless sequences like /rp/ in *carpet* are not counted here, since /r/ has no voiceless homorganic counterpart.

/p/ are neutralized after /s/, and can then be represented by the archiphoneme P, which would indicate the "common element" of both: /sPin/ instead of /spin/. This did not in itself prove to be a productive method of description. In the first place, most cases of "neutralization" involve not merely two phonemes that directly neutralize each other. Usually several phonemes occur in a given position while several others do not, and "neutralization" may be said to exist between the two whole classes of phonemes; thus after word-initial /s/ we find /p, t, k, f, l, w, y, m, n/ and the vowels, but not /b, d, g, v, θ, ð, š, ž, s, z, r, ŋ, h/. To select /p/ and /b/ out of the two lists and assign them to a separate archiphoneme P implies some further and hitherto unformulated method of phonemic classification on phonetic grounds. And what shall we do with /θ/ or /š/ or /z/?[3]

Related to these limitations of individual phonemes are other distributional facts. In a particular language, certain positions have the greatest number of phonemic contrasts, and others have the least: in Swahili every phoneme may occur in the position after pause, but only the five vowels ever occur before pause or between consonants. There are also limitations upon clustering: in English, not more than three consonants occur in succession initially, nor more than four or five (depending on the inclusion of foreign names) medially in a morpheme. These clusters may be further limited in the order of the phonemes: /t/ occurs after /p/ and /k/ before word-juncture, but not before them. In our present descriptions, facts of this type are not automatically derivable from any other information given. They must be separately stated, and are not represented in the phonemic writing itself.

A less important point in which our present method of description is inadequate is the phonetic similarity among the allophones of various phonemes. Thus English /p, t, k/ all have identically varying allophones in identically varying positions (strongly aspirated initially, unaspirated after /s/, etc.); /k, g, ŋ/ have identical places of articulation in identical environments (fronted allophones after front vowels, etc.). These similarities are recognized in the grammar when we describe the variation in allophones of all the analogous phonemes in one statement, as was done above. But the similarities among these phonemes are not explicit in the phonemic inventory or directly marked in the transcription.

2.3 Breaking an Allophone into Two Phonemes Whereas the two previous types of treatment have been fairly clear-cut, there is a group of linguistic facts in which the usual treatment is ambiguous: in some cases simultaneous elements are separated out and in other cases they are not, with no very clear criteria to decide whether the separation is to be performed or not.

It is customary to divide an allophone x into two successive allophones x_1 x_2 if we can then assign x_1 and x_2 to two otherwise recognized phonemes whose sequence is complementary to x. Thus we may break up English [č] into two successive phonemes /tš/, considering the retracted [t] as a positional variant of /t/ and the fronted [š] off-glide as a positional variant of /š/. We do this because phonemes /t/ and /š/ have already been recognized in English, but do not (except here) occur next to each other. We therefore consider the two successive parts of [č] as the allophonic values of the two phonemes /t/ and /š/ when they do occur next to each other. Certain accessory criteria influence us in deciding to consider the allophone as a combination of the allophones of two phonemes. The positions in which [č] occurs should be such in which sequences of the same type as /tš/ also occur. The new allophones, back [t] before a palatal spirant /š/, and [š] off-glide after a stop /t/, should have some phonetic similarity to other allophones of the phonemes to which they will be assigned, and should if possible have the same relation to them that analogous allophones have in analogous positions. Finally, the original allophone [č] should have some of the phonetic qualities which characterize a sequence of two phonemes in English (e.g., it should be longer than a single phoneme; or should have the tongue moving not directly

[3]The Prague Circle more closely approached the technique of dividing elements into simultaneous components, but purely on arbitrary phonetic grounds, when they said that the difference between two phonemes was not *a* vs. *b*, but *a* vs. *a* + *x* (where *x* is a Merkmal denoting the extra features which differentiate *b* from *a*). See N. S. Trubetzkoy, *Grundzüge der Phonologie* 67 (*Travaux du Cercle Linguistique de Prague* 7; 1939).

from the alveolar stop to the position of the next sound, but going out of its way via the spirant off-glide).

In practice, however, this last criterion is often disregarded. Among speakers who distinguish the initials of *tune* and *tool,* many pronounce in *tune* a simple consonant—a palatalized post-dental blade stop with no recognizable [y] off-glide; nevertheless we consider that allophone to represent the phonemic sequence /ty/. Similarly the nasalized alveolar flap in *painting,* which contrasts with the alveolar nasal continuant in *paining,* is not considered a new phoneme occurring only after loud-stressed vowel and before zero-stressed vowel, but is assigned to the sequence /nt/.[4] Analyses of this type constitute an important departure in method, because we are here analyzing a sound segment into two simultaneous parts and assigning one part to one phoneme and the other to another. In the case of /ty/ we may say that the post-dental occlusion is the allophone of /t/ and the simultaneous palatalization is the allophone of /y/. In the case of /nt/, we may say that nasalization combined with obstruction of the breath in the dental-alveolar area is the allophone of /n/, and the alveolar flap movement is the normal allophone of /t/ between loud and zero-stressed vowels. In each case we have avoided the introduction of a new phoneme with defective distribution, by assigning the sound to a sequence of previously recognized phonemes.

In all these cases we have an allophone broken up into components each of which we consider an allophone of phonemes which had already been recognized in other positions. As an extension of this analysis we have the occasional setting up of a new suprasegmental phoneme to account for a whole sequence of allophones which always appear together. Thus in Moroccan Arabic a new suprasegmental emphatic phoneme[5] is set up to account for the emphatic allophones. Phonetically, we

have [ṣog] 'drive' (with cerebral [ṣ]) but [flus] 'money' (with post-dental [s]); [ḍar] 'house' (with cerebral [ḍ] and [r̩]), but [dær] 'he built'; [lanba] 'lamp' (with low back [a]), but [læbs] 'dressing'. We could write this phonemically by considering [ṣ, o, ḍ, a, r̩] to be different phonemes from [s, u, d, æ, r] respectively. But we notice that to say this would indicate a greater phonemic distinction than actually exists. In [lanba] ~ [læbs], the difference between [a] and [æ] is phonemic; for there is nothing in the neighboring phonemes to indicate that the vowel is [a] in one word and [æ] in the other. But in [ḍar] ~ [dær] the difference between [a] and [æ] need not be considered phonemic; for [æ] never occurs next to [ḍ], and we could say that [a] is the positional variant of the /æ/ phoneme next to /ḍ/ and other emphatics (i.e., cerebrals). This crux is avoided by breaking each emphatic phoneme into two simultaneous parts: a regular consonant or vowel, and an emphatic component: [ṣ] is analyzed as /s/ plus /'/, [o] as /u/ plus /'/, etc. It is then shown that when this emphatic component occurs after consonants it affects a sequence of phonemes, but when it occurs after vowels it affects only the preceding phoneme: /s'ug/ = [ṣog], /d'ær/ = [ḍar], /læ'nba/ = [lanba]. But it must be noted that this new phoneme was not inescapable. We could have written each of the Moroccan emphatic sounds as a new emphatic phoneme, and added a statement that in certain positions emphatic phonemes occur with each other to the exclusion of non-emphatic phonemes. However, such a statement would be at least as complicated as the equivalent statement which gives the domain of the single emphatic phoneme, and would leave us with a large number of extra and defectively distributed phonemes instead of the single emphatic /'/.

INTRODUCTION OF
SIMULTANEOUS COMPONENTS

3.0 The various linguistic situations mentioned in §§2.1–3 can all be compactly described by the use of simultaneous components. In order to introduce these components, all we need do is to permit the segmental elements of our linguistic description to be resolved into any number of simultaneous component sub-elements.

3.1 This is not a new operation in lin-

---

[4] Y. R. Chao gives other "cases of one homogeneous sound represented by two or three piece symbols, each of which represented some aspect or aspects of the sound" in his article "The Non-Uniqueness of Phonemic Solutions of Phonetic Systems," *Bulletin of the Institute of History and Philology* 4.371 (Academia Sinica; Shanghai, 1934).

[5] Z. S. Harris, "The Phonemes of Moroccan Arabic," *JAOS* 62.309–318 (1942).

guistics: it is used implicitly when pitch and stress features are extracted as separate phonemes, and it is used when we analyze English flapped [n] as /nt/. There is no particular reason to admit such analysis in these cases and to deny it in such cases as the Greek aspiration (which, like stress, occurred in most forms only once within a word) or English voicelessness (which, like the Moroccan Arabic emphatic, occurs over a sequence of phonemes). No new methods or postulates are therefore required to extend the analysis of simultaneous components into all the phonemes of a language.

3.2   It may also be noted that this operation involves us in no theoretical difficulties. It does not prevent us from having a statable physical character for our linguistic elements. The traditional phonemes indicate explicit physical events: time-stretches of sound (sound-waves), or sets of simultaneous motions of the "vocal organs." The new component elements also indicate explicit physical events: time-stretches of sound-waves,[5a] or motions of particular vocal organs.[6] The only difference is that phonemes are elements which can, in general, occur only after one another, while components are elements which can also occur simultaneously with each other (as well as after each other).

3.3   If we are to permit our segmental elements to be resolved into components, we must bear in mind that there are many different ways in which any elements can be broken down into sub-elements. There are a great many ways in which components—various numbers of them and variously grouped— can be arranged so that every combination of components recognized in the arrangement will yield a particular phoneme. Such expressions of phonemes in terms of components are not in themselves of value to linguistics. The advantage they offer in reduction of the number of elements may be more than offset if connecting them with the distributional and phonetic facts requires more complicated statements than are required for regular phonemes. We consider the possibility of such analysis into components only because, as will be shown below, we can select the components in a way that will enable us to give simpler statements of the facts about phonemes.

3.4   We can now say in general terms what we must do when we analyze phonemes into components. We take a list of phonemes, each with its phonetic and distributional description; we select a number of components; we select some method for combining these components simultaneously (e.g., not more than three components at a time), in such a way that each combination permitted by the method will identify a phoneme, and that the grammar becomes simpler and briefer when written in terms of the components.

PROPERTIES OF THE COMPONENTS
4.0   Since the components are to be physical elements (§3.2), we must consider the phonetic values that they can have (§4.1). Furthermore, it will be seen that in special cases a component (or its phonetic value) may extend over more than one phoneme; and it will be important to note what happens when we get such *long components* (§4.2). The work that a component can do in the description of a language depends on its length. Components whose length is that of one phoneme can be used to describe the phonetic composition of phonemes (§5.4) or the dissection of a single allophone into two or more phonemes (§5.3). Components whose length is that of two or three phonemes (or thereabouts) can be used to indicate the limitations of distribution of any phoneme which contains them (§5.2). And components which can extend over long sequences of phonemes are used in the descriptions of intonational and other contours (§5.1).

4.1   *Phonetic Values*   Since the components are to identify phonemes, or more generally speech sounds, each component must have a stated phonetic value in each environment in which it occurs. As in the case of phonemes, there is no reason to require that

---

[5a]It is possible, by Fourier analysis, to replace periodic waves by a sum of simpler periodic waves. The original waves (e.g., sound waves) can then be considered the resultants which are obtained by adding together all their component waves.

[6]E.g., vibration of the vocal cords, giving "voice." This might be the phonetic value of a particular component in a particular position, whereas the phonetic value of a particular phoneme in a particular position might be, for example, voice plus closing off of the nose plus closing of the lips (English /b/). A phonetic system of this kind without the phonemic limitation is Otto Jespersen's analphabetic system, presented in his *Lehrbuch der Phonetik* (2d ed. Leipzig and Berlin, 1912) and elsewhere.

its phonetic value be identical in all the environments. The component can therefore have different phonetic variants (allophones) in various positions, and the environmental factor which determines the particular allophone may be anything outside the component itself: other components with which it is concurrent, neighboring components or pauses, position of the component within the sequence of segments, etc.

Again as in the case of phonemes, it is not required that components have a constant phonetic value throughout their duration. A component may have a phonetic value which changes in a fixed way in respect to its endpoints: e.g., falling tone, increase in nasality, voiceless beginning and voiced ending.

Finally, if we are ready to admit partial overlapping among phonemes,[7] we may agree to have different components in different environments represent the same phonetic value. So long as we do not have a component in one environment represent two phonetic values which are not freely interchangeable, or two components or component-combinations in the same environment represent the same phonetic value, we are preserving the bi-unique one-to-one correspondence of phonemic writing. (The term bi-unique implies that the one-to-one correspondence is valid whether we start from the sounds or from the symbols: for each sound one symbol, for each symbol one sound.)

4.2 Length Values Whereas the considerations of phonetic value are comparable for phonemes and for components, we find that in the matter of length there is an important restriction upon phonemes which can be lifted in the case of components. In the operations which lead to the setting up of phonemes, one of the most important steps is segmenting the flow of speech into successive unit lengths, such that every allophone or phoneme consists of exactly one of these lengths.[7a] In analyzing out the components, we make use of this segmentation, because what we break down are phonemes or allophones, not just

random parts of the speech flow. However, there is no reason for us to restrict every component to the length of one phoneme. If a component is always common to a sequence of phonemes, we can say that its length is the length of the sequence. This will enable us to describe the limitations of phoneme sequences. When particular phonemes occur next each other (e.g., English /sp/ in /spin/), while others do not (e.g., /sb/), we will say that the phonemes which occur next to each other all have some one component in common. The length of a component will therefore always be an integral number of phoneme-lengths—1, 2, 3, etc.—but need not be just one.

It follows that just as a component may have different phonetic variants in different positions, so it may have different lengths in different environments. When the Moroccan Arabic emphatic occurs after a vowel, it affects only the preceding vowel; when it occurs after a consonant, it affects a whole neighborhood, including several consonants and vowels.

OBTAINING THE COMPONENTS

5.0   The greatest advantage from the analysis into components comes from the components with a length of two or more phonemes. These components enable us to express situations which could not be symbolized by the fixed-length phonemes. We shall investigate these components first. The first technique we shall use will yield the syntactic contours. The second will yield a way of treating the limitations of distribution of phonemes. The third will yield special cases of segmental phonemes. Finally we shall consider the components whose length is that of only one phoneme.

5.1 Automatic Sequences Expressed by Long Components Our first operation is to extract those components which appear only in fixed patterns.

INTONATIONS   We first consider the case where some connection among particular successive components in successive allophones is readily noticeable to us—that is, where we do not have to conduct a search to find a series of components which we can extract. Since we are assuming that no simultaneous elements have as yet been extracted, we have our language material in the form not of phonemes but of allophones, with each future phoneme,

---

[7]Bernard Bloch, "Phonemic Overlapping" [8], *American Speech* 16.278–284 (1941).

[7a]The lengths are not absolute (so many hundredths of a second) but relative. This means that an allophone [p], for instance, is not composed of two shorter allophones "p-closure" and "p-release."

or at least each vowel, represented by many allophones:[7b] loud and middle-pitched [a], loud and high-pitched [a], very loud and middle-pitched [a], soft and low-pitched [a], etc. As a result of our past experience with languages, we may tend to scrutinize particularly the various stresses or pitches of each successive allophone in an utterance. However, we may also happen to note fixed patterns in the sequence of other features in successive allophones: e.g., a decrease in sharpness of articulatory movements from the beginning to the end of English utterances. Or we may notice a fixed pattern composed of several phonetic features of successive allophones: decrease in sharpness plus level tone during most of the utterance, followed by a falling tone at the end, in certain types of English statement.

In any case, we look for successions of phonetic features which recur in various utterances. We note that the occurrence of these features is limited: only certain sequences appear. For instance, we find the relative pitch sequence 1221130 (where 3 = highest pitch and 0 = lowest) in *I don't know where he's going.* | *We can't tell when they're coming.* | etc. Among utterances with the same stress positions we do not find other pitch sequences ending in 30. For utterances with these stresses then, we tentatively count the above pitch sequence as one of the fixed patterns. We then see if we can in any way reduce the number of fixed patterns. We note that before the final 30, the slightly raised pitch 2 occurs wherever a mildly loud stress occurs; we therefore consider pitch 2 to be an allophone of pitch 1 in stressed position. Other pitch sequences can also be considered special cases of this one: occurrences of relative high pitch 4 at one or more places in such utterances will always be accompanied by a loud contrastive stress (*Wé can't tell when they're coming.* 4221130), and can therefore also be considered an allophone of pitch 1. As a result of such manipulations

a large number of pitch sequences ending in 30 become identical. They are all cases of one fixed sequence: as many relatively low tones as vowels (with slightly raised tones under stress and fairly high tones under contrastive stress) followed by a middling high tone on the last stressed vowel with a drop to zero (lowest) pitch on the vowels or consonants after it.

In English, a number of other sequences will not be reducible to this. For instance, there is the sequence in which every loud-stressed vowel, and every vowel or consonant after the last loud stress, has a higher pitch than the preceding one, while every zero-stressed vowel has the same pitch as the preceding loud stressed: *You're not going over to Philadelphia?* 012233333456.

By investigating all these intonations, we obtain a small number of pitch-sequence patterns, occurring over whole utterances or over sections of utterances (phrases, etc.). In phonemics, if we were dealing with a fixed sequence of segmental phonemes as long as these sequences of pitch, we should have to consider it as composed of the observable successive elements; and the fact that only a very few of the possible sequences of these elements occur could only be stated as a limitation upon their distribution. Since, however, components are not restricted as to length, we can say in this case that each of these pitch sequences is a single component whose length is that of a whole utterance or phrase. This is permissible, since the successive parts of the sequence are not independent of each other (e.g., before 30, only 1's occur) and may all be considered parts of one element. And it is advantageous, since we thus avoid having to state limitations of distribution for individual phonemic tones.

The essential operation here is to put two successive sounds or sound features into one unit if they always occur together in a particular environment. This is often done in phonemics, as when we consider the aspiration after initial [p, t, k] to be not a separate phoneme but part of the allophones of /p, t, k/ in that position.[8] Similarly, in these few fixed

---

[7b]We will assume that these allophones satisfy all the criteria for phonemes—that is, that complementary allophones have been grouped together—except that allophones having different stress and pitch have been considered different sounds and hence not grouped together under one symbol. It is impossible to obtain the conventional phonemes until intonational components have been extracted from the allophones.

[8]This operation is used implicitly throughout phonemics to keep us from breaking sounds down into smaller and smaller segments ad infinitum. We do not consider the lip closing and the lip opening

sequences of pitch or the like, we consider the parts of each sequence to be automatically dependent upon each other, so that the whole sequence is one phonemic element.[9]

COMPONENTS OF COMPONENTS If we wish to reduce the number of such dependent-sequence elements, we analyze them in turn into components on the basis of phonetic similarity (since there are no limitations of distribution among them) in the same way that this will be done for segmental phonemes (see §5.4 below). That is, we break up the sequences into any simultaneous components which seem most convenient, and the combinations of which uniquely identify each sequence: e.g., the direction of pitch change after the last loud stressed vowel, the degree of change there, etc.

STRESS An analogous operation is performed when we have word or morpheme junctures phonemically established and note that some feature always occurs exactly once between each two junctures, or that some phonetic feature has fixed patterns between junctures. Thus we may note that there is never more than one loud stress between word junctures in English, and that the other vowels between these junctures have medium or weak stress, usually in fixed patterns: e.g., 1030 in *distribution, independent,* etc. Certain facts about the stresses are thus automatic: the number of loud stresses, the occurrence of some of the weak stresses. We therefore mark as phonemic only the remaining nonautomatic facts: the place of the loud stress, and where necessary the place of any secondary stress. In a similar way, English contrastive stress (1040 in *distribution, not production*) would be discovered, since when it does occur it hardly ever appears more than once between two word junctures. This operation, however, will not discover features which do not appear in a limited number of fixed sequences, e.g., pitch in languages where all sequences occur and where the different sequences cannot be reduced into special cases of one another.

In dealing here with dependent sequences,

it has been assumed that the phonetic features comprising the sequences would be readily noticed by the linguist. This is usually the case not only because pitch and stress are so frequently the features concerned, but also because it is relatively easy to notice phonetic features which show recurrent patterns in many sequences of allophones. Nevertheless, the analysis in no way depends upon a lucky finding of these phonetic features. It is possible to discover any fixed sequences methodically by the laborious process of taking each allophone (or each of a class of allophones, e.g., vowels) in many utterances and seeing in what respect the allophone after it is limited: e.g., given a low-pitched, sharply-articulated, weak-stressed vowel at the beginning of various utterances, can we find examples of every grade of pitch, sharpness, and stress in the vowel after it, or do only certain grades occur?

SEGMENTAL ALLOPHONES The net result of this operation has been not only to produce a number of phonemic sequences of phonetic features (e.g., pitch-sequence phonemes), but also to extract these same phonetic features (e.g., pitch) from the recorded flow of speech. The recurring fixed patterns helped us to notice these phonetic features and gave us the basis for extracting them as a single independent element. But by doing so we are left with the original sequence of allophones minus these features. If we now go back to the allophones, we shall find that the extraction of these dependent-sequence elements (e.g., pitch) has reduced the allophones, which had originally differed in these features, to the conventional phonemes: the variously stressed and pitched [a]'s are now identical /a/, since they no longer represent classes of actual sounds but only features of sounds—namely, all the features except stress and pitch. What we thus obtain out of our original allophones equals the conventional phonemes merely because it has been customary for linguists to extract pitch and stress features, so that our usual phonemes are even now not classes of sounds but classes of sounds minus their pitch and stress features. The original allophones with which we began here were pure classes of freely varying or complementary sounds, and when we extracted the dependent sequences, which in most cases are composed of the pitch

---

of intervocalic /p/ to be separate phonemes, because they always occur together in that position.

[9]A fuller discussion of the character of these contour components is given in fn. 22a below.

and stress features, we obtained the conventional phonemes.

The fact that most of these fixed sequences of sound components have meanings, or correlate with morphological constructions, is a matter apart. This fact is independently recognized by including them in the list of morphemes of the language. Dependent sequences may turn out to be phonemic without being morphemes, e.g., word-stress, varying rhythms and melodies of speech.

5.2 Limitations of Distribution Expressed by Long Components In our second operation we consider the usual type of limitation of distribution, in which a phoneme that occurs in most environments is limited by never appearing in certain positions. Here no solution is possible within the methods of segmental phonemics. The difficulty with the archiphoneme device, and with the statements about distributional relations between phonemes, is that they seek only to find a relation or common factor among the phonemes that can or cannot occur in a given environment. But there also exists a relation between the phonemes which occur in a given environment and that environment itself, namely the fact that they occur next to each other. That relation exists, for instance, between English /ŋ/ and /k/, but not between /ŋ/ and /t/. If we are willing to break phonemes up into simultaneous components, we restate this relation as a factor common to /ŋ/ and /k/ but not to /t/; and we say that /ŋ/ and /k/ each contain a certain component (say, back position) and that this component spreads over the length of two phonemes when the first is nasal. /ŋt/ therefore does not occur, nor /nk/, because the component of mouth position always extends identically over both phoneme places. If we mark N for nasal without regard to mouth position, and s for stop without regard to mouth position, and ‾ for alveolar and ＝ for velar position, then we say that the latter two marks always have 2-phoneme length when the first is /N/.[9a] Thus /N̅s̅/ = /nt/ and /N̿s̿/ = /ŋk/;

there is no way to write /nk/, since ‾ is so defined that it cannot be stopped after the /N/.

By the use of components which are defined so as to extend over a number of phoneme places, we thus circumvent the limitation in distribution of the phonemes. This is not merely a trick, concealing the limitations of the phonemes in the definitions of the components. For the components are generalized phonemes: they appear concurrently with each other as well as next each other, and they may have a length of several phoneme-places as well as of one phoneme-place. And when we write with these components it is natural that various ones will have various lengths; each of them has to have some stated length, and the components symbolized by ‾ and ＝ are simply among those that in some situations have 2-phoneme length.

Since we should like our new elements, the components, to have as general a distribution as possible, we try to select them in such a way that the components which occur under (or together with) a two-length component should also occur without it. Thus given English morpheme-medial /sp/ but not /sb/, we say that the component common to /s/ and /p/ is unvoicing, or fortisness, and that its length is that of the cluster in which it is present. /sp/ is then a sequence of sibilant plus stop, with overriding unvoicing. The same sequence occurs with the unvoicing absent: /zb/ in *Asbury*. As in the case above, /sb/ and /zp/ cannot be written in terms of components, because of our definition of the length of the unvoicing.

GENERAL FORMULA The procedure of obtaining these 2-length (and longer) components can be stated generally. If we have a sequence of two phonemes *xy*, we can select

---

[9a]Linguistic forms which are written in components will be set between diagonals, in the same way as forms written phonemically. It is convenient to use identical brackets for these two systems, because many linguistic forms cited in this paper are written partly in phonemes, partly in components: e.g., /†sz'r/ 'tree'. We write in components only those

parts of a form which are under discussion. This is permissible because phonemics is merely a special case of component analysis; the extension from phonemics into components can be carried out to any degree desired. In the analysis of Moroccan Arabic cited in fn. 5, the phonemes are of the usual kind except for the component /'/ (§2.3 above), which is included among the phonemes.—In some cases, where it is clear that a symbol indicates a component, the diagonals are omitted. The use of non-alphabetic marks like the horizontal bar (§5.2) is not in general desirable; but only such marks can depict on paper the effect of a long component that extends over more than one phoneme.

any number of factors which they have in common (both may be oral, both articulated in a certain position, both voiced or both voiceless, both explosive as against implosive, etc.). If one of these two phonemes does not occur with some third phoneme (say xc does not occur), we can then say that xy have significantly that component in common which c lacks. We call this component γ, and say that it has 2-phoneme length. Then x consists of this component γ plus some residue w, and y consists of the same γ plus some other residue u; thus $/s/$ = unvoicing plus sibilant articulation, $/p/$ = unvoicing plus lip and nose closing. We try to identify some other sequence of phonemes with these residues, and in particular to have the phoneme c equal the residue u, since the phoneme c is already known as lacking the component γ; in this case such a sequence would be $/zb/$, where $/z/$ = sibilant articulation, $/b/$ = lip and nose closing.[10]

> If xy occurs   then $xy = \gamma + (wu)$
> xu does not occur $x\ = \gamma + (w)$
> wu occurs $y\ = \gamma + (u)$

Then our new elements are w, u, and the 2-length γ, and all possible sequences of them occur. There is no longer any limitation of distribution: w and u occur alone (intervocalic $/z/$ and $/b/$) and together as wu (cluster $/zb/$), and each of these occurs with γ in the combinations $\gamma + w = /s/$, $\gamma + u = /p/$, $\gamma + wu$ = cluster $/sp/$.[11] If we represent unvoicing by a small circle, we may paraphrase our general formula as follows:

> Since $/sp/$ occurs $/sp/ = \circ + (zb)$
> $/sb/$ does not occur $/s/ = \circ + (z)$
> $/zb/$ occurs $/p/ = \circ + (b)$

ASSIMILATIONS   In Moroccan Arabic, the clusters $/šš/$, $/žž/$, $/šž/$ all occur, as well as the clusters $/ss/$ and $/zz/$; and there are morphemes which contain both $/š/$ and $/ž/$, or both $/s/$ and $/z/$, not contiguous to each other and in any order. But no morpheme containing $/s/$ or $/z/$ ever contains also $/š/$ or $/ž/$ anywhere within its bounds, nor does $/s/$ or $/z/$ ever occur in a morpheme with $/š/$ or $/ž/$. This complete statement of limitations[12] can be eliminated if we extract the feature † as a component and define it as having the length of a morpheme[13] and the phonetic value of retracting the tongue when in sibilant position (and as having zero phonetic value when the tongue is not in sibilant position). In doing this we can simply follow the formula above. $/š ... ž/$ occur in one morpheme and represent our xy; $/š ... z/$ do not occur in one morpheme and represent our xc. The factor common to $/š, ž/$ and absent in $/z/$ (our γ component) is †, a component of morpheme length. Then $/ž/$ (our y) consists of † (our γ) plus a residue (our u), and we identify this residue with $/z/$ (our c), which fits in with the fact that $/š ... z/$ does not occur. And since $/s ... z/$ does occur, we consider $/s/$ to be the residue of $/š/$ when the † component is extracted: $/š/ = † + /s/$, $/ž/ = † + /z/$, $/šž/ = † + /sz/$, etc. We now have three elements $/s/$, $/z/$, and †, each with its stated length and phonetic value, and all sequences of them occur:[14] $/s/$ in $/iams/$ 'yesterday', $/zz/$ in $/zzit/$ 'the olive', $/sz/$ in $/†sz'r/$ (= $/šž'ṛ/$) 'tree', $/ss/$ and $/z/$ in $/†ssrzm/$ (= $/ššržm/$) 'the window', etc.

> $/šš/$ occurs $/šš/ = † + (ss)$
> $/šs/$ does not occur $/š/ = † + (s)$
> $/ss/$ occurs $/s/ =\ \ \ \ (s)$

Note that † has a defined phonetic value when it occurs with some phonemes (the sibilants) and zero phonetic value when it occurs with other phonemes within its length.

Frequently the $\gamma + u$ and the u, i.e., the phonemes which do and which do not occur next to the $\gamma + w$, represent whole classes of phonemes. In Swahili, $/t, d, k, g, s, z, l, r, n/$ occur after $/n/$, but the other consonants $/p, b, f, v, m, h, \theta, ð, \gamma/$ do not.

> $/nt/$ occurs $/nt/ = \bar{\ } + (mp)$
> $/np/$ does not occur $/n/ = \bar{\ } + (m)$
> $/mp/$ occurs $/t/ = \bar{\ } + (p)$

---

[10]More briefly: Given that xy occurs, we select u such that xu does not occur. Then $y = \gamma + u$ (where γ has 2-phoneme length, when two phonemes are present), and $x = \gamma + w$, where w is selected so that wu occurs.

[11]Note that in this example γ does not occur alone.

[12]Aside from an unrelated limitation between $/s/$ and contiguous $/z/$.

[13]Or of a word, except for one enclitic. That is, when † occurs, it extends from one word juncture to the next.

[14]See fn. 12.

We call /n/ a 2-length component having the value of a dental nasal when occurring by itself, and stated other values (mostly, retarding of the tongue) when occurring simultaneously with various other components. Hence the n-component by itself = /n/. When the n-component is simultaneous with a labial, its value is tongue retarding, so that (n + p) = /t/. Since the n-component has the length of two phonemes, it will always stretch over the p whenever n occurs before it, so that /n p/ = /n (n + p)/ = /nt/. In terms of fixed-length phonemes, the distributional statements seem paradoxical: we are saying that p occurs after /n/, but when it does, it isn't /p/ at all but /t/. This apparent paradox brings out the difference, and the profit, in speaking in terms of components. For in terms of components we have two statements: 1. t = (p + n), d = (b + n), etc.; 2. n has 2-phoneme length when over consonants. Initially, or after m or vowels, we may have the components which constitute /p/, or those which constitute /t/ (i.e., the p components plus the n component): /paka/ 'cat', /tatu/ 'three'. After /n/, the components which comprise /p/ may indeed occur, but they then fall under the length of the n component, and their conjunction with that component yields /t/ : /amentizama/ 'he saw me'. If we take an /n/, we can say that the /p/ components may follow it (in which case the n component extends over them); or we may say that the /t/ components follow it, since the segment following /n/ will actually contain precisely the /t/ components (/p/ components plus the n component). It makes no difference which we say, since either statement describes the same situation. This type of description, which cannot differentiate between /np/ and /nt/ in Swahili, corresponds exactly to the Swahili situation where /np/ does not exist phonemically as against /nt/. When we speak in terms of components, therefore, we do not have to make statements of limitation of distribution such as that the phoneme /p/ does not occur after the phoneme /n/.

A component may have a particular length when it occurs in one environment, and another when it is in other positions. In the case of the Moroccan Arabic emphatic (§2.3), we find the following sequences: /tæ/, /ta/ (rare), /ṭa/ (the /ṭ/ being domal unaspirated), but not /ṭæ/ (except across word juncture). We say

that /ṭ/ and /a/ each contain a 2-place component ' whose phonetic value in general is to pull consonants and vowels to central position. The lack of /ṭæ/ is explained by the fact that /æ/ does not contain the ' component. We call /æ/ the residue of /a/ after the ' is extracted. Then since /tæ/ does occur, we call /t/ the residue of /ṭ/ after ' is extracted. Now /a/ = ' + /æ/, /ṭ/ = ' + /t/, /ṭa/ = ' + /tæ/, and every combination occurs. We write /mæt/ 'he did' but /gæt'/ for [gaṭ] 'pliers', and /t'ab/ for [ṭab] 'he repented'. However, in this case we also have /ṭa/ occurring, though rarely, as in [banka] 'bank'. The only way to write it is to restrict our previous statement: ' is a 2-place component only when it appears with a consonant; on the rare occasions when it appears concurrently with a vowel (written after the vowel) it is a one-place component. Now we add /ṭa/ = /tæ/ + '; we write /bæ'nka/ 'bank'.

/ṭa/ occurs	/ṭa/ = (t'æ)
/ṭæ/ does not occur	/ṭ/ = (t')
/tæ/ occurs	/a/ = (æ')
/ṭa/ occurs rarely	/ṭa/ = t(æ')

This situation is repeated for all the vowels and nine of the consonants, and the length of ' when placed after a consonant turns out to be several phonemes, not all contiguous. However, all these additional results can be obtained merely by repeating the investigation sketched above.

The technique of using these components to express limited distribution may simplify the description of morphophonemic alternation. For example, German has (to take only one pair) contrasting /t, d/ before vowels, as in *bunte* 'colored ones', *Bunde* '(in) the group', but only /t/ before open junction (- or #, and in certain types of clusters). The lack of the sequence /d-/ involves morphophonemic complications, since morphemes ending in /d/ before a vowel, end in /t/ before open juncture: /bunt/, /bunde/ 'group'. The /t-/ is the *xy* of our formula, and /d-/ is the *xc* which does not occur. We recognize a 2-place component having the phonetic value of unvoicing (but having zero value on certain phonemes such as /e/) which is common to /t/ and open juncture /-/ but lacking in /d/. If we write this component as ⁻, we can say that open juncture equals ⁻, and /t/ = /d/ + ⁻. Since /e/ does not contain the ⁻ component, /d/ is free to occur before it. However, since we also have /t/ before /e/, we must define ⁻ as having 2-place length only when it occurs by itself (i.e., when it equals open juncture) and as having one-place length otherwise. We now have /bund̄ ͞ ‚ bund̄e ͞ / = *bunt, bunte,* and /bund̄ ͞ , bunde ͞ / = *Bund, Bunde* (where the overhanging ⁻ is the phonemic open juncture). The writing is still phonemic; /bund̄ ͞ / 'group' and /bund̄ ͞ / 'colored' are still identical. But now we need not say that there is a morphophonemic alternation in the word for "group." The morpheme is /bund/ in both environments; the unvoicing heard before open juncture is not part of the morpheme /bund/ but is an automatic part of open juncture. This juncture consists of the component ⁻, which is a 2-place component in this position. Note that since open juncture is phonemic, we should have to write it one way or another, if in no other way than by a space. We can equally well write this open juncture with one or more of the new components, so long as the sum of their phonetic values in that position equals the phonetic value of open juncture (and pause). In contrast with this, the morpheme 'colored' is /bund̄/, as in the inflected form /bund̄er/; when it occurs before open juncture the ⁻ component of the juncture and the ⁻ component of the last place in the morpheme coincide, and we have /bund̄ ͞ /.

/t-/ occurs	/t-/ = · + (d + vowel)
/d-/ does not occur	/t/ = · + (d)
/d/ + vowel occurs	open juncture = ·

In view of the possibilities of a component coinciding with a 2-length component extending over the next place, this case does not eliminate the practical lexical problem: given /bund̄ ͞ / we do not know whether the morpheme is /bund/ or /bund̄/. But in terms of components we need no longer say that /Bùnd/ has two forms.

DISSIMILATIONS In all the foregoing cases there has been a physical similarity between the phonemes that occur together, which is not shared by the phonemes that do not occur in such combinations. The matter is somewhat more difficult when it is the dissimilar phonemes that occur together while the similar ones do not.

In classical Greek, only one aspirate occurs in a stem with its affixes, except for a very few morphemes, and there is a morphophonemic alternation between aspirates and nonaspirates, as when an aspirate-initial stem is reduplicated with the homorganic non-aspirate: φύω 'I produce', pf. πέφῡκα. We analyze φ into /p/ plus a component ' having the length of a stem plus its affixes, and the phonetic value of aspiration after one of the voiceless stops (which one, to be stated in terms of the phonetic structure of the word) and zero after every other phoneme. It is now possible to write /ˈpépūka/, with the ' component anywhere in the word, and with no need for morphophonemic statements.[15]

In Moroccan Arabic, double consonants are common (e.g., /tt/ in /fttš/ 'he searched', etc.), but no two different phonemes pronounced in the same mouth position (labial, dental, palatal, laryngal) ever occur next each other (with certain exceptions): there is no /fb, bf, td, gx, çh/,[16] etc. If we try to pin this limitation upon a component of one of the phonemes, say /f/ among the labials, we must recognize that component in all the other homorganic phonemes—/b/ and /m/—since the limitation applies equally to them. In order to enable the component to have any effect upon the neighborhood of the labial (so as to preclude another labial there), it must be present also in the neighboring position. We are thus faced with the need for a component which occurs in all the labials and in the place next to each labial, and which permits only a doubling of that labial, or a non-labial, to occur, but no different labial. This can be done by a 3-length component whose phonetic value is defined as follows: in its middle length, labial (so that this component serves to distinguish, say, the labial voiced stop /b/ from the dental voiced stop /d/); in its first and third lengths, labial if

---

[15]The morphophonemic alternation of φ for π + ' (e.g., in ἀφ' ὧν) can also be avoided, if the ' component is written where it is heard. In the few cases of two aspirates within a word, a second ' would have to be written over the extra aspirate, and the statement of the length of ' would have to be adjusted accordingly. In the case of the reduplication there is a real elimination of a morphophonemic statement: the stem initial in /ˈpépūka/ (or /pépˈūka/) is /p/, which is duly present in the reduplication.

[16]For the phonetic values of these phonemes see *op.cit.* in fn. 5.

the other components are identical with those of the middle length, and laryngal otherwise. If this component is simultaneous in its middle length with the components for voiced stop, it will yield /b/ in that position; and if on either side there are again the voiced-stop components alone, this component will yield with them another /b/; while if the components there are anything else, say voiceless continuant, this component, extending over them, will with them yield a corresponding laryngal voiceless continuant, /ḥ/.[17]

If, as in English, there are no double consonants, we have to say that certain components, one or another of which is present in every consonant, have 3-phoneme lengths and have some stated value in their middle length and some contrary value in their end lengths, if the other components are identical with those of the middle length.

CLUSTERINGS Further extensions of our method are necessary when we treat some of the more complicated limitations upon clusters, especially when limitations of order are present, i.e., when certain phonemes occur in one order but not in another. For example, English has morpheme-medial clusters like /rtr/, /ndy/, as in *partridge, endure,* but never clusters like /trt/, with any one of the consonants /r, l, m, n, ŋ, y, w/ in the middle. We cannot say simply that phonemes in the class of /r/ do not occur after stops, because in clusters of two consonants we have /rt, kr, lr, pt/ (*curtain, secret, walrus, reptile;* but no stop other than /t/ or /d/ after another stop). We require, therefore, a component extending over the length of a cluster and having the following phonetic values: in first position, general consonant value (serving incidentally to distinguish consonants from vowels; this because any consonant may occur here); in second position, continuant or /t, d/ if it follows a stop, otherwise general consonant value; in third position, continuant if it follows a stop (but

if the stop is /t, d/, this value only if a continuant precedes it), otherwise, vocalic value. This value of the consonant-component permits any clusters of two except stop plus /p, b, k, g/, and then permits the third place to have continuant value (and to remain a member of the cluster) only if the preceding two are continuant and stop; otherwise the component has non-consonant value and thus changes the third position into a vowel. This statement does not allow for clusters with middle /s/, as in *sexton,* and omits several details which would be taken care of in the other components for the individual phonemes. However, it is included here to show that even fairly complicated clusterings can be described by single components.

SUMMARY The net result of this technique is the extraction of 2-length and longer components from all sequences that can be matched against non-occurring sequences (a sequence being an environment and the phoneme that occurs in it); e.g., from English /rtr/ matched against /trt/. These components do part of the work of identifying and phonetically describing the phoneme over which they extend (e.g., the ' gives the aspiration component of Greek φ), so that only a residue of the original phoneme is required to accompany them (in this case /p/ to accompany ': /ʻp/ = φ). This residue in turn can designate another phoneme which occurs without the component (/p/ = π). Meanwhile, the length of the component, covering an environment and the phoneme that occurs in it, takes care of the original limitation in distribution. In the simplest cases this may be just a special limitation between contiguous phonemes, when in a given environment only such phonemes occur as are similar in some respect to that environment: the extracted component then has a single phonetic value throughout its length (so /n̄s̄/ for English /nt/). In other cases, the phonemes which occur in an environment may be no more similar to it than those which do not; in fact, it may be precisely the phonemes similar to the environment that never occur in it: the extracted component will then have different phonetic values in different parts of its length (so the Moroccan labial component). More generally, these components can be set up to express the fact that particular phonemes occur in one order and not in another (English morpheme-medial /pt/

---

[17]The laryngal value for the ends of the labial component is not essential, though it seemed most convenient for various reasons. It would also be possible to assign merely a "non-labial" value to the ends of the labial component, leaving it to the components in the neighboring positions to decide whether they are laryngal, dental, or palatal. They cannot be labial because a "non-labial" component extends over them.

occurs, /tp/ does not), and that only certain types of clusters occur; in such cases the phonetic values of the components may vary according to what phonemes or components adjoin it (just as allophones of phonemes vary in value according to what phonemes adjoin them).

Where two groups of phonemes are completely separated, so that no member of one group occurs with a member of the other, the extracted component always keeps its particular length (e.g., when in Moroccan Arabic neither /š/ nor /ž/ occurs near either /s/ or /z/). Where the separation is not complete (so that Moroccan /ṭ/, for example, occurs with /a/ but not with /æ/, while /t/ occurs with both /a/ and /æ/), the extracted component must have different lengths in different positions: with /ṭ/ it has 2-phoneme length so as to exclude /æ/, but with /a/ it has 1-phoneme length so as not to exclude /t/.[18] Where the limitation of distribution operates only between adjoining phonemes, their common component extends only over the sequence in question (i.e., the environment, and the phoneme which occurs in it to the exclusion of some other phoneme): so in English /ŋk/ or in Swahili consonant clusters. Where the limitation operates across unaffected phonemes, or throughout some stated limits such as a cluster or a morpheme, then the extracted component has zero value over those phonemes which happen to occur in its length but are not party to the limitation which it expresses: e.g., the Moroccan limitation on the occurrence of /š, ž/ and /s, z/ is operative throughout word limits; and the voiced–voiceless separation in English morpheme-medial clusters applies only to phonemes with voiced or voiceless homorganic counterparts and hence does not affect /r, l, m, n, ŋ, y, w/ if they occur in the same cluster (thus /ŋgz/ in *anxiety*, but /ŋkš/ in *anxious;* there is no /ŋkz/).

5.3   Defective Distribution Expressed by Simultaneous Components   Our third operation is to try to break up into simultaneous components any allophones which cannot be assigned to the existing phonemes and which have a very defective distribution in themselves. This is the case with the nasalized al-

veolar flap of *painting,* which occurs only after loud-stressed and before weak-stressed vowels. In this position it contrasts with all the consonant phonemes, so that we would be forced to recognize it as a new phoneme occurring only in this one environment.[18a] Since we cannot set up this restricted allophone as complementary to some single previously recognized phoneme, we ask if it may not be complementary to some sequence of previously recognized phonemes. We find that /nt/ is one of the very few sequences which occur between vowels under other stress conditions without also occurring after loud and before weak-stressed vowels. The nasalized flap is therefore in complementary distribution with this sequence and is analyzed into two simultaneous components, one an allophone of /n/ in this position (V́-tV) and the other an allophone of /t/.

There is, of course, a morphophonemic consideration: *painting* can be divided into two morphemes, the first of which would have a morphophonemic alternation between /nt/ and the nasalized flap if we recognized the latter as being anything but /nt/. This consideration is not important here, but might be resorted to in other cases. In any event, it is not essential to such analysis. When we break up the palatalized post-dental blade stop into simultaneous allophones of /t/ before /y/ and of /y/ after /t/ (/tyuwn/ for *tune*), we have no morphophonemic advantage, since when a morpheme ending with /t/ comes before a morpheme beginning with /y/, we get not the palatalized stop but /č/ (or /tš/) by morphophonemic alternation.

From the point of view of relations between allophones, this operation means that we extend complementary distribution to apply not only to single allophones but also to sequences of allophones. From the point of view of the physical nature of allophones, it means that we no longer require an allophone to be an observable complete sound; we extend the term to include observable components of a sound. The net result is to eliminate some potential phonemes of exceptionally limited distribution.

---

[18]Or we may say that with /t/, absence of that component has 1-phoneme length so as not to exclude /a/ (which contains the component).

[18a]Rather than include it in one of the vowel phonemes, which would confuse all the general statements about the distribution of vowel phonemes and their allophones.

5.4 Phonetic Similarity Expressed by Short Components In carrying out the distributional analysis, we shall have extracted components from various phonemes in whatever language we investigate. It may be profitable to continue this extraction until all phonemes have been reduced to combinations of components.

When long components have been set up for all the important distributional limitations, we proceed to analyze those phonemes which have not been broken up, or the residues of the phonemes which have been broken up. Each of these phonemes or residues may be analyzed into simultaneous components so chosen as to distinguish the phonemes phonetically one from the other in the simplest manner. "Simplest" can be determined with the aid of a few obvious criteria: where possible we should utilize components already recognized in the previous analysis, stating that in this position (or in this combination) the component has only 1-phoneme length, since it affects only the phoneme which it identifies phonetically. For example, if in a particular language we have had to recognize front, middle, and back consonants because they follow /m, n, ŋ/ respectively, whereas all vowels occur after each of these three nasals, we may nevertheless use the front, middle, and back components to differentiate vowels, with the proviso that they do not have 2-component length when they occur with vowels, and hence do not preclude the occurrence of a front vowel (say /i/) after a back nasal /ŋ/.[19] This means in effect that the limitations of distribution among certain phonemes are used as a partial guide to show us what phonetic differences among the other phonemes are the relevant ones.

Another criterion is the parallelism of allophones among different phonemes. If the allophones of English /p, t, k/ are all analogous in that they all have comparable differences of aspiration in identical environments (as [pʰ, tʰ, kʰ] after word-juncture but [p, t, k] after /s/, etc.), we can say that a particular component γ is contained in each of them and that this γ (which may be the combination of the unvoicing and the stop components) is strongly

aspirated after word-juncture, unaspirated after /s/, etc.

The physical movements of articulation may also offer certain absolute factors common to various phonemes: /p, t, k/ are generally voiceless, fortis, stopped. Since the components will in the last analysis have to identify articulatory (as well as acoustic) events, it is desirable to reflect these as closely as possible. However, as is well known, the correlation with articulatory events will rarely coincide completely with our other criteria, not even with our criterion of complementary distribution for phonemes. To take the simplest example, there are sounds in the /t/ phoneme which are not stops (in *butter,* etc.).

Some components which are commonly extracted by linguists merely because they consist of pitch or stress features have no basis for being thus extracted except the phonetic considerations of this section. Such, for example, are the tones in languages where each vowel in a morpheme has an arbitrary phonemic pitch.[20] As far as distributional simplicity goes we could just as well state that a language has not, say, 5 vowels and 3 tones, but 15 vowel phonemes (high /í/, mid /i/, low /ì/—all of which might differ in quality as well as pitch; high /é/, etc.). If these vowels have not already been completely broken down into components on distributional grounds, we may now extract the tones as components on grounds of phonetic simplicity.

5.5 Manipulating the Components When all the phonemes of a language are completely analyzed into components, various additional problems are met. A set of components which conveniently express certain limitations of distribution (e.g., of the voiced–unvoiced group in English as against /r, l, m, n, ŋ, y, w/) may conflict with a different analysis which results from a different limitation but which involves some of the already-analyzed phonemes of the first group (e.g., /s/ which in certain respects behaves like /r, l, m, n, ŋ, y, w/). Sometimes the only way to resolve such difficulties is to reconsider the phonemic system. This is, of course, permissible since in grouping allophones together into

---

[19]In varying measure, this is the case in English (within a morpheme), Swahili, and Fanti.

[20]E.g., Fanti. See W. E. Welmers and Z. S. Harris, "The Phonemes of Fanti," *JAOS* 62.319 (1942).

phonemes there are often alternative ways of grouping within the basic phonemic criteria.[21] We choose one way for our phonemic statement, but a slightly different grouping of some of the allophones may be more convenient for the component analysis. Furthermore, we sometimes obtain an extremely complicated component analysis for the distributional limitations and clusterings of the phonemes throughout the vocabulary of the language, where a much simpler system may be possible if we eliminate from consideration certain morphemes (often borrowed ones) which have a different phonetic structure from the rest.[22] It is often possible to identify phonemically the parts of the vocabulary which we wish to exclude from consideration, and perhaps to give them a separate component analysis. For all these reasons, any attempt at a component analysis of a whole phonemic system requires considerable attention to the detailed facts of the language. No examples of such systems will therefore be presented here. It has been possible, however, to carry out the analysis for a few languages, and to obtain sets of components which had only mildly complicated phonetic values, and which required very few statements about distribution (so that practically every combination or sequence of components occurred).

ARE THE COMPONENTS USABLE?

6.1 Their Status in Descriptive Linguistics Having worked through specific cases of analysis into components, we may now ask: What is the status in linguistic science of the new techniques and the new elements which they produce? At present the phonemic elements of linguistic analysis are obtained by segmenting the flow of speech and calling each group of mutually substitutable segments ("free variants") an allophone. Now the components described in this paper are not complete physical events; therefore, they cannot actually be substituted for each other to see if any two of them are free variants or "repetitions" of each other. First, therefore, we must move as before from unique sounds

to allophones, which in general have the relative length of a phoneme (that is, are not composed of smaller segments which in turn are allophones of phonemes). Only then can we proceed to analyze the allophones into simultaneous components, producing a new set of elements instead of the previous allophones. The operation of complementary distribution can be performed upon the new elements as well as upon the old. Theoretically, therefore, we could break the allophones into components and then do all the complementary grouping on the components. Actually, it is more efficient to group the complementary allophones into tentative phonemes, and to analyze these tentative phonemes into components. We can then try to group the components by complementary distribution in order to get fewer components, each having wider coverage. If certain limitations of occurrence exist for some components, we may even try to express their limitations in turn by a second extraction of components, on much the same grounds that we used in expressing phonemic limitations by components, in order to obtain the most general and least limited set of elements.

We thus obtain for the language a new set of elements, each of which occurs with fewer limitations than the original phonemes. This is so because each setting up of a component of more than one-phoneme length takes care of at least one limitation of phonemic occurrence; this is equally true of the automatic-sequence components (§5.1) which replace the highly limited distribution of phonemic pitch and stress.[22a] In some cases the components

---

[21]Y. R. Chao, *op.cit.* in fn. 4.

[22]Leonard Bloomfield, "The Structure of Learned Words," *A Commemorative Volume Issued by the Institute for Research in English Teaching* 17–23 (Tokyo, 1933).

[22a]We have seen that the 2- and 3-place components of §5.2 and the fixed-sequence components of §5.1 differ in effect, in that the former describe limitations of distribution and the latter describe contours. It is of interest to notice wherein these two types of long components differ structurally and wherein they are similar.

They are similar in that they are all expressions for limitations of distribution of different segments. In the case of the pitch contours, we begin with allophonic segments that contain pitch and stress features in them. We notice that there are limitations upon the distribution of these segments. For instance, after a sequence of segments in which each loud-stressed segment is higher-pitched than the preceding, we never get a low-pitched segment: after *Is your brother?* we never get a low *going*, but only a *going* which is pitched even higher than

can be so selected that practically every possible combination and sequence of the components actually occurs. Any combinations and sequences that do not occur will, of course, have to be stated.

The new elements are still, like the phonemes, in bi-unique correspondence with speech events: given the writing we know uniquely what sounds to pronounce, and given the sounds we know uniquely how to write

---

brother. And in *Is your brother going?* we do not get a low pitched *ing*. We express this limitation of distribution by saying that all the segments of the utterance contain a particular component in common, and that this component has various phonetic values at various parts of its stretch: low pitch on the first low-stressed vowel, higher pitch on the next, etc. Exactly this is what we do with the 2- and 3-place components: We notice that after /s/ we never have /b/, but only /p/. We express this by saying that both successive segments have a particular component in common, and that this component has fortis value throughout its stretch.

The differences between the two types of long components are four. First, the phonetic values of the contour components are usually all pitch and stress features, which we are accustomed to consider a thing apart, while the phonetic values of the other components may seem to us to be arbitrarily extracted from the rest of the segment, as when we distinguish the closure of /b/ from its lip position.

Second, since the contour components are often constituents of simultaneous morphemes (e.g., the question intonation), we often cannot obtain the phonemes of the segmental morphemes (e.g., *your* or *brother,* without regard to intonation) until after the contour components have been extracted. Therefore we usually extract the contour components while working on sequences of allophonic segments, whereas we extract the other long components by working on sequences of phonemes.

Third, whereas the long components usually extend over a definite small number of phonemes, the contour components usually extend over a variable (and much larger) number—as many as there may be in a linguistic form or utterance of a particular type.

Fourth, we usually have many more positional variants of a contour component than of a 2- or 3-place component. The 1221130 of *I don't know where he's going.* (§5.1) and the 2230 of *Bud Clark fumbled* are positional variants of the 230 in *He told him.* The phonemic component environment, which determines the number of 1's and the number and place of 2's in all these variants, is the simultaneous sequence of stress contours. The 2- or 3-place components usually have fewer though more complicated positional variants, as when the Swahili n component indicates tongue retarding with labial components, but velar occlusion with h (n + p = t, n + b = d, n + h = k).

them.[23] The components are essentially similar to phonemes in that both are distributional symbols with phonetic values. That is to say, the observed physical events are always sounds, and the criteria for classifying them into linguistic elements—whether phonemes or components—are always distributional.

The components are merely generalizations of the phonemes, extending the very development which gives us phonemes out of sounds. In writing allophones we have one distinguishable sound per symbol (hence closely abiding by the physical event); but there are many symbols and each usually has a highly restricted occurrence. In writing phonemes we often have several distinguishable sounds per symbol, usually but not always having considerable phonetic similarity (hence abiding rather less closely by the physical event); but there are fewer symbols with a wider distribution for each. In writing components we usually have more distinguishable sounds per symbol, sometimes with no common feature (hence abiding much less by the physical event); but there are fewer symbols yet, with much wider distribution for each. It follows that analysis into components completes what phonemics can only do in part: the transfer of the limitations of sounds from distributional restriction to positional variation in phonetic value. This is not an argument for the use of components: phonemics is undoubtedly the more convenient stopping point in this development, because it fits alphabetic writing; but we must recognize the fact that it is possible to go beyond it.

6.2   Practical and Historical Considerations   The use of components will clearly be practicable only within narrow limits. Components which enter into supra-segmental morphemes (e.g., sentence intonations) are now extracted and must be extracted in order to permit isolation of morphemes in general. Components which resolve major distributional limitations, e.g., Moroccan ' or †, can easily be extracted and written among the segmental phonemes. Such components are espe-

[23]If only the first of these were true, we should have morphophonemic writing. We may permit partial overlapping among our components, i.e., the same sound feature may be represented in different environments by different components, but that is no bar to phonemic writing.

cially worth extracting if many morphophonemic statements are thereby eliminated.[24] One-length components produce little saving and would not normally be extracted except for cases like vowel tones (§5.4), where the extraction is due chiefly to tradition or is desirable because the tones have morphophonemic alternations under various syntactic pitches.

Analysis into components may be of interest to linguists even where it is not used to simplify the writing system, for components may offer correlations with historical change, and may in a sense quantify the structural importance of various phonemic limitations. The connection with linguistic change derives from the fact that many phonemic limitations are produced by single historical changes[25] or by a related series of them, so that the long components may represent the effect of events in history. The structural quantification derives from the fact that some non-occurrences of phonemes are represented by long components and others merely by the non-occurrence of one component with a particular other component in a position where the first component otherwise occurs. Let us take the non-occurring */sbin/ and */stend/ in English. If the cluster-long unvoicing component is ⎺, we may say that *spin* is /z̄bin/; the sequence /z̄b/ (= /sb/) is impossible since ⎺ always extends over the whole cluster in which it occurs. On the other hand the general vowel component contained in /e/ occurs after /st/, but only with the particular quality component of /æ/ and not that of /e/: *stand* but not **stend*. There is no long component excluding the /e/-quality component from the position after /t/ or before /n/ or between clusters, since the /e/-quality component occurs in those positions: *tend*, *spend*. Therefore all we have is the fact that while the general vowel component occurs in between /st/ and /nd/, it does not occur there with the /e/-quality component, although it does occur with that component elsewhere. We may then say that forms like */sbin/ are excluded from the phonetic structure as it is described by our components, while forms like

*/stend/ are not excluded. True, the same considerations which led us to set up a long component in the first case and not in the second could have led us directly to such a judgment concerning these two forms. But no form of expression creates new information: the only question is the availability and organization which it gives to the information. The difference in terms of components is perhaps more clear-cut than a direct discussion of each form, and in setting up the components we may have used relevant considerations which we should not have thought of in a direct discussion.[26]

SUMMARY

7   This paper has tried to show that many linguistic facts can be discovered and described by the application of a single operation: the analysis of speech into simultaneous components. Automatic sequences of phonetic features yield intonations, word stresses, and the like. Defectively distributed phonemes complementary to sequences of phonemes are broken up into allophones of those sequences. Limitations of phonemic distribution, including neutralization, cluster limits, and certain automatic morphophonemic changes, are resolved by components having a length of more than one phoneme. Phonemes and residues not otherwise broken up are analyzed into components of one-phoneme length on the basis of phonetic considerations. The length of a component can vary in different positions, and can be bounded by phonemic environment or by junctures. The phonetic value of a component can vary in different positions, and can be determined by its concurrent components, or its neighboring components, or the section of the component's length. Whole phonemic systems can be replaced by component systems.

No one technique is essential, but rather

---

[24]This will in general happen only in cases of automatic morphophonemic alternation.

[25]See now Henry Hoenigswald, "Internal Reconstruction," *Studies in Linguistics* 1944.

[26]Various other facts about the phonetic structure also transpire from a component analysis. One can tell, by looking at the combinations of components representing the phonemes, which phonemes ever occur next to each other and which never do (i.e., whether they have a long component in common), which phonemes replace each other in complementary environments (i.e., whether all their one-length components are identical), which phonemes have the smallest number of different phonemes next to them (i.e., the ones that contain the largest number of long components).

the method of attack. Different devices will have to be used in different situations. For each language, it will be necessary to state what system of combination of the components is being used, what the length and phonetic value of each component is, and what limitations of occurrence remain among the components.

It has been shown that this analysis creates a new set of elements out of the original allophones or phonemes, and that these elements have the same status as phonemes and are, indeed, merely generalized phonemes. Analysis into simultaneous parts is the only operation aside from segmentation into allophones that produces usable elements for descriptive linguistics.

BIBLIOGRAPHY 7
Componential Analysis

HARRIS, Z. S. (1942) "The Phonemes of Moroccan Arabic"

HOCKETT, C. F. (1947) "Componential Analysis of Sierra Popoluca"

HARRIS, Z. S. (1948) "Componential Analysis of a Hebrew Paradigm"

HAUGEN, E. (1949) "Phoneme or Prosodeme?"

HAMP, E. P. (1954) "Componential Restatement of Syllable Structure in Trique"

LONGACRE, R. E. (1955) "Rejoinder to Hamp's 'Componential Restatement of Syllable Structure in Trique'"

VOEGELIN, C. F. (1956) "Linear Phonemes and Additive Components"

GARVIN, P. L., and M. MATHIOT (1958) "Fused Units in Prosodic Analysis"

See also Parts II and III.a of this volume.

13

THE PITCH PHONEMES
OF ENGLISH*
RULON S. WELLS

[A system of four pitch phonemes enables us to differentiate all the phonemically (i.e., perceptually and meaningfully) different pitch contours of English that have come to the writer's notice. If new contours should come to light, they could probably be treated without the introduction of any additional pitch phonemes. The system applies to the problem of English pitches the methods already applied to segmental phonemes as well as to stresses and junctures.]

1. Orientation Ordinary phonemics adheres, with a few exceptions, to the segmental principle.[1] This principle may be thus formulated: all the utterances of a dialect can be divided into segments ("phones") such that (1) each segment is continuous; (2) each segment belongs to just one phoneme; (3) only segments belong to phonemes; (4) the segments are as short as a phonemic analysis warrants. The principle of phonetic similarity is likewise respected: (1) if a phone A belongs to a phoneme, any phone B indistinguishable therefrom belongs to the same phoneme, whether B occurs in the same environment as A or another environment; (2) allophones which are in complementary distribution belong to the same phoneme if and only if they are phonetically similar to one another, and are more similar to each other than to allophones of any other phonemes. The first half of this principle forbids overlapping, even partial overlapping;[2] the second half makes complementation a necessary but not a sufficient ground for uniting allophones into one phoneme. Mere reliance upon the demand for contrasts (non-complementary distribution) and bi-uniqueness[3] does not yield a methodical and determinate analysis of any given language.[4]

Some of the frequently admitted exceptions to the segmental principle are as follows: (1) The extraction of a nasalizing phoneme in languages such as Bengali and Hindustani, which have certain vowel qualities existing both nasalized and unnasalized, where the nasalizing makes a phonemic difference. (2) Extraction of a length phoneme in languages with significant length, and of a syllabifying phoneme where semivowels and continuants function as syllabics. Whether such phonemes are to be extracted is determined by distri-

[1]Zellig S. Harris and Henry M. Hoenigswald, by their suggestions and questions, have greatly helped to improve the adequacy of this system. It was outlined in a paper read before the Linguistic Society in New York in December 1944. The following books and papers are cited by authors' names only:

Bernard Bloch and George L. Trager, *Outline of Linguistic Analysis,* 1942.

G. L. Trager and Bernard Bloch, "The Syllabic Phonemes of English" [9], *Language* 17.223–246 (1941).

Leonard Bloomfield, *Language,* 1933.

Charles F. Hockett, "A System of Descriptive Phonology" [11], *Language* 18.3–21 (1942).

George L. Trager, "The Theory of Accentual Systems," *LCP* 131–145 (1941).

[2]Bernard Bloch, "Phonemic Overlapping" [8], *American Speech* 16.278–284 (1941).

[3]Yuen Ren Chao, "The Non-Uniqueness of Phonemic Solutions of Phonetic Systems," *Bulletin of the Institute of History and Philology* (Academia Sinica) 4.363–397 (1934).

[4]Hockett 9[103]; Morris Swadesh, "The Phonemic Interpretation of Long Consonants" [6], *Language* 13.1–10 (1937). See especially the first page of Swadesh's article.

*Reprinted from *Language* 21.27–39 (1945) by permission.

butional more than by phonetic facts; but the extraction is always possible.

Another exception to the segmental principle is (3) necessary in dealing with languages which have significant features called "prosodic"[5] or "suprasegmental"[6]—for instance pitch, stress, and juncture in English. To avoid this third exception is for many languages not feasible. Certain pitches and stresses in English are unquestionably phonemic; yet they occur not by themselves but simultaneously with vowel and consonant qualities; physically and acoustically, they are not parts of phones but features or qualities of phones. In this sense they are suprasegmental; but no phonemicist would dream of regarding two English phones with the same vowel quality but significantly different pitches as belonging to different vowel phonemes; rather, they would be assigned to the same vowel phoneme but to different pitch phonemes.[7]

This paper studies the pitch phonemes of American English. Stress and juncture, the other two features usually regarded as suprasegmental,[8] have been analyzed by the same phonemic methods that are applied to vowels and consonants; but the systems hitherto published (Palmer, Bloomfield, Bloch and Trager, Harris) have denied a like treatment to pitches. Instead, whole pitch patterns have been analyzed as single phonemes. This paper tries to apply to pitches, mutatis mutandis, all the principles and methods of segmental phonemics. There is interest in seeing what the mutanda are; and there is interest also in deciding between conceivable alternative analyses. Some prima facie plausible analyses turn out to be mere tricks whose advantages are only apparent.

2. Meaning of "Suprasegmental" In effect, the term "suprasegmental[9] phoneme" as used in recent discussions[10] simply denotes phonemes which are neither vowels nor consonants.[11] The term SS has also been used in several other senses:

PHONETIC   Let us suppose that, by some stated procedure, an utterance has been divided into pieces which we may call segments; each segment has, during all or part of its duration, various qualities or features. Now let each segment be of such length that it is a phone, i.e., a member of a segmental phoneme. Then a feature is called SS if it is contained without interruption in two or more successive segments,[12] whether it be automatically conditioned or phonemically significant.

PHONETIC-PHONEMIC   A feature is called SS if every segment or sequence of segments having it is assigned to a certain phoneme, but if it occurs simultaneously with other features such that every segment possessing them belongs to some other phoneme. The feature in question may or may not be SS in the purely phonetic sense. For example, if every vowel quality occurs both with and without nasal resonance (as in Bengali, etc.), and if the difference is phonemic, we may extract a phoneme of nasal resonance. Then one segment may belong to two phonemes: by virtue of its vocalic features it belongs to a vowel phoneme, by virtue of its nasalization it belongs to the nasal phoneme.[13]

PHONEMIC   A phoneme is called SS if the feature which determines the assignment of segments or sequences to that phoneme is always or sometimes SS in the phonetic sense —e.g., ancient Greek rough and smooth breath-

---

[5]Trager 132, paragraph 4.

[6]Hockett §5.31.

[7]The fact that vowels and consonants, as well as pitches and stresses, are abstracted features rather than segments does not require us, with Hockett (8[103]), to regard phonemes as classes of classes of features, or even as classes of features, instead of as classes of segments. One segment can be assigned to two phonemes at once, provided the two phonemes are of different dimensions. Suppose that there are just two pitches, P and Q, and just two vowel or consonant qualities, A and E. Then as primary classes there will be AP (segments with the quality A and the pitch P) AQ, EP, and EQ. The phoneme $A = AP + AQ = A(P + Q)$, since $P + Q$ is the total class of pitches; likewise the pitch phoneme $P = AP + EP = P(A + E)$, since $A + E$ is the total class of qualities.

[8]Hockett 9[103], §6; Bloch and Trager 34; Trager and Bloch §2.

[9]Hereinafter abbreviated SS.

[10]Trager 131 (par. 5), 132 (par. 4); Bloch and Trager, implied 39 (par. 2), 41, 47–52.

[11]It is chiefly in this negative sense that juncture phonemes (Bloch and Trager 41; Hockett §6, §§7.74 ff.) are to be regarded as SS, though Bloch and Trager (34–36) regard the members of juncture phonemes as phonetically SS in some sense.

[12]Hockett §§5.31–32.

[13]Cf. Trager 135 (par. 2).

ing as analyzed by Trager,[14] the English stress phonemes, and (as we shall argue) pitch; or if the feature is SS not in the phonetic but in the phonetic-phonemic sense—e.g., the Bengali nasal phoneme; or third, if it does not affect patterning of segmental phonemes. Where P and Q are any two segmental phonemes and R is another phoneme, the statement that R is SS means that in whatever environment PRQ occurs, PQ also occurs.

GRAMMATICAL   The phonemes belonging to a certain set (e.g., stresses; pitches or pitch-contours) are called SS if, whatever their phonetic character, they behave grammatically like a separate system. For instance, in English the pitch and stress phonemes do not mix with segmental phonemes to form morphemes; each set forms morphemes separately; yet every complete utterance must contain at least one segmental morpheme (i.e., a morpheme composed wholly of segmental phonemes) and at least two SS morphemes: one pitch morpheme and one stress morpheme.[15] This is one of Bloomfield's[16] grounds for regarding pitch and stress phonemes as "secondary."

Since the grammatical differences between English pitch and stress on the one hand and segmental morphemes on the other are tied up with differences in the kinds of meanings which they respectively convey, the problem here arises[17] of drawing the line between linguistic meanings and cultural or conventional (non-linguistic) meanings.

There are in English (as in many other languages) various features, other than those characterizing vowels and consonants, which serve to convey standardized meanings. All of these features are, presumably, organizable into phonemes, provided only that their meanings and the modes in which the features convey the meanings are such that we are willing to regard the features as falling within the province of linguistics. All such phonemes would be SS not only in the strictly phonemic sense, but no doubt in the grammatical sense as well. A list of the more obvious features of

this kind, apart from pitch and stress, might include timbre, rate of speed, and style. They are mentioned only to clarify the meaning of the term SS; they will not be dealt with here. For stress and juncture, Bloch and Trager's system[18] is accepted as correct.

3.   The System   As in segmental phonemics, pitch contours admit of alternative phonemic analyses. This is due not to a lack of principles, but to ignorance of how to apply them. Specifically, we try to choose the simplest system, but we have no criteria which are applicable in difficult cases.[19] We shall first outline the system which seems to us the most faithful to the purpose of phonemics, and then delineate the two or three alternatives which have been previously suggested.

In the first place, we observe the principle of segmentation: the pitch contour of an utterance is not treated as a continuum, nor as an atom; it is broken up into segments. Phonetically, a pitch segment is rarely if ever homogeneous, i.e., constant throughout its length. But in the sequence of pitches, certain ones are key pitches; the others may be regarded as functions of these. Each utterance is divided into segments in such a way that every segment contains a key pitch at the beginning, and no other. Often the duration of the key pitch is very short compared with the length of its segment; many features of pitch contour are automatically conditioned.

The distinctive feature of the segments assigned to the pitch phonemes is pitch relative to the speaking-range of the speaker's voice. There are four pitch phonemes, designated by Arabic numerals from *1* (lowest) to *4* (highest). Thus, the phonemic pitch contour of the sentence *The telephone's ringing!* would be rendered as follows: *²The ³tel-²ephone's ringing!* This means that pitch phoneme *2* is initial; pitch phoneme *3* begins at about the beginning of *telephone;* pitch phoneme *2* begins again after the first syllable of *telephone.* All the rest of the utterance belongs, phonemically, to pitch phoneme *2.*

---

[14]Reported by Hockett §7.61.

[15]The argument in favor of regarding pitch contours as morphemes is given below in Part 4.

[16]116; cf. 163.

[17]Bloomfield 114 (par. 2).

[18]Trager; Trager and Bloch; Bloch and Trager.

[19]Mere number of phonemes, as proposed by Hockett §6.12, is not always an acceptable measure of simplicity, nor is simplicity always a last resort as a criterion. Often economy and pattern (distribution) favor different analyses.

For simplicity's sake, the examples in this paper are not written in a phonemic transcription except for the pitch phonemes. As a further aid to easy comprehension, the standard English punctuation signs are used. Furthermore, we take advantage of the standard orthographic division into syllables, and write our pitch symbols at the beginning of the orthographic syllables to which they apply. This is done merely for the reader's convenience. The system does not presuppose the existence of phonetic syllables, nor even of syllabics. (The reason will become clearer as more examples are presented.) Phonetically, the significant pitches may or may not exactly coincide with vowels; but we may assume that phonemically they do, for there is no contrast between a pitch beginning on a vowel and one beginning on a consonant between that vowel and the following vowel. (We assume that Bloomfield's syllabifier phoneme [see his *Language* 92, 120–123] is phonemically a vowel, i.e., virtually equivalent to Bloch and Trager's /ə/.)

Considered phonetically in relation to the segmental phonemes, the length of a pitch phoneme is variable. It can coincide in time with any number of segmental phonemes. Its effect will continue until replaced by another pitch phoneme, or until the end of the utterance. A corollary of this statement is that a pitch phoneme cannot immediately follow itself. For instance, *22* would be merely a notational lapse for *2*.

THE SPECIFIC PITCH CONTOURS OF ENGLISH

Some of the most common contours are herewith exemplified. Minimal contrast between pitch phonemes *1* and *2* is seen by comparing Nos. 14 and 19; between *1* and *3* by comparing Nos. 1 and 2; between *1* and *4* by comparing Nos. 24 and 25; between *2* and *3* by comparing Nos. 11 and 26; between *2* and *4* by comparing Nos. 18 and 24; between *3* and *4* by comparing Nos. 24 and 27.

1. ²*Are you* ³*positive?* (also: ²*Are you* ⁴*positive?*)
2. ²*I brought it* ³*home* ¹*with me.*
3. ²*Who* ³*did* ¹*it?*
4. ²*He doesn't lend his books to* ³*an*¹*ybody.*
5. ²*He doesn't* ³*lend* ¹*his books to* [*just*] ³*an*²*ybody.*

6. ²*If* ³*you* ²*go, then I'll go* ³*with* ¹*you.*
7. ²*Naught*³*y,* ⁴*naught*³*y!* (monitory, to children)
8. ²*I'll* ³*be* ⁴*an*³*gry!* (monitory, to children)
9. ²*I'm* ⁴*sure* ¹*I brought it home.*
10. ²*Take* ⁴*me* ¹*there!*
11. ²*The* ⁴*tel*²*ephone's ringing!*
12. ²*Where were* ⁴*you* ²*last night, my* ³*friend?*
13. ²*I was talking a*⁴*bout* ²*him, not* ³*with* ¹*him.*
14. ³*I* ¹*did it.*
15. ³*That's* ¹*not* ²*funny* [—*that's* ³¹*mean.*]
16. ³*At*¹*ta*²*boy!* (expression of encouragement)
17. ³*I* ²*didn't do it* [*I don't know who did*].
18. [²*Go ahead and* ³*do* ¹*it*—] ³*I* ²*don't mind.*
19. ³*I* ²*didn't ask you, did I?*
20. ³*Talk*²*ing!* (on the telephone, to identify oneself as the person asked for)
21. ³*Well,* ²*well,* ¹*well!* (sarcastic, etc.)
22. ³*My* ²*good*¹*ness!*
23. ³*Oh* ²*my* ³*good*¹*ness!*
24. ³*Give* ⁴*him the money?!* [²*I should* ⁴*say* ¹*not.*]
25. [*You've charged me fifty cents extra*—] ³*how* ⁴¹*come?*
26. ³*How did it* ⁴*hap*²*pen?*
27. ⁴*Who did you say did it?* (great surprise)
28. ⁴*Go*²*ing!* [²*Why, you've just* ³¹*come.*]
29. ⁴*Yoo-*²*hoo!* (woman's call to hail a person)

These examples illustrate nineteen different pitch contours:

23	(No. 1)
231	(Nos. 2, 3, 4)
23132	(No. 5)
23231	(No. 6)
2343	(Nos. 7, 8)
241	(Nos. 9, 10)
242	(No. 11)
2423	(No. 12)
24231	(No. 13)
31	(No. 14)
312	(Nos. 15, 16)
32	(Nos. 17, 18, 19, 20)
321	(Nos. 21, 22)
3231	(No. 23)
34	(No. 24)
341	(No. 25)
342	(No. 26)
4	(No. 27)
42	(Nos. 28, 29)

It must be borne in mind that a contour like *231* contrasts minimally with *23*, if the spacing of the phonemically identical segments (i.e., here *2* and *3*) is the same. This is because iteration of pitch phonemes does not occur in this system; *231* contrasts with what would be *233* if such a contour could occur. Thus the contrast between *1* and *3* is as well exemplified by *23* and *231* as by *23* and *21*.

In proving the existence and distinctness of the four pitch phonemes by minimal contrasts, we ought to consider the same string of segmental phonemes with minimally contrasting pitch contours imposed on it; but it is difficult to find one such string equally well adapted to two minimally contrasting contours. In most of the examples, therefore, the contrast is minimal only so far as the contours are concerned.

Under circumstances to be stated below (Semantic Values), a single vowel may be affected by two pitch phonemes, but never by more than two. Each of the above examples consists of what would be called, on the basis of the structure of its segmental morphemes, a single clause. One of them contains a single pitch phoneme; most of them contain two or three. These contours may be called the simple pitch contours. One such simple pitch contour may be followed in the same utterance by one or more others; the result may be called a compound pitch contour. The basis of this classification is not intrinsic; it is not the contours themselves, but their correlation with sequences of segmental morphemes. If we were to define a simple contour as a contour of which no part (initial, middle, or final) ever characterizes an independent utterance, this definition would exclude certain contours, such as *231*, which we wish to include. Moreover, this definition would give us no criteria; it would not always enable us to break up a given compound contour in a unique manner into its immediate constituents—two or more simple contours—just by considering the pitch phonemes alone; we should have to take into account stress and juncture phonemes and morphemes also, and sometimes syntactical structure as well. Besides compound contours, there also occur what we may call intrusive contours. Such are modifications due to emphasis and the contours characterizing parenthetical phrases.

In the discussion of distributions and allophones, only the simple contours need be taken into account.

DISTRIBUTION

As was noted above, each pitch contour can be separated into two components: the bare sequential order of pitch phonemes, and their spacing with respect to segmental phonemes. The same could be said of segmental phonemes with respect to each other; compare the usual statements about consonants with respect to vowels in Semitic languages. The reason is grammatical (and semantic) only; just as consonants and vowels form separate morphological systems in Semitic, so segmental phonemes and pitch phonemes form separate morphological and syntactical (and semantic) systems in English. That is, a sequence of segmental morphemes and a sequence of pitch morphemes are partially independent: the segmental sequence may be accompanied by any one of a number of pitch sequences, and each pitch sequence may accompany an indefinitely large number of segmental sequences. When only the order of pitch phonemes is specified, all we know about the spacing is that the first vowel is accompanied by the first-mentioned pitch phoneme. In discussing distribution of pitch phonemes, it is sufficient to consider their selection and order, while ignoring their spacing. Any order which occurs (e.g., *241*) usually admits of an indefinite variety of spacings.

Pitch phoneme *1* does not occur initially. This is the principal limitation upon distribution. Examination of the examples shows that *2, 3,* and *4* occur initially; that each pitch phoneme occurs medially, preceded by any other pitch phoneme; and each pitch phoneme occurs finally. Subordinating clauses generally end in *2*, but it is a mistake to think that pitch phoneme *2* before juncture is always or even usually a sign that the utterance is unfinished. Not all possible orders occur. The list of examples is by no means complete; for instance, of the twenty-seven possible orders of three pitch phonemes PQR, where P is initial and therefore not *1*, and where $Q \neq P$ and $Q \neq R$, only ten are exemplified in the list. Again only one pitch phoneme (*4*) is exemplified in isolation. Occurrences of the other pitch phonemes in isolation are rare, except that *2* is often used in slow and deliberate counting.

ALLOPHONES

The two main facts about allophones[20] are these:

1. Pitch phonemes *2, 3,* and *4,* when final, are subject under certain circumstances to a rise at the very end. This is clearly shown in the following example: (a) *I didn't?*—(b) [*No,*] *I didn't.* In both these, *I* belongs to pitch phoneme *2* and *did-* to *3.* In (a), the *-n't* is on an appreciably higher pitch than *did-;* in (b) it belongs to pitch phoneme *1.* We could assign *-n't* in (a) to pitch phoneme *4,* in which case it would be a low allophone of *4,* lower than the allophone in *⁴go²ing!* (Ex. 28). But Ex. 27 shows us that *4* is subject to a similar final rise, unless we wish to set up a pitch phoneme *5* just to account for this rise. The necessity is obviated by treating the pitch of *-n't* as a high allophone of *3; 2* and *4* have similar allophones.

2. Unstressed vowels sometimes have lower allophones than stressed vowels; the exact conditions of occurrence have not been investigated. Example: *³He who ²hesitates is ³¹lost.* In *hesitates,* the syllables *-si-* and *-tates* are lower-pitched than *he-; -tates* in addition has a very slight rise at the end, less than the rise before pause juncture.

It seems likely that besides allophony, there is considerable free variation in phonemically identical pitch contours. Such is the frequent phonetic approximation or assimilation of the actual phonetic value of one pitch phoneme to that of the following, remarked by Palmer and others.

How faithfully we have observed the principle of phonetic similarity cannot be known until the present phonemic analysis has been compared with phonetic graphs from the laboratory—a comparison which however is not necessary for establishing the validity of the phonemic analysis itself. But whether or not the second proposition of this principle (see Part 1) has been observed, we have not violated the fundamental doctrine. Within one utterance by one person, if segment A has

been assigned to pitch phoneme P, then every other segment indistinguishable from A in pitch is also assigned to P.

SEMANTIC VALUES

The pitch phonemes, like segmental phonemes, do not in general have meaning by themselves. They are organized into meaningful sequences called pitch morphemes, which are the strict analogues of segmental morphemes composed of segmental phonemes. But pitch morphemes are so few in number that it seems unnecessary to regard them as in turn organized into syntactical arrays, except in the case of compound sentences. The morphemes into which pitch phonemes enter contain no other kind of phonemes. In the following attempt to state the meanings of the pitch contours or morphemes previously exemplified, no concern need be felt that the meanings given for each morpheme are not particularly unified. These meanings reduce to two main kinds: *emphasis* and *attitude.* Emphasis is a modification of attitude; any attitude can be emphasized or merely expressed without emphasis.

Every utterance contains at least one main emphasized word; and within this word it is one vowel or diphthong which receives the emphasis. The emphasis is marked by maximum stress and by the pitch features which are now to be described.

Let us first consider the favorite contour.[21] As has been remarked, this consists of an order: *231,* and a spacing. Consider the following examples:

(a) *²Where shall we go TO³¹DAY?*
(b) *²Where shall we ³GO ¹today?*
(c) *²Where shall ³WE ¹go today?*
(d) *²Where ³SHALL ¹we go today?*
(e) *³WHERE ¹shall we go today?*

The pitch phoneme *2,* if it occurs, accompanies the first vowel; the phoneme *1* occurs immediately after *3.* We could, then, take *3* as a function of *1* or vice versa. If *3* is a function of *1,* we say that *3* occurs one vowel before *1,* except that both *3* and *1* occur on a final stressed vowel. If *1* is a function of *3,* we say that *1*

---

[20]Allophones of pitch phonemes can, of course, differ from each other only in the one dimension or respect of pitch.

[21]Cf. Bloomfield §11.2 on favorite sentence-types.

occurs one vowel later than *3,* with the same exception. The phoneme *2* occurs on the first vowel except when *3* occurs there, in which case *2* does not occur at all. It is slightly easier to take *2* as a function of *3* than of *1;* hence *1* will also be taken as a function of *3.* The position of *3* then is the independent variable, and the positions of *1* and *2* are the dependent variables.

This fact might be symbolized by writing the symbols of all the pitch phonemes before one vowel; e.g., (c′) *Where shall* [231]*WE go today?* If the utterance has only one loud stress, the place of the independent pitch phoneme coincides with the place of the loud stress. In other words, the independent pitch variable is independent only in relation to the other pitch phonemes; its place is dependent on that of the loud stress (or partially dependent, if there is more than one loud stress). This is a fact of phonemic distribution.

Some utterances have more than one main emphasis; e.g.,

(f) [*Oh dear,*] [2]*what* [32]*SHALL we* [31]*DO?*
(g) [3]*WHAT* [2]*shall we* [31]*DO?*

We may regard the order *23231* in example (f) as a sub-type of the order *231* in examples (a) to (d), with the sequence *232* replacing the phoneme *2.* This pitch rise is not an inevitable result of the extra stress; the extra stress could occur without the pitch modification.

Elaborate discussion of the semantics of pitch phonemes (qua morphemes or constituents of morphemes) is outside the scope of this paper. It will suffice to note that pitch phoneme *4* is a morpheme in itself, with the meaning 'surprise'. As the final pitch phoneme in a sequence, it indicates surprised questioning; when followed by *1,* it indicates a surprised assertion.

4. Some Possible Alternative Systems

The system which has been presented has retained as many as possible of those principles which govern standard segmental phonemics. The systems now to be described desert one or another of these principles.

BLOOMFIELD'S SYSTEM

Bloomfield (92) lists five pitch phonemes: /. ¿ ? ! ,/. These, together with the stress pho-

nemes and the syllabifier, he terms "secondary phonemes." Each of these pitch phonemes characterizes a sentence as a whole, and a single utterance often contains just one of them. As his example /'sevṇ o "klɑk?!/ (92) shows, the phoneme /!/ may occur simultaneously with one of the others.

Whether or not these phonemes will account for all the contrasting pitch contours, they do contrast with each other: translated into the present system, /./ usually equals *231;* /¿/ usually equals *32* or *342;* /?/ usually equals *23;* /!/ signifies the presence of *4* somewhere in the pattern; and /,/ usually equals *232.* But in setting up these phonemes, the principle of segmentation has been abandoned. The segments are not as short as they could be; it is as if we showed /kæ/ and /æk/ in a minimal contrast, ignoring the fact that they are themselves composed of the same parts in two different orders.

It will be noticed that the pitch morphemes are not always used in an economical way in English; very often they are mere auxiliaries. (Or, if we prefer to express it so, segmental morphemes and grammatical arrays of such morphemes are often merely auxiliary to pitch morphemes.) Thus the use of the auxiliary verb *do* without any special pitch morpheme would sufficiently indicate that *Do you have a cold* is a question, in contrast with the statement *You have a cold;* or the use of the pitch morpheme without the use of *do* would equally well signalize the question. A third way of expressing the difference would be by word order alone: by the difference between *You have a cold* and *Have you a cold.* Thus a difference which is expressible lexically (e.g., by the presence or absence of *do* or of a pitch morpheme) is also expressible syntactically. This may have lent plausibility to the view that pitch phonemes are not morphemic (lexical) but grammatical (in particular, syntactical). But as the case of *do* shows, the fact that a meaning is expressible grammatically does not imply that whatever expresses that meaning must be grammatical itself.

There is, then, no reason why pitch morphemes should not be treated as composed of pitch phonemes, just as other morphemes are composed of segmental phonemes. It is true that pitch morphemes are fewer in number, so that it is feasible to treat them as unanalyzed units; but it is still more convenient to analyze them. A further point is that if any new distinctive[22] pitch contours should be discovered, Bloomfield's method could deal with them only by admitting them as absolutely new contours. Just this is done by Bloch and Trager (52); they add /../ ("suspensive") and /¡/ ("contrastive") to Bloomfield's list; the latter phoneme combines features of pitch and stress. The method of this paper, however, would probably be able to deal with any newly noticed pitch contours by analyzing them as other sequences of the same four pitch phonemes. Though it is always possible that a fifth phoneme might be required, it is much less likely. For so far as has yet been observed, many of the possible combinations of the pitch phonemes are not actually used.

PALMER'S SYSTEM

Harold E. Palmer[23] virtually sets up a system of pitch phonemes, which are intermediate in character between Bloomfield's and those of the present system. An utterance is divided into as many units as there are "maximums of prominence" (loudest stresses). A syllable containing such a loudest stress is called a *nucleus;* the preceding part of the unit is called the *head,* the following part of the unit is called the *tail.* No criteria for finding the division between the tail of one unit and head of the next are stated, but they are partially implied by the automatic limitations which Palmer ascribes to tails. Tails are non-distinctive, their pitch contours being automatically determined by their respective nuclei; but the pitch patterns of heads are independently variable and distinctive. Palmer lists one set of pitch phonemes for nuclei (8),[24] and another set for heads (17–18). The nucleus phonemes are I falling, II high-rising, III falling-rising, and IV low-rising. Ignoring differences between British and American pitch patterns, his I usually equals *31;* II usually equals *24,* III usually

equals *32,* and IV usually equals *23.* Then the head phonemes are the equivalent of groups of pitch phonemes which precede the pairs here named.

If pitches be compared to writing, we may say that what Palmer has given is a syllabary rather than an alphabet. Furthermore, tying up pitches with stresses in one system engenders not merely repetitions but difficulties (cf. his p. 69).

HARRIS'S SYSTEM

In conformity with standard phonemic methods, Z. S. Harris's system,[25] like ours, aims to break up pitch contours into segments just short enough to provide enough phonemes to mark the difference between the phonemically different pitch contours which actually do occur. Yet the phonemes of the two systems are quite different.

The following example shows this point. In the sentence [2]*Don't you* [32]*dare do that* *a*[31]*gain!,* the pitch is fairly level on the first two words; then comes a bump or hump (a sharp rise and fall) on the first part of the vowel in *dare,* followed by another level stretch and by another bump on the first part of the vowel in *-gain.* Harris divides a sentence of this kind into two segments: *don't you dare* and *do that again.* The pitch of the first segment is analyzed into two phonemes. One, a "scope" phoneme, represents the level-bump-level contour, without regard to where the bump occurs; the other represents the exact location of the bump (in this example, near the end of the first segment). The second segment is analyzed similarly. Our system of four pitch phonemes resembles Harris's system in that it distinguishes between the sequence of phonemes and their spacing.

The principal difference between the two systems is that Harris allows his phonemes to occur simultaneously. Thus, the difference between two contours which is expressed in our system by symbolizing one as *232* and the other as *343* could be expressed in another way. Let us set up a phoneme R whose effect is to raise each following phoneme except *4* one step; this effect will continue until the end

---

[22]Distinctive, and having a kind of meaning which we will agree (cf. Bloomfield 114) is not merely cultural but linguistic.

[23]*English Intonation,* 1922.

[24]In the *Grammar of Spoken English* by himself and F. G. Blandford (2d ed. 1939), Palmer divides his former No. I into two: a high-falling and a low-falling (§§20–39). This is a change of details, not of method.

[25]"Simultaneous Components in Phonology" [12], *Language* 20.181 [115] ff. (1944).

of the utterance, or until halted by another phoneme T. Then *343 = R232.* Now if we choose to treat the sequence *232* as one phoneme S, *343* would consist of two: RS. This is in conformity with an analysis into components or scope phonemes, such as Harris has propounded in his paper. But it deviates considerably, as any analysis of phonemes into components will, from the principles of segmentation and phonetic similarity.

TWO OTHER POSSIBILITIES

Finally, two modifications of our system are possible. Each has a prima facie lure; but each violates a useful principle of phonemics and is therefore rejected.

1. If we set up a system which assumes syllables, we could treat each syllable as containing at least one pitch phoneme; for instance, ^{2}*Why* ^{2}*did*^{2}*n't* ^{2}*he* ^{31}*come?* This system would allow iteration of pitch phonemes; and, as a notational device, we could perfectly well write all the pitch phonemes first, enclosing any two which occur in the same syllable in parentheses; thus, 2222(31) *Why didn't he come?*

The disadvantages of this system are two. It would demand the recognition of many morpheme alternants—contours differing only in the number of times the respective pitch phonemes are iterated; and it would not take account of the automatic elements in the pitch contour. We should have to say, in general, that where P is a pitch phoneme, PP is a morpheme alternant of P. The alternation would be automatic, i.e., predictable; but there is no need to have alternants at all.

2. The other modification to be considered looks like a trick. We reduce the number of pitch phonemes from four to two, P and Q, as follows: P may be iterated two, three or four times:

P	= phoneme *1*
PP	= phoneme *2*
PPP	= phoneme *3*
PPPP	= phoneme *4*

Successive occurrences of P operate simultaneously, backwards and forwards, until stopped by an occurrence of Q or of pause in either direction.

Obviously, any system containing any number of phonemes can be "analyzed" into two phonemes in this way: one iterable, the other punctuative. Yet in this particular case, the analysis can be made to appear not unplausible. P, we may say, has one value throughout: a raising value. By itself it raises zero to pitch phoneme *1;* operating on *1* it raises this to *2;* and so on. Q, like any ordinary phoneme, halts the effect of what precedes (and of what follows). So the pattern *231* (as analyzed by the system of this paper) could be reanalyzed as PPQPPPQP. P and Q would contrast minimally; PPPP (i.e., *4*) would contrast phonemically with PPQP (i.e., *21*); Q would not occur initially or finally; and there would be limitations of pattern exactly analogous to those of the four-phoneme system: just as *212* does not occur, so PPQPQPP also would not occur.

We have already (Part 2) found reason to admit phonemes which act simultaneously with each other; but here we have a special case of a phoneme acting simultaneously with another occurrence of itself. And this is no doubt the reason why this two-phoneme system would be rejected by most phonemicists: the fact that, of the two phonemes, neither one has segments—actual phones—as its members.

This study does not profess to delineate a general method for analyzing the suprasegmental phonemes of every language; still less does it purport to reveal whether or not a given language has suprasegmental phonemes. All that has been done is to apply the received methods of phonemics to a phase of English phonology where, so far as we are aware, they have not been applied in quite the same way before. And a phonemicist quite ignorant of English would doubtless, sooner or later, stumble upon the fact that English phonemes are profitably divided into segmental and suprasegmental, and that stress and pitch are among the latter; but no method has been devised which will automatically, even if laboriously, lead him to this discovery.

Attention to the facts of distribution (patterning) is a close approach to such a method; and we may take the pragmatic view that the success of the theory here presented is independent of its general validity, that is, of its applicability to any language whatever.

BIBLIOGRAPHY 8
Suprasegmentals

TRAGER, G. L. (1941) "The Theory of Accentual Systems"

BLOCH, B., and G. L. TRAGER (1942) *Outline of Linguistic Analysis*

PIKE, K. L. (1945) *The Intonation of American English*

Reviewed by: WELLS, R. S. (1947)
BOLINGER, D. L. (1947)

NEWMAN, S. S. (1946) "On the Stress System of English"

MOULTON, W. G. (1947) "Juncture in Modern Standard German"

COWAN, J. M., and B. BLOCH (1948) "An Experimental Study of Pause in English Grammar"

PIKE, K. L. (1948) *Tone Languages*

Reviewed by: BLACK, J. W. (1948)
HERZOG, G. (1949)
TRAGER, G. L. (1949)
LI, F.-K. (1950)

BOLINGER, D. L. (1951) "Intonation: Levels Versus Configurations"

PIKE, E. V. (1951) "Tonemic-Intonemic Correlation in Mazahua (Otomí)"

STETSON, R. H. (1951) *Motor Phonetics*

TWADDELL, W. F. (1953) "Stetson's Model and the 'Supra-Segmental Phonemes'"

SHARP, A. E. (1954) "A Tonal Analysis of the Disyllabic Noun in the Machame Dialect of Chaga"

BOLINGER, D. L. (1955) "Intersections of Stress and Intonation"

SPRIGG, R. K. (1955) "The Tonal System of Tibetan (Lhasa Dialect) and the Nominal Phrase"

CHAO, Y. R. (1956) "Tone, Intonation, Singsong, Chanting, Recitative, Tonal Composition, and Atonal Composition in Chinese"

STOCKWELL, R. P., J. D. BOWEN, and I. SILVA-FUENZALIDA (1956) "Spanish Juncture and Intonation"

CHOMSKY, N., M. HALLE, and F. LUKOFF (1956) "On Accent and Juncture in English"

MARCKWARDT, A. (1962) "'On Accent and Juncture in English'—A Critique"

BOLINGER, D. L., and L. J. GERSTMAN (1957) "Disjuncture as a Cue to Constructs"

SPRIGG, R. K. (1957) "Junction in Spoken Burmese"

BOLINGER, D. L. (1958) "A Theory of Pitch Accent in English"

GARVIN, P. L., and M. MATHIOT (1958) "Fused Units in Prosodic Analysis"

JENSEN, M. K. (1958) "Recognition of Word Tones in Whispered Speech"

KINGDON, R. (1958) *The Groundwork of English Intonation*

SHARP, A. E. (1958) "Falling-Rising Intonation Patterns in English"

LEHISTE, I., and G. E. PETERSON (1959) "Vowel Amplitude and Phonemic Stress in American English"

GRIMES, J. E. (1959) "Huichol Tone and Intonation"

WELMERS, W. E. (1959) "Tonemics, Morphotonemics, and Tonal Morphemes"

LEHISTE, I. (1960) *An Acoustic-Phonetic Study of Internal Open Juncture*

STOCKWELL, R. P. (1960) "The Place of Intonation in a Generative Grammar of English"

BOLINGER, D. L. (1961) "Contrastive Accent and Contrastive Stress"

HILL, A. A. (1961) "Suprasegmentals, Prosodies, Prosodemes: Comparison and Discussion"

SHARP, A. E. (1961) "The Analysis of Stress and Juncture in English"

JOOS, M. (1962) "The Definition of Juncture and Terminals"

POTTER, S. (1962) "Syllabic Juncture"

BOLINGER, D. L. (1963) "Length, Vowel, Juncture"

HAUGEN, E. (1963) "Pitch Accent and Tonemic Juncture in Scandinavian"

LEHISTE, I. (1965) "Juncture"

PIKE, K. L. (1967) "Suprasegmentals in Reference to Phonemes of Item, of Process, and of Relation"

WANG, W. S.-Y. (1967) "Phonological Features of Tone"

LEHISTE, I. (1970) *Suprasegmentals*

14

ON THE PHONEMIC STATUS
OF ENGLISH DIPHTHONGS*

KENNETH L. PIKE

This paper[1] presents evidence to show that in certain dialects of American Speech —in "General American"—phonetic [ɪⁱ], [ʊᵘ], [eⁱ], [oᵁ] are not structurally parallel to [aⁱ], [aᵁ], [ɔⁱ] (or [oⁱ]), but that the first group act as phonetically complex single units (single phonemes), whereas the second group function as sequences of two units (two phonemes).

Various other writers deny this dichotomy, and treat the two sets as parallel. One approach treats all seven items as single phonemes; Swadesh[2] is one of the principal exponents of this analysis. Trager and Bloch,[3] on the other hand, consider these diphthongs to constitute sequences of two phonemes each. A symbolization more closely reflecting an analysis like the present one, but without detailed discussion of the problem, is seen in Kenyon's[4] material.

EVIDENCE FROM THE REACTION OF AMERICAN STUDENTS OF PHONETICS

In the last ten years, with approximately seven hundred students of phonetics in the Summer Institute of Linguistics,[5] my colleagues and I have observed the following fact: It is relatively easy to teach these students

to notice that [aⁱ] is phonetically composed of two parts—a vowel somewhat similar to the [a] of *father* and an [ɪ] somewhat similar to the [ɪ] of *bit* or the [i] of *beet;* [aᵁ] and [ɔⁱ] act like [aⁱ]. Occasionally, to be sure, one of these students will confuse [aⁱ] with a single simple letter "i" on the analogy of the spelling of *bite* and the like, but even in these rather rare cases it is quite simple to point out to the student the two phonetic elements in [aⁱ].

On the other hand, practically without exception, the students have considerable difficulty in learning to recognize two elements, or a glide, in the [oᵁ] of *boat, toe,* and similar words. Most of them do so only with considerable effort, by watching for lip movements in a mirror, or by hearing exaggerated slow pronunciations. The diphthongization is hard for them to learn to hear; many of the students never do learn to recognize such diphthongization easily and consistently. A similar situation exists for the [eⁱ] of *bait, may,* and the like, except that the difficulty is possibly a bit greater because it is harder to see the tongue movements that occur in [eⁱ] than it is to observe the corresponding lip movements in [oᵁ]. For [ɪⁱ] and [ʊᵘ] as in *beet* and *boot,* even greater difficulty exists for the students, presumably because the diphthongization is phonetically less pronounced than for [eⁱ] and [oᵁ]. The few students who have had no difficulty with such diphthongization appear to have been those who took our courses after having had previous phonetic instruction which emphasized the contrast between diphthongized and nondiphthongized vowel types, or who came with a language background in which nondiphthongized vowel types occurred. In general, however, the students quickly learned to hear diphthongization in [aⁱ], [aᵁ],

[1] Prepared as part of the work done as Lloyd Post-Doctoral Fellow of the University of Michigan.
[2] Morris Swadesh, "The Vowels of Chicago English," *Language* 11.148–151 (1935). Swadesh gives references to similar analyses.
[3] G. L. Trager and Bernard Bloch, "The Syllabic Phonemes of English" [9], *Language* 17.223–246 (1941).
[4] J. S. Kenyon, *American Pronunciation: A Textbook of Phonetics for Students of English*[6]; Ann Arbor, 1935.
[5] Of Glendale, Calif., with academic sessions on the campus of the University of Oklahoma.

*Reprinted from *Language* 23.151–159 (1947) by permission.

[oᴵ], but had to have considerable training to hear it in [eᴵ], [oᵁ], [ɪᴵ], [ᵁᵘ].

Controlling the pronunciation of the diphthongs brought problems related to those in hearing them. The students could readily be taught to begin with the pronunciation of [aᴵ] (or [aᵁ] or [ɔᴵ]) and then to omit the second element so as to obtain a level (nondiphthongized) vowel [a] (or [ɔ]). With [eᴵ] and [oᵁ], however, they had much greater difficulty. Speakers who diphthongized [eᴵ] and [oᵁ] found it awkward to eliminate the vocalic glide of the second part of the diphthong while preserving the phonetic character of the first part. The difficulty of controlling and modifying the diphthongal character of the pronunciation of [eᴵ] and [oᵁ] but not of [aᴵ], [aᵁ], [ɔᴵ], helps to establish the fact that native speakers of the dialect react differently to the group [eᴵ], [oᵁ], [ɪᴵ], [ᵁᵘ], and to the group [aᴵ], [aᵁ], [ɔᴵ].

Moreover, if we taught students to write *bait, boat, beet, boot* with dual symbols "ey," "ow," "iy," "uw" (or "eᴵ," "oᵁ," "ɪᴵ," "ᵁᵘ," or the like), then when they reached a field of investigation where the language concerned had nondiphthongized vowel types, they were very likely to write a nondiphthongized [e] or [o] in the same way that they had written their diphthongized English sound of *bait* or *boat*. For example, they were likely to write Spanish *bebe* as "beybey" even though the Spanish sounds have little or no diphthongization. On the other hand, if the students were taught to write English *bait, boat, beet, boot* as "bet," "bot," "bit," "but," then they tended also to write the pure vowels of a foreign language with single letters.

Similarly, some of these same students whom we were later able to observe in field work had difficulty in recognizing a sequence of [e] plus [i] in languages where such a sequence contrasts with a pure vowel. They were inclined to write such sequences also in whatever way they had learned to write the English vowels of *bait, boat, beet,* and *boot*.

For [aᴵ], [aᵁ], [ɔᴵ], the same problem did not exist. Speakers of General American English had little or no difficulty in these foreign languages in recognizing the two parts in a sequence of [a] plus [i] (or [ɪ]), or of [a] plus [u] (or [ᵁ]), or of [o] plus [i] (or [ɪ]).

From the difficulty which American students have in hearing the diphthongized nature of [eᴵ], [oᵁ], [ɪᴵ], [ᵁᵘ] but not of [aᴵ], [aᵁ], [ɔᴵ], from their difficulty in learning to produce level nondiphthongized vowels, and from their problems of transfer of transcription to languages with pure and diphthongized vowels, we conclude that in the structure of General American the phonetic sequences of [aᴵ], [aᵁ], [ɔᴵ] are structurally not comparable to the phonetic sequences [eᴵ], [oᵁ], [ɪᴵ], [ᵁᵘ]. The two sets evoke different native reactions.

The question arises: what are the characteristics of the English structural system that force this difference in students' reaction to the two sets? Are structural data available to support the difference, or is the evidence of the native speaker's reaction invalid, not paralleled by other facts in the language?

It appears to me that certain other evidence does exist. Not all kinds of evidence are necessarily conclusive or equally valuable. One kind, however—the bearing of intonation upon the problem—does not seem to have come to the attention of persons discussing the question and may be of sufficient weight to make them reconsider their conclusions.

EVIDENCE FROM INTONATION

Not all parts of a sentence are spoken with equal speed; some parts of an English sentence are faster than others. Certain of these differences in rate—those which we will consider here—are conditioned by the placement of an intonation contour or contours upon the sentence.

The first primary contour[6] in an utterance begins with the first heavily stressed syllable of that utterance. By a heavily stressed syllable we mean one which in traditional terminology has "sentence stress," although it need not have that especially strong accentuation which comes with emphatic stress. A lexical stress becomes considerably reduced in intensity if it does not occur as the beginning point of a primary contour. In the sentence

---

[6]For a full discussion of the parts of American intonation contours and for detailed illustrations, together with definitions of the meanings of these contours and frequency counts of their usage in selected bodies of text, see K. L. Pike, *The Intonation of American English* (University of Michigan Publications in Linguistics, Vol. 1); Ann Arbor, 1945.

The 'gentleman de'sires a 'ticket but not
3-   °2- -3 3- °2-
a reser'vation.
-3-   °2-4//

lexical stresses occur on *gentleman, desires, ticket,* and *reservation;* sentence stresses occur on *ticket, not,* and *reservation.* On *ticket* and *reservation* the sentence stresses constitute the beginning of a primary intonation contour and reinforce lexical stresses. On *not,* the sentence stress occurs on a word which need not be considered to have lexical stress. *Gentleman* and *desires* have lexical stresses partially reduced because they are not the beginning of a primary contour.

Primary contours begin on the syllables *tic-, not,* and *-va-,* as indicated by the degree sign under them, and these primary contours end with the syllables which are connected by hyphens following the degree sign; that is, the first primary contour includes *ticket,* the third includes *-vation,* and (as a special case which will not be discussed in detail here) the second is *not a.* The numbers indicate relative pitch of the voice. Pitch 1 is highest, pitch 4 is lowest, pitches 2 and 3 are intermediate. Syllables which have no number beneath them need not occur on one of these relative levels but are more or less evenly distributed between the pitches preceding and following them.

Preceding the first and last primary contours are certain precontour syllables; in this sentence they are the phrases *the gentleman desires a* and *but not a reser-.* Now it is the precontour of the total intonational contour which is the most rapid section.[7] Vowels which occur there are pronounced more rapidly than the same vowels when they constitute an entire primary contour. Compare, for example, the difference in rate of [æ] of *man* in the two sentences following, each of which is marked with emphatic sentence stress, but not with lexical stress.

Why the man over there won't 'do it!
3-   °1- -4//
You say you saw a 'man?! I don't
3-   °2-4-3/ 3-
be'lieve it!
°2- -4//

In the first of these sentences *man* is pronounced rapidly; in the second it is pronounced slowly. If now the types [a^i], [a^u], [ɔ^i] and the types [e^i], [o^u], [ɪ^i], [u^u] are placed in a position where they constitute the entire primary contour, both sets appear strongly diphthongized. Note, for example, the diphthongization in the words *bike, bout, quoits, bait, boat, meat,* and *suit* in the following intonation contexts. (In each sentence, the last word has the same contour, °2-4-3/, as the word *man* in the second of the two sentences above; each sentence can be followed by the sentence *I don't believe it!,* with the same intonation as noted above.)

[a^i] *You say you bought a 'bike?!*
[a^u] *You say you saw the 'bout?!*
[ɔ^i] *You say you bought some 'quoits?!*
[e^i] *You say you paid for the 'bait?!*
[o^u] *You say you bought a 'boat?!*
[ɪ^i] *You say you want some 'meat?!*
[u^u] *You say you bought a 'suit?!*

The vowels are not quite so long if they constitute only the first part of the primary contour, but nevertheless each type may be heard as diphthongized. Compare:

[e^i] *It's 'bait that I want.*
3-   °2   -4//
[a^i] *It's a 'bike that I want.*
3-   °2-   -4//

When, however, these words are found in a rapidly pronounced precontour, it appears[8] to me that there is a sharp difference in their phonetic action. The set [a^i], [a^u], and [ɔ^i] always retain a strong diphthongization even when they are pronounced rapidly. Note the same set of words in the intonational precontours of the following sentences:

---

[7]For references to Classe, who gives instrumental measurements of these differences, see Pike, *Intonation* 38 and 187. In statements of intrumental data, such as that given by C. E. Parmenter and S. N. Treviño, "The Length of the Sounds of a Middle Westerner," *American Speech* 10.129–133 (1935), the intonation is not indicated. Otherwise such studies could be used for checking the statements given here.

[8]Here again instrumental testing is needed. Such testing would prove valid, however, only if the sample of speech studied were actually illustrating the intonation structure here portrayed.

[aᶦ] *The bike that 'you have is the 'best.*[9]
     3-   °2- -4-3 3-   °2-4//

[aᵁ] *The bout for the 'championship*
     3-   °2   -4-3

will come next 'month.
     3-   °2-4//

[ɔᶦ] *The boy over 'there is my 'brother.*
     3-   °2-4-3 3-   °2- -4//

In the set [eᶦ], [oᵁ], [ɪᶦ], [ᵁᵘ], however, the diphthongization is sharply diminished or in some instances possibly even eliminated when the words containing them become part of the precontour. Note the following sentences. (In reading these sentences aloud, the reader must be sure that the stress on the words *bait, boat, meat,* and *suit* is largely or completely reduced. If he stresses these words, he will introduce a further primary contour.)

[e] *The bait is 'spoiled.*
     3-   °2- -4//
    (Not: *The 'bait is 'spoiled.*)
           3- °2- -3- °2- -4//

[o] *'Why   does the boat 'leak?*
     °2-3 3-   °2-4/

[i] *He buys meat for the 'dog here.*
     3-   °2-3 °2-4//

[u] *If he tries to buy a suit to'day*
     3-   °2-3

he'll be disap'pointed.
     3-   °2- -4//

From this evidence we draw the following conclusions. (1) The set [aᶦ], [aᵁ], [ɔᶦ] acts differently from the set [eᶦ], [oᵁ], [ɪᶦ], [ᵁᵘ] in that the first set retains its strongly diphthongal character even in the rapid part of an intonational contour, while the second set

[9]This sentence, like some of those given earlier, is of a contrastive type. The same principle holds for other kinds of sentences, provided that the intonation is read as written; but the contrastive type is most likely to be pronounced with the primary contour in the desired place. Note the special attention given to *arrive* and the lack of stress on *bike* in the following sentence:

[aᶦ] *The bike will ar'rive to'morrow.*
     3-   °2- -3-°2- -4//

Nouns tend to be pronounced with their lexical stress reinforced by sentence stress, except in cases of special attention like this one.

tends to lose most of its diphthongal character in such a position. (2) In the set [aᶦ], [aᵁ], [ɔᶦ], each sound is a sequence of two units, of which the second does not disappear even in a rapid pronunciation; but in the set [eᶦ], [oᵁ], [ɪᶦ], [ᵁᵘ], each sound is structurally a single unit (phonetically complex), which may be modified according to the intonational environment in which it occurs.[10] (3) The difference in students' reactions to the two sets is substantiated by the fact that these sets show different ranges of variation in the degree to which they remain diphthongal in various intonation contours. (4) Since the configurational reality of the difference between the two sets is attested both by the occurrence of different variants in similar contexts and by different native reactions, it appears that the latter type of evidence can be legitimately used to support other evidence for grouping sounds in a linguistic system: namely, the manner in which speakers of one language react to the sounds of a second language in their attempts to hear, pronounce, and record them, is valuable and valid evidence to be considered in analyzing the phonemic system of the first language.

EVIDENCE FROM MODIFICATION
UNDER VARYING STRESS CONDITIONS

Once such a distinction has been established for English by evidence of the kind that has just been presented, it is convenient to state that the intonational conditioning is paralleled by conditioning by stress, or possibly that the two factors of stress and intonation work together to produce the observed result (inasmuch as the primary contour includes a stressed syllable and the precontour reduces or eliminates stress or has no lexical stress at all). In a word like *obey,* for example, where the first vowel is unstressed, the tendency is to lose the diphthongization of *o-.* Diphthongization of [eᶦ], [oᵁ], [ɪᶦ], [ᵁᵘ] tends largely to disappear in unstressed syllables, but to be retained in the stressed syllables. In the set [aᶦ], [aᵁ], [ɔᶦ], however, the unstressed syl-

[10]Some time ago I presented this suggestion to W. F. Twaddell. He thought that instrumental study might be able to establish a significant difference in the range of variation between the two sets: even though neither set becomes actually monosyllabic, one set loses appreciably more of its diphthongization than the other. Compare footnote 15 below.

lables tend to have the diphthongization retained; cf. [a$^\text{I}$diə] *idea.*

We find, then, some tendency to reduce the diphthongization in unstressed syllables, and to do so considerably more for [e$^\text{I}$], [o$^\text{U}$], [I$^\text{i}$], [U$^\text{u}$] than for [a$^\text{U}$], [a$^\text{I}$], [ɔ$^\text{I}$]. It is a little difficult, however, to postulate this as complete conditioned variation by stress, since with an increase of length and a very slight increase of stress the diphthongization of more or less unstressed [e$^\text{I}$], [o$^\text{U}$], [I$^\text{i}$], [U$^\text{u}$] may be considerably increased (as in a slow pronunciation of the first syllable of *obey*).

For this reason it may prove convenient to handle even those differences which at first sight appear to be lexical as actually caused or conditioned by intonation placement, instead of trying to treat them as conditioned varieties according to stress placement. This possibility is made more tenable in that intonation placement involves stress placement: as was seen in the preceding section, precontours have either no lexical stresses or only reduced lexical stresses, whereas all primary contours begin with a heavy (i.e., normal) lexical or sentence stress. With this in mind, it might prove easier to handle the difference between [o$^\text{U}$be$^\text{I}$] and [o$^\text{I}$be$^\text{I}$] as conditioned by the optional variation in the intonation contour, or by an optional variation in the speed of the precontour, rather than (a) as a subphonemic difference conditioned by stress placement or (b) as the optional occurrence of one sound unit [o] or of two sound units in sequence [o$^\text{U}$].

This discussion of the stress does not attempt to force a final decision as to whether reduction of diphthongization is best handled in terms of conditioning by stress, or by intonation, or possibly even by rate, or by a combination of these speech characteristics, but it does add further evidence that there exists a structural difference between the two sets [a$^\text{I}$], [a$^\text{U}$], [ɔ$^\text{I}$] and [e$^\text{I}$], [o$^\text{U}$], [I$^\text{i}$], [U$^\text{u}$], in that the second has a much greater range of variation in its optional or conditioned loss of diphthongization. In the set [a$^\text{I}$], [a$^\text{U}$], [ɔ$^\text{I}$], both parts of the diphthong must be retained in all places in the intonation contour and under varying stress conditions,[11] whereas [e$^\text{I}$],

[o$^\text{U}$], [I$^\text{i}$], [U$^\text{u}$] are single units which may be phonetically complex or phonetically simple with optional or conditioned fluctuation between the diphthongal and monophthongal varieties.

EVIDENCE FROM THE PHONETIC NATURE OF THE SOUNDS

Up to this point we have assumed that [e$^\text{I}$], [o$^\text{U}$], [I$^\text{i}$], [U$^\text{u}$] are in General American speech always diphthongized at the beginning of a primary contour. Yet this assumption is not completely valid. In some dialects of General American speech [I$^\text{i}$] and [U$^\text{u}$], less commonly also [e$^\text{I}$] and [o$^\text{U}$] lack this diphthongization[12] even in stressed position at the beginning point of a primary contour. For [a$^\text{I}$], [a$^\text{U}$], [ɔ$^\text{I}$], however, one finds diphthongized varieties in all positions in the sentence.[13] From this we conclude that the phonetic evidence substantiates a significant difference between [a$^\text{I}$], [a$^\text{U}$], [ɔ$^\text{I}$] on the one hand, and [e$^\text{I}$], [o$^\text{U}$], [I$^\text{i}$], [U$^\text{u}$] on the other, in that some of the latter for many speakers of General American are seldom or never diphthongized.[14]

There may be further physical characteristics[15] differentiating [e$^\text{I}$], [o$^\text{U}$], [I$^\text{i}$], [U$^\text{u}$] from [a$^\text{I}$], [a$^\text{U}$], [ɔ$^\text{I}$].

EVIDENCE FROM LEXICAL CONTRASTS

It may be of value to point out further that for [a$^\text{I}$] and [a$^\text{U}$] one can show contrasts

---

[11] Unless of course both types are completely eliminated by the substitution of an entirely different vowel, as in *write* [a$^\text{I}$] : *written* [I].

[12] Cf. Kenyon 36 and 34; Trager and Bloch, *Language* 17.235 [81], fn. 21.

[13] We are not here discussing dialects of southeastern American English, where the number and the nature of diphthongs are often different from the situation assumed for this paper.

[14] In dialects where the vowel of *bet* is diphthongized as [ε$^\text{I}$] or [ε$^\text{ə}$], this vowel has a structural similarity with the vowel of *bait,* [e$^\text{I}$]. In such dialects this relationship may be a further reason for treating the two sounds as parallel in phonemic structure also, and for considering each of the phonetic diphthongs to be a single phonemic unit.

In such dialects, also, it becomes clear that the first part of the diphthong [e$^\text{I}$] is not a phoneme [ε], since the vowels [e] and [ε] contrast as the differentiating characteristics of the diphthongs [e$^\text{I}$] and [ε$^\text{I}$].

[15] It is to be hoped that the new approaches through "Visible Speech" may produce data that will answer some of the problems raised by this article and will test the theories propounded in it. Note, for example, the diphthongs portrayed on p. 82 of G. A. Kopp and H. C. Green, "Basic

between a single vowel and a diphthong beginning with the same (or practically the same) vowel. Note the words *pa* [pa] and *pie* [paᴵ]; *pa* [pa] and *pout* [paᵁt]; *raw* [rɔ] and *Roy* [rɔᴵ] (or, for speakers who use a higher vowel in the diphthong of *Roy*, the pair *beau* [boᵁ] and *boy* [boᴵ] or [boᵁᴵ]). For [eᴵ], [ɪᴵ], [ᵁᵘ] such contrasts cannot be obtained.[16] This again seems to point to a difference between [aᴵ], [aᵁ], [ɔᴵ] on the one hand, and [eᴵ], [oᵁ], [ɪᴵ], [ᵁᵘ] on the other.

In the light of these data, how can one reconcile the fact that other writers, with strong arguments based on the structural distribution of sounds, analyze [eᴵ], [oᵁ], [ɪᴵ], [ᵁᵘ] as two units instead of one, or [aᴵ], [aᵁ], [ɔᴵ] as single units?[17] Is there not some phonemic principle, as yet perhaps unstated, which would account for such apparently conflicting conclusions, and which would permit the dis-

---

Phonetic Principles of Visible Speech," *JASA* 18.74–89 (July 1946). For [aɪ], [ɔɪ], [aʊ] there is a shift of direction, quite noticeable, in the middle of the glide from the first to the second part of the diphthong; for [eɪ] and [oʊ] the glide is practically continuous. This evidence is of course inadequate, and will be greatly complicated by transitional modifications to and from other sounds. Nevertheless, we venture to propose the following hypothesis: "Diphthongs" composed of two phonemes tend to show a sharp change of direction in their "Visible Speech" pattern; but "diphthongs" comprising single phonemes tend—when transitional modifications to and from other sounds are discounted—to show a less prominent break.

Unfortunately, the Kopp-Green article contains too little evidence to test the changes postulated here for diphthongs in precontours—first, because the range of stress differences is deliberately modified by the recording techniques so as to make weak items legible (Kopp-Green 75), and second because the phrases were not chosen to contrast sounds in different positions of a controlled intonation contour.

[16] I avoid including [oᵁ] in this statement, since some investigators might suggest the parallel *raw* : *row*. For my own dialect, such a parallel would assume a phonemic relation between the [ɔ] in *raw* and the first part of the [oᵁ] in *row*—that is, between sounds that are phonetically quite different. It appears to me that such an assumption should be avoided wherever possible.

[17] The first view is taken by Trager and Bloch (cf. fn. 3), the second by Swadesh, *Language* 11.148–151 (1935). I am informed that Swadesh has now written another article on the same question, with a different conclusion, which is to appear in the same issue of this journal. [See Swadesh 1947 —VBM]

covery of some definite unity within the complexity of phonemic structure?

It seems to me that such a principle can be found. Phonemes may occur in structural layers, in series of immediate constituents; a close-knit inner layer comprising a sequence of phonemes may act, in a larger structural layer, as a single but phonemically complex unit.

If, now, we assume that the reasoning in this paper is substantially correct, /ai/, /au/, /ɔi/ would be sequences of phonemes in an inner layer, but would serve in larger sequences as (phonemically complex) nuclear units; on the other hand, /e/, /i/, /o/, /u/ would constitute single phonemes in the inner layer, and would serve in larger sequences as (phonemically simple) nuclear units somewhat similar in distribution to the complex nuclear units /ai/, /au/, /ɔi/.

In other words, I would agree that Swadesh was partially right in his earlier treatment of [aᴵ] as a unit—provided, however, that the unity of [aᴵ] is described on a higher level of structural sequence than that of phonemes as such; and at the same time I would agree with Trager and Bloch in pointing out various distributional parallels among the seven nuclear items [eᴵ], [oᵁ], [ɪᴵ], [ᵁᵘ], [aᴵ], [aᵁ], [ɔᴵ]—provided that in spite of their all being phonetically complex, the first four are shown by the evidence here presented to be phonemically simple.

One should note, furthermore, that within the nuclear unit /ai/, the first and second phonemes of the sequence have distinct functions. The first is the more prominent; it seems to carry (or to be the domain of) the major part of a significant stress, as in *isolate* /ˈaisolet/. The second, on the other hand, is less prominent. Within a complex nucleus the various phonemes need not all have the same function.

The phonemic principle suggested here may well find application in other languages.[18]

---

[18] Thus in Totonaco a sequence of vowel + glottal stop could be treated as a nuclear sequence of two phonemes which acts, in distribution, frequency, morphology, morphophonemic alternations, and dialect borrowings, much like a single vowel. The interpretation suggested here would seem to account for Aschmann's data (see Herman P. Aschmann, "Totonaco Phonemes," *IJAL* 12.34–43 [1946]), most of which I have checked with his in-

Unfortunately, we still lack some of the criteria needed for the analysis of immediate constituents on the phonemic level; but this limitation does not destroy the fact of structural layers. Rather, it should spur us on to learn how the principle here stated can be uniformly handled by different investigators.

---

formant. At the same time it would account for the unitary action of the nucleus, while making the treatment of the phonetic data more satisfactory than Aschmann's analysis of [Vʔ] as a single phoneme —a laryngealized vowel.

For a detailed analysis of Mazateco from this point of view see K. L. Pike and E. V. Pike, "Immediate Constituents of Mazateco Syllables," *IJAL* 13.78–91 (1947). In this article, various types of symbolism are developed to indicate the structural layers of phonemes; some of these might be adapted to English.

BIBLIOGRAPHY 9
The Syllable

SOMMERFELT, A. (1931) "Sur l'importance générale de la syllabe"
—— (1936) "Can Syllable Divisions Have Phonological Importance?"

STETSON, R. H. (1936) "The Relation of the Phoneme and the Syllable"

FIRTH, J. R., and B. B. ROGERS (1937) "The Structure of the Chinese Monosyllable in a Hunanese Dialect (Changsha)"

HJELMSLEV, L. (1939) "The Syllable as a Structural Unit"

VOGT, H. (1940) "The Structure of the Norwegian Monosyllables"

ELIASON, N. E. (1942) "On Syllable Division in Phonemics"

HARDEN, M. (1946) "Syllable Structure in Terena"

EDGERTON, W. F. (1947) "Stress, Vowel Quantity, and Syllable Division in Egyptian"

PIKE, K. L., and E. V. PIKE (1947) "Immediate Constituents of Mazateco Syllables"

KURYŁOWICZ, J. (1948) "Contribution à la théorie de la syllabe"

STETSON, R. H. (1951) *Motor Phonetics*

TWADDELL, W. F. (1953) "Stetson's Model and the 'Supra-Segmental Phonemes'"

O'CONNOR, J. D., and J. L. M. TRIM (1953) "Vowel, Consonant, and Syllable—A Phonological Definition"

HAMP, E. P. (1954) "Componential Restatement of Syllable Structure in Trique"

LONGACRE, R. E. (1955) "Rejoinder to Hamp's 'Componential Restatement of Syllable Structure in Trique'"

MALMBERG, B. (1955) "The Phonetic Basis for Syllable Division"

HAUGEN, E. (1956) "The Syllable in Linguistic Description"

15

GRAMMATICAL PREREQUISITES
TO PHONEMIC ANALYSIS*
KENNETH L. PIKE

0. In recent years various phonemicists seem to have set as an ideal of phonological description and analysis the elimination of all reference to or reliance upon facts about the grammatical structure of the language being investigated. Possibly the most specific rejection of grammar in phonemics is made by Charles F. Hockett: "No grammatical fact of any kind is used in making phonological analysis." Also: "There must be no circularity; phonological analysis is assumed for grammatical analysis, and so must not assume any part of the latter. The line of demarcation between the two must be sharp."[1]

The present article holds that it is impossible for such claims to be realized completely, and that even were it possible it would at times prove undesirable. It assumes that the best description of any set of data is that statement about them (1) which accounts fully and accurately for all the facts and (2) which at the same time is the most concise and simple and convenient. Since the convenience of a description varies somewhat with the purposes to which it may be placed, the goal of phonemic description for the present discussion is taken to be the purely scientific presentation of the phonology of languages as part of their structural delineation. To eliminate the facts of grammatical relationship and structure from the analysis and presentation of phonological structure is frequently undesirable because many of the phonological facts are inextricably interwoven with grammatical facts and structural relationships; avoiding the portrayal

of this relationship means omitting, completely or at least temporarily, an important part of the total structure of the language. When phonological and grammatical facts are mutually dependent, the treatment of phonology without reference to grammar is a concealment of part of a most important set of structural facts pertinent to phonology. The apparent gain in compartmentation or systematization of data at the expense of an early indication of such structural phenomena within the total phonological arrangement is too high a price to pay for neatness of statement.

Furthermore, it may prove unnecessarily complex to establish in every instance a distinct terminology to differentiate the phonological structure and grammatical structure, if the same set of facts and relationships may apply to each. If, for example, a grammatical entity is discovered which is clearly a minimum unit of free expression, and which may be conveniently labelled a "word," and if phonological distributions can only conveniently be described in reference to these same sections of utterances, one has lost something of convenience, simplicity, and clarity of presentation of the language as a whole if in the grammatical discussion these units are called "words" but in the phonological discussion they are called, let us say, "intrajunctures." Distinct terminology for distinct "levels of analysis" is valuable only when the facts and relationships are likewise distinct. An artificial distinction based upon different approaches to a single set of data may result in a sharp artificial dichotomy which has no reality.

Such an unfortunate exaggerated distinction already exists within grammatical analy-

---

[1]Charles F. Hockett, "A System of Descriptive Phonology" [11], *Language* 18.20–21 [112] (1942).

*Reprinted from *Word* 3.155–172 (1947) by permission.

sis in the traditional terminological cleavage between syntax and morphology in those characteristics of grammatical analysis which may be similar for both phases of the analysis. This terminology proves especially inconvenient, and is most likely to lead to error, in those languages in which no such basic structural dichotomy can readily be demonstrated.[2]

Altho Hockett held that he used "no grammatical fact of any kind" in his analysis, it appears to me that one must inevitably utilize—however unintentionally—facts which are linked so closely to grammatical phenomena that an attempt to separate completely a phonological analysis from a grammatical one proves impossible.

1. Field Procedure   The first fact to be noted, which indicates an essential relation between phonological and grammatical analysis, is that the field procedure of linguists in general is to conduct some grammatical research simultaneously with phonemic analysis. Hockett himself admits doing so:[1] "Analytical procedure is a trial-and-error process, in which the analyst makes successive approximations. He gathers phonological and grammatical material at the same time, tho he may emphasize now one, now the other. He makes errors of omission and commission, and later corrects them."

This dual research, I maintain, is essential, not accidental; phonemes cannot be analyzed without some knowledge—tho it may be very slight—of grammatical facts. Furthermore, it appears to me that one must assume that any elements of unavoidable procedure must in turn reflect something of the structure being analyzed. Generally used field procedures imply that phonemes can be analyzed only in reference to grammatical facts.

[2]On overlapping morphology-syntax nomenclature see K. L. Pike, "Taxemes and Immediate Constituents," *Language* 19.76 (1943); for a language without pronounced cleavage between morphology and syntax, see K. L. Pike, "Analysis of a Mixteco Text," *IJAL* 10.113–138 (1944), esp. 113, 125–128, 131–132; for problems in English, see *idem.* p. 128, fn. 8, and K. L. Pike, *The Intonation of American English*, University of Michigan Publications in Linguistics 1.81 (Ann Arbor, 1945). Also note M. Swadesh, "Nootka Internal Syntax," *IJAL* 9.77 ff. (1939) esp. 78: ". . . the combination of morphemes into a single word in a synthetic language has the same function as the juxtaposition of independent words in an analytic language."

B. Bloch and G. L. Trager[3] take a different view in saying: "The procedure by which we analyze the grammar of a language is in principle the same as that used in phonemics. Here again we examine a collection of utterances, list the recurrent fractions, and establish classes by grouping together parts of different utterances which are alike in form and function. Phonemic analysis must come first (cf. §3.2); for the utterance fractions listed and compared in grammatical analysis are not sounds but meaningful forms phonemically recorded."

Their assertion that phonemic analysis must come first is, indeed, partially true: A succint, adequate, complete statement of the grammar can only be given when the forms are presented phonemically; otherwise, many postulated minor "rules of grammar" might prove to be nothing more than statements regarding subvarieties of phonemes (allophones) where occurrences are determined by the phonetic environments as they change with substituted or added grammatical elements.[4]

If, however, one interprets their statement to mean that *no* grammatical analysis can precede phonemic analysis, or to mean that a *complete* phonemic analysis either *can* or *must* precede even a partial grammatical one (and these are implications of their statement as given), then serious errors are involved. Many of the most significant grammatical facts of a language can be deduced from a crude and inaccurate phonetic transcription: Morphemes can often be identified even by rough similarity in form and meaning; indeed, even accurate phonemic transcriptions sometimes show the morphemes in variant forms. Once the morphemes are identified, they can be grouped into major and minor form classes: into stems, affixes, and the like; into tenses, aspects, etc.; into words, compounds, or phrases; into structural layers of immediate constituents. Boundaries between morphemes, words, clauses, utterances and so on, may then usually be

[3]*Outline of Linguistic Analysis* 53 (Baltimore, 1942).

[4]It is to these difficulties which Bloch and Trager call attention in §3.2, referred to in the previous quotation. These facts are not sufficient, however, to justify their sweeping instructions to the beginner that *all* phonemic analysis be completed before *any* grammatical research be undertaken.

established. That is to say, many of the most important structural facts which differentiate two languages can be discovered from crude phonetic data, subject to some omissions if pertinent sounds are overlooked, or unnecessary complexity of form at those points where allophones, instead of phonemes, are transcribed.

These facts seem sufficiently pertinent, at least, to counterbalance somewhat the hyperbole of Bloch and Trager (*Outline* 39): "In short, a purely phonetic description makes it impossible to distinguish the really significant features of the vocabulary and the grammar from the accidental and personal features which inevitably form part of every utterance; as a scientific procedure it is about as fruitful as it would be for a biologist to assign two cats to different species because one had more hairs in its tail than the other." Hockett, however, (*Language* 18.20 [112]) admits that "Grammatical work is carried on, of course, in cases where phonological information is incomplete, either slightly deficient as it is for Old English, or sadly inadequate as for ancient Egyptian."

2. Identification of Morphemes The phonemic analysis cannot be completed until some initial grammatical steps are taken. Perhaps the most important of these is the identification of at least a limited number of morphemes. Thus Hockett,[5] and Bloch and Trager[6] utilize pairs of utterances which (1) have different meanings, and (2) are minimally different in their pronunciation.

Recognizing that the utterances are different in meaning is a grammatical process,[7] not a phonemic one. It is thus absolutely essential that a minimal grammatical identification be achieved before phonemic analysis can be carried on: the irreducible minimum

---

[5]*Language* 18.7 [102].

[6]*Outline* 38, 40.

[7]Hockett himself (*Language* 18.20 [112]) acknowledges this fact, without noting that it contradicts a statement in his succeeding paragraph to the effect that "no grammatical fact of any kind is used in making phonological analysis." He says: "The criteria for grammatical classification are (1) recognition of morpheme, word, and construction, and of borders between them, (2) the phonemic shape of morphemes, words, and constructions, and (3) biosocial function, or meaning; the third is used in determining the first."

prerequisite is that the investigator know enough about two items to be certain that they are "different." One might at first conclude that morpheme identification is a lexical problem instead of a grammatical one. This objection, in my opinion, is overruled by at least three facts: (1) Many morphemes, to be identified at all, must be studied in larger utterances, since they do not occur in isolation. In longer sequences the processes of grammatical comparison, and structural classification become very evident; the abstraction of these morphemes is not a mere listing of lexical items. (2) Even in situations commonly called isolation, morphemes must be abstracted, by processes of grammatical comparison of occurrences in the same or different practical situations, from a host of speech characteristics such as intonational modifications, variable voice qualities and the like. (3) Meanings can be determined only in context. The pertinent contexts may be practical (gestures and so on) or linguistic. Especially in matters of linguistic context, grammatical analysis must be used in finding the meanings.

The phonemic analyst must have some knowledge of when he is hearing repeated pronunciations of the same morpheme or sequence of morphemes. If this were not true, he might sometimes think he heard variation in the pronunciation of what he assumed was a single "word" whereas he had actually heard two different words with two different sound sequences. M. Swadesh evidently recognizes the need for knowing what constitute repetitions of the same word in such a methodological statement as:[8] "Except for word variants . . . different occurrences of the same word have the same phonemic make-up. If differences are observed in different pronunciations of the same word, these are to be taken as showing the range of deviation of the component phonemes." The identification of repetitions of a morpheme involves the grammatical segmentation of the utterances containing it.

Based upon this field procedure, is another highly important one even tho subject to abuse: the gathering of clues as to positional variation of a phoneme by noting the changes of a morpheme in different grammatical con-

---

[8]"The Phonemic Principle" [3], *Language* 10.123 [35] (1934).

texts. If, for example, a certain suffix ends in voiceless *l* when that morpheme comes at the end of an utterance, but ends in a voiced *l* when a further suffix is added to it,[9] the investigator assumes that *l* and *l* are submembers (or allophones) of a single phoneme unless or until he finds these two sounds in direct contrast elsewhere, in phonetically and grammatically analogous positions. There must be something wrong with present-day phonemic theory if workers agree on the practical value and validity of a procedure (and of evidence) in the field which they then rule out in theoretical discussion and in presentation.

Certain types of phonemic description require considerable grammatical knowledge— more than a mere differential knowledge of morphemes. An example is L. Bloomfield's "Stressed Vowels of American English,"[10] whose introductory summary describes it as a "Description of the stressed vowel phonemes of Central Western Standard-English as spoken in Chicago. The article possesses a more general interest as an example of the technique of analyzing phonemically the structure of a dialect." In giving a description "of the combinations in which the phonemes occur," the author states, for example: *"Type 1.* As the basis of our description we take morphologically simple one-syllable words ... *Type 1a.* Such combinations are made with suffixes and enclitics of the form [s, z, t, d], added without phonetic modification . . ." One should also note that Bloch and Trager (*Outline* 54) treat identification of free forms in their morphological analysis, not their phonemic one.

3. Contrasts in Utterance-Initial A field which receives wide usage,[11] tho not as much attention as word pairs, is the study of sounds in contrast at the beginning of utterances. At

the outset in the phonetic study of a language it is no arbitrary whim which dictates the observation of the sounds occurring at the beginning of utterances. Rather, at that place the analyst can be certain that he is at the beginning of a phoneme, of a syllable, of a stress or rhythm group, of an intonation contour, of a phonological sequence of some type. These facts eliminate some of the variables and uncertainties which he would inevitably face in the middle of an utterance. At no other place, except at the end of utterances, can he be certain, before he has studied the structure of the language, that he will find such dependable conditions.

By studying sounds at the beginning of utterances the analyst also knows that they are simultaneously at the beginning of a word, and at the beginning of a construction.[12] These positions are grammatical. By the mere focusing of his attention on the phonological characteristics at the beginning of utterances, the analyst does not thereby eliminate the grammatical characteristics at that same point. The value of utterance-initial position in phonological analysis is in part due to the potential influence of these grammatical units on the sounds, not just to the potential phonological conditioning factors. The assumption that one can treat utterance-initial sounds without being affected by grammatical relations seems therefore to be incorrect.

4. Junctures Now, what are so-called junctures? Are they phonemes in their own right, or are they special kinds of joints between phonological units, or are they joints between grammatical units with occasional phonological characteristics?

I cannot recall having seen a careful discussion of the problem.[13] I am under the impression, however, that some workers in the field are tending toward the conclusion that junctures are phonemes of some sort. Thus

[9]A situation existing in some of the Mayan languages, including Cakchiquel of Guatemala (data from W. C. Townsend). For a problem in which this type of evidence proves important, see N. Weathers, "Tsotsil Phonemes with Special Reference to Allophones of b," *IJAL* 13.108–111 (1947).

[10]*Language* 11.97–116 (1935).

[11]Note, for example, references in Bloch and Trager, *Outline* 40–41; also M. Swadesh, "A Method for Phonetic Accuracy and Speed," *American Anthropologist* 39.728–732 (1937), esp. p. 730, step 2.

[12]See K. L. Pike, *Phonemics, A Technique for Reducing Languages to Writing* 63–65 (Glendale, 1946). In that edition, as well as the editions of 1943 and 1945, I have presented phonemic techniques with reference to grammar.

[13]Hockett, however, states (*Language* 18.15 [108]) that "Junctural phones are not matters of grammatical segmentation, though a junctural situation may define phonological segments which are of grammatical significance."

junctures appear in lists of phonemes in the writings of Z. S. Harris,[14] C. T. Hodge,[15] and others.

If one wishes to treat junctures as phonemes, one must be ready to answer the following questions: Are junctures phonemes similar to segmental and prosodic ones? If not, how do they differ? If a juncture is a phoneme, can one describe its variant forms or indications as allophones? And how will one treat allophones of a juncture phoneme if they have nothing physically in common with each other, or if close "juncture" is phonetically zero?[16] Most important of all, what must be done when the analyst is convinced that a space should be written because of morphological parallels at a place where no known phonological justification exists for placing a "juncture phoneme"?

The last question is a serious one. At the moment, those investigators treating junctures as phonemes seem to be writing spaces at such points and calling them junctures, but postulating the existence of phonological data which they have as yet been unable to hear but assume—on grammatical grounds—that it must be there. Bloch, for example, says of Japanese:[17] "Pauses do not occur within a word: every pause marks a word boundary. On the other hand, many word boundaries are never marked by pauses. In our transcription we separate words by spaces, but these have no phonetic value." Since Bloch has claimed that phonemic analysis must precede a grammatical one, where does he obtain this morphological transcription? Since he states that only a phonemic transcription is constructive for grammatical description, why does he include nonphonemic—even nonphonetic—elements in his transcription?

Several other quotations can be given of a similar nature: Trager says of Taos,[18] "Word-division has here been determined by morphological criteria when the available phonemic description does not suffice."

W. E. Welmers says of Fanti,[19] "However, for practical purposes, since such junctures will always parallel morpheme boundaries, it may be pointed out that, in learning Fanti and most other languages, the recognition of morphemes proceeds more rapidly than the recognition of the minute phonetic details that may possibly be present to establish junctures in such cases . . . for the time being then, such junctures are written arbitrarily but without apology." This statement occurs in the paragraph immediately following one which begins thus: "It must also be pointed out that the establishment of phonemic junctures is independent of any considerations as to morpheme boundaries."

Harris, for Moroccan Arabic,[20] states that "The segments of various length (word, etc.) are not defined by the morphological terms used in this section, but by the points in which the junctures are placed, and the place of the junctures is in turn determined by the sound types in whose environment junctures are included." Contrast this quotation with others taken from the page immediately preceding it in the same article: "The junctures are not in themselves heard as sounds . . . We have to count as phonemic those junctures which are necessarily mentioned as environments of sound types which we consider automatic or include as positional variants of phonemes . . . it is only because we recognize a morpheme juncture after l 'the' that the u in [l-u̯ŭžh] 'the face' does not contrast with the u in [kursi] 'chair' . . . The advantage of these junctures is that in addition to helping set up successive (linear) and simultaneous (contour) phonemes, they also divide the flow of speech into morphologically distinct segments: morphemes, words, and the like."

For Kingwana-Swahili, Harris and F. Lukoff[21] likewise utilize some grammatical junctures, with attempted or implied phonemic justification for them: "In order to establish the tone-stress sequences, we have had to rec-

---

[14]"The Phonemes of Moroccan Arabic," *JAOS* 62.318 (1942).

[15]"Serbo-Croatian Phonemes," *Language* 22.112 (1946).

[16]Note, for example, Bloch and Trager, *Outline* 47—varieties of phenomena preceding and following open juncture.

[17]"Studies in Colloquial Japanese II: Syntax," *Language* 22.202 (1946).

[18]"An Outline of Taos Grammar" 189, *Linguistic Structures of Native America*, Viking Fund Publications in Anthropology 6 (New York, 1946).

[19]*A Descriptive Grammar of Fanti* 21 (Language Dissertation 39, Baltimore, 1946).

[20]*JAOS* 62.318.

[21]"The Phonemes of Kingwana-Swahili," *JAOS* 62.337 (1942).

ognize word juncture / # /. We may now recognize junctures which mark the boundary of utterance intonations . . . No other junctures have had to be recognized on phonemic grounds."

We must now ask ourselves the following questions: If phonemic analysis, including junctural phonemics, must be completed before grammatical analysis is begun, as Bloch and Trager imply, how does it happen that Bloch and Trager in analytical publications utilize junctures established by grammatical procedures instead of by phonetic data? If junctures are phonemes, and if the allophones of such a phoneme have some underlying phonetic characteristic, why is it that Trager and Welmers failed to find such characteristics and were forced to use grammatical ones? If, as Bloch implies, a phonemic analysis is the only convenient one for grammatical description, why do Harris, Lukoff, and Bloch himself write spaces bolstered by grammatical analysis?

If phonemic analysis is the most practical one as a background for grammatical description, there must be something amiss with any statement of phonemic theory (1) which must be abandoned in difficult spots, or (2) contradicted by actual field procedure, or (3) executed with dependence upon extremely obscure phonetic data which elude even expert observers and which are called upon to support junctures set up by other (grammatical) procedures rather than for serving those practical advantages claimed for phonemic transcription.

I am inclined to believe that, when research workers such as Bloch, Trager, and Harris fail to find phonetic data at these points, then (1) either no such data exist, or (2) the data are so obscure, and so minute, as to be below the threshold of useful signals for communication, or transcription by the analyst.[22]

What constitutes the mysterious element which forces investigators to write junctures in contradiction to their theories? In my opinion it is grammatical structure. Hockett asserts that, for phonological analysis and grammatical analysis, "The line of demarcation between the two must be sharp." Why? If it can be demonstrated that a grammatical approach to phonemics gives a simpler, easier, accounting for *all* of the *facts,* why should we follow an a priori separation of the two?[23] If language actually works as a unit, with grammatical configurations affecting phonetic configurations, why should we not describe the language and analyze it in that way? If forced to do so, why pretend we are avoiding it?

I conclude that in many languages certain grammatical units—say "words"—have as one of their characteristics the induction of subphonemic modification of some of the sounds. When modifiable sounds happen to occur at the borders of such units, the juncture becomes phonologically recognizable. If no modifiable sounds happen to occur at a grammatical boundary, the boundary is not phonetically perceptible but is nontheless present and just as important in the total structure of the language. The phonemics of a language, in other words, cannot be presented completely until something is known of the grammar, just as the grammar cannot be presented completely until something is known of the phonemics.

5.   Optional or Potential Phenomena   As a corollary of these statements I conclude that grammatical units such as words, or grammatical borders, may carry various potentials which are not actualized as phonetic data at every occurrence of these words or borders, but which are important to practical ortho-

---

[22]This does not completely eliminate the possibility of groupings of a physiological type, which at present elude us but which may ultimately be isolated in such a way that we can train ourselves to record them. R. H. Stetson (*Bases of Phonology* 57, Oberlin, 1945) says: "The foot includes one or more chest pulses, syllables, grouped by abdominal-diaphragmatic contraction of expiration. This is the movement which binds the syllables together and gives junctures and the main stress." Can this involve something in addition to what we respond to in writing stress, pause, intonation, and the like?

[23]Hockett (*Language* 18.9 [104]) sets up simplicity, under economy, as a criterion. In the following quotation from his writing (*Language* 18.15–16 [108]), simplicity seems to be on the side of grammatical, not phonological, definition (I have no description by Hockett, available to me at the time of writing, of a modern language as a whole): "Our phonetic information for Latin is defective, but it seems quite possible that the stress in early classical Latin was not an accent but part of a junctural phone. It can be located mechanically if certain borders are assumed. Grammatically these borders are clear, but without adequate material it is impossible to tell whether they were also phonological or not."

graphical symbolization of a language and to its phonemic analysis.[24]

Perhaps the most important of such potentials—long recognized and utilized by other workers, but not under the arguments presented in this paper—is the ability of certain grammatical items to occur as free forms. Such items are usually called words, and are frequently set off by spaces in the orthography.[25] The point I wish to emphasize here is that the potentiality of free occurrence remains in force even when the words are included in longer utterances, and that the grammatical unit is capable of affecting phonemic structure even tho it may not in every instance be phonologically definable or observable in terms of stress, characteristic clusters of sounds, or other objective phenomena. Presumably it is this potential which, in part, led Trager, Bloch, Welmer, and Harris to set up certain word junctures without phonological evidence, and to symbolize them with "phonemic" spaces in their orthographies.

In many languages it seems to be these word units which control the types of permitted sequences of phonemes or of the specific allophones which occur in various positions within the words. Thus M. Swadesh says,[26] "Each language has a characteristic word and syllable structure. Some of the limitations of occurrence of phonemes are best accounted for as connected with principles of word structure . . . The limits of the word are often marked in special ways . . . Such elements [e.g., aspiration, glottal stop, accent] are not phonemes, but mechanical signs of the limits of the word units."

A second type of potential which is highly important for English,[27] and possibly for some other languages, is that the end of an intonation contour may occur at the end of any word. The end of every word is potentially the end of such a contour whether the word is found in isolation or included in a longer phrase. Note the following set of sentences; the numbers indicate pitch from 1 as highest to 4 the lowest; the degree sign indicates the beginning of a primary contour, and the syllable carrying it is stressed; hyphens link the elements of a single total intonation contour; the accent mark indi-

cates innate lexical stress, which is reduced or eliminated unless a degree sign occurs with the same syllable—but syllables with accent mark and no degree sign are potentially stressed, so that the actual stress may reappear normally on that syllable at any time that the intonation is modified:

```
'Thomas  is  'coming, (but . . .)
 °2 -4-3 3-   °2 -4
'Thomas  is  'coming, (but . . .)
 °2-        -4 -3
'Thomas  is  'coming, (but . . .)
 °2 -4   °2-4  °2 -4
```

In the first sentence an intonation contour ends with the word *coming;* in the second, with the word *Thomas* as well; in the third, another contour is completed on the word *is.* The potential for a contour end existed on the words *Thomas,* and *is,* in the first two sentences as well as the third. This potential helps to establish grammatical junctures (word junctures in this instance) which are phonologically pertinent, even tho perhaps not phonetically marked, between the words in the first sentence in rapid speech.

Another type of pertinent potential may be illustrated with these same sentences: Pauses may optionally occur between words; usually, but not essentially, an intonation contour ends at every pause—but many contours end where no pause occurs. The intonation break is often accompanied by a change of speed. In the third sentence, repeated here, note the pauses, symbolized by a virgule:

```
'Thomas  is  'coming, (but . . .)
 °2 -4/  °2-4/  °2 -4/
```

These English potentials of permitted placement of pause and end of intonation contour normally occur at word ends. The potentials are lost in compound words.[28] This formulation eliminates the necessity of postulating a "compounding stress," which appears difficult to maintain in the light of occasional homophonous phrases and compounds.

A further kind of potential occurs in the illustration above, but does not seem to affect English junctures so directly: Lexical stress may be reduced considerably in intensity or, with sufficient speed of utterance,—reduced

[24]See my *Phonemics* 66–67.
[25]E.g., Bloch and Trager, *Outline* 54.
[26]*Language* 10.122 [35].
[27]See Pike, *Intonation*, esp. 78–88 and 29–39.
[28]See Pike, *Intonation* 79–88.

below the threshold of contrast perceptually discernable. Note, for example, loss of stress on the word *coming,* in the first sentence, if the word *Thomas* is heavily stressed. Nevertheless, if an intonation of the type seen in sentence two is then given to the utterance, the stress returns to the word *coming,* and—be it noted—reappears on the same syllable as before. This potential (for reappearance of stress on a specific syllable of a specific word) can be predicted only if the word is known from other contexts, or if the stress is not completely eliminated in the other pronunciations.

In a somewhat different analysis one may note that so-called "secondary stress" on words like *vaccination* may be (1) very weak or (2) nondetectable by auditory analysis, or (3) moderately weak, or (4) as strong as the primary stress. Even in the weak pronunciations, however, the potential remains for the recurrence of stress in other contexts.

So also various nonphonemic modifications of sounds, such as "drawling" of voiced consonants or vowels at word ends, are potentially but not essentially present. Likewise the phrase *an aim* may be phonetically distinct from the phrase *a name,* but optionally, or with rapid pronunciation, the phrases may be homophonous. If the grammatical juncture is symbolized with a space (and the options or potentials at such borders defined in a phonemic statement), the total admissible series of pronunciations is symbolized. If, however, one insists on writing a space only where phonetic criteria can be heard, the problem of the writing of the space would be complicated by the necessity to decide at what point the phonetic characteristics of the one juncture had faded into the other, or disappeared altogether. The failure to treat optional but normal pronunciations of various kinds is a deficiency in Bloch and Trager's discussion[29] of "internal open juncture."

6. Problems of Transcription It appears necessary to solve two problems before grammatical junctures can be utilized as such in phonemic analysis and presentation:

(1) How could a beginner, given a phonemic alphabet and a statement of allophones by an early worker in the field, take dictation in the language and write all the sounds and junctures, if the junctures are grammatical and at times reflect no positive phonetic characteristic?

The answer is: He could not. The beginner would have to be able to recognize some of the morphemes, and know something of the grammatical structure, before he could correctly leave spaces in places where phonetic clues were not present. But can he do any better with a phonologically defined set of juncture symbols if, as in the cases presented by Welmers and Trager, certain spaces are written morphologically in spite of the definition? The answer is again: No. If, however, phonetic phenomena characterize the presence of a certain juncture, the beginner has as good a chance to record it whether it is defined in terms of a "phonemic phrase"[30] with phonetic markers, or of a grammatical "word" with the same markers.

(2) If one uses grammatical units or their borders for the description and analysis of phonemes, which kinds of units must one use and symbolize? Morphemes? Words? Short constructions? Long constructions? Noun constructions? Verb constructions? Suffixes? Or what? And how can he know when he has symbolized enough kinds of grammatical units?

A partial answer: the analyst studies grammar and phonology simultaneously, allowing phonemic hypotheses to give him clues for finding grammatical facts, and grammatical hypotheses to give him clues for finding phonemic facts; grammatical analysis can be begun with phonetic data, and phonemic analysis can be begun with a small amount of grammatical data plus the phonetic data. He assumes that any specific phone is a phoneme in its own right unless he finds two similar sounds occurring in mutually exclusive phonetic environments, in which he concludes that they are allophones of a single phoneme and writes the two with a single phonemic symbol. Similarly, if two similar sounds are restricted to mutually exclusive grammatical environments, he concludes that they are members of a single phoneme; he then uses a single symbol, but he must also symbolize in some way the gram-

[29]"The Syllabic Phonemes of English" [9], *Language* 17.228 [76].

[30]Term used by Bloch and Trager, *Language* 17.226 [75].

matical environment causing the modification.

Three rules, related to the preceding statements, may help the beginning analyst:

(a) Phonemes must be defined, in so far as grammatically conditioned varieties are concerned, only in terms of those grammatical borders which are symbolized in some way —such as by space, or by hyphen.

(b) Symbols for grammatical borders should be utilized only for those types of junctures by which the analyst wishes to define subphonemic variation or for highly important nonphonetic potentials such as ability to occur in isolation.

(c) Once a certain kind of juncture is symbolized at one point in the language, the investigator must write that same symbol at every occurrence of the same kind of border, even tho no phonetic modification is there observed.

Experience seems to show that a fourth rule should be added:

(d) The investigator should avoid utilizing small or (even large) specific grammatical categories for these purposes. Altho one may conceive, for example, of a situation in which the symbolization of every noun in a way different from every verb would reduce the number of phonemes postulated,[31] this type of transcription should be avoided. I shall not attempt to state here the reasons which give rise to this practical conclusion. In any event, the previous rules hold: a noun-verb distinction must not be used for defining the environments of allophones unless the analyst is prepared to symbolize this distinction at every occurrence of a noun or a verb; such a symbol should not be set up unless needed for phonological reference; once used at all, the symbols must be used consistently thruout the language. It is because of the uncertainty with regard to rule number (d), that I have called this discussion a partial answer, only, to the last question proposed. When, however, the analyst (1) has accounted for all his phonetic data, (a) by symbols for the phonemes themselves, or (b)

by symbols for those grammatical junctures which modify the phonemes and produce subphonemic phonetic phenomena, and (2) has symbolized all highly important and widespread potentials such as possibility of occurrence in isolation, he needs no further analysis of the grammar for phonemic purposes.

7. Phonological Characteristics of Mixteco Morphemes

In previous sections of this paper I have affirmed that morphological units could affect phonemic units. I now wish to indicate several ways in which the Mixteco morpheme unit (a) is sometimes marked and (b) controls sequences of vowel phonemes.[32]

7.1 Every Mixteco morpheme in its full form consists of one of the following bisyllabic sequences (c represents a consonant, v a vowel, *n* nasalization of final vowel): cvcv, cv$^{\textrm{?}}$cv, cvv, cv$^{\textrm{?}}$v; cvcv*n*, cvv*n*, cv$^{\textrm{?}}$v*n*. Any medial consonant may be optionally but nonphonemically (noncontrastively) lengthened. If the listener hears a long consonant, he knows that he is at the middle of a morpheme, since such consonants do not occur elsewhere. If the consonant is extra long it signals general intensity or emphasis. In this form one might choose to analyze out a prosodic phoneme superimposed on the phrase. However, it is probably best treated as a type of socially significant gradation[33] rather than as a contrastive phoneme since there seems to be no line of demarcation between the normal and the emphatic lengthening.

The first syllable of any morpheme may optionally be marked by stress. The second syllable is never stressed. If the listener hears a stressed syllable he knows that he is at the beginning of a morpheme. The first syllable nevertheless, is not necessarily stressed; frequently I can detect no extra intensity on it whatever.

It is the morpheme unit which controls these two optional phenomena. When neither special length nor stress is present, the potential must still be symbolized by an indication of morpheme beginnings since the reader without such symbolization would tend to make

---

[31]Harris and Welmers considered and rejected such a possibility in "The Phonemes of Fanti" (*JAOS* 62.325): "If we could indicate by their form which words are verbs, we would not have to mark tones on them. However, it is not quite possible to make a phonemic distinction between verbs and nouns, for there are a few possible cases where the same form could be either . . ."

[32]I am discussing in these paragraphs morphemes of native origin only. Loan words introduce new sequences.

[33]See Pike, *Intonation* 98–99.

some syllables more intense than others but would frequently stress the wrong ones. This type of mispronunciation by foreigners frequently leads to misunderstanding by the natives.

The indication of potential initial stress and potential medial lengthening is complicated by the phenomenon of morpheme reduction, by which the basic two-syllable form is reduced to a monosyllabic proclitic or enclitic that attaches to another full morpheme. To set all morphemes apart equally by space would not show whether a reduced element goes with the preceding or following full morpheme, with consequent confusion of meaning. To place a stress mark at the beginning of every morpheme would misrepresent the facts by insisting on a feature that is frequently absent. My solution has been to use spaces and hyphens.[34]

7.2   Once the morpheme unit has been recognized in Mixteco, one finds that there are systematic restrictions in the sequences of vowels that may occur within it. The vowel sequences are correlated with the syllabic pattern of the morpheme, cvcv, for example, being less restricted than cv?vn. Contiguous sequences (as in cvv) are much more heavily limited than noncontiguous ones (as in cvcv), and the types found with final nasalization (cvcvn, cvvn, cv?vn) are more limited than corresponding types without nasal. There are also restrictions in consonant sets, but these have not yet been fully worked out. Also toneme sequences and sandhi changes of tone are not treated here.[35]

---

[34]See texts published in *IJAL* 10.113–138, 11.129–139, 219–224, 12.22–24. In *cuendu ñánga* [*Funny Stories*] (San Miguel el Grande, Oaxaca, Mexico, 1946), designed for native readers, I use hyphens to set off postclitics but spaces after proclitics; this cuts down the number of hyphens without creating ambiguity.

[35]For Mixteco tone, see Pike, *Tone Languages* (Glendale, 1945). The treatment of morpheme makeup as attempted here would be "morphophonemics" in Hockett's definition (*Language* 18.20 [112]): "the branch of grammar which deals with the phonemic shape of morphemes, words, and constructions, without regard to their meaning." However, Bloch and Trager (*Outline* 57) define morphophonemics as "the study of the alternation between phonemes in morphemes related to each other by internal change." The data given here were presented at Ann Arbor to

The six vowels, *i a u ə e o,* fall into two groups according to the freedom with which they occur in sequences within stems. The first three, forming the outer points in the vowel triangle, are relatively unrestricted. The second three, occupying inner points in the vowel triangle, are very considerably restricted. Examples illustrating all the sequences that occur in the different stem patterns are given below.

cvcv with unrestricted vowels: *?ini* 'to become late', *?ísá* 'day after tomorrow', *lítú* 'a kid'; *čáká* 'a fish', *kačì* 'cotton', *?añú* 'heart'; *žúžú* 'dew', *ⁿduči* 'bean', *žùča* 'river'. None lacking.

cvcv with one or two restricted vowels: *meke* 'brain', *žeha* 'craw', *lelu* 'lamb'; *səkə̀* 'back', *tə̀ka* 'grasshopper', *tə̀ñí* 'mouse', *ñìtə́* 'sand', *kata* 'shade', *kuta* 'short'; *sókó* 'a spring', *?oⁿdè* 'up to', *víló* 'lizard', *kʷažo* 'rubbish'. Some speakers add: *təku* 'for sewing'. Lacking sequences: *a-e, i-e, ə-e, u-e, e-i, o-i, e-ə, o-ə, e-o,ə -o, u-o, o-u.*

cv?cv with unrestricted vowels: *kʷi?ñì* 'a crack', *kʷi?nà* 'the devil', *či?ⁿdù* 'an oak ball', *sa?ma* 'cloth', *ka?ni* 'sweat' (from illness), *ña?mù* 'tuber', *su?nù* 'shirt', *ku?ni* 'to wring', *su?mà* 'tail'.

cv?cv with restricted vowels: *té?ⁿdé* 'torn', *ⁿdə̀?ži* 'a sore', *sə́?bə̀* 'a name', *kó?ⁿdó* 'frog'. Some speakers: *li?lò* 'rabbit'.

cvv with unrestricted vowels: *níí* 'you' (polite), *kʷià* 'year', *bìu* 'green sprout'; *náá* 'I' (polite), *kai* (short form of *kahi*) 'eat', *žau* 'century plant'; *ⁿdúú* 'both', *ⁿdua* 'arrow'. *cui* is lacking.

cvv with restricted vowels: *bèe* 'heavy'; *nə́ə́* 'whole', *hiò* 'griddle', *róó* 'you' (familiar).

cv?v with unrestricted vowels: *lí?i* 'rooster', *kʷi?à* 'expensive', *ⁿdi?ù* (or *ⁿdi?bù*) 'closed', *na?a* 'thatch pole', *ⁿda?ì* 'to cry', *bá?ù* 'coyote'; *žu?u* 'mouth', *ⁿdu?a* 'a plain'. *cu?i* is lacking.

cv?v with restricted vowels: *kʷe?è* 'illness', *sə́?ə́* 'female', *hí?o* 'spice', *žo?o* 'root'.

---

a summer meeting of the Linguistic Society of America about eight years ago. I have been able to add several specific vowel sequences which have since been discovered by my colleague, Donald Stark.

CVCV*n* with unrestricted vowels: *ⁿdihìn* 'wing', *ⁿdihàn* 'sandal', *tisùn* 'June bug', *kakàn* 'ask', *žahìn* 'gourd', *kasùn* 'to bake'; *čúkún* 'a fly', *a-ⁿduhìn* 'last year', *žuhan* 'dough'.

CVCV*n* with restricted vowels: *žə́kə́n* 'infantile', *ⁿdoson* 'breast'.

CV*ʔ*CV*n* does not occur at all.

CVVV*n* with unrestricted vowels: *sìin* 'side'; *čaàn* 'forehead', *taìn* [*tañì*] 'sweat' (from working); *tùun* 'feather'; others lacking.
CVVV*n* with restricted vowels: *ʔəən* 'one'.

CV*ʔ*V*n* with unrestricted vowels: *kiʔin* 'take', *síʔàn* 'eagle'; *saʔàn* 'doctrine', *saʔùn* 'fifteen'; *kuʔun* 'put on' (clothing); others lacking.
CV*ʔ*V*n* with restricted vowels: *səʔə́n* 'a post': also, as an alternate of *cuʔun, tòʔon* 'word'.

Examination reveals a considerable amount of patterning in the sequences that occur and fail to occur. Except for the two least frequent of the stem types ending in nasality (CVVV*n* and CV*ʔ*V*n*), there are occurrences for all stem patterns of: (a) all repeat sequences (*i-i, e-e,* etc.) both for outer and inner vowels; (b) all possible sequences of outer vowels (*i-a, i-u, a-i, a-u, u-i, u-a*). Sequences of inner vowels with each other are almost completely lacking: *o-e* in the morpheme *ʔoⁿde* 'up to' is the only case that has been found. The most usual combination of inner vowels is the repeat: *ə-ə, e-e, o-o.* No simple general rule for the occurrence of inner with outer vowels can be given. The vowel *e* is the most restricted of all, occurring only in *ceca.* No combinations of *o* with *u* are found; since the same is true of *e* with *i*, one can generalize to the extent of pointing out that (except for repeat sequences) no combinations of palatal with palatal vowel or of labial with labial vowel occur.

The different patterns of stem form can be graded from high to low in terms of the number of vowel sequences they admit. The pattern CVVV*n* shows the least number (only *a-i* in addition to repeat sequences, and even two of the latter, *ceen* and *coon,* are lacking). Slightly better is CV*ʔ*V*n*. Then follow CV*ʔ*V and CVV; then CV*ʔ*CV; and finally CVCV, with the greatest number of sequences. Using arrows to show the combinations that occur

(other than repeat sequences) and the order of the vowels, the following diagram shows the occurrences for the CVCV pattern. Since this is the type that has the maximum possibilities, the diagram at the same time can serve as the total for all patterns except for one item, *ciʔo.*

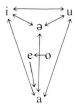

8. Summary Grammatical analysis of an initial kind is prerequisite to phonemic analysis.

Field procedures of necessity carry on grammatical and phonemic analysis more or less simultaneously.

Partial identification of morphemes is one of the grammatical prerequisites to phonemics; utilization of contrasts in utterance-initial position, so as to be certain of initial position in various grammatical units, is another.

The fact that the proponents of phonological juncture phonemes are by their own admission forced in their analytical work to symbolize many nonphonetic but grammatical junctures indicates that grammatical juncture should be one of the bases of phonemic analysis. Various optional phonetic phenomena need to be symbolized; these potentials are most readily indicated by symbolizing grammatical junctures. All grammatical junctures which are used as a basis for describing modification of sounds must be symbolized.

Mixteco morphemes show a highly organized phonological structure. The morpheme is marked by optional initial stress and optional length of medial consonant. In its phonemic make-up it is marked by a complicated series of permitted vowel sequences involving restricted and unrestricted vowels.

If a language structure is to be described realistically, the interweaving of grammatical and phonemic facts must not be ignored. A language system represents a structural whole which one cannot compartmentalize mechanically without doing violence to the facts.

A NOTE ON ZERO ALLOPHONES Since this paper was submitted for publication, two articles have appeared which suggest or utilize "zero allophones" of juncture and bearing closely on matters discussed in §4 of the present paper.

Thus Rulon S. Wells, in "Immediate Constituents," *Language* 23.108 (Apr.–June 1947), says in fn. 45, "If we could reckon the silence at the beginning and end of an utterance as one allophone of juncture, we would be justified in positing another allophone, a zero-allophone, which occurs for example in *night-rate*." It appears doubtful that such a solution would be completely consistent with his general phonemic approach, concerning which he says (*Language* 23.271, July–Sept. 1947), while reviewing *The Intonation of American English* (italics mine):

Phonemics takes the point of view of the hearer. Now the hearer, in order to interpret correctly an utterance that he hears, must rely on two separate sources of information: (a) the *heard sounds* (supplemented, it may be, by the sounds of previous or following utterances); (b) the extra-linguistic context (including his knowledge of what the utterance may or must mean). For the purpose of sharply distinguishing between what can be learned from one source and what can be learned from the other, phonemics makes a point of recording *nothing but what is conveyed by (a)*. All else belongs to grammar (and lexicography). This is why one wishes to avoid intersection (overlapping) in phonemics but not in grammar. And a fortiori, "potentialities" (as of stress to become totally suppressed, and of an intonation break or a pause to be inserted into a rhythm unit) are not indicated in a purely phonemic transcription. We do not say that phonemics and grammar must be separated, but only that the separation is feasible and serves the above purpose. . . . Pike's system of transcription is not purely phonemic. (1) Extra-phonemic information is sometimes required to determine the boundaries of his complexes, particularly the primary contours (§11). (2) Pike proposes (cf. §16, §26) to take morpheme boundaries into account in determining the stress phonemes.

Now Wells does not illustrate in detail how such a proposed zero allophone would work, so it may be that he ultimately would prevent its being written at any place except where phonological clues occurred preceding or following it. On the other hand, he might himself be tempted to write such zero allo-phones of juncture where the phonetic clues were zero, and thereby utilize the very procedure to which he elsewhere objects (*Language* 23.107): "The validity of juncture phonemes is open to grave doubts on phonetic grounds. Linguists find themselves tempted to institute 'junctures' simply as notational devices for reducing the number of phonemes." It is difficult to see how a strictly phonetic zero could be considered part of the "heard sounds" which Wells postulates as the only data pertinent to phonemics.

A more detailed treatment of proposed zero allophones is given in "Juncture in Modern Standard German" (*Language* 23.212–226, July–Sept. 1947) by William G. Moulton, following out a suggestion from Bernard Bloch (see p. 220, and fn. 13). "This segmental phoneme + has the following allophones: at the beginning or end of an utterance it appears as a pause of indeterminate duration: +'tail+, +ta'blet+; within an utterance it appears either as a pause of brief duration or, in *free variation with this* [italics mine, KLP], as zero: +'ʔan+ˌtra:t+, +ʔix,ʔantvorte+te'rase+." A similar statement is given on 223, Section 4.2; however a limitation is indicated later (225): "only the zero allophone occurs at morphological boundaries within words (usually only between the constituents of compound words)." By these statements, one might gather that the phonemic symbol + reflects a *potential* placing of pause, rather than actual phonetic data. Such symbolization of potentials must in turn reflect morphemic structure, since it is the morphemic or grammatical structure which controls such options.

Moulton gives a grammatical statement of the occurrence of the postulated phoneme (224): "The places where + occurs usually coincide with syntactic and morphological boundaries. The only exceptions are a few words (all of foreign origin) in which open juncture and onset of strong stress precede a voiceless stop or a vowel: +pa+'pi:r+ 'paper', . . . +ru:+'i:nen+ 'ruins', etc." In a fn. on 225 he asks, "Should we accept syntactic and morphological boundaries as part of our phonemic analysis if, by so doing, we can limit the scope of—or even avoid assuming—open juncture?" His answer is negative, as follows:

First—and this is a purely methodological reason—I believe that the phonemes of a language should be analyzed without reference to syntax or morphology. . . . Secondly, we could not do so successfully even if we tried, because of the cases (noted above [i.e., the words of foreign origin]) in which open juncture does not coincide with a syntactic or morphological boundary. Finally, it would seem that the phonetic marking of morphological and syntactic boundaries is more clearly described precisely by the assumption of open juncture.

The present paper implies that the first of Moulton's reasons is arbitrary and conceals, rather than reveals, total linguistic structure. The third line of reasoning is weakened by his occasional use of perplexing phrases such as that on p. 225: ". . . words which are not separated by a syntactic boundary . . ."—but, we ask, are not all words so separated, by definition? The second reason is serious, but one should hesitate to allow a small residue of words of foreign origin to prevent a general formulation, at least until vigorous attempts have been made to follow the analysis which otherwise would more easily represent the total grammatical-phonological structure of the language; possibly a descriptive expedient might be found which would preserve the easier formulation without doing violence to the facts.

Such an attempt is especially in order here when the difficulties of a residue from a grammatical approach are offset, in part at least, by difficulties of a residue within Moulton's nongrammatical approach. His Section 5 discusses the problem of a certain few items which do not follow the rules for distribution of allophones as he has set them up, but which might respond with less difficulty to an attempt to describe them in terms of grammatical rather than phonological junctures. In "the sequence r plus unstressed vowel," the "one phoneme behaves as if it were followed by a pause, but the following phoneme does not behave as if it were preceded by a pause . . . (In the speech of my informant, r behaves in this way at the end of any word or constituent of a compound word.)"

One other question should be asked of Moulton's material, for which I did not find an adequate answer within the article (but see his §4.31 for a partial answer): Does the "brief pause" "in free variation with [zero]" ever occur within the sentence at points where the preceding or the following sounds do not indicate its phonemic presence? That is to say, if aspiration, or glottal stop, or a fronted x, or some other marker is not present, but the zero allophone as a free variant of pause does so occur, then Moulton's entire structure falls. In any such instance the writing of the + for representing the zero allophone would be accompanied by no phonological mark of its presence; the reason for its occurrence would then be (1) the potential occurrence of the pausal allophone, or (2) a grammatical juncture. In either case, grammar would enter, since the potential for pause would be controlled by the morphemic structure.

An attempt to utilize grammatical junctures for the symbolization in his phonemic orthography would presumably have necessitated at least the following: (1) the writing of spaces between words; (2) the writing of hyphens within certain types of words, such as compounds; (3) the writing of a phoneme of pause at the time it actually occurred, especially in slow speech (but not when it was an unactualized potential),—and all spaces might be points of potential pause. If it be objected that this is more complicated than the writing simply of + to represent pause and nonpause, one may answer that we are not after simplicity first, but rather a representation of the structure of the language as it functions, whether the result be simple or complex.

BIBLIOGRAPHY 10
Grammar and Meaning versus Phonology

PIKE, K. L. (1944) "Analysis of a Mixteco Text"

PIKE, K. L., and E. V. PIKE (1947) "Immediate Constituents of Mazateco Syllables"

WELMERS, W. E. (1947) "Hints from Morphology for Phonemic Analysis"

VOEGELIN, C. F. (1948) "Distinctive Features and Meaning Equivalence"

JAKOBSON, R. (1949) "The Phonemic and Grammatical Aspects of Language and Their Interrelation"

SMALLEY, W. A. (1955) "A Problem in Phoneme Identification without Differential Meaning"

PIKE, K. L. (1958) "Interpenetration of Phonology, Morphology, and Syntax"

See also the following articles in this volume:

PIKE, K. L. (1947) "On the Phonemic Status of English Diphthongs" [14]

BLOCH, B. (1948) "A Set of Postulates for Phonemic Analysis" [16]

HOCKETT, C. F. (1949) "Two Fundamental Problems in Phonemics" [17]

PIKE, K. L. (1952) "More on Grammatical Prerequisites" [18]

BLOCH, B. (1953) "Contrast" [19]

ROBINS, R. H. (1957) "Aspects of Prosodic Analysis" [24]

LYONS, J. (1962) "Phonemic and Non-Phonemic Phonology" [25]

FROMKIN, V. (1965) "On System Structure Phonology" [26]

16

A SET OF POSTULATES
FOR PHONEMIC ANALYSIS*
BERNARD BLOCH

INTRODUCTORY

0.1 Leonard Bloomfield was the first to state explicitly some of the assumptions that underlie the methods of linguistic science; his formulation of these axioms in the second volume of *Language*[1] has remained for more than twenty years the only attempt of its kind. We may find it necessary now, in the light of recent theoretical discussions,[2] to make certain changes of detail in his list of assumptions; but the importance of his article as a contribution to linguistic theory is undiminished. Whoever undertakes, in future, to apply the postulational approach to linguistics, will find his task made easier by the model that Bloomfield has provided.

The validity of such an approach is best set forth in Bloomfield's own words:[3]

The method of postulates (that is, assumptions or axioms) and definitions is fully adequate to mathematics; as for other sciences, the more complex their subject-matter, the less amenable are they to this method, since, under it, every descriptive or historical fact becomes the subject of a new postulate.

Nevertheless, the postulational method can further the study of language, because it forces us to state explicitly whatever we assume, to define our terms, and to decide what things may exist independently and what things are interdependent.

Certain errors can be avoided or corrected by examining and formulating our (at present tacit) assumptions and defining our (often undefined) terms.

Also, the postulational method saves discussion, because it limits our statements to a defined terminology; in particular, it cuts us off from psychological dispute. Discussion of the fundamentals of our science seems to consist one half of obvious truisms, and one half

---

[1] Leonard Bloomfield, "A Set of Postulates for the Science of Language," *Language* 2.153–164 (1926). In December 1925, a paper of the same title was presented by Bloomfield at the second annual meeting of the Linguistic Society of America in Chicago (*Language* 2.73).

[2] The following works deal with phonemic theory: Leonard Bloomfield, *Language* 74–138 = Chaps. 5–8 (New York, 1933; reviewed by Kent and Bolling, *Language* 10.40–52); Edward Sapir, "La réalité psychologique des phonèmes" [2], *Psychologie du langage* 247–265 (Paris, 1933); Yuen Ren Chao, "The Non-Uniqueness of Phonemic Solutions of Phonetic Systems," *Bulletin of the Institute of History and Philology (Academia Sinica)* 4.363–397 (1934); Morris Swadesh, "The Phonemic Principle" [3], *Language* 10.117–129 (1934); W. Freeman Twaddell, *On Defining the Phoneme* (Language Monograph No. 16, 1935); Swadesh, "The Phonemic Interpretation of Long Consonants" [6], *Language* 13.1–10 (1937); N. Van Wijk, *Phonologie: een hoofdstuk uit de structurele taalwetenschap* ('s-Gravenhage, 1939; reviewed by

Trager, *Language* 16.247–251); N. S. Trubetzkoy, *Grundzüge der phonologie (TCLP* 7: Prague, 1939; reviewed by Harris [27], *Language* 17.345–349); George L. Trager and Bernard Bloch, "The Syllabic Phonemes of English" [9], *Language* 17.223–246 (1941); Bloch and Trager, *Outline of Linguistic Analysis* 38–52 = Chap. 3 (Baltimore, 1942; reviewed by Sturtevant, *Language* 19.42–44, and Emeneau, *JAOS* 63.208–209); Charles F. Hockett, "A System of Descriptive Phonology" [11], *Language* 18.3–21 (1942); Kenneth L. Pike, *Phonemics* (Glendale, Calif., 1943); Zellig S. Harris, "Simultaneous Components in Phonology" [12], *Language* 20.181–205 (1944); Rulon S. Wells, "The Pitch Phonemes of English" [13], *Language* 21.27–39 (1945); Pike, *The Intonation of American English* (Ann Arbor, 1945; reviewed by Wells, *Language* 23.255–273).

[3] *Language* 2.153–154.

---

*Reprinted from *Language* 24.3–46 (1948) by permission.

of metaphysics; this is characteristic of matters which form no real part of a subject: they should properly be disposed of by merely naming certain concepts as belonging to the domain of other sciences.

0.2 Bloomfield's fourth assumption and the definition based on it read as follows:[4] "Different morphemes may be alike or partly alike as to vocal features. . . . A minimum same of vocal feature is a *phoneme* or *distinctive sound.*" The criterion by which different morphemes are to be called alike is not mentioned, and cannot be inferred from the assumptions leading up to this one. Moreover, Bloomfield's view of the phoneme as a feature present in the sounds or soundwaves has been shown to be untenable,[5] and is no longer widely accepted among descriptive linguists. It will be useful, therefore, to re-examine those of our postulates that underlie phonemic analysis, and to state, so far as we can, the theoretical groundwork of its methods.

In attempting this task, we do not mean to offer any facts hitherto unknown, or to set up rules for the guidance of workers. Practical work in a science does not begin with a statement of postulates; rather, such a statement is a form of stocktaking: a pausing, at some crucial point in the development of a science, to look more closely into the substructure of its methods and to repair whatever logical flaws may appear in it.[5a]

That we have reached a crucial point in the development of phonemics is clear from the first published results of sound spectrog-

raphy.[6] The implications of the sound spectrograph for phonemics are of the utmost importance; and it may well be that when more linguists have worked with this machine and have published its answers to their questions, we shall have to abandon some of our present assumptions in favor of new ones to accord with newly discovered facts.

But a statement of postulates is more than merely stocktaking. As Bloomfield points out, it saves discussion, or at least puts discussion on a firmer basis. When our hitherto tacit assumptions have been put on paper and our terms have been defined, we may hope to escape a good deal of fruitless argument over differences in method. Two linguists will find either that they subscribe to the same set of postulates, or that they do not; and in the latter case they cannot argue profitably until they have compared their assumptions.

0.3 We shall try to state here some of the postulates—not all of them—that underlie the methods of phonemic analysis.[7] Our point of departure is the following definition of the phoneme, which most American linguists would probably accept at least as a basis for discussion:

A phoneme is a class of sounds in the utterances of a given dialect, such that (a) all members of the class contain a feature absent from all other sounds, (b) the differences among them are in complementary distribution or free variation, and (c) the class belongs to a set of

[4]*Language* 2.157, §15 and §16.
[5]Twaddell, *op.cit.* 17–25.
[5a]Compare the statement by Edna Heidbreder, *Seven Psychologies* 368 (New York and London, 1933): "Science, of course, is not above muddling through. Scientific practice often runs ahead of theory; it often proceeds unwittingly and unintentionally on assumptions that it discovers only after it has used them. But the justification for this procedure is that in the actual business of acquiring and interpreting its data, those assumptions eventually do come to light. Somewhere along the line there is a point where the scientist encounters recalcitrant facts that force him to examine the assumptions to which they refuse to conform. Such a point is always an important one in the development of science."

[6]See R. K. Potter, "Visible Patterns of Sound," *Science* 102.463–470 (1945) = Bell Telephone System Technical Publications, Monograph B-1368; R. K. Potter and others, "Technical Aspects of Visible Speech," *Journal of the Acoustical Society of America* 17.1–89 (1946) = BTSTP, Monograph B-1415; R. K. Potter, G. A. Kopp, and H. C. Green, *Visible Speech* (New York, 1947). In an unpublished mimeographed booklet of 58 pages, entitled *Basic Notions for Acoustic Phonetics*, Martin Joos has summarized a course of lectures given at the 1947 session of the Linguistic Institute, in which he developed some of the linguistic implications of sound spectrography. See now his new book, *Acoustic Phonetics* (Language Monograph No. 23, 1948).
[7]In arriving at the present formulation of these postulates, I have profited immeasurably from the criticisms and suggestions of many colleagues. I am especially indebted to Yuen Ren Chao, Charles F. Hockett, Henry M. Hoenigswald, Martin Joos, W. Freeman Twaddell, and—above all—Rulon S. Wells.

classes that are mutually contrasting and conjointly exhaustive.

By a sound we mean here any auditory fraction, of whatever length, that occurs as part of an utterance. This term and all the others in the definition will themselves be defined as we go on.

Our postulates are intended to state either empirical facts or what are assumed to be facts. They are *not* intended to delineate procedures, or to constitute a list of practical rules to be followed step by step in one's work with an informant. On the other hand, the methods of analysis by which linguists usually proceed in arriving at the phonemic system of a dialect are implied in these postulates and can be justified by them.

In our wording we shall avoid all semantic and psychological criteria. The implication is, of course, that such criteria play no part, or at least need not play one, in the theoretical foundation of phonemics. But we do *not* imply —in view of what has just been said—that appeals to meaning, or even (in desperate cases) to the informant's own judgment of like and unlike sounds, are therefore necessarily ruled out as practical devices in the actual work of making a phonemic analysis. The basic assumptions that underlie phonemics, we believe, can be stated without any mention of mind and meaning; but meaning, at least, is so obviously useful as a shortcut in the investigation of phonemic structure—one might almost say, so inescapable—that any linguist who refused to employ it would be very largely wasting his time.[8]

[8]Theoretically it would be possible to arrive at the phonemic system of a dialect entirely on the basis of phonetics and distribution, without any appeal to meaning—provided that in the utterances of the dialect not all the possible combinations of phonemes actually occurred. Given a sufficient sample of the dialect—say twenty or thirty hours of connected speech by an informant, recorded either on a high-fidelity machine or in a minutely accurate phonetic transcription—a linguist could probably work out the phonemic system without knowing what any part of the sample meant, or even whether any two parts meant the same thing or different things. (But he would need some kind of guarantee that every part of the sample meant *something*.) Whether his final description of the sample turned out to be an adequate description of the dialect as a whole would of

0.4 Postulates will be numbered serially throughout the set, from 1 to 57. For convenience in reading, they will be divided into twelve groups, each with a heading to serve as a mnemonic device, as follows:

   I. Dialect (1–4)
  II. Articulation (5–10)
 III. Segmentation (11–16)
 IV. Classification (17–20)
  V. Position (21–22)
 VI. Duration (23–24)
VII. Distribution (25–31)
VIII. Distinctiveness (32–43)
 IX. Congruence (44–46)
  X. Features (47–52)
 XI. Phonemes (53–54)
 XII. Order (55–57)

Each postulate is followed by the corollaries and the definitions that proceed from it, together with necessary comments and illustrations.[9]

From §21.1 to the end of the set, each postulate is to be read as beginning with the

---

course depend on how inclusive and how representative the sample was; but this would be true to some extent even if he followed the usual (and more sensible) method of asking what each part of the sample means.

It is worth noting that Daniel Jones's definition of the phoneme, for all its want of precision, is essentially non-semantic; see for instance *An Outline of English Phonetics*[3] 48, §191 (Cambridge, 1932). Especially striking is this passage, in *Le Maître Phonétique* 3.7.44 (1929): "An important point to notice is that the phoneme is essentially a phonetic conception. The fact that certain sounds are used in a language for distinguishing the meanings of words doesn't enter into the definition of a phoneme. It would indeed be possible to group the sounds of a language into phonemes without knowing the meaning of any words." Cf. Twaddell, *op.cit.* 25–27 and fn. 11.

[9]For the larger postulational framework of science in which the present set must be supposed to appear, see Twaddell, *op.cit.* 36 and 37. As for the precise number of postulates in any set, this is determined largely by stylistic considerations; for whether a given fact or complex of facts is to be covered by one postulate or by more than one depends at least in part on how easy it is to state the matter clearly in a single sentence. The number of our postulates could have been increased by dividing certain of them into two or more separate statements, or reduced by combining certain others into one.

words: "In any dialect"; except that each postulate marked with a dagger (†) is to be read as beginning with the words: "In any of certain dialects." The presence or absence of a dagger thus marks the distinction between those postulates that hold only for some dialects and those that are thought to hold for all.

I. DIALECT

1.1. Postulate 1 There are communities of human beings who interact partly by the use of conventional auditory signs.

Since our approach differs in some respects from Bloomfield's—chiefly in that Bloomfield invokes meaning as a fundamental criterion and arrives at his definition of the phoneme without stating in detail the intermediate assumptions that lead to it—we shall begin at the very beginning, instead of attaching our postulates to his. Our first assumption contains six undefined terms: community, human being, interact, conventional, auditory, and sign. The meaning of these terms is guaranteed for us by the sciences of sociology and psychology.

1.2. Definition Such a community is a *speech-community*.

1.3. Definition The totality of the conventional auditory signs by which the members of a speech-community interact is the *language* of the community.

1.4. Definition A member of a speech-community is a *speaker* of the language.

1.5. Definition The activity of a speaker in using a language or some part of it to interact with other members of a speech-community is *speech*.

1.6. Definition A single instance of speech is an *utterance*.

It is true that this definition, like Bloomfield's,[10] leaves the limits of an utterance completely vague, and therefore fails to tell us just how much of speech an utterance is supposed to include. For our purpose, however, the length or inclusiveness of utterances can be ignored. It makes no difference here whether the term "utterance" is taken to cover only the speech activity carried on between two respirations of a speaker, or the total speech activity carried on in the course of a day. We require

---

[10] "An act of speech is an *utterance*" (*Language* 2.154, §1). Here the term "speech" is used without a definition.

---

only that an utterance include less than *all* the speech activity of a given speaker; and so much at least is implied in our definition.

1.7. Definition The totality of the possible utterances of one speaker at one time in using a language to interact with one other speaker is an *idiolect*.

As Bloomfield says in a similar connection (*Language* 2.155, §4), we are obliged to predict; hence the word "possible." An idiolect is not merely what a speaker says at one time: it is everything that he *could* say in a given language. As for the words "at one time," their interpretation may safely vary within wide limits: they may mean "at one particular moment" or "on one particular day" or "during one particular year"; they are included in the definition only because we must provide for the fact that a speaker's manner of speaking changes during his lifetime. The phrase "with one other speaker" is intended to exclude the possibility that an idiolect might embrace more than one *style* of speaking: it is at least unlikely that a given speaker will use two or more different styles in addressing a single person.

Our definition implies (a) that an idiolect is peculiar to one speaker, (b) that a given speaker may have different idiolects at successive stages of his career, and (c) that he may have two or more different idiolects at the same time.

2.1. Postulate 2 The utterances of an idiolect are various arrangements of different auditory fractions, whose number is less than the number of utterances.

By an auditory fraction we mean any segment or stretch of sound that occurs as part of an utterance.

2.2. Corollary Some utterances contain auditory fractions that are the same.

Compare Bloomfield's first assumption: "Within certain communities successive utterances are alike or partly alike" (*Language* 2.154, §2).

This corollary and the assumption from which it proceeds are crucial; for they open the way to identifying parts of successive utterances. Bloomfield's phrasing does not tell us in what respect successive utterances are alike; his discussion states that the likeness lies partly in "vocal features" (auditory fractions), partly in "stimulus-reaction features" (meaning), but gives no clue to its essential character. In framing our present assumption, we have made the partial sameness of successive utterances depend on the fact that the utterances are more numerous than the different auditory fractions that compose them. While we grant that this sameness is no doubt ultimately a matter of biosocial equivalence,[11] we prefer to account for it here simply in terms of recurrent auditory fractions that are (by assumption) the same.

2.3. Definition The process of discovering the different auditory fractions of an idiolect and their different arrangements is *phonological analysis.*

2.4. Definition The totality of different auditory fractions in the utterances of an idiolect, and of their different arrangements, is the *phonological system* of the idiolect.

We use the word "phonological," rather than "phonemic," because the auditory fractions of which we are now speaking are not necessarily members of phonemes. They may be sections of any length—whole syllables or combinations of syllables at one extreme, "components" at the other:[12] we have not yet established the criteria for choosing fractions of the most useful dimensions. Accordingly, our definitions imply that phonological analysis can be carried on, and a phonological system arrived at, regardless of the length or complexity of the auditory fractions that we deal with—provided only that they satisfy the requirement of our second postulate in being less numerous than the utterances which they compose.

3.1. Postulate 3 In some speech-communities there are some speakers whose idiolects have the same phonological system.

In some communities, not necessarily in all. A language on the point of extinction may survive only in the speech of two or three persons, all speaking idiolects with different phonological systems.

3.2. Definition A class of idiolects with the same phonological system is a *dialect.*

This definition gives both a wider and a narrower meaning to the term "dialect" than it has in most linguistic discussions. In terms of it, speakers who differ in vocabulary and grammar may still speak idiolects belonging to the same dialect; while on the other hand, speakers who agree in all respects but some small detail of pronunciation will speak idiolects belonging to different dialects. Our intention is not to change the accepted meaning of the term "dialect," or to propose that the meaning here given to it be carried over into other discussions, but simply to define the term for our immediate use in the present context.

4.1. Postulate 4 Some languages include two or more dialects.

4.2. Corollary Phonological analysis of two idiolects belonging to the same dialect reveals the same phonological system.

This statement is not meant to exclude the possibility that two investigators, working with two speakers of the same dialect, and both following the procedures implied in the present set of postulates, may arrive at very different formulations of the phonological system which they discover. However, such formulations will always be mechanically convertible, one into the other, and will therefore be scientifically equivalent.[13]

4.3. Corollary Phonological analysis of a given idiolect does not reveal the phonological system of any idiolect belonging to a different dialect.

This, of course, is why the investigator finds it wise, in the early stages of his work with a new language, to concentrate on a single informant. The introduction of a second informant, before the phonological system of the first one's idiolect is known at least in part, is always a possible source of confusion.

4.4. We might insert here another postulate, to read as follows: The phonological analysis of any dialect is possible in the present state of our knowledge and equipment. We must, of course, assume this to be true; for if it were not, we should have no warrant for proceeding any further. However, such a postu-

---

[11]See Hockett, *Language* 18.5–6 [101–102], §4–§4.4.

[12]On components as parts of single sounds, and on their possible value in phonological analysis, see Harris, *Language* 20.186–201 [118–130], §3.0–§5.5.

[13]The possibility of different but equally valid formulations of a phonological system is the point of the article by Chao, *Bulletin of the Institute of History and Philology (Academia Sinica)* 4.363–397.

late would be on a different level of assumption from all the others, and would not form a link in the chain of statements leading to our final definition of the phoneme.

II. ARTICULATION

5.1. Postulate 5 Every utterance is an auditory event produced entirely by movements and positions of some or all of the following organs in a speaker's body: the lungs, together with the diaphragm and the other muscles that control them, the larynx, the vocal cords, the arytenoid cartilages, the pharyngeal musculature, the faucal pillars, the velum, the uvula, the buccal walls, the lower jaw, the tongue, the teeth, and the lips.

This postulate, as well as the three that follow, is taken over from the domain of practical phonetics.

5.2. Definition Each of these organs, or any part of one of them that moves independently during an utterance, is a *vocal organ.*

5.3. Definition Collectively, all of these organs and their parts are the *vocal apparatus.*

5.4. Definition Each movement or position of a given vocal organ during an utterance is an *articulation* of that organ. An organ performing an articulation is said to *articulate.*

5.5. Definition Collectively, the simultaneous articulations of all the vocal organs are a *phonation.*[14]

6.1. Postulate 6 Some successive articulations of each of the vocal organs are the same.

Throughout this paper, the term "successive" is applied to events that occur at different times. If two events follow one another without the intervention of another event belonging to the same class, we call them "immediately successive."

6.2. Definition Successive phonations composed wholly of the same articulations are *the same.* Other successive phonations are *different.*

7.1. Postulate 7 Two or more phonations that are the same produce the same auditory result.

7.2. Corollary Any difference between utterances or between parts of utterances is due to a difference in the articulation of one or more of the vocal organs.

8.1. Postulate 8 Some different phonations produce the same auditory result.

8.2. Definition Such phonations are *equivalent.*

The fact of equivalent phonations is well known to phoneticians, and has been recently confirmed in the laboratory.[15]

8.3. Corollary Every utterance can be uniquely identified in terms of articulations.

If some fraction of an utterance is of the kind that can be produced by two or more equivalent phonations, that part will still be uniquely identified by naming any of the phonations that can produce it. The articulations in terms of which an utterance is identified are therefore not always necessarily the articulations by which it was actually produced.

8.4. Definition The identification of an utterance or of any part thereof in terms of articulations is *phonetic description.*

9.1. Postulate 9 An observer can be trained to make a phonetic description of the utterances of any dialect, or of a sufficient sample thereof, without the aid of laboratory devices, that will be adequate and valid for the purposes of phonological analysis.

In a sense this postulate is on the same level as the one mentioned in §4.4; but it forms an important link in our chain and must therefore be included. Essentially, the postulate means that our present methods of pursuing phonological (specifically phonemic) analysis are sound: that a linguist can be trained to hear all that he needs to observe in his informant's speech; that he needs to rely only on his ears and eyes; and that his results will have scientific value even if he records only a

---

[14]I take this term from a forthcoming monograph by R. S. Wells, to be entitled *History of the Phoneme Concept* [never published—VBM].

[15]In an experiment conducted at the 1947 session of the Linguistic Institute (cf. fn. 6), the sound spectrograph produced nearly identical records for two "retroflex" or "*r*-colored" vowels (as in *bird*) pronounced by the same speaker—one formed with simultaneous raising of the tongue tip toward the middle of the hard palate, the other formed without such raising but with retraction and lateral spreading of the main body of the tongue. The differences between the two spectrograms were well below the threshold of audibility; and a group of trained observers agreed that they could detect no difference between the two sounds as heard.

sampling of all the possible utterances that his informant might make.

9.2. Definition Any part of an utterance is *perceptible* if an observer so trained can identify it in terms of articulations; and any articulation is *perceptible* if he can identify in terms of it some part of an utterance. Other parts of an utterance and other articulations are *non-perceptible.*

In practice, a trained observer—if his training qualifies him to make a phonological analysis, as we have assumed—will be able to identify at least some component of every auditory fraction in the utterances of his informant: there will be no fraction, of whatever length, in which there is nothing at all that he can identify as the product of one or more articulations. But there are sure to be components among the "gross acoustic features" that he cannot thus identify—either because he has failed to observe them, or because he does not know how they were produced. In terms of our assumptions, such unidentified components of auditory fractions can safely be neglected: if it were essential, for the purposes of phonological analysis, to identify them in terms of articulation, they would be among the parts of an utterance that we have assumed to be perceptible.

It might be supposed that a pause—a "moment of silence"—would be a fraction of the kind that we have excluded: one in which there is nothing at all that an observer can identify in terms of articulation. We prefer to regard a pause, however, as produced by the total absence of articulations, and therefore as falling outside the class of auditory fractions in the stricter sense; see Part V below. Another kind of "silence"—the kind that occurs during the formation of a voiceless stop—is of course easily identified in terms of articulation.

Our use of the term "perceptible" refers to the observer's perception, not to the speaker's. We assume, of course, that the observer will hear at least as much of the "gross acoustic features" as the speaker does, and probably more; and that his description of the phonological system of the dialect will turn out to coincide, more or less, with whatever statements about it the speaker might make intuitively. But this assumption—essentially a profession of faith in the biosocial validity of our analyses—need not be included as a separate formal postulate.

10.1. Postulate 10 Some articulations of some vocal organs are non-perceptible.

10.2. Corollary Some vocal organs perform both perceptible and non-perceptible articulations.

We need not separately assume that some articulations are perceptible, since this is clearly implied by Postulates 5 and 9.

The articulations of the velum are perceptible throughout the utterance *mitten* ['mɪtn̩]; that is, there is something in the utterance at every point that a trained observer can identify as the result of a certain position assumed by the velum. During the [m] and the [n̩] (perhaps also during the first part of the [ɪ]) the velum is lowered; during the [ɪ] (or the last part of it) and the [t], the velum is raised. On the other hand, the articulation of the velum is non-perceptible at one point of the utterance *mitten* ['mɪʔn̩] pronounced with a glottal stop instead of [t]: during the formation of the glottal stop, there is nothing in the utterance that the observer can identify as the result of any position of the velum, whether lowered or raised. Similarly, the articulations of the tongue tip are perceptible in many parts of an utterance, but not, for example, during the formation of the [p] in *dumpcart.*[16]

III. SEGMENTATION

11.1. Postulate 11 The series of perceptible articulations of any given vocal organ during an utterance can be divided without a residue into successive parts such that each part occupies the time-interval during which the organ (a) remains in one position without perceptible movement, (b) moves without perceptible change of acceleration or direction, or (c) is set into vibration by a passing air current.

Note that we are speaking of perceptible

[16]The phonetic transcriptions in this paper are not intended to be full or accurate recordings of any real utterances; in other words, they are not really transcriptions at all, but abstractions from possible transcriptions. The phonetic symbols have the values usually assigned to them. We follow in this paper the practice introduced in *Language* 17.229 [76] and now generally accepted, of placing phonetic symbols between square brackets, but phonemic symbols between diagonals.

articulations only; we assume nothing here about non-perceptible articulations.

Phoneticians have long known that the movements of the vocal organs from one "position" to another proceed by continuous, uninterrupted flux; that in fact the concept of "position" has no basis in physiological reality, and that each movement of an organ flows imperceptibly into the next. This was demonstrated as early as 1936 by the Janker-Menzerath X-ray motion pictures;[17] recently it has been still more graphically shown in spectrograms of connected speech (cf. fn. 6). Such instrumental data, however, need not be taken as evidence that speech *as perceived* cannot be segmented; every phonetician has had the experience of breaking up the smooth flow of speech into perceptibly discrete successive parts. In Postulate 11 we do not imply that the vocal organs assume static positions or move in unidirectional ways at constant acceleration; rather, we imply that a phonetically trained observer can interpret the auditory fractions of an utterance in terms of articulations that seem (to his perception) to be static or unidirectional.

11.2. Definition Such a part is a *phase* in the articulation of the organ.

11.3. Corollary A non-perceptible movement or position of an organ is not a phase.

11.4. Corollary Some phases in the articulation of some organs are separated by movements or positions that are not phases.

12.1. Postulate 12 Some phases in the articulation of some vocal organs are not separated by any non-perceptible movements or positions of those organs.

12.2. Definition A point of time at the beginning or at the end of a phase in the articulation of a given organ is a *change-point* in the articulation of that organ.[18]

Such a point may be the boundary between two contiguous phases, or between a phase and an interval of non-perceptible movement or position that is not a phase.

12.3. Definition A fraction of an utterance between any two immediately successive change-points is a *segment*.

The change-points that define the limits of a segment may both be change-points in the articulation of the same organ, or they may be change-points in the articulation of two different organs. Change-points in the articulation of the same organ define the limits of a segment only if the time-interval between them does not include any change-point in the articulation of some other organ.[19]

Throughout this paper, the term "segment" will be used to denote a particular fraction of a particular utterance—an event unique in time and space. This meaning of the term should be borne in mind when we come to define the various kinds of similarity among segments, and to call certain segments in various respects "the same" (§16.2, §23.6, §42.5), and especially when we adopt the convention, in §24.2, of using the term to denote any of a class of segments sharing certain characteristics.

12.4. Corollary Every utterance consists wholly of segments.

Segments, as we have defined them, are one of the possible kinds of auditory fractions that we spoke of earlier; accordingly, they fulfill the requirements of our second postulate, which might now be restated as follows: The utterances of an idiolect are various arrangements of different segments, whose number is less than the number of utterances. Cf. §20.4 below.

12.5. Corollary Some segments are perceptible.

In view of our scholium to §9.2, it is doubtful that any segment will be non-perceptible; but all that follows logically from our assumptions is that *some* segments, at least, will be perceptible. From this point on we shall

---

[17]See Paul Menzerath, "Neue Untersuchungen zur Wortartikulation," *Actes du IVe congrès international des linguistes* 67–75 (Copenhagen, 1938); and cf. Menzerath and A. de Lacerda, *Koartikulation, Steuerung und Lautabgrenzung* (Berlin and Bonn, 1933).

[18]See Hockett, *Language* 18.5 [101], §3.3.

[19]Our segments are thus established by a different method from Pike's; see his book *Phonetics* 107–120 and *passim* (Ann Arbor, 1943). We define segments by first defining their boundaries; Pike defines them by concentrating on their centers. His definition: "A *segment* is a sound (or lack of sound) having indefinite borders but with a center that is produced by a crest or trough of stricture during the even motion or pressure of an initiator . . ." (107). The terms in this definition are defined earlier in his book.

use the term "segment" to designate only perceptible segments.

Segments are said to occur in utterances; utterances are said to contain segments.

12.6. Definition An uninterrupted succession of two or more segments is a *sequence*.

12.7. Definition A sequence of only two segments is a *dyad*.

Dyads, then, are a subclass of sequences. Our reason for defining this term is that we shall have use for it later on, whereas we shall not need additional terms like "triad," "tetrad," or the like.

12.8. Definition A succession of two or more segments interrupted by one segment or dyad is a *disjunction*.

Again our reason for defining this term, and for defining it in just this way, is that we shall need it later on. Note that a disjunction consists of two segments or sequences with a gap between them to accommodate the interrupting element (a segment or dyad): if *ABCDEF* is a sequence, then *A...CDEF*, *A...DEF*, *AB...DEF*, *AB...EF*, *ABC...EF*, and *ABC...F* are disjunctions, but *A...EF* and *AB...F* are not.

As a matter of practical convenience, we shall apply the term "disjunction" also to a segment or sequence that immediately precedes or follows such a gap, even when there is no other segment or sequence on the other side of the gap to complete the disjunction. Thus, we shall sometimes apply the term to a succession like *ABCDE...* or *ABCD...* or *...BCDEF* or *...CDEF*, when for some reason we are more interested in the gap than in the surrounding segments.

13.1. Postulate 13 Some synchronous phases in the articulation of different vocal organs are not coterminous.

Restated in less forbidding terminology, this means that one phase in the articulation of some one organ may overlap in time with part or all of several phases in the articulation of some other organ; or (still more simply), phases in the articulation of different organs may overlap instead of exactly coinciding.

For example, the phonation (§5.5) of the utterance *Come back* [ˌkʌm'bæk] includes three phases in the articulation of the velum: (1) raised position for [kʌ], (2) lowered position for [m], (3) raised position for [bæk]; and

at least three phases in the articulation of the lips: (1) opening to a certain aperture for [kʌ], (2) closure for [mb], (3) opening to a different aperture for [æk]. The second phase in the articulation of the velum (lowered position) begins—let us suppose—at the same time as the second phase in the articulation of the lips (closure), but ends much sooner, while the lips are still closed. The lowered position of the velum is therefore synchronous with the closure of the lips, but not coterminous with it. If the vowel in *come* is nasalized, the lowering of the velum overlaps in time with both the first and the second phase in the articulation of the lips: it begins before the lips have closed, and ends before they have opened again.

13.2. Definition Any phase or fraction of a phase that is coterminous with a given segment is an *aspect* of that segment.

An aspect of a segment is a complete phase only if the limits of the segment are defined by the change-points at the beginning and end of that phase—in other words, if the change-points that define the limits of the segment are both change-points in the articulation of the same organ (cf. §12.2, §12.3). Otherwise an aspect of a segment includes only so much of a given phase as coincides with the segment in time.

Reverting to the example in §13.1, let us suppose that the [m] in *Come back* is a segment, and that the vowel in *come* is not nasalized. One of the aspects of the segment [m] is then a *complete* phase in the articulation of the velum; for this phase—the lowered position of the velum—begins and ends at the same times as the segment itself. Another aspect of the segment [m] is a *fraction* of a phase in the articulation of the lips; for this phase—the closure of the lips—begins at the same time as the segment itself but continues after the end of the segment.

13.3. Corollary Some aspects are fractions of whole phases; but no aspect is more than a single phase.

The second clause of this corollary follows from the fact that two phases in the articulation of a given organ are (by definition) separated by a change-point, and every change-point marks the beginning or end of a segment.

13.4. Corollary The perceptible phonation of every segment consists wholly of aspects.

Aspects are said to occur in segments; segments are said to contain aspects. We adopt this terminology for convenience, in spite of the fact that aspects are not properly parts of segments but of phonations: segments are auditory units (fractions of utterances), aspects are physiological units (articulations or parts of articulations).

In speaking of aspects, we shall say that an aspect is *defined* by a given vocal organ, or by a given articulation, or by both together. Thus, the segment [m] contains an aspect that is defined by the lips, or by the position of closure, or by closure of the lips.

Not only the articulations of the lips, the tongue, the velum, and the vocal cords are to be stated in terms of aspects, but also such "qualities" as pitch and stress. The aspect of pitch in a given segment is defined by the position of the arytenoid cartilages, which control the tension of the vocal cords and hence their rate of vibration; the aspect of stress is defined by the motion of the diaphragm and the other muscles that control the lungs.

13.5. Definition Aspects defined by the same articulation of the same vocal organ are *the same;* other aspects are *different.*

On "same articulations" see §6.1. In determining whether two aspects are the same or not (in the sense just defined), we disregard their temporal duration. The subject of longer and shorter segments will be treated in Part VI below.

13.6. Definition Any number of aspects contained in a single segment, from one to one less than the totality of aspects in that segment, is a *combination.*

Therefore, when we speak of a combination we shall mean one or more of the aspects contained in a given segment, but not *all* the aspects contained in it. Two or more combinations are the same if they consist wholly of aspects that are the same (§13.5).

13.7. Corollary Some successive segments (including some immediately successive segments) contain combinations that are the same.

We shall say that such segments contain a combination in common.

The interrelationship of phases, aspects, combinations, and segments can perhaps be clarified by an ideal diagram. Let us suppose that the phonation of a certain utterance consists of the articulations of only four vocal organs (identified simply as A, B, C, D), and that each of these organs performs only two different kinds of perceptible articulation. The accompanying diagram represents the articulations of the four vocal organs by lines on a horizontal time-scale: for each organ, a straight line represents one kind of perceptible articulation, a wavy line represents the other kind; a dotted line represents an interval during which the articulation of the organ is nonperceptible. The phases and the non-perceptible intervals are identified by small letters. As

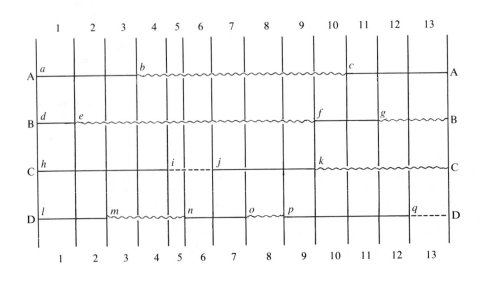

the diagram shows, the phonation of this utterance includes three phases in the articulation of organ A (*a, b, c*) four phases in the articulation of B (*d, e, f, g*), three phases in the articulation of C (*h, j, k*), and five phases in the articulation of D (*l, m, n, o, p*); in addition, there are two intervals (*i* and *q*) during which the movement or position of C and D respectively is non-perceptible.

The utterance is divided into segments (numbered 1–13) by drawing a vertical line through every change-point—i.e., through every point at the beginning or end of a phase. Of the thirteen internal change-points in the utterance (excluding those at the beginning and at the end), only two are simultaneous: the boundary between phases *e* and *f* coincides in time with the boundary between *j* and *k*. Except for the dividing line between segments 9 and 10, therefore, every such line is determined by only a single change-point.

Segments 1–4 and 7–12 contain four aspects each; segments 5, 6, and 13 contain only three; for the two intervals *i* and *q* are not phases, and therefore cannot be aspects either. Each aspect is represented by the part of a horizontal line that lies between two verticals. Only two of the aspects shown in the diagram consist of whole phases: the second aspect of segment 1 (reading down from the top) and the fourth aspect of segment 8; all the other aspects consist of parts of phases.

Combinations can be read from the diagram by taking together any set of lines or fractions of lines representing aspects in the same segment—for instance, in segment 1, by taking the first alone, or the first and second, or the second and third and fourth, and so on.

Note, finally, that the segments are shown to occupy time-intervals of different lengths. At this point in our discussion, such differences are irrelevant: each of the segments in the diagram is co-ordinate with every other.

14.1. Postulate 14 If a given vocal organ defines an aspect in one segment, the same organ defines an aspect also in some other segment.

14.2. Corollary No vocal organ articulates only once in producing the utterances of an idiolect.

15.1. Postulate 15 Some vocal organs articulate in two or more perceptibly different ways.

15.2. Definition Each of the perceptibly different ways in which a given vocal organ articulates is an *articulation type* of that organ.

Among the articulation types of the tongue tip are closure, as for [t, d, n]; raising to form a groove-shaped aperture, as for [s, z]; raising to form a slit-shaped aperture, as for [θ, ð]; raising to form an arch- or crescent-shaped aperture, as for [ɹ]; and raising to form a contact in the median line with lateral opening, as for [l].

15.3. Definition Different aspects defined by the same vocal organ are *homorganic*.

It follows from this definition that we do not apply the term "homorganic" to two or more aspects that are the same (§13.5). Combinations are homorganic if they consist wholly of homorganic aspects; thus, the combination consisting of labial closure and lowering of the velum in [m] is homorganic with the combination consisting of labial aperture and raising of the velum in a bilabial spirant [v].

15.4. Corollary No segment contains two or more homorganic aspects.

15.5. Corollary Some segments contain one or more aspects that are not matched by any homorganic or identical aspects in some other segments.

This follows from §10.2, §11.3, §11.4, and the diagram in §13.7. The segments that compose the utterance *mitten* ['mɪtn̩] all contain an aspect defined by the velum; but the glottal stop in ['mɪʔn̩] contains no such aspect.

15.6. Corollary Some segments contain different numbers of aspects.

16.1. Postulate 16 No segment contains a totality of aspects that does not occur as the totality of aspects in some other segment.

That is, no segment is unique in its phonation; no phonation is used only once by a speaker. Cf. §14.2.

16.2. Definition Segments containing the same totality of aspects are *organically same;* other segments are *organically different.*

We must qualify the words "same" and "different" by some adverb, because we have not yet taken account of possible differences in duration. See Part VI below.

16.3. Corollary Immediately successive segments are organically different.

16.4. Corollary The number of organically different segments in the utterances of any idiolect is finite, and less than the number of utterances.

Compare Postulate 2 and its corollary (§§2.1, 2).

IV. CLASSIFICATION

17.1. Postulate 17 The lower lip and some parts of the tongue articulate by touching or approaching the upper lip, the upper teeth, various parts of the hard and soft palate, and the rear wall of the pharynx.

Another assumption based on the findings of practical phonetics.

17.2. Definition The lower lip and such parts of the tongue as articulate independently are *primary organs*.

17.3. Definition The parts or surfaces of the upper jaw and the pharynx that are touched or approached in the articulations of primary organs are *points of articulation*.

Just as we say that an aspect is defined by a given vocal organ, or by a given articulation, or by both together (§13.4), so we may say that an aspect is defined by a given point of articulation, when such a point is mentioned in a complete description of the aspect. Thus, the aspect of tongue-tip raising in English [ɹ] is defined by the alveolar ridge (or the forward part of the hard palate, etc.).

18.1. Postulate 18 The articulation types of any primary organ form an ordered series according to the width of the aperture between the organ and a point of articulation.

On the term "articulation type" see §15.2.

18.2. Definition The place of each articulation type in such a series is its *rank*.

The highest rank in each series is that of the articulation type characterized by the smallest aperture—the limit of aperture being zero, i.e., complete closure. Articulation types characterized by successively wider apertures have successively lower ranks. Thus, among the articulation types of the tongue tip (§15.2) the highest rank is assigned to the closure seen in [t, d, n], and the lowest rank to the so-called position of rest seen in [æ] or [a].

Homorganic aspects defined by a primary organ are said to have ranks corresponding to the ranks of the articulation types that also

define them. Aspects not defined by a primary organ have no rank.

19.1. Postulate 19 Some different primary organs have some articulation types that are the same.

Since this is an assumption, the sameness of different articulation types requires no proof. It is this assumption that underlies our habit of calling both [p] and [k] stops, both [f] and [x] spirants, both [i] and [u] vowels, and so on.

19.2. Definition Aspects defined by the same articulation type of different primary organs are *homotypical*.

An aspect is not, by this definition, homotypical with itself. Examples of homotypical aspects: closure of the lips in [b] and closure between the tongue tip and the palate or teeth in [t]; raising of the lip to form a slit-shaped aperture in [f] and raising of the back of the tongue to form a (slit-shaped) aperture in [x].

19.3. Corollary No two aspects are both homotypical and homorganic.

Homorganic aspects are defined (§15.3) by different articulation types of the same vocal organ; homotypical aspects are defined (§19.2) by the same articulation type of different organs.

19.4. Definition If the aspects of highest rank in two organically different segments are homotypical, the segments are *homotypical*.

19.5. Definition If the aspects of highest rank in two organically different segments are homorganic, the segments are *homorganic*.

19.6. Definition If the aspects of highest rank in two organically different segments are the same, the segments are *both homotypical and homorganic*.

Pairs of homotypical segments: [p] and [k], [f] and [x], [i] and [u]; pairs of homorganic segments: [p] and [f], [k] and [x], [i] and [e]; pairs of segments both homotypical and homorganic: [p] and palatalized [p'], [t] and [n], clear [lᵢ] and dark [lᵤ] (as in *let* and *tell* respectively), [a] and nasalized [aⁿ]. On the other hand, palatalized [p'] and palatalized [s'] are neither homotypical nor homorganic, even though the front of the tongue is raised in both; for the aspect defined by this organ is not the aspect of highest rank in either segment. Similarly, a nasal consonant [m] and a nasalized vowel [aⁿ] are neither homotypical nor homorganic, even though the velum is lowered in both; for the velum is not a primary organ (§17.2), and hence aspects defined by the velum have no rank (§18.2).

20.1. Postulate 20 Of the segments that compose the utterances of an idiolect, not all are homotypical with each other, and not all are homorganic with each other; but there are some segments that are homotypical, and some that are homorganic.

That is, no dialect is known in which all the sounds are stops (or spirants, or vowels, etc.), or in which all the sounds are labials (or dentals, or velars, etc.). On the other hand, no dialect is known in which there is only one stop, one spirant, one vowel, etc., or only one labial, one dental, one velar, etc.

20.2. Definition Any vocal organ, articulation type, or point of articulation that defines a given aspect is a *component* of that aspect and of the segment in which the aspect occurs.

20.3. Corollary If two segments are homotypical or homorganic or both, they contain at least one component in common; but some segments that are neither homotypical nor homorganic also contain one or more components in common.

Thus, palatalized [p'] and palatalized [s'], though they are neither homotypical nor homorganic (§19.6), contain a number of aspects in common (raising of the front of the tongue, raising of the velum, voicelessness, etc.) and hence also a number of components.

20.4. Corollary Every aspect, every segment, and hence every utterance can be described wholly in terms of components.

Components, then, like segments (§12.4), are one of the possible kinds of auditory fractions mentioned in our second postulate.[20]

V. POSITION

21.1. Postulate 21[20a] Some utterances contain a perceptible time-interval during

---

[20]Harris, *Language* 20.181–205 [12]. A description of a phonological system in terms of components is attempted by Hockett, "Componential Analysis of Sierra Popoluca," *IJAL* 13.258–267 (1947); but what Hockett there calls "components" are rather what in the present paper we call aspects.

[20a]As announced in §0.4, each postulate from this point on is to be read as beginning with the words: "In any dialect"; except that each postulate marked with a dagger is to be read as beginning with the words: "In any of certain dialects."

---

which none of the vocal organs perceptibly articulates.

21.2. Definition Such a time-interval is an *internal pause*.

By simply assuming that some utterances contain internal pauses, we escape the necessity of deciding how long an interval of silence may intervene between two parts of the same utterance, and hence of distinguishing between one utterance and several immediately successive utterances.

21.3. Definition The absence of speech before or after an utterance is an *external pause*.

21.4. Definition Any fraction of an utterance between two immediately successive pauses (internal or external) is a *phrase*.

21.5. Corollary Every utterance contains an integral number of phrases, and every phrase contains an integral number of segments.

We can now abandon the rather vaguely defined term "utterance" (§1.6), and use instead the term "phrase" to designate a unit with unambiguously defined limits.

21.6. Definition The serial order of a given segment *X*, reckoned as the number of segments intervening between the preceding pause and *X*, or between *X* and the following pause, or both, is the *position* of *X* in the phrase.

A segment is said to fill a position.

21.7. Definition The serial order of a given sequence *XYZ*, reckoned as the number of segments intervening between the preceding pause and *X*, or between *Z* and the following pause, or both, is the *position* of *XYZ* in the phrase.

A sequence, like a segment, is said to fill a position. As a graphic shortcut, a sequence *XYZ* filling a given position *P* will be written as *XYZ(P)*.

21.8. Corollary Two segments or sequences occurring in phrases that contain the same number of segments, and separated from the preceding (or following) pause by the same number of intervening segments, have the same position in the two phrases.

22.1. Postulate 22 Some phrases contain different numbers of segments.

22.2. Definition Two segments or sequences occurring in phrases that contain different numbers of segments, and separated from the preceding pause (or from the following pause) by the same number of intervening segments have *the same position* in the two phrases *relative to the beginning* of the phrase (or *relative to the end* of the phrase).

22.3. Definition   Other segments or sequences (not covered by the provisions of §21.8 or §22.2) have *different positions*.

VI. DURATION

23.1. Postulate 23   †Some organically same segments filling the same position in successive phrases occupy time-intervals of noticeably different length.

The expression "noticeably different" implies that the difference is great enough to be noticed by a trained observer without the aid of mechanical measuring-devices (cf. §9.1).

23.2. Definition   Such segments *differ in duration*.

23.3. Definition   If two segments differ in duration, the longer contains an *aspect of duration* that is absent from the shorter.

For the purpose of this paragraph and the other paragraphs in Part VI, the expression "aspect of duration" is to be taken as a unit term, not as the name of a special kind of aspect as previously defined (in §13.2). Note that aspects of duration, unlike aspects in the ordinary sense, are relative: they are discoverable only by comparing the segments in which they occur with certain other segments from which they are absent.

The second segment in *bid* (i.e., the vowel) is noticeably longer than the one in *bit;* and in some dialects of English the second segment in can_1 'tin' is noticeably longer than the one in can_2 'is able'. Since the vowels in *bid* and *bit* and the vowels in can_1 and can_2 respectively are organically same, we say that the vowels in *bid* and can_1 contain an aspect of duration that is absent from the vowels of *bit* and can_2. (The fact that the difference in duration between can_1 and can_2 is on a different footing from the difference between *bid* and *bit* plays no part in the definition here proposed for aspects of duration. It will be dealt with later, in §42.4.)

23.4. Definition   If three or more segments all differ in duration, each one except the shortest contains a separate *aspect of duration* that differentiates it from all the others.

This provision applies to languages where it is necessary to distinguish two or more degrees of length as opposed to short sounds.

23.5. Definition   If two segments each contain an aspect of duration but do not differ in duration from each other, they contain *the same aspect of duration*.

The long vowel in *bid* contains the same aspect of duration as the long vowel in *rib* or *fig;* and it contains the same aspect of duration as the long vowel in can_1 'tin' or the long vowel in *balm*. Segments need not be organically same in order to contain the same aspect of duration; all that is required is that each of them contain an aspect of duration and that they do not differ in duration from each other, in the sense defined in §23.1.

23.6. Definition   Organically same segments containing the same aspect of duration or containing no aspect of duration are *phonetically same;* other segments are *phonetically different*.

23.7. Corollary   All phonetically same segments are organically same, but not conversely; and all organically different segments are phonetically different, but not conversely.

23.8. Definition   Two sequences, phrases, or utterances composed wholly of phonetically same segments in the same positions are *phonetically same;* two sequences, phrases, or utterances not so composed are *phonetically different*.

24.1. Postulate 24   Some organically different segments, and some organically same segments filling different positions in a phrase or in successive phrases, occupy time-intervals of noticeably different length.

24.2. Definition   Such segments *do not differ in duration*.

That is, we shall not regard them as differentiated from each other by the presence or absence of what we have called an aspect of duration: their difference in length is simply irrelevant. This provision allows us to disregard, for example, the fact that in American English the vowel [æ] is usually longer than other vowels in comparable surroundings, and that [m] and [n] are longer at the end of a phrase than at the beginning. To differ in duration (as we have here defined such a difference), two segments must be organically same and must fill the same position in successive phrases.

N.B.—From this point on, the term "segment" will be used to designate any of a class of phonetically same segments; an expression of the form "the segment X" will denote either a particular X or any other segment that is phonetically the same as X. (Compare §12.3, end.) Also, the term "aspect" will henceforth include both aspects as previously defined (in §13.2) and aspects of duration.

VII. DISTRIBUTION

25.1. Postulate 25 Some phonetically same segments occur in phonetically different phrases.

25.2. Corollary Some phonetically same segments occurring in successive phrases are immediately preceded, or immediately followed, or both immediately preceded and immediately followed, by two or more phonetically different segments or sequences.

The segment [m] in the phrases *come* and *home* is preceded by [kʌ] and by [how]; in the phrases *mitten* and *mutton* it is followed by [ɪtṇ] and by [ʌtṇ]; in the phrases *coming* and *hammock* it is preceded by [kʌ] and by [hæ], followed by [ɪŋ] and by [ək].

25.3. Definition If A and B are given segments or sequences (except that one of them may be zero), P is a given position in the phrase, and X is a segment or dyad occurring in the sequence $AXB(P)$, the disjunction $A...B(P)$ is an *environment* of X.

For the term "disjunction" see §12.8; for the writing $AXB(P)$ see §21.7.

In the phrase *hammock*, the segment [m] has an environment [hæ...ək] or [hæ...ə] or [æ...ək] or [æ...ə]: all four of these disjunctions are environments of [m]. In practice, one of them would no doubt be chosen in preference to the rest as the crucial or essential environment of the segment in this phrase; the choice will depend on which one turns out to be most useful in comparing the environments of different segments.[21]

In the phrase *come*, the segment [m] has an environment [kʌ...] or [ʌ...]; here the B of our definition is zero (i.e., nothing). In the phrase *mitten*, the segment [m] has an environment [...ɪtṇ] or [...ɪt] or [...ɪ]; here the A of our definition is zero.

[21]It would of course be possible to frame special postulates to cover such a choice, but we shall not attempt the task here. See the first sentence in §0.3.

If X and Y are phonetically different segments or dyads occurring in the sequences $AXB(P)$ and $AYB(P)$, they both have an environment $A...B(P)$. In such a case we say that X and Y have the environment $A...B(P)$ in common, or that the disjunction $A...B(P)$ is a common environment of X and Y. Thus, in the phrases *mitten* and *mutton* the segments [ɪ] and [ʌ] have the environment [m...tṇ] or [m...t] in common; in the phrases *inner* and *under* they have the environment [...n] in common.

If the disjunction $A...B(P)$ is an environment of X and if the sequence $AB(P)$ also occurs without X, the segment or dyad X is said to have the environment $A...B(P)$ in common with zero; that is, both X and zero (= nothing) occur between A and B in the position P. For example, in the phrases *smash* and *sash*, the segment [m] has the environment [s...æš] in common with zero.

25.4. Definition If X is any member of a given class of phonetically same segments or dyads, one or more of the environments in which X occurs is a *set of environments* of X.

The disjunctions [hæ...ək] and [...ɪtṇ] are a set of environments of the segment [m], and so also is either of these disjunctions alone. The set can be enlarged by adding other environments in which [m] occurs—i.e., in which a segment phonetically the same as the [m] of *hammock* or *mitten* occurs: [kʌ...], [s...æš], etc.

26.1. Postulate 26 †There are phonetically different segments that have no environment in common.

26.2. Definition Such segments are in *complementary distribution* with each other.

In English, the segments [h] and [ŋ] are in complementary distribution with each other, because there is no environment in which both of them occur. Occasionally two segments will appear to have some of their environments in common, if the environments in which they occur are stated merely in terms of immediately preceding and following sequences; but will prove to be actually in complementary distribution, if the description of their environments is expanded so as to include a differentiating segment or sequence that is not contiguous with the segments in question. Thus, the segments [u·] and [ü·] in pre-English are in some phrases immediately preceded and immediately followed by the same sequences, and hence appear to have some of their environments in common—for instance in *[mu·s] 'mouse' and *[mü·si] 'mice'; but if we state the environments of [u·] and [ü·] in such a way as to include the following vowel, the two segments turn out to be in complementary distribution: [ü·] occurs only in environments that contain the segment [i] or [j] in the following sequence, [u·] occurs only in environments that do not contain such a segment.[22]

26.3. Definition If such segments contain a combination or a component in common and different residual combinations or components, the latter are *in complementary distribution* with each other.

For the term "combination" see §13.6; for the term "component" see §20.2.

The segments [h] and [ŋ], mentioned above, contain no aspect and no component in common. On the other hand, there are several pairs of segments in English that are in complementary distribution with each other and at the same time contain one or more aspects in common. Thus, voiceless [L] occurs after initial [p] and [k], as in *please* and *clean,* and in some dialects also after initial [s] and [f], as in *sleep* and *fleece,* and in some other environments; voiced [l], on the other hand, never occurs in precisely these environments. Voiceless [L] and voiced [l], then, are in complementary distribution with each other. But the two segments contain a combination in common: in both, the tongue tip is raised to form a closure in the median line with lateral opening, the back of the tongue (let us suppose) is slightly raised toward the soft palate, and the velum is raised. The residual combinations by which they are differentiated from each other consist of only one aspect each: separation of the vocal cords (voicelessness) in [L], vibration of the vocal cords (voicing) in [l]. Accordingly, we say not only that the two segments [L] and [l] are in complementary distribution with each other, but also that in these segments the aspects of voicelessness

and voicing are in complementary distribution with each other.

27.1. Postulate 27 †There are phonetically different segments that have all their environments in common.

27.2. Definition Such segments are *in free variation* with each other.

Many American speakers pronounce words like *sit, pin, fist,* etc., indifferently with the vowel [ɪ] and with a slightly lower vowel, approaching in quality the vowel of *set* and *pen* but remaining everywhere distinct from it: in any environment where they pronounce the one, they will also sometimes pronounce the other. In such a dialect, the two segments, higher and lower [ɪ], therefore have all their environments in common, and are accordingly in free variation with each other.

27.3. Definition If such segments contain a combination or a component in common and different residual combinations or components, the latter are *in free variation* with each other.

There are speakers of American English who pronounce words like *ram, ran, rang,* and also words like *rat, cab, fast,* indifferently with an oral vowel [æ] and with a weakly nasalized vowel [æⁿ]. The two segments are thus in free variation with each other; but they contain a combination in common: in both, the lips are open to a certain degree and somewhat spread, the tongue tip is "at rest" behind the lower front teeth, the front of the tongue is slightly raised toward the hard palate, and the vocal cords are in vibration. The residual combinations by which they are differentiated from each other consist of only one aspect each: raised position of the velum (oral articulation) in [æ], lowered position of the velum (nasalization) in [æⁿ]. Accordingly, we say not only that the two segments [æ] and [æⁿ] are in free variation with each other, but also that in these segments the aspects of oral articulation and nasalization are in free variation with each other.

The same is true of the aspects of lip-rounding and lip-spreading in two kinds of [u] in the speech of many Japanese.

28.1. Postulate 28 †If *A* and *B* are given segments or sequences (except that one of them may be zero) and *P* is a given position in the phrase, there are phonetically different

---

[22]This is, of course, a grossly oversimplified statement of the situation, but it will serve as an example. Cf. Bloomfield, *Language* 381, §21.7 (New York, 1933); W. F. Twaddell, "A Note on Old High German Umlaut," *Monatshefte für deutschen Unterricht* 30.177–181 (1938).

segments X and Y occurring in the environment $A...B(P)$, such that for every phrase containing the sequence $AXB(P)$ there is an otherwise phonetically same phrase containing $AYB(P)$, and conversely.

28.2. Definition Such segments are *in free variation* with each other in the given environment.

The customary statement is that two segments are in free variation in a certain environment if successive occurrences of the same word show sometimes one segment, sometimes the other, without any difference in meaning.[23] But in terms of our postulates up to this point we do not know what is meant by "the same word," and in any case we have undertaken to frame these postulates without invoking semantic criteria (§0.3). Now if it is true that certain pairs of segments alternate with each other in successive occurrences of the same word regardless of the larger environments in which the word is used, then obviously the provisions of our present postulate are an adequate statement of the situation: if a given word is pronounced indifferently with X and with Y, then—provided we take a sufficiently large sample of the idiolect under investigation—any phrase containing the word in its X variant will be matched somewhere in the record by an otherwise identical phrase containing the word in its Y variant, and conversely. It is granted, of course, that in practical work with an informant one can hardly hope to accumulate a collection of utterances large enough to exclude the danger of incompleteness in this respect, and that a direct appeal to meaning is a more efficient way of establishing free variation than the painstaking scrutiny of the record implied in our postulate; but such practical considerations do not affect the theoretical groundwork which it is our present purpose to establish.

In some varieties of American English the segments [k] and [t] are in free variation with each other when they occur initially before voiceless [ʟ], e.g., in *clear, clean, class,* etc., all pronounced by speakers of these dialects indifferently with [kʟ-] and with [tʟ-]. Again, many speakers pronounce words like *milk, elk, welcome,* etc., indifferently with a

tongue-tip lateral [l] and with a totally different sound—a lateral formed by raising the back of the tongue to touch the soft palate in the median line with an opening at the side. In such dialects the tongue-tip lateral and the tongue-back lateral are not in free variation with each other everywhere; for in words like *let, fellow, tell,* etc., only the tongue-tip sound occurs. Rather, the two segments are in free variation with each other only in a particular environment, namely, [...k].

28.3. Definition If such segments contain a combination or a component in common and different residual combinations or components, the latter are *in free variation* with each other in the given environment.

In the illustration of §27.3, we referred to speakers in whose idiolects the segments [æ] and [æⁿ] are in free variation with each other in all their environments. More numerous, however, are speakers who pronounce these two segments in free variation only before a nasal consonant, in words like *ram, ran, rang* (not also in words like *rat, cab, fast*). In the speech of these persons, the aspects of oral articulation and nasalization in [æ] and [æⁿ] are in free variation with each other only in the set of environments [...m, ...n, ...ŋ].

29.1. Postulate 29 †There are phonetically different segments that are in free variation with each other in a given set of environments E, and also occur elsewhere, but that have no environments in common except the set E.

29.2. Definition Such segments are *partially in complementary distribution, partially in free variation* with each other.

This is the situation in some dialects of British English with respect to the voiced frictionless continuant [ɹ] and the voiced alveolar flap [r]: only the continuant occurs initially, in words like *red, roof, rain,* and after initial voiced stops, in words like *brain, drain, grain;* and only the flap occurs after initial [θ], in words like *three, throw, through;* but both segments occur, in free variation with each other, between vowels, in words like *very, carry, spirit.* In such dialects we say that [ɹ] and [r] are partially in complementary distribution, partially in free variation with each other.

29.3. Definition If such segments contain a combination or a component in common

---

[23]For instance in Bloch and Trager, *Outline of Linguistic Analysis* 42, §3.4.

and different residual combinations or components, the latter are *partially in complementary distribution, partially in free variation* with each other.

To illustrate this we have only to modify the example in §26.3—in other words, to choose a slightly different dialect of English. Let us suppose that in some dialect voiceless [L] occurs after initial [p] and [k], voiced [l] occurs initially and after the voiced stops [b] and [g], and both occur, in free variation, after initial [s] and [f]:[24] the words *please* and *clear* always contain [L], the words *lead, bleed,* and *glee* always contain [l], but the words *sleep* and *fleece* contain sometimes [L], sometimes [l]. Then the aspects of voicelessness and voicing in these two segments are partially in complementary distribution, partially in free variation with each other.

29.4. Definition Two or more segments, combinations, or components that are (a) in complementary distribution with each other, (b) in free variation with each other, or (c) partially in complementary distribution, partially in free variation with each other, are said to be *non-contrastive* with each other.[25]

30.1. Postulate 30 There are phonetically different segments that have some but not all of their environments in common, and are not in free variation with each other.

30.2. Definition Such segments are *in contrast* with each other in their common environments.

The segments [ɪ] and [æ] have many environments in common, e.g., [p'...n] in *pin* and *pan,* [s...l] in *silly* and *salad,* [...kt] in *ictus* and *actor;* but each has certain environments where the other does not occur, e.g., [w...š] and [f...lθ] as environments of [ɪ] in *wish* and *filth,* [f...ð] and [θr...ks] as environments of [æ] in *fathom* and *anthrax.* Since the two segments are not in free variation anywhere, we say that they are in contrast with each other in those environments where they both occur.

31.1. Postulate 31 †There is a segment that has some but not all of its environments in common with zero, but is not in free variation with zero.

31.2. Definition Such a segment is *in contrast with zero* in their common environments.

The segment [m] has the environments [s...æš] and [li...p] in common with zero in the phrases *smash* and *sash, limp* and *lip;* but only [m] occurs in the environment [kʌ...ɪŋ] (*coming*), and only zero occurs in the environment [š...ɪp] (*ship*). Accordingly, we say that the segment [m] is in contrast with zero in those environments where they both occur.

VIII. DISTINCTIVENESS

32.1. Postulate 32 †There is a segment that occurs in a set of environments where it is not in contrast with any other segment or with zero.

32.2. Definition Such a segment is *determined* in such a set of environments.

The word "determined," as here defined and as used throughout this paper, is equivalent to "non-distinctive" or "non-significant."

It is customary to base the difference between distinctive and non-distinctive sounds on meaning: to say, for instance, that any interchange of distinctive sounds will affect the meaning of a word or phrase, while any interchange of non-distinctive sounds will leave the meaning unaffected.[26] But a definition based on absence of contrast (in the sense defined in §30.2 and §31.2) covers exactly the same cases that are covered by the customary semantic definition, and fits better into our set of postulates.

The following four postulates (33 to 36) deal with special instances of the general situation defined above.

33.1. Postulate 33 †There is a segment that is in free variation with zero in some or all of its environments.

Although we have not formally defined free variation with zero, the meaning of this phrase is clearly implied by the statements in §25.3, §27.2, and §28.2. The implication can be made explicit as follows. A segment *X* is everywhere in free variation with zero if it

---

[24]Once again an oversimplified statement will serve as an example. We have not, of course, listed here all the environments in which the two segments [l] and [L] occur.

[25]This term is adopted from Hockett, "Problems of Morphemic Analysis," *Language* 23.328, §8 (1947).

[26]For instance in Bloch and Trager, *op.cit.* 38, §3.1.

has all its environments in common with zero; it is in free variation with zero in an environment *A...B(P)* if for every phrase containing *AXB(P)* there is an otherwise phonetically same phrase containing *AB(P)*, and conversely.

33.2. Definition Such a segment is *determined* in the environments where it is in free variation with zero.

Two examples from American English dialects. (1) Some speakers occasionally use a glottal stop initially before vowels, in phrases like *Oh!, Outside!, Eat it!, All of them,* but also pronounce the same phrases without this segment. Since the glottal stop occurs nowhere in this dialect except in this one set of environments, it is in free variation with zero wherever it occurs, and therefore is everywhere determined. (2) Many speakers pronounce words like *dance, fence, mince,* and also words like *pants, tents, hints* indifferently with [-nts] and with [-ns]: the environment [n...s] at the end of a phrase is common to both [t] and zero. Accordingly, the segment [t] is determined when it occurs in this particular environment.

34.1. Postulate 34 †There are phonetically different segments that occur in free variation with each other in a set of environments where they are not in contrast with any other segment or with zero.

34.2. Definition Every such segment is *determined* in such a set of environments.

Some speakers, especially in New York and other metropolitan centers, pronounce words like *cat, sit, bet* indifferently with a weakly aspirated final [-t'], with a strongly aspirated final [-t^h], with an affricated final [-t^s], and with an unreleased final [-t]: The segments ['], [^{h}], [^{s}] are in free variation with each other and with zero. Accordingly, each of these segments is determined when it occurs in this environment.

35.1. Postulate 35 †If *A* and *B* are given segments or sequences (except that one of them may be zero) and *P* is a given position in the phrase, there is a segment *X* occurring in the sequence *AXB(P)* such that the sequence *AB(P)* does not occur without *X*, and that no other segment than *X* occurs in the environment *A...B(P)*.

35.2. Definition Such a segment *X* is *determined* in the given environment.

In Japanese there is a palatalized [t'] (phonetically different from non-palatalized [t]) that is always followed by [š]: the sequence [t'ša], for example, occurs, but not the sequence [t'a] and not any sequence in which some other segment than [š] intervenes between the [t'] and the [a]. In such an environment, then, the segment [š] is determined.

36.1. Postulate 36 †If *A* and *B* are given segments or sequences, *P* is a given position in the phrase, and *H* is a class of phonetically different but homotypical segments, there is a segment *X*, not homotypical with any member of the class *H*, occurring in the environment *A...B(P)*, such that the sequence *AHB(P)* occurs also, but that the sequence *AB(P)* does not occur without either *X* or some member of the class *H*.

For the term "homotypical" see §19.2 and §19.4.

This postulate is included as an example of the rather specialized assumptions that are sometimes required to cover situations in particular languages.

36.2. Definition Such a segment *X* is *determined* in the given environment.

In Japanese the sequence [ts] occurs only before [u]: there is [tsu] but not [tsa, tse, tso]; moreover, the sequence [tu] does not occur. We cannot apply to this case the postulate of §35.1, because it is not true that [s] is the only segment that ever occurs between [t] and [u]: there are also, for instance, the sequences [tau] in the word *taue* 'rice planting' and [tou] in the word *tou* 'pay a visit', where the segments [a] and [o] respectively intervene between the [t] and the [u]. Since [a] and [o] are homotypical (both vowels), whereas [s] is not homotypical with either of them, we invoke our present assumption ad hoc to cover this case, and say that the [s] in [tsu] is determined.

37.1. Postulate 37 †There is a segment containing a combination or component *Q* and a residue of aspects or components *R*, that is in contrast in some environments with one or more segments not containing the residue *R*, but nowhere with any phonetically different segment containing *R*.

37.2. Definition In such a segment the combination or component *Q* is *determined*.

Let us suppose that in a certain dialect of English voiced [m] occurs but its voiceless counterpart does not. We can say that [m] contains an aspect of voicing (vibration of the vocal cords) and a residue of aspects consisting of lip closure, lowered position of the velum, and some others. Now [m] is in contrast with several other segments (for example with [n] in *mail* and *nail,* with [l] in *smile* and *sly*), but not with any segment that has the aspects of lip closure and lowered velum but is phonetically different from [m]—i.e., not, in this dialect, with a voiceless labial nasal. Accordingly, the aspect of voicing in [m] is determined.

38.1.   Postulate 38   †Some phonetically different segments, containing a combination or component Q in common and a residue of different aspects or components R, occur in a set of environments where they are non-contrastive with each other but in contrast with one or more segments not containing the combination or component Q.

38.2.   Definition   In every such segment, the residual combination or component R is *determined.*

We illustrate this by the example of voiceless [L] and voiced [l], already mentioned in §26.3 and §29.3. The two segments contain in common the aspects of lateral articulation by the tongue tip, slight elevation of the tongue back, and raised position of the velum; and they contain a residue of different aspects, namely voicelessness in [L] and voicing in [l]. Since they are non-contrastive with each other, as already shown, but in contrast with other segments that lack their common combination (for example with [s] in *let* and *set,* with voiceless [R] in *play* and *pray*), we say that the aspects by which they differ (voicelessness and voicing) are determined.

39.1.   Postulate 39   †Some phonetically different segments, containing a combination or component Q in common, occur in a set of environments E where they are in contrast with each other and where no other phonetically different segment occurs.

39.2.   Definition   In every such segment, the combination or component Q is *determined.*

In a dialect of English where vowels occurring before nasal consonants are nasalized but vowels in any other environment are not, we find, for example, nasalized [I^{n}], [$\mathrm{æ}^{\mathrm{n}}$], and [Λ^{n}] in contrast with each other in words like *pin, pan, pun.* All three vowels contain an aspect of nasalization (lowered position of the velum) in common; and no segment that is not a nasalized vowel ever occurs in the environment [p'...n]. Therefore the nasalization in these vowels is determined.

40.1.   Postulate 40   †Given the provisions of the foregoing postulate, there is one segment containing the combination or component Q and occurring in the given set of environments E, that is phonetically the same as a determined segment in some other environment.

40.2.   Definition   Such a segment is *determined* in the given set of environments E.

This is the basis on which we say that the aspiration after initial [k] is determined. The segments that occur after initial [k] satisfy the provisions of Postulate 39; we find a segment of voiceless aspiration ['] as in *coo,* voiceless [L] as in *clue,* voiceless [R] as in *crew,* and voiceless [J] as in *cue.* These segments are in contrast with each other in this environment, and no other phonetically different segment occurs there. According to §39.2 we can say at once that the aspect of voicelessness in these segments is determined; but we can go further. One of the segments that occur after initial [k], namely ['], occurs in at least one other environment—namely at the end of a phrase after [t], as in *sat*—where we have already shown it to be determined (§33.2, §34.2). Hence—according to §40.2—the segment ['] is determined also in the environment where the other voiceless segments occur, that is, after initial [k].

41.1.   Postulate 41   †There are two phonetically different segments X and Y occurring in the dyad XY, such that every segment phonetically the same as X is followed by a segment phonetically the same as Y, and every segment phonetically the same as Y is preceded by a segment phonetically the same as X.

In looser terms, there is a dyad XY such that X is never followed by any other segment than Y and Y is never preceded by any other segment than X.

41.2.   Definition   In such a dyad XY, the segment Y is *determined.*

It would be just as satisfactory to say that

X is determined instead of *Y*. Our choice is a matter of convenience and brevity.

The English affricate in *chin, church, butcher* commonly consists of a palatalized stop [t'] plus an alveolo-palatal spirant [ś], and is thus different from the combination of non-palatalized [t] plus palatal or cacuminal [š] in *hat-shop* and *courtship*. The segment [t] is followed by other segments than [š] (e.g., in *train*) and the segment [š] is preceded by other segments than [t] (e.g., in *marsh*); but the two segments [t'] and [ś] occur only in the dyad [t'ś]. Accordingly, we say that the spirant [ś] in this dyad is determined.

42.1. Postulate 42 Some segments, combinations, and components are not determined.

42.2. Definition A segment, combination, or component occurring in an environment where it is not determined is *distinctive* in that environment.

In the segment [m] in English, the aspect of voicing is determined (§37.2). But in the segment [z] of *zeal, busy, maze,* the aspect of voicing is distinctive; for there is a phonetically different segment [s], as in *seal, missing, mace,* that lacks this aspect, and the difference between the two segments [s] and [z] cannot be shown by any of our preceding assumptions to be determined.

Once the facts of distribution have been described for a particular dialect, a statement of the distinctive elements that occur in any phrase will include, by implication, a statement of all the determined elements that occur in it. If we know the distinctive segments, aspects, and components in a given phrase, and the patterns of distribution, we can infer the presence of every determined element that occurs in the phrase. In a sense, therefore, we can say that the determined elements of a dialect are *predictable* in terms of distinctive elements.

42.3. Definition The total set of environments in which a given segment is distinctive is the *range* of the segment.

Note that the term "segment" is used here to mean a class of phonetically same segments. Cf. §24.2, end.

42.4. Definition A segment that contains a distinctive aspect of duration (§23.3) is a *long segment.* A segment that is organi-

cally the same as a long segment but lacks the aspect of duration is a *short segment.* Other segments are neither long nor short.

If three or more segments differ distinctively in duration (§23.4), it will be necessary to use still other terms in speaking about them, such as *half-long* and *over-long.*

The vowels of *bid* and *bit,* and in some dialects also the vowels of *can₁* 'tin' and *can₂* 'is able', differ in duration; the vowels of *bid* and *can₁* contain an aspect of duration. According to §26.2, the longer and the shorter [ɪ] of *bid* and *bit* are in complementary distribution with each other, and the aspect of duration in the vowel of *bid* is therefore determined. On the other hand, the longer and the shorter [æ] of *can₁* and *can₂* are in contrast with each other, and the aspect of duration in the vowel of *can₁* is therefore distinctive. The vowel of *can₁,* accordingly, is a long segment, and that of *can₂* is a short segment; the vowels of *bid* and *bit* are neither long nor short.

42.5. Definition Segments containing the same totality of distinctive aspects or components are *distinctively same;* other segments are *distinctively different.*

Compare §16.2 and §23.6.

42.6. Corollary All phonetically same segments are distinctively same, but not conversely; and all distinctively different segments are phonetically different, but not conversely.

Compare §23.7.

42.7. Corollary A segment is distinctive in any environment where it is in contrast with another segment or with zero.

43.1. Postulate 43 †Some segments, aspects, and components are determined wherever they occur.

43.2. Definition Such segments, aspects, and components are *irrelevant;* other segments, aspects, and components are *relevant.*

The glottal stop mentioned in §33.2 is irrelevant by this definition. So also is any aspect or component that appears as a constant or nearly constant element in a given speaker's pronunciation, distinguishing his voice quality from that of another speaker.

IX. CONGRUENCE

44.1. Postulate 44 †Some phonetically different segments and some phonetically different dyads have the same or nearly the same range.

For the term "range" see §42.3. Whether two segments or dyads can be shown to have exactly the same range depends, of course, on just how their separate environments are described; cf. §25.3. Thus, if the environments of [ɯ] in *hammock* and of [n] in *cannon* are both described as [æ...ə], the possibility that they have the same range is not excluded; but if the environments are described as [hæ...ək] and [kæ...ən] respectively, this possibility is excluded from the outset. We therefore subjoin to this postulate the assumption that it is possible, in practical work with a given dialect, to describe environments in some useful way that will show certain phonetically different segments to have the same range.

The expression "nearly the same range" is of course open to a wide variety of interpretations; but again we assume that in practical work a line can somehow be drawn between ranges that are nearly the same and those that are clearly different. Problems of procedure, as already mentioned, do not concern us here.

44.2. Definition Segments and dyads that have the same or nearly the same range are *congruent* with each other.

The two following postulates (45 and 46) are included as illustrations of what can be done toward establishing the theoretical basis of the criterion commonly known as patterning or pattern congruity, the most elusive but in some ways the most valuable of all criteria used in the practical work of phonemic analysis. These two assumptions by no means exhaust the possibilities of applying the concept of congruent sounds; but they may be useful in suggesting the type of statements needed to clarify our notions about patterning.

45.1. Postulate 45 †There are two segments X and Y occurring in the dyad XY, and a segment A that is homotypical with either X or Y and congruent with XY.

For the term "homotypical" see §19.2 and §19.4.

45.2. Definition Such a dyad XY constitutes a single *binary segment.*

The German affricate [pf] is an example. If we compare its range with that of the segment [k] (choosing a segment that is homo-typical with the first segment in the dyad [pf]) we find that there is a considerable resemblance. Both [pf] and [k] occur initially before a vowel (*Pfote, Kohl*), before [r] (*Pfropf, Kropf*), and before [l] (*Pflug, klug*), as well as in other environments; but there are some environments where only [k] occurs—for instance after initial [s] (*Skizze*). Although the ranges of [pf] and [k] are not identical, we might perhaps consider them sufficiently alike to justify us in saying that [pf] and [k] are congruent, and therefore that [pf] is a binary segment.[27]

As a practical convention, we shall say that the distinctive aspects occurring in each part of a binary segment are common to both parts, and thus occur simultaneously.

46.1. Postulate 46 †There are the following segments: a long segment L, a short segment S organically the same as L, and a segment A organically different from S and occurring in the dyad SA or AS, such that this dyad is congruent with the long segment L.

For the terms "long segment" and "short segment" see §42.4; for the terms "organically same" and "organically different" see §16.2.

46.2. Definition Such a long segment L is composed of two *conjugate segments,* of which at least one is distinctively the same as the short segment S.

In some varieties of northeastern American English, words like *balm, father, Pali* contain a long segment [ɑ·], while words like *bomb, bother, Polly* contain a short segment [ɑ]. The range of the long segment is on the whole similar to that of a dyad consisting of the short segment plus a consonant—say [t]; e.g., [ɑ·] in *pa*, [ɑt] in *pot*. Accordingly, we say that the long segment [ɑ·] is composed of two conjugate segments, of which at least one is [ɑ].

To decide which of the two conjugate segments is distinctively the same as the corresponding short segment, we use the following

---

[27]If we had chosen some other segment than [k] for comparison—say [t], which is also homotypical with [p], or [š], which is homotypical with [f] —we might have been able to demonstrate a still closer similarity between the range of the dyad [pf] and that of the chosen segment. In practical work, the investigator must choose the segment that will give him the best results; and this he can sometimes do only after repeated trials.

criteria. (1) If *A* and *S* in §46.1 are *not* homotypical, then (a) if *L* is congruent with a dyad *SA,* the first of the two conjugate segments is *S;* but (b) if *L* is congruent with a dyad *AS,* the second of the two conjugate segments is *S.* (2) If *A* and *S* are homotypical, each of the two conjugate segments is *S,* and *L* accordingly is *SS.*

In our American English example, the long segment [ɑ·] is congruent with a dyad of the type of [ɑt]. Therefore the first of the two conjugate segments in [ɑ·] is [ɑ].

In a language where a long consonant such as [k·] is congruent with a dyad of homotypical consonants such as [pt] or [tk], we say instead that each of the two conjugate segments in [k·] is [k], so that the long segment is [kk].

Further postulates will be necessary to cover the interpretation of the remaining conjugate segment where only one is the same as the corresponding short segment.

From this point on, the term "segment" will include binary and conjugate segments.

X. FEATURES

47.1. Postulate 47 Some distinctively different segments contain a distinctive combination, or one or more distinctive components, in common.

47.2. Definition The distinctive aspects or components of a segment constitute one or more *features* of the segment.

We use the term "feature" for what is commonly called a distinctive or significant feature of a sound. Features are said to occur in segments; segments are said to contain features (cf. §13.4).

48.1. Postulate 48 †Distinctive aspects of stress or of pitch or of both occur in some segments that contain also other distinctive aspects or components.

On aspects of stress and pitch cf. §13.5, last paragraph.

48.2. Definition Every distinctive aspect of stress or of pitch is a *prosodic feature* of the segment in which it occurs.

Accordingly, if a segment contains both a distinctive aspect of stress and a distinctive aspect of pitch, it contains *two* prosodic features. (The term "prosodic feature" is intended merely to name one kind of feature, as defined in §47.2.)

This definition (admittedly ad hoc in its phrasing) allows us to abstract the qualities of stress and pitch from the totality of distinctive aspects in a segment, without obliging us at the same time to abstract certain other qualities that we do not usually wish to treat in the same way—for instance voicing and vowel color. For a language like Hindustani, where nasalization acts very much like pitch or stress in the more familiar languages,[28] Postulate 48 can be rephrased or supplemented by a further postulate so as to allow this quality also to be abstracted as a prosodic feature. For still other languages, where still other qualities act in a similar way, still other modifications or extensions of our postulate will be required.

An example from English. In the utterance *Coming?* (spoken as a question), the segment [ʌ] contains three distinctive aspects: the position of the back of the tongue resulting in a particular vowel color, the position of the arytenoid cartilages resulting in lower-mid pitch, and the movement of the diaphragm and other muscles that control the lungs resulting in loud stress; the segment [ɪ] contains only two distinctive aspects: a different position of the tongue resulting in a different vowel color, and a different position of the arytenoid cartilages resulting in higher-mid or high pitch. (We may regard the aspect of stress in [ɪ] as determined.) Accordingly, the segment [ʌ] contains two prosodic features (in addition to any other features that may occur in it), and the segment [ɪ] contains one.

49.1. Postulate 49 †There is a segment *X* whose distinctive aspects or components can be divided without a residue (or with a residue consisting only of prosodic features) into smaller combinations or groups of components, such that each smaller combination or group occurs in some other segment as the totality of its distinctive aspects or components (or as the totality except for prosodic features).

49.2. Definition In such a segment *X,* each of the smaller combinations or groups of components is a separate *feature* of the segment.

---

[28] I am indebted for this information to Henry M. Hoenigswald. Cf. his manual *Spoken Hindustani* 71 (U. S. Armed Forces Institute, EM 544, 1945).

The "retroflex" or "*r*-colored" vowel [ɚ] commonly heard in American English in *father, better, pattern* contains only two distinctive aspects (aside from any prosodic features that may occur in it). One is the position of the surface of the tongue, raised about halfway to the middle of the palate; the other is the position of the tongue tip, raised toward the alveolar ridge or the hard palate, or else the retraction and lateral spreading of the whole body of the tongue (cf. fn. 15). Each of these aspects occurs in other segments as the only distinctive aspect: the former in the second vowel of *sofa, bacon, hammock;* the latter in the initial segment of *red, roof, rain.* Accordingly, the two distinctive aspects in the retroflex vowel of American English are separate features of that segment.

In Japanese there is a segment [š] (not the one shown to be determined in §35.2) that contains three distinctive aspects: raising of the tongue tip or blade to form a groove-shaped aperture behind the upper teeth, raising of the surface of the tongue toward the hard palate, and separation of the vocal cords (voicelessness). The first and third of these occur together as the totality of distinctive aspects in the segment [s]; the second appears alone as the only distinctive aspect in the segment [j]. The three distinctive aspects in [š], therefore, constitute two separate features of the segment.

50.1. Postulate 50 There are segments to which the provisions of the foregoing postulate do not apply.

50.2. Definition Such a segment has only *one feature,* aside from any prosodic features that may occur in it.

In many languages this is the statistically normal case. For example, English [k] contains three distinctive aspects: closure between the back of the tongue and the soft palate, raised position of the velum, and separation of the vocal cords; but none of these occurs in any segment as the only distinctive aspect.

50.3. Definition Features that consist of the same totality of distinctive aspects or components are *the same;* other features are *different.*

50.4. Corollary Distinctively different segments contain different features or different synchronous groups of features. (Cf. §42.5.)

50.5. Corollary No aspect or component is part of two or more features in the same segment.

50.6. Corollary No segment contains a given feature more than once.

This statement may not be so superfluous as it sounds. The suggestion has been put forward that the loudest stress in English might be interpreted as a doubling of the second-loudest—that is, that in a word like *blackbird* both vowels carry the same phonemic degree of stress, but that the first vowel carries it twice over. If our postulates are valid, such an interpretation is ruled out.

50.7. Corollary A determined segment contains no feature.

51.1. Postulate 51 Some features do not appear together in the same segment.

In English, no segment contains both the feature present in [k] (the three aspects mentioned in §50.2) and the feature of lower-mid pitch present in the first vowel of the utterance *Coming?* (§48.2).

51.2. Definition A segment containing a totality of features *T* is *open to* a given feature *F* (where *F* is not included in *T*) only if there is at least one segment that contains both *F* and *T*, or both *F* and such aspects of *T* as are not homorganic with *F*.

In the utterance *This but not that,* the segment [ʌ] in *but* contains only two features: one of vowel color, one of pitch; it contains no distinctive aspect of stress. However, this segment is open to the feature of loud stress, because there is another segment that contains the same two features and in addition the feature of loud stress—for instance the segment [ʌ] in the utterance *Can you cut it?.* On the other hand, a segment [k] is not open to any feature of pitch, because there is no segment that contains both the [k]-feature and a pitch feature (§51.1).

52.1. Postulate 52 †In some sequences all the segments contain one or more features in common.

In the utterance *It's a blackbird,* all the segments in the sequence [blæ] contain in common a feature of higher-mid pitch, and all the segments in the sequence [bɚ·d] contain in common a feature of low pitch.

52.2. Corollary Some synchronous features are not coterminous.

52.3. Definition A sequence composed of segments containing a given feature *F* in common (and any number of other segments not open to *F*), and bounded at each end either by a pause or by a segment open to *F*, is a *span.*

A span can be described as the total domain of a given feature that extends through more than one segment. It may include segments that are not open to the given feature; but the occurrence of any segment that is open to it (i.e., any segment that might contain the feature but does not) marks a boundary of the span.

In the example of §52.1, the sequences [blæk] and [bɚ·d] are both spans;[29] but the sequence [ækbɚ·] is not, because there is no feature common to all the segments that occur in it.

52.4. Definition A feature that is common to all the segments of a span (or to all the segments that are open to it) is *a feature of the span itself,* not of any segment in the span.

Such a feature is said to occur in the span only once, synchronously with all the features contained in the individual segments of the span. Thus, in the span [blæk] of *It's a black-bird,* the feature of higher-mid pitch occurs only once, synchronously with the features of [b], of [l], of [æ], and of [k] respectively.

A feature of a span is very often a prosodic feature (§48.2), but need not be one. If such a word as *cat* is pronounced with "falling intonation," the vowel will consist of two segments: an [æ] with loud stress and higher-mid pitch (let us say), and an [æ] with loud stress and low pitch. The features of pitch, being different in the two parts of the vowel, are features of the individual segments; but the features of loud stress and of [æ]-color, being common to both parts, are features of a span. Although aspects of stress constitute prosodic features, aspects of vowel color do not.

XI. PHONEMES

53.1. Postulate 53 No segment or span contains a totality of features that does not occur as the totality of features in some other segment or span.

53.2. Definition The class of all segments and spans containing a given feature is a *phoneme.*

A segment or span is said to belong to every phoneme in which it is classified; a phoneme is said to correspond to any segment or span that is classified in it.

53.3. Corollary A phoneme is a class of events.

In spite of this fact, it is convenient to speak of a phoneme as occurring in a phrase or an utterance if it corresponds to a segment or span that occurs there. The logical error of saying that a class occurs can be corrected if we adopt the convention that an expression of the form "the phoneme *X*" is usually a class name, but a variable (indicating a member of the class) when the verbal context requires this meaning.[30]

53.4. Corollary A determined segment belongs to no phoneme. (Cf. §50.7.)

53.5. Corollary Every distinctive segment belongs to at least one phoneme, either by itself or as a member of a span.

53.6. Corollary A segment or span that contains two or more features belongs to two or more phonemes simultaneously.

If a segment *X* contains the features *e* and *f,* another segment *Y* contains the features *e* and *g,* and a third segment *Z* contains only the feature *e,* all three segments (by the provisions of §53.2) will belong to the same phoneme /E/. In addition, the segment *X* will belong also to a phoneme /F/, and the segment *Y* to a phoneme /G/. Thus, in English, every segment that contains the feature of [æ]-quality (a distinctive aspect defined by a certain position of the front of the tongue) will belong to the /æ/ phoneme; and some of these segments will belong simultaneously to other phonemes as well, by virtue of such additional features as pitch and stress of various degrees.

The provision that a given segment may belong simultaneously to two or more phonemes does not violate the well-known principle that phonemes must not intersect.[31]

---

[30]Compare the similar convention (on which ours is modeled) by which Hockett justifies his use of "morpheme" as a variable, *Language* 23.324, fn. 12.

[31]Cf. Bernard Bloch, "Phonemic Overlapping" [8], *American Speech* 16.278–284 (1941)—a statement in some respects now seriously antiquated.

---

[29]The first span is [blæk], not merely [blæ]; for the segment [k], not being open to the feature of pitch, does not mark a boundary of the span.

Intersection of phonemes is the result of assigning a given segment X to a certain phoneme /A/, and another segment that is phonetically the same as X to a different phoneme /B/—for instance, of assigning the segment [ə] in *sofa* to the phoneme /a/, and the phonetically same segment in *circus* to the phoneme /ʌ/.[32] The treatment here proposed is quite different from this: all phonetically same segments are assigned to the same phoneme, or to the same group of phonemes.

53.7. Corollary Except for determined segments, every phrase consists wholly of members of phonemes.

Or more loosely, every phrase consists wholly of phonemes; cf. §53.3. We cannot safely make the same statement about utterances, because we have not yet taken account of the pauses that may occur in an utterance (§21.1).

53.8. Corollary Every member of every phoneme is in contrast with some member of at least one other phoneme, or with zero.

This implies that the phoneme itself, as a class, is in contrast with at least one other class, or with zero, in every environment where some member of it occurs.

53.9. Corollary No member of a given phoneme is in contrast with any other member of the same phoneme.

53.10. Corollary The number of phonemes is smaller than the number of phonetically different segments, and therefore still smaller than the number of utterances.

Compare §2.1 and §16.4. The distinctively different segments and spans that make up the utterances of an idiolect thus turn out to satisfy the requirements of our second postulate. In §§2.3–4 we proposed the terms "phonological analysis" and "phonological system" to denote in general any process leading to the discovery of different auditory fractions and any statement of the results of such a process. The particular kind of phonological analysis that leads to the discovery of distinctively different segments and spans, we can now say, is to be called *phonemic analysis;*

and a statement of the results of such a process in terms of phonemes is to be called the *phonemic system* of the idiolect.

53.11. Corollary The phonemic system of any idiolect is determined solely by the utterances of that idiolect itself, and can be discovered only through phonemic analysis of these utterances or of a sufficient sample thereof.

This follows ultimately from §4.3. The corollary implies that the phonemic system of any dialect is unique, and furnishes no clue to the phonemic system of any other—not even to that of a closely related dialect in the same language.

53.12. Definition The feature common to all members of a given phoneme is the *characteristic* of the phoneme.

This is what logicians would call the defining attribute of the class. In view of our last corollary, it is clear that a combination, component, or group of components that is a characteristic of a phoneme in one dialect is not necessarily a characteristic of any phoneme in some other dialect.

In his book *Language,* Bloomfield defines a phoneme as "a minimum unit of distinctive sound-feature" (79; cf. the definition quoted in §0.2 above). From the discussion that follows, it is clear that by "sound-feature" Bloomfield means a particular configuration in the sound-waves produced by a speaker's movements, "recurring in recognizable and relatively constant shape in successive utterances." If we may reinterpret "sound-feature" to mean instead a recurrent movement or position in the articulations of a speaker's vocal organs (one or more aspects or components), Bloomfield's phoneme turns out to be identical with what is here called the characteristic of a phoneme. Accordingly, all that Bloomfield says (*Language* 79–84) about the practical importance of phonemes to the speaker, applies to the phoneme as defined in this paper no less than to the phoneme as defined by Bloomfield himself.

54.1. Postulate 54 Some members of the same phoneme are phonetically different.

If this were not true, the term "phoneme" would mean merely a class of phonetically same segments or spans. It is of course a commonplace that phonemic analysis very often

---

[32]Bloomfield's treatment of American English vowels is open to precisely this objection. See for instance his *Language* 112, §7.4, where in successive lines the sound [ə] is represented by the symbol /o/ (= ʌ) in *concerted* and by the symbol /e/ in *address.*

groups together in the same phoneme sounds that are objectively different.

54.2. Definition A class of phonetically same segments, or of spans consisting wholly of phonetically same segments in the same order, is an *allophone.*

By this definition, an allophone is what we commonly call simply "a speech-sound" (in the narrowest meaning of the term) or "a set of identical sounds." In practice we apply the term "allophone" to a class of segments or spans only when we are thinking about the phonemic status of the class. In other words, an allophone is a class of phonetically same sounds regarded collectively as members of a particular phoneme.

54.3. Corollary All members of a given allophone belong to the same phoneme (or group of phonemes).

54.4. Corollary Phonetically different segments or spans that belong to the same phoneme (or group of phonemes) belong to different allophones.

It is usual to speak of such allophones as "allophones of the same phoneme." When we talk about a particular member of some phoneme, what we commonly have in mind is the allophone as a whole, rather than one of the individual segments or spans that constitute the allophone.

54.5. Corollary The determined combinations or components in different allophones of the same phoneme (or group of phonemes) are non-contrastive with each other.

For the term "non-contrastive" see §29.4.

The definition of a phoneme in §53.2, together with the additional statements concerning phonemes and allophones in the following sections, should now be compared with our preliminary definition in §0.3. If we replace the term "sounds" in the preliminary definition by the more precise term "segments and spans," we find that our statements from §53.2 to §54.5 state explicitly all that is implied in the preliminary formulation.

XII. ORDER

55.1. Postulate 55 In any phrase, the phonemes occur in a particular order.

For the term "phrase" see §21.4; for the expression "phonemes occur" see §53.3.

55.2. Corollary Any phrase is uniquely identified by a list of the phonemes that occur in it and a statement of their order.

Compare §8.3. This kind of identification is the function of what is called *phonemic transcription:* we choose symbols to represent phonemes, and we write them down in the order in which the phonemes occur in the phrase to be transcribed. Since every phoneme is defined as a class of auditory fractions (segments and spans) that contain a particular feature—that is, ultimately, a particular grouping of articulations—and since all determined segments, aspects, and components can be inferred from the occurrent phonemes and their order (§42.2), it is clear that a phonemic transcription implies exactly as much about the "gross acoustic features" of any utterance as the most minute impressionistic transcription that the observer could devise. All arguments about the relative accuracy of impressionistic and phonemic transcriptions are therefore meaningless: each is implied in the other.

56.1. Postulate 56 The order of phonemes is either successive or simultaneous.

56.2. Definition A phoneme that corresponds to a given span *S* occurs simultaneously with every phoneme corresponding (a) to a segment included in *S,* (b) to a smaller span included in *S,* (c) to a larger span of which *S* is a part, and (d) to the same span *S.*

This definition can be restated in terms of a generalized illustration. Suppose a particular sequence of five segments *ABCDE.* Each of the segments contains one feature and thus belongs to one phoneme: the segment *A* contains a feature *a* and belongs to a phoneme /A/, *B* contains *b* and belongs to /B/, and so on. The whole sequence is a span containing a feature *f* and belonging to a phoneme /F/; and the sequence *BCD* (included as part of the larger sequence) is also a span, containing two features *x* and *y* and belonging to two phonemes /X/ and /Y/. We now say that the phoneme /X/, corresponding to the span *BCD,* occurs simultaneously with the phonemes /B/, /C/, and /D/ (corresponding to the segments *B, C,* and *D* respectively), with the phoneme /F/ (corresponding to the larger span *ABCDE*), and with the phoneme /Y/ (corresponding to the same span *BCD* that belongs also to /X/).

56.3. Definition All other phonemes *occur successively.*

In our generalized illustration, the phonemes /A/, /B/, /C/, /D/, and /E/ (corresponding to the individual segments) occur successively in the order listed; the phoneme /X/ (corresponding to the span *BCD*) occurs after /A/ and before /E/.

56.4. Definition   The serial order of a given phoneme /X/, reckoned as the number of phonemes intervening between the preceding pause and /X/, or between /X/ and the following pause, or both, is the *position* of /X/ in the phrase.

Compare §21.6.

56.5. Corollary   The position of a given phoneme, relative to preceding and following phonemes in the same phrase, is the same as the position of the segment or span to which the phoneme corresponds, relative to preceding and following distinctive segments.

56.6. Corollary   Two or more phonemes that occur simultaneously have the same position.

57.1. Postulate 57   †There are the following segments: a segment *X* containing the two features *e* and *f*, a segment *A* containing *e* but not *f*, and a segment *B* containing neither *e* nor *f* but sharing a distinctive aspect or component with *X*, such that the segment *X* is congruent with a dyad *AB* or *BA*, but not with both *AB* and *BA*.

The purpose of this statement is to clarify the procedure commonly followed in determining the order of two phonemes that correspond to a single segment.

57.2. Definition   The two phonemes /E/ and /F/ to which the segment *X* belongs (by virtue of its two features *e* and *f* respectively) *occur successively:* in the order /EF/ if *X* is congruent with a dyad *AB*, but in the order /FE/ if *X* is congruent with a dyad *BA*.

The retroflex vowel [ɚ] of American English (§49.2) contains two features: raising of the surface of the tongue (= *e* in our postulate) and raising of the tongue tip (= *f*). The segment [ə] in *sofa* (=*A*) contains the first of these features alone. The segment [l] in *dull* (= *B*) contains neither of them, but shares with [ɚ] the distinctive component of tongue-tip articulation. We ask, now, whether the segment [ɚ] is congruent with [əl] (=*AB*) or with [lə] (= *BA*), or with both or neither.

It can be shown that [ɚ] is congruent (in the rather liberal sense defined in §44.2) with [əl] but not with [lə], although both dyads occur frequently. Note, for example, the common environments of [ɚ] and [əl] in the following phrases: *eager* and *regal, awkward* and *equaled, periphery* and *polygamy, arouse* and *aloud, hammers* and *camels*. The dyad [lə] can hardly be found in any of these environments.

Accordingly, the two phonemes /ə/ and /r/ to which the segment [ɚ] belongs (by virtue of its two features) occur in the order /ər/.

Another example is the Japanese segment [š] (§49.2). By virtue of one feature (raising of the tongue tip or blade, and voicelessness) it belongs to the phoneme /s/; by virtue of the other (raising of the surface of the tongue) it belongs to the phoneme /y/. The order /sy/ rather than /ys/ is established by the following argument. The segment [j] contains the second feature by itself (and thus belongs to the phoneme /y/ also). The segment [k'] contains neither of the two features in [š], but shares with [š] the distinctive aspect of voicelessness. There is a dyad [k'j] that is congruent with [š]; but no dyad [jk'] occurs anywhere.

Similar postulates can be formulated to cover the order of phonemes when one segment contains three or more features.

CONCLUSION

58.1   The foregoing set of postulates is obviously not complete: here and there (as in §44.2, §46.2, §57.2) we have called attention to the need for further assumptions to cover special procedures. It is safe to say that the peculiar facts of each new dialect will call for new postulates, supplementing though not replacing those that we have listed (cf. §36.1, §48.2). Such minor gaps are no blemish in our system; for they could hardly have been filled in advance without knowing all the special situations existing in all the dialects of the world.

58.2   In addition to such gaps, however, there are several more serious omissions. We have nowhere defined the term *syllable*, which is often useful as the name of a structural unit determined by phonemic analysis; and we have included no postulates on which a definition might be based. That such postulates are statable (even if not here stated) is implied by the fact that in the description of some languages—not all—there emerges a unit of one or more phonemes whose role in the formation of larger units (phrases and utterances) is analogous to the role of individual phonemes in the formation of this unit itself.[33] If this is a fact in some languages, there must be a way of stating the fact—and such a statement would be a postulate on the same footing as the others in our set.

58.3   Again, there is nothing in our assumptions to cover the use of the term *juncture*. Indeed, we may go so far as to say that the so-called juncture phonemes of English and German, as they have hitherto been described,[34] are not phonemes at all in the sense of our definition (§53.2): they are not, or at least not obviously, classes of segments or spans containing a given feature, but rather fictions created ad hoc to account for the difference between certain sets of phonetically different segments. The concept of juncture can probably be salvaged without violating any of our assumptions—perhaps by reinterpreting what is called "open juncture" as an allophone of a pause phoneme (a "zero allophone")[35] or even as merely the border between two spans belonging to a phoneme of "close juncture." Or it may be that the definitions of *pause* and of *allophone* given above (§§21.2–3, §54.2) can be developed, by the aid of additional postulates, into a sufficient basis to support our present view of juncture phonemes.

[33]On the syllable as a phonemic—not a phonetic—term, see Henry M. Hoenigswald, *JAOS* 64.155 and fn. 5 (1944).

[34]On juncture in English see Trager and Bloch, *Language* 17.225–226 [73–75], §4 and fn. 5; Bloch and Trager, *op.cit.* 35–36 and 47, §2.14 and §3.7. On juncture in German see William G. Moulton, "Juncture in Modern Standard German," *Language* 23.212–226 (1947). Cf. also Rulon S. Wells, "Immediate Constituents," *Language* 23.107, §64 (1947): "The validity of juncture phonemes is open to grave doubts on phonetic grounds."

In his work on American intonation, Pike does not operate with juncture phonemes as such, but treats some of the same phenomena that Trager and Bloch regarded as juncture. See the discussion of this book by Wells, *Language* 23.257–259 and 262–263, §8, §11, and §15 (1947), and the references there given.

[35]This is Moulton's solution, *Language* 23.220, §3.14; cf. Wells, *Language* 23.108 fn. 45. The terms "pause phoneme" and "zero allophone" of course call for separate postulates, as yet unformulated.

58.4   No assumptions are included in our set that would warrant the use of such terms as *fortis* and *lenis*—terms referring to the character of a phonation as a whole, not to any particular aspect or component. In terms of our assumptions, the English phoneme /p/ is characterized by a certain statable feature, and the phoneme /b/ by another; the features, in turn, can be defined wholly in terms of distinctive aspects or components. If we agree that the difference between /p/ and /b/ is one of voicing, we define the feature of /p/ as consisting of the aspects of lip closure and open glottis, and the feature of /b/ as consisting of the aspects of lip closure, raised position of the velum, and vibrating vocal cords. (None of these aspects occurs in any segment as the only distinctive aspect.) But if we decide, in view of "voiced *t*" and the unvoicing of final [b, d, g], that the crucial difference between /p/ and /b/ is one of muscular tension—that /p/ is a "fortis" labial stop and /b/ is a "lenis" labial stop—how are the features of these two phonemes to be defined? Degrees or states of muscular tension are not either movements or positions of the vocal organs—at least not in the sense in which we have used these terms in our definitions above—and therefore cannot serve to define aspects. No doubt this difficulty can be resolved; but the necessary axioms are still to be formulated.

58.5   The last and possibly the most important omission concerns the large question of *patterning* (cf. §44.2). Few languages are so simple that their phonemic system can be economically described without invoking at least some of the criteria that are currently grouped under this head—for the most part, criteria based on the parallel distribution of phonetically parallel segments and dyads.

Suppose, for example, a language in which the following situation exists. The voiceless unaspirated stops [p, t, k] and the voiced unaspirated stops [b, d, g] occur initially, medially, and finally; so does the segment [h]; and so do the dyads [ph, th, kh] and [dh, gh]. The dyad [bh], however, occurs only medially and finally, not initially. The only voiced spirant in the language is bilabial [v], and this occurs only initially—i.e., in complementary distribution with the dyad [bh]. If there is nothing in the rest of the phonetic data to forbid the interpretation, most phonemicists would agree in classifying the segment [b] in a phoneme /b/ and the segment [h] in a phoneme /h/, and in regarding the dyad [bh] as a succession of two phonemes /b/ and /h/. Furthermore, most phonemicists would interpret the segment [v] as representing the same succession; they would state this, perhaps, by saying that the phonemic succession /bh/ corresponds to the dyad [bh] medially and finally, but to the single segment [v] initially. On the basis of patterning—the parallel distribution of [bh] and [v] together on the one hand and of [dh] or [gh] on the other—this would be a perfectly normal analysis. And yet, in terms of only those postulates that we have listed, we should be obliged to reject it. For suppose further that the phonemes /b/ and /h/ in this language are characterized by the following features: /b/ by lip closure and voicing, /h/ by a slight separation of the vocal cords resulting in voicelessness or weak voice (murmur). Are both of these features present in [v]? If they are, the segment will belong to the phonemes /b/ and /h/ simultaneously, and their order will be determined by that of the phonemes corresponding to [dh] or [gh] (see Postulates 49 and 57). But [v] cannot be fully voiced like [b] and at the same time voiceless or murmured like [h]: clearly it is impossible to find the features of both /b/ and /h/ in the segment [v]; and since our postulates make no other provision for analyzing a single segment as belonging to two phonemes, the normal solution must be given up.[36]

Once more there is no doubt that our usual procedures and our appeals to pattern congruity can be clarified by a statement of suitable axioms. Any procedure for which no tenable assumption can be found is for that very reason open to the gravest suspicion; for to the extent that our procedures depend on the facts of a language, those facts can be put into words. It will not always be easy: the assumptions underlying our use of pattern congruity are likely to be more difficult than any others to state simply and clearly. But the stylistic difficulty is only superficial. What is more important—what is indeed essential, if we are to put phonemics on a solid theoretical basis—is to know what we are assuming, and

[36]The imaginary situation here described is modeled on a situation said to exist in Bengali.

to make sure that we assume nothing that is contrary to fact.

59.1   Given our premise that the theoretical groundwork of phonemics can be established without any mention of mind and meaning (§0.3), is the approach that we have used the only one conceivable? Specifically, is it necessary (in theory) to define the characteristics of phonemes in terms of articulation? By no means. Two other approaches are possible, both (in theory) equally valid and usable.

The raw material of phonemic analysis is a set of utterances—instances of the use of conventional auditory signs by the members of a speech-community (§§1.1–6). By Postulates 5–8 we arrive at the conclusion that every utterance can be uniquely identified in terms of articulations (§8.3)—in other words, that there is a one-to-one correspondence between the auditory fractions of an utterance and the articulations of the speaker. From the moment that we arrive at this conclusion, we are free to speak wholly in terms of the vocal organs and their activity, knowing that whatever is alike or different in articulation is also alike or different in sound. But the postulates leading to this conclusion are not necessary: they are included precisely to make it possible for us to speak in terms of articulation. If they were modified or omitted, we should have to speak in other terms; but we could still say—in some terms—what we assume about the constitution of an utterance.

59.2   Suppose first that Postulate 5 were omitted, together with the three postulates that directly follow it (6–8). We should be thrown back, in this case, upon the utterances themselves; and we should have to speak about them, in all that followed, in auditory terms. This would be exceedingly difficult to do: phoneticians have developed no terminology for dealing with the auditory impressions that sounds make on the hearer's ear and brain. But it is at least conceivable that a terminology might be evolved, and that we might use it to isolate the parts of an auditory whole, defining segments, aspects, and so on entirely from the hearer's point of view. The definition of the phoneme at which we should arrive in such a case would be completely equivalent to the one that we have actually given; it might even be framed in the same words.

59.3 Or suppose instead that Postulate 5 were modified to read as follows: Every utterance is an auditory event produced entirely by sound waves resulting from the activity of certain organs in a speaker's body. (The organs could be enumerated as in §5.1, or left unnamed.) We should then proceed to show that a one-to-one correspondence exists between the auditory fractions of an utterance and the successive fractions of the sound-waves that produce it; and we should go on to base all the rest of our terminology on particular configurations of sound-waves or on particular distributions of acoustic energy.

It is true that the manipulation of acoustic terminology is beyond the ability of all but a very few linguists; but it is also true that the development of the sound spectrograph (fn. 6) promises to bring it within the grasp of many more. Again it is at least conceivable that our postulates might be phrased entirely in acoustic terms, and that acoustic records—oscillograms and spectrograms—might substitute, in practical work, for the phonetic transcriptions that we now use. And again the definition of the phoneme at which we should arrive by such a path would be the same.

Our reasons for adopting the physiological approach are practical. Linguists are already familiar with the vocal organs and their behavior; the correspondence between articulations and auditory fractions is easily observed and easily tested in controlled experiments; and a full terminology based on the speaker's movements is ready to our hand. But it should be clearly understood that our reasons for adopting this approach in preference to the other two are *only* practical: they have no theoretical significance.

60.1 We conclude by describing a sample utterance in terms of our postulates: the sentence *I'd rather not,* spoken with loudest stress and sharply falling pitch on the last word. The distinctive segments in this utterance, together with their distinctive aspects, are the following: (1) a vowel [ɑ] with low-central tongue position, medial stress,[37] and lower-mid pitch; (2) a consonant [j] with a rela-

tively higher and more forward tongue position,[38] and lower-mid pitch; (3) a consonant [d] with apico-alveolar closure, raised velum, vibrating vocal cords, and lower-mid pitch; (4) a consonant [ɹ] with "retroflexion" of the tongue tip, reduced-loud stress, and lower-mid pitch; (5) a vowel [æ] with low-front tongue position, reduced-loud stress, and lower-mid pitch; (6) a consonant [ð] with slit-shaped aperture between tongue blade and upper teeth, vibrating vocal cords, and lower-mid pitch; (7) a vowel [ɚ] with mid-central tongue position, "retroflexion" of the tongue tip, and lower-mid pitch; (8) a consonant [n] with apico-alveolar closure, lowered position of the velum, loud stress, and higher-mid pitch; (9) a vowel [ɑ] with low-central tongue position, loud stress, and higher-mid pitch; (10) a vowel [ɑ] with low-central tongue position, loud stress, and low pitch; (11) a consonant [t] with apico-alveolar closure and separation of the vocal cords.

A transcription of the utterance in terms of the individual distinctive segments that compose it—no longer a phonetic transcription but not yet phonemic—might look like this:[39] [₃ˋɑ-₃j-₃d-₃ˈɹ-₃ˈæ-₃ð-₃ɚ-₂ˈˈn-₂ˈˈɑ-₄ˈˈɑ-t].

60.2 There are five sequences in this utterance, some of them overlapping, in which all the segments contain a feature in common. Such segments are spans, and in each span we say that the common feature occurs only once (§§52.3–4).

Two spans have a feature of stress. Segments 4 and 5 are a span [ɹæ][40] with reduced-loud stress. Segments 8–10 are a span [nɑɑ] with loud stress. (Since we are free to regard the weak stress that is common to segments 2

[37]The terms referring to stress (loud, reduced-loud, medial, weak) are taken from Bloch and Trager, *op.cit.* 47–48, §3.7.

[38]The definition of an aspect in relative terms ("higher and more forward") involves an assumption that we have not stated—one of the special assumptions needed to cover the facts of a particular language (cf. §58.1).

[39]Distinctive aspects of pitch are denoted by inferior numerals before the letter: [₂] for higher-mid, [₃] for lower-mid, [₄] for low. Distinctive aspects of stress are denoted by superior ticks before the letter: ["] for loud, ['] for reduced-loud, [ˋ] for medial; weak stress, regarded here as determined, is not marked. Other distinctive aspects are implied by the usual phonetic values of the letters themselves. Segments are separated by hyphens for greater ease in reading; but these have no phonetic or phonemic significance.

[40]In this section we simplify our transcription by omitting marks of stress and pitch.

and 3 and again to segments 6 and 7 as merely the absence of any distinctive aspect of stress, we do not set up the sequences [jd] and [ðɚ] as spans.)

Two spans have a feature of pitch. Segments 1–7 are a span [ɑjdɹæðɚ] with lowermid pitch. Segments 8 and 9 are a span [nɑ] with higher-mid pitch.

One span has a feature of tongue position. Segments 9 and 10 are a span [ɑɑ] with low-central tongue position.

Notice that two segments contain two features apiece (aside from any features they may share with other members of a span). Segment 1 contains the feature of low-central tongue position and the feature of medial stress. Segment 7 contains the feature of mid-central tongue-position and the feature of "retroflexion"; we have already shown (§57.2) that the two phonemes to which this segment belongs occur in the order /ər/.

60.3 The segments and spans of the utterance *I'd rather not,* as we have described it, belong to seventeen phonemes.[41]

We name first the phonemes that correspond to single segments: corresponding to segment 1, the phoneme /a/ and the stress phoneme /ˋ/; to segment 2, /y/; to segment 3, /d/; to segment 4, /r/; to segment 5, /æ/; to segment 6, /ð/; to segment 7, /ə/ and /r/; to segment 8, /n/; to segment 10, the pitch phoneme /4/; to segment 11, /t/. There is no phoneme corresponding to segment 9 by itself: this segment belongs to three different phonemes (see below), but only as a member of three different spans (cf. §53.5).

The following phonemes correspond to spans of two or more segments: corresponding to segments 4–5, the stress phoneme /ˈ/; to segments 8–10, the stress phoneme /ˈˈ/; to segments 1–7, the pitch phoneme /3/; to segments 8–9, the pitch phoneme /2/; to segments 9–10, the phoneme /a/.

To express these facts in a concise phonemic notation, we first adopt a set of orthographic conventions.[42] We agree, for example, to call phonemes of stress and pitch "diacritic phonemes" and all others "letter phonemes";[43] and we agree to write letter phonemes with letters of the alphabet, diacritic phonemes with various other symbols, inferior and superior. Any span belonging to a letter phoneme will be written with only one letter, though spans belonging to diacritic phonemes will be written with two letters or more. Any symbol for a diacritic phoneme will be placed immediately before the letter denoting a segment that belongs to it, or the first segment of a span that belongs to it. If a given span *X* belonging to a letter phoneme contains segments that belong to two or more diacritic phonemes, the symbols for the latter will all be placed together before the letter denoting the span *X*. (If the first of such diacritic phonemes corresponds to a span that overlaps the beginning of the span *X,* its symbol will appear twice: once at the head of its own span, and again, together with one or more other diacritic symbols, at the head of the span *X.*) The four pitch phonemes will be represented by inferior numerals, from 1 (high) to 4 (low). The three stress phonemes will be represented by superior ticks: /ˈˈ/ for loud, /ˈ/ for reduced-loud, /ˋ/ for medial. If a pitch symbol and a stress symbol both precede the same letter, the pitch symbol is written first.

With these conventions in mind, we now write a phonemic transcription of the utterance *I'd rather not* as follows: /$_3$ˋayd'ræðər-$_2$ˈˈn$_{24}$at/.

60.4 To ask whether this is a "correct" or a "true" transcription of the given utterance is meaningless. The transcription either is, or is not, an accurate record of the phonemes that we believe to occur in this utterance, and of their order. And the analysis on

---

[41]There are only fifteen different phonemes in the utterance, but two of them occur twice.

[42]Cf. Wells, *Language* 23.107 §63, 110 fn. 52, 116 §84, 117 §88.

[43]These terms have no meaning beyond what we have just assigned to them. We purposely avoid the terms "suprasegmental" and "segmental," because their traditional meaning is irrelevant here. In the traditional sense, any feature that extends over more than one segment is suprasegmental as compared with any feature that occurs in one segment only. Thus, in our present example, pitch is suprasegmental as compared with vowel color in segment 1, but vowel color is suprasegmental as compared with pitch in segment 10. Such a reversal of status shows that the distinction between suprasegmental and segmental has no useful meaning within the framework of our postulates.

which the transcription is based either is, or is not, in accord with our set of postulates.

Any objections to such a transcription (aside from esthetic or practical objections to the orthographic conventions that we adopted) must therefore be stated and answered wholly in terms of these postulates. Whoever prefers a different transcription (not merely one re-sulting from a different set of conventions) must show either that our analysis violates one or more of the postulates that we have stated, or else that these postulates are untenable. If he takes the latter position, we may reasonably ask him to state his own assumptions in equal detail, and put off all argument until he has done so.

17

TWO FUNDAMENTAL PROBLEMS
IN PHONEMICS*

CHARLES F. HOCKETT

0 This article was originally planned as a review of several recent works of Kenneth L. Pike.[1] Although it has grown somewhat beyond the bounds of a review, the writer has found it useful to retain the procedure of using Pike as an advocatus diaboli—not, it is hoped, as a straw man.

Pike and his co-workers are engaged in the difficult task of making linguistic field workers out of large numbers of people—who come to them with no previous linguistic training and often with little apparent linguistic ability. In order to get anywhere near their goal, the Pike staff have had to prepare their own textbooks: teaching materials in which the whole task of analyzing a language is broken down into the smallest possible separate steps, for individual discussion and practice. This, of course, is a good idea for any beginner. The Pike-trained student will face a practical job: he must learn an "obscure" language, analyze its structure, devise a practical orthography, conduct literacy campaigns, and, above all, translate highly refractory material into the language. In training such students, Pike and his co-workers must keep these practical considerations constantly in mind. As a result, many definitions and concepts assume a guise somewhat different from what would result in a purely scientific context.

Of this we shall give two preliminary examples. By "phonemics" Pike apparently means just what he says in the subtitle of his book on that subject (Pike, 1947a): a set of operations that can be performed with the end product of a practical orthography (save, at most, for the choice of graphic shapes with which to represent whatever it is one represents). The scientific approach, as the writer sees it, would keep the following two matters separate: (1) the task of determining the phonemic structure of a language, and (2) the task of devising a practical orthography for use by the speakers of the language. True enough, the second involves the first; and the first involves something related to the second, in the sense that we have to develop notations with which to handle our material at every stage.[2] In one way these alternatives are perhaps only arbitrary preferences for one or another use of a term, but behind this lurk some real differences of method to be discussed presently.

Again: from the scientific point of view, the expression "tone languages" (Pike, 1948

[1]Those cited below. References to the following works are made in text and footnotes by name of author and year of publication, with page number if needed:

Bernard Bloch, 1948: "A Set of Postulates for Phonemic Analysis" [16], *Language* 24.3–46.

J. B. S. Haldane, 1945: "A New Theory of the Past," *American Scientist* 33.129–145.

Charles F. Hockett, 1947: Review of Nida, *Morphology*. *Language* 23.273–285.

Lillian Lieber and Hugh Gray Lieber, 1944: *The Education of T. C. Mits.* New York.

Kenneth L. Pike, 1947a: *Phonemics, A Technique for Reducing Languages to Writing.* Ann Arbor. University of Michigan Publications, Linguistics, volume III.

——, 1947b: "Grammatical Prerequisites to Phonemic Analysis" [15], *Word* 3.155–172.

——, 1948: *Tone Languages.* Ann Arbor. University of Michigan Publications, Linguistics, volume IV.

C. F. Voegelin, 1949: Review of Pike, *Phonemics. IJAL* 15.75–85.

Norbert Wiener, 1948: *Cybernetics.* New York.

[2]Prof. William G. Moulton, reading an earlier draft of this paper, pointed out that this constant development of notations with which to handle one's data is a part of every science.

*Reprinted from *Studies in Linguistics* 7.29–51 (1949) by permission of the Editor and of the author.

—title of book) may be no more meaningful than, say, "velar spirant languages" or "triangular five-vowel-system languages." Such terms may form no part of an objective linguistic taxonomy. And again the justification for the expression is practical. Pike's students are speakers of English, for whom the various phenomena subsumed roughly under the rubric "tone" constitute a special kind of difficulty.

An elementary textbook should not be expected to constitute a contribution to scientific knowledge. In chemistry, such a textbook is built on a broad base of accepted doctrine, and a reviewer passes judgment only on the effectiveness of the pedagogical devices used. Linguistics does not yet stand with chemistry; in writing an elementary textbook one has to choose in some cases between different and incompatible fundamental theories. A reviewer can still discuss pedagogical merits, but such discussion is sometimes only of secondary importance. It would be in the case of Pike's recent books. Here we shall discuss only those two points in Pike's theoretical frame of reference which seem weakest: the avowed use of "grammatical" criteria in phonemic analysis, and the notion of "potentials."[3]

1 Pike's volume *Phonemics* makes use of "little-language" problems, sometimes coined quite a priori, sometimes derived by restriction from some actual language. The contrast between Pike's point of view and that which we are going to defend here can best be shown by starting with one of his problems. We choose problem 208 (Pike, 1947a, p. 159—further page references are to this work). The raw data are:

[op] 'horse'   [basop] 'the big horse'
[bas] 'big'   [opzuMbas] 'the horse is big'
[zuM] 'is'   [opmazuMbas] 'his horse is big'.
[ma] 'his'

We are to assume either that these seven utterances are the whole language, or else that any

conclusions we base on these data will not be controverted by further data; and we are to assume that the phonetic transcription is correct and complete. Pike's instructions to the student are "1. Rewrite phonetically the last three utterances, adding spaces in the appropriate places. 2. Rewrite the same data phonemically." His solutions are, phonetically [bas op], [op zuM bas], [op ma zuM bas]; phonemically /baz ob/, /ob zum baz/, and /ob ma zum baz/.

In the preceding discussion he says (159): "It is frequently convenient to write spaces between items which themselves may be found elsewhere as constituting complete utterances." Later: "Any morpheme or close-knit sequence of morphemes which can occur at the beginning, end and middle of utterances should be preceded and followed by a space." That is, we are to determine where grammatical boundaries of certain types fall, write them with spaces, and then regard these spaces as parts of environments in determining distribution of sounds and achieving our final notation. This is clearly what he means; yet in the first quoted passage there is no explicit reference to grammatical forms and borders—he uses the colorless term "item," which might be purely phonological. We shall show presently that if "item" is so interpreted, then the passage shows us how to introduce *purely phonological* junctures, without ringing in any grammatical considerations.

If we ignore Pike's instructions for problem 208, and simply examine distributions, we observe that [b] and [p], and likewise [m] and [M], are in complementary distribution, since the voiceless member of each pair occurs only before another consonant or at end of utterance. We could therefore replace the paired symbols by single symbols, say /b/ and /m/, and have an entirely satisfactory phonemic notation, in which the seven utterances would appear as /ob/, /bas/, /zum/, /ma/, /basob/, /obzumbas/, and /obmazumbas/. Note that it is still necessary to keep [z] and [s] separate, since they contrast intervocalically. Now it is unlikely that Pike intended the problem to be so simple. He probably meant for the contrasts between [b] and [p], [m] and [M], to appear distinctive until the introduction of spaces. In all fairness, therefore, let us modify his data in such a way as to make this so. Let us add to

---

[3]Pike's article (1947b) [15] is devoted to the former of these points. I have not dealt piecemeal with his arguments as given there, since most of those arguments lose their weight once their fundamental underpinning is removed—and the latter is the task of the present paper.

the raw data the utterances [ba] 'not', [za] 'cow', [opop] 'many horses', [mazuMop] 'his is a horse', [opzuMbabas] 'the horse isn't big', and [zama] 'his cow'. The enlarged corpus appears, without meanings, in column I of the Table. In this new assemblage, [b] and [p] contrast between vowels, as do [m] and [M], but otherwise there are no essential changes of apparent structure.

If we follow Pike's instructions—first inserting spaces between "free forms," and then "phonemicizing" in terms of the modified environments in which our symbols appear—we obtain the solution given in column IV of the Table.

If again we ignore Pike's instructions, then we must conclude that the enlarged corpus appears already, as raw data, in a notation which by the reviewer's definition of the term must be considered phonemic. That is, the notation indicates in each position all the contrasts which are distinctive there, and no others; it indicates each such contrasting element with a single and consistent symbolization. However, the notation of column I is only one of a great many possible phonemic notations in this sense, and we may profitably discuss what other purely phonemic notations are also possible. We shall derive three others, each no more and no less phonemic than that of column I.

(1) First we take advantage of the fact that in utterance-final only [s p M] occur, to the exclusion of the paired voiced sounds [z b m]. We break [s p M] into two simultaneous components each, respectively /z b m/ and *unvoicing*. We then agree to use no special symbol for devoicing in utterance-final, since it is automatic there; medially, we will write it with a space placed directly after the symbol representing the affected consonant. The utterances then appear as given in column II. When columns II and IV are compared, it will be noted that without bringing in any grammatical criteria we have introduced spaces at nine of the thirteen points where Pike's procedure would introduce them, and nowhere else; the four exceptions are in utterances (9), (11), (12), and (13).

(2) Next (starting over again), we take advantage of the fact that in utterance-initial only [z b m] occur, to the exclusion of the paired voiceless sounds. We break [z b m] into

two simultaneous components each, respectively /s p M/ and *voicing*. We then agree to use no special symbol for voicing in utterance-initial, since it is automatic there; medially, we will write it with a space placed directly *before* the symbol representing the consonant affected. In this notation, the utterances appear as given in column III. Comparing columns III and IV, we note that there is a one-to-one correspondence between the /s p M/ of III and the /z b m/ of IV, so that the difference is merely one of shape of individual symbol, and quite irrelevant; and beyond this that without bringing in any grammatical criteria we have once again introduced spaces in most of the places in which the Pike solution introduces them (ten of his thirteen places), but nowhere else; the three exceptions are in utterances (7), (10), and (11).

(3) Finally, we go a step further, and extract from the pairs [z : s, b : p, m : M] *both* voicing *and* unvoicing. What is left in this case is a concatenation of articulatory features that can only occur in a simultaneous cluster with one or the other of our two components; this need disturb us no more than that most "consonants" in most languages can occur only in sequential clusters with "vowels." Choosing the symbols /z b m/ for these abstracted concatenations of features—purely so that the results will look more like Pike's—we define them respectively as apico-dental groove position (?—the phonetic details are of course not supplied), bilabial closure with velic closed, and bilabial closure with velic open. Since initially and finally in utterances the presence, respectively, of voicing and of unvoicing is automatic, we agree not to use any extra symbol in these positions for either feature. Medially, we agree that voicing will be written by a space *before* the symbol representing the consonantal articulation affected, unvoicing by a space *after* the symbol; and we agree that where these conventions would lead us to write two spaces in succession, we will write only one—no ambiguity can result. The utterances appear in this notation in column IV— that is, precisely in the shape that Pike would give them. We have thus achieved an identical symbolization without bringing any grammatical considerations to play.

The reader at this point may be inclined to ask: Why go all around Robin Hood's barn

TABLE

Utterance	I	II	III	IV
(1)	[op]	/ob/	/op/	/ob/
(2)	[bas]	/baz/	/pas/	/baz/
(3)	[zuM]	/zum/	/suM/	/zum/
(4)	[ma]	/ma/	/Ma/	/ma/
(5)	[ba]	/ba/	/pa/	/ba/
(6)	[za]	/za/	/sa/	/za/
(7)	[basop]	/baz ob/	/pasop/	/baz ob/
(8)	[opzuMbas]	/ob zum baz/	/op suM pas/	/ob zum baz/
(9)	[opmazuMbas]	/ob mazum baz/	/op Ma suM pas/	/ob ma zum baz/
(10)	[opop]	/ob ob/	/opop/	/ob ob/
(11)	[mazuMop]	/mazum ob/	/Ma suMop/	/ma zum ob/
(12)	[opzuMbabas]	/ob zum babaz/	/op suM pa pas/	/ob zum ba bas/
(13)	[zama]	/zama/	/sa Ma/	/za ma/

if it gets us just where Pike gets us more directly? Our route, it is true, is a seemingly lengthy one, and his apparently direct; but ours lies entirely on firm ground, whereas the Pike "shortcut" may turn out to lead across a bog in which we can lose our way irretrievably. I cannot resist an analogy: Most people would agree with Euclid that it is perfectly clear intuitively which is the "inside" of a triangle, which the "outside"; but unless one provides formally for a definition of "inside" and "outside," it is possible to prove Euclidean plane-geometric propositions which are patently not the case (Lieber and Lieber, 1944). Now, in linguistic analysis, suppose we are confronted with the following set of forms:

[ga] 'this'   [gali] 'that'
[lima] 'boy'   [ma] 'stone'
[galima] 'this boy' [galima] 'that stone'

Following Pike's procedure, we would first insert spaces to get [ga lima] and [gali ma] respectively. But it is obvious that the phonetic sequence [galima] is identical regardless of whether it means 'this boy' or 'that stone'. Introduction of border markers on the basis of grammatical considerations, it would seem, can conceal identities of environment and thus lead analysis astray. This does not mean that we might not insert the spaces in these last forms; it does mean that we would find no *phonemic* reason for inserting them, and consequently would be putting them in at some later point in the whole operation of developing a "practical orthography," not during the process of phonemicization. In other words, there are languages where there are phono-

logical data susceptible of a kind of interpretation that would lead us to write spaces, and other languages where there are not.

This brings us to a consideration of the two different kinds of "word" and "morpheme" current today. Pike seems to accept a definition of word involving meaning: a minimum free form which occurs as a whole utterance with approximately the same meaning it has when in included position. But it is also possible to define a *phonological word:* any stretch of phonemes which occurs as a whole utterance, and which cannot be broken into two or more shorter stretches which also so occur, quite regardless of meanings. If in the modified problem 208 [basop] meant 'bishop' instead of 'the big horse', then Pike would presumably not choose to retranscribe it as [bas op] or /baz ob/, since /baz/ and /ob/ do not occur (according to the corpus) with any meanings such that the sum of the meanings could be 'bishop'. But our procedure would apply exactly as before, and with the same results. Our phonological inspection has revealed the structuring of the longer utterances of the corpus in terms of sequences of "phonological words," has revealed that the borders between phonological words in longer utterances are phonetically marked, and has made the most of that fact to develop a notation which uses symbolisms in a mnemonically convenient way. In the case of [galima], our procedure would show that this is not a phonological word, since there exist shorter phonological words such that [galima] can be taken as a sequence of two of them in either of two ways; it would show, however, that there is *not* any phonetic marking of the borders between phonological words in included position, so that on the phonological level there would be no justification for any retranscription with spaces or other border markers.

I should not hesitate to call the complex of phenomena symbolized by spaces in our third rephonemicization of the modified problem 208 a *phoneme;* specifically, a junctural phoneme or simply a juncture.[4] It is, so to speak, an utterance-medial event parallel to what happens between the end of one utterance (providing it ends with a consonant) and the beginning of the next (providing it begins with a consonant), with the sole difference that in the latter situation there is a pause, lasting anywhere from a second to a day or week, whereas in the former there is no pause. We can define our juncture in this problem as transition from voicelessness to voicing, when it occurs flanked by consonants; if no consonant precedes, then the juncture has, as another allophone, inception of voicing without any preceding interruption of voicing; if no consonant follows, similarly; the juncture of course does not occur with neither preceding nor following consonant. Indeed, this is a good simple example of what I should mean by "junctural phoneme": If some particular phenomenon is predictable at the ends of utterances, either always or whenever certain other features are found there, but is not predictable medially, and if its successive occurrences seem to mark fairly well the borders between *phonological* words, then that phenomenon is junctural; similarly for such a phenomenon predictable initially but not medially. (In

many languages—perhaps in most actual languages, in contrast to the simplified languagettes of Pike's book—some modification of the above definition is needed, along the line of relaxing the requirements to be met by a stretch of phonemes for it to be considered free.[5] Thus in English we will get one set of junctural phenomena with the definition as originally given; if we then "lift off" intonation phonemes and define phonological words relative to the abstracted remainder, we get another set; if, then, we also abstract from all stress differences except that between no stress at all and a non-zero stress level, and define phonological words relative to the remainder, we get still a third set.) A juncture *phoneme* is then a grouping of such phenomena which makes for unambiguous and simple linear transcription. If this last statement seems arbitrary, it is no more so than is, for me, the definition of any kind of phoneme. One can derive, from the totality of distinctive features in the utterances of a language and the arrangements in which they occur, various different sets of bundles to be represented by unit symbols in a linear transcription, and any such derivation establishes what I should call a phonemicization. A phoneme is a phoneme only as part of a stated phonemicization. The "phonemic structure" of a language is not to be equated to any such phonemicization; rather it is the "least common denominator" of every possible sufficient phonemicization:[6] that which must be subsumed by *any* set of phonemic symbols with accompanying instructions for use. We have already demonstrated four different phonemicizations of modified problem 208, which will illustrate the point just made. It also follows that juncture is never forced upon us; it is always possible to phonemicize without junctures, though perhaps only sometimes possible to phonemicize in a way that gives us juncture phonemes.

Juncture phonemes, as set up on the above basis, may indeed have one property which is superficially different from the properties usually ascribed to phonemes. We do

[4]This and the following two paragraphs are directed as much at Bloch (in the light of Bloch, 1948 [16], and subsequent discussions) as at Pike. Bloch and Pike seem to stand together in considering juncture a grammatical matter; beyond this, they are poles apart, for while Pike considers this ample basis for bringing in all kinds of grammatical criteria for phonological analysis, Bloch considers it sufficient reason to eliminate juncture from phonological analysis. I am confident that Bloch's postulates could be modified, along lines suggested here, in such a way as to allow for junctures, but can hardly attempt a full demonstration of this here. As to the difficulty Bloch cites in telling how much speech constitutes a single utterance—we could easily enough begin with an arbitrary minimum length of pause which we shall consider sufficient to mark inter-utterance boundary, say one second, and then modify this as further work suggested.

[5]Cf. Hockett 1947, p. 277.
[6]One might perhaps better say: the phonemic structure of the language is that which remains invariant under all possible transformations from one sufficient phonemicization to another.

not ordinarily classify a group of allophones into a single phoneme unless all the allophones have some configuration of phonetic features in common, however much they may differ as to other phonetic features. But the various allophones grouped into a single juncture phoneme may have nothing in common. Two of the allophones of the juncture phoneme introduced into the third solution of modified problem 208 have, it would seem, no feature in common: i.e., the allophone consisting of momentary cessation of voicing on a consonant without resumption of voicing on a second consonant, and the allophone consisting of voicing on a consonant without momentary cessation of voicing on a preceding consonant. Now, mathematically, a *class* is considered to be *defined* when, if presented with any object, we can say whether or not that object is a member of the class. One way to set up a class is to specify a *property,* so that possession of that property by an object puts it in the class, lack of that property leaves it out of the class. Thus "even integer" is a property which establishes a class including 2, 4, 6, etc., but not 1, 3, 5, etc., nor a leaf nor a nose. But another perfectly satisfactory way to define a class is by *itemization.* Thus I can establish a class consisting of the first three even integers, all the leaves on the tree outside my window, and the third word on this page. A class so defined is a perfectly good class; it even has properties that can be investigated, e.g., it consists of a certain number of objects. If we insist on tying up a class with a property, in the case of a class of this kind we can regard the property of *membership in the class enumerated* as the associated property. That is, a class can be defined in terms of a property, or vice versa. So we see that the failure of all the allophones of some juncture phonemes to have some (articulatory or acoustic) property in common is no logical defect. We may with perfect validity define a juncture phoneme as consisting of all occurrences in certain specified contexts of certain specified phenomena. It may be well doubted whether we would wish to extend this type of class-definition to other phonemes, although perhaps we do in actual practice: in certain dialects of English we class [ʔ] into a /t/ phoneme, though in doing so we may have to admit that the only "property" all our /t/ allophones

share is "non-[k]-ness" and "non-[p]-ness." Juncture phonemes, where recognized, do consist of allophones with a *structural* property in common; ultimately this may actually be more important.

In the above lengthy defense of juncture I have not intended, of course, to claim that all juncture "phonemes" or "junctures" set up so far for various languages, or even all set up in previous discussions by myself, would really pass the tests here established. Where they would not, however, I should now feel that the analysis is defective.

There are two different approaches to morphemes just as there are two different kinds of words. Pike accepts a semantic definition: "A MORPHEME is the smallest meaningful unit of linguistic structure, such as *boy* and *-ish* in *boyish*" (60, right-hand column, fn. 2). But there also exists a more formal definition, of the Harris type: a morpheme is an arrangement of phonemes such that the occurrence of phonemes in utterances (long as well as short) is most efficiently stated in terms of the phonemic structure of morphemes and the morphemic structure of utterances, rather than directly in terms of the phonemes themselves.[7] True enough, even with morphemes defined this way, we often find that meanings seem to be more or less regularly attached to them, and we can use meanings as hints to tell us what the morphemes of a language *may* be, without thereby abandoning the fundamental purely formal definition. And when morphemes are defined formally, it becomes perfectly obvious that use of position in morphemes or relative to morpheme borders as a criterion in phonemic analysis is completely circular.

The formal definition of morpheme also brings out the importance of the phonological word, and, where possible, of junctures defined in terms of phonological words. From the very definition of phonological word, such sequences of phonemes are going to be maximally useful units in stating the structures of whole utterances. Phonological words (with or without phonetically marked boundaries) are larger units capable, by definition, of the

---

[7]This definition is a paraphrasing of one by H. Hoenigswald in an unpublished manuscript entitled *Meaning.*

greatest amount of reshuffling from utterance to utterance. There are of course limits to this shuffling—otherwise "syntax" would be easy —but the degree of freedom is none the less great. They are, in fact, the "items" to which we wish Pike were referring in the passage already quoted ("It is frequently convenient to write spaces between items which themselves may be found elsewhere as constituting complete utterances.").

I should say that it is not yet certain whether formally defined morphemes are actually what concern us more, rather than semantically defined morphemes; perhaps the two are simply different units, with some correlation between them but without identity. The formal morpheme needs much further investigation. But even with the semantic definition, it would seem clear to me from the above considerations that use of morpheme borders in *phonemic* analysis is unproductive. To take up again the "short cut" analogy, we will do better to regard Pike's "short cut" through grammatical territory not as a shorter route to the same goal at all, but rather as a direction in which we can *look* (without venturing to proceed for fear of the bog) before taking the long but safe road around, and from time to time while en route.

2   Now so far in our discussion we have been accepting one of Pike's procedural premises and framing our argument within it. That is, we have agreed to handle small corpora of data on the assumptions he gives: either that such a corpus constitutes the whole language, or that nothing found elsewhere in the language will ever controvert conclusions based on the small corpus; and, in either case, that the data given are phonetically accurate and complete. Except for one factor, this is a reasonable enough assumption. Given time enough, a field worker can arrive at a transcription which has the characteristics of Pike's problem corpora, although the experienced field worker is apt to reach a tentative phonemicization long before he observes and provides for all the phonetic details that turn out to be relevant (Voegelin, 1949). There is, however, one factor in the small corpora which tends to invalidate the approach unless great care is taken: their size. If we accept one of the alternative assumptions, namely that the small

corpus is the whole language, then we are obviously unrealistic. If we accept the other alternative, that nothing else we may later add to the corpus will contradict any conclusions based on it, it is possible to demonstrate that this assumption actually precludes there being any other utterances in the language, and we are back again with the first assumption. For from the data of modified problem 208, we could quite validly conclude that [b] occurs only before [a], that [o] occurs only before [p], and so on; in fact, that [b] occurs initially only when the remainder of the utterance is [as], [a], or [asop]. The brighter beginning student is often very much inclined to reach such conclusions; we have to muddle up our instructions in order to prevent it. The unrealism of such conclusions does not lie in the logic; it lies in the smallness of the corpus and in the accompanying assumption. Actually, *no* corpus is ever complete. We work by a method of successive approximations. We state what seems to be the case in terms of the material gathered up to a given time, involving intuitions gathered from experience with other languages; when the material gathered is sufficiently extensive, we can venture to predict with some hope of verification that certain additional things will in time be observed, certain other additional things will not. Only by a recurrent cycle of prediction, checking, gathering of new data, modification of predictions, and rechecking, can we eventually arrive at a description which is accurate to within any prescribed amount of tolerance.

In this sequence of operations, the fundamental assumption of the field worker is Bloomfield's fundamental assumption of descriptive linguistics: In any speech community (and a fortiori for any single speaker) *some utterances are alike.* "Utterance" here means "utterance-event," a unique historical event, at a given time and place. Bloomfield's postulate is an *existential* assumption rather than an operational one; it is the shape taken in linguistics of a general principle of science recently formulated (Wiener, 1948, p. 62–63) as follows: "For the existence of any science, it is necessary that there exist phenomena which do not stand isolated. In a world ruled by a succession of miracles performed by an irrational God subject to sudden whims, we should be forced to wait each new catastrophe in a state of perplexed passiveness. We have a picture of such a world in the croquet game in *Alice in Wonderland,* where the mallets are flamingoes; the balls, hedgehogs, which quietly unroll and go about their own business; the hoops, playing-card soldiers, likewise subject to locomotor initiative of their own; and the rules are the decrees of the testy, unpredictable Queen of Hearts. The essence of an effective rule for a game or a useful law of physics [or any other science] is that it be statable in advance, and that it apply to more than one case. Ideally, it should represent a property of the system discussed which remains the same under the flux of particular circumstances. In the simplest case, it is a property which is *invariant* to a set of *transformations* to which the system is subject."

An existential assumption, such as Bloomfield's version for linguistics of the general principle of science just stated, unfortunately does not tell us how to discover which utterance-events *are,* as a matter of fact, the same; it merely assures us, as does common sense, that some of them are. Harris only apparently carries us closer when he prescribes that we look for *repetitions;*[8] that is, we hear someone say something, and perhaps record it, and then ask him to say the same thing again, or even try to say it back to him, thus, if we are lucky, producing a repetition ourselves. In a way, we are really quite uninterested in the individual utterance-event with its date and place of occurrence; and yet that is all we can ever observe. Harris's advice leaves the fundamental problem unsolved, for how can we be sure that the second event is actually a repetition of the first? Imagine such a dialog as this:

MARY: I thought I'd go downtown today.
JOHN (looking up from *SIL*): What's that, dear?
MARY: I said I thought maybe if you could leave the car with me I'd go do some shopping today.

Mary's second utterance is not a falsehood, and yet the portion after "said" is not a repetition for our purposes. Suppose she had an-

---

[8]The procedure is proposed in Harris's forthcoming book *Methods in Descriptive Linguistics.* [See Harris 1951, *Methods in Structural Linguistics* —VBM.]

swered in "the same words" she used the first time, but with a different speed and intonation. Would her second utterance in this case have been a repetition of the first?

In order to tell, we have to compare different utterances as specific historical events. In Newton's day people worried about the problem of measuring duration. It was claimed that you couldn't know that the minute from midnight to 12:01 lasted as long as that from 8:00 AM to 8:01, since you couldn't lay one of them alongside the other the way you could compare two objects as to length in space. This problem was solved by common sense and clocks. Two intervals of time are *defined* as of the same duration if a clock ticks the same number of times during one as during the other. We could use someone's heart as our clock if we wanted to (Haldane, 1946, p. 130); that we do not, but instead use planets and develop intricate and delicate apparatus which will move in a prescribed way with them, is only because the mathematics of our description of the universe is so much simpler this way. The problem of comparing two distinct historic events, be they utterances or other cultural manifestations, is the same. We cannot put one alongside the other. If we have two forms which we think are almost the same, and suspect may be identical, and therefore ask our informant to say one and then the other, we are not comparing any *other* historical events; we are simply comparing the two we elicit at that moment. Even in this case the informant does not utter two utterances simultaneously; he produces one and then the other. The analyst has to make use of his short-term memory, the type of memory which establishes the "specious present," to make the comparison. And for events that occur at greater temporal separation, the technique that has to be used is still that of memory.

Memory can be a device within a human nervous system, or it can be some externalized device: written records of all kinds, and electronic recordings, are all external memory devices. When a given utterance-event occurs, we can produce an *icon* of it with the latter type of apparatus, or a *record* of it with the former. When, later, we consult our icons and records, the playback in one case, our own speech mechanism in the other, must indeed produce a new historic event in order for there to be any comparison within the specious present with some new or some other old occurrence; but the pattern of sound waves produced by the playback, in particular, is far more closely similar to the pattern of the original event than is anything we might, early in a field enterprise, reproduce from internal memory; or, at least, the distortion is of a quite different nature. And with any such internal or external memory devices, the most that can be accomplished is the production of more or less accurate images of the original events, in close succession, for comparison within the specious present; our *short-term memory* is still indispensable.

In general, we find it quite feasible to dispense with any electronic apparatus, and rely on our own nervous systems supplemented by pencil and paper. That this will suffice is guaranteed by the fact that the first part, unsupplemented, is enough for the newly arrived child in a community, who comes eventually to participate in the linguistic behavior of the community on a par with everyone else.

As practical working criteria, as we compare utterances, we use such as the following, in various specific forms: Do the two utterances seem very similar, to our ears, in their phonetic configuration? Do the two seem to occur in somewhat the same context? Do similar stimuli produce them, and do they produce similar responses? As we begin work on a language, we hardly ever put anything down on paper until after we have asked for "the same" form several times; sometimes we do not actually get "the same" form, but except in obvious cases we ignore possible deviations and leave corrections for later. The given criteria, as stated, can be summarized as similarity of *sound* and of *meaning*. As we start, we can trust neither our ears nor our apperception of the culturally defined meanings of forms. So we proceed by trial and error. Regardless of how much rationalization of analytical procedures we may indulge in, there is an irreducible minimum of *language-learning* involved in any linguistic field project. An entity cannot function as a linguistic field worker and analyst unless it is endowed with the language-learning apparatus and ability that human beings have, which implies, of course, that for the present only human beings can be trained as linguists—we cannot yet construct a machine to analyze languages on the basis of the really raw data which comes from the lips of speakers. This is also the fundamental source of disagreement between descriptions. Equally competent observers with comparable points of view can produce descriptions of a language that differ widely, and which, as the work of each proceeds, will only approach complete agreement, without ever reaching it. This is an analog of the fact that two infant arrivals in a speech community will never grow up to speak entirely identical idiolects. That is, the area of indeterminacy is not necessarily in the analyst or the technique; it is in the data. This is the nature of the flux within which we must seek the invariants which we call utterances (not utterance-events), and then, later, distinctive features, phonological words, phonemes, and all the rest.

One more remark must be made here before we turn to Pike's "potentials." It has been granted above—nay, proclaimed—that we cannot decide which utterance-events are "the same" for purposes of further analysis without using meaning (as defined). This use of meaning is (1) differential, rather than specific, in the sense that we use it to tell us whether two utterance-events had more or less similar meanings or not, but are not then concerned (at this stage) with just what those meanings were;[9] and (2) applied to *whole utterance-events,* not to parts of utterances. Having once concluded which utterance-events should be classed as "the same" utterance, and having thus assembled a corpus of utterances (not utterance-events) for further analysis, that further analysis can proceed without any further reference to meaning. Our avowed use of meaning here, therefore, does not constitute a concession to Pike's desire to use meaning for the comparison of recurrent parts of utterances. That is one procedure which can be followed in due time; we claim that Pike introduces it at the wrong point in the sequence of analytical observations.

Now it is to be noted that however long an analyst may have been observing a language, the problem as to whether historical utterance

---

[9]Meaning, so defined and so used, is it seems to me not avoided in Bloch's postulates (Bloch, 1948) [16].

A and historical utterance B are linguistically identical or not—if answerable at all with the memory devices at hand—is open to two and only two answers: "yes" and "no." Heuristically, there is the middle ground of "I don't know yet, so I'll record the features I think I hear which seem to differentiate them, and suspend judgment until further evidence is in." But logically there is no middle ground; every such question must in due time be resolved one way or the other. One cannot eat one's cake and have it too. This, however, is precisely what Pike attempts to do with his "potentials."

Pike's problem 212 (p. 163) consists of four short utterances and two longer bracketed sequences of symbols:

['tato'lala'lo'tomo'mara] 'I saw Tom and Mary'
['tato'lala'lo/'tomo'mara] (repeated) 'I saw Tom and Mary'.

(The slant line stands for short pause.) His "phonemic" solution is /tato lala lo tomo mara/ for both. Since all utterances in the corpus begin with onset of stress, and most segments bounded by stress are phonologically free, taking the stress as junctural would be in accord with our definition of juncture. Pike's discussion includes the following remarks: *"Spaces should be written in normal utterances at points where pauses occur, since pauses in natural speech tend to occur only between large grammatical and phonological divisions which are highly pertinent to the language."* And: "There were alternate pronunciations of the first sentence—one with pause and one without pause. In either case *one should normally write a space at points where pauses may optionally be given*, that is, at POTENTIAL PAUSE POINTS."

We have no way of knowing whether or not pauses might be inserted at other points in "the same" utterance. We are limited again by the corpus size; we should have to conclude that this particular "single" utterance can be said in either of the two ways transcribed, but not, say, ['tato/'lala'lo'tomo'mara]. Pike's slant-lined notation therefore writes two different things with the same symbol (space)—point of onset of stress, on the one hand, and point of onset of stress plus possibility of pause on the other. The real problem is: are these two utterance-events actually the same linguistically? Perhaps the first means 'I saw Tom and Mary', the second 'I saw Tom [23 intonation], and Mary'. In this case, we would be led to doubt that the two are actually the "same" utterance—highly similar utterances, true enough, but not identical. Analytically, (1) we cannot assign phonemic status to something when it is not present, and therefore "potential pause" cannot be phonemic; (2) we cannot decide *both* that (actual) pause is phonemic *and* that it is not. Suppose we used a comma instead of no special symbol, but otherwise accepted Pike's slant-lined notation, giving /tato lala lo, tomo mara/, the comma meaning 'pause here if you want to'. The comma cannot, so defined, represent a phoneme. If we decide that internal pause is not phonemic, then it should not be symbolized. If it is phonemic, then the two utterance-events are not linguistically identical, and cannot be transcribed by a single array of symbols in a purely phonemic notation. We should rather have to define /,/ as *actual* pause, and transcribe the first utterance without a comma, the second one with one.

To summarize: If contrasts are not considered, at a particular stage in our observation of a language, to be distinctive, then they must not be noted in a phonemic transcription. If contrasts are distinctive, then two utterances which differ in terms of such a contrast cannot be transcribed at the same time in a phonemic notation. There is, in other words, no place for "potentials" in a phonemic transcription.

Does this mean that there is no place at all for "potentials"? It does not. It is Pike's preoccupation with the aim of a practical orthography which leads him methodologically astray. No language has yet had a generally used writing system in which a single array of graphic symbols stands unambiguously for a single utterance (i.e., for any member of a class of linguistically identical utterance-events). Some linguistically relevant features are always left out, so that the single array of graphic symbols stands for two, three, or many more linguistically different utterances; context, and the special conventions of writing, remove any possible ambiguity (except sometimes when they do not).[10] The reader can read aloud the first English sentence on this page with a dozen different intonations, which will prove the point. It is probably desirable for practical orthographies to have this property. In the task of supplying an illiterate speech community with an effective writing system, it is therefore desirable for the technician to give serious thought to which distinctive features in utterances should *not* be regularly written. At *this* step in his operations, he rightly takes into consideration such items as Pike subsumes under the rubric "potentials."

3 We have gone to some pains to build a thorough foundation for our objections to Pike's phonemic theories. We may now summarize what the differences in point of view seem essentially to be.

It is important to keep clearly in mind the distinction between *theoretical frame of reference* and *actual sequence of operations in the field*. A theory which cannot guide practice is idle speculation; a practice not guided by a carefully and logically elaborated theory— itself subject to constant revision in the light of practical experience—cannot be considered part of science. Like the sailing ship which sets a course due west but must tack north and south in order to follow that course, the field worker must know where he is ultimately going, without being inflexible to the impact of the various more or less favorable winds he encounters. When a mathematician is working out a proof of a theorem, he goes where the winds blow him, he follows his "intuition," he analogizes on the basis of previous mathematical experience; but he has not *established* the proof and the theorem until it comes out as a series of statements of a specified logical

shape. Many an apparent disagreement on method has been resolved when it has become clear that the participants were not talking about the same thing (theory or practice) at the same time. I have tried to avoid any source of such confusion in the foregoing discussion.

It will be noted that we have not objected to any specific criterion or procedure that Pike proposes as of importance in the total task of achieving a practical orthography. The objections which have been raised here concern the *sequence* in which the various criteria are applied, the various procedures undertaken. And here I mean sequence in the theoretical frame of reference (in the shape of the mathematician's final proof) rather than in actual field work (the mathematician's search for the proof), though the latter is involved by implication.[11] Accepting the definition of the overall task as the practical needs of Pike's students shape it, it seems clear that Pike's frame of reference is inefficient and misleading, not atomistically, but as a system. The best of his students will learn anyway, as English-speaking children learn to read despite all the confused "methods" of the educators; the less gifted students will not learn as well as would be possible if they were given theoretically more logical guidance. The really serious danger is that Pike (as a colleague has put it) has over-institutionalized himself, thereby losing the flexibility, the openmindedness towards new evidence and new theory, that any practitioner of our science or any other must constantly maintain.

---

[10]This, of course, is why we speak of *"reducing"* a language to writing.

[11]In his paper before the 1948 Christmas meeting of the LSA, M. Joos pointed out that a given operation can occur more than once in a sequence —even in the logical sequence which constitutes one's frame of reference. But this is still something different from the trial-and-error process of actual field work.

18

MORE ON GRAMMATICAL PREREQUISITES*

KENNETH L. PIKE

0. Introduction A few years ago I wrote an article[1] in which I stated (GPPA 155 [153]) that:

To eliminate the facts of grammatical relationship and structure from the analysis and presentation of phonological structure is frequently undesirable because many of the phonological facts are inextricably interwoven with grammatical facts and structural relationships; avoiding the portrayal of this relationship means omitting, completely or at least temporarily, an important part of the total structure of the language. When phonological and grammatical facts are mutually dependent, the treatment of phonology without reference to grammar is a concealment of part of a most important set of structural facts pertinent to phonology. The apparent gain in compartmentation or systematization of data at the expense of an early indication of such structural phenomena within the total phonological arrangement is too high a price to pay for neatness of statement.

The present paper, by citing a number of recent articles, attempts to show that the validity of a rigid separation of phonemic and grammatical levels in analysis and presentation has not yet been adequately demonstrated.

1. Structure in Relation to Interpenetrating Layers The separateness of phonemics and grammatical layers appears to me to have become for many of our most capable linguists an assumption based on an unwarranted *a priori* judgment: Thus Moulton[2] says:

I believe that the phonemes of a language should be analyzed without reference to syntax or morphology.

This kind of position, it seems to me, has been taken rather to construct aesthetically satisfying compartmentalized systems than to report the manner in which an existing language system is seen to be operating.

Hockett insists that:[3]

a language is what it is, it has the structure it has, whether studied and analyzed by a linguist or not.

Yet in phonemics, it seems to me, he in fact repudiates this conclusion when he claims[4] that a specific language may have

a great many possible phonemic notations—

even though, we note, such solutions lead in that hypothecated language to radically different lists of phonemes,[5] distributions of phonemes, contrastive relations between pho-

---

[1]"Grammatical Prerequisites to Phonemic Analysis" [15], *Word* 3.155–172 (1947); hereafter referred to as GPPA.

[2]"Juncture in Modern Standard German," *Language* 23.225 fn. 14 (1947).

[3]"A Note on 'Structure,'" *IJAL* 14.271 (1948).

[4]"Two Fundamental Problems in Phonemics" [17], *Studies in Linguistics* 7.33 [202] (1949).

[5]Further evidence that Hockett believes that a language does not contain one and only one specific list of phonemes is seen in his statement in "Problems of Morphemic Analysis," *Language* 23.325 (1947):

A notation is phonemic if it indicates, in every position, only those phonemic contrasts which occur in that position, but indicates all of them. Once one has found the morphemically most desirable notation . . .

and (324):

. . . we may discover that a phonemic notation other than the one we have used—for there are always several mutually convertible possibilities—would simplify the task.

*Reprinted from *Word* 8.106–121 (1952) by permission.

nemes, and even kinds of phonemes. Hockett himself attempts to avoid this difficulty by stating (38) [204] that

A phoneme is a phoneme only as part of a stated phonemicization. The "phonemic structure" of a language is not to be equated to any such phonemicization; rather it is the "least common denominator" of every possible sufficient phonemicization: that which may be subsumed by *any* set of phonemic symbols with accompanying instructions for use.

In Hockett's treatment of juncture, one can see most easily the fact that he is unconvinced that a specific list of phonemes exists as part of the structure of a language, but that his phoneme lists are orthographic devices rather than a report of discovered structural units:[6]

A juncture *phoneme* is then a grouping of such phenomena which makes for unambiguous and simple linear transcription. If this last statement seems arbitrary, it is no more so than is, for me, the definition of any kind of phoneme.

Specifically, it appears to me that Hockett, in placing highly diverse elements into a juncture "phoneme," fails to seek such existing structure;[7] his analysis becomes a mechanism to avoid describing interpenetration of levels. His defense in terms of classes is to me unconvincing:

Juncture phonemes, as set up on the above basis, may indeed have one property which is superficially different from the properties usually ascribed to phonemes. We do not ordinarily classify a group of allophones into a single phoneme unless all the allophones have some configuration of phonetic features in common, however much they may differ as to other phonetic features. But the various allophones grouped into a single juncture phoneme may have *nothing in common* [italics mine, K.L.P.] . . . Now, mathematically, a *class* is considered to be *defined* when, if presented with any object, we can say whether or not that object is a member of the class. One

way to set up a class is to specify a *property,* so that possession of that property by an object puts it in the class, lack of that property leaves it out of the class. Thus "even integer" is a property which establishes a class including 2, 4, 6, etc., but not 1, 3, 5, etc., nor a leaf nor a nose. But another perfectly satisfactory way to define a class is by *itemization.* Thus I can establish a class consisting of the first three even integers, all the leaves on the tree outside my window, and the third word on this page. A class so defined is a perfectly good class; it even has properties that can be investigated, e.g., it consists of a certain number of objects. If we insist on tying up a class with a property, in the case of a class of this kind we can regard the property of *membership in the class enumerated* as the associated property. That is, a class can be defined in terms of a property, or vice versa. So we see that the failure of all the allophones of some juncture phonemes to have some (articulatory or acoustic) property in common is no logical defect. We may with perfect validity define a juncture phoneme as consisting of all occurrences in certain specified contexts of certain specified phenomena. . . . Juncture phonemes, where recognized, do consist of allophones with a *structural* property in common; ultimately this may actually be more important.

Although, as the last quoted sentence suggests, Hockett would presumably not concur in these conclusions—and might still feel that he were searching for existing structure in phonemics as well as in grammar—he seems to me to have rejected the existence of a specific limited number of phonemic units. Further, I suggest that this rejection may be related to a rejection, on inadequate grounds, of a methodology which early shows *structural interpenetration of structural levels* of analysis. I see no theoretical reason why the interpenetration of layers cannot be as much a part of structure as the layers themselves.

2. Silent Transitions in Relation to Heard Sounds
In GPPA (161) [157] I pointed out that Trager had described Taos in 1946 in a manner inconsistent with his theory of separate phonemic/grammatical levels. He said:

Word-division has here been determined by morphological criteria when the available phonemic description does not suffice.

[6]*SIL* 7.38 [204] (1949).
[7]*SIL* 7.38–39 [204–205] (1949).

In 1948 Trager published a revision[8] of this study, in which he says (155):

Revisiting Taos after ten years enabled me to hear the things which I *knew had to be there* [italics mine, here and below, K.L.P.] in order to analyze fully the phonological limits of utterances and parts of utterance.

Later, (158) he insists that his statements:

furnish a *purely objective* basis for morphemic and syntactic analyses, based on *things heard* when the language is spoken.

When one seeks in his article a statement of the phonetic elements heard thus objectively at the alleged juncture points, one finds (157):

A phrase may have within it one or more points at which the movements of the organs stop as if before pause, and then begin again as if after pause, but without any actual pause. At such points there is said to occur the phoneme of *plus-juncture* (marked by a hyphen in ordinary orthography and by /+/ in formulas).

If, now, one seeks further a statement of things "heard" pre-pausally and post-pausally —since they are not discussed at the place just quoted—one finds (156):

The pause of greater or less length preceding an utterance and at the points marked by space, comma, or period, with its accompanying *silent transitions* from the pre-pausal to the post-pausal positions of the speech organs, is the phoneme of *external juncture*.

To me it appears dangerously easy to fall into error when to support a theory, a linguist must hear things that "had to be there"— particularly when the items "heard" are silent.

3. Grammatical Techniques in Relation to Grammatical Units
In a review of my *Intonation of American English,* Wells[9] was disturbed (269) by:

a basic and pervasive confusion, in Pike's book, concerning the relation between the work of phonemics and the work of grammar.

Wells objected (259) to my use of grammatical analysis to find the beginning points of intonation contours:

Contour beginning-points [in Pike's analysis] are not determined by phonemics alone, not even by the "impression of a single unified contour" referred to in §3. (insofar as that impression has a purely auditory basis), but by meanings—by grammatical analysis. It follows that if we desire a clear-cut separation of phonemics from grammar, Pike's system must be accordingly modified.

Now Wells, following Harris, had earlier[10] treated intonation contours as morphemes. It follows then, that Wells, in objecting to the use of grammatical techniques for the finding of intonation contours, was objecting to the use of *grammatical techniques* for the finding of *grammatical units.* Such a position, once clearly seen, would appear to me to be untenable. What then was the source of such an objection? To me it appears to have been an *a priori* judgment that "levels" should be kept apart, an assumption which in fact was given precedence by Wells over an acceptance of the report in that volume of the observed data and the observed interrelationships between those data.

4. Potentials (and Meaning) in Relation to Phonological Words
In the process of objecting to the use of grammatical considerations in phonemic analysis, Hockett,[11] for analyzing a phonemic system, rejects the use of meaning *within* utterances, even though accepting a differential use of meaning for utterances as a whole. Thus: (46) [208]

One more remark must be made here before we turn to Pike's "potentials." It has been granted above—nay, proclaimed—that we cannot decide which utterance-events are "the

---

[8]"Taos I: A Language Revisited," *IJAL* 14.155–160 (1948). The earlier quote was from "An Outline of Taos Grammar" 189, *Linguistic Structures of Native America,* Viking Fund Publications in Anthropology 6 (New York, 1946).
[9]*Language* 23.255–273 (1947).

[10]"The Pitch Phonemes of English" [13], *Language* 21.29 [137] (1945): "The argument in favor of regarding pitch contours as morphemes is given below in Part 4."
[11]*SIL* 7.29–51 (1949) [17].

same" for purposes of further analysis without using meaning (as defined). This use of meaning is (1) differential, rather than specific, in the sense that we use it to tell us whether two utterance-events had more or less similar meanings or not, but are not then concerned (at this stage) with just what those meanings were; and (2) applied to *whole utterance-events,* not to parts of utterances. . . . Our avowed use of meaning here, therefore, does not constitute a concession to Pike's desire to use meaning for the comparison of recurrent parts of utterances. That is one procedure which can be followed in due time; we claim that Pike introduces it at the wrong point in the sequence of analytical observations.

In addition to rejecting the use in phonemic analysis of meaning within utterances, Hockett rejects the use of potentials for phonemic analysis, though accepting them at later stages—e.g., the formation of practical orthographies. I find it difficult to select adequate quotations to demonstrate fairly his position, but note the following (47) [209]:

One cannot eat one's cake and have it too. This, however, is precisely what Pike attempts to do with his "potentials."

and (48) [209]:

To summarize: If contrasts are not considered, at a particular stage in our observation of a language, to be distinctive, then they must not be noted in a phonemic transcription. If contrasts are distinctive, then two utterances which differ in terms of such a contrast cannot be transcribed at the same time in a phonemic notation. There is, in other words, no place for "potentials" in a phonemic transcription.
    Does this mean that there is no place at all for "potentials"? It does not. It is Pike's preoccupation with the aim of a practical orthography which leads him methodologically astray.

and (49) [210]:

In the task of supplying an illiterate speech community with an effective writing system, it is therefore desirable for the technician to give serious thought to which distinctive features in utterances should *not* be regularly written. At *this* step in his operations, he rightly takes into consideration such items as Pike subsumes under the rubric "potentials."

I shall now try to demonstrate that Hockett brings in by the back door both the use of such utterance-included meanings and the use of *certain* potentials, in his proposed phonemic approach.
    Hockett gives a basic definition of a phonological word (36) [203]:

But it is also possible to define a *phonological word:* any stretch of phonemes which occurs as a whole utterance, and which cannot be broken into two or more shorter stretches which also so occur, quite regardless of meanings.

I would maintain that the expression "which cannot be broken into two or more stretches which also so occur" is *reference to a potential.* The phrase "also so occur" refers to *distribution elsewhere,* or occurrence elsewhere than in the phrase at hand; this, from the point of view of the one phrase, is reliance on a positive or negative potential for so occurring.
    Nor is this all. To me the term "phonological word" means, if it means anything, a unit phonetically delineated. Hockett seems to mean that also. Thus (36) [203]:

Our phonological inspection . . . has revealed that the borders between phonological words in longer utterances are phonetically marked.

Yet this conclusion seems contradicted in the artificial problem proposed by Hockett (35) [203]:

Now, in linguistic analysis, suppose we are confronted with the following set of forms:
    [ga]   'this'   [gali]   'that'
    [lima]   'boy'   [ma]   'stone'
    [galima] 'this boy' [galima] 'that stone'
. . . But it is obvious that the phonetic sequence [galima] is identical regardless of whether it means 'this boy' or 'that stone'.

Now, however, in spite of the fact that [galima] 'this boy' and [galima] 'that stone' are "identical" phonetically—so that there could be no distinction of internal phonetic markings— Hockett nevertheless handles *each* of these homophonous forms as a sequence of *two* phonological words, with the implication of an (unwritten) phonological *border at a different place* within each. Thus (36) [203–204]:

In the case of [galima] [here representing both sequences, K.L.P.], our procedure would show that this is not a phonological word, [i.e., not a single one, but an ambiguous sequence of two, K.L.P.] since there exist shorter phonological words [by potential for isolated occurrence elsewhere, K.L.P.] such that [galima] can be taken as a sequence of two of them in either of two ways; [i.e., as the phonological word ga 'this' plus the phonological word lima 'boy'—or the phonological word gali 'that' plus the phonological word ma 'stone', K.L.P.]; it would show, however, that there is *not* any phonetic marking of the borders between phonological words in included position . . .

Here, then, we find phonetic (phonological) words which are not phonetic, and we note that the existence of two phonological words in the ambiguous [galima] could only be known (1) after the included items were recognized by their meanings—in spite of Hockett's rejection of that expedient—and (2) after their potential for occurrence elsewhere (i.e., in isolation) was also known.

If we try to discover the reason why Hockett did not notice and correct this contradiction, the answer would seem to lie in the remainder of the sentence last quoted, which ends thus:

. . . so that on the phonological level there would be no justification for any retranscription with spaces or other border markers.

Here Hockett, though aware of the danger that one's orthography may lead one "methodologically astray," seems to have overlooked his implication of non-phonetic but phonological borders within the ambiguous sequence [galima], simply because he had chosen to leave the borders without spaces to mark them.

In his materials on Potawatomi, Hockett shows much more clearly a use of potential—this time, potential for pause.[12]

From utterances we extract *words* (essentially, stretches before and after which the informant will pause on occasion; but see [section] 3).

[12]"Potawatomi I," *IJAL* 14.2 (1948).

In addition (6, §3), morphophonemic phenomena are used:

We now supplement that. Certain successive morphemes in an utterance are joined together by internal morphophonemics, others by external morphophonemics. *Word juncture* is any border between successive morphemes between which internal morphophonemics does not apply. A word is a segment between successive word junctures.

This test and the first do not always correlate perfectly. Occasionally an informant will pause at a point where the phonemic and morphophonemic construction of the elements involved does not permit us to say for sure whether internal or external morphophonemics is involved . . . Occasionally no pause has been observed at a point where clearly external morphophonemics are involved . . . When the two tests do not agree, we follow whichever one calls for postulation of word juncture. In some neither test clearly demands word juncture, and yet we posit it on the (more or less vague) analogy of similar forms, providing our statements of morphophonemics would not be thereby disrupted.

Hockett, however, states that his analysis was largely made by the year 1939, without revision at time of publication to allow for new theory. This probably accounts for the fact that the status of space as a phoneme—or something else—is not too clear, although (216):

phonemically and morphophonemically the hyphen and space have the same status.

and even though the symbol of space here contributes to an unambiguous linear orthography and hence is a juncture phoneme under his recent definition.[13]

5. Meaning in Relation to Phonemic Analysis

If, as I maintained in GPPA, 158–159 [155–156], "the recognition of meanings is a grammatical process"[14] then, as I claimed there, an essential use of differential meaning in phonemic analysis is automatically a grammatical prerequisite to phonemic analysis.

[13]Quoted above, p. 107 [212].
[14]Note, also, Wells in *Language* 23.259: ". . . by meanings—by grammatical analysis."

Bloch attempted[15] to prove, on a strictly theoretical plane, that the use of meaning is not such a necessity (5) [169]:

The basic assumptions that underlie phonemics, we believe, can be stated without any mention of mind and meaning; but meaning, at least, is so obviously useful as a shortcut in the investigation of phonemic structure—one might almost say, so inescapable—that any linguist who refused to employ it would be very largely wasting his time.

Also (fn. 8):

Theoretically it would be possible to arrive at the phonemic system of a dialect entirely on the basis of phonetics and distribution, without any appeal to meaning—provided that in the utterances of the dialect not all the possible combinations of phonemes actually occurred. Given a sufficient sample of the dialect—say twenty or thirty hours of connected speech by an informant, recorded either on a high-fidelity machine or in a minutely accurate phonetic transcription—a linguist could probably work out the phonemic system without knowing what any part of the sample meant, or even whether any two parts meant the same thing or different things.

As the first quotation implies, Bloch himself uses[16] meaning in his actual field work. Yet I suggest that such a procedure is not only "almost inescapable" on a practical plane, but is probably so on a theoretical plane as well—with the investigator's knowledge of *some* semantic differential between *some* utterances as a prerequisite for certainty in phonemic analysis.

The crucial pivot point in Bloch's theoretical framework seems to be his attempt (26) [184] to establish contrast by distribution of sounds without resort to semantic differentia, in Postulate 30. I expect to show that this postulate is weakened[17] because Bloch uses the phrase "free variation," with two vitally dif-

ferent meanings, apparently without being aware that he has substituted one phrase (which I shall hereafter call "free variation type-2"—i.e., with *some* but not all environments in common) for a crucially different homophonous phrase, one which I shall call "free variation type-1"—i.e., with all environments in common. Free variation type-2 is not a member of the class of free variation type-1.

Note (24) [182] Postulate 27, which leads to the definition of free variation type-1:

Postulate 27. There are phonetically different segments that have *all* [italics mine, K.L.P.] their environments in common.
   27.2 Definition. Such segments are *in free variation* with each other.

Many American speakers pronounce words like *sit, pin, fist,* etc., indifferently with the vowel [ɪ] and with a slightly lower vowel, approaching in quality the vowel of *set* and *pen* but remaining everywhere distinct from it: in any environment where they pronounce the one, they will also sometimes pronounce the other. In such a dialect, the two segments, higher and lower [ɪ], therefore have all their environments in common, and are accordingly in free variation with each other.

After noting that in free variation type-1, the segments have all their environments in common, we turn again to Postulate 30:

There are phonetically different segments that have some *but not all* [italics mine, K.L.P.] of their environments in common, and are not in free variation with each other.
   30.2 Definition. Such segments are *in contrast* with each other in their common environments.

It is evident, now, that if "free variation" here means free variation type-1, the phrasing is redundant, and would read thus: "There are phonetically different segments that have some but not all of their environments in common, and do not have all their environments in com-

---

[15]"A Set of Postulates for Phonemic Analysis" [16], *Language* 24.3–46 (1948).
   [16]Such usage may of itself constitute evidence of theoretical importance; see GPPA 156–157 [154].
   [17]Other approaches can also be used to suggest that his attempt is abortive. Thus it may be argued that he has admitted meaning into the system when

he says (8) [171] that "this sameness is no doubt ultimately a matter of biosocial equivalence."
   Miss Eli Fischer-Jørgensen in "Remarques sur les principes de l'analyse phonémique" (TCLC *Recherches structurales* 5.219 [1949]) has argued that variants of a phoneme are never quite identical, and hence the necessary condition of the recurrence of Bloch's defined variants could never be fulfilled.

mon." The use of "free variation [type-1]" adds nothing whatever.

Why, then, was it added? What type of objection was it designed to forestall? The answer perhaps is this: that Bloch hoped to show that sounds occurring in only *different* environments are the same phoneme (i.e., conditioned variants); those in only *same* environments are the *same* phonemes (i.e., in free variation type-1), and those in *partly same* and *partly different* environments would be *different* phonemes. But in the latter is a severe difficulty: if in a particular language [t] but not [d] were to occur initially in utterances, and [d] but not [t] medially in utterances, but both [t] and [d] optionally finally in utterances, the [t]–[d] difference would turn out as phonemic contrast by Postulate 30—whereas experience based on use of semantic criteria would indicate that the [t] varied freely and noncontrastively with [d] in utterance-final position. If, however, such variation type-2 could be *first* eliminated, then Bloch's rule might hold, contrast might be established, and there might possibly be no further grammatical prerequisites to phonemic analysis. This would appear to be the reason for the addition, in Postulate 30, of the phrase "and are not in free variation with each other"; the contrast part was handled there, and the other type—variation type-2— was to be handled (25) [183] in a separate postulate, No. 29:

Postulate 29. There are phonetically different segments that are in free variation with each other in a given set of environments *E*, and also occur elsewhere, but that have no environments in common except the set *E*.
29.2. Definition. Such segments are *partially in complementary distribution, partially in free variation* with each other.

In fact, however, Bloch set up no means for differentiating, without meanings, between the two kinds of situations where distribution is partly alike and partly different. Instead, Postulate 29 and Postulate 30 were written in such a fashion that they *include the same essential conditions*, under different nomenclature. This double use of the same conditions is difficult to see because of the use of the phrase "free variation" in Postulate 30. Actually, "free variation" must there be interpreted as "free variation type-2,"[18] which is the same as in the phrase "partially in complementary distribution, partially in free variation" as set up in Postulate 29.

In order to show that Postulate 29 is not in its underlying conditions essentially different from Postulate 30, note that the illustration given for Postulate 30 can with appropriate re-phrasing be used to illustrate Postulate 29. First we give the illustration as Bloch has it (26) [184] where he uses it to demonstrate contrast:

The segments [ɪ] and [æ] have many environments in common, e.g., [p'...n] in *pin and pan,* [s...l] in *silly* and *salad,* [...kt] in *ictus* and *actor;* but each has certain environments where the other does not occur, e.g., [w...š] and [ˈ...lθ] as environments of [ɪ] in *wish* and *filth,* [f...ð] and [θr...ks] as environments of [æ] in *fathom* and *anthrax.* Since the two segments are not in free variation[19] anywhere, we say that they are in contrast with each other in those environments where they both occur.

Now we repeat the same illustration, chosen from Postulate 30 but reworded to fit the phrasing of the illustration of Postulate 29. We first repeat Postulate 29 for convenience; the reader must determinedly ignore all meanings and lack of phonetic similarity in order to test the postulate as given:

Postulate 29. There are phonetically different segments that are in free variation with each other in a given set of environments *E*, and also occur elsewhere, but that have no environments in common except the set *E*.
29.2 Definition. Such segments are *partially in complementary distribution, partially in free variation* with each other.

Re-phrased illustration:

This is the situation in some dialects of English with respect to [ɪ] and [æ]: only the higher vowel occurs in environments like [w...š] and

---

[18]Note that this *cannot* be free variation type-1, because the segments do not each occur at *every* place where the other occurs. It *can* represent free variation type-2, however, since the two occur in some same environments.

[19]If this is to be read "free variation type-1" (occurrence in all same environments), it adds nothing to the first sentence.

[f...lθ] of the words *wish* and *filth,* and only the lower vowel in environments like [f...ð] and [θr...ks] in the words *fathom* and *anthrax;* but both segments occur, in free variation [type-2] with each other, medially in the environments like [p'...n], and [s...l], and [...kt] in the words *pin* and *pan, silly* and *Sally, ictus* and *actor.* In such dialects we say that [ɪ] and [æ] are partially in complementary distribution, partially in free variation [type-2] with each other.

It may be argued (as suggested to me by Alan Healy, of Melbourne) that the postulates are valid if one uses *free variation* only in reference to the given environment *plus* the larger phrase in which it occurs, as in Postulate 28. That postulate, however, would bring in a free variation type-3; type-2 having *no* environment in common except that set where there is free variation (§29.1), but type-3 *having* other immediate environments in common. Then in my dialect [a] and [ɔ] are in free variation type-3 in *fog* but with common non-free-variation environment [k...t] in *cot* versus *caught.* If Bloch tidies up this difficulty, Postulates 27–30 may look stronger.

Trager and Smith recently have tried a related approach for eliminating the necessity of using meaning—not only by implication from the identification of phonemes but explicitly on a theoretical plane for the identification of morphemes as well: They make "statements" that place morphemes (and/or phonemes, by extension) and meaning on different levels of theory, insisting that they are theoretically separate, and then proceed to ignore the difficulty by using "shortcuts" which allegedly do not destroy the theory of the essentiality of separate analytical levels but which in practice are their actual method of operation without such separation. I fail to find any place where they attempt to teach us *how* to go the long way around, eliminating their own short cut. I am troubled by this use of "statements" where I need demonstration or evidence to appreciate and to utilize their material. In my experience problems assumed or defined out of existence have a troublesome habit of reappearing. Until a theory is translateable into *workable procedure,* i.e., until it is testable by experience in the face of a *hard core of reality in communication,* I do not assume it to be proved.

If I understand Trager correctly, meaning for him is on a metalinguistic level of analysis, beyond microlinguistics (i.e., beyond linguistics as such). Thus, in *The Field of Linguistics* he says:[20]

The full statement of the point-by-point and pattern-by-pattern relations between the language and any of the other cultural systems will contain all the "meanings" of the linguistic forms, and will constitute the metalinguistics of that culture.

In 1951 writing with Smith in *An Outline of English Structure,*[21] meaning is similarly treated by him, in the chapter on metalinguistics (81):

Thus, the morpheme has been defined hitherto in terms of meaning, and all the work done to date in syntax could be termed "meaning syntax." The procedure followed in this *Outline* has endeavored to use the meaning of recurring partials *only as a short cut* [italics mine, K.L.P.] to the establishing of contrasting structural features, as pointed out in 4, and to go forward on the assumption that microlinguistic analysis can and must deal with statements about the distributions of the elements rigidly observed on ascending levels of complexity of organization.

By the time one reaches section 4, referred to in the last quotation—both the phonemes and the morphemes have already supposedly been established—presumably without the theoretical use of meaning. Now it is the analysis of higher levels for which the analytical necessity of meaning is denied (68):

Utterances are analyzed syntactically about as follows: A phonemic transcription is made first. . . . When all the allologs and words are established, we then resort to the usual substitution techniques. After that, statements can be made describing the constructions that occur, in terms of classes of words, allologic changes in the presence of phrase superfixes, classes of superfixes, intonation patterns, and order and concord. It is emphasized that *all this is done without the use of "meaning":*

[20]Occasional Papers No. 1, *Studies in Linguistics* (Norman, 1949), 7.
[21]Occasional Papers No. 3, *Studies in Linguistics* (Norman, 1951).

[italics mine, K.L.P.] it is formal analysis of formal units. In fact, it becomes evident that any real approach to meaning must be based upon the existence of such an objective syntax, rather than the other way round.

Earlier (54), note reference to morpheme identification:

In the present state of morphemic analysis it is often convenient to use the meanings of utterance fractions as a general guide and short-cut to the identification of morphemes. This is especially so in the case of languages that are more or less well known to the analyst, as has been true for most morphemic work done up to now. When we are confronted, however, with a language that we know little about[22] in terms of the relation of the linguistic behavior of the speakers to the rest of their cultural behavior, it becomes clear that *meaning can be of little help as a guide* [italics mine K.L.P.]. The theoretical basis of the analysis

[22]Compare, for an opposite view, Bloomfield ("Meaning," *Monatshefte für Deutschen Unterricht* 35.102 [1943]):
In language, forms cannot be separated from their meanings. It would be uninteresting and perhaps not very profitable to study the mere sound of a language without any consideration of meaning. Even in laboratory phonetics one specifies what word or what part of a word is being analyzed. In studying a language, we can single out the relevant features of sound only if we know something about the meaning. This appears plainly when one confronts an unfamiliar language. An observer who first hears the Chippewa of Wisconsin or Michigan will note down such forms as [gi:žik, gi:šik, ki:žik, ki:šik], and he will not know whether he has recorded one, two, three, or four different words. Only when he learns that all four indifferently mean 'sky' and when he finds similar variations for other unit meanings, will he realize that these variations are not significant. On the other hand, the difference between the final consonants of such forms as [ki:šik] and [ki:šikk] will perhaps at first escape the observer or seem to him to be trifling or irrelevant, until he realizes that this difference goes hand in hand with a gross difference of meaning, since only the forms with a shorter and weaker final consonant mean 'sky', while the others mean 'cedar'. It is only the differences of meaning which decide that most of the inevitable variations of sound are irrelevant and only certain ones play a part in communication. In short, the significant features of sound (the *phonemes*) of a language are, of course, those which involve a difference of meaning.

then becomes evident: it consists of the recognition of the recurrences and distributions of similar patterns and sequences.

Note, finally, (85):

As we have shown in our microlinguistic analyses, the stress phonemes, juncture phonemes, and pitch phonemes are used in English as parts of superfixes and intonation patterns, these being morphemes. On the microlinguistic level, *it was preeminently clear* that the *analysis* [italics mine, K.L.P.] of these entities as morphemes was in no way dependent on their meaning. . . . Intonation patterns, however, do have meanings, and when they have been described microlinguistically, it is possible to begin to examine these meanings.

After having searched to find where Trager and Smith with preeminent clarity demonstrate how they identify and analyze morphemes without the use of meaning, I fail to do so. Their "short cuts" by using meaning still appear to be their own prerequisite procedure to their goal.

6. Field Procedure in Relation to Interpenetrating Levels of Analysis

In GPPA I maintained (156) [154] that:

The first fact to be noted, which indicates an essential relation between phonological and grammatical analysis, is that the field procedure of linguists in general is to conduct some grammatical research simultaneously with phonemic analysis.

and:

Furthermore, it appears to me that one must assume that any elements of unavoidable procedure must in turn reflect something of the structure being analyzed.

Hockett grants[23] the *usefulness* of gram-

[23]"Peiping Morphophonemics," *Language* 26.69–70 (1950). Compare also W. E. Welmers, "Hints From Morphology for Phonemic Analysis," *Studies in Linguistics* 5.91–100 (1947):
In short, *every detail of our phonemic analyses must be justified on the basis of phonetic considerations alone* . . . a shove along the road of phonemic analysis by our knowledge of morphology. However, the final test of our phonemic analysis must be that of phonetic justifiability; yet our choice of one out of several possible phonemic analyses may be determined by the morphology.

mar in phonemic analysis, but not its *essentiality:*

We have been led to this rephonemicization through grammatical considerations; but once discovered the new analysis is established purely on phonological grounds.

Also (fn. 10):

This is a statement of historical fact. Since the discovery of the possible rephonemicization obviously came about before this paper was ready for publication, it would have been possible to introduce it before, rather than after, the discussion of morphophonemics. But it seemed worthwhile to retain the ordering of matters as above, as a fairly elaborate demonstration of the way in which grammatical considerations can serve as *clues* for phonological analysis without implying that the latter is *logically* built on the former; there are still no grammatical "prerequisites" for phonemic analysis.

Hockett also grants[24] that:

Pike's non-phonetic criteria in phonemics . . . do not belong in phonemics by my definition, but most of them belong somewhere in the total task of linguistic analysis and practical application, and the problem is one of sorting out and reordering, rather than of rejection.

In 1942 Bloch and Trager insisted:[25]

The procedure by which we analyze the grammar of a language is in principle the same as that used in phonemics. Here again we examine a collection of utterances, list the recurrent fractions, and establish classes by grouping together parts of different utterances which are alike in form and function. Phonemic *analysis must* come *first* [italics mine, K.L.P.] (cf. §3.2); for the utterance fractions listed and compared in grammatical analysis are not sounds but meaningful forms phonemically recorded.

It is important that the reader note that it is phonemic analysis—not phonemic presentation—which Bloch and Trager here affirm must come first. In GPPA[26] I pointed out the untenable nature of this position. Bloch now argues[27] that it is *presentation* of phonemics which must come before presentation of grammar:

Such a record [ignoring all features that are distinctive but not immediately observable in the stream of speech, such as morpheme boundaries, word structure, and morphophonemic relations] is the only safe and adequate basis for further investigations of linguistic structure; the analyst who attempts to study the morphemes or the grammatical constructions of a language in terms of a transcription that is either less or more than phonemic— a raw phonetic transcription on the one hand, or on the other a transcription that tacitly relies on non-phonetic evidence—will either be lost in a confusion of irrelevant details or overlook significant correlations between the phonemic structure and the structure of other linguistic levels. This does not mean (though it has now and then been misunderstood [with fn. referring to my GPPA, K.L.P.]) that the analyst should shut his eyes to all morphemic and grammatical facts until he has completely worked out the phonemics of a new language. Facts of all kinds come to his attention from the very beginning of his first interview with an informant, and should be filed away as they appear, even if some of them cannot be imme-

---

[24]C. F. Hockett, "Which Approach in Linguistics is 'Scientific'?" *Studies in Linguistics* 8.55 (1950).

[25]Bloch and Trager, *Outline of Linguistic Analysis,* 53.

[26]P. 157 [154–155]:
Since "Many of the most significant grammatical facts of a language can be deduced from a crude and inaccurate phonetic transcription: Morphemes can often be identified even by rough similarity in form and meaning; indeed, even accurate phonemic transcriptions sometimes show the morphemes in variant forms. Once the morphemes are identified, they can be grouped into major and minor form classes: into stems, affixes, and the like; into tenses, aspects, etc.; into words, compounds, or phrases; into structural layers of immediate constituents. Boundaries between morphemes, words, clauses, utterances and so on, may then usually be established. That is to say, many of the most important structural facts which differentiate two languages can be discovered from crude phonetic data, subject to some omissions if pertinent sounds are overlooked, or unnecessary complexity of form at those points where allophones, instead of phonemes, are transcribed."

[27]"Studies in Colloquial Japanese IV," *Language* 26.124 (1950).

diately accommodated in a larger system. . . . Finally, when he comes to write down his description of the language so that others may see the structure that he has discovered, he must group the many facts *to be presented* [italics mine, K.L.P.] (since he cannot present them all at once) into separate compartments or levels, each one organically distinct from the others; and here the requirements of good method and good style demand that the statements made on any given level be as independent *as possible* [italics mine; just how impossible is "as possible"? K.L.P.] of those made at other levels—in particular, that they assume as known only what has been said earlier, nothing that is to be said later.

Trager and Smith in 1951 also admit that in actual procedure phonological and morphological materials are handled together.[28]

This is not to say that in the *actual*[29] [italics mine, K.L.P.] procedure of analyzing a language there is not a constant going back and forth between phonology and morphemics, with refinements and corrections being made in either direction. But the analyst must at all times be aware of the level-differences, and the systematic presentation must always be made in terms of the logical sequence, in one linear order, with the levels carefully distinguished.

Bloch goes much farther. In spite of his statement in our last quotation from his material that a phonemic transcription (as defined by him) is the only safe and adequate basis for further investigation of linguistic structure, he in the next paragraph of the article (124–125) states that a non-phonemic orthography of a certain type, when used for the writing of connected texts "reveals more of the linguistic structure"! The entire paragraph is worth quoting:

However, it does not follow that a rigorously phonemic transcription must be retained throughout all the levels of a descriptive treatment, or that forms cited near the end of the work in the exposition of syntax must be written in the same way as those cited in the exposition of morphemics near the beginning. Once the transcription has been used in the study of morphemes (in particular, of morpho-

phonemic alternations), it may be legitimately modified, elaborated, or normalized on the basis of new facts now first made fully available to the reader. A normalized notation, still firmly based on the phonemic analysis but incorporating the most common or the most important morphophonemic relations—especially those that are automatic—and such grammatical features as word boundaries and pitch morphemes, approaches the character of a practical orthography. It is usually *far better* [italics mine, K.L.P.] adapted to the discussion of morphology and syntax than a wholly unmodified transcription; when used for the writing of connected texts it *reveals more of the linguistic structure;* [italics mine, K.L.P.] and those who already know the language find it easier to read.

Bloch, as I pointed out in GPPA 160–161 [157], had in his earlier materials[30] used a "phonemic" transcription which according to his own definition was nonphonemic, since it brought in word borders symbolized by spaces which have no phonetic value. Bloch now[31] grants this. But a curious fact remains: according to his recent theory just quoted, the earlier orthography, now repudiated, may have been "better adapted to the discussion of morphology and syntax" than the newer, supposedly more "adequate" one is.

7. Circularity There seems to be one major objection[32] to the utilization of grammatical considerations in phonemic analysis: the alleged circularity of the techniques: Thus Hockett:[33]

And when morphemes are defined formally, it becomes perfectly obvious that use of position in morphemes or relative to morpheme borders as a criterion in phonemic analysis is completely circular.

This objection seems to me invalid.

---

[28]*An Outline of English Structure,* 54.
[29]Contrast their *theory,* quoted above.

[30]"Studies in Colloquial Japanese II," *Language* 22.202 (1946).
[31]*Language* 26.86 (1950).
[32]Apart from the desire to keep levels apart.
[33]*Studies in Linguistics* 7.40 [205] (1949). Compare, also, his discussion of proposed phonemes of speed in "Peiping Morphophonemics" (*Language* 26.76–77 [1950]), and note his uncertainty as to the circularity of his argument at that point (especially in his fn. 16).

Bloch,[34] Trager,[35] and Hockett[36] have now all acknowledged explicitly or implicitly that some grammatical analysis can be made with phonetic data—as I contended in GPPA 157 [154–155].[37]

It is precisely because of this fact that it is possible to utilize in phonemic analysis certain grammatical facts (in addition to differential meanings) in some languages without being circular.

The investigator (1) first listens to utterances—which, as the analyst knows,[38] simultaneously contain phonological and grammatical facts. These (2) he records with rough impressionistic phonetic symbols. In these data, (3) he makes numerous kinds of grammatical (including semantic) discoveries—as to contrastive utterances, grammatical borders, meanings of total utterances or parts of utterances, and the like. With these data, (4) he can tentatively determine some phonemic contrasts and phoneme units. (5) He rewrites his earlier data phonemically insofar as these partial phonemic conclusions allow him to do so. Then (6) he reaches further phonemic conclusions based upon (a) the remainder of the initial impressionistically recorded material, (b) the tentative grammatical and semantic discoveries, and (c) the tentative partial phonemicization of the early data; or he makes further grammatical structural discoveries within the phonetically recorded or quasi-phonemically recorded material; or he proceeds to record further data, utilizing either the original impressionistic orthography or the quasi-phonemic orthography. From this, (7) he continues taking further steps in analysis, reaching further phonemic conclusions and further grammatical conclusions. (8) He continues working thus, from phonetics to grammar; and from grammar and phonetics to phonemics; and from phonemics, phonetics, and grammar to progressively revised and amplified phonemics and grammar. Eventually, (9) he is finished, when all data are accounted for and his analysis has reached a state of equilibrium, with no changes needed to account for old or new recorded data or analytically obtained units.

Such a procedure need not be circular; rather it is a *spiral* procedure, building higher conclusions on earlier conclusions and data, moving where necessary from one type of data to another and back again. Of course, errors may creep in, during the application of the spiral approach. A possibility of error in the application of a procedure, however, invalidates no procedure as such—else no procedure existing or conceivable would be valid. If errors or infelicities have entered the descriptions made by particular individuals—in mine, for example—these errors should be eliminated and the procedure refined.[39] But one should not throw out valid spiral procedure (with grammatical considerations or valid non-

[39]See, for example, the discussion in my "A Problem in Morphology-Syntax Division" (*Acta Linguistica* 5.125–138 [1950]), especially pp. 137–138, where fusion in English phrases prevents certain grammatical borders from being co-terminous with certain phonological ones. For a recent European reaction to the problem, see E. M. Uhlenbeck, "The Structure of the Javanese Morpheme," in *Lingua* 2.254–255 (1950):

> In determining what are phonemes in a language we do not accept the point of view that one should draw a distinct dividing-line between the grammatical and the phonological analysis. Some American linguists favour this point of view. . . . Thus—purely by means of criteria of a phonal nature—he [Hockett] arrives at the phonemes, which therefore for him and other American linguists can be nothing but relevant "features of sound," whereas according to our definition phonemes are relevant moments of the form of the word and the morpheme. This aversion from the use of grammatical distinctions in phonological analysis has been—and in our opinion rightly—criticized by Pike.

See also Roman Jakobson, "The Phonemic and Grammatical Aspects of Language and Their Interrelation," in *Proceedings of the Sixth International Congress of Linguists* (Paris, 1948), 5–18.

[34]*Language* 26.124 (1950): "This does not mean (though it has now and then been misunderstood) that the analyst should shut his eyes to all morphemic and grammatical facts until he has completely worked the phonemics of a new language. Facts of all kinds come to his attention from the very beginning . . ."

[35]*An Outline of English Structure,* 54 (1951): "This is not to say that in the actual procedure of analyzing a language there is not a constant going back and forth between phonology and morphemics, with refinements and corrections being made in either direction."

[36]*Language* 26.69 (1950): "We have been led to this re-phonemicization through grammatical considerations . . ." so some grammatical analysis, or non-phonemic data, was known first.

[37]See fn. 26, above.

[38]See GPPA 159–160 [156].

phonetic considerations in phonemic analysis) with any particular error discovered in particular descriptions.

A systematic statement of the relation between the levels of analysis, however, is needed. Such a statement I have in preparation as part of a volume on the nature of linguistic structure—a project which has been absorbing a large part of my attention for the past several years.

19

CONTRAST*

BERNARD BLOCH

Contrast between sounds can be defined, I think, on the basis of distribution alone, without the customary appeal to meaning. On two earlier occasions I tried to formulate such a definition,[1] but both times without success—largely because the essential criterion was not yet clear to me. A number of readers, fastening on the weak spot in my argument, have quite properly refused to accept the conclusions based on it.[2] This third attempt to state my position has the excuse that I now think I know what the position is.

The range of an allophone[3] in some finite sample of a dialect (theoretically also in the dialect as a whole) is defined by a list of all the environments in which members of the allophone occur. Less precisely but more usefully, the range of an allophone can also be defined in general terms, by reference to the features of position, accent, or surrounding sounds that are common to the environments of the member phones or to particular subsets of member phones, but without specific mention of any individual environments. What

such a *general definition* defines is not the exact range of the allophone in question, but rather a class of possible environments, including the range of the allophone and also some environments in which members of the allophone do not occur. By making the number of features referred to in the definition large enough, it is possible to reduce the otiose environments to a practicable minimum, a point at which their existence does not impair the diagnostic value of the definition for the purposes of phonemic analysis. But although these otiose environments can be reduced in variety, they cannot be eliminated altogether so long as the definition of the range does not list the constituent environments one by one.[4]

Comparing the range of one allophone

---

[1] "A Set of Postulates for Phonemic Analysis" [16], *Language* 24.3–46 (1948), esp. 22–26 [181–184]. Postulates 25–31, and the definitions prefixed to an account of Japanese phonemes, *Language* 26. 89–90 (1950).

[2] See Eli Fischer-Jørgensen, "Remarques sur les principes de l'analyse phonémique," *TCLC* 5.214–234 (1949); John Lotz, "Speech and Language," *Journal of the Acoustical Society of America* 22.712–717 (1950); Kenneth L. Pike, "More on Grammatical Prerequisites" [18], *Word* 8.106–121 (1952).

[3] For the definition of technical terms, see the two passages cited in fn. 1. Specific references: for *allophone*, *Language* 24.38 [193] (§54.2); for *dialect*, 24.8 [171] (§3.2); for *environment*, 24.22 [181] (§25.3), 26.89; for *phone*, 26.89, and cf. 24.12 [174] (§12.3), 24.35 [191] (§52.3); for *range*, 24.30 [187] (§42.3).

[4] Thus, the range of [ň] (the class of all voiced nasalized apical flaps or one-tap trills) in some sample of English can be very simply defined: members of the allophone occur after a vowel or semivowel and before a weak-stressed vowel (as in *winter, painting, counter, carpenter, Mount Olympus*). The range of [ŋ′] (the class of all front or prevelar voiced nasals), again in some sample of English, requires a general definition somewhat more complex: members of this allophone occur (1) final in a syllable after a front vowel (as in *bingo, sang, making*) or after the semivowel [j] (as in *boing* or a monosyllabic pronunciation of *being, saying, trying*); (2) after a front vowel or [j] before prevelar [k′] in a strong stressed syllable (as in *think, winked, jinx, Schenck, Jenks, bank, Manx, Schumann-Heinck, oink-oink*); and (3) after the vowel [ɛ] before [þ] in a strong-stressed syllable (as in *length*). If the choice of defining features is correct, any environment in which a member of one of the allophones occurs will be found to exhibit one of the features referred to in the definition. But there will be countless environments, both among those that actually occur in the sample studied and among the vastly greater number that do not occur but can be invented, which exhibit one of these features and yet contain no member of the allophone in question.

*Reprinted from *Language* 29.59–61 (1953) by permission.

(however defined) with the range of another allophone in the same dialect or sample, yields a statement of the relation between the two ranges, or the *relative distribution* of the two allophones. For any pair of allophones P and Q, there are four possible types of relative distribution:

(1) Complementary: the ranges of P and Q are mutually exclusive. If the environments are listed in full, the two lists have no member in common; if the ranges are defined in general terms, the two definitions have no feature (of position, accent, or surrounding sounds) in common.

(2) Coincident: the ranges of P and Q are the same. Every environment of P is also an environment of Q,[5] and conversely.

(3) Incorporating: the whole range of P is a part of the range of Q. That is, the range of P is wholly included within the range of Q, but not conversely. Every environment of P is also an environment of Q, but Q has environments in which P does not occur.

(4) Overlapping: a part but not all of the range of P is a part but not all of the range of Q. The two ranges have some environments in common, but each range includes environments which are not in the other.

---

[5]Provided that each environment is interpreted as composed of allophones rather than phones. The statement in the text can be more pedantically paraphrased as follows: To any environment of P consisting of the phones $a_1b_1c_1$ . . . there corresponds an environment of Q consisting of the phones $a_2b_2c_2$ . . . , such that a_1 and a_2, b_1 and b_2, c_1 and c_2, etc., belong respectively to the same allophones —and conversely.

If we speak of the environments common to a pair of ranges as the (pars) *communis,* and of the environments in one range not shared by the other as the (pars) *propria,*[6] we can characterize the four types of relative distribution as follows: in complementary distribution, there is no communis; in coincident distribution, there is no propria in either range; in incorporating distribution, one range has a propria but the other has not; in overlapping distribution, each range has a propria in addition to the communis.

The rest of this paper will be stated in postulational form.[7]

Postulate In any dialect there are pairs of allophones P and Q in overlapping or incorporating distribution, such that the communis of their ranges cannot be distinguished from either propria by any general definition.

Corollary For any such pair of allophones P and Q, the communis of their ranges can be distinguished from either propria only by a complete listing of the individual environments.

Definition Such allophones P and Q are *in contrast* with each other, and any member of P is *in contrast* with any member of Q.

Definition Any pair of allophones P' and Q' to which the provisions of this postulate do not apply are *noncontrastive* with each other, and any member of P' is *noncontrastive* with any member of Q'.

---

[6]These terms are adopted from Rulon S. Wells, "Automatic Alternation," *Language* 25.99–116 (1949), esp. 104. (Wells uses the terms communis and propria for parts of morphs.)

[7]This postulate is intended to replace the seven postulates referred to in fn. 1. Other parts of my 1948 set of postulates are similarly in need of restatement and simplification.

THE BINARY INTERPRETATION
OF ENGLISH VOWELS*
A Critique
HANS KURATH

1 The first question to be considered here is whether the traditional view concerning the positional restriction of the phoneme /h/ in Modern English has been successfully challenged or not. Before considering the evidence and the arguments advanced in favor of a new doctrine, we shall give an outline of the traditional view in structural terms and point out the factual basis on which it rests. In doing so, we shall have occasion to call attention to structural facts in support of the traditional view that have either been overlooked or underrated.

Briefly stated, the traditional view is as follows.

Old English had an /h/ phoneme in two positions only: before vowels, semi-vowels, and sonorants, as in *hūs, hwīt, hlāf* (pronounced as [h]), and after vowels, as in *sih, niht*, and *plōh, brōhte* (pronounced as palatal and velar fricatives respectively). Between vowels, /h/ had been lost prehistorically, as in *sēon* 'see' (corresponding to OHG and OS *sehan*). In addition, OE had a long /hh/ phoneme, as in *hliehhan, hlæhhan* 'laugh' (corresp. to OHG *hlahhan*, Goth. *hlahjan*) and *cohhetan* 'cough', pronounced as a palatal or velar fricative, which occurred only between vowels (like all other long consonants of OE).

In ME this situation persisted until phonemically long consonants were eliminated (before 1200 in parts of the Midland and the North, after 1400 elsewhere).[1] Thereafter ME

[1]See H. Kurath, "The Loss of Long Consonants and the Rise of Voiced Fricatives in Middle English," *Language* 32.435–445 (1956).

had an /h/ phoneme in all positions, pronounced as [h] before vowels and /w/, and as a palatal or velar fricative after vowels and between vowels: *hŏus, whīt; hīgh, night, plŏugh, broughte; laughen, coughen.*

In Early MnE, according to the traditional view, the phoneme /h/ was lost in all positions except before vowels, before the semivowel /w/ as in *white*, and before the semivowel /y/ as in *hew, huge* (which arose through the change of ME *eu* and *ū* to /yu/ in MnE). In Standard British English (and in American English spoken in a narrow belt along the Atlantic coast), /h/ was later lost also before /w/ and /y/.

If this view is accepted, most varieties of American English have the phoneme /h/ only before vowels and before the semivowels /y, w/, and Standard British English only before vowels.

This prevocalic /h/ is voiceless if the following vowel has full stress or half-stress; it may or may not be partially or fully voiced before a weakly stressed vowel, as in *prohibition, annihilate*, and in the unstressed allomorphs of *he, her, have*, etc., as in *if he can't, I'll tell her, I have seen it*, unless it is dropped entirely. The voiced variant is clearly a prosodic allophone of the phoneme /h/. Hence, the absence or presence of voice is not a distinctive feature of /h/; its distinctive feature is friction.

This phoneme /h/ is traditionally grouped with the voiceless fricatives /f, θ, s, š/, although it has, as a unique feature, a prosodic voiced allophone. The distinctive feature of friction justifies this classification.

*Reprinted from *Language* 33.111–122 (1957) by permission.

Like other fricatives, /h/ enters into initial clusters with the semivowels /y, w/, as in *hew, white,* with which compare the initial clusters of *few, thwart, swim.* If MnE /h/ does not form clusters with sonorants, as other fricatives do (cf. *from, flow, throw, slow, snow, smell, shred*), one may point out that no two fricatives of MnE have precisely the same clustering habits (witness the unique /sp-, st-, sk-/).

Therefore, neither with regard to its distinctive feature, friction, nor with respect to clustering (pattern congruity) can this /h/ be grouped with the semivowels /y/ and /w/, as in *yell* and *well,* which are frictionless and occur in initial clusters after sonorants, fricatives, and stops (e.g., in *mute, few, swim, twice*), positions in which /h/ never appears. No structuralist can overlook these patent facts.

2 Postvocalic /h/ was first posited for Modern English by George L. Trager and Bernard Bloch in 1941, in their article "The Syllabic Phonemes of English" [9] (*Language* 17.223–246), shortly thereafter reasserted in their *Outline of Linguistic Analysis* (Baltimore, 1942). Owing to the fact that the *Outline* served as an introduction to structural linguistics for the many young linguists who were trained to prepare descriptions, text books, and dictionaries of various languages during the war years and after, this doctrine has been widely accepted.

It will be well to quote the substance of the statements made by Bloch and Trager concerning the English vowels and the posited semivowels /y, w, h/ in their *Outline of Linguistic Analysis* 50–51. I have inserted the numbers [1] to [10] for convenience in commenting on specific points in this passage.

. . . English syllabics can be completely and accurately described in terms of six vowel phonemes, which occur as peaks of syllables either alone or in combination with a following semivowel [1]. In the distribution of these vowels and diphthongs, English dialects differ more than in any other feature. For the dialect here analyzed the facts are classified as follows.

Simple vowels with strong stress occur only in checked syllables . . . in *pit* /i/, *pet* /e/, *pat* /a/, *pot* /o/, *cut* /ə/, *put* /u/ . . .

Diphthongs occur both in checked and in free syllables: /ej/ . . . in *bay, bait* . . . ; /aj/ . . . in *buy, bite* . . . ; /oj/ . . . in *boy, boil;* /aw/ . . . in *cow, bout;* /ow/ . . . in *go, boat* . . . /ij/

. . . in *see, beat* . . . ; and /uw/ . . . in *too, boot* . . .

Long vowels [2] occur both in checked and in free syllables: /a·/ in *calm, father;* /o·/ in *caught, law* . . . ; /e·/ . . . occurs . . . in some varieties of our dialect in words like *bad, adds, jazz, (tin) can* . . . The most efficient [3] analysis is to regard the element which we have written here with a raised dot as a separate phonemic unit, which calls for a special allophone of the preceding vowel phoneme—longer and qualitatively different from the allophones in other positions [4]; after certain vowels, the element /·/ appears as a nonsyllabic [ə].

This unit is in complementary distribution with [h]: the latter occurs only initially and medially after a weak-stressed vowel or certain consonants, the other never in these positions. Phonetically, the element /·/ is a voiced continuation of the preceding vowel, with the same or a progressively centralized tongue position; it is thus, except in the matter of voicing, the converse of /h/, described above as partial or complete voiceless anticipation of a following voiced sound. On the basis of distribution and phonetic similarity [5], we may simplify our transcription [6] by classing [h] and the "lengthening element" together in one phoneme, written /h/; and we may accordingly write the combinations discussed in the preceding paragraph as /ih, eh, ah, oh, uh/. Since /h/ here acts like /j/ and /w/ in forming compound syllabics with a preceding vowel [7], we group /h, j, w/ together in a structural set . . . and label them semivowels, even though the phonetic definition of this term . . . does not apply to [h] [8].

Before /r/, the simple vowels occur with strong stress only if a weak-stressed vowel immediately follows the consonant, as in *mirror, merry, marry, sorry, hurry, jury.* Before final /r/ we find six contrasting syllabics, as in *beer, bear, bar, bore, burr, boor,* which appear also in such words as *dearer, Mary, starry, story, furry, Jewry.* None of the words in this last series rimes with any of the words in the series *mirror–jury.* Noting the resemblance of some of the syllabics [9] in the series *beer–boor* and *dearer–Jewry* to those analyzed above as consisting of a vowel + /h/, we write the series *beer–boor* as /bihr, behr, bahr, bohr, bəhr, buhr/.

In regarding the syllabics of *pat, bite, cow, calm* (or of *pot, boil, boat, law,* or of *cut, burr*) as phonemically related, we do not of course mean to imply that they all contain phonetically identical vowels. The analysis we have made means only that we have classed to-gether, for the purpose of simplifying and sys-tematizing our description of the language, cer-tain objectively different categories of sounds; it neither denies the difference between them nor considers it unimportant. Phonetic diver-sity among allophones of the same phoneme is after all not uncommon; we ask only that such allophones be complementarily distributed, and characterized by a phonetic feature or combination of features absent from the mem-bers of all other phonemes. For each of our six vowel phonemes, we establish as the char-acterizing feature a certain range of tongue po-sitions, according to the following descriptions: /i/ high non-back; /u/ high non-front; /e/ mid front; /a/ low non-back; /o/ non-high back; /ə/ mid central, or perhaps rather all remaining vowel qualities, including the syllabicity of syllabic consonants [10]. Note that our de-scriptions leave the exact tongue position, as well as the position of the lips, unspecified; these vary from one allophone to another, but always within the limits of the range we have defined.

I shall comment briefly on the ten points identified by the numbers I have inserted in the passage quoted above.

(1) The authors tell us on p. 47 that "only the finished classification is presented, usually without reference to the phonetic material on which it is based." No reference is provided to their article [9] in *Language* 17.223–246, where one might expect to find a justification of "the finished classification." In fact, one looks there in vain for any satisfactory evi-dence.[2] All we have, then, is the dogmatic as-sertion that "English syllabics can be com-pletely and accurately described in terms of six vowel phonemes."

[2]There is only one point in this paper that calls for separate comment. The statement (233–234) [80] that *being, buying, going, booing,* etc., "exhibit a syllabic structure exactly parallel to that of such words as *bidding, bedding ... budding, pudding*" is an extremely doubtful assertion, and cannot be used as evidence either for or against a unitary or a binary phonemicization of the diphthongal phones in *be, buy, go, boo,* etc. Hence it cannot be cited in sup-port of the assumption that the "free vowels" of *be, bay, go, boo,* etc., are phonemically complex, and that therefore "a strong-stressed short vowel cannot end a syllable." The authors admit that in English unstressed syllables do end in a vowel (e.g., *sofa*); why not also stressed syllables? Why set the principle of pattern congruity aside in this instance?

(2) "Long vowels" here means "phoni-cally long vowels." It is at best doubtful whether the vowels of *calm* and *law* are phoni-cally longer under the same prosodic condi-tions than the other low or lowish vowels, as in *odd* and *man,* which the authors treat as "simple vowels."[3] Hence the phonic (phonetic) basis for assuming that *calm* and *law* have "simple vowels" plus [·] = /h/ is anything but secure.

(3) "Efficient" is a weasel word. If the phonemicization does not square with observ-able facts, it must be rejected, no matter how "efficient" the solution may appear. See (5), (6), and (7) below.

(4) How can a phoneme whose phonic character depends wholly upon the preceding phoneme (as the authors themselves state) determine the allophonic character of that pho-neme? Allophonic variants are produced, as everyone admits, by the (partial) anticipation or prolongation of an articulatory (hence acoustic) feature of a following or preceding sound. Clearly, this postulated /h/ cannot af-fect a preceding vowel. I would urge the ac-ceptance of this methodological principle: if two phonemic solutions appear to be equally probable or equally doubtful, the solution that facilitates the tie-up between the synchronic and the diachronic treatment of the language should be adopted.

(5) Prevocalic [h] and the "lengthening element" said to occur after vowels cannot be "classed together . . . on the basis of . . . pho-netic similarity," even though they are in com-plementary distribution. The distinctive phonic feature of [h] is friction, not tongue and lip position, which are incidental, depending upon the following vowel. The incidental (allo-phonic) feature—variation in tongue position —cannot be regarded as the distinctive feature of the authors' postulated postvocalic /h/.

(6) A "transcription" cannot be simpli-fied arbitrarily. We must establish the pho-nemes before we assign symbols to them, i.e.,

[3]On objective vowel length in two varieties of American English, see Roe-Merrill S. Heffner and Winfred P. Lehmann, *American Speech* 12.128–134 (1937). On the devastating implications of these ob-jective data for the system of six "short" vowels asserted by Bloch and Trager, see Einar Haugen and W. F. Twaddell, "Facts and Phonemics" [10], *Lan-guage* 18.230 [92] ff. (1942).

decide upon a transcription. The authors' statement is persuasive, not cognitive.

(7) This is an inference from an unsupported prior decision. If [·] and [ə] are not /h/, they cannot be classed with the postulated /y/ and /w/ as the semivowel /h/.

(8) The authors obviously rank a clearly distinctive phonic feature below an arbitrarily postulated "structuring" feature—for the sake of a neat vowel scheme?

(9) This is an inference from points (7) and (8), which I have rejected above. Note also that *starry* and *calm* are said to have the same vowel as *marry* and *pat*, and that *law, go, boy,* and *bore* are said to have the vowel of *pot*. See also their table on p. 52. I have commented on this point in my review of the *Outline*.[4]

(10) The authors make their apology, it seems, for their loose and arbitrary handling of phonic features. They undertake to justify their procedure by telling us that "simplifying and systematizing" their "description of the language" was their purpose, and they remind us that "phonetic diversity among allophones of the same phoneme is after all not uncommon." As to the former, I reply that it is the aim of structural analysis to discover the system of the language, not to impose a system on it, however neat and symmetrical. As to the latter, I ask whether it is not incumbent upon the structuralist to account for the assumed allophones in phonic terms as well as in terms of distribution. To be specific, if *law* /loh/ and *boil* /bojl/ are assumed to have the same vowel phoneme as *pot*, we should be told how the [ɑ]-like allophone of *pot* /pot/ is related to the [ɔ]-like allophones occurring in *law* and *boil*. Do /y/ and /h/ raise and round [ɑ] to [ɔ], or do all other consonants lower and unround [ɔ] to [ɑ]?

3 The *Outline of English Structure* by G. L. Trager and H. L. Smith Jr. (Norman, Okla., 1951) presents no new evidence in support of postulating postvocalic /h/. The authors find "nine simple vowel phonemes [1] in English as a whole," and

complex nuclei beginning with one of the nine vowel qualities, and ending with offglides of

[4] *American Journal of Philology* 66.209 (1945).

three kinds: a glide to a higher and fronter position . . . one to a higher, back, more rounded position . . . one to a more central, unrounded position . . . [2] Within each of these contrasting sets, there is a complementary distribution, and the three show pattern congruity with each other . . . If each complex is to be taken as a unit, there must be 27 phonemes involved [3]. But the beginnings of the complex nuclei are clearly like allophones of the nine already identified phonemes . . . and the ends of them show patterns and distributions expected of separate phonemes [4]. The conclusion is inescapable [5] that the complex nuclei consist each of two phonemes, one of the short vowels [6] followed by one of three glides (20).

I shall comment briefly on five points indicated by the numbers I have inserted in the quotation.

(1) The evidence presented by the authors (12–14) for the nine "simple vowels," which are said to constitute a neat three-by-three system (14), is deficient. The well known ingliding diphthongs used by many Americans in *give, bed, good, sun,* etc., are disregarded in this "over-all" analysis of American English. If postvocalic [ə] is phonemicized as /h/ elsewhere, why not also here? From the point of view of the analysis presented by Trager and Smith, such diphthongal pronunciations can certainly not be regarded as phonemically "simple." Nor can these posited simple vowels be called "short," as the authors do at point [6]. See footnote 3.

(2) This statement glosses over the monophthongal vowels occurring in various American English dialects in such words as *bee, beat, go, goat,* etc., in which the authors later discover a feature of length, which they combine with [ə] in the postulated phoneme /h/.

(3) One cannot object in principle to a large number of phonemes, if the language has them. However, the authors really mean that there are 27 (9 times 3) theoretical possibilities for English "as a whole," if one regards such diphthongs as unit phonemes. Bloomfield found only 8 (actually 7) in Chicago English (*Language* 90–91); the authors record only 13 "complex nuclei" as clearly established in Trager's speech (22–24), including 6 with /h/. The authors' statement is deterrent, not factual.

(4) The ends of the so-called "complex nuclei" do not "show patterns and distribu-

tions expected of separate phonemes." They are allophonic offglides, as pointed out below.

(5) The conclusion is not "inescapable," since the premises are false. It is untenable.

If the statements criticized above are theory-ridden, negligent in the treatment of easily observable facts of pronunciation, and persuasive rather than objective, the attempt made in the following passage (21–22) to get /h/ into the fold of the "semivowels" is nothing short of reckless. The passage reads as follows:

The allophones of the prevocalic phonemes /y w h/ parallel in quality and distribution those of the post-vocalic glides /F B C/ [1] . . . In the case of /y w/ the allophones are each a little higher than the corresponding ones of /F/ and /B/, and the highest often have some friction noise [2]. For /h/, the allophones are partly voiceless and have friction-noise onset, while those of /C/ are usually fully voiced, and even when ending voiceless (in utterance-final, for some speakers) are frictionless [3]. There is thus phonetic similarity, the allophones of /y w h/ being onglide mirror images of the off-glides /F B C/. In addition, /y w h/ are in complementary distribution with /F B C/. Finally, the two sets show exact pattern congruity in all their allophones . . . There is thus no doubt that the only possible *phonemic* analysis is to put /F B C/ into the phonemes /y w h/ respectively [4].

Can anyone fail to see the weakness of the arguments advanced here? Let us look at them one by one, as I have numbered them in the passage quoted.

(1) This statement is a half-truth as far as /y/ and /w/ are concerned. Many Americans pronounce the syllabics of *night* and *out* as [ai] and [au], raising the tongue from low to high in the process—as high as in their syllabics of *eat* and *boot*. These speakers do not have allophones of postvocalic /y/ and /w/ of the sort imputed by the authors. Others do, of course. As far as their postulated /h/ is concerned, the terminal position in articulating the syllabics of *beer, bear, boor, boar* is always [ə]-like, if there is a noticeable glide at all. Hence, although prevocalic /y/ and /w/ may be "onglide mirror images of the offglides /F B/" in the speech of many, prevocalic /h/ is not an "onglide mirror image" of the off-glide /C/. The parallelism between /y w/ and /h/ asserted by the authors simply does not exist.

(2) Do prevocalic /y w/ ever have "some friction noise," say before the high vowels in *yield* and *woo?* Are the authors thinking of the clusters /hy, hw/ as in *huge, wheat?* If so, why did they fail to notice—and to mention—that in initial position /h/ can be followed by a semi-vowel, but not /y/ or /w/? If /h/ is a semivowel, why does it not act like one here? The fact is, as everyone knows, that consonants of the same type do not enter into initial clusters in English: a stop never follows a stop, a fricative never a fricative, a sonorant never a sonorant. If such initial clusters as /pt, fθ, ml/ do not occur initially, how can one justify the authors' assumption—implied if not expressed—that semivowels do form such initial clusters, namely /hy/ and /hw/?[5]

(3) The authors grant—if half-heartedly—that the prevocalic allophones of /h/ are "partly [!] voiceless and have friction-noise onset, while those of /C/ are usually [!] fully voiced" and "frictionless." Why be so sensitive about the presence or absence of friction, when friction is not regarded as the distinctive feature of /h/, though it actually is? The behavior of /h/ in initial clusters alone shows that it cannot be classed as a semivowel or as a sonorant. Since it cannot be classed as a stop, it must be either a fricative or unique. I see no reason for excluding it from the class of fricatives, although it has relatively weak friction, possesses a unique voiced prosodic allophone, and is not paired with a voiced fricative phoneme like /f θ s š/, the other members of this class.

(4) In the passage discussed in (3) above, the authors appear to speak with tongue in cheek. But that does not prevent them from jumping to this conclusion: "There is thus no doubt that the only possible *phonemic* analysis is to put /F B C/ into the phonemes /y w h/."

How much confidence do such procedures arouse in a scholarly reader?

4 When we ask ourselves what would be achieved if the occurrence of postvocalic /h/ could be demonstrated, we make these sober-

[5] I do not overlook the fact that initial clusters of fricatives occur in English in a few learned words taken from Greek, as *sphinx, sthenic, phthisis.* But I do not admit that this oddity is a part of the English system, and therefore do not regard it as a suitable basis for assuming that English has initial clusters of semivowels.

ing discoveries with regard to the most widely used types of American English, including the authors' own: (1) this /h/, voiced and frictionless, occurs only before /r/, whereas /y/ and /w/ turn up before any other consonant as well as finally; i.e., /y/ and /w/ appear in complementary distribution with this /h/; (2) this /h/, though varying allophonically with the preceding vowel, quite miraculously deflects the phonic character of the preceding vowel, i.e., it produces allophonic variation in the vowel. Confronted with these indisputable observations concerning the result achieved by the authors, we may well wonder whether the game was worth the candle.

The answer to this puzzle is quite simple. As soon as one breaks down the upgliding diphthongal syllabics into clusters of vowel plus /y/ or /w/, as Bloch, Trager, and Smith do, one creates a troublesome problem. To illustrate: if *boat, bait* are taken as /bowt, beyt/, containing the same syllabics as *pot, pet,* then *four, fair* must have a phoneme between the syllabic and the /r/ in many dialects of American English, including the authors' own. If it is not /w/ or /y/, what is it? /h/ is the answer we receive. From the point of view of the three authors discussed in this paper, it is perhaps the most "convenient" answer, although one might postulate an unsyllabic /ə/ instead. This /h/ is thus a necessary corollary to the postulated /y/ and /w/. Conversely, if /h/ cannot be established in postvocalic position, the analysis of the upgliding diphthongs into vowel plus /y/ or /w/ becomes questionable.

I am convinced, and hope to have shown, that the authors have failed to make out a satisfactory case for positing postvocalic /h/, and therefore regard also their postvocalic /y/ and /w/ with suspicion. With Bloomfield and others, before and along with him, I treat the upgliding diphthongs of English as unit phonemes and the ingliding or monophthongal vowels before /r/ in *beer, bear, bar, boor, boar* as allophones of the "free vowels" in *bee, bay, do, doe, law,* or of the "checked vowels" in *bit, bet, bat, pot, put,* depending on the dialect. Since the incidence of vowels before tautosyllabic /r/, and even before intersyllabic /r/, is restricted in all dialects and varies greatly from dialect to dialect, special handling of the vowels in this position is required; but I see no serious difficulties.

5 Leonard *Bloomfield's* position with regard to the so-called "complex nuclei" of English seems to be widely misunderstood, partly because of the distinction he makes between "simple primary phonemes" and "compound primary phonemes," partly—largely, one suspects—because Bloch and Trager failed to mention their fundamental departure from Bloomfield's treatment in their *Outline of Linguistic Analysis,* which, after all, is largely a digest of Bloomfieldian structural linguistics. If such an omission is perhaps excusable in this little practical manual intended as an introduction to linguistic analysis, it is rather unfortunate in a scholarly paper published in *Language.* Should not the authors of "The Syllabic Phonemes of English" [9] (*Language* 17.223–246) have at least mentioned the fact that their analysis of the English syllabics— the crucial problem in English phonemics— differed sharply from Bloomfield's solution? Should they not have indicated how scholars trained in Bloomfieldian structuralism could arrive at radically different solutions of the same problem?

Since Bloomfield's solution is passed over in silence by Bloch, Trager, and Smith, and their own doctrine has been so widely accepted by younger scholars, especially by those who were introduced to the method of structural analysis during and after the war by the two *Outlines* and their authors, a review of Bloomfield's position is clearly called for.

In his *Language* (New York, 1933), Bloomfield states (90–91) that "Standard English, as spoken in Chicago" has eight "simple primary [vowel] phonemes," exemplified in *pin, egg, add, alms, odd, ought, up, put,* and eight "compound primary [vowel] phonemes," exemplified in *buy, bough, bay, bee, few, go, boy, do.* On 124 we read: "In English, successions like [je] in *yes* or [we] in *well* are treated as two phonemes, like any sequence of consonant plus vowel, but combinations of vowels plus semivowels are treated as compound phonemes . . . . In the phonetic structure of our speech-forms, these groups play the same part as simple vowel phonemes." Can one doubt that Bloomfield takes the "compound primary phonemes" as unit phonemes? The expression "combinations of vowels plus semivowels" in the second passage clearly refers to the phonic character of these "compound phonemes" and cannot be interpreted as meaning "combinations of phonemes," a notion he explicitly rejects in this context. Further confirmation of the fact that Bloomfield regarded the diphthongs of English as phonemic units may be gathered from the following passage (124): "Another non-distinctive peculiarity of our diphthongs is their divergent sound, in most American types of pronunciation, before /r/: in this position they approach the character of a single long and rather tense vowel."

Bloomfield does not discuss the nondiphthongal vowels occurring in some varieties of American English in such words as *bee, bay, do, dough,* but it is certain that he would have taken them as unit phonemes, whether long or not. Witness the following statements: "Features of duration distinguish primary phonemes in German" (109); and: "In German the combinations [aj] as in *Eis* . . . [oj] as in *neu* . . . and [aw] as in *Haus* . . . are treated, structurally, as unit phonemes" (125). Bloomfield would presumably have written such "long" vowel phonemes of English as /iː, eː, uː, oː/, and regarded them as diaphones, i.e., as regional or social variants, of the phonemes /ij, ej, uw, ow/, etc., occurring in his (Chicago) English.

There is one passage in Bloomfield's *Language* that seems to contradict his unitary phonemicization of the diphthongs and "long" vowels of English. It reads as follows (103–104): "The Central-Western type of American English distinguishes nine vowel phonemes. One of these, /r/ . . . is peculiar in its inverted tongue-position. The other eight form what we may call a *two-four system,*" i.e., a system contrasting front and back on four tongue levels. He adds that "some Central-Western types of American English lack the distinction" exemplified in *alms : odd* of Chicago English; i.e., they have only one low vowel, and hence do not have a neat "two-four system."

The passage is ambiguous as it stands, but must, I feel sure, be taken to refer only to the "simple primary [vowel] phonemes" mentioned on p. 91 and the "r-vowel" of *bird.* If Bloomfield had changed his mind about the "compound primary [vowel] phonemes" before going to press, he surely would have revised the passages that I have quoted above.

Bloomfield adheres to his unitary phonemic interpretation of phonically complex vowels in his article "The Stressed Vowels of American English," *Language* 11.97–116 (1935). However, in a footnote (101) he admits the possibility of a binary analysis in these words:

The customary alternative statement is this: The phonemes [i, e, a, ɔ] occur before [j], as in *bee, bay, buy, boy,* and the phonemes [u, o, a] occur before [w], as in *do, go, now,* but in these combinations both the syllabic and the following [j, w] deviate acoustically from their usual shape, especially before [r], as in *fear, fair, fire, poor, pour, sour.* This statement is equivalent to the one in the text above, and preferable in the way of brevity and clearness, but it annoys some students.

A few years later, in his *Linguistic Aspects of Science = International Encyclopedia of Unified Science* 1:4 (Chicago, 1939), he leaves the question open (22–23):

The number of phonemes which will be stated as existing in any one language depends in part upon the method of counting. For instance, we shall recognize an English phoneme [j] which appears initially in forms like 'yes,' 'year,' 'young,' and another phoneme [e] in the vowel sound of words like 'egg,' 'ebb,' 'bet.' The longer vowel sound in words like 'aim,' 'say,' and 'bait' may then be counted as another phoneme, or else one may describe it as a combination of the phonemes [e] and [j]. This option would not exist if our language contained a succession of [e] plus [j] which differed in sound, and as to significant forms in which it occurred, from the vowel sound of 'aim,' 'say,' 'bait.' . . . The count of phonemes in Standard English will vary, according to economy, from forty-odd to around sixty.

From this statement it would appear that Bloomfield found no conclusive evidence for his unitary interpretation of phonically complex vowels, nor for a binary analysis. One could, therefore, adopt either "method of counting" the stressed vowel phonemes of English. His followers, attempting a binary solution first in terms of six vowels (Bloch and Trager) and then in terms of nine (Trager and Smith), have certainly not succeeded in establishing their solution.

6 It will not be irrelevant to point out a number of serious problems that are created if /y, w, h/ are postulated in postvocalic position.

(1) The six-vowel system of Bloch and Trager (1941, 1942) commits one to admitting that the vowel of *pat* is lowered before /y, w/ in *buy, cow*, although /y, w/ favor high tongue position; that the vowel of *pot* /pot/ is rounded before /y/ in *boy*, although /y/ favors unrounding; that the vowel of *pat* is lowered before /h/ in *calm, car* while the vowel of *pot* is raised and rounded before /h/ in *law, bore*, although the authors explicitly state that the "semivowel" /h/ mimics the tongue and lip position of the adjoining vowel. Such admissions run counter to all we know about the way in which adjoining sounds affect each other—the spectrograph merely confirms and emphasizes what has long been observed.

(2) This disregard of clearly observable articulatory and acoustic facts turns such well-known phenomena as the splitting and merging of phonemes and the realignment of allophones into a complete mystery. We cannot sacrifice reliable observations and proven principles of linguistic behavior to the ideals of "simplicity" and "symmetry," however captivating they may be, without introducing a fatal split between synchronic and diachronic linguistics and endangering linguistics as a science.

(3) The unscientific handling of allophones mentioned in (1) and the fascination with the "simplicity" and the "symmetry" of a six-vowel system or a nine-vowel system (which is, at best, a seven-vowel system with two strays[6]) lead to a highly arbitrary identification of the vowels in the so-called "complex syllabic nuclei." For example, *buy* is said to have the vowel of *pat* (Bloch-Trager, 1941, 1942) or of *pot* (Trager-Smith, 1951); *boat* that of *cut* (1941), of *pot* (1942), or of *home* as pronounced by some speakers in eastern New England (1951); to *law* is assigned the vowel of *pot* (1941–1942) or that of eastern New England's *home* (1951); to *calm, bar* the vowel of *pat* (1941) or of *pot* (1951). Do not such arbitrary manipulations in themselves demonstrate the untenability of these "simple" systems?

7 I shall now summarize my findings with regard to the postulated postvocalic /h/ and the six-vowel or nine-vowel systems assumed for Modern English.

(1) The phoneme /h/ of Modern English is a fricative, not a semivowel. Its distinctive stable feature is friction. It enters into initial clusters with a following semivowel, as other voiceless fricatives do. These two features of /h/, phonic similarity and pattern congruity, clearly put it into the class of voiceless fricatives. If further proof were needed, one could point out the fact that consonants of the same class do not enter into initial clusters in Modern English; hence the clusters /hy, hw/ cannot contain two semivowels.

---

[6]In 1941 and 1942 Trager found only six vowels (simple nuclei) in his idiolect of English, exemplified in *bit, bet, bat, put, cut, cot*. A decade later he found three more (*Outline* 14): two rounded back vowels, /o/ and /ɔ/, and a high central vowel, /ɨ/.

Trager reports that he has /o/ in *whole* "most of the time" and in *home* "about one-fourth of the time"; that he has /ɔ/ in *boss* (a hump) and in *gloss* (translation); that he uses /ɨ/ in the expression *the willies*, the preposition *until, till*, nearly always in *twenty*, "75% of the time" in the adverb *just*, and "part of the time" in *this* (22–23). H. L. Smith is said to have /o/ in the phrase *gonna* (going to), /ɔ/ "most of the time" in the last syllable of *alcohol*, /ɨ/ "more than half the time" in *children* and "40% of the time" in the adverb *just* (24).

If this is the best evidence the authors of the *Outline* can offer, it is shaky indeed—whether it is intended to be exhaustive or indicative of the evidence which they would adduce in support of positing three additional "simple nuclei." The examples cited in support of /ɨ/ actually have prosodic or positional allophones of the vowel in *bit;* Trager's /o/ in *whole, home* is either a rare relic or an isolated acquisition from another dialect, Smith's /o/ in *gonna* a prosodic allophone of the vowel in *bone;* on the meager evidence offered, the status of /ɔ/ is obscure, but it would seem that in any "simple"-vowel system a rounded low-back or mid-back vowel must be included.

The plea in support of adding /o/ and /ɨ/ to the vowel system for the sake of achieving an analysis of "the total pattern of all the dialects" (9) is irrelevant. There is no such thing as a "total pattern" that can be imposed upon all dialects of American English (not to mention the dialects of England, Scotland, and Ireland). The linguist must analyze the system of each dialect separately before he can know what systematic features are shared by all dialects, or by groups of dialects. He must distinguish between the systematic features and sporadic unsystematized features of each dialect, since every dialect has elements that are not built into the system. To regard unsystematized features as part of a "system" and to impose an "over-all pattern" are spurious notions that must be rejected.

(2) The three authors assert that their postulated /h/ in postvocalic position behaves like their postulated postvocalic semivowels /y, w/, completely ignoring the fact that /y, w/ have as their distinctive feature a certain tongue and lip position (which, to be sure, varies allophonically with the preceding vowel to a certain extent), whereas the postulated /h/ has no distinctive tongue and lip position, but varies in this respect allophonically with the preceding vowel (and, according to the authors, nevertheless produces allophonic variation in the preceding vowel). All that the authors actually demonstrate, despite their persuasive presentation, is that the inglide and the assumed lengthening of the vowel before tautosyllabic /r/, which they phonemicize as /h/, is in complementary distribution with the upglides [y, w], which do not occur before this /r/.

It should be clear that the existence of a postvocalic semivowel /h/ has not been demonstrated; hence the question of joining this voiced and frictionless phonic feature occurring after vowels with the voiceless fricative [h] before vowels and semivowels as allophones of one and the same phoneme does not even arise. It is equally clear that such a semivowel, if it had been established by sound procedures, could not be regarded as an allophone of initial /h/, since the latter is unquestionably a fricative.

(3) Since the unsuccessfully postulated postvocalic /h/ is a necessary corollary to the postulated postvocalic semivowels /y, w/, the latter should also be abandoned as phonemes, if we are to deal adequately with the vowels of English, their allophonic variations, and their regional and social diaphones. If we treat the phonically diphthongal vowels of *day, fair, dough, door, nine, now,* etc., as unit phonemes, as Bloomfield did among others, we shall not have to resort to questionable methods to attain questionable results.

(4) Finally, I must repeat my warning against the arbitrary handling of allophones imposed by a six-vowel system or any oversimplified vowel system for English. It makes sport of what we know about the physiological and the acoustic nature of such variations and makes phonemic change utterly unintelligible. We cannot run the risk of creating an insurmountable barrier between structural linguistics and historical and area linguistics.

8 Serious objections to the procedures by which the six (or nine) vowel system of Modern English and the concomitant postvocalic /h/ are postulated were raised by reputable American scholars more than a decade ago, but none of the proponents have met them.

The most telling blows against the six-vowel system and postvocalic /h/ were delivered by Einar Haugen and W. F. Twaddell in a paper entitled "Facts and Phonemics" [10], *Language* 18.228–237 (1942). They make the following points: (1) the assertion that *bid, bed, bad, odd, bud, good* have phonically "short" vowels does not square with objective measurements of vowel length (230–232) [92–94]; (2) this assertion of shortness, based upon "admittedly subjective . . . judgments of length," is not a sound point of departure for dealing with the vowels of *pa, far, law, more,* etc., which are claimed to be "long" and are therefore phonemicized as clusters of vowel plus /h/ (235) [96]; (3) the assignment of vowels to such words as *bite, balm, law, bore,* etc., is "capricious"; the so-called allophones "move up and down, or counterclockwise, at the command of the following 'semivowels'" (232–233) [94]; (4) "the authors are not disturbed by the rather considerable phonetic dissimilarity of prevocalic and postvocalic *h;* they even manage to turn it into a 'striking similarity'" (233) [95]; (5) the introduction of /h/ in such words as *bear, boar, law* is "meaningless," i.e., it is "not a contribution to linguistic knowledge" (236) [97].

To these serious objections Trager and Bloch had only this to say (237) [98]: "Although we have modified our views on one or two points, we still regard our classification of the English vowels and diphthongs as fundamentally sound. This, however, is not the place to attempt a refutation of our critics' objections." To my knowledge, they have never squarely met the challenge.

Other scholars look rather favorably upon the more recent nine-vowel system, but they do not feel entirely at ease with it.

Charles F. Hockett, in *A Manual of Phonology* (Baltimore, 1955), admits the theoretical possibility of treating the phonically diphthongal vowels of English as unit phonemes (160); but he seems to prefer the nine-vowel system of Trager and Smith, which implies the acceptance of postvocalic /h/ (197–200). He offers no new evidence in support of this solution of the problem.

In his review of the Trager-Smith *Outline, Language* 31.312 ff. (1955), James H. Sledd concludes: "Very tentatively, as the best available working hypothesis, the analysis [i.e., of the vowel system of English] in the *Outline* may well be accepted and used with some confidence that it can produce good results much of the time" (324). He offers this qualified endorsement of the nine-vowel system as a working hypothesis after pointing out some of its weaknesses: loose handling of the criteria of complementary distribution, phonetic similarity, and pattern congruity (which one overrides the other?); the application of the criterion of pattern congruity to subphonemic features (how much validity does this have, if any, in establishing a system of phonemes?); the chameleon-like character of /h/ and its uneasy status in Sledd's dialect, basically of Atlanta, Ga.; and the need for recognizing a tenth vowel in his dialect.

Sledd overlooks the clustering habits of /h/, to which I attach great importance; he underestimates the damaging evidence of the arbitrary identification of vowels in "complex nuclei"; and he restricts the concept of allophones to monosyllabic morphemes (as others do, quite unjustifiably). If these points are admitted, the six-vowel system of Trager-Bloch and the nine-vowel system of Trager-Smith must be discarded.

21

VARIOUS KINDS
OF PHONEMES*
ARCHIBALD A. HILL

The concept of the phoneme has never been unified, having been applied to contrasting classes in individual speech, or to items in a general pattern, sometimes without much attention to contrast. Nevertheless for a generation there was sufficient agreement on basic concepts so that analysts could communicate with each other. Now the phoneme has split into at least three varieties, giving off the heat that can be expected to accompany fission.

The first variety of phonemics is orthodox, or to borrow and reapply a British term, narrow phonemics. The narrow system presents contrasts with the maximum of completeness, so that a contrast, no matter how rare, still appears in the phonemic inventory. Further if a difference is a contrast once, the difference is always written even in the many instances where it is redundant. Thus in my speech post-vocalic /h/ in final position in stressed syllables contrasts with /y/, /w/, and /r/ only in *idea*. It occurs commonly elsewhere without contrastive value. Yet by orthodox principles I must write /h/ even when it is the mere product of full stress and slow pronunciation in such a form as *bit*. The use of maximum completeness and maximum consistency together make up the principle of bi-uniqueness so often denounced by the generative grammarians.

Narrow phonemics also makes use of symmetry as a heuristic and presentational device. The well-known example is the re-examination of the data which resulted in the addition of a high central vowel to the English phonemic inventory, after symmetry of contrast-arrangement had suggested its possibility. And the last characteristic of narrow pho-

nemics is that it admits only physical entities, unified by identifiable distinctive features, into its phonemic inventory. No use is made of such a syntactic concept as word boundary, and juncture to be acceptable, has to be defined as a phoneme.

Broad phonemics is the second variety. It is variously practiced, but the variety which concerns me here is that which is like narrow phonemics except that rare contrasts are excluded from the inventory. The rare contrasts are not ignored, they are merely relegated to the lists of exceptions. Omission of contrasts also affects the use of symmetry, which becomes much more nearly valueless. Broad phonemics is sometimes practiced to the exclusion of narrow phonemics, but more often it is treated as a pedagogical tool, not at all in conflict with narrow analysis. I have myself recently completed a considerable body of learner's drills in a systematically designed broad phonemic transcription, though I continue to present narrow phonemics to my linguistic students.

The third approach to phonemics is that of the generative grammarians. If I understand them rightly, they describe phonemics altogether as a set of rules for the pronunciation of entities syntactically defined. For instance, both Lees and Stockwell have defined phonemic entities as points in the chain of utterance where the speaker has a choice, the allophonic entities as points where the speaker's course is obligatory. Such an approach works downward from a fully constructed and "well-formed" sentence as the original datum. This approach therefore makes full use of nonphysical syntactic entities in both analysis

*Reprinted from *Studies in Linguistics* 16.3–10 (1962) by permission of the editor and of the author.

and notation. This kind of phonemics is therefore extremely close to morphophonemics as practiced by a narrow phonemicist. There are differences, and in consequence I shall here call this new type of phonemics production-phonemics. The name is one of convenience, adopted for purposes of clarity in discussion. What I mean by it is that this type of phonemics is concerned with how speakers and even hearers form and manipulate sentences, giving them a final form which consists of sounds.

Production-phonemics goes even further than broad phonemics in rejecting bi-uniqueness and symmetry altogether. There is also rejection of a good deal of the respect ordinarily paid to phonetic consistency. Probably the most important characteristic of production-phonemics, however, is that it insists on the use of a syntactic concept of word-boundary, and also insists that a phonemic juncture is at worst impossible, and at best useless. Since the term juncture is used for both the physical phoneme and the syntactic word-boundary, there is danger of confusion. I shall therefore keep the term juncture for the physical entity and phoneme. I shall devise a second term of convenience, and call the syntactic entity a coupling. I define a coupling as a point in the chain of utterance where items can be separated or uncoupled, and then coupled anew after manipulation and shuffling, without damage to the entities thus manipulated. The analogy is a train, or lengths of hose—any chain which has joints or couplings permitting separation and joining. The term is intended to indicate something operationally identified, and is neither the audible phoneme of juncture, nor the visible white space between written words. A coupling may be accompanied by either a juncture or a word-space or both, but need not be. The introduction of couplings into production-phonemics introduces great simplification into the phonemic inventory, as the well-known work of Chomsky, Halle, and Lukoff on English stress fully demonstrates. The notion of the utility of couplings in various kinds of phonemics is not new, however. Couplings have long been used by many Europeans and not inconsiderable numbers of Americans, though it has never been the orthodox American position. The use of couplings in production-phonemics is new primarily in the way in which they are systematically exploited and made to fit into a tightly knit and integrated system of analysis.

Presumably, speakers in some sense know what they are saying and are going to say, since they manipulate the items of speech and therefore must control them. Even more, Martin Joos has formulated the relation of hearer to speaker so as to show that the hearer, too, is a producer. The hearer treats the speaker's talk as a stimulus to produce sentences of his own, but silently. When there is a match between the hearer's and the speaker's sentence, understanding takes place. Furthermore, the hearer often matches on the basis of largely a priori probabilities, backed by only inadequate phonetic evidence of identity. The formulation certainly gives us insight into the nature of understanding, and makes plain the virtue of production-phonemics as a description of a process central to all phases of communication. For both speaker and hearer when we describe production, it therefore seems to me legitimate to speak of "emic" points as choices, as Lees and Stockwell have done.

These are the three varieties of phonemics which I consider most important and most useful. I should now describe the relationships betwen them in more detail.

First narrow and broad phonemics. I have said that broad phonemics is useful in practical situations. I can also add that narrow phonemics does indeed have a complicated inventory, and makes for great waste in transcription. Both faults are avoided in systems of broad phonemics. Yet I do not believe that broad phonemics in any way invalidates narrow analysis. Surely the analyst must collect all the contrasts he can find, even the rare ones and those believed to be rare, if contrasts are what he is studying. He must also be consistent in recording differences which are capable of making contrasts, if he is to discover the functional load that contrasts bear. At the very least, narrow phonemics is a necessary heuristic technique, and one which imposes on the user a duty to investigate both inventory and functional loads to the fullest. Further, when the investigation is completed, the investigator must present his results in an adequate description which presumably follows the inventory.

If the analyst wishes, on the contrary, to

practice broad phonemics he must possess exactly the same information which is the narrow phonemicist's goal. He must, in short, have a complete inventory and exact description of the functional load of all contrasts. He can then devise a systematic broad analysis and transcription. But when he has done so, he must also give a careful account of all contrasts which he has rejected as exceptional.

Typically, the treatment of exceptions goes into the footnotes. I do not believe that the difference between narrow and broad phonemics amounts to much more than a dispute over terminology and whether the most detailed description belongs in text or footnotes. There are only two statements about the relation which seem to me important. Narrow phonemics should precede any broad phonemic presentation, since the reduction of inventory can not be properly accomplished by guess and common sense. It can only be done after careful survey. Also, it is clear that the practitioners of broad phonemics are under obligation to describe what the threshold for admission into the broad phonemic inventory should be. I have heard some statements which set this threshold so high that it seems to me all the description would be in the footnotes. On the other hand, if the threshold is set so low as to admit any contrast which occurs twice—as is sometimes done—the amount of simplification will be negligible.

Much more important than resolution of the unnecessary conflict between narrow and broad phonemics is consideration of the relations between either of these kinds and production-phonemics. It is frequently assumed that because both speaker and hearer are producers, production-phonemics is all that is necessary. To achieve a match the hearer must first produce a test sample. This he does by making full use of all probabilities in guessing what the speaker is saying and is going to say. We know also, that as soon as the hearer thinks he has a match, he quits listening. Yet often the supposed match produces unsatisfactory results. Here I believe the hearer turns on his silent playback and rematches. The process may be slow and conscious, a deliberate trial of several possible forms judged by probability. More interestingly, it may be rapid and not fully conscious. In any case the sentences must match upon examination. This statement suggests that narrow phonemics is still useful, though it now needs a new definition. A phonemic contrast can be defined as a minimal non-match. An analysis of what constitutes minimal matches and non-matches is surely useful to the analyst, just as practical command of them must be necessary to all users of language.

The remaining matter is the use of nonphysical couplings together with rejection of juncture phonemes. The production-phonemicists' position has been several times presented making use of the same example. English /t/, /d/, and voiced alveolar flap are stated to be impossible to reduce to two phonemes satisfactorily unless a coupling is used to describe their distribution.

The first version of this statement known to me is in Noam Chomsky, "A Transformational Approach to Syntax," *Third Texas Conference on Problems in the Analysis of English,* Austin, mimeographed, 1958 [see now Chomsky 1962a—VBM], pp. 286–287, and footnote 29, pp. 298–299. The second version was delivered in a lecture at the University of Texas, summer 1960, by Robert B. Lees. The third version is by Noam Chomsky, in *Explanatory Models in Linguistics,* Cambridge, mimeographed, n.d. (1961?) [see now Chomsky 1962b—VBM], footnote 23, page 4 of footnotes. The three versions do not all agree, though the Lees version seems to have been derived from the second Chomsky version. In the first version, Chomsky states the stress limitations on the effectiveness of prediction of coupling by occurrence of the alveolar flap. In that version he recognized the occurrence of a flap occurring after stress without following coupling. In the second and third versions this stress limitation, though necessary for the understanding of the working of the prediction rules, is left out.

I shall summarize the several statements rather than quote any of them entire. First for juncture as a phoneme, I give Chomsky's most recent opinion:

There has been an attempt . . . to define juncture [read coupling] in purely phonetic terms, e.g., by considering features internal to an utterance that are similar to those at utterance boundary. It does not seem likely that any such attempt can succeed. (Chomsky, *Explanatory Models,* fn. 23.)

As a statement of what I believe to be the nature of phonemic juncture, this quotation is inadequate. It states the way in which juncture is searched for; it does not state its nature when found. It describes juncture as a convenient fiction for sorting out medial sounds from sounds which occur at boundaries. Such a juncture would be a phoneme with no reality and no distinctive features, and would in itself be quite unidentifiable by any means. I am well aware that this is a club that orthodox phonemicists have given to their enemies, since not long ago many analysts were despairingly defining juncture as a zero phoneme. Sins always come home, perhaps most embarrassingly when we are no longer sinning. If juncture is merely a convenient zero, it would be useless to defend it, and far better to set up zeroes for a more superficially tractable entity like the coupling. I think, in fact, that this is exactly what the production-phonemicists have done.

Chomsky says that phonemic junctures fall before stressed syllables, and quotes a number of examples to show this common distribution. Yet one of his examples is *today,* where according to his analysis there is a flap, which most users of juncture would define as a form with the product of smooth transition. Also, when stress falls before an intervocalic /t/ Chomsky recognizes that the flap is predictable, and does not suggest a coupling, as in *rider* and *writer* (the consonants are alike in his speech). If this flapped variety is then taken as the junctureless form, he finds its distribution exactly reversed if the stress follows. Here he says the presence of a flap is "more general" as a signal of a coupling after the consonant. His examples are *at Ed's, at Ellen's,* and *at all.*

Chomsky also gives examples of junctures without couplings. These are *po+tato* and *fi+nancial, a+ttend* and *a+dept.* All difficulties are solved for Chomsky if the coupling is written, and if, as is implied but not fully stated, variant stress conditions are also taken into account.

My own phonemic analysis for all these examples is that the aspirated stop follows juncture, and that the flap is the intervocalic variety when juncture neither precedes nor follows. I define the juncture as a physical event and a phoneme which has distinctive features of timing. It is not to be confused with the allophones of the sounds on each side of it, and its occurrence is physically identifiable.

Chomsky's examples fall into three groups, the most interesting of which is *at Ed's, at Ellen's, at all.* For me these are all without juncture, though there is a coupling present in each after the consonant, which is symbolized by the word-space. There are for me no other examples which bear out Chomsky's statement that a flap occurs generally before a coupling in the situation described. Note such pronunciations as *adequate aid,* and *basket edge* where, in my speech, the flap does not occur. In all versions of the Chomskyan statement that I know, the examples are limited to use of *at,* yet it is curious that not all uses of *at* before a stressed vowel agree in showing a flap. Note "Look *at Ed!"*

The second group of examples are forms like *adept, attend.* For these I should like to substitute the contrastingly written pair, *a tack* and *attack.* These ought, one would suppose, to supply a junctural contrast. They do not do so, in isolation at least. Chomsky is therefore right in supposing that the couplings distinguish the isolated forms better than do the junctures. For that matter, so do the spellings. Yet in sentences a junctural difference emerges. I once had it experimentally demonstrated to me that, in my speech at least, the following sentences were audibly distinguishable when normally pronounced.

It's under a tack.   *It's under attack.*

One has a juncture only after the weak vowel —this is *a tack.* The indefinite article attaches itself to what precedes. The second sentence, with *attack,* has junctures before and after the weak vowel (cf. "The Audibility of /+/," *Journal of the Canadian Linguistic Association* 5.81–82, 1959 [by Archibald A. Hill— VBM]). About the last group, forms such as *potato,* I will say nothing except to point out that juncture, word-space and coupling can all occur where they are not needed—witness such a form as *good bye.*

I believe that the production-phonemicists are throwing away information which would be of use to them when they reject phonemic juncture. Chomsky has often said that the purpose of grammatical study is to investigate our common intuitive knowledge about language.

Whenever an observable event can be shown to correlate with intuitive knowledge, successful investigation has taken place. A part of our intuitive knowledge is where couplings fall. If an observable phonemic event correlates with the intuitively placed couplings, knowledge is thereby made more precise. I think Chomsky's own examples suggest this sort of correlation.

My intuitive knowledge places a major coupling before, not after, *at* in *at Ed's,* and *at all.* The word groups are operational unities. The absence of juncture bears out my intuition because it correlates with it. Contrariwise, my intuition places a major coupling after *at* in "Look at Ed!" Again the occurrence of juncture bears my intuition out. For me, at least, *at* is a clitic—a proclitic in *at Ed's,* and an enclitic in *look at.*

Similarly, *attack* and *a tack* show the expected difference in couplings which I should predict intuitively. And once again, since the juncture distribution shows the indefinite article as an enclitic, juncture is giving me knowledge of intuition. The junctures not only tell me about the relative looseness of couplings, I think they also bear out my intuitive belief that the first syllable of the verb is not the same entity as the first syllable of the phrase, which is an article.

I do not wish to press the matter further, but it is considerations of this sort that make me feel that attacks on the orthodox phoneme are at least premature. I am sure that all three kinds of phoneme are valid, useful, and different. A little tolerance all around would help linguistics. To quarrel over which kind of practitioner is alone entitled to the name phoneme, is to quarrel solely over who owns words. It is a quarrel of the sort that is most common, most embittered, most useless, and most avoidable.

22

THE CURRENT RELEVANCE
OF BLOCH'S "POSTULATES"*
ARCHIBALD A. HILL

The continuing relevance of Bernard Bloch's "Postulates for Phonemic Analysis" [16] lies in the facts that they point to the basis of the minimal-pair identification test, the most powerful tool in phonological analysis, and that they further point to the basic necessity of sound-discrimination in the development of human language.

Bernard Bloch's postulates (1948) occupy a curious place in current linguistic discussion. Since the whole concept of a phonological base for grammatical recognition and interpretation is now under vigorous attack, one might expect that the article would be forgotten or dismissed as of only antiquarian interest. Instead, the usual position seems to be that it was a work so painstakingly explicit that it revealed all the weaknesses of the neo-Bloomfieldian position. It is certainly true that the work was explicit, and that by being so it raised important issues, but it seems to me that to regard it as no more than a brave but inevitable failure is a curiously roundabout way of bringing it into line with currently fashionable thinking. I shall discuss some aspects of the work, not assuming that its conclusions are untenable, but believing that it is a work important to the analysis of sound and the way sound is used as a physical trigger for the processes of recognition and interpretation. The work is still, it seems to me, important for outlining the relevant phonetics of idiolects, dialects, and languages.

Bloch's corollary to Postulate 2 (pp. 7–8 [170]) reads as follows: "Some utterances contain auditory fractions which are the same. Compare Bloomfield's first assumption: 'Within certain communities successive utterances are alike or partly alike' (*Language* 2.154, §2). This corollary and the assumption from which it proceeds are crucial; for they open the way to identifying parts of successive utterances." It is my belief that this statement is even more important than Bloch stated it to be. It is on this assumption that the most powerful tool that phonological analysis possesses, the minimal pair test, must rest. A generation of work in phonological analysis has convinced me that the human ear hears by comparison, and not primarily by identification of isolated sounds. That is, a group of Spanish learners of English will relatively easily hear that "I saw a big sheep" and "I saw a big ship" are different sentences if they are placed side by side. On the other hand, if asked to identify *sheep* by pointing to one of two pictures, their results are random.

The minimal pair test alone merely tells us that two sounds can be identified as different when they are set in a framework of identity. This fact is sometimes used nowadays to argue against the importance of such testing, as when a contemporary scholar points out that his daughter can hear and distinguish five degrees of aspiration. Yet even if the minimal pair test is not refined beyond the point where it does no more than identify acoustic differences, it still gives us some insights into hearing and identification of sound. Ability to hear differing sounds must include all distinctions used as identifiers anywhere in the world, at any time, since children of any hereditary background have always succeeded in learning the language of the community in which they were brought up. The ability to distinguish pairs is thus a constant for all normally

*Reprinted from *Language* 43.203–207 (1967) by permission.

equipped human beings—though, of course, it does not remain constant for individuals throughout life, since we know that gradual deafening is normal. Not only, however, does the ability to distinguish paired sounds include all the distinctions which have ever been used, it must include more, since for the human ear to accomplish what it does in all language communities, there must be a safety factor. That is, each learner of his native language must be able to hear more than his native language uses; he must be able to hear more than any language uses. It is this fact that accounts for the linguist's daughter, who hears more grades of aspiration than I believe have ever been used as identifiers.

To be linguistically relevant, however, the pair test must be used as an identification test; that is, pairs of sentences, containing different items suspected of being identifiable by their pronunciation, must be presented to a jury. The jury may be made up of nearly mythical "naïve expert speakers," or it may be made up of linguists. For the test to prove linguistic difference, the jury must be able to identify which sentence is which, without reference to context. If "I saw a big sheep" and "I saw a big ship" are given to a native jury, there is always convergence on identification, since this is an extremely easy distinction for natives, though it is not so for my Spanish-speaking learners. Suppose, however, that the situation is different. A learned Choctaw linguist (to use one of Bloch's favorite fictions) has heard the word *hat* pronounced sometimes with release of the /t/, sometimes without. He makes the guess that there is a difference of identity between *hat*$_1$, which is released and is made of straw, and *hat*$_2$, which is not released and is made of felt. He asks a native speaker to use the sentence "Here's your hat," meaning a straw hat, and "Here's your hat," meaning a felt hat, and asks the native jury to tell which sentence is which. Note that he does not merely pronounce the sentence with released /t/ and with unreleased /t/, asking the jury whether the two utterances sound different. If that had been the question, he might well have gotten merely identification of the difference between release and its absence. In the method I am describing, the tester is asking "are these two utterances instances of the same sentence, or of different sentences?" It is true, of course, that a single pair test, like that of *hat* just given, does not tell our Choctaw linguist that there is not some other pair, like a *pot*$_1$ and a *pot*$_2$, where the presence or absence of the release is a difference marker, but at least he knows that there is no difference between a supposed *hat*$_1$ and *hat*$_2$.

Though I think the suspected minimal-pair identification test is the one essential tool in analysis, it is surpisingly seldom used. For extensive use of it, I know only the experimental study by Ilse Lehiste on internal open juncture (1960). What is often used, instead, is introspective testing. That is, the linguist decides that he makes a difference between, say, *atom* and *Adam,* says it over several times, and regards the difference as confirmed. Such testing is the kind of activity that John Firth used to dismiss contemptuously as "fishing in your own pond." I am sure that a good many of the distinctions insisted on by phonological analysts in the forties and fifties may have been artifacts of just this sort. I am further convinced that phonological analysis without frequent use of the identification test is vulnerable to the attacks of non-Bloomfieldians, who point out that it is easy and economical to give exact specifications of pronunciation morpheme by morpheme, and word by word, selecting from universal acoustic qualities. That is, current phonological analysis rejects the notion of relevant phonetics altogether, as is quite possible if identification is overlooked. I have never heard a convincing argument, however, which escapes the fact that *knotty* and *naughty* show a relevant difference in many dialects of English, and that whether or not it is relevant for a given dialect can be shown by whether or not a jury can identify which sentence ("It's knotty" vs. "It's naughty") a given speaker is saying.

The minimal-pair identification test does not, of course, solve all problems. One persistent problem springs from the fact that distinctions in one environment are not the same as distinctions in another. This is a problem that troubled Bloch, of course; he discusses it on page 25 [183], where he says: "In some varieties of American English the segments [k] and [t] are in free variation with each other when they occur initially before voiceless [L], e.g., in *clear, clean, class,* etc., all pronounced by speakers of these dialects indifferently with [kL-] and with [tL-]." The problem represented by such "neutralization of opposition" was also discussed at length by Twaddell (1935), and is with us today. The fact of the matter seems to me to be that a description of differences, environment by environment, with no attempt to collapse these environments into classes believed to be comparable, would be intolerably unwieldy. It would be unwieldy not merely for the analyst, trying to make a phonological statement for a given language, but for the learner of that language trying to master the distinctions so as to make his words and sentences identifiable.

All analysts, and all learners, are faced with the problem of deciding whether what occurs before voiceless [L] is to be classed with /k/ or with /t/. There will, I believe, always be a certain amount of looseness in these cross-environment classifications, so that we will never be able to say that we have achieved a final and unalterable analysis of the phonological structure of any language. We can only say that one analysis is better than another, since it achieves the goals of completeness, consistency, and economy more nearly than another. The fact that all classifications are subject to discussion and improvement should not lead the analyst to give up trying to make them, as has happened sometimes.

One of the ways in which Bloch's article has been definitely affected by the passage of time is that we now have adequate means of acoustic analysis, so that it is now possible to describe sounds in terms of how they look on sound-spectrograms, whereas eighteen years ago it was only possible to describe distinctive features in articulatory terms. Yet the effect is on the whole a not very important one, since it remains true that the basic discriminatory tool is the human ear. I do not wish to go into theoretical discussion of whether sound discrimination is necessarily binary; the important fact is that the ear discriminates among sounds which have acoustic characteristics and that these acoustic characteristics are produced by articulations. Without going further than this, it would seem that comparison and cross-environment classification can profitably and perhaps most accurately be done by use of the machine, though it is a truism that the machine must work on a prior basis of human discrimination collected experimentally. The machine can tell us that A and B, stated to be different in environment Y ... Z, have certain features in common with A' and B', stated to be different from each other in environment W ... X. A and A', B and B' can be classed together on the basis of their similarities, which are then further stated to be distinctive features. I have labored these rather obvious points at such length because it seems to me that the nature of distinctive features, as the qualities used to class sounds into groups, is often misunderstood. Very often it is argued that such and such a quality—say the voicelessness of a prevocalic [t] in contrast with the voice of a prevocalic [d]—cannot be a distinctive feature, because the voice is less audible than the aspiration. Such statements fail to recognize that what we hear is an identificational clue, whereas the "distinctive features" so called, are abstractions for classification only, and do not have to be sharply audible. For instance, the closure of intervocalic [t] and [k] is usually taken to be the distinctive feature of the two types of sound, yet during the phase of closure, there is no sound at all to be heard, or to show a trace on the spectrogram. From this point of view, a better name than "distinctive feature" might be classificatory feature.

I have tried to develop the notion that all users of language discriminate between sounds, environment by environment; and because this type of classification develops an unwieldy number of different classes, all users also carry out a considerable amount of cross-environment classification, less exact than the differentiation in separate environments, but at least serviceable. I have also tried to show that this activity rests on Bloch's "crucial statement" that utterances contain identities and differences. A complete statement of the importance of these views, however, cannot be made in the framework of description of language today. Chomsky is fond of describing the task of linguistics as that of analyzing and accounting for the acquisition of linguistic competence by the human individual. Such a goal is a dazzling one, and at present one can only say that its very recognition is the chief step so far taken towards achieving it. Yet dazzling and even perhaps unreachable as it may be, it is not a completely adequate goal for our activity. Quite obviously, anything that can be brought to bear on the origin of the species-specific linguistic competence is of great value. Hockett and Ascher (1964) have carried us a long step toward knowledge of the acquisition of this competence by homo sapiens, in that they have pointed to the dual organization of all human language into recurrent meaningless elements, plus larger meaningful elements containing and characterized by these meaningless smaller elements. It would seem that this duality is one of the language universals, though not precisely of the sort that is at present exciting scholarship. I believe that sound-discrimination, and cross-environment classification, is still another language universal, even more basic than the duality pointed to by Hockett and Ascher.

Chomsky has recently given a concise description of animal communication, and pointed out that it is different in kind, not degree, from language (1966:78):

Modern studies of animal communication so far offer no counterevidence to the Cartesian assumption that human language is based on an entirely distinct principle. Each known animal communication system either consists of a fixed number of signals, each associated with a specific range of eliciting conditions or internal states, or a fixed number of "linguistic dimensions," each associated with a non-linguistic dimension in the sense that selection of a point along one indicates a corresponding point along the other. In neither case is there any significant similarity to human language. Human and animal communication fall together only at a level of generality that includes almost all other behavior as well.

It seems clear that, in these terms, language can be described as a system which breaks up the "dimensions" and "fixed signals" into discrete entities, and which classifies the entities of one dimension or signal with those of another, thus giving rise to the possibility of the Hockett and Ascher duality.

If sound-discrimination and cross-environment classification can be accepted as a language universal, a number of implications follow. One is that ability to perceive differences in sound must have preceded their use as markers of linguistic identity. That is, ability to hear differences must have preceded, ontogenetically at least, the creation of grammatical classes of sounds, or morphophonemes. Not that morphophonemes may not be the most currently interesting type of sound class, but

Bloch at least was concerned solely with difference-classes of sound, and it is interesting that his concern is one which can still be defended.

Nor is the importance of his statement to be found alone in the justification of the minimal-pair identification test, and of its relation to sound-discrimination and cross-environment classification. His insistence on similarity and difference leads as well to interest in another basic problem and activity, also currently unfashionable. This is segmentation. The whole third section of his article (pp. 12–17 [173–178]) is taken up with this problem. We do not need to discuss the details of his procedure and results, but it is important to point out that it was right that so much attention should have been given to the problem. Recognition of identity without segmentation is to leave human language like animal communication, a correspondence between linguistic and nonlinguistic dimensions, where "selection of a point along one indicates a corresponding point along the other." The breakdown of continuous dimensions into discrete entities necessitates segmentation, and the analyst who carries on segmentation as a part of his analytic procedure is drawing a model of the construction of language. To be sure, the higher levels of syntactic and semantic analysis as carried on in 1967 are more exciting than the muddy work of carrying the stones and mixing the mortar for foundations. But even the most elaborate building requires a firm footing, and Bernard Bloch was one of those delighted to work in ways which seem unrepaying, sure that others would build on the courses he laid.

REFERENCES

BLOCH, BERNARD. 1948. "A Set of Postulates for Phonemic Analysis." *Language* 24.3–46 [16].

CHOMSKY, NOAM. 1966. *Cartesian Linguistics: A Chapter in the History of Rationalist Thought.* New York, Harper and Row.

HOCKETT, CHARLES F., and ROBERT ASCHER. 1964. "The Human Revolution." *Current Anthropology* 5.135–147.

LEHISTE, ILSE. 1960. *An Acoustic-Phonetic Study of Internal Open Juncture.* (*Phonetica,* vol. 5, supplement.) Basel, Karger.

TWADDELL, W. FREEMAN. 1935. *On Defining the Phoneme.* Language Monograph 16. Baltimore, Linguistic Society of America.

II

PROSODIC ANALYSIS

INTRODUCTION

Although there is a long tradition of phonetic studies in England, it is my purpose here to present in detail that approach which has attracted the most interest and adherents in America, namely prosodic analysis.

Other schools of thought existed in England long before the advent of prosodic analysis, particularly that of Daniel Jones and his followers. Jones's conception of the phoneme differed from those used by Bloomfieldian linguists in that, as he stated in *The Phoneme: Its Nature and Use* (1950), his phoneme is a "physical" one since the phoneme is treated as a "family of sounds," while the phoneme of other linquists is either "mentalistic" or else "functional" or "structural." By "physical" he did not mean articulatory. Rather, his is a system of auditory distinctions, which only secondarily is based on presumed articulatory positions. Jones's system has not met with much favor in this country, although he has acquired many followers in England. See the bibliography that follows this Introduction for some of his more important writings. Also see Peter Ladefoged's "The Value of Phonetic Statements" (1960) for a brief explanation of Jones's system.

J. R. Firth was working in the area of phonology, as well as in other areas of linguistic analysis, from the early 1930s on, although it was only in 1948 with his "Sounds and Prosodies" [23] that the idea of prosodic analysis as such was specifically formulated. Already in 1937 in "The Structure of the Chinese Monosyllable in a Hunanese Dialect (Changsha)" he and B. B. Rogers had advanced the idea of listing those phonetic features that extend over entire syllables and hence are better regarded as properties of the syllables rather than of elements within the syllable. By 1948 Firth referred to these as "prosodic units" and suggested that they should also include phonological phenomena extending over whole phrases and sentences. The remainders, after prosodic units had been extracted, he called "phonematic units." This article gave the impetus for a wide variety of writings on prosodic analysis, mostly exemplifications of the theory based on many different languages, and pointing out its particular usefulness in handling such phenomena as vowel harmony, nasalization, pharyngealization, and all sorts of phonologically conditioned alternations, in addition to such elements as stress and pitch, which were already being treated as "suprasegmentals" by most linguists.

The similarity of prosodic analysis to Harris' idea of long components ("Simultaneous Components in Phonology" [12], 1944) was mentioned in Part I. In fact, it appears that many practitioners of prosodic analysis believe that there is very little difference between the two. But W. S. Allen in his "Aspiration in the Hārautī Nominal" (1957) finds a significant difference. He says (p. 71), "Harris's method is . . . entirely unprosodic in its phonemic presuppositions, which lead to such pseudo-problems as that admitted on p. 132, n. 7: 'One of the major difficulties in deciding whether to extract a component is the requirement that if we extract a component from the sequence /XY/ by saying that it equals /$\overline{WU}$/, we must extract it from /X/ and from /Y/ even when they are not in the same sequence.'" In prosodic analysis, Allen argues, there is no such requirement and thus no problem arises.

R. H. Robins in "Aspects of Prosodic Analysis" (1957) [24] set down some of the basic principles of prosodic analysis as it had come to be applied by that time and compared it to the treatments of similar phenomena by Bloomfieldian and Prague school linguists. He specifically discussed the points of difference between prosodic analysis and Harris' long components.

John Lyons' "Phonemic and Non-Phonemic Phonology: Some Typological Reflections" (1962) [25] (originally delivered as a lecture at Indiana University in 1961) was an explanation and illustration of the workings of prosodic analysis for the benefit of American linguists, along with some observations on the implications of such analysis for phonological typologies.

Victoria Fromkin's "On System-Structure Phonology" (1965) [26] illustrates the possibility of incorporating some of the features of prosodic analysis into a transformational study. Although her views on the subject have since changed, the article nevertheless argues convincingly for the view that occasionally an eclectic approach in linguistics may result in the simplest and best analysis.

For a detailed account of the development of Firth's ideas on phonology and a discussion of several examples of prosodic analysis, see D. Terence Langendoen, *The London School of Linguistics: A Study of the Linguistic Theories of B. Malinowski and J. R. Firth* (1968).

BIBLIOGRAPHY 11
The English School
of Phonetics

SWEET, H. (1877) *A Handbook of Phonetics*
—— (1913) *Collected Papers of Henry Sweet*
—— (1923) *The Sounds of English* (2d ed.)
JONES, D. (1931) "On Phonemes"
—— (1931) "The 'Word' as a Phonetic Entity"
—— (1932) *An Outline of English Phonetics* (3d ed.)
SWEET, H. (1932) *A Primer of Spoken English* (4th ed.)
VACHEK, J. (1932) "Professor Daniel Jones and the Phoneme"
FIRTH, J. R. (1934) "The Word Phoneme"
—— (1935) "The Use and Distribution of Certain English Sounds: Phonetics from a Functional Point of View"
FIRTH, J. R., and B. B. ROGERS (1937) "The Structure of the Chinese Monosyllable in a Hunanese Dialect (Changsha)"
JONES, D. (1939) "Concrete and Abstract Sounds"

—— (1944) "Chronemes and Tonemes"
—— (1944) "Some Thoughts on the Phoneme"
FIRTH, J. R. (1947) "The English School of Phonetics"
JONES, D. (1950) *The Phoneme: Its Nature and Use*

Reviewed by: MCDAVID, R. I. (1952)
O'CONNOR, J. D. (1957) "Recent Work in English Phonetics"
LADEFOGED, P. N. (1960) "The Value of Phonetic Statements"
ABERCROMBIE, D., D. B. FRY, P. A. D. MAC-CARTHY, N. C. SCOTT, and J. L. M. TRIM (eds.) (1964) *In Honour of Daniel Jones*
LANGENDOEN, D. T. (1964) *Modern British Linguistics: A Study of Its Theoretical and Substantive Contributions*
—— (1968) *The London School of Linguistics: A Study of the Linguistic Theories of B. Malinowsky and J. R. Firth*

BIBLIOGRAPHY 12

Prosodic Analysis

A. THEORETICAL DISCUSSION

HAUGEN, E. (1949) "Phoneme or Prosodeme?"

FIRTH, J. R. (1951) "General Linguistics and Descriptive Grammar"

ALLEN, W. S. (1954) "Retroflexion in Sanskrit: Prosodic Technique and Its Relevance to Comparative Statement"

—— (1957) "Aspiration in the Hārautī Nominal"

BURSILL-HALL, G. L. (1960–1961) "Levels Analysis: J. R. Firth's Theories of Linguistic Analysis"

HILL, A. A. (1961) "Suprasegmentals, Prosodies, Prosodemes: Comparison and Discussion"

HILL, T. (1966) "The Technique of Prosodic Analysis"

B. APPLICATIONS OF THE THEORY

CARNOCHAN, J. (1948) "A Study in the Phonology of an Igbo Speaker"

SCOTT, N. C. (1948) "A Study in the Phonetics of Fijian"

HENDERSON, E. J. A. (1949) "Prosodies in Siamese: A Study in Synthesis"

ALLEN, W. S. (1950) "Notes on the Phonetics of an Eastern Armenian Speaker"

—— (1951) "Some Prosodic Aspects of Retroflexion and Aspiration in Sanskrit"

CARNOCHAN, J. (1951) "A Study of Quantity in Hausa"

HENDERSON, E. J. A. (1951) "The Phonology of Loanwords in Some South-East Asian Languages"

CARNOCHAN, J. (1952) "Glottalization in Hausa"

HENDERSON, E. J. A. (1952) "The Main Features of Cambodian Pronunciation"

ROBINS, R. H., and N. WATERSON (1952) "Notes on the Phonetics of the Georgian Word"

ROBINS, R. H. (1953) "The Phonology of the Nasalized Verbal Forms in Sundanese"

ALLEN, W. S. (1954) "Retroflexion in Sanskrit: Prosodic Technique and Its Relevance to Comparative Statement"

SHARP, A. E. (1954) "A Tonal Analysis of the Disyllabic Noun in the Machame Dialect of Chaga"

PALMER, F. R. (1956) "'Openness' in Tigre: A Problem in Prosodic Statement"

SCOTT, N. C. (1956) "A Phonological Analysis of the Szechuanese Monosyllable"

WALLIS, E. (1956) "Simulfixation in Aspect Markers of Mezquital Otomi"

WATERSON, N. (1956) "Some Aspects of the Phonology of the Nominal Forms of the Turkish Word"

ALLEN, W. S. (1957) "Aspiration in the Hārautī Nominal"

BERRY, J. (1957) "Vowel Harmony in Twi"

CARNOCHAN, J. (1957) "Gemination in Hausa"

PALMER, F. R. (1957) "Gemination in Tigrinya"

ROBINS, R. H. (1957) "Vowel Nasality in Sundanese: A Phonological and Grammatical Study"

SPRIGG, R. K. (1957) "Junction in Spoken Burmese"

BENDOR-SAMUEL, J. T. (1960) "Some Problems of Segmentation in the Phonological Analysis of Tereno"

CARNOCHAN, J. (1960) "Vowel Harmony in Igbo"

SPRIGG, R. K. (1961) "Vowel Harmony in Lhasa Tibetan: Prosodic Analysis Applied to Interrelated Vocalic Features of Successive Syllables"

BOADI, L. A. (1963) "Palatality as a Factor in Twi Vowel Harmony"

CRYSTAL, D., and R. QUIRK (1964) *Systems of Prosodic and Paralinguistic Features in English*

BENDOR-SAMUEL, J. T. (1966) "Some Prosodic Features in Terena"

HENDERSON, E. J. A. (1966) "Towards a Prosodic Statement of Vietnamese Syllable Structure"

C. BIBLIOGRAPHIES AND BIBLIOGRAPHICAL STUDIES

FIRTH, J. R. (1957) "A Synopsis of Linguistic Theory 1930–1955"

O'CONNOR, J. D. (1957) "Recent Work in English Phonetics"

BURSILL-HALL, G. L. (1960–1961) "Levels Analysis: J. R. Firth's Theories of Linguistic Analysis"

SEBEOK, T. A. (1963) "Selected Readings in General Phonemics (1925–1964)"

LANGENDOEN, D. T. (1964) *Modern British Linguistics: A Study of Its Theoretical and Substantive Contributions*

PIKE, K. L. (1967) *Language in Relation to a Unified Theory of the Structure of Human Behavior*

LANGENDOEN, D. T. (1968) *The London School of Linguistics: A Study of the Linguistic Theories of B. Malinowski and J. R. Firth*

D. COLLECTIONS AND ANTHOLOGIES

FIRTH, J. R. (1957) *Papers in Linguistics 1934–1951*

Reviewed by: HAUGEN, E. (1958)

Studies in Linguistic Analysis (1957)

Reviewed by: STOCKWELL, R. P. (1959)
                LANGENDOEN, D. T. (1964)

BAZELL, C. E., J. C. CATFORD, M. A. K. HALLIDAY, and R. H. ROBINS (eds.) (1966) *In Memory of J. R. Firth*

Reviewed by: LANGENDOEN, D. T. (1969)

23

SOUNDS AND PROSODIES*
J. R. FIRTH

The purpose of this paper is to present some of the main principles of a theory of the phonological structure of the· word in the piece or sentence, and to illustrate them by noticing especially sounds and prosodies that are often described as laryngals and pharyngals. I shall not deal with tone and intonation explicitly.

Sweet himself bequeathed to the phoneticians coming after him the problems of synthesis which still continue to vex us. Most phoneticians and even the "new" phonologists have continued to elaborate the analysis of words, some in general phonetic terms, others in phonological terms based on theories of opposition, alternanceś, and distinctive differentiations or substitutions. Such studies I should describe as paradigmatic and monosystemic in principle.

Since de Saussure's famous *Cours,* the majority of such studies seem also to have accepted the monosystemic principle so succinctly stated by Meillet: "chaque langue forme un système où tout se tient." I have in recent years taken up some of the neglected problems left to us by Sweet. I now suggest principles for a technique of statement which assumes first of all that the primary linguistic data are pieces, phrases, clauses, and sentences within which the word must be delimited and identified, and secondly that the facts of the phonological structure of such various languages as English, Hindustani, Telugu, Tamil,[1] Maltese,[2] and Nyanja[3] are most eco-

nomically and most completely stated on a polysystemic hypothesis.

In presenting these views for your consideration, I am aware of the danger of idiosyncrasy on the one hand, and on the other of employing common words which may be current in linguistics but not conventionally scientific. Nevertheless, the dangers are unavoidable since linguistics is reflexive and introvert. That is to say, in linguistics language is turned back upon itself. We have to use language about language, words about words, letters about letters. The authors of a recent American report on education win our sympathetic attention when they say "we realize that language is ill adapted for talking about itself." There is no easy escape from the vicious circle, and "yet," as the report points out, "we cannot imagine that so many people would have attempted this work of analysis for themselves and others unless they believed that they could reach some measure of success in so difficult a task." All I can hope for is your indulgence and some measure of success in the confused and difficult fields of phonetics and phonology.

For the purpose of distinguishing prosodic

---

in the discussion which followed, I pointed out my own findings in Tamil and Telugu for both of which languages it is necessary to assume at least three phonological systems: non-brahman Dravidian, Sanskrito-dravidian, and Sanskritic.

[2] See J. Aquilina, *The Structure of Maltese: A Study in Mixed Grammar and Vocabulary.* (Thesis for the Ph.D. degree, 1940. University of London Library.)

[3] See T. Hill, *The Phonetics of a Nyanja Speaker, with Particular Reference to the Phonological Structure of the Word.* (Thesis for the M.A. degree, 1948. University of London Library.)

[1] At one of the 1948 meetings of the Linguistic Society of America, Mr. Kenneth Pike suggested that in certain Mexican Indian languages it would be convenient to hypothecate a second or phonemic sub-system to account for all the facts. Taking part

*This article first appeared in *Transactions of the Philological Society 1948,* pp. 127–152. It was reprinted in J. R. Firth, *Papers in Linguistics 1934–1951,* Oxford University Press, 1957. Reprinted here by permission.

systems from phonematic systems, words will be my principal isolates. In examining these isolates, I shall not overlook the contexts from which they are taken and within which the analyses must be tested. Indeed, I propose to apply some of the principles of word structure to what I term *pieces* or combinations of words. I shall deal with words and pieces in English, Hindustani, Egyptian Arabic, and Maltese, and refer to word features in German and other languages. It is especially helpful that there *are* things called English words and Arabic words. They are so called by authoritative bodies; indeed, English words and Classical Arabic words are firmly institutionalized. To those undefined terms must be added the words *sound, syllable, letter, vowel, consonant, length, quantity, stress, tone, intonation,* and more of the related vocabulary.

In dealing with these matters, words and expressions have been taken from a variety of sources, even the most ancient, and most of them are familiar. That does not mean that the set of principles or the system of thought here presented are either ancient or familiar. To some they may seem revolutionary. Word analysis is as ancient as writing and as various. We A.B.C. people, as some Chinese have described us, are used to the process of splitting up words into letters, consonants and vowels, and into syllables, and we have attributed to them such several qualities as length, quantity, tone, and stress.

I have purposely avoided the word *phoneme* in the title of my paper, because not one of the meanings in its present wide range of application suits my purpose and *sound* will do less harm. One after another, phonologists and phoneticians seem to have said to themselves "*Your* phonemes are dead, long live *my* phoneme." For my part, I would restrict the application of the term to certain features only of consonants and vowels systematically stated *ad hoc* for each language. By a further degree of abstraction we may speak of a five-vowel or seven-vowel phonematic system, or of the phonematic system of the concord prefixes of a Bantu language,[4] or of the monosyllable in English.[5]

By using the common symbols **c** and **v** instead of the specific symbols for phonematic consonant and vowel units, we generalize syllabic structure in a new order of abstraction eliminating the specific paradigmatic consonant and vowel systems as such, and enabling the syntagmatic word structure of syllables with all their attributes to be stated systematically. Similarly we may abstract those features which mark word or syllable initials and word or syllable finals or word junctions from the word, piece, or sentence, and regard them syntagmatically as prosodies, distinct from the phonematic constituents which are referred to as units of the consonant and vowel systems. The use of spaces between words duly delimited and identified is, like a punctuation mark or "accent," a prosodic symbol. Compare the orthographic example "Is she?" with the phonetic transcript iʒʃiy? in the matter of prosodic signs. The interword space of the orthography is replaced by the junction sequence symbolized in general phonetic terms by ʒʃ. Such a sequence is, in modern spoken English, a mark of junction which is here regarded as a prosody. If the symbol *i* is used for word initial and *f* for word final, ʒʃ is *fi*. As in the case of **c** and **v**, *i* and *f* generalize beyond the phonematic level.

We are accustomed to positional criteria in classifying phonematic variants or allophones as initial, medial, intervocalic, or final. Such procedure makes abstraction of certain postulated units, *phonemes,* comprising a scatter of distributed variants (allophones). Looking at language material from a syntagmatic point of view, any phonetic features characteristic of and peculiar to such positions or junctions can just as profitably and perhaps more profitably be stated as prosodies of the sentence or word. Penultimate stress or junctional geminations are also obvious prosodic features in syntagmatic junction. Thus the phonetic and phonological analysis of the word can be grouped under the two headings which form the title of this paper—sounds and prosodies. I am inclined to the classical view that the correct rendering of the syllabic accent or the syllabic prosodies of the word is *anima vocis,* the soul, the breath, the life of

[4]See T. Hill, *The Phonetics of a Nyanja Speaker.*

[5]Miss Eileen M. Evans, Senior Lecturer in Phonetics, School of Oriental and African Studies, has work in preparation on this subject, as part of a wider study of the phonology of modern English.

the word. The study of the prosodies in modern linguistics is in a primitive state compared with the techniques for the systematic study of sounds. The study of sounds and the theoretical justification of roman notation have led first to the apotheosis of the sound-letter in the phoneme and later to the extended use of such doubtful derivatives as "phonemics" and "phonemicist," especially in America, and the misapplication of the principles of vowel and consonant analysis to the prosodies. There is a tendency to use one magic phoneme principle within a monosystemic hypothesis. I am suggesting alternatives to such a "monophysite" doctrine.

When first I considered giving this paper, it was to be called "Further Studies in Semantics." I had in mind the semantics of my own subject or a critical study of the language being used about language, of the symbols used for other symbols, and especially the new idioms that have grown up around the word "phoneme." Instead of a critical review of that kind, I am now submitting a system of ideas on word structure, especially emphasizing the convenience of stating word structure and its musical attributes as distinct orders of abstractions from the total phonological complex. Such abstractions I refer to as prosodies, and again emphasize the plurality of systems within any given language. I think the classical grammarians employed the right emphasis when they referred to the prosodies as *anima vocis*. Whitney, answering the question "What is articulation?" said: "Articulation consists not in the mode of production of individual sounds, but in the mode of their combination for the purposes of speech."[6]

The Romans and the English managed to dispense with those written signs called "accents" and avoided pepperbox spelling. Not so the more ingenious Greeks. The invention of the written signs for the prosodies of the ancient classical language were not required by a native for reading what was written in ordinary Greek. They were, in the main, the inventions of the great scholars of Alexandria, one of whom, Aristarchus, was described by Jebb as the greatest scholar and the best Homeric

critic of antiquity. The final codification of traditional Greek accentuation had to wait nearly four hundred years—some would say much longer—so that we may expect to learn something from such endeavours.[7] It is interesting to notice that the signs used to mark the accents were themselves called $\pi\rho o\sigma\omega\delta\iota\alpha\iota$, prosodies, and they included the marks for the rough and smooth breathings. It is also relevant to my purpose that what was a prosody to the Greeks was treated as a consonant by the Romans, hence the "h" of hydra. On the relative merits of the Greek and Roman alphabets as the basis of an international phonetic system of notation, Prince Trubetzkoy favoured Greek and, when we talked on this subject, it was clear he was trying to imagine how much better phonetics might have been if it had started from Greek with the Greek alphabet. Phonetics and phonology have their ultimate roots in India. Very little of ancient Hindu theory has been adequately stated in European languages. When it is, we shall know how much was lost when such glimpses as we had were expressed as a theory of the Roman alphabet.

More detailed notice of "h" and the *glottal stop* in a variety of languages will reveal the scientific convenience of regarding them as belonging to the prosodic systems of certain languages rather than to the sound systems. "h" has been variously considered as a sort of vowel or a consonant in certain languages, and the glottal stop as a variety of things. Phonetically, the glottal stop, unreleased, is the negation of all sound whether vocalic or consonantal. Is it the perfect minimum or terminus of the syllable, the beginning and the end, the master or maximum consonant? We have a good illustration of that in the American or Tamil exclamation ˀaˀa! Or is it just a necessary metrical pause or rest, a sort of measure of time, a sort of mora or matra? Is it therefore a general syllable maker or marker, part of the syllabic structure? As we shall see later, it may be all or any of these things, or just a member of the consonant system according to the language.

We have noticed the influence of the Roman and Greek alphabets on notions of sounds

---

[6]Amply illustrated by the patterns to be seen on the Visible Speech Translator produced by the Bell Telephone Laboratories.

[7]See *A Short Guide to the Accentuation of Ancient Greek,* by Postgate.

and prosodies. The method of writing used for Sanskrit is syllabic, and the Devanagari syllabary as used for that language, and also other forms of it used for the modern Sanskritic dialects of India, are to this day models of phonetic and phonological excellence. The word analysis is syllabic and clearly expressive of the syllabic structure. Within that structure the pronunciation, even the phonetics of the consonants, can be fully discussed and represented in writing with the help of the prosodic sign for a consonant closing a syllable. For the Sanskritic languages an analysis of the word satisfying the demands of modern phonetics, phonology, and grammar could be presented on a syllabic basis using the Devanagari syllabic notation without the use of the phoneme concept, unless of course syllables and even words can be considered as "phonemes."

In our Japanese phonetics courses at the School of Oriental and African Studies during the war, directed to the specialized purposes of operational linguistics, we analyzed the Japanese word and piece by a syllabic technique although we employed roman letters. The roomazi system, as a system, is based on the native Kana syllabary. The syllabic structure of the word—itself a prosody—was treated as the basis of other prosodies perhaps oversimplified, but kept distinct from the syllabary. The syllabary was, so to speak, a paradigmatic system, and the prosodies a syntagmatic system. We never met any unit or part which *had* to be called a phoneme, though a different analysis, in my opinion not so good, has been made on the phoneme principle.

Here may I quote a few of the wiser words of Samuel Haldeman (1856), first professor of Comparative Philology in the University of Pennsylvania, one of the earlier American phoneticians, contemporary with Ellis and Bell. "Good phonetics must recognize the value for certain languages 'of alphabets of a more or less syllabic character,' in which 'a consonant position and a vowel position of the organs' are regarded 'as in a manner constituting a unitary element.'"[8] Sir William Jones was the first to point out the excellence of what he called the Devanagari system, and also of the Arabic alphabet. The Arabic syllabary he found almost perfect for Arabic itself—"Not a letter," he comments, "could be added or taken away without manifest inconvenience." He adds the remark, "Our English alphabet and orthography are disgracefully and almost ridiculously imperfect." I shall later be using Arabic words in Roman transcription to illustrate the nature of syllabic analysis in that language as the framework for the prosodies. Sir William Jones emphasized the importance as he put it of the "Orthography of Asiatic Words in Roman Letters." The development of comparative philology, and especially of phonology, also meant increased attention to transliteration and transcription in roman letters. Sir William Jones was not in any position to understand how all this might contribute to the tendency, both in historical and descriptive linguistics, to phonetic hypostatization of roman letters, and theories built on such hypostatization.

In introducing my subject I began with sounds and the Roman alphabet which has determined a good deal of our phonetic thinking in Western Europe—as a reminder that in the Latin word the letter was regarded as a sound, *vox articulata*. We moved east to Greek, and met the prosodies, i.e., smooth and rough breathings, and the accents. The accents are marks, but they are also musical properties of the word. In Sanskrit we meet a syllabary built on phonetic principles, and each character is əkṣərə, ultimate, permanent, and indestructible. Any work I have done in the romanization of Oriental languages has been in the spirit of Sir William Jones, and consequently I have not underestimated the grammatical, even phonetic, excellence of the characters and letters of the East where our own alphabet finds its origins. On the contrary, one of the purposes of my paper is to recall the principles of other systems of writing to redress the balance of the West.

And now let us notice the main features of the Arabic alphabet. I suppose it can claim the title "alphabet" on etymological grounds, but it is really a syllabary.[9] First, each Arabic letter has a name of its own. Secondly, each one is capable of being realized as an art figure in itself. Thirdly, and most important of all,

---

[8] Cf. Firth, "The English School of Phonetics," *Transactions of the Philological Society, 1946.*

[9] Or rather Arabic writing is syllabic in principle. Professor Edgar Sturtevant has stated this view and recently confirmed it personally in conversation.

each one has syllabic value, the value or *potestas* in the most general terms being consonant plus vowel, including vowel zero, or zero vowel. The special mark, *sukuun,* for a letter without vowel possibilities, i.e., with zero vowel, or for a letter to end a syllable not begin it, is the key to the understanding of the syllabic value of the simple letter not so marked, and this is congruent with the essentials of Arabic grammar. Like the **hələnt** in Devanagari, **sukuun** is a prosodic sign. The framework of the language and the etymology of words, including their basic syllabic structure, consist in significant sequences of radicals usually in threes. Hence a letter has the potestas of one of these radicals plus one of the three possible vowels **i**, **a**, or **u** or zero. Each syllabic sign or letter has, in the most general terms, a trivocalic potentiality, or zero vowel, but in any given word placed in an adequate context, the possibilities are so narrowly determined by the grammar that in fact the syllable is, in the majority of words, fully determined and all possibilities except one are excluded. The prosodies of the Arabic word are indicated by the letters if the context is adequate. If the syllabic structure is known, we always know which syllable takes the main prominence. It is, of course, convenient to make the syllabic structure more precise by marking a letter specially, to show it has what is called zero vowel, or to show it is doubled. Such marks are prosodic. And it is even possible to maintain that in this system of writing the diacritics pointing out the vowels and consonants in detail are added prosodic marks rather than separate vowel signs or separate sounds in the roman sense; that is to say, generalizing beyond the phonematic level, **fatha, kasra, ðamma, sukuun, alif, waw, ya, taʃdiid** and **hamza** form a prosodic system.

In China the characters, their figures and arrangement, are designs in their own right. Words in calligraphy are artefacts in themselves of high aesthetic value, for which there is much more general respect than we have in England for the Etonian pronunciation of the King's English. For my purpose Chinese offered excellent material for the study of institutionalized words long since delimited and identified. With the help of Mr. K. H. Hu, of Changsha, I studied the pronunciation and

phonology of his dialect of Hunanese.[10] Eventually I sorted out into phonological classes and categories large numbers of characters in accordance with their distinguishing diacritica. Diacritica were of two main types, phonematic and prosodic. The prosodic diacritica included tone, voice quality, and other properties of the sonants, and also yotization and labiovelarization, symbolized by **y** and **w**. Such diacritica of the monosyllable are not considered as successive fractions or segments in any linear sense, or as distributed in separate measures of time.[11] They are stated as systematized abstractions from the primary sensory data, i.e., the uttered instances of monosyllables. We must distinguish between such a conceptual framework which is a set of relations between categories, and the serial signals we make and hear in any given instance.[12]

Before turning to suggest principles of analysis recognizing other systems of thought and systems of writing outside the Western European tradition, let me amplify what has already been said about the prosodies by quoting from a grammarian of the older tradition and by referring to the traditional theory of music.

Lindley Murray's *English Grammar* (1795) is divided in accordance with good European tradition,[13] into four parts, viz., Orthography, Etymology, Syntax, and Prosody. Part IV, Prosody, begins as follows: "Prosody consists of two parts: the former

[10]See my "The Structure of the Chinese Monosyllable in a Hunanese Dialect (Changsha)," *BSOS.,* vol. viii, pt. 4 (1937) [with B. B. Rogers].

[11]In the sending of Japanese morse ak = ka, the first signal being the characteristic sonant. (Joos, *Acoustic Phonetics,* L.S.A., pp. 116–126, and conclusions on segmentation.)

[12]See also N. C. Scott, "A Study in the Phonetics of Fijian," *BSOAS.,* vol. xii, pts. 3–4 (1948), and J. Carnochan, "A Study in the Phonology of an Igbo Speaker," *BSOAS.,* vol. xii, pt. 2 (1948). Eugénie Henderson, "Prosodies in Siamese," in *Asia Major,* N.S. Vol. I, 1949.

[13]Cf. *Arte de Escribir,* by Torquato Torío de la Riva, addressed to the Count of Trastamara, Madrid, 1802. The four parts of grammar are etimología ó analogía, syntaxis, prosódia, or ortografía. Prosódia teaches the quantity of syllables in order to pronounce words with their due accent. There are three degrees in Spanish, acute or long, grave or short, and what are termed *común* or *indiferentes.*

teaches the true *pronunciation* of words, comprising *accent, quantity, emphasis, pause,* and *tone;* and the latter, the laws of versification. Notice the headings in the first part—*accent, quantity, emphasis, pause,* and *tone.*"

In section 1 of *Accent,* he uses the expression the *stress of the voice* as distinguishing the accent of English. The stress of the voice on a particular syllable of the word enables the number of syllables of the word to be perceived as grouped in the utterance of that word. In other words, the accent is a function of the syllabic structure of the word. He recognizes principal and secondary accent in English. He recognizes two quantities of the syllable in English, long and short, and discusses the syllabic analysis and accentuation of English dissyllables, trisyllables, and polysyllables, and notices intonation and emphasis.

The syntagmatic system of the word-complex, that is to say the syllabic structure with properties such as initial, final and medial characteristics, number and nature of syllables, quantity, stress, and tone, invites comparison with theories of melody and rhythm in music. Writers on the theory of music often say that you cannot have melody without rhythm, also that if such a thing were conceivable as a continuous series of notes of equal value, of the same pitch and without accent, musical rhythm could not be found in it. Hence the musical description of rhythm would be "the grouping of measures," and a measure "the grouping of stress and non-stress." Moreover, a measure or a bar-length is a grouping of pulses which have to each other definite interrelations as to their length, as well as interrelations of strength. Interrelations of pitch and quality also appear to correlate with the sense of stress and enter into the grouping of measures.

We can tentatively adapt this part of the theory of music for the purpose of framing a theory of the prosodies. Let us regard the syllable as a pulse or beat, and a word or piece as a sort of bar length or grouping of pulses which bear to each other definite interrelations of length, stress, tone, quality—including voice quality and nasality. The principle to be emphasized is the *interrelation of the syllables,* what I have previously referred to as the *syntagmatic relations,* as *opposed to the paradigmatic or differential relations* of sounds in

vowel and consonant systems, and to the paradigmatic aspect of the theory of phonemes, and to the analytic method of regarding contextual characteristics of sounds as allophones of phonematic units.

A good illustration of these principles of word-analysis is provided if we examine full words in the spoken Arabic of Cairo, for which there are corresponding forms in Classical Arabic. Such words (in the case of nouns the article is not included) have from one to five syllables. There are five types of syllable, represented by the formulae given below, and examples of each are given.

SYLLABIC STRUCTURE IN CAIRO COLLOQUIAL[14]

(*i*) CV: open short. C + *i, a,* or *u.*
  (*a*) **fíhim nízil**
  (*b*) **zálamu ʃitláxam dárabit**
  (*c*) **ʕindáhaʃu** (*cvc-cv-cv-cv*)

(*ii*) CVV: open medium. C + *i, a,* or *u,* and the prosody of vowel length indicated by doubling the vowel, hence VV—the first V may be considered the symbol of one of the three members of the vowel system and the second the mark of the prosody of length. Alternatively **y** and **w** may be used instead of the second **i** or **u**.
  (*a*) **fáahim fúulah nóobah***
  (*b*) **muṣíibah ginéenah*** **misóogar***
  (*c*) **ʕiʃtaddéenah*** (*cvc-cvc-cvv-cvc*)
  (*d*) **ʕistafáad náahum**

(*iii*) CVC: closed medium. C + *i, a,* or *u.*
  (*a*) **ʕáfham dúrguh**
  (*b*) **yistáfhim duxúlhum**
  (*c*) **mistalbáxha** (*cvc-cvc-cvc-cv*)

(*iv*) CVVC: closed long. C + *i, a,* or *u* and the prosody of vowel length—see under (*ii*).
  (*a*) **naam ṣuum ziid baat ʃiil xoof***

---

[14]See also Ibrahim Anis, *The Grammatical Characteristics of the Spoken Arabic of Egypt.* (Thesis for the Ph.D. degree, 1941. University of London Library.) ʈ ɖ ʂ ʐ = **t d s z** (I.P.A.)

(b) kitáab yiʃíil yiṣúum
(c) ʕistafáad yistafíid
     yifhamúuh
(d) ʕistalbaxnáah tistalbaxíih

(v) CVCC: closed long. C + i, a, or u and the prosody of consonant length in final position only, the occurrence of two consecutive consonants in final position.

(a) ʃadd bint
(b) ḍarábt yimúrr
(c) ʕistaӡádd yistaӡídd
     (cvc-cv-cvcc)

In the above words the prominent is marked by an accent. This is, however, not necessary since prominence can be stated in rules without exception, given the above analysis of syllabic structure.

Though there are five types of syllable, they divide into three quantities; short, medium, and long. When vowel length is referred to, it must be differentiated from syllabic quantity—vowels can be short or long only. The two prosodies for vowels contribute to the three prosodies for syllables.

* The special case of ee and oo In most cases Colloquial **ee** and **oo** correspond to Classical *ay* and *aw,* often described as diphthongs. There are advantages, however, in regarding *y* and *w* as terms of a prosodic system, functioning as such in the syllabic structure of the word. **xawf** and **xoof** are thus both closed long, though *cvwc* is replaced by *cvvc.* Similarly **gináynah** and **ginéenah, náy** and **née** are both medium, one with *y*-prosody and one with vowel length. Though the syllabic quantities are equivalent, the syllabic structure is different. Two more vowel qualities must be added to the vowel system, **e** and **o**, different from the other three in that the vowel quality is prosodically bound and is always long.

There are other interesting cases in which, quite similarly, colloquial C + **ee** or **oo** with the prosody of length in the vowel in such words as **geet** or **ʃuum**, correspond to equivalent classical monosyllables **jiʕt, ʃuʕm.** The phonematic constituents of the pairs of corresponding words are different, but the prosody of equipollent quantity is maintained. Many such examples could be quoted including some in which the prosodic function of ʕ (glottal stop) and "**y**" are equivalent.

Classical		Cairo Colloquial
ðiʕb		diib
qaraʕt	[Cyrenaican: garayt]	ʕareet
faʕs		faas
daaʕim		daayim
naaʕim		naayim
maaʕil		maayil
ḍaraaʕib		ḍaraayib

The prosodic features of the word in Cairo colloquial are the following:—

In any word there is usually such an interrelation of syllables that one of them is more prominent than the rest by nature of its prosodies of strength, quantity, and tone, and this prominent syllable may be regarded as the nucleus of the group of syllables forming the word. The prominent syllable is a function of the whole word or piece structure. Naturally therefore, the prosodic features of a word include:—

1. The number of syllables.
2. The nature of the syllables—open or closed.
3. The syllabic quantities.
4. The sequence of syllables ⎫ [radicals and
5. The sequence of consonants ⎬ flexional elements separately
6. The sequence of vowels ⎭ treated.]
7. The position, nature, and quantity of the prominent.
8. The dark or clear qualities of the syllables.

There is a sort of vowel harmony and perhaps consonant harmony, also involving the so-called emphatic or dark consonants.

I think it will be found that word-analysis in Arabic can be more clearly stated if we emphasize the syntagmatic study of the word complex as it holds together, rather than the paradigmatic study of ranges of possible sound substitutions upon which a detailed phonematic study would be based. Not that such phonematic studies are to be neglected. On the contrary, they are the basis for the syntagmatic prosodic study I am here suggesting. In stating the structure of Arabic words, the prosodic systems will be found weightier than the phonematic. The same may be true of the Sino-Tibetan languages and the West African tone languages.

Such common phenomena as elision, liaison, anaptyxis, the use of so-called "cushion" consonants or "sounds for euphony," are involved in this study of prosodies. These devices of explanation begin to make sense when prosodic structure is approached as a system of syntagmatic relations.

Speaking quite generally of the relations of consonants and vowels to prosodic or syllabic structure, we must first be prepared to enumerate the consonants and vowels of any particular language for that language, and not rely on any general definitions of vowel and consonant universally applicable. Secondly, we must be prepared to find almost any sound having syllabic value. It is not implied that general categories such as vowel, consonant, liquid, are not valid. They are perhaps in general linguistics. But since syllabic structure must be studied in particular language systems, and within the words of these systems, the consonants and vowels of the systems must also be particular to that language and determined by its phonological structure.

Let us now turn to certain general categories or types of sound which appear to crop up repeatedly in syllabic analysis. These are the weak, neutral, or "minimal" vowel, the glottal stop or "maximum" consonant, aitch or the pulmonic onset—all of which deserve the general name of laryngals. Next there are such sounds as ħ and ʕ characteristic of the Semitic group of languages which may also be grouped with "laryngals" and perhaps the back γ. Then the liquids and semi-vowels **l, r, n** (and other nasals), **y** and **w**.

Not that prosodic markers are limited to the above types of "sound." Almost any type of "sound" may have prosodic function, and the same "sound" may have to be noticed both as a consonant or vowel unit and as a prosody.

First, the neutral vowel in English. It must be remembered that the qualities of this vowel do not yield in distinctness to any other vowel quality. The term neutral suits it in English, since it is in fact neutral to the phonematic system of vowels in Southern English. It is closely bound up with the prosodies of English words and word junctions. Unlike the phonematic units, it does not bear any strong stress. Its occurrence marks a weak syllable including weak forms such as **wəz, kən, ə**.

Owing to the distribution of stress and length in Southern English words, it is often final in junction with a following consonant initial. Two of the commonest words in the language, *the* and *a,* require a number of prosodic realizations determined by junction and stress, ðə, ði, **'ðiy, ə, ən, 'ey, æn**. In other positions, too, the neutral vowel often, though by no means always, marks an etymological junction or is required by the prosodies of word formation, especially the formation of derivatives. The distribution of the neutral vowel in English from this point of view would make an interesting study. The prosodic nature of is further illustrated by the necessity of considering it in connection with other prosodies such as the so-called "intrusive" *r,* the "linking" *r,* the glottal stop, aitch, and even *w* and *y.* Examples: *vanilla ice, law and order, cre'ation, behind, pa and ma, to earn, to ooze, secretary, behave, without money.* The occurrence of Southern English diphthongs in junctions is a good illustration of the value of prosodic treatment, e.g.:—

(*i*) The so-called "centring" diphthongs, iə(r), eə(r), ɔə(r), uə(r).

(*ii*) What may be termed the "y" diphthongs, **iy**,[15] **ey, ay, oy**.

(*iii*) The "w" diphthongs **uw, ow, aw**.

It may be noted that e, æ, ɔ do not occur finally or in similar junctions, and that ɔ:, a:, and ə: all involve prosodic *r.*

Internal junctions are of great importance in this connection since the verb *bear* must take -*ing* and -*er,* and *run* leads to *runner up.* Can the r of *bearing* be said to be "intrusive" in Southern English? As a prosodic feature along with *ə* and in other contexts with the glottal stop, aitch and prosodic *y* and *w,* it takes its place in the prosodic system of the language. In certain of its prosodic functions the neutral vowel might be described temporarily as a pro-syllable. However obscure or neutral or unstressed, it is essential in *a bitter for me* to distinguish it from *a bit for me.* In contemporary Southern English many "sounds"[16] may be pro-syllabic, e.g., tsn̩'apl, tstuw'mʌtʃ, sekrrtri or sekətri, s'main, s'truw. Even if '*s true*' and *strew* should happen to be homophonous, the two structures are different:

---

[15]It is, I think, an advantage from this point of view to regard English so-called long *i:* and *u:* as *y*-closing or *w*-closing diphthongs and emphasize the closing termination by writing with Sweet *ij* or *iy,* and *uw.*

[16]In the general phonetic sense, not in the phonematic sense.

ç'cvw and 'cvw. "Linking" and "separating" are both phenomena of junction to be considered as prosodies. In such a German phrase as ʔin ʔeinem ʔalten 'Buch, the glottal stop is a junction prosody. I suppose Danish is the best European language in which to study the glottal stop from the prosodic point of view.[17] Unfortunately, I am not on phonetic speaking terms with Danish and can only report. The Danish glottal stop is in a sense parallel with tonal prosodies in other Scandinavian languages. It occurs chiefly with sounds said to be originally long, and in final position only in stressed syllables. If the word in question loses its stress for rhythmical or other reasons, it also loses the glottal stop. It is therefore best considered prosodically as a feature of syllabic structure and word formation. The glottal stop is a feature of monosyllables, but when such elements add flexions or enter compounds, the glottal stop may be lost. In studying the glottal stop in Danish, the phonematic systems are not directly relevant, but rather the syllabic structure of dissyllabic and polysyllabic words and compounds. In Yorkshire dialects interesting forms like 'fɔʔti occur. Note however 'fɔwər and 'fɔwə'tiyn. A central vowel unit occurs in stressed positions in these dialects, e.g., 'θəʔti, 'θəʔ'tiyn.

There may even be traces of a prosodic glottal stop in such phrases as t 'θədʔ'dɛɛ, t 'θədʔ'taym. Junctions of the definite article with stressed words having initial t or d are of interest, e.g., ɔntʔ'tɛɛbl, itʔ'tram, tətʔ-'tɛytʃə, fətʔ'dɔktə, witʔ'tawil. These are quite different junctions from those in 'gud 'dɛɛ or 'bad 'taym. Compare also Yorkshire trɛɛn (cvvc) t'rɛɛn (c'cvvc), tət'ʃɔp, tə 'tʃɔp, and especially witʔ'tak (with the tack) and wid 'tak (we'd take), also witə'tak (wilt thou take). In London one hears 'θə:ʔ'tsiyn and 'θə:t'ʔiyn, where the two glottal stops have somewhat different prosodic functions.

The glottal stop as a release for intervocalic plosives is common in Cockney, and is a medial or internal prosody contrasting with aspiration, affrication, or unreleased glottal stop in initial or final positions. Such pronunciations as 'kɔpʔə, 'sapʔə, 'wintʔə, 'dʒampʔə are quite common. I would like to submit the

following note of an actual bit of conversation between two Cockneys, for prosodic examination: i 'ʔo:ʔ ʔə 'ʔɛv iʔ 'ʔo:f, baʔ i "wawʔ ʔɛv iʔ o:f.

I have already suggested the y and w prosodies of English, including their effect on the length prosody of the diphthongs and their function in junctions when final. After all, human beings do not neglect the use of broad simple contrasts when they can combine these with many other differentiations and in that way multiply phonetic means of differentiation. In the Sino-Tibetan group of languages the y and w element is found in a large number of syllables—there are many more y and w syllables than, say, b or d or a syllables. In the many Roman notations used for Chinese, these two elements are variously represented and are sometimes regarded as members of the paradigm of initials, but, generally as members of the paradigm of finals. They can be classified with either, or can be simply regarded as syllabic features. Sounds of the y or w type, known as semi-vowels or consonantal vowels, often have the syllable-marking function especially in initial and intervocalic position. In Sanskrit and the modern languages affiliated to it, it is clear that prosodic y and v must be kept distinct from similar "sounds" in the phonematic systems. The verbal forms **aya, laya, bənaya** in Hindustani are not phonematically irregular, but with the y prosody are regular formations from **a-na, la-na,** and **bəna-na.** In Tamil and other Dravidian languages y and v prosodies are common, as markers of initials, for example, in such Tamil words as **(y)enna, (y)evan, (y)eetu, (v)oor, (v)oolai, (v)ooṭṭu.** However, the prosodies of the Dravidian languages present complicated problems owing to their mixed character.

Other sounds of this semi-vowel nature which lend themselves to prosodic function are **r** and **l,** and these often correspond or interchange with y or w types of element both in Indo-European and Sino-Tibetan languages. Elements such as these have, in some languages, such pro-syllabic or syllable-marking functions that I think they might be better classified with the syntagmatic prosodies rather than with the overall paradigmatic vowel and consonant systems. Studies of these problems in Indo-European and Sino-Tibetan languages are equally interesting.

The rough and smooth breathings are

---

[17]See Sweet, "On Danish Pronunciation" (1873), in Collected Papers, p. 345, in which he makes a prosodic comparison with Greek accents. (On p. 348 he uses the term "tonology.")

treated as prosodies or accentual elements in the writing of Greek. It is true that, as with accents in other languages, the rough breathing may imply the omission of a sound, often **s,** or affect the quality and nature of the preceding final consonants in junction. "h" in French is similarly connected with junction and elision. Even in English, though it has phonematic value in such paradigms as *eating, heating; eels, heels; ear, hear; ill, hill; owl, howl; art, heart; arming, harming; anchoring, hankering; airy, hairy; arrow, Harrow;* and many others, it is an *initial signal* in stressed syllables of full words having no weak forms. English **h** is a special study in weak forms, and in all these respects is perhaps also to be considered as one of the elements having special functions, which I have termed prosodic. In English dialects phonematic "h" (if there is such a thing), disappears, but prosodic "h" is sometimes introduced by mixing up its function with the glottal stop. I have long felt that the aitchiness, aitchification, or breathiness of sounds and syllables, and similarly their creakiness or "glottalization" are more often than not features of the whole syllable or set of syllables. Indeed, in some of the Sino-Tibetan languages, breathiness or creakiness or "glottalization" are characteristic of prosodic features called tones. In an article published in the *Bulletin* of the School of Oriental and African Studies, Mr. J. Carnochan has a few examples of aspiration and nasalization in Igbo as syntagmatic features of a whole word, rather like vowel harmony, which is prosodic.

Apart from the fact that nasals such as *m, n, ŋ* are often sonants—that is to say, have syllable function—they are also quite frequently initial or final signals, and in Bantu languages such signals have essentially a syntagmatic or syllable or word-grouping function. In a restricted prosodic sense, they can be compared with the glottal stop in German.

In bringing certain types of speech sound into consideration of the prosodies, I have so far noticed the neutral or weak vowel, the minimal vowel, which often becomes zero; the glottal stop, the maximal consonant which unreleased is zero sound; aitch, the pulmonic onset, and the liquids and nasals. The first two, I suggest, deserve the name of laryngals, and perhaps **h.** There remain such sounds as **h, ʕ, γ,** and χ, characteristic of the Semitic group of languages. These sounds are certainly phonematic in Classical Arabic. But in the dialects they are often replaced in cognate words by the prosody of length in change of vowel quality, generally more open than that of the measure of comparison.

When words containing these sounds are borrowed from Arabic by speakers of non-Semitic languages, they are usually similarly replaced by elements of a prosodic nature, often with changes of quality in the vowels of the corresponding syllable.

Hindustani and Panjabi provide interesting examples of phonematic units in one dialect or style being represented in another by prosodies. Instances of interchanges in cognates between phonematic units of the vowel system and units of the consonant system are common, and examples and suggestions have been offered of interchanges and correspondences between phonematic units of both kinds and prosodies. The following table provides broad transcriptions to illustrate these principles.

TABLE I

h

Hindustani, Eastern, careful	Hindustani, Western, quick	Panjabi, (Gujranwala)
pəhyle	pəyhle	pâylle
bəhwt	bəwht	bâwt
pəhwŋcna	pəwhŋcna	pâwŋc
bhəi		bəi
kər rəha həy	kərrahəyh	
rəhta (ræhta)		râynḍa

In **pəhyle** we have a three-syllable word in which **h** is phonematic (*cvcvcv*). In **pəyhle** there are two syllables by a sort of coalescence in which əyh indicates an open "h"-coloured or breathy vowel of the æ-type (*cvhcv*). Similarly in the phrase **bəhwt‿əccha** there are four syllables (*cvcvc‿vccv*), in **bəwht‿əccha** three, the vowel in the first of which is *open* back and "h"-coloured (*cvhcvccv*).

In Panjabi **pâylle** the open vowel carries a compound high falling tone and the structure is prosodically quite different (*cv̂ccv*) which, I think, is equipollent with *cvhcv* (**pəyhle**). **bâwt** similarly is *cv̂c*, reduced to a monosyllable with initial and final consonant and a tonal prosody. In Hindustani verbal forms like **rəhna, rəhta; kəhna, kəhta;** the ə vowel in the h-coloured syllable immediately followed by a consonant is open with a retracted æ-like quality. yɪh is realized as **ye**, vwh as **vo**, in both of which there is a similar lowering and potential lengthening in emphasis.

TABLE II

Arabic ʕ in Urdu Loan-words

Spelling Transliterated	Transcription of Realization in Speech
məʕlum	malum
bəʕd	bad
dəfʕ	dəfa
mənʕ	məna
məʕni	məani, mani
ystʕmal	ystemal

In all these cases the vowel realized is open and fairly long. In Maltese, words which in Arabic have **h** and which still retain **h** in the spelling are pronounced long with retracted quality, e.g., **he, hi, ho, eh, ehe**, as in **fehem, fehmu, sehem, sehmek, qalbhom**. These long vowels may be unstressed. Similarly all the **għ** spellings (transliterated γ) are realized as long slightly pharyngalized vowels which may also occur in unstressed positions, which is not possible with vowels other than those with the Semitic **h** and **għ** spellings. E.g., γa, aγ, aγa, γo, oγ, oγo, γi (γey), γe, γu (γəw) in such words as **għidt, għúda, maghmul, bálagħ**. In the phrase **balagħ balgħa** (he swallowed a mouthful) the two forms are pronounced alike with final long **a** (for form, cf. **ħataf   atfa**, he snatched). **h** and **għ** are often realized in spoken Maltese as a prosody of length.

In Turkish the Arabic ʕ in loan-words is often realized as a prosody of length in such pronunciations as **fiil** (*verb, act*), **saat** (*hour*), and similarly Arabic γ, in **iblaa** (*communicate*), and Turkish **ğ** in **uultu** (*tumult*). We are reminded again of Arabic ʕ which is also realized as a prosody of length in the colloquials, e.g., Classical **jiʕt** is paralleled by **geet** in Cairo, **jɛɛt** in Iraqi, and **ʒiit** in Cyrenaican Saʿadi. In Cairo and Iraqi the prosody of length is applied to an opener vowel than in Classical, but this is not always the case.

The study of prosodic structures has bearing on all phonological studies of loan-words, and also on the operation of grammatical processes on basic material in any language. Taking the last-mentioned first, elision or anaptyxis in modern Cairo colloquial are prosodically necessary in such cases as the following:

misíkt + ni = misiktíni, where the anaptyctic **i** is required to avoid the junction of three consonants consecutively which is an impossible pattern. The prominence then falls on the anaptyctic vowel by rule. Pieces such as **bint + fariid** are realized as **bintifaríid**. With the vowels **i** and **u**, elision is possible within required patterns, e.g.,: **yindíhiʃ + u = yindihʃu, titlíxim + i = titlíxmi**, but not with **a**, **ʕitlaxam + it = ʕitlaxamit**.

Amusing illustrations of the effect of prosodic patterns on word-borrowing are provided by loan-words from English in Indian and African languages and in Japanese. Prosodic anaptyxis produces **səkuul** in Panjabi and prothesis **iskuul** in Hindi or Urdu. By similar processes **səṭeʃən** and **iṣṭeʃən** are created for *station*. In Hausa *screw-driver* is naturalized as **sukuru direba**. Treating **skr** and **dr** as initial phonematic units, English *screw-driver* has the structure 'cvw-cvycə, the prosodies of which Hausa could not realize, hence cvcvcv-cvcvcv, a totally different structure which I have carefully expressed in nonphonematic notation, to emphasize the fallacy of saying Hausa speakers cannot pronounce the "sounds," and to point to the value of studying prosodic structure by a different set of abstractions from those appropriate to phonematic structure. It is not implied that there is one all-over prosodic system for any given language. A loan-word may bring with it a new pattern suited to its class or type, as in English borrowings from French, both nominals and verbals. When completely naturalized the prosodic system of the type or class of word in the borrowing language is dominant. In Japanese strange prosodic transformations take place, e.g., **bisuketto** (biscuit), **kiromeetoru**, **kiroguramu**, **supittohwaia**, **messaasyumitto**, **arupen-suttoku**, **biheebiyarisuto**, **doriburusuru** (to dribble).

Linguists have always realized the importance of the general attributes of stress, length, tone, and syllabic structure, and such considerations have frequently been epoch-making in the history of linguistics. Generally speaking, however, the general attributes have been closely associated with the traditional historical study of sound-change, which, in my terminology, has been chiefly phonematic. I suggest that the study of the prosodies by means of ad hoc categories and at a different level of abstraction from the systematic phonematic study of vowels and consonants, may enable us to take a big step forward in the understanding of synthesis. This approach has the great merit of building on the piece or sentence as the primary datum. The theory I have put forward may in the future throw light on the subject of Ablaut which, in spite of the scholarship expended on it in the nineteenth century from Grimm to Brugmann, still remains a vexed question and unrelated to spoken language. I venture to hope that some of the notions I have suggested may be of value to those who are discussing laryngals in Indo-European, and even to those engaged in field work on hitherto unwritten languages. The monosystemic analysis based on a paradigmatic technique of oppositions and phonemes with allophones has reached, even overstepped, its limits! The time has come to try fresh hypotheses of a polysystemic character. The suggested approach will not make phonological problems appear easier or oversimplify them. It may make the highly complex patterns of language clearer both in descriptive and historical linguistics. The phonological structure of the sentence and the words which comprise it are to be expressed as a plurality of systems of interrelated phonematic and prosodic categories. Such systems and categories are not necessarily linear and certainly cannot bear direct relations to successive fractions or segments of the time-track of instances of speech. By their very nature they are abstractions from such time-track items. Their order and interrelations are not chronological.

An example is given below of the new approach in sentence phonetics and phonology[18] in which the syntagmatic prosodies are indicated in the upper stave and the phonematic structure in the lower stave, with a combination text between. Stress is marked with the intonation indicated.

Prosodies

cy vcə vcə cəz mvtʃ bvcə vy cvcc

[18]For a fuller illustration of the scope of sentence phonology and its possible applications, see Eugénie Henderson's "Prosodies in Siamese."

ðy ʌðə[19] ɔfə wəz mʌtʃ betə ay θiŋk

Phonematic Structure

ð— ʌð— ɔf— w–z mʌtʃ bet— a— θiŋk

Prosodies

cvy hvz ʃvy əccvccic cvc cvc

way hæz ʃiy əkseptid ðis wʌn

Phonematic Structure

wa — æz ʃi — ksept-d ðis wʌn

It is already clear that in cognate languages what is a phonematic constituent in one may be a prosody in another, and that in the history of any given language sounds and prosodies interchange with one another. In the main, however, the prosodies of the sentence and the word tend to be dominant.

To say the prosodies may be regarded as dominant is to emphasize the phonetics and phonology of synthesis. It accords with the view that syntax is the dominant discipline in grammar and also with the findings of recent American research in acoustics. The interpenetration of consonants and vowels, the overlap of so-called segments, and of such layers as voice, nasalization and aspiration, in utterance, are commonplaces of phonetics. On the perception side, it is improbable that we listen to auditory fractions corresponding to uni-directional phonematic units in any linear sense.

Whatever units we may find in analysis, must be closely related to the whole utterance, and that is achieved by systematic statement of the prosodies. In the perception of speech by the listener whatever units there may be are prosodically reintegrated. We speak prosodies and we listen to them.

[19]The use of ə as a prosodic symbol in such final contexts implies potential r or ʔ according to the nature of the junction.

24

ASPECTS OF
PROSODIC ANALYSIS*

R. H. ROBINS

The object of this paper is to give some account and illustration of what would seem to be certain of the general principles of prosodic analysis, as being developed among the group of linguists working in London in association with Professor J. R. Firth. Prosodic analysis falls under the general rubric of phonology, and this in turn comes within the compass of descriptive linguistics.

The modern era of general and descriptive linguistics may perhaps be said to begin with the great Swiss scholar Ferdinand de Saussure, whose lectures, published postumously in 1916 (*Cours de linguistique générale,* Paris, 1949 [4th edition]), more than any one other factor served to broaden the academic study of language from its 19th century preoccupation with the comparative and historical aspect, and to establish as well as christen the discipline of synchronic linguistics. In establishing synchronic linguistics de Saussure did much to inaugurate the application of structural analysis to language, which is emphasized by almost all schools of linguistics today.

Many of the main features of structural linguistics, on which the literature is now very extensive, can be traced back to de Saussure, whose ideas were developed on different lines by the Prague school and by Hjelmslev; cp. especially Karl Bühler, "Das Strukturmodell der Sprache," *TCLP* 6, 1936, pp. 3–12; Ernst A. Cassirer, "Structuralism in Modern Linguistics," *Word* 1, 1945, pp. 99–120; Louis Hjelmslev, "Structural Analysis of Language," *Studia Linguistica* 1, 1947, pp. 69–78, *Prolegomena to a Theory of Language*

(tr. Whitfield, as Supplement to *IJAL* 19.1, 1953), pp. 13–17.

In developing the structural approach to language, de Saussure drew attention to the two dimensions that must be taken into account in linguistic analysis, the syntagmatic and the associative, in his own terms (*Cours,* pp. 170–175) rapports syntagmatiques and rapports associatifs, the former referring to the relations obtaining between elements in parallel to the stream of speech ("in praesentia"), the latter to the relations ("in absentia") between different elements in the language that are associated in some way with the items at various points in stretches of speech. This latter set of relations was more appropriately designated paradigmatic by Hjelmslev (*Actes du Quatrième Congrès International de Linguistes,* 1938, p. 140), thereby avoiding the latent psychologism of de Saussure's term.

In connection with these two sets of relations, syntagmatic and paradigmatic, it is desirable to keep apart on the same lines the terms *structure* and *system,* so often used almost interchangeably, and to employ *structure* and its derivatives (*structural,* etc.) to refer to the syntagmatic relations and pieces in parallel with stretches of utterance in a language, and to reserve *system* and its derivatives (*systemic,* etc.,) for the paradigms of comparable and contrastive elements relevant to the various places in structures (see further Robins (3), p. 109, Allen (5), p. 556. Publications listed at the end of this paper will be referred to by name (and number) only). Thus syllables, words, and sentences constitute structures, and the relations between and with-

*Reprinted from *Proceedings of the University of Durham Philosophical Society* 1.1–12 (1957) by permission.

in them are structural relations; the familiar vowel triangles and quadrilaterals of languages, and sets of consonants or consonant clusters applicable to particular places in syllables or words are examples of phonological systems, and the word classes (parts of speech) of a language and its sets of inflectional categories are grammatical systems.

During the period in which de Saussure's thought was making its impact on linguistics, the synchronic study of phonology was expressing itself in the development of the phoneme theory, or, as we might better put it from the standpoint of today, the various phoneme theories. The dominance of the phoneme concept on phonology at the present time may be seen in the array of phoneme derived terms currently in use, particularly in the writings of American linguists (phonemic, allophone, phonemicize, rephonemicize, etc.).

The origin of the phoneme as a linguistic concept must be seen in the search for economical "phonetic transcriptions" of the type of Sweet's Broad Romic and Daniel Jones's Broad Transcription (cp. Henry Sweet, *Handbook of Phonetics,* Oxford, 1877, pp. 100–108, 182–183; Daniel Jones, *Outline of English Phonetics,* 6th edition, Cambridge, 1947, pp. 48–51). Since these early days different interpretations and theoretical developments have made such growth that the need has been felt to formulate explicit statements of principle in regard to phonemic analysis; one may instance in particular Trubetzkoy's *Grundzüge der Phonologie* (*TCLP* 7, 1939, tr. Cantineau, Paris, 1949); Bloch's "Set of Postulates for Phonemic Analysis" [16] (*Language* 24, 1948, pp. 3–46); Daniel Jones's *Phoneme: Its Nature and Use* (Cambridge, 1950); and the all too néglected monograph by W. Freeman Twaddell, *On Defining the Phoneme* (Language Monograph 16, 1935).

During the development of the phoneme theories, considerable discussion took place on the status of the phoneme as an analytical term, on the classical lines of the philosophical disputes between realists, conceptualists, and nominalists. According to the realist view, espoused by Jones and others (cp. Jones, "Concrete and Abstract Sounds," *Proceedings of the Third International Congress of Phonetic Sciences,* 1939, pp. 1–7), the phoneme has actual existence as an "abstract sound" or structural entity in the language to which it belongs; on the conceptualist view, favored by Trubetzkoy for a time (cp. "La phonologie actuelle," in *Psychologie du langage,* Paris, 1933, pp. 227–246, "Zur allgemeinen Theorie der phonologischen Vokalsysteme," *TCLP* 1, 1929, pp. 39–67. But note his later views, *Principes de phonologie* [tr. Cantineau], pp. 41–46), the phoneme is a mental entity or conception as against the sound, which is a physiological and acoustic entity. The nominalist attitude, in contrast to both the above viewpoints, is that the phoneme, like any other element of scientific analysis, is no more than an appropriate term or operational fiction, with which to handle the mass of observations and to make orderly statements about the gross data, in the case of phonetics, the sounds of a language (cp. Twaddell, *op. cit.,* pp. 33–36).

It might be said that this controversy is of no concern to linguists as such; but it has a relevance to linguistic work, not as an aspect of philosophical thinking, but as one of method and attitude to linguistic science. In a fairly recent statement of the realist position, Pike writes (*Phonemics,* Ann Arbor, 1947, pp. 57–58): "It is assumed in this volume that *phonemes exist as structural entities or relationships,* and that *our analytical purpose is to find and symbolize them.* This implies that there is only one accurate phonemic analysis of any one set of data" (author's italics). This says in effect that phonemes exist in some way in languages apart from the work of the analyst, who is finding an existing structure or system lying behind the phenomena of utterance, and that this structure or system is organized in phonemes, which the linguist must discover and in his description and symbolism represent as accurately as he can.

Methodologically there is much to be said for the nominalist point of view. Such an attitude, which has been somewhat flippantly labelled "hocus-pocus" in contrast to the "God's truth" or realist position (cp. Fred W. Householder in *IJAL* 18, 1952, pp. 260–268) does not imply any levity towards language as an object of study, nor any scientific irresponsibility or disregard of the need for the most meticulous observation and painstaking analysis that is possible. All that adherents of this view of the subject would claim is that existence or reality are not properly predicable of anything other than the actual phenomena or data under observation. Terms and concepts used in analysis are in the nature of a set of words, and no more, employed by the analyst to talk about his data, and in so talking to make summary statements and analyses which account for and explain not only the data from which they are made, but also further data from the same field, in the case of the linguist, from the same language. Phonemes, like all other technical terms in linguistics, take their place as part of the linguist's "language about language," and no more than that. In linguistics we are, in fact, putting language to an unfamiliar and relatively uncomfortable task, that of talking about itself. To summarize, one may quote Firth ("Personality and Language in Society," *Sociological Review* 42, 1950, p. 42): "In the most general terms we study language as part of the social process, and what we may call the systematics of phonetics and phonology, of grammatical categories or of semantics, are ordered schematic constructs, frames of reference, a sort of scaffolding for the handling of events. . . . Such constructs have no ontological status and we do not project them as having being or existence. They are neither immanent nor transcendent, but just language turned back on itself."

The attitude summed up here is relevant to the purpose of this paper. If the terms and categories employed by the linguist are, as it were, imposed on the language in the process of analysis, it follows that linguistic structures and systems must likewise be thought of not as pre-existing or discoverable in any literal sense, but rather as the product of the linguist in working over his material. No one analysis, or mode of analysis, is the only one accurate or sacrosanct, but any account of the language, in any terms, is an adequate statement and analysis, provided that, and to the extent to which, it comprehensively and economically explains what is heard (and read) in the language, and "renews connection" with further experience of it. Questions of truth and falsity of "what is there" and "what is not there," only arise on the view here set out at the level of the barest phonetic observation and recording, before any analysis has taken place.

The last few paragraphs may seem like an unnecessary methodological digression, but it is necessary to make it clear that in developing phonological analysis on prosodic lines there is no suggestion that phonemic analysis is wrong, invalid, or untrue. In terms of the general theory of linguistic analysis just outlined, such statements have no meaning. Nor is it suggested that phonemic analysis is inapplicable or unhelpful.

It is however, legitimate to claim that from its origin the phoneme concept has been primarily tied to transcription, the representation of a language in terms of its phonic material by means of discrete and consecutive letters or symbols on paper (cp. the subtitle of Pike's book *Phonemics: A Technique for Reducing Languages to Writing*), and that in consequence of this, phoneme theories have necessarily concentrated on minimal contrast in identical environment, emphasizing the paradigmatic aspect of phonological relationships at the expense of the syntagmatic or structural aspect (in the narrower sense of *structural* referred to at the beginning of this paper). Where a language is unwritten, or where the orthography is far from adequate as a key to pronunciation, a phonemic analysis may well be indispensable as the basis of a workable transcription unburdened with the excess of different symbols required in a narrow impressionistically "accurate" phonetic transcription. But phonological analysis need not stop at or be based on phonemic transcription.

The aim of prosodic analysis in phonology is not that of transcription or unilinear representation of languages, but rather a phonological analysis in terms which take account not only of paradigmatic relations and contrasts, but also of the equally important syntagmatic relations and functions which are operative in speech. These syntagmatic factors should be systematized and made explicit in phonology, no less than paradigmatic contrasts.

The theory of prosodic analysis was put forward in a paper read to the Philological Society by Firth in 1948 [23], and since then applications of the method there presented and theoretical developments have been undertaken with reference to a variety of individual languages. An attempt will be made here to state the principles of this sort of analysis very briefly and then elaborate them in the light of recent work and with the aid of examples.

Prosodic analysis is, in fact, an abbreviated designation of an analysis that makes use of two types of element, prosodies and phonematic units (cp. Firth (2), pp. 150–152 [262–263], Allen (5), p. 556); the latter are not phonemes or phonemic units, and the analysis is carried out in terms other than phonemic. In this analysis, abstractions adequate to a full analysis of the phonological working of the language are made from the phonic data, or the raw material of the actual utterances, and these abstractions fall into the two categories of prosodies and phonematic units. Phonematic units refer to those features or aspects of the phonic material which are best regarded as referable to minimal segments, having serial order in relation to each other in structures. In the most general terms such units constitute the consonant and vowel elements or C and V units of a phonological structure. Structures are not, however, completely stated in these terms; a great part, sometimes the greater part, of the phonic material is referable to prosodies, which are, by definition, of more than one segment in scope or domain of relevance, and may in fact belong to structures of any length, though in practice no prosodies have yet been stated as referring to structures longer than sentences. We may thus speak of syllable prosodies, prosodies of syllable groups, phrase or sentence-part prosodies, and sentence prosodies; and since grammatically defined elements may also be characterised by prosodic features (cp. Sharp, pp. 168–169) we may have in addition word and morpheme prosodies. A structure will thus be stated as a syntagmatic entity comprising phonematic or segmental units and one or more prosodies belonging to the structure as a whole.

This abstract statement of principle may be illustrated from the application of prosodic analysis to Siamese (Henderson (1)), a basically monosyllabic and tonal language with fairly rigid patterns of syllable structure. Phonological analysis of a Siamese sentence involves among others, the following prosodic and phonematic elements:

Sentence Prosody: Intonation;

Prosodies of Sentence Pieces: Length, Stress, and Tone relations between component syllables;

Syllable Prosodies: Length, Tone, Stress, Palatalization, Labiovelarization;

Prosodies of Syllable Parts: Aspiration, Retroflexion, Plosion, Unexploded closure.

Phonematic Consonant and Vowel units, 'in such classes as Velar, Dental, Bilabial, Nasal, Front, Back, Rounded, Unrounded.

After this very summary and incomplete illustration, more may be said in explanation and justification of the methods of prosodic analysis. Phonemic analysis essentially involves the allotment of all the phonic material that is regarded as relevant to individual segments or segmental phonemes, except for the special case of suprasegmental phonemes which are of limited application (cp. below, p. 8 [271–272]). But a great deal of the phonic material of languages seems clearly to belong to structures longer than single segments, and is very probably so perceived by the native speakers. Broadly speaking this may come about in two ways.

In the first case a feature may be spread or realized phonetically over a structure, such as a syllable, as a whole; examples of this type of syllable prosody are stress, pitch, and length, nasalization, in languages in which a nasal consonant is always followed by a nasalized vowel and a nasalized vowel is only found after a nasal consonant, and palatalization and velarization, when front or palatally articulated consonants are associated in the syllable with front type vowels and back type consonants with back articulated vowels, as in some Slavonic languages. In languages with "vowel harmony" as a feature of word structure, for example Turkish and Hungarian, this is well treated as a prosodic feature of the word as a whole or word prosody; these word prosodies may be put in such categories as Front, Back, and Lip-rounded, and apply to the words concerned as structures, the articulation of the consonants being determined by the relevant prosodies no less than that of the vowels (cp. Waterson, pp. 578–580). Intonation sequences or "tunes" that are associated with sentences or with divisions within sentences (clauses and the like) are stated as prosodies of sentences or of sentence parts. The typical English intonation tunes 1 and 2, as described by Daniel Jones (*Outline,* pp. 258–276), are obvious examples.

Features of the type that have just been instanced can, of course, be analysed phonemically, but in such an analysis there is the risk of misrepresenting or distorting important aspects of the phonic material. Where a feature belongs in the manner described above to a syllable (for example) as a whole, this of necessity involves the phonemicist in saying that at one point in the syllable, say the consonant, the distinction between (say) palatalization and non-palatalization is phonemic or relevant (in Prague terms pertinent) (cp. Trubetzkoy, *Principes* [tr. Cantineau], p. 34), while the same feature in the vowel, being a constant concomitant of the consonantal feature, must be relegated to non-significance, non-pertinence, or "redunancy." Yet at what point are we to tell, if at any point, that the feature involved is perceived and so functions for the native listener? It is not, of course, implied that linguistic analysis can or should be based on the Sprachgefühl or sentiment linguistique of native speakers; but it is desirable that the analysis should not be in violent disagreement with it. This may be illustrated from Jones's treatment of the palatalized (soft) and non-palatalized (hard) consonants in Russian (Daniel Jones, *The Phoneme,* pp. 50–53, cp. pp. 25–26). Any phonemic analysis of Russian, it would appear, must recognize as phonemic the difference between the two sets of consonants in that language; this being so, the concomitant differences in the quality of adjacent vowels will necessarily be non-distinctive phonemically. But we are told that the difference between a palatalized and a non-palatalized consonant is in many words easier to recognise by the difference in the adjacent vowel than in the consonant itself. Thus we are involved in listening to the non-distinctive or irrelevant feature in order to catch what is distinctive or relevant. An analysis of palatalization and non-palatalization as syllable prosodies with phonetic realization in the syllable as a whole helps to avoid this rather paradoxical form of statement, though it is obviously necessary to differentiate, by the concept of focus, (cp. Allen (3), p. 943), or

otherwise, palatalized syllables with initial palatalized consonants, those with final palatalized consonants, and those with both.

We must not be slaves to our machines in preference to the observations of the human ear, for which in the first instance speech is given utterance, but it may be relevant to notice that the tracings of the kymograph show scant regard for the phonemic segmentation of each and every phonetic feature that requires phonological notice. In kymograph tracings made of the utterances of a Georgian speaker (Robins (1), pp. 66, 70; see also the kymograph tracings on p. 11 [273], below) it is clearly shown that the glottalized consonants, p', t', tʃ', k', and q', are followed in the syllable by vowels of a constricted or glottalized tamber, a feature also noticeable in listening. Glottalization in such syllables may be treated as a feature of the syllable and abstracted as a syllable prosody.

The above examples are intended to illustrate the first case of prosodic treatment mentioned earlier, in which prosodies are abstracted as elements of structures in view of the extended realization of a feature therein.

In the second case may be mentioned features which are not realized phonetically over the whole or large part of a structure, but which nevertheless serve to delimit it, wholly or partly, from preceding and following structures, thus entering into syntagmatic relations with what goes before or after in the stream of speech. By virtue of their syntagmatic relations in structures, such features may be treated as prosodies of the structures they help to mark or delimit (cp. Firth (2), p. 129 [253]; for examples of prosodies of both types, with respect to monosyllables, see Scott).

Examples of these demarcative prosodies are found in the analysis of Siamese mentioned above. In Siamese, as in some other languages of South-east Asia, the audible release of stop consonants, or plosion, is confined to syllable initial position, final stop consonants being unexploded. In this language, therefore, plosion serves as a syntagmatic signal of syllable initiality and helps delimit the syllable. So also do aspiration, affrication, and some other articulatory features (Henderson (1), pp. 192–193). These are abstracted as prosodies of syllable initiality; though they may be realized phonetically at one place in the syllable, their relevance extends over the whole structure which they serve to mark off and bind together as a functional unit. In a similar manner features invariably associated with the final place in syllable structures may be abstracted as prosodies of syllable finality.

Obviously phonetic features which in one language are treated as prosodic may not be so treated, or may be so with reference to different structures, in other languages. It is the task of the analyst to decide what and how many prosodic elements and phonematic units he requires, to state the syntagmatic and paradigmatic relations relevant to the phonology of the language as completely, economically, and elegantly as he can.

The grammatical unit referred to as the word, fundamental to the traditional distinction between syntax and morphology, is in many languages marked off in speech, to a greater or less extent, by prosodic features of this second type. In English no word in normal speech has more than one full stress. Orthographically hyphenated words like *home-made,* which in certain contexts bear two full stresses, may for that reason be regarded structurally as two words, behaving phonologically like other comparable sequences of two words (cp. "This parsnip wine is ¹home-¹made/¹well ¹brewed" and "This is a ¹home-made/¹well brewed parsnip wine") and the difference between *greenhouse* and *green house, blackbird* and *black bird, Maryport* and *Mary Port,* can be at least partially explained in these terms. On the other hand the converse is not true; in connected discourse many words are not fully stressed, and certain words, such as the definite and indefinite articles, never bear stress in the forms in which they are most frequently found in speech (ðə and ə(n)). In at least two languages, which are quite unrelated, Swahili and Sundanese, full stress is confined in words of more than one syllable to the penultimate syllable (a few exceptions to this rule occur in Sundanese and may be covered by a separate statement [cp. Robins (3), pp. 125–126]). In these languages, stress, which is a prosody by extension of the syllable which it characterizes, is a prosody by demarcation of the word whose boundaries it helps to delimit. Similar prosodic significance may be assigned to the word-initial stress of Hungarian and Czech.

In some languages particular aspects of consonantal articulation, which would be regarded as allophonic or phonemically irrelevant in a phonemic analysis, exhibit this demarcative function. In English word divisions falling between a final consonant and an initial vowel (*e.g., an ocean, an aim*) are, potentially at least, distinguishable from word divisions falling between vowel and consonant (*e.g., a notion, a name*). The distinguishing features, which include greater duration and laxer articulation of the word-final consonant as against the tenser and shorter articulation of the word-initial consonant, may be treated as prosodic word markers, and set English off as prosodically different in this respect from French, where the feature of liaison in similar phonetic contexts is no respecter of grammatical word divisions.

Some further examples of the application of prosodic analysis to various languages may serve to illustrate both types of prosody that have been referred to in the preceding paragraphs. (It may be felt that these examples are mostly drawn from relatively unfamiliar and little known languages. This should not be taken as implying that prosodic analysis is more readily applicable to such languages than to more familiar ones; the choice of languages is governed by the fact that the linguists whose work is being described are, or have been, members of the staff of the School of Oriental and African Studies in the University of London, with the consequent concentration of their attention in the main on languages coming within the purview of the School. It is greatly to be hoped that the attention of linguists in Great Britain will progressively be turned to the languages that form the basis of our general educational system.) The well known feature of Sanskrit word structure usually referred to as cerebralization has been re-examined prosodically (Allen (3)). This feature, which concerns the relations between certain retroflex consonants in Sanskrit words, is generally expressed in such terms as these (A. A. Macdonnell, *Sanskrit Grammar,* second edition, London, 1911, p. 28): "A preceding cerebral ṛ, ṝ, r, ṣ (even though a vowel, a guttural, a labial, y, v, or Anusvāra (a nasal consonantal unit whose precise phonetic value is obscure [cp. Allen (4), pp. 39–46]) intervene) changes a dental n (followed by a vowel or n, m, y, v) to cerebral ṇ." It is an unsuitable metaphor to say that one sound operates at a distance over intervening sounds to exert a force on another sound, and change it from something which in fact it never was (in the words concerned) into something else. It is indeed generally desirable that synchronic description and analysis should as far as possible avoid the use, even metaphorically, of terms and concepts more appropriate to the diachronic study of the history and development of languages and linguistic features (cp. C. F. Hockett, "Two Models of Grammatical Description," *Word* 10, 1954, pp. 210–234).

In the re-examination of retroflexion in Sanskrit, it is suggested that an R-prosody, or prosody of retroflexion, be abstracted from the words concerned as a structural feature. This prosody was no doubt marked by a retroflex articulation not only of the lingually articulated consonants but also of the intervening vowels, though the traditional treatment makes no mention of this. Such a retroflex "coloring" of vowels in juxtaposition to retroflex consonants is certainly a feature of many Indian languages today (cp. Allen (3), p. 942).

The analysis proposed requires no concept of action at a distance of one sound on another, but simply posits a non-linear, non-segmental feature, retroflexion, as part of the structure of the words, or portions of the words, concerned, realized at all points where it is phonetically possible, that is where the tongue tip is one of the organs of articulation.

Mention has already been made of the relevance of prosodic abstractions in several languages to grammatical units. It is interesting in this connection to see that in more than one language what may appear at first sight as a miscellany of separate phonetic features characterizing a particular grammatical category can all be shown to be the exponents of a single prosodic feature, which thus serves as the marker of a category in the grammar of the language. Such a congruence between the different levels of analysis (cp. Firth, "The Technique of Semantics," *TPS* 1935, pp. 36–72) of a language, as it operates between speakers, is surely an important desideratum of our linguistic operations. Two examples may be cited from widely separated languages. In Bilin (Palmer (3)), a language of Eritrea, the morphology of the very complex tense system of

the nine verb classes that have been set up for that language may be analysed in terms of a single set of statements involving the prosodies of centrality, frontness, backness, and openness, realized in the consonantal and vocalic articulations of the verb forms concerned. In Sundanese (Robins (2)), two types of verb root are found for nearly all verbs, and these two types are used both by themselves, roughly speaking as active and passive verbs respectively, and as bases for a very large number of derived forms involving prefixation, infixation and suffixation, with extensive functions in the language. The relation between these two verbal roots can be simply stated by showing that the active form is always characterized by an N- prosody, or prosody of nasalization, the precise realization that the N-prosody takes being determined by the phonological structure, involving other prosodic components, of each type of verb.

One may find instances, which future research is likely to multiply, of prosodic treatment bringing into the analysis phonetic features either not noted before or dismissed as phonologically (*i.e.,* phonemically) irrelevant. Examples of the demarcative prosodic function of some "allophonic" features have already been given. Fixed place word stress for example, and consonantal features invariably associated with syllable initial or syllable final position, are frequently treated as differentially irrelevant since they are positionally determined, but they are, for just that reason, prosodically relevant and functional. That phonemic analysis may let slip many phonologically relevant features is illustrated from the following observation by Leonard Bloomfield, *Language,* London, 1935 (p. 84): "Practical phoneticians sometimes acquire great virtuosity in discriminating and reproducing all manner of strange sounds. In this, to be sure, there lies some danger for linguistic work. Having learned to discriminate many kinds of sounds, the phonetician may turn to some language, new or familiar, and insist upon recording all the distinctions he has learned to discriminate, even when in this language they are nondistinctive and have no bearing whatever." *Distinctive* in the context of phonemic analysis often means *capable of differentiating one word from another* (cp. Bloomfield, *op. cit.,* pp. 77–78, Jones in *TPS* 1944, pp. 127–132), the implication being that phonetic differences not serving such a purpose are functionally and phonologically irrelevant. This implication is unjustified. In addition to the examples already given we may consider the phonological status and functions of the glottal stop in Sundanese (Robins (3)). This is a frequent phonetic component of utterances in the language, and a failure to use it properly may lead to misunderstanding and would certainly mark the speaker as a foreigner; but it is not a phoneme on a par with the other phonemes that would be set up in a phonemic analysis of the language, and it would not be easy to devise a satisfactory allophonic treatment of its occurrences (though structurally the two are very different, cp. Jones's remarks on the glottal stop in English [Outline, pp. 138–139]). The Roman orthography currently in use in Java today for Sundanese, which comes very near to a phonemic transcription, has no symbol for the glottal stop, except in certain, mostly Arabic, loan words, where it is represented by an apostrophe. As a prosodic element, however, the Sundanese glottal stop has several functions in words other than loans, and in various contexts serves as a syntagmatic marker of the junction of syllables, morphemes, words, and clauses.

Between like vowels, syllable division, when not marked by any other consonant, is marked by the glottal stop. Between unlike vowels, not separated by any other consonant, the glottal stop is only found at points corresponding to certain morpheme boundaries within a word, whose morphological structure it thus helps to indicate. A glottal stop between a consonant and a vowel signals either a morpheme boundary or a word boundary; a glottal stop between a vowel and a consonant, usually in conjunction with other features, signals a clause division within the sentence.

The glottal stop in Sundanese is, in fact, an example of a phonetic feature which should be treated less as a member of a paradigm of consonants than as a marker of certain syntagmatic relations between one structure and another, at both the phonological and grammatical levels. It is the syntagmatic or structural dimension of language that phonemic analysis may be felt to neglect, or to subordinate to the paradigmatic dimension of overall contrast in identical environment, a lack of balance that prosodic theory and practice attempts to redress.

After the description and illustrations of prosodic analysis that have been given, mention should be made of some relatively recent developments in phonemic theory that partially at least seem to cover the same ground in phonology.

One of the first phonetic features of a strictly non-segmental character to be brought into phonemic analysis was that of pitch, whether in the category of intonation or in the category of tone, in the so-called tone languages (cp. Pike, Tone Languages [Ann Arbor, 1948], p. 3). In either case pitch phenomena clearly belong to the syllable as a whole, though in transcription pitch is frequently marked over the vowel letter. Pitch (or tone), stress, and sometimes length (as distinct from shortness) are now fairly generally treated (at least in America) as suprasegmental phonemes, a self-explanatory and self-justificatory category which would seem at first sight to apply to the same field as syllable prosodies of the first type mentioned above, where the phonetic feature treated prosodically was phonetically realized over the whole syllable (pp. 4–5) [267–268]. The terms prosodic phoneme and prosodeme are sometimes used instead of suprasegmental phoneme, with no difference in technical meaning.

There are, however, two differences. Firstly, in prosodic analysis any phonetic feature whose realization extended over the whole or greater part of a syllable could be eligible for treatment as a syllable prosody of this type, irrespective of the nature of its articulation. Examples have already been given of nasalization, palatalization, and glottalization, as well as pitch, stress, and length, being prosodically analysed. But suprasegmental phonemic treatment has in practice been confined to these last three phonetic features, and Pike explicitly limits the term suprasegmental to "quantitative characteristics . . . some modification of a sound which does not change the basic quality or shape of its sound waves" (Phonemics, p. 63; for a suggestion that other features might be treated suprasegmentally, see G. L. Trager in Language, Culture, and Personality, ed. L. Spier, Menasha, 1941, pp. 131–145), i.e., pitch, stress, and length, and nothing else. Secondly, suprasegmental is simply non-segmental, with the implied domain of the syllable; a syllable prosody is an abstraction of a specific order in a separate dimension (the syntagmatic), taking its place in a system of prosodies intended to cover the analysis of syntagmatic relations generally, within linguistic structures.

The demarcative aspect of prosodies (see pp. 5–6 [268–269], above) is foreshadowed by the Grenzsignale of the Prague school and the juncture phonemes of some American linguists. It is certainly the case that the Prague discussion of these junction features (see Trubetzkoy, *Anleitung zu phonologischen Beschreibungen*, Brno, 1935, pp. 30–32, *Principes* [tr. Cantineau], pp. 290–314) was one of the first factors drawing the attention of linguists to the neglected syntagmatic aspect of phonology, but the Prague treatment of them, left where Trubetzkoy left it, does not fully exploit the analytic and structural potentialities of these features, and the status of the Grenzsignale, partly phonemic (phonematische) and partly non-phonemic (aphonematische), remains rather in a phonological limbo, as a sort of appendage rather than a fully integrated part of a complete theory.

Structurally similar features to those treated under the category of Grenzsignale by Trubetzkoy are analysed in terms of juncture phonemes. It may be said that this aspect of phonemic analysis is somewhat complicated by the involvement of two separate questions: firstly, the phonological analysis of the features and their functions in the language, and secondly, their symbolization in a unilinear transcription. Juncture phonemes, like other phonemes in current theories, are also subject to the general rule that the phonemic analysis and transcription of a phonetic element or feature at any point necessarily implies the same analysis of that feature at all other points in structures, despite the quite different relations that it may contract at different places. Alone among phonemicists, it would seem, Twaddell explicitly challenged the assumptions that phonological relations were the same throughout all places in the structures of a language, and that the needs of a full phonological analysis and those of an economical transcription could be satisfied with one and the same procedure and with the same basic elements or concepts (*On Defining the Phoneme*, pp. 54–

55. For this reason phonemic analysis may be considered basically "monosystemic" (Firth (2), pp. 127–128 [252])).

Perhaps symptomatic of the unsettled state of juncture analysis in phonemic terms are the wholly contrasting natures of the juncture phonemes of Harris and of Hockett (cp. Zellig S. Harris, *Methods in Structural Linguistics*, Chicago, 1951, pp. 79–89; Charles F. Hockett, *A Manual of Phonology*, IJAL 21.4, part 1, 1955, pp. 167–172). For Harris juncture phonemes are zero phonemes, with no phonetic realization, put into the analysis to complete the picture, and the border phenomena involved in the analysis are assigned to the allophones of the phonemes in the new environment created by the insertion of the juncture zero phonemes. For Hockett, on the other hand, juncture phonemes are bundles of all the phonetic features, of whatever nature, associated with the boundaries or borders to be analysed.

In general, juncture phonemes tend to be associated with word and morpheme boundaries in American phonemics, just as suprasegmental phonemes are generally confined to the domain of the syllable. In this way junctures have a particular relevance to current American linguistic theory, which holds that grammatical features and grammatical units cannot be used as part of the defining environment of phonemes. (The principal opponent among American linguists to this methodological attitude is Pike; see his "Grammatical Prerequisites to Phonemic Analysis" [15], *Word* 3, 1947, pp. 155–172, and "More on Grammatical Prerequisites" [18], *Word* 8, 1952, pp. 106–121.) It is, therefore, highly advantageous if convenient grammatically defined elements, such as word and morpheme, can be for the most part matched by phonemically defined juncture marked stretches of the same length, even though the correlation between the two in a language may not be complete. As has already been said, prosodic analysis sees no objection to the use of analysis at the grammatical level for the stating of contexts in analysis at the phonological level, and prosodies may be abstracted and stated of grammatical elements as well as of more purely phonological elements (p. 4, above [267–268]: cp. Palmer (1), pp. 548–549).

Finally mention should be made of phonemic long components, which are intended as a means of stating syntagmatic relations and structural implications between successive segmental phonemes in stretches of utterance (cp. Harris, *Methods,* pp. 125–149). There are at least three differences between abstractions of this type and the prosodies of prosodic analysis: firstly, abstraction of a component from a phoneme in one environment implies its abstraction from that phoneme in all other environments (*op. cit.,* p. 128); secondly, long components are not all associated with specific phonological or grammatical structures; thirdly, no one phonetic feature can be stated as the mark or exponent of the long component over its domain in the way that prosodies statable of a whole structure are associated with phonetic features exhibited by that structure as a whole (*op. cit.,* p. 129).

The remarks on certain recent developments in phonemic analysis in the last few paragraphs must not be taken as a comprehensive review of contemporary phonemic theories, and still less as a disparagement of the work of other linguists. They are merely intended to help place prosodic analysis in its context of relations with current phonological doctrine and methods elsewhere.

BIBLIOGRAPHY

The following publications have a direct bearing on prosodic analysis as treated in this article:

W. S. ALLEN
(1) "Notes on the Phonetics of an Eastern Armenian Speaker," *TPS* 1950, pp. 180–206.
(2) "Phonetics and Comparative Linguistics," *Archivum Linguisticum* 3, 1951, pp. 126–136.
(3) "Some Prosodic Aspects of Retroflexion and Aspiration in Sanskrit," *BSOAS* 13, 1951, pp. 939–946.
(4) *Phonetics in Ancient India,* London, 1953.
(5) "Retroflexion in Sanskrit: Prosodic Technique and Its Relevance to Comparative Statement," *BSOAS* 16, 1954, pp. 556–565.

J. CARNOCHAN
(1) "A Study of Quantity in Hausa," *BSOAS* 13, 1951, pp. 1032–1044.
(2) "Glottalization in Hausa," *TPS* 1952, pp. 78–109.

J. R. FIRTH
(1) "The Semantics of Linguistic Science," *Lingua* 1, 1948, pp. 393–404.

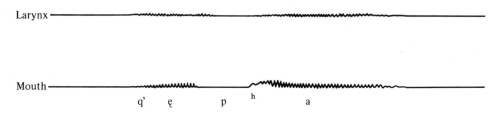

FIG. I.—*qepʻa* to bark.
Tracings of vowels immediately following glottalized consonants exhibit a distinctive shape, the maximum amplitude of the vowel being reached late in the vowel segment. Such vowels were heard with some constriction.

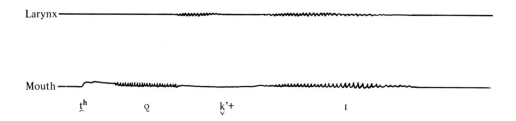

FIG. II.—*tʻoki* rope.
The vowel tracing following the glottalized consonant exhibits a shape similar to that in Fig. I.

(2) "Sounds and Prosodies," *TPS* 1948, pp. 127–152 [23].

(3) "General Linguistics and Descriptive Grammar," *TPS* 1951, pp. 69–87.

E. J. A. HENDERSON

(1) "Prosodies in Siamese," *Asia Major* (new series) 1, 1949, 189–215.

(2) "The Phonology of Loanwords in Some South-East Asian Languages," *TPS* 1951, pp. 131–158.

(3) "The Main Features of Cambodian Pronunciation," *BSOAS* 14, 1952, pp. 149–174.

T. F. MITCHELL

"Particle-Noun Complexes in a Berber Dialect (Zuara)," *BSOAS* 15, 1953, pp. 375–390.

F. R. PALMER

(1) "The 'Broken Plurals' of Tigrinya," *BSOAS* 17, 1955, pp. 548–566.

(2) "'Openness' in Tigre: A Problem in Prosodic Statement," *BSOAS* 18, 1956, pp. 561–577.

(3) "The Verb in Bilin," *BSOAS* 19, 1957, pp. 131–159.

R. H. ROBINS

(1) "Notes on the Phonetics of the Georgian Word" (with Natalie Waterson), *BSOAS* 14, 1952, pp. 55–72.

(2) "The Phonology of the Nasalized Verbal Forms in Sundanese," *BSOAS* 15, 1953, pp. 138–145.

(3) "Formal Divisions in Sundanese," *TPS* 1953, pp. 109–142.

N. C. SCOTT

"A Phonological Analysis of the Szechuanese Monosyllable," *BSOAS* 18, 1956, pp. 556–560.

A. E. SHARP

"A Tonal Analysis of the Disyllabic Noun in the Machame Dialect of Chaga," *BSOAS* 16, 1954, pp. 157–169.

R. K. SPRIGG

(1) "Verbal Phrases in Lhasa Tibetan," *BSOAS* 16, 1954, pp. 134–156, 320–350, 566–591.

(2) "The Tonal System of Tibetan (Lhasa Dialect) and the Nominal Phrase," *BSOAS* 17, 1955, pp. 134–153.

At the time of writing an article by Mitchell is to be published in the André Basset Memorial Volume, and articles by Allen, Carnochan, Firth, Mitchell, Palmer, Robins, and Sprigg will appear in *Studies in Linguistic Analysis,* to be published by the Philological Society [both volumes published in 1957 —VBM].

25

PHONEMIC AND NON-PHONEM
PHONOLOGY: SOME TYPOLOGIC
REFLECTIONS*

JOHN LYONS

American linguistics has proudly and more or less consciously adopted the pragmatic position; the philosophy of justification by results, of first getting things done and only then, if at all, asking what in fact has been done.[1] In the preface to his collection of articles by American linguists, Martin Joos brings out this point well. He goes on to remark: "Altogether there is ample reason why both Americans and (for example) Europeans are likely on each side to consider the other side both irresponsible and arrogant. We may request the Europeans to try to regard the American style as a tradition comme une autre; but the Americans can't be expected to reciprocate: they are having too much fun to be bothered, and few of them are aware that either side has a tradition."[2] As a representative of one European tradition in the enviable position of having secured a captive American audience for an hour or so, I propose to put before you views that absorption in the fun might otherwise prevent you from considering. To those of you who, having heard these views, might feel inclined to say that they are "of only theoretical interest" and that the linguist's job is to describe what actually occurs in particular languages without troubling himself about what might occur (for I have heard this said), I would suggest that the history of science is full of examples to support the opinion that the actual cannot be properly described, perhaps not even recognized, except in the framework of what has previously been envisaged as possible. At the same time, of course, the sphere of what is thought of as possible is being constantly revised under the impact of discoveries made in the description of actual languages. Such is the relation between the theoretical and the applied. And, as a consequence of this, linguistic typologies should be built of a judicious mixture of induction and deduction. This view is at least defensible; and it underlies what I have to say here on phonological typologies.

The concept of the phoneme is so widely accepted nowadays, especially in America, that it may seem perverse to question it. The use of the same terminology, it is true, tends to conceal a number of differences both of theory and of practice among the several schools of phonemicists. These differences, however, important though they are, do not concern us in the present connection. There is a common core of doctrine upon which all phonemicists are agreed and which sets them apart from non-phonemicists: this is expressed in their aim to describe language-utterances, on the phonological level, as a unidimensional se-

[1]This paper was given at one of the regular Ethnolinguistic Seminars at Indiana University in March 1961. In preparing it for publication, at the kind invitation of C. F. Voegelin, I have left the exordium more or less unchanged, although I realize that its style is more appropriate to a seminar talk than to a formal article. My intention is quite selfish: I wish to be reminded more vividly, whenever I see this paper later, of the enjoyable and instructive year I spent at Indiana University and of the seminars that form such a vital part of linguistic activity there.

[2]*Readings in Linguistics* (Washington, 1957), p. vii.

*Reprinted from *International Journal of American Linguistics* 28.127–134 (1962) by permission.

quence of discrete units, every one of which is in opposition with every other of the inventory in at least one pair of distinct utterances of the language.[3]

A radically different kind of phonological analysis has been developed and practised in recent years by what might be called "the London school" of linguists headed by J. R. Firth.[4] To this they give the name "the Prosodic Approach."[5] Since this type of phonological analysis is less familiar to American linguists than the phonemic, I shall first give a brief exposition of what seem to me to be its main distinguishing characteristics. Though this cannot claim to be either an authoritative or an adequate statement of prosodic theory, it will have served its main purpose if it arouses the interest of readers sufficiently for them to turn up and study the several articles listed in the bibliography. After discussing and illustrating the prosodic approach by comparison with the phonemic I shall suggest that neither the one nor the other is completely satisfactory as a general theory of phonological structure, but rather that the applicability of the one rather than the other model to the description of a particular language can be used as a means of typological classification along

a continuous scale ranging from one extreme point, the cardinally phonemic, to the other, the cardinally prosodic and that, in fact, there is probably no language that is either cardinally phonemic, or cardinally prosodic.[6] Other independent variables may then be sought for the typological classification of the phonology of different languages. If this approach is pursued we are led to the view that the phonological system of a given language (or its phonological subsystems) may be thought of as a point (or set of points) in a multidimensional space—the number of selected variables giving the number of dimensions in the hyperspace. Classical phonemic theory would fit perfectly only languages whose phonological systems were placed by this kind of classification at one "corner" of the hyperspace. That there is probably no such language does not mean that phonemic description is never appropriate: it will be more or less appropriate according as the language being described is more or less close to the phonemic "corner"; and in no language will each of the phonemes have equal claim to legitimacy.[7]

The two main differences between the prosodic approach and the phonemic seem to be these: (1) whereas the phonemicist maps the phonic data onto a unilinear sequence of phonological segments (phonemes), the prosodist describes the data in terms of two fundamentally different kinds of elements, *phonematic units* and *prosodies,* the former being ordered with respect to one another in terms of successivity, the latter having as their "domain" a variable, but determinate, number of phonematic units; (2) the prosodist, unlike the phonemicist, does not set up one overall inventory of phonological units for the language he is describing, but a number of different *subsystems,* each relevant for different phonological structures or for different places in these structures.[8] These differences may be

---

[3]As used throughout, the term "phoneme" is to be understood as referring to what are generally called "segmental" phonemes in America, as distinct from the so-called "suprasegmental" phonemes. It is in any case doubtful whether the extension of the term "phoneme" to include phonologically distinct degrees of stress, tone and quantity is justifiable: for it tends to obscure the important distinction between paradigmatic opposition and syntagmatic contrast. (Cf., e.g., R. Jakobson and M. Halle, *Fundamentals of Language,* pp. 25–26, on the comparison of "inherent" and "prosodic" features.)

[4]Most of the linguists practising this kind of analysis are, or have been, at the School of Oriental and African Studies in the University of London and have published their work generally in either *Transactions of the Philological Society* (*TPS*) or *Bulletin of the School of Oriental and African Studies* (*BSOAS*). A list of such works is given at the end of this article.

[5]It should be emphasized that the term "prosodic" as used in this connection covers much more than, and something different in kind from (though it may include), what is generally held to fall within the scope of the term by other linguists. For the London school usage cf. primarily J. R. Firth, "Sounds and Prosodies" [23], *TPS* 1948, 127–152; for the more general usage cf., e.g., Jakobson and Halle, p. 22.

[6]This approach to typological classification may be compared with that exemplified for morphology in C. E. Bazell, *Linguistic Typology* (London, 1958).

[7]The practical advantages of phonemic description for typing and printing should not of course be allowed to influence the theory of phonological structure. It has been argued that phonemic theory has been built on the "hypostatization" of letters of the Roman alphabet: cf. Firth, *op. cit.,* p. 134 [255].

[8]A terminological distinction is made by pro-

summarized by saying that the phonemic model is *unidimensional* and *monosystemic,* and the prosodic *two-dimensional* and *polysystemic.* Though both of these characteristic features of prosodic analysis have been associated with it from the beginning and are insisted upon equally by prosodists, they are clearly independent of one another and may be discussed separately.

The idea of describing the phonology of a language in terms of a two-dimensional model is not new to American linguists. In an early article, Zellig Harris pointed out that "Two independent breakdowns of the flow of speech into elements are physically and logically possible. One is the division of the flow of speech into successive segments. . . . The other is the division of each segment into simultaneous components."[9] He went on to show that in many languages the "simultaneous components" recognized in the analysis extended over more than one segmental phoneme and could frequently be associated with the whole of a higher-level structure: e.g., tongue-retraction in Moroccan Arabic, nasality in Swahili, etc. This point of view, which is essentially that of the prosodist, does not seem to have commended itself to the majority of American linguists; and Harris himself appears unwilling to draw from it its full implications, at least in the practical description of languages.[10]

To illustrate the difference between the phonemic and the prosodic approach to analysis we may briefly consider what is generally called "vowel harmony" in Turkish. It seems that any phonemically-based analysis of Turkish must recognize eight vowels: viz., /i ï u ü e a o ö/. Any one of these vowels may occur in monosyllabic words: in words of more than one syllable, however, there are systematic restrictions on the co-occurrence of the several vowel phonemes. Thus, in words of native Turkish origin, front vowels, /i ü e ö/, and back vowels, /ï u a o/, do not occur together; nor do rounded vowels, /ü ö u o/, and unrounded vowels, /i e ï a/. Moreover, the phoneme /o/ occurs generally only in the first syllable of a word (with the exception of certain verbal forms). A phonemic representation of polysyllabic words is therefore very highly redundant, since it represents each vowel in the structure as a selection from eight contrasting units, whereas all but two of the eight vowel phonemes are excluded from occurrence by the occurrence of any other given vowel phoneme of the word. The phonemicist may of course take account of the limitations upon the co-occurrence of vowel phonemes in his statement. It is to be noticed, however, that the redundancy is of his own making, and the corrective distributional statement a consequence of the phonemic preconceptions of the analysis in the first place. Redundancy at a particular point in a language can be measured only by reference to the set of "choices" permitted by the language at that point.[11] By introducing the

---

sodists between "structure" and "system." Briefly, the distinction is this: a *system* is a set of *terms* in paradigmatic opposition (a substitution set); a *structure* is a sequence of *items* occurring in the stream of speech and considered as a unit at some level of analysis (a syllable, morpheme, word, phrase, etc.). Cf. R. H. Robins, "Formal Divisions in Sundanese," *TPS* 1953, 109; W. S. Allen, "Retroflexion in Sanskrit: Prosodic Technique and its Relevance to Comparative Statement," *BSOAS* 16.556 (1954).

[9]"Simultaneous Components in Phonology" [12], *Language* 20.181–205 (1944) = Joos, *Readings,* pp. 124–138. The quotation is from Joos, p. 124 [115].

[10]His reason is interesting: "The components are merely generalizations of the phonemes extending the very development which gives us phonemes out of sounds. . . . Analysis into components completes what phonemics can only do in part: the transfer of the limitations of sounds from distributional restriction to positional variation in phonetic value. This is not an argument for the use of components: phonemics is undoubtedly the more convenient stopping point in this development, *because it fits alphabetic writing;* but we must recognize the fact that it is possible to go beyond it." (Joos, p. 137 [131]:

my italics—J. L.). The prosodist would deny that the recognition of "long components" (prosodies) is an extension of phonemic analysis and subsequent to it.

[11]It may be observed in passing that many of the generalizations made about the degree of redundancy in languages are vitiated by the failure to allow for redundancy artificially introduced into the description by the choice of model for the analysis. As an instance of this, cf.: "a maximally efficient code, in the information-theory sense, would employ just the number of features necessary to distinguish its phonemes, e.g., the 32 phonemes of English would require only five distinctive binary features. . . . However in English nine binary features are actually employed. The efficiency of English in respect to phonology is therefore about five-ninths, or 56%. Investigation of several languages suggests the generalization that the phonetic efficiency of languages is distributed around the 50% point." J. H. Greenberg, Ch. Osgood, James Jenkins, "Memo-

two binary *prosodic* contrasts of front/back and rounding/non-rounding, and admitting only two contrasting segmental *phonematic units,* high/low, not only do we secure economy in the inventory of phonological elements, but we produce a much more satisfying description of the language—one based on the patterns actually operative in the language.[12]

The advantages of the prosodic approach in a description of Turkish are especially apparent as soon as one moves from phonology to morphology. The phonemicist must either make use of morphophonemes in his representation of the Turkish suffixes or list the allomorphs of each suffix and append a statement of the rules governing the automatic conditioning in different *phonological* environments. C. F. Voegelin and M. E. Ellinghausen, in their account of the structure of Turkish, set up two morphophonemic variables to handle "vowel harmony" in the suffixes, x^2 and x^4, the former taking the two phonemic "values" /e/ and /a/, and the latter the "values" /i ü ï u/. The "value" taken by the variables is then said to depend on the phonemic shape of the preceding vowel. "The phonemic shape of the determined vowel may be any of the four high vowels or either of the two unrounded low vowels . . . ; the rounded low vowels o and ö are never determined in vowel harmony, but may serve as influencing vowels." Determination by the preceding vowel is expressed graphically as follows:

(a) in vowel harmony of the x^2 type:

$$\begin{array}{cc} \text{i} \quad \text{ü} & \text{ï} \quad \text{u} \\ \downarrow \swarrow & \downarrow \swarrow \\ \text{e} \leftarrow \text{ö} & \text{a} \leftarrow \text{o} \end{array}$$

e.g., with the plural suffix -lx^2r: /kibritler/ : /kollar/, etc.

(b) in vowel harmony of the x^4 type:

$$\begin{array}{cccc} \text{i} & \text{ü} & \text{ï} & \text{u} \\ \uparrow & \uparrow & \uparrow & \uparrow \\ \text{e} & \text{ö} & \text{a} & \text{o} \end{array}$$

e.g., with the possessive suffix -x^4m: /kibritim/

: /evim/ : /üzümüm/, etc.[13] For comparison, we may consider a prosodic representation of words containing the same suffixes, using lower case letters for phonematic units and upper case for prosodies. Prosodies will be put before phonematic units: but this, it may be noted, is simply a matter of arbitrary decision—they might just as well be written above or below, at the end of the word, or even in the middle.[14] For the phonematic contrast between the high vowel and the low vowel, I use $i : a$; for the prosodies of front/back and rounding/non-rounding, I use $F : B$ and $R : N$ respectively. (One might equally well, of course, treat one of each pair of prosodies as the absence of the other and so dispense with two symbols.) With the exception of R when it "combines" with a, the domain of these prosodies is the whole word (independently definable in Turkish in terms of stress): in combination with a the domain of R is the first syllable, in succeeding syllables N necessarily occurs (and, therefore, need not be written).[15]

The following table brings together for comparison the morphophonemic, phonemic and prosodic representation of selected words:

gözlx²r	/gözler/	FRgazlar
evlx²r	/evler/	FNavlar
kollx²r	/kollar/	BRkallar
adamlx²r	/adamlar/	BNadamlar
güllx²r	/güller/	FRgillar
kibritlx²r	/kibritler/	FNkibritlar
bulutlx²r	/bulutlar/	BRbilitlar
kïzlx²r	/kïzlar/	BNkizlar
gözx⁴m	/gözüm/	FRgazim
evx⁴m	/evim/	FNavim
kolx⁴m	/kolum/	BRkalim
adamx⁴m	/adamïm/	BNadamim
gülx⁴m	/gülüm/	FRgilim
kibritx⁴m	/kibritim/	FNkibritim
bulutx⁴m	/bulutum/	BRbilitim
kïzx⁴m	/kïzïm/	BNkizim

[13]C. F. Voegelin and M. E. Ellinghausen, "Turkish Structure," *JAOS* 63.34 ff. (1943). The quotation is from p. 37.

[14]Prosodists usually write the prosodies above or below the phonematic units and make their domain explicit in the symbolization.

[15]Cf. Waterson, p. 580, where the domains of these prosodies are described, together with the additional fact that R may occur with *i* in a syllable following one in which N occurs with *a*, provided that there is labiality before the *i* in question. (Thus: BNkarRpiz, /karpuz/, etc. This fact, of course, re-

randum Concerning Universals," Preprint for the SSRC Conference on Language Universals held at Dobbs Ferry (April 1961).

[12]For a more complete account of Turkish phonology in terms of prosodic analysis, cf. N. Waterson, "Some Aspects of the Phonology of the Nominal Forms of the Turkish Word," *BSOAS* 18.578–591 (1956).

It will be observed that the prosodic representation here, and elsewhere, does away with the need for morphophonemics. And this still holds true (with a few exceptions, which must be treated as exceptional in any description) however many suffixes occur: thus what is morphophonemically $g\ddot{o}zlx^2rx^4mx^4zdx^2n$ and phonemically /gözlerimizden/, is prosodically ERgazlarimizdan. That is to say, both stems and suffixes have everywhere the same phonological form. That this gives a "truer" picture of the language seems impossible to deny. If it is objected that prosodic formulae are difficult to read, it may be replied that it is worth making the effort, if thereby we come to see things as they are.[16] If it is objected that the prosodic formulae are longer than the phonemic, it may be pointed out that even shorter formulae than the phonemic may be secured by using a syllabic notation. The only relevant criterion is that of phonological opposition; and if this is consistently applied in the analysis of Turkish, it will lead us to something like the statement given here, according to which the prosodies are "long components" (not of sequences of phonemes, but of words as structural units on the phonological level of analysis) and phonematic units are minimal segmental elements following one another in serial order within morphemes and words.[17]

What is customarily called "dissimilation" is no less suggestive of prosodic treatment than is "assimilation," of which "vowel harmony" is one instance. Suppose, for instance, there was a language in which (phonetically speaking) the occurrence of a front vowel in any given syllable excluded the occurrence of a front vowel in contiguous syllables within the same word, and likewise in the case of back vowels. It would seem to be quite justifiable to set up a pair of contrasting word-length prosodies whose phonetic realization would be contrasting frontness and backness in alternate syllables: that is $P_1 : P_2 = bfbfb \ldots$: $fbfbf \ldots$, where P_1 and P_2 are the prosodies in question, $=$ denotes phonetic realization and f/b represents a syllable marked by frontness/backness. And of course we can envisage prosodies with a far more complex phonetic "realization." There is no reason to fight shy of recognizing phonological units of a quite "abstract" nature or of great phonetic complexity.[18]

Enough has been said to make clear the distinction between phonemic and prosodic analysis. It should be clear also that some languages are more satisfactorily described by the one than the other. This being so, it may be suggested that the goodness of fit of one model of analysis rather than the other should be made a criterion in the typological classification of the phonology of languages. It will be evident that there will be a continuous "line" separating the cardinally phonemic from the cardinally prosodic languages.

We may now ask whether there is not good reason to divide what the London school handles under the head of prosodies into two different kinds of phonological units. The one would comprise those features that are called "prosodic" in the more general usage of linguists (namely: tone, quantity and stress); the other would cover suprasegmental consonantal and vocalic features operating as "long components." If this division is made, we may decide to restrict the term "prosody" to the former, and the term "suprasegmental" to

---

quires a slight, though general and systematic, modification of the statement given above, where it was omitted for the sake of simplicity.)

[16]Prosodists seem generally to prefer the "hocus pocus" philosophy of language (cf., e.g., R. H. Robins, "Aspects of Prosodic Analysis" [24], *Proceedings of the University of Durham Philosophical Society,* Series B (Arts), 1.2–3 [265–266] (1957)). It seems, however, that on this question (as on so many theoretical questions of linguistics) it is possible to adopt an intermediate position. Where the structure of the language being described is clearly determinate and all linguists can reach agreement on the "facts," one might claim to be dealing with "God's truth"; but where the language is indeterminate and does not compel one analysis rather than another, the linguist may choose arbitrarily one of the alternative solutions, providing that he makes clear what he is doing. This, if I understand him correctly, is the position of C. E. Bazell in *Linguistic Form* (Istanbul, 1953) and in many articles. At the same time it should be emphasized that a good deal of "hocus pocus" is rendered unnecessary by the proper choice of linguistic model.

[17]In a full prosodic analysis of Turkish phonology further consonantal and junctural prosodies are required: cf. Waterson, *op. cit.*

[18]There is abundant exemplification from the analysis of real languages in the articles listed in the bibliography. Of particular interest is R. H. Robins, "Vowel Nasality in Sundanese: A Phonological and Grammatical Study," *Studies in Linguistic Analysis* (Philological Society, Oxford, 1957) pp. 87–103.

the latter, kind of phonological unit. The division itself is justified by the fact that prosodies (the term now and henceforth being used in the restricted sense) rest upon syntagmatic contrast, while suprasegmentals, like phonematic units, depend upon paradigmatic opposition, being what Jakobson calls "inherent" features.[19] Indeed, if the matter is pressed, there seems to be no reason to group together prosodies and suprasegmentals as against phonematic units. We may therefore use three, rather than two, cardinal points for the phonological typology, each point representing the employment of one of the phonological variables to the exclusion of the others. It is easy to construct at least rudimentary languages that make exclusive use of only one of the phonological variables (and this establishes their theoretical independence). It is improbable in fact that there exists any natural language that is cardinally of any one of the three types: but this does not invalidate the proposed typology, any more than the fact that few languages, if any, are purely agglutinating, isolating or fusional invalidates the particular morphological typology implied by these terms.[20] The phonological systems or subsystems of given languages can be represented as points within the triangle formed by lines joining the cardinal extremities. To the present writer at least, this appears to be a much more satisfactory system of typological classification than that of forcing all languages into the same phonemic mold, often at the price of arbitrariness, and then comparing them as to the number of phonemes, the ratio of consonants to vowels, etc. That it is always *possible* to phonemicize a language does not prove that one always *should* phonemicize.[21]

There are at least two other theoretical questions touching on phonological analysis upon which linguists are divided. The first is the question of "coexistent phonemic systems,"[22] or, better, coexistent *phonological* systems: the second is that of "grammatical prerequisites."[23] As has been said above, the view that the phonology of a language cannot be described satisfactorily in terms of one, overall system, but should be considered as a set of subsystems, is an integral part of the London school approach; and it is accepted by linguists of the London school that the sphere of relevance of a given subsystem may be, though is not necessarily, grammatically, as well as phonologically determined. The "orthodox" American view seems to be: (a) that the phonology of any given language is a uniform system; and (b) that phonological analysis can, and should, be carried out independently of grammatical analysis. Neither of these propositions is acceptable.[24] A more reasonable point of view would be that the phonology of a given language may or may not form a uniform system and that, in a given case, it may or may not be desirable to do the phonological analysis independently of the grammatical. In Turkish, for example, it would be desirable to set up a different phonological system or different systems to handle those words to which "vowel harmony" does not apply (in the manner described above), since such words form a minority and, being loanwords, may have other "non-Turkish" features. Methodological differences among linguists may here again reflect an inherent difference in languages. And, if this is so, the possibility or non-possibility of (a) describing the phonology of a language satisfactorily in terms of a uniform system and (b) carrying out the phonological analysis independently of the grammatical could be used to provide a further pair of (two-valued) variables in the phonological typology. And of course these variables could be given more values by quantizing the complexity of the phonological subsystems and of the grammatical correlations.

[19]Cf. note 3 above.

[20]Cf. Bazell, *Linguistic Typology*.

[21]C. F. Hockett observes: "The danger which we encounter in letting ourselves become too firmly attached to any one arbitrary unit (feet; Trubetzkoy's principle; Bloch's postulates) is that we fail to realize the extent to which our generalizations are dependent on the frame of reference." (*Manual of Phonology* (1955) pp. 2–3). The attachment of most linguists, including Hockett himself, to the concept of the phoneme would seem to fall within the scope of this warning.

[22]Cf. C. C. Fries and K. L. Pike, "Coexistent Phonemic Systems," *Language* 25.29–50 (1949).

[23]Cf. K. L. Pike, "Grammatical Prerequisites to Phonemic Analysis" [15], *Word* 3.155–172 (1947) and "More on Grammatical Prerequisites" [18], *Word* 8.106–121 (1952).

[24]Hockett's argument that the use of grammatical criteria in phonological analysis necessarily involves circularity is not convincing (cf. *SIL* 7.40 [205], 1949).

Further variables may suggest themselves: but the five mentioned above, especially the first three, would seem to have a good claim to inclusion in any reasonably comprehensive phonological typology of languages.

SELECT BIBLIOGRAPHY

When citing journals, abbreviations will be used as follows: *TPS* = *Transactions of the Philological Society; BSOAS* = *Bulletin of the School of Oriental and African Studies,* University of London; *SILA* = *Studies in Linguistic Analysis,* Special Volume of the Philological Society, Oxford, 1957.

W. S. ALLEN
"Notes on the Phonetics of an Eastern Armenian Speaker," *TPS* 1950.180–206.

"Phonetics and Comparative Linguistics," *Archivum Linguisticum* 3.126–136 (1951).

"Some Prosodic Aspects of Retroflexion and Aspiration in Sanskrit," *BSOAS* 13.939–946 (1951).

Phonetics in Ancient India. (London, 1953).

"Retroflexion in Sanskrit: Prosodic Technique and its Relevance to Comparative Statement," *BSOAS* 16.556–565 (1954).

"Aspiration in the Hāṛautī Nominal," *SILA* 68–86.

"Structure and System in the Abaza Verbal Complex," *TPS* 1956.127–176.

J. CARNOCHAN
"A Study of Quantity in Hausa," *BSOAS* 13.1032–1044 (1951).

"Glottalization in Hausa," *TPS* 1952.78–109.

"Gemination in Hausa," *SILA* 149–181.

J. R. FIRTH
"The Semantics of Linguistic Science," *Lingua* 1.393–404 (1948).

"Sounds and Prosodies," *TPS* 1948.127–152 [23].

"General Linguistics and Descriptive Grammar," *TPS* 1951.69–87.

"A Synopsis of Linguistic Theory 1930–1955," *SILA* 1–32.

E. J. A. HENDERSON
"Prosodies in Siamese," *Asia Major* (new series) 1.189–215 (1949).

"The Phonology of Loanwords in Some South-East Asian Languages," *TPS* 1951.131–158.

"The Main Features of Cambodian Pronunciation," *BSOAS* 14.149–174 (1952).

T. F. MITCHELL
"Particle-Noun Complexes in a Berber Dialect (Zuara)," *BSOAS* 15.375–390 (1953).

"Long Consonants in Phonology and Phonetics," *SILA* 182–205.

F. R. PALMER
"The 'Broken Plurals' of Tigrinya," *BSOAS* 17.548–566 (1955).

"'Openness' in Tigre: A Problem in Prosòdic Statement," *BSOAS* 18.561–577 (1956).

"The Verb in Bilin," *BSOAS* 19.131–159 (1957).

"Gemination in Tigrinya," *SILA* 139–148.

R. H. ROBINS
"Notes on the Phonetics of the Georgian Word" (with Natalie Waterson), *BSOAS* 14.55–72 (1952).

"The Phonology of the Nasalized Verbal Forms in Sundanese," *BSOAS* 15.138–145 (1953).

"Formal Divisions in Sundanese," *TPS* 1953. 109–142.

"Vowel Nasality in Sundanese: A Phonological and Grammatical Study," *SILA* 87–103.

N. C. SCOTT
"A Phonological Analysis of the Szechuanese Monosyllable," *BSOAS* 18.556–560 (1956).

A. E. SHARP
"A Tonal Analysis of the Disyllabic Noun in the Machame Dialect of Chaga," *BSOAS* 16.157–169 (1954).

R. K. SPRIGG
"Verbal Phrases in Lhasa Tibetan," *BSOAS* 16.134–156, 320–350, 566–591 (1954).

"The Tonal System of Tibetan (Lhasa Dialect) and the Nominal Phrase," *BSOAS* 17.134–153 (1955).

"Junction in Spoken Burmese," *SILA* 104–138.

NATALIE WATERSON
"Some Aspects of the Phonology of the Nominal Forms of the Turkish Word," *BSOAS* 18.578–591 (1956).

BIBLIOGRAPHY 13
Typology and Universals in Phonology

VOEGELIN, C. F., and J. YEGERLEHNER (1956) "The Scope of Whole System ('Distinctive Feature') and Subsystem Typologies"

BAZELL, C. E. (1958) *Linguistic Typology*

JAKOBSON, R. (1958) "Typological Studies and their Contribution to Historical Comparative Linguistics"

SPANG-HANSSEN, H. (1958) "Typological and Statistical Aspects of Distribution as a Criterion in Linguistic Analysis"

GREENBERG, J. H. (1962) "Is the Vowel-Consonant Dichotomy Universal?"

FERGUSON, C. A. (1963) "Assumptions about Nasals: A Sample Study in Phonological Universals"

GREENBERG, J. H. (ed.) (1963) *Universals of Language*

SAPORTA, S. (1963) "Phoneme Distribution and Language Universals"

GREENBERG, J. H. (1966) "Synchronic and Diachronic Universals in Phonology"

AOKI, H. (1968) "Toward a Typology of Vowel Harmony"

KIPARSKY, P. (1968) "Linguistic Universals and Linguistic Change"

CAIRNS, C. E. (1969) "Markedness, Neutralization, and Universal Redundancy Rules"

26

ON SYSTEM-STRUCTURE PHONOLOGY*

VICTORIA FROMKIN

In 1934, when Yuen-Ren Chao discussed the nonuniqueness of phonemic solutions,[1] he demonstrated that different phonological analyses presuppose different underlying concepts. The thirty years since the publication of that paper have not produced any one phonological theory to which even most linguists will subscribe. The situation is not unusual in the history of science. Scientific theories are constantly submitted to change and revision; in an empirical science, the structure is never completed. Experiments become more precise, new phenomena are revealed, new concepts are developed. At all times we must be prepared to abandon our theory, remodel the foundations, and erect a new structure. But the history of science shows also that theories which turn out to be inaccurate can yet lead to the discovery of new facts; and each new theory retains some elements of the one it has supplanted. Acceptance of one theory does not require one to reject a rival theory in toto.

It is in this spirit that the present paper attempts to describe certain characteristics of Twi phonology.[2] It suggests that the incorporation of certain principles of the British system-structure or prosodic approach into the phonological component of a transformational grammar of Twi may provide a simpler and more revealing description.

The phonological inventory of Twi, as it might look in a transformational grammar modeled after Morris Halle, *The Sound Pattern of Russian*,[3] is presented in Tables 1 and 2 as a matrix of morphonemes and a branching diagram to represent them. According to this view, speech consists of a series of segments, specified by distinctive features (DF) and boundaries (#) characterized by their effect on the features.[4]

No nasal consonants are included in the list of contrasting segments, because all vowels are nasalized after nasal consonantal phones, and no nasalized vowels follow the −tense consonants /d, b, g/.[5] A few phonological rules (P rules) can handle nasalization and assimilation of nasal consonants.[6]

As can be seen in Tables 1 and 2, eight distinctive features are needed to specify the

---

[4]Halle 19.

[5]There are two exceptions to the rule. *Gã* is the name of a language spoken in Ghana and may be considered a loan-word, outside the system. *Mo* 'good', though widely used, is best handled by a special rule.

[6]These rules include the following.

$$(1) \quad -\text{tense consonants} \rightarrow +\text{nasal} \, / \, \text{———} \, \begin{Bmatrix} V \\ \# \end{Bmatrix},$$

where # = morpheme final. (A morpheme-structure rule limits the final nasal to [m] or [ŋ].)

$$(2) \quad C \rightarrow \alpha \text{ compact}, \, \alpha \text{ grave}, \, +\text{nasal} \, / \, \text{———} \, C.$$

(α = 'the same as'.) Thus $C \begin{Bmatrix} b \\ p \\ f \end{Bmatrix} \rightarrow m \begin{Bmatrix} b \\ p \\ f \end{Bmatrix}$, $C \begin{Bmatrix} t \\ s \end{Bmatrix} \rightarrow$ n $\begin{Bmatrix} t \\ s \end{Bmatrix}$, etc.

Rule 2 applies after other P rules have specified the feature as + or − grave wherever it was left unspecified in the lexical matrix, and after certain nonpalatal consonants have been specified as −grave by other P rules.

$$(3) \quad -\text{tense } C \rightarrow +\text{nasal} \, / \, N \, \text{———} \, (\text{where } N = C$$

nasalized by rule 2; e.g., mb → mm, nd → nn, ŋg → ŋŋ.

Note. Throughout the paper symbols used have the following meanings. The arrow (→) = is rewritten as; the slant line (/) = in the environment of; the braces ({ }) indicate a choice of items.

---

[1]Yuen-Ren Chao, "The Non-Uniqueness of Phonemic Solutions of Phonetic Systems," *Bulletin of the Institute of History and Philology, Academia Sinica* 4.363–397 (1934).

[2]The dialect described is Akuapem Twi. My informant was Kwaku Asenso.

[3]The Hague, 1959.

*Reprinted from *Language* 41.601–609 (1965) by permission.

TABLE 1
Matrix representing the morphonemes of Twi

	w	y	yʷ	d	b	t	p	s	f	g	k	h	gʷ	kʷ	hʷ	ɪ	ĩ	i	ĩ	ʊ	ũ	u	ũ	ɛ	a	ã	e	ɔ	o	r
1. vocalic	−	−	−	−	−	−	−	−	−	−	−	−	−	−	−	+	+	+	+	+	+	+	+	+	+	+	+	+	+	+
2. consonantal	−	−	−	+	+	+	+	+	+	+	+	+	+	+	+	−	−	−	−	−	−	−	−	−	−	−	−	−	−	+
3. compact	−	+	+	−	−	−	−	−	−	+	+	+	+	+	+	−	−	−	−	−	−	−	−	−	+	+	+	+	+	0
4. flat	0	−	+	0	0	0	0	0	0	−	−	−	+	+	+	−	−	−	−	+	+	+	+	−	−	−	−	+	+	0
5. continuant	0	0	0	−	−	−	−	+	+	−	−	+	−	−	+	0	0	0	0	0	0	0	0	0	0	0	0	0	0	0
6. tense	0	0	0	−	−	+	+	0	0	−	+	0	−	+	0	−	−	+	+	−	−	+	+	−	−	−	+	−	+	0
7. grave	0	0	0	−	+	−	+	−	+	0	0	0	0	0	0	0	0	0	0	0	0	0	0	−	+	+	0	0	0	0
8. nasal	0	0	0	0	0	0	0	0	0	0	0	0	0	0	0	−	+	−	+	−	+	−	+	0	−	+	0	0	0	0

TABLE 2
Branching diagram representing the morphonemes of Twi as specified in Table 1. The numbers at each node refer to the features as listed in the matrix. Left branches represent minus values, right branches plus values.

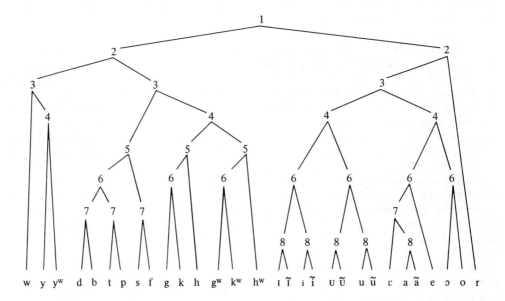

thirty contrasting morphonemes.[7] But only 164 of the possible 240 total features are needed to specify the morphonemic contrasts. This is most clearly seen in the tree diagram of Table 2, which shows each phoneme with its distinct branching. For any one morphoneme, only the nodes (i.e., features) leading to that segment need to be specified.

The matrices of distinctive features representing the individual lexical morphemes, on which the rules of the phonological component operate, include additional zeros to represent features predictable from neighboring segments. These zeros will be rewritten by morpheme structure rules. By thus eliminating redundancies, we state the distributional constraints of the language.

The zeros or blanks which are not specified by the morpheme structure rules, but which must be specified for final phonetic realization, are supplied by the P rules. By eliminating the phonemic level, traditionally required between the morphophonemic and the phonetic, we achieve a simplification of the phonological system. For instance, a traditional phonemic analysis would demand the inclusion of the phoneme /ky/, since the following

[7]Twi is a tone language, with both lexical and grammatical tone. The tonal system is outside the scope of this paper; tone is therefore unspecified in the DF matrix and in the examples.

contrasts can be found: [kyi] 'to hate', [kita] 'to hold', [kye] 'to divide', [kɛsɪ] 'big', [kɛntɛŋ] 'to straggle', [kyɪnɪ] 'salt'. By simple ordered P rules we can rewrite the morphophonemic transcription to produce the correct phonetic values:

(1)
$$A \begin{bmatrix} +\text{compact} \\ -\text{flat} \\ -\text{continuant} \\ +\text{tense} \end{bmatrix} C \rightarrow$$

$$-\text{grave} / \underline{\quad\quad} \begin{bmatrix} -\text{flat} \\ \begin{Bmatrix} - \\ 0 \end{Bmatrix} \text{grave} \end{bmatrix} V \text{ not followed by}$$

$$(N) \begin{bmatrix} -\text{compact} \\ -\text{grave} \end{bmatrix} C.$$

Written in phonemic symbols this rule reads: /k/ →

[ky] / ——— front vowels not followed by (n)$\begin{Bmatrix} s \\ t \end{Bmatrix}$.[8]

(2) /i/ preceded by /k/ and followed by /a/ → Ø, e.g., /kiam → kyiam → kyam/.

These rules work only if one considers grammatical boundaries or junctures, since /k/ before a front vowel does become palatal if the vowel is followed by a morpheme boundary followed in turn by (n)$\begin{Bmatrix} s \\ t \end{Bmatrix}$. Thus, /kɛ # sika/ 'to divide money' is rewritten as [kyɛ # sika],[9] but /kɛsɪ/ 'big' is not [kyɛsɪ].

Reduplicated stems further illustrate the point. Reduplication is the doubling of the stem by prefixing, with a change of the stem vowel and sometimes loss of nasalization in the prefix. A rule may be written to generate the reduplicated prefix vowel: prefix V → −compact. By this rule the −flat stem vowels /ɪ, i, ɛ, e, a/ are reduplicated in the prefix as /ɪ/ or /i/ and the +flat stem vowels /ʊ, u, ɔ, o/ are reduplicated in the prefix as /u/ or /ʊ/. The same applies to the nasalized vowels. Using this rule, the stem /ki/ [kyi] 'to hate' is reduplicated as [kyikyi], but the stem /ka/ 'to say' is reduplicated as [kɪka] since /k/ is not palatalized before front vowels in reduplicated stem prefixes. It is evident that the morpheme structure rule stated earlier must be applied before the reduplication of the stem.

It seems clear that the distinctive feature

[8]In the rules the parentheses represent optional segments.
[9]By a later P rule [kyɛ] will be rewritten as [kye].

matrix in Table 1, when compared to a traditional phonemic analysis, both reduces the inventory of contrasting segments and reveals certain regularities in the language. The question remains, however, whether alternate solutions (i.e., alternate matrices and branching diagrams) are possible with the same number of specified features. Tables 3 and 4 present such a matrix. The same number of features are specified, but not the same features. Is there then no unique solution, even when using one phonological theory? Halle has written[10] that "Economy should be measured by the number of Distinctive Features utilized. The fewer features mentioned in a description the greater its economy." This, of course, refers to the overall description and not to any isolated part of the grammar. The selection of the proper matrix must depend on the rules which comprise the phonological component rather than on an arbitrary choice between two matrices. The discussion below will attempt to show that a unique solution is in fact possible.

Only two aspects of Twi phonology will be discussed in this paper. The first is the relation between morpheme classes and phonological structure. What I have already said about reduplicated stems shows that the phonological structures of disyllabic simple and of reduplicated stems are subject to different constraints. Similarly the Twi verb stem differs from the noun stem. In the disyllabic verb stem, of the structure C_1VC_2V,[11] C_1 may be any C, but C_2 is limited to /r, s, N, t/, e.g., *ware* 'to marry', *tena* 'to sit', *suro* 'to fear', *bisa* 'to ask'.[12] In nouns, on the other hand, C_2 is unrestricted, e.g., *a-bofra*[13] 'child', *o-nipa* 'person', *sika* 'money', *mako* 'pepper', *nantwi* 'beef'.

This relation between morpheme classes and phonological structure is not made explicit

[10]Morris Halle, "On the Role of Simplicity in Linguistic Descriptions," *Proceedings of Symposia in Applied Mathematics* 12.90 (1961).
[11]For the rest of this paper, except where specified, C = any segment that is −vocalic and +consonantal, and V = any segment that is +vocalic and −consonantal. N = C which by virtue of P rules is rewritten as +nasal.
[12]The italicized forms are printed in the official orthography.
[13]In these forms, the hyphen represents the boundary between prefix and stem.

TABLE 3
Alternate matrix of Twi morphemes

	w	y	yʷ	d	b	t	p	s	f	g	k	h	gʷ	kʷ	hʷ	ɪ	i	ĩ	ĩ	u	u	ũ	ũ	ɛ	a	e	ã	ɔ	o	r
1. vocalic	−	−	−	−	−	−	−	−	−	−	−	−	−	−	−	+	+	+	+	+	+	+	+	+	+	+	+	+	+	+
2. consonantal	−	−	−	+	+	+	+	+	+	+	+	+	+	+	+	−	−	−	−	−	−	−	−	−	−	−	−	−	−	+
3. compact	−	+	+	−	−	−	−	−	−	+	+	+	+	+	+	−	−	−	−	−	−	−	−	+	+	+	+	+	+	0
4. flat	0	−	+	0	0	0	0	0	0	−	−	−	+	+	+	−	−	−	−	+	+	+	+	−	−	−	−	+	+	0
5. nasal	0	0	0	0	0	0	0	0	0	0	0	0	0	0	0	−	−	+	+	−	−	+	+	−	−	−	+	0	0	0
6. continuant	0	0	0	−	−	−	−	+	+	−	−	+	−	−	+	0	0	0	0	0	0	0	0	0	0	0	0	0	0	0
7. tense	0	0	0	−	−	+	+	0	0	−	+	0	−	+	0	−	+	−	+	−	+	−	+	−	−	+	0	−	+	0
8. grave	0	0	0	−	+	−	+	−	+	0	0	0	0	0	0	0	0	0	0	0	0	0	0	0	0	−	+	0	0	0	0

TABLE 4
Branching diagram representing the morphemes of Twi as specified in Table 3

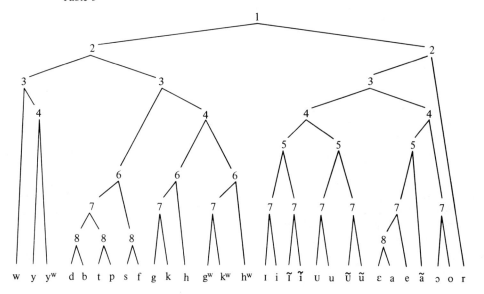

w   y   yʷ   d   b   t   p   s   f   g   k   h   gʷ   kʷ   hʷ   ɪ   i   ĩ   ĩ   u   u   ũ   ũ   ɛ   a   e   ã   ɔ   o   r

in the transformational model. Differences between the phonological structures of different morpheme classes can only be inferred by going through the entire lexicon and the various sets of rules. The phonological component can be viewed as a transducer which converts the lexical and grammatical formatives into speech sounds. While only permissible verb roots are generated in a transformational grammar, the differentiation of verbs and nouns in phonological structure is given no more status than the trivial fact that a certain specific number of words in the language begin with /k/.

Adherents to the Firthian approach do not consider this sufficient. Their theory starts with the assumption that language is patterned activity, and requires that all the patterns which occur must be made explicit.[14] According to Firth,[15] "The first principle of phonological and grammatical analysis is to distinguish between structure and system." Structure consists of elements in syntagmatic or horizontal relation; systems consist of commutable terms in paradigmatic, vertical relation. Since their approach is polysystemic, a basic requirement is to differentiate between the phonological structures of verbs and nouns, and to reveal the fact that in C_1VC_2V verbs, the C_2 system

[14]M. A. K. Halliday, "Categories of the Theory of Grammar," *Word* 17.241–292 (1961).

[15]J. R. Firth, "A Synopsis of Linguistic Theory 1930–1955," *Studies in Linguistic Analysis* 30 (Oxford, 1957).

(consonants which commute as terms) is different from the C_2 system in C_1VC_2V nouns.

I have already shown that the differentiation between simple and reduplicated stems is both revealing and simplifying. If syntactic information is utilized in the morpheme structure rules, the polysystemic nature of the language, as suggested by followers of Firth, will be further revealed, and more of the features can be left unspecified in the lexical matrices as redundant. Two ordered rules will specify:

(1) A segment $\begin{bmatrix} -\text{vocalic} \\ +\text{grave} \end{bmatrix}$ / $+$vocalic ──

in a verb morpheme is $\begin{bmatrix} +\text{consonantal} \\ -\text{tense} \\ -\text{compact} \\ -\text{continuant} \end{bmatrix}$

(This permits [m] or [n] to occur as C_2. The $+$nasality feature is added by a later P rule; cf. footnote 6.)

(2) A $-$vocalic segment / $+$vocalic ── $+$vocalic

in a verb morpheme is $\begin{bmatrix} +\text{consonantal} \\ +\text{tense} \\ -\text{compact} \\ -\text{grave} \end{bmatrix}$

(This rule permits [s] or [t] to occur as C_2.)

Two examples of such verbs, *tumi* 'to be able' and *bisa* 'to ask', are shown below with the distinctive features of the second consonant as they would be listed in the lexicon, and as they would be listed after the application of the two rules.

Another interesting aspect of Twi phonology is the phenomenon known variously as vowel harmony, vowel raising, or euphony, which restricts the serial cooccurrence of vowel qualities. In monosyllabic morphemes nine oral vowels contrast: /si/ *si* 'to sit', /sɪ/

-se 'father-in-law', /se/ *se* 'to say', /sɛ/ *sɛ* 'to equal', /so/ *so* 'to seize', /sɔ/ *sɔ* 'to drop', /su/ *–su* 'rain', /sʊ/ *so* 'to wear', /sa/ *sa* 'to cut into'.

Stem morphemes which contain more than one vowel are divided into two groups. In the first, one of the vowels is tense /i, e, o, u/; they are preceded only by another tense vowel or by /ɛ/, and followed only by a tense vowel or by /a/. The second group contains the lax vowels /ɪ, ɛ, ɔ, ʊ, a/.

Group I
/sika/ *sika* 'money'
/o-buroni/ *oburoni* 'European'
/gʷini/ *adwini* 'art'
/sie/ *sie* 'to guard'
/onipa/ *onipa* 'person'

Group II
/a-tadɪ/ *atade* 'cloth'
/a-burɔfu/ *aborofo* 'Europeans'
/mpʊanu/ *mpoano* 'coast'
/sɛɪ/ *sɛe* 'to destroy'
/anɔpa/ *anɔpa* 'morning'

This phenomenon occurs also across morpheme boundaries, with certain constraints. A tense vowel occurring as the first vowel of a stem morpheme conditions a change in a lax vowel occurring as the final vowel of the morpheme before the grammatical boundary: /ɪ, ɛ, ɔ, ʊ, a/ → /i, e, o, u, ɛ/ / ── #C $+$tense V. By such a process, /atadɪ/ becomes /atadi # yi/ 'this cloth'.

The phenomenon can be handled in the phonological component by the following rules.

MORPHEME STRUCTURE RULES
M1. If a V segment is $+$tense, all preceding V segments are either $+$tense, or, if $-$tense,

	Lexicon matrix #tubi# vb		by rule 1	Lexicon matrix #bisa# vb		by rule 2
1. vocalic	−		−	−		−
2. consonantal	0	→	+	0	→	+
3. compact	0	→	−	0	→	−
4. flat	0		0	0		0
5. continuant	0	→	−	+		+
6. tense	0	→	−	0		0
7. grave	+		+	0	→	−
8. nasal	0		0	0		0

−grave. (Only /i, e, o, u, ɛ/ precede /i, e, o, u/.)

M2. If a V segment is +tense, any −tense V segment which follows it is +grave. (/a/ occurs after tense vowels.)

P RULES:

P1. $A \begin{bmatrix} -\text{tense,} \\ \begin{Bmatrix} 0 \\ - \end{Bmatrix} \text{grave} \end{bmatrix} V \rightarrow +\text{tense} / \underline{\quad} \# C +\text{tense V.}$

P2. A +grave V →

$-\text{grave} / \underline{\quad} \# C +\text{tense V. (a} \rightarrow \varepsilon.)$

The P rules are noncyclic, i.e., they apply only once, before grammatical boundaries are removed. Without this restriction, a −tense preboundary vowel which has been rewritten +tense would condition the rewriting of the −tense vowels preceding it. Since vowel raising occurs across morpheme boundaries for just one preceding vowel, the rule must be applied only once.

These rules would be applied to a terminal string, after the grammatical morphemes have been specified in terms of distinctive features:

	1	2	3	4	5	6	7	8
Terminal string:	# ɔ	# b u r o	d ī	# t ɪ	# a	# b u r i	#
1. vocalic	+	+ + +	+ +	+	+	+ +	
2. consonantal	−	− − −	− −	−	−	− −	
3. compact	+	− − +	−	+	−	− +	
4. flat	+	+ + +	−	−	−	+ −	
5. continuant	0	0 0 0	0 0	0	0	0 0	
6. tense	−	0 0 +	− −	0	+		
7. grave	0	0 0 0	0	+	0	0	
8. nasal	0	− 0 +	− 0	−	−		

'A European lives in Aburi'

By applying M1, the following unspecified features are specified: segments 2 u, 3 o, 7 u → +tense.

By applying P1, segment 1 ɔ → +tense, and segment 6 a → −grave.

Since these rules also apply to nasalized vowels, if we select the matrix as shown in Table 3, other rules must be included as follows.

M2′. If a V segment is +tense, a following V is +tense, or +grave, or +compact and +nasal. (To account for /ã/ following tense Vs.)

P3: $A \begin{bmatrix} +\text{compact} \\ +\text{nasal} \end{bmatrix} V \rightarrow$

$\begin{bmatrix} -\text{tense} \\ -\text{grave} \end{bmatrix} / \underline{\quad} \# C +\text{tense V.}$

It now becomes apparent that the alternate matrix must be rejected in favor of the matrix in Table 1.

If we incorporate into our grammar another of the concepts first developed by Firth, a new matrix with fewer morphonemes and fewer specified features will result. This will prove worthwhile only if such a solution is more revealing and in an overall view simpler.

By such an analysis, speech consists of more than the designated segments and boundaries. Phonological features which refer to structures larger than single segments are called prosodies.[16] These are realized phonetically over a whole structure, or else mark the beginning or end of words, morphemes, or syllables.[17]

Using this concept, we extract a prosody of vowel raising.[18] This calls for a new symbol R to be added in the matrices of certain morphemes; but it reduces the number of morphonemes from 30 to 24, and the number of specified features from 164 to 151.

The specification of the features can be left to the P rules, as follows.

P1′. Nongrave (0 or −grave) Vs in the

sequence $\begin{Bmatrix} C \\ \# \end{Bmatrix} V \# V^n R \# \rightarrow +\text{tense.}$

(V^n = one or more Vs.)

P2′. +grave V in the sequence $\begin{Bmatrix} C \\ \# \end{Bmatrix} V \# V^n R,$

but not $/ \underline{\quad} R \# \rightarrow -\text{grave.}$

(Final /a/ is not rewritten as /ɛ/ if the V after # is not raised by the presence of R.)

[16]Firth 24.

[17]R. H. Robins, "Aspects of Prosodic Analysis" [24], *Proceedings of the University of Durham Philosophical Society*, series B 1.5 [268–269] (1957).

[18]This phenomenon has been treated prosodically in J. Berry, "Vowel Harmony in Twi," *Bulletin of the School of Oriental and African Studies* 19.124–130 (1957); L. Boadi, "Palatality as a Factor in Twi Vowel Harmony," *Journal of African Languages* 2.133–139 (1963); and J. Carnochan, "Vowel Harmony in Igbo," *African Language Studies* 1.155–163 (1960).

The terminal string cited earlier is now specified as

	1	2	3	4		5	6		7	8
Terminal string:#	o #	b	u	r	o	d	ī R #	t	i #	a # b u r i R #
1. vocalic	+	+	+	+		+	+		+	+
2. consonantal	−	−	−	−		−	−		−	−
3. compact	+	−	+	−		−	+		−	−
4. flat	+	+	+	−		−	−		+	−
5. continuant	0	0	0	0		0	0		0	0
6. tense	0	0	0	0		0	0		0	0
7. grave	0	0	0	0		0	+		0	0
8. nasal	0	−	0	+		−	−		−	−

By rule 1, segments 1, 2, 3, 4, 7, 8 → +tense
By rule 2, segment 6 → −grave.

Extracting the R prosody is justified by more than the desire for economy. As I showed above, the constraints on vowel sequences can be handled in the phonological component without extracting a vowel-raising prosody. But in that case one segment is marked as +tense, and the other V segments are specified as +tense only by virtue of their sequential relation to the marked V. The arbitrary assignment of the feature +tense to one segment obscures the more interesting fact that tenseness is a property of a phonological structure larger than a single segment, which may be called the unit of vowel harmony. By using one of the concepts in the system-structure theory we not only achieve economy in the inventory of phonological elements and features, and a simplification of the rules, we also arrive at a more satisfying description of the language, one that reveals the patterning of Twi morphemes and the phonological relations among them.

This paper does not deny the main aims of a transformational grammar. Rather, it attempts to show that by incorporating two concepts of the system-structure approach—the polysystemic nature of language and the phonological prosody—the phonological component reveals more about the language, and does so without violating the criterion of simplicity.

The existence of multiple theories does not necessarily argue for the abandonment of all but one of them. At the present stage of linguistics it may be profitable to be eclectic, taking concepts from various theories where they seem to add to the descriptive and explanatory power of the grammar.

III

DISTINCTIVE FEATURES AND GENERATIVE PHONOLOGY

INTRODUCTION

This section is divided into two parts—the first illustrating the formation of the principle of distinctive feature analysis by members of the Prague school, the second showing the development of transformational-generative phonology and its incorporation of the distinctive feature principle.

At the same time that the phonemic principle was being discussed in America by Sapir, Bloomfield, and others, Roman Jakobson, and others in Europe following his lead, were working out a different approach to the phoneme. Whereas in America the main emphasis was placed on the distribution of phonemes and their allophones, Prague school linguists were more interested in stating the phonetic contrasts among the phonemes, that is, in noting those features that serve to distinguish one phoneme from another. Already in his *Novejšaja russkaja poèzija* (published in Prague in 1921 but written in Moscow two years before), Jakobson emphasized the importance of the phoneme concept. His early writings show that right from the first he was concerned with the distinguishing function of phonemes. In 1927 he talked about "the repertory of meaningful distinctions among the acoustico-motor images proper to a given language" (in "The Concept of the Sound Law and the Teleological Criterion"), and in his "Proposition au Premier Congrès International de Linguistes" (1928) he said, "Une corrélation phonologique est constituée par une série d'oppositions binaires définies par un principe commun et qui peut être pensé indépendamment de chaque couple de termes opposés." Thus he was already thinking of the differences among phonemes in terms of binary oppositions. In his *Remarques sur l'évolution phonologique du russe comparée à celle des autres langues slaves* (1929) Jakobson introduced the idea of the archiphoneme, which was taken up and discussed at great length by other members of the Prague school. Jakobson himself later gave up the idea in favor of a treatment in terms of distinctive features.

N. S. Trubetzkoy and others of the Prague school, under the influence of Jakobson, worked on classifying the sounds of language in terms of phonological oppositions, and this became one of the main concerns of Prague school phonology. Trubetzkoy died in 1938 but his *Grundzüge der Phonologie*, published posthumously in 1939, is a classic statement of Prague school phonology as it then stood. Zellig Harris' review of this book in 1941 [27] characterizes the system briefly and points up the objections of the Bloomfieldian linguists to this kind of approach. (See Part I for Harris' own later treatment of "Simultaneous Components.")

The same year that Trubetzkoy's book appeared, Jakobson, in "Observations sur le classement phonologique des consonnes" [28], proposed revisions in the theory. Here for the first time he attempted to systematize the application of the distinctive feature approach by defining the phonemes entirely in terms of an exhaustive set of distinctive features. Also, up until this time the features had been articulatory, but now they became acoustic features, making it possible to do away with some of the vagueness of oppositions stated in articulatory terms, and to apply the binary principle much more widely. But not everything was binary yet at this stage; the vowels were not yet analyzed in binary terms, and the treatment of liquids and glides was still not worked out. There was as yet no insistence on economy in the number of distinctive features.

Charles F. Hockett's 1951 review [29] of André Martinet's *Phonology as Functional Phonetics* (1946) serves as an excellent comparison of Trubetzkoyan phonology, as presented by Martinet, and neo-Bloomfieldian phonemics, including a comparison of the terminologies of the two schools.

Jakobson wrote no more about distinctive features until the appearance of his article "On the Identification of Phonemic Entities" [30] and Jakobson and Lotz' "Notes on the French Phonemic Pattern," both in 1949. These two articles used, for the first time, tables of the distinctive features of each pho-neme. And it was the first time that all the phonemes in a language were treated system-atically in terms of features. In the original version of "On the Identification of Phonemic Entities" there were no minus signs but only pluses, blanks, and the combination sign ± (making the features thus represented actually ternary). At this stage Jakobson did not dis-tinguish between the absence of a feature and redundancy—his prime concern was to mark the positive features, and the fewer of these one had to have, the better the analysis. In the version of this article reprinted here, Jakobson has revised the table to correspond to his cur-rent thinking, in which a minus represents ab-sence of the feature, whereas a blank repre-sents redundancy.

Jakobson, Fant, and Halle's *Preliminaries to Speech Analysis* (1952) provided the first full-scale account of the acoustic properties of distinctive features. The claim was made here for the first time that there is a limited number of distinctive features which can be used to describe all the languages of the world. This claim has since become one of the major argu-ments given for the superiority of the distinc-tive feature approach. Parallels were drawn here also between acoustic distinctive features and the characterization of each in terms of the shape and size of the resonators involved, but with the insistence that the acoustic statements are linguistically more relevant.

The ± sign was still used in *Preliminaries,* while in Cherry, Halle, and Jakobson's "To-ward the Logical Description of Languages in Their Phonemic Aspect" (1953) [31] the sign had been done away with. Concern with econ-omy in the number of features needed had given way to the desire to make all the features binary. This article was an application of some of the concepts of statistical communication theory to distinctive feature analysis, using colloquial Russian as an example.

Morris Halle's "The Strategy of Pho-nemics" (1954) [32], on the other hand, went back to using the ± sign again. In this article he outlined a procedure for phonemic analysis done in terms of distinctive features rather than allophones.

Noam Chomsky's 1957 review [33] of Jakobson and Halle's *Fundamentals of Lan-guage* (1956) consisted primarily of an explica-tion and evaluation of the essay "Phonology and Phonetics," which made up the first part of the book. The interest of transformational-ists in distinctive features was already begin-ning, although it would be several years before a complete theory of generative phonology based on distinctive features was formulated.

In the meantime the study of distinctive features as such, apart from their use in trans-formational grammar, has continued, and sev-eral objections to the theory have been raised. In "A Criticism of Distinctive Features" (1966) [34] Robert D. Wilson formulated some of the main objections and offered suggestions for the improvement both of the theory itself and of its use in transformational grammar.

Gunnar Fant, in "The Nature of Distinc-tive Features" (1967) [35], replied to some of the major objections to distinctive feature anal-ysis and presented some revisions in his own thinking on the matter.

Morris Halle's *The Sound Pattern of Rus-sian* (1959) was the first attempt to give a com-plete phonological description of a language based on the principles of transformational grammar and employing distinctive features. In the accompanying theoretical discussion, Halle set forth six basic conditions which he felt a phonological analysis should satisfy. These conditions, and the book as a whole, were reviewed and evaluated in 1962 by Charles Ferguson [36]. At that time generative phonology was generally poorly known and understood by many Bloomfieldian linguists, and this review served to bring it to their atten-tion and to point out some of the ways in which it departed from structuralist methodology—for example, the argument that phonology is not autonomous but is inextricably tied up with grammar and cannot be described indepen-dently of the grammar as a whole.

Halle's "Phonology in Generative Gram-mar" (1962) [37] was a further attempt to ac-quaint linguists with the way the phonological rules of a generative grammar are formulated and an effort to show that historical as well as descriptive phonology is reflected in such rules —a radical departure from the traditional view that synchronic and diachronic facts must not be mixed.

Halle's "On the Bases of Phonology" (1964) [38], a revised version of an article that first appeared in 1958, is a presentation of the terminology customarily used in distinctive feature discussions, with a description of the "articulatory correlates" of each—not in terms of points of articulation but rather of the shape, degree of narrowing, and so on, of the vocal tract. Halle then goes on to show how morphemes in a generative grammar are represented directly by distinctive features, entirely eliminating the traditional phoneme. In a final section he discusses the way that distinctive features fit into the over-all theory of generative phonology.

In 1962 Noam Chomsky presented his "The Logical Basis of Linguistic Theory" to the Ninth International Congress of Linguists. In 1964 a revised and expanded version of this report appeared under the title *Current Issues in Linguistic Theory*. The portion of that book which deals with phonology is reproduced here [39]. Chomsky presents the form that the phonological component of a generative grammar should take, followed by a critique of what he calls taxonomic phonemics (i.e., phonemics that is primarily concerned with segmentation and classification), which he characterizes as being tied to conditions of linearity, invariance, biuniqueness, and local determinacy. His brand of phonemics, which he terms systematic phonemics, does not observe these conditions and is not based on such things as complementary distribution. It was in this work that he introduced the ideas of systematic phonemics and systematic phonetics and showed how they relate to each other and to the syntactic component of the grammar.

Vachek's "On Some Basic Principles of 'Classical' Phonology" (1964) [40] was a critique of some of the arguments of Chomsky in the above work, particularly as they apply to Prague school phonology. (Vachek's article was based on Chomsky's original report, but the differences involved here are ones of detail only.)

F. W. Householder, Jr., in his article "On Some Recent Claims in Phonological Theory" (1965) [41], also registered objections to the views of Chomsky and Halle as expressed in the above report and in "Phonology in Generative Grammar." Chomsky and Halle countered with "Some Controversial Questions in Phonological Theory" (1965) [42], followed by Householder's "Phonological Theory: A Brief Comment" (1966) [43].

In his "Distinctive Features and Phonetic Features" (1967) [44], Householder took exception to the claim that generative grammar uses distinctive features, arguing that nothing in generative grammar corresponds to the original idea of binary distinctive features as envisaged by Jakobson.

In the meantime Sydney M. Lamb's "Prolegomena to a Theory of Phonology" (1966) [53] had appeared, with its critique of the transformationalist position on phonology and presentation of the stratificational view (see Part IV).

Henry Kučera, in "Distinctive Features, Simplicity, and Descriptive Adequacy" (1967) [45], found fault with some of the underlying assumptions of generative phonology and suggested that some revisions in the theory are in order.

E. C. Fudge, in "The Nature of Phonological Primes" (1967) [46], pointed up some of the problems involved in the application of a generative distinctive feature approach (illustrated with examples from the phonology of Tswana) and suggested some alternatives to the usual distinctive feature description within a generative framework.

James D. McCawley also compared Jakobson's distinctive features to the features used by Halle and Chomsky, and re-examined the role that features should play in generative grammar, in his "The Role of a Phonological Feature System in a Theory of Language" (1967) [47].

Chomsky's "Some General Properties of Phonological Rules" (1967) [48] was a presentation of the principles underlying the form, organization, and interpretation of phonological rules in a generative grammar and a reply to some of the criticisms of the theory made by Sydney M. Lamb.

David A. Johns, in "Phonemics and Generative Phonology" (1969) [49], attempted to resurrect a phonemic level in generative phonology, arguing that the reasons given for eliminating such a level are unconvincing and that, in fact, it would add considerably to the understanding of how language works.

BIBLIOGRAPHY 14
Distinctive Oppositions and Distinctive Features

A. THEORETICAL DISCUSSION
JAKOBSON, R. (1921) *Novejšaja russkaja poèzija*

—— (1927) "The Concept of the Sound Law and the Teleological Criterion"

—— (1928) "Proposition au Premier Congrès International de Linguistes: Quelles sont les méthodes les mieux appropriées à un exposé complet et pratique de la grammaire d'une langue quelconque?"

—— (1929) *Remarques sur l'évolution phonologique du russe comparée à celle des autres langues slaves*

TRUBETZKOY, N. S. (1929) "Zur allgemeinen Theorie der phonologischen Vokalsysteme"

—— (1931) "Die phonologischen Systeme"

—— (1933) "La phonologie actuelle"

—— (1935) *Anleitung zu phonologischen Beschreibungen*

—— (1936) "Die Aufhebung der phonologischen Gegensätze"

—— (1936) "Essai d'une théorie des oppositions phonologiques"

POS, H. J. (1938) "La notion d'opposition en linguistique"

TRUBETZKOY, N. S. (1939) *Grundzüge der Phonologie;* French translation: (1949) *Principes de phonologie* translated by J. Cantineau

MARTINET, A. (1948) "Où en est la phonologie?"

VOEGELIN, C. F. (1948) "Distinctive Features and Meaning Equivalence"

MARTINET, A. (1949) *Phonology as Functional Phonetics*

JAKOBSON, R., C. G. M. FANT, and M. HALLE (1952) *Preliminaries to Speech Analysis: The Distinctive Features and Their Correlates*

Reviewed by: GARVIN, P. L. (1953)

MOL, H., and E. M. UHLENBECK (1954) "The Analysis of the Phoneme in Distinctive Features and the Process of Hearing"

PRIETO, L. J. (1954) "Traits oppositionnels et traits contrastifs"

CHERRY, E. C. (1956) "Roman Jakobson's 'Distinctive Features' as the Normal Co-ordinates of a Language"

JAKOBSON, R., and M. HALLE (1956) *Fundamentals of Language,* especially "Phonology and Phonetics," pp. 1–51.

REICHLING, A. (1956) "Feature Analysis and Linguistic Interpretation"

BAR-HILLEL, Y. (1957) "Three Methodological Remarks on *Fundamentals of Language*"

JAKOBSON, R. (1962) "The Phonemic Concept of Distinctive Features"

JAKOBSON, R., and M. HALLE (1962) "Tenseness and Laxness"

TRNKA, B., et al. (1964) "Prague Structural Linguistics"

VACHEK, J. (1966) *The Linguistic School of Prague*

CONTRERAS, H. (1969) "Simplicity, Descriptive Adequacy, and Binary Features"

B. APPLICATIONS OF THE THEORY
TRNKA, B. (1935) "A Phonological Analysis of Present-Day Standard English"

JAKOBSON, R., and J. LOTZ (1949) "Notes on the French Phonemic Pattern"

MARTIN, S. E. (1951) "Korean Phonemics"

MALÉCOT, A. (1960) "Vowel Nasality as a Distinctive Feature in American English"

BROZOVIĆ, D. (1967) "Some Remarks on Distinctive Features Especially in Standard Serbocroatian"

COURT, C. (1967) "A Distinctive Feature Analysis of the Phonemes of Měntu Land Dayak"

C. BIBLIOGRAPHIES AND BIBLIOGRAPHICAL STUDIES
SEBEOK, T. A. (1963) "Selected Readings in General Phonemics (1925–1964)"

VACHEK, J. (1964) "Prague Phonological Studies Today"

IVIĆ, P. (1965) "Roman Jakobson and the Growth of Phonology"

PIKE, K. L. (1967) *Language in Relation to a Unified Theory of the Structure of Human Behavior* (esp. pp. 344–363)

D. COLLECTIONS AND ANTHOLOGIES

TCLP Vols. 1–8 (1929–1939)

HALLE, M., H. G. LUNT, H. MACLEAN, and C. H. VAN SCHOONEVELD (eds.) (1956) *For Roman Jakobson*

JAKOBSON, R. (1962) *Selected Writings I: Phonological Studies*

VACHEK, J. (ed.) (1964) *A Prague School Reader in Linguistics*

To Honor Roman Jakobson (1967)

BIBLIOGRAPHY 15
Transformational-Generative Phonology

A. THEORETICAL DISCUSSION

CHOMSKY, N. (1957) *Syntactic Structures*

Reviewed by: LEES, R. B. (1957)

CONTRERAS, H., and S. SAPORTA (1960) "The Validation of a Phonological Grammar"

STOCKWELL, R. P. (1960) "The Place of Intonation in a Generative Grammar of English"

LIGHTNER, T. M. (1963) "A Note on the Formulation of Phonological Rules"

UHLENBECK, E. M. (1963) "An Appraisal of Transformation Theory"

CHOMSKY, N. (1964) *Current Issues in Linguistic Theory*

KATZ, J. J., and P. M. POSTAL (1964) *An Integrated Theory of Linguistic Descriptions*

CHOMSKY, N. (1965) *Aspects of the Theory of Syntax*

LAMB, S. M. (1967) Review of Chomsky's *Current Issues in Linguistic Theory* and *Aspects of the Theory of Syntax*

WINTER, W. (1965) "Transforms without Kernels?"

CARMONY, M. D. (1966) "Surface and Deep Phonology"

CHOMSKY, N. (1966) *Topics in the Theory of Generative Grammar*

MCCAWLEY, J. D. (1967) "Sapir's Phonologic Representation"

STANLEY, R. (1967) "Redundancy Rules in Phonology"

CHAFE, W. L. (1968) "The Ordering of Phonological Rules"

POSTAL, P. M. (1968) *Aspects of Phonological Theory*

CAIRNS, C. E. (1969) "Markedness, Neutralization, and Universal Redundancy Rules"

MAKKAI, A. (1969) "On the Validity and Limitations of Generative Morphophonemics"

SAMPSON, G. (1970) "On the Need for a Phonological Base"

B. APPLICATIONS OF THE THEORY

HALLE, M. (1959) *The Sound Pattern of Russian*

LEES, R. B. (1961) *The Phonology of Modern Standard Turkish*

SAPORTA, S., and H. CONTRERAS (1962) *A Phonological Grammar of Spanish*

Reviewed by: GARCIA, E. C. (1963)

CHOMSKY, N., and M. HALLE (1968) *The Sound Pattern of English*

JACOBS, R. A., and P. S. ROSENBAUM (1968) *English Transformational Grammar*

MCCAWLEY, J. D. (1968) *The Phonological Component of a Grammar of Japanese*

Reviewed by: OKUDA, K. (1970)

SCHANE, S. A. (1968) *French Phonology and Morphology*

Reviewed by: SMITH, N. V. (1969)

STOCKWELL, R. P., P. SCHACHTER, and B. PARTEE (1969) *Integration of Transformational Theories on English Syntax*

C. BIBLIOGRAPHIES AND BIBLIOGRAPHICAL STUDIES

BOYD, J. C., and H. V. KING (1962) "Annotated Bibliography of Generative Grammar"

SEBEOK, T. A. (1963) "Selected Readings in General Phonemics (1925–1964)"

PIKE, K. L. (1967) *Language in Relation to a Unified Theory of the Structure of Human Behavior* (esp. pp. 344–363)

SCHANE, S. A. (1967) "Bibliographie de la phonologie générative"

D. COLLECTIONS AND ANTHOLOGIES

FODOR, J. A., and J. J. KATZ (eds.) (1964) *The Structure of Language: Readings in the Philosophy of Language*

REIBEL, D. A., and S. A. SCHANE (eds.) (1969) *Modern Studies in English*

JACOBS, R. A., and P. S. ROSENBAUM (eds.) (1970) *Readings in English Transformational Grammar*

III.a

The Development
of Distinctive
Feature Analysis

27

REVIEW OF
*GRUNDZÜGE DER PHONOLOGIE**

BY N. S. TRUBETZKOY.
(*Travaux du Cercle Linguistique de Prague,* No. 7.
Pp. 271. Prague, 1939.)

ZELLIG S. HARRIS

In this unfinished study, his last work, Trubetzkoy presents a final version of his phonological theories and applies them to the phonemic systems of a large number of languages. The book discusses the relation of phonology to other studies (5–30), the nature of phonemes (30–41), how to determine the phonemes of a language (41–59), relations between phonemes in general analysis (59–80) and in particular languages (80–206), neutralization (206–218), phonemic combinations (clusters, 218–230), phonological statistics (230–241), and boundary-markers (junctures, 241–261).

This volume shows, even more than did his shorter works, the breadth of Trubetzkoy's knowledge and the intricacy and incisiveness and cerebral character of his scientific analysis. However, precisely because this is the last statement of his theoretical work, it is desirable to criticize here some features of the Prague Circle's terminology. The point at issue is the Prague Circle's occasionally mystical use of philosophical terms. Now, it is not necessary for us to agree on our idea of the nature of a phoneme: whether we are to understand it as a class of sounds (each sound being itself a slice out of a continuum of sound), or regard it as some new entity containing a "characteristic" sound plus an on-glide and an off-glide. For linguistic work it suffices to know how to recognize the phonemes of a language. But Trubetzkoy offers a specific picture of the phoneme as a "functional" sound: "The phonologist considers in the sound only that

which fills a specific function in the language system" (14). And having established such units of function, he speaks of language structure, in contrast to speech, as "something general and constant" (5). Such talk may be considered a matter of taste. It makes no difference what picture each linguistic worker has of a phoneme, so long as each performs the same operations upon it.

The Prague Circle terminology, however, has two dangers: First, it gives the impression that there are two objects of possible investigation, the Sprechakt (speech) and the Sprachgebilde (language structure), whereas the latter is merely the scientific arrangement of the former. Second, talking about function, system, and the like, without defining them in terms of operations and relations, fools even the linguistic worker. For by satisfying him with undefined psychological terms it prevents him from continuing his analysis. Thus Trubetzkoy says that each word is, in the language structure, a Gestalt, and that it therefore "always contains something more than the sum of its parts (i.e., of the phonemes), namely a unity (Ganzheitsgrundsatz) which holds the sequence of phonemes together and gives the word its individuality" (35). Had he not been satisfied with such words, he would have been forced to seek for the physical events which enable us to consider the word as a unity and not merely a sequence of phonemes. And he would undoubtedly have realized that this physical event is usually the "zero juncture" (see below) defined as the juncture between

*Reprinted from *Language* 17.345–349 (1941) by permission.

phonemes of one morpheme (or the like) in contrast to other junctures. Had he recognized this he could not have written his next sentence: "In contrast to the individual phonemes, this word-unity cannot be localized in the body of the word."

In his introductory material Trubetzkoy gives a general approach to phonology. On pp. 17–18 he follows Bühler's division of the act of speech into three "aspects": features of sound characteristic of the speaker, features constituting the appeal to the hearer, features referring to the content of discourse. He indicates that phonology can build only upon the third of these divisions. On p. 29 he distinguishes three phonological functions: "distinctive or meaning-distinguishing" (phonemes proper), "culminative or crest-making" (stress, etc.), "boundary-marking" (junctures).

The definition of the phoneme given here is typical for the Prague Circle. The instructions on how to recognize the phonemes of a language closely follow, with some improvements, Trubetzkoy's important pamphlet *Anleitung zu phonologischen Beschreibungen* (1935).

This review will discuss the three chief contributions of the present volume: 1. Trubetzkoy's method of phonemic patterning; 2. neutralization; 3. junctures.

1. The main point at issue is Trubetzkoy's method of phonemic patterning. Looking at his whole theoretical work, we can find in it three steps: first, the recognition that phonemes are not absolute but relative, that what is relevant in phonemics is only the contrast between one group of sounds and another; second, the selection of a particular contrast-criterion in terms of which to compare the phonemes; third, studying the relations between the contrasts and working out a pattern which describes these relations.

The first step is basic to phonemics, and Trubetzkoy and the Prague Circle performed a great service in clarifying and stressing it. Trubetzkoy was always keenly aware that phonology, like any science, dealt only with what was relevant to it. And he stressed, perhaps more than anyone else, that no feature or group of sounds was relevant in itself, but only if it contrasted with another to distinguish morphemes. For example, lengthening of vowels is phonologically irrelevant in English,

where it is positionally conditioned, but phonologically relevant in several European languages, where its presence or absence yields different morphemes.

The second step will be discussed later.

The third step, charting the relations between the contrasts, is complexly and competently handled, although few of us would accept Trubetzkoy's particular system of charting. Trubetzkoy studies the relations between phonemic contrasts in terms of a rather old-fashioned logic of limited scope. Modern logic and especially modern mathematical methods have developed much more powerful procedures of analysis, although the question whether and in what way they can be applied to linguistic relations cannot be discussed here.

Since many linguistic workers in America may want to have some idea of Trubetzkoy's method, a few of its lines will be indicated here. Phonemes are points in a network of contrasts. Two phonemes which have no features in common (in respect to the criterion chosen; see the second step below) cannot be contrasted. Two phonemes which have in common some feature which no other phoneme has are in *unidimensional* contrast. Two phonemes whose common feature is also common to some other phoneme are in *pluridimensional* contrast. The unidimensional contrasts are fewer but more interesting than the other. Pluridimensional contrasts are *homogeneous* if they obtain between phonemes which are endpoints of a chain of unidimensional contrasts; otherwise they are *heterogeneous*. Homogeneous pluridimensional contrasts are *linear* if only one chain can be constructed; otherwise they are *non-linear*. Pairs of phonemes having similar contrasts between them may be equated in a *proportional* formula. Various proportional chains may criss-cross, thus presenting a network pattern. Two phonemes in particularly close and limited contrast form a *relation-pair*. The difference between them is a *relation-marker*. The two phonemes are considered identical except that one has the marker of their private relation while the other does not; they would be represented not as A : B but as A : (A + a). A closed network of relations among a group of phonemes constitutes a *relation-bundle*.

This is but the skeleton of Trubetzkoy's system, and it seems confusing indeed. It is vaguer and more difficult to keep in mind than would appear necessary. But complexity alone does not suffice to condemn it; any logical or mathematical analysis would seem complicated as long as it is strange. The test of its value should primarily be: What results does it give? In answer we must note that its only results are a patterning of the phonemes (which cannot be checked against anything else) and a correlation with the incidence of neutralization (70–76). Other procedures of studying the relations among phonemic contrasts may produce more important results.

It is in the second step, selection of the contrast-criterion, that Trubetzkoy's work falls wide of the mark. For in order to study the relations between phonemic contrasts one must first have selected what kind of contrast to investigate. Those which Trubetzkoy studies are the phonetic contrasts. He does not say that he is intentionally selecting these rather than any other. He merely uses them as though they were the natural and necessary ones to consider. He sets up certain phonetic criteria: localization and degree of the obstacles to passage of air; "co-articulation" features such as palatalization; resonance chamber; etc. It is in these terms that he lists phonemic contrasts. E.g., English [t] and [d] contrast unidimensionally in respect to voicing, the other phonologically relevant phonetic features being common to both of them.

But there are other criteria in terms of which one may study the contrasts between phonemes. Chief among these is the positional distribution ("privileges of occurrence" in Bloomfield's *Language*). It is possible to contrast the positions in which each phoneme of a language may and may not occur, to see which phonemes differ much or little in this respect. Trubetzkoy was quite aware of this. On p. 206 he discusses the importance of considering these distributional contrasts, and in the following section he modifies the patterning of the phonetic contrasts by some results from distributional contrasts.

However, it is pointless to mix phonetic and distributional contrasts. If phonemes which are phonetically similar are also similar in their distribution, that is a result which must be independently proved. For the crux of the matter is that phonetic and distributional contrasts are methodologically different, and that

only distributional contrasts are relevant while phonetic contrasts are irrelevant.

This becomes clear as soon as we consider what is the scientific operation of working out the phonemic pattern. For phonemes are in the first instance determined on the basis of distribution. Two positional variants may be considered one phoneme if they are in complementary distribution; never otherwise. In identical environment (distribution) two sounds are assigned to two phonemes if their difference distinguishes one morpheme from another; in complementary distribution this test cannot be applied. We see therefore that although the range of phonetic similarity of various occurrences of a phoneme is important, it is the criterion of distribution that determines whether a given sound is to be classified in one phoneme or another. And when, having fixed the phonemes, we come to compare them, we can do so only on the basis of the distributional criterion in terms of which they had been defined. As in any classificatory scheme, the distributional analysis is simply the unfolding of the criterion used for the original classification. If it yields a patterned arrangement of the phonemes, that is an interesting result for linguistic structure.

On the other hand, the types and degrees of phonetic contrast (e.g., whether all the consonants come in voiced and unvoiced pairs) have nothing to do with the classification of the phonemes; hence they do not constitute a necessary patterning. This is not to say that phonetic comparisons of the phonemes may not be interesting. It may indeed be desirable to work out patterns of the phonetic relations between phonemes and see how they compare with the distributional pattern. But that would be a new correlation, interesting for diachronic linguistics and for linguistic psychology, e.g., for the question: How do the physical (phonetic) differences within the ranges of phonemes (events to which people conventionally react uniformly) compare with the differences between different phonemes (events to which they react differently)? In synchronic linguistics, it is only the distributional pattern that would show what work each phoneme can do, what operations can be performed upon each, i.e., what its place is in the structure.

Valuable and suggestive as Trubetzkoy's work has always been, the selection of phonetic criteria vitiates the structural value of his phonemic patterns.

2. The two most important contributions of Trubetzkoy's last volume are his detailed (though not complete) discussions of neutralization and junctures. Both of these are fairly new terms in linguistics, representing procedures of analysis which have only recently become explicit.

Two phonemes may be contrasted in some positions but not in others, if in these other positions only one of them can occur. For example, English [b] and [p] are not contrasted after [s], because only one of them can occur after [s]. Neutralization (Aufhebung) is the term for such lack of contrast in specific positions. It is a relation analogous to positional variants and is central in the description of phonemic distribution. This is the only distributional problem analyzed by Trubetzkoy. Like other European linguists, he discusses whether the phoneme in neutralized position should be regarded as representing one of the neutralized phonemes or both together, and so on. For example, is the second phoneme in English *spin* [p] or [b], or [P] representing both? Trubetzkoy also notes (217–218) that for each language there are certain phonemic environments with maximum phonemic contrasts and others with maximum neutralization.

The value of Trubetzkoy's discussion is limited by the fact that he groups together all neutralizations, both those which would be eliminated in morphophonemic formulae (in cases where the neutralized and contrasted positions of a phoneme occur in two forms of the same morpheme) as well as those which constitute the purely phonemic positional limitations of the phoneme in question (where no morpheme could have it in both neutralized and contrasted positions).

3. In the final section Trubetzkoy discusses boundary-markers (Grenzsignale). He lists various negative markers, phonetic and phonemic forms that can occur only medially in a morpheme or word: e.g., certain clusters in some languages, and positional variants which foreshadow the following phoneme only if it is in the same morpheme or word. He also lists positive markers which, in various languages, betray the presence of a morpheme or word boundary: e.g., positional variants or clusters which occur only at morpheme or word initial or final, clusters which occur only across such boundaries, bound accent, and change of vowel-harmony.

Much of this is included in the analysis of what we call junctures, namely the type of contact between phonemes. In such analysis of a given language the contact between phonemes within a morpheme might be called zero juncture, while contacts across morpheme, word, and other boundaries, if they differ from zero, are given successive names. This method not only organizes all the boundary-markers which Trubetzkoy recognizes, but also reveals certain relations which Trubetzkoy's method would probably miss. For example, morphemes of a given class may combine with certain morphemes without any boundary indication (zero juncture), whereas they undergo morphophonemic alternations when combined with certain other morphemes (e.g., Nootka junctures of stems with suffixes; see Sapir and Swadesh, *Nootka Texts,* grammatical survey). In Trubetzkoy's system morphophonemic alternations which don't yield non-medial clusters may be overlooked; in a juncture analysis a special juncture must be recognized to account for the alternation.

These remarks suggest that a different approach may yield results beyond those of Trubetzkoy. However, this can in no way detract from the value of Trubetzkoy's vanguard work, since discussion of neutralization and junctures is so recent that no writer can give a complete presentation. Even where his method was unsatisfactory, Trubetzkoy's knowledge and interest and intuition in phonology were so great as to bring out most of the important points.

OBSERVATIONS SUR LE CLASSEMENT PHONOLOGIQUE DES CONSONNES*

ROMAN JAKOBSON

On ne pourrait mieux définir la thèse fondamentale de la phonologie qu'en citant la formule classique de Ferdinand de Saussure: "Les phonèmes sont avant tout des entités oppositives, relatives et négatives." Nous délimitons les phonèmes d'une langue donnée en découpant dans la chaîne parlée les plus petites tranches phoniques susceptibles de différencier les significations des mots. Nous identifions les phonèmes d'une langue donnée en les décomposant en leurs caractères phonologiques constitutifs, c'est-à-dire que nous établissons pour chaque phonème quelles *qualités* l'opposent aux autres phonèmes du système en question. Ainsi le vocalisme du turc-osmanli avec ses huit phonèmes ne comprend que trois différences spécifiques: à savoir l'opposition des voyelles ouvertes et fermées, celle des voyelles palatales et vélaires et enfin celle des arrondies et des non-arrondies.

Par opposition aux voyelles fermées, les voyelles ouvertes possèdent, du point de vue acoustique, une *perceptibilité* majeure et un son plein. Deux oppositions de timbre distinctes correspondent à la division des voyelles en vélaires et palatales d'une part, en arrondies et non-arrondies de l'autre. La différence des deux oppositions est manifeste pour l'acoustique tant objective que subjective. Pour désigner le contenu acoustique des voyelles palatales et vélaires, nous nous servirons des termes *"aiguës"* et *"graves,"* acceptés par M. Grammont. On pourrait dire en se basant sur l'analyse de Stumpf: 1° qu'une voyelle palatale complète la formante de la

vélaire correspondante par une formante supérieure et, 2° qu'une voyelle arrondie ne se distingue de la non-arrondie correspondante que par un rabaissement de sa formante supérieure ou unique. Les nouveaux spectrogrammes des voyelles compliquent un peu ces formules sans pourtant dissimuler leur netteté.

Si la note caractéristique d'une voyelle arrondie est moins haute que celle de la non-arrondie correspondante, c'est qu'on rétrécit l'orifice antérieur du résonateur buccal. En émettant une voyelle palatale, on divise le résonateur buccal et on élargit le pharynx, son orifice postérieur. La note caractéristique de la palatale est par conséquent plus haute que celle de la vélaire correspondante munie d'un résonateur indivis avec le pharynx rétréci.

Tout le vocalisme de l'osmanli et tout système vocalique en général obéit au principe de la *dichotomie* et se laisse réduire à un nombre restreint de qualités phonologiques formant des oppositions binaires. La logique distingue deux espèces d'oppositions. Le premier type, opposition des termes *contradictoires,* est une relation entre la présence et l'absence d'un même élément. Exemple: voyelles longues s'opposant aux voyelles sans longueur. Le second type, opposition des termes *contraires,* est une relation entre deux éléments "qui font partie d'un même genre, et qui diffèrent le plus entre eux; ou qui, présentant un caractère spécifique susceptible de degrés, en possèdent respectivement le maximum ou le minimum." Exemple: voyelles aiguës s'opposant aux graves. De même dans le do-

*This article was first published in the *Proceedings of the Third International Congress of Phonetic Sciences* (Ghent, 1939), pp. 34–41. Reprinted here from Roman Jakobson, *Selected Writings I* (Mouton, 1962), pp. 272–279, by permission.

maine du consonantisme comme l'a surtout mis en relief le prince Trubetzkoy, toutes les différences phonologiques du mode d'articulation, de l'intensité et du travail phonatoire secondaire se décomposent intégralement en des oppositions binaires des deux types signalés. Il ne reste que les *distinctions des consonnes d'après le lieu de leur articulation.* Seraient-elles en contradiction avec la dichotomie du système phonologique? Présenteraient-elles ainsi une exception unique?

Imaginons une série de consonnes qui ne se distinguent prétendument que par le lieu de leur articulation, par exemple les six occlusives sourdes du tchèque ou du hongrois. Nous avons été jusqu'ici portés à croire que la totalité des traits communs à deux de ces consonnes se rencontre aussi dans les autres consonnes de la même série. Mais cela revient à admettre que chaque point d'articulation dont on chercherait vainement à définir l'équivalent acoustique immédiat, constitue une qualité phonologique indécomposable. Il en résulterait d'autre part que les six phonèmes en question forment entre eux suivant la formule mathématique des combinaisons quinze oppositions disparates, partant quinze qualités différentielles, et que la disposition de ces phonèmes les uns par rapport aux autres dans le système reste indéterminée. Mais dans ce cas il n'y aurait à vrai dire ni système ni même oppositions, puisque le système exige un enchaînement ordonné des parties et que l'opposition présuppose des termes contradictoires ou contraires.

D'ordinaire on essaye au moins de ranger les consonnes en question d'après le voisinage de leurs zones d'articulation, de sorte que les vélaires d'un côté et les labiales de l'autre terminent la série. Mais comment expliquer, dans ce cas, des phénomènes si fréquents et répandus dans les langues du monde que les changements de vélaires en labiales et vice-versa et leurs substitutions acoustiques réciproques? On invoque le principe des extrêmes qui se touchent, mais à moins que ce ne soit de la mystique ou de l'arbitraire pur, la question se pose de savoir si ces deux extrêmes ne se trouvent pas unis dans le cadre d'un *genus proximum,* opposé au reste des consonnes.

Il se trouve effectivement que les vélaires et les labiales prennent leur qualité dans un

résonateur buccal long et indivis; par contre, pour les palatales et les dentales, la langue partage la cavité buccale en *deux courtes caisses de résonance.* De plus, les expériences, et en particulier les admirables radiographies des sons tchèques, que l'on doit à M. Hála, montrent que *le pharynx se rétrécit* pour les vélaires et les labiales, tandis qu'il *s'élargit* pour les palatales et les dentales correspondantes.

De même, c'est une différence spécifique qui oppose les vélaires et les palatales y compris toutes les chuintantes aux labiales et aux dentales. En unissant les premières sous le nom de *postérieures* et les secondes sous celui *d'antérieures* on peut énoncer la formule suivante: pour les postérieures le point d'articulation se trouve être en arrière et pour les antérieures en avant de la caisse de résonance unique ou dominante.

Ainsi les différences entre quatre types de consonnes (vélaires, palatales, dentales, labiales) se réduisent en fait aux deux oppositions de qualités phonologiques, que nous venons de définir au point de vue de la phonation et que nous allons examiner maintenant du point de vue acoustique.

Les consonnes postérieures s'opposent aux antérieures correspondantes par un plus haut degré de *perceptibilité,* souvent accompagné *ceteris paribus* d'un plus haut degré de durée. Ainsi dans des expériences de Rousselot sur les consonnes françaises, p et t sont par ordre de compréhensibilité au dessous de k; de même b et d au dessous de g et les constrictives f et s au dessous de la chuintante correspondante. La filtration acoustique (Abbau) des sons pratiquée par Stumpf a donné des résultats analogues.

C'est au résonateur long et indivis et à son orifice postérieur rétréci qu'est due la note caractéristique des consonnes vélaires et labiales, *note relativement basse,* correspondant à celle des voyelles vélaires et opposée à celle des consonnes palatales et dentales. Cette dernière est *relativement haute* et correspond à peu près à la note caractéristique des voyelles palatales. La différence de hauteur en question est démontrée non seulement par de nombreuses observations acoustiques, mais aussi par les expériences de Stumpf qui en filtrant un s obtient un f. L'exemple du sourd, cité par Rousselot, qui confond les voyelles et les consonnes graves avec les aiguës correspondantes est également très instructif.

Pour l'ouïe de la parole, comme le fait justement remarquer Köhler, il ne s'agit pas sans doute de hauteurs musicales absolues, mais uniquement d'une *opposition de deux timbres indécomposables* et dans notre cas en particulier, il s'agit d'une opposition de consonnes aiguës et graves. Les deux catégories opposées sont présentes avec netteté dans le sentiment linguistique. Ainsi par exemple les onomatopées hésitent souvent entre les consonnes postérieures et antérieures du même timbre et d'autre part dans la langue poétique la nuance affective diffère sensiblement selon que les vers mettent en relief les consonnes aiguës ou les graves.

Des faits longuement discutés comme le passage roumain de *k* en *p* devant *t* et *s* (*direct* → *drept,* etc.) trouvent facilement leur explication en connexion avec les deux oppositions considérées: par assimilation partielle, la consonne grave postérieure se change devant les aiguës antérieures en une consonne antérieure sans perdre sa gravité.

Les consonnes graves peuvent se changer en aiguës correspondantes devant les voyelles aiguës. Le passage des vélaires aux palatales dans cette position est bien connu et nous nous bornons à signaler le changement de *p, b* et *m* en *t, d* et *n* devant *i* dans le tchèque de l'Est. D'un autre côté, comme l'a constaté l'éminent phonéticien Thomson, les consonnes aiguës et les consonnes graves influent en deux sens opposés sur le timbre des voyelles contiguës, et les données abondantes de la phonologie historique sur le traitement divergent des voyelles accompagnées d'une consonne grave ou au contraire d'une consonne aiguë, confirment cette observation et y trouvent leur explication.

"On dit, qu'une consonne est mouillée," enseigne M. Grammont, "quand à son timbre habituel vient s'ajouter un timbre particulier qui rappelle ce qu'il y a de spécifique dans celui du *j.*" *Mutatis mutandis* on pourrait répéter la même formule par rapport aux consonnes arrondies, dont le timbre particulier rappelle ce qu'il y a de spécifique dans celui de la semi-voyelle labiale. L'orifice antérieur du résonateur buccal est rétréci et par conséquent une note basse caractérise le timbre en question; au contraire la note caractéristique

de la mouillure est haute, grâce au résonateur aplati. Un timbre particulier vient en effet "s'ajouter"—autrement dit les consonnes mouillées s'opposent aux consonnes sans mouillure et les arrondies aux consonnes sans arrondissement; ce sont donc des oppositions de termes contradictoires, tandis que l'opposition des consonnes *aiguës* et *graves* est une opposition de termes contraires ainsi que celle des *postérieures* et des *antérieures* ou du point de vue acoustique, l'opposition des perceptibilités majeure et mineure. Ces deux oppositions de même que celle des consonnes *nasales*[1] et *orales,* dues toutes les trois à la place et à la structure différentes des *résonateurs,* constituent le noyau du système phonologique des consonnes et trouvent un équivalent acoustique exact dans le vocalisme.

Rappelons que c'est à ces trois oppositions consonantiques que se borne, si on laisse de côté les liquides, sur lesquelles on reviendra ci-dessous, un type archaïque des langues primitives et de même, selon la comparaison heureuse de M. Sommerfelt, le language enfantin (tel qu'il se présente vers la fin de la première année, ainsi que le précise M. Grégoire). A l'exception de quelques idiomes indiens, les consonnes à perceptibilité mineure se divisent toujours en graves et en aiguës, c'est-à-dire en labiales et dentales. Quant aux consonnes à perceptibilité majeure, c'est-à-dire les vélo-palatales, leur scission en graves et aiguës ou en d'autres termes, en vélaires et en palatales correspondantes reste inconnue à un nombre considérable, sinon à la majorité des langues du monde. Les langues de l'Océanie possèdent les deux variétés de consonantisme oral dans leur forme pure, d'un côté le triangle $\begin{smallmatrix} k \\ p \quad t \end{smallmatrix}$ "système consonantique le plus simple" suivant l'observation précise du P. van Ginneken, et de l'autre le *carré* $\begin{smallmatrix} k \quad c \\ p \quad t \end{smallmatrix}$ représenté par l'aranta que vient d'analyser M. Sommerfelt.[2] Les deux structures offrent, par leur composition et par leur rapport mutuel, une analogie des plus frappantes avec les deux types du *système vocalique*—le carré et le triangulaire.

---

[1] Les nasales par opposition aux orales sont dues à un tuyau bifurqué.

[2] *c* = consonne palatale occlusive, suivant la transcription de l'Association phonétique.

L'abîme que creusaient les manuels d'autrefois entre la structure des consonnes et celle des voyelles est contesté à juste raison par l'acoustique moderne et apparaît surmonté dans l'étude phonologique.

La distinction entre les consonnes dentales, palatales, labiales et vélaires est fondée sur les caractères différents de leur résonateur buccal. Mais les classes mentionnées peuvent se diviser chacune en deux séries de consonnes correspondantes. Ainsi on distingue les linguo-dentales et les sifflantes, les palatales proprement dites et les chuintantes, les bilabiales et les labiodentales, les vélaires proprement dites et les uvulaires. On range d'ordinaire toutes ces consonnes d'après la région de leur articulation, bien que les descriptions phonétiques aient permis d'observer à maintes reprises que, de ce point de vue, la délimitation des séries en question est à peine possible. Quelle est donc la différence spécifique qui détermine ces subdivisions?

Un *frottement énergique* de l'air expiré provoquant un ton tranchant (le "Schneidenton" de Stumpf) oppose les sifflantes, les chuintantes, les labio-dentales et les uvulaires, en un mot les consonnes *stridentes* à leurs "partenaires" mentionnés, qu'on peut qualifier de consonnes *mates*. Une paroi supplémentaire participant à ce frottement distingue l'articulation des constrictives stridentes de celle des mates: ainsi au fonctionnement des lèvres qui seul intéresse l'émission des bilabiales celle des labio-dentales vient ajouter l'action des dents; outre le fonctionnement de la langue et des dents supérieures, propre aux linguo-dentales, la phonation des sifflantes comporte de plus une action des dents inférieures, et c'est elle également qui intervient dans la production des chuintantes; le fonctionnement du palais mou et du dos de la langue qu'exigent les vélaires proprement dites est complété par celui de la luette dans la prononciation des uvulaires. Le même frottement intense distingue les occlusives stridentes des occlusives mates. Les premières sont d'ordinaire des affriquées, c'est-à-dire des occlusivo-fricatives, alors que les secondes sont des occlusives proprement dites, ou à plus exactement parler des occlusivo-explosives.

L'opposition des dentales stridentes et mates existe par exemple dans la langue anglaise qui distingue les constrictives sifflantes et linguo-dentales. L'opposition des labiales stridentes et mates existe par exemple dans la langue ewe qui distingue les constrictives labiodentales et bilabiales. En allemand cette opposition a lieu pour les dentales et pour les labiales grâce aux couples *t-"ts"* (*Tauber-Zauber*) et *p-"pf"* (*Posten-Pfosten*). En français l'opposition des stridentes et des mates coïncide avec celle des constrictives et des occlusives: toutes les constrictives sont stridentes et toutes les occlusives sont mates. A l'exclusion des liquides, le système triangulaire des consonnes françaises avec ses quinze phonèmes se réduit à cinq oppositions de qualités phonologiques contraires: l'opposition des consonnes postérieures et antérieures, l'opposition des consonnes nasales et orales, l'opposition des antérieures graves et aiguës, l'opposition des orales occlusives et constrictives et celle des orales sonores et sourdes.

Il nous reste à examiner deux espèces rares de consonnes que, d'habitude, on range également d'après le lieu de leur articulation. Toutes les consonnes que nous venons d'examiner sont articulées *soit en arrière soit en avant* de leur résonateur buccal unique ou dominant. Cependant certaines langues leur opposent des consonnes dont le point d'articulation se trouve *à la fois en arrière et en avant du résonateur cardinal.* Pour les consonnes au résonateur long et indivis, cela signifie deux points d'articulation—l'un derrière et l'autre devant le résonateur. C'est le cas des labio-vélaires opposées dans certaines langues africaines aux consonnes vélaires et labiales. D'autre part aux consonnes palatales et dentales divisant la cavité buccale en deux résonateurs dont l'un prédomine, viennent s'opposer les rétroflexes correspondantes, divisant le canal buccal en deux résonateurs, tous deux également cardinaux.

Quelle est la place qu'occupent dans le système phonologique total toutes les oppositions consonantiques passées en revue?

Les phonèmes d'une langue donnée se divisent en *voyelles* et en *consonnes*. D'après leur fonction primaire ou constante les premières sont sonantes et les secondes consonantes.

Les *voyelles déterminées* s'opposent à la voyelle indéterminée ou *neutre*. Ce "*chva*," selon la formule judicieuse de M. Brøndal, est défini "par la non-application des éléments définisseurs, c'est-à-dire par l'absence de toute détermination à part celle qui constitue la nature même des voyelles." Nous retrouvons une opposition toute pareille dans maints systèmes consonantiques, où un phonème laryngal fonctionne comme *consonne neutre.* La position des organes pour ces deux phonèmes neutres est à peu près celle du repos.

Les *liquides* s'opposent au reste des consonnes déterminées. L'opposition de r et de l peut se neutraliser dans certaines conditions comme c'est le cas en grec moderne; il y a des langues, par exemple le coréen, où ce ne sont que deux variantes d'un même phonème: il est beaucoup plus facile à reconnaître l'affinité évidente des consonnes liquides que de dégager les caractères objectifs de cette affinité. Il semble que c'est le fait du *glissement* qui est décisif pour l'impression acoustique des consonnes en question: pour les latérales, le souffle qui rencontre un barrage sur la ligne médiane du canal buccal s'écarte et "s'échappe sur les côtés de la langue où il glisse," selon l'expression de M. Grammont, "comme un liquide qui s'écoule." Pour les r intermittents c'est l'obstacle élastique qui glisse écarté par le souffle et rappelle ainsi la formation du ton dans les tuyaux à anche. On pourrait aussi dire en suivant M. Menzerath que les liquides s'opposent aux autres consonnes par l'ouverture et fermeture simultanées du canal buccal: pour les latérales les deux actions dites simultanées se réalisent effectivement en même temps mais à deux lieux divers, tandis que pour les intermittentes ces deux actions se réalisent au contraire tour à tour au même lieu. C'est à l'acoustique physique de confronter la phonation des l et des r. Peu s'en faut que la présence des liquides dans le système phonologique soit universelle, tandis que le dédoublement de cette classe en r et l manque à une quantité de langues. Ainsi une zone étendue des langues bordant le Pacifique ne connaît qu'un phonème liquide unique. La subdivision phonologique du type latéral ou du type intermittent est un fait relativement rare. Le cas échéant, l'opposition des liquides graves et aiguës se trouve fusionner avec celle des liquides antérieures et postérieures. Les intermittentes, de même que les latérales, peuvent se dédoubler en des phonèmes mats et stridents. Comme spécimens de ces dernières citons d'une part les fricatives et les affriquées latérales des langues caucasiques-septentrionales et de l'autre la fricative intermittente dite "r chuintant" (ř) du tchèque et des parlers grecs ou bien celle de l'arménien et le "r mi-occlusif malgache," étudié par Rousselot.

La théorie phonologique, fidèle aux suggestions de F. de Saussure, a toujours insisté sur le fait que ce n'est pas le phonème, mais *l'opposition,* et par conséquent la *qualité différentielle,* qui est l'élément primaire du système; il apparaît de plus en plus nettement que non seulement la diversité des phonèmes est beaucoup plus limitée que celle des sons de la parole, mais également le nombre des qualités différentielles est beaucoup plus restreint que celui des phonèmes. C'est la réponse que donne la phonologie à la question embarrassante de l'acoustique: comment se fait-il que l'oreille humaine distingue sans difficulté toutes les consonnes si nombreuses et si imperceptiblement variées de la langue.

Communication présentée d'abord au Cercle Linguistique de Prague (v. le résumé dans *Slovo a slovesnost,* IV [1938], p. 192), puis au Troisième Congrès International des Sciences Phonétiques, Gand 1938, et publiée dans les *Proceedings of the Third International Congress of Phonetic Sciences* (Ghent, 1939).

29

REVIEW OF
PHONOLOGY AS
*FUNCTIONAL PHONETICS**
Three Lectures Delivered
before the University of London
in 1946

BY ANDRÉ MARTINET.
(Publications of the
Philological Society; published with the aid
of a subvention from the University of
London Publication Fund.) Pp. [iii], 40. London:
Oxford University Press, 1949
[reprinted 1950].

CHARLES F. HOCKETT

The first two of these lectures are in English; they are printed as a single article, bearing the same title as the whole booklet. Pages 1–21 deal with synchronic aspects of the matter, 21–27 with diachronic. The third lecture is in French, entitled "Les traits généraux de la phonologie du français." The lectures were prepared and delivered not long after the author had ended a period of internment in a German prison camp for French officers. He had been out of touch with developments in linguistics for several years, particularly with developments in England and the United States. One apparent purpose of the lectures was to reestablish contact by "feeling out" contemporary British colleagues: he presented them with a systematic discussion of the phonological point of view, and an example of that point of view in action, in order to observe their reactions. Martinet is apologetic about the possibility that the ideas he is presenting may already have achieved general acceptance in England. I must be similarly apologetic about any unfavorable remarks in the body of this review: they apply to Martinet-1946, perhaps not at all to Martinet-1951.

By and large my impression is extremely favorable. Martinet presents an outline of fairly orthodox Trubetzkoyan phonology, but by no means implies slavish adherence thereto on his own part. The presentation is as clear and convincing as any I have ever read. Martinet's main emphasis is to show the contrast between "pure" phonetics, carried on without regard to the functional relevance of sounds, or even (it is implied) the fairly unsystematic phonemics of Daniel Jones, and the functional interpretation of phonetic data implicit in the

*Reprinted from *Language* 27.333–342 (1951) by permission.

Prague approach. There is, he says, another way of conceiving Prague phonology: the way of Louis Hjelmslev, who concentrates on the system as system, expunging all possible reference to the fact that a phonological system is normally "realized" in "phonic substance"; this approach Martinet nods to in a friendly manner, but avoids in these lectures. In arguing his main point, Martinet is quiet and unbelligerent, but devastatingly successful. Neither "pure" phonetics nor Jonesian phonemics stands the ghost of a chance with anyone who is prepared to be convinced by evidence. The booklet should be widely read; it ought to be read in this country, with a more open mind than we sometimes grant our European colleagues.

The bulk of this review will be devoted to the first part of the first article. The essential contribution of the second part (21–27) is the suggestion that the freedom of phonemic changes[1] in a language over a given period of time may well be conditioned by the communicative importance of the distinctions between the sounds involved—a stimulating thesis worthy of extended investigation. The second article is a brief survey of the most important of the results of Martinet's internment-camp work, reported in greater detail elsewhere.[2] The brevity of these comments should not be interpreted as meaning that those parts of the book are unimportant; I simply want to pass on to the main task.

A relevant point of departure for our present discussion is the differences between Martinet's way of looking at things and the ways most current in this country. We must begin with a quotation which shows Martinet's admirable flexibility of approach and lack of dogmatism (21): "But should we happen to meet a structure where [no features of a certain kind] are to be found and where it would seem more adequate to put on the same plane successive and concomitant relevant features, we should not hesitate, for the time being, to abandon the concept of phoneme and replace it by any other operative concept which would appear more suitable in that particular case." Obviously such an orientation is scientific in the best sense of the word; it implies that any hypothesis, however effectively it has worked and whatever "authority" it may have behind it, is always subject to modification or rejection in the light of new evidence. There are members of our profession on both sides of the Atlantic who seem sometimes not to remember this.

Only in one place does Martinet refer to "American" practices with any overt disapproval. Since the practices in question are those of the early forties or even earlier, many of us might be expected to disapprove too, perhaps in quite similar ways. However, the points which Martinet criticizes seem to turn principally on terminological differences.

He says (10): "A serious disadvantage of the term 'phonemics' extensively used in America to designate the new branch of phonetics [i.e., 'phonology'] is first of all that, by emphasizing so much the importance of the phoneme, it suggests that phonologists or rather phonemicists content themselves with a schematic delineation of phonic structures, leaving to others, probably the phoneticians properly so called, the task of describing those structures." I am not sure that this criticism is relevant. It is true that many very brief phonemic descriptions have been published in this country—often, however, at the beginning of an article devoted primarily to some other matter, so that brevity was desirable. But there are also some fairly extensive treatments, with a great deal of phonetic detail. Yet it may be that Bloomfield's influence has been too strong in some cases; Bloomfield, as is well known, considered the indication of subphonemic phonetic detail hardly worth while because it is so subject to the accidents of the analyst's experience and training, whereas phonemic contrasts can be determined by objective procedures free from such influence. We now know that Bloomfield was both right and wrong: right in that accidents of training can indeed lead to irrelevancies of detailed phonetic description, but wrong in his identification of the unit below which the influence of such acci-

[1]"Phonemic" or "phonological" change is the alteration of the phonological system of a language between a given time and a given later time. "Phonetic" change is one mechanism of that alteration. This distinction ought to be maintained with care; I failed to do so in *Language* 24.117–131 (1948). The broader term is used above because Martinet's suggestion is made for the whole, not just for the one mechanism.

[2]Martinet, *La prononciation du français contemporain* (Paris, 1945).

dents is unavoidable. The relevant unit in this connection is not the Bloomfieldian building-block type of phoneme, but the distinctive feature.

Martinet continues: "But another serious drawback lies in the fact that 'phonemics' necessitates the use of another term 'tonemics' for the study of all those relevant features, which since Trubetzkoy have been called prosodical. First of all, the word 'tonemics' is hardly comprehensive enough, as it seems to imply a study restricted to only the pitch elements of languages, leaving out of consideration stress phenomena. More generally, when we give a name to the second chapter of phonology, we should avoid a term suggesting that the study is restricted to a definite phonic substance." Martinet's positive remarks are quite right, and "tonemics" is hardly of any value save as a loose preliminary term for certain half-phonetic, half-phonological problems. Apart from this, there is a misunderstanding of terminology. Martinet misinterprets the American meaning of the term "phoneme" because of European usage. (The reverse error is by no means unrecorded.) We can equate Trubetzkoyan and American terms of the early forties about as follows:

TRUBETZKOYAN	AMERICAN
phonology	phonemics (sometimes phonology)
phoneme	segmental or linear phoneme
phonemics (phonematics)	segmental or linear phonemics
prosodics	suprasegmental or supralinear phonemics
prosodic feature (or accent)	accentual phoneme (or accent)

If we go no further into detail, the two terminologies are isomorphic down to the level of the shape of the term in a given position—that is, they are really a single terminology.

In the early forties perhaps the greatest objection that most American linguists would have had to Martinet's systematization would be to the notions of "opposition," "neutralization," and "archiphoneme." This deserves some discussion, for supporters of both sides of this argument need to pay more heed to what is said on the other side.

Unlike Bloomfieldian phonemics, Trubetzkoyan phonology does not stop when phonemes—the smallest *successive* units, essentially the "primary" phonemes of Bloomfield's *Language*—have been determined. Analysis continues in terms of the articulatory (or otherwise identified) features, simultaneous bundles of which constitute phonemes or allophones of phonemes. Such componential analysis has gained currency in this country too by now, and some of it was done here before 1946.[3] Trubetzkoyan workers then take another step. In French and in Russian, for example, there occur pairs of phonemes, such that the members of each pair share all distinctive features save one, and differ only in that one: thus, *p : b, t : d*, and so on, the distinguishing feature here being the voicing of the second member of the pair. Each such pair constitutes an *archiphoneme*. In French, there are no positions (or no important ones) in which *p* is found but *b* is not, or conversely; and similarly for the members of each other voiceless-voiced archiphoneme. In Russian, on the other hand, though both voiced and voiceless members occur initially and medially, only a single type is found finally. The difference between voiced and voiceless makes a difference initially and medially, given the proper assortment of other features in a bundle; finally however, that difference is not functional. Thus *byl'* 'a fact' and *pyl'* 'dust' are different words; *zabivát'* 'to thrust' and *zapivát'* 'to start drinking' are different words; but corresponding to [pόp] 'priest' there is no *[pόb], nor is any other such pair to be found.[4] The Trubetzkoyan way of stating this situation is to say that in final position the opposition—which is simply a synonym of the American term "contrast"—between voiced and voiceless is "neutralized," and that the [p] that one hears finally, despite its objective similarity to initial and medial [p], is not to be interpreted as phonemically the same, but rather as an occurrence of the *p/b* archiphoneme. The term "realize" comes in

[3]Hockett, "A System of Descriptive Phonology" [11], *Language* 18.3–21 (1942).

[4]The forms are those given by Martinet (4). I assume that the italicized forms are transliterations rather than transcriptions, because of the use of *y* and of the lack of a mark of palatalization after the medial *p* and *b* of the second pair.

here too: in Russian, the *p* and *b* phonemes are "realized" in certain positions, whereas in another only the *p/b* archiphoneme is "realized"; in French, there is no position in which the *p/b* archiphoneme is "realized" as such, even though it exists there just as much as in Russian.[5]

The traditional American way of stating the same situation is at least superficially different: in Russian, the phonemes *p* and *b* both occur initially and medially, but finally only the phoneme *p* occurs; that is, voiceless phonemes, of those that are paired with voiced phonemes, occur in final position to the exclusion of the latter.

The usual American objections to the Trubetzkoyan way of stating the situation seem rather trivial. It is sometimes said that speaking of "neutralization" shirks the necessary task of discovering the bases for phonemic identification, on the one hand, and on the other multiplies entities beyond necessity, since in addition to phonemes, one has to introduce a supplementary set of things called archiphonemes.

The first objection is certainly quite pointless. A great deal of careful study has to precede any clear final statement as to what is subject to neutralization in a given language, and the positions where it is found. If sloppy jobs have been done within this framework, that is no objection to the framework, any more than are some of the slipshod American "phonemic" analyses to their framework.

The second part of the objection is equally pointless, for it equates "simplicity" with "minimum number of different units," which is only one possible way of getting "simplicity"; or else the objection reflects a search for a neater "phonemic" notation, which can be achieved just as well within the Trubetzkoyan system simply by establishing certain conventions of representation. Thus it would be perfectly valid to establish the convention of writing Russian obstruent archiphonemes with the same letters used for Russian voiceless obstruent phonemes—e.g., *póp* 'priest', where the two *p*'s represent different units quite unambiguously; this would be inefficient only

in a context in which the phonological facts themselves were under discussion.[6]

There is a different objection, which I think deserves more attention. It may be suspected that "neutralization" is too simple a notion to handle all the relevant types of distributional phenomena which deserve mention in a phonological description. Martinet himself gives an example. The non-occurrence of initial *tl* in English, he says, is no ground for saying that initially before *l* the contrast *p : t* or the contrast *k : t* is neutralized. The reason for this is that *p* and *t* do not both consist in part of a bundle of relevant features which does not recur elsewhere, and, for the rest, of some single feature present in one and absent in the other; nor do *k* and *t*. The three, *p, t,* and *k,* are alike stops, voiceless, and nonnasal; *t* and *p* differ from each other in much the same way as do *t* and *k,* namely by position of articulation.

This means that the notion of neutralization can handle only some of the distributional limitations in a language. There is a class of facts which can be subsumed under "neutralization"; this class includes the non-occurrence of final voiced stops in Russian but not the non-occurrence of initial *tl* in English. There is a larger class of facts which includes all facts in the first class and also all facts like the non-occurrence of English *tl*. This larger class of facts needs formal recognition. The "informational value" of initial *p* in English is greater when *l* does not follow than when it does, because if no *l* follows then *p* is a choice from a larger number of alternatives. Similarly, a final *k* in Russian (be it "phoneme" or "archiphoneme") has less "informational value" than a medial *k*, because in the former case it is a selection from only about half as many possible alternatives as in the latter.[7] Quite similarly, if one is transmitting messages in a code which allows, during each second of transmission-time, only one or the other of two signals, less information can be transmitted per unit of

---

[5]Martinet (7): "But as this archiphoneme is, in that language, never realized as such, it is probably just as well not to mention it."

[6]It is also sometimes said that neutralization involves invalid use of morphophonemic considerations on the phonemic level; cf. *SIL* 8.99 (1950). This is at least not true of Martinet's use of the term, except in the much more general way to be discussed later in this review.

[7]This way of putting the matter stems from Shannon and Weaver, *The Mathematical Theory of Communication* (Urbana, 1949).

time than when the code being used allows a selection from three or more alternative signals each second. I think that considerations of this kind must have lain at the bottom of Trubetzkoy's development of the "neutralization" idea; certainly Martinet's discussion is full of just this kind of reasoning. And if these considerations are relevant for the cases which can be handled by "neutralization," then they are equally relevant for those cases which cannot.

There is no reason why we should not recognize, within this identical overall framework, the difference between the case where "neutralization" will apply and the case where it will not; and I can see no reason why the "neutralization" terminology should not be used for those cases which it does handle. But we should not lose sight of the more general problem.

Both the Trubetzkoyan tradition and the "American" tradition have made contributions towards the solution of the more general problem. The contributions are somewhat different. Trubetzkoy and some of his followers have been so concerned with the structure of phonemes in terms of distinctive features that some aspects of linear distribution have tended to escape them. Americans were for a long time so concerned with the details of linear distribution that they tended, in their turn, to lose sight of the structure of individual phonemes. The difference in emphasis can be illustrated by comparing what would probably happen in a specific case. Imagine a High German dialect in which the older apical trill has passed not only to a uvular trill but on to a voiced velar spirant. There is a voiceless velar spirant in German; the Trubetzkoy approach would immediately pounce on the new voiced velar spirant as affording a new voiced-voiceless pair, on a par with $b : p$, and so on. The American approach, on the other hand, though possibly noting the different phonetic nature of the descendant from older r, would concentrate on the fact that the distribution of the new voiced velar spirant relative to other phonemes is in no way like the distribution of x, or of a voiced spirant like z, but rather is closer to the distribution of l than of any other single phoneme. The American approach would conclude that, despite its phonetic nature, γ is nevertheless in a functional

class with l rather than with x. In this particular instance, the American's conclusion would be of more functional relevance than the Trubetzkoyan's, but other examples could be given where the opposite would be true.

There is at least one way in which the merits of the Trubetzkoyan emphasis and those of the American emphasis can be combined. Let us recall the characterization of all phonemes (and all archiphonemes, when "realized" as such) as simultaneous bundles of distinctive features, and temporarily let us use the term "bundle" instead of either "phoneme" or "archiphoneme." Now in some cases limitations of distribution are best stated in terms of features, and in others they are best stated in terms of whole bundles. The non-occurrence in standard British English of initial sr is of the latter sort: the convenient statement is "the bundle s does not occur after pause before the bundle r," and nothing is gained by speaking, in this particular case, of the features which constitute the bundle s.[7a] The non-occurrence of English initial tl is not quite of this sort, because it is matched by the non-occurrence of initial dl, so that the simplest description is one which mentions what d and t have in common, rather than their points of difference: "an initial bundle involving the features of stop and of apico-alveolar position of articulation does not occur before the bundle l." The Russian situation can be handled in terms of bundles and features as follows: Russian bundles are vocalic or consonantal; consonantal bundles are obstruents if they involve stop or spirant articulation (without nasalization), otherwise they are sonorants. Every Russian bundle is voiced or voiceless, but the contrast is non-distinctive (that is, determined or predictable) save only in non-final obstruent bundles. Even there, in any sequence of non-final obstruent bundles which does not have the features of labiodental and spirantal articulation in the last bundle, the contrast between voiced and voiceless is

---

[7a]It might seem advisable to subsume the non-occurrence of zr- and sr- in the same statement, putting this in the same class as the non-occurrence of tl- and dl-. Perhaps this is so. But the absence of zr- seems to be more easily subsumed under the non-occurrence of any initial bundle involving voicing and spirantal articulation (v, ð, z, ž) before any consonantal bundle.

distinctive only for the whole sequence, not for each bundle individually. If the last bundle of such a sequence involves labiodental and spirantal articulation, then it may be voiced independently of the voicing or voicelessness of the preceding bundles of the sequence, but if it is voiceless so are all the preceding bundles of the sequence.

This way of speaking needs considerable refinement and abbreviation before it can become very "elegant"; for one thing, the first two examples discuss arrangements that do not occur instead of arrangements that do, and only in crucial cases (where the rest of the pattern would lead one to expect certain arrangements) are such negative statements worth while. But this way of speaking does indeed afford the machinery for taking care both of all the cases that are classifiable as "neutralization" and of all the cases that are not. Let there be no mistake about it: the Trubetzkoyan contribution to such a more complete schema is just as essential as anything that might seem to stem from the "American" tradition. We are not suggesting a "better American" way to handle what Trubetzkoy failed to handle; we are suggesting a synthesis, no more American than it is Trubetzkoyan or anything else.

There is a far more fundamental objection to the system which Martinet outlines than anything mentioned so far. Up to the early 1940s, the only kind of phonology that anyone dealt with was a kind that operates in terms of words and word-boundaries as given points of reference. This kind of phonology is still practiced, by various linguists in Europe and at least by K. L. Pike and some of his students in this country. So far as I know, the first published protest against the assumptions implicit in such phonology appeared in 1942.[8] Since then a different approach has gained considerable ground.

The difference is easily illustrated. Suppose we have a language in which voiceless stops occur only initially and finally in words, voiced stops only medially. The conclusion immediately to be drawn, by the older rules, is that voicing is phonematically[9] non-distinc-

tive for stops. The occurrence of such sequences as, let us say, [pat adak] and [padat ak], where word-boundary is written with a space, does not disturb this conclusion; an acceptable phonematic transcription would be *pat atak* and *patat ak*.

By the newer system, the first thing that disturbs us is the spaces in the phonetic transcriptions given first above. These spaces do not represent anything that we can hear, even after experience, as we listen to the language. And a primary rule is that we pretend (if necessary—it may well actually be the case) that we know nothing about words and word-boundaries. Since the spaces represent nothing, they have to be taken out: our phonetic transcriptions must be [patadak] and [padatak]. But now voiced and voiceless stops are in contrast, since both occur medially between vowels. We are forced to phonemicize as /patadak/ and /padatak/.

By the newer approach, this is all there is to the matter on the strictly phonological level: we have systematized everything which is capable, in the language, of distinguishing utterances from each other, and we are done. There remain other levels of analysis. When we proceed to these other levels, one of the first things we do is to discover words and word-boundaries (or to stop pretending that we don't know anything about them). We are concerned with any correlation there may be between words and phonemic structure; we are also concerned with a fairly simple notation for further analysis, or, perhaps, for other uses such as native literacy. If in the phonemic notation that we have now achieved we introduce (non-phonemic) spaces at word-boundaries, we discover the very interesting fact that the distribution of voiceless and voiced stops, although not predictable for whole utterances, is indeed predictable for individual words. We find that if such spaces are written, we can profitably use a single series of stop symbols instead of two, writing *pat atak* and *patat ak*. This looks like the acceptable phonematic transcription achieved by the earlier rules, but it has a completely different status. When confronted with anything written in this transcription, we can de-

[8]See fn. 3.

[9]I have tried to use "phonematic," as Martinet does, with reference to Trubetzkoyan phonemes = American segmental phonemes, and "phonemic"

in the usual American sense. This is tricky, and there may be some slips.

duce very easily what the phonological structure of the utterance is, simply by interpreting stop-symbols flanked by a space (or by the beginning or end of the utterance) as representing members of the voiceless-stop phoneme series, and other stop-symbols as representing members of the voiced-stop phoneme series. But if we hear an utterance and wish to transcribe it, we do not in general know how to do so on the basis of the phonemic data and nothing else. Suppose we hear /padatak/. If we know that there is no word /pada/, or no word /tak/, or that, both of these words existing, they would not occur in this sequence, then we can conclude that the proper representation would be *patat ak,* as before. Suppose, on the other hand, that both of the words just mentioned do exist and that they occur in the sequence given. Then we do not know whether to transcribe what we have heard as *patat ak* or as *pata tak.* Both of these are phonemically /padatak/. In other words, the relation between the phonemic structure of the language and our special transcription with spaces for word-boundaries is a one-many relation. For a notation to be phonemic, we require a bi-unique one-one relation rather than a one-many relation.[10]

It is not to be thought that the Trubetzkoyan system presented by Martinet rests content once everything has been tabulated that keeps words apart. Further steps are taken. If they were not, then such a distinctive feature as the Czech accent would never be discovered. This accent does not keep words apart, since it is bound to the first syllable of each word; it is, in Trubetzkoyan terminology, not phonematic. But it is distinctive, since

when one has an utterance consisting of several words the accents tell where each word begins (or each "full word"—there are a few difficulties). By thus plowing over the same ground enough times, from different directions, Trubetzkoyan methods are eventually going to turn up and categorize, for any one language, everything that the newer scheme will find.

The essential differences are twofold. First, there is the obvious difference in the sequence of operations. Here I mean logical sequence—what is allowed to take logical priority over what—not sequence of field procedure, where one gets a little of everything at the same time. In the older approach, one recognizes words first and then phonologizes (and then puts words back into context and phonologizes over again). In the newer approach, one phonologizes first, using whole utterances, and then recognizes words. Done with proper care, neither procedure will miss anything that the other turns up. But there is a second, less obvious, difference that stems from the first. This is that when Trubetzkoyan analysis is complete, one has an array of facts on several different structural levels, not properly sorted out according to level but in a hodgepodge arrangement; when the newer analysis is complete, one knows quite definitely to what level each fact applies. This might be paraphrased in Hjelmslev's terms: the newer phonology is a much purer analysis of the level of expression, and thus affords a better frame of reference for the analysis of content or of expression and content taken together, than is the old, which is an analysis of expression with traces of content left in.[11]

There is some historical perspective in all this that ought to be seen. Pre-Trubetzkoyan phonology, and early Trubetzkoyan phonology too, concentrated wholly on words. A terminology arose which was adapted to the discussion of such word-phonology. Trubetzkoy himself was one of the first to see that a feature may play no role in keeping words apart and yet be linguistically distinctive; he systema-

---

[10]A good illustration of the difference between the old-style and the new-style phonological treatment is the contrast between Bernard Bloch's short outline of Japanese phonemics in "Studies in Colloquial Japanese II: Syntax," *Language* 22.200–248 (1946), specifically fn. 3 and the text of pp. 200–204, and the lengthy discussion of the same topic in "SCJ IV: Phonemics," *Language* 26.86–125 (1950). What is deceptively simple in the earlier treatment turns out to be quite complicated in the later—but the more complicated treatment is also obviously more accurate. At the end of the latter article (§9, 122–125) Bloch discusses the derivation of a simpler (not purely phonemic) notation for purposes of further analysis of the language; this matches my own discussion in *Language* 26.63 ff., particularly 68–70 and 73.

[11]If I follow Hjelmslev's discussion at all, his "expression" level is my "phonological"—as characterized above—and his "content" level, so far as it is worked out in terms of form and not of substance, is my "tactical." My "morphophonemics" is then the set of rules which relate expression and content.

tized this sort of thing, but developed a supplementary terminology for it and did not rework the older word-phonology to be of a piece with the new addition. In history, and in the Trubetzkoyan system as it finally emerged, there is this discontinuity: part of it looks like an afterthought. Very much the same sequence of events took place in this country, in a partly but not wholly independent manner. Our aim in the newer synthesis is not to throw out what Trubetzkoy contributed, on this score any more than on the score of "oppositions." Rather, it is to remove the discontinuity, to develop a scheme by which the successive operations are in clear logical relation to each other instead of hanging together in a lopsided way determined by the accidents of history. Perhaps it would be a not too distant analogy to say that Trubetzkoyan phonology stands to the newer phonology much as Euclidean geometry stands to the more general modern geometry; in each case the latter would be impossible without the former, and in each case the rules of the former take their place as operative under special conditions within the more general framework.[12]

One might ask why such an extended discussion should be included in a review of Martinet's booklet. My justification is that Martinet's succinct exposition can very well stand as the last and best summary of Trubetzkoyan methods, an excellent point d'appui for moving from the Trubetzkoy phase of the history of phonological theory into the new phase which we are now collectively engaged in developing.[13]

[12]For a more extended discussion of the differences between the two approaches see my article "Two Fundamental Problems in Phonemics" [17], *SIL* 7.29–51 (1949).

[13]The "we" includes Martinet himself: see his "Où en est la phonologie?" *Lingua* 1.34–58 (1948).

ON THE IDENTIFICATION
OF PHONEMIC ENTITIES*
ROMAN JAKOBSON

As phonemes are linguistic elements, it follows that no phoneme can be correctly defined except by linguistic criteria, i.e., by means of its function in the language. No extra-lingual criteria can be relevant, i.e., neither physical nor physiological nor psychological criteria.

This motto, extracted from Louis Hjelmslev's address to the Second International Congress of Phonetic Sciences (London, 1935),[1] is one of the most stimulating of the many ideas which he contributed to the development of structural linguistics. May I now briefly trace here the corollaries of this sagacious methodological requirement as I, for my part, conceive them.

"Both phonematic, grammatical and lexical elements," the cited paper insists, "are at the same time inner and outer phenomena." As a matter of fact, this twofold nature of any phonemic entity, uniting it with all the superordinated linguistic constituents, was ascertained at the very outset of phonemic inquiry. Beginning in the early eighties, Baudouin de Courtenay repeatedly stated that from the semantic point of view "the utterance breaks up into sentences, sentences into significative words, words into morphological components or morphemes and morphemes into phonemes." For "a morpheme is divisible only into components which are of the same nature as itself: they, too, must be significative." Thus, a dissociation of the morpheme into physical or physiological elements, i.e., into sounds, would be, according to Baudouin de Courtenay, "an unjustified and paralogical jump in division."

Likewise for Ferdinand de Saussure any linguistic constituent is necessarily a "twofold entity" ("entité à deux faces"). "Une unité matérielle n'existe que par le sens, la fonction dont elle est revêtue; ce principe est particulièrement important pour la connaissance des unités restreintes, parce qu'on est tenté de croire qu'elles existent en vertu de leur pure matérialité. . . . Inversement . . . un sens, une fonction n'existent que par le support de quelque forme matérielle."

The lesson taught by both great discoverers of the primary concepts of structural linguistics is quite unequivocal. But when the time came for linguistics to utilize these fundamentals and to build up a total conception of language far removed from tradition both in theory and in descriptive technique, it proved much more difficult to heed the cited methodological warnings than merely to admit their validity.

The 1930s witnessed an impetuous and promising international development of phonemic studies, and Hjelmslev's polemic fervor in focusing attention on and vindicating the strictly *linguistic criteria* was most appropriate and expedient.

However various were the definitions of the phoneme offered by different scholars and schools, all of these formulations aimed at essentially one and the same thing, and, in broad outline, the practical task of enumerating the stock of phonemes for any given language found its approximate solution. The difficulties began with the attempts at the in-

---

[1] *The Proceedings of the Second International Congress of Phonetic Sciences* (Cambridge, 1936), p. 49.

*This article was first published in the *Travaux du Cercle Linguistique de Copenhague* 5.205–213 (1949). Reprinted here from Roman Jakobson, *Selected Writings I* (Mouton, 1962), pp. 418–425, by permission.

ward characterization of any of these phonemes, and two diverse attitudes are most indicative for the whole initial period of phonemic investigation. Either the student limited himself to registering the number of distinct phonemes in the given language and to symbolizing graphically the mere fact of this distinctness, or he made the obviously paralogical jump from a purely linguistic analysis to the raw sound-matter: he defined, e.g., the French phoneme *g* as a postpalatal stop, *ɲ* as an antepalatal nasal, and *ʒ* as a palato-alveolar spirant, without asking himself whether, *ceteris paribus,* the difference between the articulation toward these three regions of the palate could be of some autonomous relevance for the phonemic distinction of French consonants.

It seems to me that the consistent application of linguistic criteria as required by Hjelmslev does not allow the discontinuation of the phonemic analysis either through a kind of agnosticism toward the proper essence of the phonemes or through a substitution of sound-physiology and physics for a thoroughly linguistic procedure.

Overcoming the one-track mind of the neogrammarian bias, F. de Saussure pointed out that beside the *axis of successiveness,* linguistics, as any science dealing with *values* does, must also tackle the other coordinate— the *axis of simultaneity* "concerning relations between coexistent things"; whereas for the traditional approach there was no science of language outside questions of succession. The neogrammarians were entirely taken up with the axis of successiveness, as if it were possible to comprehend the sequence without seizing upon the consecutive modes of being.

The two axes underlie not only language as a whole, but also any single linguistic form. On this level, however, the neogrammarian attitude, which eliminates the axis of simultaneity, has survived in the Saussurian doctrine which postulates "the linear character of the signifier (*signifiant*)." The attempt to warrant this "fundamental principle" by a reference to the impossibility of implementing two phonemes at the same time is nothing but a vicious circle, since the phoneme is defined by the impossibility of implementing two such units simultaneously. This arbitrary thesis prevented both its author and the phonemicists following in his tracks from solving the pivotal

problem which he himself astutely foresaw: the task of "determining the distinctive features (*éléments différentiels*) of the phonemes." The group relations were still examined only in terms of sequences and not at all in terms of bundles. Long ago the neurologists distinguished two kinds of complexes (*Simultankomplexe* und *Sukzessivkomplexe* in K. Kleist's terminology) which underlie our speech-ability, which are differently located in the brain and which may be respectively compared with the chords and sequences in music. Meanwhile the science of language continued to treat the phoneme as the most minute (further indivisible) linguistic unit.

However, as the phonemes of a given language form a system of sequences, so the system of phonemes, in turn, is formed by their constituents, i.e., by distinctive features. And the breaking up of the phonemes into distinctive features follows precisely the same tested devices as the division of the morphemes into phonemes. "By studying the possible *commutations*" we obtain, e.g., a French phonemic "paradigm" /bu/ 'boue' : /mu/ 'mou' : /pu/ 'pou' : /vu/ 'vous' : /du/ 'doux' : /gu/ 'goût', and thus we find out that the phoneme *b* in /bu/ can be decomposed into five commutable elements: b/m, b/p, b/v, b/d, b/g. In examining the same phoneme in other environments we confirm this scheme. Cf. /bo/ 'beau' : /mo/ 'mot' : /vo/ 'veau' : /po/ 'peau' : /do/ 'dos' : /go/ 'gau', etc. Having ascertained a set of "micro-features," as we could call them after the model of Twaddell's "micro-phonemes," we may broach the question of the "macro-features," and we easily detect a set of ratios, as for instance—/bu/ : /mu/ = /du/ : /nu/ 'nous'; /bu/ : /pu/ = /du/ : /tu/ 'tout' = /gu/ : /ku/ 'cou' = /vu/ : /fu/ 'fou' = /zuzu/ 'zouzou' : /su/ 'sou' = /ʒu/ 'joue' : /ʃu/ 'chou'; /bu/ : /du/ = /pu/ : /tu/ = /vu/ : /zuzu/ = /fu/ : /su/ = /mu/ : /nu/; and finally /bu/ : /gu/ = /pu/ : /ku/ = /vu/ : /ʒu/ = /fu/ : /ʃu/ — cf. /bõ/ 'bon' : /gõ/ 'gond' = /võ/ 'vont' : /ʒõ/ 'jonc' = /mõ/ 'mon' : /ɲõ/ 'gnon'. In this way the distinctive features constituting the French consonantal phonemes come to light: nasality vs. the absence of nasal resonance; tenseness vs. laxity; continuousness vs. brokenness; gravity (due to a vaster and more unified resonator with a contracted orifice) vs. acuteness; higher vs. lower saturation (respectively due to a back and a front articulation).[2] *Entia non sunt multiplicanda:* higher saturation (correspondingly, back articulation) presents one single indivisible feature in the pattern of French consonants, and it is phonemically irrelevant, toward which part of the palate this back articulation is produced; the variants are due to the environment: the articulation is antepalatal when combined with nasality, palatoalveolar in combination with continuousness, and postpalatal elsewhere. Thus the question of contextual variance is quite as pertinent for bundles as for sequences.

Only when brought up to the level of distinctive features, does the linguistic analysis enable us to verify Saussure's cardinal statement on phonemic units as first and foremost *"entités oppositives."* The phoneme by itself is not a term of opposition. E.g., the phoneme *b* does not call unequivocally, irreversibly, and necessarily for a definite opposite, while any distinctive feature does. There is no possible distinctive tenseness without laxity, no gravity without acuteness, no higher without lower saturation, or, as Saussure pointed out, no presence of nasal resonance without its absence, and *vice versa.* The dichotomous principle applies here in full force.

Let us exemplify the results of breaking up phonemes into bundles of distinctive features. The inventory of Standard Serbocroatian totals 29 qualitatively distinct phonemes, and if we add the phonemes distinguished by prosodic features the amount of phonemes swells to 47. The whole pattern is based on eight dichotomous properties; among them six *inherent* (or *qualitative*) features concerning the axis of simultaneity only (vocality, nasality, saturation, gravity, continuousness, and voicing), and two *prosodic* features involving also the axis of successiveness (length, and high-tone). We mark the presence of a feature by a plus sign; its opposite, the distinctive absence of the given feature, is indicated by a minus. A complex combining both opposite terms is represented by the ± sign. To avoid longer comments, the current Croatian spelling form is used for denoting the Serbocroatian phonemes.

Prosodic features divide any vowel, as well as *r,* into four distinctive varieties: high-toned long, high-toned short, low-toned long, and low-toned short.[3]

Thus there must be added to the analytic records of *r* and of any vowel the following four commutable characteristics:

	1	2	3	4
High-tone	−	−	+	+
Length	−	+	−	+

This analytic phonemic transcription, when applied to connected speech-utterances, exhibits the distribution of the different distinctive features throughout the sequences.

On the level of phonemes there are 1081 "significant differentiations" in Serbocroatian, according to W. F. Twaddell's formula: "If *x* is the maximum number of significant phonological differentiations within a given articulatory range in a language, then $2x = n(n-1)$, where *n* is the maximum number of phonemes in that range, and $(n-1)$ is the number of consecutive phonological relations within that range."[4]

In dissociating the phoneme into distinc-

	t	d	c	s	z	p	b	f	v	ć	đ	č	ǧ	š	ž	k	g	x	n	m	ń	r	l	ľ	i	u	e	o	a
Vocality																						±	±	±	+	+	+	+	+
Nasality	−					−				−									+	+	+								
Saturation	−	−	−	−	−	−	−	−	+	+	+	+	+	+	+	+	+	+	−	−	+		−	+	−	−	±	±	+
Gravity	−	−			−	+	+	+	+	−	−			−		+	+	+	−	+					−	+	−	+	
Continuousness	−	−	±	+	+	−	−	+	+	−	−	±	±	+	+	−		+				−	+	+					
Voicing	−	+		−	+	−	+	−	+	−	+	−	+	−	+	−	+												

[2] Cf. R. Jakobson and J. Lotz, "Notes on the French Phonemic Pattern," *Word* 5 (1949).

[3] Without an adjacent vowel, *r* is syllabic. Without an adjacent consonant, *r* is non-syllabic. When *r* adjoins both a vowel and a consonant, the phonemic opposition long/short is in force and is implemented as syllabic/non-syllabic. The non-syllabic *r* is prosodically undifferentiated.

[4] *On Defining the Phoneme* (Baltimore, 1935), p. 53.

tive features we isolate the ultimate linguistic constituents charged with semiotic value. When determining their specific essence, do we slip from the linguistic level into physical or physiological criteria and sin thereby against the epigraph of this paper? One must recognize that language obviously pertains to the domain of culture and that even the minutest element charged with semiotic value is a manifestation of culture, for instance, the "functional role" played by the opposition of voiced and unvoiced consonants in Serbocroatian. But as far as the phonic essence of this opposition is concerned, one would be tempted to assign it not to culture but to nature as a purely material phenomenon.

Certainly the existence of sound production with or without glottal vibrations is conditioned by the structure of our vocal apparatus, and the subsequent difference of the acoustic effect is a physical phenomenon. The phoneticians have ascertained that the emission of consonants presents an infinity of degrees and shades with regard to the participation of voice: the glottis can be closed to a greater or lesser degree; the vibrations of the vocal cords can be of different amplitude; and the phase at which they begin or cease can vary. Thus, the glottis is capable of producing diverse nuances in the matter of consonantal voicing, but only the opposition "presence vs. absence of voicing" is utilized to differentiate word meanings.

Since the sound matter of language is a matter organized and formed to serve as a semiotic instrument, not only the significative function of the distinctive features but even their phonic essence is a cultural artifact. Of course, it must reckon with natural limitations; it is, to use Saussure's apt expression, *"en quelque sorte imposé par la nature."* But at the same time our organizing activity superimposes its own rules. Phonemic entities draw on the gross sound matter but readjust this extrinsic stuff, dissecting and classifying it along their own lines. Above all, the procedure is one of selection. Among a multitude of acoustico-motor possibilities, there is a restricted number upon which language chooses to set a value.

Where nature presents nothing but an indefinite number of contingent varieties, the intervention of culture extracts pairs of opposite terms. The gross sound matter knows no oppositions. It is human thought, conscious or unconscious, which draws from this sound matter the binary oppositions for their phonemic use. The term *opposition* (or correspondingly, *contrast*) is currently used in modern linguistic literature, but it is still opportune to recall the vital implications of this concept as, for instance, H. J. Pos neatly formulated them: "L'opposition n'est pas un fait isolé: c'est un principe de structure. Elle réunit toujours deux choses distinctes, mais qui sont liées de telle façon, que la pensée ne puisse poser l'une sans poser l'autre. L'unité des opposés est toujours formée par un concept, qui, implicitement, contient les opposés en lui et se divise en opposition explicite quand il est appliqué à la réalité concrète. . . . L'opposition dans les faits linguistiques n'est pas un schéma que la science introduit pour maîtriser les faits, et qui resterait extérieur à ceux-ci. Son importance dépasse l'ordre épistémologique: quand la pensée linguistique range les faits d'après les principes d'opposition et de système, elle rencontre une pensée qui crée ces faits mêmes."[5]

As music imposes upon sound matter a graduated scale, similarly language imposes upon it the dichotomous scale which is simply a corollary of the purely differential role played by phonemic entities. The consonantal opposition of strong and weak is achieved by varying degrees of air ouput (*débit* in Rousselot's terminology). Speech sounds present an ample progression in output: the latter is higher in aspirated than in nonaspirated consonants, in fortes than in lenes, in voiced than in unvoiced, in stops than in corresponding spirants. In different positions the relation strong/weak can be implemented by different variants: for instance, in a strong (stressed, initial, etc.) position, by an aspirated fortis stop vs. a lenis stop (voiced or unvoiced), and in a weak position by matching two nonaspirated stops—a fortis and a lenis one, or two spirants—an unvoiced and a voiced one. In Danish this opposition strong/weak is implemented, for example, by *t* vs. *d* in strong position, and by *d* vs. *ð* in weak position, so that the weak phoneme in the strong position *materially* coincides with

[5] "La notion d'opposition en linguistique," *Onzième Congrès International de Psychologie* (Paris, 1938), p. 245.

the strong phoneme in the weak position. The relation strong/weak in any position is perfectly measurable both physically and physiologically, as in general every phonemic opposition presents in all its manifestations, a common denominator both on the acoustic and the articulatory level. But if one should measure the sound matter without reference to the rule of dichotomy imposed upon it by language, the conclusion would be that there are "overlapping" phonemes, in the same way as a physicist with his acoustic instruments, according to H. Frei's felicitous comparison, fails to explain why, in a given piece of music, F-flat and E represent two different values.[6] The dichotomy of distinctive features is, in essence, a logical operation, one of the primary logical operations of a child and—if we pass from ontogeny to phylogeny—of mankind. The question arises as to whether it is justifiable to admit a kind of logical operation which escapes the attention of the speech-community and which unfolds outside our consciousness. But it is sufficient to recall Ribot's focal thesis: "the reasoning, whether conscious, subconscious or unconscious, remains identical, save in differing degrees of clarity of representation."[7]

And now to return to our starting point: since phonemes are linguistic elements, they are subject to a strictly linguistic analysis which must *specify* all the underlying oppositions and their interrelations. The specific property of any opposition, the phonic nucleus utilized semiotically, must be exactly identified. Otherwise even a rudimentary listing of the phonemes of a given language becomes a *scientifically* insoluble problem. What enables us to treat two units appearing each in a different environment ("microphonemes" in Twaddell's conception), e.g., the Spanish initial stop *d* and the intervocalic spirant *ð*, as pertaining to the same phoneme (Twaddell's "macrophoneme")? If we did not submit the phonemes to the analysis sketched above,

what would authorize us to consider these units equivalent? Their identification is then, patently or latently, based on the precarious criterion of outer (physical or physiological) "resemblance," or on an even more wavering criterion of subjective feeling for "sameness."

But these difficulties, particularly striking on the "macrophoneme" level, begin already on the "microphoneme" level, when the "method of commutation" is used. Without the advocated internal analysis of the phoneme one can scarcely know which of the three contiguous variations is a phonemic distinction in such a set of Russian words as [v′era] 'belief' (Nom.)—[v′ér′æ] 'believing', [v′ɛru] 'belief' (Acc.)—[v′ér′y] 'I believe', [v′ɛru] 'belief' (Gen.)—[v′ér′i] 'belief' (Dat.).[8] A reference to the r in final position would help somewhat ([ʒár] 'heat'—[ʒár′] 'roast!') but the matching of the intervocalic trill r and the more flap-like final r returns us to the embarrassing "macrophoneme" problem, and in such a set as [sláva] 'glory' (Nom.) − [sláv′æ] 'glorifying', [sláv u] 'glory' (Gen.) − [sláv′i] 'glory' (Dat.), no reference to other positions is of assistance since the opposition v/v′ is always prevocalic.

Only in resolving the phonemes into their constituents and in identifying the ultimate entities obtained does phonemics arrive at its basic concept (which insures the consistent use of linguistic criteria sought by Hjelmslev) and thereby definitely breaks with the extrinsic picture of speech vividly summarized by L. Bloomfield: a *continuum* which can be viewed as consisting of any desired, and, through still finer analysis, an infinitely increasable number of successive parts.[9]

Linguistic analysis, with its concept of ultimate phonemic entities, signally converges with modern physics, which has revealed the granular structure of matter as composed of elementary particles.

[8]The phonetic transcription used is approximate (and without special signs for reduced vowels). The same series as transcribed phonemically: /v′éra/ − /v′ér′a/, /v′éru/ − /v′ér′u/, /v′éri/ − /v′ér′i/.
[9]*Language* (New York, 1933), p. 76.

[6]"Monosyllabisme et polysyllabisme dans les emprunts linguistiques," *Bulletin de la Maison Franco-Japonaise* 8, No. 1 (Tokyo, 1936), p. 146.
[7]See also E. Sapir, "The Unconscious Patterning of Behavior in Society," *The Unconscious* (New York, 1928).

Written in Hunter, N.Y., Summer 1949, and published in *Travaux du Cercle Linguistique de Copenhague* 5 (1949), pp. 205–213, dedicated to Louis Hjelmslev.

31

TOWARD THE LOGICAL DESCRIPTION OF LANGUAGES IN THEIR PHONEMIC ASPECT*

E. COLIN CHERRY, MORRIS HALLE, and ROMAN JAKOBSON

Distinctive features occur in lumps or bundles, each one of which we call a phoneme. The speaker has been trained to make sound-producing movements in such a way that the phoneme-features will be present in the sound-waves, and he has been trained to respond only to these features and to ignore the rest of the gross acoustic mass that reaches his ears.

Leonard Bloomfield (1933).

The number of different phonemes in a language is a small submultiple of the number of forms.

Leonard Bloomfield (1926).

The logical demand that a science speak in quantitative terms is met by linguistics because it speaks in terms of phonemes.

Leonard Bloomfield (1927).

1. INTRODUCTORY

This paper, an attempt to contribute to a logical description of the phonemic structure of a language, employs some of the elementary concepts of statistical communication theory.[1] A concrete illustration is provided by a statistical analysis of colloquial Russian;[2] the material studied was the Russian urban conversations recorded by Peškovskij, comprising in the latter's phonetic transcription ten thousand sounds.[3]

In analyzing Russian or any other language, we must ascertain which and how many *distinctive features* are needed to differentiate the meaningful units of its code, i.e., the smallest meaningful units, termed morphemes, and their combinations into words. Words are the maximum units that are expected to be entirely provided by the code. We must determine the minimum set of such features that the listener needs in order to recognize and distinguish all except homonymic morphemes, without help from context or situation. Once this set is determined, all other phonetic differences among morphemes or words of the given language can be shown to be predictable and therefore redundant.[4]

If we compare, for example, the Russian words (1) [bɨt] 'way of life', (2) [b,it] 'beaten',

---

[1]See, in particular, C. E. Shannon and W. Weaver, *The Mathematical Theory of Communication* (Urbana, 1949); D. M. Mackay, "In Search of Basic Symbols," *Cybernetics: Transactions of the Eighth Conference* (New York, 1952); *id.*, "The Nomenclature of Information Theory," *ibid.*

[2]This analysis was made as part of the research on contemporary Russian conducted by the Department of Slavic Languages and Literatures at Harvard University under a grant from the Rockefeller Foundation.

[3]A. Peškovskij, "Desjat' tysjač zvukov russkogo jazyka," *Sbornik statej*, 167–191 (Leningrad, 1952).

[4]For further information on distinctive features and their acoustic and articulatory correlates, see R. Jakobson, C. G. M. Fant, and M. Halle, *Preliminaries to Speech Analysis* (MIT Acoustics Laboratory, Technical Report No. 13, 1952).

*This article, first published in *Language* 29.34–46 (1953), is reprinted here from Roman Jakobson, *Selected Writings I* (Mouton, 1962), pp. 449–463, by permission.

(3) [bɨt,] 'be', and (4) [b,it,] 'beat',[5] we observe that words (1) and (2), or words (3) and (4), differ from each other in two respects: [ɪ] is farther forward than [ɨ] (i.e., has a higher second formant), and [i] is farther forward than [ɨ]; while [b,] is distinguished by its palatalization from [b]: it is produced with a flattening of the mouth cavity and a simultaneous widening of the pharyngeal channel, which results in an upward displacement of energy along the frequency axis. Words (1) and (3), or words (2) and (4), also differ from each other in two respects: [ɨ] and [i] are closer than [ɨ] and [ɪ], respectively; while [t,] differs from [t] in its palatalization.[6]

If, now, the presence as opposed to the absence of consonantal palatalization is viewed as the distinctive feature, this one feature (which we call sharp vs. plain) suffices to differentiate the four words in question. If, on the other hand, the distinctive function were to be assigned to the vowels, we would have to postulate two independent features, front vs. back and close vs. open. This superfluous multiplication of features is reason enough for rejecting the second solution. In Russian there is an additional reason for adopting the first solution, for in this language, in certain positions, the presence or absence of consonantal palatalization can by itself distinguish sequences otherwise identical, and must therefore in any case be considered an autonomous distinctive feature; compare [voʃt,] 'leader' with [koʃt] 'outlay', or [sel,t,] 'herring' with [k,el,t] 'Kelt'. On the other hand, the distribution of the advanced and retracted varieties of vowels, as well as that of the close and open ones, is entirely predictable from the presence or absence of palatalized consonants before and after the vowel.

Proceeding consistently in this way, we find in the code of contemporary Standard Russian eleven distinctive features, grouped by superposition into forty-two phonemes.[7] These eleven distinctive features suffice to differentiate all but homonymic morphemes and words in Russian.

We leave aside here sound features that perform other functions, namely *configurational* features, which signal the division of the utterance into grammatical units of different degrees of complexity, and expressive (or more precisely *physiognomic*) features, which signal solely the emotional attitudes of the speaker. Examples of configurational features signaling the division of the sound chain into word units: [dəv'ol,nɨj] /da v'ol,nij/ 'free besides' : [dav'ol,nɨj] /dav'ol,nij/ 'content'; [t,'e·n,it'am] /t,'en,i tam/ 'shadows are there' : [t,'en,ɪt'am] /t,'e n,i-t'am/ 'they are elsewhere'; [jix'ɨ·də jix,'idə] /j'ix 'ida. jix'ida/ 'their Ida is malicious'. Physiognomic features are illustrated by the different ways of pronouncing the word for 'yes' (simply [d'a] when unemphatic) according to the degree and kind of emphasis. These features convey subsidiary information similar to that which is carried by such graphic equivalents of configurational features as spaces or punctuation marks, and such equivalents of physiognomic features as underlining or italicizing. The *redundant* features, on the other hand, operate in conjunction with the distinctive features, thereby facilitating the selective process on the part of the listener and lessening the burden on his attention.

For our computations, the text was split up into phoneme sequences consisting of two successive vowels and the consonants (if any) between them. In this way each vowel appears twice in our corpus, once as the initial and once as the final phoneme of a sequence. We chose these sequences "from vowel to vowel"

---

[5]Cf. A. Isačenko, *Fonetika spisovnej ruštiny,* 177, 182 (Bratislava, 1947).

[6]We follow the IPA system of transcription, except in three respects: we use a comma after a letter to indicate palatalization; we place the accent mark immediately before the vowel letter; and we render the strident stop by the same letter as the corresponding constrictive with the addition of a circumflex.

[7]There are two competing varieties of contemporary Standard Russian. The more conservative is codified in *Tolkovyj slovar' russkogo jazyka,* ed. by D. Ušakov (Moscow, 1935–1940); the other is advocated by S. Obnorskij, and is presented in *Slovar' russkogo jazyka,* ed. by S. Ožegov (Moscow, 1949). In general, we accept Ušakov's norms; but in order to include all the phonemic discriminations possible in Standard Russian, we add to his traditional repertory of phonemes a new phoneme /g,/ as distinguished from /g/. Such new gerund formations as /b,ir,ig,'a/ 'taking care', distinct from /b,ir,ig'a/ 'banks', are admitted into Standard Russian by Obnorskij and his followers.

because phonemic conditioning is confined, in Russian, to consonantal clusters and to combinations of a vowel with preceding or following consonants; there is no apparent influence on consonants following a given vowel by those preceding it or vice versa. The compulsory syntactic pause (both initial and final) was denoted by a period and equated with a vowel.

Three sets of counts are of interest: (A) those that take into consideration both the word boundaries (symbolized by a space) and the junctures between the immediate constituents of compound words[8] (symbolized by a hyphen); (B) those that are concerned only with the word boundaries; and (C) those that deal neither with the word boundaries nor with the junctures, but break up a sequence only at the points of compulsory pause. The three ways of dividing a text into elementary sequences are illustrated in the accompanying table, based on the following passage: *Vot, na tebe na obed. Pojdës'* . . . /.v'ot. n'a t,ib,'e na-ab,'et. pa-jd,'oʃ./ 'Here, that's for your dinner. You'll go . . .' The computations in this paper are made according to the first way of counting.

(A) #v'o'ot# #n'a'a# #t,iib,'e'e# #na a#
 #a ab,'e'et# #pa a# #jd,o'oʃ#

(B) #v'o'ot# #n'a'a# #t,iib,'e'e# #na aa ab,'e'et#
 #pa ajd,'o 'oʃ#

(C) #v'o'ot# #n'a 'at,i ib,'e 'ena aa ab,'e'et#
 #pa ajd,'o 'oʃ#

2. THE FEATURE PATTERN AS A LOGICAL DESCRIPTION OF THE PHONEME

In the description that follows, language will be treated as a Markoff process.[9] The phonemes will be considered uniquely identifiable; but their order, in the sequences that compose our sample, can be described only statistically.

For the purpose of identifying one particular phoneme out of the set employed by the language, the distinctive features may be regarded as questions to be answered yes or no. Thus one may ask, Is the phoneme vocalic? —yes or no; Is the phoneme consonantal? —yes or no; and so on through the entire list of features. For the language under consideration here, a total of eleven such questions is necessary to identify any one phoneme uniquely. Table A illustrates these questions answered yes (+) or no (−); a zero (○) means either. This suggests that the logic is three-valued, a point that will be taken up again later.

A simple illustration of such a logical description is provided by Fig. 1, which shows a set of eight "objects" A, B, . . . H, to be identified by yes (+) or no (−) answers. Thus the group is first split in two, and we begin by asking, Is the object that we want on the right side (+) or not (−)? Successive subdivisions eventually identify any object in a set. If there are N objects in the set, and if N happens to be a power of 2, the number of yes-or-no answers necessary to identify each of the objects in the set is $\log_2 N$. The complete identification of any object is then a chain of plus and minus signs; thus, the object G in Fig. 1 is identified by the chain (+ + −).

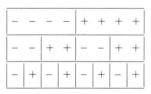

Fig. 1
The Logical Identification
of Objects in a Set of Eight

[8]Among Russian compound words we include all words with a non-initial root: words with more than one root, e.g., /adna-abr'aznij/ 'uniform'; words with prefixes, e.g., /za-astr,'it,/ 'to sharpen', /iz-vad,'it,/ 'to exhaust'; and words with preceding prepositions which are phonemically treated like prefixes, e.g., /za-akn'o/ 'behind the window', /iz-vad'i/ 'out of the water'.

[9]Cf. Shannon and Weaver 102: "A system which produces a sequence of symbols . . . according to certain probabilities is called a *stochastic process,* and the special case of a stochastic process

in which the probabilities depend on the previous events, is called a Markoff process or a Markoff chain." In his "Essai d'une recherche statistique sur le texte du roman *Eugène Onĕgin,* illustrant la liaison des épreuves en chaine," *Bulletin de l'Académie Impériale des Sciences de St. Pétersbourg,* Vol. 7 (1913), A. A. Markov studied the distribution of vowel and consonant *letters* in a part of Puškin's famous poem and showed that the transitional probabilities between the letters were not those of a random sequence but rather depended on the preceding letter or letters.

Even when N is not a power of 2, the quantity $\log_2$ N can still be used as a measure. In such cases the fractional result must not be taken to imply a fraction of a question; it means, rather, that the N members of the set will not all necessarily require the same number of answers for identification. The fraction results from averaging.

The quantity $\log_2$ N is conventionally expressed in *bits;* the name for this unit is derived from *binary digit* (i.e., yes-or-no choice).

In Fig. 1 each successive division has been consistently into two equal subgroups; this method allows us to achieve complete identification with the smallest possible number of answers (i.e., the shortest chain of plus and minus signs). Subdivision into unequal subgroups requires, on the average, more questions and answers.

We shall now apply this process to the list of forty-two Russian phonemes listed in Table A. But first, let us consider a purely hypothetical description of any one phoneme out of the forty-two, as though these were not phonemes but merely objects without linguistic significance. If they were successively subdivided as in Fig. 1, the description of any one object would require, on the average, $\log_2$ 42 questions, or 5.38 bits per phoneme. In our analysis of language we are concerned, however, not only with questions of logic but also with matters of fact; hence the answers yes or no in Table A are provided for us by considerations of the natural process of speaking.

One might ask, Why cannot a type of feature pattern be invented which employs, on the average, only 5.38 questions per phoneme, in a manner analogous to the hypothetical case discussed? This could perhaps be done; but the distinctive features used at present (Table A) serve other purposes and are intimately related to the physical production of speech. They number eleven, implying an average of 5.62 extra questions per phoneme (11 − 5.38). This means that redundant or extra plus and minus signs are brought in. Nevertheless, these features, as they have been proposed for earlier linguistic analyses, fit into the logical descriptive system, though apparently with some inefficiency. Can the efficiency of our empirical description be improved by simplification of Table A?

Table A shows the simplest possible description of the 42 phonemes in terms of the given eleven features. There are several points of difference between this table and Fig. 1. First, the successive questions have phonetic significance; they do not merely ask Right or Left? like those in Fig. 1. The answer to the first question (vocalic—yes or no?) does not split the 42 phonemes into two equal groups, but into 12 pluses and 30 minuses; Russian phonemes simply happen to have this characteristic. The second question (consonantal—yes or no?) again parts each of these groups into unequal subgroups; and so on.

Moreover, some of the questions in the list need not be answered at all for some of the phonemes, because the identification is complete without them. In Table A we use a zero to indicate "either"—that is, either plus or minus. For example, the phoneme /t/ is represented by the chain (−+−○−−−−−−○). Each of the zeros can be replaced by either plus or minus without affecting the identification; in either case, the chain of symbols for /t/ remains unique. Since every zero may thus be regarded as either a plus or a minus, the total number of questions answered here is eleven per phoneme. This is a measure of the "information" conveyed when the speaker selects any particular phoneme out of the 42, at least on the basis of the feature pattern here presented. But as we have seen, the true "information" is rather to be expressed by an average of 5.38 questions (bits); the extra 5.62 bits represents the redundancy that would result from the replacement of the zeros by plus or minus signs. (It must be emphasized that our measure of "information" has up to this point been based upon the assumption that all 42 phonemes have an equal probability of occurrence and that they are wholly independent units. Since language has, of course, a much more complex structure than this, our definition of "information" will later have to be modified.)

The term "redundancy" should not be taken to imply wastefulness; it is a property of speech (and, in fact, of every system of communication) which serves a most useful purpose. In particular, it helps the hearer to resolve uncertainties introduced by distortion of the signal or by disturbing noises. For example, the feature of nasality is marked ○ for all vowels. If these zeros were changed to

TABLE A
The phonemes of Russian, showing their distinctive feature patterns
as represented by the answers yes (+), no (−), either (○).

	k	k,	g	g,	x	c	ʃ	ʒ	t	t,	d	d,	s	s,	z	z,	ŝ	n	n,	p	p,
VOCALIC	−	−	−	−	−	−	−	−	−	−	−	−	−	−	−	−	−	−	−	−	−
CONSONANTAL	+	+	+	+	+	+	+	+	+	+	+	+	+	+	+	+	+	+	+	+	+
COMPACT	+	+	+	+	+	+	+	+	−	−	−	−	−	−	−	−	−	−	−	−	−
DIFFUSE	○	○	○	○	○	○	○	○	○	○	○	○	○	○	○	○	○	○	○	○	○
GRAVE	+	+	+	+	+	−	−	−	−	−	−	−	−	−	−	−	−	−	−	+	+
NASAL	○	○	○	○	○	○	○	○	−	−	−	−	−	−	−	−	−	+	+	−	−
CONTINUANT	−	−	−	−	+	−	+	+	−	−	−	−	+	+	+	+	−	○	○	−	−
VOICED	−	−	+	+	○	○	−	+	−	−	+	+	−	−	+	+	−	−	−	−	−
SHARP	−	+	−	+	○	○	○	○	−	+	−	+	−	+	−	+	○	−	+	−	+
STRIDENT	○	○	○	○	○	○	○	○	−	−	−	−	○	○	○	○	+	○	○	○	○
STRESSED	○	○	○	○	○	○	○	○	○	○	○	○	○	○	○	○	○	○	○	○	○

	b	b,	f	f,	v	v,	m	m,	'u	u	'o	'e	'i	i	'a	a	r	r,	l	l,	j
VOCALIC	−	−	−	−	−	−	−	−	+	+	+	+	+	+	+	+	+	+	+	+	−
CONSONANTAL	+	+	+	+	+	+	+	+	−	−	−	−	−	−	−	−	+	+	+	+	−
COMPACT	−	−	−	−	−	−	−	−	−	−	−	−	−	−	+	+	○	○	○	○	○
DIFFUSE	○	○	○	○	○	○	○	○	+	+	−	−	+	+	○	○	○	○	○	○	○
GRAVE	+	+	+	+	+	+	+	+	+	+	+	−	−	−	○	○	○	○	○	○	○
NASAL	−	−	−	−	−	−	+	+	○	○	○	○	○	○	○	○	○	○	○	○	○
CONTINUANT	−	−	+	+	+	+	−	−	○	○	○	○	○	○	○	○	−	−	+	+	○
VOICED	+	+	−	−	+	+	−	−	○	○	○	○	○	○	○	○	○	○	○	○	○
SHARP	−	+	−	+	−	+	−	+	○	○	○	○	○	○	○	○	−	+	−	+	○
STRIDENT	○	○	○	○	○	○	○	○	○	○	○	○	○	○	○	○	○	○	○	○	○
STRESSED	○	○	○	○	○	○	○	○	+	−	○	○	+	−	+	−	○	○	○	○	○

pluses, the new symbols would not imply that a Russian speaker always nasalizes his vowels: normally he does not; but even if he did, the nasality would have no phonemic significance. In some cases a zero appears in a place where the substitution of plus or minus would imply an impossible articulation; but even here the point is that the phoneme is uniquely identified without this feature.

If the data given in Table A can be recast so as to eliminate the necessity of using the ambiguous symbol ○, then the number of questions needed to identify any one phoneme will, on the average, be reduced. That is, the description of the phonemes in terms of features will be less redundant.

3. REMOVAL OF THE AMBIGUOUS ZERO SIGNS

One might suppose that by re-ordering the feature questions, it would be possible to remove all the zero signs in Table A, or at least to shift them to the end of every phoneme column so that they could be omitted (the phoneme then being identified only by the chain of plus and minus signs). It turns out, however, that this cannot be accomplished by any simple re-ordering.

The whole problem may be changed by regarding the table of signs (+, −, ○) as a code book for identifying the various phonemes. In this view there is no reason why the order of the feature questions should not be different for different phonemes. In fact, the order could change during the identification of a particular phoneme, at certain stages depending upon the answers to earlier questions. Thus a sequence of different code books would be required. Table B shows the result of such a recoding.

As an example, consider the identification of the phoneme /'o/. The answers to the questions Vocalic? Consonantal? Compact? are respectively +−−, which identifies the phoneme as belonging to the group /'u u 'o 'e 'i i/.

TABLE B

The phonemes of Russian, re-ordered to eliminate the ambiguous zero.

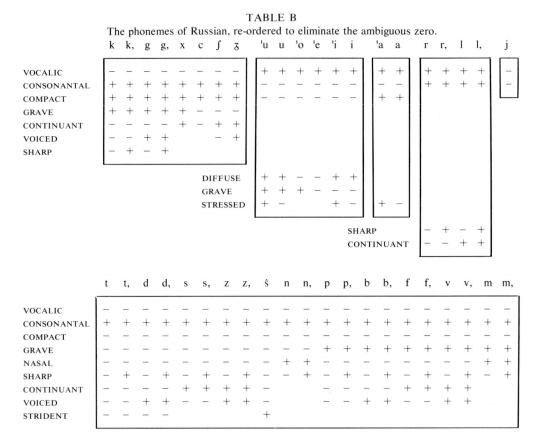

	k	k,	g	g,	x	c	ʃ	ʒ	'u	u	'o	'e	'i	i	'a	a	r	r,	l	l,	j
VOCALIC	−	−	−	−	−	−	−	−	+	+	+	+	+	+	+	+	+	+	+	+	−
CONSONANTAL	+	+	+	+	+	+	+	+	−	−	−	−	−	−	−	−	+	+	+	+	−
COMPACT	+	+	+	+	+	+	+	+	−	−	−	−	−	−	+	+					
GRAVE	+	+	+	+	+	−	−	−													
CONTINUANT	−	−	−	−	+	−	+	+													
VOICED	−	−	+	+			−	+													
SHARP	−	+	−	+																	
DIFFUSE									+	+	−	−	+	+							
GRAVE									+	+	+	−	−	−							
STRESSED									+	−			+	−	+	−					
SHARP																	−	+	−	+	
CONTINUANT																	−	−	+	+	

	t	t,	d	d,	s	s,	z	z,	ŝ	n	n,	p	p,	b	b,	f	f,	v	v,	m	m,
VOCALIC	−	−	−	−	−	−	−	−	−	−	−	−	−	−	−	−	−	−	−	−	−
CONSONANTAL	+	+	+	+	+	+	+	+	+	+	+	+	+	+	+	+	+	+	+	+	+
COMPACT	−	−	−	−	−	−	−	−	−	−	−	−	−	−	−	−	−	−	−	−	−
GRAVE	−	−	−	−	−	−	−	−	−	−	−	+	+	+	+	+	+	+	+	+	+
NASAL	−	−	−	−	−	−	−	−	−	+	+	−	−	−	−	−	−	−	−	+	+
SHARP	−	+	−	+	−	+	−	+	−	−	+	−	+	−	+	−	+	−	+	−	+
CONTINUANT	−	−	−	−	+	+	+	+	−			−	−	−	−	+	+	+	+		
VOICED	−	−	+	+	−	−	+	+	−			−	−	+	+	−	−	+	+		
STRIDENT	−	−	−	−					+												

This requires that a new code book be used for the subsequent questions. These, as we see from Table B, are asked in the order Diffuse? Grave? Stressed? The code books are known a priori and represent, in this case, the independent phoneme structure of Russian; they themselves contain the "information" provided by the zeros in Table A.

This process of recoding may be regarded as a *transformation*. The number of signs (bits) required to identify any phoneme uniquely is now less than before by the number of zeros eliminated from Table A. Although it is different for different phonemes, on the average it is 6.5 bits per phoneme, a value considerably lower than our original 11 and nearer to the ideal value of 5.38. The description in terms of features has thus been made efficient.

4. CONSIDERATIONS OF PHONEME PROBABILITIES

(A) Individual Frequencies of Occurrence   The next step in our description of the language will be to consider the relative frequencies of the individual phonemes. The "information" in bits per phoneme obtained previously has the hypothetical minimum value of 5.38 (log₂ 42), a result obtained by successively subdividing the set of phonemes into two equal groups. When their frequencies of occurrence are unequal, however, the required average (bits per phoneme) is obtained by successively subdividing the set into two groups of equal total probability. The result then is that the average number of questions needed to identify a phoneme (in terms of bits per phoneme) is H_1, where

$$H_1 = -\Sigma\, p_i \log p_i \qquad (1)$$

summed over all phonemes i. This is the "expected" value of $-\log p_i$. (Remember that p_i is always less than 1). The relative frequencies of the individual Russian phonemes have been counted from samples of the language, as described in Section 1; they are listed in Table C. From these frequencies p_i we may readily

TABLE C

a = Phoneme (i); $b = p_i \times 10^4$; $c = -\log_2 p_i$; $d = -p_i \log_2 p_i$;
e = number of features listed in Table B (i means "any given
phoneme"; p_i means "the probability of a given phoneme")

a	b	c	d	e	a	b	c	d	e
a	1316	2.94	.387	4	d	177	5.81	.100	9
i	977	3.35	.328	6	l,	162	5.95	.096	4
t	602	4.05	.244	9	'u	153	5.96	.091	6
'a	539	4.23	.228	4	r,	133	6.20	.083	4
j	457	4.45	.202	2	z	130	6.25	.081	8
n	392	4.66	.183	6	d,	126	6.30	.080	9
'o	379	4.72	.179	5	b	119	6.39	.075	8
s	359	4.80	.172	8	x	102	6.60	.067	5
'e	343	4.86	.167	5	g	91	6.80	.062	7
k	284	5.14	.146	7	v,	89	6.84	.061	8
v	273	5.15	.140	8	ž	89	6.84	.061	6
'i	243	5.38	.131	6	f	85	6.86	.058	8
u	240	5.40	.129	6	s,	85	6.86	.058	8
p	232	5.42	.126	8	š	59	7.40	.044	9
r	230	5.45	.125	4	m,	56	7.50	.043	6
n,	221	5.50	.121	6	b,	52	7.60	.039	8
l	212	5.55	.118	4	p,	50	7.64	.038	8
ʃ	207	5.56	.115	6	k,	36	8.10	.029	7
m	202	5.64	.114	6	z,	21	8.90	.018	8
c	197	5.65	.111	5	f,	8	10.30	.008	8
t,	196	5.65	.111	9	g,	7	10.50	.008	7

calculate the hypothetical "information" H_1 given by (1). This is

$$H_1 = 4.78 \text{ bits/phoneme} \qquad (2)$$

On the other hand we may calculate the average number of features, i.e., the binary choices per phoneme, knowing the probabilities p_i of the individual phonemes. If N_i is the number of features required to identify the ith phoneme in Table B, then the rate of feature choices which actually occurs is

$$\Sigma N_i p_i = 5.79 \text{ features/phoneme} \qquad (3)$$

which may be compared to the ideal given by (2).

In a recent article,[10] Huffman has de-

---

[10]David A. Huffman, "A Method for the Construction of Minimum Redundancy Codes," *Proceedings of the IRE,* 40:9.1098–1101 (1952).

scribed a method for devising the most efficient code possible for a set of independent messages of known frequency distribution. In such a code "the average number of coding digits per message is minimized." If we regard the phonemes of our language as independent messages, we can apply Huffman's method and compute from the probabilities given in Table C the number of digits which in an optimal code would be necessary to identify each phoneme uniquely. This can be compared to the number of features necessary to identify each phoneme in Table B. It must be pointed out, however, that these are not strictly comparable: as we stated in Section 3, the description in terms of distinctive features presupposes that the digits are interpreted differently depending on the answers given in a preceding stage of the analysis, while in Huffman's code all digits have the same interpretation. In the following table we compare the number of phonemes having a given number of digits in the optimal code with the number of phonemes having the same number of distinctive features in Table B.

NUMBER OF DIGITS OR DISTINCTIVE FEATURES	2	3	4	5	6	7	8	9	10
In an optimal code	0	2	2	11	13	8	3	1	2
In the actual case (Table B)	1	0	6	4	10	4	12	5	0

Regarded purely as a descriptive process, then, the method of listing the distinctive features is rather efficient.

So far we have been regarding the phonemes of the language as independent. But the natural process of speech consists not merely of choosing a chain of independent phonemes; at the very least it consists of a succession of choices, where each choice is in part conditioned by the preceding phoneme chosen. It may be a truer description of the natural process of speech to say that phonemes are chosen in groups. Thus, the simple analysis that we have made so far must be regarded as a somewhat artificial though quite efficient description of the language in its simplest aspect.

Before concluding this section on individual phonemes, it may be of interest to note a few statistical facts gathered from Table C.

Probability of a vowel occurring = 0.4190; of a liquid = .0737; of a glide /j/ = 0.0457; of a consonant proper = 0.4616.[11]

In the accompanying table, the plus and minus probabilities of each feature were calculated by adding the probabilities of all phonemes showing a plus for that feature in Table B and of all those showing a minus. Thus the probability of a yes-answer to the question Voiced? is the sum of the probabilities of /g–g,–ʒ–d–d,–z–z,–b–b,–v–v,/, while the probability of a no-answer is the sum of the probabilities of /k–k,–ʃ–t–t,–s–s,–ŝ–p–p,–f–f,/. (We omit the data concerning nasality,

stridency, compactness, and diffuseness; for here the pluses are much fewer than the minuses, and the lower probability of the former is obvious.)

	PROBABILITY OF	
	+	−
Voiced	.1174	.1920
Sharp	.1242	.3445
Stressed (vowels only)	.0935	.2533
Continuant	.1822	.2530
Grave (vowels)	.0772	.1563
Grave (consonants)	.1684	.2861
Totals	.2456	.4424

These figures are significant, especially since the pluses and minuses were assigned without considering their relative frequency, entirely on the basis of an examination of the features and their interrelations.

But the phonemic structure of a language is not defined entirely by the total probabilities of feature occurrence; their distribution in time is also significant. These distributions measure what might be termed the continuity of each feature; they can be obtained from the analysis of joint probabilities presented below. Thus, if we know the probabilities p(a b c ⋯ n) of various chains of n phonemes, we can readily assess the probability that a certain distinctive feature exists uninterrupted for a duration greater than m phonemes, where m = 1, 2, ⋯ n. It is not our purpose here to execute such an analysis in detail, but rather to point out its potentialities as a basis for language description.

(B) Phoneme Groups, Syllables In the preceding section we paid attention mainly to what may be termed phonemic monograms— that is, to individual phonemes, with some reference also to phoneme groups and to their joint probabilities of occurrence. These groups may be digrams, trigrams, and so on. Another type of probability which is of interest to the student of language structure is the *transition probability* that a particular phoneme will follow a given phoneme or phoneme group. Thus, if p(a b ⋯ n) is the probability of the phoneme group (a b ⋯ n), then

$$p(a\ b\ \cdots\ n) = p(a)p_a(bc\ \cdots\ n)$$
$$= p(a)p_a(b)p_{ab}(cd\ \cdots\ n)$$
$$= p(a)p_a(b)p_{ab}(c)p_{abc}(d\ \cdots\ n),\ \text{etc.} \quad (4)$$

[11]Markov, in his study of *letter* distributions in a Russian poem, obtained the value 0.4317 for vowels and 0.5683 for consonants. His figures are remarkably close to ours, especially if we make allowance for the fact that Markov counted some instances of /j/ as vowels and others not at all.

In this way the joint probability of a group is related to the transition probabilities of the successive phonemes a, b, c, etc. occurring in the group.

Given a particular phoneme (a) of a language, or a possible group of phonemes (ab $\cdots$ n), the phonemes (m) which can occur next in the chain have a set of probabilities $p_{ab...n}(m)$. The fact that these probabilities vary according to the character of m implies that a certain degree of prediction is possible. This property provides another form of "redundancy" in the language, a quality which is of great importance in aural recognition, as when we follow a conversation in a noisy room.

For instance, if one hears a palatalized /v,/ in a Russian utterance, one can be sure that no unstressed vowel except /i/ will follow. After a palatalized /b,/, the probability of an unstressed /a/ is extremely low; the sequence /b,a/, as in /g'olub,a/ 'pigeon' (gen.-acc. sing.) and /gal'ub,a/ 'fondling', is exceptional. In our count we have found the following phonemes after palatalized /s,/, with the indicated frequencies:

i	33	'a	6	u	1
'e	16	m	2	j	1
'o	9	'u	1	a	1
'i	8				

Note especially the almost complete absence of consonants and the very low frequency of unaccented /a/. On the other hand, after non-palatalized /s/ the unaccented /a/ was the most frequent of all the vowels in our material, and consonants occurred very freely. Our figures for phonemes after /s/ are these:

t	76	p	9	k,	3
a	37	u	6	j	2
t,	30	v	6	'i	1
k	27	i	5	m,	1
l	20	m	5	r	1
'a	16	n,	5	'u	1
'o	11	p	5	v,	1
l,	10	x	3	r,	1
n	10				

Since the inequality of the transition probabilities makes possible a certain degree of prediction, the information conveyed by one phoneme in the chain of connected speech is less than that conveyed by one phoneme in isolation. Unless it is the first in the chain, we know something about it, so to speak, before it arrives. This information can be strictly defined, in the technical sense of the earlier sections; we can even derive formulae, analogous to equation (1), which will be applicable to connected groups of phonemes. Suppose, for example, that we have computed the probabilities p(ab) of all the phoneme digrams of a language; then the information conveyed by any digram of the language is, on the average, $H_{1,2}$:

$$H_{1,2} = -\Sigma p(ab) \log p(ab) \text{ bits/digram} \qquad (5)$$

Similarly for trigrams:

$$H_{1,2,3} = -\Sigma p(abc) \log p(abc) \text{ bits/trigram} \qquad (6)$$

But if, instead, we have computed the various transition probabilities $p_a(b)$, the information conveyed by the occurrence of each successive phoneme is $H_1(2)$:

$$H_1(2) = -\Sigma p(ab) \log p_a(b) \qquad (7)$$

Again, if we know the transition probabilities $p_{ab}(c)$:

$$H_{1,2}(3) = -\Sigma p(abc) \log p_{a,b}(c) \qquad (8)$$

Clearly these various information rates, based on different probability tables, are connected. To show this, consider equation (4); take logs of both sides and then average over all possible groups (ab $\cdots$ n):

$$-\Sigma p(ab \cdots n) \log p(ab \cdots n) =$$
$$-\Sigma p(ab \cdots n) [\log p(a) + \log p_a(b) + \log p_{ab}(c) \cdots] \text{ or}$$
$$H_n = H_1 + H_1(2) + H_{1,2}(3)$$
$$+ H_{1,2,3}(4) \cdots \text{bits/n-gram} \qquad (9)$$

This means that the information conveyed by groups of phonemes is, on the average, equal to the sum of the information obtained from each successive phoneme.

We have computed the values for the digrams and trigrams in our material according to the first count—the one that takes account of the boundaries between words and between the parts of compounds. The values were found to be 8.45 bits/digram and 9.15 bits/trigram. If the phonemes were independent, the corresponding values would be 9.54 bits/digram and 14.31 bits/trigram. As expected, the values are lower when the units in the chain are not regarded as independent.

Another very promising approach, which for the present must remain unexplored, is to calculate the distributions of the distinctive features in time, as already proposed in Section 4(a). Given a long sample of text transcribed phonemically, we write under each symbol a column of pluses, minuses, and zeros representing its distinctive features in some regular order (as in Table A). The horizontal sequences of pluses, minuses, and zeros produced in this way can then be used to measure the "continuity" of the various features. The probabilities of such sequences may be written $p_{+}(m)$, $p_{-}(m)$, $p_0(m)$, where m = 1, 2, 3, etc. It is obvious that such distributions may provide a basis for the statistical specification of the phonemic differences between one language and another.

The statistical analysis of the phonemes and their sequences in connected messages must be supplemented by a similar analysis of the dictionary, in order to understand the distribution of phonemes in the lexical code of the given language.[12] The comparison of the two sets of data is certain to be most instructive. The statistical analysis of the dictionary permits us to draw conclusions about the phoneme sequences peculiar to different types of morphemes and to words of different grammatical categories.[13] Furthermore, it forms the basis for definitive statements about phoneme combinations with probabilities of 1 and 0; for no phoneme sequence can occur in messages if it is not provided by the code.

Finally, among the problems which remain to be investigated are those transitional probabilities which operate backwards, i.e., which depend not on earlier but on subsequent events, or, in linguistic terms, not on the progressive but on the regressive action of phonemes in a sequence. The comparison of these two sets of statistics is very important, because it is obvious that for different types of sequences the predictability is greater in one direction than in the other. Analysis of such data will provide the most solid basis for setting up a statistical model of the syllable as a recurrent link in the chain of speech.

---

[12]In R. Carnap's terminology, the occurrences of phonemes, having been studied in the Russian word-*events*, are to be investigated in the word-*designs*, just as we have here studied the occurrences of distinctive features in the phoneme-*designs*; cf. *Introduction to Semantics*, 3 (Cambridge, Mass., 1946). Charles S. Peirce, the founder of modern semiotics would say that besides the application of the phonemic *legisigns* within the lexical *sinsigns*, such an application must be scrutinized again within lexical *legisigns;* cf. his *Collected Papers*, 2.245– 247 (Cambridge, Mass., 1932).

[13]An exhaustive statistical analysis of the phonemic structure of Russian root morphemes has been prepared by Robert Abernathy within the framework of the research program mentioned in footnote 2.

Written jointly in Cambridge, Mass., 1952; published in *Language* 29 (1953).

32

THE STRATEGY OF PHONEMICS*
MORRIS HALLE**

I. INTRODUCTION.
DISCRETE OR CONTINUOUS?

From the time of the invention of alphabetic writing until the end of the nineteenth century, students of language accepted without question the view that speech consisted of sequences of discrete sounds which are tokens of a small number of basic types. It was generally held that we speak in a manner quite similar to the way in which we write, and the idea that there might not be any simple, one-to-one correspondence between letters and sounds did not seem as obvious to an earlier generation as it does to us. The learned Baron van Helmont even believed that the Hebrew letters represented the position of the tongue during the production of the corresponding sounds and to illustrate this, published a set of completely imaginary articulation profiles which have a somewhat gruesome quality about them.[1]

The achievements of the natural sciences in the last century permitted as well as forced students of language to make much more detailed observations of the speaking process, with the result that grave doubts were cast on the validity of practically all the standard notions firmly held by preceding generations. Speech was shown to be not a sequence of clearly separated, discrete events, but rather a continuous flow of sound, an unbroken chain of movements.[2]

Although the view of language as a continuous phenomenon is simple and straightforward from a strictly physical standpoint, it has certain inherent difficulties which make it undesirable as a basis for descriptions, and investigators of language, phoneticians as well as physicists, have usually preferred to describe language as a sequence of discrete events.[3]

Furthermore it is not necessary that a physical phenomenon be actually discontinuous in order to break it up into a sequence of discrete events. It is possible to divide it into segments if we can show exactly how it is to be done. We shall later state some of the conditions as they apply to speech (see Chapter II). At this point in the argument it is only necessary for us to establish the possibility of segmenting into discrete events the continuous acoustical phenomenon that is speech. A person taking dictation is performing just such an operation. His eardrums receive the continuous acoustical wave, his hand writes (types, if you will) sequences of discrete symbols, the letters. The acoustical wave, therefore, must contain clues which enable human beings to perform this operation. If we could state what these clues are, we could presumably build a machine to perform the same operation. In sum, both the continuous and the discrete representation of speech can—at least in principle—be achieved by a set of

[1]Cf. reproduction of one of his figures in H. Dudley and T. Tarnoczy, "The Speaking Machine of Wolfgang von Kempelen," *Journal of the Acoustical Society of America* 22.151–167 (1950).

[2]P. Menzerath and A. de Lacerda, *Koartikulation, Steuerung und Lautabgrenzung* (Berlin-Bonn, 1933).

[3]The major exception is the work of some communications engineers on long time spectra of speech; e.g., H. K. Dunn and S. D. White, "Statistical Measurements on Conversational Speech," *Journal of the Acoustical Society of America* 11.278–288 (1939), and L. G. Kraft, "Correlation Function Analysis," *ibid.*, 22.762–764 (1950).

*Reprinted from *Word* 10.197–209 (1954) by permission.
**I wish to acknowledge my indebtedness to those of my colleagues and students who have served as none too passive guinea pigs on whom the ideas expressed in this essay were tested at various stages of maturation. In particular I want to thank Roman Jakobson, whose influence ought to be apparent on every page, and Noam Chomsky, whose illuminating and penetrating discussions of many problems have greatly influenced my views. This work was supported in part by the Signal Corps, the Air Materiel Command, and the Office of Naval Research.

physical operations. We can, therefore, assert that both views are meaningful in an empirical, physical sense.[4]

It is now necessary for us to show why the discrete picture of language is preferable. Our answer is that it enables us to account for many facts which on the assumption of continuity would be extremely difficult, if not impossible, to explain. The grossest of these is the well-known fact that speech is perfectly intelligible in the presence of very great disturbances. We shall call this property of speech "resistance to noise."

In a recent paper B. Mandelbrot[5] has shown that it is impossible to account for the high resistance to noise of speech on the basis of a continuous view. If linguistic messages (utterances) be thought of as continuous, the correction of errors in the reception cannot begin until the entire message is received, which would make correction well nigh impossible, certainly infinitely more difficult than it actually is. On the other hand, if a discrete view be adopted, correction of errors can begin upon receipt of each discrete unit (quantum), since the discrete units in the language are just a small fraction of all possible things that the ear can receive.

Mandelbrot investigated in detail the consequences of the discrete character of language only on one level, that of words. The necessity for discrete units on other levels is implicit in his argument. The words themselves are thus viewed as being composed of discrete components, usually known as *morphemes,* which in turn consist of other discrete units, the *phonemes.*

The reasons for our using the phoneme as the smallest quantum of language in preference to other units that have been suggested, as, e.g., the syllable, are as follows:

(1) Since the larger units (words, morphemes, syllables) can usually be subdivided into phonemes, it follows that the number of different phonemes necessary for describing a given set of messages will be smaller than that of the larger units.

(2) The phonemes are extremely useful (if not the only possible) units when it is necessary to describe other facts of languages, such as rules of grammar, regularities of linguistic change, development of language in children, pathological manifestations of language, poetic devices such as rime, assonance, etc. One can easily convince oneself of this by trying to state such a simple grammatical rule as the distribution of the English past tense suffixes /-d/, /-ɪd/ or /-t/ in terms of syllables or words.

We want to insist on this point in particular. To us the major criterion for the applicability of a certain category to linguistic description is whether or not this category yields simple statements not only on the particular level for which it was introduced, but on all levels which are pertinent to descriptions of a language. It always must satisfy a multiplicity of criteria.

We have chosen to represent language as a sequence of discrete events and thereby to complicate our description on the physical level, because the physically simpler, continuous view would have made impossible other statements about language which we would like to make; e.g., to give a simple description of grammar. The nonlinguist need not follow us there, and as a matter of fact a high-fidelity recording of human speech involves neither phonemes nor words nor any other linguistic quantization.

In sum, then, the traditional view of language as a sequence of discrete events of phoneme length is empirically meaningful and has certain clear advantages not only over the purely physical view of language as consisting of utterances which themselves are continuous, but also over other proposed schemes of quantization (syllable, for instance).

II. THE PHONEME

It is now necessary to sketch a procedure whereby we would be guaranteed to arrive at answers to two questions: (1) How many phonemes does our language possess? (2) What acoustical properties are used for the identification of the phonemes?

Since in our view the most important property of language is that it serves as an

---

[4]"A term (predicate) is a legitimate scientific term (has cognitive content, is empirically meaningful) if and only if a sentence applying the term to a given instance can possibly be confirmed to at least some degree." R. Carnap, "Truth and Confirmation," in H. Feigl and W. Sellars, *Readings in Philosophical Analysis* (New York, 1949), p. 123.

[5]B. Mandelbrot, "Structure formelle des langues et communication," *Word* 10.1–27 (1954).

artifact for the transmission of information, it is evident that we must be able to record those features of the speech wave which by themselves serve to convey information. It is to be stressed that "information" is used here in its technical meaning, which involves a selection of one from an ensemble of possible messages. In other words, we must be able to detect those properties of the speech wave which enable us to tell that a particular utterance is *bill* and not *pill* or *dill* or *gill,* etc.[6] We have placed ourselves hereby in the position of the receiver, and our description is to be made primarily from the receiver's point of view.[7]

In the preceding paragraph we have spoken of "an ensemble of *possible* messages." This means that we must be prepared to deal only with those sound sequences which are possible in our language, and not with all sounds that man might emit; i.e., we need to establish the conditions sufficient for decoding the messages which we might receive, for speakers of a language are in the position of people who communicate by means of a common code. The linguist's role is in part similar to that of the cryptanalyst who must describe the code from observations made on both the messages and the behavior of the users of the code (not excluding his own).[8]

Since, if taken as physical events pure and simple, no two utterances are alike, the decision of whether two utterances are the same or different can only be made on another level, namely, by observing the behavior of the users of the code, including their verbal behavior. It has been shown by Harris[9] that this decision

can be established without recourse to "meaning" or "difference of meaning." Two utterances as spoken by the same informant are recorded on tape and a test tape is prepared by re-recording the original two utterances in a random order. The test tape may thus contain fifty or sixty re-recordings of the original utterances. The two original utterances are played to an audience of native speakers who are instructed to make a check on their ballots (or signify in some other manner) whenever they hear the first utterance during the playing of the test tape. If the utterances are "different," i.e., phonemically distinct, the audience will obtain an almost perfect score; if the utterances are homophonous the score will be in the vicinity of 50 percent. Since all linguistic descriptions are based on analyses of a finite number of utterances, it is possible, at least in principle, to subject the entire corpus to this test. This is, however, not necessary since shortcuts can be easily devised and justified. A particular advantage of this method is the neat solution which it provides for the difficulties connected with phonemically distinct utterances having the same meaning, like /ekən'amɪks/ and /ikən'amɪks/.

Having thus established *sameness* and *difference* among the utterances in his corpus, the linguist must next outline a procedure for the identification of the elementary discrete units that compose the utterances; i.e., of the phonemes.

In the past, the problem of identification has been approached essentially from two directions. The first approach is formulated in Potter and Steinberg's article, "Toward the Specification of Speech": "If different speakers are asked to speak one of the vowels, the utterances will, of course, be different. *The problem is to determine those physical properties that are invariant in the several utterances that enable the ear to identify them as a given vowel.*"[10] In other words, these investigators assume that from a study of the physical

---

[6]Cf. F. de Saussure, *Cours de linguistique générale* (Paris, 1949), p. 163: "Ce qui importe dans le mot, ce n'est pas le son lui-même, mais les différences phoniques qui permettent de distinguer ce mot de tous les autres, car ce sont elles qui portent la signification."

[7]For a detailed discussion of this point see B. Mandelbrot, *op. cit.*

[8]Whether the linguist can "break the code," just by investigating records without recourse to observations of the speakers' behavior, has been the subject of spirited debate. While I doubt the possibility I do not take a definite position in this matter.

[9]Z. S. Harris, *Methods in Structural Linguistics* (Chicago, 1951), pp. 32 ff. It is to be noted here that in Harris' presentation recourse is had to meaning

in the instructions given the original speaker, where the two utterances are identified "by translation or otherwise." On the relation between meaning and translation cf. R. Jakobson, *Sound and Meaning* (in preparation).

[10]*Journal of the Acoustical Society of America* 22.807 (1950).

characteristics of a great number of utterances of a given vowel they will be able to isolate the invariant properties which presumably serve the human being as cues for the correct identification. The attention is focused here on the properties which all repetitions of a given phoneme have in common, a sort of common denominator.

The second approach to the problem of identification was already foreshadowed in the quotation from de Saussure (footnote 6); we can add another which reads: "Or ce qui les [the phonemes] caractérise, ce n'est pas, comme on pourrait le croire, leur qualité propre et positive, mais simplement le fait qu'ils ne se confondent pas entre eux." Primary attention is here directed not to the properties which all repetitions of a given phoneme may possess in common, but rather to the properties which differentiate each repetition of a given phoneme from all other possible phonemes which might have been uttered in its stead; i.e., the focus is on the distinctive differences instead of the similarities. Focusing on the distinctive difference presupposes, of course, a knowledge of all the possible judgments which one might be expected to make; it presupposes a knowledge not only of the phoneme under investigation but also of all the phonemes in the language.

The two approaches might be illustrated by the following analogy: It is necessary to find a car in a parking lot. If it is not known what other cars are in the parking lot, then the only sufficient way to specify the wanted car is by giving its total description: make, year, model, color, and such other distinguishing characteristics as bumps, scratches and broken windshield. If on the other hand, it were known that the wanted car is the only red car in the parking lot it would be sufficient to specify this one distinctive property in order to find the wanted car. It is, of course, true that the first specification is sufficient in all cases—however, under the given conditions the second method is doubtless the more economical. In the case of language it is evident that the second method, i.e., concentration upon distinctive differences rather than upon common properties, is a more reasonable approach.

One technique for establishing the number and properties of the phonemes of a language consists in arranging the utterances in *minimally different sets*. These are sets of different utterances (preferably of short words) which differ from one another by only one phoneme but are alike in every other respect; for example, sets like:

(a) *bin, pin, kin, Lynn, tin, din, sin, thin, fin,* etc.
(b) *bin, bean, boon, bun, ban, Ben,* etc.
(c) *bin, bit, big, bill, bib, bid, bing,* etc.

It may be objected that the ability to make such an arrangement necessarily presupposes a knowledge of the solution: one cannot arrange utterances in sets in which each member differs from all others by one phoneme without first knowing the phonemes.

The objection overlooks one other way in which this particular arrangement might be arrived at, namely, by an exhaustive examination of all possible arrangements. Since the number of utterances on which our analysis is based is finite, there is also a finite number of ways in which these can be arranged; i.e., in a finite time we could generate all possible arrangements. If we now possessed criteria for determining which arrangement actually consists of minimally different sets, we might conceivably check through all possible arrangements with the guarantee that in a finite time we should end up with the desired arrangement.

As a matter of fact we possess such criteria (see the following discussion), and it is by means of these criteria that we establish the minimally different sets. The procedure is as follows: each arrangement is provisionally assumed to contain nothing but minimally different sets; i.e., all words in it are assumed to differ from one another by one phoneme only and to be alike in every other respect. In the overwhelming majority of cases the incompatibility of this assumption with the requirements for simple solutions are immediately obvious. Thus, for example, we never consider minimally distinct, sets like *bee, antidisestablishmentarianism,* and *psychic,* for it is immediately apparent that no conceivable manner of segmentation of these words will yield units which even remotely resemble phonemes. (Cf. requirements of physical uniformity stated below.) In more difficult cases, as, e.g., whether

the affricate [tʃ] as in *chew* should be considered as one or two phonemes (or in our
terminology, whether *chew* belongs in the set
shoe, sue, too, do, etc., or both in the set *true,
tew,* and in the one-member set *chew*), both
assumptions are actually tested and the interpretation yielding the simpler over-all description is chosen.[11]

The criteria which phonemes have to meet
are the following:[12]

(*1*)   They must be of relatively simple physical
structure: within a phoneme segment
there cannot be (a) turning on and off of
the exciting source or sources; (b) a
switching on and off of the nasal resonances; (c) sudden severe drops in over-all
level; (d) certain changes in the formant
positions; (e) sharp changes in the band-
widths of the formants (exact specifications have still to be given here).

(*2*)   The segments considered different must
be replaceable in the members of the set
without destruction of intelligibility; i.e.,
by careful cutting and splicing it must be
possible to transform minimally different utterances like *bill* and *mill* into each
other, as has been done by P. Menzerath,[13]
Carol Schatz[14] and others.

(*3*)   There must be as many phoneme intervals
in each utterance as will enable us to distinguish each utterance from each other

utterance which is not a repetition of the
former, and no more.[15]

(*4*)   The identification in terms of the distinctive features (see below) must be possible
and show no inconsistencies.

It is to be noted that in the above specifications there are involved both physical and
distributional properties. In recent years the
former have tended to be under-emphasized
with the result that phonemic solutions often
have had a very artificial appearance.

By application of criteria 1, 2, and 4,
above, we establish where the phoneme boundaries approximately lie. However, we have not
as yet identified a single phoneme.

III. DISTINCTIVE FEATURES

It has already been stated that the method
of identification to be adopted here will concentrate on the differences existing between
the phonemes, and not upon the properties
common to all utterances of a given phoneme.
Our first step is to characterize the differences between the members of a minimally
different set: we intend to state how *bin* differs
from *pin,* from *tin,* from *din,* etc.

Given *n* entities there may be as many as
$n(n - 1)/2$ differences between them. This
would be the case if none of them had any
properties in common: e.g., if we assumed that
the following eight phonemes /p/, /t/, /f/, /s/,
/b/, /d/, /v/, /z/ had no properties in common,
then in order to characterize each one of them
by the method of differences adopted here, we
would need a total of $8 \times 7/2 = 28$ statements.
We would have to be prepared to answer
questions of the form "Is the phoneme under
consideration /p/ or /t/, /p/ or /b/, etc.?" Once
we have discovered, however, that some of the
phonemes possess common properties which
others lack, we can pose much more "perceptive questions"; e.g., "Is the phoneme under
consideration voiced? continuant?"

Since to each of the questions two answers (yes or no) are possible, we can identify
by means of three questions eight different
entities corresponding to the eight phonemes

---

[11]The necessity of setting up a special set containing just the phoneme in question (since stops
cannot precede fricatives in English unless the affricate be considered a cluster) would incline us towards a monophonematic interpretation. Further
complications which arise in other parts of the description would cause us to prefer this interpretation
even more.

[12]The first two requirements are of a physical
nature and are introduced specifically to account for
two facts: (a) that a fairly rough segmentation, the
so-called phonetic transcription, can be made just
by listening to samples of the language, and (b) the
remarkable agreement of various phoneticians on
how to segment a sequence. On this point see the
discussion in K. L. Pike, *Phonetics* (Ann Arbor,
1943), pp. 42–55.

[13]"Neue Untersuchungen zur Lautabgrenzung
und Wortsynthese mit Hilfe von Tonfilmaufnahmen," *Mélanges de linguistique et de philologie
offerts à Jacques van Ginneken* (Paris, 1937), pp.
35–41.

[14]Verbal communication.

[15]This is a slightly paraphrased version of a
statement by Z. S. Harris, *op. cit.,* p. 43. On homo-
phones see *ibid.,* pp. 32 ff.

of our sample. Add a ninth phoneme to our example—/t͡s/, for instance—and the three questions no longer suffice. We now have a choice to complicate our description in one of two ways, either by admitting more than two answers to some or all of our questions (e.g., instead of asking "continuant? yes? or no?" we may now pose the question in the form "continuant? stop? or something in between?" thereby accepting three answers) or by increasing the number of questions (e.g., by introducing an additional "yes or no" question, like "Is it strident?"). We shall refer to the first method as an increase in the *accuracy of measurement;* we shall refer to the second method as an increase in the *dimensionality of measurement.*

In conformity with our requirement that our terms be empirically meaningful, the "questions" in the preceding paragraph are of a kind to which answers can be provided by physical measurement; i.e., they are questions regarding the presence of certain definite physical properties. Thus if we ask whether a certain phoneme is voiced we have in mind definite acoustical measurement procedures to determine it.[16]

It is to be noted that the number of questions is considerably smaller than the number of phonemes. The minimum number of "yes or no" questions necessary to identify n phonemes is $\log_2 n$. In the language of communications engineering such a description would be said to possess minimal redundancy.[17] In a natural language we should not expect minimal redundancy, for redundancy is one of the factors that makes language resistant to noise. On the other hand, we would expect natural languages not to have excessive redundancy, for a very redundant language is an inefficient language.

The physical properties whose discovery is the purpose of the "questions" of the preceding paragraphs have received a detailed discussion in another place.[18] They are referred to there by the term *distinctive features,* which will also be used in the remaining part of this essay.

It may justifiably be asked: "How does the linguist know what 'questions' to pose?" The answer is much like the one we gave when we discussed the establishment of phoneme boundaries. As yet, we have no procedure for arriving at the correct set of "questions"; we can only guess. We do, however, possess a method for checking whether or not any proposed set fits our requirements for a simple description of language on all levels.

Many distinctive features, though under different names, have long been used in phonetics. They are implicit in the work of the Hindu grammarians as well as in the works of Western phoneticians. In spite of their apparently independent development these two major traditions show certain striking similarities. Both traditions agree in assigning great importance to the "point" of articulation, the place in the vocal tract where the stricture is narrowest. They also agree to some extent in their treatment of the "manner" of articulation and of nasality. There is, however, one striking difference between the two traditions. The Hindus used the "point" of articulation for the classification of both the vowels and the consonants, while in the West the vowels were classified according to the so-called "vowel triangle" (a two-dimensional classification).

Thus the picture which the classification of the sounds presented was a mixed one: most features were two-valued (for example, sounds were said to be either nasal or nonnasal; voiced or unvoiced; aspirated or unaspirated, etc.); a few others were multivalued. Further complications were introduced in the course of the nineteenth and twentieth centuries when it was discovered that sounds which had been thought to differ only in their manner of articulation differed also in their place of articulation. There were even suggestions in the literature to make the place of articulation the primary variable and to consider the other features as redundant. This led,

---

[16]For details of the acoustical measurement procedures see M. Halle and L. G. Jones, *The Russian Phonemes* (in preparation). [See now M. Halle, *The Sound Pattern of Russian* (1959)—VBM.]

[17]On the concept of redundancy see C. Shannon and W. Weaver, *The Mathematical Theory of Communication* (Urbana, 1949), and R. Jakobson, C. G. M. Fant, and M. Halle, *Preliminaries to Speech Analysis,* Technical Report No. 13, Acoustics Laboratory, M.I.T., May 1952, pp. 4–8.

[18]R. Jakobson, C. G. M. Fant, and M. Halle, *loc. cit.*

however, to complications, once it was actually put into practice. For example, in French it may be said that the difference between /g/ and /ɲ/ lies in their different points of articulation: /g/ is velar and /ɲ/ prepalatal. It was thought that by this increase in the number of points of articulation, the introduction of an additional dimension, i.e., nasality, would be avoided. French also possesses the phonemes /b/ and /m/, which have identical points of articulation. The dimension of nasality, therefore, must be introduced anyway to distinguish between /b/ and /m/ and might as well be used in the case of /g/ and /ɲ/, for it is patently uneconomical to describe the labial consonants differently from the velars, especially if it is possible to avoid this.

These difficulties were resolved by Roman Jakobson.[19] In making descriptions one usually has the choice between using few dimensions with many significant values and using many dimensions with few significant values. In other words one can trade accuracy of measurement for dimensionality. Reduced to its simplest terms, Jakobson's fundamental argument was that the most satisfactory description of a language would be obtained by using as many dimensions (features) as necessary, but decreasing the accuracy of measurement, i.e., the number of significant decisions which have to be made with regard to each dimension. The dichotomous scale, which underlies the distinctive features, has minimal accuracy of measurement: it is in this sense that it is the simplest possible.[20]

Jakobson suggested that the consonants be subdivided into "strident" vs. "mellow." He thus obtained a fourfold division of consonants where formerly there was only a two-fold one: the stops and the continuants were each subdivided into strident and mellow. The increase in dimensionality brought with it a corresponding decrease in the number of "significant" points of articulation. (As a matter of fact it was shown that four such points sufficed for all languages.)

Then, as if taking his cue from the old Hindu grammarians but turning them upside down, Jakobson ordered both vowels and consonants according to a single principle, which, in conformity with his fundamental demand for a substitution of dimensionality for accuracy, he found in the two-dimensional vowel triangle rather than in the one-dimensional, multivalued "points of articulation" parameter.[21]

Finally Jakobson demanded an acoustical classification of the sounds of speech. *Preliminaries* is a step in the implementation of this program, for there the attempt is made to state all the dimensions of phonetic descriptions in terms of acoustical as well as articulatory criteria.

Traditional phonetics was primarily an articulatory phonetics. From time to time attempts were made to translate the articulatory terms into acoustical. Since results were not always convincing, doubts were voiced as to whether this could be done at all.[22] There are two arguments in favor of the possibility of translating into acoustical terms uniformities which have been observed most clearly and first on the articulatory level. The first argument is quite simple: given a certain geometrical configuration and excitation of a resonator, its acoustical output is entirely predictable. Hence, all other things being equal, any uniformity on the articulatory side *must* have a statable acoustical counterpart. The second argument appeals to the fact that the phoneticians who picked a particular articulatory uniformity as a distinctive feature over a whole series of others which they might have chosen were guided by the observation that these functioned as perceptually distinctive marks, and hence must also have existence on the acoustical level.

The distinctive features in the formulation which is given in *Preliminaries* are, with one

---

[19]R. Jakobson, "Observations sur le classement phonologique des consonnes" [28], *Proceedings of the Third International Congress of Phonetic Sciences* (Ghent, 1939), pp. 34–41, and *Kindersprache, Aphasie und allgemeine Lautgesetze, Språkvetenskapliga sällskapets i Uppsala förhandligar* (1940–1942).

[20]I. Pollack's recent work in *Journal of the Acoustical Society of America* 25 (1953) and 26 (1954) (see footnote 24 below) provides interesting evidence relevant to this problem.

[21]For details see *Preliminaries* and R. Jakobson's forthcoming *Sound and Meaning.*

[22]Cf. E. Fischer-Jørgensen, "The Phonetic Basis for Identification of Phonemic Elements," *Journal of the Acoustical Society of America* 24. 614–615 (1952).

exception, binary in structure. This is to be understood as an empirical proposition: If the differentiating phonemes in a minimally different set were to be measured for a certain distinctive feature (e.g., degree of voicing), the results would cluster about two values: one for the voiced and the other for the unvoiced consonants. E. Zwirner's experiments with German vowels[23] do not constitute a counter-example that proves the incorrectness of the hypothesis of binarity, because Zwirner did not compare vowels in identical context only (he plotted all vowels in his sample on a single graph) and the above proposition applies only to minimally different sets, i.e., to contexts identical by definition.

The success of the distinctive features as a framework for linguistic descriptions in terms of which a host of difficult linguistic problems can be readily explained is the major reason for their adoption. Recent work in psycho-acoustics has provided further support for the distinctive feature model. Studies by Pollack and others on the transmission of information by multidimensional auditory stimuli show that best results "are obtained when each dimension [is] crudely subdivided into two alternative states. Finer subdivision of each dimension does not produce a proportional gain in information transmission with the display."[24] It is only reasonable to assume that natural languages are constructed in a way fairly closely approximating optimal conditions for auditory transmission of information among human beings.

To justify still further the use of the distinctive features as descriptive parameters we have given in *Preliminaries* under the subheading "Occurrence" examples from the most diverse languages in which the distinctive features provide a convenient framework for the expression of observations which otherwise would require much more complicated statements.

Finally comparisons have been made between the economy of a code utilizing the distinctive features and that of a theoretical code having minimal redundancy. The distinctive-feature code is, as expected, somewhat lower in economy than the optimal code, but not very far below it.[25]

IV. PROCEDURE OF ANALYSIS

The procedure of analysis by means of the distinctive features is as follows: The segments which were established as signalizing phonemic differences are subjected to an analysis in terms of the entire list of distinctive features. We obtain answers to questions such as: "Is the segment under consideration voiced? Is it a continuant? Is it fortis (aspirated)? . . . ." through the entire list of features. Each segment in each of the words in our catalogue is so characterized. Segments which have the same answers are said to be the same phoneme[26] and are symbolized by the same letter.

In the course of this analysis it will turn out that certain questions are not necessary for identification: i.e., in the language under consideration there will be no pair of words which are distinguished by the differences which the given question has in view. Thus, for example, we shall find that in the set *bin, pin, din, tin,* etc., all voiceless stops are fortis (aspirated), while in the set *spin, skin,* etc., none of the voiceless stops is aspirated. Since this difference is associated with different contexts it is not a primary but a redundant difference and can, therefore, be disregarded (at least as far as stops are concerned) for the present purpose, which is to establish the minimal conditions for identification.

On the other hand, if in a given minimally different set a certain distinction is not represented, it cannot be disregarded if it functions distinctively in another context: e.g., in English there is no *stin* opposed to *spin* although

[23]E. Zwirner, "Phonologische und phonometrische Probleme der Quantität," *Proceedings of the Third International Congress of Phonetic Sciences* (Ghent, 1939), pp. 57–66.

[24]I. Pollack and H. Ficks, "The Information of Elementary Multidimensional Auditory Displays," *Program of Meeting of the Acoustical Society of America, B, 2,* May 7–9, 1953, Philadelphia. This paper has now been published in full in *Journal of the Acoustical Society of America* 26.155–158 (1954).

[25]Cf. E. C. Cherry, M. Halle, and R. Jakobson, "Toward the Logical Description of Languages in Their Phonemic Aspect" [31], *Language* 29.41 [328] (1953).

[26]This constitutes a definition of "phonetic similarity."

the difference between /p/ and /t/ functions in many other contexts, and hence a statement about the quality of gravity (distinctive feature characterizing the difference between /p/ and /t/) must be made.[27]

The method of minimally different sets avoids the difficulties connected with allophones and eliminates the need for reference to "phonetic identity" as was already pointed out in 1935 by Twaddell.[28] Since the members of minimally different sets are by definition identical contexts, we are always comparing things which are otherwise the same, and the question of identifying phonemes purely by complementary distribution is entirely eliminated. The much discussed problem of whether we should consider the English [h] and [ŋ] as one or two phonemes does not arise at all, because the answers from analyzing *hill* in a minimally different set like *hill, pill, till, bill*, etc., differ completely from those obtained by analyzing *sing*, in a set like *sing, sin, sick, sit*, etc.

V. IDENTIFICATION OF PHONEMES

The analysis just described permits us to establish the inventory of the phonemes of the language. We can write our results in the form of a matrix in which each phoneme is given with the distinctive features which are necessary for its identification.

The identification of phonemes can then be thought to proceed as follows:

(*1*) The speech is segmented according to principles outlined above.

(*2*) Each segment is analysed in terms of distinctive features. In order to establish the correct answer it may often be necessary to refer to adjacent segments.

(*3*) Each segment is identified by reference to the matrix (see table) with the following instructions: If the analyzer output for any given feature is positive, disregard all phonemes which in the matrix are marked negative for that feature. If the analyzer output is negative for any given feature, disregard all phonemes which are marked positive for that feature. Do nothing about phonemes for which the particular feature is not distinctive (i.e., which have noughts in the table).[29] At the end of such an analysis there will be only one phoneme which has not been excluded from consideration —it is the phoneme under analysis.

VI. CONCLUSION: FUNDAMENTAL PROPERTIES OF NATURAL LANGUAGES

The model of language which has been presented here has the following properties:

(*1*) Language consists of discrete units of short duration which meet certain physical requirements (the phonemes).

(*2*) In their function as signaling devices the phonemes can be viewed as simultaneous implementations of a number of attributes —the distinctive features.

(*3*) The distinctive features are, with a single exception, binary.

(*4*) No language utilizes all the distinctive features.

(*5*) No language has as many phonemes as there are possible combinations of the utilized distinctive features.

---

[27]In cases where a feature is neutralized in a certain context, as, e.g., in English in the above example, the question arises: To which phoneme, /p/ or /t/, is the above consonant to be assigned? I believe that this is to be decided by physical measurement.

[28]W. F. Twaddell, *On Defining the Phoneme*, Language Monograph No. 16 (1935). See also R. Jakobson, "On the Identification of Phonemic Entities" [30], *Travaux du Cercle Linguistique de Copenhague* 5.205–213 (1949).

[29]This provision does two things: it establishes the status of the noughts in our matrix tables and makes allowance for what is known as "free variation," where a feature, being nondistinctive, may or may not be present in various utterances of a given phoneme, e.g., nasality in vowels in Midwestern dialects of American English.

TABLE I

Matrix Showing the Phonemes and the Distinctive Features of Standard Literary German

	m	p	b	f	v	f̂	n	t	d	s	z	ŝ	k	g	x	ʃ	r	l	u	o	a	ü	ö	i	e	æ	h
Vocalic vs. non-vocalic	−	−	−	−	−	−	−	−	−	−	−	−	−	−	−	−	+	+	+	+	+	+	+	+	+	+	−
Consonantal vs. non-consonantal	+	+	+	+	+	+	+	+	+	+	+	+	+	+	+	+	+	+	−	−	−	−	−	−	−	−	−
Compact vs. diffuse	0	−	−	−	−	−	0	−	−	−	−	−	+	+	+	+	0	0	−	±	+	−	±	−	±	+	0
Grave vs. acute	+	+	+	+	+	+	−	−	−	−	−	−	+	+	+	−	0	0	+	+	+	−	−	−	−	−	0
Flat vs. plain	0	0	0	0	0	0	0	0	0	0	0	0	0	0	0	0	0	0	+	+	0	+	+	−	−	0	0
Nasal vs. non-nasal	+	−	−	−	−	−	+	−	−	−	−	−	−	−	−	−	0	0	0	0	0	0	0	0	0	0	0
Continuant vs. interrupted	0	−	−	+	+	−	0	−	−	+	+	−	−	−	+	0	−	+	0	0	0	0	0	0	0	0	0
Strident vs. mellow	0	−	0	0	0	+	0	−	0	0	0	+	0	0	0	0	0	0	0	0	0	0	0	0	0	0	0
Tense vs. lax	0	+	−	+	−	0	0	+	−	+	−	0	+	−	0	0	0	0	0	0	0	0	0	0	0	0	0

The symbol ± indicates an intermediate degree of compactness, for the feature of compactness is ternary for vowels.

The vowels are further differentiated into long vs. short. Among short vowels the distinction between /e/ and /æ/ is non-phonemic.

33

REVIEW OF
*FUNDAMENTALS OF LANGUAGE**

BY ROMAN JAKOBSON AND MORRIS HALLE.
('S-Gravenhage: Mouton and Co. [Janua Linguarum,
No. 1], 1956. ix + 87 pp.)

NOAM CHOMSKY

This monograph, the first volume of a new linguistic series, contains a joint essay on phonology summarizing various theoretical and empirical investigations that these authors have reported on during the last few years[1] and an individual contribution of Jakobson's that ranges widely over many problems of language and pathological disturbances, literature, and general symbolic behavior. Both essays are written in a rather picturesque and inexplicit style which, to me at least, presents a bar to comprehension. It is difficult to determine which statements are empirical hypotheses and which are true by definition, or just what conditions the authors require a phonemic transcription to meet. Furthermore, the justification that the authors give for their own positions is often vague and unconvincing. I think that this is unfortunate, since it seems to me that much can be said for their approach to phonological problems. At the risk of possible misunderstanding of their position, I will try to state what I think it is, concentrating on the essay entitled "Phonology and Phonetics," and to see where in fact it diverges from certain other phonological theories.

Suppose that we have a set of utterances belonging to some language. Suppose further that we know which pairs of utterances are phonemically distinct[2] in this language; i.e., a test is available for classifying utterances into sets of repetitions. In addition, we have available a set of physically defined features or phonetic qualities that can be used in describing these utterances. We may now divide the utterances into segments, assigning to each segment as its *value* the set of features that characterize it. The utterances must be segmented in such a way that the following condition is met:

(1) If two utterances are phonemically distinct, then the sequences of values assigned to these utterances must differ in at least one place.

Practically all approaches to phonological analysis have at least this much framework in common. Differences appear when we go on to investigate the nature of the physical features and the principles by which segments are assigned to the same phoneme. These are of course interrelated problems.

Jakobson and Halle proceed in the following way. First, they present a certain set of physical features, defined independently of any particular language. That is, these features are part of the general definition of Language— they are part of the conceptual framework, the

[1]Cf., particularly Jakobson, Fant, and Halle, *Preliminaries to Speech Analysis,* M.I.T. Acoustics Laboratory, Technical Report, No. 13, 1952; Halle, "The Strategy of Phonemics" [32], *Word* 10.197–209 (1954); and Cherry, Halle, and Jakobson, "Toward the Logical Description of Languages in Their Phonemic Aspect" [31], *Language* 29.34–46 (1953).

[2]I.e., nonrepetitions. The notion "phonemically distinct" does not presuppose the notion "phoneme."

*Reprinted from *International Journal of American Linguistics* 23.234–242 (1957) by permission.

theoretical apparatus which the linguist brings to the analysis of each particular language, very much as the general notions "phoneme," "word," "immediate constituent," etc., are defined independently as general analytic devices available for the organization of data in the case of each particular language. Twelve of these distinctive features are listed and described in §3.6 in both articulatory and acoustic terms, and it is asserted that these are sufficient (with the addition of prosodic features) for phonological analysis of all languages. This is an empirical claim. We can seek to determine whether in fact, in each language, utterances can be segmented in such a way that condition (1) is met, when values composed of these features are assigned to segments. Since the Jakobson-Halle distinctive features constitute a small subset of the features that are assumed, implicitly or explicitly, in most approaches to phonemic analysis (e.g., at most four points of articulation are available for any language), substantiation of this claim would in itself be an interesting result. The authors would wish to claim further that (1) can be met in a significant way for each language, in the sense that the redundancy of the feature description (cf. below) is low. This amounts to a claim, again empirically testable, that there will be a considerable amount of symmetry in the feature description.

A second important aspect of the Jakobson-Halle approach is that certain of the distinctive features are defined in relative, not absolute terms. Thus the grave-acute distinction is one of higher versus lower pitch. There is no absolute point for which we can say that concentration of energy in the frequency spectrum above this point signifies acuteness, while concentration below it signifies gravity. This means that these features must be determined for a given segment relative to a certain class of segments (which we will call an "opposition set") to which the given segment is assigned. This necessitates some modification of the fundamental condition on segmentation stated above. We now require that the utterances of a language must be segmented in such a way that:

(2) The segments can be assigned to opposition sets in such a way that if two utterances are phonemically distinct, then the sequence of values assigned to these utterances

must differ in at least one place, where values are assigned to a segment with respect to the opposition set to which that segment belongs.

It would furthermore be important to state certain conditions on these opposition sets. Thus we could require that:

(3) Segments occuring in the same phonemic environment[3] must belong to the same opposition set, so that, in particular, phonemically identical utterances would be associated with the same sequence of opposition sets.[4] With this revision, the claim that the given twelve distinctive features suffice for all languages retains its operational testability. Notice that two segments may be assigned the same value even if they are phonetically quite dissimilar, and may be assigned different values even if they are phonetically quite similar. This is quite important, as we will see below.

Certain of the distinctive features are, however, defined in absolute terms. This is true, for example, of the consonant-vowel distinction (the features consonantal-nonconsonantal and vocalic-nonvocalic). This means that segments will be assigned these features irrespective of the opposition sets to which they belong (i.e., whether or not there is a consonant-vowel opposition in the language). Since phonemes are defined in terms of feature content, it is thus misleading to speak of a phoneme as an endpoint in a network of oppositions or to state that "when analyzing a given language into its ultimate constituents, we seek the smallest set of distinctive oppositions which allow the identification of each phoneme in the messages framed in this language" (p. 45). These statements may not be accurate beyond the point where relative features enter into the identifications of the phoneme.

[3]Despite appearances, this requirement can be stated without circularity as one of a set of conditions of compatibility relating the notion "phoneme" to various other concepts of linguistic theory.

[4]We would surely not require that occurrence in the same phonemic environment be a necessary condition for membership in a single opposition set, however. Thus, e.g., the [l]'s of *helicopter, alimony,* etc., would be assigned to the same opposition set, along with the [r] of *arid,* etc. The problem of constructing opposition sets is essentially that of determining "relevant contexts."

Suppose that we have now succeeded in segmenting, forming opposition sets, and assigning values to segments. Notice that certain features may not be assignable in certain opposition sets. Thus there may not be any oppositions with respect to a certain relative feature, or a feature may exhibit free variation in some position in a set of phonemically identical utterance tokens. We must, therefore, distinguish between the case where a segment lacks a certain feature (e.g., the /p/ of *pin* lacks voicing) and where a certain feature is not assignable to a given segment as a result of, e.g., lack of opposition, or free variation. To clarify terminology, we say that a segment has the value 0 with respect to a given feature if that feature is not assignable to it, and that otherwise it has the value + (if it has the feature) or − (if it lacks the feature). It is not difficult to state conditions under which the sequence of pluses and minuses associated with a segment will identify it, with zeros omitted, and we can regard this sequence as the value of the segment. We see, then, that certain segments may be assigned values of fewer than twelve elements. It is natural to seek an even more economical description by showing that certain of the feature indications are predictable in terms of others in the same segment. For example, in English, voicing is predictable for nasals and vowels, and can thus be considered a redundant feature for these segments. More generally, we may label as redundant (in given segments) those features which are not necessary for the identification of these segments. Thus voicing, though not predictable for English /l/,[5] does not serve to distinguish any /l/ from a segment in the same opposition set that has, otherwise, the same features. We now try to find the most economical assignment of values to segments that will preserve distinct representation for phonemically distinct utterances. If this is unique, we can speak significantly of *the* distinctive and *the* redundant features in certain positions, or throughout the language.

Given a minimal, nonredundant valuation as above, we can define a phoneme as a set of segments with identical values. A segment X and a segment Y are thus members of the same phoneme just in case their distinctive feature composition (in terms of the given, nonredundant valuation) is identical—just in case X and Y are identified in the same way in their respective opposition sets.

The authors would presumably agree that the distinctive features are not set rigidly for all time. If a distinctive framework with different physical reference turned out to be more useful, they would undoubtedly accept it, just as they have revised and redefined their features in the past. In this respect, too, the distinctive features have very much the same status in linguistic theory as does the notion "phoneme" itself. Distinctive features and the notion "phoneme" are taken to be given in the analysis of any particular language as part of the theoretical apparatus brought to bear in the analysis. But, of course, pragmatic considerations can lead to revision of this apparatus—i.e., to a different conception of Language.

It is instructive to compare this approach to phonemic analysis with other widely held conceptions. Commonly, the phonemes of a language are held to be a set of elements meeting the following conditions:

(4) a. Two phones[6] belong to (are allophones of) the same phoneme only if they are in free variation or complementary distribu-

---

[5]Since we find both voiced and voiceless /l/'s (e.g., *leer, clear*). Of course, context enables us to predict the occurrence of voicing in /l/, but we run into difficulties in attempting to determine redundancy of features in terms of contextual factors. For example, the presence of voicing is predictable in the context /−rin/, but we would not want to say that it is a redundant feature of the /g/ that occurs in that context. On the other hand, Jakobson-Halle would

presumably take context into account in some circumstances in determining redundancy—thus they might say that voicing is redundant in the context /s−/. The difficulty of specifying relevant contexts is of course not unique to the Jakobson-Halle approach. The natural way to attack this problem in their terms is by specifying more carefully the conditions on opposition sets and defining a "nonredundant valuation" of a segment as a minimal set of feature indications that distinguishes the segment in question from every phonemically distinct segment in the same opposition set.

[6]By a "phone" here I mean a set of indistinguishable or "sufficiently similar" phone tokens. One cannot speak of the distribution of phone tokens. The clearest formulations of such principles of phonemic analysis with which I am acquainted are those of B. Bloch in "A Set of Postulates for Phonemic Analysis" [16], *Language* 24.3–46 (1948), "Studies in Colloquial Japanese IV: Pho-

tion. b. Allophones of the same phoneme are phonetically similar. c. The set of phonemes must meet certain requirements of "pattern congruity" and "distributional similarity."

Free variation figures in the Jakobson-Halle approach, as indicated above, at the point where we determine the feature valuation of segments. Given a set of phonemically identical utterances, if we find that some distinctive feature appears with either of its values in a certain segment, then this feature is not assignable to this segment, which is said to exhibit free variation with respect to this feature.

Jakobson-Halle never appeal directly to the principle of complementary distribution. I think that there is much justification for their avoidance of this principle, for its status and value are quite questionable. It is a commonplace that complementary distribution is not a sufficient condition for assigning two phones to the same phoneme. It has not been sufficiently emphasized, however, that it is also not a necessary condition, and in fact, that the principle is frequently violated with no unacceptable consequences. Two phones X and Y are said to be in complementary distribution in a given corpus if there is no context in which both X and Y occur. Suppose that X and Y both occur (contrast) in a class A of contexts, and that Y and Z contrast in a class B of contexts, where A and B have no common member. There are many circumstances under which any phonemicist would choose to assign X in the contexts A and Y in the contexts B to one phoneme, while assigning Y in the contexts A and Z in the contexts B to a second phoneme. But these perfectly natural phonemic solutions are ruled out by the principle of complementary distribution, since X and Y are not in complementary distribution in this case. To exclude such solutions is not only extremely arbitrary and unmotivated (since these solutions preserve the biunique relation between utterances and representations which is the strongest demand that it seems reasonable to place on phonemic analysis), but they also lead to unwieldy and complex phonemic

solutions in many familiar cases. This familiar phenomenon of partial overlapping has often been brought forward as an argument in favor of defining features in relative instead of absolute terms; i.e., as an argument against too strict and absolute a formulation of the requirement (4b) of phonetic similarity. As we see, however, its consequences for (4a) are just as severe, since partial overlapping and the principle of complementary distribution are incompatible. Whatever is of value in this principle can be preserved by appropriate conditions on opposition sets; e.g., by (2) and (3), above. Beyond this it seems ad hoc and unacceptable.

Instead of requirement (4b) that allophones of a single phoneme be phonetically similar, Jakobson-Halle require that these allophones, in their respective opposition sets, have associated with them the identical sequence of feature indications, i.e., the same *value,* in the sense characterized above. As we pointed out, two segments may be assigned to the same phoneme even if they are not phonetically similar in an absolute sense, and two closely matching segments may (in the case of partial overlapping) be assigned to different phonemes if they are identified in their respective opposition sets by different feature indications. Similarly, two occurrences of the same phoneme may differ in redundant features.

With respect to criteria (4a, b), the Jakobson-Halle approach seems to compare quite favorably with alternative versions of phonemic structure. Given a set of distinctive features as part of the definition of language, it seems possible to meet the requirement of phonetic similarity in a natural way while avoiding some of the difficulties inherent in the use of such notions as complementary distribution. The Jakobson-Halle neglect of distributional considerations and, more generally, of considerations of patterning and simplicity (4c), however, leads to certain difficulties. Although this position is never explicitly stated, it seems clear that in their view there is a very direct, in fact, order-preserving relation between a phonemic representation and the associated sequence of speech segments. That is, speech is taken to be literally constituted of a sequence of phonemes, each with its distinctive and redundant features; accordingly, the phonetic value of a sequence of phonemes

nemics," *Language* 26.86–125 (1950), and "Contrast" [19], *Language* 29.59–61 (1953); and Z. S. Harris, *Methods in Structural Linguistics* (Chicago, 1951).

is the sequence of phonetic values of these phonemes. But this view has consequences which few would be willing to accept.

Consider, for example, the case of an English dialect where medial post-stress /t/ and /d/ merge in a tongue flap [D] and where only the normally redundant feature of vowel length distinguishes *writer* (phonetically, [ráyDɨr]) from *rider* (phonetically, [rá·yDɨr]). Jakobson-Halle would be forced to consider length to be a distinctive feature for vowels in such a variety of English, though its appearance (as distinctive) would be limited to this position and to the phonemic opposition /a/-/a·/.[7]

A weaker condition on the relation between phonemic representation and phonetic qualities would allow a much simpler and more natural solution. Irrespective of the *writer-rider* opposition, the rules of English grammar that convert sequences of phonemes into sequences of phones will have to contain the following:

(5) a. Vowels are automatically lengthened before voiced consonants. b. Medial, post-stress /t/ and /d/ become [D].

If we give /ráydɨr/ as the phonemic transcription of *rider* and /ráytɨr/ as the phonemic transcription of *writer,* rules (5a–b), applied in the given order, will automatically yield the correct phone sequences [rá·yDɨr], [ráyDɨr]. We can accordingly dispense with the heavily restricted phoneme /a·/ and the distinctive feature of vocalic length. But this solution violates the condition that the phonetic value of a sequence of phonemes is the sequence of phonetic values.

I think it is clear that this implicit assumption that phonemes literally occur in sequence in speech must be rejected. It does not seem difficult, in fact, to revise the Jakobson-Halle theory along lines that they themselves suggest in a different context, without sacrificing the general framework of their approach. In discussing style of speech, the authors argue that "when analyzing the pattern of phonemes and

distinctive features composing them, one must resort to the fullest, optimal code at the command of the given speakers," treating the "slurred fashion of pronunciation [as] . . . but an abbreviated derivative from the explicit clear-speech form which carries the highest amount of information" (p. 6). In other words, in the description of the total linguistic behavior of an individual we can most efficiently account for his normal speech as a deviation from a more explicit standard which he could use if occasion demanded. But this last requirement, that the standard be actualized in some overt behavior, is really superfluous.[8] There is no reason why one should not attempt to account for the linguistic behavior of an individual in terms of a hypothetical constructed standard, if this leads to a more economical and revealing description, just as one sets up unactualized base forms, zero elements, etc., in morphology. One could object to this only on the basis of a kind of pseudo-objectivity that would rule out theoretical constructs throughout science. Following this line of reasoning, we can retain the Jakobson-Halle assumption of order-preserving correspondence, and accept the /ráytɨr/ — /ráydɨr/ phonemic analysis as the description of a hypothetical, unspoken standard to which any actual speech (in these dialects) is related by such rules as (5).

Equivalently, and less misleadingly, we can accept the /ráytɨr/ — /ráydɨr/ solution along with the whole Jakobson-Halle distinctive feature framework, but change our conception of the relation between phonemic representation and speech. The distinctive feature table, which assigns zeroes, pluses, and minuses to phonemes, would become a system of classification with no direct physical meaning. This abstract system is related to actual speech by a set of rules which we try to make as simple as possible. The optimal situation from the point of view of simplicity arises when we can interpret the value given to a phoneme in the distinctive feature table directly in physical

---

[7]This and similar examples are discussed in Harris, *op. cit.* M. Halle has brought to my attention a similar case in certain varieties of German where *reiss, reis,* etc., are distinguished, but only by the normally redundant difference in the vowel. Cf. P. Martens, "Einige Fälle von sprachlich relevanter Konsonantendauer im Neuhochdeutschen," *Le Maître Phonétique,* No. 103, Jan.–June 1955.

[8]In fact, it immediately suggests many problems and objections. Under sufficiently artificial conditions one can elicit not only special citation forms, but also morphophonemic and spelling pronunciations which can only lead to confusion and complication.

terms; for example, if we can state that every phone of a phoneme with a plus value for the voicing feature is physically voiced. But occasionally, the total description can be simplified if we give such indirect rules as (5) instead. Although this must be worked out much more carefully, I think that the significant part of the Jakobson-Halle approach can be retained under this interpretation of the distinctive feature analysis as an abstract underlying system of classification related, perhaps indirectly, to the physical facts of speech. The complexity of this relation will be an important element in the evaluation of a particular phonemic analysis.

The sole criterion that Jakobson-Halle propose for evaluation of a phonemic solution is redundancy; the phonemic system for a language is the one with minimal average number of feature indications per phoneme, i.e., with the smallest number of pluses and minuses in the distinctive feature table. We have now suggested that some consideration of simplicity is also required. There are other reasons to suspect that their limitation of evaluation procedures to considerations of redundancy is too severe. Jakobson-Halle argue (p. 47) that this consideration answers affirmatively the question whether there is a unique phonemic solution for each language. This, however, is doubtful. For one thing, there is every reason to expect that there will in many cases be alternative systems of equal "optimality" in this sense. Elsewhere[9] the authors argue that the statistics of phoneme distribution should

also be considered; we then can evaluate a phonemic solution by the average number of feature specifications per phoneme in actual text (not the average number per phoneme). This extension will undoubtedly cut down the number of equally valued alternatives, but in a rather arbitrary way. The nonstatistical measure discussed above has considerable motivation; it gives a good explication of one aspect of the symmetry which most linguists would seek in phonemic analysis. The extension to include statistical information seems to be just one of any number of rather arbitrary and unmotivated ways to choose among alternatives.

More seriously, the Jakobson-Halle evaluation procedure applies only when segmentation is fixed. But some of the most important problems of nonuniqueness concern the choice among alternative segmentations.[10] It thus appears that the authors have overstated the ability of their approach to eliminate nonuniqueness, and that if they wish to arrive at unique phonemic solutions in a nonarbitrary manner, they will very likely have to appeal to the kinds of simplicity considerations that are employed (in some still vague and unformulated manner) elsewhere in linguistic description.

Equal in importance to the problem of nonuniqueness, in the authors' view, is the question (also attributed to Chao) "whether the dichotomous scale is the pivotal principle which the analyzer can profitably impose upon the linguistic code or whether this scale is inherent in the structure of language" (p. 47). They consider that "there are several weighty arguments in favor of the latter solution."

---

[9]Cherry, Halle, and Jakobson, *op. cit.* [31]. The authors point out that in the case of Russian, the average number of feature indications per phoneme of text is less than the average number per phoneme. In other words, the phonemes with shorter "codings" into features are used more frequently, as would be the case in an efficient code. This might be taken as support for the analogy between coding and distinctive feature analysis, and as indirect evidence for rating a phonemic system more highly if it assigns shorter values to more frequent phonemes. But a closer analysis of the Russian case seems to show that there is a simpler structural explanation for the gain in efficiency of the distinctive feature coding when frequency is considered. The syllabic structure of the language requires a frequency of vowels which is greater than the proportion of vowel phonemes to phonemes. Since there are fewer vowels than consonants, and since vowel-consonant is the basic distinctive feature subdivision, vowels have shorter

values (codings) than consonants. Hence there is a structural requirement that the phonemes with shorter codings be used more frequently, and I think that this accounts for the gain in efficiency noted. This fact can thus not be used as even indirect support for the view that statistical considerations of this sort are relevant to the choice among phonemic solutions.

[10]In fact, these are perhaps the most striking examples brought up in Chao's paper, "The Non-Uniqueness of Phonemic Solutions of Phonetic Systems," *Bulletin of the Institute of History and Philology, Academia Sinica,* vol. 4, part 4 (1934), where the issue of nonuniqueness is raised most clearly, and around which the Jakobson-Halle discussion of this problem centers.

Phrased in this way, this statement is at worst pointless—at best, misleading. If we take it literally, it seems to raise a pseudo-issue. It is hard to imagine what possible evidence could count for one of these positions and against the other. It is not clear what could be meant by saying that the dichotomous scale is "inherent in the structure of language" other than that this scale is the one that can most profitably be imposed upon the linguistic code. These are just two ways of describing the same thing; the choice between them is only a matter of temperament.

From the arguments that Jakobson and Halle adduce in support of their position, however, it appears that they interpret this controversy in the following terms: are there extra-linguistic reasons for choosing the dichotomous scale (e.g., independent psychological reasons) or is the only motivation the resulting convenience in describing the linguistic data? They argue for the former view. This interpretation of their remarks yields a meaningful question, but one which is posed in a very misleading way. If we find extra-linguistic evidence for the dichotomous scale we may, if we like, say that we have shown that it is inherent in the structure of language. Or we may, with equal justification, say that the most profitable and economical way to view language as part of human behavior is in terms of the dichotomous scale. The question of the relevance to phonemics of extra-linguistic data is a meaningful and important one, but there is no issue of truth versus convenience here. This phrasing of the problem has perhaps been suggested in part by the recent "God's truth-hocus pocus" discussions, which seem to me to be quite empty and sterile in just the same way.

The question of the significance of the dichotomous scale has been obscured by a certain inexplicitness in characterizing the distinctive features. A feature can be defined as a property or as a scale. In the first case (e.g., voicing, nasality), a given phone either has the property or fails to have it,[11] just as every object is either red or nonred. Such distinctive features are thus binary by definition,

and we learn nothing by being told that these features demonstrate a principle of polarity. If a feature is defined as a scale (e.g., compactness), then we can measure each phone (or, in the case of a relative feature, each phone in an opposition set) against this scale, and ask whether there are two, three or more clusters of points along this scale. If there are two, we can say (this time significantly) that the scale is dichotomous, as a matter of fact, not definition. I have not been able to determine where exactly the authors consider the polarity to be significant (i.e., an empirical fact about clustering of points along a physically defined scale) and where it is simply a tautology. Until this is clarified, the problem of "binarity" will remain confused.

In summary, then, it appears that the phonological theory under review is conceptually sound, in its essentials, and that it embodies certain empirical claims that are subject to confirmation. Its ultimate acceptability will hinge on the results of such investigations as the following:

1. Precise physical definition of the distinctive features along the lines qualitatively suggested in the monograph under review and more carefully described in other publications.[12] Clarification of the status of these features as properties or scales.

2. Specification of the conditions on opposition sets.

Given the results of 1 and 2, we can check to see whether the empirical criterion (2) is in fact met, for many or all languages.

3. Further clarification of the criteria for determining which features are redundant. There is some discussion of this in the monograph, but it is not completely adequate.

4. Clarification of the nature of the relation between the distinctive feature analysis and the physical facts of speech, and determination of criteria of simplicity, patterning,

---

[11]Assuming that the property is assignable to the phone in question. Cf. the discussion of redundancy, above.

[12]Cf. footnote 1. Also Hughes and Halle, "Spectral Properties of Fricative Consonants," *Journal of the Acoustical Society of America* 28. 303–310 (1956): Halle, Hughes, and Radley, "Acoustic Properties of Stop Consonants," *Journal of the Acoustical Society of America* 29 (1957); and Halle and Jones, *The Phonemes of Russian*, to appear. [See now Morris Halle, *The Sound Pattern of Russian* (1959)—VBM.]

etc., to aid in the choice among alternative analyses.

5. Investigation of prosodic features and clarification of their relation to the remainder of the phonological and grammatical structure. There is some discussion of this problem, but it is very sketchy, and it remains to be seen whether the proposals made can do justice to the full range of intonational phenomena.

6. Investigation of the efficacy of these phonological theories in accounting for the development of language in children, pathological linguistic disturbances, and other aspects of linguistic behavior. For many years

Jakobson has urged that these problems are of utmost importance for linguistics and that they provide crucial tests for the adequacy of phonological theory. These topics are discussed at length in the monograph (particularly in the second part, entitled "Two Aspects of Language and Two Types of Aphasic Disturbance") in a manner which is suggestive and insightful, though still far from conclusive. It is very much to be hoped that these lines of inquiry will be further pursued. They are sure to provide a very fruitful orientation for linguistic research.

34

A CRITICISM
OF DISTINCTIVE FEATURES*
ROBERT D. WILSON

1. Introduction The relationship between segment and sound is a central concern of phonology.[1] A framework for the definition of this relationship is that of distinctive features —proposed by Roman Jakobson and developed by Morris Halle. This framework may be looked at as having two parts: the substantive and the formal. The substantive is made up of the small number of features which, it is claimed (Halle, 1957: 67 ff.), are all that are necessary for describing all the languages of the world—fifteen by the latest count (Halle, 1964a: 329 [396]). The formal consists of a number of concepts which appear to have contributed to the definition of the relationship between segment and sound in transformational theory (Chomsky, 1964: 86 [401–402]). Only incidentally will I be concerned with the substantive part of the framework.

The following concepts are said to be the formal properties of distinctive features (Jakobson and Halle, 1956): (1) they are binary; (2) they make up segments in the form of "complexes of features" rather than in the form of "indivisible units"; (3) they are relational. I shall discuss each of these properties in two ways: first, as part of the framework itself and, second, as part of transformational theory. Unfavorable criticisms will be followed by alternative proposals, which should perhaps be less ambitiously called suggestions, pending a fuller treatment in a separate paper.

2. Binary Choice The basic idea behind the distinctive feature framework is said to be the

binary choice confronting the receiver of the message (Jakobson *et al.*, 1956: 44–49). The choice is prompted by a yes/no question and is formalized by the marks: + for *yes*, − for *no*, and o for either, but because this suggests that "the logic is three-valued" (Cherry, Halle and Jakobson, 1953: 37 [325], a re-ordering of the marks—called transformation—makes it possible to get rid of most of the zero marks.

Transformation is the procedure by which the usual table of columns (representing the segments) and rows (representing the features) which defines all the segments of a language with a single ordering of the features is replaced by several similar tables. Each of the new tables has the features ordered in a different manner and each of the new tables has a smaller subset of the features required for the language as a whole. This procedure is said to be made possible by regarding these tables (the original and the new) as "code books" (Cherry *et al.*, 1953: 39–40 [327]).

The new code books retain several zeros, however (Cherry *et al.*, 1953: 40; but note the inconsistency in Cherry 1961: 95–96). Does this not suggest that "the logic remains three-valued"?

The transformation involved is merely a procedure and not part of the formalization: "the code books are known *a priori* and represent here the independent phoneme structure of Russian; they themselves contain the 'information' provided by the zeros in Table A [=the original code book]" (Cherry *et al.*, 1953: 40 [328]). This view of the code book fails to distinguish between two different zeros:

[1]Helpful comments were made by Kalon Kelley, Peter Lackowski, Peter Ladefoged, Terence Moore, and Robert P. Stockwell.

*Reprinted from *Journal of Linguistics* 2.195–206 (1966) by permission of the author and Cambridge University Press.

(1) the zero which represents a redundant feature that is language specific, e.g.,

Just because one feature opposition is left blank, such as the nasal-oral feature of all the vowel phonemes, this does not mean that English speakers necessarily differ in their nasalizing of their vowel sounds. It implies rather that we do not need to know whether or not they do, to be able to identify the vowels, provided that we know certain other features (Cherry, 1961:94).

and (2) the zero which represents a feature that is universally redundant, e.g.,

Since all *compact* consonants are *non-diffuse* and all *diffuse* consonants, *non-compact,* only one of the two features functions distinctively in the consonants. We therefore describe labials and dentals as *non-compact;* palatals, velars, gutturals, etc., as *compact,* and *omit reference* [RDW] to feature *diffuse-nondiffuse* (Halle, 1957: 71).

I will call (1) the *specific zero,* (2) the *universal zero.* The latter is said to occur when "in some cases a zero appears in a place where the substitution of plus or minus would imply an impossible articulation" (Cherry *et al.,* 1953: 39 [327]). I intend to show in the following subsection that there is a very natural way of characterizing these two zeros. And in section 2.2 I propose to show how these two zeros might be represented in transformational grammars.

2.1. The Meaning of the Minus (−) Symbol   I should like to clear up the terminological confusion that has appeared in the literature regarding the minus (−) symbol. The following passages are relevant to the discussion:

In using the distinctive feature system one commits oneself to the view that all features are of a simple, binary type: i.e., one restricts oneself to asking about the phonetic features of a language only questions that can be answered by "yes" or "no" (Halle, 1957: 66).
    This framework differs from others in that it consists exclusively in terms of binary properties. If we adopt the distinctive features as our classificatory scheme, we commit ourselves to speaking about speech sounds exclusively in terms of two-valued attributes; i.e., of properties which a given sound may or may not possess (Halle, 1961: 89).

In accepting the distinctive features one commits oneself to characterizing all segments in terms of a restricted check list of attributes like "nasality, voicing, palatalization, etc.," with regard to which the only relevant question is "does the segment possess the particular attribute?" It follows, therefore, that differences between segments can be expressed only as differences in their feature composition and that consequently segments (even in different languages) can differ from each other only in a restricted number of ways (Halle, 1959: 19).

It would appear from the phrase "may or may not possess" that in answering the question "Is it continuant?" the answer minus (−) means that the segment in question does not possess the feature of open or close approximation (Halle, 1964a: 327 [395]). But the answer minus (−) does not mean mere absence. It also means that the segment in question is a stop (rather than a nasal, for example): "produced with a vocal tract in which the passage from the glottis to the lips is effectively closed by *contact*" (Halle, 1964a: 327 [395]). Put differently, the minus mark indicates a feature which the segment in question does possess. If this is the sense in which the questions are to be asked of each segment, then the proper characterization of the questions is not as yes/no questions but as disjunctive either/or questions, e.g., "Is it continuant or interrupted?" (cf. Fischer-Jørgensen, 1958: 472).
    Jakobson and Halle (1956: 4) speak of both yes/no questions and either/or questions: "the listener is obliged to choose either between two polar qualities of the same category, as in the case of grave vs. acute, or between the presence and absence of a certain quality such as voiced vs. voiceless, nasalized vs. non-nasalized, sharp vs. plain." But the choice between voiced and voiceless is not merely between the presence and absence of vibrating vocal cords but between two states of the glottis. The choice between nasalized and non-nasalized is not merely between the presence and absence of a nasal resonator but between two states of the velum. The choice between sharp and plain is not merely between the presence and absence of palatalization but between palatalization and all the other tongue positions. It is misleading to speak of the presence or absence of a feature when the basic

concept is the following: "Each of the distinctive features involves a choice between *two* [RDW] terms of an opposition" (Jakobson *et al.,* 1956: 4).

An important consequence of the view that the series of questions involved in determining a phonological segment are disjunctive either/or questions is the rejection of the distinctive feature framework as a "check list of attributes." Implied in this view is not merely the presence or absence of an attribute "X" but that the absence of "X" means the presence of another attribute "Y" and that the presence of "X" means the absence of the other attribute "Y." Formally, this would mean the adoption of an explicit rule which would incorporate such a property, e.g., "Is it continuant?/If *no* (−), then it is interrupted" (cf. Jakobson, 1958: 20).

This opens a new dimension. This is the dimension of implicational rules. Such rules would make it possible—unlike the transformation procedure mentioned in section 2— to characterize the two kinds of zeros. For example, (1) "In English, if the segment is plus (+) vocalic and minus (−) consonantal, then do not ask the question 'Is it nasalized?'" for specific zeros;[2] (2) "If the segment is plus (+) vocalic and minus (−) consonantal, then do not ask the question 'Is it strident?'" for universal zeros.

The value of implicational rules over a check list may be further demonstrated by an inadequacy in the framework of distinctive features itself. It appears that two minus (−) marks may imply a third unstated feature:

the close vowels are characterized as diffuse and non-compact; the open vowels like [a] and [æ] are classified as compact and non-diffuse; the vowels of intermediate degree of openness—e.g., [e], [ø], and [o]—are both non-compact and non-diffuse (Halle, 1961: 71).

The intermediate vowels, in fact, are neither non-compact nor non-diffuse, that is, they are neither horn shaped nor shaped like a Helmholtz resonator (for the open and close vowels, respectively), but are of a different shape altogether (cf. Fischer-Jørgensen, 1958: 452). Observe that the description of the intermediate vowels as non-compact and non-diffuse is not parallel to the description of a segment as a "bundle of features" where every feature present in the bundle is assumed to be an explicit member of the "restricted check list of attributes." It seems quite clear that the two terms non-compact and non-diffuse are meant to imply a third term. This is the job of an implicational rule. It might be argued that an exegesis of the literature expounding the distinctive feature framework would show precisely what I have suggested: the adoption of implicational rules. Be that as it may, an implicit commitment is hardly sufficient.

2.2. Zeros and Transformational Theory
In transformational grammars the relationship between segment and sound is made with the use of two matrices, one for the segments— called the classificatory matrix—the other for the sounds—called the phonetic matrix. In the classificatory matrix "the columns stand for what we can call 'segments' and the rows, for categories; the entry in the ith row and the jth column indicates whether the jth segment belongs to the ith category" (Chomsky, 1964: 85 [401]). In the pnonetic matrix "columns represent phones and rows, phonetic features. . . . The entry in the ith row and the jth column indicates whether the jth phone of the generated utterance possesses the ith feature, or the degree to which it possesses this feature" (Chomsky, 1964: 86 [401]). Furthermore, "the rules of the phonological component modify . . . the matrices of the phonological representation [=classificatory matrix]: the rules supply value to non-phonemic features, they change the values of certain features, and they assign a phonetic interpretation to the individual rows of the matrix [i.e., convert the classificatory matrix into a phonetic matrix]" (Halle, 1964a: 333 [399]).

The adoption of the distinctive feature framework in transformational grammars has brought about an important formalized restriction: "In the phonemic representation [=classificatory matrix] the different features [=categories] are allowed to assume only two values, plus or minus" (Halle, 1964a: 332 [399]). This means that a category may (1) not assume both plus and minus values (but rather plus or minus) and (2) not assume neither plus nor

---

[2]In transformational theory the characterization of specific zeros implied by the example will be represented in the classificatory matrix only; cf. §2.2.

minus, i.e., have no value at all. An empty cell in the matrix (i.e., zero) which is to be filled in by some rule—called a redundancy rule—is said to be either plus or minus as the formalization requires (cf. Cherry *et al.*, 1953: 37 [325]; Halle, 1959: 32). Such an empty cell is said to represent a non-phonemic feature (=category). Unlike the classificatory matrix, the phonetic matrix may not have empty cells except for those features which are in free variation (Halle, 1959: 30, 37).

It appears to be the case that the distinctive feature framework necessarily requires empty cells in the classificatory matrix which no redundancy rule can fill in with a plus or minus value. Halle himself has provided a case in point (1959: 30):

Certain features are non-phonemic because they can be predicted from certain other features in the same segment. Thus, for instance, in Russian the feature diffuse-nondiffuse is non-phonemic everywhere except in vowels; i.e., its distribution can be predicted in all segments which are non-vocalic and/or consonantal.

How then is the diffuse-nondiffuse row to be specified in consonants? Either a plus or a minus would not so much be incorrect as irrelevant since, by definition[3] (Halle, 1959: 53), the diffuse-nondiffuse opposition is distinctive only for vowels or, put even more strongly, "restricted to vowels" (Halle, 1964*a*: 327 [395]; cf. fn. 2 above). In fact, Halle (1959: 43) has actually retained the mark o (=an empty cell) for the diffuse-nondiffuse row under the consonants in the phonetic representation of a Russian utterance. The diffuse-nondiffuse feature cannot be in free variation in a segment where it cannot even occur; free variation, then, cannot be used as an explanation. Other similar objections might be made, e.g., how is the strident-nonstrident row to be specified in vowels when, by definition (Halle, 1964*a*: 327 [395]), this feature is restricted to consonantal sounds? Halle answers this question by picking the other horn:

[3]In Halle, 1959: 53, the diffuse-nondiffuse opposition is restricted to vowels; on the other hand, in Halle, 1964*a*: 327 [395], it is the compact-noncompact opposition which is restricted to vowels and not the diffuse-nondiffuse.

he writes a P-rule which fills in a minus (−) value (1964*b*: 339–340 [383–384]), in effect regarding the vowel as non-strident.

It might be noted in passing that the transformation procedure applied to an original code book for the purpose of deriving a set of new code books which could characterize subsets of phonemes in a language (cf. section 2) cannot be applied to a classificatory or phonetic matrix (and, of course, no one has claimed otherwise) because these matrices define morphemes and morphemes do not have the same composition as the code books. Morphemes will mix classes of segments which the code books will not, e.g., vowels and consonants, so that no amount of reordering and judicious choice of features will succeed in avoiding as many zeros as the code books can—and probably none.

Observe that, like the code books, the classificatory and phonetic matrices of distinctive features as they have been incorporated into transformational theory by Chomsky and Halle will not reflect the difference between specific and universal zeros. The empty cells (=zeros) which redundancy rules may fill in do not distinguish between specific and universal zeros nor do different types of rules distinguish between them. The empty cells remaining in some phonetic matrices are said to represent free variation.

Recall that an empty cell (=zero) is not a nothing but either a plus or a minus. This means, more appropriately, that an empty cell in a classificatory matrix is a disjunct ±, that redundancy rules delete either the plus (+) or the minus (−), and that the remaining empty cell in a phonetic matrix is a disjunct ±. This is in accord with the statement that "the zeros [=empty cells] are auxiliary symbols utilized for purposes of exposition only; they have no function in the phonological system of the language" (Halle, 1959: 30). It follows that a matrix, which is a set of empty cells, has no function in the phonological system either. Chomsky (1964: 85–86 [401]) speaks of it as a representation.

I would like to suggest that zeros be part of the derivational history of a generated sentence and that some of them may be allowed to remain as zeros, that is, as nothings, in the output to the phonological component, namely the phonetic matrix. This requires the adoption of a matrix as a notation defined by the meta-theory (like braces and parentheses for the syntactical component) such that, among other things, the empty cells in a matrix represent the absence of a feature. It will probably be objected that this suggestion involves the adoption of ternary choices: a plus value, a minus value, and a non-value. This objection is aimed at the wrong target. The formalization proposed here involves three terms but it represents binary choices—given the features. It should be pointed out that the binary choices confronting the grammar involve only the fea-tures present in a given segment. This implies further that there will be implicational rules which will prevent the grammar from asking certain questions, i.e., from making certain choices. Given the segment as a bundle of features, the grammar asks an ordered set of disjunctive either/or questions. For example, in distinctive feature terms there must be two initial questions and their concomitant impli-cational rules, that is, those implied in "vocalic-nonvocalic" and "consonantal-nonconsonan-tal"; if the answers to these questions are vo-calic and nonconsonantal, then a rule instructs the grammar not to ask the question "strident-nonstrident." This instruction, which in a manner of speaking is the correlate of the third term in the formalization, the empty cell, is not a choice but an obligatory restriction on the set of possible questions. Each question, when asked, involves a binary choice, characterizing the assumption that communication[4] is a binary process.

In this view specific zeros in a transfor-mational grammar will be filled in with a minus or plus value by redundancy rules. Universal zeros will remain in the matrices—prevented from being filled in by implicational rules of the sort described above. Thus, in the derivational history of a sentence the remaining empty cells will reflect the metatheoretic redundancies. And the empty cells which have been filled in by redundancy rules will reflect the redun-dancies which are language specific.

Free variation will be represented by the mark ± in the appropriate cell—placed there by an implicational rule which is language specific. Free variation of two features and

free variation of a segment with its absence will be handled in the following manner. The latter will be represented by the mark ± in the row named *segment*.[5] The eventual choice (in a model of performance) of the mark + would indicate the presence of the segment while the eventual choice of the mark − would indi-cate the absence of the segment. The former (free variation of two features) will be repre-sented by the mark ± in the appropriate row, e.g., continuant/interrupted for those instances of free variation between the interdental frica-tive and the interdental stop in a Colombian dialect of Spanish. The eventual choice (in a model of performance) of the mark + would indicate the presence of the feature continuant (and the absence of the feature interrupted) while the eventual choice of the mark − would indicate the presence of the feature interrupted (and the absence of the feature continuant).

3. Complexes of Features   The explicit break with the view that segments are indivisible units was made by Jakobson (1962: 635–636) in 1932 by proposing the view that segments are "complexes of features." The latter view would *not* require that a phoneme (whether of the taxonomic or systemic variety) be repre-sented by a phone having independent theo-retical status before finally being described with the bundle of features it is composed of, e.g., /d/ (or /D/) is to be rewritten as [d], and [d] is to be rewritten as "voiced alveolar stop" (or with the equivalent distinctive feature terms). Rather, the latter view would require that a phoneme be represented directly by the features which make it up, e.g., /d/ (or /D/) is to be rewritten as "voiced alveolar stop" (or with the equivalent distinctive feature terms).

I shall not repeat here Halle's convincing argument (1964b: 335–337 [380–382]) that greater simplicity is achieved by the definition of "natural class" made possible by the notion "complexes of features" (Householder's ob-jections notwithstanding; 1965: 16–17 [444–445]). However, it should be noted that in ac-cepting the view that a phonological segment is to be represented as a complex of properties, one does not necessarily have to commit one-

---

[4]That is, a (non-performance) competence model of communication.

[5]*Segment* is to be added to the list of features—from a suggestion by Halle in a letter to Peter Lackowski.

self to the substantive elements of the distinctive feature framework. This appears to be admitted by Halle when in a footnote to the discussion comparing complexes of features with indivisible units he states (1964*b*: 336 [381]):

I shall use here the Jakobsonian distinctive features as the properties in terms of which segments are to be characterized. The choice of a different phonetic framework, however, would not affect the outcome of the present comparison.

In the same article he goes on to make the following claim, however (1964*b*: 337–338 [382]):

I shall attempt to justify the proposed view of phonological segments, i.e., as complexes of features or properties by examining some of its consequences. These consequences will incidentally provide ample justification for the decision to operate with the Jakobsonian distinctive feature framework rather than with one of the other phonetic frameworks (IPA or Jespersen's antalphabetic notation, and so on).

As far as I can make out from the rest of Halle's paper, the "consequences" which are meant to provide the justification for operating with the Jakobsonian distinctive features are the simplifications and explanations of linguistic phenomena made possible by (1) redundancy rules and/or (2) ordered rules. The question is whether redundancy rules or ordered rules are consequences of the view of segments as complexes of *Jakobsonian distinctive features*. It is unarguable that the view of segments as complexes rather than indivisible units makes redundancy rules (and the simplifications they effect) possible. But it is arguable whether the substantive elements of the Jakobsonian distinctive feature framework contribute to the advantages credited to redundancy rules. Any phonetic framework which makes it possible to define "natural class" (Halle, 1964*a*: 328 [396]) and to describe all languages in a consistently similar manner can make redundancy rules possible. This is a function of the formal properties of phonetic frameworks, not of their substantive terms.

Next, it seems to me extremely doubtful that the imposition of order on the phonological rules is a consequence of the view of segments as complexes of properties—whether

of distinctive features or of any other phonetic framework. Both ordered and unordered rules may be devised with the distinctive feature framework, as Halle (1964*b*: 347–348 [389]) himself has shown. And both ordered and unordered rules may be devised without the distinctive feature framework, as Halle (1964*b*: 338 [382–383]) himself has shown. Furthermore, one might trivially object that, unlike redundancy rules, ordered rules are not even associated with the conception of distinctive features but with transformational theory (Chomsky, 1955).

The foregoing arguments are not meant to deny the usefulness of the substantive part of the distinctive feature framework in so far as the universal statements therein will hold. The universality of the statements contributes to the function of the framework in describing all languages in a similar manner, and it contributes to the measurement of simplicity (Halle, 1961). The arguments were merely meant to prevent the unwarranted rejection of phonetic frameworks with different substantive terms.

Whatever the substantive elements of the theory, full advantage should be taken of the view of segments as complexes of properties. To this end the introduction of matrices as notational conventions (cf. §2.2) should make for rules with more power. With an empty cell as an extra term, there will be rules which will specify o (for empty cell) besides the usual minus (−), plus (+), and zero—that is, if Halle's (1959: 30) zeros are regarded as equivalent to my ±.

4. Relation vs. Accuracy The importance of the third formal property of the distinctive features is that it supports the universal claims of the substantive part of the framework. This property, the relational character of the features, is such that "the 'minimum same' of a feature in its combination with various other concurrent or successive features lies in the essentially identical relation between the two opposite alternatives" (Jakobson *et al.*, 1956: 14). For example:

A pair of palatal vowel phonemes . . . may in some languages be implemented in one position as [ae]–[e] and in another position as [e]–[i], so that the same sound [e] in one position implements the diffuse, and in another, the compact term of the same opposition. The relation in both positions remains identical. Two degrees of aperture and, correspondingly, of concentration of energy—the maximal and the minimal—oppose each other in both positions (Jakobson *et al.*, 1956: 14–15).

However the stops in *tot* may differ from each other genetically and acoustically, they are both high-pitched in opposition to the two labials in *pop,* and both display a diffusion of energy, as compared to a greater concentration of energy in the two stops of *cock* (Jakobson *et al.,* 1956: 14).

It is this sort of consistent relationship between two terms of an opposition which makes the universal statements of the substantive part of the framework possible. For example, it is the consistent relationship between grave and acute which makes it possible to collapse all peripheral type sounds (back vowels, labial and postpalatal consonants) under the heading of grave and all non-peripheral type sounds (front vowels, dental and palatal consonants) under the heading of acute (cf. Halle, 1961: 67–71).

For phonetic theory the alphabet of distinctive features defined in terms of relational properties on the binary scale provides a simplification at the expense of accuracy:

Jakobson's fundamental argument was that the most satisfactory description of a language would be obtained by using as many dimensions (features) as necessary, but decreasing the accuracy of measurement, i.e., the number of significant decisions which have to be made with regard to each dimension. The dichotomous scale, which underlies the distinctive features, has minimal accuracy of measurement; it is in this sense that it is the simplest possible (Halle, 1954: 205 [339]).

If phonetic theory were to include general laws of measurement besides "a fixed set of features . . . [and] general laws concerning possible combinations and contrasts" (Chomsky, 1964: 86 [402]), then the price of the simplification achieved by Jakobson may not have to be paid. For example, if the term flat of the opposition flat/plain were to be further subdivided into pharyngealization, velarization, retroflexion, and labialization (that is, into a second set of yes/no questions and implicational rules), then it would be possible for the description of a particular language which real-

izes flat as labialization to so interpret the fact while the description of another language which realizes flat as velarization to so interpret the facts—thus increasing the accuracy of the measurement in the descriptions of these languages. Observe that the suggestion is not to substitute the four-way division for the term flat of the flat/plain opposition but to supplement it.

The inclusion of the additional dimensions in the metatheory will make it possible to compare, to that extent, the phonological structure of languages. Thus, if both language L_1 and language L_2 were said to manifest the feature rounding (=labialization), then the statement could be made that the separate manifestations of rounding in the two languages exhibit the feature rounding as it is defined in the metatheory. On the other hand, if the feature rounding as a realization of flat were to be defined not in the metatheory but only in the particular descriptions of language L_1 and language L_2, then they cannot be said to be similar in an explicit and natural way. Without a general definition of rounding there is no unequivocal basis for comparison. (It should be noted that the foregoing does not make the suggestion that the metatheory will include definitions of the degrees to which a feature may be possessed.)

The relational property of the distinctive features, while making possible certain universal statements, presents a fundamental problem in transformational theory. Halle has apparently ruled out the possibility of increasing the accuracy of the measurements of the distinctive features when he says (1964*a*: 333 [399]):

The phonetic interpretation assigned to rows of the matrix is uniform for all languages; i.e., some row in the matrix will be associated with the feature *vocalic-nonvocalic,* another with the feature *consonantal-nonconsonantal,* and so on. This fact explains our practice of designating the rows in the phonemic matrices [=classificatory matrices] which represent abstract differential markers, by names of the different phonetic features. When we designate a given row in the phonemic matrix by the name of a particular phonetic feature, we imply that the grammar will ultimately associate this row with the phonetic feature in question.

It should be noted that allowing the phonetic

matrix to contain entries specifying the degree to which a feature is possessed (cf. §2.2; Halle, 1964a: 333 [399]) is not the same as adding dimensions such as velarization, labialization, etc. Degrees to which a feature is possessed are necessarily language specific since the metatheory cannot deal with continuum as a property (cf. Halle, 1964a: 324–325 [393–394]). Examples of degrees of a feature are stress (Chomsky, 1964: 86 [401]; Halle, 1959: 44) and the following: "English [ʌ] as in *pup* is less grave ('back') than English [u] as in *poop*" (Halle, 1964a: 333 [399]). Dimensions are universal—whether broad like grave or narrow like velar—reflecting "the fact that the articulatory apparatus of man is the same everywhere, that men everywhere are capable of controlling the same few aspects of their vocal tract behavior" (Halle, 1964a: 333 [399]).

A transformational grammar is required to generate all and only the sentences of a language. If a particular language is described as having the feature flat/plain and if a plus value for this feature means in this language labialization (=rounding), then transformational theory requires that labialization be specified in order that the sentences which the particular grammar generates (that is, those said to contain labialized segments) BE sentences of that language. For example, describing some of the vowels of French as flat and having them come out as pharyngealized instead of rounded will not make those vowels French vowels—to that extent violating the requirement imposed on grammars by transformational theory. The objection here is of a different order from that above (where the loss of accuracy is pointed out). There only comprehensiveness was questioned; here an essential formal property of the theory in which the distinctive feature framework is to relate segment to sound is not being conformed to. At the most crucial joint the parts do not fit.

An alternative would be to increase the number of dimensions in the metatheory—as I suggested earlier—such that gross features like flat might be allowed to be rewritten as any of the secondary articulations. The only other machinery needed will be implicational rules (already justified on other grounds) such as: "If plus flat, ask the following set of four questions" and extra questions for the added dimensions, e.g., "Is it pharyngealized? labialized?" etc. Their effect would be to rename the row in question—either the row in the phonetic matrix or in the classificatory matrix, whichever turns out to be simpler—as "flat: labialized" for the French vowels, for example. Perhaps a parallel sort of approach to the problem might be inferred from Chomsky's remark (1964: 85 [401]):

Some squares in the classificatory matrix may be blank, where the feature in question can be supplied by a general rule (e.g., the entry for Rounding in the case of English Lax Front Vowels, which become, automatically, unrounded).

It might not be wholly unnecessary to point out that my suggestion to increase the number of features is not to be taken as implying a decrease of systemic relationships. On the contrary, every new dimension must find its place in the system (even a list of exceptions plays a role in the system), thus creating new relationships.

5. Summary I have tried to show (1) that the binary property of distinctive features, if it is to be properly understood, must be viewed not as a pair of terms, plus (+) and minus (−), but as a choice prompted by disjunctive either/or questions (that is, by yes/no questions with concomitant implicational rules); (2) that the notion "complexes of properties" is not necessarily tied to the distinctive features; (3) that the relational property of distinctive features should not and need not mean the loss of descriptive accuracy. I have also made the following suggestions: (1) the adoption of implicational rules; (2) the adoption of matrices as notational conventions having the same status as braces and parentheses in the general theory; (3) a representation for distinguishing between (a) two general classes of redundancies, the specific and the universal, (b) two sorts of free variation, i.e., variation between two features and between a segment and its absence.

REFERENCES

CHERRY, C. (1961). *On Human Communication.* New York: Science Editions.

CHERRY, C., HALLE, M., and JAKOBSON, R. (1953). "Toward the Logical Description of Languages in Their Phonemic Aspect," *Language* 29.34–46 [31].

CHOMSKY, N. (1955). "The Logical Structure of Linguistic Theory," mimeographed unpublished manuscript.

CHOMSKY, N. (1957). Review of Jakobson and Halle's *Fundamentals of Language, IJAL* 23. 234–242 [33].

CHOMSKY, N. (1964). "Current Issues in Linguistic Theory," in Fodor and Katz (1964: 50–118) [39].

FISCHER-JØRGENSEN, E. (1958). "What Can the New Techniques of Acoustic Phonetics Contribute to Linguistics?" *Proceedings of the 8th International Congress of Linguists.* Oslo: Oslo University Press. 433–480.

FODOR, J. A., and KATZ, J. J. (1964). *The Structure of Language.* Englewood Cliffs: Prentice Hall.

HALLE, M. (1954). "The Strategy of Phonemics," *Word* 10.197–209 [32].

HALLE, M. (1957). "In Defense of the Number Two," *Studies Presented to Joshua Whatmough.* The Hague: Mouton. 65–72.

HALLE, M. (1959). *The Sound Pattern of Russian.* The Hague: Mouton.

HALLE, M. (1961). "On the Role of Simplicity in Linguistic Descriptions," *Structure of Language and Its Mathematical Aspects.* Providence: American Mathematical Society. 89–94.

HALLE, M. (1964a). "On the Bases of Phonology," in Fodor and Katz (1964: 324–333) [38].

HALLE, M. (1964b). "Phonology in Generative Grammar," in Fodor and Katz (1964: 334–352) [37].

HOUSEHOLDER, F. W. (1965). "On Some Recent Claims in Phonological Theory," *Journal of Linguistics* 1.13–34 [41].

JAKOBSON, R., and HALLE, M. (1956). *Fundamentals of Language.* The Hague: Mouton.

JAKOBSON, R. (1958). "Typological Studies and Their Contribution to Historical Comparative Linguistics," *Proceedings of the 8th International Congress of Linguists.* Oslo: Oslo University Press. 17–25.

JAKOBSON, R., FANT, C. GUNNAR M., and HALLE, M. (1961). *Preliminaries to Speech Analysis.* Cambridge, Massachusetts: The MIT Press.

JAKOBSON, R. (1962). *Selected Writings I: Phonological Studies.* The Hague: Mouton.

THE NATURE OF
DISTINCTIVE FEATURES*
GUNNAR FANT

INTRODUCTION

The following essay is intended as a review of my own thinking on distinctive features. Of all that has been written on this topic I have followed up only a part. I am more practically oriented than linguists and less bound to orthodox acceptance of working principles but I still find it a rather fascinating subject to sit down and work out alternative solutions, e.g., for ordering of Swedish vowels which was one of my early interests.

I certainly feel that a substantial revision of our old *Preliminaries* (15) has long been overdue. The major principles are still valid but I feel we need much more factual data before a substantial revision can be undertaken. Till then the following material may serve as an expression of my views on the subject.

Specialists in language and speech have displayed rather diverging reactions to the theory of distinctive features and misunderstandings have been frequent. Does it provide a condensed presentation of the most useful facts about speech or is it just an intellectual game, a purpose of itself for the structural linguist? High initial expectations of finding new and simple solutions to central problems of speech analysis, such as automatic speech recognition, have been followed by distrust. Now, the theory of distinctive features is not intended as a working recipe for technical application but it can provide some organizational principles and suggestions. The rather specific terminology does not stand for either radically new or very special features. The articulatory, acoustic, or perceptive correlates of distinctive features should comprise condensed transforms of the most relevant information from any of these stages within the complete speech communication system. A continued study of alternative solutions and descriptive forms is needed in the development of the distinctive feature theory as in speech analysis in general.

What is then really the concept of distinctive features? How are they defined, from the speech wave, from articulation, or from perception? Are they simply a part of the linguistic code for decomposition of phonemes in a bundle of smaller units? Reading the *Preliminaries* one finds that the distinctive features operate on all four levels but from which one do you start the analysis? Here as in phonemic analysis the set of distinctive features constitutes abstract units of the message code. The distinctive feature is a choice between one of two alternatives. In the *Preliminaries* distinctive features are referred to by terms as "discriminations," "choice," and "selection" stressing the linguistic level. A distinctive feature generally recurs as a choice situation in several minimal distinction pairs within a language and it is of course required that the physical or physiological manifestations be consistent, i.e., one and the same feature shall have qualitatively the same articulatory, acoustic, and perceptive correlates independent of context of other features within the bundle. The modification "qualitatively" here implies that the relation between the two opposites is the same in all contexts. Absolute values of descriptive parameters, however, generally vary with context. Failure to recognize the role of contextual bias is a frequent source of misunderstanding of the nature of

*Reprinted from *To Honor Roman Jakobson* (Mouton, 1967), pp. 634–642, by permission.

distinctive features. A distinctive feature is by definition the same in all contexts. The underlying physical phenomena, on the other hand, referred to as "correlates," "cues," or "parameters" need exhibit only relational invariance.

Distinctive features are really distinctive categories or classes within a linguistic system but just like in accepted phonemic analysis it is required that they are consistent with the phonetic facts and these phonetic facts on various levels have lent their name to the features. It is not within my competence to discuss the generality of distinctive features but it is apparent that they comprise, as they should, the essentials of the framework of classical phonetics and in addition some categorizations of a seemingly more novel appearance.

I shall now proceed to some specific points concerning distinctive features some of which are often brought up in discussions.

HOW IMPORTANT IS THE BINARY PRINCIPLE?

The binary principle obviously has its basis in the presence versus absence of an articulatory or phonatory event, e.g., presence versus absence of voicing, nasality, occlusion, etc., or in a selection of one of two polar alternatives along a continuous parameter scale, e.g., more open as opposed to less open. In the analysis of vowels it can be motivated to recognize more than two significant levels of one and the same parameter, cf. the discussion on compactness in the *Preliminaries*, paragraph 2.414. As indicated in the analysis of the Swedish vowel system later in this paper one could conceive of instances, where up to four distinct levels of one and the same feature might be considered. In these instances a decomposition in terms of two binary categories is generally undertaken in order to allow a consistent use of the binary principle within the whole system.

The distinctive feature represents the linguist's condensed view of the minimal units for composing speech messages. If properly applied, categorization according to binary principles need not come in conflict with the physical reality. It is a matter of coding convenience only.

ECONOMY BUT AT WHAT PRICE?

If alternative solutions of distinctive features are possible it is established policy to adopt the one providing the best economy in terms of the smallest number of features or rather the least redundancy minimizing the number of alternatives that can be generated by the specific set of categories. However, this requirement can come in conflict with the principle of consistency, i.e., there is the risk that one or more minimal pairs in which a feature is supposed to operate do not conform sufficiently well with the rest of the system. Seemingly elegant solutions may thus have to be rejected by failures to apply in specific contexts. It is also apparent that the economy gained in treating consonants and vowels with the same features at times leads to somewhat remote analogies.

ARE DISTINCTIVE FEATURES ALWAYS ORTHOGONAL?

Distinctive features are handled as independent units on the linguistic level but their phonetic manifestations often lack orthogonality. The phonetic quality of a vowel may to a first approximation be specified by F1 and F2. In the F_1, F_2 plane, however, gravity, compactness, flatness, and tenseness all occupy specific vectors and interdependency is thus unavoidable. Even when such parameters as F_3, F_0, overall intensity, and duration are added in order to provide a better approximation it is not phonetically realistic to choose a consistently orthogonal set of features.

HOW ARE DISTINCTIVE FEATURES DISTRIBUTED IN TIME?

People who lack training in experimental phonetics are generally rather surprised when they learn that the acoustic speech wave does not stand up very well to the ideal concept imposed by our intuitive phonemic view of speech as a sequence of discrete units with distinct boundaries. One major shortcoming of the *Preliminaries* is the lack of a realistic discussion of the time-varying aspects of speech patterns and the temporal distribution of the acoustic articulatory and perceptual characteristics underlying the distinctive features which might have saved phonetically inexperienced people from developing an oversimplified, often naive, view of the segment structure of speech.

It is said in paragraph 2.14 of the *Preliminaries* that "For practical purposes each phoneme can be represented by a quasi-stationary spectrum in which the transfer function is invariable with respect to time, except in the manner stated for transient effects." Phoneme boundaries are said to be related to rapid changes either in the source function or in the vocal transfer function. It is also said that inherent features in contrast to prosodic features are definable without a reference to the sequence. These rules are oversimplified and need to be reformulated and expanded.

The speech spectrogram displays a mixture of continuous and discontinuous elements. A successivity of "segments" is to be seen but what from the spectrogram appears to be a natural unit may constitute only a fraction of a phoneme, e.g., the aspiration segment or the occlusion segment of a noninitial unvoiced stop. In other instances a piece of speech that stands out from the rest of the sequence as a separate unit, e.g., in virtue of a continuity of voicing, may be associated with several successive phonemes.

No unique and simple rule exists for segmentation of speech on the basis of nonphonemic criteria. I would claim, however, that a non-phonemic segmentation (1, 2) could be of value as a rationale for articulatory or spectrographic systematizations per se and as an introductory form of transcription before imposing the linguistic message concepts on the signal data. The outcome of such confrontations of preconceived linguistic structure with the observed acoustic-phonetic structure is that the number of physical sound segments comes out to be larger than the number of phonemes. Because of coarticulation effects one sound segment generally carries information on two or more successive phonemes. Conversely, a single phoneme exerts an influence on several successive sound segments of the signal structure.

When it comes to discussing the distribution of distinctive features in time one must make clear if it is the abstract message structure or the physical manifestation of speech signals that is intended. In the former case distinctive features are bounded as the phonemes although there can be continuity of a feature from one phoneme to the next. It is thus said in paragraph 1.1 of the *Preliminaries* that "The difference between the distinctive features of continuous bundles permits the division of a sequence into phonemes. This difference may be either complete, as between the last two phonemes /i/ and /ŋ/ in the word *wing* (which has no distinctive features in common), or partial as between the last two phonemes of the word *apt*."

This statement is correct on the message level. Indeed, the phoneme /i/ is categorized as nonconsonantal, vocalic, nongrave, acute, and noncompact whereas the phoneme /ŋ/ is labelled consonantal, nonvocalic, nasal, compact. One would accordingly expect a maximum of acoustic contrast between the /i/ and the /ŋ/ of *wing*.

In a multidimensional articulatory or acoustic space, however, the contrast between the two corresponding segments is minimal only. The place of tongue articulation is identical or almost identical in American English, and both segments are produced with a lowered velum, the anticipatory nasalization being a normal feature generally affecting the entire segment assigned to the /i/. The raising of the tongue against the palate closing off the mouth cavity does not affect the sound much since a substantial part is directed through the nose already in the /i/ segment. In the case of a more reduced articulation the tongue never reaches the stage of full contact with the palate and the phoneme /ŋ/ is signaled merely as the nasalization of the sound segment. The perceptual importance of nasalization of a vowel as a cue for identification of an adjacent nasal phoneme is considerable (3).

The theory of segmentation of speech on various levels is a well worth object for further research and descriptive studies. The essential point to consider is that we can measure the duration of physical events such as sound segments in a spectrogram but there exists no unique method or convention of measuring the duration of a phoneme or of a distinctive feature.

SPECIFIC FEATURES: VOCALIC AND CONSONANTAL

One of the weaker parts of the distinctive feature theory is that of defining consonants and vowels. It is in my opinion quite motivated to categorize liquids as being both vocalic and consonantal but the classification of the consonant *h* (and glides) as being nonvocalic and nonconsonantal is a more arbitrary construction although arguments can be raised in favor of such a classification. The physical criteria for the vocalic and consonantal features have not been very rigid. A small damping of vowel formants has been one of the requirements in all versions of the system. The first edition of the *Preliminaries* stressed the voiced source of vocalic sounds but the Addenda and Corrigenda chapters of the later edition turned the emphasis on the formant pattern and formulated the consonantal feature as almost the negative of the vocalic feature in terms of formant reduction.

In *Fundamentals of Language* Jakobson and Halle (4) limit the consonantal feature to a low intensity alone. In a study of the classification of Swedish phonemes (5) I introduced a new formulation retaining the concept of formant reduction in defining the consonant feature but with intensity associated with the vocalic feature. One gain of this formulation is that the phoneme /h/ accordingly contrasts with vowels as being less intense. Also /h/ differs from other consonants in the lack of pattern contrast with adjacent vowels, motivating the minus consonantal feature.

The study of Fant (1960) (5) also includes comments on the theory of the syllable. The syllable nucleus must possess the vocalic feature and it displays a *temporal contrast* with respect to adjacent sounds in terms of either higher intensity or a more vowel like structure. Syllabicity should not be ascribed to intensity alone.

TENSE/LAX AND VOICED/VOICELESS

The subject of tense and lax vowels and consonants has been given a thorough treatment by Jakobson and Halle (6). Their view on the subject does not depart substantially from that expressed in our earlier joint work. The tense versus lax opposition is intended to operate in vowels as well as in consonants. Tenseness is phonetically described by an "articulation with greater overpressure behind the place of the active source; in the case of vowels a higher subglottal pressure and in the case of stops and constrictives a higher pressure behind the place of articulation. Further-

more tenseness is associated with a more extreme articulation and with a greater time spent in an extreme articulatory position."

The two last mentioned characteristics were mentioned in our earlier work but I am somewhat sceptic about the higher overpressure. This factor when present indeed adds emphasis to tense consonants but in my opinion it has not been sufficiently well documented in experimental work. Recent studies of Malécot (17) suggest that the combined effect of pressure and duration expressed as a pulse integral could have a role in proprioceptive feedback. In my experience Swedish voiced and unvoiced stops are produced with the same subarticulatory pressure at the instance before release. This does not prove anything for English but it seems probable that the pressure factor, if present as a constituent in the opposition between American English unvoiced and voiced stops, is of relatively small significance and a secondary effect of glottal articulation. Several recent studies support the view of Lisker and Abramson (7) that it is the glottal articulation that is the basic factor.

The longer duration and higher intensity of the noise interval following at the release of an unvoiced stop is physiologically due to a delayed closing of the vocal cords compared with the voiced stops. The pulmonary pressure appears to be the same. Studies of subglottal pressure in Swedish speech does not reveal any difference in the pulmonary activity comparing voiced and unvoiced consonants or short and long vowels. I really doubt that subglottal pressure would have anything to do with the tense-lax opposition among English and French vowels.

On these grounds I hesitate to accept the use of the tense-lax opposition among American English consonants as well as vowels suggested by Halle (8) [37]. In vowels it would be motivated if the pressure factor is forgotten. Within consonants it would be just as motivated to use the voiced-voiceless distinction as the tense-lax distinction. The economy gained by one and the same feature operating in vowels as well as in consonants is of course desirable but I find it more important that the match between phonetic facts and feature criteria is optimized. We need more experimental data to illuminate this very interesting problem.

DISTINCTIVE FEATURES AND PERCEPTION[1]

I do not hold the view that the decoding of speech in the brain up to the level of phonemic identification has to follow a functional scheme strictly conforming with a distinctive feature system of language analysis. This does not imply that I consider distinctive features unimportant in speech perception. Distinctive features as phonetic classes are a psychological reality as judged from confusion tests under varying types of distortion or mental disturbance. Even in rapid mimicking (9) the decoding proceeds along phonetic classes so that, e.g., place of articulation may be confused whilst the category of stop sound is correctly recognized.

When constructing models of speech perception we should not limit our choice to a representation in terms of either allophones or features. On the contrary it seems reasonable that a decoding in terms of phonetic classes (distinctive features) is paralleled by a direct attempt of allophone decoding. I am thus more in favor of a parallel analysis of features than of a serial analysis with a succession of decisions.

The question whether a translation to equivalent motor instructions precedes phonemic identification is not important. Of greater importance is to study what aspects of known features are of primary importance to perception (10). It is observed that in some instances it is the *temporal contrast* of two successive sound segments (e.g., stops, laterals, nasals) rather than the inherent quality of each of the segments that evokes the particular auditory sensation associated with the particular class (feature). The pertinent problem is to find what transforms we should apply to the speech wave data in order to extract the information bearing elements that operate in speech perception. Attempts to avoid the search for auditory relevant sound characteristics by an uncritical acceptance of the view that perception is merely a reconstruction of the production does not appear very fruitful.

Recent studies of Chistovich et al. in Stockholm have revealed interesting results concerning vowel perception. These studies

[1]A more detailed treatment is contained in the *QPSR* article (16).

(11) support the view of a categorical perception of isolated vowels and the existence of an F_1F_2 quantization in accordance with our working principles of acoustic phonetic analysis.

SWEDISH VOWELS

The Swedish vowel system is generally presented in terms of nine long and nine short phonemes. Special pre-*r* variants of the open unrounded and rounded front vowels, in Swedish orthography ä and ö, stand out as well recognized allophones of an especially "open" quality.

The following phonemic symbols referred to as the STA alphabet will be used for the nine vowels. Approximate IPA symbols are included as examples of phonetic values in contexts other than before [r].

GROUP	STA	IPA	STA	IPA
I. Back vowels	o_1	ʉ:	o_2	U
	$å_1$	o:	$å_2$	ɔ
	a_1	ɑ:	a_2	a-a
II. Unrounded front vowels	i_1	i:	i_2	I
	e_1	e:	e_2	e-ɛ
	$ä_1$	ɛ:	$ä_2$	ɛ
III. Rounded front vowels	y_1	y:	y_2	Y
	$ʉ_1$	ʉ:	$ʉ_2$	θ
	$ö_1$	ø:	$ö_2$	ø-œ

In my first attempt of ordering (12) I chose to oppose group I to groups II and III in terms of the grave/acute distinction and group III was naturally opposed to group II in terms of the flat/plain feature. So far my views have not changed. However, a division within the three major groups in terms of articulatory opening, i.e., the compactness feature classifying not only /å₁/ and /e₁/ but also by an intermediate ± degree of compactness did not conform well with phonetic facts, the F_1 of /ʉ₁/ being the same as the F_1 of /y₁/. Also within the short vowels the F_1 of /u₂/ was generally not significantly different from the F_1 of /ö₂/. I therefore chose in later works (5, 13, 14) to use three degrees of flatness assigning an intermediate value of flatness to the phonemes /y/ and /ö/ and to the phoneme /ʉ/ the maximal degree of flatness. This conforms well with the flatness criteria of low $F_1 + F_2 + F_3$ and the extreme degree of lip-rounding in the /ʉ/ and /o/ phonemes. In group I either flatness or compactness in three levels can be used for the further division.

An alternative solution which perhaps comes closer to the views of Roman Jakobson would be the following. In group I flatness is used to separate phonemes /o/ and /å/ from /a/, and /å/ is opposed to /o/ by the greater compactness. Now in group II and group III the opposition sharp/plain is introduced[2] to differentiate /i/ and /e/ from /ä/ and /y/ and /ö/ from /ʉ/. The criterion of sharpness is higher F_2 and F_3 everything else being equal. In this sense sharpness is given a function similar to that of diffuseness in Halle's vowel analyses (8) [37]. By this arrangement one avoids introducing three degrees of flatness or compactness and four binary features specify the entire system as shown below.

FEATURE[3]	o	å	a	i	e	ä	y	ʉ	ö
grave	+	+	+	−	−	−	−	−	−
flat	+	+	−	−	−	−	+	+ ᵒ	+
compact	−	+	+	−	+	+	−	−	+
sharp				+	+	−	+	−	+

In this solution /ʉ/ differs from /ö/ by two features. Within the system of short vowels /ö₂/ is opposed to /ʉ₂/ primarily by the sharpening (palatalization) whereas within the long vowels /ö₁/ differs from /ʉ/ primarily in terms of greater compactness.

In terms of economy this new system is superior to my previous system. Four binary classes versus one binary and two ternary distinctions of 16 versus 18 maximal number of combinations of the code. However, the more redundant system may be phonetically simpler and more realistic. Further studies are needed to evaluate the various alternatives.

REFERENCES

(1) FANT, G., "Descriptive Analysis of the Acoustic Aspects of Speech," *Logos* 5 (1962), 3–17.

(2) FANT, G., and LINDBLOM, B., "Studies of Minimal Speech Sound Units," *STL-QPSR* 2/1961, 1–11.

(3) MÁRTONY, J., "The Role of Formant Amplitudes in Synthesis of Nasal Consonants," *STL-QPSR* 3/1964, 28–31.

(4) JAKOBSON, R., and HALLE, M., *Fundamentals of Language* ('s-Gravenhage, 1956).

(5) FANT, G., "Structural Classification of Swedish Phonemes," *STL-QPSR* 2/1965, 10–15.

(6) JAKOBSON, R., and HALLE, M., "Tenseness and Laxness," in R. Jakobson, *Selected Writings*, I ('s-Gravenhage, 1962), 550–555.

(7) LISKER, L., and ABRAMSON, A. S., "A Cross-Language Study of Voicing in Initial Stops: Acoustical Measurements," *Word* 20 (1964), 384–422.

(8) HALLE, M., "Phonology in Generative Grammar," *Word* 18 (1962), 54–72 [37].

(9) KOZHEVNIKOV, V. A., and CHISTOVICH, L. A., *Speech: Articulation and Perception* (English translation), US Dept. of Commerce, *JPRS: 30, 543* (Washington, 1962).

(10) FANT, G., "Auditory Patterns of Speech," published in the *Proceedings of the Symposium on Models for the Perception of Speech and Visual Form*, Boston, Mass., Nov. 11–14, 1964.

(11) CHISTOVICH, L., et al., "Mimicking of Synthetic Vowels," *STL-QPSR* 2/1966, 1–18, and CHISTOVICH, L., et al., "Mimicking and Perception of Synthetic Vowels, Part II," *STL-QPSR* 3/1966, 1–3.

(12) FANT, G., "Phonetic and Phonemic Basis for the Transcription of Swedish Word Material," *Acta Oto-Laryngologica, Suppl.* 116 (1954), 24–29.

(13) FANT, G., "Acoustic Analysis and Synthesis of Speech with Applications to Swedish," *Ericsson Technics* 15 (1959), 1–106.

(14) FANT, G., "Modern Instruments and Methods for Acoustic Studies of Speech," *Acta Polytechnica Scandinavica* 246 (1958), 84 p.

(15) JAKOBSON, R., FANT, G., and HALLE, M., *Preliminaries to Speech Analysis: The Distinctive Features and Their Correlates*," Acoustics Laboratory, MIT, Technical Report No. 13 (1952), 58 pp.; 4th printing, published by the MIT Press (Cambridge, Mass., 1963).

(16) FANT, G., "The Nature of Distinctive Features," *STL-QPSR* 4/1966, 1–14 (the topics of speech perception and vowel classification are expanded in this edition).

(17) MALÉCOT, A., "Mechanical Pressure as an Index of 'Force of Articulation,'" *Phonetica* 14 (1966), 169–180.

[2]Suggested by S. Öhman.
[3]In terms of the compactness and sharpness features, the vowel [e] may be either + + or − −.

III.b

Transformational-Generative Phonology

36

REVIEW OF

THE SOUND PATTERN
*OF RUSSIAN:**
A Linguistic and Acoustical
Investigation

BY MORRIS HALLE.
(With an excursus on the contextual variants
of the Russian vowels by Lawrence G. Jones.
[Description and Analysis of Contemporary
Standard Russian, Vol. 1.] Pp. 206.
's-Gravenhage: Mouton & Co., 1959.)

CHARLES A. FERGUSON

1. Contents This important book is both disappointing and highly rewarding. It is disappointing because it makes no significant new contribution to our understanding of the Russian sound system. It is rewarding because it contains a very clear, persuasive account of a new approach to linguistic theory which is rapidly gaining ground, and because it provides an impressive body of information on the acoustic specification of phonological units.

The Introductory Note by the editors, Roman Jakobson and C. H. van Schooneveld (5–8), is an eloquent programmatic statement depicting the aims of the whole series of studies of Contemporary Standard Russian (CSR) of which the present volume is the first. There can be no doubt that this series, which has arisen from the research project directed by Jakobson at Harvard 1950–1958, will be a major landmark in linguistic science, and one can only hope that other languages will be

treated as thoroughly and as imaginatively by other scholars before long.

The Foreword by the author (11–15) explains that the original aim of the study was "to establish the acoustical correlates of various entities that have traditionally been used in the description of the phonic aspects of languages" (11). It then proceeds to make clear that the study developed into an attempt to exemplify a new theory of linguistics, which views the phonological description of languages as one chapter of a set of rules which will specify all and only the grammatical utterances of the language. In addition, this particular study, by providing "acoustical measurements on various linguistic entities," attempts to establish "the link between the theoretical entities of linguistic descriptions and the real world of sound" (13).

In this Foreword, Halle makes a great point, following Chomsky, of explicitly rejecting "discovery procedures" in phonology,

*Reprinted from *Language* 38.284–298 (1962) by permission.

or for that matter in all linguistic analysis. He seems to consider it almost immoral to try to describe the procedures an investigator should follow in determining the phonological structure of a language. This point is hard to understand. When Halle says that the identification of the method by which Newton discovered the principles of gravitation belongs to the philosophy of science and not to science itself, this seems quite reasonable. Similarly it seems quite reasonable to turn over to psychologists or philosophers of science the investigation of the methods by which a given innovating linguist has arrived at a concept like the phoneme, the language family, glottochronology, or transformational grammar. But this is quite different from trying to provide techniques for linguistic analysis. Once the innovator has arrived at a new concept it is presumably his duty or the duty of his followers to communicate it to others and then to help devise techniques for putting the concept to work in actual linguistic analysis. The more detailed, the more explicit these techniques are, the better, i.e., the more success investigators will have in applying them and in testing the usefulness and validity of the new concepts. Halle himself sometimes carries out this duty very well. For example, he gives three pages of careful instructions (34–36) on how to construct a branching diagram before announcing (37) that "The phonological system of a language will be presented by means of a branching diagram." The reviewer for one is grateful for this kind of helpful explanation of a new discovery procedure and cannot understand why Halle does not want such help from others.

The main body of the book consists of two parts, Phonology and Acoustics. The first part contains an explanation of the new theory of phonology (19–44) and an application of the theory to Russian (44–75). The second part consists of an introduction to acoustic science for linguists (79–90), a history of the acoustic investigation of speech sounds (91–109), and the description of the acoustic correlates of the distinctive features of Russian (111–153). Jones's excursus on the contextual variants of Russian vowel phonemes follows (157–197), and the book is completed by a bibliography. There is no index.

Since in the Chomskian view of grammar

writing the phonology of a language is presented only in the final (and relatively unimportant?) chapter of the whole grammar, and since the organization of the phonology chapter is determined by the requirements for simplicity, consistency, and so on of the total grammar rather than by internal consideration of the phonological material, the publishing of a phonology such as Halle's of Russian, separate from the rest of the grammar of the language, is a very poor way of demonstrating the merits of the Chomskian approach to linguistic description. The very virtues that are claimed for the organization of the phonological material could be fully apparent only if one had the whole grammar at hand to relate it to. As it is, one can only compare it with other presentations of Russian phonology which have been done from other points of view, and in this comparison it suffers: it seems less simple, less clear, less useful for most of the purposes for which one consults phonological descriptions than several previous presentations.[1]

2. Phonological Theory The author characterizes phonological analysis by listing the six basic conditions which he feels it must fulfill. He states these conditions clearly and straightforwardly, and he has done linguists a service in doing so. The examination of his list of conditions offers a very direct way to understand and evaluate the author's views.

Condition (1): In phonology, speech events are represented as sequences of entities of two kinds: *segments,* to which specific phonetic (articulatory as well as acoustical) properties

---

[1]For those of us who still regard the phonology of a language as deserving autonomous description, there are various ways of treating it in a fashion parallel to Chomskian grammars. One might select, for example, certain basic syllables, analogous to the kernel sentences of Chomskian grammar, describe their structure essentially by immediate constituents, and then formulate rules of transformation which would provide as terminal strings all and only the phonologically possible syllables, analogous to Chomskian grammatical sentences. It is even conceivable that approaches of this sort would be more than just interesting exercises, since they might produce results which would show correlations, at present unsuspected, with other aspects of language structure or with the process of language learning.

are assigned, and *boundaries,* which are characterized solely by their effects on the former. (19)

This full recognition of these two fundamental entities in phonology is to be welcomed: the author has avoided the difficulties of those who spend time and effort trying to show that junctures are really like regular phonemes and of those who prefer to brush junctural phenomena aside. One may regret somewhat the choice of the term "boundary," since this has usefully served as the colorless, everyday word for points of grammatical segmentation without further technical specification in phonological terms. For the colorless, unspecified term Halle is now forced to use other expressions, most often "morpheme junction."

The one real difficulty with Condition (1) is that it offers no satisfactory home for the so-called suprasegmentals. Many such phenomena, including English stress, Japanese pitch-fall, and Danish stød can be analyzed as prosodic features of segments (i.e., with /a/, /á/, and so on as separate phonemes) although many would prefer to analyze them as phonological entities in their own right. But what about intonation? If Halle means to exclude intonation from phonology, then he presumably regards it as a part of grammar, or as a third system apart from phonology and grammar, or as altogether outside linguistics. Linguists can be found who maintain each one of these positions. If, on the other hand, Halle means to include intonation in phonology, then presumably he is opting for the pitch-level approach, but with the pitch levels as prosodic features of segments so that *a* on pitch level 1 is a separate phoneme from *a* on pitch level 2 and so on.

Condition (2): The phonetic properties in terms of which segments are characterized belong to a specific, narrowly restricted set of such properties called the *distinctive features.* All distinctive features are binary. (19)

The first sentence of this could possibly be interpreted or rephrased in such a way as to include such different approaches as that of Trubetzkoy's *Grundzüge,* Pike's *Phonemics,* or Bloch's "Postulates" [16]. At any rate, in one form or another this condition is met in most approaches to the structural analysis of

phonology. The view expressed in the second sentence, however, is not so wide-spread, and is probably limited in its extreme form to Roman Jakobson and his followers. Jakobson and others have certainly shown that it is possible and instructive to analyze languages in purely binary terms, but they have not yet convinced other linguists that this is always desirable or that it is in any sense "natural" or necessary. There is no need to discuss this point here. If the case of the pure binarists is really sound, the superiority of their analyses of real languages will eventually persuade other linguists. If it is not completely sound, criticism from others will eventually lead to modification or abandonment of the view.

Condition (3): A phonological description must provide a method for inferring (deriving) from every phonological representation the utterance symbolized, without recourse to information not contained in the phonological representation. (21)

This condition is quite rightly accepted as fundamental by Halle. It may be noted, however, that when he reformulates it as "all distinctively different utterances are represented by different symbol sequences" (21) he neglects the problem of lexical homonymy. In leading into his discussion of the next condition he touches on conditioned homonymy, such that a given morpheme has an allomorph homophonous with an allomorph of some other morpheme under certain phonological or grammatical conditions, but he does not mention the problem of full homophony between two morphemes (e.g., the two utterances *He bought us a pair* and *He bought us a pear,* which are distinctively different but may be phonologically identical). It may safely be assumed that every language has cases of this kind which point up the fundamental duality of linguistic structure: phonemic contrasts serve to distinguish grammatically distinct utterances, but not all grammatically distinct utterances are distinguished by phonemic contrasts.

Halle then moves on to the fourth condition, which he numbers 3a, presumably so that later on he can reject it without interfering with the numbering system. It reads:

Condition (3a): A phonological description

must include instructions for inferring (deriving) the proper phonological representation of any speech event, without recourse to information not contained in the physical signal. (21)

The author notes that linguists have added certain limitations to this condition by requiring for each language that a minimum total number of symbols be used for such representations and that the sounds represented by each symbol should be phonetically similar. Representations which satisfy Conditions (3) and (3a) are called "phonemic," and those which satisfy only (3) are "morphophonemic." This formulation seems quite adequate. He then asserts, however, on the basis of a Russian example and alleged parallels in analytical procedures of other sciences, that Condition (3a) should be dispensed with, being an "unwarranted complication which has no place in a scientific description of a language" (24).

Halle's Russian example is concerned with the voicing of /c č x/ before voiced obstruents. The problem is the familiar one, found in many languages, of a conditioned variation in sound feature (e.g., voicing before voiced obstruent, intervocalic spirantization, final devoicing) which is regarded as allophonic for some segments but as phonemic alternation for others. Halle's point is that it is more economical (and more natural?) to describe the variation once for all in the grammar than to separate it out on two levels reported in two different parts of the grammar. Lees in his panoramic review of Chomsky's *Syntactic Structures* uses this same kind of example (final devoicing in Turkish).[2] Halle refers to this with approval (22 fn. 12), and since Lees' explanation is fuller it may be examined here for support of Halle's position.

Lees says, "final morphophonemic b, d, ǰ, g, ɢ, r, and l are devoiced to [p, t, č, k, q] and [r̥, l̥]. Since the traditional treatment recognized [r̥, l̥] . . . as allophones of /r, l/, but [p, t, č, k, q] as separate phonemes, the rule of devoicing must be stated twice . . ." Leaving aside the fact that final devoicing in Turkish is neither so general nor so clearcut as Lees suggests (e.g., final voiced and voiceless spirants contrast, final nasals are devoiced

slightly or not at all), we must note that the devoicing of the final stops and affricates is functionally different from the devoicing of final /r l/. When a Turk hears a new word (e.g., a proper name or new technical term) ending in a voiceless stop or affricate he does not know how to treat that word morphophonemically, i.e., whether the consonant in question may be voiced elsewhere in the paradigm. When a Turk hears a new word ending in voiceless [r] or [l̥] he "knows" that elsewhere in the paradigm the voiced allophone appears. The former is phonemic neutralization, the second is subphonemic variation. The /r l/ are more nearly parallel to final /s z f v m n/ than to final voiceless stops and affricates. It is, of course, the duty of the analyst to point out that final /r l/ are devoiced just as final morphophonemic *b d* etc. are devoiced and that this is a significant parallel. It is just as important for him, however, to point out that these two kinds of final devoicing are quite different in the phonological and grammatical structure of the language.[2a]

The effect of Condition (3a) is to set a careful line between phonology and grammar, and it is the abandonment of this condition and erasure of its dividing line which constitute the greatest break between the current approaches to phonological analysis and that of Chomsky and Halle. It may seem plausible, as they suggest, that the sound system of a language is so intimately tied up with its grammar, and functions so completely as a tool of the grammar, that any attempt to treat it separately from the grammar is fundamentally mistaken. The autonomy of phonology, however, is a concept arrived at as a result of over a century of linguistic research, and the concept is not to be discarded lightly: to discard it would surrender some of the most striking achievements of linguistic science.

First, the autonomy of phonology was forced upon investigators in historical linguistics in the nineteenth century by the facts of language change. The discovery of Verner's law made clear that, in general, phonological

---

[2]*Language* 33.389–390 (1957).

[2a]It is a pleasure to note that Lees, in his new *Phonology of Modern Standard Turkish* (Bloomington, 1961), which became available after this review was written, lists these two devoicings in different places.

change takes place under conditions and within limitations which are in phonological terms and not in grammatical or semantic terms. The conditions under which these particular changes took place involved features such as voicing or voicelessness of neighboring sounds and the position of accent with regard to the sound in question, and the changes took place not only not in terms of grammatical conditions but in many cases in direct opposition to "natural" grammatical parallels and analogies.

A synchronic analysis which ties phonology and grammar up in a neat bundle not only falsifies the current situation but makes it impossible to understand the diachrony. One area of flux which is of importance diachronically is the borderline between phonology and grammar, where the fit of the two segmentations shifts and structural changes take place.

An illustration may make the point clear. Chomsky and Halle prefer to derive phonological junctures from grammatical information. Obviously junctures often serve to indicate grammatical boundaries of one kind or another, and indeed this may with considerable justification be regarded as their fundamental purpose; but the fact is that the fit between junctures and grammatical boundaries in a language is always shifting, and such shifting can be well described only if the two are separately analyzed. For example, it has often been noted that English has a contrast between two pronunciations of the cluster *dr,* one in which the two consonants are closely amalgamated into an affricate-like sound and the other in which the two sounds have values very similar to those of utterance-final *d* and utterance-initial *r*.[3] The first kind of pronunciation is normal for cases like *Audrey,* the second for cases like *bedrock.* Current analytical procedures regard the former as /dr/ and the latter as /d+r/, where the + represents a phonemic juncture. Chomsky and Halle, while recognizing the phonetic difference, would prefer to derive it from the difference in grammatical structure, since words like *bedrock* have a morpheme boundary and words with the affricate have not. An analysis of this sort makes it very difficult to account for cases where the

same grammatical structure yields different juncture patterns. Many speakers of English regularly use /d+r/ in the word *bedroom;* others use /dr/. In either case most analysts would still recognize a morpheme boundary between *bed* and *room.* For the speakers who have no /+/ in *bedroom* the way is now open for the formation of a new compound with /+/, contrasting with the old one, and in fact such speakers may use the pronunciation *bed+room* to mean 'space for beds' so that a sentence can occur like *There's not enough bed+room in this bedroom.* Any analysis of English which fails to provide machinery for describing this kind of variation is not an adequate analysis of the language, since this kind of variation occurs throughout the English-speaking world and has apparently been occurring for many centuries, though of course not necessarily in this particular item.

Halle shows awareness of this kind of phenomenon at one point, where he says (64), "... in a slow, solemn style of speech ... there is a tendency to treat every accented word as a separate phonemic phrase and hence to pause between words ...." Since he maintains elsewhere that the occurrence of phonetic "boundaries" is determined by the grammatical structures, either he means that the sentences with more such boundaries have a different grammatical structure, nowhere referred to, or he is inconsistent.

In the second place the autonomy of phonology has repeatedly been brought home to us in synchronic work, most obviously perhaps in studies of the principles of language learning but also in dialect studies and ordinary description and analysis of languages. People who are learning to speak a second language may develop excellent pronunciation but poor control of grammar and lexicon or, perhaps more frequently, the reverse. A second-language learner generally finds it easy to use phonological distinctions he already has in his native language to serve quite different grammatical and lexical ends in the second language. In child speech there is, apart from the earliest stages, a surprisingly independent development of the phonological structure and the grammatical structure. Finally, in plotting phonological and lexico-grammatical isoglosses it is often quite clear that subareas of different phonological systems do not coincide well with

[3] Cf. D. Jones, *Outline of English Phonetics*[8] 167 (London, 1957).

subareas of grammatical systems and lexical inventories.

Condition (4): The phonological description must be appropriately integrated into the grammar of the language. Particularly, in selecting phonological representations of individual morphemes, these must be chosen so as to yield simple statements of all grammatical operations—like inflection and derivation—in which they may be involved. (24)

This condition is neither explained nor justified; it is simply used as an excuse for presenting the theory of grammar which Halle wishes to follow in this book. That theory regards a grammar as a kind of postulate set and every possible sentence in the language as a theorem which can be derived from the postulates by the application of definite rules of inference.[4] A grammar according to Halle consists of several sets of rules. The highest set, the phrase structure rules, begin with the symbol "Sentence" and produce a specification of it in terms of other symbols. The final set, the phonological rules, produce a representation of the actual phonetic features of a sentence. Between these two sets of rules there is a set of transformational rules which take the results of the phrase structure rules and turn them into something on which the phonological rules can operate.

The phrase structure rules which Halle believes appropriate for Russian (though of course they are only illustrated, not fully explained, and presumably have yet to be worked out) produce terminal strings of quasiphonemic representations of lexical morphemes but morpheme class symbols for grammatical morphemes—e.g., &{pj'an}&Masc.&Nom.&, which represents p,j'anij 'drunk'. Halle's phonological rules for Russian (although not necessarily for other languages) are split into two sets, the MS rules, which are actually applied *before* the transformation rules, and the P rules, which are applied *after* the transformation rules. The MS rules result in a represen-

tation of lexical morphemes in morphonemes while leaving the grammatical morphemes and boundaries in morphemic notation—e.g., &{-+-+---*-- +--++-+---+-}& Masc.&Nom.&, which represents p,j'anij 'drunk'. The transformational rules result in a representation consisting entirely of morphonemes and boundaries, of which each morphoneme is shown by an ordered sequence of pluses and minuses (e.g., {|-+-+---*-- +--++-+---+- +-+-- --%}, which represents p,j'anij 'drunk' between a phonemic phrase boundary and a word boundary). The P rules result in full specification of the distinctive features present in each segment of the sentence, i.e., a "transcription of the sentence, which can be directly converted into sound" (42) (e.g., |fči³ra¹|p,ja²ni³jbra³d,a¹gə⁴| žžo²kce¹rkə⁴f,|, which represents the Russian sentence presumably translatable as 'Yesterday a drunk tramp burned down the church').

Halle gives all the phonological rules for Russian, thirty MS rules, numbered 1a to 11e (58–61) and thirty-nine P rules, numbered 1a to 19 (63–75). It is a remarkable feat for the author to provide the phonological rules without the rest of the grammar, and it is impossible for the reviewer to evaluate the degree of appropriate integration into the grammar without seeing the total grammar.

Condition (5): In phonological representations the number of specified features is consistently reduced to a minimum compatible with satisfying Conditions (3) and (4). (29, 30)

This condition turns out to be very troublesome. The author for some reason wants to play his game of phonological analysis in such a way that the transcription of morphemes identifies each phonological segment only to the extent that its component features are not predictable from the nature of the segment itself (some features imply the presence of others in the same segment), from the nature of the segments on either side of it, or from certain grammatical rules (e.g., placement of accent in declension).

For more orthodox descriptivists the result that Halle reaches could be more directly described as a dictionary entry form for each morpheme of the language, or at least each stem, with the following characteristics: (a) all its allomorphs can be derived from it by fol-

---

[4]The reviewer has long been convinced that this is a very useful way to regard a grammar. It must be pointed out, however, that such a view by no means requires a number of the other features of the theory of grammar followed by Halle. Many ways of constructing the postulates can be imagined.

lowing a set of general rules, (b) the transcription and the rules are in terms of segments of phoneme length, (c) the segments are identified in terms of distinctive features, and (d) only those distinctive features are specified which cannot be inferred from the set of general rules.

There can be no question that it is possible to operate with a morphophonemic level of this type in Russian, but it is by no means clear that it is always possible to cover all allomorphs by a single morpheme spelling or that it is wise to limit morphophonemic transcription and rules to segments of phoneme length. One can readily imagine languages where this approach would not be very helpful, such as a language with a great deal of suppletion or a language where allomorphy is largely in segments longer or shorter than phonemes. Also, it must be noted that it is insistence on Condition (5) that forces Halle to split his phonological rules into two levels, the MS rules and P rules, a misfortune not too different from that of having final devoicing and similar phenomena in two places in a grammar which keeps Condition (3a).

The system of notation which results from Halle's requirements growing out of Condition (5) is so complicated that it defied repeated attempts on the part of the reviewer to master it. One problem is the use of numerous starred symbols to indicate incompletely specified segments, e.g., *'a for unspecified accented nondiffuse vowel, *A for unspecified nondiffuse vowel,[5] # for unspecified vowel alternating with zero, *s for either *s ~ s*, or *s ~ s, ~ z ~ z,* (examples of both uses 49). Another problem is the use of italic and roman type within braces, which is explained (30 fn. 23, 32), but which does not seem to agree with the explanation; e.g., why {*iv'anu*} in italics (37) or {*l*es} in roman (41)? Possibly many of the questionable transcriptions are misprints, but if so this is especially regrettable in the pages explaining the system (30–41). Sample uncertainties: 30, last paragraph, line 2: Why the third asterisk in {*a*u*}? 31, top diagram: Why is *u* listed as vocalic minus? 33, table: Why is the *r* in *fčira* incompletely specified *r*

while the *r* in *brod* is completely specified *r* when they have identical matrices?

One result of such complicated rules and complicated notation is that inconsistencies and errors are likely to arise in the analysis. To take a simple example, Halle's P rules provide no way to get from {*dožž*}, the morpheme 'rain', to [d'oš,š,], its transcription in fully specified morphonemes, since final devoicing (rules P1b, P2, P3a) is prescribed *before* the sharping of {*žž*} (rule P4). Such minor mistakes cannot be used as an argument against the validity of the approach, but they certainly can be cited as evidence of the difficulty of carrying out and presenting an analysis of this kind.

Condition (6): The & markers are translated by the rules of morphology into phonological boundaries or altogether eliminated. (41)

This condition is simply a statement of one requirement that Halle has set up for grammar writing, and it is difficult to interpret it as a condition which a phonological description must satisfy. It seems totally out of place here. In fact, Halle's entire treatment of Russian junctures, while showing some interesting and original features, is very sloppily presented. Of the five phonological boundaries he lists (41), two are clearly in complementary distribution, numbers 3 and 4. The symbol = is frequently used within square brackets where it does not belong. The dash boundary is not well thought out: it invalidates the statement "nor are there 'phonological' words with more than one accented vowel" (49) and it could have been used to advantage in the discussion of voicing in foreign words (74). Finally, no attempt is made to analyze the boundaries as bundles of binary distinctive elements, perfectly possible and surely desirable from Halle's point of view.

3. Russian Phonology Turning now to the merits of Halle's description of Russian phonology, it can be reported that he provides a list of the phonemes/morphonemes, an identification of each in terms of distinctive features, a fairly full statement of the distributional "constraints" of the phonemes, and a moderately full statement of the range of phonetic variation of the phonemes. These last two are

---

[5]Wrongly defined (57 fn 2a) as unspecified diffuse vowel.

provided in the form of sets of rules—the MS rules and the P rules referred to above. But all this information is of course available elsewhere; what is new is the organization and presentation of the material, and the wealth of acoustic data, which will be discussed separately below.

A definitive statement of Russian phonology, however, could well have gone beyond a mere rehashing of the existing information, no matter how thoroughly or how brilliantly rehashed. First, one could have hoped for an assembling of all the fundamental information previously available and a filling in of the gaps. This was not done. For example, there is very little detail on the articulatory side from the experimental phonetics tradition. There is no treatment of frequency of occurrence of the various phonological elements. The suprasegmental phenomena are given only the most cursory treatment: accent is discussed at some length and rules for five phonetic levels of prominence in terms of accent and juncture are given (74–75), but there is not even a statement on the possible positions of stress in a "phonological word" or "phonological phrase." Intonation is not mentioned.

Second, one could have hoped for full discussion of the moot points of Russian phonological analysis: the points which raise interesting questions either for the general theory of sound systems or for understanding of the diachronic and dialectological facts of Slavic languages. All these moot points are ignored except for two: whether the affricates are to be regarded as clusters or unit phonemes/morphonemes (50–51) and whether the palatal sibilants, š and ž are independent phonemes/morphonemes (51–52).

One of the most interesting features of Russian phonology is the role of palatalization or sharping of consonants and vowels. In view of the pervasive effects of this phenomenon in Russian and its central role in the phonology, its analysis deserves full discussion. Alternative analyses in terms of distinctive vowel phonemes, distinctive consonant phonemes, Harris's long components, and Firthian prosodies are worth examining, not only to find the most useful description of Russian for its own sake but also to point up the differing roles of such phenomena as "emphasis" in Arabic, nasality in South Asian languages, and so on, which are

somewhere between ordinary distinctive feature components of segmental phonemes and more clearly accentual phenomena such as Danish stød or Japanese pitch-fall. The reader must try to discover the fundamental facts from some of the remarks on vowel allophones and the description of sequential constraints in consonant clusters. The only discussion of this interesting and important analytic problem as such in the book is a very brief but clear statement in Jones's excursus (159) of some reasons for regarding palatalization as a consonant feature and not a vowel feature in Russian.

Closely connected with this problem is the perennial debate—at least among Russian phoneticians—on the phonemic status of [i] and [ɨ]; Halle does not mention the question at all. It has become customary among structuralists of almost all persuasions (including Daniel Jones, Jakobson, Trager, Hjelmslev, and Boyanus) to regard them as allophones of a single phoneme. The only investigators who call them separate phonemes seem to be scholars who are not fully aware of the principles and procedures of structural analysis. Yet there is more to the problem than this. The phenomenon in question is one found in various languages and not adequately recognized or discussed by phonologists, the opposition which is just barely in existence. It is safe to assume that for many millions of Russian speakers [i] and [ɨ] are in full complementation, with their respective occurrences conditioned by the nature of the surrounding consonants. Yet monolingual speakers of Russian can apparently be found who have occurrences of these sounds in "wrong" positions, whether from pronunciations of foreign proper names which have become Russianized, or from dialect forms in their standard Russian, or from quite different sources. Russians seem to hear the i–ɨ difference more readily than e–ɛ and others; some Russians are even reported to recite the alphabet using [i] for и and [ɨ] for ы. In a definitive treatment of Russian phonology one would welcome data on these points, again not only to get the full picture for Russian but to learn more of the surprising stability of phenomena of this kind where two sound types continue in an uncertain relationship instead of becoming definitely allophones or separate phonemes throughout the speech community (cf. *s–ś* in Bengali, *e–æ* in Turkish, and so on). A fuller treatment of this phenomenon would throw light on such problems as "overall" phonological analysis of languages and the origin of new phonemes.

Another moot question or set of moot questions in Russian phonology is the analysis of the affricates. The questions, phrased in the most uncompromisingly phonemic way, are these. (1) Are the sounds spelled ц ч unit phonemes rather than clusters? (2) If they are unit phonemes are there voiced counterparts? (3) Is the sound spelled щ a unit phoneme (vs. a cluster of some kind, geminate or other)? (4) If it is a unit phoneme is there a voiced counterpart? Halle answers (1) affirmatively. His answer to (2) is that there is only nondistinctive voicing in voiced obstruent clusters. Questions (3) and (4) he answers negatively by deriving the phonetic facts of one variety of Russian from the morphonemes {š ž č} and various boundaries by his P rules.

The present review is not the place to offer answers to these questions, but it *is* the place to express regret that Halle discusses them in such an inadequate way. One wonders, for example, about his statements that "the compact acute (palatal) consonants raise special problems only in the Moscow literary standard" and that "the facts are well known" (51). The facts are variously reported and the phonological interpretation is a problem in other varieties of standard Russian and in dialects. He eliminates, perhaps quite properly, some occurrences of palatalized [š,] and [ž,] as foreignisms (73), but he does not comment on the status of [dz] and palatalized [dž,], which are infrequent but certainly present in varieties of Standard Russian; e.g., thousands of people use the Dzeržinskaya subway stop in Moscow each day; many Russians are said to pronounce Tadžik with [i]. Since this is an area of flux it is particularly important to describe the facts accurately and to examine alternative structural analyses.

Another point that goes unmentioned is the voiced velar fricative which is used by some speakers in a handful of words. It is by no means clear from the fragmentary descriptions of this phenomenon in the grammars just how frequent the usage is and in what words it occurs. It is often attributed only to old people or very pious people, but it can hardly be ex-

cluded from CSR when apparently there are millions of speakers who use it and even the most recent pronouncing dictionary of Avanesov and Ožegov lists this variant pronunciation for a fair number of entries. This problem, too, is of general linguistic interest: the phoneme that is well integrated into the phonemic system of a language but occurs only in a very few words, at least one of which is a very common one (cf. Arabic /ḷ/, Tunica /g/).

4. Distinctive-Feature Analysis   The distinctive-feature analysis of Russian phonemes is presented by Halle in the customary table of pluses, minuses, and zeros. The table (45) calls the entities involved "morphonemes," but since they are listed in their fully specified form and seem to be identical with the entities between slant lines which are discussed in the acoustic analysis of Chapter 5, we may assume that they are equivalent to traditional phonemes. Questions were raised on points of Russian phonemic analysis in the preceding section of this review; in this section it will be assumed that Halle's phonemic analysis is satisfactory, and the discussion will be concerned only with evaluation of his distinctive-feature analysis.

Halle has 43 phonemes, 11 distinctive features, and a total of 271 distinctive-feature statements, i.e., pluses or minuses on the chart.[6] In offering a critique one could suggest various alternative analyses, either more economical (i.e., with fewer distinctive features or fewer statements) or having statements more in accord with phonetic or distributional facts of the language. Let us take an example of each type to illustrate the possible lines of reworking the analysis.

At first glance the chart shows several distinctive features in complementary distribution, viz., accent and diffuseness are distinctive only for the vowels; stridency, nasality, continuantness, voicing, and sharping are distinctive only for the consonants. In trying to match up these complementary features to re-

---

[6]The reviewer accepts the figure 271 on faith. Halle says "271 distinctive feature statements (pluses or minuses in Table I-3, or branches in Figure I-1)" (44). Actual count shows 272 pluses and minuses in the chart and roughly a third this number of branches in the diagram.

duce the total number, we must bear in mind that distinctive-feature analysis is supposed to have cross-language validity and therefore the matching must not be done in a way which would not work for other languages. Thus, nasality in some languages is distinctive for both consonants and vowels; hence consonantal nasality in Russian could not be identified with some other distinctive feature of vowels. But one identification seems immediately plausible: accent and voicing.

Orthodox distinctive-feature analysis maintains that voicing is never distinctive in vowels (i.e., phonemes that are vocalic + and consonantal −) and that accent is never distinctive for consonants (vocalic −, consonantal +) although in some languages it may be distinctive for liquids (vocalic +, consonantal +) and nasals. Surely it would be possible to find some kind of acoustic resemblance between voicing and accent at least as plausible as that between compactness in consonants and compactness in vowels (cf. the strikingly different characterizations of compactness 127–128, 133–134, and 136). This alternative analysis, which would make accent and voicing the same distinctive feature, would not, of course, reduce the total number of distinctive feature "statements," since the 31 pluses and minuses under the two features would simply appear under the same feature, but it would reduce the number of distinctive features by one[7] and would suggest an interesting insight into the functioning of sound systems. Various other alternative analyses of this kind deserve consideration.

As an example of the other type of alternative analysis, which attempts to bring the statements more into line with the phonetic and distributional facts, let us take the analysis of /j/. For some reason, apparently connected with a-priori notions of distinctive-feature analysis, /j/ is interpreted as a "glide," i.e., nonvocalic and nonconsonantal and thus the only completely isolated, unpaired phoneme in the language. Would it not be better to recognize it as similar to unaccented /i/ in distinctive features except for being conso-

nantal? In such an analysis the values of /j/, /i/, and /'i/ would be:

	/j/	/i/	/'i/
vocalic	+	+	+
consonantal	+	−	−
diffuse	+	+	+
low tonality	−	−	−
accented	0	−	+

It is true that this analysis would add two more "statements" to the distinctive-feature analysis, but the analysis would now fit the phonetic and distributional facts much better. Halle ignores the resemblance between /i/ and /j/ in the linguistic parts of the book, but he is forced to note the close resemblance in the acoustic sections, where he says (125), "The glide /j/ resembles the vowel /i/. In a great many instances it was impossible to be sure from the sonogram that the subject had actually uttered /j/ and not the vowel."

This reclassification of /j/ as a liquid would necessitate some changes in the MS rules of pp. 58–59, but the net change might well be toward simplicity because of certain similarities in the distribution of /j/ and the other liquids /l l, r r,/. For example, MS 5d would be unnecessary, being included in MS 7a. In many languages semivowels of the type *j w* show striking phonetic and distributional parallels with vowels and/or liquids or are in close morphophonemic relation with vowels, and it would be desirable to have a distinctive-feature system which accounted for this in some way.

5. Acoustics In Part II of the book Halle does an excellent job of explaining many of the acoustic properties of Russian speech sounds and providing background information on acoustics and the acoustical analysis of speech. The style and content are carefully controlled to be intelligible to the professional linguist who lacks extensive training and experience in acoustics. Only occasionally are there slips in the form of misleading oversimplifications or the use of unexplained technical terminology. An example of the former is the apparent confusion between the actual percussion and the sound of the tapping of a pane of glass (82, 84). An example of the latter is the last two sentences of page 116, which would prob-

---

[7]It would not affect the basic structure of the branching diagram except to call the number 11 branches number 9 and move them up a little higher.

ably be quite unintelligible to the average linguist: "This made it possible to cascade the two sections of the filter and to obtain an attenuation of 36 db per octave. . . . The filtered output was then passed through a calibrated attenuator, amplified and fed into a square law device."

The first step in the procedures of investigation was to have four native speakers of Russian record three kinds of material: all possible CV and VC syllables of Russian, polysyllabic words with unaccented vowels in various positions, and some connected discourse. The recorded material was then subjected to analysis of sonograms and, for consonants, to analysis of power spectra by a specially devised technique. The procedures employed seem to have been well worked out and highly appropriate, and Halle gives a fully satisfactory defense of the use of "artificial" material for his purposes.

In the detailed discussion of the acoustic specification of Russian sounds (and often by implication sounds of other languages) important refinements and clarifications are offered on the features of vocalicity, compactness/diffuseness, consonant nasality, interruptedness, and sharpness. It is clear that the experimental work reported by Halle is making significant progress toward fuller understanding of the physical nature of speech sounds, and it is exciting to think of the future result of continued investigation of this kind in the form of a solid body of acoustical knowledge which would be an integral part of the elementary training of all phoneticians and linguists.

One of the most encouraging developments in Halle's treatment is the tacit abandonment of the assumption that there is an acoustical property, no matter how complex, corresponding to each distinctive feature. Halle's discussion is in terms of sets of cues, disjunctions (this property under these circumstances, that one under those), and even negative characterizations. From time to time, too, there is acknowledgement that even a characterization along these lines is difficult or uncertain. Symptomatic of this more empirical approach is the almost complete predominance of terminology such as "the vowels as a class are characterized by" (118) and "to separate the compact strident phonemes from the noncompact the following set of criteria . . ." (133) over phrasings like "compactness is signaled by" (127), which were characteristic of the earlier, more aprioristic approach to distinctive-feature theory. Two examples of candid, unemotional statements of present difficulties in acoustic investigation of distinctive features will suffice to show the general tone of the presentation: "It thus appears that in the case of the feature of gravity in the nasal consonants, we are dealing with a multiplicity of cues, none of which can clearly be said to be necessary" (139); "The procedure for separating compact from noncompact stops differs in some details from that used to separate compact from noncompact continuants. . . . Both procedures, however, have so much in common that with further work it should prove possible to combine them into a single operation." (136)

Finally, Jones's excursus forms a useful supplement to the book. He reviews the framework of vowel allophones described by Trofimov and Daniel Jones, revises it, and adds valuable acoustic information, largely in confirmation of the articulatory identifications used by them.

37

PHONOLOGY IN
GENERATIVE GRAMMAR*
MORRIS HALLE**

A generative grammar is formally a collection of statements, rules or axioms which describe, define or generate all well-formed utterances in a language and only those. The theory of generative grammars consists of a set of abstract conditions which determine the form of the statements admitted in such grammars and which govern the choice among alternative descriptions of a given body of data.[1]

In the part of the grammar that is of interest here, all statements are of the form

(1a)   A→B in the environment X___Y
$$\phantom{(1a)\quad A\to B \text{ in the environment } X}Z$$

where A, B, X, Y, Z are symbols of a particular alphabet or zero, and "→" can be read "is to be rewritten as." The statements are, moreover, subject to a special notational convention which allows us to coalesce partly identical statements by factoring the parts that are identical. For instance, (1a) and

(1b)   C→D in the environment X___Y
$$\phantom{(1b)\quad C\to D \text{ in the environment } X}Z$$

can be coalesced into

(1c) $\begin{Bmatrix} A\to B \\ C\to D \end{Bmatrix}$ in the environment X___Y
$$\phantom{(1c)\quad\begin{Bmatrix} A\to B \\ C\to D \end{Bmatrix} \text{ in the environment } X}Z$$

The theory of generative grammar postulates, moreover, a mechanical procedure by means of which preferred descriptions are chosen from among several alternatives. The basis of this choice, which in accordance with common usage is termed *simplicity,* must be some formal feature of the set of statements. In many obvious cases, simplicity can be equated with brevity. Thus, a short formula, like that embodied in Verner's Law, for example, is normally regarded as simpler, and hence preferred over a list of all forms implied by the formula. It would seem, therefore, natural to attempt to extend this notion of simplicity to all cases. In order to accomplish this, it is necessary to define a formal measure of length of descriptions which would appropriately mirror all considerations that enter into simplicity judgments. For example, in all cases where independent grounds exist for preferring one of several alternative descriptions, the preferred description must also be judged shorter than the rest by the proposed measure of length.

The measure of length that apparently possesses the desired properties is the number of alphabetic symbols (capital letters in (1a)–(1c) or the symbols by which these are

---

[1]For more detailed discussions of generative grammars see:

N. Chomsky, *Syntactic Structures* (The Hague, 1957); M. Halle, *The Sound Pattern of Russian* (The Hague, 1959); R. B. Lees, *A Grammar of English Nominalizations* (Bloomington, Indiana, 1960); N. Chomsky and M. Halle, *The Sound Pattern of English* (in preparation). [See now Chomsky and Halle, 1968—VBM.]

---

*Reprinted from *Word* 18.54–72 (1962) by permission.
**This work was supported in part by the U.S. Army (Signal Corps), the U.S. Navy (Office of Naval Research), and the U.S. Air Force (Office of Scientific Research, Air Research and Development Command), and in part by the National Science Foundation. I want also to express my gratitude to the Center for Advanced Study in the Behavorial Sciences, Stanford, California, and to the J. S. Guggenheim Foundation for providing me with a year that could be fully devoted to study, of which the present essay is one tangible result.

replaced in later examples) appearing in the description. Given two alternative descriptions of a particular body of data, the description containing fewer such symbols will be regarded as simpler and will, therefore, be preferred over the other.

In the rest of this paper, I shall outline in detail some consequences of these abstract conditions on the form of phonological descriptions and exhibit the manner in which, by mechanical application of the proposed simplicity measure, certain formulations are chosen from among several alternatives. The plausibility and intrinsic appeal of the descriptions so selected will provide the primary justification not only for the proposed simplicity criterion, but also for the theory of generative grammar, of which the criterion is an integral part.

1 It has been noted above that the symbols appearing in the statement of a generative grammar belong to a restricted alphabet. In phonology, the majority of statements deal exclusively with segments or segment sequences. In order to simplify the discussion, I shall consider here only statements of this type and exclude from consideration state-

ments involving junctures, morpheme class markers, etc. In the present discussion, the capital letters will, therefore, represent phonological segments, classes of segments, or sequences of these.

There are basically two ways in which phonological segments have been treated in linguistic descriptions. In some descriptions they are represented as further indivisible entities; in others, as complexes of properties. In order to choose between these two manners of representation, I propose to compare them in situations where the preferred solution is self-evident. The statement:

(2)   /a/ is replaced by /æ/ if followed by /i/

is evidently simpler than the statement:

(3)   /a/ is replaced by /æ/ if followed by /i/
                           and preceded by /i/.

Translating into the standard form of (1), and regarding phonological segments as indivisible entities, we obtain

(2′)   /a/→/æ/ in the env. _____/i/

(3′)   /a/→/æ/ in the env. /i/_____/i/

Alternatively, if we regard phonological segments as complexes of properties,[2] we obtain

(2″)

$[+\text{grave}]\rightarrow[-\text{grave}]$ in the env.
$\begin{bmatrix} \underline{\hspace{1.5cm}} \\ +\text{vocalic} \\ -\text{consonantal} \\ -\text{diffuse} \\ +\text{compact} \\ -\text{flat} \end{bmatrix} \begin{bmatrix} +\text{vocalic} \\ -\text{consonantal} \\ +\text{diffuse} \\ -\text{compact} \\ -\text{flat} \\ -\text{grave} \end{bmatrix}$

(3″)

$[+\text{grave}]\rightarrow[-\text{grave}]$ in the env.
$\begin{bmatrix} +\text{vocalic} \\ -\text{consonantal} \\ +\text{diffuse} \\ -\text{compact} \\ -\text{flat} \\ -\text{grave} \end{bmatrix} \begin{bmatrix} \underline{\hspace{1.5cm}} \\ +\text{vocalic} \\ -\text{consonantal} \\ -\text{diffuse} \\ +\text{compact} \\ -\text{flat} \end{bmatrix} \begin{bmatrix} +\text{vocalic} \\ -\text{consonantal} \\ +\text{diffuse} \\ -\text{compact} \\ -\text{flat} \\ -\text{grave} \end{bmatrix}$

[2] I shall use here the Jakobsonian distinctive features as the properties in terms of which segments are to be characterized. The choice of a different phonetic framework, however, would not affect the outcome of the present comparison. In view of the decision to operate with the distinctive feature framework, all references below to segments as "/s/" or as "labial stops" are to be understood as unofficial circumlocutions introduced only to facilitate the exposition, but lacking all systematic import.

Either reformulation of statement (2) is to be preferred by the proposed simplicity criterion over the corresponding reformulation of statement (3), since the equivalents of (2) utilize three (respectively 13) symbols, vs. four (respectively, 19) symbols utilized in the equivalents of (3).

Consider, however, the following pair of statements for a language possessing the three front vowels /æ/ /e/ /i/:

(2)   /a/ is replaced by /æ/, if followed by /i/

(4)   /a/ is replaced by /æ/, if followed by
                                       any front vowel.

Here (4) is the more general rule, and is, therefore, to be preferred over (2). Translating the two statements into the standard form, and viewing phonemes as indivisible entities, we obtain

(2′)   /a/→/æ/ in the env._____/i/

(4′)   /a/→/æ/ in the env. ———— $\begin{Bmatrix} /i/ \\ /e/ \\ /æ/ \end{Bmatrix}$

Regarding phonemes as complexes of features, we obtain

(2″)

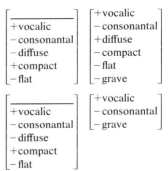

                [+grave]→[−grave] in the env. $\begin{bmatrix} \underline{\qquad} \\ +\text{vocalic} \\ -\text{consonantal} \\ -\text{diffuse} \\ +\text{compact} \\ -\text{flat} \end{bmatrix} \begin{bmatrix} +\text{vocalic} \\ -\text{consonantal} \\ +\text{diffuse} \\ -\text{compact} \\ -\text{flat} \\ -\text{grave} \end{bmatrix}$

(4″)

                [+grave]→[−grave] in the env. $\begin{bmatrix} \underline{\qquad} \\ +\text{vocalic} \\ -\text{consonantal} \\ -\text{diffuse} \\ +\text{compact} \\ -\text{flat} \end{bmatrix} \begin{bmatrix} +\text{vocalic} \\ -\text{consonantal} \\ -\text{grave} \end{bmatrix}$

The alternative reformulations of (2) and (4) are not consistent with each other: statement (2′) utilizes fewer symbols than (4′), whereas (2″) utilizes more symbols than (4″). Since we know on independent grounds that (4) is more general than (2) and must, therefore, be preferred over the latter, the results obtained in the reformulations (2′) and (4′) are also inconsistent with the results obtained in (2′) and (3′), where the preferred statement required fewer symbols. It follows, therefore, that if we wish to operate with the simplicity criterion that has been proposed here, we must regard

phonological segments as complexes of properties.

It is, of course, conceivable that a simplicity criterion may be formulated that yields the proper results even when segments are represented as indivisible entities. The burden of proof, however, is clearly on those who reject the view that segments are complexes of phonetic properties. Rather than explore here alternative simplicity criteria, I shall attempt to justify the proposed view of phonological segments by examining some of its consequences. These consequences will incidentally provide ample justification for the decision to operate with the Jakobsonian distinctive feature framework rather than with one of the other phonetic frameworks (IPA or Jespersen's antalphabetic notation, etc.)

2 Significant simplifications can be achieved by imposing an order on the application of the rules. Consider in this connection the rules which constitute the essence of the Sanskrit vowel sandhi. In Whitney's *Grammar,* where order of application is not a factor, the vowel sandhi is described by means of the following four rules:

(5)   "Two similar simple vowels, short or long, coalesce and form the corresponding long vowel . . . (§126)

(6)   "An *a*-vowel combines with a following *i*-vowel to *e*; with a *u*-vowel, to *o* . . ." (§127)

(7)   "The *i*-vowels, the *u*-vowels and the *r* before a dissimilar vowel or a diphthong, are each converted into its own corresponding semi-vowel, *y* or *v* or *r*." (§129)

(8) "Of a diphthong, the final *i-* or *u-*element is changed into its corresponding semivowel, *y* or *v*, before any vowel or diphthong: thus *e* (really *ai* ...) becomes *ay*, and *o* (that is *au* ...) becomes *ay* ... (§131)

If the first three rules are applied in the order (5) (7) (6), two important economies can be effected. First of all, in rule (7), the qualification "before a dissimilar vowel or a diphthong" can be simplified to "before a vowel," for at the point where rule (7) applies only sequences of dissimilar vowels remain, since rule (5) replaces all sequences of identical vowel by single long vowels. Moreover, rule (8) can be dispensed with altogether. Since rule (7) converts /i/ and /u/ in position before vowel into /y/ and /v/, respectively, no sequences of /ai/ and /au/ in position before vowel will ever be turned into /e/, or /o/, respectively, by the subsequent application of rule (6). Inasmuch as rule (6) is the only source of /e/ and /o/ in the language, there is now no need for rule (8), whose sole function is to convert /e/ and /o/ into /ay/ and /av/ in those cases where by the proposed ordering of the rules, /e/ and /o/ could not have arisen. Thus, the forms quoted by Whitney as requiring rule (8) are handled properly without it: /naia/ and /bʰaua/ are turned by rule (7) into /naya/ and /bʰava/ to which rule (6) does not apply. The same stems without the suffix /a/, on the other hand, are not subject to rule (7) and are, therefore, affected by (the later) rule (6), which converts /nai/ into /ne/ and /bʰau/ into /bʰo/.

In sum, rule (8) is superfluous as long as the proposed ordering of the rules is maintained. Should we choose to allow random access to the rules or impose a different order on the rules, we should have to pay for it by admitting rule (8). Our simplicity · criterion leaves us no alternative but to choose the former solution.

3 A complete description of a language must evidently include a list of all actually occurring morphemes; i.e., the dictionary of the language. Being part of the description, the dictionary is also subject to the notational conventions and simplicity criterion that have been outlined above. The items in the diction-

ary will, therefore, be given in the form of sequences of distinctive feature complexes. For instance, in place of an entry /dɔg/, our dictionary might contain the entry

(9)

$$
\begin{bmatrix}
-\text{vocalic} \\
+\text{consonantal} \\
-\text{strident} \\
-\text{compact} \\
-\text{grave} \\
-\text{continuant} \\
-\text{nasal} \\
-\text{tense} \\
+\text{diffuse} \\
-\text{flat} \\
+\text{voiced}
\end{bmatrix}
\begin{bmatrix}
+\text{vocalic} \\
-\text{consonantal} \\
-\text{strident} \\
+\text{compact} \\
+\text{grave} \\
+\text{continuant} \\
-\text{nasal} \\
+\text{tense} \\
-\text{diffuse} \\
+\text{flat} \\
+\text{voiced}
\end{bmatrix}
\begin{bmatrix}
-\text{vocalic} \\
+\text{consonantal} \\
-\text{strident} \\
-\text{compact} \\
+\text{grave} \\
-\text{continuant} \\
-\text{nasal} \\
-\text{tense} \\
-\text{diffuse} \\
-\text{flat} \\
+\text{voiced}
\end{bmatrix}
$$

This representation contains an excessive number of features. As can be seen in (10), English vowels—i.e., segments that are $\begin{bmatrix} +\text{vocalic} \\ -\text{consonantal} \end{bmatrix}$—are all non-nasal, non-stri-

(10)

	u	o	ɔ	a	i	e	æ
vocalic	+	+	+	+	+	+	+
consonantal	−	−	−	−	−	−	−
nasal	−	−	−	−	−	−	−
continuant	+	+	+	+	+	+	+
strident	−	−	−	−	−	−	−
flat	+	+	+	−	−	−	−
compact	−	−	+	+	−	−	+
diffuse	+	−	−	−	+	−	−
grave	+	+	+	+	−	−	−
voiced	+	+	+	+	+	+	+

The distinctive feature composition of vowels in certain dialects of modern English. The feature of tenseness has not been specified since the system contains 7 tense and 7 non-tense vowels.

dent, voiced and continuant. Moreover, compact (low) vowels are always non-diffuse (non-high); while all flat (rounded) vowels are always grave (back). Non-flat (unrounded) vowels, on the other hand, are invariably non-grave (front) only if they are also non-compact (non-low). This suggests that the redundant features be omitted in all dictionary entries in which the respective vowels figure and be introduced by a special rule[3]:

$$
(11) \quad
\left\{
\begin{array}{ll}
\text{a.} & [+\text{compact}] \rightarrow [-\text{diffuse}] \\[4pt]
\text{b.} & [X] \rightarrow \begin{bmatrix} -\text{nasal} \\ -\text{strident} \\ +\text{continuant} \\ +\text{voiced} \end{bmatrix} \\[10pt]
\text{c.} & [+\text{flat}] \rightarrow [+\text{grave}] \\[4pt]
\text{d.} & \begin{bmatrix} -\text{flat} \\ -\text{compact} \end{bmatrix} \rightarrow [-\text{grave}]
\end{array}
\right\}
\text{ in the env. } \begin{bmatrix} \overline{+\text{vocalic}} \\ -\text{consonantal} \end{bmatrix}
$$

where [X] represents an arbitrary feature complex.

Given (11), the vowel in (9) can be represented by the feature complex

$$
\begin{bmatrix} +\text{vocalic} \\ -\text{consonantal} \\ +\text{compact} \\ +\text{flat} \\ +\text{tense} \end{bmatrix}
$$

i.e., by five instead of eleven features.

The simplicity criterion clearly demands that this procedure be followed in the representation of every dictionary entry, for it allows us to shorten the dictionary, which is an integral part of a grammar, by many hundreds of features at the slight additional cost represented by the 13 features utilized in rule

(11). In general, we must omit features in all dictionary representations, whenever these can be introduced by a rule that is less costly than the saving it effects.

4 Among the redundancies that must be eliminated are those where the appearance of a given feature in a segment is contextually determined. Thus, for instance, /tsaym/, /gnayt/ and /vnig/ are not English words, since English words to not begin with the sequences /ts/, or /gn/, or /vn/. As a matter of fact, it is generally true that if an English word begins with a sequence of two consonants, the first is invariably /s/: /st/, /sp/, /sk/, /sm/, /sn/ are the only two-consonant—i.e., $\begin{bmatrix} -\text{vocalic} \\ +\text{consonantal} \end{bmatrix}$— sequences admitted in word initial position. This suggests immediately that in the dictionary representation of all items beginning with two consonants, we omit in the first consonant all but the features $\begin{bmatrix} -\text{vocalic} \\ +\text{consonantal} \end{bmatrix}$; i.e., all features that differentiate that consonant from all other consonants of the language. The omitted features are then introduced by the following rule:

$$
(12) \quad \begin{bmatrix} -\text{vocalic} \\ +\text{consonantal} \end{bmatrix} \rightarrow \begin{bmatrix} +\text{strident} \\ -\text{compact} \\ -\text{grave} \\ +\text{tense} \\ +\text{continuant} \end{bmatrix} \text{ in env. } \# \begin{bmatrix} \overline{} \end{bmatrix} \begin{bmatrix} -\text{vocalic} \\ +\text{consonantal} \end{bmatrix}
$$

---

[3]In order to shorten the formulaic representations of the rules and to make them more perspicuous, expressions in the form

$$
[X] \rightarrow [A] \text{ in the env. } [B] \begin{bmatrix} \underline{} \\ C \end{bmatrix} [D]
$$

where X is an arbitrary feature complex, and A, B, C, D are specific feature complexes or zero, will usually be given in the following form:

$$
[C] \rightarrow [A] \text{ in the env. } [B] [\underline{}] [D]
$$

As a result of rule (12) the description is shortened by five features for every dictionary item beginning with two consonants. Thus, a very great saving is realized in the dictionary at the cost of the nine features mentioned in rule (12).[4]

Consider now such sequences as /bik/, /θōd/, or /nis/. Like the aforementioned /tsaym/, /gnayt/, and /vnig/ none are actual English words. If, however, we attempted to exclude them by means of a rule like (12), we should discover that the cost of the rule—i.e., the number of features mentioned in the rule—would exceed that of the saving that might be effected in the dictionary. For instance, since *big, bin, bid, bit, bib, biff* are all English words, the rule that excludes /bik/ would have to read:

$$
(13) \quad
\begin{bmatrix}
-\text{vocalic} \\
+\text{consonantal} \\
-\text{compact} \\
-\text{strident}
\end{bmatrix}
\rightarrow [-\text{tense}] \text{ in the env.}
\begin{bmatrix}
-\text{vocalic} \\
+\text{consonantal} \\
-\text{strident} \\
+\text{grave} \\
-\text{compact} \\
-\text{nasal} \\
-\text{tense}
\end{bmatrix}
\begin{bmatrix}
+\text{vocalic} \\
-\text{consonantal} \\
+\text{diffuse} \\
-\text{compact} \\
-\text{tense} \\
-\text{grave}
\end{bmatrix}
[\text{\textemdash}]
$$

And at the cost of the 18 features mentioned in rule (13), we could effect a saving of one feature in the dictionary. The simplicity criterion, therefore, does not allow us to include rule (13) in a description of English.

The presence of rule (12) and the absence of rule (13) in a description of English mirrors the English speaker's intuition about his language. The presence of rule (12) corresponds to the fact that speakers of English will regard /vnig/, /tsaym/ and /gnayt/ as not only meaningless, but also as totally un-English; impossible by the rules of their language. The absence of rule (13) and a host of similar rules

corresponds to the fact that English speakers will accept the equally meaningless /bik/, /θōd/ and /nis/ as possible English words, perhaps as words found in an unabridged dictionary rather than in the vocabulary of the average speaker.

In attempting to satisfy the simplicity criterion, we are, thus, forced to incorporate into every complete generative grammar a characterization of the distinction between admissible and inadmissible segment sequences. This fact effectively cuts the ground out from under the recent suggestion that generative grammars be supplemented with special phonological grammars,[5] since the sole purpose of phonological grammars is to characterize the distinction between admissible and inadmissible segment sequences.

5   In the study of dialects, it has been common in recent years to focus primary attention on the facts of the utterance and to concern oneself primarily with such questions as the mutual intelligibility of two dialects, the similarities and differences of cognate utterances, of their phoneme repertories, distributional constraints, etc. Instead of following this procedure, we propose to focus here on the grammars of the dialects, i.e., on the ordered set of statements that describe the data, rather than on the data directly.

That the two approaches are distinct in quite fundamental ways can be seen if we examine the manner in which "Pig Latin," a "secret" language popular among schoolchildren in the United States would be described from these two points of view. If we compared utterances in Pig Latin with their cognates in

[4]This saving has the additional effect of ruling out forms such as /vnig/, /tsaym/, and /gnayt/. It may be noted that the idea of representing segments in a given form by less than their normal complement of features is essentially identical with the "archiphoneme" concept that was first proposed by Jakobson in *Travaux du Cercle Linguistique de Prague* 2 (1929) and was used for a time by the Prague School. Since the Prague School did not operate consistently with features but rather regarded the phoneme as the ultimate phonological entity, great difficulties were soon experienced with this concept, which ultimately led to its official abandonment.

[5]Cf. F. Householder, "On Linguistic Primes," *Word* 15 (1959) 231–239, and H. Contreras and S. Saporta, "The Validation of a Phonological Grammar," *Lingua* 9 (1960) 1–15.

General American, we should be struck by the extreme differences between them; e.g.,

General American	Pig Latin
/str'īt/	/'ītstrē/
/str'īts/	/'ītstrē/
/k'æt/	/'ætkē/
/k'æts/	/'ætskē/
/r'ōz/	/'ōzrē/
/r'ōzɨz/	/'ōzɨzrē/

We observe that the distribution of phonemes in Pig Latin differs radically from that in General American, for in the former all words end in the vowel /ē/, and very unusual consonant clusters abound. We note also that infixation rather than prefixation and suffixation is the major morphological device. In view of this, we are hardly surprised to find that Pig Latin is incomprehensible to the uninitiated speaker of General American. Since these are precisely the observations we would expect to make if we compared the utterances in two totally unrelated languages, we are led to conclude that Pig Latin and General American are unrelated, or, at best, only remotely related tongues; a conclusion which is patently false.

The picture would be radically different if instead of "hugging the phonetic ground closely" we were to compare the grammars of General American and Pig Latin. From this point of view, the difference between the two is that Pig Latin contains a morphophonemic rule that is absent in the more standard dialects:

(14) Shift initial consonant cluster to end
of word and add /ē/

Since rule (14) is the only difference between the grammars of Pig Latin and General American, we conclude that Pig Latin is a "ciphered" form of General American, a somewhat special dialect of the latter, a conclusion which is obviously right. But this result follows only if instead of concentrating on the utterances, we shift primary attention to the grammars that underlie the utterances.

6 Since grammars consist of ordered sets of statements, differences among grammars are due to one or both of the following: (a) different grammars may contain different rules; (b) different grammars may have differently ordered rules. The case of Pig Latin exemplifies difference (a). An interesting example of difference (b) was discussed by M. Joos in a paper entitled "A Phonological Dilemma in Canadian English."[6] In certain Canadian dialects "the diphthongs /aj/ and /aw/ . . . each have two varieties. One . . . begins with a lower-mid vowel sound; it is used before any fortis consonant with zero juncture . . . *white, knife, shout, house*. The other is used in all other contexts: . . . *high, find, knives; how, found, houses*. Note the difference in singular and plural of irregular nouns, including *wife : wives*." To account for this difference, Joos suggests the rule

(15) "/a/ is a lower-mid vowel . . . in diphthongs
followed by fortis consonants."

Moreover, like in many other American dialects, these dialects contain the rule that

(16) in intervocalic position /t/
is voiced and lenis /d/

Joos notes that the speakers of these dialects "divide into two groups according to their pronunciation of words like *typewriter*. Group A says [tʌɪprʌɪdɚ] while group B says [tʌɪpraɪdɚ]. . . . Group A distinguishes *writer* from *rider, clouting* from *clouding* by the choice of the diphthong alone. . . . Group B has shifted the articulation of all vowels alike before the new /d/ from earlier /t/ . . . from *write* to *writer* there is both the phonemic alternation from /t/ to /d/, and the phonetic alternation from [ʌɪ] to [aɪ]."

The dilemma referred to in the title of Joos' paper is, therefore, a lawful consequence of the fact that in the grammar of group A, rule (15) precedes rule (16), while in the grammar of group B, the reverse order obtains. Hence in the speech of group A /taɪpraɪtɚ/ is converted by rule (15) into [tʌɪprʌɪtɚ] which then is turned by rule (16) into [tʌɪprʌɪdɚ]. In the speech of group B, on the other hand, /taɪpraɪtɚ/ is first turned by rule (16) into [taɪpraɪdɚ] and then by rule (15) into [tʌɪpraɪdɚ].[7]

[6]*Language* 18 (1942) 141–144.
[7]Joos notes that in the speech of group A, the observed phenomenon is restricted to certain classes of words. This restriction does not affect the point illustrated here, viz., that data of the kind described

Since ordered rules are all but unknown in present day synchronic descriptions, the impression has spread that the imposition of order on statements in a synchronic description is always due to an oversight, to an unjustifiable confusion of synchronic and diachronic.[8] I must therefore stress that, in the preceding examples, order is determined by the simplicity criterion alone and that no historical considerations have entered in establishing it.

7   A complete scientific description of a language must pursue one aim above all: to make precise and explicit the ability of a native speaker to produce utterances in that language. We can, therefore, enquire how the acquisition of this ability is viewed within the framework of a generative grammar. It has been suggested by Chomsky that language acquisition by a child may best be pictured as a process of constructing the simplest (optimal) grammar capable of generating the set of utterances, of which the utterances heard by the child are a representative sample.[9] The ability to master a language like a native, which children possess to an extraordinary degree, is almost completely lacking in the adult. I propose to explain this as being due to deterioration or loss in the adult of the ability to construct optimal (simplest) grammars on the basis of a restricted corpus of examples. The language of the adult—and hence also the grammar that he has internalized—need not, however, remain static: it can and does, in fact, change. I conjecture that changes in later life are restricted to the addition or elimination of a few rules in the grammar, and that a wholesale restructuring of his grammar is beyond the capabilities of the average adult.

The addition of rules may—though it need not invariably—result in a grammar that is not optimal (the simplest) for the set of utterances that it generates. As an example, consider the consequences of expanding rule (11) by the addition of subpart (e):

$$
(11')\quad
\left\{
\begin{array}{ll}
\text{a.} & [+\text{compact}] \rightarrow [-\text{diffuse}] \\[4pt]
\text{b.} & [X] \rightarrow \begin{bmatrix} -\text{nasal} \\ -\text{strident} \\ +\text{continuant} \\ +\text{voiced} \end{bmatrix} \\[20pt]
\text{c.} & [+\text{flat}] \rightarrow [+\text{grave}] \\[4pt]
\text{d.} & \begin{bmatrix} -\text{flat} \\ -\text{compact} \end{bmatrix} \rightarrow [-\text{grave}] \\[12pt]
\text{e.} & \begin{bmatrix} -\text{flat} \\ +\text{compact} \end{bmatrix} \rightarrow [-\text{grave}]
\end{array}
\right\}
\ \text{in the env.}\
\begin{bmatrix} +\text{vocalic} \\ -\text{consonantal} \end{bmatrix}
$$

---

by Joos can best be accounted for by postulating different orders of rules in grammars of different dialects.

[8]Thus, for example, Hockett confesses to being unable to conceive of ordered statements in terms other than historical: ". . . if it is said that the English past tense form *baked* is 'formed' from *bake* by a 'process' of 'suffixation,' then no matter what disclaimer of historicity is made, it is impossible not to conclude that some kind of priority is being assigned to *bake* as against *baked* or the suffix. And if this priority is not historical, what is it?" ("Two Models of Grammatical Description," *Word* 10 [1954] 233.) Synchronic ordering was used by both Bloomfield and Sapir and to a certain extent also by younger linguists (Joos, *op. cit.,* Voegelin, Swadesh) who later abandoned it, however.

[9]This view of language learning was once almost a commonplace among linguists. I have found clear statements to this effect in the writings of linguists as diverse as Humboldt, Hermann Paul and Meillet. Cf. for example, the following comment made by Meillet in 1929: ". . . chaque enfant doit acquérir par lui-même la capacité de comprendre le parler des gens de son groupe social et de l'employer. La langue ne lui est pas livrée en bloc, tout d'une pièce. Il n'entend jamais autre chose que des phrases particulières, et ce n'est qu'en comparant ces phrases entre elles qu'il arrive à saisir le sens des paroles qu'il entend et à parler à son tour. Pour chaque individu, le langage est ainsi une recréation totale faite sous l'influence du milieu qui l'entoure." *Linguistique historique et linguistique générale* II (Paris, 1952), p. 74.

As can be readily seen from (10), the addition of subpart (e) amounts to a coalescence of /a/→/æ/. The distribution of gravity in vowels is, therefore, completely determined, and rule (11′ a—e) must be replaced by the following, simpler rule (12 vs. 10 features):

(17)

$$
\left\{
\begin{array}{lll}
\text{a.} & [+\text{compact}] \rightarrow [-\text{diffuse}] \\
\text{b.} & [X] \rightarrow \left[\begin{array}{l} -\text{nasal} \\ -\text{strident} \\ +\text{continuant} \\ -\text{grave} \\ +\text{voiced} \end{array}\right] \\
\text{c.} & [+\text{flat}] \rightarrow [+\text{grave}]
\end{array}
\right\}
\text{ in the env. } \left[\begin{array}{l} +\text{vocalic} \\ -\text{consonantal} \end{array}\right]
$$

Observe that rule (11′e), which was the cause of the whole upheaval, does not even figure in (17), which nevertheless generates precisely the same set of utterances as (11′ a—e).[10]

Since every child constructs his own optimal grammar by induction from the utterances to which he has been exposed, it is not necessary that the child and his parents have identical grammars, for, as we have just seen, a given set of utterances can be generated by more than one grammar. In the case where rule (11′e) was added to the grammar, I should therefore postulate that the adult, who of necessity is maximally conservative, would have a grammar containing rule (11′ a—e), whereas his children would have grammars with the simpler rule (17). It is clear that such discontinuities in the grammars of successive generations must exercise a profound influence on the further evolution of the language.[11]

[10]For a discussion of further consequences of the addition of rules such as (11e), see sections 10–12.

[11]The significance of discontinuities in the transmission of language from generation to generation was discussed over fifty years ago by A. Meillet: "Il faut tenir compte tout d'abord du caractère essentiellement discontinu de la transmission du langage: l'enfant qui apprend à parler ne reçoit pas la langue toute faite: il doit la recréer tout entière à son usage d'après ce qu'il entend autour de lui. . . . Cette discontinuité de la transmission du langage ne suffirait à elle seule à rien expliquer, mais, sans elle, toutes les causes du changement auraient sans doute été impuissantes à transformer le sens des mots aussi radicalement qu'il l'a été dans un grand nombre de cas: d'une manière générale d'ailleurs, la discontinuité de la transmission est la condition première qui détermine la possibilité et les modalités

8 Linguistic change is normally subject to the constraint that it must not result in the destruction of mutual intelligibility between the innovators—i.e., the carriers of the change—and the rest of the speech community. Except in such special cases as "secret languages" like Pig Latin or different varieties of thieves' argot, all changes must preserve comprehensibility for the rest of the speech community. This restriction clearly affects the content of the rules to be added; e.g., a rule such as (14) has little chance of survival under normal conditions, for it renders the utterances incomprehensible to the rest of the community. It is equally obvious that the number of rules to be added must also be restricted, for very serious effects on intelligibility can result from the simultaneous addition of even two or three otherwise innocuous rules.

It may be somewhat less obvious that the requirement to preserve intelligibility also restricts the place in the order where rules may be added. All other things being equal, a rule will affect intelligibility less if it is added at a lower point in the order than if it is added higher up. I am unable at present to characterize the place in the order where rules may be added with a minimum impairment of intelligibility. Such additions, however, seem characteristically to occur at points where there are natural breaks in the grammar.[12]

Because of the intelligibility constraint

de tous les changements linguistiques." *Linguistique historique et linguistique générale* I (Paris, 1948), p. 236. I am indebted to E. S. Klima for drawing my attention to the quoted passage.

[12]E.g., before the first morphophonemic rule involving immediate constituent structure of the utterance (i.e., at the end of the morpheme structure (MS) rules); at the end of the cyclical rules which eliminate the immediate constituent structure of the utterance from the representation; before the phonological rules that eliminate boundary markers (junctures) from the representation.

the type of change most likely to survive is the one involving the addition of a single, simple rule at the end of certain natural subdivisions of the grammar. It can readily be seen that in cases where the addition of such a rule does not affect the over-all simplicity of the grammar, the order of rules established by purely synchronic considerations—i.e., simplicity—will mirror properly the relative chronology of the rules. This fact was noted by Bloomfield in his important "Menomini Morphophonemics" [7]:

The process of description leads us to set up each morphological element in a theoretical *basic* form, and then to state the deviations from this basic form which appear when the element is combined with other elements. If one starts with the basic forms and applies our statements . . . in the order in which we give them, one will arrive finally at the forms of words as they are actually spoken. Our basic forms are not ancient forms, say of the Proto-Algonquian parent language, and our statements of internal sandhi are not historical but descriptive, and appear in a purely descriptive order. However, our basic forms do bear some resemblance to those which would be set up for a description of Proto-Algonquian, some of our statements of alternation . . . resemble those which would appear in a description of Proto-Algonquian, and the rest . . . , as to content and order, approximate the historical development from Proto-Algonquian to present-day Menomini.[13]

9 It has been proposed here that the primary mechanism of phonological change is the addition of rules to the grammar with special (though not exclusive) preference for the addition of single rules at the ends of different subdivisions of the grammar. It seems to me that this view is implicit in much of the work in historical linguistics; in fact, I believe that the successes and failures of linguistics in its attempts to reconstruct the history of different languages can best be understood in the light of the model discussed here.

As is well known, in reconstructing the history of a language, it is customary to postulate a proto-language from which subsequent (documented) stages are derived by the operation of "phonetic laws"[14] and a few other processes which need not concern us here. In the terms of this study, reconstructing the history of a language would be described as deriving the grammars of later (attested) languages from that postulated for the proto-language by the addition of new rules. I have tried to show elsewhere that considerations of simplicity (in the precise sense defined here) usually play an important role in reconstruction.[15] The all but universal agreement on the relative chronology of Grimm's and Verner's Laws is no doubt due to the fact that simplicity considerations clearly demand that Verner's Law apply after Grimm's Law. When simplicity considerations do not dictate a particular order, there is often also no agreement about the relative chronology. For instance, the chronological position within Grimm's Law of the shift of Indo-European voiced aspirate stops to voiced non-strident continuants (bh→β; dh→ð; gh→γ) is still under discussion[16] and is likely to remain so for a long time, since no particular order for this rule is dictated by the simplicity criterion, which, in view of the absence of documentary or other external evidence, is the only remaining basis for establishing the chronology.

10 It was noted in **8** that as a result of the requirement that linguistic change not disrupt mutual intelligibility between the innovators and the rest of the speech community, the new rules are ordinarily added at the end of the

---

[13]*Travaux du Cercle Linguistique de Prague* 8 (1939) 105–115. This study is unaccountably omitted in C. F. Hockett's "Implications of Bloomfield's Algonquian Studies," *Language* 24 (1948) 117–131. Cf. also Bloomfield's comments on "descriptive order" in his *Language* (New York, 1933), pp. 213 and 222.

[14]"Pour tous les groupes actuellement établis et étudiés d'une manière méthodique, le moyen de faire le rapprochement est de poser une 'langue commune' initiale." A. Meillet, *La méthode comparative en linguistique historique* (Oslo, 1925), p. 12.

[15]"On the Role of Simplicity in Linguistic Descriptions," *Structure of Language and its Mathematical Aspects: Proceedings of Symposia on Applied Mathematics,* vol. XII (Providence, 1961) pp. 89–94.

[16]For a review of this problem see W. G. Moulton "The Stops and Spirants of Early Germanic," *Language* 30 (1954) 1–42, and L. L. Hammerich, "Die germanische und die hochdeutsche Lautverschiebung," *Beiträge zur Geschichte der deutschen Sprache und Literatur* 77 (1954) 1–29.

grammar or of one of its major subdivisions. The addition of rules at other places is not, however, completely excluded. In such instances the order of rules in the synchronic description will not properly mirror their relative chronology. This situation is well illustrated by the Middle English dialects in which both tense (long) /ǣ/ and /ā/ became /ē/ simultaneously with tense (long) /ɔ̄/ becoming /ō/.[17] The tense vowel system of these dialects was originally like that in (10), and was also subject to the phonetic rules given in (11). The change in question can be accounted for very elegantly if we assume that (11) was modified as shown in (18) by the addition of subpart (e*) before rather than after subpart (d); i.e., at a place other than the end of the grammar:

netic contrast between the phonemes /a/ and /æ/ in all utterances of the dialect, the question naturally arises whether such a suppression of a phonetic contrast necessarily leads also to simplifications in the dictionary. In other words, since /æ/ and /a/ are not in contrast phonetically, must this contrast also be eliminated from the dictionary representation of lexical items? One's first reaction is to answer this question in the affirmative, for it seems pointless to use different feature complexes to represent segment types that are never distinguished phonetically. And yet there are cases where this would not be so, where simplicity considerations force us to maintain distinct representations of segment types that never contrast phonetically.

(18)
$$
\left\{
\begin{array}{ll}
\text{a.} & [+\text{compact}] \rightarrow [-\text{diffuse}] \\
\text{b.} & [X] \rightarrow \begin{bmatrix} -\text{nasal} \\ -\text{strident} \\ +\text{continuant} \\ +\text{voiced} \end{bmatrix} \\
\text{c.} & [+\text{flat}] \rightarrow [+\text{grave}] \\
\text{e*.} & [+\text{compact}] \rightarrow [-\text{compact}] \\
\text{d.} & \begin{bmatrix} -\text{flat} \\ -\text{compact} \end{bmatrix} \rightarrow [-\text{grave}]
\end{array}
\right\}
\ \text{in the env.}\
\begin{bmatrix} +\text{vocalic} \\ -\text{consonantal} \\ +\text{tense} \end{bmatrix}
$$

Rule (18e*) converts the three compact non-diffuse (low) vowels to their non-compact (mid) cognates; i.e., /ǣ/→/ē/, /ā/→/γ̄/, and /ɔ̄/→/ō/. Since the resulting vowels are still subject to (18d), /γ̄/ is immediately fronted to /ē/. Thus the falling together of /ā/ and /ǣ/ in /ē/ does not require us to assume a separate fronting of /ā/→/ǣ/, provided that we allow rules to be added to places other than the end of the grammar or the end of its major subdivisions.

11   In discussing (under 7) the effects of the addition of subpart (e) in rule (11'), it was observed that the addition of rules may result in a grammar which is not the simplest for the set of utterances it generates, and that the identical set of utterances may be generated by a simpler grammar. Since the addition of subpart (e) to rule (11') eliminates also the pho-

In certain Russian dialects, non-diffuse (non-high) vowels preceded by sharp (soft) consonants in pretonic position are actualized as /i/ or as /a/ depending on the vowel under the accent. Of interest here are those among the dialects which possess the so-called seven vowel system, a system that is substantially identical with that presented in (10).[18] In some of these dialects, the distribution of the pretonic vowel is governed by the rule:

(19) After sharp consonants, non-diffuse vowels in pretonic position are pronounced /i/ if the accented vowel is compact (/ɔ a æ/), otherwise they are pronounced /a/.

In these dialects, which are subject to what is technically known as "dissimilative jakan'e

---

[17]Some scholars believe that the change /ā/→/ē/ was later by 50 years than the changes /ǣ/→/ē/ and /ɔ̄/→/ō/. If they are right, my example is a hypothetical, rather than an actually attested instance. This does not affect its validity, however, since the example does not violate any known constraints on the structure or on the evolution of language.

[18]The phoneme that derives historically from /o/ under rising tone is represented in (10) as /o/ and the reflex of the so-called *jat'* is represented in (10) as /e/. Other reflexes of Old Russian /o/ and /e/ and of the strong *jers* are represented in (10) by /ɔ/ and /æ/ respectively. I regard therefore the distinction between the two types of /o/ and of /e/, as one of non-compact vs. compact, rather than as one of tense vs. lax, as is done in most dialectological studies. I hope to justify this departure from tradition in a study now in preparation, in which, inci-

of the Obojansk type," we find, therefore, that /s,ɔl'o/ 'village' (nom. sg.) is pronounced [s,al'o], whereas /s,ɔl'ɔm/ 'village' (instr. sg.) is pronounced [s,il'ɔm]. In some of these dialects, the distinction between compact /ɔ/ and /æ/ and non-compact /o/ and /e/ is lost, yet the vowels in pretonic position are treated as before; e.g., [s,il'ɔm] but [s,al'ɔ]. In such dialects, therefore, phonetically identical segments—[ɔ]—produce distinct results in the distribution of the pretonic vowel. If the distinction between these etymologically distinct yet phonetically identical vowels were to be eliminated from the representation of morphemes, the statement of the distribution of the pretonic vowel (rule (19)) would become hopelessly complex.[19] Considerations of simplicity would dictate that the distinction between the respective segment types be maintained and that their phonetic coalescence be accounted for by adding to the end of the grammar the rule:

(20) [−compact]→[+compact]

$$\text{in the environment} \begin{bmatrix} +\text{vocalic} \\ -\text{consonantal} \\ -\text{diffuse} \end{bmatrix}$$

12 The two possibilities discussed in **10** and **11**—that of adding rules to the grammar at places other than the end and that of maintaining a phonemic distinction in the dictionary even when the distinction is not directly present in any utterance—suggest that phonemes that have fallen together at one stage in the evolution of a language may at a later stage emerge again as completely distinct entities. The point being made here is that it is not only that phoneme types that have merged at one stage may reappear at a later stage, but that the re-emerging phonemes correspond precisely to their historical antecedents which had previously coalesced. The latter development has usually been regarded as impossible on theoretical grounds, yet if our theory is correct such developments are anything but impossible.

As an hypothetical example, consider a language containing the seven vowel system shown in (10) which is subject to the phonetic rule (17) causing all reflexes of /a/ to merge into /æ/. Suppose that rule (17) were to be modified as shown below in (21) by the addition of subpart (d*) before subpart (b) rather than after subpart (c):

(21)

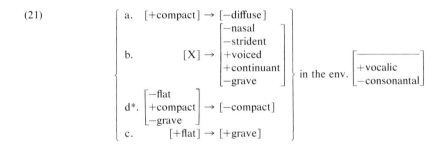

dentally, I shall also try to show that in the so-called seven vowel dialects, only five vowels are actually distinctive.

[19]These phenomena have recently been discussed by K. F. Zaxarova "Arxaičeskie tipy dissimiljativnogo jakan'ja v govorax Belgorodskoj i Voronežskoj oblastjax," *Materialy i issledovanija po russkoj dialektologii* (Moscow, 1959), with the significant comment that "*jakan'e* of the Obojansk type can continue to exist in dialects in which the system of stressed vowels corresponding to [this type of *jakan'e*—M. H.] is being or has already been lost." (p. 21).

Cases where distinct morphophonemic pro-

cesses take place in what from a phonetic point of view are indistinguishable contexts are by no means rare. An intricate example is discussed by N. Chomsky and me in our forthcoming *Sound Pattern of English*. [See now Chomsky and Halle, 1968—VBM.] We show that, in order to account for the different stress patterns of such pairs as *hyperbola* and *avocado,* for the difference in vowel length in such pairs as *balm* and *bomb,* and for a few other phenomena, it is necessary to maintain a distinction between lax /ɔ/ and tense /ā/ even in General American where these two segment types are phonetically never distinct.

A third example is provided by those Northern

Observe that before the addition of subpart (d*) the original seven vowels are phonetically actualized as follows:

(22)

As a result of adding (d*), which coalesces /æ/→/e/, the original seven vowels are implemented as follows:

(23)

As a result of adding (d*), which coalesces /æ/→/e/, the original seven vowels are implemented as follows:

Observe that the changes cannot be explained if it is assumed that because rule (17) eliminates the phonetic distinction between /æ/ and /a/, this distinction is also lost in the representation of all morphemes, so that the phonemic system corresponding to (17) is that given in the lower row of (22). No difficulties are experienced in accounting for the change if we postulate that, for reasons of the kind discussed in section 11, /a/ and /æ/ remained distinct entities even though every /a/ was actualized phonetically as /æ/. Subpart (d*), which was introduced at a later point in time, could then affect the original seven vowels as shown in (23).[20]

The example just reviewed suggests a possible solution to some of the traditional puzzles of historical linguistics. Thus, for example, it is well known that in Elizabethan English, the reflexes of Middle English long /ǣ/ rime with the reflexes of Middle English long /ā/, both of which are assumed to have become /ē/; e.g., *beat* rimes with *late* rather than with *feet*. In the late seventeenth century, a radical change is found; reflexes of /ǣ/ now

rime with those of /ē/ rather than with those of /ā/. To account for this, we assume that Middle English had a tense vowel system like that in (10) and, moreover, that in the Early Modern English period, this tense vowel system was subject to rule (17), now appropriately modified to affect tense vowels only, which caused /ā/→/ǣ/ [cf. (22)]. We then postulate that the Great Vowel Shift operated on this system, thereby yielding the following reflexes of the original seven vowels:

(24)

which are the long vowels of Shakespeare and his contemporaries. Assume further that the various morphophonemic processes of English, in particular the shortening of long vowels which played such a major role in derivational morphology, required the maintenance of the original seven vowel system in spite of the rather radical transformations effected by the phonetic rules which now include not only (17) but also the analogue of the Great Vowel Shift. The changes in the late seventeenth century can then be accounted for by postulating the addition of (d*) to (17); i.e., the replacement of (17) by (21). Operating on the original seven vowel system of (10), (21) followed by the Vowel Shift rule yields the following correspondences:

(25)

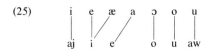

which are the reflexes of the Middle English long vowels in the language of today.[21]

Russian dialects in which the affricate /c/ has become /s/. The distinction between affricate and continuant must, however, be marked in the dictionary in order to account for the fact that in position before /e/, the /s/ which is the reflex of the affricate /c/ is not sharped, whereas the reflex of the continuant is sharped; e.g., prep. sg. /l,is'e/ 'fox' and /l,ic'e/ 'face' are implemented phonetically as [l,is,'ɛ] and [l,is'ɛ], respectively. Cf. V. G. Orlova, *Istorija affrikat v russkom jazyke* (Moscow, 1959), especially pp. 164–166.

[20]We are not taking into consideration here the fact that after the addition of subpart (d*), simplicity

considerations may lead us to postulate a six vowel system like that in the lower row of (23) and to revise radically rule (21). This would not affect the grammar of the carriers of the change, but only that of their children. Since it is the change itself that is of interest here, rather than its consequences for the speech of the next generation, the simplifications in the grammar of the later generations must be disregarded.

[21]The comments on the history of English are meant to be merely suggestive. A detailed study of this topic is being planned by my colleague S. J. Keyser.

ON THE BASES OF PHONOLOGY*
MORRIS HALLE

I

Our central concern in this section is the framework to be used for characterizing speech in a linguistic description. It is required of such a framework that it not only make it possible to represent the observed data with a sufficient degree of accuracy, but also that this representation lead to reasonable, fruitful, insightful, and simple descriptions of the relevant facts. As an illustration consider the following example.

It is an easily observed fact that speakers of English can produce plural forms of nouns regardless of whether or not they have ever heard the noun before. This bit of linguistic behavior is usually described by saying that in forming the regular plural [ɨz] is added if the noun ends in [s z š ž č ǯ] (e.g., *busses, causes, bushes, garages, beaches, badges*); [s] is added if the noun ends in [p t k θ f] (e.g., *caps, cats, cakes, fourths, cuffs*); and [z] is added in all other cases.

Underlying this rule is the assumption that the speech signal is a linear sequence of discrete entities variously termed phonemes, sounds, segments, allophones, and so on. It is this assumption which makes it possible to give the concise account quoted above. Without making use of the phoneme these facts can be expressed only with the greatest laboriousness as one can easily convince oneself by trying to give the rule in terms of syllables, words, or such clear acoustical properties as periodicity, formant behavior, noise spectrum, and the like.

The layman .may regard as somewhat paradoxical our terming as an assumption the proposition that speech is a linear sequence of sounds. It does not seem to be widely known that when one examines an actual utterance in its purely physical manifestation as an acoustical event, one does not find in it obvious markers which would allow one to segment the signal into entities standing in a one-to-one relationship with the phonemes that, the linguist would say, compose the utterance.[1]

The inability of instrumental phoneticians to propose a workable segmentation procedure has, however, not resulted in a wholesale abandonment of the phoneme concept. Only a few easily frightened souls have been ready to do without the phoneme. The majority has apparently felt that absence of a simple segmentation procedure does not warrant abandoning the discrete picture of speech. The most important justification that could perhaps be offered for this stand is that almost every insight gained by modern linguistics from Grimm's Law to Jakobson's distinctive features depends crucially on the assumption that speech is a sequence of discrete entities. In view of this fact many linguists have been willing to postulate the existence of discrete entities in speech even while accepting as true the assertion of instrumental phoneticians that there are no procedures for isolating these entities. There are numerous precedents in science for such a position. For instance,

---

[1]For discussion of some of the evidence, see P. Ladefoged's contribution to the Teddington Symposium, *The Mechanization of Thought Processes*, National Physical Laboratories, Symposium #10 (London 1959). Analogous observations have been made also with regard to other physiological, motor aspects of speech; cf. the report by Menzerath on his x-ray moving pictures of speech at the Fourth International Congress of Linguists (Copenhagen, 1938).

*Morris Halle, "On the Bases of Phonology," from *The Structure of Language* by Jerry A. Fodor and Jerrold J. Katz, © 1964, pp. 324–333. Reprinted by permission of Prentice-Hall, Inc., Englewood Cliffs, New Jersey. This is a revised version of M. Halle, "Questions of Linguistics," published in the supplement to *Il Nuovo Cimento* 13, Series 10 (1958), 494–517.

Helmholtz postulated that electric current is a flow of discrete particles without having isolated or even having much hope of isolating one of these particles. The status of the phoneme in linguistics is, therefore, analogous to that of electrons in physics, and since we do not regard the latter as fictional, there is little reason for applying this term to phonemes. They are every bit as real as any other theoretical entity in science. It now appears, moreover, that the insurmountable difficulties encountered in the attempt to state a procedure for segmenting the speech signal are no bar to constructing a device which will transform (continuous) speech into sequences of discrete entities.[2]

In addition to viewing utterances as composed of phonemes, the phonemes themselves shall be regarded here as simultaneous actualizations of a set of attributes. This view can be traced back almost to the very beginnings of abstract concern with language since rudimentary schemes for classifying speech sounds are implicit already in the earliest alphabets. This is hardly surprising, for it is all but self-evident that speech sounds form various intersecting classes. Thus, for instance, the final sounds in the words *ram, ran, rang* share the property of nasality; i.e., the property of being produced with a lowered velum, which allows air to flow through the nose. In a similar fashion, the sound [m] shares with the sounds [p] and [b] the property of being produced with a closure at the lips, or, as phoneticians would say, of having a bilabial *point of articulation.*

The proposed frameworks differ, of course, from one another, and up to the present, phoneticians have not agreed on any single framework that is to be used in all linguistic descriptions. In the present study I shall utilize the *distinctive feature framework* that is due primarily to R. Jakobson. Since the distinctive features have been described in detail elsewhere, I shall present here only the articulatory correlates of the most important

features and comment briefly on some of them.[3]

ARTICULATORY CORRELATES OF THE DISTINCTIVE FEATURES (PARTIAL LIST)

In the description below four degrees of narrowing in the vocal tract will be distinguished.

The most extreme degree of narrowing, termed *contact,* is present when two opposite parts of the vocal tract touch. Stop consonants such as [p] [d] or [k] are articulated with *contact* at different points in the vocal tract.

A less extreme degree of narrowing, termed *occlusion,* is one capable of producing turbulence. *Occlusions* are characteristically involved in the production of fricatives such as [v] [s] or [š].

The next degree of narrowing, termed *obstruction,* is exemplified in the articulation of glides such as [w] or [j].

The fourth degree of narrowing, termed *constriction,* is that manifest in the articulation of diffuse ("high") vowels such as [i] or [u].

VOCALIC—NONVOCALIC: vocalic sounds are produced with a periodic excitation and with an open oral cavity, i.e., one in which the most extreme degree of narrowing is a *constriction;* nonvocalic sounds are produced with an oral cavity narrowed at least to the degree of an *obstruction* or with an excitation that is not periodic.

CONSONANTAL—NONCONSONANTAL: consonantal sounds are produced with *occlusion* or *contact* in the central path through the oral cavity; nonconsonantal sounds are produced with lesser degrees of narrowing in the central path of the oral cavity.

GRAVE—NONGRAVE: grave sounds are articu-

---

[2]For a discussion of these procedures see D. MacKay "Mindlike Behaviours of Artefacts," *British Journal for the Philosophy of Science* 2 (1959) 105–121, and M. Halle and K. N. Stevens, "Speech Recognition: A Model and a Program for Research," pp. 604–612 in this volume [i.e., Fodor and Katz, 1964—VBM].

[3]The fact that in the following list, reference is made only to the articulatory properties of speech and nothing is said about the acoustical properties, is not to be taken as an indication that the latter are somehow less important. The only reason for concentrating here exclusively on the former is that these are more readily observed without instruments. If reference were to be made to the acoustical properties of speech it would be necessary to report on experimental findings of fair complexity which would expand this paper beyond its allowed limits. For a fuller discussion, see R. Jakobson, C. G. M. Fant, M. Halle, *Preliminaries to Speech Analysis,* Cambridge, Mass.: M.I.T. Press, 1963.

lated with a primary narrowing located at the periphery of the oral cavity (i.e., at the lips or in the velar or pharyngeal region); nongrave sounds are articulated with a primary narrowing located in the central (i.e., dental-alveolar-palatal) region of the oral cavity.

FLAT—NONFLAT: flat sounds are produced with a secondary narrowing at the periphery of the oral cavity; nonflat sounds are produced without such a narrowing.[4]

DIFFUSE—NONDIFFUSE: diffuse sounds are produced with a narrowing which in degree equals or exceeds that of a *constriction* and is located in the front part of the vocal tract; nondiffuse sounds are articulated with narrowings which are either of a lesser degree or are located in the back part of the vocal tract. The dividing line between *front* and *back* is further retracted for vowels than for other sounds: for the vowels, *front* includes almost the entire oral cavity, while for other sounds, the dividing line between *front* and *back* runs between the alveolar and palatal regions.

COMPACT—NONCOMPACT: this feature is restricted to vowels. Compact vowels are produced with a forward flanged oral cavity which contains no *constrictions* or narrowings of higher degree; noncompact vowels are produced with an oral cavity that is not forward flanged.

STRIDENT—NONSTRIDENT: this feature is restricted to consonantal sounds. Strident sounds are produced by directing the air stream at right angles across a sharp edged obstacle or parallel over a rough surface, thereby producing considerable noisiness which is the major acoustical correlate of stridency. Nonstrident sounds are produced with configurations in which one or several of the factors mentioned are missing.

VOICED—VOICELESS: voiced sounds are produced by vibrating the vocal cords; voice-

less sounds are produced without vocal vibration.

NASAL—NONNASAL: nasal sounds are produced by lowering the velum, thereby allowing air to pass through the nasal pharynx and nose; nonnasal sounds are produced with a raised velum which effectively shuts off the nasal pharynx and nose from the rest of the vocal tract.

CONTINUANT — INTERRUPTED: continuant sounds are produced with a vocal tract in which the passage from the glottis to the lips contains no narrowing in excess of an *occlusion;* interrupted sounds are produced with a vocal tract in which the passage from the glottis to the lips is effectively closed by *contact.*

The first two features on the above list produce a quadripartite division of the sounds of speech into (1) vowels, which are vocalic and nonconsonantal; (2) liquids, [r], [l], which are vocalic and consonantal; (3) consonants, which are nonvocalic and consonantal; and (4) glides, [h], [w], [j], which are nonvocalic and nonconsonantal. This division differs from the traditional one—into vowels and nonvowels (consonants).

A further difference between most standard systems and the distinctive feature system lies in the treatment of two major classes of segments, the vowels and the consonants. In most standard systems these two classes are described in terms of features which are totally different: consonants are described in terms of "points of articulation," whereas vowels are described in terms of the so-called "vowel triangle." In the distinctive feature system, on the other hand, these two classes are handled by the same features, *diffuse-nondiffuse,* and *grave-acute.*[5]

The manner in which individual speech sounds are characterized in terms of distinctive features is illustrated in Table 1. As can be seen there, [s] is characterized as nonvocalic, consonantal, nongrave, diffuse, strident, nonnasal, continuant, voiceless; or [m] is char-

---

[4]Sounds produced with a single narrowing which is located at the periphery of the oral cavity may be classed either as flat or nonflat; they are, of course, grave. Sounds articulated with two narrowings, of which one is central and the other peripheral, are acute and flat; whereas sounds articulated with two narrowings both of which are peripheral are grave and flat.

[5]Over 2000 years ago, Hindu phoneticians had the idea of treating vowels and consonants together. Their solution differs from the one proposed here in that it classified vowels as well as consonants in terms of their points of articulation.

TABLE 1

Distinctive Feature Representation of the Consonants of English

	p	b	m	f	v	k	g	t	d	θ	ð	n	s	z	č	ǯ	š	ž
VOCALIC	−	−	−	−	−	−	−	−	−	−	−	−	−	−	−	−	−	−
CONSONANTAL	+	+	+	+	+	+	+	+	+	+	+	+	+	+	+	+	+	+
GRAVE	+	+	+	+	+	+	+	−	−	−	−	−	−	−	−	−	−	−
DIFFUSE	+	+	+	+	+	−	−	+	+	+	+	+	+	+	−	−	−	−
STRIDENT	−	−	−	+	+	−	−	−	−	−	−	−	+	+	+	+	+	+
NASAL	−	−	+	−	−	−	−	−	−	−	−	+	−	−	−	−	−	−
CONTINUANT	−	−	−	+	+	−	−	−	−	+	+	−	+	+	−	−	+	+
VOICED	−	+	+	−	+	−	+	−	+	−	+	+	−	+	−	+	−	+

acterized as nonvocalic, consonantal, grave, diffuse, nonstrident, nasal, noncontinuant, voiced. The alphabetic symbols [s] and [m], by which we conventionally designate these sounds are therefore, nothing but abbreviations standing for the feature complexes just mentioned. It is as feature complexes, rather than as indivisible entities, that speech sounds will be regarded hereinafter.

It is obvious that we can use the features to refer conveniently to classes of speech sounds. Thus, for instance, all sounds represented in Table 1 belong to the class of consonants, and as such they share the features *nonvocalic* and *consonantal*. We note moreover that the consonants [s z č ž š ž] are the only ones that share the features *nongrave* and *strident;* or [p b f v m] alone share the features *grave* and *diffuse*. On the other hand, [m] and [s] share no features which would distinguish them from all other consonants. If we wanted to designate the class containing the sounds [m] and [s] in distinctive feature terminology, we should have to give a long, cumbersome list of features. We shall say that a set of speech sounds forms a *natural class* if fewer features are required to designate the class than to designate any individual sound in the class. Hence, the first three sets of sounds cited above form natural classes, whereas the set containing [m] and [s] is not a natural class.

Jakobson has shown that in describing the most varied linguistic facts we commonly encounter sets of sounds which form natural classes in the distinctive feature framework and that only rarely does one meet sets of sounds which require long, cumbersome lists of distinctive features for their characterization. As a case in point consider again the formation of English noun plurals. As was

noted above, [ɨz] is added if and only if the noun ends in [s z š ž č ž]. But as we have already seen it is precisely this class of consonants that is exhaustively characterized by the features *nongrave* and *strident*. Similarly, the nouns to which the suffix [s] is added end in consonants all of which are characterized by the feature *unvoiced*. These coincidences are important, for the distinctive features were evidently not postulated with the express purpose of affording a convenient description of the rules for forming the English plural.

The total number of different distinctive features is quite small; there seem to be about fifteen. These 15 attributes are sufficient to characterize all segments in all languages. Since we cannot have knowledge of all languages—e.g., of languages which will be spoken in the future—the preceding assertion must be understood as a statement about the nature of human language in general. It asserts in effect that human languages are phonetically much alike, that they do *not* "differ from one another without limit and in unpredictable ways." Like all generalizations this statement can be falsified by valid counter-examples. It can, however, not be proven true with the same conclusiveness. The best that can be done is to show that the available evidence makes it very likely that the statement is true. Most important in this connection is the fact that all investigations in which large numbers of languages have been examined—from E. Siever's *Grundzüge der Phonetik* (1876) to Trubetzkoy's *Grundzüge der Phonologie* (1939)—have operated with an extremely restricted set of attributes. If this can be done with about a hundred languages from all parts of the globe, there appears good reason to believe that a not greatly enlarged catalogue of attributes will be capable of handling the re-maining languages as well.

If it is true that a small set of attributes suffices to describe the phonetic properties of all languages of the world, then it would appear quite likely that these attributes are connected with something fairly basic in man's constitution, something which is quite independent of his cultural background. Psychologists might, therefore, find it rewarding to investigate the phonetic attributes, for it is not inconceivable that these attributes will prove to be productive parameters for describing man's responses to auditory stimuli in general. It must, however, be noted that for purposes of linguistics, the lack of psychological work in this area is not fatal. For the linguist it suffices if the attributes selected yield reasonable, elegant, and insightful descriptions of all relevant linguistic data. And this in fact they accomplish.

II

It has been noted that in linguistic descriptions utterances are represented as sequences of discrete segments, which themselves are characterized by means of distinctive features. Although in many instances there is a one-to-one relationship between the segments and specific stretches of the acoustical signal, there are many instances where this relationship is anything but simple. The part of linguistics that is concerned with the relationship between segment (phoneme) and sound is called *phonology*.

A complete description of a language must include a list of all existing morphemes of the languages, for without such a list the grammar would fail to distinguish a normal English sentence such as "it was summer," from the jabberwocky "'twas brillig." Our purpose in preparing a scientific description of a language is, however, not achieved if we give only an inventory of all existing morphemes; we must also describe the structural principles that underlie all existing forms. Just as syntax must be more than an inventory of all observed sentences of a language, so phonology must be more than a list of its morphemes.

In order to generate a specific sentence it is obviously necessary to supply the grammar with instructions for selecting from the list of morphemes the particular morphemes appearing in the sentence. Instead of using an arbitrary numerical code which tells us nothing about the phonetic structure of the morphemes, it is possible—and also more consonant with the aims of a linguistic description—to utilize for this purpose the distinctive feature representation of the morphemes directly. In other words, instead of instructing the grammar to select item (#7354), we instruct the grammar to select the morpheme which in its first segment has the features *nonvocalic, consonantal, diffuse, grave, voiced,* and so on; in its second segment, the features *vocalic, nonconsonantal, diffuse, acute,* and the like; in its third segment the features *vocalic, consonantal,* and so forth. Instructions of this type need not contain information about all features but only about features or feature combinations which serve to distinguish one morpheme from another. This is a very important fact since in every language only certain features or feature combinations can serve to distinguish morphemes from one another. We call these features and feature combinations *phonemic,* and we say that in the input instructions only phonemic features or feature combinations must occur.[6]

Languages differ also in the way they handle nonphonemic features or feature combinations. For some of the nonphonemic features there are definite rules; for others the decision is left up to the speaker who can do as he likes. For example, the feature of aspiration is nonphonemic in English; its occurrence is subject to the following conditions:

All segments other than the voiceless stops [k], [p], [t] are unaspirated.
The voiceless stops are never aspirated after [s].
Except after [s], voiceless stops are always aspirated before an accented vowel.
In all other positions, aspiration of voiceless stops is optional.

A complete grammar must obviously contain a statement of such facts, for they are of

---

[6]The requirement to represent morphemes in the dictionary by phonemic features only is a direct consequence of the simplicity criterion discussed on pp. 335 [380] ff. in this volume.

crucial importance to one who would speak the language correctly.

In addition to features which, like *aspiration* in English, are never phonemic, there are features in every language that *are* phonemic, but only in those segments where they occur in conjunction with certain other features; for example, the feature of voicing in English is phonemic only in the nonnasal consonants—all other segments except [h] are normally voiced, while [h] is voiceless.

So far we have dealt only with features which are nonphonemic regardless of neighboring segments. There are also cases where features are nonphonemic because they occur in the vicinity of certain other segments. As an example we might take the segment sequences at the beginning of English words. It will be recalled here that the features *vocalic-nonvocalic* and *consonantal-nonconsonantal* distinguish four classes of segments: vowels, symbolized here by *V*, that are vocalic and nonconsonantal; consonants, symbolized by *C*, that are nonvocalic and consonantal; liquids [r], [l], symbolized by *L*, that are vocalic and consonantal; the glide [h], symbolized by *H*, that is nonvocalic and non-consonantal.[7] We shall be concerned solely with restrictions on these four classes; all further restrictions within the classes are disregarded here.

English morphemes can begin only with *V, CV, LV, HV, CCV, CLV,* and *CCLV: odd, do, rue, who, stew, clew, screw.* A number of sequences are not admitted initially—e.g., *LCV, LLV*. These constraints are reflected in the following three rules which are part of the grammar of English:

RULE 1: If a morpheme begins with a consonant followed by a nonvocalic segment, the latter is also consonantal.
RULE 2: If a morpheme begins with a sequence of two consonants, the third segment in the sequence is vocalic.
RULE 3: If between the beginning of a morpheme and a liquid or a glide no vowel intervenes, the segment following the liquid or the glide is a vowel.

[7]We consider the semivowels [j] as in *you* and [w] as in *woo,* to be positional variants of the lax vowels [i], [u], respectively; cf. N. Chomsky and M. Halle, *The Sound Pattern of English* (to appear). [See now Chomsky and Halle, 1968—VBM.]

These rules enable us to specify uniquely a number of features in certain segment sequences:

vocalic	−	−		
consonantal	+		+	

is converted by rules 1, 2, and 3 into

vocalic	−	−	+	+
consonantal	+	+	+	−

which stands for a sequence *CCLV,* e.g., *straw.*

The above rules must be applied in the given order. If no order is imposed, they will have to be given in a much more complex form. An interesting illustration of the effects of ordering on the complexity of the rules is provided by the Finnish vowel system, which shall now be examined. Finnish has eight vowel sounds which can be characterized by means of the following distinctive feature matrix.

	[æ]	[a]	[e]	[ö]	[o]	[i]	[ü]	[u]
flat	−	−	−	+	+	−	+	+
compact	+	+	−	−	−	−	−	−
diffuse	−	−	−	−	−	+	+	+
grave	−	+	−	−	+	−	−	+

This matrix is clearly redundant, since it utilizes four binary features to characterize eight entities. The redundant features have been omitted in the table below.

	[æ]	[a]	[e]	[ö]	[o]	[i]	[ü]	[u]
flat	−	−	−	+	+	−	+	+
compact	+	+	−			−		
diffuse			−	−	−	+	+	+
grave	−	+		−	+		−	+

The omitted nonphonemic features are supplied by the following rules:

RULE 4:   Flat vowels are noncompact.
RULE 5:   Compact vowels are nondiffuse.
RULE 6:   Noncompact nonflat vowels are nongrave.

The treatment just proposed has an interesting further consequence. In Finnish there is a restriction on what vowels can occur in a given word (vowel harmony). The Finnish word can contain a selection either from the set [i e ü ö æ] or from the set [i e u o a]. If [e i] are temporarily set aside, one could propose that Finnish is subject to

RULE 7:   In a word all vowels are either grave or nongrave, depending on the nature of the root morpheme.

If [e i] are included, Rule 7 leads to incorrect results, since in words with *grave* root morphemes, [e] and [i] would be turned by Rule 7 into grave vowels, whereas in fact they remain nongrave. This incorrect result is immediately avoided if we let Rule 6 apply after, rather than before Rule 7, for Rule 6 makes all nonflat noncompact vowels nongrave and Rule 7 does not affect either flatness or compactness of any vowel.

III

In the preceding, the distinctive features have been utilized for two separate purposes. On the one hand, they have been used to characterize different aspects of vocal tract behavior, such as the location of the different narrowings in the vocal tract, the presence or absence of vocal cord vibration, lowering or raising of velum, and so forth. On the other hand, the features have functioned as abstract markers for the designation of individual morphemes. It is necessary at this point to give an account of how this dual function of the features is built into the theory.

As already noted the rules that constitute the phonological component of a grammar relate a matrix consisting of abstract markers—the phonemic representation—to a matrix where each marker represents a particular aspect of vocal tract behavior. The latter matrix is our counterpart of the conventional phonetic transcription. In the phonemic representation the different features are allowed to assume only two values, plus or minus. In this representation, however, no phonetic content is associated directly with the features which function here as abstract differential markers.

The rules of the phonological component modify—at times quite radically—the matrices of the phonological representation; the rules supply values to nonphonemic features, they change the values of certain features, and they assign a phonetic interpretation to the individual rows of the matrix. The phonetic interpretation assigned to the rows of the matrix is uniform for all languages; i.e., some row in the matrix will be associated with the feature *vocalic-nonvocalic*, another with the feature *consonantal-nonconsonantal*, and so on. This fact explains our practice of designating the rows in the phonemic matrices which represent abstract differential markers, by names of the different phonetic features. When we designate a given row in the phonemic matrix by the name of a particular phonetic feature, we imply that the grammar will ultimately associate this row with the phonetic feature in question.

The statement that the assignment of phonetic interpretations to phonemic matrices is uniform for all languages reflects the fact that the articulatory apparatus of man is the same everywhere, that men everywhere are capable of controlling the same few aspects of their vocal tract behavior. The phonetic features represent, therefore, the capacities of man to produce speech sounds and constitute, in this sense, the universal phonetic framework of language. Since not all phonetic features are binary, the phonological component will include rules replacing some of the pluses and minuses in the matrices by integers representing the different degrees of intensity which the feature in question manifests in the utterance. Thus, for instance, the fact that the English [ʌ] as in *pup* is less grave ("back") than English [u] as in *poop* will be embodied in a phonological rule replacing the plus for the feature gravity by a higher integer in the vowel in *poop* than in the vowel in *pup*.

In the light of the above, the extensive discussion concerning the claim that the distinctive features are binary appears to have been due primarily to an identification of abstract phonemic markers with the phonetic features with which they are associated by the rules of the grammar. Once a distinction is made between abstract phonemic markers and phonetic features, there is little ground for disagreement, for the fact that there are many more than two phonetically distinct degrees of gravity does not invalidate the claim that in the abstract phonemic representation of morphemes there are only binary features.

THE NATURE OF
STRUCTURAL DESCRIPTIONS*
NOAM CHOMSKY

4.2. THE PHONOLOGICAL COMPONENT

The phonological component of the grammar can be regarded as an input-output device which operates on a string of formatives, provided with a structural analysis by the syntactic component, and assigns to this string a representation as a string of phones. It is, in part, an open question to what extent structural information on the syntactic level is relevant to determining the phonetic form of a string of formatives. There is no doubt that information of the kind provided in the derived Phrase-marker is essential,[5] and there are scattered examples that suggest that deeper syntactic features may also play a role in determining the details of phonetic shape.

A rather classical view of the structure of the phonological component might be something like this. Formatives are of two types: grammatical and lexical (among the grammatical we count, as subtypes, class markers and junctural elements introduced by syntactic rules, e.g., word boundary). Each grammatical formative is represented by a single symbol. Each lexical formative is represented in a systematic orthography as a string of symbols, each of which is assigned to certain categories (Vowel, Consonant, Voiced, etc.). Each symbol can, in fact, be regarded as an abbreviation for the set of categories to which it belongs, and each lexical item can thus be represented by a *classificatory matrix* in which the columns stand for what we may call "segments" and the rows, for categories; the entry in the ith row and j^{th} column indicates whether the jth segment belongs to the ith category. These categories we may call (classificatory) distinctive features. Some squares of the matrix may be blank, where the feature in question can be supplied by a general rule (e.g., the entry for Rounding in the case of English Lax Front Vowels, which become, automatically, unrounded).

The rules of the phonological component are ordered, and apply in sequence to the string of formatives (utilizing, when this is relevant, the associated syntactic information) until ultimately a representation in terms of a universal phonetic alphabet is reached. The symbols of this alphabet are specified in terms of a set of phonetic features; hence the output of the phonological component can again be regarded as a matrix in which columns represent phones and rows, phonetic features of the universal system. The entry in the ith row and j^{th} column indicates whether the jth phone of the generated utterance possesses the ith feature, or the degree to which it possesses this feature (in the case of such features as stress). Classificatory distinctive features are by definition "binary"; phonetic features may or may not be. A representation in terms of phonetic features we may call a *phonetic matrix,* again regarding the symbols of the universal phonetic alphabet as mere conventional abbreviations for sets of feature specifications.

The universal phonetic alphabet is part of a universal phonetic theory. In addition to a

[5]See the references of note 6, §1, and notes 4 and 5 of §2 for details. All of these studies are based on the notion "transformational cycle" sketched in §1.

*The present selection comprises all but the first six pages of Chapter 4 ("The Nature of Structural Descriptions") of *Current Issues in Linguistic Theory* by Noam Chomsky (Mouton, 1964). Pages 65–110 reprinted by permission. (In order to avoid confusion in cross-referencing, the original section and footnote numbers have been retained.)

fixed set of features, such a theory should contain general laws concerning possible combinations and contrasts. Steps toward such a theory are found in the work of the classical British phoneticians (Bell, Ellis, Sweet); in the "phonologie" of de Saussure's 1897 lectures[6] and again in Jakobson's theory of distinctive features and phonetic universals (e.g., Jakobson, Fant, and Halle, 1952). This theory constitutes a part of general linguistic theory, exactly as do the restrictions on the form of rules and the other constraints on the structure of a generative grammar. We will refer to the requirement that a general linguistic theory must incorporate a universal phonetic theory,

---

[6]Thus, for example, he claims that Nasalization is never distinctive for liquids in any language (1916, 74), and consequently need not be specified in the representation of, e.g., the nasalized /l/ of French "branlant." If this is true, then Nasalization need not be specified for liquids in the phonetic matrix for any language, just as Rounding need not be specified for Lax Front Vowels in the classificatory matrices of English. It is worth noting that there are much earlier studies of articulatory phonetics with a view towards establishing a universal phonetic theory, for example, in the English grammatical tradition, the extensive distinctive features analysis developed by Wallis, Wilkins and others in the seventeenth century. It is difficult to imagine what might be the basis for the fairly commonly held view that Western scholars, prior to the nineteenth century, "had not observed the sounds of speech, and confused them with the written symbols of the alphabet" (Bloomfield, 1933, p. 8). In fact, Aristotle observes that "spoken words are the symbols of mental experience and written words are the symbols of spoken words" (*De Interpretatione*), and the truism that writing is a derivative system is repeated frequently in grammatical studies. Furthermore, there was serious investigation of articulatory phonetics, as noted above, well before the nineteenth century. In the same connection, it is worth mentioning that the widely held view (cf. again Bloomfield, 1933, Chapter 1) that early modern "general grammar" was typically prescriptive and wedded to a Latin model (or a "logical model") is also quite false. Thus, for example, the *Grammaire générale et raisonnée* (often taken as the prototype of this tendency) suggests interesting analyses of the syntax of French, and (so far as "prescriptiveness" is concerned) establishes the following maxim (82–83) which "ceux qui travaillent sur une langue vivante, doivent toujours avoir devant les yeux," namely, "que les façons de parler qui sont authorisées par un usage général et non-contesté, doivent passer pour bonnes, encore qu'elles soient contraires aux règles et à l'analogie de la langue" (though it goes on, quite correctly, to warn against the absurdity of misuse or misevaluation of such "bizarreries de l'usage").

with a fixed alphabet, as the condition of *phonetic specifiability*. Note that a universal phonetic alphabet is the counterpart of a substantive theory of syntactic categories (see note 1, §4) that assigns a fixed significance to the labels used in the syntactic component; but in the case of a phonetic alphabet, the construction of a concrete and substantive theory has, of course, been much more fully realized.

Let us assume that at a certain stage in the application of the rules of the phonological component, all grammatical formatives except junctures will have been eliminated and we have a representation in terms of classificatory matrices and junctures alone (with derived phrase structure indicated). At this point, for example, English "saw," which at the input stage is /sī/ + *past,* might be represented /sɔ̄/ (though English "heard," which at the input stage might be /hīr/ + *past,* might be represented /hīr#d/, since the general rules that convert ī to e in many contexts, and that convert lax, non-compact vowels to [ɨ] before final /r/ (+ Consonant), would presumably not yet have applied). Similarly, at this stage, such a phrase as "telegraphic code" (at the phonetic level, perhaps [tʰelɨgrǽfikkʰɔ̄wd]) would still be represented /tele + græf + ik # kōd/, or, more fully,

(19) $[_{NP}[_{Adj}[_N[_{Pre}$ tele $]$ $[_{Stem}$ græf$]]$ ik$]$ # $[_N$ kōd$]]$,

where the notation $[_A$ x$]$, with paired brackets, indicates that the bracketed string x is a string of the category A. This representation in terms of segments and junctures, with the derived constituent structure of the string still marked (since it plays a role in the determination of phonetic shape by subsequent phonological rules), we will call, tentatively, the level of *systematic phonemics,* implying by the word "systematic" that the choice of elements at this level is deeply determined by properties of both the syntactic and the phonological component. The representation in terms of phones (and, possibly, phonetic junctures) that constitutes the output of the phonological component, we will call the level of *systematic phonetics.*

So far as I can see, there is no other significant level of representation that can be isolated in the phonological component. The input to the phonological component is, in effect, the lowest level of syntactic representation ("l'étage inférieur de la morphologie" of de Saussure, cf. Godel, 1957, 166) where segments are classified in terms of what will ultimately be phonetic characteristics ("caractères phoniques," op. cit.). The output of this component, as mentioned above, is essentially de Saussure's "phonologie," or the "narrow transcription" of the British phoneticians. The level of systematic phonemics is, essentially, the "phonological orthography" of Sapir (cf. Sapir, 1933 [2]), his "ideal sounds" and "true elements of the phonetic pattern" (cf. 1925 [1], note 2); whereas systematic phonetics is his "phonetic orthography" (1933) or "objective phonemes" (1925). Similarly, systematic phonemics seems to be, in essence, the phonemics of Bloomfield's practice (1933) (in particular, when his "secondary phonemes" are not represented), though it is difficult to say whether it is in accord with his phonological theory, which is hardly a model of clarity.[7] Systematic

phonemics would now generally be called "morphophonemics," in one of the several senses of this term. This terminological innovation is justified if there is a third, intermediate level of systematic representation, more closely related to sound and quite independent of syntactic structure, such as the system of representation now called "phonemic." However, as I will attempt to show below, the existence of an additional level is highly dubious, and for this reason I have preferred to keep the older term, modified by "systematic" to avoid confusion.

In general, we can say, with Palmer (1958), that the place of the phonological component is "that of an ancillary technique; it provides a bridge between the grammatical statement and the direct observations that are reported in phonetics." For linguistic theory, the significant questions concerning the phonological component have to do with the choice of phonetic features (and, more generally, the universal phonetic theory), and with the conditions on the form and ordering of rules. The latter question, in particular, is of great importance, and phonological theory has suffered seriously from its neglect. As soon as the attempt to construct explicit rules to determine the phonetic shape of a string of formatives passes the most superficial and introductory stage, it becomes obvious that a fairly strict ordering must be imposed on phonological processes, if they are to be describable in full generality. Thus most of the examples in Sapir (1933) involve ordering, though he does not explicitly mention this fact. Bloomfield was much concerned with questions of ordering[8] and his "Menomini Morphophonemics" (1939) [7] is the first modern example of a seg-

---

[7] It is instructive, in this connection, to recall the controversies aroused by Bloomfield's *Language*. In particular, Kent's review (1934) criticized it from the point of view of traditional (systematic) phonetics. Kent argues that "the difference between [s] and [š] is functional in English: shall we disregard it in citing Japanese, because it is not functional—even though we have the machinery for marking the distinction?" In this vein, he criticizes Bloomfield's phonemicization of "secretary" [sekṛiterij] as /sekretejrij/ (which Bloomfield justifies, presumably, by reference to "secretarial" [sekṛitejrijɨl]), etc. In responding to the review, Bolling (1934) comments that to mark predictable phonetic variants, in particular, reduced variants of unstressed vowels, "would be like the meaningless underlining of a schoolgirl"; and he supports Bloomfield's phonemicizations by the argument that they mark only what is not predictable. It is interesting to note that the position that Bolling is attacking is, on many points, just the one that is adopted by the "neo-Bloomfieldian" linguists of the 1940's and 1950's, who characteristically criticize Bloomfield for failure to separate levels, and who return to a much "narrower" transcription. In particular, the marking of reduced variants of unstressed vowels is considered one of the major innovations in this development. We return to this issue directly.

The controversy between Kent and Bloomfield-Bolling concerns the choice between systematic phonetics and systematic phonemics. But it is clear that these are not alternatives, and that in fact both levels are significant in the description of a language. It was Bloomfield's summary rejection of phonetics as without scientific value or status, rather than his development of a higher level of representation, that should really have been at issue here.

---

[8] Cf. Bloomfield (1933, 213). He regarded ordering of rules as an artifact—an invention of the linguist—as compared with order of constituents, which is "part of language." But this depreciation of the role of order of synchronic processes is just one aspect of the general antipathy to theory (the so-called "anti-mentalism") that Bloomfield developed and bequeathed to modern linguistics. This tendency fitted well with the operationalism, verificationism and behaviorism that formed a dominant intellectual mood in the early 1930's. Harris showed (1951a, 237) that some of Bloomfield's examples of ordering can be handled by unordered rules that state the phonemic composition of a morphophoneme *in a strictly morphophonemic context*. But his method does not generalize to such examples as the one

ment of a generative grammar with ordered rules. Bloomfield does not discuss the extent or depth of ordering in this grammar, and it is not easy to determine this from the examples that he gives. It apparently does not exceed five (cf. Bever, 1963). In the segment of the phonological component for Modern Hebrew presented in Chomsky (1951), a depth of ordering that reaches the range of twenty to thirty is demonstrated[9] and this is surely an underestimate. Recent work (see note 5, p. 65 [401]) gives strong support to the belief that ordering relations among phonological processes are quite strict; and, furthermore, it provides evidence that the ordering is not strictly linear, but is in part cyclic (see §1). Resolution of these questions seems to me the outstanding problem for contemporary phonology. Although several cases of ordering will be presented below, it is important to bear in mind that scattered examples cannot give an accurate indication of the extent or significance of ordering in a full grammar.

To make the discussion somewhat more concrete, consider the following simple example from English. We find such phonological regularities as the following (where the notation $[s_1, s_2]$ is used for the "archiphoneme" consisting of the features common to s_1, s_2)[10]

$$(20) \quad (i) \quad \begin{Bmatrix} k \\ t \end{Bmatrix} \rightarrow s \text{ in the context: } \underline{\qquad} + [i, y]$$

$$(ii) \quad [s,z] + [i,y] \rightarrow [š,ž]$$
$$\text{in the context: } \underline{\qquad} \text{ Vowel.}$$

Thus we have "opaque" – "opacity," "logic" – "logicism," "democrat" – "democracy," "pirate" – "piracy," in case (i); "race" – "racial," "express" – "expression," "erase" – "erasure," "enclose" – "enclosure," "revise" – "revision," in case (ii). Although various qualifications are needed, clearly rules such as these belong to English grammar. But if these are regarded as purely classificatory, unordered rules to the effect that "mophophoneme" X has the "phoneme" Y as member (or realization, etc.) in the context Z—W, then they must be supplemented by the additional rule

$$(21) \quad \begin{Bmatrix} k \\ t \end{Bmatrix} + [i,y] \rightarrow š \text{ in the context: } \underline{\qquad} \text{ Vowel,}$$

to account for "logician," "delicious" (cf. "delicacy"), "relate" – "relation," "ignite" – "ignition," etc. But clearly this rule is unnecessary if (20ii) can apply to the result of application of (20i), that is, if the rules are ordered as in (20).

The grammar containing just (20i), (20ii), in that order, will provide such derivations as[11]

(22)	lajik + yin	prezident + i	prezident + i + æl
	lajis + yin	prezidens + i	prezidens + i + æl
			(by (20i))
	lajišin		prezidenš + æl
			(by (20ii)).

The top line in (22) is the systematic phonemic representation, in each case, and the last line becomes the systematic phonetic by additional rules. But none of the intermediate stages has any systematic status at all, apparently. For each linguistic form, the number of intermediate representations will depend on the number of rules in the ordered sequence that apply to it, and this number will differ for different forms, indeed, for different subparts of the same sentence, phrase, or word.

Clearly a grammar that contains (21) as a rule is missing a generalization. In fact, con-

_____

given directly below; and, furthermore, it is not clear whether the italicized condition on morphophonemic rules is compatible with the procedures by which they are established, since these procedures set up morphophonemes (similarly, phonemes) in terms of phonemic (respectively, phonetic) or mixed environments. There are important questions of principle here that have not been sufficiently clarified.

[9]That is, it is shown that a sequence of some twenty-five rules can be formed such that any interchange of adjacent rules will lead to a reformulation that increases complexity (and hence reduces generality). In the light of more recent work, the grammar presented there would have to be modified in many respects, but the conclusion concerning ordering, so it appears, would, if anything, be strengthened.

[10]A natural evaluation measure ("simplicity" measure) for the phonological component (cf. Halle, 1961) is the number of feature specifications it contains. In particular, then, the grammar is more

_____

highly valued (and more general) if rules are stated in terms of archiphonemes (and, furthermore, "generalized archiphonemes" such as C, V, etc.) rather than segments.

[11]As throughout, irrelevant details are omitted. In particular, for reasons beyond the scope of this discussion, the first vowel in "logic" should actually be not /a/ but the archiphoneme [ă, ɔ̃] (cf. note 19 on p. 90 [413]), and /ɨ/ should actually be the "archiphoneme" lax vowel.

sideration of additional examples shows immediately that several generalizations are being missed. Thus observe that alongside of (20) there is also the rule

(23) z → s in the context: —— + iv,

as in "abuse" – "abusive." But consider the forms "persuade" – "persuasive" – "persuasion," "corrode" – "corrosive" – "corrosion," etc. In a taxonomic grammar with no provision for applying rules in sequences, these regularities must be accounted for by two entirely new rules, independent of (20), (21), (23), namely:

(24) (i) d → s in the context: —— + iv
     (ii) d + [i,y] → ž in the context: —— Vowel.

If we allow rules to apply in sequence, the rules (24) are entirely superfluous. It is simply necessary to generalize (20i) to apply to [d,t] instead of simply /t/,[12] thus giving for "persuasive" the derivation (25) and for "persuasion" the derivation (26):

(25) perswēd + iv, perswēz + iv (by (20i)),
                              perswēsiv (by (23))

(26) perswēd + yɨn, perswēz + yɨn (by (20i)),
                              perswēžɨn (by (20ii)),

where again the first is the systematic phonemic and the last the systematic phonetic representation (details omitted).

to be preferred, on grounds of descriptive adequacy, to one which contains in addition the rules (21), (24). The latter grammar is simply leaving significant generalizations unexpressed. But a descriptively adequate grammar in this case again requires that the rules be applied in the sequence given.

Finally, let us extend the analysis to include the forms (27), illustrating a point to which we will return below:

(27) (i) decide [dīsa·yd]
     (ii) decided [dīsa·yDɨd] – [D] = alveolar flap
     (iii) decisive [dīsaysiv]
     (iv) delight [dīlayt]
     (v) delighted [dīlayDɨd].

To account for such facts as these, we must add to the phonological component containing the rules (20) and (23), the rules (28) and (29), where the order is now: (20i), (20ii), (23), (28), (29).

(28) a → a· in the context: —— (Glide) Voiced
(29) [t,d] → D in the context:
        Stressed Vowel —— Unstressed Vocalic.

Again, these can be generalized in familiar ways, and each is required, independently, by many other examples. With the rules so ordered we have such derivations as the following:

(30)	*decide*	*decided*	*decisive*	*delight*	*delighted*	*Rule*
(a)	dīsayd	dīsayd#d	dīsayd+iv	dīlayt	dīlayt#d	
(b)	dīsayd	dīsayd#d	dīsayz+iv	dīlayt	dīlayt#d	(20i)
(c)	dīsayd	dīsayd#d	dīsays+iv	dīlayt	dīlayt#d	(23)
(d)	dīsa·yd	dīsa·yd#d	dīsays+iv	dīlayt	dīlayt#d	(28)
(e)	dīsa·yd	dīsa·ydɨd	dīsays+iv	dīlayt	dīlaytid	
(f)	dīsa·yd	dīsa·yDɨd	dīsays+iv	dīlayt	dīlayDɨd	(29)

Again, it is obvious that a grammar that accounts for this variety of phonetic facts by the rules (20) (suitably generalized) and (23), which are independently motivated, is much

Again details and well-known rules are omitted. Line (a) is the systematic phonemic and line (f) the systematic phonetic representation. At no other stage does the set of representations have any systematic character that I can detect. Perhaps (c) is what would be called "phonemic" by many structural linguists (though not, e.g., by Bloch). If so, it is to be observed that ordering of rules is also necessary to convert the "phonemic" representation to the phonetic one, in the optimal way, since clearly if (28) and (29) are not given in this order, the correct output will not be achieved. Thus the [D] of "delighted" is phonetically

---

[12]To this extent, this adjustment of (20i) simplifies the grammar (cf. note 10). Several qualifications are needed, however, which make the effect of the adjustment neutral, as regards complexity. Note that these rules should properly be stated strictly in terms of features. Thus, for example, rule (23) should assert, simply: [+ Continuant] → [– Voiced] in the context: —— + iv.

voiced, but is functionally Voiceless, for the application of rule (28)—thus it has the classificatory distinctive feature of Voicelessness and the phonetic feature of Voiced, in the framework proposed above.

As we enlarge the range of examples considered, the depth of required ordering increases (as does its intricacy, when we introduce the transformational cycle). Investigation of this question has, so far, failed to reveal any systematic set of representations that might be taken as constituting a level of representation at any intermediate point in the operation of the phonological component, and therefore it seems necessary to conclude that systematic phonemics and systematic phonetics are the only two levels of representation that appear in structural descriptions provided by the phonological component. To fortify this conclusion, I would like to consider briefly the status of modern taxonomic phonemics, as seen from this point of view.

4.3. TAXONOMIC PHONEMICS

Sound pattern has been taken as the primary object of study in modern, structural linguistics; it has, furthermore, been studied in relative or complete isolation from the syntactic setting within which phonological processes operate.[13] In both of these respects, structural linguistics marks a departure from a more traditional point of view, which again emerges in recent work in generative grammar, as sketched above. Though modern phonologists have not achieved anything like unanimity, a body of doctrine has emerged to all or part of which a great many linguists would sub-

---

[13]I naturally cannot hope to survey all contemporary points of view in the space of this paper, and I will concentrate on those that seem to me the clearest, referring to Troubetzkoy, Harris, Bloch, and Jakobson, among others. I will not consider glossematics (which, for reasons unclear to me, is often referred to as extremely rigorous and of high "operational preciseness"—cf., e.g., Haugen, 1951; Diderichsen, 1958), or the prosodic analysis of the London school, since I have been unable to find formulations of these positions that are explicit enough to show what evidence might count either for or against them, though the latter, in particular seems to have certain relations to the point of view sketched above in §4.2. See Langendoen (1964a) for a discussion of prosodic analysis, and an interpretation of its results within a framework of the kind proposed here.

scribe. Abstracting away from much variation, let us coin the term "taxonomic phonemics" to refer to this body of doctrine, thus emphasizing its striking reliance, in almost all versions, on procedures of segmentation and classification (identification of variants).

Taxonomic phonemic theory constitutes the first attempt to formulate a linguistic theory with sufficient clarity and care so that questions of theoretical adequacy can seriously be raised. The development of taxonomic phonemics has led to standards of explicitness and precision that had rarely been attained in previous linguistic description, and to many new insights into sound structure. Furthermore, the period of its dominance has also been one of unparalleled extension of the range of linguistic investigation. For these reasons, the methodological and substantive assumptions that underlie this theory deserve careful and critical scrutiny. It seems to me, however, that they have not received the kind of critical appraisal that this position merits. In this discussion of taxonomic phonemics, I will attempt to show that several of the major methodological and substantive assumptions that have played a crucial role in taxonomic phonemics are invalid, and that, in several important respects, the theory of taxonomic phonemics, as it has emerged during the last thirty years, is less adequate than the phonemic theory that was implicit in the work of such pioneers of modern phonology as, for example, Edward Sapir.

Under discussion, then, are four potential levels of representation associated with the phonological component, namely, the levels of:

(31) (i) physical phonetics
      (ii) systematic phonetics
      (iii) taxonomic phonemics
      (iv) systematic phonemics

Physical phonetics is the study referred to by Troubetzkoy (1939) as "the science of the sounds of *parole*," a study with methods and goals entirely different from those of phonology (the "science of the sounds of *langue*"). It provides Bloomfield's "mechanical record of the gross acoustic features, such as is produced in the phonetics laboratory" (1933, 85); its status is not in question here, and no further attention will be given to it.

I will assume, for the purposes of this discussion, that the status of systematic phonemics ("morphophonemics," in one sense of the more usual modern phrase) is also not in question.

The status of systematic phonetics and the condition of phonetic specifiability (cf. p. 67 [402], above), however, has been very much in question, and it has, in fact, been explicitly repudiated in many theoretical discussions. Thus for Bloomfield (1933, 85), the only kind of linguistic record that is "scientifically relevant," aside from that provided by physical phonetics, "is a record in terms of phonemes, ignoring all features that are not distinctive in the language." Phonetic transcription is dismissed as haphazard, limitless, accidental, and of no scientific value; and Bloomfield maintains that in phonology "we pay no heed to the acoustic nature of phonemes but merely accept them as distinct units and study their distribution" (p. 137). Troubetzkoy sometimes refers to phonemes as completely "abstract" units serving only a distinctive function. But elsewhere, he pays a great deal of attention to the systematization of the universal phonetic features that play a distinctive role in some language (structural phonetics—cf. 1939, 93f.). Bloomfield's apparent rejection of the level of structural phonetics reappears in an extreme form in Joos' (1957) summary of what he takes to be the characteristic view of American linguistics, namely, that "languages could differ from each other without limit and in unpredictable ways" (96), that "distinctive features are established ad hoc for each language or even dialect," and that "no universal theory of segments can be called upon to settle the moot points" (228). Similarly, Hjelmslev appears to deny the relevance of phonetic substance to phonological representation.

Nevertheless, it seems to me correct to regard modern taxonomic phonemics, of all varieties, as resting squarely on assumptions concerning a universal phonetic theory of the sort described above. Analysis of actual practice shows no exceptions to the reliance on phonetic universals. No procedure has been offered to show why, for example, initial [pʰ] should be identified with final [p] rather than final [t], in English, that does not rely essentially on the assumption that the familiar phonetic properties (Stop, Labial, etc.) are the "natural" ones. Harris might be interpreted

as suggesting that a non-phonetic principle can replace reliance on absolute phonetic properties when he concludes (1951a, 66) that "simplicity of statement, as well as phonetic similarity, decide in favor of the p-pʰ grouping"; but this implication, if intended, is surely false. The correct analysis is simpler only if we utilize the familiar phonetic properties for phonetic specification. With freedom of choice of features, any arbitrary grouping may be made simpler. From innumerable examples of this sort, it seems that we must conclude that, despite disclaimers, all varieties of taxonomic phonemics rely essentially on the condition of phonetic specifiability. Furthermore, actual practice shows remarkable agreement as to which features constitute the universal phonetic system that is implicitly assumed.

It appears, then, that the status of systematic phonetics is also beyond dispute, though there is room for much discussion as to what is the actual character of the universal phonetic theory that underlies all descriptive practice. In any event, we can assume that each utterance of any language can be uniquely represented as a sequence of *phones,* each of which can be regarded as an abbreviation for a set of features (those that constitute the universal theory in question), in terms of which "phonetic similarity," "simplicity of statement," "pattern congruity," and so on, are defined.

Let us turn then to a more detailed investigation of taxonomic phonemics, taking this to be a theory that requires that phonological representations must, in addition to the condition of phonetic specifiability, meet conditions which, for the sake of this discussion, I will designate by the following terms:

(32)   (i)   linearity
             (ii) invariance
             (iii) biuniqueness
             (iv) local determinacy.

The linearity condition (32i) requires that each occurrence of a phoneme in the phonemic representation of an utterance be associated with a particular succession of (one or more) consecutive phones in its representing matrix, as its "member" or "realization"; and, furthermore, that if A precedes B in the phonemic representation, then the phone sequence associated with A precedes (is to the left of) that associated with B in the phonetic matrix. This condition follows from definitions of the phoneme as a class of phone sequences (as in post-Bloomfieldian American linguistics, typically[14]) or as a bundle of distinctive features (Bloomfield, Jakobson) or a minimal term in a phonological opposition (Prague circle).

The invariance condition (32ii) asserts that each phoneme P has associated with it a certain set $\varphi(P)$ of *defining features* (that is, P = Q if and only if $\varphi(P) = \varphi(Q)$) and that wherever P occurs in a phonemic representation, there is an associated occurrence of $\varphi(P)$ in the corresponding phonetic representation. The invariance condition has no clear meaning unless the linearity condition is also met; I will assume, then, that it is inapplicable when linearity is violated. The invariance condition, in the form stated above, is required explicitly by Bloomfield, Troubetzkoy, Jakobson and Bloch, for example, and appears to be implicit in many other conceptions. Where linearity and invariance are both met by a taxonomic phonemic representation, the string of phones is segmented into successive segments, each of which contains, along with redundant (determined) features, the defining features $\varphi(P)$ of some phoneme P, and the phonemic representation is just the sequence of these phonemes.

One can distinguish two versions of the invariance condition, depending on whether the features are taken to be *relative* (i.e., more or less along a certain phonetic dimension) or *absolute*. Jakobson explicitly accepts the relative version of the invariance condition, and Bloch, as I understand his account, seems to accept the absolute version. Under the absolute invariance condition, partial overlapping is excluded. If a certain occurrence of a phone P is assigned to a phoneme Q, then every other occurrence of P must be assigned to Q. Under the relative version of the invariance condition, certain cases of partial overlapping are permissible.

There are, however, some unresolved conceptual difficulties concerning the formulation of the relative invariance condition. Consider, e.g., a binary feature F such that a phone P in a certain context X-Y is assigned the feature [+F] or [−F] depending on its relation, in terms of the feature F, to some other phone Q in the context X-Y. But how is the context X-Y in question to be specified? If in terms of phones, then in general we can expect that the contrasting element Q will not appear in the context X-Y, but in a context X'-Y', where X' belongs to the same phoneme as X and Y' to the same phoneme as Y. If in terms of phonemes, then what happens when features that define X and Y are again relative to a context which, in this case, includes P and Q? For some discussion, see Chomsky (1957b) [33].

Technically, the biuniqueness condition (32iii) asserts that each sequence of phones is represented by a unique sequence of phonemes, and that each sequence of phonemes represents a unique sequence of phones.[15] The biuniqueness condition is very widely maintained by modern phonologists, in particular, by those mentioned above. However, it is very difficult to formulate this condition in a manner that is actually in accord with their intentions. Consider, for example, Hockett's explicit discussion of it (1951) [29]. He considers a hypothetical language with no mor-

---

[14]In the case of Bloch's very careful system of definitions (cf. Bloch, 1950, for a lucid sketch), the linearity condition is not necessarily met, but it is met, apparently, insofar as linear order is defined on phonemes at all. There are various unclarities here, despite the care of Bloch's presentation. Thus as the definitions stand, it is impossible for English [pʰ] to be a member of the phoneme /p/ (with [p]), since the defining qualities for /p/ are not coextensive with [pʰ] (or if a defining quality need qualify only part of a phone, it would follow that, e.g., [sp] could be assigned to /p/ and to /s/). It is also unclear what is meant by the statement that the phonemes of a dialect must "accommodate all the phones." Thus English "solely" has a doubled [l], phonetically. By definition, this pair of successive segments constitutes a phone. Must this phone be a member of a phoneme, or can the phonemic representation have two /l/'s, given the requirement that the phonemes must accommodate the phones? Bloch's work illustrates an important point, namely, that as the explicitness of formulation of taxonomic phonemics increases, the difficulty of giving a consistent and descriptively adequate interpretation also increases. Thus as compared with the other phonemic theories under consideration here, Bloch's is quite explicit; but the difficulty of determining whether the conditions (32) are met is at least as great in the case of his phonological theory as in the case of the others.

[15]In this form, the condition is of course rarely met. What is intended, rather, is that each sequence of phonemes represents a sequence of phones that is unique up to free variation.

phophonemic contrast between voiced and voiceless stops and with the rule:

(33)   Stop → Voiced, medially, in words.

Thus morphophonemic pat#atak becomes phonetic [patadak], while morphophonemic patat#ak becomes phonetic [padatak]. But, Hockett argues, if we hear [padatak] we do not know whether to transcribe /patat#ak/ or /pata#tak/. Consequently the morphophonemic representation fails the biuniqueness condition, and cannot be taken as the phonemic representation, which, in this case, must mark the distinction between voiced and voiceless consonants. This illustrative example, however, leaves many questions unanswered. Suppose, following Hockett, "that there is no word /pada/, or no word /tak/, or that, both of these words existing, they would not occur in this sequence." Or, suppose that there is a general rule to the effect that no word ends in a vowel. In any such case, "we can conclude that the proper representation would be *patat ak*" (/patat#ak/), and the morphophonemic representation would, technically, meet the biuniqueness condition and would thus qualify as phonemic, if we take this condition literally.

Hockett does not state whether he would accept this system as phonemic, in this case, but it is fairly clear from the context that he would not. In fact, a decision to accept it as phonemic would seem to be inconsistent with his principle of separation of levels, to which we return below, under any reasonable interpretation of this. It is fairly clear that linguists who accept the so-called biuniqueness condition would regard the situation just described as still being a violation of "biuniqueness" in the intended sense. That is, they do not mean by "biuniqueness" simply one-one correspondence, but rather a correspondence such that the unique phonemic representation corresponding to a given phonetic form can be determined by "purely phonetic" considerations, or perhaps, considerations involving only "neighboring sounds." This convention, which is rather difficult to state precisely, is what I have called the condition of local determinacy (32iv). Apparently it is this, rather than literal biuniqueness in the technical sense, that is required in taxonomic phonemics.

Notice that from the linearity and absolute invariance conditions one can deduce a particularly strong form of the biuniqueness and local determinacy conditions, namely, as noted above, the condition that the phoneme corresponding to a particular phone can be determined independently of the context of this phone. That is, even partial overlapping is disallowed, and (32iv) is vacuous. Although, as noted above, the situation is still somewhat confused in the case of the relative invariance condition, it is clear that proponents of such positions (e.g., Jakobson, Harris) would disallow complete overlapping but not partial overlapping, since however they interpret the invariance condition, they do insist on some sort of "biuniqueness."

Although conditions (32i-iv) are (with a qualification to which I return below in §4.3) quite generally accepted, and though they do follow from familiar definitions of the phoneme, there are many examples showing that they are untenable. Consider first the linearity condition. Of the many examples that illustrate its incorrectness,[16] perhaps the simplest is one presented in a recent paper by Malécot (1960). He observes that Lax Vowel + Nasal is often realized as Nasalized Vowel before Unvoiced Stop, in English, so that e.g., phonemic /kænt/ is phonetic [kæ̃t], though phonemic /hænd/ is phonetic [hæ̃nd]. In the face of this evidence, no linguist would conclude that vowel nasalization is distinctive in English, and "can't" – "cat" constitute a minimal pair, while "can't" – "canned" do not. Rather, in such a case, the linearity condition would be disregarded. Furthermore, there can be no doubt that this decision is correct. The phonetic representation can be derived from the phonemic, in this case, by the phonetic rules (34), ordered as given:

(34) (i) Vowel → Nasalized in the context:
                   —— Nasal + Consonant
     (ii) Nasal → Ø in the context:
                   Lax Vowel —— Unvoiced Stop.

Though perfectly general and straightforward, these rules happen to lead to a violation of the linearity condition.

A second and more extreme example of the violation of linearity is the case of the a-a· contrast, discussed above (p. 74 [405], §4.2). The rules (28), (29), applied in this order, con-

---

[16]For several, see Harris (1951a, Chapters 7, 9).

vert the systematic phonemic representations of row (I) of (35) first to row (II) and then to the systematic phonetic representation of row (III):

(35) (I)   rayt#r   rayd#r
                        ('writer', 'rider', respectively)
     (II)   rayt#r   ra·yd#r   (by (28))
     (III) rayDɨr   ra·yDɨr   (by (29), etc.).

But here words which differ phonemically only in their fourth segments differ phonetically only in their second segments. Hence if phonemic representation is to play any significant role in linguistic description (if it is to be part of a grammar that achieves descriptive adequacy), the linearity condition must be rather grossly violated.

These violations of the linearity condition incidentally show, in yet another way,[17] the

[17]For further discussion, see Chomsky (1957c). Notice, for example, that such a pair as [r], [D] are in free variation and are assigned to the same phoneme in the context /θ-Vowel/ ("three," "throw," etc.) in many English dialects, but replacement of one by the other in /bæ-l/ leads to a meaning difference ("battle," "barrel") (whereas, on the other hand, /t/ and /d/ can replace one another in the context /bɨrn-/ ("burned," "burnt") with no change in meaning, though they would never be assigned to the same phoneme), so that the semantic criterion is falsified from right to left. And [ə], [r], though phonetically similar, clearly cannot be assigned to the same phoneme (cf. below) though they never contrast (with or without change of meaning), so that the criterion is falsified from left to right.

The history of the notion "contrast" in modern linguistics is very curious. Bloomfield (1926) took it as a primitive notion, and Harris provided a fairly effective operational test (1951a, 32f.), which is the only known device that can be used when the problem of determining contrast actually arises in practice. The only coherent attempt to define "contrast" has been Bloch's careful distributional definition. This has been frequently criticized, mainly on grounds of impracticality. Insofar as the criticism is valid, it shows only that "contrast" must be taken as a primitive notion. However, the criticism has almost universally been taken as showing that "contrast" must be defined in terms of "synonymy of utterance tokens" (e.g., Diderichsen, 1958), and in the background of the entire development has been the assumption that there is such a definition. Obviously, however, difficulties in one analysis do not show that another analysis is correct. And in fact there is no proposal for defining "contrast" in terms of "synonymy" that does not have obvious objections to it. In fact, the only definition I have been able to find or to construct that does not immediately fail (Chomsky, 1957c, 95–96) not only requires (with Bloch) that each token appear in each possible

incorrectness of the claim that phonology can (or, even more unaccountably, that it must) be based on synonymy, in its usual formulation to the effect that phonetically similar sounds are not assigned to the same phoneme if and only if replacement of one by the other in some context leads to a change of meaning (cf., e.g., Diderichsen, 1949). If what is meant by "context" is "phonetic context" then the criterion would give the result that V-Ṽ and a-a· constitute a phonological opposition (contrast) in English. If what is meant is "phonemic context," then obviously the question at issue is simply being begged. In general, it should be observed that "minimal pair" is not an elementary notion. It cannot, in any interesting sense, be defined in phonetic terms, but only in terms of a completed phonemic analysis. Consequently, the "commutation test" is of little significance if formulated, in the usual manner, as a procedure for phonemic analysis.

Such violations of the linearity condition have not gone unnoticed by careful taxonomic phonologists, and it is instructive to consider the steps that have been taken to meet them. Troubetzkoy gives an example quite analogous to (34) both in the *Anleitung* and the *Grundzüge* (1939, 46). He observes that the following phonological rules operate in Russian:

(36) (i) o → ǫ in the context: —— l
     (ii) l → Ø in the context:
                        Vowel —— Nasal + Consonant.

Thus phonemic /sólncǎ/ ('sun') is phonetic [sǫ́ncə], and there is no necessity to set up /ǫ/ in contrast to /o/ as a new phoneme. Here the linearity condition is violated, as in (34); and, furthermore, the rules must be ordered as given. To account for such violations of linearity, Troubetzkoy proposes a general rule for phonemicization which we can state as follows:

(37) If the phone A is phonetically similar to the phone sequence BC, and A-BC are in

context, but that it occur in each possible context with each "meaning," so that the "impracticality" of Bloch's proposal is compounded many-fold. Perhaps some semantic criterion for "contrast" exists. This we will not know, however, until proponents of this view take the same care in formulating their proposal as Bloch did in formulating his. Until such time, it can only be dismissed as a totally unsupported claim.

free variation or complementary distribution, and BC is a realization of the phoneme sequence PQ, then A is to be regarded as a realization of PQ.

Thus [o] is phonetically similar to and in complementary distribution with [o̦l], which is a realization of /ol/; thus [o̦] is a realization of /ol/.[18] Similarly, nasalized vowels, in some English dialects, are in complementary distribution with Vowel + Nasal, and could thus be regarded as a realization of Vowel + Nasal, thus dealing with the violation of linearity caused by (34), in these dialects. Similarly, one might use the same argument to justify representing intervocalic and word final English [ŋ] as /ng/ (though to apply the argument in this case, complementary distribution would have to be defined in terms of phonemically specified, rather than phonetically specified contexts).

However, the rule (37) seems to me not at all satisfying. It is entirely ad hoc, and it can only be taken as indicating that the definition of the phoneme as a minimal term of a phonological opposition is incorrect. More seriously, it cannot be applied in general, without absurdity. Thus, in English, the pairs [n]-[ny], [yū]-[y] are phonetically similar and in complementary distribution, but it would be absurd, following the rule, to phonemicize [kitn̩] ('kitten') as /kitny/ or [yat] ('yacht') as /yūat/. Even more serious for the taxonomic phonemicist, is the fact that this rule can lead to a violation of biuniqueness. Thus consider the English [ǎ]-[a·] contrast ("write" – "ride"), discussed above. [ǎy] appears only initially or after a consonant, and before an unvoiced consonant; [y] can never appear in this position. Since [y] and [ǎy] are phonetically similar and [ǎy] is a realization of /ay/, by Troubetzkoy's rule, [y] is a realization of /ay/. Aside from the absurdity, this leads to a violation of biuniqueness, in this case, since /y/ and /ay/ contrast ('ion' /ayan/ – 'yon' /yan/). Hence aside from being ad hoc, this rule cannot be regarded as an extension of the notion "phoneme" to deal with the case of violation of linearity.

Troubetzkoy's informal comments and

discussion of examples indicate that the rule, as he stated it, perhaps does not conform to his actual intentions. Suppose, in fact, that we were to restrict application of the rule (37) to the case in which B is a Lax Vowel and C a Liquid or Nasal. Then the violations of linearity in the Russian example (36) and the English example (34) (but not the example of English /ng/) would still be handled, while the counterexamples of the preceding paragraph would be ruled out. But now the entirely ad hoc character of the rule becomes even more clear, and surely with such a restrictive formulation as this no one would seriously regard it as constituting part of the definition of the fundamental concept "phoneme." Furthermore, it is still not difficult to construct counterexamples. Thus in many American dialects, [e] of "get" is in complementary distribution with [ɛr] of "berry," which is a realization of /er/; so that by the rule, even as amended, [e] must be regarded as a realization of /er/, and "get" must be phonemicized /gert/.

The rule (37) is a typical example of an ad hoc device invented to remedy an inadequacy of some general notion of "taxonomic phoneme," and this discussion of difficulties that it faces could be duplicated for other principles of this sort. These ad hoc revisions of a basically inadequate notion do not succeed in reaching the central issue. In such cases as those discussed above, it is clear that the acceptability of an analysis hinges on its effect on the grammar as a whole. Thus the rules (34i) and (34ii) are quite general and are independently motivated. A grammar that incorporates them is materially simpler than one that does not. But the rules: /yu/ → [y] before Vowels, or /er/ → [e] before Consonants, as in the absurd examples given above, obviously do not simplify the grammar of English. Similarly, Troubetzkoy's Russian example is well-motivated by general systematic considerations; e.g., by the existence of such forms as /sólnešnij/, [so̦ln,išnij], and by the fact that were (36) not incorporated in the grammar, then each occurrence of /o/ in the lexicon would have to be marked as distinct from /o̦/, greatly complicating the grammar (cf. note 10). Similarly, the necessity of assigning English [ŋ] to /n/ (more accurately, to the archiphoneme Nasal) becomes obvious only when the full range of examples involving Nasal + Stop in

---

[18]Note that Troubetzkoy's rule must be modified, for adequacy, since as it stands it would require that [o̦l] be regarded as a realization of /oll/.

various syntactic positions comes under investigation. The fact that considerations of this sort are crucial suggests that any such "atomistic" rule as the one that Troubetzkoy suggests will fail.

General systematic considerations are, however, foreign to the point of view of taxonomic phonemics, and, in fact, they have often been criticized as circular (cf., e.g., Twaddell, 1935, 66). This criticism is correct, given the general "procedural" bias of modern phonology; but it shows only that the attempt to develop a taxonomic phonemics on the basis of analytic procedures of segmentation and classification, supplemented by such ad hoc rules as (37), is ill-conceived from the start.

The more extreme case of violation of linearity posed by "writer" – "rider" (which is beyond the range of (37) or any modification of it) is discussed by Harris (1951a, 70). He proposes that [ayD] be assigned to /ayt/ as a unit, and [a·yD] to /ayd/ as a unit, on general grounds of symmetry of distribution. But this is a rather vague notion, and it is not at all clear how it would fare once clarified. Furthermore, suppose that somehow a criterion of distributional symmetry can be formulated that has just the desired effect in this case. This result would still seem to be accidental and beside the point, since clearly in this case the critical factors are, once again, the generality and independent motivation of the rules (28), (29), and the relation of the forms in question to others; in particular, the relation of "writer" to "write" and "rider" to "ride," which would surely be expressed, on syntactic grounds, in the systematic phonemic representation. But these factors have nothing directly to do with distributional symmetry. They are, once again, of a general systematic character, and thus lie beyond the narrow scope of taxonomic phonemics. Finally, notice that Harris' proposal appears to involve an inconsistency with respect to the notion "distribution." Phonemes are to be established in purely distributional terms. If the distribution is with respect to *phonetic* contexts, then the definition of "phoneme" is violated by his assignment of [a] and [a·] to /a/, since these phones contrast in the phonetic context [—yD]. If the distribution is with respect to *phonemic* contexts (an assumption difficult to reconcile with a procedural approach, as noted above), then the definition

is violated by the assignment of [D] to either /t/ or /d/, depending on the phonetic context, in this case.

It seems to me, then, that the ad hoc devices for dealing with the violations of linearity are not defensible, and that the definition of a phoneme as "a bundle of [phonetic] distinctive features," "a class of phones in free variation or complementary distribution," or a "minimal term in a phonological opposition" can be maintained only if we are willing to tolerate such absurdities as the phonemic representations /kæt/, /rayDɨr/, /ra·yDɨr/ for 'can't', 'writer', 'rider', and so on, in many other cases.

Consider now the invariance condition. Notice first that it fails in the case of violations of linearity such as those discussed above. However, it seems to me untenable even when linearity is preserved. Phonemic overlapping provides the clearest example of this. Thus consider an English dialect in which [D] is the allophone of /r/ in "throw" and of /t/ in "Betty" (where it contrasts with the /r/ of "berry"— cf. Bloch, 1941 [8]). Following the principle of invariance, we must assign [D] to /t/ in the context #θ—, counter not only to the speaker's intuition but also to the otherwise valid rules of consonant distribution. The situation is worse in dialects in which [D] and [r] are in free variation in this context and in intervocalic contrast, in which case no coherent solution is possible within the framework of (32), although the description of the facts is perfectly straightforward. The situation is still worse if we accept the absolute invariance condition, particularly if (as in Bloch, 1950) the features ("qualities") are defined in auditory terms. For it is known that in this case, not even the correct analysis of English stops is tenable, since /p/, /t/, and /k/ overlap (Schatz, 1954). For reasons such as these, then, it seems that the invariance condition cannot be accepted, however the condition of linearity is treated.

The biuniqueness condition is difficult to discuss because of the unclarity of formulation noted above. Nevertheless, certain consequences of accepting it are clear, and it seems to me that these are quite devastating, for anyone concerned with descriptive adequacy. Halle has pointed out that it is generally impossible to provide a level of representation meeting the biuniqueness condition without destroying the generality of rules, when the sound system has an asymmetry. Thus he gives the following, quite typical example from Russian (Halle, 1959). In (38) the four forms in column I are given in systematic phonemic representation and in column III in systematic phonetic representation:

(38)

I	II	III
d'at, l,i	d'at, l,i	d'at, l,i
d'at, bi	d'ad, bi	d'ad, bi
ž'eč l,i	ž'eč l,i	ž'eč l,i
ž'eč bi	ž'eč bi	ž'ej bi.

The forms of column III are produced from those of column I by the general rule:

(39) Obstruent → Voiced in the context:
——— Voiced Obstruent.

But the representations in column I fail the condition of biuniqueness as usually construed (in terms of local determinacy), and consequently would not be accepted as taxonomic phonemic. The representations in column II would be accepted as "phonemic" by taxonomic phonologists, because of the fact that t, - d, contrast while č - ǰ do not. But if the grammar is to provide II as a level of representation, then it cannot incorporate the general rule (39), but must have in its place the two rules (40i) and (40ii), the first of which is taken as a rule relating "morphophonemic" to "phonemic" representation, and the second as relating "phonemic" to phonetic representation:

(40) (i) Obstruent → Voiced in the context:
——— Voiced Obstruent, except for c, č, x;
(ii) c, č, x → Voiced in the context:
——— Voiced Obstruent.

It seems to me that the force of this example has not been sufficiently appreciated by taxonomic phonemicists. Where it has been noted at all, the discussion has not been adequate. Ferguson, in his review (1962) [36] of Halle (1959), discusses not the example given in the book under review (and reproduced above), but instead a Turkish example that had at first been proposed by Lees as analogous to Halle's, and then withdrawn by Lees as inappropriate (Lees, 1961, p. 63). Insofar as Ferguson's discussion carries over to the correct example that Halle gives, it amounts only to the observation that from the phonetic record alone it is possible to determine the

underlying systematic phonemic (in his terms, morphophonemic) form in the case of c, č, x, but not in the case of the other obstruents. This is correct but irrelevant, since this information is provided just as explicitly in the grammar which incorporates only systematic phonemics and systematic phonetics as in the grammar which, in addition, adds an intermediate level of taxonomic phonemics. Thus the fact remains that in this case, the only effect of assuming that there is a taxonomic phonemic level is to make it impossible to state the generalization.

In the face of Halle's example, I do not see how one can fail to be uncomfortable in attributing to Russian a level of taxonomic phonemics. Furthermore, similar examples are not difficult to find in other languages. Bloch, in fact, gave a rather similar example in his discussion of phonemic overlapping (Bloch, 1941) [8]. In his dialect of English there are forms that might have the systematic phonemic representations of column I and the systematic phonetic representations of column III of (41):

(41)

	I	II	III
'nod' :	nad	na·d	na·d
'knot' :	nat	nat	nat
'bed' :	bed	bed	be·d
'bet' :	bet	bet	bet.

Column I does not meet the biuniqueness condition because of such contrasts as "balm" – "bomb," "starry" – "sorry," "father" – "bother," and because of the fact that the vowel of "Pa'd (do it)" is that of "pod," phonetically. Column III can be derived from column I by the familiar rule of lengthening before voiced segments (of which (28) is a special case).[19] But Bloch is forced, by the bi-

[19]This discussion is quite unaffected by the residual cases of a-a· contrast. For Bloch's dialect, "father" and "bother" have different vowels, quite independently of how we analyze the forms of (41). In fact, it is no accident that the short vowel in the a-a· pairs is generally spelled "o" while the long one is spelled "a." A good case can be made for the conclusion that the vowel phoneme of "nod," "knot," "bomb," etc., is actually [ă, ɔ̆], which in certain dialects goes to [a·] (merging with the variant of /a/), in others goes to [a] (giving the a-a· contrast), and in others becomes [ɔ]. This assumption is required by many other considerations, e.g., to describe in the most general way the familiar ē → æ and ō → a alternations. Cf. Halle and Chomsky (forthcoming) [see now Chomsky and Halle, 1968—VBM] for a detailed discussion. The issue is further complicated

uniqueness condition, to accept II as the phonemic level of representation. Thus a full grammar of English, meeting this condition, would have to replace the general rule of vowel lengthening by two rules, the first of which applies only to /a/ and the second to all other vowels. The first would relate "morphophonemic" and "phonemic," and the second "phonemic" and phonetic representations. The situation is exactly analogous to the Russian example just given, and again we see that the effect of the biuniqueness condition is to complicate the grammar, that is, to prevent it from achieving descriptive adequacy.

The complicating effect of the biuniqueness condition has been commented on by several of its proponents. Thus Bloch remarks at once, in discussing the preceding example, that it leads to a loss of symmetry. Similarly, he remarks (1950, note 3) that the National Romanization which influenced his earlier, non-biunique analysis of Japanese, though "neat and systematic," is not as close to a "phonemic notation" as the Hepburn Romanization, "unsystematic and cumbersome as it seems to be." Similarly, Hockett (1951) [29] compares Bloch's "deceptively simple" non-biunique analysis with his later "quite complicated . . . but obviously more accurate" taxonomic phonemic analysis. In fact, however, the "greater accuracy" of the latter seems to reside in nothing other than its observance of conditions (32i-iv). We return below to the question of why this is regarded as a sign of greater accuracy.

We have, as yet, said nothing about the principle of complementary distribution, which is the central concept of taxonomic phonemics as developed, for example, by Jones, Troubetzkoy, Harris, and Bloch. This principle is, basically, the principle of biuniqueness converted into a procedure. Regarded as an analytic procedure, its goal is to provide the minimally redundant representation meeting the conditions of biuniqueness and local determinacy. We will show, however, that it is in general incapable of providing the mini-

mally redundant analysis meeting these conditions, and furthermore, that it may even lead to a non-biunique analysis.

We can formulate the principle in this way (following Harris, 1951a, Chapter 7): Given a set of representations in terms of phones, let us define the distribution D(x) of the phone x as the set of (short-range) phonetic contexts in which x occurs. The relation of complementary distribution holds between phones x and y if D(x) and D(y) have no element in common. A *tentative phoneme* is a class of phones related pair-wise by the relation of complementary distribution. Some would require further that a defining phonetic property be associated with each tentative phoneme, marking each of its members and no other phone (the invariance condition).[20] A *tentative phonemic system* is a family of tentative phonemes meeting a condition of exhaustiveness. We find *the* phonemic system (or systems) by applying additional criteria of symmetry.

But consider the example of phonemic overlapping due to Bloch that was discussed above, namely, the case of a dialect with [D] as the realization of /r/ in "throw" and of /t/ in "Betty," where it contrasts with the [r] of "berry." The requirement of biuniqueness is preserved if we set up the phonemes /t/, with the allophone [D] in intervocalic, post-stress position, and /r/, with the allophone [D] after dental spirants. Given a phone in a phonetic context, we can now uniquely assign it to a phoneme; and given a phoneme in a phonemic context we can uniquely determine its phonetic realization (up to free variation). However, this solution, which is the only reasonable one (and the one Bloch accepted in his 1941 paper [8]), is inconsistent with the principle of complementary distribution. In fact, the allophones [D] and [r] of /r/ are not in complementary distribution since they both occur in the context [be-iy] ('Betty', 'berry'). Hence complementary distribution is not a necessary condition for biuniqueness. Furthermore, the class of "tentative phonemic systems" as defined in the preceding paragraph will not include the optimal biunique system as a mem-

by dialects (cf. Sledd, 1959) in which liquids drop pre-consonantally (giving long variants of short vowels in such words as "absolve" /æbsɔlv/—cf., "absolution"—etc.). This is just one of the many examples that show how wide a range of information is necessary to determine what is in fact a minimal pair.

[20]This would be required by Troubetzkoy, Jakobson, and Bloch, but not by Harris (cf. 1951a, 72, note 28). He maintains that "any grouping of complementary segments may be called phonemic," and that further criteria have to do only with convenience, not with linguistic fact.

ber, so that no supplementary criteria will suffice to select it from this class.

But now observe further that the class of tentative phonemic systems, as defined, will contain systems that fail the principle of biuniqueness. Thus, for example, [k] and [ă] are in complementary distribution in English (and, furthermore, share features shared by nothing else, e.g., in Jakobson's terms, the features Compact, Grave, Lax, Non-Flat). Hence they qualify as a tentative phoneme, and there is a tentative phonemic system in which they are identified as members of the same phoneme /K/. But in this phonemic system, 'socked' [săkt] and 'Scot' [skăt] will both be represented phonemically as /sKKt/. Similarly, [ə] and [r] are in complementary distribution (and share defining features) and thus qualify as a potential phoneme. But if they are identified as variants of /R/, we will have 'prevail' /pRRvēl/ [prəveyl], 'pervade' /pRRvēd/ [pərveyd], which is a violation of local determinacy, and of biuniqueness as generally construed. Nor is adjacency a crucial feature of such counter-examples. Suppose, for example, that we set up the "phoneme" /D/ consisting of the allophones of /d/ and the pre-[r] allophone of /ī/, which are pair-wise in complementary distribution and meet the invariance condition. Then we have /DrD/ in "(two-)eared," "drea(ry)," which is again a violation of biuniqueness, in the usual interpretation. Or, if an exact contrast is wanted, consider the analogous argument with the Low, Back Vowel, and the pair "order" - "drawer." The same kind of problem might well arise in cases of "dissimilation at a distance," which are not rare. In short, we see that the principle of complementary distribution does not even provide a sufficient condition for biuniqueness. Since it provides neither a necessary nor a sufficient condition for biuniqueness, and, apparently, has no motivation except for its connection with biuniqueness, the principle of complementary distribution appears to be devoid of any theoretical significance.

Related questions have been discussed by taxonomic phonemicists, but the general problem has received little attention. Troubetzkoy considers the example of English [r] and [ə], and gives a rule (1935, Rule IV; 1939, Rule IV) that would prevent them from being as-signed to the same phoneme in case the sequence [ər] is in contrast with [ə]. This rule, as formulated, is not pertinent to the problem of preserving biuniqueness, and does not cover the examples of the preceding paragraph. It is, furthermore, entirely ad hoc, and thus simply serves to indicate a theoretical inadequacy of taxonomic phonemics.

Among linguists who rely primarily on distributional definitions of the phoneme, apparently only Harris has considered a special case of this problem explicitly. He points out (1951a, 62, note 10) that we might have phonetic representations [t̯ray], [kray] for 'try', 'cry', where t-k and r̯-r are in complementary distribution. But if we were to set up a tentative phonemic system in the manner described above, we could have a phoneme /T/ with allophones [t̯] before [r̯] and [k] before [r], and a phoneme /R/ with allophones [r̯], [r]. But now both 'try' and 'cry' would be represented /TRay/. To avoid this, Harris suggests that we first group [r̯] and [r] into /r/, and then redefine distributions in terms of the newly specified contexts, in which [t̯] and [k] now contrast before /r/. This procedure will avoid the difficulty in the particular case of 'try', 'cry', but not in the cases described above. Furthermore, the same procedure could just as well be used to group [t] and [k] into /T/, thus keeping [r̯] and [r] phonemically distinct (in further justification, we could point out that this regularizes distributions, since now /t/ occurs neither before /r/ or /l/, instead of, asymmetrically, only before /r/). Hence, as in the case of the procedures discussed above, it fails to distinguish permissible from impermissible applications. Finally, the procedure as stated is inconsistent with Harris' general requirement on the set of linguistic procedures (1951a, 7), namely, that operations must be "carried out for all the elements simultaneously" without any "arbitrary point of departure." In fact, this requirement was what made it possible for Harris to avoid Bloomfield's use of descriptive order (cf. note 35, above). But it is violated by the procedure just discussed.

It is interesting to note that well before the principle of complementary distribution was proposed as the basis of a procedure for phonemic analysis, Jakobson (1931a) pointed out the inadequacy of any such principle with a Czech example of exactly the "Scot"-"socked" type given above, and stated as a condition on phonemic analysis that if the phone sequence AB contrasts with BA (see note 17, p. 83 [410]), then A and B represent different phonemes (I am indebted to T. Lightner for this reference). Even this condition does not guarantee biuniqueness, because of the adjacency requirement (see above), and is therefore theoretically inadequate. It should be replaced by the simpler condition C: if phone sequences X and Y contrast, then their phonemic representations must differ (Jakobson's condition being a useful special case of this).

To summarize, both taxonomic and systematic phonemic representations must (by definition) meet condition C of the preceding paragraph. But there are no known distributional procedures for defining phonemes that guarantee that this condition will be met, and, in particular, the principle of complementary distribution fails in actual cases. Furthermore, there are no known distributional procedures that permit all analyses meeting condition C and, in particular, the principle of complementary distribution excludes the optimal system meeting C in many real cases. In brief, known procedures of phonemic analysis are unacceptable, and the existence of (still undiscovered) procedures of anything like the sort that have been sought by taxonomic phonemicists is highly dubious.

4.4. CRITERIA FOR SYSTEMATIC PHONEMICS

Systematic phonemics in the sense of Sapir or of §4.2 does not observe the conditions (32) and is not based on such techniques as complementary distribution or, for that matter, on any analytic procedures of segmentation and classification.[21] Furthermore, construction of the set of ordered rules constituting the phonological component cannot be undertaken in isolation from the study of syntactic processes, just as study of the syntactic component cannot be carried to a conclusion without regard for the simplicity and generality of the rules that convert its output into a phonetic representation.

In analyzing a particular language, we

[21]In the case of Sapir, it seems that the choice of examples in his important psychological reality paper (1933) [2] was motivated by his rejection of these (at the time, still unformulated) conditions.

must assume given a theory of generative grammar that specifies abstractly the form of grammars and a measure of evaluation for grammars. To fix the level of systematic phonemics for this language, we must attempt to construct the most highly valued grammar compatible with the primary data from this language (cf. §1). The level of systematic phonemics will consist of the set of representations that appear in derivations provided by this grammar at the point where grammatical morphemes other than junctures have been eliminated. It is certainly conceivable that there exist procedures of some sort that would facilitate the task of selecting this level of representation, but they are not, to my knowledge, available today. It is hardly likely that elementary taxonomic procedures of the kind that have been studied in modern structural linguistics can lead to the discovery of this level of representation. For the present, it seems that the most promising way to give a closer specification of this level of representation and the criteria that determine it is by refining the abstract conditions on the form of generative grammar, the measure of evaluation and the universal features that define the phonetic matrices in terms of which the primary data is represented.

We observed in §4.2 that if a grammar is to achieve the level of descriptive adequacy, the rules of its phonological component must be ordered; and, in general, a derivation will contain many representations between the systematic phonemic and the systematic phonetic. We suggested that there is no set of intermediate representations that has any systematic significance. Whether or not this is true, we have now, in §4.3, accumulated evidence showing that if a level meeting the conditions associated with taxonomic phonemics is incorporated in a grammar, then many generalizations will not be expressible and descriptive adequacy cannot be achieved. It is important, then, to see whether there is some way of justifying the assumption that a level of taxonomic phonemics actually constitutes a part of linguistic structure.

4.5. THE MOTIVATION FOR TAXONOMIC PHONEMICS

We are now concerned with the question: why should it be assumed that a grammar must generate representations meeting the conditions (32), as part of the structural descriptions of utterances? What, in other words, is the justification for the theory of taxonomic phonemics, in any of its modern varieties?

Many linguists would perhaps take a position of the sort expressed by Twaddell (1935). In opposition to the "mentalistic" approach of Sapir (that is, the approach that is concerned with descriptive and explanatory adequacy), he proposes a method of phonemic analysis for which the following is "the only defense that may be offered": "this procedure . . . appears to be characterized by a minimum of the undemonstrable. With one coherent set of assumptions and conventions, which are indispensable to all scientific linguistic study, and one sound laboratory generalization, we may apply strictly mathematical methods and deduce a logically unimpeachable definition of some entity" (74). Thus the phoneme is "a mere terminological convenience" (68). There is no necessity for demonstrating "psychological reality" (i.e., descriptive adequacy), because "this demonstration would be a convenience rather than a necessity for linguistic study: it would represent a summary of the behavior of native speakers, a behavior which is already available for the student of language, though in less concentrated form" (58). The only legitimate activity is "the study of phenomena and their correlations" (57—this value judgement Twaddell regards as a principle of "scientific methodology"); attempts to provide explanations on the basis of "mentalistic assumptions" are characterized as "fraud." Thus all that may be asked of a linguistic notion or a linguistic description is that it meet the requirement of *consistency* and what we may call *convertibility* (namely, the account must be explicit enough to be convertible into some other, equally arbitrary framework) and, perhaps, in some sense, *simplicity* and *convenience*.

In part, Harris seems to take a similar position in his *Methods* (1951a, Chapter 1). He describes his procedures as "merely ways of arranging the original data." The only general condition that they must meet is the bi-uniqueness condition, which is not justified on any external count, but simply is taken as defining the subject. The procedures must be "based on distribution, and be unambiguous, consistent and subject to check." The criteria for selecting phonemes are stated only "to make explicit in each case what method [of data arrangement] is being followed" (63). Thus only consistency and convertibility (and convenience, for one or another purpose) is required of a linguistic theory or a grammatical description. But Harris also states (372–373) that "the work of analysis leads right up to the statements which enable anyone to synthesize or predict utterances in the language," that is, to a generative grammar. This constitutes a truth claim for the procedures, a claim which surely cannot be maintained if conflicting procedures meeting the conditions of consistency and convertibility are equally valid, and which would appear to be incompatible with Harris' earlier remark that the "overall purpose . . . [of the procedures] . . . is to obtain a compact one-one representation of the stock of utterances in the corpus" (366). Furthermore, there are no known procedures which lead to this more ambitious, and far more significant goal. These conflicting remarks concerning what Hockett has called "metacriteria" (1955) illustrate a general ambivalence concerning goals that makes evaluation of modern taxonomic linguistics on its own terms rather difficult.

Insofar as consistency and convertibility are taken as the only valid metacriteria, linguistic theory is concerned only with the level of observational adequacy. This theory makes no claim to truth; no evidence conflicts with it, just as none can be offered in its support. The only criticism that is relevant is that taxonomic phonemics, as indicated above, seems more of an inconvenience than a convenience, if embedded within a full grammatical description. This point of view takes a theory to be, essentially, nothing more than a summary of data. In contrast, it has been repeatedly pointed out (most forcefully, by Karl Popper) that the prevailing attitude in the sciences is to regard data as of interest primarily insofar as it has bearing on the choice among alternative theories, and to search for data, however exotic, that will be crucial in this sense. In any event, there is surely no reason why the linguist must necessarily limit himself to "the study of phenomena and their correlations," avoiding any attempt to gain insight into such data by means of an explanatory theory of language, a theory which is, of course, "mentalistic," in that it deals with the character of mental processes rather than with their physical basis.

If one is unwilling to settle for just consistency and convertibility, what further justification can be offered for taxonomic phonemics? I have tried to show above that the internal linguistic evidence does not support taxonomic phonemics. Taxonomic phonemic representations do not contribute to the simplicity or generality of a grammar, but, in fact, have just the opposite effect. Therefore one must search for external evidence. In particular, it is important to ask whether reasonable requirements for a perceptual model ((1a) of §1.3) or a learning or discovery model ((1b) of §1.3) have any bearing on the validity of taxonomic phonemics. Considerations of this sort may actually have been at the core of some theoretical and methodological studies.

One might try to justify the conditions (32) by arguing that speech perception involves two successive and entirely separate stages: the hearer first uses only local phonetic cues to identify the invariant criterial attributes that determine the successive taxonomic phonemes; and he then goes on to determine the deeper structure of the utterance (in particular, its systematic phonemic representation and its syntactic structure). This clearly seems to be the view of Jakobson (cf. Jakobson, Fant, and Halle, 1952) and of Joos (1957, 92)[22] among others. However, there is no real basis for this account, and it is scarcely in accord with what little is known about complex perceptual processes, or, for that matter, about speech perception. Thus it is well-known that intelligibility is preserved under gross phonetic distortion, which may be completely unnoticed when grammatical constraints are met; and brief exposure to an unfamiliar dialect is often sufficient to overcome unintelligibility or even an impression of strangeness (note that related dialects may differ greatly, sentence by sentence, in phonetic and taxonomic phonemic representations, though perhaps hardly at all on the level of systematic pho-

nemics—cf. in this connection Halle, 1962 [37]; also Chomsky, 1959, for an analysis of some of the data presented by Sledd, 1955, 1958, from this point of view). Sapir is the only linguist to have presented careful observations of native perceptual responses relevant to this question, in his classic paper on psychological reality (1933) [2], and his reports are directly counter to the taxonomic account of speech perception. Surely one would expect that in identifying an utterance, the hearer will bring to bear the full grammatical apparatus that determines the space of possibilities from which this utterance is drawn and the nature and interrelations of these objects. That is, one would naturally expect that, as in the case of other perceptual processes, the hearer's knowledge will provide a complex schema within which the actual signal is interpreted. To the extent that this is true, the "atomistic" view of the taxonomic phonologists will be in error. In any event, presently available evidence does not support the taxonomic model given above as an adequate general account of speech perception.[23]

It remains to consider the status of taxonomic phonemics with respect to a model of acquisition of language. There is, in fact, an approach to the question on these grounds.

Suppose that we impose on the acquisition model the condition of *separation of levels*, which we can interpret as requiring that the level of systematic phonetic representation must be "rationalized" and converted to a level of taxonomic phonemic representation without reference to any morphological or syntactic information.[24] Observe that this con-

---

[22]To illustrate his point, Joos cites the example of someone who responded to "he has poise" with "what's a poy?" But this seems rather dubious support for his position, since the hearer in this case was puzzled by the apparent application of the unfamiliar lexical rule: N → poy, and had clearly assigned a full syntactic structure to the utterance. Thus this example does not support the independence of phonemic representation from syntactic structure in perception.

[23]For further discussion, see Halle and Stevens (1964), Miller and Chomsky (1963), and references there cited. For discussion in a similar vein on the syntactic level, see Matthews (1961).

[24]One or another form of this is implicit in all substantive discussions of linguistic procedures that I have been able to locate. Some linguists (e.g., Pike and Harris) would allow restricted use of certain higher level information in phonology, where this can be obtained by "cyclic" or "spiral" procedures (cf. Pike, 1947a [15], 1952 [18]; Harris, 1951a), but many American linguists insist on strict separation. Glossematicians also mention successive and intricately interwoven procedures of analysis and synthesis (Diderichsen, 1958). The kinds of procedures they have in mind also allow for some sort of interdependence of levels, but the reference to procedures is too vague for the extent of permitted interdependence to be determinable, in this case.

dition is not to be confused with the conditions of biuniqueness and local determinacy. These (as all of the conditions (32)) pertain to the "perceptual model"; they assert that the phonemic correspondent to a given phonetic sequence must be determinable by operations involving only neighboring sounds, *once the phonemic system is fixed.* But the condition of separation of levels is not a formal condition on a phonemic system and the rules that relate it to sound; it is a methodological condition on information relevant to determining the correct choice of a phonemic system. It thus pertains to an acquisition model such as (1b), rather than to a perceptual model such as (1a).

Nevertheless, there is a connection between the condition of separation of levels and the conditions of biuniqueness and local determinacy. If no higher-level information is relevant to determining what is the taxonomic phonemic system, it is natural to require that once the taxonomic phonemic system is fixed, on purely phonetic grounds, no higher-level information should be relevant to determining what is the sequence of taxonomic phonemes corresponding to a given sequence of phones. Consequently, an argument in support of the condition of separation of levels would, indirectly, provide a motivation for imposing the conditions of biuniqueness and local determinacy on the perceptual model as formal conditions on the notion "phoneme."

This is apparently the line of reasoning that has been followed insofar as justification for the conditions of biuniqueness and local determinacy has actually been attempted. Thus, for example, Hockett gives only one argument in support of these conditions in the review cited above (Hockett, 1951 [29]), namely, that given these conditions "one knows definitely to what level each fact applies." Otherwise, we have a "hodge-podge arrangement." He is concerned here with the context of discovery, not perception, and is offering an argument in support of the condition of separation of levels rather than in support of the biuniqueness and local determinacy conditions directly. Similarly, in his important paper on phonemic overlapping (1941) [8], Bloch offers only one argument (an argument that Joos, in his comment, 1957, considers conclusive) to show why the biuniqueness condition must be maintained, namely, this: "Suppose that we are studying a new and un-

familiar dialect of English, and that we have succeeded in pairing the stressed and the unstressed vowels of such words as *at, them, could, will, so* and the like; if we now hear a phrase like *oút of tówn,* with the unstressed vowel of the second word perceptually the same as those which we have already identified with various stressed alternants, how are we to treat this? We must defer the phonemic analysis until we chance to hear a stressed form of the same word, which may not occur in the dialect we are studying, or which, if it does occur, we may fail to recognize as 'the same word.'"

Both Bloch and Hockett are proposing that the condition of biuniqueness must be imposed on the notion "phoneme" because the model for acquisition must meet the condition of separation of levels. But it is important to observe that both of them are presenting an argument that is methodological rather than substantive. They do not suggest that an accurate model of the process of acquisition of language must incorporate the condition of separation of levels—that this is a fact about the design of language and about the intrinsic characteristics of an organism capable of learning a language under the empirically given conditions of time and access. They are considering rather the problems of gathering and organizing data, and thus their indirect argument for the conditions of biuniqueness and local determinacy at most shows that it would be convenient for the linguist if there were a level of representation meeting these conditions, but it does not bear on the question of the existence of this level as a part of linguistic structure.

Let us turn to the question of separation of levels as a substantive issue. As in the case of the conditions (32), two kinds of considerations are relevant: external considerations pertaining, in this case, to language acquisition rather than perception; and purely internal linguistic considerations. As to the former, Hockett has in fact suggested in various places (e.g., 1948a) that the successive steps of the analyst should in some way parallel those of the language learner. But clearly the child does not master the phonology before proceeding to the syntax, and there is no possible justification for the principle of separation of levels from considerations of this sort.

It remains then to ask whether this condition can be justified (thus indirectly providing a justification for the biuniqueness and local determinacy conditions) on internal linguistic grounds, that is, by a demonstration that it contributes to the clarity, generality or coherence of a full grammar. But it seems clear that this principle has rather the effect of detracting significantly from these qualities, and, in fact, that adherence to this principle makes it impossible to attain the levels of descriptive or explanatory adequacy. Consequently, the principle seems to be entirely superfluous, in either its stronger or weaker forms (see note 24 on pp. 100–101 [418]).

The effects of strict application of a principle of separation of levels have often been discussed. The matter of word boundary that Hockett cites in his invented example discussed above on pp. 80–81 [408–409] illustrates the problems that arise when it is adopted. It has long been recognized that a phonemic system is quite unacceptable if no junctures are recognized. Consequently, linguists who adopt the principle of partial or complete separation of levels have attempted to devise analytic procedures that would make it possible to place junctures in appropriate places on the basis of phonetic evidence alone. These procedures make use of phonetic features that appear at utterance boundary to determine the position of junctures medially in utterances. Thus a juncture would be marked in "night rate" because it contains an utterance-final allophone of /t/ followed by an utterance-initial allophone of /r/. Apart from the counterexamples that have already been offered to this principle (and that remain unanswered—cf., e.g., Leopold, 1948; Harris, 1951a, 87; Chomsky, Halle, Lukoff, 1956, §2) it is clear that it cannot succeed because of examples of the following kind. In many dialects of English, /t/ has the allophone [D] in word final position after a weak stress and before a main stress—thus we have [ɨDédz] ('at Ed's'), [ɨDǽwr] ('at our'), [ðæDǽd] ('that ad'), contrasting with [ɨténd] ('attend'), [ɨtǽk] ('attack', 'a tack') and with [ɨdépt] ('adept'), [ɨdǽpt] ('adapt'). But [D] occurs only medially, never finally. Thus any consideration involving utterance boundary will place junctures at exactly the wrong places. Alternatively, if no junctures are placed, [D] must be taken as a third alveolar stop, giving an equally unacceptable

phonemic analysis. We must conclude, then, that there is no known method for assigning junctures in terms of phonetic evidence alone. Present methods do not distinguish permissible from impermissible applications, and, consequently, are useless as they stand. It seems unlikely that this difficulty can be remedied, and unless it is, the principle of separation of levels is entirely untenable.

As a second example, consider the much debated subject of English vocalic nuclei. According to a view that is widely held among American structuralists,[25] these are to be analyzed as short vowels plus one of the glides /y/, /w/ or /h/. On the purely phonetic grounds on which the question must be discussed by those who accept the principle of separation of levels, this is a very neat and well-motivated description. In particular, the post-vocalic /h/, representing a centering glide, can be used to account for such contrasts as "real" /rihl/, "really" /rihliy/ versus "reel" /riyl/, "Greeley" /griyliy/, etc.

If, however, we are concerned with selecting a phonemic system that will be compatible with a full descriptively adequate grammar, this analysis becomes quite unacceptable. Thus observe that on the level of systematic phonemics, the words "real," "really" will be represented /riæl/, /riæl+li/ (because of "reality"), just as "total," "totally" are represented /tōtæl/, /tōtæl+li/ because of "totality," and "mobile" is represented /mōbil/ because of "mobility." Furthermore, the glide of "real," "really" is the same on the level of systematic phonetics as the reduced vowel of "total," "totally," "mobile" (or, for that matter, "dialect," "betrayal," "refusal," "science," etc.), namely, [ɨ] (there is dialectal variation with respect to height of this vowel that is not relevant here). Hence in all of these cases the systematic phonetic representation can be derived from the systematic phonemic by the very general rule of English phonology that:

(42) Vowel → ɨ when unstressed.[26]

[25]For an account of its background, see Gleason (1961, Chapter 19). An important critique is presented in Sledd (1955).

[26]This rule is of course incorrect as stated (cf. "relaxation" [rɨlǽkséyšɨn], "condensation" [kàndɨnséyšɨn], etc.) if it is one of a set of unordered rules of a taxonomic grammar. But it is correct if it is embedded into a transformational cycle of the

If, however, we wish to provide the taxonomic phonemic representations /rihl/, /rihliy/, /towtɨl/, /towtɨliy/, /mowbil/, /dayɨlekt/, /biytreyɨl/, etc., as an intermediate stage of formal description, we must replace the general rule (42) by the three rules:

(43) (i)   Vowels → ɨ post-consonantally,
                      when unstressed
       (ii) Vowels → h post-vocalically,
                      when unstressed
       (iii) h → ɨ post-vocalically,

where the first two relate "morphophonemic" and "phonemic" representations, and the third relates "phonemic" and phonetic representations. Thus again we find that what may very well be the optimal taxonomic phonemic system is not incorporable into a descriptively adequate grammar. The failure to achieve descriptive adequacy, in this case, is traceable to the requirement of separation of levels in the underlying theory.

In his review of Halle (1959), Ferguson (1962) [36] criticizes Halle for his rejection of the biuniqueness and local determinacy conditions (condition (3a) in Halle's presentation), and offers a defense of these conditions. But he presents the issue incorrectly, and as a result neither his critique of Halle's position nor his arguments in support of biuniqueness and local determinacy are to the point. Since Ferguson's is the only recent discussion of this issue from the point of view of taxonomic phonemics, it is important to trace the argument with some care. Ferguson argues for what he calls "the autonomy of phonology," that is, the view that phonology is entirely independent of syntax and morphology, and that the biuniqueness and local determinacy conditions are thus reasonable. Halle's position —and the one that I have advocated here—is the direct contradictory of this, namely, the view that *some* phonetic processes depend on syntactic and morphological structure so that phonology as a whole cannot be studied, without distortion, in total independence of higher level structure. Let us call this the view that phonology is "non-autonomous." A third possible position we may call the assumption of "inseparability of phonology," that is, the view that *all* phonetic processes depend essentially

on syntactic and morphological structure. This view has certainly never been advocated by anyone, and it is unnecessary to refute it. But it is the assumption of inseparability of phonology, not the assumption of non-autonomy of phonology, that Ferguson imputes to Halle, and against which he presents a series of arguments (to which we return directly). These arguments against the inseparability of phonology have no bearing on the question of autonomy of phonology. This failure to observe the distinction between inseparability of phonology and non-autonomy of phonology in fact vitiates Ferguson's argument entirely.

Specifically, Ferguson cites in favor of his position the undeniable fact that syntactic and morphological structure are not involved in certain sound changes and in certain aspects of language learning and dialectal variation. This observation is irrelevant to the issue of autonomy or non-autonomy of phonology (though it successfully demolishes the absurd thesis of inseparability of phonology). It also seems apparent that morphology and syntax play an important role in specifying the range and character of certain sound changes (cf. much of Kuryłowicz' recent work, or e.g., Twaddell, 1935, p. 79, etc.), of certain aspects of phonological development in language learning, and of certain aspects of phonological dialectal variation. Consequently, to the extent that considerations of the sort that Ferguson adduces are relevant, they show nothing more than the untenability of the thesis of autonomy of phonology. It is true that in plotting isoglosses, "it is often quite clear that subareas of different phonological systems do not coincide well with subareas of grammatical systems and lexical inventories" (Ferguson, 290 [373–374]), just as it is clear that isoglosses drawn for vocalic systems often do not coincide with those drawn for consonantal systems. The argument from this to autonomy is equally apposite in both cases. Similarly, in the case of Ferguson's other examples.[27]

---

kind discussed above. Cf. references of note 6, p. 14, for details.

[27]Ferguson's claim that a phonological theory that does not observe Halle's condition (3a) (biuniqueness and local determinancy) makes diachronic change incomprehensible is particularly astonishing. Would anyone really be willing to maintain that the phonology of, e.g., Sapir and Bloomfield, cannot accommodate sound changes that have been exhibited and explained by the post-Bloomfieldian linguists who have insisted on these conditions? His

Finally, I should like to comment on Ferguson's assertion that Halle's theory (as also the theory of the present paper) does not provide machinery for describing phonetic data that is accounted for adequately by his autonomous phonology. He cites, e.g., the word *Audrey* with the cluster /dr/ as compared with *bedrock* with /d+r/ and *bedroom* with variation between /dr/ and /d+r/. In this case, a "non-autonomous" generative grammar would give rules stating that in *bedroom* the morpheme boundary sometimes does and sometimes does not become a phonetic juncture (depending on dialect or style, as the facts indicate). It would, on the other hand, make no such statement about *Audrey* (with no boundary) or *bedrock* (where the boundary always becomes phonetic juncture). I do not see what is the problem here, or how an autonomous phonology of the type that Ferguson proposes would handle the situation any differently. Ferguson's example simply shows the absurdity of the claim that *every* morphemic boundary is a phonetic juncture, but surely no one has ever maintained this. What has been maintained is that syntactic and morphological considerations must be taken into account in determining when to handle phonetic facts by placement of junctures and when to handle them by postulation of new phonemes, and Ferguson's remarks have no bearing on this question.

Summarizing, then, it seems that if we are concerned with descriptive and explanatory adequacy, only two levels of representation can be justified in structural descriptions provided by the phonological component, namely, the levels of systematic phonemics and systematic phonetics. The level of taxonomic phonemics is not incorporable into a descriptively adequate grammar. As noted in §4.2, this conclusion is close to the position of de Saussure and Sapir, and is close to Bloomfield's practice, though perhaps not his theory.

It is interesting to consider the kinds of criticism that have been offered by taxonomic linguists against de Saussure, Sapir, and Bloomfield. Wells (1947c) criticizes de Saus-

sure for not making use of the principle of complementary distribution with respect to a particular language in his "phonologie" (but only the analogous principle with respect to all languages). In his long review of Sapir's collected papers (1951b), Harris devotes very little attention to Sapir's theoretical papers on phonology (Sapir, 1925 [1]; 1933 [2]), and remarks only (293) that they confuse phonology and morphophonemics. Similarly Joos comments (1957, 92) that "when we look back at Bloomfield's work, we are disturbed at this and that, but more than anything else Bloomfield's confusion between phonemes and morphophonemes disturbs us." In the same vein, Twaddell, 1935, in his attempt to counter Sapir's arguments for the psychological reality of the phoneme, dismisses several of Sapir's examples as irrelevant on the curious grounds that they involve morphological, syntactic and lexical information, basing himself, apparently, on the assumption that if certain evidence does not support his own grammar-free concept of the phoneme, then it must also be irrelevant to Sapir's grammar-dependent concept. It is important to observe that these and other critics have not actually demonstrated that the position of de Saussure, Sapir or Bloomfield is in any way confused. The criticism relies on the assumption that systematic phonetics has no significant status (so that de Saussure's phonologie goes only "half way" towards Wells' taxonomic phonemics), and that taxonomic phonemics is a significant intermediate level of linguistic structure (so that Sapir and Bloomfield appear to be confusing morphophonemics and taxonomic phonemics in their systematic phonemics). Hence the criticism amounts only to the comment that de Saussure, Sapir, and Bloomfield have not developed the level of taxonomic phonemics, but only the levels of systematic phonetics and systematic phonemics. The criticism, then, is only as well-founded as is the status of taxonomic phonemics.

There is, in fact, a real confusion in Bloomfield, and this has perhaps played a role in the development of taxonomic phonemics in its American version, at least. Bloomfield's assertion that only two kinds of representation are scientifically relevant on the level of sound (cf. above, p. 76 f. [407]) has had a significant impact on later developments. One of Bloom-

assertion that the principles of biuniqueness and local determinacy (note that it is just these that are at issue at this point in his discussion) underlie the achievements of the last century represents a curious interpretation of the history of linguistics.

field's significant levels is physical phonetics. The other, if we follow his descriptive practice, is close to Sapir's systematic phonemics; or, if we follow his "bundle of distinctive features" theory (1933, 79), it is close to post-Bloomfieldian taxonomic phonemics. In any event, he explicitly denies any status to systematic (universal) phonetics. (Similarly, Troubetzkoy, despite his thoroughgoing reliance at every step on a universal phonetics, tends to disparage it in his theoretical remarks.) However, as we noted above, phonology of any sort is unthinkable without assumptions involving phonetic universals, and Bloomfield uses them constantly, as do all phonologists. Hence there are implicit assumptions concerning systematic phonetics in his descriptive and theoretical work. Furthermore, from the rejection of a level of systematic phonetic representation as the "lowest level" of representation to be provided in a grammar, post-Bloomfieldian linguists were forced to the conclusion that the phonemic level must be the lowest level of representation. Consequently, phonemic representation must be much closer to actual

sound than in the case of the systematic phonemics of Sapir or of much of Bloomfield's practice. In particular, the conditions (32) become well-motivated, for this lowest level of representation, and the principle of complementary distribution is invoked to eliminate obvious redundancy (supplemented by various ad hoc, and ineffective rules of the kind we have discussed above to take account of cases where the representations meeting (32) are too unintuitive).

In short, we find that there is a gradual return in phonological theory, both American and European, from the systematic phonemics of Sapir and (to a large extent) Bloomfield to a much "narrower" system not too far removed from that of the phoneticians who were Bloomfield's critics (see note 7). It is in this sense that modern taxonomic phonemic representations are "more accurate" (cf. page 91 above [414]), and it is for this reason that they are far more complex than the earlier systematic phonemic representations. In this way, the fundamental insights of the pioneers of modern phonology have largely been lost.

40

ON SOME BASIC PRINCIPLES
OF "CLASSICAL" PHONOLOGY*

(In margine N. Chomsky's "Logical Basis of
Linguistic Theory")

JOSEF VACHEK

I In his comprehensive report presented to the Ninth International Congress of Linguists held in 1962 in Cambridge, Mass., Noam Chomsky[1] drew a distinct line of demarcation not only between the so-called taxonomic, traditional grammar and the grammar of the new type, generative and transformational, but also between what he calls taxonomic phonology and the phonology of his own conception. He accuses traditional phonology of mistakes analogous to those which he has found in traditional grammars: followers of traditional phonology have only been enumerating and classifying the facts of the phonic level, and they have taken no notice of the relations existing between phonological and other linguistic facts. Chomsky[2] himself tries to do justice to such relations by his typical method of establishing a set of ordered rules whose gradual application can lead from the morphematic structure of an utterance to the phonic structure of the latter. There exists, e.g., a rule according to which

(20i) $\begin{cases} [k] \\ [t] \end{cases} \rightarrow$ [s] in the context —— + [i, y][3]

(cf., e.g., *opaque − opacity,*
democrat − democracy)

(20ii) [s, z] + [i, y] → [š, ž] in the context — Vowel

and further rules linking up with the preceding one,

(23) [z] → [s] in the context —— + [iv]

(24i) [d] → [s] in the context —— + [iv]

(24ii) [d] + [i, y] → [ž] in the context —— Vowel

Examples: *persuade* → *persuasive, persuasion;* in Chomsky's terms:

perswēd + iv → perswēz + iv → perswēsiv
perswēd + y∔n → perswēz + y∔n → perswēžin.[4]

The third form in both lines is termed by N. Chomsky as "systematic phonetic representation," the first form as "systematic phonemic representation" (see p. 534 [405]).

The quoted instance calls for some comment. First, it should be pointed out that the above-quoted rule (20) has not a general validity: it can only be applied to the lexical layer of synchronically foreign English words (taken mostly from French or Latin),[5] while in the

---

[1]N. Chomsky, "The Logical Basis of Linguistic Theory," *Preprints of Papers for the Ninth International Congress of Linguists,* Aug. 27–31, 1962 (Cambridge, Mass.), pp. 509–574. [See here article 39—VBM.]

[2]To quote Chomsky's own words (p. 536 [406]): "Sound pattern has been taken as the primary object of study in modern, structural linguistics; it has, furthermore, been studied in relative or complete isolation from the syntactic setting within which phonological processes operate."

[3]The symbol y here denotes [i̯].
[4]The symbol ∔ stands here for the unstressed [ə]-vowel.
[5]On synchronical foreignisms see V. Mathesius, "Zur synchronistischen Analyse fremden Sprachguts," *Englische Studien* 71, 1935, pp. 21–35.

*Reprinted from *Zeitschrift für Phonetik, Sprachwissenschaft und Kommunikationsforschung* 17.409–431 (1964).

synchronically domestic words, forming the core of ModE vocabulary, it does not assert itself at all. This is shown by instances like *rock — rocky, fat — fatty, risk — risky, mist — misty*, etc., not to speak of common morphological formations of the type *kick — kicking, fit — fitted, fitting* (these instances might be disputed away by the American pronunciation of the derived forms, in which the vowel is [ɨ] rather than [i]; this would, of course, necessitate the establishment of different "grammars" for American and British English).

Second, the above-quoted instances reveal that Chomsky's procedure does not result in the establishment of the phonological structure of the utterance, and, consequently, of the system of phonemes of the given language; the phonological inventory is obviously regarded as already known. This conclusion is borne out by Chomsky's transcription symbols, reminding one of the Yale inventory (found, e.g., in G. L. Trager's, H. L. Smith's or C. F. Hockett's books and papers).

Third, the example quoted above shows clearly that Chomsky's conception of phonology is really limited to one single section of the vast field of phonological problems, viz., to morphonology (as a matter of fact, Chomsky himself recalls the term "morphophonemics," identifying it with what he himself calls "systematic phonemics" (cf. p. 532 [403])).[6]

Under the term "taxonomic phonology" Chomsky brings together—rather inorganically —various currents of pre-1960 phonology, including the theories of the Yale and Prague groups. His information about the Prague theory, however, seems to be somewhat super-

ficial; this is clearly connected with the fact that out of Chomsky's very extensive bibliographical list, containing no less than 102 items, only two reflect the views of the Prague group. The author of both was N. S. Trubetzkoy; one of them is *Grundzüge der Phonologie*—in the French version provided by Cantineau—the other is the small handbook *Anleitung zu phonologischen Beschreibungen* (Brno, 1935). Surprisingly enough, Chomsky does not quote here a number of important writings by R. Jakobson; he should have registered at least *Remarques sur l'évolution phonologique du russe*, published as early as 1929 in *TCLP* 2, and the important paper on principles of historical phonology from *TCLP* 4 (the French version of which was annexed to Cantineau's translation of *Grundzüge*), not to speak of many outstanding contributions from other Prague writers, pre-war and post-war alike, documenting the Prague conception of language as a system of systems. Greater familiarity with at least some of such contributions would have convinced Chomsky that the Prague conception of phonology cannot be flatly dismissed as taxonomic, i.e., as limited to mere enumeration and classification of the established phonic phenomena. It should be emphasized that since the very beginning of its activities the Prague group has been laying particular stress not only on the interrelation of the items forming the phonological system of language but also on the interrelations existing between the elements of this particular system taken as a whole and the elements of other systems (or, better, sub-systems or levels) found within the language, such as the levels of morphology, syntax, etc. Mainly in the post-war period a number of interesting interdependences were pointed out, and it was shown that such inter-level relations may play an important part in the historical development of language. If then, the derogatory epithet "taxonomic" can be applied to some other phonologically oriented currents (perhaps to the Yale group, although even there some effort at establishing the relations among the phonemes of the given language distinctly stands out),[7] the Prague group is placed, very

---

[6]Chomsky's viewpoint is expressed even more clearly in the (so far) unpublished paper, N. Chomsky and G. A. Miller, "Introduction to the Formal Analysis of Natural Languages" [see now Miller and Chomsky, 1963—VBM], which says: "It is assumed . . . that there is a level of representation intermediate between phonetic and morphophonemic, this new intermediate level being generally called phonemic. However, there seems to us good reason to reject the hypothesis that there exists an intermediate level of this sort . . ." (duplicated copy, p. 64). Chomsky states that his usage of the term phoneme is "much like that of Sapir" (*ibid.*); this does not seem well compatible with Sapir's recognition of the "sound pattern," which has much in common with what the Prague group has been calling "the phonological system."

[7]For criticism of the Yale group, undertaken from Prague phonological positions, see J. Vachek,

obviously, outside the reach of the said qualification. Obviously, the Prague group not only does not limit itself to mere enumeration and classification but tries to penetrate more deeply into the inter-level connections found in language. The Prague scholars are just as opposed to the "separation of levels," typical of most American descriptivist scholars, as Chomsky's himself appears to be.[8]

It appears, indeed, that Chomsky's chief merit in the history of world linguistics will rest in his realization of what was too one-sided in the conception of language held by American descriptivist scholars, including their ban on the "mixing of levels." It cannot be denied that Chomsky's approach to problems of grammar has duly called the linguists' attention to the importance of inter-level relations in language (especially of the relations between the levels of morphology and syntax, and those existing between phonology and morphology). An altogether different problem is, of course, whether Chomsky is right in asserting that the "ordered set of rules" generating correct sentences in the given language can fully exhaust the meaning of the term "grammar." As this question is too complex to be handled in its entirety in the limits set to this paper, we will try to make our position clear in a few remarks concerning what we take to be some of the crucial points of the question.

II The major source of Chomsky's inspiration in building up his theory of grammar seems to have been the following: a language system, which can be mastered by a child in a relatively short time, must be statable as a set of relatively not too complicated rules, starting from simple, basic sentences (called kernel sentences by Chomsky)[9] and capable of generating from them all sorts of more complicated sentences of the language, and only these. The idea which inspired Chomsky is, of course, not entirely new to our linguistic public. Its premises—though not the "generativist and transformationist" conclusion— were formulated in Prague by B. Havránek as early as in 1956, i.e., one year before the publication of Chomsky's *Syntactic Structures,* in the discussions held at the Prague linguistic conference on the research-work in contemporary languages.[10] It might be doubted, of course, whether from the unquestionably correct premises one may deduce exactly that kind of conclusion as one finds with Chomsky. Some time ago A. Reichling expressed[11] well-founded doubts on the point that a speaker would master the grammar of a language by a process whose stages would constitute a sequence analogous to the sequence of rules established by Chomsky. It is hardly open to doubt that the acquisition of the system of language by a child is primarily an inductive, not a deductive process (though deduction comes in, secondarily, too), and that this induction does not operate very systematically, but rather tentatively and alternatively on various points and sections of the system. Here, however, Reichling's objections might be faced with the assertion that a theoretician has the right, and the duty, to express in rationalistic and deductive terms the process which in the child progresses empirically and inductively. This may be true to some extent, but this admission at the same time considerably invalidates the premises which have often been regarded as particularly strong evidence for the adequacy of the Chomskyan method.

A thorough consideration of the gradual, inductive procedure by which the child proceeds in building up his or her language patterns[12] rather appears to show that what Chomsky and his followers denote by the term

---

"Yaleská škola a strukturalistická fonologie" [The Yale School and Structuralist Phonology], *SaS* 11, 1949, pp. 36–44.

[8]See Chomsky's *Syntactic Structures* ('s Gravenhage, 1957), p. 56.

[9]In his Cambridge lecture Chomsky uses a different term, viz., matrix sentences.

[10]See the proceedings of the conference, published under the title *O vědeckém poznání soudobých jazyků* [On Research into Contemporary Languages] (Praha, 1958), p. 387: "If one realizes that every child of eight (or even younger) has managed to master his or her mother tongue, i.e., to master the system of its language, then it is clear that language and its system cannot be so complex as to be incomprehensible except to people who have long been trained in complex and deep abstract thinking."

[11]A. Reichling, "Principles and Methods of Syntax: Cryptanalytical Formalism," *Lingua* 10, 1961, pp. 1–17.

[12]On this point see some interesting remarks by E. M. Uhlenbeck, "An Appraisal of Transformation Theory," *Lingua* 12, 1963, pp. 1–18.

"grammar" cannot pretend to exhaust the actual semantic content of the latter term. We feel inclined to believe that the Chomskyan procedure is not so much an attempt at establishing the grammar of a language as an attempt —certainly an ingenious one—at fixing the plan of what might be denoted by the Saussurean term *parole*.[13] The Chomskyan "grammar," that is, summarizes a number of selective processes by which the means placed at the disposal of the speaker are selected and mobilized for the purpose of mutual communication and expression in the given language community. But one should not overlook the fact that such a system of means, from which the selection is taken, *"langue,"* undoubtedly exists as a social and psychological reality in the consciousness of the speakers. In other words, processes, though most important, should not make one blind to the existence of entities, for it is only with and upon the latter that processes can operate. To put the matter still differently, just as *parole* cannot exist without *language* (and, of course, *vice versa*), so it appears impossible to reduce the scope of grammar to the processual aspect alone, without due consideration of the entitative aspect. That the opposite reduction of the scope of grammar to the entitative aspect alone is not feasible, has been unmistakably demonstrated exactly by the brilliant, if one-sided, work of Chomsky's.

There is, however, another important source of inspiration that, too, must have played a major part in the rise of the generative and transformational grammar (and modeling in linguistics in general). This other source has been the effort to make linguistics an "exact" science by formalizing and axiomatizing its rules; an ideal linguistic theory, in this conception, should be able to predict such language phenomena as have not yet been concretely met with. This ideal very obviously lies at the bottom of the effort of the "transformationists" to formulate their sets of rules in such a way as to make them capable of generating all sentences possible in language (and only these), even those which have never

yet occurred in actual utterances. This ideal goal is methodically most interesting and respectable; but the transformationists honestly admit that they still have a very long way to go to reach that goal—so far only relatively small sections of concrete language systems could be formalized, and a full-fledged generative and transformationist grammar of any concrete language still seems to be a matter of very distant future.[14]

Moreover, it is necessary to realize some other difficulties which may render the formalization and the axiomatization of the language system rather difficult. One is faced here with the basic question of the extent to which the method of mathematical modeling can be applied in social sciences. There can be no doubt that mathematical models will most adequately express the regularity of the phenomena examined by natural sciences, in which one has to do with a regularity that might be called stable or even static. (Admittedly, it is taken for granted that natural laws are not subject to changes, at least as long as we keep within our own cosmic limits.) But the problem becomes less clear in the domain of social sciences. The regularities observable in the latter are rather of dynamic character, in other words, the examined structures are subject to "laws" which are not necessarily stable but are apt to be changed in the course of time. The basic difference between the "sound laws," whose operation is limited both in time and in space, and the natural laws of physics, chemistry,

---

[13]The need for "linguistique de la parole," unwritten by Saussure, has long been felt—see particularly V. Skalička, "The Need for a Linguistics of la Parole," *Recueil linguistique de Bratislava* 1, 1948, pp. 21–36.

[14]It should also be noted that attempts at the formalization of even relatively limited sections of language, when based on Slavonic materials, often lead to so complicated sets of rules as almost to defeat their own purpose. (See, e.g., B. Palek's paper "Informace o transformační gramatice" [Information on Transformational Grammar], *SaS* 24, 1963, pp. 140–151; its complicated rules for the generation of Czech sentences strikingly contrast with the simplicity of the corresponding rules of English. And yet one could hardly assert that a Czech child learning how to form sentences is faced with greater difficulties than an English child in the analogous position. Only two conclusions appear to be possible: either the rules for the generation of Czech sentences are unduly complicated (but it is difficult to see how they could be expressed more simply in a language whose grammar is of the "synthetic" type), or the acquisition by the child of the language is effected on lines different from those indicated by the grammarian's set of rules.

etc., whose operation is not subject to such limitation, is too commonplace to need further comment (just as the fact that the regularities observable on "higher" language levels reveal more stability than those typical of the phonic level). General, unlimited validity of the kind found in natural sciences could only be claimed in linguistics by panglottic and panchronic laws.

It would be certainly unwise to deny the existence of such laws; an effort aimed at their formulation has been found in the Prague group since its early days and today's world linguistics shows an intensified interest in these problems.[15] But the purport of such universal laws is too abstract (and often can be expressed rather in negative than in positive terms) to be able to give a complete account of the development of the examined language. For the greater part, this development seems to be governed by regularities and interdependences of non-general, partial character, the validity of which is limited both in time and in space, and without due regard to them the development of language cannot be satisfactorily grasped. Besides, one should not overlook the well-known fact that the structural reshapement, observable in the course of development of any language, proceeds relatively very quickly, and that traces of this reshapement are observable in any language system at any moment of its development. The Prague group has repeatedly stressed this fact (for the first time in the above-mentioned volume 2 of the *TCLP*, published as early as in 1929), explaining why at any moment of its history any language is characterized by a number of archaisms as well as neologisms, constituting elements of peripheral nature in its system. In other words, at any moment of its development language constitutes a structure in motion; and it is certainly remarkable that—as far as we know—the existing models of language, including that of Chomsky's—have failed to do justice to this particular and certainly typical, feature of language. Incidentally, the inadequacy of language models in the said point has been noted, more or less

clearly, by N. D. Andrejev and Punya Śloka Ray; in this country, the problem was touched upon by I. Poldauf.[16]

Admittedly, some rare attempts have been made at finding such models as would do justice to the fact of language development. Thus I. I. Revzin quotes the well-known conception of A. Martinet, who is of the opinion that the phonological system of language tends to eliminate the "cases vides" that occasionally emerge in such systems.[17] One may leave aside as meaningless the question whether Martinet, in formulating his theory stressing the economic aspect of language development, actually meant it as a sort of language model. What is really essential here is the fact that the developmental factor emphasized by Martinet (the tendency striving at the elimination of the "cases vides") is, for all its importance, only one of a large series of factors influencing the development of language. As the present writer pointed out elsewhere,[18] the development of the phonological level is not necessarily motivated by the needs and wants of that same level alone, but, at least occasionally, by the needs and wants of other language levels, e.g., the morphological one. But there are other possible motivations of phonological development. Sometimes it appears necessary to take into consideration the regularities to which speech organs are subjected *qua* physiological factors; finally, one should not forget the possibility of some, however remote, influence of outer factors on the phonological develop-

[16]N. D. Andreyev, "Models as a Tool in the Development of Linguistic Theory," *Word* 18, 1962, pp. 186–197, very aptly observes: "Those who create schemes for language phenomena must always remember that the object of their research is in perpetual flux and cannot, therefore, be identified with any constant structure" (p. 197). Similar, if not so precisely formulated, are the standpoints of Punya Śloka Ray ("The Logic of Linguistics," *Methodos* [*Language and Cybernetics*] 13, 1961, pp. 239–254, and I. Poldauf, "Strukturalismus a americký deskriptivismus [Structuralism and American Descriptivism], in: *Problémy marxistické jazykovědy* [Problems of Marxist Linguistics] (Praha, 1962), pp. 79–110 (esp. p. 103).

[17]I. I. Revzin, *Modeli jazyka* (Moskva, 1962), p. 35 f.; A. Martinet, *Économie des changements phonétiques* (Berne, 1955), esp. p. 111.

[18]J. Vachek, "Dvě vyznamné fonologické publikace zehraniční" [Two Important Foreign Books on Phonology], *SaS* 19, 1958, pp. 52–60.

[15]See, e.g., *TCLP* 2, 1929, pp. 17 f.; most recently, the collective volume *Universals of Language,* ed. by J. H. Greenberg, Cambridge, Mass., 1963.

ment of language (and on the development of language in general).[19]

This comment, however brief, will have shown that the development of language (and even the development of one single of its levels, the phonological one) is an affair far too complicated to be adequately grasped and explained on the basis of Martinet's principle of economy alone; though certainly important, this principle is only one of a number of factors that are at work in the process of that development. If we regarded, with Revzin, Martinet's conception as a kind of model of the development of language, then undoubtedly the model would be a very imperfect one and could not claim to mirror, with due adequacy, the structures and the processes which it was intended to formalize.

What has been said above should not, of course, be interpreted as a flat refusal of the idea of language modeling, which is certainly able to throw unexpected light on some aspects of the life of language. It has only been thought useful to point out that it is exactly the language events that will put more obstacles in the way of the modeling procedure than events studied by some natural sciences (and perhaps some social sciences). It is well known that the supporters of the cause of modeling have honestly admitted that, in the long run, any model can do only approximate justice to the reality it models; it should only be added that for the modeling of language this honest admission will have to be kept in mind more cautiously than for modeling in most branches of other sciences.

III Our above analysis has disclosed that Chomsky's theory of grammar appears to be too static, not taking due account of the fact that language—and particularly its phonological level—must be conceived as a structure in motion.[20] This general disclosure is fully endorsed by a more detailed analysis of some of the objections adduced by Chomsky as arguments against the principles and procedures of the "taxonomic" phonology. The remain-

ing part of this paper will be devoted to the analysis of the most important of these objections.

Chomsky blames "taxonomic" phonologists for proclaiming the principle of linearity (i.e., the principle that a sequence of the phonemes A and B is phonetically implemented by the corresponding sequence of phones [a] and [b]) but for frequently ignoring this principle in their practice. As a specimen of such inconsistency Chomsky quotes A. Malécot's example of the Anglo-American nasal vowel [æ̃] in words of the type *can't* (*op. cit.*, p. 540 [409]). This vowel is phonologically interpreted as /æn/, despite the obvious phonic opposition [kæ̃t] : [kæt]; in consistently observing the linearity principle one would have to regard the nasality of the vowel as a superimposed distinctive feature, and to ascribe to [æ̃] the status of a phoneme. In other words, [kæt] would have to be interpreted not as /kænt/, but as /kæ̃t/. Chomsky is perfectly right in stating that no linguist will ever draw this conclusion, in view of its obvious inadequacy. But he uses the case as an argument for his thesis that the principle of linearity as a working hypothesis of "taxonomic" phonology is untenable in practice.

The above argumentation fully endorses our general conclusion presented here above, viz., that Chomsky visualizes language as a static fact, as what might be called a self-contained whole. This sort of conception of language is, naturally enough, incompatible with an idea that some analytical procedure might be applied to language only in part, not indiscriminately. If, however, language constitutes a system which is not self-contained, i.e., constitutes a structure not fully closed—and this has been held by the Prague group for decades—it will hardly be surprising to find that some analytical procedures cannot be applied to that structure indiscriminately; it is, of course, absolutely imperative to offer a satisfactory explanation of each of the cases in which the application has not proved feasible. In the above quoted instance (of the type [kæ̃t] : [kæt]) such an explanation is not difficult to find. As Chomsky himself admits, the nasality of [æ̃] is found in a single contextual situation, which is specified by a rather limited phonematic environment, viz., in a position before a voiceless stop; another limi-

---

[19]For a discussion of these problems see J. Vachek, "On the Interplay of External and Internal Factors in the Development of Language," *Lingua* 11, 1962, pp. 433–448.

[20]See also N. D. Andreyev's statement quoted here above, note 16.

tation is that the nasality only occurs with short ("lax"), not with long ("tense"), vowels. Chomsky himself points out the fact that besides forms like [kǣt] there exist forms like [hænd], which reveal that before a voiced stop the nasality of the vowel is evidently a mere concomitant, irrelevant phenomenon, due to the immediately following nasal consonant. This very limited positional distribution of the demonstrably relevant [ǣ]-vowel must raise legitimate doubts of the possibility of the independent phonematic status of that vowel. These doubts are further borne out by the fact that while an opposition of the type [kǣt] : [kæt] undoubtedly exists, there is no trace of an opposition of the type [kǣt] : [kænt]. All this very urgently forces the phonologist working with the functionalist methods of the Prague group to interpret the American English [ǣ]-vowel as /æn/.

The said interpretation is also justified by the simultaneous presence in the sound [ǣ] of the same two component elements as are found to exist, successively, in the sound combination [æn], viz., [æ] + nasal articulation. The admission of an independent phonematic status of [ǣ] could only be indicated if the functionally relevant opposition of the type [ǣ] : [æ] were coupled with an equally relevant opposition, nonconditioned by the phonic environment, of the type [ǣ] : [æn]. This, incidentally, is the situation in Modern French where, aside of oppositions like [trɔ̃] : [trɔ], one also meets functionally relevant oppositions of the type [bɔ̃] : [bɔn]. Here it is worth pointing out that French, too, must have passed through a stage in which the nasalization of the vowel in a word like *bon* was a mere concomitant, functionally irrelevant phonic fact, which only later, after the loss of the final -*n*, was to be revaluated into a functionally relevant, distinctive feature. It should be noted that when French was passing through that transitional stage, it must have also proved impossible to apply the principle of linearity to its contexts with absolute consistency. It is of course clear why this proved impossible: the following stages of the development of French show unmistakably that in the. transitional stage the phonological system was in motion, in a "state of flux," and so must have revealed some inconsistencies in a number of its points. To go back to American English

again, although we, naturally, cannot forecast the direction of the future development of its phonological system, so much at least is obvious that here, too, the phonological system of the language proves to be in motion, which accounts for the impossibility of applying to it the principle of linearity with absolute consistency.

Another point deserves stressing in this connection: the instances to which the principle of linearity cannot be applied constitute, as a rule, a very small minority if compared with those instances to which the principle can be consistently applied without any difficulty. This very fact should persuade the analyst to proceed with utmost caution: if a certain principle works in a predominant majority of the involved instances, it appears methodologically more advisable, *faute de mieux,* to try and find separate explanations of the instances defying the concerned principle than flatly to denounce that principle as inoperative and, therefore, untenable.

In some of his arguments Chomsky is undoubtedly right, but the inferences he draws from such arguments are hardly justified. Thus one can only agree with his statement that Trubetzkoy's rule explaining the phonematic interpretation of the closed [ǫ]-vowel in Russian words like [sǫ́ncə] as /ol/[21] is not formulated satisfactorily (p. 544 [411]). In Trubetzkoy's conception, if a sound A is phonetically similar („nahesteht") to a sequence of sounds BC and if, at the same time, the mutual relation of A and BC is one of free variation or of complementary distribution, and if, finally, BC implements the sequence of phonemes PQ, then it is necessary to evaluate also the sound A as an implementation of the phonematic sequence PQ.

This formula calls for some qualification in two points. First, it should be emphatically underlined that the sound A, if found in complementary distribution with the sequence of sounds BC, has a strictly limited occurrence, being a minority phenomenon, while the sequence BC is found in all other positions which make up a clear majority. Second, the

---

[21]*Grundzüge der Phonologie,* pp. 55–56. In the above text we start from Chomsky's slightly adapted formulation of the rule, as the adaptation does not substantially alter the meaning conveyed by Trubetzkoy's own formula.

rather vague formula "phonetic similarity" of the sound A and the sequence BC should be made more exact. One should emphasize here the closest possible articulatory and acoustic similarity of the two compared phonic facts: Such an improvement of the formula would eliminate the possibility of such instances of *reductio ad absurdum* of Trubetzkoy's rule, as can be met with in Chomsky's commentary on that rule.

Chomsky argues, that is to say, that Trubetzkoy's rule, as it stands, would allow of a phonematic interpretation of ModE syllabic [n̩] as /nj/, because the sound [n̩] and the sound group [nj] are "phonetically similar" and, as to the positions of their occurrences, mutually complementary. In other words, it is suggested that Trubetzkoy's formula might allow to draw from it the obviously wrong conclusion that the English word spelt *kitten* has the phonematic structure /kitnj/. Chomsky himself brands such interpretation as absurd, but blames Trubetzkoy's conception for the absurdity. But the blame is not due to the conception but to its inadequate formulation which needs such emendation as shown here above. It is, of course, perfectly clear how arbitrary would be the phonological identification of English [n̩] and [nj]; the "phonetic similarity" of these two phonic facts is demonstrably much smaller than that existing between the syllabic [n̩] and some other phonic facts with which it stands in complementary distribution. It is, above all, the non-syllabic [n], which goes infinitely better with [n̩] as its variant partner than the [nj] foisted into this function by Chomsky; the other possible candidate for the partnership, backed by the authority of Trubetzkoy himself, would be the sound group [ən],[22] which, too, stands in complementary distribution with [n̩] and displays a much closer "phonetic similarity" to it than [nj]. Whichever of the two possibilities is adopted, it goes much better with the spirit (though, of course, not with the letter) of Trubetzkoy's principle than the admittedly absurd interpretation of the type /kitnj/.

Analogous criticism might be applied to

the other English example used by Chomsky to reduce Trubetzkoy's rule *ad absurdum,* viz., the English sound [j] and the sound combination [ju]. As these two phonic facts, too, stand in complementary distribution, it is suggested that the English word *yacht,* pronounced [jat] in American, might be phonematically interpreted as /jŭat/. The absurdity of this kind of interpretation (and of some others which cannot be discussed here in detail) would have been obvious not only to Chomsky but to Trubetzkoy himself who would never have asserted the variant partnership of [j] and [ju] in view of the fact that [ju], taken as a whole, is not a partner of [j]; it is only its first component part [j], which is very naturally identified with [j] on a phonological basis, while the phonematic value of the other element [u], for all its specific phonic qualities in some American types of pronunciation, makes a separate problem, quite independent of the phonematic status of [j]. (The most obvious solution of that problem is, naturally, the phonological identification of [u] preceded by [j] with the sound [u] found in other positions.)

It is, however, fair to admit that sometimes Chomsky's objections to Trubetzkoy's procedure are not quite unsound. Thus, in connection with the above-discussed problem of the American English [æ]-sound, he directs the reader's attention to the possibility, suggested by Trubetzkoy's rule, of interpreting the ModE word-final and intervocalic [ŋ]-sound as /ng/. The whole context clearly shows that Chomsky does not favor such interpretation. Still, a finer analysis of the ModE phonological situation, together with the examination of the historical processes involved, proves quite conclusively that the biphonematic interpretation of ModE [ŋ] is not so absurd as it might seem at first sight. In another of his papers[23] the present writer tried to demonstrate that since the beginning of the Early ModE period two opposed conceptions of the [ŋ]-sound have been conflicting in the phonological system of English. One of the two interpretations has been monophonematic

[22]In his *Grundzüge* (p. 56) Trubetzkoy suggests this as an interpretation of the Modern German [n̩]-sound, but it is equally well applicable to the analogous sound of Modern English.

[23]J. Vachek, "Notes on the Phonematic Value of the Modern English [ŋ]—Sound," *In Honour of Daniel Jones* (London, 1964), pp. 191 ff.; also *Brno Studies in English* 4, 1964, pp. 46–54.

(i.e., /ŋ/), the other one, however, biphonematic (i.e., /ng/). It appears that, in the long run, the monophonematic interpretation managed to prevail, but there is some evidence that the position of the /ŋ/-phoneme in the phonological system of ModE has not been settled for good, because a number of facts in the phonological structure of ModE still appear to favor rather the biphonematic interpretation /ng/. In short, /ŋ/ remains one of the "fuzzy points" of the ModE phonological system, an indicator of the fact that, at the given time, the system has some structural problems to solve, in other words, that far from being a static structure, it is a structure in motion.

IV   Another case, a particularly interesting one, by which Chomsky wants to demonstrate the illegitimacy of the "taxonomic" principle of linearity, is concerned with the word-pair *writer — rider* in most types of the American pronunciation of English. As is commonly known, in this kind of pronunciation the intervocalic[24] [t] is pronounced as "a single tap" of the tongue tip against the upper alveoli. The quickness of the articulation and the intervocalic position of the consonant appear to have caused the assimilation of the voiceless tap to its voiced surroundings. One might thus expect that members of word-pairs like *writer — rider, latter — ladder,* etc., would appear as perfect homonyms, in view of what might be called, in Prague terminology, the neutralization of the phonological opposition of /t/ : /d/ in such pairs. And yet the matter proves to be much more complex. Already Kenyon, in his above-quoted handbook (see note 24) pointed out the fact that the speakers who have effected the above-mentioned assimilation of [t] in their pronunciation continue to discern very distinctly between the original intervocalic stops [t] and [d], so that members of word-pairs like *latter — ladder* are not evaluated as homonyms by such speakers (§163).

Various scholars have tried to account for this continued differentiation; thus, e.g., I. C. Ward[25] attributed it to the difference in the

energy of articulation, which is weaker in [d] than in [t]. But this explanation is far from satisfactory, as one might well wonder why an analogous difference does not make itself felt in the other pairs of stops. In this connection Chomsky's explanation of the difference is certainly worth considering. In his opinion, the members of the American English word-pair *writer — rider* are phonetically manifested as [raiṭəʳ] — [rai·ṭəʳ], respectively (in Chomsky's transcription, [rayDɨr] — [ra·yDɨr]; in the following sections of the present paper we will be using this latter type of transcription too, to make reference easier). This means, in Chomsky's interpretation, that the opposition of /t/ and /d/ is manifested not in the consonantal articulation but in the articulation of the preceding vowel (or diphthong): in our concrete instance, the prolonged articulation of the diphthong [a·y], signalizes that a voiced consonant follows, while the non-prolonged articulation of [ay] signalizes the (original) voicelessness of the following consonant.

Chomsky's observation is in full agreement with what phoneticians of English have been pointing out since Henry Sweet's and E. A. Meyer's times, viz., that the quantity of one and the same vowel (or diphthong) is markedly longer before an immediately following voiced consonant than before its immediately following voiceless counterpart. Chomsky's new contribution is that this quantitative differentiation of the vowel can be observed even in those instances in which, to all appearances, the opposition of voice in the following consonant has become neutralized by merging the original [t] and [d] into [D]. Chomsky's main concern is, of course, his conclusion that "if phonemic representation is to play any significant part in linguistic description . . . , the linearity condition must be rather grossly violated" (p. 541 [410]). This statement should be understood in the sense that, in Chomsky's conception, the phonological structures of the two words continue to be /rayt#r/ — /rayd#r/ but that the opposition of the phonemes /t/ and /d/ is implemented not by the opposition of the consonant sounds but by that of the diphthongal articulations preceding these consonants, i.e., [ay] : [a·y].

However persuasive Chomsky's argumentation may seem, a more detailed analysis of the matter is bound to reveal that here, too,

---

[24]The discussed type of pronunciation also occurs in some other positions which, however, do not concern us here (see, e.g., J. S. Kenyon, *American Pronunciation,* 9th ed., Ann Arbor, 1946, §379).

[25]I. C. Ward, *The Phonetics of English,* 4th ed. (Cambridge, 1945), §370.

Chomsky fails to do justice to the dynamic character of the system of language, which is far from constituting a self-contained whole. The analysis of the instances shows that in this particular point the phonological sub-system of the language has been slightly shifted, in consequence of the neutralization of two of its phonemes in one specified position. As is well known, in some other words that are semantically and grammatically closely allied to the members of the examined word-pair the phonological opposition /t/ − /d/ has not been neutalized because it is functioning in a position exempt from such neutralization. Thus, alongside the forms of the nouns of agents *writer* and *rider,* there exist forms of their infinitival bases *write* and *ride* (and also homophonous forms found in the present indicative) in which the phonological opposition of /t/ and /d/ has never been neutralized. One should also keep in mind that in the phonetic implementation of the forms *write* and *ride* one always finds the same quantitative difference of vowels standing before the final consonant as was pointed out above in the pair *writer − rider.* In other words, in the phonetic implementation of the form /rayt/ the diphthong [ay] will (*caeteris paribus*) always be objectively shorter than the phonetic implementation of /ay/ in the corresponding form /rayd/. As, then, the close semantic and grammatical relationship of the forms *write* and *writer* (or, for that matter, *ride* and *rider*) is a fact notorious to any user of the language, it is by no means surprising that the quantity of the vocalic or diphthongal articulation common in the basic word is also preserved in the derived word, despite the fact of consonant neutralization which should discard any motivation of the quantitative difference in the preceding vowels.

But, as a matter of fact, some motivation of the quantitative difference of vowels persists, though not on the phonological level. The motivation, this time, has its grounds in morphology: need is felt to signalize, by phonic means, the close morphological relationship of the forms *write − writer,* and so to prevent their phonic merger with the analogous pair *ride − rider.* (An analogous difference, due to analogous motivation, might presumably be found in instances like *writing − riding,* and the like.) This need is satisfied by revaluating

the originally concomitant variation of vocalic (or diphthongal) quantity into a kind of relevant signal-like opposition.

If all consequences are derived from the above observation, one notices that the difficulties connected with the phonematic interpretation of the American English word-pair *writer − rider* are due to the conflicting interests of two language levels, phonological and morphological. While the developmental tendencies of the former appear to tend to (or, at least, not to be opposed to) the phonematic neutralization of the intervocalic /t/ and /d/, the tendency of the latter level is to preserve the morphematic distinction of /rayt-/ and /rayd-/ unimpaired even in word-forms like *writer − rider* (or *writing − riding,* etc.). The conflict appears to be settled by a sort of compromise: the tendencies of the phonological level are satisfied in so far that the implementations of /t/ and /d/ in the compared words do become merged (which is a necessary prerequisite for phonological neutralization). But the full assertion of the phonological tendencies is barred by the tendencies of the morphological level which insist on the preservation of phonic difference in the concerned word-bases. These other tendencies are satisfied, in their turn, by the preservation of the quantitative differences of the preceding vocalic (or diphthongal) articulations.

It will be easily seen that the resulting compromise is at variance with the structural laws and regularities of English viewed as a systematic whole. The fact that the phonic opposition [rayDɨr] − [ra·yDɨr] is associated with two different kinds of extra-linguistic reality might seem to point to the existence of a phonological opposition between [ay] and [a·y] (or, possibly, between [a] and [a·]).[26] But this kind of opposition would be limited to one single phonological situation (before [D], whatever its phonological evaluation may be), while in all others the quantitative difference of [ay] and [a·y] (or, for that matter, of [a] and [a·]) is functionally irrelevant, being motivated

[26]The parenthesized alternative does not appear very probable, in view of the difficulties connected with the biphonematic interpretation of ModE diphthongs (see, most recently, J. Vachek, "The Phonematic Status of Modern English Long Vowels and Diphthongs," *Philologica Pragensia* 6, 1963, pp. 59−71).

exclusively by the voiced or voiceless quality of the following consonant. And it is exactly this exceptionality of occurrence of the supposed phonological opposition which calls for utmost caution. All other possibilities of phonological interpretation should be tried before we decide to accept an interpretation so exceptional from the point of quality and quantity alike.

It appears that in the given situation one is faced with two alternative possibilities of phonological interpretation. The first of the two rests on the assumption that, after all, the consonant [D] is not articulated in exactly the same way in both examined word-forms, *writer* and *rider*. If any objective difference can be established between [D] in *writer* and [D] in *rider,* then it should be evaluated as implementation of the phonological opposition of /t/ and /d/. This alternative might be supported by the observation of I. C. Ward referred to above (perhaps for some variants of American English). If no such objective difference between the two [D]-sounds should be detected (and this seems to be the case of the variant of English described by Chomsky), one will have to resort to the other alternative. It may be briefly expressed as interpreting the [D]-sound either as /t/ or as /d/, according as it is preceded by a short or long vocalic (or diphthongal) allophone. This interpretation would be supported by the psychological situation in which the speaker finds himself placed when pronouncing the discussed words. As the speaker is certainly fully conscious of the closest formal and semantic relation of the forms *write — writer — writing,* it can be taken for granted that in the second and third members of this series he proceeds to the phonation of the intervocalic /t/ with the same intention as in the first member. This supposition is borne out by the fact that an important accessory feature of the vocalic articulation preceding the stop consonant, and regularly predicting its voiced or voiceless quality, is found to be the same in all the three elements of the series. (Analogous argumentation might be applied—*mutatis mutandis*—to the other series, viz., *ride — rider — riding.*) To sum up, the undoubted identity of the morpheme coupled with the objective identity of the accessory vocalic feature supply, if anything, conclusive evidence of the identical phona-

tional intention of the phoneme placed at the end of that morpheme.

Here we must be ready to face the well-known objection (to be certainly raised from some descriptivist quarters) that by drawing upon a morphological argument we commit the methodological offense of the "mixing of levels" of language. But such an objection can be squarely met. As already pointed out, the conception of language as a system of systems (or, better, sub-systems or levels), held by the Prague group, emphasizes the fact that no level of language can be fully understood if its structure is isolated from the structures of the other levels co-existing with it in the same language. The mutual interdependence of the levels of language was repeatedly demonstrated by instances taken from the historical development of languages.[27] It should also be recalled that Chomsky himself was emphatically critical of the descriptivist maxim of the inadmissibility of the "mixing of levels," and that he was by no means alone in this (see, e.g., K. L. Pike's criticism of the approach, which he aptly terms "compartmentalization").[28]—We are, of course, fully aware of the unusual features of the interpretation suggested here, but insist on the fact that the unusualness is a necessary consequence of the fact that one is faced with an unusual feature of the phonological structure of American English—indeed, with what might again be termed one of its "fuzzy points."

Our analysis of the *writer — rider* case, presented by Chomsky as a particularly convincing argument against the principle of linearity held by "taxonomic" phonologists, has revealed that the position of the analyzed phenomena in American English is far more complex and the problem of their phonological interpretation far more delicate than Chomsky can realize. It is certainly true that the difficulties connected with the structural analysis of such complex and delicate problems can be by-passed by establishing a set of generating and transformational rules leading from the morphematic build-up of the examined form

[27]For particulars, see J. Vachek, "Prague Phonological Studies Today," *Travaux linguistiques de Prague* 1, 1964, and the literature there quoted.

[28]*Proceedings of the Eighth International Congress of Linguists* (Oslo, 1958), pp. 363–371.

to its phonological, and finally phonetic, implementation (or, to use Chomsky's term, representation). Such a set of rules may be most useful, in its own sphere—it may, indeed, throw the much-needed light on some problems of the "linguistique de la parole" (as pointed out here above). On the other hand, such a set will never be able to solve the given problem of the place of the analyzed oppositions in the phonological structure of language. Such problems may be ignored, they may be perhaps stigmatized as pseudoproblems, but all this does not bring them an inch nearer their solution. Our own analysis has shown that the place of the *writer* − *rider* opposition is, in a way, anomalous, so that it can be justly denoted as a fuzzy point of the system. The structural anomaly of the oppositions of this type lies in the above-noted fact that hand in hand with the neutralization of the phonological opposition /t/ : /d/ in a certain type of environment one concomitant phonic variation of the preceding vocalic sounds appears to be raised to the status of phonological opposition. The anomaly is clear to anyone who realizes that the said variation would obtain this phonological status in a very specific type of its environment, while in all other positions the said variation would remain as concomitant and as functionally irrelevant as ever.

It might be argued that instances of revaluation of a concomitant variation into a phonological opposition are fairly frequent in phonological histories of concrete languages, and that, moreover, there is nothing very extraordinary in such revaluation starting in a specific type of environment from which it afterwards spreads into other positions in which the variation can occur. All this is perfectly true; but the interesting point of our case is that the supposed revaluation of our concomitant variation into phonological opposition does not spread into other positions (e.g., it does not emerge before labials, velars, etc., but only before alveolar stops). In addition to this, it is certainly remarkable that in the only position where the supposed revaluation has taken place, its newly acquired phonological value appears to be canceled by the pressure of the morphological level of the language. As was shown here above, this pressure charges the old concomitant variation with a new function, viz., with the signalization of the original

presence or absence of voice in the immediately following neutralized consonant phoneme. To sum up, it appears clear that there was indeed a start opening up a certain phonological change. That change, however, not only did not have free course, but the very opposite thing happened: it was halted by the impact of the morphological system of the language. This system not only prevented any further spread of the phonological change, but was even strong enough to alter the result of the change in the very position in which it had originally emerged.

The above analyses will have shown that some typical instances adduced by Chomsky as arguments against the methods of "taxonomic" phonology are, in reality, only indicators of the fact that in the particular points the analyzed phonological system proves to be in motion, in a "state of flux," i.e., of imperfect balance. And it is only too clear that this system in motion cannot be adequately handled by the indiscriminate application of the current phonological methods such as have been established for the "macroscopic" phonological analysis. The analysis of the above-discussed fuzzy points will, naturally, require finer and more delicate methods, paying due regard to all the inner and outer complexities in which the structure of language has to function, and some specimens of which were pointed out in the above lines.

V All the instances so far analyzed here were used by Chomsky as arguments against the "taxonomic" principle of linearity. Another such "taxonomic" principle is that of invariance. In Chomsky's formulation, "the invariance condition . . . asserts that each phoneme P has associated with it a certain set $\varphi(P)$ of defining features . . . and that wherever P occurs in a phonemic representation, there is an associated occurrence of $\varphi(P)$ in the corresponding phonetic representation" (*op. cit.*, p. 538 [408]). This principle, too, is declared to be inadequate, as is shown by the well-known instances of the overlapping of phonemes. One such instance is singled out by Chomsky and it will be found useful to comment on it briefly here, too.

The case of overlapping to be discussed was pointed out more than twenty years ago by B. Bloch.[29] It is again concerned with the sound [D] which, in a certain type of American English, constitutes not only an allophone of the phoneme /t/ (see the *writer — rider* case, discussed here above) but also an allophone of the phoneme /r/, as in the form *throw,* phonetically [θDou]. It should be noted, besides, that there exists a functional opposition of [D] and [r] in form-pairs like *Betty — berry,* phonetically [beDi] — [beri]. The principle of invariance would, naturally, enforce (as Chomsky, too, aptly notes) a consistent phonological interpretation of [D] as /t/, so that the form [θDou] would have to be interpreted as /θtou/. Such an evaluation, however, would contradict not only the speakers' consciousness ("intuition," as Chomsky calls it) but—which is much more important—"the otherwise valid rules of consonant distribution" (*op. cit.,* p. 544 [412]). This latter contradiction, based on an objective fact of the non-existence of the sequence "/θ/ + discontinuous phoneme," is certainly too serious to be overlooked. An attempt to solve the problem by suggesting some kind of neutralization of the phonological opposition of /r/ : /t/ is doomed to fail as contrary not only to the laws of phonological structure of English (there is, in fact, no positive phonematic basis common to the two phonemes) but also to the laws of its morphology and morphonology: there is no morphological alternation in English of the type [θD] : [θVt], and the like (where the symbol V stands for any vowel). Thus, the phonic identity of the [D]-sounds in *throw* and *writer, Betty,* etc., must necessarily appear as overlapping of the phonemes /t/ and /r/. But this overlapping is obviously not motivated by the structural needs of the American English phonological system (or of the higher levels of that language). It seems more probable that we are faced here with a sort of collision caused by the operation of non-phonological (and non-grammatical) factors—more concretely, by an intervention of physiological laws and regularities, governing the work of the organs of speech *qua* physiological factors.

A brief analysis will prove this: in the sound sequences of the type [θrou], [θri·], etc.,

one is faced with consonantal clusters consisting of two apical, non-explosive consonants, one of which, at that, has a retroflex articulation. There is every reason to suppose that such sequences prove rather uncomfortable to pronounce, so that a dissimilative change appears to be indicated. The dissimilative process abolishes the second non-explosive, retroflex sound by changing it into an explosive articulation. It is worth recalling that an analogous dissimilation of a non-explosive into an explosive sound in the neighborhood of [θ] has occurred in some English words of foreign provenience, in which the cluster [fθ] has been replaced by [pθ] (cf. words like *diphthong, diphtheria*). The fact that in these latter words one finds the regressive dissimilation while in words like *three, throw* the change acted in the opposite direction may be due, among other things, to the commonly admitted importance, and the resulting stability, of the initial phoneme of the word.

There is no doubt that the discussed dissimilation has brought about some structural anomaly, or, in other words, has given rise to another "fuzzy point" in the structure of the concerned type of American English. As in the above-analyzed *writer — rider* case, one is faced here with a conflict of interests of two different structures, each of which is characterized by its own problems and regularities. The difference between the *writer — rider* case and the *throw — Betty* case is that in the former the conflicting structures were two different levels of the given system of language (the phonological and morphological) while in the latter the conflicting sides are the regularities of the phonological system on the one hand, and those governing the work of the organs of speech *qua* physiological factors on the other hand. A conflict of this type calls for prompt and radical solution in case that its duration jeopardizes the basic function of language, that of mutual communication. A decade ago we pointed out a case of the kind in the history of Early Middle English, where purely physiological, functionally unmotivated soundchanges went on unhampered until a certain moment, i.e., the moment of the rise of the structurally unacceptable phoneme /J/, implemented as [ç] (see the process *hēo > heǭ >*

[29]B. Bloch, "Phonemic Overlapping" [8], *American Speech* 16, 1941, 278–284.

$h\underline{i}\bar{o} > hj\bar{\varrho} > \varsigma\bar{\varrho}$, 'she').[30] There the conflict was abolished by substituting the /š/-phoneme for the slightly charged, and thus structurally unremunerative, phoneme /J/, which was thus disposed in a manner analogous to that by which previously the phonemes /R, L, N/ had been eliminated from the same phonological system.

The confrontation of the *throw* case with the *she* case very naturally raises the question why in the former no attempt at some kind of solution of the existing conflict appears to be in sight. As regards the regularities governing the phonological system, it should be added that one has to consider here not only the postulate of invariance (i.e., the observation of the principle of invariance, referred to here above) but also another postulate, that of biuniqueness. The principle of biuniqueness, in Chomsky's conception another objectionable methodological maxim of "taxonomic" phonology, "asserts that each sequence of phones is represented by a unique sequence of phonemes and each sequence of phonemes represents a unique sequence of phones" (Chomsky, *op. cit.*, p. 539 [408]). In other words, mutual overlapping of phonemes obviously contradicts the principle of biuniqueness, and such contradiction is, naturally, also inherent in the mutual overlapping of /t/ and /r/ in the discussed variant of American English: as was shown above, the sound [D] implementing the two is in most instances an allophone of /t/, in some exceptional cases, however, an allophone of /r/.

It appears that it is exactly in the exceptionality of the phonological value /r/ of the [D]-sound that a satisfactory solution of our problem might be found. It appears, that is to say, that the given structural anomaly has not yet overstepped the limits beyond which it might become unacceptable to the structural build-up of the system and to severely jeopardize its frictionless functioning. It appears, that is, that when situated after [θ], the sound [D] is still safely evaluated as an allophone of /r/, not of /t/. This can be inferred from the fact that when [D] is undoubtedly an allophone of /t/ (as in instances like *write — writer — writing,* see above), its occurrence is clearly motivated by its intervocalic position, so different from the position of [D] after [θ]; besides, in the latter kind of position no morphological evidence is available that might testify to the identity of the phonational intention present in [D] to that of [t] in some closely related word (on this point, as well as on the necessity to avoid the "separation of levels," see here above).

Another noteworthy difference by which the two [D]-sounds are distinctly kept apart may be seen in the phonetic processes by which they have originated. While the [D]-sound in words like *writer, Betty* has resulted from an assimilating process, the rise of the [D]-sound in *throw, three,* etc., has been due to dissimilation. It should also be remembered that this dissimilative motivation, confronted with the assimilative motivation found in *writer, Betty,* etc., certainly stands out as something exceptional, which fact may well harmonize with the exceptional phonological interpretation of this particular type of the [D]-sounds. Last but not least, one should not forget that the interpretation of [D] as /r/ in instances like *throw, three* is also psychologically supported by the written norm of English and, of course, by the existence in these words of the non-assimilated [r]-sound in other varieties of English.[31]

The above analysis of the *throw, three* case will have convincingly revealed that even their apparent non-susceptibility to the principles of invariance and biuniqueness can be satisfactorily explained. These "exceptions" to the said principles are, again, only indicative of the dynamicity of the given language system, coping with its inner contradictions and with structural problems resulting from them, in short, of the non-static system, of the system in motion. Chomsky's arguments, at least in so far as they are directed against the Prague theory, cannot thus be regarded as convincing; they would only be so if the

---

[30]Cf. J. Vachek, "Notes on the Phonological Development of the Modern English Pronoun *she,*" *Sborník Filosofické Fakulty Brno* A 2, 1954, pp. 67–80.

[31]Why the [r]-sound in these other varieties has not become dissimilated is another question which outsteps the limits of the present paper (it can only briefly be noted that the non-American [r] is not a retroflex sound).

Prague group defined language as a static, fixed and immobile system, which is definitely not the case. For this reason, too, one cannot subscribe to the flat refusal of the principle of complementary distribution which, in Chomsky's opinion, "appears to be devoid of any theoretical significance" (*op. cit.*, p. 547 [415]). In reality, that principle remains fundamental for both phonological theory and practice. Even in those instances which it seems incapable of solving satisfactorily, the principle of complementary distribution has major heuristic significance. Its apparent inability to arrive at a clear and strict delimitation of phonemes is, in reality, an invaluable indicator of those points in which the examined language system has been, for this or that particular cause, brought into some kind of motion. To endorse Chomsky's flat refusal of the principle of complementary distribution would, indeed, result in throwing away a most valuable tool of linguistic analysis, a tool enabling the student to identify what appears to be one of the most typical aspects of language, viz., its dynamism and potential variability within the frame of its basic stability—in brief (to use V. Mathesius' felicitous term), its elastic stability.[32] And it should be particularly stressed that this tool enables the student to do so on the phonic level, whose structural relations, examined with the view of ascertaining how the said elastic stability is reflected in them, prove to be most elusive and most difficult to grasp.

VI   Let us note here another case of the lack of structural balance in American English, this time the well-known opposition *bomb* : *balm* (phonologically, /bam/ : /ba·m/), which again was discussed by B. Bloch more than twenty years ago and is again considered by Chomsky. He points out that, in view of the above opposition /a/ : /a·/, the "taxonomist" analyst is forced to evaluate differently the vocalic oppositions [nat] : [na·d] (i.e., *not* — *nod*) on the one hand, and, e.g., [bet] : [be·d] (i.e., *bet* — *bed*) on the other hand. In the former of the two cases the "taxonomist"

analyst is bound to admit the existence of a functional opposition of the phonemes /a/ and /a·/ (established in the language on the basis of the above-mentioned opposition /bam/ : /ba·m/), while in the latter case he will only ascertain the presence of a non-phonological, concomitant variation. It should be noted, that the quantitative difference has the same motivation in both word-pairs: the long vowels got their long quantity under the influence of the following paired voiced consonants. Here Chomsky argues, very aptly, that in his own procedure the phonetic implementations [na·d, be·d] can be derived from the phonological structures /nad, bed/ by using one single rule, stating that a short vowel becomes lengthened when followed by a voiced consonant. On the other hand, the "taxonomist" interpretation, clinging to the principle of biuniqueness, is forced to give different phonological interpretations of the lengths in [a·] and [e·] (which are evaluated phonologically as /a·/ but /e/, respectively), so as to avoid the overlapping of the phonemes /a/ and /a·/. As a consequence of this, Chomsky argues, the "taxonomists" necessarily need two generating rules where his theory can do with a single one. The first of the two rules would only concern the vowel /a/ and would produce a phonological fact, i.e., /a·/; the other rule would concern all other short vowels and produce mere phonetic facts, i.e., lengthened allophones of the original short phoneme. Hence Chomsky concludes that the condition of biuniqueness only complicates grammar, as it prevents it from reaching descriptive adequacy.

If the *bomb* — *balm* case is to be commented upon from Prague positions, it must again be said that here, too, one is faced with another instance in which the American English system of phonemes appears to be in motion. It must again be recalled that history of languages has recorded very many instances in which a phonic difference that was originally irrelevant functionally becomes functionally relevant in some specific environment.[33] After this has happened, the concerned language

---

[32]See V. Mathesius, "O požadavku stability v spisovném jazyce" [On the Postulate of Stability in the Standard Language], in the volume *Spisovná čeština a jazyková kultura* [Standard Czech and Culture of Language] (Praha, 1932), pp. 14–31.

[33]For instances of such "phonemication," see R. Jakobson, "Prinzipien der historischen Phonologie," *TCLP* 4, 1931, pp. 252 ff.; for the French version of the paper, see the Appendix to Cantineau's translation of Trubetzkoy's *Grundzüge*.

finds itself in a situation which again must, from the structural viewpoint, be evaluated as anomalous: alongside of such oppositions as have already turned phonological, there exist phonetically identical oppositions that have not yet been "phonemicized" and still clearly reveal their being exclusively motivated by the phonic environment of the sounds standing in the opposition. In such situations the phonemic system is faced with the problem which calls for some future solution—whether for a consistent phonemicization of the given phonic difference or, possibly, for some phonological revaluation of that difference in those positions in which it had already been "phonemicized." One cannot foretell which course the language is likely to take in the future; all that can be said is that here again the language system proves to be in motion.

Chomsky may be perfectly right in his claim that disregard of the problems of phonological entities sometimes results in simplification of structural descriptions, which, in its turn, may prove useful for some practical purposes (e.g., for the purposes of language teaching in schools). One cannot, however, overlook the fact that some price has to be paid for this: in doing so, one necessarily distorts, at least to a degree, the actual situation in the given language: one unduly simplifies the fine and delicate complexity of the system, the specific feature of which is that it is never static but subject to continuous motion. Even practical language teaching should, at least in rough outlines, do justice to this fact (at least in pointing out archaisms and neologisms). Admittedly, an analyst is fully entitled, for the sake of experiment, to disregard some problems existing in language, but he should be aware of the fact that the problems disregarded have not ceased to exist.

VII The above discussion of some of the typical arguments advanced by Chomsky in criticizing "taxonomic" phonology and its methods has shown that such arguments miss the point, at least as far as the label "taxonomic" phonology is meant to cover the conception and methods of the Prague group. It has been shown that, at least to a degree, Chomsky misinterprets the Prague position by not considering some of Prague basic theses (especially that of language constitut-

ing a system in motion). Undoubtedly, one of the chief causes that have led to this misinterpretation has been Chomsky's inadequate familiarity with the Prague conception of language in general and of its phonic plane in particular.[34] This can be easily understood if one takes into account the difficulties connected with obtaining Prague linguistic publications (most of which, dating from pre-war years, have long been out of print). Incidentally, one can find, at times, that Chomsky does not seem to be quite correctly informed even of the full import of the phonological teachings of some American linguistics. This is shown by another concrete objection adduced by Chomsky in support of his assertion that the principle of complementary distribution appears to be "devoid of any theoretical significance." In the concluding paragraphs of the present paper we want to mention this objection, with our own brief comment.

Following the principles of Z. S. Harris (*Methods in Structural Linguistics*, Chicago, 1951, Chapter 7), Chomsky defines the principle of complementary distribution as follows (p. 546 [414]): "Given a set of representations [i.e., implementations, J. V.] in terms of phones, let us define the distribution $D(x)$ of the phone x as the set of (short-range) phonetic contexts in which x occurs. The relation of complementary distribution holds between phones x and y if $D(x)$ and $D(y)$ have no element in common." Chomsky also defines the concept of the "tentative phoneme," which is said to be "a class of phones related pairwise by the relation of complementary distribution." We will not dwell upon the adverbial "pairwise," overlooking the fact that in very many instances complementary distribution relates in one phoneme three or more allophones. Let us proceed further. The "tentative phonological system" is defined as "a family of tentative phonemes meeting a condition of exhaustiveness."

Starting from these definitions, Chomsky points out that "the class of tentative phonemic systems, as defined, will contain systems that fail the principle of biuniqueness."

[34]Some idea of this conception can now be conveniently obtained from J. Vachek and J. Dubský's *Dictionnaire de linguistique de l'école de Prague*, Utrecht-Anvers, 1960.

Thus, in his opinion, the American English sounds [k] and [a] (corresponding to Southern British [ɔ]) stand in complementary distribution and, besides, "share features shared by nothing else, e.g., in Jakobson's terms, the features Compact, Grave, Lax, Non-Flat." Hence, Chomsky infers "they qualify as a tentative phoneme and there is a tentative phonemic system in which they [= both these sounds, J. V.] are identified as members of the same phoneme /K/." Very naturally, Chomsky finds it very easy to disprove this absurd conclusion, which would obviously lead to the phonological identification of sequences like *Scot* and *socked*. Such identification, however, would not only contradict the principle of biuniqueness (as it would efface the limit separating /k/ from /a/), but also the principle of "local determinacy," urging that the occurrence of this or that allophone of one and the same phoneme is determined by its phonic environment. In addition to this, however, Chomsky draws a surprising conclusion: the principle of complementary distribution provides "neither a necessary nor a sufficient condition for biuniqueness" (p. 547 [415]).

It is clear that the preceding argumentation cannot be found convincing at all. Admittedly, Harris' conception of the tentative phonemes and tentative phonological systems contains some loop-holes, and it might be attacked as it stands. If, however, Harris' conception is combined with that of the Harvard group (by making use of some of the Harvard inventory of distinctive features), one should be on one's guard to do full justice to this latter conception as well. It is obvious that Chomsky's argumentation here misrepresents the Harvard conception of the phoneme as a bundle of distinctive features. If Chomsky had duly observed the Harvard line of argument, he would not have found it feasible to arbitrarily select, from all the distinctive features of /k/ and /a/, exactly the four enumerated above, and to completely overlook at least two others, viz., Vocalic/Non-Consonantal for /a/, and conversely, Consonantal/Non-Vocalic for /k/. The importance of these two features lies in their classificatory capacity: it is they that are primarily resorted to for the purpose of elementary classification of phonemes as wholes. One should carefully note the fact that in the Harvard conception the oppositions of distinctive features are not placed all on the same level but that there exists some hierarchy of these oppositions.

In this hierarchy, the most important place is taken exactly by the two oppositions mentioned above, i.e., vocalic–non-vocalic and consonantal–non-consonantal. That this is indeed so, is clearly evidenced by the treatment of distinctive features found in Jakobson, Fant, and Halle's *Preliminaries* (1952), where distinctive features are classified into fundamental source features (among which one finds exactly the vocalic and consonantal features), further the so-called secondary consonantal features, and finally the resonance features; it is only in this last category that one finds features like compact–diffuse, grave–acute, flat–plain, etc. Besides, the Harvard tables, demonstrating the structures of concrete phonemes as bundles of distinctive features, regularly place the reference to the opposition vocalic–non-vocalic and consonantal–non-consonantal in the top lines of the tables.[35] All this clearly points to one necessity: if the Harvard list of distinctive features is to be employed for the purpose of establishing the tentative phonemes of language, one must respect the hierarchies of these features established by the Harvard scholars. It is certainly not feasible to select, for the purpose of establishing such tentative phonemes, the distinctive features of the lower order without any regard to how the compared phonic phenomena appear if compared with reference to the distinctive features of the higher order. If this maxim is duly borne in mind, no such obviously wrong conclusion can be reached as the one regarding [k] and [a] as allophones of one and the same phoneme.

What, however, should especially be noted is that unsatisfactory results obtained in the establishing of tentative phonological systems are not caused by the principle of complementary distribution but by the wrong application of that principle, which in itself is perfectly sound and most valuable. To sum up,

[35]Also in the list of oppositions of distinctive features in Jakobson and Halle's monograph *Fundamentals of Language* ('s Gravenhage, 1956) the two above-discussed oppositions occupy the first two places.

here, too, Chomsky's arguments against one of the basic principles of "taxonomic" phonology obviously miss the point.

Technical reasons have prevented us to analyze, from the Prague point of view, more than a limited number of arguments advanced by Chomsky against what he calls "taxonomic" phonology. As, however, the analyzed arguments can be denoted as typical of Chomsky's approach to the involved problems, it may be hoped that the thematic limitation has not impaired the validity of the conclusions presented here. It appears that Chomsky's highly original and meritorious approach to phonological problems does not invalidate the essence of Prague phonological theory and practice. Moreover, the Prague approach to the given problems appears to remain superior to that of Chomsky's in one particular aspect which has been surprisingly alien to Chomsky's analysis: in the conception of language as a system whose very essence is dynamic, non-static, and whose continuous motion is always reflected in some irregularities, "fuzzy points" of its structure.

41

ON SOME RECENT CLAIMS
IN PHONOLOGICAL THEORY*
F. W. HOUSEHOLDER, JR.

In 1962, on the occasion of the Ninth International Congress of Linguists, an article by Morris Halle (1962) [37] appeared in the special issue of *Word,* and Noam Chomsky (1964) [39] appeared before a plenary session of the Congress to defend some remarks which had previously been distributed in the *Preprints*.[1] These two papers were perhaps intended as a sort of one-two punch to knock old-fashioned linguistics out of the ring; at any rate, on matters of phonology, their claims and assertions, if all wholly true, would tend to make all phonological work impossible on any known lines (curiously, they fail to reveal their own methods).

It is not usual in a scientific paper to enter evidence of disinterestedness, but since the members of this sect tend to be thin-skinned (this is not true of the founders, as far as I am aware), I will waste a few inches of valuable space. (1) I am not an opponent of generative grammar, never have been, and never will be. Theses directed or influenced by me which show this in various ways include those of Mary Sleator (1958), George Sholes (1958), Ernesto Constantino (1959), Chalao Chaiyaratana (1960), Don Leuschel (1960), Gerd Fraenkel (1961), A. K. Ramanujan (1962), R. L. Gunter (1962), David Reibel (1963),

S. Agesthialingom Pillai (1963). This is also clear in most of my published reviews and articles since 1958; in fact one earlier article (Householder, 1947) is clearly generative if not transformational. (2) I am not an opponent of transformational grammars or of the use of transformational rules; this can be attested by the students who heard my lectures beginning in the summer of 1954 (including one at Michigan to Professor Waldo Sweet's class, and in 1957 at Cornell in a seminar class which included E. Constantino, and again in 1958 at Michigan in the course in Morphemics) as well as by the evidence already cited. I have never quarrelled with Noam Chomsky or Morris Halle in public or in private, and my files will show some friendly correspondence with Chomsky. I am not an opponent of distinctive features; in fact, I first learned about them from a minute study of Trubetzkoy at Columbia in 1939, and a few years later attended two seminars there conducted by Roman Jakobson, whom I continue to respect and admire. The influence of this appears in several of my published reviews and articles as well as in numerous lectures (including those at Cornell in 1957 and Michigan—in a course on Latin phonological structure—in the summer of 1958) and in several of the Ph.D theses already alluded to. So the following discussion can in all fairness be blamed only on my obtuseness or perhaps pique, not on animosity.

Since there are many points to be discussed I will depart somewhat from my usual free-association style and try to impose some organization, taking up first an assortment of purely philosophical points, matters which

[1]Let me add here that I quite agree with a great deal of what both Chomsky and Halle have to say, including, e.g., the importance of ordered rules in phonology. I must here also acknowledge the partial support of the National Science Foundation (Grant GS-108) and the helpful comments of colleagues and students, especially Peter H. Matthews, Andreas Koutsoudas, George M. Landon, George Lakoff and Robert Stockwell. Let no one assume that any of these men agree with anything I say, however.

*Reprinted from *Journal of Linguistics* 1.13–34 (1965) by permission of the author and Cambridge University Press.

one either believes or doubts without justification since they are not capable of proof or disproof, then turn to certain specific claims about phonemes and features made by Chomsky or Halle, and finally consider a few particular details other than those related directly to the above claims.

The most general philosophical tenet involved here, and one upon which various other problems depend, is the famous principle of three adequacies. In the Congress speech these are stated as follows (Chomsky, 1964: 923–924):

(1) A grammar that aims for observational adequacy is concerned merely to give an account of the primary data (e.g., the corpus) . . .
(2) A grammar that aims for descriptive adequacy is concerned to give a correct account of the linguistic intuition of the native speaker . . .
(3) A linguistic theory that aims for explanatory adequacy . . . aims to provide a principled basis, independent of any particular language, for the selection of the descriptively adequate grammar of each language.

As these are expressed here, only number one "observational adequacy" is intelligible (at least to me), and the gratuitous "merely" in that definition shows the animosity which Chomsky feels toward this principle. It is clear from this paragraph and many other passages in this speech that Chomsky feels that "observational adequacy" is completely "uninteresting" (and whatever Chomsky himself may intend by this term, his followers without exception interpret it as meaning "bad," "scientifically unsound," "to be avoided at all costs," etc.). This has the unfortunate effect that mere mistakes of fact, no matter how gross and glaring, tend to be looked upon as trivial, and no votary would admit publicly that he spends any time avoiding them. I am sure Chomsky did not mean to exert such an influence, but it is unquestionable that he does. And here is my plainest philosophical disagreement with Chomsky: I feel that until a given level of "observational adequacy" (combined, of course, with a respectable level of economy, and based on a corpus which has been repeatedly enlarged at specific test points) is reached, it is sheer braggadocio to talk about descriptive ade-

quacy, even if one knew how to discover what a "correct account of the linguistic intuition of the native speaker" is. No doubt Chomsky means "descriptive adequacy" to include "observational adequacy" somehow, but he does not say so, and the result is unquestionably the notion that data are unimportant to the linguist. I find the word "correct" here particularly puzzling, and regard the "linguistic intuition of the native speaker" as extremely valuable heuristically, but too shifty and variable (both from speaker to speaker and from moment to moment) to be of any criterial value.[2] In the account of explanatory adequacy I am distrustful of the definite article "*the* descriptively adequate grammar of each language," which seems to imply that there can be only one. This appears to me an unwarranted assumption, and prima facie unlikely.

The definitions are followed by some examples which make them somewhat clearer; it turns out that observational adequacy means that the grammar gives back the data *and no more*. This is surely not an acceptable goal to any linguist, even though Chomsky ascribes it to (all?) "post-Bloomfieldian" Americans and to "the London School of Firth." It appears also to be impossible to attain in any other manner than by simply reproducing the corpus; since the number of sentences to be excluded as ungrammatical must be infinite, while the corpus is finite, and neither set has a rational structure. The examples for descriptive adequacy show that it means, for phonology, the inclusion of general rules of phoneme combination (or, stated otherwise, eliminates all systematic redundancies, distinguishing them "correctly" from accidental ones; but surely the Firthians were keen on this long before Halle), and for syntax, the inclusion of means for identifying all pairs of structures which have a transformational relationship to each other. This last is fine, and I'm all for it, but I would say it is equally required by econo-

[2]In scientific discourse it seems to be a fact that all arguments based on bare intuition, whether the linguist's or the native speaker's, constitute a hindrance to communication, since there is no way of evaluating conflicting claims. The situation resembles that which arose in phonetics in the thirties, when rival linguists made conflicting claims about what their trained and decisive ears could detect.

my and observational adequacy (in a reasonable sense). The examples for explanatory adequacy (which is primarily a property of a particular linguistic theory, and only secondarily a property of grammars written according to the precepts of that theory), however, do not make matters much clearer to me, except that, in some vague way, a linguistic theory should be able to demonstrate why one grammar is correct and all others incorrect. This, too, strikes me as fine, if it is possible, and if there really is in all cases a demonstrably unique correct grammar. Maybe an old God's truth man like myself ought to believe this, but I am more inclined to the view that two inconsistent and irreconcilable descriptions of a language may each convey some important "intuition" about the language which cannot be conveyed by the other, nor both by any third. I do not think we should assume that there is always one point of vantage from which we can equally well see the front and the back, the inside and the outside, the left and the right. Maybe there is, but I'm against assuming this.

To sum up these points: I believe that a respect for determinable facts is the first duty of the linguist, and that to tie one's hands in advance by assumptions about uniqueness of correct solutions is a mistake. I believe that, whatever Chomsky's actual intentions may be, his remarks about observational adequacy can only lead to disrespect for data, while those about the other adequacies must lead to narrow orthodoxy and a contempt for all who have not been saved, and that neither of these emotional states will contribute much to the progress of linguistics.[3]

The second bit of philosophy I would like to take up comes from Halle's article (1962: 56–57 [381–382]) where it provides the needed basis for a proof that a grammar which contains from two to four times as many symbols as another is "in fact" the more economical. He does not there state the principle explicitly, but I should word it thus:

"No symbol-system may be judged economical unless it is always the case that the more general statement, when expressed in it, is the shorter."

Where Halle got the idea for this principle, I cannot discover. My friends in various other fields (including philosophy of science) have not heard of it, and obvious counterexamples come readily to mind. In arithmetic, for example, a proposition about every odd number is surely more general than one about the number three; yet the former is written "$2n+1$ for integral n" or the like and the latter is "3." "Prime number," to take another very general notion, may be expressed as "$P \neq ab$ for any integral values of a or b > 1." The numbers 3 and 1013 are equally prime, yet differ in length. In Chomsky's sketch (1957: 112) a rule like 16 (the negation transformation) is obviously more general than 12 (the passive transformation), yet requires at least five or six more symbols.

Halle further interprets his principle as meaning that all expressions to be compared for simplicity must contain only symbols of the terminal alphabet, as otherwise his rule (4')

$$/a/ \rightarrow /ae/ \text{ in the env.} \underline{\qquad\qquad} \begin{matrix} /i/ \\ /e/ \\ /ae/ \end{matrix}$$

would normally be written

$$/a/ \rightarrow /ae/ \text{ in the env.} \underline{\qquad\qquad} F$$

or the like, where F is a non-terminal[4] symbol

---

[3]It is interesting, in this connection, to consider the five measures of excellence in grammar recently proposed by I. A. Mel'chuk (1963). The five are "Completeness of Description" (i.e., how nearly does it give *all* the data?); "Adequacy of Description" (*only* the data); "Economy of Description" (small inventory of symbols); "Simplicity of Description" (small number of rules); and "Compactness of Description" (small size of grammar). He adds two modified measures for various reasons, "Calculated Specific Economy" (size of inventory measured in bits) and "Calculated Specific Simplicity" (size of the rules in bits), though I don't quite understand the difference (in practice) between the last measure and the "Compactness" measure. Note that all these are at the observational level of Chom-

sky. It is only fair to mention that many followers believe they in fact have a practical test for explanatory adequacy: (1) if it's not from MIT, it's wrong; (2) of two from MIT, the one O.K.'d by Chomsky or Halle is correct. On many points they must remain in suspense for a time, of course. Nothing ever needs retraction; only exegesis.

[4]Non-terminal only in a pure generative phonology, with rules like V→F,B   F→i,e,æ. Otherwise it is a cover-symbol and would still count as three.

including /i/, /e/, and /ae/, and the rule would be exactly equal to (2′) in number of symbols. But think of the consequences of this interpretation for the rules of syntax, if every instance of N must be counted not as one but as several thousand symbols, for instance! But his statement (57) [382]

It follows, therefore, that if we wish to operate with the simplicity criterion proposed here, we must regard phonological segments as complexes of properties

clearly depends upon these two assumptions, (1) that the more general must always be the shorter, and (2) that the only possible phoneme class-symbols are features or feature-complexes. My own point of view is that both assumptions are improper (one cannot say "false" since they are not falsifiable), and that features and small feature-sets provide one excellent source of class-symbols, but not the only one. But the notation imposed by Halle upon his followers is surely the world's clumsiest, and I cannot conceive a non-linguist who would regard the assertion that (e.g.) rule (3″) on p. 56 [381] was simpler than rule (3′) as anything but an obscure joke. Generality is often useful, and it is indeed easy, using 11 distinctive features, as Halle does for English, to construct 175,099 ($3^{11} - 2^{11}$: 3^{11} being the combinations of the values +, − and "unspecified" for each of 11 features, 2^{11} being the same for the values + and − only, which specify 2048 individual phonemes) different phoneme classes,[5] but the sense in which all this may be considered maximally simple is surely Pickwickian.

The third general point of philosophy raised by both Halle and Chomsky concerns a question which I would regard as one of strategy, but which Halle (at least) seems to make a matter of orthodox faith. The question is simple: "Is it possible, and (if possible) is it wise to put all the structural information there is about a given language into a single set of ordered rules?" My own answer (given in

Householder, 1959 for instance) is that it is neither possible nor wise; their answer is that it is obligatory. I would now tend to add that it is also counter-intuitive to do this.

In that article, I proposed the following types of grammar: (1) The sentence-grammar (in two parts, the first part using "morphemes" or "idioms" as primes—i.e., symbols of the terminal alphabet—and including phrase-structure rules and transformational rules, the second using "phonemes" as primes and converting the output of the first part, by means of rules which again would be largely transformational, from strings of morphemes into strings of phonemes); (2) a phonological grammar, generating grammatical strings of phonemes which might be termed phonological words; (3) a descriptive etymology grammar, generating grammatical words from nameless units derived (mainly) from morphs of the classical languages, differing from the phonological grammar in supplying vague semantic suggestions along with the output words; (4) a phonaesthetic grammar, resembling the last-named except for the character of the output, which consists of words involving sound symbolism. I regard both 3 and 4 as small sub-grammars belonging to a collection (5) containing various other similar sub-grammars for derivation of lexical items (exclusive of a few types which may legitimately, because of their productivity, be included in the main sentence grammar), including the categories customarily dealt with in traditional grammars under the heading of word-formation. I also mentioned the possibility of (6) a verse-grammar or perhaps a verse-forming attachment to the sentence-grammar, and (7) a continuous text-g.ammar, whose output would be dialogues or paragraphs. About these last possibilities Halle and Chomsky are silent, but the grammars 2 and 5 (2, 3, and 4, etc.) are somehow to be included in 1.

Since our announced topic is phonology, I will consider only the incorporation of grammar 2, its motivation and its consequences. The question is sometimes asked this way: "Is phonology independent?" or "Are there two levels of structure in language?" Halle's answer (Chomsky isn't quite so firm on this point) seems to be "No; phonology is wholly dependent on grammar, and there is only one structure." Note that this question has nothing

[5] Of course not all are usable because of co-occurrence restrictions on the features, but about a tenth of them are. The enormous wastefulness of this scheme seems to be due to the effort of simultaneously hugging the phonetic ground and allowing for as much morphophonemics as possible.

whatever to do with the old Pikean heresy, which merely concerned the advantages of knowing the language when choosing between alternative phonemic analyses. Almost everyone seems to be agreed on this matter nowadays. In a way this is the exact converse of the Tragerian attempt to base syntax directly on phonology (this is probably no coincidence, as Tragerian influence on Halle is evident elsewhere), and this resemblance was noted by one of the discussants at the Congress, though the suggestion would probably horrify Trager. Halle believes he has *proved* the unity of grammar with phonology (and, alas, many of his young admirers believe this also). The steps are as follows:

(1) The inevitable grammar must be simple (measured by counting symbols).
(2) To be eligible even to have its symbols counted, more general rules must be shorter than less general. Only feature notation permits this.
(3) Feature notation multiplies the number of symbols in the lexicon by 11 (e.g., from 50,000 to 550,000) so ways of economizing are obligatory.
(4) Elimination of all redundant features in the lexicon and addition of rules to restore them cuts the number of symbols in the lexicon by half (more or less; say 280,000 instead of 550,000).
(5) But these rules for inserting predictable features constitute the morpheme structure rules of a so-called independent phonological grammar.
(6) Therefore phonology cannot be independent.[6]

Since the whole chain of argument depends

[6]Here are Halle's words (1962: 61 [385]): "In attempting to satisfy the simplicity criterion, we are, thus, forced to incorporate into every complete generative grammar a characterization of the distinction between admissible and inadmissible segment sequences. This fact effectively cuts the ground out from under the recent suggestion that generative grammars be supplemented with special phonological grammars."

Peter Matthews suggests that the motivation for step (2) comes from syntactic rules, where it is the case that rules involving early and more general symbols like NP and VP are in fact shorter than rules involving ones which are later and less general.

upon our acceptance of step 2, and since no reasoning or evidence has been offered to support step 2, it is perhaps uninteresting to look at any of the others. I will, however, add a few words about the last two steps. In regard to step 5 one may observe (1) that the addition of *certain* "morph structure rules" cannot be motivated by the considerations Halle drags in, e.g., rules concerning the number of segments in a morph (since this must already be specified in the lexicon); (2) that there will have to be some arbitrary decisions which can be avoided in a separate phonological grammar, where, e.g., feature a in segment A is solidary with feature b in segment B, so that either may be used to predict the other, but for each individual morph one or the other has to be specified. In regard to step 6, it is perhaps essential to say what one means by a statement about the independence of phonology. What Halle means is not at all clear to me; what I mean I have said already (Householder, 1962) but will repeat briefly here. If it is the case that the phonological structure (inventory, distribution, shapes of all individual morphs, morph structure rules, etc.) can be changed completely without altering any of the syntactic structure of a language, then the two are independent. All the evidence so far available indicates that this is actually the case. In fact, it is difficult to imagine how it could be otherwise; suppose that the presence of a direct object in a sentence entails the aspiration of all unaspirated voiceless stops and the deaspiration of all aspirates. Immediately this behavior is no longer phonological, but represents a morpheme of some kind, which could equally well be represented in some other way (say by voicing every third voiceless fricative). The converse is equally true; a given phonological system (inventory, distribution, rules, etc.) can be mated to two quite dissimilar syntactic systems. This, in fact, is the reasonable interpretation of the old slogan about the arbitrariness of the sign. Notice that this has no connection with "grammatical prerequisites," nor with the use of labeled brackets to predict English stress distributions.

It is possible to carry the argument further and suggest that even in the composite grammar phonology does not necessarily follow syntax; perhaps a better picture is of two parallel structures with a final stage of selecting matching pairs, one half from each output. But even if that is not accepted, the mere fact that the phonological rules follow the syntactic rules does not show dependence in the ordinary understanding of the word. Nor does the fact (if it is a fact, and no evidence has yet been offered to make it one) that all the structural specification of a language can be crammed into a grammar which is somehow single and monolithic mean that it is improper or impossible to devote special sub-grammars to individual aspects of structure.[7]

The one remaining philosophical point is a real puzzler (for me, at least), although its antecedents seem to go back to Aristotle. This is the assertion made by Chomsky and Halle that ordinary alphabetic symbols used by a linguist (old-fashioned phonemes or Chomsky's systematic phonemes or phones) are to be regarded as arbitrary ad hoc symbols substituted conventionally for certain complexes of distinctive features, and utterly without status themselves,[8] i.e., belonging neither to the terminal alphabet (the phonological primes, which must now be features only) nor to the non-terminal alphabet (like such symbols as *NP* or *Comp* in the syntactic component). In fact, for Halle at least, all operations in the phonological component are conducted in terms of the terminal alphabet, the features. Chomsky carefully distinguishes two kinds of features: what might be called morphophonemic distinctive features (used, e.g., in the lexicon and up to the last level of rules), on the one hand, and universal international phonetic distinctive features (used in the final output) on the other; and even though most features remain apparently the same from the beginning to end,

this conceals a conventionally omitted set of rules of the form

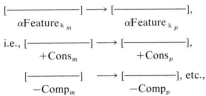

where the subscript m indicates members of the set of morphophonemic features, while p indicates the phonetic set. This is exactly parallel to the old-fashioned mapping of morphophonemes into phonemes, where a set of rules of the form $*p* \longrightarrow /p/$, etc., is understood (in which the double-asterisk notation encloses morphophonemic transcriptions). Now what does it mean to say that symbols like $/p/$ are "mere abbreviations" without "systematic import"? One thing it means, in a marginal sense of the word, is that in symbol-counts to determine simplicity (as proposed by Halle), each instance of $/p/$ will constitute eleven symbols (or possibly six, if redundancies are omitted), whereas each instance of [− continuant] will, of course, count as one, as will [~α continuant] (read: "the feature 'continuant' takes the opposite value to one which occurs somewhere nearby, being plus if there it is minus and minus if there plus"). But this is "meaning" in the sense of justification or motive. Is it or is it not the same as saying, "Every time I speak of a 'pencil' this is to be understood as a mere abbreviation for the collection of properties 'useful for writing,' 'containing a slim rod of graphite,' 'stick-like in shape,' 'easily held in the fingers,' 'approximately 3−9 inches long,' 'a quarter-inch or so in diameter,' etc.?" This seems to take us back to Aristotle's *Categories* and the difference between substance and all the other categories (see, e.g., *Cat.* 2a−2b). This difference amounts, in the main, to the fact that substance is expressed by concrete nouns, while all the rest are either adjectives, verb-forms, phrases, or at any rate abstract nouns. Primary substance, in which the difference is most absolute, means names, proper nouns (in general). The question then is, can substance be dispensed with? Or rather, perhaps, *should* substance be dispensed with? Are all names covert descriptions? Can a thing be distinguished from the totality of its properties? A

---

[7]Halle's is not the only way to incorporate the complete phonological grammar into a sentence-grammar; a more obvious place is in a series of rules of the form Name$_k \rightarrow$———, where the only constraints on the right-hand side are phonological. The subscript (k) indicates that this is true of many different classes of names—personal, geographical, mathematical, names of English words [see Lackowski (1963) and Hiorth (1963), though they don't fully seem to understand what they're talking about], names of non-English words rendered with an English accent, etc.

[8]Halle (1962: 56 [381], fn. 2), "unofficial circumlocutions . . . lacking all systematic import." Chomsky (1964: 945 [401]), "mere conventional abbreviations."

phoneme is a thing, in this sense, while a feature is a property or set (class, group in a non-
technical sense) of things.[9] Is there behind this
decision of Halle and Chomsky a general
philosophical principle to regard all "thing"
words as illegitimate abbreviations for descriptions in terms of "property" words? If so, I
would greatly appreciate an exposition of the
principle, and a justification of it.[10] I am familiar with an exactly opposite contention (though
I do not subscribe to it myself), according to
which *only* thing-words are legitimate, while
property-words and other class names are
purely utilitarian abbreviations. From this
viewpoint (which certainly has much to justify
it) an instance of /p/ is real, whereas "voicelessness" is a conventional name for the class
ptkfθssč and cannot occur except in so far as
one of its class members occurs. Similarly,
"nasality" *means* [m, n, ŋ] and "labiality"
means [p, b, f, v, m]. From this point of view
it's as preposterous to say that only features
have status, while phonemes are merely conventional abbreviations, as it would be (if all
the men in Bloomington could be uniquely
specified by the organizations to which they
belonged) to say that only the club-member-
ships are real, and the individual men are
merely conventional abbreviations.

The nearest thing I have yet come upon
to a situation where this notion might apply

[9]Two quotations from Quine (1953) are apposite here:
107: "Now what sets attributes apart from classes
is merely that whereas classes are identical when
they have the same members, attributes may be distinct even though present in all and only the same
things."
156: "Attributes, as remarked earlier, are individ-
uated by this principle: two open sentences which
determine the same class do not determine the same
attribute unless they are analytically equivalent."
I might say here that I feel a lot happier with classes
than I do with attributes (and I think Quine does
too). But if a feature is a class of phonemes and a
phoneme is a bundle of features, we seem to be
caught in an odd sort of circle. George Lakoff feels
that all general scientific statements are about attributes rather than entities or substances, and hence
linguistics should choose a language in which only
attributes may be named.
[10]In the realm of epistemology a somewhat
similar view has been upheld especially by a number of English philosophers from Berkeley and

with some theoretical validity is the case of the
sub-atomic particles.[11] All these particles appear to share certain properties such as position, motion, acceleration, etc., but to differ in
mass, charge, baryon number, isotopic spin,
spin angular momentum, etc.; and when these
quantities have been fully specified, nothing
more remains to be said about any particle.
The authors of the cited article do not make
any such proposal, of course, but it would truly
appear possible to argue that there are not
really any such "things" as pi mesons, muons,
protons, etc., but only more or less transient
bundles of the aforesaid properties, and that
the numerous decay and transmutation phenomena are really just spatial reshufflings of
the properties. Such a way of considering the
matter may perhaps be fruitful; we must leave
that decision to the physicists. Returning to
linguistics, it is interesting to note the differing extents to which followers make use of
these conventional abbreviations. Chomsky
seems to use them nearly all the time; many
unpublished pieces of work emanating from
the group use them quite frequently (after all,
they are much more economical of printer's
ink and space as well as easier to understand),
whereas Halle avoids them as much as possible, and tries to use matrix notation exclusively.[12] It is perhaps curious that no one has
yet been able to devise a notation in which one
Halle-count symbol can be represented by a
single mark on the page. A binary numerical
notation (writing, say 01001100100 for /p/
and 10000010010 for /e/), where a fixed order
is used for the features, a zero for minus values
and a one for plus, has certain advantages but
requires abandonment of the strictly binary
claim since every place must be occupied by
something, and if it cannot be zero or one, it
must be (say) x for redundant, y for unspecified, α for harmonizing, ᾱ for anti-harmonic,
and we end up with 6 possible values instead
of two. It would, further, place a considerable

Hume to Russell; we do not perceive and cannot
know "things" but only "properties."
[11]My information here comes mainly from
Chew, Gell-Mann, and Rosenfeld (1964).
[12]It is, however, a baseless rumor that he intends to found a linguistic periodical (*Le Maître
Distinctif*) in which all the contributions must be
written in this notation.

burden on the memory and the attention. So the status-less conventional abbreviations continue to be used even though a considerable gain in economy would result if they were granted the status of non-terminal symbols. Assume a lexicon of 50,000 morphs averaging 5 phonemes in length, total 250,000 symbols, plus the 300 or so needed for rules rewriting phonemes into features; in distinctive features, using an average of 4 features per phoneme (which is probably on the low side; 5 or 6 is more likely) this means a total of 1,000,000 symbols. Some saving in physical bulk can of course be achieved by actually writing all the rules with phonemes and convenient arbitrary morphophonemes, but pretending all the while that you are really (in some metaphysical sense) using feature matrices.

If it were a matter of only 4 or 5 genuinely binary features, some notation with letters (e.g., C and V) plus assorted diacritics could be managed; but with eleven features, each of which must be capable of being assigned one of 4 values, it becomes impossible. (The eleven can easily be reduced to seven, by the way.)

So I must give up the attempt; I can see neither any philosophical justification for regarding "phonemes" as status-less abbreviations, nor the motive for desiring such a principle, but I can see many reasons for not desiring it, from the viewpoints of ease of use, clarity, and effective economy.

Let us take a brief further look at the morphophonemic use of features, and at other ways of writing morphophonemic rules and of eliminating redundancies in morph structure. (For convenience I will throughout use morphophonemic in the broad sense, to include both "phonotactic" rules in general and strictly morphophonemic rules as well.) The symbols that are needed here are those indicating classes of phonemes which co-occur, do not co-occur, commute, condition various changes, condition resistance to various changes, and so on. As many people have remarked (including Çhomsky) many of these classes are "natural" classes, sharing some phonetic feature or features. Consequently, it is often easy to specify such classes in terms of Jakobsonian features. Sometimes it is not so easy, however. Chomsky (1964: 948 [404], rule 20,i) wants to rewrite k or t as s before i

or y. Unfortunately, k is opposed to t in both compactness and gravity (in the analysis Halle and Chomsky were following two years ago), so that in order to include k and t but exclude p, a disjunctive class is needed:

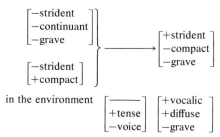

in the environment

This certainly seems clumsy, as well as difficult to understand, even though I have tried to make use of all available redundancies. In some cases the necessity for disjunctive classes can be eliminated by discreet extrapolation. Consider, for instance, the familiar rule that in Latin a long vowel is shortened before final m, t, l and r. This would require a threefold disjunction to state in this form; but if one extends the rule to cover all phonemes except s and f (and counterinstances are either nonexistent or easily listable), then it's not hard at all:

$+$length $-$length

in the environment ——————— ~ $\begin{bmatrix} +\text{Continuant} \\ -\text{Nasal} \end{bmatrix}$ #

Even this would be difficult without the use of the negation sign, however. The implied inclusion of vowels here does no harm because shortening also takes place before vowels, whether final or non-final, with a few special exceptions.

The extent to which unavoidable disjunctive (in Jakobsonian features) classes will be needed in the phonological rules varies, of course, from one language to another. A rapid check of Sanskrit sandhi rules indicates about 5 (out of some 25 or so) classes of this sort; one set of rules for Latin nouns requires 4 out of 10. In most cases this could be avoided by a willingness to abandon Jakobsonian features, but (though a few daring souls may *add* an extra feature to the "systematic phonemic" set) no one seems to be anxious to construct features from scratch for each language, specifically to be maximally useful in the description of that language. There is a kind of orthodoxy which no one dares violate because no one understands the reasons behind it. We noted above that an 11-feature system allows the specification of 175,099 different classes of phonemes, if fully utilized. It does seem awkward that 4 of the 10 classes needed for a specific segment of a grammar are nowhere to be found among those 175,099. Purely ad hoc phoneme classes in the traditional manner would seem, superficially at least, to be more efficient. We could say: "For the purposes of these rules 'i, e, æ' constitutes a single non-terminal symbol, representing the class whose members are i, e, and æ," if we wish to avoid the unnecessary nuisance of creating special symbols to be used only once or twice for very small classes. This is certainly handy for such classes as English "i, æ, ʌ, a" (the vowels which are grammatical before [ŋ]), where the feature specification is:

$$\left\{ \begin{array}{l} \begin{bmatrix} -\text{consonantal} \\ +\text{compact} \end{bmatrix} \\ \begin{bmatrix} +\text{diffuse} \\ -\text{grave} \end{bmatrix} \end{array} \right\}$$

One criticism leveled against distinctive feature analysis is that it treats as equal things which are equal and things which are unequal alike. In other words, many linguists are willing to grant a feature-like nature to "voicing" or "nasality" or "interruptedness," but consider that (e.g.) consonants and vowels are entities rather than features. Instead of a binary distinction between units and prosodies or between segments and components, MIT linguistics seems to suggest a hierarchy of features, with "vocalicness," "consonantality," and "stridency" near the top, but "flatness," "voicing," and "tenseness" (e.g.) near the bottom. I have heard it suggested that there is some non-arbitrary basis for this ranking, but have never learned what it is (the question "to how many phonemes is the feature relevant?" is obviously not a question of fact, but of definition, and is, besides, often indecisive). The psychological motivation, however, is obvious; a sneaking feeling (or "intuition") that some things are more independently variable than others. It is certainly fairly easy (physiologically speaking) to vary the values of "nasality," "voicing," "flatness" (i.e., lip-rounding), and

in some measure "tenseness" and "continuancy," while holding everything else constant, and these are precisely the features ranked near the bottom of the (inverted) "tree." It is clearly impossible (except in rare instances) to accomplish such a feat with "vocalicity," "consonantality," "stridency," "compactness," "diffuseness," or "gravity." From this point of view, too, a dichotomy seems more realistic than a hierarchy. The question is academic, however, since rank in the hierarchy appears to perform no function in an actual set of phonological rules. The elimination of redundancy which makes Halle so happy (1962: 58 [383]) when he shows the theoretical necessity of spelling *dog*

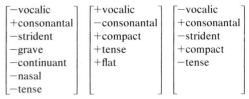

using only 17 symbols (by his reckoning) instead of

with 33, involves all features but the top two and tenseness. The spelling /dɔg/, one should remember, also counts as 17 (or perhaps 33?), since each letter is a conventional notation for the corresponding set of features. The elimination of redundancy achieved in other cases (e.g., vowel-harmony languages) is similar to or identical with that accomplished by prosodic analysis. For the vowels, at any rate, "gravity" (i.e., front vs. back), "diffuseness" (high vs. non-high) and "compactness" (low vs. non-low) are almost as subject to voluntary control as nasality and voicing, suggesting perhaps a trichotomy of features for vowels as against the dichotomy evidently presented in consonants.

Let us turn now to the big shocker in

Chomsky's paper (1964) [39], the assault on complementarity. Two quotations will suffice:

The definition of a phoneme as . . . "a class of phones in free variation or complementary distribution" . . . can be maintained only if we are willing to tolerate . . . absurdities. (1964: 959 [412])

Since it provides neither a necessary nor a sufficient condition for biuniqueness, and, apparently, has no motivation except for its connection with biuniqueness, the principle of complementary distribution appears to be devoid of any theoretical significance. (1964: 963 [415])

This is, of course, part of a general attack on *all* the defining characteristics of the conventional phoneme, which Chomsky lists (p. 953 [407]) as: (1) linearity (by which Chomsky means that the mapping of phonemes onto phones has to be exhaustive and order-preserving); (2) invariance (either absolute, i.e., without partial overlapping, or relative, with some permissible partial overlapping); (3) biuniqueness (that the mapping of phonemes onto phones be unique and reversible, i.e., you don't need to know the language to transcribe correctly); and (4) local determinacy (Chomsky says so little about this that I can't quite make out how this differs from linearity or perhaps a combination of linearity with biuniqueness). As we have seen, he does not treat complementary distribution separately, but as a technique for achieving biuniqueness. The form in which he states the principle (1964: 962 [414]) is adapted from Harris, and would perhaps not be universally accepted; certainly the link Chomsky makes with biuniqueness is quite puzzling to me. I should find the motivation for complementary distribution rather in the goal of adequacy—observational adequacy plus "descriptive adequacy" (which is mainly "native speaker's reaction")—with a major second goal of economy. Let me state the principle of complementary distribution (which is merely the principle of phonological opposition or contrast looked at negatively) as I understand it. "If two phonetically distinct segments (of any reasonable length) are not everywhere in free variation or complementary distribution, they cannot be phonemically the same." That is, if the sequence XAY contrasts with the se-

quence XBY, then XAY and XBY cannot be represented by the same sequence of phonemes. This is the principle of complementary distribution as ordinarily understood. Even as stated here, this principle would exclude Chomsky's most amusing example, the complementarity of [k] and [a], since the sequence in "Scot" does contrast with that in "socked,"[13] and makes unnecessary the Trubetzkoy provision which Chomsky finds arbitrary and ad hoc. This I would state as follows: "If a sequence of two segments contrasts with either of the two segments separately or with the two in reverse order, then they contrast with each other." I.e., [AB] may contrast with [BA], or [B] or [A], and all these are instances of a B vs. A contrast.

This rule will not take care of the Pleistonesian case which I once cited (Householder 1952: 262), where [ka] can quite easily be [kk], unless a zeroing rule is applied first: "If no single phone contrasts with zero in any environment, one of the phones must be counted as phonetic (or 'tentative phonemic') zero before any other steps of phonemicizing are taken." After this has been done, [ka] will either contrast with /k/ or with /a/ or else will be represented as /k/ or as /a/. The rule may extend to two phones if they never contrast or occur in sequence (e.g., a language may have both a predictable schwa and a predictable glottal stop). All this does not seem as narrowly ad hoc to me as it does to Chomsky, and is closely related to another familiar rule: "If [XABY] is much more frequent than [XAY] or [XBY] for all values of X and Y, then the advantages of treating AB as a unit phoneme should be considered."

The other "ad hoc" rule of Trubetzkoy's objected to by Chomsky is worth mentioning here, though Chomsky regards it as concerned with "linearity" rather than complementarity directly. This is the rule for "diphonematic interpretation" of single segments, which I will state as follows: "If, after tentative phonemicization has been completed, there is a single tentative phoneme C of limited distribution, in complementary distribution with a sequence AB, and if at least some speakers are

---

[13]As a matter of fact my dialect seems to have a minimal pair in *chaos* as opposed to *cakes,* but this is not relevant to Chomsky's point.

found who tend to substitute AB for C on some occasions, and if the rephonemicization of C as AB will regularize the distribution of A or B or both, then C may be regarded as a realization of AB." Regularizing the distribution of a phoneme is understood to mean making it more like that of other phonemes belonging to the same general distributional class (in feature terms, sharing such features as the vocalic and consonantal, and among vowels as many features as possible; sets like [m, n, r, l, w, y] are rather awkward to specify, however). This is indeed a rather elaborate procedure, but something like it seems to be necessary, even if (like Chomsky) we are unwilling to make it explicit. The wording I have given evades Chomsky's counterexamples, but others could (no doubt) be devised.

Many of Chomsky's arguments imply the existence of some solid basis for phonetic identity which is unknown to me. For instance (1964: 962 [414]) he discusses the assumed overlapping allophones of /t/ and /r/ in *throw* and *Betty* as if he had some way of knowing that the flaps were identical (possibly he simply accepts this from Bloch); I should say that they must be invariably different enough so that the linguist should have no qualms about choosing to regard them as different phones in the first place. As a matter of fact, the same is obviously true of the [k]'s in *Scot* and *socked*. I have never yet seen a good example of phonemic overlap where this escape route was not open. Of course, if the phonetic identification is restricted to a small number of distinctive features specified in advance, some of these escapes may be blocked, but contrariwise some of the nice points of advanced rules written by Chomsky are excluded at the same time. He wants to describe a dialect in which the sole difference between *writer* and *rider* lies in the portion immediately after the initial r: [rayDɨr] and [ra·yDɨr].[14] The question here is, what kind of length is represented? If it is instrumentally measured length, i.e., if it is the case that *all* instances of *writer* spoken so as to be accurately distinguished from instances of *rider* by a speaker of this dialect have an [a] segment which is measurably

shorter, and nothing else different, why this is obviously nonsense. There may be an *average* difference (if so, it would be something of the order of 6 cs. for the short one to 6.2 cs. for the long one), but this is irrelevant here. If it is perceptible distinctive length, like that found in some dialects between (say) *Pa'd* and *pod,* then we have an oddity in our "descriptive adequacy," that the same speakers perceive a difference in two inconsistent ways. But obviously no speaker *does* perceive it as length. If we revert now to instrumental measurements, I can tell you from experience that you will, if the words are in fact consistently distinguished, invariably find one or more of several other differences: the flap in *writer* may differ in length from that in *rider* (it would be longer in my speech: 2.5–3.0 cs. as against 1.5–2.0, more or less); the second syllable of *rider* may be longer than in *writer* (14 cs. or so to 10 cs. or so in fairly rapid speech); the rate of change of F[1] or F[2] may be more gradual in *writer* than in *rider;* the quality of the first parts of the diphthongs may differ; the drop in amplitude for the flap in *writer* may be greater than for the one in *rider;* and so on. And, incidentally, how does Chomsky know where to draw the line between the [a] and the [y] for his length measurements? It was exactly this morass of phonetic hair-splitting that the phonemic principle was intended to extricate us from long ago; and it was to some extent successful. Let's not voluntarily throw ourselves back in. I should be inclined, therefore, to stick by my position (Householder, 1959, 1961) that the terminal alphabet of the phonological grammar (*and* of the phonological "component" of a sentence grammar) should be, in the main, phonemic, including (at the most) only such allophones as are distinguished by the native speaker (and isn't that "descriptive adequacy"?), but not the fine phonetic distinctions required for exact international communication. Chomsky is by no means clear (and Halle says nothing at all) about how fine he intends this phonetic specification to be, but at least some of his examples clearly are below the level of Jakobsonian features and also below the perceptible level (as to localization, at any rate). Halle (1962: 71 [392]) achieves the remarkable position of specifying distinctions which are present (apparently) only in the brains of speakers: "/a/ and /æ/

14(Chomsky, 1964: 950, 956 [405, 410]). Halle uses a similar example in which the difference is qualitative (1962: 63 [386]), [a] vs. [ɑ]. This is more realistic.

remained distinct entities [sc. for several generations] even though every /a/ was actualized phonetically as /æ/." But this presumably belongs to the "systematic phonemic" rather than the "systematic phonetic" level.

Let us examine these two levels a bit more. In *Primes* (Householder, 1959: 238–239) I said that we wanted among our phonological primes (1) features, such as voicing; (2) cases where two primes had the same phonetic mapping; (3) archiphoneme-like units; (4) prosodies and intonation-units. Here I may have been lumping together terminal and nonterminal symbols, though there are perhaps occasions where "voice" or "voicelessness" is a useful terminal symbol; I specifically excluded some non-terminal symbols (e.g., the F in some systems which represents an /f/ alternating with a /v/ as in /wayF/ 'wife' as opposed to the ordinary /f/ of the noun *safe* or the /v/ of *brave*) as having no place in an independent phonological grammar, but only in the phonological component of a sentence-grammar. Do terminal symbols of the kind I had in mind correspond to Chomsky's s. phonemic level or to his s. phonetic level or to neither? He examines (1964: 947–953 [403–408]) the question whether there is any significant level between the two and comes to the conclusion that there is none. I think (judging from his examples) that he is wrong; at least he clearly has two kinds of rules (and possibly two kinds of symbols), one designed to account for the non-productive alternations enshrined in our Latin loans (and, no doubt, a few similarly dead relations in the native vocabulary, linking say *mould* to *mildew* or *wake* to *watch*), which are morphophonemic in the narrower sense which I called irrelevant in a phonological grammar, and others intended to handle living or at worst moribund phenomena like vowel reduction and accent demotion. In all cases the Latin rules precede the properly English ones; consequently, an intermediate level might very easily be defined at the conclusion of the first set of rules. This would, in fact, correspond very closely to the representation which I had in mind as the final one of a phonological grammar, with a few obvious exceptions. For example, Chomsky introduces all words of Latin origin whose spelling begins with *de-* in a systematic phonemic shape beginning with /dī/, even those whose first syllable is never stressed, like *decide, delight* and their derivatives. He does this, I presume, on the ground that there is a morpheme boundary after the *de-* (which is a prefix, not a stem), which will enable him to predict stress on the stem and eventual reduction of the /dī/ to /dɨ/. I relegated such facts as these (Householder, 1959: 237) to a special idiom grammar, rather than recognize a host of unusable morphemes, and in the lists of my sentence grammar would introduce *decide* as a single morph /d'sayd/ or /dsayd/, containing only one vowel to begin with. The prediction of phonetic [ɨ] in such cases would be in terms of consonant sequences or the symbol /'/, and would be subphonemic, that is would belong to that layer of fine phonetic specification to which there is no end. Clearly Chomsky's systematic phonetic level is also intended to avoid some fine detail, and as it includes no morphophonemic notations, it seems to be the closest thing to my phonemic level. This also seems to be indicated by the inventories and decision-trees of phonemes (?) with their feature specifications which appear to emanate from Chomsky and Halle.[15] But these lists do not seem to include some of the terminal symbols used by Chomsky, e.g., [D], ['], [ɨ]; nor, on the other hand, do they include some of the "systematic phonemic" symbols that would seem to be needed to distinguish, e.g., those k's and t's which undergo rule 20 (Chomsky, 1964: 948 [404]) as in *democrat-democracy* or *opaque-opacity* from those which do not, as in *racket-rackety* or *monarch-monarchy,* or the unchanging f's and v's in nouns from the f's that become v's in the plural. No doubt careful ordering of rules can save some trouble, but unless the vocabulary is going to be interspersed among the rules (and the last report my spies could give me was that the lexicon is still way back at the end of the phrase-structure) some such morphophonemes (and morphophonemic fea-

---

[15]The inventory for English seems to include h, d, t, n, ð, θ, b, p, m, g, k, s, z, f, v, č, j, š, ž, e, ē, o, ō, i, ī, u, ū, æ, ǣ, a(=ə), ā, ɔ, ɔ̄, l, r. Some lists add y, w. Possibly details of this analysis are open to discussion; at any rate there are some obvious inadequacies. Why, for instance, is the lax vowel of *but* matched with the tense one of *balm* instead of *boat,* in view of Miller (1956), which shows clearly that *hud* matches *head* as *hoed* matches *hayed,* or *hood* matches *hid?*

tures) are going to be needed. So if Bloch's phonemes or my phonemes won't fit in between Chomsky's first rules (in systematic phonemic notation) and his last ones (in systematic phonetics), where do Halle's "phonemes" fit?

The trees and inventories raise another interesting question. Presumably they are not legitimate parts of the one and only complete monolithic grammar; how, then, can a brother linguist find them in the grammar? If you check through all the items in the lexicon, you can eventually compile a list of all the feature-combinations to be found there, but this does not seem very systematic. Similarly, by inspecting all the right-hand sides of rules not altered by later rules (and determining which ones these are is not always easy) one could eventually compile a list of all the terminal feature combinations. But this, of course, is only a part of the phonological information that has no motivated place in the Grammar; information on canonical stem-shapes or syllable-types is similarly concealed or missing. This is aside from the various sorts of statistical information which all hands are ready to exclude from the grammar or grammars in the narrow sense.

Another interesting question is raised by Chomsky's remark (1964: 964 [416]) "It is certainly conceivable that there exist procedures of some sort that facilitate the task of selecting this level of representation, but they are not known today." ("This level" here means the level of systematic phonemics, which Chomsky seems to prefer to compare with traditional phonemics.) How do the MIT school arrive at (a) a set of phonemes (by whatever name they may be called) and (b) a set of features? I mean, how theoretically? In practice, of course, the procedure is simple; one makes a phonemic analysis in the old-fashioned way, making stout use of complementary distribution ("devoid of significance" though it be) and the commutation test ("of only marginal interest"; Chomsky, 1964: 957), and then one looks around for some similar phoneme system which has received a canonical feature analysis and follows it as closely as possible, checking against one or two other officially approved analyses. If /D/ is then to be distinguished from /d/ in the terminal alphabet, it must be by means of the available features,

which in this case limits the choice to stridency, compactness, diffuseness (but there may be a strict ukase forbidding diffuseness to be used for consonants), gravity, or flatness.[16] For if extra features must be called in *both* at the systematic phonetic level *and* at the systematic phonemic level (the only place I have seen them used in documents emanating from MIT), to what level does the analysis belong which is implied in Halle's article (1962) [37]? I think it must be taken to be the systematic phonetic level, and certainly that appears to be the one which corresponds best to my phonemic level (from which true morphophonemes are excluded). The main dispute between Halle and Chomsky, then, appears to concern the amount of detail which is to be included in that level; Halle wants only details which can be specified with the official features, while Chomsky wants more (but we don't know how much more; evidently less than a traditional Finno-Ugric transcription would have). What principles lead one to stop adding more detail? We are not told.

Let us sum up. Halle (1962) [37] appears to offer a demonstration that feature matrix notation is more economical than phonemic notation. This is seen to be clearly false; it undoubtedly has many advantages and merits, but economy is not one of them. One advantage seems to be the ability to provide convenient symbols for phoneme classes. Unfortunately, though it readily provides thousands of such symbols, most of them are quite useless, and (for many languages) important classes are not constructible except by disjunction, a very awkward device in using matrices. The claim is also made that economy will require the incorporation of a complete morpheme-structure grammar into the phonological component of a sentence grammar. Since the economy achieved by doing this does not begin to approach the economy of phonemic notation in the lexicon, and since, furthermore, certain rules of morpheme structure are unmotivated in such a context, this claim must be rejected. Since this is also the argument designed to prove that linguistic

---

[16]One may also increase the number of values for any given feature, distinguishing [D] from [d] by differing plus values of (e.g.) "interrupted" or "voiced" or "lax."

structure is monolithic, we may safely go on believing that phonology has a structure which is independent of the syntactic structure of a language. Chomsky (1964) [39] lends his weight to the entire programme offered by Halle and then attempts to show that there are no reasonable motives or methods for phonemic analysis. Again our verdict must be that he has failed to make his case, though many individual points are sound. We conclude that something very like traditional phonemes must continue to be part, at least, of the terminal alphabet of the phonological grammar, even if something like a few phonetic distinctive features or Firthian prosodies are also included.

Chomsky's distinction between the morphophonemic or "systematic phonemic" level, where only distribution is relevant and phonetic substance does not exist, and the phonemic or "systematic phonetic" level, where phonetic substance is relevant, is of course sound and should not be forgotten, though Halle seems to overlook it entirely. Finally, the utility of some sort of internationally accepted inventory of phonetic features to help in comparing phonological structures and statements of changes in structure cannot be denied, but the existence of at least two and perhaps three distinct categories or types of features must not be forgotten. I do not say that it is impossible to write grammars as Halle wants to do them, nor that it is scientifically wrong to do so; but I do say that there are other ways which are in some respects preferable. Let us not block the path of inquiry.[17]

REFERENCES

CHEW, G. F., GELL-MANN, M., and ROSENFELD, A. H. (1964). "Strongly Interacting Particles," *Scientific American*, February 1964. 74–93.

CHOMSKY, N. (1957). *Syntactic Structures.* (Janua Linguarum, No. 4.) 's-Gravenhage: Mouton.

CHOMSKY, N. (1964). "The Logical Basis of Linguistic Theory," *Proceedings of the Ninth International Congress of Linguists.* The Hague: Mouton 914–1008. [See here article 39—VBM.]

HALLE, M. (1962). "Phonology in Generative Grammar," *Word* 18.54–72. [37]

HIORTH, F. (1963). "Hypostasis," *Lingua* 12.211–216.

HOUSEHOLDER, F. W. (1947). "Descriptive Analysis of Latin Declension," *Word* 3.48–58.

---

[17]After this article was entirely written and had been submitted, I had the privilege of listening to Chomsky's exposition of some of the points discussed in this paper. (1) Chomsky (if I understand him) believes that the only reasonable motivation for the study of linguistics is the desire to know how it is that all children develop essentially the same built-in grammar from different but relatively small collections of utterances. This sameness, he believes, can only be explained as the result of a neurological evaluation procedure. Some earlier discussions of the evaluation of grammars is therefore irrelevant, since the goal is not to determine the best grammar of a language, but the precise one internalized by the native speaker. This bears mainly on my discussion of explanatory adequacy. I confess to being almost as much in the dark as ever; I realize that Chomsky regards this argument as crystal clear and quite unanswerable, but I find many things to doubt and little to agree with here. (2) The distinctive feature counting method proposed by Halle is such a simple and obvious evaluation procedure (for phonology) that it must be the precise one built into us. Phonemes as units cannot be taken seriously because they have no built-in evaluation procedure. This argument again seems to me a little question-begging. For instance, if only phonemes were countable entities (class-symbols being mere conventional abbreviations), then the measure $\Sigma \frac{1}{n}$—i.e., the reciprocals of the numbers of phoneme-symbols in each rule—should give substantially the same rank-order as Halle's method. It also seems to me perfectly possible to apply Halle's evaluation procedure without alleging that only features exist. It should be pointed out here, however, that the question of the relative economy of features and phonemes was not discussed by Halle; many people incorrectly assume that Halle claims to have proved feature notation to be more economical than phoneme notation (and it must be admitted that Halle sounds at first reading as if he were saying just that). The criterion of evaluativeness takes precedence over the criterion of simplicity or economy.

Though Chomsky vehemently rejects the charge of dogmatism, it remains a fact that he *knows* certain things for sure that I do not know and appear incapable of learning; this knowledge enables him to say what linguists must do to remain linguists (or become linguists). I am almost the opposite; I do not believe I know very much or that it is possible to know very much. My chief preachment is always to say "X may be described as Y" rather than "X is Y." If there are unique correct descriptions of languages, I do not believe we can hope to approximate them for any given language within our life-times, and should strive meantime to give the best descriptions we can by whatever standards we can find; Chomsky seems to believe that we already know much of the truth and should find the rest very shortly, after which linguists can go out of business.

HOUSEHOLDER, F. W. (1952). Review of Harris's *Methods in Structural Linguistics. IJAL* 18. 260–268.

HOUSEHOLDER, F. W. (1959). "On Linguistic Primes," *Word* 15.231–239.

HOUSEHOLDER, F. W. (1961). "On Linguistic Terms," in *Psycholinguistics, A Book of Readings.* Edited by Sol Saporta, 15–25. New York: Holt, Rinehart and Winston.

HOUSEHOLDER, F. W. (1962). "On the Uniqueness of Semantic Mapping," *Word* 18.173–185.

LACKOWSKI, P. (1963). "Words as Grammatical Primes," *Language* 39.211–215.

MEL'CHUK, I. A. (1963). "On the Standard Form and Quantitative Characteristics of Several Linguistic Descriptions," *Foreign Developments in Machine Translation and Information Processing.* No. 120. Translated from *Voprosy Jazykoznanija* No. 1, 1963, 113–123. This translation is available from the Superintendent of Documents, U.S. G.P.O., Washington 25, D.C.

MILLER, G. A. (1956). "The Perception of Speech," *For Roman Jakobson.* The Hague: Mouton. 353–360.

QUINE, W. V. O. (1953). *From a Logical Point of View.* Cambridge, Mass.: Harvard University Press.

42

SOME CONTROVERSIAL QUESTIONS IN PHONOLOGICAL THEORY*
NOAM CHOMSKY and MORRIS HALLE

In the first issue of this journal, Fred W. Householder discussed two papers of ours[1] which he found defective in various respects. We feel that the issues involved are important and deserve the fullest clarification. We will therefore discuss Householder's objections and the underlying issues in some detail, re-iterating points that have been made in the aforementioned papers and elsewhere and making no attempt to avoid redundancy if this can contribute to clarity.

In the two papers under discussion, we were concerned with the phonological component of a generative grammar. A generative grammar contains a system of rules that assign structural descriptions to the sentences of a particular language and thereby express a fundamental aspect of what the speaker of this language knows. The phonological component of a generative grammar relates the phonetic representation of an utterance to its syntactic structure. This syntactic structure consists of a string of formatives (minimal syntactically functioning elements) with a Phrase-marker determining the Immediate Constituent structure (the labeled bracketing) of this string. Applying the rules of the phonological component to a syntactic structure in a fixed and predetermined order, we derive the phonetic representation corresponding to this structure. In studying the organization and functioning of this system of rules, we found that we were able to isolate two levels of representation, corresponding to what Sapir called phonological and phonetic representation. We suggested the names *systematic phonemic* and *systematic phonetic* for these levels of representation. The systematic phonemic representation includes in addition to purely phonological elements also information about the morphological and syntactic structure of the utterance. The rules that relate the systematic phonemic representation to sound are *transformational* in that they take into account the

This work was supported in part by the Joint Services Electronics Program under Contract DA36-039-AMC-03200(E); in part by the National Science Foundation (Grant GP-2495), the National Institutes of Health (Grant MH-04737-05), the National Aeronautics and Space Administration (Grant NsG-496), and the U.S. Air Force (ESD Contract AF19(628-2487).

[1]Delays in publication as well as other factors have led to what may be a rather confusing situation, with regard to the paper by Chomsky to which Householder refers. It appeared at approximately the same time in three different versions under two different titles. The *Preprints* paper (Chomsky, 1962) appears in the *Proceedings of the Ninth Congress* in a revised version submitted for publication in 1962; its title is that of the session at which it was presented (Chomsky, 1964a). A revised and ex-panded version was submitted for publication in 1963 and has now been published (Chomsky, 1964b) in Fodor and Katz (1964). A still later and further revised and expanded version was submitted for publication in late 1963 and has now appeared as a separate monograph (Chomsky, 1964c [39]). We will give page references in a double form, referring to the *Proceedings* and the separate monograph. The latter page reference is only for the convenience of the reader; the various versions do not differ in any way relevant to this discussion.

Halle's paper (1962) [37] also appears (Halle, 1964b) in a revised version in Fodor and Katz (1964). This anthology also contains a revised and expanded version of an earlier article (Halle, 1958–1964a [38]). For the convenience of the reader we will give page references to Halle's paper also in double form (1962 and 1964b).

*Reprinted from *Journal of Linguistics* 1.97–138 (1965) by permission of the authors and Cambridge University Press.

Phrase-marker of the string. "Higher-level" considerations play an important role in determining the choice of this system, which is selected in such a way as to contribute to an optimal generative grammar of the language. The systematic phonetic representation utilizes a universal phonetic alphabet, based on a theory of distinctive features. For this purpose, we have adopted with some modifications Jakobson's theory of distinctive features, since this seems to us to be by far the best theory of universal phonetics now available. We showed that for a wide range of linguistic data, which otherwise would have to be treated as isolated fact without systematic import, we could offer partial explanations if we consistently formulated all rules and representations (both systematic phonemic and systematic phonetic) strictly in terms of features. Systematic reliance on features thus permits a deepening of insight into the nature of linguistic competence and makes possible an analysis of the notion "linguistically significant generalization," a notion which underlies all descriptive practice but has, so far, resisted clear and general formulation. We also discussed some of the consequences of this phonological theory for historical linguistics, and showed how certain otherwise knotty problems can be handled in what appears to be a natural and effective way.

In addition, we studied various theories of sound structure that have been developed since Sapir. We called these *taxonomic phonemic theories* so as to bring out their reliance on procedures of segmentation and classification and their essential independence of "higher levels." Taxonomic phonemics, in one or another form, has been almost universally regarded as either supplanting phonology in Sapir's sense or as constituting a new and fundamental level intermediate between systematic phonemics (often called "morphophonemics") and systematic phonetics. We tried to show that neither claim is justified—that taxonomic phonemics is an artifact and does not constitute a level of linguistic structure. That is, a taxonomic phonemic representation simply cannot be incorporated into a fully explicit grammar that expresses phonological processes in full generality, and therefore cannot be justified on internal linguistic grounds. We also argued that

it has no support on external grounds (of perception or language use or acquisition), and that the procedures of analysis that have been proposed (in particular, insofar as they rely on "complementary distribution") are seriously defective and ineffective as analytic devices. Consequently, we concluded that taxonomic phonemics has no place in a grammar that describes the competence of the speaker or in a model of language use. Its sole justification is that it may allow sentences to be read or written in an economical notation by someone who does not understand the language; and, whatever the utility of such a system may be, there is no reason to assume that it plays any role in language use or has a place in grammar.

This, in brief, is the content of the articles that Householder is discussing. Our comments will refer directly to his discussion of these points, and are intended to be read in conjunction with his paper. We shall classify Householder's major criticisms under the following seven headings: (i) the goals of linguistic theory; (ii) evaluation procedures; (iii) independence of phonology; (iv) the status of phonemes vs. features; (v) the adequacy of Jakobson's theory with respect to natural classes; (vi) the validity of procedures of taxonomic linguistics; (vii) the phonetic basis of phonemic analysis. We will discuss these in turn. In each case, we will first briefly restate our position, as given in Halle (1962 [37] and 1964*b*) and Chomsky (1964*a* and *c* [39]). We will next try to state Householder's version of our position. Unfortunately, this version often has little relation to what we have stated and, correspondingly, is unsupported by reference or quotation. We will then discuss his criticisms in the cases where the criticism does relate to some position we have taken.

I. The Goals of Linguistic Theory   In Chomsky (1964*a* and *c*) three roughly delimited goals are suggested as a framework for the discussion. We say that a grammar meets the level of *observational adequacy* if it correctly describes the data on which it is based and nothing more—if, in other words, it gives a compact one-one organization of this data. We say that a grammar meets the level of *descriptive adequacy* to the extent that it gives a correct account of the speaker's "tacit knowledge."[2] We say that a linguistic theory (n.b., not a grammar) meets the level of *explanatory adequacy* to the extent that it provides a principled basis for the selection of descriptively adequate grammars. We remarked that these three levels of adequacy can be clarified by describing them in terms of the problem of developing an acquisition model for language. An acquisition model can be regarded as a device AM:

primary linguistic data $\rightarrow$ $\boxed{\text{AM}}$ $\rightarrow$ grammar

This device takes as input the kind of data used by the child who acquires the language and gives as output the grammar which is internally represented by the child in some way, and which expresses his implicit knowledge. A linguistic description meets the level of observational adequacy if it gives a correct account of the input to AM, and meets the level of descriptive adequacy if it gives a correct account of the output of AM. A linguistic theory meets the level of explanatory adequacy insofar as it succeeds in describing the internal structure of AM and thus shows how the descriptively adequate grammar arises from the primary linguistic data. Such a linguistic theory is explanatory in that it accounts for the linguistic intuition (the underlying competence, tacit knowledge, *langue*) of the

speaker on the basis of a certain assumption about the form of language (i.e., about the internal structure of AM) and about the data that was available to the speaker. Clearly the assumption about the form of language embodied in an explanatory theory of this sort must be universal—that is, we take it for granted that a child is not genetically predisposed to learn one human language rather than another. Consequently a strong assumption about the device AM is easily falsifiable if incorrect (and thus is an interesting claim) by a demonstration that it fails to give a descriptively adequate grammar for some new language.

Thus the levels of observational adequacy, descriptive adequacy, and explanatory adequacy relate, respectively, to the input, output, and internal structure of AM. Clearly language is acquired (i.e., a grammar is developed) by an organism with fixed initial constraints that delimit the class of possible grammars. It is acquired on the basis of some sort of data; therefore, interest in the data, the acquired grammar, and the fixed initial structure (that is, interest in observational, descriptive and explanatory adequacy, respectively) is surely legitimate. There is, in particular, a right answer to the question: what is the basis for the acquisition of linguistic competence? A linguist may choose to disregard these questions, but there is surely no conceivable reason for him to object to the attempt of others to investigate them.

For concreteness, let us consider an actual example of linguistic material analyzed at these three levels of adequacy. The simplest example, and the one that Householder takes as central to his critical discussion, is the case of "possible, non-existent forms" in a particular language. Thus in English there is a form *brick* (/brik/), but no /blik/ or /bnik/. Nevertheless, a speaker of English knows that /blik/ is an admissible form in a sense in which /bnik/ is not. This distinction is, furthermore, not a matter of universal phonetics. These are the facts of the matter. So far as we know, no one challenges them; certainly Householder seems to accept the distinctions in question.

A description of English will achieve the level of observational adequacy, in this case, if it distinguishes /brik/, as an occurring form, from /blik/ and /bnik/, as non-occurring forms.

---

[2]We assume, with no further discussion, the distinction of *langue-parole* (except that we do not accept the Saussurian limitation of *langue* to "system of elements," but regard it also as a system of rules—for discussion, cf. Chomsky (1964a: 914–923 and 1964c: 7–27. That is, we consider here only such linguistic grammars as attempt to reveal the principles (which are, obviously, in general, unconscious and may even be beyond the level of possible consciousness) that determine how utterances are interpreted in the language, and what structures are assigned to them by the speaker-hearer, idealizing away from the various factors irrelevant to the system of grammar (lapses of attention, etc.) that interact with this tacit knowledge to determine actual performance. Notice that there is no "moral imperative" in our concern with grammars that describe *langue* in this sense. One who has no interest in these traditional questions will simply not be concerned with *descriptive adequacy,* in the sense in which we are using this term, but only with what we have called *observational adequacy.* Such a linguist (if he exists) would find our concerns (as those of Saussure, Sapir, and others) rather exotic, as we would find his overly limited. There is no question of right or wrong here, but only of goals and interests.

Thus a lexicon—a list of all occurring forms—meets the level of observational adequacy. It correctly presents the data available to the child, the input to the acquisition model AM. The description will meet the level of descriptive adequacy if it distinguishes /brik/ and /blik/, as admissible forms, from /bnik/, as an inadmissible form. In this case, it will state what the speaker knows (unconsciously—cf. note 2) to be true; it gives correctly the output of AM. To meet the level of explanatory adequacy, a linguistic theory must justify the descriptively adequate grammar on internal grounds. That is, it must show on what basis the device AM (or the linguist) selects a grammar admitting /blik/ and excluding /bnik/. It must, in other words, justify the inclusion in a grammar of English of the rule (1) but not the rule (2):

(1) Consonantal Segment→Liquid in the context: # Stop − Vowel
(2) Consonantal Segment→/r/ in the context: # /b − ik/

Both rules (1) and (2) are true of English, at the level of observation. That is, both correctly state facts about occurrence and nonoccurrence. Rule (1) excludes /bnik/ as inadmissible, but permits /blik/. Rule (2) excludes both /bnik/ and /blik/ as inadmissible. To achieve the level of explanatory adequacy, a linguistic theory must present some general grounds for requiring the grammar to include rule (1) but not allowing it to include rule (2), despite the correctness of (2) at the level of observation. One natural way to achieve this result is to devise a measure for evaluating grammars within general linguistic theory in such a way that rule (1) will contribute to the value of English grammar, as so defined, but rule (2) will detract from the value of English grammar. This problem has never, to our knowledge, been raised in traditional or modern taxonomic phonology. The only attempt that we know of to achieve the level of explanatory adequacy is the proposal, discussed in Halle (1962 [37] and 1964b) and Chomsky (1964a and c [39]) and earlier publications, to construct an evaluation procedure based on systematic feature analysis. We return to the details in section 2 of our discussion. For the moment, we are only concerned to distinguish the three levels of adequacy, in this particular case.

As noted in Chomsky (1964a and c [39]), almost all linguists, in their actual practice, are concerned with descriptive adequacy. But taxonomic linguistic *theory* has generally limited itself to observational adequacy. That is, it has been concerned to develop procedures that rearrange and organize the data of a corpus in various ways, for economy and perspicuity. This has often been stated explicitly (cf., e.g., Harris, 1951: 1, 3, 12, 361, 366); often it is implicit in the definition of procedures. There have been some attempts to develop procedures that go beyond organization of data in a corpus.[3] However, these fail badly to give grammars that achieve the level of descriptive adequacy.

To summarize, we are concerned only with grammars that attempt to meet the level

[3]For example, see Harris (1951: Chapter 15); Chomsky (1953); or, consider the various attempts to develop procedures of morphemic analysis during the forties and early fifties. These attempts presuppose intuitive knowledge of the correct morphemic analysis, and are concerned to develop procedures that give the intuitively correct analysis. Thus these are attempts to raise linguistic theory to the level of explanatory adequacy. However, these attempts met with little success. Invariably, it is necessary to apply the procedures "intelligently," in some sense, if they are to give the desired (intuitively correct) results. Hence the procedures, as formulated, do not succeed in capturing the notion "morpheme," in the desired intuitive sense. And the same is true of the explicit procedures designed to isolate other linguistically significant units.

It seems to us that the repeated failures of attempts to develop adequate procedures in taxonomic linguistics reflect an inherent limitation of this approach, namely, its adherence to the Saussurian view that repeated segmentation and classification exhausts the domain of linguistic structure. This is an empirical claim about the nature of language, which, in fact, seems clearly to be false. It seems that the underlying base forms and the linguistically significant abstract structures cannot be revealed by segmentation and classification but are, rather, related to phenomena only by intricate sets of ordered rules that violate the formal conditions presupposed in taxonomic methodology. We in no way disparage these attempts; rather, they are notable in that they are serious attempts to achieve explanatory adequacy. But their failure, and the reasons for this failure, suggest that it is necessary to approach the problem of developing an adequate linguistic theory in an entirely different way; and our purpose in Halle (1962 [37] and 1964b) and Chomsky (1964a and c [39]) and elsewhere has been to outline a different and, we feel, much more hopeful direction for the development of a linguistic theory that can approach the level of explanatory adequacy.

of descriptive adequacy and with linguistic theories that attempt to meet the level of explanatory adequacy: Only such grammars and theories are empirically significant in the sense that evidence can be brought for or against them, in that they can be right or wrong. Hence our decision to limit attention to these topics seems quite justifiable.

One of the most common objections to the program just outlined (and one that reappears explicitly in Householder's paper) has to do with the statement that a descriptively adequate grammar must give a correct account of the tacit knowledge (linguistic intuition) of the native speaker. We have discussed these objections at various times in the past, but as they recur in Householder's paper, it may not be out of place to repeat once again that which seems to us entirely obvious. Without reference to this tacit knowledge there is no such subject as descriptive linguistics. There is nothing for its descriptive statements to be right or wrong about. Taxonomic linguistics has been unhappy with this state of affairs. Since Bloomfield conferred upon linguistics the first place among the social sciences for having freed itself of the yoke of the "elusive spiritistic-teleologic words of our tribal speech" (Bloomfield, 1927), it has been thought undignified to pay attention to such a "mentalistic horror" as linguistic intuition. Nevertheless, tacit knowledge of the speaker's language is at every stage and every point precisely what the linguist is dealing with. No one, surely, is content simply to rearrange the data in a corpus. Every linguistic description attempts, at least, to extract "patterns" or "regularities" from a corpus, or to abstract from it principles that will apply to other linguistic material as well. But statements of "patterns," "regularities," and "underlying principles" go beyond the data. They are based on some assumption about the nature of linguistic patterns or regularities. Without such assumptions (which, unfortunately, are rarely made explicit), innumerable "patterns" and "regularities" can be found in any data, all mutually conflicting, and most of them, for some reason, quite ridiculous. All linguistic work is, obviously, guided by certain assumptions about the nature of linguistic structure and linguistic patterns; and such assumptions, which are the heart of linguistic theory, can be tested for adequacy in only one way, namely, by determining whether the de-

scriptions to which they lead are in accord with tacit knowledge concerning the language. Whatever may have been said in methodological discussions, this ultimate reference to the speaker's tacit knowledge of his language is quite apparent in all actual linguistic work.

Consider again the successive attempts to develop procedures of analysis in taxonomic linguistics (cf. note 3). These were, obviously, guided by assumptions about what is the correct result—intuitively correct, that is. Otherwise, the successive attempts to develop refinements and improvements would be quite unintelligible. Without reliance on tacit knowledge as an ultimate criterion, there could be no possible objection to a "phonological grammar" (e.g., a chart of the type given by Whorf, 1940) that excludes /blik/ along with /bnik/, just as there could be no objection to the rigorous definition of "morpheme" as "sequence of three phonemes," or the rigorous definition of "juncture" as "boundary inserted before a voiced stop," etc. Even operational tests, were they available, would not eliminate the reliance on linguistic intuition. On the contrary, an operational test must be tested for conformity to linguistic intuition before it becomes acceptable. Otherwise there would be no objection to some operational test that characterizes "morpheme," let us say, in terms of GSR fluctuation (averaged, perhaps, to obtain uniformity).

There is only one way to avoid complete reliance on linguistic intuition (i.e., tacit knowledge) in descriptive practice. This is to develop operational tests and explanatory linguistic theories that correctly characterize linguistic intuition in a mass of clear cases, so that we then have some basis for relying on their results in new or unclear cases.

In any event, there is no basis for disagreement between Householder and us insofar as reliance on linguistic intuition or concern for correctness is concerned. His belief that he somehow escapes this necessity is a simple consequence of his willingness to use such terms as "systematic redundancy," "economy," "generality," etc., as if they were clear and well-understood in advance. But this is quite false. These terms have no clear meaning. One cannot rely on them to escape the responsibility of facing up to the problems of descriptive and explanatory adequacy. To characterize these notions correctly is, on the contrary, one of the major problems of linguistic theory. There is no necessity for everyone to be interested in linguistic theory, of course, but one must remain aware of the fact that he is solving no problems by uncritical use of just those notions that the theory of language is concerned to analyze and clarify.

Householder further objects that we assume the existence of a unique correct grammar. This strikes us more as a quibble than as a serious issue. It is logically possible that for English, for example, two different grammars will some day be discovered, neither of which is falsifiable on any conceivable empirical grounds. It is logically possible that two linguistic theories will be constructed that are perfectly consistent with all obtainable empirical evidence, and that fully justify, with equal effectiveness, all descriptively adequate grammars. Similarly, it is logically possible that several incompatible theories of motion, or light, will some day be developed, none of which is falsifiable on any empirical grounds. We agree, then, that to state that the goal of linguistic theory is to determine the choice of "*the* descriptively adequate grammar" (or that the goal of linguistics is to discover "*the* theory of linguistic form") is as misleading as it is to describe physics as concerned with discovering "*the* theory of motion," "*the* theory of light," "*the* theory of the chemical bond," etc. Having stated this, we propose to return to the use of these locutions, and we assume that the physicist, biologist, etc., will continue to do so as well, as they invariably have in the past.

In fact, even to raise these questions is to betray a misconception of the problems that actually face the linguist, or, for that matter, the physical scientist. The real problem for the linguist is to find a theory (actually, a small part of a theory) that will come somewhere near accounting for some domain of linguistic fact; the problem for the grammarian is to develop some small fragment of a grammar that is adequate for some part of the language that concerns him. Where two equally effective fragments can be constructed, the grammarian will attempt to choose between them by enriching the domain of relevant fact or deepening linguistic theory; where two linguistic theories are equally adequate, he will attempt to adjudicate between them by bringing additional facts to bear, facts which can be accounted for by one but not by the other. This is the only way in which the grammatical descriptions of particular languages or the general theory of linguistic structure can progress. Those who prefer to contemplate the abstract possibility that at some time in the future it will be impossible to make any further progress (because all theories will be so perfect as to be unfalsifiable) are welcome to do so.

To conclude the discussion of this point, we should like to comment on Householder's notion of "correctness." On p. 16 [444] of his paper, he gives the following summary of his views:

I am more inclined to the view that two inconsistent and irreconcilable descriptions of a language may each convey some important "intuition" about the language which cannot be conveyed by the other, *nor both by any third*. I do not think we should assume that there is always one point of vantage from which we can equally well see the front and back, the inside and the outside, the left and the right. Maybe there is, but I'm against assuming this. (Our emphasis.)

This is the most general expression that he gives to views that apparently dominate his paper throughout, and seem to be distressingly common in recent methodological discussion by descriptive linguists.

We may begin by eliminating the false analogy presented in the second sentence of the quotation. A view from the front is not inconsistent with a view from the back, etc. The importance of giving a full description of an object from many vantage points has never been at issue, and does not bear on Householder's view expressed here and elsewhere; namely, that there is no reason to "assume" the possibility for a consistent description of a language.

Consider now the first sentence of the quotation. Once again, there is no issue about the question of whether two inconsistent descriptions may each convey some important "intuition" about the object under investigation. It is significant that there are no known examples of this in the case of language (and Householder cites no linguistic evidence to justify his beliefs), but it is certainly possible in principle that each of two inconsistent descriptions may, in some vague sense, shed some light on the actual character of what is being described, whether this is a language or any other object of study and research. In any serious field of investigation, the discovery of two mutually inconsistent descriptions, each somehow suggestive, would be taken as posing a problem for research, a challenge to the investigator to be resolved by showing how the two inconsistent "suggestive" descriptions can be replaced by a single, consistent description that goes beyond mere suggestiveness and actually expresses a precise view about the nature of the object of study. But this is because in all serious intellectual pursuits, whether those of the historian, the psychologist, the biologist, the physicist, the literary scholar, etc., it is taken for granted that the goal of research is to discover the truth about the object under investigation. This truism is rarely discussed; it is a deeply-engrained assumption that one finds no need to emphasize because it has not been challenged for centuries, within scholarship and science.

But Householder seems to take a different view. If the comment we have singled out for emphasis, in the passage from his article quoted above, reflects his actual views, he believes that there is no truth to be discovered. If the optimal description of a language consists of two mutually inconsistent parts, then this description cannot be proposed as a significant and verifiable assumption concerning the language—that is, no claim to empirical truth can be made for the description that is presented, and no evidence can conceivably be relevant for or against what the linguist does. In place of a proposal with content concerning the language he is studying, Householder's linguist has to be satisfied with the following assertion: "I have a description D_1 and a description D_2, each of which is somehow suggestive and conveys some intuition; the two are inconsistent, but this is no problem, since in any event there is no reason to try to find a consistent description of a language, or to assume that one exists—language, in other words, may be an undescribable object, beyond the possibility of rational discussion."

Notice that this question can arise at the level of either descriptive or explanatory adequacy. In the case of the former, the linguist may or may not be concerned with giving a correct account of the rules of the language that he is describing and of the way in which sentences are formed and understood, on the basis of this system of rules, by speakers of this language. In the case of the latter, he may or may not be interested in giving a correct account of the nature of language, the *faculté de langage* that underlies the acquisition of linguistic competence, the linguistic universals that define the general form of human language. A linguist, who, like Householder, is willing to accept inconsistent accounts—in fact, claims that such inconsistency is ineliminable—has disavowed any concern for the topic of descriptive or explanatory adequacy. He has simply given up the attempt to find out the facts about particular languages or about language in general. His work is immune to criticism, of course, as an automatic consequence of his tolerance of inconsistency.

II. Evaluation Procedures Our approach to the question of evaluation procedures is, briefly, this. Suppose that we are concerned to develop a linguistic theory that meets the level of explanatory adequacy. It seems that a two-pronged attack on this problem offers some hope of success. In the first place, we attempt to enrich the structure of linguistic theory so as to restrict the class of grammars compatible with the data given—in other words, we attempt to make the strongest legitimate universal claim about the structure of language. Secondly, we attempt to construct an evaluation procedure for selecting one among the various grammars permitted by the proposed linguistic theory and compatible with the given data. The narrower the class of grammars permitted (as possible hypotheses), the easier it will be to select among them by an evaluation procedure. The broader the class of permitted grammars, the more difficult it will be to construct an effective procedure of evaluation.

Let us return, for concreteness, to the linguistic example discussed above. The child is presented with /brik/ but not with /blik/ or /bnik/. He somehow constructs a grammar that contains rule (1) but not rule (2), so that he then knows (see note 2) that /blik/ is admissible but /bnik/ is not. It is this fact that the linguist is attempting to explain. He can try to do so by making a strong assumption about the form of grammar—about the class of hypotheses that the child is free to sample—and developing an evaluation procedure for selecting among them. In Halle (1962 [37] and 1964b) and elsewhere two specific proposals are made, relating to this question. The first concerns the form of grammar; it states in particular, that phonological rules should be stated completely in terms of features. The second concerns the evaluation measure; it states that a grammar should be evaluated by minimizing the total number of features specified in the lexicon and in the phonological rules.[4] It is then pointed out that these two assumptions jointly lead to the selection of the descriptively adequate grammar and exclude the descriptively inadequate grammar in a variety of interesting cases. These proposals thus stand as an empirical hypothesis concerning general linguistic theory—concerning the language acquisition model AM discussed above—a hypothesis which (like any empirical assumption) is to be tested by its consequences.

It is furthermore pointed out by Halle that various other proposals will not work. For example, the evaluation procedure cannot be stated in terms of minimization (or maximization) if the theory of grammatical form permits rules to be stated in terms of phonemes rather than (or along with) features. This observation is offered as an argument in favor of the hypothesis that features, rather than phonemes, are the linguistically significant elements. To meet this objection to the use of phonemic notation in grammar, a linguist who doubts our empirical assumption must develop a theory of the form of grammar permitting phonemic notation and an associated evaluation procedure which, jointly, have the same effect as the proposals in terms of features. We do not maintain that this is *a priori* impossible. However, it must be done in a serious way. Nu-

merology of the sort to which Householder treats us is entirely irrelevant.[5]

We stress once more that choice of an evaluation measure is an empirical matter. The problem of discovering an evaluation measure is much like that of evaluating a physical constant. We are given a certain pairing of empirical facts: primary linguistic data D_1 leads to descriptively adequate grammar G_1, D_2 leads to G_2, etc. One can no more give an *a priori* argument for a particular evaluation measure than one can for a particular value of the gravitational constant.

An evaluation measure is probably best regarded as a procedure for assigning an integer to a grammar, the smaller integer corresponding to the higher value. It should be designed in such a way that the greater the degree of linguistically significant generalization achieved in a grammar, the higher the value and the smaller the assigned integer. It should,

---

[4]This was a first approximation. We now know of various ways in which it can be refined and improved. For further discussion of this and other related questions, see Chomsky and Halle (to appear) [now 1968—VBM]. In general, it is an extremely difficult problem to construct an evaluation procedure that gives the desired results, and it is a pity that so little attention has been paid to the problem of justifying correct descriptions. We emphasize once again that the uncritical use of such notions as "systematic redundancy," "economy," "general rules," etc., is largely responsible for this failure on the part of Householder and others to face this and other problems of linguistic theory.

[5]In a supplementary footnote added after his article was written, Householder proposes that "the reciprocal of the numbers of phoneme symbols in each rule should give substantially the same rank-order as Halle's method." This very proposal has been considered and refuted by Halle. Halle considered the following three rules (the numbering is that of Halle, 1962: 56–57 [381–382]; cf. also Halle, 1964b: 336):

/a/→/æ/ in the env. /i/ —— /i/   (3')
/a/→/æ/ in the env.   —— /i/   (2')

/a/→/æ/ in the env.   —— $\left\{\begin{matrix} /i/ \\ /e/ \\ /æ/ \end{matrix}\right\}$ (4')

He noted that in the sense of generality that is commonly accepted in linguistics, (3') is less general than (2'), which in turn is less general than (4'). Halle showed then that this rank ordering will be obtained by using the number of features as an evaluation measure, but that if phonemes are used in place of features an evaluation measure based on counting symbols will give results that fail to correspond to the correct rank order. For example, following Householder, let us calculate "the reciprocal of the numbers of phoneme symbols in each rule." Our results are:

(3') . . . 1/4
(2') . . . 1/3
(4') . . . 1/5

This clearly does *not* "give substantially the same rank order as Halle's method."

The rest of the supplementary footnote, which purports to summarize the main points of Chomsky's lectures at Bloomington in 1964, is as inaccurate as the part examined directly above. Since little purpose is served by correcting these additional inaccuracies we refrain from further comment.

in other words, be a measure of the degree of linguistically significant generalization achieved. As a first approximation, it seems reasonable to take the measure to be length. But if this is the selected measure, then the theory of grammatical form must permit only such notations as convert considerations of generality into considerations of length. (If notations are invented freely, any desired grammar can be made the shorter and the measure collapses.) This, in fact, is the motivation for the particular decisions that have been made concerning notations in the work in generative grammar in the past ten or fifteen years. Notations were selected in such a way that what seemed to be linguistically significant generalizations gave rise to shorter, hence higher valued grammars. The proposal to write grammars in terms of features rather than phonemes also has just this effect, and hence fits in rather nicely with what has been, so far, a moderately successful approach to the problem of explanatory adequacy. The notations that have been selected constitute an empirical hypothesis as to what is a significant generalization, a hypothesis which can be falsified on grounds of descriptive inadequacy, if it is incorrect.[6]

The notion of "simplicity" with which we have been concerned is internal to linguistic theory. That is, a simplicity measure (evalua-

tion measure) is an empirical hypothesis about the form of grammar, ultimately, about the native intellectual capacity ("faculté de langage") that makes language acquisition possible and, correspondingly, that justifies the linguist's attempt to describe what it achieves (to construct a descriptively adequate grammar). In this usage, "simplicity" is a technical term of linguistic theory, on a par with "phoneme," "grammatical transformation," "distinctive feature," etc. There is another sense in which one talks of the simplicity, elegance, etc., of theories (relativistic physics is more elegant—simpler—than Newtonian physics, Copernican astronomy is simpler than Ptolemaic, etc.). We do not deny the interest of this notion, but we have nothing to say about it. It is a concept that belongs not to linguistics, nor to any particular scientific discipline, but rather to general epistemology or philosophy of science. Our concern, as linguists, is to clarify the status and the precise content of the evaluation measure (simplicity measure, in the technical terminology that has now become familiar) that is internal to linguistics and that plays a role in the determination of a descriptively adequate grammar. We emphasize, once again, that such a measure is relative to a particular form of grammatical statement. It is not of the slightest importance to us that the simplest grammar, in our sense, may be difficult for some linguists to read, or that it may be wasteful of printer's ink. We do assume that a grammar has a physical representation in the speaker's brain, but obviously neither we nor anyone else has the slightest idea about this. But evidence about this, if it will some day be forthcoming, is the only relevant evidence relating to physical representation of grammars.

Householder is not alone in assuming some absolute notion of "simplicity" that can be relied upon to choose among linguistic theories. As another example, consider the discussion of ordering of rules in Lamb (1964) [52]. Lamb compares two theories of generative grammar, each of which contains rewriting rules of the form: $A \rightarrow X/Z - Y$. The two

---

[6]Householder's notion of "evaluation" is rather different from ours, so far as we can make out from his comments. He objects (1965: 19–20 [446–447]) to the evaluation measure presented in Halle (1962 [37] and 1964b) because the form of grammar on which it is based, with systematic use of features, is clumsy, difficult for linguists to read, wasteful of printer's ink, burdensome to the memory and attention. If we may assume that Householder is using our terms as we do, then we are forced to attribute to Householder the following empirical hypothesis: a descriptively adequate grammar is selected (by the child, or linguist—i.e., by the acquisition model AM, above) on the basis of an evaluation measure involving amount of printer's ink, ease of reading, etc. Of course, he intended no such absurd claim. We conclude, then, that his criticism of our notion of evaluation is not based on what we have stated.

In fact, it is not difficult to see where Householder has gone astray in his criticism. An evaluation measure is often called by the technical term *simplicity measure*. As we noted above, Householder (along with many others) has fallen into the unfortunate habit of using the terms "simplicity," "economy," "generality," etc., as if they are somehow clear in advance and require no analysis. Hence when he sees the term "simplicity measure" used in

the technical sense described above, he concludes that what is intended is the vague, intuitive notion that he has in mind, and he is naturally taken aback to see that what we call the simplest (highest-valued) grammar does not meet his *a priori* conception of "simplicity."

systems differ in the way in which these rules are organized. The first theory is the one we have been considering (for this discussion, we will refer to the grammars it permits as *mutation grammars,* following Lamb's terminology). In a mutation grammar the rewriting rules are linearly ordered, and apply in the given sequence. The second theory requires that the rewriting rules be unordered, except that the rules that rewrite the same symbol form a linearly ordered bloc, and are to be applied in the given order with the additional constraint that only one may apply. The rules of such a grammar (following Lamb, we call it a *realization grammar*) convert a representation on a "higher level" to one on a lower level; each rule applies to the higher level representation, not to the representation as it appears after application of previously selected rules. Except for the condition on ordering of subrules, Lamb's realization grammars are identical to those considered by Harris (1951: Appendix to 14.32), in his demonstration of how one of Bloomfield's examples of descriptive order can be restated with a different condition on rule-application, not involving ordering.[7]

How can one decide between mutation systems and realization systems? Obviously, one must turn to questions of empirical import. One must try to discover phenomena that can be adequately described by one of these systems but not the other. For example, it has been pointed out by Chomsky that although certain examples of descriptive order can be handled by realization systems (cf. 1964a: 946, n.34 and c: 70 [403], n.8), such systems are inadequate for slightly more complex examples of a sort easily found, and illustrated there. Lamb does not try to show how these defects can be overcome (in fact, he makes no reference to the earlier discussion of realization systems); nor does he show how certain phenomena can be handled by realization systems that are beyond the scope of mutation systems. In short, he does not attempt to deal with the question of empirical import. Instead, he argues for realization systems on

two grounds: one, on the ground that mutation systems are appropriate only for diachronic linguistics; two, on grounds of absolute simplicity. The first statement we shall not discuss. It is simply an ex cathedra pronouncement, for which no justification is offered. The second argument is the one that concerns us here. Lamb claims that some theory-independent absolute notion of simplicity favors the organization of rules allowed by realization grammars over that of mutation grammars. Furthermore, he is quite explicit about some of the details of this universal measure. For example, each rule in a mutation system must be supplied with exactly one extra symbol, for this universal measure to be applied (viz., an integer indicating its position in the ordering); the statement of a negative context (i.e., a context of the form "except for . . .") is exactly as complex as the statement of the corresponding positive context (cf. Lamb, 1964: 114 [600]); the absolute number of symbols in a mutation grammar is commensurable with the absolute number in a realization grammar; etc. Needless to say, he makes no attempt to validate this absolute measure nor to develop it in any systematic way; nor does he show any awareness that such justification is necessary, that these particular arbitrary decisions are not obvious *a priori* truths.[8]

We can perhaps clarify this question still further by considering the one actual linguistic example that Lamb presents. He considers a language (Monachi) in which both /w/ and /kʷ/ are realized as [qʷ] in the context $V_1h—V_2$ (where V_1 and V_2 are two classes of Vowels,

---

[7]In fact, Lamb's "hypothetical morphophonemic example," invented to illustrate this property of realization grammars, is identical, except for choice of symbols, with the Menomini example of Bloomfield's discussed by Harris in his illustration of the same point, and Lamb's treatment of this example is identical with Harris's.

[8]Notice that even if this absolute notion of "simplicity" could somehow be justified, this would have little relevance to the problem of choosing among linguistic theories. Suppose it were true that a grammar that derives Y from X by a sequence of rules, each applying to the last step of the derivation (i.e., a mutation grammar), is more "complex," in some sense, than a grammar that derives Y from X by an unordered set of rules, each available at every stage of the derivation and each applying to X rather than to the last step of the derivation so far produced (a realization grammar). This conclusion would still leave open the question whether the system used in natural language is "maximally simple" in this absolute sense. There is not the slightest reason to expect natural languages to be "maximally simple," assuming that some content can be given to this curious notion. The relevant constraints are those of physical realizability, not "absolute simplicity," whatever this may mean.

the membership of which is of no further relevance here), /w/ being realized as $[k^w]$ elsewhere after /h/. In a mutation grammar, the facts are stated in the form (3); in a realization grammar, in the form (4).

(3) $w \rightarrow k^w/h$—   (i)
      $k^w \rightarrow q^w/V_1h$—V_2 (ii)

(4) $w \rightarrow \begin{Bmatrix} q^w/V_1h$—$V_2 \\ k^w/h$— \end{Bmatrix}$ (i)
                                                          (ii)
      $k^w \rightarrow q^w/V_1h$—V_2 (iii)

In the grammar (4), the only requirement on order of application of rules is that (i) must precede (ii). In the grammar (3), the rule (i) must precede (ii).

In the mutation grammar (3), the vocalic environment determining $[q^w]$ is stated once; in the realization grammar, it is stated twice. But, Lamb argues, the relatively greater economy of the mutation grammar is only apparent, since "this economy is achieved at the cost of making these rules ordered," (1964: 119 [603]).[9] We agree with Lamb in denying that (3) is "simpler" than (4), but not for his reasons. It is not that an extra symbol must be added to each rule in (3), to be counted in measuring "economy" along with the symbols in the rules themselves; rather, the point is that comparison of (3) and (4) in "economy" is entirely meaningless until some cross-theoretical absolute notion of "economy" is produced, and no such measure is known.

There is a real difference between (3) and (4). It is not a matter of "economy," however, but of empirical import. The theory of mutation grammar claims, in effect, that there is a linguistically significant generalization underlying the phenomena described by (3) and (4); it claims, in other words, that there is a significant relationship between the realization of /w/ and /k^w/ as [q^w]. The theory of realization grammar takes this to be a mere accident, of no linguistic significance. This difference between the two theories becomes obvious if we consider a language identical to the one just discussed except for the fact that /w/ is realized as [x^w] after /h/ except in the context of

(4i), and /k^w/ is realized as [q^w] not in the context of (3ii) and (4iii), but in some entirely new context V_3h—V_4, where $V_1 \neq V_3$ and $V_2 \neq V_4$. For this language, both the mutation grammar and the realization grammar would have the form (5):

(5) $w \rightarrow \begin{Bmatrix} q^w/V_1h$—$V_2 \\ x^w/h$— \end{Bmatrix}$ (i)
                                                          (ii)
      $k^w \rightarrow q^w/V_3h$—V_4 (iii)

Assume now that each of the theories under discussion has some reasonable evaluation measure internal to it (e.g., symbol counting under specified notational transformations, as described above). Then the mutation grammar (5) is more complex than the mutation grammar (3), but the realization grammar (5) is identical in complexity to the realization grammar (4). This comparison brings out one of the empirically significant differences between mutation grammar and realization grammar. For the former, the facts described by (3) exhibit a systematic arrangement, in comparison with those of (5). For realization grammar, neither set of facts falls into any systematic arrangement—the actual language of Lamb's example and the invented language are identical, with respect to the possibility of finding significant generalizations.[10]

The crucial point, once again, is that the issue between the alternative theories is an

---

[9]Actually, Lamb's conclusion is incorrect even on his own grounds, since exactly one statement of relative order is required in both (3) and (4). However, this inconsistency is unimportant, in the light of the meaninglessness of his attempted comparison.

[10]Of course, Lamb is no more willing to accept this absurd conclusion than any other linguist would be, and so he then goes on to propose a further modification of realization grammar, suggesting new mechanisms that permit organization of rules beyond the ordering allowed in the system described above. No doubt he would claim that these new principles of organization are still "simpler" in his absolute sense than the kind of organization permitted in linearly ordered mutation grammars. If so, this claim would be as meaningless as the claim he makes for realization grammar as opposed to mutation grammar. In any event, it would serve no purpose to undertake an investigation of the further principles of organization he proposed. They are designed, *ad hoc*, to account for the inability of realization grammars to express the distinction between the facts of (4) and those of (5), and they do not overcome the defects of realization grammars that have been discussed in the literature. Cf. pp. 110–111 [598]. Once again, since Lamb does not attempt to deal with these difficulties and suggests no compensating advantage for the new mechanisms he proposes, there is little point in discussing them any further.

empirical one. In the particular case that Lamb discusses, the issue is whether there is a real generalization underlying the phenomena described by (3) and (4), as compared with the unsystematic arrangement of (5). There is no question of the "relative complexity" of (3) and (4). There is no known absolute measure of complexity that can be called upon to make such a comparison among linguistic theories. If each of two theories has an evaluation measure *internal to it,* then the question of empirical consequences can be raised and fruitfully discussed. We can, in particular, determine what sorts of configurations of data count as "systematic" in terms of the competing theories, and, to the quite considerable extent to which independent agreement is possible on this matter, we can adjudicate between these theories. We can, for example, reject the theory of realization grammar on the grounds of its inability to distinguish (4) from (5). But in the present state of our knowledge, a comparison of two theories in terms of their "absolute complexity" or "economy," in the sense of Lamb and Householder, is entirely without significance.

In general, the absolute "size" of a grammar is a matter of no linguistic importance, and, in the abstract, it makes no difference how it is measured. If we decide to use length, under certain "notational transformations," as an evaluation measure, then relative length becomes important. A decision concerning notational transformations (e.g., a convention for the use of brackets, parentheses, etc.) will be of some interest if it affects different systems of rules in different ways; otherwise, it will be of no interest. For example, the now common use of brackets is an important empirical hypothesis about the nature of language, because it shortens a grammar and hence assigns it a higher value if this grammar contains successive rules which are similar in form in a certain well-defined way, but does not shorten a grammar containing similar rules that are not successive, or successive rules that are not similar in the way which is implicitly defined by these conventions. Thus conventions for use of brackets amount to the assumption that certain formal properties of a grammar (in this case, a certain sort of similarity among successive rules) count in its favor, and that an acquisition model will prefer

grammars with these properties—will select grammars with these properties over others that are also compatible, on the level of observation, with the data presented to it. There is no *a priori* reason why this assumption should be correct—it is, in other words, a nontrivial assumption. Similarly, the proposal to minimize the number of features in the lexicon and redundancy rules is an interesting hypothesis, since it selects certain grammars (in particular, the grammar containing rule (1)) over others (in particular, the grammar containing both rule (1) and rule (2)) which are equally compatible with the data, and it thus contributes directly to explanatory adequacy, as defined above. It is important to avoid mere arithmetical fetishism, and to bear in mind that an evaluation procedure is important only insofar as it contributes to an understanding of the notion "linguistically significant generalization" and to the extent that it distinguishes among grammars that provide different hypotheses as to linguistic competence.

III. Independence of Phonology The next point raised by Householder (1965: 17–20 [445–447]) concerns the "independence of phonology." The high point of this discussion is a six step deduction (p. 19 [446]) which is Householder's reconstruction of an argument which he attributes to Halle (with no specific reference), purporting to show that phonology cannot be independent of grammar. We agree with Householder in finding the argument inconclusive. Furthermore, we find its separate steps largely unintelligible. We observe, however, that the argument as presented by Householder is totally unrelated to anything we have ever proposed or would ever think of proposing. We do not recognize it or any of its steps. We therefore omit all further discussion of it. Instead we briefly outline our position as stated in Halle (1962 [37] and 1964b) and Chomsky (1964a and c [39]) on the questions of how the phonological component of the grammar relates to the syntactic component, and whether a "phonological grammar" is needed as a new and independent part of a full grammar.

We assume that the phonological component of the grammar is purely interpretive. The syntactic component generates a "surface structure" which consists of a string of formatives (minimal syntactically functioning elements) and a Phrase-marker (labeled bracketing) of this string. The formatives are represented completely in terms of features. The phonological rules fall into three basic types. The redundancy rules (morpheme structure rules) state general properties of formatives, and thus make it possible to eliminate redundant feature specifications from lexical entries. The transformational phonological rules apply in a cycle, as determined by the Phrase-marker (see Chomsky (1964a and c [39]) and references cited there for details). The nontransformational phonological rules apply, in sequence, just once—namely, at the stage when word boundaries are reached in the transformational cycle. Since the Phrase-marker determines the functioning of the phonological rules, we would say that phonology is not independent of syntax, but we have no idea whether we agree or disagree with Householder about this. In particular, when he attributes to Halle the view that "'phonology is wholly dependent on grammar'" (p. 18 [445]) (with no citation or reference despite his use of quotes), we are quite surprised. Taken literally, this presumably means that all phonological rules are transformational, in our sense. This we deny. It is obviously false, and we have never even hinted at such an absurd claim.[11] Perhaps Householder has in mind something else, but once again we have no way of knowing. On the other hand, when he attributes to us (and our "young admirers") the claim to have established "the unity of grammar with phonology," we accept this attribution, if it means that transformational rules involving the Phrase-marker of a string are a fundamental part of the phonological component (we do not know what else it might mean). This seems to us to be established beyond reasonable doubt.[12]

Furthermore, as argued in detail in Chomsky (1964a and c [39]), there seems to be no systematic linguistic level intermediate between systematic phonemic (see above, pp. 97–99 [457–458]) and systematic phonetic, the former (but not the latter) requiring transformational (i.e., syntax-dependent) rules to relate it to physical fact. If this implies that "phonology is united with syntax," in Householder's sense of this phrase, then again we accept this as a fair statement of our present view, a view, furthermore, that we feel that we have supported by strong and valid arguments.

Consider now the need for an independent "phonological grammar." Perhaps it will clarify matters to trace the brief history of the notion. In his review of *Syntactic Structures,* Lees pointed out (1957), correctly, that grammars of the type considered there failed to achieve descriptive adequacy in that they made no distinction between admissible and inadmissible phonological forms. To remedy this, he proposed that the grammar contain a separate system of rules to generate the admissible forms.[13] With such additional rules, the grammar would achieve descriptive adequacy. This suggestion has now been repeated by Householder in several places, although he has made no attempt, to our knowledge, to go beyond Lees' suggestion by developing either some sort of specific theory of rules of this type, or some concrete linguistic example of them.[14]

Shortly after Lees' review appeared, Halle pointed out (1959a, 1962 [37], and 1964b) that a grammar of the *Syntactic Structures* type can achieve descriptive adequacy in this respect even without the addition of a new and *ad hoc* phonological grammar. If we state the phonological rules strictly in terms of features

---

[11]The identical mistake was made by Ferguson (1962) [36] in his review of Halle (1959b). Like Householder, Ferguson mistakenly assumes that a denial of the autonomy of phonology from the rest of the grammar implies the claim that all of phonology is totally dependent on grammar; cf. Chomsky (1964a: 31 and 1964c: 105–107 [421]).

[12]Of course, we can claim no originality in this respect. The fact that phonological processes must be stated in terms of syntactic structure (for example, lexical category) was a commonplace until challenged by modern structural linguistics. Cf., for example, Postal (1964).

[13]In the same place, Lees also suggested that an independent sub-grammar might be necessary to account for non-transformational morphology. This suggestion Householder has also adopted without, however, elaborating, extending, or exemplifying it in any way. As distinct from the question of "phonological grammar," this problem seems to us very much open. For some inconclusive discussion see Chomsky (1965: Chapter 4).

[14]The problem of developing Lees' suggestion has been taken up by Contreras and Saporta (1960). However, in the light of the remarks that we present directly, we feel that there is no necessity for an independent phonological grammar in the first place.

and include among them redundancy rules (morpheme structure rules) that extract regularities from individual lexical matrices, then the distinction of admissible versus inadmissible is already made by the grammar which generates just the occurring forms. For example, if the lexicon lists only occurring forms (e.g., /brik/) and the grammar contains rule (1) as a redundancy rule, then this grammar distinguishes the non-occurring but admissible /blik/ from the non-occurring but inadmissible /bnik/ in the following way: there exists a possible but non-occurring distinctive feature matrix which is converted by the phonological rules into /blik/, but there is no possible matrix that is converted by these rules into /bnik/. We can therefore define the admissible forms as those that can be generated by the rules from some (possibly non-occurring) matrix. Consequently, the rules that generate the occurring forms also make the distinction between admissible and inadmissible, and it is unnecessary to add a new system of rules (an independent phonological grammar) for the grammar to achieve descriptive adequacy, in this respect.

This observation alone is sufficient to rule out the suggestion that the grammar must be supplemented by an independent phonological grammar. But actually, the approach we have adopted goes well beyond this. It is possible to achieve not only descriptive, but (in part) also explanatory adequacy in this way, as is pointed out explicitly in Halle (1962 [37] and 1964*b*) and elsewhere. Suppose, in fact, that the grammar is stated strictly in feature notation, and that the minimization procedure mentioned above is taken as an evaluation measure. If we add rule (1) to the grammar, as a redundancy rule, we may delete from the lexical entry of each item of the form /Consonant + Liquid + . . ./ the feature (namely, [+Vocalic]) that indicates that the second segment is a Liquid rather than a true Consonant. In this way, many features are saved in the lexicon, many more than are added by the rule (1), stated in feature notation. On the other hand, if we were to add rule (2) to the grammar we would save one feature specification for each entry /brik . . ./ (more generally, in fact, every entry /bri + Velar . . ./), since the second segment would not have to be lexically distinguished from /l/, but this would not amount

to the number of features added by rule (2) itself. Consequently, the grammar that contains rule (1) is higher-valued than the grammar not containing this redundancy rule; but a grammar that contains rule (2) is lower-valued than the grammar not containing this rule. In this way, we can account for the selection of a grammar containing rule (1) and excluding rule (2)—we can account, in other words, for the intuitive knowledge that /blik/ has a different status from /bnik/. In short, the distinction between admissible and inadmissible forms results automatically from the attempt to extract all possible generalizations from the lexicon and to state these as redundancy rules, *under a highly specific definition of "generalization,"* given jointly (and implicitly) by the decision to use strict feature notation in grammar and to count features in evaluating grammars. It is also pointed out in Halle (1962 [37] and 1964*b*) and elsewhere that these assumptions have many other merits as well.

Incidentally, it goes without saying that our assumptions about the form of grammar and about an appropriate evaluation measure are surely defective in many ways, and will require refinement and modification as additional empirical evidence is obtained (see notes 4 and 15). This is a first approximation, a first step towards the problem of defining "linguistically significant generalization." But it seems to us a promising first step, which already has some achievements to its credit. So far as is now known, the suggestion that an independent phonological grammar be added to the grammar takes no step at all towards a solution of this problem, and is, therefore, to be rejected.

Our claim, then, is the following. If we construct a grammar to generate the occurring forms (more precisely, to generate the well-formed sentences involving attested lexical items), then this grammar already makes a distinction between admissible and inadmissible. Furthermore, by applying a rather well-motivated evaluation measure to grammars of the type to which we restrict ourselves, we can even achieve partial explanatory adequacy; that is, we can offer a general explanation for the intuition of the native speaker that certain forms are admissible and others, inadmissible. We can thus take certain preliminary steps towards establishing a hypothesis about the internal structure of the acquisition model AM discussed above—about the general character of the distinction in question. In the light of this, we see no point in adding to the already descriptively adequate grammar a new, unjustified, *ad hoc* system of rules that simply repeats what this grammar already establishes, and does so in a way that permits of no explanation or justification, so far as is known. In short, we see no need for an independent phonological grammar.

To justify an independent phonological grammar it would be necessary to show one of two things: either that it can achieve descriptive adequacy in a way in which the grammar to which it is added cannot, or that it is possible to motivate its rules in a way that is more far-reaching than is possible in the case of phonological redundancy rules. The second question is beyond Householder's concerns altogether, since he nowhere indicates any interest in explanatory adequacy. As to the first, he does suggest that a phonological grammar will be superior to the kind of system that we have described in detail. On p. 19 [446] he cites two examples of rules that can be handled more easily in a phonological grammar than by means of "the considerations Halle drags in." The first of these involves "rules concerning the number of segments in a morph (since this must already be specified in the lexicon)." We have no idea what this comment means, and therefore make no attempt to discuss it. The second concerns a hypothetical case in which "feature a in segment A is solidary with feature b in segment B, so that either may be used to predict the other, but for each individual morph one or the other has to be specified." Such a case is certainly logically possible; whether it exists is not so clear. In real cases, there are usually many considerations that determine the choice one way or another. However, let us assume that such an example can be found. Then a grammar of the sort we have described would (by hypothesis) have to make an arbitrary decision, and from our point of view this would be a defect in our theory.[15]

[15]Why it should be a defect from Householder's point of view is unclear. This is a case in which there are (by hypothesis) two equivalent grammars, indistinguishable on empirical grounds, and this is what he takes to be the normal situation (see the discus-

Householder assures us that in this case, the arbitrary decision "can be avoided in a separate phonological grammar" of the sort he has in mind. Since he has never presented an example of such a separate phonological grammar, nor described its properties in any way, we have no idea whether his claim is justified. If it is, and if real examples of this sort of case exist, then this would be an argument in favor of the theory that he has in mind. Obviously such discussion of hypothetical examples and how they would be handled by still unformulated theories has little bearing on real issues and can not outweigh the empirical evidence we have presented above. We persist, therefore, in our belief that a separate phonological grammar is superfluous.

IV. The Status of Phonemes Versus Features
This "remaining philosophical point is a real puzzler" to Householder. He cannot understand why we propose that phonological rules be stated completely in terms of features, rather than in terms of phonemes or in a mixed notation. The only possible explanation that he can concoct for this strange perversity of ours is that we are entangled in some sort of phenomenalist metaphysics, and therefore believe that physical objects are really sets of properties (1965: 20–23 [447–449]). We omit completely any discussion of this digression.

The explanation for our conclusion that so puzzles Householder is given in a clear and straightforward fashion in Halle (1962 [37] and 1964*b*), and we have repeated it above. To repeat once again, if we state rules strictly in terms of features, then we can propose an ef-

sion of uniqueness of grammar above, and on p. 16 [444] of his paper).

Cases of this sort are interesting, and we have considered them several times in our various attempts to develop an adequate phonological theory, but without arriving at a satisfactory proposal. One feature of redundancy rules that seems to us somewhat questionable is precisely their "directionality," that is, the fact that they select one position as independent and characterize the feature composition of other segments in terms of it. A possible modification of our theory would be to replace these "directional" rules by schemata that simultaneously fill in unspecified features in various positions in a phonological matrix. There are various ways to realize this proposal, but we have no strong empirical examples that motivate one or another decision, and prefer therefore to leave the question open.

fective evaluation procedure which distin-guishes true generalizations in terms of natural classes (in the sense in which linguists have always intuitively relied on these notions) from linguistically nonsignificant pseudo-generaliza-tions, and which makes the distinction be-tween admissible and inadmissible forms in an interesting class of cases. With a mixed nota-tion, or a purely segmental notation without features, we know of no way to construct an evaluation procedure that will have these prop-erties. For detailed argument, see Halle (1962 [37] and 1964*b*). Furthermore, the grammar must obviously somewhere contain a specifi-cation of elements in terms of features. As has frequently been observed (see note 24 below), all phonology breaks down if we do not as-sume analysis on the phonetic level in terms of universal phonetic features.

We conclude, therefore, that only feature notation has linguistic significance, and that segments are simply to be regarded as con-ventional abbreviations, utilized to cope with the exigencies of printing but having no lin-guistic significance in themselves. The argu-ments for this position are purely linguistic, and are based neither on metaphysical com-mitments nor analogies to elementary particle theory, as Householder supposes (p. 22 [448]). To refute them, it will be necessary to show how equally good or better results can be achieved by a different theory that allows sepa-rate status to "phonemes" or other segmental units. This Householder does not even at-tempt. His only argument for such units is that they save ink or "physical bulk" in printing, and are easier for him to read. We fail to see the linguistic significance of these comments, the correctness of which we certainly do not challenge.

V. The Adequacy of Jakobson's Theory with Respect to Natural Classes   The next section of Householder's paper (1965: 23–26 [449–450]) concerns the use of distinctive features (in Jakobson's sense) to specify the classes of elements that play a role in phonological[16] rules.

[16]The reader will recall that our use of the word "phonological" (= "systematic phonemic") is that of Sapir, not that of post-Bloomfieldian taxonomic phonemics. Thus it incorporates what is now desig-nated "morphophonemics," in some of the many

This is an interesting and important topic, but unfortunately, in Householder's treatment of it few of the serious questions are even touched.

It is important to be clear about the var-ious roles played by distinctive features in our adaptation of Jakobson's theory.[17] In the first place, they provide a universal phonetic theory that determines all possible "outputs" of the phonological component of any generative grammar. That is, the feature system deter-mines the class of "possible sentences" from which the sentences of any human language are drawn, and, furthermore, imposes an intrinsic classification, in terms of feature composition, on the sounds that constitute utterances. Hence the theory provides an empirical hy-pothesis about the phonetic constitution of any human language and the organization and structure of the system of sounds and of pos-sible phonetic contrasts that a human lan-guage can utilize.

In the second place, the features indirectly determine the classification of lexical entries.[18] Each lexical entry must be classified in terms

and various senses of this loose cover term. Our de-cision to return to more traditional terminology is motivated by what we take to be an empirical find-ing, namely, that only two levels of representation (systematic phonemic and systematic phonetic— see above, pp. 97–98 [457], and references cited there) can be isolated in the phonological component. The new term "morphophonemic" is justified if there is a third level, intermediate between systematic phonemic and systematic phonetic, to which the term "phonemic" might be applied. But since the exis-tence of any such intermediate level has not been demonstrated, so far as we can determine, we see no justification for the terminological innovation and therefore suggest a return to earlier usage.

[17]To simplify the discussion, we will not raise the question of how our adaptation of Jakobson's theory conforms to Jakobson's views. In fact, we feel that our position is in no way different from his in any respect relevant to this discussion. But since we limit ourselves here to Householder's critique of our papers, we will not discuss this further question.

[18]Householder proposes (1965: 17 [445]) that as an alternative to feature analysis, phonological rules be presented in terms of "non-terminal sym-bols" analogous to the non-terminal symbols Noun, Verb, Noun Phrase, etc., of syntax. Thus we will have such rules as Vowel→V-Front, V-Front→ [i, e, æ], etc., in a pure generative phonology, analogous to the rules Verb→Verb$_{\text{Transitive}}$, Verb$_{\text{Transitive}}$→*eat, read, see,* etc., in syntax. Actually, precisely the op-posite decision must obviously be made: that is, the syntactic rules used as an analogon must be restated in terms of features (see Chomsky, 1965, for discus-

of a variety of syntactic, semantic, and phonological categories. We consider here only the latter. For example, the lexical entry *bee,* in English, must be so represented in the lexicon that the phonological rules will assign to it the phonetic representation [bīy].[19] Thus, *bee* must be assigned to the category of forms that have an initial Voiced nonContinuant, the category of forms that have a Diffuse, non-Grave Vowel following the initial Consonant, and so on. The natural way to represent this categorization of *bee* (and, in general, of all lexical items) is by a matrix in which columns stand for "segments" and rows correspond to features. Each feature corresponds to a pair of opposed categories, membership in one being indicated by a + and membership in the other being indicated by a −. These paired categories are mutually exclusive but not necessarily exhaustive. Thus certain entries may be blank, indicating that no information is given as to the membership of the segment in question with respect to the paired categories corresponding to the row in question. The phonological rules then fill in the blanks, modify entries where necessary, and replace the +'s and −'s by integers indicating degree, where the features correspond to phonetic scales. Thus the lexical entry *bee* might be represented by the phonological matrix (6) (we modify this below), which is converted by phonological rules to the fully specified feature matrix conventionally abbreviated as [bīy].

---

sion of this point which summarizes and generalizes the many proposals that have been made during the last five or six years for remedying the defect of grammatical theory illustrated by such rules as Verb→Verb$_{Transitive}$, etc.). The reason is that cross-classification of the sort that is typical on the phonological level (as on the lexical level, in syntax) is inexpressible in terms of rewriting rules. Thus if we want to introduce both Frontness and Height, let us say, which intersect in [i], it is impossible to use the device of rewriting rules with non-terminal symbols, in the way that Householder suggests.

[19]In citing examples, we will omit phonetic detail irrelevant to the discussion. Our discussion of phonological rules will also omit details and refinements that have no bearing on the issues being raised. The reader will recall that the phonetic symbols, in our view, are nothing other than conventional abbreviations for feature complexes. Furthermore, we maintain that in practice this is everyone else's view too, and has been for many centuries.

(6)

Vocalic	−	+
Diffuse	+	+
Grave	+	−
Nasal	−	
Continuant	−	
Voice	+	

The representation (6) is a lexical categorization; the representation [bīy] (in its full, matrix form) is a phonetic specification of the corresponding item. In this unusually simple case, it may seem that the phonological rules simply contribute further specification to (6); for example, one rule assigns the feature [+Tense] to the Vowel because of the fact that it is in final position, a second rule of equal generality (*the diphthongization rule,* to which we return below) adds a Diffuse Glide to the Tense Vowel, the Glide sharing the categorization of the Vowel with respect to Gravity (thus [w] is added to Grave Vowels and [y] to nonGrave Vowels), and so on. But in general, phonological rules will also modify entries, as, for example, when an unstressed Vowel, in various contexts, is reduced to [ɨ], in English. It is, in fact, quite common for the lexical categorization of a segment to appear in none of the corresponding phonetic matrices, without change. For example, for reasons that we cannot detail here, the second Vowel of *demon* must be entered lexically as /ɔ/ (nonTense, Grave, Rounded, Compact) although it appears phonetically, in most American English dialects only as [ɨ] (nonCompact, nonRounded) or /ā/ (Tense, nonRounded), as in *demon, demonic,* respectively. In fact, we will see below that even in the case of *bee,* the phonological rules modify as well as expand feature content.

Notice, incidentally, that there is no need to incorporate in a grammar rules that convert phonological to phonetic features (the rules discussed on pp. 16−17 [444−445] of Householder's paper. Rather, we may think of the phonetic features as inducing a lexical categorization, in the sense described above. Notice further that lexical items may be assigned to additional categories beyond those provided by the phonetic features. Thus, for example, the word *see* in English must be assigned a categorial (phonological) representation that indicates that it takes irregular inflections, etc.

Implicit in Jakobson's theory is another interesting and non-trivial empirical assumption, namely, that the lexical categorization induced by the phonetic theory will be "natural," from the point of view of the functioning of phonological rules; that is, that the rules will apply to classes of segments which can, in general, be easily and simply specified in terms of feature composition. There is no *a priori* reason why this should be true. The framework we have just described presupposes that it is true in general; otherwise, it would be quite unmotivated and pointless.

Householder challenges this empirical assumption, and suggests that very often the classes of elements that are referred to in phonological rules are not natural in the sense just outlined. He also draws some curious conclusions concerning the universality of a feature system from this purported demonstration of the inadequacy of the Jakobsonian framework. We return to his conclusion below, but first investigate the six examples that he offers to show that the classes that appear in rules are not natural. We shall see that none of his examples has any bearing on this quite interesting question—in most cases, because he has simply paid little attention to the linguistic facts.

His first example is the rule that converts /k/ and /t/ to [s] before high front Vowels (e.g., *democrat-democracy, electric-electricity*). But /k/ and /t/ differ in Diffuseness and Gravity. Therefore the rule does not apply to a natural class.

Notice, however, that in the positions where /k/ goes to [s], which is Diffuse and nonGrave, /g/ generally goes to [ǰ] (e.g., *pedagogue-pedagogic*), which is nonDiffuse and nonGrave. It seems to us that the simplest way to describe these alterations is by a sequence of rules: the first applies to [k, g] (that is, the archi-segment consisting of the features common to [k] and [g]) in certain contexts, changing the Gravity of the consonant to nonGrave; a second rule raises the nonGrave variant of /k/ to Diffuse; a third rule converts all of the nonGrave stops to Strident Continuants, in certain contexts. This brief account omits details, but, so far as we have been able to discover, it extracts whatever generality there is in this set of consonant alternations. (For details, see our *Sound Pattern of English*, forthcoming. [See now Chomsky and Halle, 1968—VBM.]) But, in fact, each rule involves

natural classes. We see no improvement that can be effected by adding new, *ad hoc* categorization to the principled categorization induced by distinctive feature theory, in this case. Furthermore, Householder suggests no way in which this set of alternations can be described more simply by using *ad hoc* features. Hence this example is apparently quite irrelevant to his claims.

Notice, incidentally, that to refute Jakobson's theory (or our version of it), it is not sufficient to point to some complicated phenomenon. It is also necessary to show that certain generalizations that are linguistically significant cannot be extracted if we restrict ourselves to the categories provided by distinctive feature theory. This Householder makes no attempt to do in this case or, as we shall see, any of the others he cites.

Householder's second example involves Vowel length in Latin, before final Consonants. The rules, in this case, seem to be the following:

(5) V→[−long] in the context:

$$\left\{ \begin{array}{ll} VC - \left[\begin{array}{l} +cons \\ -strid \end{array} \right] & (i) \\[2em] \#C - \left[\begin{array}{l} -strid \\ +diff \\ -voc \end{array} \right] \end{array} \right\} \#$$

$$(ii)$$

Case (i) applies to polysyllables, and asserts that Vowels shorten in this case before non-Strident Consonants or Liquids. Case (ii) asserts that in monosyllables, the Vowel shortens before a nonStrident Diffuse true Consonant (i.e., before Liquids there is no shortening, in this case). Probably, Diffuseness need not be specified in case (ii), since the examples with final Velars (which are, in any event, sparse) have an elided final -e, and proper ordering of rules can thus eliminate these cases. Furthermore, it does not seem difficult to extend the rules to final clusters.[20] In any event, the rule is quite simple and involves

[20]It seems that before double Consonant, the Vowel is Long if one of the Consonants is Strident; otherwise Short. In particular, then, before Nasal plus Strident, the Vowel will be Long (e.g., *mōns, mēns*). The Nasal then is dropped in this position (possibly, post-classically), giving a Long, presumably Nasalized Vowel before the single Strident Consonant. We have not discussed the problem of

only natural classes. It must therefore be regarded as an example supporting the distinctive feature framework and it is entirely unclear why Householder brings up this example at all.

Householder's third and fourth examples we quote in full: "A rapid check of Sanskrit Sandhi rules indicates about five (out of some 25 or so) classes of this sort [i.e., of the sort that involve unavoidable disjunctive classes: NC/MH]; one set of rules for Latin nouns requires four out of ten." Since one cannot refute a serious theory by a "rapid check of . . . rules," or by mentioning "one set of rules" (which may be the wrong set) we shall not discuss these examples. We cannot resist observing that such unwillingness to deal with linguistic data ill becomes one who takes it upon himself to lecture others on their disregard for facts (cf. Householder, 1965: 14 [443]).

Householder's fifth example involves a hypothetical rule that applies only to i, e, and æ. Just why he gives this example is rather unclear, since these constitute a natural class (nonGrave, nonRounded), as noted incidentally in Halle (1962 [37] and 1964b) (see also fn. 5 above).

Householder's final example is the most interesting of all. He discusses the Vowels that occur before final [ŋ], and notes that they do not form a natural class. That is, we have the Diffuse nonGrave Vowel [i] (as in *sing*) and all the Compact Vowels ([æ], as in *sang*; [ʌ], as in *sung*; [ɔ] as in *song*).[21] Thus we have the class: Compact, or Diffuse nonGrave. And this is not a natural class.

There is, however, not the slightest reason why the phonetic data should fall into natural classes. The theory presumes only that phonological rules will apply to natural classes. Furthermore, one would expect that underlying phonological (systematic phonemic) forms will be symmetrically arranged, in general. In this case, one would expect the natural class /i, u, æ, ɔ/ (i.e., the class $\begin{Bmatrix} [+\text{Diffuse}] \\ [+\text{Compact}] \end{Bmatrix}$) instead of the nonnatural class /i, ʌ, æ, ɔ/, which appears in the phonetic representations. And, in fact, if we look at the situation more closely, this is exactly what we find.[22]

Notice first that phonetic [ŋ] is clearly phonological /ng/, (or, more properly, /Ng/). The reasons are well-known, and we will not take the space to discuss them here.

Notice further that the problem that Householder mentions is not unique to final /ng/, but involves *all* final Consonant clusters. That is, in the context −CC#, we have phonetic [ʌ] instead of the expected [u] and thus fail to have a natural class. Hence the gap has nothing to do with [ŋ], but is a matter that involves all final phonological clusters. Thus instead of [luŋ] we have [lʌŋ], instead of [bump] we have [bʌmp], instead of [tusk] we have

---

shortening before /d/, as in Ablative and Accusative of personal pronouns, where the /d/ drops finally. It may be that dropping of the final /d/ precedes (synchronically) the shortening rule. Note, incidentally, that shortening before /t/ is attested late.

As in any real linguistic example, there are numerous facts to consider before one arrives at a hypothesis as to the grammatical description. We have made no attempt to exhaust the problem of Classical Latin shortening, obviously. But we see, at the moment, not the slightest relevance of this phenomenon to the question of inadequacy of the Jakobsonian framework, and are therefore mystified by Householder's reference to it.

[21]There is a dialectal variation here which we will overlook, since it is irrelevant to the main point. The main point is the departure from naturalness in the phonetic data, and this concerns only the fact that [u] does not appear.

[22]For our speech, the situation is even more simple, since only /e/ is excluded (phonologically) before [ŋ] (= /ng/) in final position. Thus *long* (phonetically, [lɔŋ]) is phonologically /long/, as we can see by the alternant *length* (involving the Gravity shift rule that we mention below). The lowering of phonological /o/ to phonetic [ɔ] in this and various other positions is automatic and fairly general. Phonological /ɔ/ also appears, as in *thong* (phonetic [θãŋ]), where /ɔ/ goes to [ã] by the general rule noted above, p. 122 [473]). Phonological /u/ also appears, as we shall see directly.

Notice that there is no Tense-Lax contrast before [ŋ#] (as there is before [n#], [m#]), but this is regular. There is a general redundancy rule specifying Vowels as Lax before Consonant clusters (more precisely, before clusters that are not fully dental or palatal). Since [ŋ#] is phonologically /Ng#/, where N is the archi-segment [+Nasal], this rule applies to the Vowel preceding it, eliminating the contrast. Hence the only gap before [ŋ#] is /e/. Here, too, the situation is of course slightly more general, since we have the same gap before [ŋk#]. Thus the gap is before Nasal+Velar.

Summarizing, no restrictions need be stated on the distribution of vowels before phonological /Ng/ except for the rule that /e/ does not occur before N+Velar. All other distributional limitations are accounted for by general rules.

[tʌsk], instead of [dukt] we have [dʌkt], etc. In each case, the phonetic data fails to form a natural class because of the absence of phonetic [u].

This observation suggests that we consider adding to the phonology of English a rule

(8)   u→ʌ

applying in the context: —CC# (and, in fact, in various other contexts—for details, see our forthcoming *Sound Pattern of English;* the historical basis for this synchronic rule is quite well known). If this rule can be justified, then the underlying phonological representations will have the symmetries expected in terms of Jakobsonian features, though the phonetic facts will not.

But, in fact, rule (8) is extremely well motivated. First, observe that it allows us to remove /ʌ/ completely from phonetic representations. The Lax Vowels will be simply /i, e, æ, u, o, ɔ/, and Rounding will now be entirely redundant for them (it will coincide with Gravity). Second, notice that this rule will immediately account for simple Vowel alternations, e.g., *reduce-reduction.* The Grave Diffuse Vowel of *reduce* becomes Lax [u] in *reduction* by general rules that we need not discuss here, and then is converted to phonetic [ʌ] by rule (8).

Similarly, we can extract subregularities from many irregular Verb alternations, by means of rule (8). Thus the rule (9), which shifts Gravity, is of fairly wide applicability in English "irregular" constructions:

(9)   [α Grave] → [− α Grave]. (α = + or −)

This rule will convert /sing/ to /sung/, which is converted by rule (8) to [sʌng], finally, [sʌŋ], and it applies similarly in other cases.

But most important is the fact that rule (8) is really a special case of a very general rule in English that is a synchronic reflection of the Great Vowel Shift. This rule converts Diffuse Vowels to Compact Vowels (and has various other effects that we will not discuss here in detail).[23] Together with the Diphthongization rule (see p. 121 above [473]), it converts phonological /ī/ to [āy] (through intermediate [īy],

by Diphthongization) and converts phonological /ū/ to [āw] (through intermediate [ūw], by Diphthongization). The reader will observe that rule (8) is simply the special case of this extremely general rule where the Vowel in question is Lax, Diffuse. The rule applies to all Tense Vowels, and to the Lax Diffuse Grave Vowel (i.e., /u/) and, in certain cases, to the Lax Diffuse nonGrave Vowel as well. Its primary motivation is to explain such Vowel alternations as *divine-divinity, decide-decision,* etc., and their well-known analogues for the other Vowels. Thus *divine* is phonologically /divīn/ and becomes /divāyn/ by Diphthongization and Vowel Shift, while *divinity* derives from underlying /divīn+ity/ by automatic Laxing before an unstressed Vowel in a nonfinal syllable. In the same way, we can account for the other alternations. But notice that this also allows us to account automatically for such alternations as *profound-profundity* from underlying /pro+fūnd/ (which becomes [profāwnd] by Diphthongization and Vowel Shift, and [profʌnd] before -*ity* by automatic Laxing and Vowel Shift, in this case, rule (8)).

We give no more details here than this, but these few comments and hints are sufficient to indicate that rule (8) is actually a special case of a very general phonological process, which is quite central to the synchronic phonology of English (and also, as is usual in such cases, reflects a historical "sound change"). Hence there is a very strong justification for the assumption that the underlying phonological representations form a natural class.

We have gone into this degree of detail to illustrate a very important though perhaps obvious point. Nothing significant can be learned from superficial phonetic observation alone. In particular, from the observation that the phonetic distribution of Vowels before [ŋ#] is defective, nothing whatsoever follows. This defective distribution may have any number of causes. A slightly more serious look at the question shows that the defective distribution (the nonnaturalness of the class) has nothing

---

[23]In particular, it converts nonDiffuse nonCompact Vowels to Diffuse, and Compact to nonCompact. Thus the phonological representation for

bee cited above is actually incorrect, and should be replaced by /bE/, where /E/ here is the archi-segment [nonGrave, nonCompact, nonDiffuse Vowel]. The Vowel Shift rule is the central rule in the synchronic nontransformational phonology of English. We discuss it in detail in *Sound Pattern of English.*

particular to do with [ŋ], but is a property of all (phonological) final clusters. A deeper investigation of the facts of English shows that the underlying systematic phonemic forms do constitute precisely a natural class, in the Jakobsonian sense, because of the centrality of the Vowel Shift rule (and its special case (8)) in the phonology of contemporary English. In this case, Householder's conclusion about the inadequacy of the Jakobsonian framework result simply from his failure to pay attention to the facts of English structure.

Having shown that none of the examples that Householder adduces has any relevance to his purpose, let us now return to the conclusion that he draws from them. In commenting on the difficulties that he believes himself to have discovered, he states (p. 24 [449-450]):

In most cases this could be avoided by a willingness to abandon Jakobsonian features, but (though a few daring souls may *add* on extra features to the "systematic phonemic" set) no one seems to be anxious to construct features from scratch for each language, specifically to be maximally useful in the description of that language. There is a kind of orthodoxy which no one dares violate because no one understands the reason for it . . .

This is a remarkable comment. Notice first that he has not shown a single deficiency in the distinctive feature system. Notice secondly that even where he thinks he has found a difficulty (because of his inattention to linguistic facts), he has not even suggested a way to avoid these presumed difficulties by abandoning Jakobsonian features. Finally, Householder not only overlooks the rich literature and serious linguistic studies that have been concerned with justifying and improving the distinctive feature system, simply asserting, casually, that this system is a mere orthodoxy which no one dares violate but for which no support has been proposed; he also confesses to inability to conceive of a reason why "no one seems to be anxious to construct features from scratch for each language,"[24] thus, in effect, he insists that there must be a new linguistic theory for each language.

[24]As has often been noted—cf., e.g., Chomsky (1964a: 944-973 and c: 65-110 [401-423])—the assumption of a universal feature structure is made (often only implicitly) in every approach to phonology that is known, and clearly cannot be avoided.

VI. The Validity of Procedures of Taxonomic Linguistics

In Chomsky (1964a and c [39]) it is pointed out that the notion of "complementary distribution" is of no theoretical significance (it permits entirely unacceptable results, including even analyses that violate biuniqueness, and excludes optimal analyses) and that the other conditions that define "taxonomic phonemics"[25] are also unacceptable.

What is at issue only is the choice of features, not their universality. To repeat the obvious once again, suppose that we were to approach, let us say, English with no assumption at all about universal features (i.e., suppose we were to follow Householder's proposal). Consider only monosyllables of the form CVC. We find certain phonetic elements in initial position and others (phonetically distinct from them) in final position. Phonemic analysis of any sort requires that we somehow identify initial and final phones. With no assumption about feature structure, we can do this in any way we like. No way is more "useful" than any other, or more "simple," in any abstract sense. For example, if we wish to show that the maximally simple system is to identify initial p with final t and initial t with final p, it is only necessary to invent a physical feature (there are innumerably many of these) which is common to initial p and final t, and excludes initial t and final p. Call this the feature A. Following Householder, there is no reason to prefer, e.g., the feature Labial to the feature A. And furthermore, having now (à la Householder) accepted A for our analysis, we can immediately demonstrate the absurdity of using the feature Labial for the analysis of English. For consider the complexity of the feature Labial. Thus a phone is Labial only if it is in initial position and has the feature A or in final position and has the feature non-A. Obviously such a disjunctive feature does not contribute to the "simplicity" or "usefulness" of linguistic description (in the vague sense of these terms that Householder apparently has in mind).

It is for such reasons as this that one does not "construct features from scratch for each language."

[25]The conditions discussed are *linearity, invariance, biuniqueness,* and *local determinacy.* Householder finds the first three clear, but states that "Chomsky says so little about [. . . local determinacy . . .] that I can't quite make out how it differs from linearity or perhaps a combination of linearity with biuniqueness." A more careful reading of Chomsky (1964a and c [39]) would have explained to Householder the source of his difficulty. As shown there in detail, linguists who refer freely to the "biuniqueness principle" apparently are not using "biuniqueness" in the technical sense of this word. It appears, from the examples they give, that what they have in mind is another principle, called "local determinacy" in Chomsky (1964a and c [39]) to distinguish it from "biuniqueness," which, after all, has a clear technical meaning. But this principle has never been clearly formulated. The unclarity is, then, the fault of taxonomic linguistics and not of the attempt in Chomsky (1964a and c [39]) to evaluate it.

Householder discusses only the criticism of "complementary distribution" but, because of an equivocation in his argument, his discussion is quite beside the point.

To clarify the issue, let us state precisely what is involved. We assume the notion "contrast" defined on utterances (i.e., *pin* contrasts with *bin, lighthouse keeper* with *light housekeeper,* etc.). All approaches to phonology with which we are familiar require of a phonemic notation that it meet condition (10):

(10) if X contrasts with Y, then the phonemic representation of X differs from the phonemic representation of Y,

where X and Y are utterances (let us assume, phonetically transcribed). Taxonomic linguistics adds various other conditions (e.g., the converse of (10)), but this does not concern us here (our feeling is, as argued in Halle (1962 [37] and 1964*b*), Chomsky (1964*a* and *c* [39]), and elsewhere, that many of these additional conditions are incorrect—that is, if imposed, they define a system of representation which is not a part of linguistic structure).

A major concern of taxonomic linguistics has been to develop procedures of analysis which will guarantee that condition (10) and others will be met by a phonemic system. Interesting and valuable accounts of such procedures have been presented by Trubetzkoy, Harris, Bloch, and others, and it is these that are discussed in Chomsky (1964*a* and *c* [39]). One notion that is central to many of these procedural accounts is the notion of *complementary distribution*. The "distribution" of a phone is the class of phonetic contexts in which it occurs (these being of some reasonable length). Two phones are said to be in "complementary distribution" if their distributions are complementary, i.e., nonoverlapping. A *tentative phoneme* is a class of phones which are pair-wise in complementary distribution. The *phonemic system* of the language is a family of tentative phonemes that meets certain other conditions. This approach can be and has been refined in various ways, and is intended as a procedure of phonemic analysis, a procedure which will, in particular, guarantee that (10) will be met.

In Chomsky (1964*a* and *c* [39]) it is pointed out that the procedure, in any of its known forms, does not guarantee that (10) will be met. For example, in English the unaspirated allophone of /k/ is in complementary distribution with Lax [a] but if the two are combined in a phoneme /K/, then both *socked* and *Scot* will be represented /sKKt/, violating condition (10). This illustrates the fact that the "principle of complementary distribution" unfortunately is not sufficiently strong to guarantee that (10) will be met. But this is its major theoretical justification (it is also pointed out in Chomsky (1964*a* and *c* [39]) that this principle fails to permit optimal "biunique" systems, so that its other theoretical justification fails). Consequently, the principle is apparently of no theoretical significance, and should be dropped from linguistic theory altogether.

Householder proposes to counter this argument against the definition of "phoneme" in terms of complementary distribution by giving condition (10) the new name "the principle of complementary distribution," and, presumably, dropping the principle of complementary distribution as defined by Harris, Bloch, and others and restated above.[26] With this termi-

[26]He points out that the version of the principle of complementary distribution given in Chomsky (1964*a* and *c* [39]) (and restated, briefly above) "is adapted from Harris, and would perhaps not be universally accepted." He does not go on to point out that the principle is given in the same form by everyone else who has defined the notion, and he also does not observe that in his own review of Harris (Householder, 1952) he found no difficulty with Harris' formulation of what is, after all, the fundamental notion in procedural taxonomic linguistics.

Householder also states that "the link Chomsky makes with biuniqueness is quite puzzling to me." This comment is quite puzzling to us, particularly in the light of the fact that he proposes to use the term "principle of complementary distribution" for (10), which (with its converse) is just the principle of biuniqueness.

To be precise, we should point out that Householder assigns the new name "principle of complementary distribution" not to the familiar condition (10), but rather to a stronger variant of it, namely, the principle that two phonetic segments (of reasonable length) must be phonemically distinct if they *ever* contrast. This is much too strong. For example, it rules out phonemic overlapping, in most cases. Thus, take Bloch's example of a dialect with alveolar flap [D] as the variant of /r/ after [θ] (as in *throw*), and assume, as is widely true, that intervocalic poststress /t/ has the variant [D]. Most formulations of taxonomic principles will permit assignment of [D] to /r/ after [θ] and to /t/ intervocalically, as is obviously correct. This leads to no violation of (10);

nological change, he is now able to avoid the conclusion that the principle of complementary distribution leads to a violation of (10), i.e., to a violation of itself. He also can conclude that the "principle of complementary distribution," as newly defined, excludes the *socked-Scot* example. This is quite correct. Since this example was specifically constructed so as to violate (10), it follows that the principle (10) excludes it. With this ingenious defense, the term "principle of complementary distribution" is saved, though of course the notion "complementary distribution" and the procedural definition of the phoneme based on it are entirely given up.

It is interesting, incidentally, to note that well before the principle of complementary distribution (for the remainder of our discussion, we return to the pre-Householder usage of terms) was formulated as a basis for phonemic analysis, Jakobson gave an example of exactly the *socked-Scot* type which shows the inadequacy of any such principle (Jakobson, 1931). He pointed out that in Czech, although [i] and [j] do not contrast, [ij] contrasts with [ji]; and he proposed the following subsidiary principle of phonemic analysis:

(11) if AB contrasts with BA, then A and B cannot be assigned to the same phoneme.

This rules out the Czech case, and also the *socked-Scot* case, but it is still ineffective. Thus in English, the pre-[r] allophone of /ī/ is apparently in complementary distribution with [d], and their assignment to the same phoneme

---

nor, for that matter, does it even necessarily lead to a violation of biuniqueness. But it does violate Householder's stronger variant of (10) (assuming that phonemes are "of reasonable length"). Since [r] and [D] sometimes contrast (namely, *berry-Betty*), they cannot be considered allophones of the same phoneme. Hence the post- [θ] phone [D] must be assigned to /t/ (giving /θtow/ as the phonemic representation of *throw,* counter both to intuition and to otherwise valid rules of morpheme structure). Householder's formulation of (10) also has a consequence which he considered an absurdity in his review (1952) of Harris. Thus he objected strenuously to Harris' treatment of q and g in Moroccan Arabic as "at all times distinct phonemes," on the grounds that they sometimes contrast, a conclusion which he finds "staggering" (1952: 263–264). But it is just this conclusion that is required by the principle he has now proposed.

is not ruled out by (11), but if we assign them to the same phoneme D, then *dreary* will be /DrDri/ and (*two*)-*eared* will be /DrD/, violating biuniqueness (in its usual interpretation, as local determinacy). Other similar examples are not difficult to construct.

In fact, no such subsidiary principle as (11) is necessary *or* sufficient. What is needed, as a defining principle for the notion "phoneme," is simply the condition (10) itself rather than any of its special cases (such as (11)). Of course, having recognized this fact, all hope of a "procedural" definition of "phoneme," in the usual sense of these terms, quite disappears.

Returning to Householder's discussion, we should like to comment on several new principles of phonemic analysis that he proposes. He suggests (p. 27 [451]) the principle

(12) "If a sequence of two segments contrasts with either of the two segments separately or with the two in reverse order, then they contrast with each other." I.e., [AB] may contrast with [BA], or [B] or [A], and all these are instances of a B versus A contrast.

Householder proposes (12) as "his statement" of a principle of Trubetzkoy's which was found wanting in Chomsky (1964*a* and *c* [39]), but the relation of (12) to Trubetzkoy's principle seems obscure. In fact, while Trubetzkoy's principle was correct so far as it went, but inadequate to its purpose, Householder's "restatement" of it is quite absurd. Thus (12) rules out the possibility of analyzing geminates as double consonants or long vowels as double vowels, in the usual cases where this is done. For example, the lengthened /l/ of English *solely* cannot be analyzed as /ll/, because it contrasts with the single /l/ of *holy;* or to take an example from Householder himself (1952: 265), his double /t/ in *thirteen* cannot be analyzed as double /t/, as he proposed, because it contrasts with the single /t/ of *thirty.* In all such cases, the usual analysis would give a sequence of two segments contrasting with one of the members of the sequence, and (12) requires that the two segments in question must be assigned to different phonemes in this case.

Householder also suggests (p. 28 [451])

such additional rules of phonemic analysis as the following:

(13) "If [XABY] is much more frequent than [XAY] or [XBY] for all values of X and Y, then the advantages of treating AB as a unit phoneme should be considered."

The only emendation we would suggest is that the advantages be considered under any other circumstances as well. As to the other rule that he discusses (p. 28 [451]), we have nothing to say. It is far too vague to discuss, and we ask only why he calls it a restatement of a rather clear (though *ad hoc*) rule of Trubetzkoy's.

In a recent paper, Vachek (1964) [40] offers a defense of Prague phonological theory against the criticisms that we have just been discussing. This defense, however, is in reality merely an acknowledgement of the justice of the criticisms. Thus Vachek admits that the principles of Prague phonology are in fact inconsistent with the facts cited as counterexamples, but he suggests that this is not important because these principles are valid for all cases except those of a certain specific category, namely, the category of cases where the language is in a "state of flux." Accepting this view, we must then ask what the defining criterion is for this category of cases. The answer is that this is the category of cases for which Prague phonological principles fail. There is no independent way of identifying this class. Conclusion: the theory in question works for all cases except those for which it fails; Vachek is claiming no more than this.

There is no disagreement between Vachek and us as to the correctness of particular analyses. Clearly, then, we share some notion of descriptive adequacy, a notion that is not captured by Prague phonological theory, and is in fact, in conflict with the assumptions of this theory in the cases mentioned. For this reason, the theory must be revised, and it is just such a revision that we have been proposing.

VII. The Phonetic Basis of Phonemic Analysis
The linguistic examples used in Chomsky (1964*a* and *c* [39]) are, for the most part, simply taken from the authors whose principles of phonemic analysis are discussed. But Householder doubts the phonetic accuracy of the analyses given by Bloch, Harris, and others, which are accepted in Chomsky (1964*a* and *c* [39]) as a basis for discussion of their principles. For example, he objects to Bloch's example of overlapping in the case of the flaps of *throw* and *Betty* (*r:tt*), claiming that the "basis for phonetic identity" is unknown to him, in such cases. He goes on to state (p. 28 [452]): "I have never yet seen a good example of phonemic overlap where this escape route [namely, the assumption that the phones in question are physically distinguishable] was not open." Thus all examples of overlapping can be eliminated, by a sufficiently fine phonetic analysis. And the same is true of all the other examples given in Chomsky (1964*a* and *c* [39]). That is, all of these examples are based on certain assumptions about phonetic identity of physically distinct occurrences, and it is always possible to insist upon a finer and more detailed phonetic representation in which these distinct occurrences are phonetically distinguished. In other words Householder is making the point that distinct physical events can (with sufficiently fine measurement) be distinguished from one another, and that certainly, two phones in different phonetic contexts can generally be shown to be physically distinct in some respect.

How can it be, then, that Bloch, Harris, and others overlooked this insight in presenting and discussing their examples? The answer is not difficult to find. They knew perfectly well, of course, that it is possible to give a phonetic analysis so fine that phones in different contexts are differently represented—so that, in particular, the flaps of *throw* and *Betty* can be distinguished. But they were also aware of the fact that no phonemic analysis can be based on a phonetic transcription so fine. This truism Householder seems to have overlooked. Obviously a very narrow phonetic transcription makes any distributional phonemics impossible, since distributional procedures will lead nowhere unless phones and contexts repeat sufficiently often. Knowing this, Bloch, Harris, and others who are concerned with developing phonemic theory base their analyses on a phonetic theory which is not so narrow as to exclude sufficient repetition, and, at the same time, gives rise to the cases of overlapping, etc., which they discuss. The dilemma that Householder has placed himself in is this:

true, he can insist on a phonetic analysis so narrow as to eliminate the examples of Chomsky (1964*a* and *c* [39]), in which case distributional phonemics of the sort he wishes to defend is also ruled out as vacuous; or he may require only a phonetic analysis of the type assumed by Harris, Bloch, etc., in which case distributional procedures will apply nonvacuously, but the counter-examples discussed in Chomsky (1964*a* and *c* [39]) will also arise.[27]

Householder concludes this discussion (p. 29 [452]) by pointing out that the difficulties presented in Chomsky (1964*a* and *c* [39]) exemplify precisely "the morass" of problems "that the phonemic principle was intended to extricate us from long ago." We agree, but we add that as shown in Halle (1962 [37] and 1964*b*), Chomsky (1964*a* and *c* [39]) and elsewhere, the phonemic principle, as developed in modern taxonomic phonemics, apparently fails in this attempt and simply introduces a rash of new problems of its own, although what

we called "systematic phonemics," a phonological theory based heavily on earlier ideas of Sapir's combined with a version of Jakobson's distinctive feature theory and various other new notions (e.g., the transformational cycle), does seem to extricate us effectively from this morass. These arguments Householder does not deal with at all.

This completes our discussion of the main issues raised by Householder. Turning now to his summary, we state his major conclusions and, briefly, the result of our analysis of them.

Householder's first conclusion (p. 32 [454]) is this: "Halle appears to offer a demonstration that feature matrix notation is more economical than phonemic notation. This is seen to be clearly false." What is false is that anyone has even attempted this absurdity. In fact, we have no idea what it might mean to show that matrix notation is more economical than phonemic notation, or the opposite. What we are interested in is an entirely different question, as discussed above.

His second conclusion is that the feature system does not provide natural classes. As we have shown, he has not given a single argument to support this conclusion.

His third conclusion is that we have given no argument to justify the incorporation of morpheme structure rules in the grammar. This conclusion is based entirely on a complete and thorough misinterpretation of what we say about evaluation procedures, and is therefore worthless. In fact, the argument for incorporating such rules, as given in Halle (1962 [37] and 1964*b*) and Chomsky (1964*a* and *c* [39]), and again above, is quite simple and straightforward.

His fourth conclusion (p. 32 [455]) is that "phonology has a structure which is independent of the syntactic structure of a language." If this means that no phonological rules refer to syntactic structure, we have given abundant (and unchallenged) evidence that he is wrong. If it means that there is a taxonomic phonemic level, independent or relatively independent (in the Pike or Harris sense) of syntax, we have, again, given so far uncontroverted arguments that this is false. If it means that a grammar must contain an independent "phonological grammar," we have argued (a) that this is superfluous, since the new addition simply repeats what is already fully accounted for by

---

[27]In the same connection, Householder discusses Harris' example of an English dialect in which the phonetic distinction of *writer-rider* is length of the Vowel. This seems to him an unacceptable example, and he gives an irrelevant disquisition on instrumental phonetics to illustrate the difficulties of defining length. The problem that disturbs him is, apparently, that some occurrences of the "shorter" phone may be physically longer than some occurrences of the "longer" phone. This is surely true. But surely it is unnecessary to repeat here the introductory lecture to an elementary phonetics class in which it is pointed out that phonetic representation is based on normalization (with respect to speed of utterance, loudness, etc.), and that phonetic features are relative rather than absolute.

In any event, the whole discussion is quite beside the point. The very same argument could have been given for the dialect in which the distinction is one of quality rather than length (i.e., with *writer* = [rʌyDr] = /raytr/ and *rider* = [rayDr] = /raydr/).

Householder comments (fn. 14) that "Halle uses a similar example in which the difference is qualitative (1962: 63 [386]) [a] vs. [ə]. This is more realistic." But this is surely a slip of the pen, for we do not doubt that he is familiar with the fact that in certain dialects of English the difference between the two variants of the diphthong is one of length (/a:/ vs. /a/) whereas in others it is one of tenseness (/a/ vs. /ə/) (cf. Kurath and McDavid, 1961: maps 26–27). If indeed Householder means what he seems to be saying and regards the latter dialects as "more realistic" than the former, then he must also regard German as more realistic than English or Latvian as more realistic than Igbo, a conclusion that seems to us as unbelievable as it is unavoidable.

the grammar to which it is added, and (b) that it leads to a loss of explanatory adequacy, and this argument, too, is so far uncontroverted. If it means (Householder, 1965: 19 [446]) that "phonological structure . . . can be changed completely without altering any of the syntactic structure of a language," then we agree, but fail to see what this remark has to do with anything we have ever said, or why it is of any interest, or why it implies that (in the usual sense of these words) phonology is independent of syntax (it seems to us, rather, that it implies that syntax is independent of phonology). What else this comment might mean we do not know.

His fifth conclusion is that taxonomic phonemics must be part of grammar. But he has given no justification for this claim and has not dealt with our counter-arguments in Halle (1962 [37] and 1964b), Chomsky (1964a and c [39]), and elsewhere. We therefore see no reason to discuss this claim.

His sixth conclusion is that distinctive feature theory is clumsy and must be revised or abandoned. No argument has been offered for this assertion, which is, therefore, simply to be disregarded.

His seventh conclusion is that Halle seems to overlook the distinction between systematic phonemics and systematic phonetics (though Chomsky is not guilty of this oversight). True, this distinction is not discussed explicitly in Halle (1962 [37] and 1964b), not being germane to the issues raised there. By the same logic, he can show that Chomsky overlooks the existence of Elizabethan English (though Halle seems aware of it (1962 [37] and 1964b)), and that both of us overlook the existence of elephants.

His eighth conclusion is that there are several different types of features. This is surely true. We do not see the relevance of this familiar observation here, and are unable to discern any new contribution to this interesting question in Householder's paper.

His final conclusion is that our approach somehow blocks the path of inquiry. We would be disturbed, naturally, if this were true, but see little reason to believe it. We think that we have presented good reasons for the belief that taxonomic linguistics of the sort that Householder defends has been far too limited

in its interests, and that these limitations have, in fact, led to the wide adoption of incorrect assumptions about the nature of language. A return to many traditional questions seems to us very much warranted; and, in fact, some of the traditional answers (in particular, Sapir's views with respect to phonology) seem to us to provide a very good basis for further progress. Taxonomic linguistics has provided a wealth of new data, higher standards of rigor, and many useful ideas. But we have tried to show that the framework within which it operated was fundamentally wrong, in many serious ways. We have tried to show that it is quite possible to transcend these limitations and to face problems of descriptive and explanatory adequacy in new and promising ways. We see no respect in which the path to inquiry is blocked either by our critique of taxonomic phonemics or by our suggestions regarding what we have tried to show is a better supported and more effective theory of sound structure.

APPENDIX

In the course of his discussion of the major issues outlined above, Householder makes many incidental remarks and observations that we would like to comment on briefly, even though they do not touch on questions of general linguistic interest.

In the first place, the reader familiar with Householder's paper will recall that much of it is concerned with defending Householder's own notions of the organization of grammar, the nature of phonemes, and so on, and with the relation of his conceptions to ours. He is especially concerned to defend his ideas from our critique of taxonomic phonemics. We have not discussed this aspect of Householder's paper above, since there is no explicit reference to any of Householder's views in our critique of taxonomic phonemics. As noted in Chomsky (1964a: 951, n. 40 and c: 75 [406], n. 13) the critique was limited to positions that are sufficiently clear and well-formulated so that critical analysis might be useful and productive. Neither in his paper (1965) [41] nor elsewhere, to our knowledge, has Householder given an account of his notion of "phoneme," for example, which meets this condition. Since many clear and careful formulations do appear in print, we saw no reason earlier and see no reason now to discuss positions such as Householder's which are only vaguely hinted at. In particular, we can suggest no answer to his question (1965: 31 [454]) as to how phonemes, as he thinks of them, fit into the phonological component, and we can offer no opinion as to whether the notion he has in mind is, as he claims, immune to objections that we have raised to taxonomic phonemics. There is no way to determine whether this is true, and the question cannot be raised seriously until his views are presented with sufficient explicitness and clarity to make critical scrutiny worthwhile.

Householder's discussion of the question of levels of adequacy leaves us somewhat in the dark as to what his actual views may be. His objections to the three levels of adequacy proposed in Chomsky (1964a and c [39]) are contained in two consecutive paragraphs (1965: 14–15 [443]). In the first paragraph, Householder declares that of the three levels of adequacy, only "'observational adequacy' is intelligible (at least to me)" and he takes Chomsky to task for viewing observational adequacy as uninteresting. In the next paragraph Householder goes over the same ground again, this time however, coming to the conclusion that observational adequacy "is surely not an acceptable goal to any linguist"; i.e., precisely the view that in the preceding paragraph he found so unacceptable when expressed by Chomsky. Moreover, observational adequacy is no longer the sole intelligible goal. According to the second paragraph, descriptive adequacy is not only intelligible, but also quite "old hat," in fact; something on which "the Firthians were keen . . . long before Halle."

Householder points out (1965: 31 [453]) that it is necessary to distinguish those occurrences of /t/ and /k/ that undergo softening to /s/ from others that do not, by a separate categorization in the lexicon. This is quite correct. Thus the lexicon must distinguish Romance words from words of Greek origin (e.g., *monarchy,* cited by Householder), and both sets from the Germanic part of the vocabulary. Obviously, these subparts of the lexicon behave rather differently with respect to phonological processes and this fact must be indicated by a lexical categorization. Unfortunately, the other example that Householder gives to illustrate this point has nothing to do with it. He states that the /t/ of *rackety* must be distinguished from the /t/ of *democrat,* because the former does not undergo softening before -*y* in *rackety,* while the latter does, in *democracy.* But the -*y* affix, in the case of *rackety* has no connection with the -*y* affix of *democracy* or *monarchy.* In fact, before the Adjective-forming -*y* of *rackety,* the t-s alternation never takes place, because this affix is one of those which has an automatic # boundary before it (as distinct from the other, Noun-forming -*y* affix). We see this from the fact that it is neutral with respect to stress, leaves final clusters in word-final phonetic form, etc.

Referring to Halle (1962: 71 [392] and 1964b: 351), Householder asserts (p. 29 [452]) that "Halle achieves the remarkable position of specifying distinctions which are present (apparently) only in the brains of speakers."[28] We see nothing strange in the conclusion that perceptual distinctions may be heavily determined by *set* and need not correspond in any simple way to physical stimuli. This is a commonplace of perceptual psychology and we fail to understand why anyone would think it remarkable that speech perception shares the properties of other perceptual processes. In the case of language, the speaker's "set" is largely a matter of his knowledge (see note 2) of the language, and this may (in fact, surely does) lead him to make perceptual judgments that are not simply related to physical fact. For example, speakers of English may be trained to record stress contours of great complexity with fair consistency, and we have no doubt that what they record is an accurate account of what they "hear." But we doubt very much that these stress contours are physically present in a degree of detail that even begins to approach what they "perceive" in the utterances that they are transcribing. Since stress contours are, apparently, largely a reflection of syntactic structure, it is sufficient, to account for the perception, that the hearer understand the utterances. Similarly, we see nothing strange about the conclusion that an underlying base form may be "perceived" (or internally represented in some way in the process of interpreting an utterance) although it corresponds to no identifiable physical part of the sound stimulus. And we see no difficulty in accepting the hypothesis, which seems so outlandish to Householder, that a systematic phonemic distinction can persist (because of its role in the system of phono-

[28]The comment is based on the following remark in Halle (1962: 71 [392] and 1964b: 351) "No difficulties are experienced in accounting for the change if we postulate that, for reasons of the kind discussed in §11, /a/ and /æ/ remained distinct entities even though every /a/ was actualized phonetically as /æ/." In quoting this, Householder leaves out the phrase "for reasons of the kind discussed in §11 . . . ." What is discussed in §11 is a Russian example that shows how "simplicity considerations force us to maintain distinct representations of segment types that never contrast phonetically," despite the fact that, superficially, "it seems pointless to use different feature complexes to represent segment types that are never distinguished phonetically." In fact there are many different considerations that might lead to the conclusion that segment types must be distinguished phonologically despite the absence of any phonetic contrast between these feature sets.

Householder does not attempt to show some error in the analysis presented by Halle but simply implies that the conclusion that he affords is, for some reason, intolerable or absurd.

logical processes) despite the fact that there is no one-one correlation of the systematic phonemes to identifiable physical phones.

Nor is this hypothesis new in linguistics. Surely every student in an elementary linguistics course is made to read Sapir's "Psychological Reality of Phonemes" [2] with its classical discussion of instances where naive speakers heard speech not in terms of actual physical sounds, but in terms of an underlying abstract form, which may correspond, in fact, to an etymological reconstruction (Sapir, 1933: 49 [24]). Hence Halle's "remarkable position" is actually a classical one within linguistics, and one that is not only supported by linguistic evidence but consistent with whatever else is known about complex perceptual processes.

Householder argues (1965: 30 [453]) against the claim in Chomsky (1964a and c [39]) that there is no level intermediate between systematic phonetic and systematic phonemic, on the basis of the fact that there are two different kinds of rules in the phonological component. But in fact, as noted by Chomsky, there are not just two but many different kinds of rules, of varying generality and function. What is pointed out by Chomsky is that there is no particular point in derivations where it seems possible to extract a new and independent linguistically significant level. Various arguments are given for this, and these Householder makes no attempt to deal with.

Householder asks (1965: 31–32 [454]) how we arrive at our systematic phonemic representation.[29] He makes no reference to the discussion of this question in Chomsky (1964a: 547–548 and c: 95–96 [416]), and simply asserts, with no shred of evidence or argument, that in practice, the procedure is first to construct a taxonomic phonemic representation ("making stout use of complementary distribution," and other taxonomic procedures), and then, presumably, to go on from this to the systematic phonemic representation. This claim raises two questions: (1) How does a taxonomic phonemic representation, once available, facilitate the discovery of the systematic phonemic representation, in particular,

since this preliminary taxonomic representation apparently has no linguistic status? (2) How does Householder know that Sapir, Bloomfield, and other linguists who presented systematic phonemic representations actually went through the intermediate step that he claims to be essential, in the light of the fact that they left no evidence of this and, furthermore, that taxonomic phonemics had not been invented at the time when they were working?

The fact of the matter is that the necessity of working through a preliminary taxonomic phonemic analysis is, so far as is known, a complete myth. A variety of arguments have been offered to show that taxonomic phonemics has no justification on *internal* linguistic grounds (quite the contrary, it can be incorporated in a grammar only at the cost of loss of generalizations) and that the principles on which it is based are faulty. No answer has been offered to these arguments. It has also been pointed out that there are no known *external* grounds (i.e., in terms of what is known concerning use of language or language-acquisition) for the assumption that taxonomic phonemics constitutes a significant linguistic level. Again, no answer is proposed to these arguments. What we are left with is a totally unsupported claim that somehow taxonomic linguistics is necessary for the practicing linguist analyzing a new language. As far as we can see, this claim is not worth discussing until some argument is given for it. Returning to the two questions raised above, we see not the slightest reason to believe that the discovery of a grammar will be facilitated by a prior careful taxonomic phonemic analysis, constructed in complete or (with Pike and Harris) partial independence of any investigation of syntactic or morphological structure and, furthermore, playing no role in the grammar, once this is constructed. And we see not the slightest reason to believe that Sapir, for example, followed this curious procedure in his field work.

In Householder's discussion of our proposed evaluation procedure, he attributes a certain general principle to Halle in a passage which we quote in full:

[Halle] does not there state the principle explicitly but I should word it thus: "No symbol-system may be judged economical unless it is always the case that the more general statement, when expressed in it, is the shorter." Where Halle got the idea for this principle, I cannot discover. My friends in various other fields (including philosophy of science) have not heard of it, and obvious counter-examples come readily to mind. (1965: 16 [444])

We are as ignorant and surprised as Householder as to the sources of this completely absurd principle. We are able to find nothing in Halle (1962 [37] and 1964b) that could lead any reader to conclude that

---

[29]And also, how we arrive at a set of features. But the two questions are not at all comparable. The set of features is provided by our general linguistic theory (along with our other notions concerning the form of grammar). The systematic phonemic representation for a particular language, on the other hand, has to be discovered by the grammarian analyzing this language.

To the question how one arrives at the hypothesis (in general linguistic theory) that a certain set of features constitutes the universal phonetic framework for language, we can offer no helpful answer, just as we can offer no suggestion as to how one discovers the proper notion of "transformation," "morpheme," etc.

such an absurd principle was being advocated, either explicitly or implicitly. In fact, the principle is a complete invention of Householder's.

In the light of the preceding discussion, it is perhaps understandable that we are unimpressed with Householder's repeated admonitions to us for leading our "followers" astray by imbuing them with disrespect for the facts. We wish only to note in this connection that here, once again, Householder cites no evidence in substantiation of his charge that linguists who have been interested in or influenced by our work have no regard for linguistic fact and fail to meet common standards of accuracy and seriousness.

REFERENCES

BLOOMFIELD, L. (1927). "On Recent Work in General Linguistics," *Modern Philology* 25.211–230.

CHOMSKY, N. (1953). "Systems of Syntactic Analysis," *Journal of Symbolic Logic* 18.242–256.

CHOMSKY, N. (1962). "The Logical Basis of Linguistic Theory," in *Preprints, Ninth International Congress of Linguists* (Cambridge, Mass.). 509–574.

CHOMSKY, N. (1964a). "The Logical Basis of Linguistic Theory," *Proceedings of the Ninth International Congress of Linguists*. The Hague: Mouton. 914–1008.

CHOMSKY, N. (1964b). "Current Issues in Linguistic Theory," in Fodor and Katz (1964:50–118).

CHOMSKY, N. (1964c). *Current Issues in Linguistic Theory*. (Janua Linguarum, Series Minor, 38.) The Hague: Mouton. [39]

CHOMSKY, N. (1965). *Aspects of the Theory of Syntax*. Cambridge, Mass.: M.I.T. Press.

CHOMSKY, N., and HALLE, M. (to appear). *The Sound Pattern of English*. New York: Harper & Row. [See now Chomsky and Halle, 1968—VBM.]

CONTRERAS, H., and SAPORTA, S. (1962). *A Phonological Grammar of Spanish*. Seattle: University of Washington Press. [Actually Saporta and Contreras—VBM.]

FERGUSON, C. A. (1962). Review of Halle (1959b). *Language* 38.284–298. [36]

FODOR, J. A., and KATZ, J. J. (1964). *The Structure of Language: Readings in the Philosophy of Language*. Englewood Cliffs, N.J.: Prentice-Hall.

HALLE, M. (1958). "Questions of Linguistics," *Nuovo Cimento* 13.494–517.

HALLE, M. (1959). *The Sound Pattern of Russian*. The Hague: Mouton.

HALLE, M. (1962). "Phonology in Generative Grammar," *Word* 18.54–72. [37]

HALLE, M. (1964a). "On the Bases of Phonology," in Fodor and Katz (1964:324–333). [38]

HALLE, M. (1964b). "Phonology in Generative Grammar," in Fodor and Katz (1964:334–352).

HARRIS, Z. S. (1951). *Methods in Structural Linguistics*. Chicago: University of Chicago Press.

HOUSEHOLDER, F. W. (1952). Review of Harris (1951). *IJAL* 18.260–268.

HOUSEHOLDER, F. W. (1965). "On Some Recent Claims in Phonological Theory," *Journal of Linguistics* 1.13–34. [41]

JAKOBSON, R. (1931). "Phonemic Notes on Standard Slovak," in *Slovenská Miscellanea*. Bratislava. (Reprinted in English translation in R. Jakobson, *Selected Writings*, Vol. I. The Hague: Mouton, 1962. 221–230.)

KURATH, H., and MCDAVID, R. I., JR. (1961). *The Pronunciation of English in the Atlantic States*. Ann Arbor: University of Michigan.

LAMB, S. (1964). "On Alternation, Transformation, Realization, and Stratification," *Monograph Series on Languages and Linguistics* 17.105–122. (Edited by C. I. J. M. Stuart.) Washington, D.C.: Georgetown University Press. [52]

LEES, R. B. (1957). Review of Chomsky, *Syntactic Structures* (1957). *Language* 33.375–408.

POSTAL, P. (1964). "Boas and the Development of Phonology," *IJAL* 30.269–280.

SAPIR, E. (1933). "The Psychological Reality of Phonemes," in *Selected Writings of Edward Sapir*. Berkeley and Los Angeles: University of California, 1944. 46–60. (English original of "La realité psychologique des phonèmes," *Journal de Psychologie Normale et Pathologique* 30. 247–265.) [2]

VACHEK, J. (1964). "On Some Basic Principles of 'Classical' Phonology," *Zeitschrift für Phonetik, Sprachwissenschaft und Kommunikationsforschung* 17:409–431. [40]

WHORF, B. L. (1940). "Linguistics as an Exact Science," *Technology Review* 43.3–8. (Reprinted in J. B. Carroll (ed.), *Language, Thought and Reality*. Cambridge, Mass.: Technology Press of M.I.T., 1956.)

43

PHONOLOGICAL THEORY:
A BRIEF COMMENT*

F. W. HOUSEHOLDER, JR.

I was flattered (and more than a little puzzled) to see the length and detail of Chomsky and Halle's recent reply to my earlier article in this journal (cf. *JL* 1(1965) 13–34 [41] and 97–138 [42]). I had hoped to take up a few of the points they raise and raise a few more of my own, but owing to exigencies of both time and space, I find I must be content to restate my three main points as clearly as I can, to reaffirm my belief in them, and to mention a few of my reasons.

(1) I still do not like the use of such strong God's truth language, saying always "such-and-such *is* X" instead of "such-and-such may conveniently be described or looked at as X." And even if I believed their assertions were as securely based as those a physicist may make about atomic nuclei, I would say that this makes no difference, and that a physicist who says what the atom *is* must be speaking in some sort of figurative language. Incidentally, one of the difficulties of intuition as a check on theory is that the problem of the self-fulfilling prediction comes in. I remember well the beautiful 4-stress 4-pitch dialects spoken by some of the Foreign Service Institute personnel some years back; and there outside observers had access at least to the physical manifestations. I am not accusing anyone of subjectivity; I am merely wishing for more secure lines of communication. When I see red and you see red, even though I have no way of knowing that the quality of your perception resembles mine, I at least am able to count votes, and devise tests which will locate red-green blindness. But here the chances of comprehension are often very low, and the will to

believe is not enough; real faith is required.

(2) On my disagreement with Chomsky about traditional phonemes and phonemics, I would like to add a little. I now see that for this level a kind of uniqueness is important, and perhaps bi-uniqueness. The name "taxonomic" is of course merely pejorative, not informative; the function of such phonemes as conceived by the pioneers of the thirties and forties was to explain the manner in which speakers can *repeat* (not just *mimic*) new words. This kind of repetition implied a systematic analysis of the sound system *without any possible reference to deep morphophonemic potential* (hence not Chomsky's systematic phonemic level) and without the kind of detail which permits international phoneticians to discuss similarities and differences between sounds in different languages (hence not Chomsky's systematic phonetic level). Indeed one point emphasized by early investigators was that what is phonetically identical in two languages (say [x] in French and German) may be at this immediate repetition level quite different (say /r/ in French but /x/ in German).

(3) My first dispute with Halle was due to a misunderstanding. I (like my students) thought he claimed to have proved that distinctive feature notation was more economical than phonemic notation. In reality he seems to have claimed merely that it is true and phonemic notation false. This I still doubt. I am quite unwilling to grant that our brain-storage has any great use for economy; instead I feel that extravagant redundancy is built in all along the line, and table look-up rather than

*Reprinted from *Journal of Linguistics* 2.99–100 (1966) by permission of the author and Cambridge University Press.

algorithm is the *normal* behavior. That a speaker every time he uses the word *straw* subliminally regenerates all other features of the initial "s" from a stored form characterized only as non-vocalic is simply beyond my intuitive capacity. I believe that our brains (unlike most computers) have no need for economizing with storage space. A linguist who could not devise a better grammar than is present in any speaker's brain ought to try another trade.

Furthermore, since I cannot believe the God's-truth arguments for this position, I am left with only convenience and communicability as criteria. On grounds of convenience I find distinctive features useful for all sorts of assimilative and dissimilative changes, but awkward for deletions, insertions and metatheses, where economy of features may sometimes be achieved by extremely counter-intuitive devices.

Incidentally, while languages like English may use long series of ordered rules (which are, to me, a nice convenient trick bearing no relation—or very little—to what goes on in a speaker's brain), others, such as Polynesian ones, need very few rules (correlating consonantality or vocality with odd or even position, determining position of peaks of pitch or amplitude, and little more). I doubt if any kind of economy can be achieved there.

Finally, let me say that beside the semantic, phonological and syntactic features stored in the lexicon I would also require for languages like English the orthographic form, and would make use of economical rules to derive most of the phonological features from that form.

44

DISTINCTIVE FEATURES
AND PHONETIC FEATURES*

F. W. HOUSEHOLDER, JR.

One of the great achievements of Roman Jakobson is admitted on all hands to be his development of the theory of binary distinctive features in phonology. In recent years Noam Chomsky and Morris Halle have proposed a theory of linguistic competence in which features called "distinctive" and named by the same names (for the most part) as those coined by Jakobson are introduced at two points, neither of which seems to be quite the same as the place envisaged for them in the first instance. In that component of the model which is called the lexicon are stored entries consisting of three parts (as last reported, at any rate): a set of values of binary syntactic features, a similar set of semantic features, and a "matrix" or string of sets of values of binary phonological features. But at this level these phonological features do not have direct phonetic links; they are considered as purely abstract, forming bundles which correspond very closely with what traditional American linguistics refers to as morphophonemes, the distributional and alternational precursors of phonemes. In other words, such systematic "phonemic" features form morphophonemic and distributional classes of segments and ultimately, therefore, of morphemes. (I say "morphemes" because they apparently do not yet have a substantial phonological shape as *morphs* traditionally do, although they nevertheless seem less abstract than conventional morphemes).

Once extracted from the lexicon, these matrices of binary features undergo a series of ordered alterations, in part corresponding roughly to traditional morphophonemic rules (and indirectly to historical phonological changes), and partly to the traditional statements specifying the allophones of the phonemes. At the end of this series the matrices are said to be "systematic phonetic" representations. What they are in between is not clear, but presumably still abstract, substance-less "systematic phonemic" representations. Do these systematic phonetic features correspond to Jakobson's distinctive features? Certainly not perfectly. For one thing, *every* possible feature must have some specified value, not necessarily binary, at this level, whereas only binary *distinctive* features are relevant for a Jakobsonian representation. The systematic phonetic features, furthermore, are absolute, their values corresponding solely to the sound, without direct reference to any other sounds in the same language, though perhaps with indirect reference to the sounds of all other languages of the world. In terms of these features, if we are interpreting Chomsky and Halle correctly (which is, I suppose, in the long run impossible even for Chomsky and Halle), it can make sense to say that a certain sound of language A is identical with one of language B, or differs slightly in such-and-such a way.

This, surely, seems to be phonetics of some sort. It is not, evidently, Hockett's beta-phonetics of 1942 [11], since beta-phonetics uses only features which are distinctive (they are not features otherwise for Hockett, but "elements" and belong to alpha-phonetics, though it must be confessed that the notion of "determined" and "indeterminate" *features* is odd). And yet it is unlike Hockett's alpha-phonetics, too, since, generally speaking, sound-tokens may be alpha-phonetically similar, but *not* wholly identical. (They may be

*Reprinted from *To Honor Roman Jakobson* (The Hague: Mouton, 1967), pp. 941–944, by permission.

488

identical in certain alpha-phonetic elements—e.g., lip closure or voicing, and perhaps in a few cases sounds may have only such elements, and no others, but this is apparently not the normal case.) It does not seem to be old-fashioned European style fine phonetics, according to which no two repetitions of the same utterance could ever be identical; certainly we are given the impression that the last rules of the grammar are not stochastic in nature—at least not always. But still, maybe they are; the early parts of Hockett's 1942 article similarly lead one to believe that allophones are specific and clear-cut, but before the end he is speaking of Spanish /k/ having a large number of overlapping allophones. There seems to be at least the possibility for Chomsky and Halle of rules like this:

$$[+ \text{nasal}] \rightarrow [k \text{ nasal}] \ (.94 > k > .32,$$
$$\text{distribution normal})$$

where k specifies the degree to which the velum is lowered or the proportion of the segment during which it is lowered, or something of the sort. If this were so, then the output of the grammar could be considered to correspond to individual utterance-tokens; it is more commonly supposed that the output should rather correspond to utterance-types, i.e., classes of utterance-tokens. Tokens would be relevant perhaps to a performance model, but not to a competence model.

But Jakobsonian distinctive features were not designed to specify and distinguish unique utterance-tokens; on the contrary, their early popularity among linguists seems to have been partly due to the very fact that they offer freedom from the minutiae of fine phonetics.

It is well known that Chomsky and Halle deny (categorically and at length) the unique relevance of any single level that might be specified between the "systematic phonemic" and the "systematic phonetic" level. And yet it seems clear that distinctive features in the true, original sense cannot belong to either level, since they are *phonological* (which is not true—in the same sense—of the systematic phonemic level) and they are *distinctive* (which is not so of the systematic phonetic level).

If we try to find the reasons for not stopping the grammar at about the point where the original distinctive features belong, we have held up to us mainly examples of phonologi-

cally conditioned changes which would be in some instances changes of *distinctive* features, in others of *redundant* features: such things as devoicing of segments before junctures (or, indeed, before other segments), assimilation of nasals in point of articulation, shift of stops to fricative articulation before juncture or other stops, and so on. In all these cases, surely the Prague notion of neutralization is correct: it is not that the voicing feature changes its value from plus to minus, but rather that, if it is plus or minus in these positions, it changes to *irrelevant,* while if it is already *irrelevant,* it remains so. (I say "relevant" and "irrelevant," not "marked" and "unmarked." The marked term of an opposition should always be identical with the +term, at least if the feature has been properly named).

If, then, a rule specifying the phonetic output (with certain probabilities attached, in many cases) is wanted, it will change the value "irrelevant" of the voicing feature to the value "minus." In Azerbaijani, for example, as spoken by two of my informants, it is the case that polysyllabic words never have any contrast between tense and lax stops in absolute final position (phonetic voicing is relevant only intervocalically), but most tokens would probably be classified as lax. Monosyllabic words may, however, show a contrast: certain ones will very rarely have an audible release ("aspiration"), while others are quite likely to, especially in situations of careful enunciation. The underlying morphophonemic shape of both longer and shorter words will include some with tense finals and some with lax finals, the difference being realized whenever vowel-initial suffixes or enclitics are added. But if no such elements are attached, then this feature must take the value "irrelevant" for polysyllables invariably, and for monosyllables optionally. The phonetic realization of the feature "irrelevant tenseness" will be brief closure and inaudible release in a large percentage of cases, perceptible voiceless release (for unknown and non-linguistic reasons) in the residue. The realization of the feature "+tense" in final position is always perceptible voiceless release, that of "−tense" always inaudible release. This situation could, if you like, be handled by a stochastic rule (using i to mean irrelevant) for polysyllabic words:

$$[i \text{ tensity}] \rightarrow \begin{cases} [- \text{ tensity}] \ /p = .95 \\ [+ \text{ tensity}] \ /p = .05 \end{cases}$$

where p means probability. A range might be safer: $.75 < p < 1$ for the first line, $0 < p < .25$ for the second, say. Later will come the "rule" (if it is right to call it that):

$$[+ \text{ tensity}] \rightarrow [- \text{ voice}, \pm \text{ length}, + \text{ aspiration}]$$

although I am skeptical about the restriction of features used on the right of such rules to any very small number (less than 25 or so), even if we allow an infinite scale of values to replace binarity here.

In conclusion, I should like to say that I believe great injustice is done to Jakobson in describing his *distinctive* features as "universal *phonetic* features." Whatever else they may be, distinctive features *must* be terms of a binary opposition. Whatever else "phonetic" may mean, it *must* pertain to sound substance in some absolute way, relative (if to anything) only to some given arbitrary measuring scale. If we are to have new features added to the list given by Jakobson (and I believe we must, just as I believe some of that list must be deleted or redefined), let us look for them in the oppositions of natural languages, not in the phonetic specifications, whether acoustic or articulatory, with which we might ultimately be able to correlate them.

REFERENCES

CHOMSKY, N., and M. HALLE, "Some Controversial Questions in Phonological Theory," *Journal of Linguistics,* 1 (1965), 97–138. [42]

HOCKETT, C., "A System of Descriptive Phonology," *Language,* 18 (1942), 3–21. (Reprinted in Joos, M., *Readings in Linguistics* [Washington, ACLS, 1957], 97–108.) [11]

45

DISTINCTIVE FEATURES, SIMPLICITY, AND DESCRIPTIVE ADEQUACY*

HENRY KUČERA

Among the many outstanding contributions of Roman Jakobson to general linguistics, his elaboration of the distinctive feature theory is one of the most important. Jakobson's phonological framework has been adopted, to be sure with certain modifications, even in those contemporary linguistic theories, such as "transformational grammar," which otherwise diverge considerably from the Jakobsonian conceptual and methodological assumptions of linguistics. This is perhaps even more interesting in view of the fact that only a few of the concepts and methods of structuralist linguistics of the last three decades have remained operative in "transformational grammar."

The present paper does not aim at a general discussion of the modified version of distinctive features which has been incorporated in the linguistic model of the transformationalists. Neither is it my aim to discuss the overall merits of the transformational model nor of the phonological component in this model. These matters are certainly in need of a careful analysis. However, I assume here simply that the procedures suggested by Halle and Chomsky represent a potentially productive linguistic theory, and I will attempt to examine some of the assumptions which underlie the structure of the phonological component in generative transformational grammar and some of the consequences of these assumptions.

I In their answer to Householder in the *Journal of Linguistics* (1965, 97–138) [42], Chomsky and Halle discuss at some length two phonological rules of English with which they illustrate their distinction between "ob-servational adequacy" and "descriptive adequacy" of grammar. Essentially, they consider that a grammar meets the requirement of observational adequacy if it correctly describes the data on which it is based and nothing more—if, in other words, it gives a compact one-one organization of this data. On the other hand, a grammar presumably meets the level of descriptive adequacy to the extent that it gives a correct account of the speaker's "tacit knowledge." The English illustrations center around the forms *brick* (/brik/) and the non-existent forms /blik/ and /bnik/. Chomsky and Halle argue that a speaker of English knows that /blik/ is an admissible form in the language in a sense in which /bnik/ is not. This distinction—as they explicitly state—is not a matter of universal phonetics but a matter of facts of English.[1] The difference between existing forms and possible, non-existent forms on one hand, and inadmissible forms on the other

---

[1]Although such designations as "non-existent," "admissible," and "inadmissible" are used by Chomsky and Halle with self-assurance, a careful consideration of the facts would show that the actual situation is more complex than these statements suggest. So, for example, one finds the forms *blickey* or *blickie* or *blicky* ('a small pail') in *Webster's Third New International Dictionary* (p. 233). If this morpheme is included in the description of English, the Chomsky-Halle example is of dubious value. If *blicky* is not admitted as an English word, one should presumably offer a justification for excluding it. This and similar details which could be cited are not necessarily of great importance for the discussion of "levels of adequacy." However, they do help to point out that there may be hidden perils in proposing generalizations about the phonological composition of the English lexicon.

*Reprinted from *To Honor Roman Jakobson* (Mouton, 1967), pp. 1114–1126, by permission.

hand, is then expressed by Chomsky and Halle in terms of two possible rules in a grammar of English:

(1) Consonantal Segment → Liquid in the context:
#Stop——Vowel
(2) Consonantal Segment → /r/ in the context:
#/b—ik/.

Chomsky and Halle argue that both rules are true of English, at the level of observation. Both rules supposedly "correctly state facts about occurrence and non-occurrence." Rule (2) excludes both /bnik/ and /blik/ as "inadmissible." Rule (1), on the other hand, excludes only /bnik/ as inadmissible, but permits /blik/. Chomsky and Halle then proceed to draw the conclusion that, in order to achieve the level of "explanatory adequacy" (that is, to provide a principled basis for the selection of descriptively adequate grammars) a linguistic theory must present some general grounds for requiring the grammar to include rule (1) but not allowing it to include rule (2), despite the correctness of rule (2) at the level of observation.

Later in the article, Chomsky and Halle use the same example to illustrate their "Language-acquisition Model" which is assumed to be the model for the child's learning of the language and his "construction" of a "grammar" for it. "The child is presented with /brik/ but not with /blik/ or /bnik/. He somehow constructs the grammar that contains rule (1) but not rule (2), so that he then knows that /blik/ is admissible but that /bnik/ is not. It is this fact that the linguist is attempting to explain" (p. 107 [463]).

II   Following another paper of Halle (1962) [37], we shall assume that a complete description of a language must include a list of all actually occurring morphemes, i.e., a dictionary of the language. As a part of the description, the dictionary is subject to the notational conventions and the simplicity criterion, as is the grammar as a whole. The two principal requirements (as restated in Chomsky and Halle, 1965 [42]) are that:

(a) phonological rules should be stated completely in terms of features;
(b) a grammar should be evaluated by minimizing the total number of features speci-

fied in the lexicon and in the phonological rules.

These two assumptions then should lead jointly to the selection of the descriptively adequate grammar.

The criterion of simplicity is then (at least as a "first approximation," cf. Chomsky and Halle, 1965, 107 [464]) equated with the concept of brevity of the description, measured by the number of discrete symbols contained in the description. Halle says: "Given two alternative descriptions of a particular body of data, the description containing fewer such symbols will be regarded as simpler and will, therefore, be preferred over the other" (Halle, 1962, p. 55 [381]).

The items in the dictionary will then be specified in the form of sequences of distinctive features and have to fulfill the requirement that features must be omitted in all dictionary representations, when "the appearance of a given feature in a segment is contextually determined" (Halle, 1962, 60 [384]).

These requirements necessitate the reformulation of the Chomsky-Halle rule (1) in something like the following form:[2]

(1′) $[+\text{consonantal}] \rightarrow [+\text{vocalic}]$

in env. #
$\begin{bmatrix} -\text{vocalic} \\ +\text{consonantal} \\ -\text{continuant} \\ -\text{nasal} \\ -\text{strident} \end{bmatrix}$ [—] $\begin{bmatrix} +\text{vocalic} \\ -\text{consonantal} \end{bmatrix}$

It should be noted that rule (1′) represents correctly the Chomsky-Halle rule (1) only if a certain configuration of features is specified in the distinctive feature matrix of English. The affricates /č/ and /ž/ have to be marked as [+

---

[2]The formulaic representation of the rules, used in this paper, follows the practice generally employed in phonological descriptions of generative grammars. Rule (1′), for example, is to be read as stating that a segment which is [+consonantal] is *also* [+vocalic] in the environment specified on either side of [———], i.e., between an initial stop and a vowel. After rule (1′) is applied, the relevant segment will be $\begin{bmatrix} +\text{vocalic} \\ +\text{consonantal} \end{bmatrix}$, i.e., a liquid. In other words, rule (1′) states that any consonantal segment is predictably a liquid if between an initial consonant and a vowel. For a general explanation of the notational convention, see Halle, 1962, 59–60 [384].

strident] in order to exclude them from the environmental statement in rule (1′), i.e., in order to exclude such initial clusters as /čr/, /čl/, /ǯr/, /ǯl/.[3] If the affricates are not marked as [+ strident] in the matrix of features, then rule (1) can be reformulated accurately only in a more complex manner than is the case in (1′). This is simply the consequence of the distinctive-feature approach in which the class of "stops" is not uniquely identified by a single feature (non-nasal non-continuants include both stops and affricates). Further discussion will show the nature of this problem.

The designation of /č/ and /ǯ/ as [+ strident] and, conversely, the specification of the other two compact non-continuants, i.e., /k/ and /g/, as [− strident] is the solution adopted in the distinctive feature matrix of English in the *Preliminaries to Speech Analysis* (Jakobson, Fant, Halle, 1961, 43). It should be noted, however, that this solution has certain consequences. Since all redundancies in the feature specification of segments must be eliminated, the specification of the feature strident/non-strident for /č/, /ǯ/, /k/, /g/ requires that the feature grave/non-grave in these four non-continuants *not* be specified. Thus a zero (or a blank) should appear in the matrix for these segments in the grave row. This is indeed the case in the *Preliminaries*.

It will be shown later that such a feature selection and redundancy elimination may have rather important consequences for the

simplicity criterion in the formulation of other phonological rules.

III   If the "minimizing of the total number of features specified in the lexicon and in the phonological rules" is one of the objectives of a descriptively adequate grammar, then rule (1′) must be reformulated as two rules, one of which states that the second segment is a liquid, and the other one stating that the non-continuant of the first segment is a stop (not an affricate or a nasal):

(1a) [+consonantal] → [+vocalic]

$$\text{in env. } \# \begin{bmatrix} -\text{vocalic} \\ +\text{consonantal} \\ -\text{continuant} \end{bmatrix} [-] \begin{bmatrix} +\text{vocalic} \\ -\text{consonantal} \end{bmatrix}$$

$$(1b) \begin{bmatrix} -\text{vocalic} \\ +\text{consonantal} \\ -\text{continuant} \end{bmatrix} \to \begin{bmatrix} -\text{nasal} \\ -\text{strident} \end{bmatrix}$$

$$\text{in env. } \# [-] \begin{bmatrix} +\text{vocalic} \\ +\text{consonantal} \end{bmatrix}$$

Rules (1a) and (1b) specify the same initial clusters as rule (1′). Although they are more complex than rule (1′), rules (1a) and (1b) achieve a greater saving of features in the dictionary, since an initial non-continuant will not need to be specified in the lexicon as to stridency or nasality before a consonantal segment.

In a complete grammar of English, additional rules would be needed to correctly state the restrictions on the initial clusters discussed above. As far as the initial [non-continuant plus liquid] clusters are concerned, a rule which admits /tr/ and /dr/ but excludes /tl/ and /dl/ will have to be added.[4] Naturally, in a complete grammar it might be advantageous to deal with these restrictions jointly with restrictions on initial clusters of [continu-

---

[3] I am assuming in this paper that a grammar must state, in one form or another, the general phonological constraints operative in the language (in the present case, the restrictions on initial clusters of consonant plus liquid). Naturally, if we reduced the requirements on grammars and defined the aim of a grammar solely as the generation of correct output, we would not need to be at all concerned with the specification of the first segment as to stridency; the dictionary would simply contain no morphemes beginning with $\begin{bmatrix} -\text{continuant} \\ +\text{strident} \end{bmatrix}$ plus [+consonantal] segments. The same is true about the specification as to nasality. This latter kind of grammar, however, would make it possible to reach the conclusion that there are no initial clusters of affricates plus liquids in English only if we inspected every relevant morpheme in the dictionary. Such a grammar thus does not make significant generalizations about the language and does not, in my opinion, meet the level of descriptive adequacy, although it may be correct at the level of observation and, moreover, contain simpler rules than a more adequate grammar.

[4] Actually, there is some evidence that the initial clusters /tl/ and /dl/ may represent still another "degree" of inadmissibility in English, different from that of /bn/. In several dialects of British English, the initial clusters /tl/ and /dl/ occur in place of the standard /kl/ and /gl/ respectively. In such dialects, however, the initial clusters /kl/ and /gl/ do not occur and no phonological contrast between the dental and the velar stops in the context: # [−]/l/ is possible. Similarly, one often finds in children's language the substitution of initial /tl/ and /dl/ for /kl/ and /gl/, again strongly pointing to a neutralization of phonological contrast of these segments in these positions.

ant plus liquid], i.e., /sl/ vs. the non-occurrent /sr/, /θr/ vs. the non-occurrent /θl/, etc.

However, in order to present my argument in reasonably simple terms, I consider in the following discussion only rules pertaining to [non-continuant plus liquid] clusters.

In order to exclude initial /dl/ and /tl/, we would have to rewrite rule (1) accordingly. Such a revision would be a relatively simple matter if segments (or phonemes) were regarded as indivisible entities:

(3a) Conson. segment → Liquid in env. #

Stop — Vowel

(3b) Liquid → /r/ in env. # $\begin{bmatrix} /t/ \\ /d/ \end{bmatrix}$ — Vowel

However, if phonological segments are regarded as complexes of properties, then the reformulation has to be based on the distinctive-features matrix of the segments. We shall first follow, for this purpose, the matrix for English consonants in the *Preliminaries*. For the sake of clarifying the problem, let us assume for the time being that no redundant features have been specified for any segment by a previous rule.[5]

The partial matrix reproduced here follows the *Preliminaries* except for the replacement of the feature *compact* by the feature *diffuse*, to conform with the prevalent present usage (Halle, 1964 [38], 327 [395]).

Matrix I

	č	ž	k	g	p	b	t	d
diffuse	−	−	−	−	+	+	+	+
grave	○	○	○	○	+	+	−	−
strident	+	+	−	−	○	○	○	○

We shall assume, first of all, the following general rule which applies to all initial consonantal clusters in English, and which states that the *first* segment of all such clusters is non-vocalic (i.e., not a liquid) and non-nasal.

[+consonantal] → $\begin{bmatrix} -\text{vocalic} \\ -\text{nasal} \end{bmatrix}$

in env. # [—] [+consonantal]

[5]For the sake of terminological clarity, I shall call a feature which is predictable solely from other features specified in the same segment a *redundant feature*, and a feature which is predictable only in terms of *other* segments in the environment a *contextually determined feature*.

We can now write the following ordered rules,[6] corresponding to the statements (3a) and (3b):

(3a′) [+consonantal] → [+vocalic] in env.

$\begin{bmatrix} +\text{consonantal} \\ -\text{continuant} \end{bmatrix}$ [—] $\begin{bmatrix} +\text{vocalic} \\ -\text{consonantal} \end{bmatrix}$

(3b′) $\begin{bmatrix} +\text{vocalic} \\ +\text{consonantal} \end{bmatrix}$ → [−diffuse] in env.

$\begin{bmatrix} +\text{consonantal} \\ -\text{continuant} \\ +\text{diffuse} \\ -\text{grave} \end{bmatrix}$ [—] $\begin{bmatrix} +\text{vocalic} \\ -\text{consonantal} \end{bmatrix}$[7]

(3c′) $\begin{bmatrix} +\text{consonantal} \\ -\text{continuant} \\ -\text{diffuse} \end{bmatrix}$ → [−strident]

in env. # [—] $\begin{bmatrix} +\text{vocalic} \\ +\text{consonantal} \end{bmatrix}$

Rule (3a′) rewrites any consonantal segment after an initial non-continuant and before a vowel as a liquid. Rule (3b′) states that the liquid is always /r/ after /t/ and /d/. And rule (3c′) specifies non-stridency in the first segment of such clusters, i.e., states that the first segment must be /k/ or /g/ if it is a non-diffuse non-continuant.

As far as the saving of symbols in the dictionary is concerned, rule (3a′) saves one feature in each liquid occurring in this position; rule (3b′) saves one additional feature for each /r/ occurring after /t/ and /d/; and rule (3c′) saves still one more feature for each initial /k/ and /g/ followed by a liquid.

The following reorganization of the matrix would permit a different set of rules. Since this reorganization does not increase the redundancy of the matrix itself, such a matrix might appear to be the basis of an adequate grammar.

[6]I shall intentionally not use in further discussion the special notational convention which allows the coalescing of partly identical statements by factoring parts which are identical. My reason is simply to make it easier to explain and compare the various rules. Nothing of substance would be changed in my argument if the coalescing convention were followed.

[7]The segment /r/ is specified as [−diffuse] in contrast to /l/ which is [+diffuse]. Both are $\begin{bmatrix} +\text{vocalic} \\ +\text{consonantal} \end{bmatrix}$. This follows Halle's current classification (personal communication, Feb. 17, 1966).

Matrix II

	č	ž	k	g	p	b	t	d
diffuse	−	−	−	−	+	+	+	+
grave	−	−	+	+	+	+	−	−
strident	○	○	○	○	○	○	○	○

We could then write:

(3a″) [+consonantal] → [+vocalic] in env.

$$\# \begin{bmatrix} +\text{consonantal} \\ -\text{continuant} \end{bmatrix} [-] \begin{bmatrix} +\text{vocalic} \\ -\text{consonantal} \end{bmatrix}$$

(3b″) $\begin{bmatrix} +\text{vocalic} \\ +\text{consonantal} \end{bmatrix} \rightarrow [-\text{diffuse}]$ in env.

$$\# \begin{bmatrix} +\text{consonantal} \\ -\text{continuant} \\ -\text{grave} \end{bmatrix} [-] \begin{bmatrix} +\text{vocalic} \\ -\text{consonantal} \end{bmatrix}$$

(3c″) $\begin{bmatrix} +\text{consonantal} \\ -\text{continuant} \\ -\text{grave} \end{bmatrix} \rightarrow [+\text{diffuse}]$

$$\text{in env. } \# [-] \begin{bmatrix} +\text{vocalic} \\ +\text{consonantal} \end{bmatrix}$$

The rules based on Matrix II are slightly shorter (by one feature) and describe the same phonological facts as adequately as the previous set of rules. When it comes to the "saving" of features in the dictionary, however, there is a difference. Both sets of rules specify the same number of features in the liquids in the relevant clusters. In the first cluster segment, however, the rules based on Matrix II specify one feature in initial /t/ and /d/ by stating that every non-grave non-continuant in this position must be [+diffuse]. Rules based on Matrix I, on the other hand, specified one feature in initial /k/ and /g/ of these clusters.

We thus have two grammar fragments, G_1 and G_2. Both appear to be entirely consistent with the same linguistic theory and may be presumably evaluated by minimizing the total number of features in the rules and in the dictionary.

In order to assign some numeric values to the overall simplicity of the two grammars, let us introduce the following notation:

i = the number of features contained in the rules of G_1

j = the number of features contained in the rules of G_2

K = the number of English morphemes beginning with /kr/, /kl/, /gr/, /gl/

T = the number of English morphemes beginning with /tr/, /dr/

P = the number of English morphemes beginning with /pr/, /pl/, /br/, /bl/

The overall simplicity S of the two grammar fragments can be expressed as

$$S(G_1) = (P + 2K + 2T) - i$$
$$S(G_2) = (P + K + 3T) - j$$

If $S(G_1) > S(G_2)$, G_1 is preferred; if $S(G_1) < S(G_2)$, G_2 is preferred; and if $S(G_1) = S(G_2)$, the simplicity criterion does not result in a unique evaluation of the two grammars.

The difference
$$S(G_1) - S(G_2) = P + 2K + 2T - i - P - K - 3T + j$$
$$= K - T + j - i$$

In our case,
$$(j\text{-}i) = -1, \text{ so that}$$
$$S(G_1) - S(G_2) = K - T - 1$$

where K is the number of English morphemes beginning with /kr/, /kl/, /gr/, /gl/, and T is the number of English morphemes beginning with /tr/, /dr/.

If $(K - T - 1) > 0$, G_1 is preferred, if $(K - T - 1) < 0$, G_2 is preferred, and if $(K - T - 1) = 0$, no evaluation can be made by this procedure.

Even a cursory inspection of an English dictionary will show that the race between G_1 and G_2 might be a fairly close one.

If it should turn out, however, that G_1 is preferred, the cause of G_2 is not entirely lost. Inspection of Matrix II shows that G_2 could easily be reformulated to contain rules of exactly the same complexity as G_1 which would save exactly the same number of features in the dictionary as the rules of G_1. This could be accomplished simply by a rule specifying the feature [+grave] in every initial non-diffuse segment in the relevant clusters. The new G_2 would then state that every initial non-diffuse segment in such clusters must be /k/ or /g/, which is the same thing stated in G_1 on the basis of non-stridency. The new G_2 could of course no longer predict any feature in the initial /t/ and /d/. As far as the clusters under consideration are concerned, Matrix II can do everything that Matrix I can, but not *vice versa*.[8]

Minimizing the total number of features contained in the grammar may thus appear to be a significant procedure for evaluating the simplicity of grammars, given the assumptions stated in this Section. One of the virtues of the procedure, in my opinion, may be the fact that it could determine the optimal organization of the distinctive feature matrix, and consequently of the dictionary, in terms of the overall structure of the grammar.

The requirement that the distinctive feature matrix must include no redundant specifications of features does not in itself offer a unique solution for the organization of the matrix because more than one feature matrix can fulfill this requirement for any particular language. Among other things, the simplicity criterion—as I attempted to interpret it above —removes this ambiguity by helping to determine the particular feature matrix which is not only non-redundant but which can also serve as the basis of the simplest possible description of the language.

This procedure might thus seem to remove the justification of the objection (which has been occasionally voiced by linguists, e.g., Householder, 1965 [41], 25 [450]) that the organization of the distinctive feature matrix is

arbitrary with regard to the decision which features should be specified in the matrix as distinctive and which should be considered redundant.

We must, however, prepare to face some of the consequences of evaluating alternative grammars by the simplicity criterion. These consequences are present even if we assume that the notion of "simplicity" is "internal to linguistic theory" (Chomsky and Halle, 1965, 109 [465]):

(1) Since the parsimony of features in the dictionary is one of the factors in making this evaluation, an accurate statistical analysis of the segment composition of the complete dictionary of a language would have to be made before any evaluation procedure of this kind could be used.

(2) Unless further modified, the evaluation procedure would compare two alternative descriptions by considering as equivalent for purposes of this count features in the rules and those in the dictionary. There is a serious question whether equating these two elements of grammar is justifiable. As will be shown later in this article, such an approach can easily result in counterintuitive descriptions.

(3) The evaluation of two complete grammars by this criterion would be an extremely complex undertaking.

IV   It should be noted again that the evaluation procedure in Section III of this paper was based on the explicit assumption, stated there, that the phonological rules of grammar refer *only* to non-redundant features of the classificatory matrix. It was this assumption which resulted in the two particular grammar fragments and made their evaluation possible.

We now consider some further consequences of this assumption. Let us say that we wish to state the distribution of the English plural suffix [ɨz] which occurs only after /s z š ž č ǯ/. All of these segments are $\begin{bmatrix} -\text{grave} \\ +\text{strident} \end{bmatrix}$; moreover, no segment *without* this exact feature configuration is followed by the suffix [ɨz]. The simplest and most revealing rule describing this fact would be one which would

[8]There may be some justification for the impression that Matrix II represents a more logical basis for the rules of English grammar with regard to initial clusters of consonants plus liquids if we consider also initial clusters consisting of a continuant plus liquid. Here we find, basically, the same pattern as in non-continuants. Both liquids are admissible after [+grave] segments, i.e., initial /fr/, /fl/ occur as do initial /pr/, /pl/, /br/, /bl/, /kr/, /kl/, /gr/, /gl/. After non-grave diffuse segments, only one or the other liquid is admissible. As far as non-continuants are concerned, only /tr/ and /dr/ occur but not /tl/ and /dl/. As for continuants, only /sl/ and /θr/ are admissible but not /sr/ and /θl/. After non-grave non-diffuse segments, the restrictions are the most severe of all; no liquids are found in such initial clusters with the exception of /šr/ which occurs in a few morphemes. There are, of course, further restrictions on initial clusters of continuant plus liquid with respect to voice (/sl/ occurs but /zl/ does not, etc.). However, in the absence of a rigorous evaluation procedure which would measure the notion of "generality of a pattern," there is no guarantee that the simplicity criterion will result in an evaluation consistent with such intuitive impressions.

state that [ɨz] occurs after non-grave strident consonants.

However, if the dictionary and the phonological rules are based either on Matrix I or on Matrix II (expanded, of course, to continuants), such a simple rule cannot be written; more complex rules would have to be substituted. This is due to the fact that not all sibilants are specified as [− grave] in Matrix I and, conversely, not all sibilants are designated as [+strident] in Matrix II. In either Matrix, there is thus no way of grouping sibilants into a single class by any unique configuration of features.

Adding two different sets of plural suffix rules to G_1 and G_2 will further increase the divergence between the two grammars and presumably necessitate a new evaluation of the two grammar fragments.

Let us now consider a linguistic theory which would not include the assumption that rules are based on non-redundant features only, but would allow the introduction of redundant features in a segment by a freely placed ordered rule of grammar. Proceeding from Matrix I, we could write such a redundancy rule which would specify that all non-diffuse strident consonants are also [−grave]. Conversely, proceeding from Matrix II, we could have a rule stating that all non-diffuse non-grave consonants are also [+strident]. The segments /s/ and /z/ must be specified, in both Matrices, as non-grave strident anyhow, in order to differentiate them from /f/, /v/ and /θ/, /ð/ respectively. As a consequence, the redundancy rules suggested here would make it possible to write the same rule for the distribution of the plural suffix [ɨz] regardless of which Matrix is the basis of the dictionary and of the rules themselves.

Rules introducing redundant features into segment specification are simple, add relatively few symbols to the grammar, and do not expand the dictionary. As far as I can judge from the published writings of Chomsky and Halle, such rules would also be permissible in their theory.

Let us therefore briefly examine the repercussions of the admissibility of redundancy rules. Inspection of Matrix I and of Matrix II clearly shows that either Matrix can be converted into a full feature matrix (i.e., one which includes redundant features) by an equally simple set of rules. Consequently, it will no longer make any difference, from the point of view of "simplicity," whether the dictionary is specified in terms of Matrix I or Matrix II. After redundant features are introduced by a rule, G_1 and G_2 can be easily reformulated so that they will be completely equal as to complexity of rules and as to the saving of features in the dictionary. The evaluation of the two new grammars by "minimizing the total number of features" will no longer be possible. If the two grammars are still to be evaluated, another criterion will have to be introduced for this purpose.

One other serious consequence of the admissibility of freely placed redundancy rules lies in the fact that the selection of a particular non-redundant feature matrix again becomes a more or less arbitrary decision. At any rate, it will be a decision which it may not be possible to justify uniquely on the basis of the overall requirements of the grammar.

I suggest that this presents a serious problem. The determination of the single optimal configuration of the feature matrix (and therefore of the dictionary) strikes me as a significant requirement for a description which is to achieve the level of "descriptive adequacy." A description which includes this requirement should not only reveal differences in the phonological structure of various languages but, more importantly, should point out the nature of the hierarchical organization of features in natural languages in general. This, in itself, might represent a significant contribution to a linguistic theory which aims at "explanatory adequacy."

V   It should be also pointed out that the consequences of admitting the introduction of redundancies by a freely placed ordered rule may be by no means trivial.

Let us assume, for example, that we were to make the decision to specify all segments in the dictionary of English morphemes as to the feature continuant/non-continuant. This would make the features [− vocalic] and [+consonantal] redundant in all non-continuants since they could be introduced by a grammar rule (which could be the first rule of the phonological component of the grammar):

(4) $[-\text{continuant}] \rightarrow \begin{bmatrix} -\text{vocalic} \\ +\text{consonantal} \end{bmatrix}$

Such an unorthodox classificatory matrix will save two symbols in the dictionary specification of every stop and affricate and one symbol in specifying the nasals. However, it will also add one symbol to the specification of each vowel, liquid and glide. There will be no difference in the number of symbols required to specify fricatives.

Curiously enough, it can be shown on the basis of studies in segment composition of English morphemes (for an approximation see Trnka, 1935, 46) that the number of symbols saved in the dictionary by this unorthodox classificatory matrix will be greater than the number of symbols added by this procedure. Actually, the elimination of the specification of the vocalic/non-vocalic and consonantal/non-consonantal features in non-continuants and the consistent specification of the feature continuant/non-continuant in all segments would shorten the dictionary by 3% or more, certainly amounting to a substantial number of symbols saved.

It should be noted that this kind of classificatory matrix can be the basis of precisely the same set of grammar rules (with the addition of the redundancy rule 4) as the more usual matrix which specifies the features vocalic and consonantal as distinctive. Both descriptions can thus be made consistent with the same linguistic theory. As was demonstrated, the simplicity criterion would favor the unorthodox solution and there is nothing in the Chomsky-Halle theory which would seem to prevent it.[9] Obviously, the solution is rather counter-intuitive. It illustrates well, however, that admission of arbitrariness in the classificatory matrix configuration may have rather serious consequences. At the very least, the simplicity criterion *together* with the admissibility of ordered rules which introduce redundant features clearly makes any procedure for discerning a possible natural hierarchy of distinctive features in a language difficult if not impossible.

In order to demonstrate more specifically the nature of the problem, let us consider the

[9]Since there is in this solution one feature for which there are no zeros in the distinctive feature matrix (namely the feature continuant/non-continuant), the possibility of mapping of the matrix into a branching diagram exists. Thus this criterion of Halle (Halle, 1959, 34) is also satisfied.

different types of phonological rules which a grammar might contain. There are essentially three types of such rules:

(x) Rules specifying the distinctive features which had been omitted from the dictionary representation because they are *contextually* determined, i.e., are predictable in terms of *other* segments in the environment (including boundaries). A rule which predicts that, in English, a [+consonantal] segment is /s/ in the environment # [—] $\begin{bmatrix} -\text{vocalic} \\ +\text{consonantal} \end{bmatrix}$, is an example of this type of rule. Another example would be Chomsky's rule (1964 [39], 948 [404]) for rewriting /k/, /t/ → /s/ before /i/, /y/ in order to account for such morphophonemic correspondences as 'opaque'–'opacity', 'democrat'–'democracy', etc.

(y) Rules specifying *redundant* features which had been omitted from the dictionary representation because they are "internally" but not contextually determined, i.e., are predictable entirely on the basis of distinctive features specified for a given segment. As an example, we can list Halle's rule (1962) [37] which states that in English all vowels (i.e., $\begin{bmatrix} +\text{vocalic} \\ -\text{consonantal} \end{bmatrix}$ segments) are also

$$\begin{bmatrix} -\text{nasal} \\ -\text{strident} \\ +\text{continuant} \\ +\text{voiced} \end{bmatrix}$$

(z) Rules which convert what Chomsky has called (1964, 944 [401]) the *classificatory matrix*—containing distinctive features which are by definition binary—into a *phonetic matrix* (*ibid.*, 945 [401])—containing phonetic features which may or may not be binary. The phonetic feature specification of a segment can then be represented, as a conventional abbreviation, by a symbol of the universal phonetic alphabet.

Phonetic features may or may not be contextually determined. For example, the feature of aspiration would have to be specified in the phonetic output of English in certain consonants in specific context only. In the Slavic languages, on the other hand, all consonants would have to be specified as phonetically non-aspirated, regardless of context. In Russian, the various degrees of articulatory fronting (probably not a binary phonetic feature) of the vowels /u/ and /o/ would have to be specified for various environments, as would the partial palatalization of certain consonants before palatalized consonants, and so on.

The Chomsky-Halle theory, if I understand it correctly, imposes no *a priori* requirement on the order in which these three types of rules should appear in the grammar.[10] As a matter of fact, it is my understanding that any requirement for such ordering is considered unjustified. As already suggested in Section IV, this has the following consequence:

If no ordering is imposed on the three *types* of phonological rules, specifically on rules (x) and (y), then there may be two or more alternative grammars, consistent with a given linguistic theory, which cannot be evaluated by "minimizing the number of features in the phonological rules and in the dictionary."

This would suggest that some adjustment in the linguistic theory is necessary. In order to evaluate grammars, the theory must either require some ordering of phonological rules of different types or, alternatively, the defini-

tion of the simplicity criterion—as used by Chomsky and Halle—must be discarded. I have not studied all the implications of the two choices and cannot, at the present time, justify a preference for one or the other solution. Nevertheless, it seems to me clear that some revision in the theory of the phonological component in transformational grammar is unavoidable.

---

[10]Halle, in his *The Sound Pattern of Russian,* specifies that the so-called morpheme structure (MS) rules are to be applied before the so-called phonological (P) rules. As far as I can see, these is no attempt in that work to justify such ordering in theoretical terms and the matter is not mentioned again in the subsequent published work of Halle and Chomsky. As utilized in *The Sound Pattern of Russian,* both MS rules and P rules may specify a *distinctive* feature which is contextually determined.

REFERENCES

CHOMSKY, N., "The Logical Basis of Linguistic Theory," in *Proceedings of the Ninth International Congress of Linguists* (The Hague, 1964), 914–1008. [See here article 39—VBM.]

CHOMSKY, N., and HALLE, M., "Some Controversial Questions in Phonological Theory," *Journal of Linguistics,* 1 (1965), 97–138. [42]

HALLE, M., *The Sound Pattern of Russian* (The Hague, 1959).

HALLE, M., "Phonology in Generative Grammar," *Word,* 18 (1962), 54–72. [37]

HALLE, M., "On the Bases of Phonology," in *The Structure of Language,* J. A. Fodor and J. J. Katz, eds. (Englewood Cliffs, N.J., 1964), 324–333. [38]

HOUSEHOLDER, F. W., "On Some Recent Claims in Phonological Theory," *Journal of Linguistics,* 1 (1965), 13–34. [41]

JAKOBSON, R., FANT, C. G. M., HALLE, M., *Preliminaries to Speech Analysis* (Cambridge, Mass., 1961).

TRNKA, B., *A Phonological Analysis of Present-Day Standard English* (Prague, 1935).

THE NATURE OF
PHONOLOGICAL PRIMES*
E. C. FUDGE

1. INTRODUCTORY

1.1 The ideas of this paper spring from an attempt to grapple with certain phonological problems in a number of languages, and in particular with the special problems which arise when one desires to use a generative, "distinctive-feature" approach.[1] The facts of Tswana phonology summarized below (§5.1) proved especially awkward to handle; when the original twelve features were taken and assigned in a "classical" manner (i.e., [+Vocalic, +Consonantal] for all Liquids, [−Vocalic, −Consonantal] for all Glides, etc.), there were found to be many different ways of characterizing the various segment-types. What was disturbing was that every one of these ways entailed writing phonological rules which failed to highlight the underlying structure, or even obscured it. Conversely, if assignments other than the "classical" were permitted, any attempt to group the segment-types into an arrangement which faithfully reflected the relationships between them (such as Table 8 below) left one with insuperable phonetic problems of feature-assignment. Both these types of difficulty are exemplified in Appendix I.

1.2 The writer became aware of these problems within the context of a generative approach, and the paper is offered mainly as a

contribution to this approach; its positive proposals are intended chiefly as an alternative to the "distinctive-feature" framework in which generative phonology is usually presented. Nevertheless we are convinced that the considerations put forward have relevance for phonology in general: the chief concern is to emphasize, on the one hand, that phonology and the various phonetic levels are logically independent of one another, and, on the other hand, that it is the phonetician's task to investigate the relations which undoubtedly hold between them.

2. DISTINCTIVE FEATURES—
ARTICULATORY OR AUDITORY?

2.1 The output of a generative grammar of a language has been aptly described as a string of systematic phonetic elements which "indicate the way the physical system of articulation is to perform" (Postal, forthcoming: Part III, §A). It would seem to follow from this description that these systematic phonetic elements should be specified in terms of *articulation* rather than in terms of *recognition* (as appears to be the case with the basic elements of the distinctive feature framework). The use of Jakobsonian distinctive features as primes on the systematic phonetic level rests therefore upon the assumption of a one-to-one correspondence between articulation and recognition. Although this correspondence frequently comes close to being one-to-one, there are points in most, if not all, languages at which certain articulatory details are irrelevant from the viewpoint of recognition; some examples of this are given in the next section.

[1] I am greatly indebted to John Lyons, E. K. Brown, and K. J. Kohler for helpful discussions in the preparation of this paper. Of the many comments and criticisms received on an earlier version, those of P. H. Matthews should be mentioned as particularly valuable.

*Reprinted from *Journal of Linguistics* 3.1–36 (1967) by permission of the author and Cambridge University Press. Footnotes 2a, 3a, and 6a were added by the author for this reprinting of his article.

2.2 There are auditory (i.e., recognition-oriented—we reserve the term "acoustic" for features on the physical-phonetic level) distinctive features which correlate with more than one articulatory feature: for example [+Flat] may indicate any one of lip-rounding, pharyngalization, or retroflexion (Jakobson, Fant and Halle, 1952: 31, 50). A generative phonology of a language based on auditory features must (if it is to achieve its aim) further specify which manifestation of Flatness appears in that language, which can only be done in articulatory terms.

Again, English /N/ (i.e., nasal in what Bloomfield (1933: 132) calls pre-final position) has differing realizations depending on the place of articulation of the following consonant (e.g., [limp], [lint], [liŋk]); two of these may be specified in the same terms as realizations of /m/ and /n/ (bilabial and alveolar nasal respectively, in main-initial or main-final positions), and a third in terms of the same place of articulation (velar) as the realizations of /k/ and /g/. There is at least one further allophone, however: the dental [n̪] as in [ten̪θ], whose difference from [n] as in [tent] can be handled only in articulatory terms; there is no auditory feature by which they can be distinguished from one another. The fact that they do not need to be auditorily discriminated does not absolve us from distinguishing them as articulations (since the aim of systematic phonetics is to "indicate the way the physical system of articulation is to perform"). Nor can such an articulatory difference be classified as completely predictable in all languages—the first nasal of the English *inform* and that of the Spanish *informe* are not pronounced identically.

2.3 Conversely, if we use articulatory features as our phonological primes, there will be a good deal of redundancy when we come to the recognition process. For example in English the articulatory feature distinguishing Dental from Alveolar will always need to be specified, although it is crucial for recognition only in fricatives. Thus any criticism of auditory features on the grounds of under-specification in the articulatory field is matched by an exactly corresponding criticism of articulatory features on the grounds of over-specification for recognitional purposes. This paper is in

part an attempt to show that a grammar in which both types of features have their place gives a more accurate picture of the facts than a grammar which excludes one of the types.

3. THE SYSTEMATIC PHONEMIC LEVEL

3.1 If neither the auditory nor the articulatory features are basic to the phonological component of a grammar, then it is obvious that we need a further level to handle the basic elements, which must fulfil the following conditions:

(a) They must be completely abstract (to facilitate the link-up with the abstract morphological elements, and to maintain neutrality as between the auditory and the articulatory),

(b) They must be capable of being linked in correspondence with features of both types, i.e., they must be "feature-sized."

The advantage of introducing a systematic phonemic level is that it enables us to generalize the phonological description beyond the limits of one speaker without having to postulate a whole series of vague abstractions *à la* Daniel Jones (see especially Jones, 1939). Just as a whole set of strings of feature-bundles can be made to correspond with one string of morphological elements (e.g., a set of varying pronunciations of the word *came* may all be assigned to {come} + {past} on the morphological level), so that whole set can be made to correspond with one string of systematic phonemic element bundles (e.g., the varying pronunciations of *came* may all be assigned to the sequence /kām/; furthermore, the whole set of initial feature-bundles from the strings may be made to correspond with one systematic phonemic element-bundle (e.g., the varying pronunciations of the initial consonant of *came* may all be assigned to /k/).

Fig. 1 represents the act of communication, and shows the steps involved in inducing the hearer to select the same phonological element E as the speaker has selected. Fig. 2 exemplifies this in terms of a tone element in Mandarin Chinese,[2] as it occurs on a monosyllable in isolation.

[2]For a more detailed discussion of the articulatory factors involved (box A), see Gray and Wise, 1959: 178–182.

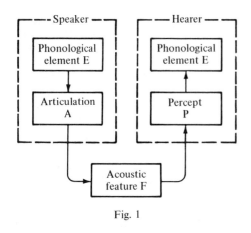

Fig. 1

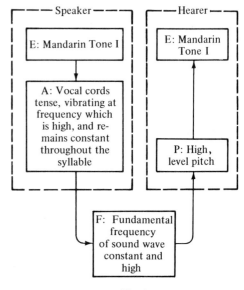

Fig. 2

3.2 Although they are closely connected with sound, it must be clearly borne in mind that the phonological elements are in themselves no less abstract than those of the syntactic and morphological levels: the actual articulation consequent upon the selection of a given phonological element is of secondary importance in the systemic context, and may in fact vary considerably between speakers. A similar statement may be made about the acoustic and auditory effects of such articulations. It is thus dangerous and misleading to say that either articulatory or auditory features *are* the phonological elements, unless they correlate so closely that no facts of language are obscured by treating them as if they were the same: there are two considerations which show that this does obscure facts:

(a) Identical articulations, even in the same environment, may best be treated as realizations of different abstract elements.
(b) Morphophonemic considerations often lead us to make groupings which are definitely counter-phonetic, and which hence cannot be handled in distinctive feature terms.

3.3 Consideration (a) is exemplified very well by Jones (1962: 98–106, also §679, p. 223), though Jones is reluctant to admit that this is

the best explanation of the facts. An even clearer example is the tone-sandhi in Mandarin whereby Tone 2 followed by Tone 3, and Tone 3 followed by Tone 3, are both realized as High Rising pitch followed by Low Rising pitch. It is not clear exactly how pitch and tone phenomena might be dealt with in terms of distinctive features: in this instance, one method might be for each Mandarin vowel carrying a full tone to have additional features as shown

TABLE 1

	Tones			
	1	2	3	4
Rising	−	+	+	−
Falling	−			+
High	−	+	−	

in Table 1. Our example of tone-sandhi could then be handled by a rule of the form:

(1) $[-\text{High}] \longrightarrow [+\text{High}] /$

$$\begin{bmatrix} \underline{} \\ +\text{Voc} \\ -\text{Cns} \end{bmatrix} \ (N) \ (N) \ (N) \ \begin{bmatrix} +\text{Voc} \\ -\text{Cns} \\ +\text{Ris} \\ -\text{High} \end{bmatrix}$$

(where each N represents any segment that is not $\begin{bmatrix} +\text{Voc} \\ -\text{Cns} \end{bmatrix}$)

One grave disadvantage of distinctive feature notation is clearly shown by this example: systematic phonemic elements and their systematic phonetic counterparts are treated in terms which are formally indistinguishable, and this often forces us to imply that one systematic phonemic element has been changed into another (Tone 3 *has become* Tone 2 in our example). This is not only undesirable, but also unnecessary, since we do not require complete biuniqueness in our phonology; our recognition component may contain rules that involve ambiguity, such as:

$$\begin{bmatrix} +\text{Ris} \\ +\text{High} \end{bmatrix} \longrightarrow$$
$$\left\{ \begin{matrix} \begin{Bmatrix} /\text{Tone 2/} \\ /\text{Tone 3/} \end{Bmatrix} / \quad \text{----- (N) (N) (N)} \begin{bmatrix} +\text{Ris} \\ -\text{High} \end{bmatrix} \\ /\text{Tone 2/} \end{matrix} \right\}$$

Lamb (1964 [52]: 111–116 [598–602]) has called rules like (1) *mutation rules;* his reservations about the use of such rules in a synchronic description of a language are, we feel, justified, at any rate in the phonological component:[2a] *realization rules* are preferable (*pace* Chomsky and Halle, 1965 [42]: 111 [466]). The two types of rule may be distinguished as follows (following the notation of Chomsky and Halle, but differentiating strictly between systematic phonemic and systematic phonetic levels):

Realization rules are unordered (though subrules are ordered within the rule), and of the form:

$$/A/ \longrightarrow \begin{Bmatrix} [P] / \text{----- } /B/ \\ [Q] \end{Bmatrix}$$
$$/B/ \longrightarrow [R]$$
$$/C/ \longrightarrow [P]$$

Mutation rules are ordered, and of the form:

1. $/A/ \longrightarrow \begin{Bmatrix} /C// \text{----- } /B/ \\ [Q] \end{Bmatrix}$
2. $/B/ \longrightarrow [R]$
3. $/C/ \longrightarrow [P]$

Notice that mutation rules do not sufficiently maintain the distinction between the systematic phonemic level and the systematic phonetic; moreover they may introduce pseudo-

[2a]See footnote 6a below.

levels between these—pseudo-levels about which Chomsky (1964 [39]: 72 [404]) has said "none of the intermediate stages has any systematic status at all, apparently."

It might be objected that we assume a stratificational position, and then criticize mutation rules for obscuring the stratification, when in fact any attempt to posit distinct levels in linguistics has no *a priori* justification and must therefore be regarded as wholly arbitrary. This objection holds water in the grammatical realm, where elements on all strata are equally abstract, but for phonology we obviously can and must distinguish several levels: the wholly abstract systematic phonemic level, the two abstract but concrete-oriented levels of articulatory and auditory systematic phonetics, and the concrete physical-phonetic level. There could be more but these at least must be differentiated.

In our Mandarin example, Tone 3 as a basic phonological element is simply Tone 3, and has absolutely no properties which are even remotely phonic—actual phonic properties only come in at the systematic phonetic levels. Rule (1) is better formulated as a realization rule:[3]

(2) $$/\text{Tone 3/} \longrightarrow \left\{ \begin{matrix} \begin{bmatrix} +\text{Ris} \\ +\text{High} \end{bmatrix} / \text{----- } /\text{Tone 3/} \\ \begin{bmatrix} +\text{Ris} \\ -\text{High} \end{bmatrix} \end{matrix} \right\}$$

$$/\text{Tone 2/} \longrightarrow \begin{bmatrix} +\text{Ris} \\ +\text{High} \end{bmatrix}$$

(or, better still, in terms of articulations).

The question of realization rules vs. mutation rules is further discussed in Appendix II below.

3.4 Consideration (b) (see §3.2) has been well stated by Rossi (1965: 515): "les résultats de l'analyse structurale ne coïncident pas avec ceux de l'analyse acoustique. Les deux plans acoustique et fonctionnel ne sont pas forcément parallèles," and by Cole (1955: 17):

[3]The rule appearing in an actual grammar would be more complex; neither (1) nor (2) will hold for strings containing three or more instances of Tone 3 in sequence. Incidentally a rule of the form (2) has the advantage of reflecting the fact that tone is a property of units larger than phonetic segments: note how much simpler it is to specify the environment in (2) than in (1).

TABLE 2

| | Front | | Central | Back |
	Lips spread	Lips rounded	Lips neutral	Lips rounded
Close	i i:	y y:		u u:
Half-close	e:	ø:		o:
Half-open	ɛ	œ		ɔ
Open			a:	ɒ

"acoustic similarity is not necessarily a criterion in determining phonemic relationships." If there are no other bases for establishing such relationships, acoustic similarity will be considered, though any other type of patterning which is indicated will be taken as more important.

Spang-Hanssen's excellent example from Czech (Spang-Hanssen, 1949: 67–68) is worth quoting here. The vowels of Czech are as follows (symbolized by the Czech orthographic units):

Short vowels: i(y)   e   a   o   u
Long vowels: í(ý)   é   á   ú (initial)
                                       ů (non-init.)
Diphthongs: ou and others

Morphophonemic alternations confirm the apparent phonetically-based correspondences:

í ⟷ /ii/, é ⟷ /ee/, á ⟷ /aa/.

The remaining vowels behave differently: morphophonemic alternations establish the groupings:

ů ⟷ /oo/, ou and ú ⟷ /uu/,

rather than those of what Spang-Hanssen calls "an ordinary phonetic description":

ú and ů ⟷ /uu/, ou ⟷ /ou/.

No matter how repugnant it may have been to their theories, linguists have always, quite rightly, worked this way in practice: Nida's treatment of the reduction of vowel clusters in Mazatec is a striking example: "For convenience in describing the relationships of the four phonemic vowels to each other, we may chart their relative positions as follows:

CHART OF VOWEL POSITIONS
	Front	Back
High	i	o
Low	e	a

This chart does not correspond precisely to the type of chart usually employed in describing the articulatory relationships of vowels, but for our purposes it is very useful, and the morphological validity of such a plotting of relationships will be evident from the correlations it reveals." (Nida, 1949: 31)

In other words, for morphophonemic purposes a phonetic classification of the vowels does not necessarily indicate what the linguist knows to be the correct structure. In the context of American phonological theory in the 1940's, of course, this called for something of an apology, since it was assumed not merely that "the articulatory relationships of vowels"

TABLE 3

| | Front | | Back |
	Unrounded	Rounded	Rounded
High	i i:	y y:	u u:
Mid	e[ɛ] e:	ø[œ] ø:	o[ɔ] o:
Low		a[ɒ] a:	

TABLE 4

	'box'	'hand'
(nominative)	/doboz/	/ke:z/
'our . . .'	/dobozunk/	/kezynk/
(3) 'your (pl.) . . .'	/dobozotok/	/kezøtøk/
(4) 'his . . .'	/doboza/	/keze/
(5) 'in his . . .'	/doboza:ban/	/keze:ben/

were basic, but also that such were the only relationships one could use in establishing phonological structure. Nida restricts himself to the claim that his "morphophonemic" chart is "useful." It is interesting to note how much stronger is Bloomfield's conclusion of sixteen years earlier, and also how it is stated without any form of apology: "A list or table of the phonemes of a language should therefore ignore all non-distinctive features. Such lists or tables are usually made on the basis of practical-phonetic classifications . . . Tables like these, even when they exclude non-distinctive features, are nevertheless irrelevant to the structure of the language, because they group the phonemes according to the linguist's notion of their physiologic character, and not according to the parts which the several phonemes play in the working of the language." (Bloomfield, 1933: 129–130).

4. EXEMPLIFICATION: HUNGARIAN
4.1 For an example illustrating this point, we shall consider the vowels of Hungarian. From the articulatory point of view they may be classified as in Table 2 (cf. Sebeok, 1943): this system reduces to the "taxonomic phonemic" vowel system shown in Table 3. This arrangement is still inadequate, since it only partially reflects vowel harmony (the assimilation of suffix vowels to stem vowels in Frontness or Backness, and in some cases in Roundedness or Unroundedness). Rows (3), (4), and (5) of

Table 4 show that the relation between /a/ and /e/ is the same as that between /o/ and /ø/; we therefore amalgamate the Mid and Low rows of Table 3, obtaining Table 5 as the result. The validity of the resultant grouping together of /a/ and /o/ is supported by the fact that the morpheme {plural} has, in the absence of possessive morphemes, the allomorphs /–øk/, /–ek/, /–ok/, /–ak/.

Notice that one of the columns headed "Unrounded" in Table 5 contains a rounded vowel (short /a/): a good example of the lack of correspondence between phonetic and phonological classifications. We could, following Chomsky (1964: 74 [405–406]), say that "short /a/" is "functionally unrounded but phonetically rounded"; this is a convenient "shorthand," but it is surely the task of phonology to make classifications on its own terms, to state explicitly what these phonetic-sounding labels ("Rounded" and "Unrounded," "Long" and "Short," etc.) are a "shorthand" for.

It will be seen that the High Back Unrounded box in Table 5 is empty. From the phonetic point of view this is unimportant, but it will easily be seen that the phonological system could tolerate this gap only if there were no suffixes containing /i/ which participated in alternations. In fact this condition is not met—the plural affix has the form /–i/ when a possessive affix is also present: /kezei/ 'his hands'. When affixed to a word containing a back vow-

TABLE 5

| | Front | | Back | |
	Unrounded	Rounded	Unrounded	Rounded
High	i i:	y y:		u u:
Low	e e:	ø ø:	a a:	o o:

el, the plural again has the form /−i/: /dobozai/ 'his boxes'. We might say that our systemic gap is filled by the corresponding front vowel, but this would entail confusing the systemic and the phonetic ("functionally back but phonetically front") in exactly the same way as we saw in the preceding paragraph. On the systemic level, the High Front Unrounded vowel and the High Back Unrounded vowel must be kept as distinct as the corresponding Rounded vowels; the fact that the articulatory movements specified by them are in this case the same must not be taken to indicate that they are themselves one and the same phonological element (an example of Consideration (a); see §3.2). In roots also the vowel /i/ may operate as either Front or Back: compare /riʒe/ 'his rice' with /di:ja/ 'his reward'. Again we must regard them as identical realizations of distinct phonological elements.

To emphasize that phonological elements are in themselves not phonic in any way, we will replace the phonetically-reminiscent labels of Table 5 by the completely neutral labels A, B, 1, 2, a, b, (i), (ii), giving the arrangement shown in Table 6. In fact Table 6 is slightly over-simplified: we need to distinguish the [e:] which alternates with [a:] (/keze:ben/ 'in his hand'—/ha:za:ban/ 'in his house') from the [e:] which has [e:] as its corresponding "B" element (as in /ha:ze:rt/ 'for a house'). However the basic argument is not affected by such simplifications.

TABLE 6

		A		B	
		a	b	a	b
1	(i)	[i]	[y]	[i]	[u]
	(ii)	[i:]	[y:]	[i:]	[u:]
2	(i)	[ɛ]	[œ]	[ɒ]	[ɔ]
	(ii)	[e:]	[ø:]	[a:]	[o:]

Such a scheme is implicit in most "Firthian" approaches to phonology (see, e.g., the presentation of Turkish vowel harmony in Waterson, 1956; Lyons, 1962 [25]) except that in these the break with phonetic or quasi-phonetic nomenclature of prosodies and phonematic units is not made.

4.2 The act of communication, as schematized in Fig. 1 (§3.1), may be accounted for by four sets of rules (corresponding to the four arrows of that figure):

1. Articulatory rules (E——→A)
2. Acoustic rules (A——→F)
3. Auditory rules (F——→P)
4. Recognitional rules (P——→E)

These will be described in §§4.3–4.5. All four types of rules are written as two expressions joined by an arrow; this arrow indicates in each case that there is a unidirectional correspondence between the two expressions. Beyond this, its implications vary from one type of rule to another, just as in the syntactic component the arrow in transformational rules implies something different from the arrow in branching rules.

4.3 Articulatory Rules These convert the strings of phonological elements selected by the syntactic component of a grammar of the language into "ideal articulations"; like Postal's phonetic transcriptions they "indicate the way the physical system of articulation is to perform" (Postal, forthcoming: Part III, §A). For the Hungarian vowels they would be as follows (simplifying somewhat— it might be preferable to specify articulatory positions by means of a three-parameter system like that of Fant (1960), which is said to be "from an acoustical point of view, more rational than the traditional highest-point-of-the-tongue reference for classifying vowels" (Fant, 1960: 210). At all events, our rules could be recast to conform with this or any other system without affecting the basic argument in any way):

1. A ——→ Front of tongue highest
2. B ——→
$$\begin{cases} \text{Front of tongue highest / ——— 1a} \\ \text{Middle of tongue highest / ——— 2a(ii)} \\ \text{Back of tongue highest} \end{cases}$$
3. 1 ——→ Tongue high
4. 2 ——→
$$\begin{cases} \text{Tongue low / B ——— a} \\ \text{Tongue half-low / ——— (i)} \\ \text{Tongue half-high} \end{cases}$$
5. a ——→
$$\begin{cases} \text{Lips rounded / B 2 ——— (i)} \\ \text{Lips neutral / B 2 ——— (ii)} \\ \text{Lips spread} \end{cases}$$
6. b ——→ Lips rounded
7. (i) ——→ Short duration
8. (ii) ——→ Long duration

There would also need to be some general rules to cover all the Hungarian vowels, specifying vocal-cord vibration, velum raised, and no contact, occlusion or obstruction (see Halle, 1964 [38]: 326 [394]). An approach similar to the above was envisaged by Harris (1944 [12]: 193 [124], and in Joos, 1957: 131), who talks of a phonological component (i.e., a feature like A, B, 1, 2, etc.) with "the phonetic value of retracting the tongue when in a sibilant position (and as having zero phonetic value when the tongue is not in sibilant position)."

It will be noticed that we have taken as logically prior not the entities /i/, /y/, /u/, etc., or [i], [y], [u], etc., but the labels A, B, 1, 2, etc.[3a] This would appear to be justified on the grounds of the close correspondence between these last and the articulatory primes: each of 2, B, and a correlates with a total of three articulatory features, while each of the remainder is always realized by the same articulatory feature. Actually our labels correspond almost exactly to Hjelmslev's *cenemes* (Hjelmslev, 1939: 271–272) or *glossemes of expression* (Hjelmslev, 1961: 100).

Questions like "How rounded is 'rounded'?" will be answered fully in the next section; for the present we will content ourselves with the rough answer "Rounded enough to be distinguished from 'neutral.'"

4.4 Acoustic Rules These are basically the ordinary language-independent laws relating shapes and resonances (or rather that subset of them determined by the range of shapes which the vocal tract is capable of forming), and would include the following (see the relevant sections of Potter, Kopp, and Green, 1947, Jakobson, Fant, and Halle, 1952, and Fant, 1960, for a more detailed account):

Lips rounded $\longrightarrow$
$$\left\{\begin{array}{l}\text{Downward shift of certain}\\\text{formants in the spectrum}\end{array}\right\}$$
Tongue low $\longrightarrow$ First formant high

[3a]I am not now certain that this is correct. Probably the phonemes are logically prior, and are postulated initially as a set of elements with no other property than that of being distinct from each other. A, B, 1, 2, etc., then represent classes of phonemes, part of whose importance is that each tends to correlate with a small set of phonetic properties (often just a single property).

Front of tongue highest $\longrightarrow$
$$\left\{\begin{array}{l}\text{Second formant closer to}\\\text{third than to first}\end{array}\right\}$$

The function of any individual rule varies from language to language, and from one part of the structure of a given language to another part. The rule may be involved in distinguishing lexical items, distinguishing allophones of one phoneme, distinguishing a normal pronunciation from a "foreign" one, or may have no function at all.

It is at this stage that the question "How rounded is 'rounded'?" can best be answered: the acoustic (cf. §2.2 above) properties of a sound wave need to be treated in terms of a series of infinitely variable parameters, and the range of values of these parameters for which a given sound is classified as acceptable by the native speaker may easily be found by experiment. "Rounded" may then be defined as that range of articulatory positions (in Hungarian: chiefly, but not necessarily exclusively, lip-positions) for which the value of the corresponding acoustic parameter falls within the "acceptable" range.

Such a system of parameters is the nearest one can get to a "universal phonetic framework": no system involving methods for recognizing what units have been signaled in the sound-wave (e.g., the Jakobsonian distinctive feature inventory) can be considered to be a universal *phonetic* framework—"distinctive features" are *phonological* and not phonetic.

4.5 Auditory and Recognitional Rules It is at this point that the Jakobsonian distinctive features operate: the sound wave (more correctly, the nerve impulses set up by the sound wave) is tested for various properties, and phonological elements selected according to the properties found. Thus in Hungarian:

(6) First formant very high $\longrightarrow$ B2a
First formant fairly high $\longrightarrow$ 2 . . . (i)
First formant fairly low $\longrightarrow$ 2 . . . (ii)
First formant very low $\longrightarrow$ 1

The four properties which figure in (6) are the same as the distinctive feature combinations $\begin{bmatrix}+\text{Compact}\\-\text{Diffuse}\end{bmatrix}$, $\begin{bmatrix}+\text{Compact}\\+\text{Diffuse}\end{bmatrix}$, $\begin{bmatrix}-\text{Compact}\\-\text{Diffuse}\end{bmatrix}$ and $\begin{bmatrix}-\text{Compact}\\+\text{Diffuse}\end{bmatrix}$ respectively; there seems no real reason, however, to maintain the necessity of binary judgments, since we have here a clear case of a continuum divided into four. Perhaps [++Compact], [+Compact], [−Compact] and [−−Compact] would be a more suitable representation.

The fact that we can write the rules in the form (6) might suggest that distinctive features in their normal form have no place in a theory of phonology and phonetics—however, this is not the case. It is important to know what set of properties of the sound wave are significant in the language concerned: in languages other than Hungarian the continuum referred to might be divided into two, three or five parts, and accordingly we need rules to state this. Thus we might have two sets of rules, (i) Auditory rules:

First formant very low $\longrightarrow$ [++Compact]
　　etc.
Certain formants in spectrum significantly low $\longrightarrow$ [+Flat]
　　etc.
All remaining acoustic features $\longrightarrow$ no auditory feature.

(ii) Recognitional rules:

1. [++Compact] $\longrightarrow$ B2a
2. [+ Compact] $\longrightarrow$ 2 . . . (i)
3. [− Compact] $\longrightarrow$ 2 . . . (ii)
4. [−−Compact] $\longrightarrow$ 1
5. [+Grave] $\longrightarrow$ B . . . b

6. $[-\text{Grave}] \longrightarrow \left\{ \begin{matrix} \left\{ \begin{matrix} A \\ B \end{matrix} \right\} / \left[\begin{matrix} \overline{} \\ --\text{Compact} \\ -\text{Flat} \end{matrix} \right] \\ A \end{matrix} \right\}$

7. $[+\text{Flat}] \longrightarrow \left\{ \begin{matrix} (i) & / \left[\overline{++\text{Compact}} \right] \\ b \end{matrix} \right\}$

8. $[-\text{Flat}] \longrightarrow \left\{ \begin{matrix} (ii) & / \left[\overline{++\text{Compact}} \right] \\ a \end{matrix} \right\}$

9. $[+\text{Long}] \longrightarrow \left\{ \begin{matrix} (ii) & / \left[\overline{--\text{Compact}} \right] \\ \text{zero} \end{matrix} \right\}$

10. $[-\text{Long}] \longrightarrow \left\{ \begin{matrix} (i) & / \left[\overline{--\text{Compact}} \right] \\ \text{zero} \end{matrix} \right\}$

The recognitional ambiguity of rule 6 might be resolved by considering whether other vowels in the same word were recognized as A or as B; in any case higher level information will lead to its resolution.

4.6 It must be emphasized here that the method of auditorily differentiating between sounds need not parallel the basic relations between the elements differentiating them on any previous level: [a:] may be longer than [ɒ], but this does not prove that they are discriminated by attending to their length differences: the reverse is indicated by the fact that the length distinction is accompanied by such marked qualitative differences; it is noteworthy that in the cases where this does not hold (i.e., the high vowels [i], [y], [u]) the length distinction is tending to disappear in the spoken language—"not so much a matter of dialectal but of age variation. I have tried to show that the length phoneme does not occur in the speech of the younger generation of Budapest." (Sebeok, 1943: 163, fn. 2) In this type of speech the recognition feature "Long" is not used; rules 9 and 10 above do not appear.

5. EXEMPLIFICATION: TSWANA
5.1 In some languages it is possible to carry out a very extensive structuring of the consonant inventory on similar lines. For example, the articulatory table of consonants in Tswana is as shown in Table 7 (adapted from Cole, 1955: 21, the page references are to this work).

Various phonological relationships may be established on the grounds of the following features of Tswana:

(i) Nasalization or strengthening. Under the influence of a preceding nasal, consonants "change"[4] as follows (39):

b $\longrightarrow$ pʔ　$\left\{ \begin{matrix} l \\ d \end{matrix} \right\} \longrightarrow$ tʔ　$\left\{ \begin{matrix} \text{zero} \\ ʔ \end{matrix} \right\} \longrightarrow$ kʔ

Φ $\longrightarrow$ ph　　r $\longrightarrow$ th　　x $\longrightarrow$ kx

　　　　　　s $\longrightarrow$ tsh　　h $\longrightarrow$ kh

　　　　　　ʃ $\longrightarrow$ tʃh　　w $\longrightarrow$ kʷʔ

(ii) Palatalization.
(a) Under the influence of the passive affix

[4]More correctly and illuminatingly "have varying realizations"; since /b/ and /pʔ/ are both realized as [pʔ] after a nasal, it would seem legitimate to infer a close relationship between the two elements, as shown by Table 8.

-*wa,* bilabial consonants are dissimilated as follows (43):

$$p? \longrightarrow t\int? \qquad ph \longrightarrow t\int h$$
$$b \longrightarrow d_3 \qquad \Phi \longrightarrow \int$$

(b) In the formation of diminutives with the suffix -*ana* (43–44):

$$p? \longrightarrow t\int^{w}? \qquad \left\{ \begin{matrix} n \\ \eta \end{matrix} \right\} \longrightarrow \text{ɲ}$$

TABLE 7

				Bilabial	Alveolar	Palatal	Velar	Glottal
Occlusives	Stops	Medial	Ejective	p?	t?		k?	?
			Aspirated	ph	th		kh	
			Voiced	b	d			
	Affri-cates	Medial	Ejective		ts?	t∫?		
			Aspirated		tsh	t∫h	kx	
			Voiced			d₃		
		Lateral	Ejective		tl?			
			Aspirated		tlh			
Continuants	Frica-tives	Medial	Voiceless	Φ	s	∫	x	h
			Voiced	β				
	Fric-tionless	Medial	Rolled		r			
			Flapped		ɾ			
		Lateral			l			
		Nasal		m	n	ɲ	ŋ	
	Semi-vowels	Medial		w		y		

Free variations: b and β (23)   d and ɾ (28)
                      ? and zero in word-initial position (21)
Complementary distribution: d/ɾ and l (28)
   (with some exceptions) x and h (25–26), kx and kh (23, 33)
Oppositions neutralized: ts?/t∫?, tsh/t∫h, s/∫, before w and rounded vowels (25, 32, 35).

TABLE 8

Systematic table of Tswana consonants: there is a further subdivision o, p, q of the whole, with the articulatory correlates lip-rounding, palatalization (roughly speaking), and plain respectively. Syllable-initial [w] and [y] will be treated as C 1 b o, C 1 b p respectively.

		A	B i		B ii		C
		x	y	f	f	g	
1	a	p?	t?	tl?	ts?	t∫?	k
	b	b	d/l			d₃	?/zero
2	a	ph	th	tlh	tsh	t∫h	kx/kh
	b	Φ	r		s	∫	x/h
3		m	n		ɲ		ŋ

$\begin{Bmatrix} ph \\ \Phi \end{Bmatrix} \longrightarrow t\int^w h$

b $\longrightarrow$ dʒ^w (t$\int^{w}$ʔ in one case) $\begin{Bmatrix} tʔ \\ d \end{Bmatrix} \longrightarrow \begin{Bmatrix} tsʔ \\ t\int ʔ \end{Bmatrix}$

l $\longrightarrow$ dʒ (t$\int^{w}$ʔ in one case)   r $\longrightarrow$ tsh

(c) In the formation of causatives with suffix
-ya (45–46):

$\Phi \longrightarrow \begin{Bmatrix} tsh \\ t\int^w h \end{Bmatrix}$ x $\longrightarrow \begin{Bmatrix} s \\ tsh \end{Bmatrix}$

(iii) Velarization (as in (ii) (a)) (46–47):

$\begin{Bmatrix} m \\ ɲ \end{Bmatrix} \longrightarrow ŋ$

5.2 On the basis of the relationships implied by the alternations listed in §5.1, we can arrange our consonant system as in Table 8 (again labeling the categories with non-phonetically-oriented terms).

Articulatory rules are as below (again, subrules are ordered within the rule, but rules are unordered among themselves). Environments are wholly within one segment unless otherwise indicated by square brackets; [. . . 3 . . .] indicates any segment containing the prime 3.

1. A $\longrightarrow \begin{cases} \text{Velar place of articulation} / \text{——— 3 o} \\ \text{Alveolar p.a.} \qquad\qquad / \begin{cases} \text{——— o} \\ \text{——— p} \end{cases} \\ \text{Bilabial p.a.} \end{cases}$

2. B $\longrightarrow \begin{cases} \text{Velar p.a.} / \text{——— 3(ii) o} \\ \text{Alveolar p.a.} \end{cases}$

3. C $\longrightarrow \begin{cases} \text{Alveolar p.a.; Palatalization} / \text{——— 1 b p} \\ \text{Glottal p.a.} / \begin{cases} \text{——— 1 b} \\ [[\text{——— 2][close vowel]} \end{cases} \\ \text{Alveolar p.a.} \qquad\qquad \text{——— p} \\ \text{Velar p.a.} \end{cases}$

4. 1 $\longrightarrow \begin{cases} \text{Ejective release} / \begin{cases} \text{——— a} \\ [[\ldots 3 \ldots][\text{——— b]} \end{cases} \\ \text{Contact} / \begin{cases} [\text{——— (i)][close vowel]} \\ \text{——— (ii)} \end{cases} \\ \text{Lateral} / \text{——— (i)} \\ \text{No articulatory effect or Contact} / \text{C ——— b q} \\ \qquad \text{(free variation)} \\ \text{No articulatory effect} / \text{C ——— b} \\ \text{Contact or Occlusion (free variation)} \end{cases}$

5. 2 $\longrightarrow \begin{cases} \text{Release with friction} / \begin{cases} [\text{C ——— a]} \\ [\ldots 3 \ldots][\text{C ——— b]} \end{cases} \text{[non-close vowel]} \\ \text{Aspirated release} \quad / \begin{cases} \text{——— a} \\ [\ldots 3 \ldots][\text{——— b]} \end{cases} \\ \text{Apical trill} / \text{B ——— b(i)} \\ \text{Occlusion} \end{cases}$

6. 3 $\longrightarrow$ Velum lowered; $\begin{cases} \text{non-syllabic} / [\text{———][vowel]} \\ \text{syllabic;} \begin{cases} \text{velar p.a. word-finally} \\ \text{same p.a. as following} \\ \text{consonant} \end{cases} \end{cases}$

7. a $\longrightarrow$ Voiceless; contact

8. b $\longrightarrow \begin{cases} \text{Voiceless; contact} / [\ldots 3 \ldots][\text{———]} \\ \text{Voiced} / \begin{cases} 1 \text{ ———} \\ 2 \text{ ——— (i)} \end{cases} \\ \text{Voiceless} \end{cases}$

9. (i) $\longrightarrow$ No articulatory effect

10. (ii) $\longrightarrow \begin{cases} \text{Palatalization} / 3\text{———} \\ \text{Groove friction} \end{cases}$

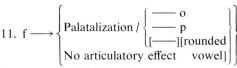

11. f ⟶ { Palatalization / { ⎰ ⟶ o ⎱ } } / { [⟶][rounded } / { No articulatory effect   vowel] } }

12. g   ⟶   Palatalization
13. x   ⟶   No articulatory effect
14. y   ⟶   Lateral release
15. o   ⟶   Lip rounding
16. p   ⟶   No articulatory effect
17. q   ⟶   No articulatory effect

6. EXEMPLIFICATION: ENGLISH

6.1 There are, however, other languages where so complete an analysis is not possible —for example, English. Morphophonemic alternations give us the following relations between consonants:

f–v	knife–knives
θ–ð	path–paths
s–z	taps–tabs
t–d	tapped–grabbed
k–s–ʃ	electric–electricity–electrician
s–ʃ	essence–essential
t–ʃ	vibrate–vibration
z–ʒ	visible–vision
d–ʒ	decide–decision

These relations give a fragmentary grouping (sometimes contradicting phonetic similarities) indicated by lines in Table 9: phonetic relations not contradicted by alternations are indicated by the relevant sounds appearing in the same row or column.

6.2 There is another, rather more complex, manifestation of phonological relatedness, which may be brought to light by studying re-strictions on what elements may co-occur within the syllable. It would be interesting to study how far morphophonemic alternations (which involve syntagmatic relations) and the relationships we are about to study (which involve paradigmatic relations) may be handled by the same set of basic elements; in the case of English this is possible, as we hope to show in the present section of our paper.

What we are attempting to do is in fact what Householder (1962: 191) has called "the specification of phonemes by distributionally defined 'distinctive features.'" Our method will be to investigate how the set of English phonemes may be partitioned into subsets on distributional grounds (compare Sapir, 1925: 49 [19–20]; also in Joos, 1957: 24).

As an example, we may say that the English /p, t, k, m, n, w, l, r (taking [ʃr] as the realization of /sr/), and f[5]/ form a group, since they are the only consonants which occur in the environment # s ————— vowel. Other groupings are listed in Table 10: notice that the definite counter-phonetic connection of /s/ with /k/ which we discovered from considering morphophonemics is confirmed. Table 11 shows the situation at this point. In terms

[5]Our own observations have led us to the conclusion that word-initial /sf/ (occurring only in Greek borrowings like *sphere, spherical, sphinx*) is felt by English speakers to be deviant—children meeting *sphere* for the first time tend to hear and say [spiə]. We can probably best regard these words as forming part of a peripheral (Pilch, 1965) "Greek loan" phonological system coexistent (Fries and Pike, 1949) with the main system in which /sf-/ does not occur.

TABLE 9

English consonants, showing morphophonemic relations. On the status of the velar nasal, see §6.4 (cf. Sapir, 1925 [1]: 49 [19], also in Joos, 1957: 24).

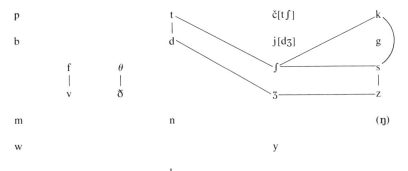

TABLE 10

Group	Occur in environment	But not in	Examples
p, t, k	# s ——— r		*spray, stray, scratch*
p, b, f	# ——— l # ——— r # ——— w	*play, blade, flake* *pray, bread, fray* (No *pw-, bw-, fw-*)
t, d, θ	# ——— w # ——— r # ——— l	*twig, dwell, thwart* *tray, drag, three* (No *tl-, dl-, thl-*)
k, g, s	# ——— w # ——— l # ——— r	*quick, Gwen,*[6] *swift* *click, glib, slick* *crab, grab, shrivel*

[6]Word-initial /gw/ occurs only in loan-words (*guano*), and a few proper names (*Gwen*) which are also borrowings; this cluster occurs freely, however, in syllable-initial position (*linguistics*), and differs from /sf-/ (see footnote 5) in that it causes no confusion. Sapir's remarks on the sound [ʒ] and its lack of difficulty in word-initial position for English speakers learning other languages would seem to be applicable in this case also (Sapir, 1925:51 [21]; also in Joos, 1957:25).

of auditory distinctive features, there is no way of indicating that /k/, /g/, and /s/ form a group corresponding to the groups /p/, /b/, /f/, and /t/, /d/, /θ/, which show obvious phonetic similarities. This would confirm that the Jakobsonian distinctive features are inadequate for the representation of the basic systematic phonemic elements of a language (cf. Householder, 1965: 24 [449]).

6.3 On similar lines we can proceed to study the continuants /w/, /l/, /r/, and /y/. Table 12 shows the possible combinations of these with the stops and voiceless fricatives in word-initial position: we have taken the initial element of the diphthong [juː] as part of the vowel, rather than as post-initial and hence part of a series of consonant clusters like [fj]

of *few* which occur only before the vowel sound [uː] (compare Householder, 1952: 266). Symmetry indicates that we should group /w/ with the "labials," /l/ with the "alveolars," and /y/ with the "palatals" (groupings which all correspond with phonetic resemblances), while /r/ should (counter-phonetically) be grouped with the "velars," giving the arrangement shown in Table 13.

6.4 [m] and [n] contrast in main-initial and main-final positions, but not when they are pre-final. If pre-final [m] and [n] are taken as realisations of one basic element /N/, we can treat main final [ŋ] as the realisation of /Ng/. Thus row 4 (the nasals) divides into two in main-initial and main-final positions, but is not subdivided at all in pre-final position.

TABLE 11

TABLE 12

	p, b, f	t, d, θ	č, j, ʃ	k, g, s
w	−	+	−	+
l	+	−	−	+
r	+	+	−	+
y	−	−	−	−

6.5 Not only is the grouping of /r/ with the velars and /s/ not capable of being handled elegantly by auditory features, but the grouping together of /w/, /l/, /y/, and /r/ is inconsistent with the "classical" allocation of the features Vocalic and Consonantal; it could conceivably be argued that

$$\begin{bmatrix} \alpha \text{ Vocalic} \\ \alpha \text{ Consonantal} \end{bmatrix}$$

defines a natural class, but this would include /h/ also, which patterns very differently in English.

6.6 The connection of /t/ with /s/ and /ʃ/ as well as with /θ/ (and the similar relation of /d/ to /ʒ/) is again (cf. fn. 5) probably best explained in terms of coexistent phonological systems—the "Germanic," shown in Table 14, and the "Latin," shown in Table 15.

7. CONCLUSION

7.1 We will conclude by attempting to answer the question "On which phonological and phonetic levels, if any, do the Jakobsonian auditory features provide a universal framework?" We will consider each level in turn.

7.2 At the Physical Phonetic Level The range of sounds which human beings are capable of uttering is in general a continuum—the acoustic features of the sound waves are infinitely and continuously variable, and are best handled in terms of parameters which also vary continuously (cf. Fant, 1960). Distinctive features handle the recognition of those features of sound waves which are distinctive in an individual language; they operate in terms of yes/no judgments, which are entirely out of place at the physical phonetic level.

7.3 At the Articulatory Systematic Phonetic Level There is a small but significant minority of articulatory differences whose corresponding acoustic differences cannot be handled in terms of auditory distinctive features. The dental and alveolar allophones of the English /N/ ([ten̪θ] vs. [tent]) exemplify this: [θ] vs. [t] involves the opposition Continuant vs. Interrupted, which cannot possibly be used to dis-

TABLE 13

		A	B	C	D
1	a	p	t	č	k
	b	b	d	j	g
2	a	f	θ	ʃ	s
	b	v	ð	ʒ	z
3		w	l	y	r
4		m	n		
5					h

TABLE 14

		A	B	C	D
1	a	p	t	č	k
	b	b	d	j	g
2	a	f	θ	ʃ	s
	b	v	ð	(ʒ)	z
3		w	l	y	r
4		m	n		
5					h

tinguish [ŋ] from [n]. Similarly with the bi-labial [m] and labiodental [M] allophones of the Spanish /N/ ([imbyérno] vs. [iMfyérno]); even if Strident vs. Mellow is used to distinguish [f] from [p], [b] and [β] (or brought in as a redundant feature), it cannot sensibly be used to distinguish [M] from [m], unless the label is used in a completely non-phonetic sense. In each case it is better to talk of distinct articulations which correlate with slight acoustic differences (best handled in parametric terms) but not with any auditory differences. Distinctive features do not cover these cases, and hence cannot provide a universal framework at this level.

7.4 At the Auditory Systematic Phonetic Level It seems likely that a system of the Jakobsonian type might apply here (cf. §4.5 above); whether the Jakobsonian system itself is adequate or appropriate is another matter, however. Phoneticians would need to investigate a large number of languages and establish for each the total inventory of acoustic cues actually used in deciding whether an uttered sound represents one phone or another. It is possible then that distinctive features may provide a universal framework at this level; however, the question must remain open until sufficient results have been obtained.

7.5 At the Systematic Phonemic Level Grammatical and lexical considerations must be taken into account at this level, as well as phonetic considerations; in fact they may override

phonetic considerations (see the examples of §§3.3, 3.4 above). Thus, although there may be individual cases where a phonetically-based system handles this level adequately, there will be others where such a system fails; hence we can say that the distinctive-feature system does not provide a universal framework at this level.

7.6 At the Taxonomic Phonemic Level The distinctive features do in fact provide some kind of universal framework in this context, since, given a taxonomic phonemic system, it can always be "translated" into distinctive feature terms, using only the "original twelve" oppositions (Jakobson et al., 1952): Abaza (see Allen, 1956) with over 60 consonant phonemes needs only eleven of these. There are frequently a large number of possible ways to "translate," and some have found this disturbing: Horálek (1965: 366) concludes "dass die Theorie der U[nterscheidenden] E[igenschaften] noch nicht in solchem Mass ausgebildet wurde, wie es für eine strenge Wissenschaft unentbehrlich ist. Man kann sogar heute von einer Krise der Theorie der UE sprechen."

7.7 *Pace* Horálek, this "crisis" has arisen not so much because this approach needs to be further developed as because it is in essence unsuited to its task. Those who originated the distinctive features held just the views on linguistic theory which have been rejected decisively (and in this writer's judg-

TABLE 15

		A	B i	B ii α	B ii β
1	a	p	t	c	qu
	b	b	d	g*	
2	a	f	s		
	b		z		
3		v	j		
4		m	n		
5			l		r

where /s/ $\longrightarrow$ $\begin{cases} [\int] & / \underline{\hspace{2cm}} \begin{cases} /iV/ \\ / y / \end{cases} & (essential) \\ [s] & (essence) \end{cases}$

/z/ $\longrightarrow$ $\begin{cases} [ʒ] & / \underline{\hspace{2cm}} \begin{cases} /iV/ \\ / y / \end{cases} & (vision) \\ [z] & (visible) \end{cases}$

/c/ $\longrightarrow$ $\begin{cases} [\int] & / \underline{\hspace{2cm}} \begin{cases} /iV/ \\ / y / \end{cases} & (electrician) \\ [s] & / \underline{\hspace{2cm}} \begin{cases} / i / \\ / e / \end{cases} & (electricity) \\ [k] & (electric) \end{cases}$

/g*/ $\longrightarrow$ $\begin{cases} [dʒ] & / \underline{\hspace{2cm}} \begin{cases} / i / \\ / e / \end{cases} & (regent) \\ [g] & (regal) \end{cases}$

ment, correctly) by those who use distinctive features today: no approach to phonology has been so "taxonomic" and phonetically-oriented as that of the Prague School. It is therefore not surprising that generative grammarians periodically feel the need to modify the system, as for example by introducing the feature Sonorant (Postal, 1964: 277; Katz and Postal, 1964: 162): this feature goes some way towards remedying the lack of fit of phonological classes with phonetic ones over the totality of the world's languages, but still fails to cover every case (see Appendix I).

The logical conclusion of this is that phonologists (above all, generative phonologists) ought to burn their phonetic boats and turn to a genuinely abstract framework. By so doing they will escape the fate of not only falling between two stools (the result of attempting to handle systematic phonemic and systematic phonetic levels in the same terms), but also ending up sitting in the very place which they have expended such strenuous and well-justified efforts to avoid.

APPENDIX I

Some problems arising in the construction of feature-matrices for Tswana.

An orthodox assignment of features to the systematic phonemes of Table 8 would begin by dividing them into three groups (Halle, 1958: 327 [395]):

(a) "Liquids": r, l; these would be assigned the features [+Vocalic, +Consonantal], then l [+Continuant], r [−Continuant].
(b) "Glides": w, y, and probably ʔ; [−Vocalic, −Consonantal], then perhaps as in Table 16.
(c) "Consonants": all the rest; [−Vocalic, +Consonantal], then perhaps as in Table 17.

TABLE 16

	w	y	ʔ
Continuant	+	+	−
Grave	+	−	

We notice straightaway that it is inappropriate to separate the "liquids" from the rest of the consonants, since from the systematic phonemic point of view they are fully integrated into the system of "consonants": [d] is a submember of /l/, while after nasals /l/ and /r/ are realized as [tʔ] and [th] respectively. It is equally inappropriate that the nasals (which may function as syllabics, and which have no morphophonemic connections with the rest of the consonants) should be allocated to the group of "consonants."

Phonological rules to handle the phenomena of §5.1 would be something like the following:

(i)   Strengthening
(b ⟶ pʔ)
$$\begin{bmatrix} +\text{Voiced} \end{bmatrix} \longrightarrow$$

$$\begin{bmatrix} -\text{Voiced} \\ -\text{Continuant} \\ +\text{Checked} \end{bmatrix} / \;[+\text{Nasal}]\; \begin{bmatrix} \\ -\text{Vocalic} \\ +\text{Consonantal} \\ -\text{Nasal} \\ -\text{Compact} \\ +\text{Grave} \end{bmatrix}$$

(Φ, s, ʃ, x ⟶ ph, tsh, tʃh, kx)
$$[+\text{Continuant}] \longrightarrow$$

$$\begin{bmatrix} -\text{Continuant} \\ -\text{Checked} \end{bmatrix} / \;[+\text{Nasal}]\; \begin{bmatrix} \\ -\text{Vocalic} \\ +\text{Consonantal} \\ -\text{Nasal} \end{bmatrix}$$

(l, r ⟶ tʔ, th)
$$\begin{bmatrix} +\text{Vocalic} \\ \alpha\,\text{Continuant} \end{bmatrix} \longrightarrow$$

$$\begin{bmatrix} -\text{Vocalic} \\ -\text{Nasal} \\ -\text{Compact} \\ -\text{Grave} \\ -\text{Strident} \\ \alpha\,\text{Checked} \end{bmatrix} / \;[+\text{Nasal}]\; \begin{bmatrix} \\ +\text{Consonantal} \end{bmatrix}$$

TABLE 17

	ŋ	ɲ	m	n	kʔ	kx	x	tʃʔ	tʃh	dʒ	ʃ
Nasal	+	+	+	+	−	−	−	−	−	−	−
Compact	+	+	−	−	+	+	+	+	+	+	+
Grave	+	−	+	−	+	+	+	−	−	−	−
Continuant					−	−	+	−	−	−	+
Voiced								−	−	+	
Checked					+	−		+	−		

	pʔ	ph	b	Φ	tʔ	th	tlʔ	tlh	tsʔ	tsh	s
Nasal	−	−	−	−	−	−	−	−	−	−	−
Compact	−	−	−	−	−	−	−	−	−	−	−
Grave	+	+	+	+	−	−	−	−	−	−	−
Strident					−	−	*	*	+	+	+
Voiced	−	−	+	−							
Continuant	−	−		+					−	−	+
Checked	+	−			+	−	+	−	+	−	

In addition, all consonants may be [+Flat] or [−Flat].

*An intermediate value of Strident seems to be the best way of specifying the lateral affricates; Strident might be applied, and then its opposite Mellow (compare Compact and Diffuse to obtain three or more distinctive vowel heights).

(? ⟶ k?)

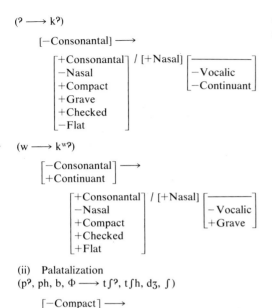

$$[-\text{Consonantal}] \longrightarrow$$

$$\begin{bmatrix} +\text{Consonantal} \\ -\text{Nasal} \\ +\text{Compact} \\ +\text{Grave} \\ +\text{Checked} \\ -\text{Flat} \end{bmatrix} \Big/ [+\text{Nasal}] \begin{bmatrix} \underline{\qquad} \\ -\text{Vocalic} \\ -\text{Continuant} \end{bmatrix}$$

(w ⟶ kʷ?)

$$\begin{bmatrix} -\text{Consonantal} \\ +\text{Continuant} \end{bmatrix} \longrightarrow$$

$$\begin{bmatrix} +\text{Consonantal} \\ -\text{Nasal} \\ +\text{Compact} \\ +\text{Checked} \\ +\text{Flat} \end{bmatrix} \Big/ [+\text{Nasal}] \begin{bmatrix} \underline{\qquad} \\ -\text{Vocalic} \\ +\text{Grave} \end{bmatrix}$$

(ii) Palatalization
(p?, ph, b, Φ ⟶ tʃ?, tʃh, dʒ, ʃ)

$$\begin{bmatrix} -\text{Compact} \\ +\text{Grave} \end{bmatrix} \longrightarrow$$

$$\begin{bmatrix} +\text{Compact} \\ -\text{Grave} \end{bmatrix} \Big/ \begin{bmatrix} \underline{\qquad} \\ -\text{Vocalic} \\ +\text{Consonantal} \\ -\text{Nasal} \\ +\text{Flat} \end{bmatrix}$$

(iii) Velarization
(m, ɲ ⟶ ŋ)

$$\begin{bmatrix} \alpha\ \text{Compact} \\ -\alpha\ \text{Grave} \end{bmatrix} \longrightarrow$$

$$\begin{bmatrix} +\text{Compact} \\ +\text{Grave} \end{bmatrix} \Big/ \begin{bmatrix} \underline{\qquad} \\ -\text{Vocalic} \\ +\text{Consonantal} \\ +\text{Nasal} \\ +\text{Flat} \end{bmatrix}$$

There are the following additional difficulties:

(a) /?/ may have a zero realization; this could be handled in terms of an additional feature Segment (see Wilson, 1966 [34]: 201 [355]).

(b) The ejectives are in fact in free variation with the corresponding unaspirated occlusives: this means that the feature Checked would need to be marked ± for these at some level, in which case they would no longer contrast with the [−Checked] of the aspirated series. We might distinguish the two by using [+Tense] for the aspirated series and [−Tense] for the others, though [−Tense] seems questionable as a specification of the ejectives. The most satisfactory solution would probably be to distinguish these two series in terms of a feature Aspirated/Unaspirated: a further addition to the inventory of features.

Other Phonological Rules
(kx ⟶ kh before high vowels)

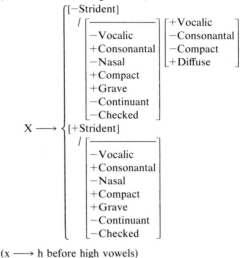

$$X \longrightarrow \begin{cases} [-\text{Strident}] \\ \Big/ \begin{bmatrix} \underline{\quad} \\ -\text{Vocalic} \\ +\text{Consonantal} \\ -\text{Nasal} \\ +\text{Compact} \\ +\text{Grave} \\ -\text{Continuant} \\ -\text{Checked} \end{bmatrix} \begin{bmatrix} +\text{Vocalic} \\ -\text{Consonantal} \\ -\text{Compact} \\ +\text{Diffuse} \end{bmatrix} \\[2ex] [+\text{Strident}] \\ \Big/ \begin{bmatrix} \underline{\quad} \\ -\text{Vocalic} \\ +\text{Consonantal} \\ -\text{Nasal} \\ +\text{Compact} \\ +\text{Grave} \\ -\text{Continuant} \\ -\text{Checked} \end{bmatrix} \end{cases}$$

(x ⟶ h before high vowels)

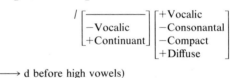

$$\begin{bmatrix} +\text{Consonantal} \\ -\text{Nasal} \\ +\text{Compact} \\ +\text{Grave} \end{bmatrix} \longrightarrow \begin{bmatrix} -\text{Consonantal} \\ -\text{Voiced} \end{bmatrix}$$

$$\Big/ \begin{bmatrix} \underline{\quad} \\ -\text{Vocalic} \\ +\text{Continuant} \end{bmatrix} \begin{bmatrix} +\text{Vocalic} \\ -\text{Consonantal} \\ -\text{Compact} \\ +\text{Diffuse} \end{bmatrix}$$

(l ⟶ d before high vowels)

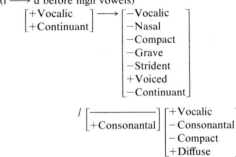

$$\begin{bmatrix} +\text{Vocalic} \\ +\text{Continuant} \end{bmatrix} \longrightarrow \begin{bmatrix} -\text{Vocalic} \\ -\text{Nasal} \\ -\text{Compact} \\ -\text{Grave} \\ -\text{Strident} \\ +\text{Voiced} \\ -\text{Continuant} \end{bmatrix}$$

$$\Big/ \begin{bmatrix} \underline{\quad} \\ +\text{Consonantal} \end{bmatrix} \begin{bmatrix} +\text{Vocalic} \\ -\text{Consonantal} \\ -\text{Compact} \\ +\text{Diffuse} \end{bmatrix}$$

(ts?, tsh, s ⟶ tʃ?, tʃh, ʃ when combined with lip-rounding, or before rounded vowels)

$$[-\text{Compact}] \longrightarrow [+\text{Compact}]$$

$$\Big/ \begin{bmatrix} \underline{\quad} \\ +\text{Strident} \\ +\text{Flat} \end{bmatrix}$$

$$\text{or } \begin{bmatrix} \underline{\quad} \\ +\text{Strident} \end{bmatrix} \begin{bmatrix} +\text{Vocalic} \\ -\text{Consonantal} \\ +\text{Flat} \end{bmatrix}$$

We will now sketch an assignment of features which, while distinctly less orthodox than the preceding one, is much more suitable for the statement of phonological relationships.

The inventory of segment-types is first subdivided as follows: using the features Vocalic and Nasal:

(a)   Vowels: [+Vocalic, −Nasal].
(b)   Syllabic Nasals: [+Vocalic, +Nasal].
(c)   Nasal Consonants: [−Vocalic, +Nasal], then as the nasals in Table 17.
(d)   Oral Consonants: [−Vocalic, −Nasal], then as in Table 18.

It is difficult to find a phonetic feature to distinguish /tlʔ/ from /tʔ/, and /tlh/ from /th/; Laterality would involve /l/ as well, and Stridency has been used already. Likewise we cannot find a phonetic feature to divide /r/ from an /l/ which has [d] as a submember; we should like to be able to use Voiced, since the relation between these two phonemes is exactly the same as that handled elsewhere by Voiced: there seems no reason why we should not say that /r/ is functionally voiceless, though phonetically voiced. Here we see clearly the advantage of breaking away from phonetic features to handle the systematic phonemic level.

The feature Tense has to be given a slightly wider definition than that of Jakobson *et al.* (1952: 36–39), but this enables the rules for Strengthening to be stated far more simply than under the preceding system:

$$\begin{bmatrix} -\text{Tense} \\ \alpha\,\text{Voiced} \end{bmatrix} \longrightarrow \begin{bmatrix} +\ \text{Tense} \\ -\alpha\,\text{Aspirated} \end{bmatrix}$$

$$/\ [+\text{Nasal}]\ \begin{bmatrix} \underline{\hspace{2cm}} \\ -\text{Vocalic} \end{bmatrix}$$

From the phonological point of view, there is no value in distinguishing the features Aspirated and Voiced, since there is no segment which needs both for its specification. If these are replaced by a nonphonetic feature F, such that [−Aspirated] and [+Voiced] are replaced by [+F], [+Aspirated] and [−Voiced] by [−F], and /l/ is [+F] while /r/ is [−F], the Strengthening rules can be still further simplified:

$$[-\text{Tense}] \longrightarrow [+\text{Tense}] \ /\ [+\text{Nasal}] \begin{bmatrix} \underline{\hspace{1.5cm}} \\ -\text{Vocalic} \end{bmatrix}$$

Palatalization:
$$\begin{bmatrix} +\text{Grave} \\ -\text{Compact} \end{bmatrix} \longrightarrow$$
$$\begin{bmatrix} -\text{Grave} \\ +\text{Strident} \\ +\text{Compact} \end{bmatrix} \Bigg/ \begin{bmatrix} \underline{\hspace{1cm}} \\ -\text{Vocalic} \\ -\text{Nasal} \\ +\text{Flat} \end{bmatrix}$$

Velarization:
$$\begin{bmatrix} \alpha\,\text{Grave} \\ -\alpha\,\text{Compact} \end{bmatrix} \longrightarrow$$
$$\begin{bmatrix} +\text{Grave} \\ +\text{Compact} \end{bmatrix} \Bigg/ \begin{bmatrix} \underline{\hspace{1cm}} \\ +\text{Nasal} \\ +\text{Flat} \end{bmatrix}$$

TABLE 18

	kʔ	kx	ʔ	x	pʔ	ph	b	Φ
Grave	+	+	+	+	+	+	+	+
Compact	+	+	+	+	−	−	−	−
Tense	+	+	−	−	+	+	−	−
Aspirated	−	+			−	+		
Voiced			+	−			+	−

	tʃʔ	tsʔ	tʃh	tsh	dʒ	ʃ	s	tlʔ	tʔ	tlh	th	l	r
Grave	−	−	−	−	−	−	−	−	−	−	−	−	−
Strident	+	+	+	+	+	+	+	−	−	−	−	−	−
Tense	+	+	+	+	−	−	−	+	+	+	+	−	−
Aspirated	−	−	+	+				−	−	+	+	?	
Voiced					+	−	−	?		?			
Compact	+	−	+	−	+	−							

In addition, all consonants may be [+Flat] or [−Flat]. [w] has been treated as the realization of /ʔw/, i.e., /ʔ/ with the additional feature [+Flat].

These two rules are similar to the preceding version. The remaining phonological rules would be somewhat simpler than before:

(kx, x ⟶ kh, h)

$$X \longrightarrow \begin{cases} [-\text{Strident}] \ / \ \begin{bmatrix} \\ -\text{Vocalic} \\ -\text{Nasal} \\ +\text{Grave} \\ +\text{Compact} \\ -F \end{bmatrix} \begin{bmatrix} -\text{Nasal} \\ -\text{Compact} \\ +\text{Diffuse} \end{bmatrix} \\[6pt] [+\text{Strident}] \ / \ \begin{bmatrix} \\ -\text{Vocalic} \\ -\text{Nasal} \\ +\text{Grave} \\ +\text{Compact} \\ -F \end{bmatrix} \end{cases}$$

(l ⟶ d)

$$X \longrightarrow \begin{cases} [-\text{Continuant}] \ / \ \begin{bmatrix} \\ -\text{Vocalic} \\ -\text{Nasal} \\ -\text{Grave} \\ -\text{Strident} \\ -\text{Tense} \\ +F \end{bmatrix} \begin{bmatrix} -\text{Nasal} \\ -\text{Compact} \\ +\text{Diffuse} \end{bmatrix} \\[6pt] [+\text{Continuant}] \ / \ \begin{bmatrix} \\ -\text{Vocalic} \\ -\text{Nasal} \\ -\text{Grave} \\ -\text{Strident} \\ -\text{Tense} \\ +F \end{bmatrix} \end{cases}$$

(tsʔ, tsh, s ⟶ tʃʔ, tʃh, ʃ)

[−Compact] ⟶ [+Compact]

$$/ \ \begin{bmatrix} \\ +\text{Strident} \\ +\text{Flat} \end{bmatrix} \text{ or } \begin{bmatrix} \\ +\text{Strident} \end{bmatrix} [+\text{Flat}]$$

It will readily be seen that, in this case, the more we relax the requirement that phonological patterning be stated in phonetic terms, the simpler becomes the statement of our rules of realization: this suggests that we should state phonological relationships in terms entirely independent of phonetics, and then frame our rules of realization so as to accommodate the phonetic facts. In this way one and the same phonological (systematic phonemic) system might be used for several phonetically very diverse dialects: any phonetically-based approach to phonology is likely to arrive at a significantly different phonemic system for each dialect. Obviously the former result accounts better for mutual intelligibility than the latter.

APPENDIX II

A more detailed consideration of mutation rules.

It is instructive to compare the set of rules in §5.2 above with the set below in which mutation rules are permitted. These rules are ordered, whereas those of §5.2, although numbered for ease of reference, are unordered (though the subrules within each rule are ordered in both cases). Notice that in these rules

(a) systematic phonemic elements appear on both sides of the arrows, not just on the left as in the realization rules,

(b) in context-sensitive rules from 12. onwards environments have increasingly to be specified in terms of articulations, as one by one the systematic phonemic elements are rewritten.

1. A . . . p ⟶ B . . . (ii) g o

2. A ⟶ $\begin{cases} C \ / \ \underline{\qquad} 3 \text{ o} \\ B \ . . . \ (ii) \ g \ / \ \underline{\qquad} o \end{cases}$

3. B . . . (ii) ⟶ C / ⎯⎯ 3 o

4. C . . . p ⟶ B . . . (ii) f q / ⎯⎯ 2 b

5. A ⟶ Bilabial place of articulation

6. B ⟶ Alveolar p.a.

7. C ⟶ $\begin{cases} \text{Glottal p.a.} \ / \ \begin{cases} \underline{\qquad} 1 \text{ b} \\ [\underline{\qquad} 2][\text{close vowel}] \end{cases} \\ \text{Velar p.a.} \end{cases}$

8. b (i) x p ⟶ a (ii) q

9. b ⟶ a / [. . . 3 . . .][⎯⎯]

10. a ⟶ Voiceless; contact

11. b ⟶ $\begin{cases} \text{Voiced} \ / \ \begin{cases} 1 \ \underline{\qquad} \\ 2 \ \underline{\qquad} (i) \end{cases} \\ \text{Voiceless} \end{cases}$

12. 1 ⟶

$\begin{cases} \text{Ejective release} \ / \ [\underline{\qquad} \text{Voiceless; contact}] \\ \text{Contact} \ / \ \begin{cases} [\underline{\qquad} (i)][\text{close vowel}] \\ \underline{\qquad} (ii) \end{cases} \\ \text{Lateral} \ / \ \underline{\qquad} (i) \\ \text{No articulatory effect or} \\ \text{Contact (free variation)} \quad /[\text{Glottal p.a.} \underline{\qquad} q] \\ \text{No articulatory effect} \quad / \ [\text{Glottal p.a.} \underline{\qquad} \ ] \\ \text{Contact or Occlusion (free variation)} \end{cases}$

13. 2 ⟶

$\begin{cases} \text{Release with friction} \\ \qquad / \ [\text{Velar p.a.} \underline{\qquad} \text{voiceless; contact}] \\ \text{Aspirated release} \ / \ [\underline{\qquad} \text{voiceless; contact}] \\ \text{Apical trill} \qquad / \ [\text{Voiced} \underline{\qquad} (i)] \\ \text{Occlusion} \end{cases}$

14. 3 ⟶

$\text{Velum lowered;} \begin{cases} \text{non-syllabic} \ / \ [\underline{\qquad}] \ [\text{vowel}] \\ \text{syllabic;} \begin{cases} \text{velar p.a. word-finally} \\ \text{same p.a. as following consonant} \end{cases} \end{cases}$

15. (i) $\longrightarrow$ Alveolar p.a.; no groove friction

16. (ii) $\longrightarrow$ $\left\{\begin{array}{l}\text{Palatalization}\\ \quad / \text{ [Velum lowered ——]}\\ \text{Groove friction}\end{array}\right\}$

17–23.   As rules 11–17 of §5.2.

Comparing the above rules with those of §5.2 we notice:

1. The mutation rules 1, 2, 3, 4, 9 above enable us to state more simply the articulatory correlates of certain elements:

Rules	simplify statement of	in rule ... above	cf. rule ... of §5.2
1, 2	A	5	1
3	B	6	2
4	C	7	3
$9\left\{\begin{array}{l}\\ \text{envt. for}\left\{\begin{array}{l}1\\2\end{array}\right.\end{array}\right.$	b	$\left.\begin{array}{l}11\\12\\13\end{array}\right.$	$\left.\begin{array}{l}8\\4\\5\end{array}\right\}$

This suggests that mutation rules might be a useful device to make clear the workings of a complicated set of realization rules, while having no systematic significance (which would explain the fact mentioned in §3.3 that any pseudo-levels introduced by mutation rules are devoid of systematic status).

2. The mutation rule 8 above which handles the realization

/ B 2 b (i) x p / ("palatalized" /r/) $\longrightarrow$ [tsh]

has no analogue in the rules of §5.2. These latter could be modified to handle this case by amending rules 5, 8, and 9 as follows:—

5.   2 $\longrightarrow$

$\left\{\begin{array}{l}\cdots\\ \text{Aspirated release} / \left\{\begin{array}{l}\text{B —— p}\\ \text{—— a}\\ [\ldots 3 \ldots][\text{C —— b}]\end{array}\right\}\\ \cdots\\ \cdots\end{array}\right\}$

8.   b $\longrightarrow$

$\left\{\begin{array}{l}\text{Voiceless; contact} / \left\{\begin{array}{l}[\ldots 3 \ldots][\text{——}]\\ \text{B2 —— (i) p}\end{array}\right\}\\ \cdots\\ \cdots \qquad\qquad \cdots\end{array}\right\}$

9.   (i) $\longrightarrow$

Alveolar p.a.; $\left\{\begin{array}{l}\text{groove friction / B —— p}\\ \text{no groove friction}\end{array}\right\}$

The additional complication introduced seems a high price to pay for the ability to handle this very isolated case; the mutation rule is perhaps preferable. This would suggest that mutation rules are useful for handling exceptions and anomalies,[6a] while alternations which are widespread and productive in the language ought to be handled by realization rules.

REFERENCES

ALLEN, W. S. (1956). "Structure and System in the Abaza Verbal Complex," *Transactions of the Philological Society* 127–176.

BLOOMFIELD, L. (1933). *Language*. London: Allen & Unwin.

CHOMSKY, N. (1964). *Current Issues in Linguistic Theory*. (Janua Linguarum, 38). The Hague: Mouton. [39]

CHOMSKY, N., and HALLE, M. (1965). "Some Controversial Questions in Phonological Theory," *Journal of Linguistics* 1.97–138. [42]

COLE, D. T. (1955). *Introduction to Tswana Grammar*. London: Longmans.

FANT, C. G. M. (1960). *Acoustic Theory of Speech Production*. (Description and Analysis of Contemporary Standard Russian, 2.) 's-Gravenhage: Mouton.

FODOR, J. A., and KATZ, J. J. (eds.) (1964). *The Structure of Language*. Englewood Cliffs, N.J.: Prentice-Hall.

FRIES, C. C., and PIKE, K. L. (1949). "Coexistent Phonemic Systems," *Language* 25.29–50.

GRAY, G. W., and WISE, C. M. (1959). *The Bases of Speech*, 3d edition. New York: Harper & Row.

HALLE, M. (1958). "On the Bases of Phonology," in Fodor and Katz (1964). 324–333. [38]

HARRIS, Z. S. (1944). "Simultaneous Components in Phonology," *Language* 20.181–205; also in Joos (1957). 124–138. [12]

HJELMSLEV, L. (1939). "The Syllable as a Structural Unit," *Proceedings of the Third International Congress of Phonetic Sciences*. Ghent: Laboratory of Phonetics of the University. 266–272.

HJELMSLEV, L. (1961). *Prolegomena to a Theory of Language*. Madison: University of Wisconsin Press.

HORÁLEK, K. (1965). "Zur Theorie der unterscheidenden Eigenschaften" ("Distinctive Features"), *Proceedings of the Fifth International Congress of Phonetic Sciences*. Basel: Karger. 365–366.

[6a]This statement unduly restricts the role of such rules. My present view is that mutation rules are of basic importance in handling alternations which are morphologically rather than phonologically conditioned, for example:

(i) $\bar{e}\rightarrow e$ / kép, slép, lén, drém, . . . / — Past

(ii) t$\rightarrow$s / — ion, ive, ial

(Although (ii) was perhaps phonologically conditioned in Latin, it cannot be so regarded in English.)

HOUSEHOLDER, F. W. (1952). Review of Harris's *Methods in Structural Linguistics. IJAL* 18. 260–268.

HOUSEHOLDER, F. W. (1962). "The Distributional Determination of English Phonemes," *Lingua* 11.186–191.

HOUSEHOLDER, F. W. (1965). "On Some Recent Claims in Phonological Theory," *Journal of Linguistics* 1.13–34. [41]

JAKOBSON, R., FANT, C. G. M., and HALLE, M. (1952). *Preliminaries to Speech Analysis.* Cambridge, Mass.: M.I.T. Press.

JONES, D. (1939). "Concrete and Abstract Sounds," *Proceedings of the Third International Congress of Phonetic Sciences.* Ghent: Laboratory of Phonetics of the University. 1–7.

JONES, D. (1962). *The Phoneme,* 2d edition. Cambridge: Heffer.

JOOS, M. (ed.) (1957). *Readings in Linguistics.* New York: American Council of Learned Societies.

KATZ, J. J., and POSTAL, P. M. (1964). *An Integrated Theory of Linguistic Descriptions.* (M.I.T. Press Research Monograph, 26.) Cambridge, Mass.: M.I.T. Press.

LAMB, S. M. (1964). "On Alternation, Transformation, Realization, and Stratification," *Georgetown Monograph Series on Languages and Linguistics* 17. Washington, D.C.: Georgetown University Press. 105–122. [52]

LYONS, J. (1962). "Phonemic and Non-Phonemic Phonology," *IJAL* 28.127–134. [25]

NIDA, E. A. (1949). *Morphology.* Ann Arbor: University of Michigan Press.

PIKE, K. L. (1948). *Tone Languages.* Ann Arbor: University of Michigan Press.

PILCH, H. (1965). "Zentrale und periphere Lautsysteme," *Proceedings of the Fifth International Congress of Phonetic Sciences.* Basel: Karger. 467–473.

POSTAL, P. M. (1964). "Boas and the Development of Phonology," *IJAL* 30.269–280.

POSTAL, P. M. (forthcoming). "On the Mentalistic Character of So-called 'Sound Change,'" *Two Studies in the Theory of Phonology.* [See now Postal, *Aspects of Phonological Theory* (1968) —VBM.]

POTTER, R. K., KOPP, G. A., and GREEN, H. C. (1947). *Visible Speech.* New York: Van Nostrand.

ROSSI, M. (1965). "Analyse spectrographique et interprétation fonctionnelle de la nasalité dans un parler de l'Italie du nord" (Rossano, prov. Massa Carrara). *Proceedings of the Fifth International Congress of Phonetic Sciences.* Basel: Karger. 512–516.

SAPIR, E. (1925). "Sound Patterns in Language," *Language* 1.37–51; also in Joos (1957) 19–25. [1]

SEBEOK, T. A. (1943). "Notes on Hungarian Vowel Phonemes," *Language* 19.162–164.

SPANG-HANSSEN, H. (1949). "On Simplicity of Descriptions," *TCLC* 5.61–70.

WATERSON, N. (1956). "Some Aspects of the Phonology of the Nominal Forms of the Turkish Word," *BSOAS* 18.578–591.

WILSON, R. D. (1966). "A Criticism of Distinctive Features," *Journal of Linguistics* 2.195–206. [34]

47

THE ROLE OF
A PHONOLOGICAL FEATURE SYSTEM
IN A THEORY OF LANGUAGE*

JAMES D. McCAWLEY

The system of phonological features used in Halle's *The Sound Pattern of Russian*[1] is essentially the same as that presented in Jakobson, Fant, and Halle's *Preliminaries to Speech Analysis*[2] eight years earlier. It is important to note, however, that the system of features played a very different role in the theoretical frameworks of these two works. In *Preliminaries,* as in Jakobson's other phonological writings, the features are intended as *distinctive* features: they are intended as a universal system of "phonemic" representation, that is, a system for representing contrasts between the utterances of any language. Jakobson sought a feature system which was not only universal but also minimal; he thus presents many cross-linguistic complementary distribution arguments for uniting various different oppositions into a single feature, e.g., uniting the oppositions rounded/unrounded and pharyngealized/non-pharyngealized into the single feature flat/plain.

If a phonemic representation as envisioned by Jakobson were incorporated into a full grammar of a language, that is, a device which specifies how semantic representation is paired with phonetic representation in that language, that grammar would have to contain both a *phonological component,* which would assign a phonemic representation to the "surface syntactic" representation of each utterance, and a *feature interpretation component,* which would specify the relationship be-

tween phonemic representation and phonetic representation in that language. The feature interpretation component would presumably have to involve (1) rules predicting "non-distinctive" values of the universal features (e.g., rules which specify the non-distinctive voicelessness of final obstruents in Russian and the non-distinctive voicedness of obstruents which are followed by a voiced obstruent), (2) rules stating which of the possible realizations of each of the universal features is utilized in a given language (e.g., a rule of English that the feature of flatness is realized as lip-rounding rather than as pharyngealization), and (3) rules specifying "ideal values" for physical parameters involved in the realization of those features (e.g., a rule in Serbo-Croatian that a long vowel is about $1\frac{1}{2}$ times as long as a short vowel, as opposed to Czech, where a long vowel is about $2\frac{1}{2}$ times as long as a short vowel).

The Sound Pattern of Russian, while utilizing almost the same feature system which Jakobson had set up for universal representation of phonemic oppositions, rejected the notion of phonemic representation. In that work Halle describes the phonological component of a grammar as consisting of an ordered system of rules for the conversion of "surface syntactic" representation into "systematic phonetic" representation. Here the "surface syntactic" representation of an utterance indicates what morphemes are involved in the utterance, what sequence they come in, how they are grouped together, and what syntactic category the various groups belong to, and

[1] Mouton (The Hague), 1959.
[2] M.I.T. Press (Cambridge, Mass.), 1951.

*This article appeared in French translation in *Langages* 8.112–123 (1967) under the title "Le rôle d'un système de traits phonologiques dans une théorie du langage." Reprinted by permission.

each morpheme is represented as a sequence of segments, each segment being a set of "underlying" specifications for phonological features. The "systematic phonetic" representation of an utterance is a representation in which each segment is assigned a value of + or − for each of the universal features, regardless of whether that value is "distinctive." The full grammar of a language would thus involve both a phonological component (which Halle describes in great detail) and a feature interpretation component (which he largely ignores), although the feature interpretation component would now only perform the second and third of the three functions listed above and would have for its input the "systematic phonetic" representation rather than a "phonemic" representation. The phonological rules operate in terms of the same system of features on which both the underlying representation of morphemes and the "systematic phonetic" representation of utterances are based. Each rule specifies the class of segments affected in terms of a formula involving those features and specifies its effect as certain changes in the feature composition of the affected segment, as in the Korean rule

$$\begin{bmatrix} +\text{obstruent} \\ +\text{closure} \\ -\text{tense} \end{bmatrix} \longrightarrow [+\text{voiced}]$$

in env. [+voiced] —— [+voiced]

which changes to + the voicing specification of a non-tense stop or affricate which is preceded by a voiced segment and followed by a voiced segment, as in [pat] + [etta] → [padetta] 'received'.[3]

Since Halle's purposes in *Sound Pattern* and subsequent works are so different from those of Jakobson in *Preliminaries*, the question obviously arises of whether Jakobson's features are adequate for Halle's purposes. It should first be noted that there are a couple

of respects in which the feature system of *Preliminaries* is inadequate even for Jakobson's purposes, in that there are languages possessing contrasts which can not be represented in that feature system. For example, the feature system of *Preliminaries* contains a feature of *stridency,* which is supposed to represent both the difference between affricates and ordinary stops and the difference between the "noisy" spirants [f, s, š, x] and the "less noisy" spirants [ɸ, θ, ś, ç]; however, the existence of languages such as Chipewyan, which has a three-way contrast between [t, tθ, ts], shows that the difference between stops and affricates and the difference between "noisier" and "less noisy" places of articulation are two independent dimensions on which sounds may differ and thus may not be subsumed under a single feature, as in *Preliminaries*. Using the terms "abrupt release" and "proximal"[4] to denote these two oppositions, the segments in question may be represented as

	θ	s	t	t	tθ	ts
				(dental)	(alveolar)	
closure	−	−	+	+	+	+
abrupt release	−	−	+	+	−	−
proximal	−	+	−	+	−	+

The above is an example of a case in which distinct articulatory oppositions which Jakobson subsumed under one feature may in fact not be so subsumed within an adequate universal theory of phonology. It is interesting to note that such may be the case even when the two articulatory oppositions never function as independent dimensions of contrast. Consider the feature of "flatness," under which Jakobson subsumes the articulatory oppositions of lip-rounding and pharyngealization. Arabic has an opposition between plain and pharyngealized consonants and has a three-vowel system [i, a, u], of which [u] is rounded; vowels are pharyngealized when adjacent to a pharyngealized consonant. Consider what phonological rules and "feature interpretation rules" would be needed to repre-

---

[3]In this paper I use square brackets to enclose all segmental transcriptions, phonetic or not, and use slashes // only to call special attention to the fact that a representation is the underlying representation. Slashes here thus do not indicate "phonemic" representation, which never figures in my examples and which I indeed reject completely. Note that in a system of ordered rules the input to and output from a rule are generally neither "underlying" nor "systematic phonetic" representation but some intermediate stage of representation.

[4]These terms are introduced in Chomsky and Halle, *The Sound Pattern of English* (Harper & Row, to appear 1967). [See now Chomsky and Halle, 1968—VBM.]

sent these facts within a theory in which the phonological component of the grammar operates in terms of the flat/non-flat opposition and "rounded" and "pharyngealized" figure only in the feature interpretation component. The phonological component would have to contain the rule

$$[+\text{syllabic}] \longrightarrow [+\text{flat}] \text{ in env.} \begin{cases} \underline{\quad} \begin{bmatrix} +\text{flat} \\ -\text{syllabic} \end{bmatrix} \\ \begin{bmatrix} +\text{flat} \\ -\text{syllabic} \end{bmatrix} \underline{\quad} \end{cases}$$

and the feature interpretation component would have to specify that "flat" is interpreted as "pharyngealized" when attached to a consonant or to a front or low vowel, as "rounded" when attached to a high back vowel, and as "rounded plus pharyngealized" when attached to a high back vowel which is adjacent to a [+flat] consonant. But note that this means that the generalization "vowel is pharyngealized when adjacent to pharyngealized consonant" must in effect be stated twice, once in the phonological component and once in the feature interpretation component. Thus, a theory of phonology in which pharyngealization and rounding are treated as the same feature throughout the phonological component suffers from exactly the same defect which Halle[5] pointed out in theories which require underlying forms to be converted into phonetic representation through an intermediate stage of "taxonomic phonemic" representation: in each case the theory may force one to treat a single phonological process as if it were rather two unrelated processes in two separate components of the grammar. I accordingly conclude that even if there are no languages in which rounding and pharyngealization function as independent oppositions, a theory which treats them as separate must still be held superior to a theory which subsumes them under a single feature.

The above examples have related to the superiority of one feature system over another on the basis of the representations which it gives as output of the phonological component, in the one case because of the inability of one of the systems to distinguish things which contrast at that level, in the other case because the mode of representation forces the feature interpretation component to duplicate

[5]*The Sound Pattern of Russian*, pp. 22–23.

rules which are already part of the phonological component. However, a system of features may be superior to another on grounds relating exclusively to the phonological component, namely relating to the role which the features play in specifying the classes of segments to which the various rules apply and the effects which these segments are subjected to. An instructive example in this connection is the comparison of the features "compact" and "diffuse" with alternative features which could be employed to represent the same contrasts. The feature of "diffuseness" has been used to oppose high vowels and alveolar, dental, and labial consonants (which are all designated as [+diffuse]) to low and mid vowels and palatal and velar consonants (which are all [−diffuse]); the feature of compactness has been used to separate the low vowels ([+compact]) from the mid and high vowels ([−compact]); there has been no uniformity on the assignment of values for compactness to consonants, which in some works (*The Sound Pattern of English*) are all said to be [−compact], whereas in others (*The Sound Pattern of Russian*) the [+diffuse] consonants are said to be [−compact] and the [−diffuse] consonants [+compact]. Suppose that a theory of language involving the feature of diffuseness is compared with an otherwise identical theory in which diffuseness is replaced by a feature in which consonants are matched with vowels in precisely the opposite fashion, i.e., a theory which differs from the former by having instead of diffuseness a feature called "high" which opposes high vowels and velar and palatal consonants ([+high]) to mid and low vowels and alveolar, dental, and labial consonants ([−high]). Crucial for choosing between these two theories is a consideration of those phonological rules in the languages of the world in which either a class containing both consonants and vowels is involved in the rule or a vowel or consonant has an unambiguously "assimilative" effect on a consonant or vowel respectively: in the former case if the one feature system allows the class to be specified with a single feature value (say, [+high]), then the latter will require a disjunction involving another feature also (say, "diffuse consonantal or non-diffuse non-consonantal"), thus providing evidence that it is the features of the former system that are functional in the rule; in the latter case the effect of the rule will in the one system be to make the two segments agree in the value of the feature in question, in the other system to disagree, thus giving evidence that the former system more correctly characterizes the notion "assimilation."

In every case which I have been able to find which is of relevance to the choice between these two theories, evidence is provided for the superiority of "high" over "diffuse." (1) In Sanskrit [s] becomes retroflexed after [i, u, r, k]. Since Sanskrit [r] has palatal place of articulation and since palatal and velar consonants other than [k, r] become something else before [s] (i.e., all consonants become voiceless and unaspirated before [s] and palatal obstruents become velars), the rule can be expressed as

$$\begin{bmatrix} +\text{obstruent} \\ -\text{grave} \\ -\text{closure} \end{bmatrix} \longrightarrow [+\text{high}]$$

in env. [+high] ——————

i.e., it is simply an assimilation of the feature of highness. If this rule were expressed in terms of diffuseness rather than highness, it would appear to do two quite distinct things: to assimilate diffuseness after a non-diffuse consonant and to dissimilate diffuseness after a diffuse vowel. (2) In Maxakalí, a language spoken in Brazil,[6] there are phonological processes by which a vowel is added after a word-final stop and the stop is either weakened or deleted entirely. The vowels added are as follows: after [p], add [o]; after [t], add [a]; after [č], add [i]; after [k], add [ɨ]. Note that the vowel added has the same "highness," i.e., the opposite diffuseness to the consonant to which it is added. Moreover, the choice of vowel is determined by an "assimilation": less movement is required of the organs of speech in passing from [p] to [o], etc., than would be required in passing to vowels of the opposite highness (i.e., the same diffuseness) as the consonant: [pɨ], [ti], [ča], [ko]. Thus the theory with highness instead of diffuseness correctly represents the assimilatory nature of this vowel insertion rule. (3) The extremely common phonological rule by which [ty] becomes [č] is universally classed as an assimilation and, in terms of the theory with highness, consists of

the stop taking on the [+high] specification of the glide; however, in terms of the theory with diffuseness this change looks like a dissimilation: [t] and [y] are [+diffuse] but [č] is [−diffuse]. (4) In the Ripuarian dialect group[7] of German, which includes the dialect of Köln, dentals have become velars after high vowels, as in [huŋk] 'dog', [kiŋk] 'child', [lūk] 'people', [tˢik] 'time', corresponding to standard German *Hund, Kind, Leute, Zeit*. This change is also an assimilation of highness.

Not only are there cases such as the above which argue for classing high vowels together with velar and palatal rather than dental and labial consonants and to my knowledge no cases which argue for the opposite classification, but it is quite easy to give a uniform articulatory characterization of the [+high] segments: they are the segments whose primary constriction or closure is above a line drawn from the rear of the alveolar ridge to the uvula,[8] whereas a uniform articulatory characterization of the "diffuse" segments may well be impossible; the articulatory definitions which have been proposed for it either do not define the class of segments enumerated above[9] or do not provide a criterion which applies uniformly to consonants and vowels.[10]

In this connection, it is worth bringing up the other feature in *Preliminaries* whose articulatory definition has never been satis-

---

[6]The facts which I cite are taken from Sarah Gudschinsky, "Phonetic Similarity and the Phonemes of Maxakalí" (unpublished, read at a meeting of the Linguistic Society of America, Aug. 1, 1964).

[7]Data from V. M. Schirmunski, *Deutsche Mundartkunde* (Akademie Verlag, Berlin, 1962), p. 121.

[8]I am grateful to Lester Rice for formulating this definition.

[9]E.g., the definition in Halle's "In Defense of the Number Two" (in *Studies Presented to Joshua Whatmough*, Mouton, The Hague, 1957, pp. 65–72): "These two extremes of vocal tract shape, the horn and the Helmholtz resonator, are taken as the defining characteristics of the features *compact–noncompact* (horn shape or not), and *diffuse–nondiffuse* (Helmholtz resonator shape or not)." (Halle, p. 71.) This definition would make not only [p, t] but also [č] "diffuse."

[10]E.g., the definition in Halle's "On the Bases of Phonology" [38] (in J. Katz and J. Fodor, eds., *The Structure of Language*, Prentice-Hall, Englewood Cliffs, 1964, pp. 324–333): "diffuse sounds are produced with a narrowing which in degree exceeds that of a constriction and is located in the front part of the vocal tract; . . . The dividing line between *front* and *back* is further retracted for vowels than for other sounds: for the vowels, *front* includes almost the entire oral cavity, while for other sounds, the dividing line between *front* and *back* runs between the alveolar and palatal regions."

factory, namely "vocalic." The definitions given in "On the Bases of Phonology" ("vocalic sounds are pronounced with a periodic excitation and with an open oral cavity, i.e., one in which the most extreme degree of narrowness is a constriction"; "consonantal sounds are pronounced with occlusion or contact in the central path through the oral cavity") appear to preclude a segment from being both [+vocalic] and [+consonantal]; nevertheless, these two features are supposed to "produce a quadripartite division of the sounds of speech into (1) vowels, which are vocalic and non-consonantal; (2) liquids . . . , which are vocalic and consonantal; (3) consonants, which are non-vocalic and consonantal; and (4) glides . . . , which are non-vocalic and non-consonantal" (*ibid.*, p. 327 [395]). One clear defect of the feature system of *Preliminaries* is that it provides no way of representing the difference between syllabic and non-syllabic liquid and nasals. Since there are languages in which utterances may differ solely by virtue of the syllabicity or non-syllabicity of a liquid or nasal (e.g., in many dialects of English the verbal noun *gambling* has a non-syllabic [l] but the present participle *gambling* has a syllabic [l̩]), an adequate phonological theory must provide some feature to distinguish between these segments. Leaving aside the difficult question of giving an articulatory characterization of syllabicity, which I will denote this feature by, I note that it is the only systematic distinction between vowels and glides and moreover that there are many cases in which an alternation between vowel and glide is governed by exactly the same rule which governs an alternation between syllabic liquid or nasal and non-syllabic liquid or nasal (e.g., Sanskrit has a rule by which high vowels become glides and syllabic liquids become non-syllabic when a vowel follows). I accordingly propose to scrap the feature of "vocalic" and assert that the features "consonantal," "syllabic," and "obstruent" more adequately distinguish between the principal classes of segments:

This system of representation has several advantages over that in terms of "vocalic," among them (1) the fact that it makes non-syllabic liquids closer in feature composition to glides than to vowels (rather than vice versa, as in the system with "vocalic"), which fits well the fact that alternations between non-syllabic liquid and glide are extremely common but alternations between non-syllabic liquid and vowel are quite rare; and (2) in the extremely common case in which the underlying forms of the morphemes of a language are all of the form "CVCV . . . ," the system with "syllabic" allows that generalization to be reflected in a redundancy rule which specifies every odd-numbered segment as [−syllabic] and every even-numbered segment as [+syllabic], whereas in the system with "vocalic," all that could be predicted about vocalicness is that even numbered segments are [+vocalic] and odd-numbered [−consonantal] segments are [−vocalic], i.e., the generalization about morpheme shape would make the vocalicness specification of glides redundant but would not make redundant any feature specification in a liquid, nasal, or obstruent.

It should be clear from the preceding portions of this paper that the optimum feature system for a theory of language such as that of *The Sound Pattern of Russian* and subsequent works will involve a considerably greater number of features than appear in *Preliminaries* and *Sound Pattern of Russian*. Indeed, on the basis of arguments such as those which I have presented above,[11] Chomsky and Halle conclude in *Sound Pattern of English* that a system containing over twice as many features as that of *Preliminaries* is needed to provide for adequate phonological description. Since the values of n binary features may be combined in 2^n different ways, the question immediately arises of whether there are as many segment types as can in principle be represented by a system of features such as that of *Sound Pattern of English*, i.e., $2^{25} = 29,434,432$. Clearly there are not: there are very sharp constraints on the way that feature specifications may combine, and the number

	vowels	glides	syllabic nasals, liquids	non-syllabic nasals, liquids	stops, spirants, affricates
syllabic	+	−	+	−	−
consonantal	−	−	+	+	+
obstruent	−	−	−	−	+

[11]Of the features which I propose, those of "syllabic" and "high" do not figure in *Sound Pattern of English*, which operates in terms of "vocalic" and "diffuse."

of combinations which will appear in the "systematic phonetic representations" of natural languages is probably no more than a couple of thousand. The fact that the feature systems (even that of *Preliminaries*) of generative phonological works allow in principle a class of feature combinations which is astronomically larger than the class which will appear in phonetic representations has been taken by some[12] as a defect of generative phonology. However, this fact merely shows that the goals of the phonologist and the electrical engineer cannot be met within the same representation: a representation in terms of the categories which play a role in phonology will not be an "optimal coding"; of course, there is no reason to expect it to be.

In actual fact, the restrictions of feature combinations which I mentioned above play an important role in the functioning of the phonological component of a language. Briefly, the universal constraints on feature combinations provide a mechanism whereby a phonological rule may have effects other than those mentioned in the rule: when a rule introduces a feature specification into a segment, the segment is adjusted so as to acquire all other feature specifications which are implied by that feature specification and the universal constraints. For example, there is a universal constraint excluding the combination of features $\begin{bmatrix} -\text{released} \\ +\text{aspirated} \end{bmatrix}$. When a rule makes a segment [−released], that segment is automatically also made [−aspirated]; likewise, a rule which makes a segment [+aspirated] would also make it [+released]. An excellent example of the important role which this principle may play in phonology is given by the following facts from Korean.

In syllable-final position in Korean the only segments which occur phonetically are [l], nasals, and unreleased stops. Corresponding to this fact, many underlying contrasts are neutralized when a consonant comes to be in syllable-final position; for example, underlying /nač/ 'day', /načʰ/ 'face', and /nas/ 'sickle', which are distinct in the locative: [naǰe], [načʰe], [nase], become homophonous in the nominative: [nat⁻] (where ⁻ means 'unre-

[12]For example, Fred W. Householder, "On Some Recent Claims in Phonological Theory," [41], *Journal of Linguistics* 1.13–34 (1965).

leased'). In this alternation, underlying obstruents become unaspirated and lax, and in addition, underlying /s, č, h/ all become [t⁻]. There are universal constraints excluding the feature combinations $\begin{bmatrix} -\text{released} \\ +\text{aspirated} \end{bmatrix}$ and $\begin{bmatrix} -\text{released} \\ -\text{closure} \end{bmatrix}$. Consequently, a rule which made consonants in syllable-final position [−released] would automatically make them also [−aspirated] and [+closure]. Thus the effect of the rule

$$[-\text{syllabic}] \longrightarrow [-\text{released}]$$
$$\text{in env.} \underline{\qquad} \left\{ \begin{matrix} [-\text{syllabic}] \\ \# \end{matrix} \right\}$$

(# means word-boundary) would be to turn [s, č, h] into [t⁻, t̆⁻, ʔ] respectively, where [t̆⁻] denotes an unreleased apico-palatal stop. The eventual effect is obtained as the result of subsequent rules which turn glottal stop into an apical stop and which make unreleased apical stops dental:

$$\begin{bmatrix} -\text{consonantal} \\ +\text{closure} \end{bmatrix} \longrightarrow [-\text{grave}]$$

$$\begin{bmatrix} -\text{grave} \\ -\text{released} \end{bmatrix} \longrightarrow [-\text{high}]$$

Korean is traditionally regarded as having a single underlying liquid, which is pronounced as flapped [r] intervocally and as [l] in syllable-final position or in a geminate; an underlying liquid at the beginning of a word is either deleted or turned into [n], depending on whether or not it is palatalized. Examples: [kʰal] 'knife (nom.)', [kʰare] 'knife (loc.)'; [täro] 'highway', [nobyen] 'roadside'; [isu] 'mileage', [oryi] 'five miles'. There are not only verbs in which morpheme-final [r] alternates with [l]: [algo] 'to know and', [aretta] 'knew', but also a large class of verbs in which morpheme-final [r] alternates with [t⁻]: [mut⁻ko] 'to inquire and', [muretta] 'inquired'. The latter verbs are traditionally regarded as irregular; however, the rules given already plus the universal constraints make it possible to assign to these verbs an underlying representation such that these alternations automatically arise. Specifically, note that [t⁻] is what would arise by the universal constraints from an underlying flapped [r] which was made unreleased. Thus, if Korean is analyzed as having two distinct underlying liquids, /l/ and /r/, and the two verbs are represented as underlying /al/ and

/mur/, the rules given already would yield all the desired forms. Note further that because of the rules alluded to whereby an intervocalic liquid becomes [r] and a word-initial liquid either is deleted or turns into [n], morpheme-final position is the one underlying segment position in which an underlying distinction between /l/ and /r/ could ever have any phonological effect. Since an underlying feature specification for laterality,[13] which distinguishes /l/ from /r/, plays no role in the phonological rules of Korean unless it is in morpheme-final position, all occurrences of liquids in other positions may be left unspecified for laterality in their underlying forms, and the value realized phonetically would be inserted by one of the phonological rules just mentioned. Consider now the fact that not only are there verbs which display the normal alternation between syllable-final [p⁻] and intervocalic [b]: [čep⁻] 'to fold', [čebe] 'to fold and', but there are also verbs which display an alternation between [p⁻] and [w]: [kip⁻] 'to mend', [kiwe] 'to mend and'. Here again underlying forms can be set up which will automatically yield the correct results thanks to the universal constraints: /čep/, /kiw/. When it is made unreleased, underlying /w/ becomes a stop as a result of the universal constraints.

An interesting point to note concerning the above discussion is that the treatment of Korean which I propose requires that "released" play a role within the phonological

component. This fact is noteworthy since no cases have been reported of a language in which the distinction between released and unreleased stops is distinctive. I point this out in order to emphasize that the system of features which play a role within the phonological component is anything but the extremely limited class of largely "distinctive" features which it until recently was generally assumed to be, and that the phonological component, rather than affecting the "more distinctive" features in the "earlier" rules and the "less distinctive" features in the "later" rules, as is sometimes supposed, must operate in terms of highly "non-distinctive" features even in very early rules of the grammar, such as the rule making syllable-final consonants unreleased indeed is.

In conclusion, it would be worthwhile to reconsider for a moment the role which the "feature interpretation component" plays in a grammar. Of the three functions which it would play in a grammar containing a "taxonomic phonemic" level of representation, one becomes unnecessary if that level is rejected. Of the two remaining functions, the domain of one, namely that of choosing between alternative modes in which a feature may be realized, has been reduced considerably in the process of the above arguments. Indeed, there remain no clear cases in which anything is gained by considering two distinct articulatory features to be identified with the same feature of universal phonology. Accordingly, then, the task of the feature interpretation component of a grammar can probably be restricted to that of supplying ideal values to the physical parameters in which the features which function in the phonological component manifest themselves.

---

[13] A feature of laterality is required in an adequate phonological theory, since in most Athabascan and Salishan (N.W. United States and S.W. Canada) languages there are minimal contrasts between laterally released and apically released segments, many of the languages having a full series of lateral obstruents exactly paralleling the apical obstruents.

48

SOME GENERAL PROPERTIES
OF PHONOLOGICAL RULES*

NOAM CHOMSKY

As the study of phonology has progressed, within the framework of generative grammar, certain principles have emerged governing the form and organization of phonological rules, and the manner in which these rules are to be interpreted. Several such principles are presented, with illustrative examples, from English, indicating the kind of evidence that supports them. Some possible alternatives are also discussed. Certain of these principles are quite abstract, and impose fairly heavy restrictions on the form and interpretation of grammars. If correct, they restrict the class of "possible human languages" in non-trivial ways. The broader context in which these principles might have more general relevance is briefly touched on.

The phonological component of a generative grammar is a system of rules that relate phonetic and syntactic representation. That a full and explicit grammar must contain such a system of rules is not in question. There are, however, many open problems concerning the nature of such rules and their systematic organization. In this paper, I will present a few of the principles that have emerged from the study of these problems in recent years, indicating the kind of evidence that bears on them and that appears, for the moment, to give them substantial empirical support.[1]

For the purposes of this discussion, I will presuppose a certain framework of assumptions. These are themselves subject to question, being empirical in nature, but seem well established; so that whatever modifications they may undergo, as increasing insight into sound structure is attained, will not affect the general conclusions based on them. I will assume, first of all, that the phonological component of a grammar is a system of rules that assigns to each syntactic structure a phonetic representation—or, in the case of free variation, several such representations; that the phonetic representation is a matrix in which rows are associated with features of a universal phonetic system, with columns corresponding to successive phonetic segments, and entries indicating the position of the segment in question along the phonetic scale (possibly a two-valued one) defined by the feature in question; that the "syntactic structures" to which phonological rules apply are surface structures, i.e., labeled bracketings of strings of formatives; and that a string of formatives within labeled brackets is itself a matrix in which rows are associated with the features of the universal phonetic system extended (a) by the feature [±segment] that distinguishes segments from junctures, (b) by a feature system for junctures, and (c) by certain "diacritic features" that express either idiosyncrasies of particular formatives and classes of formatives, or phonologically relevant syntactic properties of these formatives, assigned by

This paper was written while the author was a visiting member of the Department of English, University of California, Berkeley, California.

[1]The material that I will present here is drawn from work that Morris Halle and I have been engaged in for a number of years, and that will appear, in much further detail and explicitness, in our *Sound Pattern of English,* now in press. [See now Chomsky and Halle, 1968—VBM.] Further work, extending and deepening the theory of generative phonology in important ways, is presented in Paul Postal's *Aspects of Phonological Theory,* also in press. [See now Postal, 1968—VBM.] I am indebted to William S.-Y. Wang and Karl Zimmer for comments on this paper.

*Reprinted from *Language* 43.102–128 (1967) by permission.

convention as features of their particular segments. I will refer to such representation of strings of formatives as "phonological representation." Furthermore, I will take for granted that the universal phonetics is based on Jakobson's feature theory, in the particular form that has been given to it by Halle in various recent publications.[2] The general assumptions just mentioned are developed in greater detail in various references (cf. Halle, 1962 [37], 1964 [38], Chomsky, 1964 [39]). None of them is self-evident, but they seem to me to provide a firm basis for further work. Other empirical assumptions will be introduced when relevant to discussion of the general principles on which attention will be focused.

Evidently, the phonological component of a grammar will in general consist of many separate rules. Each rule will in some manner modify the string to which it applies. Full operation of all applicable rules, in accordance with certain general principles of organization that must be discovered and exactly formulated, will convert a surface structure of a string in phonological representation to a phonetic representation, with no labeled brackets.

To my knowledge, every study of phonology (in the sense just outlined) that goes beyond the most superficial observations has shown that there are certain general conditions of ordering that determine the application of these phonological rules (cf. references in Chomsky, 1964 [39]). The serious empirical issue is to determine the actual facts of ordering in particular languages, and to discover whatever general principles may underlie these facts.

Consider the following two tentative general principles of organization of phonological rules:

Principle 1: The rules may be linearly ordered.
Principle 2: The rules must be linearly ordered.

Princ. 2 asserts that the rules of a grammar must be given in a linear sequence 1, ..., n, and applied in this order, where each rule ap-

[2]In *Sound Pattern*, we present a further elaboration of this theory, but the matter of correct choice of features, though highly significant in itself, is not directly relevant to the problems I will be discussing here.

plies to the string that is produced by application of the preceding rule (where a rule is said, if inapplicable, to apply vacuously). Princ. 1 makes the weaker assertion that such an ordering is possible, with no loss of generality.

Notice that neither principle is in any sense obviously true. For example, Princ. 1 (and hence Princ. 2) would be false in a language containing formatives /XAY/ and /XBY/ where the first is realized phonetically as [XBY] and the second as [XAY]. Assuming no other relevant complications, this language would be based on the phonological rules (1) and (2):

(1) A → B / X—Y
(2) B → A / X—Y

In accordance with familiar conventions, which I will henceforth presuppose, rule (1) will assign to underlying segment /A/ the phonetic form [B] and to underlying segment /B/ the phonetic realization [A] when these segments appear in the context X—Y. Clearly, if the principle of application of rules is as defined above, with each rule applying to the string resulting from application of the preceding rule, either the ordering (1, 2) or the ordering (2, 1) will give one incorrect phonetic output. Many similar cases can be invented that would refute Princs. 1 and 2. Therefore it will be an important finding if principles such as 1 and 2 can be supported on empirical grounds.[3]

Although Princ. 1 has never been challenged, it is, in fact, incorrect as it stands, since there are real examples of exactly the sort just mentioned. Consider, for example, the phenomenon of vowel shift in English, which underlies such alternations as *divine-divinity, serene-serenity,* etc. This phenomenon involves several rules, two of which are the following:

$$(3)\ [+\text{diffuse}] \rightarrow [-\text{diffuse}] / \begin{bmatrix} \\ +\text{tense} \\ +\text{stress} \end{bmatrix}$$

$$(4)\ [-\text{diffuse}] \rightarrow [+\text{diffuse}] / \begin{bmatrix} \\ +\text{tense} \\ +\text{stress} \end{bmatrix}$$

Using the variable α, ranging over the values +, minus (where minus + = minus and minus

[3]Analogous considerations apply in other areas of grammar.

minus = +), we can formulate these rules as

$$(5)\ [\alpha \text{diffuse}] \rightarrow [-\alpha \text{diffuse}]\ /\ \begin{bmatrix} \underline{\hphantom{xx}} \\ +\text{tense} \\ +\text{stress} \end{bmatrix}$$

Thus the string [divíyn] becomes [divéyn] by rule (3) and the string [seréyn] becomes [seríyn] by rule (4).[4]

Clearly, we have a situation exactly like that illustrated in connection with rules (1) and (2). Therefore, granting that the postulated processes of English are correctly formulated (as I believe they are, to the degree of detail relevant here), Princ. 1 is untenable.

In what follows, I will discuss various other examples that violate Princ. 1. It appears that there is a certain rather abstract but quite well-defined property that characterizes all and only such examples. As we shall see, we can formulate this abstract property, in a very natural way, as a certain subsidiary principle of ordering. Subject to this qualification, then, Princ. 1 seems to be a well-established and non-trivial empirical hypothesis concerning phonological structure.

Let us then consider the much stronger Princ. 2. As stated, it is imprecise. We may interpret it as implying that there is a unique ordering of phonological rules that preserves fullest generality; if this ordering is violated in any respect, then some linguistically significant generalization is lost.[5] Furthermore, to give strong empirical backing to Princ. 2, it would be necessary to provide such evidence for a variety of languages. Clearly, such a demonstration is out of the question at the moment, even for one language. Hence, even if Princ. 2 is correct, we would certainly not be able to provide sufficient evidence to support it with any reasonable security, as matters now stand. Furthermore, from what is now known it seems unlikely that it is true, since there are

reasonably clear cases where ordering of two rules is irrelevant to output. Therefore it seems that Princ. 2 should be replaced by Princ. 2′, which now stands alongside Princ. 1 as a hypothesis concerning the phonological component of a grammar:

Principle 2′: The rules of the grammar must be partially ordered.

If Princs. 1 and 2′ are correct, it would be reasonable to reach the further conclusion that the rules of a grammar are, in fact, linearly ordered (in the sense defined earlier), but that the data in particular languages may not be rich enough to uniquely determine this ordering. Hence the language learner may be free, within limits, to establish various orderings. We would expect, then, that different speakers might be using slightly different orderings of rules, though these orderings effect the same mapping from surface structure to phonetic representation. Such different orderings might be detectable in various ways. It is possible, for example, that this might be one factor in divergence of dialects (cf. Halle, 1964 [38]); or it might even be demonstrated by experiment, if it proves possible to devise techniques of "extending" a given language in such a way as to bring out latent consequences of underlying rules.

Evidence in support of Princ. 2′ is by now so familiar that it is hardly necessary to cite examples. Simply for illustration, I will cite one typical case involving, once again, English vowel shift. Clearly, vowel shift is involved in such alternations as those found in the forms *varIous-varIety, hystErical-hystEria, germAnic-germAnium*, in the positions indicated by capitals. Justification for this particular analysis will be found in *Sound Pattern;* it is sufficient here to state that underlying these alternations is a process of tensing, formulated to first approximation as in (6), followed by processes—incorporating, in particular, rule (5)—that give the quality shift described by (7):

$$(6)\ V \rightarrow [+\text{tense}]\ /\ \begin{cases} -V & \text{(a)} \\ -C\bar{\imath}V & \text{(b)} \end{cases}$$

$$(7)\ \begin{cases} \bar{\imath} \rightarrow \bar{a}y \\ \bar{e} \rightarrow \bar{\imath}y \\ \bar{æ} \rightarrow \bar{e}y \end{cases}$$

---

[4]The underlying forms are /divīn/, /serēn/, respectively, the glide being introduced by a general rule of diphthongization for tense vowels. The form [divēyn], resulting from application of rule (3), becomes finally [divāyn], by other rules. The forms *divinity* and *serenity* (with [i] and [e], respectively, in the second syllable) are derived from the underlying lexical representations by a general laxing rule. There is more to be said about the vowel of the first syllable, but it is irrelevant here. For details, see *Sound Pattern.*

[5]At issue here is the matter of extrinsic and intrinsic ordering, discussed in Chomsky, 1965: 223.

As noted earlier (3–5), the quality shift (7) is, in fact, restricted to stressed positions, and the high front vowel in the context of (6b) is, as indicated, unstressed. Involved in (7) is, of course, the process of diphthongization mentioned in fn. 4, which is independent of stress. With these rules, we will have such derivations as the following:

(8) væri+ɔs   væri+ity
     vǣrī+ɔs   vǣrī+ity
     vēyrīy+ɔs   værāy+ity

     hister+icæl   hister+iæ
          histēr+īæ
          histīyr+īyæ

     germæn+ic   germæn+ium
          germǣn+īum
          germēyn+īyum

The top line, in each case, is (approximately) the phonological representation. The second line is given by application of rule (6), either case (a) or (b). The third line results from the processes summarized in (7) (with only diphthongization, and not quality shift, taking place in the unstressed positions). Other rules, here irrelevant, give the final phonetic representations.

Notice that rule (7) cannot precede rule (6); it is only the tense vowels, not their lax counterparts, that undergo the modifications of (7) in full generality. But this observation is not in itself enough to support Princ. 2′, as we see by stating it more explicitly, decomposing it into two assertions that it combines:

Principle 2′a: The rules are partially ordered, and no rule applies after a rule that follows it in this partial ordering.

Principle 2′b: Each rule applies to the string resulting from the application of the last rule that has applied.

The example of (6–8) is, in fact, consistent with the assumption that rules are unordered (contrary to Princ. 2′a), and that each rule can apply, at any time, to the string resulting from the application of the last rule that has applied. Thus the example really serves only to establish Princ. 2′b. To go beyond this and establish 2′a as well, and hence Princ. 2′ in full, we must consider slightly more complex examples, such as the following. Alongside the phenome-

non of vowel shift, discussed briefly above, English also contains a rule of velar softening that converts [k] to [s] and [g] to [j] before non-low front vowels. Thus we have a rule that can be roughly formulated as (9):

$$(9) \quad \begin{Bmatrix} k \to s \\ g \to \check{j} \end{Bmatrix} \Big/ \underline{\hphantom{xxxx}} \begin{bmatrix} -\text{grave} \\ -\text{compact} \end{bmatrix}$$

This is the rule that is involved in such alternations as those indicated by capitals in *electriC-electriCity, riGid-riGor, leGislate-leGal,* etc., that accounts for the intervocalic [s] in such words as *recess,*[6] and that applies in many similar examples. Vowel shift and velar softening are, clearly, independently motivated as rules of English phonology.

Now consider such words as *critiCize, mediCate.* What is at issue is the phonological representation of the segments given in capitals in these words. We know, in fact, that the phonological representation must be /k/ in both cases (cf. *critic, critical, medic, medical*). But there are two problems. First, the segment in question should *not* undergo velar softening in the case of *criticize,* since it does not precede a non-low front vowel, but rather the low back vowel [ā]. Second, the segment in question *should* undergo velar softening in *medicate,* since it precedes a non-low front vowel, namely [ē].

Suppose, however, that the rule (9) of velar softening precedes the rules (7) involved in vowel shift. Since the underlying representations of *criticize* and *medicate* are /kritikīz/ and /medikǣt/ respectively, velar softening will apply only to the former case. Afterwards, the vowel-shift rule will give [āy] from /ī/ in *criticize* and [ēy] from /ǣ/ in *medicate,* but this fact will be irrelevant to velar softening, if we accept this ordering and Princ. 2′a.

Many similar examples have appeared in the literature. They serve to establish Princ. 2′ as, it seems to me, one of the best-supported general principles of phonology. Consequently,

---

[6]Observe that the underlying form for *recess* cannot be /re+ses/, with medial /s/, or the phonetic form would be [rīyzes], since /s/ voices intervocalically in such forms (compare *consist-resist, subsume-resume,* etc.) Since we have phonetic [s] medially in *recess,* we know that we cannot have underlying /s/; therefore we must have underlying /k/, this being the only assumption that does not require new, otherwise unmotivated rules.

it seems reasonable to propose as a general principle of phonology that the rules are linearly ordered and applied strictly in the given order, each rule applying to the string formed by application of the last rule that has applied. This general principle provides a rational explanation for the facts which support its two consequences, Princs. 1 and 2'.

Before turning to other principles of organization, it might be useful to consider some alternatives to Princs. 1 and 2' that have been proposed in recent discussion. Actually, no one, to my knowledge, has questioned Princ. 1 on empirical grounds, although it has been questioned on "conceptual" grounds in a series of articles by Sydney Lamb. Lamb proposes that, on a priori grounds, unordered systems are simpler than ordered systems; furthermore, he states, again as an a priori truth, exactly how much simpler they are (one symbol extra for each ordered rule, where complexity of a system of rules is equal to the total number of symbols involved). In fact, his position is that the simplest system, on a priori grounds, is one that rejects both 2'a and 2'b. In the face of such apriorism, argument and evidence are beside the point. There can be no question that Princs. 1, 2'a, and 2'b are factual hypotheses, and that empirical evidence can be used to confirm or disconfirm them, along the lines sketched above. It is mere dogmatism to refuse to judge factual issues in terms of empirical evidence and simply to assert what the answer must be, independently of what any facts may suggest.[7]

[7]For additional discussion of Lamb's views on these questions, see Chomsky and Halle, 1965 [42] and Postal (in press). [See now Postal, 1968—VBM.] A similar example of apriorism can be found in a recent discussion of phonology by Householder (1966) [43], who states that, in his view, information is organized in the brain in systems of highly redundant lists, the basic retrieval device being table look-up. To be sure, there is no neurological evidence for this idea (just as there is none against it), but he regards alternatives as unacceptable ("beyond [his] intuitive capacity"). Study of language may reveal deep-seated rules and principles of an abstract sort, but, Householder argues, this is a mere artifact, because in fact the brain operates quite differently. From his a priori assumptions about neural organization, it seems to follow that a language could perfectly well be a huge system of lexical items and sentences, with little internal structure or organization, and that it is a mere accident if this is not so, in general.

Actually, in a recent article, Lamb (1966) [53] does propose a certain "principle of simplicity" which might be taken to provide some basis for his assertions about ordering. This principle, which he presents as a general principle of scientific method, is as follows: "Suppose that there are two descriptions or parts of descriptions . . . which are equivalent in effective information . . . and which differ only in that the first states a certain relationship repeatedly . . . while the second, abstracting the relationship, states it only once" (554 [619]). In this case, the second is simpler. Put this way, however, the principle is empty. If a certain theory yields a description in which something is stated several times, we can always replace it by a description in which this statement appears only once, by inventing an appropriate ad hoc notation. If a grammar contains a certain rule in five separate places, we can replace it by a grammar in which the rule appears once, and we can devise (ad hoc) an appropriate coding procedure that will tell us, as a universal principle, that when this rule appears once in the grammar in question it is to be interpreted as if it appeared five separate times in just the required positions. The grammar is now "as simple as possible" in Lamb's sense. It is evident that Lamb's proposal would make sense only if notations and coding procedures are fixed. But then the empirical content of his proposal would be determined by the choice of notations and coding procedures. Since surely no one can claim any special a priori insight into the correct choice, this choice should be settled on empirical grounds, by determining whether the grammars that it selects on the basis of given data are empirically adequate. But we are now speaking not of a principle of "simplicity" as part of "general scientific method," but of a specific empirical hypothesis of linguistics, to be judged for adequacy in terms of evidence. I will not elaborate further, since the matter has been discussed at length in earlier literature on generative grammar.

There are serious issues related to the question of "simplicity." Consider, for example, the question whether the lexicon of a generative grammar should consist of feature matrices, as presupposed above and in the work referred to there, or rather should consist of elements in a kind of orthography, where the symbols of the orthography are then given a feature analysis. Thus the word *sane* might either be represented directly by an abstract phonological feature matrix, or "orthographically" as /sæn/, where each of the symbols /s/ /æ/ /n/ is then specified in terms of abstract phonological features, at which point we have the feature matrix of the former alternative. The choice between these alternatives need not be an entirely empty one, if formulated within a significant theory of evaluation of a sort that has been frequently discussed. One cannot simply argue that the "orthographic" solution is preferable because the other multiplies symbols in the grammar (Lamb, 555–556 [621]). With an appropriate ad hoc notational definition, we can reduce the most ridiculous grammatical description to one symbol, if we wish; and, depending on choice of notations, we can have any other number of symbols we like and can support any arbitrary decisions about collapsing of matrices (e.g., consonant clusters as "phonemes," etc.). But there is a real point in the background of the discussion, namely, that a grammar is surely simpler in some important sense if its lexical entries are "coherent," one aspect of this coherence being that the entries utilize the same set of segments. Thus we would complicate English more if we added a new lexical item with a pharyngealized dental stop /ṭ/ than if we introduced an otherwise identical item with a /t/; and if we measure degree of significant generalization (i.e., "simplicity") by number of symbols in a fully specified lexicon, then a system that uses features will not reflect this difference, whereas a system that uses "phonemes," later specified in terms of features, will reflect the difference. This observation shows that it would be absurd to measure the degree of significant generalization by the number of symbols in a fully specified lexicon, a fact which has always been clearly recognized. It is for reasons of this sort that there has been a good deal of study of redundancy rules of a sort that would reflect such considerations as the one just mentioned, and that would lead to an empirically appropriate definition of "simplicity." Clearly Lamb's proposal to replace feature matrices by "phonemic" spelling will not do at all. Thus, although his proposal would make possible a distinction between a new item /tem/ and a

new item /tem/ in English, it would not make possible the perfectly analogous distinction between two items /trem/, /tlem/, or two items /trkv/, /trem/, etc. There are, in fact, many interesting open problems about what makes a lexicon "coherent" in the appropriate sense. Whatever superficial plausibility Lamb's remarks about phonemic representations may have derives from their loose connection to this set of problems. There is no indication, however, that the direction he suggests can lead to an answer to any of these problems. Hence I think that the proposals concerning "phonemic" representation must also be dismissed as irrelevant to the empirical issue, so far as is now known. It is, furthermore, quite clear what kind of work would have to be done and what kind of results achieved to give this proposal some plausibility.

Returning to the main theme, what of the question of alternatives to Princ. 2'? Suppose, following Lamb, that we reject Princs. 2'a and 2'b. Thus we adopt the empirical hypothesis that rules are unordered, that each can apply at any point, and that each applies to the underlying representation, not to the string formed by application of the last applied rule. As an empirical hypothesis, this must be faced with data, and, so far as evidence is now available, rejected for empirical reasons of the sort just discussed. However, there is one way to save this hypothesis in the face of the evidence for rule ordering. This method is to set up intermediate "strata" between lexical and phonetic representation, and to argue that Lamb's principle of application holds between successive strata. If we allow an arbitrary number of "strata," we have, of course, simply another version of the theory expressed by Princ. 2'. Thus, if a grammar contains 25 ordered rules, we can set up 24 intermediate strata, each derived from the preceding by one of these rules, Lamb's principle of application now holding (vacuously) between each pair of strata. For example, given just the rules of velar softening, tensing, and vowel shift discussed above, we could set up an intermediate stratum that is determined, from the level of phonological representation, by tensing and velar softening (which are unordered with respect to one another, in this oversimplified example), and which is mapped onto phonetic representation by vowel shift. In the intermediate stratum, the examples in (8) would be represented by the middle row (the first row, for the words that did not undergo tensing), and the effect of velar softening would also be indicated. An approach of this sort would be perfectly sensible if two empirical conditions were met:

(10) (a) There is a fixed number n of "strata," each with certain definite formal properties, in addition to phonological and phonetic representation;

(b) when the rules of a grammar are partially ordered in the empirically determined way, they are found to fall into n + 1 blocks of rules,[8] where the blocks can be ordered in such a way that if rule R_1 precedes rule R_2, then the block to which R_1 belongs precedes the block to which R_2 belongs (hence, in particular, there is no ordering internal to a block).

To establish (10a), one would have to construct a theoretical apparatus specifying strata and their properties. To establish (10b), it is necessary to provide certain factual evidence. Having established the two parts of (10), one would be justified in rejecting both parts of Princ. 2′, although a more accurate way of stating the matter would be that this new discovery (10) actually provides a refinement of Princ. 2′ for the whole system of phonological rules. However, there has been no published attempt to take serious steps towards (10a), and what evidence we have does not support the kind of organization suggested in (10b). To study the questions raised in (10) in a serious way, one has to investigate a real language system with dozens (if not hundreds) of phonological rules, with complex ordering conditions among them determined on empirical grounds; in the nature of the case, it is of no use to study a subsystem with three or four rules. A good bit of real linguistic material is available in the literature, much of it selected so as to bear on questions of ordering. In general, then, it is clear what steps one who is serious about a "stratificational" theory would have to take, and a good deal of data has already been accumulated that would be useful to anyone willing to take these steps.

Lamb has in fact taken one step toward the problem posed by (10a), proposing that one of the intermediate strata will have the properties of "classical phonemics." This matter bears directly on one of the conclusions that has repeatedly been reached in work on generative phonology, namely that no such level can be introduced without loss of linguistically significant generalization. Therefore his recent discussion of this matter should be carefully examined. What are the distinguishing properties of the stratum of "classical phonemics"?[9] According to Lamb, the fundamental property of this level is provided by the "distinctiveness principle," which he formulates (543 [611]) as follows:[10]

More precisely, the distinctiveness principle is that a correct C-phonemic solution treats

[8]We might permit fewer than n + 1 blocks, if some "strata" can be missing in certain languages.

[9]Obscuring the issue is unclarity over the actual character of "classical phonemics." Lamb rejects my characterization of its basic ideas (Chomsky, 1964 [39]) on the grounds that it is "fictitious," that no one accepted exactly that position in practice. He offers no characterization of his own, however, beyond the one that we discuss in a moment. It is correct, but irrelevant, to observe that "taxonomic phonemics," in the sense of Chomsky, 1964, is fictitious. As was pointed out there, the theory of taxonomic phonemics was formulated in an attempt to capture what was essential to the approach of classical phonemics, eliminating the inconsistencies and the debilitating unclarities of the various approaches that are developed in the literature. As an interpretation, it might be incorrect; but to reject attempts at such interpretation is pointless, since the only alternative is to reject what exists as inconsistent and vague, overlooking the important insights embedded in it. The only point at which Lamb offers a particular criticism is in connection with my condition of "linearity." He points out correctly, but irrelevantly, that tones (or suprasegmentals in general) were never presumed to meet this condition; this is, of course, why I restricted the discussion to the adequacy of the principle for segmental phonemics and did not offer suprasegmentals as counterexamples to the linearity condition. He also claims that I characterized Bloch's position inaccurately, since Bloch does allow violations of linearity; but he overlooks n. 14 (78–79 [408]), in which I pointed out just this, and where I modified the condition in the case of Bloch's quite careful and explicit theory—noting, however, unclarities that make precise interpretation impossible as to where Bloch does allow violations of linearity.

[10]Later, it is argued that the distinctiveness principle follows from the simplicity principle; but since the latter is vacuous, as noted, we can disregard this matter.

two units (i.e., segments, syllables, or the like) as phonemically different if and only if there is a distinctive phonetic difference between them. By distinctive phonetic difference I mean a difference in at least one distinctive phonetic feature; a phonetic feature is distinctive if its presence is not determined by the immediate environment.

Putting it concisely, then, the "distinctiveness principle" asserts that:

(11) Units X and Y are phonemically different if and only if there is a phonetic feature F such that:
    (a) X and Y differ with respect to F, and
    (b) F is not determined by its immediate environment.

The fundamental property of a "correct C-phonemic solution" is that it treats two units as phonemically different under just this condition.

It is clear, however, that this principle is untenable. This can be demonstrated by the use of familiar examples. Consider the following case presented by Jakobson in 1931, which I have used (Chomsky, 1964: 95 [416]) to illustrate difficulties in the existing definitions of complementary distribution. Assume a language containing units /i/ and /y/, differing only in the feature [±vocalic], and containing a context ...—... in which /iy/ occurs distinctively from /yi/, although there is no context in which /i/ and /y/ contrast. According to Lamb's distinctiveness principle, /i/ and /y/ are not phonemically different. The only feature F in which they differ is the feature [±vocalic], which is determined in all of the contexts ...—y..., ...—i..., ...y—..., ...i—.... Hence there is no F meeting conditions (11a, b); therefore the units in question are phonemically identical. And, still worse, we can continue (following Jakobson) with the observation that once we have identified /i/ and /y/ as /Y/, then both ...yi... and ...iy... are represented "phonemically" as ...YY..., despite the fact that they contrast. Putting the matter in Lamb's framework, the "units" /iy/ and /yi/ are phonemically different, in terms of (11), since there is a phonetic feature F meeting both (a) and (b), specifically the feature defined as the sequence of [+vocalic], [−vocalic]. We now have a situation in which X and Y are

phonemically identical, but XY is phonemically different from YX. Under obvious assumptions about "phonemic difference" of units, this conclusion will not only be untenable, but also inconsistent.

Other familiar examples lead to the same conclusion. Consider a case discussed by Bloch, and again used in Chomsky, 1964, namely an English dialect in which an alveolar flap [D] is the variant of /r/ in the context /#θ—V.../ (three, through, etc.) and of both apical stops in intervocalic post-stress position (butter, medal, etc.). Let X be the [D] of three and Y be the [D] of butter. Since they differ in no feature F not determined by the environment, they are phonemically identical by virtue of the distinctiveness principle. Evidently, the same absurdity will arise in every case of partial overlap.

Actually, the situation is still worse than this. Consider any English dialect in which [r̩] is the only segment that can appear in the context [#st—V...] and [u] is the only segment which can appear in the context [#Cy—w...]. Thus nothing contrasts with [r̩] in street or [u] in feud. Setting X as [r̩] and Y as [u], in these contexts, we see that there is no feature F meeting conditions (11a, b)—since all features in which X and Y differ are determined by the environments—so that [r̩] and [u] are phonemically identical. By similar reasoning, we can prove that [s] in string is identical with [r̩] in string (so that the correct phonemicization is /XtXing/, where /X/ has the allophones [s] and [r̩]), and so on, in many similar cases.

It seems pointless to pursue discussion of (11) any further. In fact, the "distinctiveness principle," as formulated by Lamb, is nothing more than a vague expression of the intuition that led early structural linguistics to search for viable principles of phonemic analysis that would overcome such absurdities as those just noted—principles which, it should be emphasized, were produced by Jakobson, Bloch, Harris, Hockett, and many other investigators in the course of the careful and serious attempts to develop a significant theory. Lamb's new theory is simply a return to the period that precedes the development of structural linguistics.[11]

[11]Similar conclusions were reached, quite correctly in my opinion, by Postal (1964) in his investi-

It is interesting to see why Lamb feels that the "distinctiveness principle" is a necessary one. He takes it to be "of fundamental importance to identify these distinctive features of difference [that are able to distinguish different meanings in a given language] and to distinguish them from those which are not distinctive [in this sense] . . . . This is the reason for separating the C-phonemic level from the phonetic in describing spoken languages" (542 [611]). But this argument is a non sequitur. No doubt it is important to distinguish features that provide contrasts in a given language from those that do not, both on the phonetic level (where, for example, vowel length functions to "distinguish meanings" in English dialects that have phonetic [rayDr], [rāyDr], derived from underlying /rayt#r/, /rayd#r/, respectively), and on the phonological level (where the same dialects use not the feature of vowel length but rather the phonological property of abstract voicing). But from this correct observation it

does not follow that it is necessary to set up a *level of representation* which makes use precisely of distinctively functioning features (of either sort).[12] To see that the conclusion does not follow, consider this perfectly analogous argument. Clearly it is important to distinguish first halves of utterances from second halves. Therefore, we must set up a level of "first-halves of utterances" in which just these are represented. Evidently, the conclusion would follow only if we were to assume that for every significant property of language, the grammar must define a level of representation in which just this property is expressed. But such an assumption is absurd. It is only necessary that the terms in which this property is expressed be definable, in a fixed and general way, by means of the notions of grammar—that the grammar determine this property in a well-defined way. Thus we can define "first halves of utterances" in terms of grammars of the usual sort, just as we can characterize features that function distinctively (in several senses of this notion) in a perfectly general way in terms of grammars containing no "phonemic level" of the sort discussed in structural linguistics.[13]

---

gation of various recent attempts to develop syntactic theory. Postal's analysis has been criticized on the grounds that he did not express accurately what was intended in the theories he was discussing; a similar comment might apply to any attempt to investigate (11). This principle, like the theories that Postal was studying, is sufficiently vague and inexplicit that an analysis of it must "distort" in the direction of further precision; any such interpretation is, surely, questionable, but unavoidable if these issues are to be discussed at all.

Given the actual status of the "distinctiveness principle" that Lamb proposes, we can return to Halle's much-discussed argument that, where a certain type of phonological asymmetry exists—as in the case of Russian /t/ /d/ [č] [ǰ]—postulation of a taxonomic-phonemic level (in the technical sense of this term as defined in Chomsky, 1964) forces the abandonment of otherwise valid generalizations in the grammar. Lamb's attempt to refute Halle's argument merely amounts to accepting it in toto, with a change of notation. But, while accepting Halle's specific analysis of Russian (in effect), Lamb objects (547 [614]) that this analysis does not refute "classical phonemics," because the real essence of classical phonemics is expressed by the distinctiveness principle, and this principle leads to the Halle-Lamb analysis for Russian. However, as we have noted, to impute the distinctiveness principle in Lamb's sense to classical phonemics is less than just, since much classical work was specifically directed to overcoming the absurdities to which this principle leads. Therefore we must still conclude that Lamb has not met Halle's argument, but has merely accepted Halle's analysis and proposed an untenable principle to justify it, all of this having nothing to do with the issue that Halle raises against classical phonemics.

[12]One might perfectly well say, however, that the phonological representation, with relevant syntactic structure indicated, does capture just this distinction, although in a highly abstract sense quite remote from Lamb's intentions.

[13]For a characterization of "free variation" in these terms and a more extensive discussion of the general matter, see Postal (in press) [See now Postal, 1968—VBM.]; for further discussion of free variation and its implications for "classical phonemics," see also Postal, 1966. Note, incidentally, another example of the very same incorrect argument that we have been discussing, this time in the domain of syntax, where Seuren (1966: 210) states that there is no "natural expression" of grammatical relations in P-markers generated by phrase-structure grammars: "they are only implied and can be extracted by some subsidiary set of defined functions." Therefore, he suggests, one should make these functions explicit in the actual representation. But it is just because the grammatical functions are determined in a quite general way by P-markers that it is quite pointless to elaborate the representation in order to express them, even where this is possible. That is, the functions are just as explicit in a P-marker (given general definitions that determine them from P-markers) as they are in "tagmemic representations" of a more elaborate kind (from which, of course, they must also be extracted by a general definition). Seuren's pattern of argument is, in fact, widespread, though quite illegitimate.

Possibly confusion over this matter results from a failure to pay sufficient attention to the fact that, without associated principles of interpretation, a generative grammar, no matter how full and explicit, says nothing at all about a language. When we say that such a grammar generates a specific phonetic representation and assigns it to an utterance with a certain syntactic and semantic representation, we are making use of principles of interpretation no less abstract than those that determine what is free variation or what are the grammatical relations, given a particular grammar. These interpretive principles determine the meaning of the formal devices of grammar. They can express the facts of free variation or grammatical relations as easily as the fact that a certain syntactically structured phonological representation is associated with a specific phonetic form. Given the rules of a grammar, in a well-defined linguistic theory, we can determine automatically the generated sentences and their structural descriptions. It is entirely pointless to complicate the grammar so as to provide representations at a certain stage of derivation that express some property which is, in any event, well-defined in a general way in terms of the grammar.

A full discussion of free variation and contrast will have to take account of the fact that this is not simply a matter of free choice of certain phonetic features. The basic issue is one of optionality in the phonological component and the lexicon. For example, there are English dialects in which the vowel that appears in the capitalized position of such words as *generAtive* may vary freely between [è̄y] and [ɨ]. Superficially, this seems to be free variation of the usual sort with respect to phonetic features, just as in the first syllable of *gradation,* for some speakers. But a more careful investigation shows that the variation of [jénɨrè̄ytiv]–[jénɨrɨtiv] is paralleled exactly by the variation of [kánsɨltē̄ytiv]–[kɨnsʌ́ltɨtiv], for example, in which case the matter cannot be stated in terms of free variation with respect to a certain feature. In fact, what appears to be involved in both cases is an optional choice at the level of phonological representation between two values for a certain feature of the juncture that precedes the affix *-ive;* the range of phonetic effects then varies widely, for reasons having to do with other, perfectly automatic principles of English phonology.

Since it is possible to define "free variation" in a general way in terms of the concepts of generative phonology, it is unnecessary to introduce a "stratum" that explicitly captures some aspect of free variation—and it is not only unnecessary but incorrect, if introduction of such a level leads to a loss of linguistically significant generalization or other unwanted modifications of the grammar. Similarly, it may be possible to characterize certain other types of psychologically meaningful types of representation in terms of these concepts. No doubt, there are other significant kinds of representation distinct from either phonological or phonetic. Suppose, for example, that it proves possible to construct experimental conditions under which a word such as *illustrative* [ilʌstrɨtiv] will be pronounced, syllable by syllable, as [í], [lʌ́], [strɛ́y], [tív]. This would demonstrate that a certain concept of "syllable" has psychological significance, that the representation [ē̄y] is somehow important with respect to the third syllable, even though it is distinct from the phonetic representation [ɨ] and the phonological representation /æ/, and so on. Possibly, such experimental results might someday provide evidence for establishment of intermediate levels; but this could only be true if the notions that seem to be significant (e.g., the syllable, and intermediate representations such as [ē̄y]) are not definable, in some general way, in terms of an unmodified theory of generative phonology. If they are definable in these terms, the results would simply serve as further corroborating evidence for this theory as it stands.

For the time being, there seems to be no plausible alternative to Princs. 1 and 2′, or to the more far-reaching assumption that the phonological rules are linearly ordered, each applying in turn to the string produced by application (possibly vacuous) of the preceding rule. Looking more deeply into phonological systems, we find still other principles of organization that are well supported by evidence. The most striking principle of this sort is the principle of the transformational cycle:

Principle 3: Each phonological rule is applied to a string bounded by paired brackets of the surface structure and containing no internal brackets; after the last rule of the sequence has applied in this way, innermost brackets are erased and the sequence of rules reapplies as before.[14]

This principle is quite intuitive, in fact almost obvious. It states that the phonetic form of a string is determined, by fixed processes, from the ideal phonetic form of its parts, where the parts in question and their arrangement are determined by the syntax. Clearly, this is a very natural principle of operation for a system of rules that must assign an interpretation to a very large number of formal objects, each of which has a (derived) phrase-marker as its formal structure.

The earliest study of the principle of the transformational cycle was in connection with intonational structure of phrases. Further work has shown that the cycle also operates to determine the phonetic form of words, making use of their internal constituent structure. To illustrate, consider the word *theatricality,* which would have the following derivation:

(12) $[_N [_A [_N \text{theatr}]_N \text{ic} + \text{al}]_A \text{i} + \text{ty}]_N$

$$\underline{\qquad 1 \qquad}$$

$$\underline{\qquad 21 \qquad}$$

$$\underline{\qquad 32 \qquad \qquad 1 \qquad}$$

The surface structure is given in the top line; thus *theatre* is a noun, *theatrical* an adjective, and *theatricality* a noun. In the first cycle, primary stress is placed on the first vowel of the innermost constituent, *theatre:* in isolation, then, the noun would be [θíyitir]. Innermost brackets are then erased in accordance with Princ. 3, and the rules now apply to the new innermost constituent, *theatrical.* The rule of stress placement, in this case, assigns primary stress to the vowel two syllables before the affix *-al.* By convention, all stresses in the word are weakened by one so that stress relationships determined in earlier cycles are preserved; thus we derive the form *theàtrical,* which in isolation would become [θìyǽtr·kil], by other rules. Innermost brackets are once

[14]This principle was first presented in Chomsky, Halle, and Lukoff, 1956. Certain criticisms of it made at the time are discussed in Chomsky, 1966, chap. 4. Additional material and expositions are presented in many references, and much of this is summarized, with new material, in *Sound Pattern.*

again erased, and we turn to the full word. The rule of stress placement once again places primary stress on the vowel two syllables before the affix (in this case, *-ty*); by convention, other stresses are weakened by one and we derive *theatricality,* which becomes [θìyàtrìkǽlìtīy] by other rules.

In English, at least, it appears that the effects of the transformational cycle are restricted to the intonational system and segmental phenomena (e.g., vowel reduction) related to the system of prosodic features, as is not unnatural. We can illustrate the range of its effects by considering such forms as those of (13) and (14):

(13)   (a) relaxation   (b) devastation
           emendation   demonstration
           condensation   compensation

(14)   (a) torment   (b) torrent
           convict   verdict
           export   effort
           progress   tigress

In my speech, the words in (13a, 14a) have an unreduced vowel in the second syllable, whereas the corresponding words in (13b, 14b) have a reduced vowel in the second syllable. The same is true of many other examples, with some dialect variation, as should be expected with such marginal phonetic phenomena as these. It is immediately clear that non-reduction, in this position, is largely explicable in terms of the operation of the transformational cycle. Thus the surface structure of the examples heading the four columns of (13, 14) would be as in (15), and the other examples are similar.

(15) $[_N [_V \text{relax}]_V \text{ation}]_N$ $[_N [_V \text{devastate}]_V \text{ion}]_N$
     $[_N [_V \text{torment}]_V]_N$ $[_N \text{torrent}]_N$

If we consider the operation of the cycle in such cases, we see that in the first cycle all the items in (13a, 14a) will receive a primary stress on the second syllable; thus in isolation, we would have the verbs *reláx, tormént,* etc. But there are no verbs **devást,* **torrént,* etc., underlying the items in columns (13b, 14b); where there is a prefinal cycle, as in the examples of (13b), it does not assign primary stress in the second syllable of the word. In the final cycle, stress is shifted to *-at,* in (13), or to the first syllable, in (14a). The result is that after the application of the final cycle, the second syllable in (13a, 14a) retains a secondary stress (which, by other processes not relevant here, weakens still further as the derivation proceeds), whereas the corresponding syllable in (13b, 14b) has no stress at all. Without going into details, it is evident that vowel reduction is contingent on stress, among other things; and, in fact, the secondary stress in (13a, 14a) is sufficient to protect the vowels in question from reduction. Thus the reduction of the vowel, in these and many other cases, is determined by the underlying constituent structure, in accordance with the principle of the transformational cycle.

There are still further segmental effects of underlying syntactic and morphological structure in such cases as these. Notice that the vowel in the first syllable of *relaxation, emendation* is [īy], whereas the corresponding vowel of *devastation, demonstration* is [e]. Both clearly derive from underlying phonological /e/. What is happening here is that the tensing rule (6) applies to [e] when the following syllable has some stress, and then rule (7) (which incorporates diphthongization and vowel shift) gives the phonetic realization [īy]. Thus we may have such free variants as [pri̇̃yzentĕyšɨn]–[prĕzɨntĕyšɨn], for example.

Many such examples indicate that Princ. 3 is well founded, and that the transformational cycle functions both within and outside the word.[15] However, there are many phonological

processes that are not cyclic; the rules of tensing, diphthongization, and vowel shift are examples. Thus if vowel shift were to re-apply on each cycle, in the case of a word such as *theatricality* (example 12), the vowel of the first syllable would become [īy] from underlying /e/ in one cycle and then [āy], by vowel shift, in the next.[16] Careful investigation shows that the non-cyclic rules all apply at the level of words. We can, therefore, distinguish two parts of phonology: cyclic phonology and word phonology. The rules of word phonology are, it seems, interspersed among the rules of cyclic phonology in the linear ordering. The formalism that suggests itself, therefore, is that certain rules of the cycle must be formulated in such a way that word boundary appears as part of the context that determines their application; thus they will apply only when the level of words is reached in the operation of the cycle, hence only once in the derivation of a phonetic representation from surface structure. The problems of defining "word" in a general and empirically adequate way are not trivial, but the general approach just sketched seems sound.

Summarizing, then, it seems that the rules of phonology are linearly ordered and apply in a cyclic manner, as determined by surface structure, forming the phonetic representations of larger units from the ideal phonetic representation of their underlying constituents, by a fixed set of principles. Certain rules apply only once in the cycle, by virtue of the fact that they are restricted to the level of words. It would be interesting to go on to characterize, in a general way, the kinds of rules that are likely to (or that may only) appear as rules of word phonology, or as cyclic rules—and, in the latter class, those that affect

[15]The principle of the transformational cycle suggests that, in normal speech perception, the hearer may sample a signal, construct a hypothesis as to its syntactic structure, project a phonetic form by the use of phonological rules operating in accordance with this and other principles, and then accept the projected phonetic representation as what he "hears" (understanding the sentence in accordance with the accepted hypothesis) if the match is sufficiently close. If this is plausible as a first approximation to a theory of speech perception, it will not be surprising that even a degraded signal can be perceived with great accuracy, and that phonetic detail may be "heard" which is not present in the signal. Thus, when utterances are understood, judgments of stress contour, which are predictable from the surface structure, appear to go well beyond any acoustic detail that can be identified. In these terms, we can also give a plausible explanation for such experimental results as those of Bolinger and Gerstman, 1957, who show that artificially introduced pauses in such constructions as *light-house-keeper* lead to one or the other interpretation, depending on the relative length of the pauses. It is certainly premature to propose, on the basis of such evidence, that

disjuncture is an acoustic cue for what is heard as stress contour. No doubt the same results would be achieved if the surface structure were suggested to the subject in other ways as well (e.g., by a change in speaker after *light* or after *house*). The simplest explanation would seem to be that the person who has enough information to understand the utterance (in particular, to make a plausible guess as to surface structure) will "hear" the phonetic representation determined by the phonological rules from this surface structure.

[16]There are, incidentally, some examples of double vowel shift, namely in the case of such semi-irregular verbs as *drive-drove, speak-spoke;* but this is another matter, not determined by the cycle.

units larger than the word, or units internal to a word. Some suggestions can be made along these lines, but evidence is still too sparse for them to carry much conviction.

It was pointed out earlier that the principle of linear ordering must in fact be qualified, since in certain cases it is untrue that a linear ordering can be imposed on phonological rules. Let us now turn to a consideration of this matter. As background to this discussion, let us consider with slightly more care the rules that place primary stress in lexical categories. The examples given above are characteristic of English, in that the basic process determining stress placement is the Romance stress rule (hereafter RSR) that assigns primary stress in the context $-C_aVC_b$ (where C_a is a string of zero or more consonants, V is a lax vowel, and C_b is either null, a single consonant, or a consonant followed by [r] or [w]) and which elsewhere assigns stress in the final syllable. This process applies under various conditions, of which three are relevant to the present discussion. First, it applies before a monosyllabic lax affix. Thus in the words *personal, dialectal, anecdotal,* RSR applies in the context —+*al,* assigning stress in the context —CCVC in *personal* and in the final syllable preceding the affix in the other two cases. Thus we have rule (16):

(16)   RSR / —+affix].

The unpaired right-hand bracket indicates the right-hand boundary of a phrase of the surface structure. Strictly speaking, this rule, as well as (17) and (18) and their later variants, should be restricted to phrases which are lexical categories, i.e., to nouns, verbs, and adjectives.

Secondly, the rule applies before a final stressed syllable. We can illustrate this process with the examples of (14). In the first cycle, primary stress is placed on the final syllable of the verbs underlying the nouns *torment, convict, export, progress* of (14a). As we have already noted, stress is shifted left in the second cycle for nouns formed from verbs.[17] The process RSR, as just described, assigns stress

to the only (hence final) vowel of a monosyllable; therefore it assigns primary stress to the residual syllable *tor-, con-, ex-, pro-,* before the stressed syllable in the second cycle.

The same process applies in the second cycle of the derivation of such words as *photograph, telephone,* and *engram.*[18] In the first cycle, primary stress is assigned by RSR to the internal stem *graph, phone, gram.* In the second cycle, it is shifted left, by RSR, before the final stressed syllable. Notice that in such forms as *photosynthesis, monomania,* where we do not have a final stressed syllable in the second cycle, primary stress is not shifted left. From many examples of this sort we establish rule (17), where Ś stands for a stressed syllable.

tions is taken for granted at the higher levels (e.g., irregular verbs), but less commonly noted, though easily attested, at a purely phonetic level. Thus, for example, the /d/ of *today* is pronounced as an alveolar flap in certain dialects, this being the only such case (contrasting with *ado, adept, to Denver,* etc.); one commonly hears, in American English, a nasalized aspirate with no dental constriction, as realization of the /θ/ of *I think so* (but not *he thinks so*); etc. Careful investigation of phonetic detail reveals many phenomena of this sort. In fact, phonology is the part of grammar that can most easily tolerate exceptions, because of its essentially finite scope.

It is surprising that many linguists seem to think the existence of exceptions a noteworthy phenomenon that somehow reflects on the search for underlying regularities—assuming, apparently, that generalizations must be abandoned because they are not maximally inclusive. Following this reasoning, one would have to exclude from a grammar the rules for regular plurals or for inflection of regular verbs because there are many well-known exceptions to them. Similarly, as just noted, one would have to give up even very low-level phonetic processes of great generality. For a recent example of this reasoning, see Winter, 1965. As has been pointed out innumerable times, exceptions such as those which Winter notes are of interest only if they lead to subsidiary or still deeper generalizations. Otherwise, they are a curiosity of no more linguistic interest than the irregular inflection of *ox, sheep, sing,* etc. There are, however, many interesting questions involved in the matter of exactly how exceptions fit into a generative (i.e., explicit) grammar. For some discussion, see *Sound Pattern,* and also the interesting study by Lakoff, 1965, which incorporates many important suggestions by Paul Postal.

---

[17]To avoid misunderstanding, it should be noted that there are many exceptions to the rules given here. This is partly because they are not formulated in sufficient detail, and partly because there are true exceptions, unique or near-unique phenomena, at every level of phonology. The existence of excep-

[18]It also applies, as can be shown by a fuller analysis, in such words as *kaleidoscope* and *heteroclite,* in which the final *-o* of the prefix actually belongs to the context for RSR, along with the final stressed syllable.

(17) RSR / — Ś]

A third case in which RSR applies is, simply, at the right-hand end of a lexical category.[19] Thus, in the words *édit, eváde, grotésque,* etc., we have a direct application of RSR to the underlying forms /edit/, /evæd/, /grotesk/. Thus, alongside (16) and (17), we have rule (18):

(18) RSR / —]

Summarizing, then, we have the three rules of (19):

(19) (a) RSR / — +affix]   (= 16)
     (b) RSR / — Ś]   (= 17)
     (c) RSR / —]   (= 18)

Observe that the process RSR itself incorporates two rules, namely (20a) and (20b), where VC_b is (as above) a lax vowel followed by zero or one consonant with an optional additional occurrence of [r] or [w], and C_a is a string of zero or more consonants:

(20) (a) V → [1 stress] / —$C_a VC_b$]

(b) V → [1 stress] / —C_a]

Thus (20a) applies to *edit* or *interpret,* and (20b) to *evade* or *grotesque,* under condition (19c). In short, (19a), (19b), (19c) really are schemata, each standing for two rules, one with (20a) replacing RSR, the other with (20b) replacing RSR.

But now consider the rules RSR of (20). Suppose that they are ordered as given. Then in the case of *edit,* (20a) will assign primary stress in the first syllable; and (20b) will then apply, switching primary stress to the second syllable, and giving (by the general convention mentioned after example 12), the incorrect form *$\overset{2}{e}\overset{1}{d}it$*. If the ordering is (20b), (20a), then application of (20b) to *edit* will give *$ed\overset{1}{i}t$*, and application of (20a) will give *$\overset{1}{e}d\overset{2}{i}t$*—which is also incorrect, since it is crucial that the final syllable should be unstressed, not secondary-stressed, if the vowel reduction rule mentioned earlier is to apply correctly. Therefore, neither order is possible, and we have a simple example of violation of Princ. 1.

What is missing in the formulation of rule (20) is, clearly, the notion "elsewhere." What

we want to say, in formulating RSR, is that case (20b) applies only in the contexts in which (20a) is not applicable, i.e., elsewhere. To put it differently, we want to say that the ordering of (20a) and (20b) is *disjunctive,* where two rules R_1 and R_2, linearly ordered so that R_1 precedes R_2, are said to be *disjunctively ordered* if R_2 cannot apply to a given string at a certain stage of the cycle if R_1 has already applied to this string at this stage of the cycle. Similarly, in the case of rules (3) and (4), we want to say that the rules are disjunctively ordered, in the same sense—either ordering of (3) and (4) now being possible. Such examples indicate, then, that a certain principle of disjunctive ordering must be added as a qualification to Princ. 1.

It is conceivable that disjunctive ordering is an ad hoc property of certain pairs of rules; if so, the grammar must be complicated quite considerably, and, furthermore, we will in effect be abandoning Princ. 1, since it could always be made to hold vacuously by a sufficiently rich assignment of ad hoc disjunctive ordering. It appears, however, that there is a rather surprising general principle that determines when rules are disjunctively ordered. If this is correct, then the grammar need not be complicated at all and Princ. 1 can be preserved, qualified now by this new principle governing disjunctive ordering.

The principle of disjunctive ordering can be formulated quite readily in terms of some familiar notational conventions. Suppose that we use braces to form (21b) as a schema abbreviating the sequence of rules given as (21a), and parentheses to form (22b) as a schema abbreviating the sequence of rules given as (22a):

(21) (a) XYZ, XWZ
     (b) X $\left\{ \begin{matrix} Y \\ W \end{matrix} \right\}$ Z
(22) (a) XYZ, XZ
     (b) X(Y)Z

Using the latter notation, RSR in (20) can be reformulated as (23):

(23) V → [1 stress] / —$C_a(VC_b)$].

Let us now tentatively assert, as a general principle, that two successive rules of the grammar are disjunctively ordered if they are formally

---

[19]To be more precise, only verbs and adjectives are affected. Stress placement in nouns is determined by a rule that falls together with (16), for reasons beyond the scope of this discussion.

related as in (22a), that is, if they can be jointly abbreviated by a schema involving parentheses. It will follow, then, that rules (20a) and (20b), the two cases of RSR, are disjunctively ordered, since they are abbreviated as (23). But consider the two rules (19a) and (19b), the first two conditions under which RSR is applied. These cannot be abbreviated by parentheses, as in (22), though they can be abbreviated by the brace notation of (21). Thus we can abbreviate (19a, b) by schema (24):

$$(24)\ \text{RSR} / - \left\{ \begin{matrix} +\text{affix} \\ \acute{S} \end{matrix} \right\} \Big]$$

Therefore (19a) and (19b) are not disjunctively ordered; let us say that they are *conjunctively ordered*. Each subcase of RSR is disjunctively ordered within (19a), as it is within (19b). Clearly, this ordering is necessary; otherwise we would derive *$\overset{2}{personal}$, *$\overset{2}{telegraph}$, just as we would derive *$\overset{2}{edit}$ if the two cases of RSR were not disjunctively ordered in (19b).

There is, however, more to the matter than this, as we can see by attempting a derivation of *personal* in accordance with (19). First, (19a) will apply, assigning primary stress to the first syllable—giving $\overset{1}{personal}$. Rule (19b) is inapplicable, and we turn next to rule (19c). This will apply, assigning primary stress to the penultimate syllable, by case (20a) of RSR. Thus we derive *$\overset{2}{personal}$, incorrectly. Clearly, the relation of disjunctive ordering must also hold between (19a) and (19c). By an analogous argument, we can also show that disjunctive ordering must hold between (19b) and (19c). However, our principle of disjunctive ordering, as it now stands, cannot accommodate these two possibilities.

The principle can easily be modified to give the correct results, namely, by permitting it to apply recursively. We have observed that (19a) and (19b) can be abbreviated by the brace notation to give (24); thus (19) is replaced by the sequence of schemata (25):

$$(25)\ (a)\ \text{RSR} / - \left\{ \begin{matrix} +\text{affix} \\ \acute{S} \end{matrix} \right\} \Big] \qquad (= 24).$$

$$(b)\ \text{RSR} / -] \qquad (= 19c)$$

But we can now apply the parenthesis notation of (22) to the sequence of schemata (25a, b): X is taken to be RSR/—; Y is the item in braces in (25a); and Z is the rightmost phrase

bracket ( ]). Applying this operation, we derive (26):

$$(26)\ \text{RSR} / - \left(\left\{ \begin{matrix} +\text{affix} \\ \acute{S} \end{matrix} \right\} \right) \Big]$$

Let us now extend the general principle determining disjunctive ordering as follows:

Principle 4: Let S be a schema X(Y)Z. Then all rules derived by expanding XYZ (or XYZ itself, if it is a rule) are disjunctively ordered with respect to each of the rules derived by expanding XZ (or XZ itself, if it is a rule).

With this formulation, disjunctive ordering is assigned to the two parts of RSR, as required, and to the pairs of rules (19a, c) and (19b, c), as is also required. Thus schema (26) expresses the following organization of rules: the sequence of actual rules of the grammar is (27); the rules are abbreviated by recursive application of notations (21), (22), in the manner indicated in (27), giving finally the representing schema (26).

(27) (a) $\text{V} \rightarrow [1\ \text{stress}] / -C_a V C_b / - +\text{affix}]$
(b) $\text{V} \rightarrow [1\ \text{stress}] / -C_a / - +\text{affix}]$ ⟩(P; 19a)
(c) $\text{V} \rightarrow [1\ \text{stress}] / -C_a V C_b / -\acute{S}]$ ⟩(B; 24)
(d) $\text{V} \rightarrow [1\ \text{stress}] / -C_a / -\acute{S}]$ ⟩(P; 19b)
(e) $\text{V} \rightarrow [1\ \text{stress}] / -C_a V C_b / -]$ ⟩(P; 26)
(f) $\text{V} \rightarrow [1\ \text{stress}] / -C_a / -]$ ⟩(P; 19c)

The meaning of (27) is as follows. Rule (27a) and rule (27b) are first collapsed by parenthesization (= P) to give (19a); similarly, rules (27c) and (27d) give (19b), and rules (27e) and (27f) give (19c). Next, schemata (19a) and (19b) are abbreviated, by bracketing (= B), to give (24). Finally, schemata (24) and (19c) are abbreviated, by parenthesization, to give (26). By application of Princ. 4, disjunctive ordering is assigned to all pairs of rules except those listed in (28):

$$(28)\ (a)\ (27a),\ (27c)$$
$$(b)\ (27a),\ (27d)$$
$$(c)\ (27b),\ (27c)$$
$$(d)\ (27b),\ (27d)$$

Only the sequences listed in (28) represent possible cases of sequential application of rules within a single cycle. Of these four cases, two are excluded as impossible by the meaning of the rules in question, namely (28a) and (28b). Therefore, the general principles we have so far established imply (subject to a qualification noted below) that when a grammar contains the sequence of rules given in (27), the only possible cases of sequential application, within a single cycle, are (27b, c) and (27b, d).

Space limitations prevent a detailed demonstration, but it is in fact the case that the stress contours of English words are determined by just these conditions on the application of the rules in (27); both permitted cases of conjunctive ordering can be attested, and all cases of disjunctive ordering can be shown to be necessary (see *Sound Pattern*). There are also a fair number of other cases beyond the example just presented where the principle is necessary; and there are none, to my knowledge, where it leads to unacceptable results. Consequently, Princ. 4 seems to be a well-founded principle of phonological organization.

The principle of disjunctive ordering, as stated, must be further generalized to account for all known cases. As it stands, it does not explain why rules (3) and (4), abbreviated as (5) in terms of a variable ranging over feature specifications, are disjunctively ordered. An explanation of this fact requires a deeper analysis of the parenthesis notation proposed in (22). What is necessary is a formal device for expressing similarities among rules more general than those captured by the parenthesis notation. It is, in fact, not difficult to develop a system for constructing rule-schemata which will include the devices presented above as a special case and which will determine the relation of disjunctive ordering in just the way that appears to be required by the available examples.[20]

That disjunctive ordering among rules should be definable in terms of recursive application of the principles for forming schemata from rules is in some respects quite surprising. For one thing, this recursive procedure may assign disjunctive ordering to rules that are not successive, as, for example, in the case of (27), where (a) and (b) are conjunctively ordered with respect to (c) and (d) but disjunctively ordered with respect to (e) and (f). One cannot tell by inspection of a sequence of rules what arrangement of conjunctive and disjunctive order holds among them; rather, this is determined by recursive application of a principle of quite an abstract sort. In this respect, the principle of disjunctive ordering, Princ. 4, must be regarded as much deeper than the principle of linear ordering and the principle of the transformational cycle. The fact that phonological rules must be at least partially ordered is almost immediately evident, when one looks at even moderately complex linguistic material. The factual evidence in support of the principle of cyclic application is less obvious, but the principle itself is entirely natural; it must surely be the first hypothesis concerning organization of rules which comes to mind when the question of mapping surface structures into phonetic representations by a fixed set of processes is formulated. The principle of disjunctive ordering is far less transparent, however. It will, therefore, be quite important to determine whether it is supported by a wider range of evidence.

It is noteworthy that the devices used in defining disjunctive ordering—namely, (21) and (22)—are just those that were developed, quite independently, in the study of evaluation of grammars. As noted earlier, a natural approach to the problem of evaluation, and the one that has been followed in all the substantive work on this subject in the past fifteen years or so, is to measure the value of a grammar as inversely proportional to the number of symbols in the sequence of schemata that results when certain notational operations are

---

[20]The extension required involves indexed parentheses which have, in particular, the meaning that ...$(X)_i$...$(Y)_i$... is an abbreviation for the sequence ...X...Y..., ...X'...Y'..., where X' is null unless X is $[\alpha F]$ (where α is + or − and F is a feature), in which case X' is $[-\alpha F]$ (where as before, $-+=-$, $--=+$), and similarly for Y'. Parenthesization, in the former sense, is the special case of indexed parenthesization in which indices differ. The variable notation of rule (5) is definable in terms of indexed parenthesization. The generalization regarding disjunctive ordering is, then, stated as in Princ. 4, but with indexed parentheses rather than the special case of simple parentheses (for details, see *Sound Pattern*.)

applied to the rules of the grammar. These notational devices define what counts as "linguistically significant generalization"; they provide an empirical hypothesis as to the kind of regularities that the language learner seeks in attempting to organize the data presented to him, and that the linguist uses in justifying a particular formulation of grammatical rules for a certain language. The fact that the study of rule application leads to the same choice of devices as the study of linguistically significant generalization is interesting and important. This convergence of two independent lines of investigation gives strong evidence for the reality of the postulated devices, for the significance of the specific type of relationship among rules expressed by these formal devices.

In reducing the sequence of rules in (27) to schema (26), we begged an important question, to which we must now turn our attention. As indicated in (27), we first applied the parenthesis notation to the pairs (a, b), (c, d), and (e, f), forming (19a), (19b), and (19c), respectively. We then applied the brace notation to schemata (19a) and (19b), forming (24). Finally, we applied the parenthesis notation to (24) and (19c), forming (26). Another possibility, equally permissible by the conventions so far established, would have been to apply the parenthesis notation to schemata (19b) and (19c), forming (29), and then the brace notation to (19a) and (29), yielding (30):

(29) $V \rightarrow [1 \text{ stress}] / —C_a(VC_b) / — (\acute{S})]$

(30) $V \rightarrow [1 \text{ stress}] / —C_a(VC_b) / — \left\{ \begin{matrix} +\text{affix} \\ (\acute{S}) \end{matrix} \right\}]$

Schema (30) has the same number of symbols as schema (26); therefore it cannot be rejected on grounds of lower value. However, it assigns an entirely different relation of disjunctive ordering to the rules and predicts different empirical consequences. For example, since the affix rule and the rule for strict final position are no longer disjunctively ordered, (30) will cause a word such as *personal* to receive primary stress on the medial syllable (see under rule 24).

We might say that (26) is selected over (30) simply on empirical grounds; schema (26) describes the facts correctly, and schema (30) does not. However, it would be much more interesting to try to find a principled reason for

the selection of (26) over (30), a principle of phonological organization that requires us, given the rules of (27), to select schema (26) rather than (30), and so to predict the empirically given facts from a set of much more restricted data that involves no successive application of the rules of (27). A general principle that suggests itself is the following:

Principle 5: The underlying representing schema is selected in such a way as to maximize disjunctive ordering.

Comparing (26) and (30), we see that Princ. 5 will select (26) over (30), as required. Furthermore, Princ. 5 is rather plausible. By maximizing disjunctive ordering we minimize the length of derivations, the amount of processing involved in production or perception of speech. It is not unreasonable to suppose that this should be a subsidiary consideration in the selection of a grammar.[21] To obtain data bearing on Princ. 5 will clearly be a difficult matter. In particular, its effects can be determined only when a phonology has been constructed in considerable depth.

Finally, let us consider a principle of a rather different kind. Notice that, in English and in many other languages, when a velar or dental becomes a palatal by some process, it also becomes strident. Thus the /g/ of *rigor* becomes [ǰ]—not [g,]—when it palatalizes in *rigid*.[22] Similarly, the /t/ of *act* becomes [č]—not [k,]—when it palatalizes in *actual*. Clearly,

[21]More precisely, this consideration bears on the interpretation of a grammar, since the sequence of rules constituting the grammar is not affected by the procedure for determining the value of the grammar and the assignment of disjunctive ordering. In studying the effect of various principles of evaluation in my *Morphophonemics of Modern Hebrew* (1951), I found that the criterion of minimizing length of derivations had only a marginal effect on determination of rule ordering, assigning an order in only one case not determined by the measure in terms of notations of the sort discussed here.

In considering Princ. 5, one must bear in mind that the question of how a grammar is used in production or perception of speech is, of course, quite open. Nevertheless, it is not unreasonable to assume, as a first approximation, that the process will increase in complexity as the number of applicable grammatical rules increases.

[22]Phonetic symbols used here include [g,] and [k,] for palatal stops, [c] for the voiceless alveolar affricate.

there is a generalization here; we should add to the grammar of English the following rule:[23]

(31) A segment which becomes a palatal
                                becomes strident.

But now consider the process of velar softening that converts /k/ to [s], as in *electric-electricity,* etc. The segment /k/ does not become palatal (i.e., [−grave, −diffuse]), but rather [−grave, +diffuse]. Nevertheless, it becomes strident. In fact, the process of velar softening that converts /g/ to [ǰ] must also convert /k/ to [c], which then becomes [s] by a further rule. Clearly, the generalization (31) must somehow also apply to the voiceless velar softening, although the segment in question does not become palatal.

If we omit reference to stridency, the rule converting /k/ to [c] is:

$$(32) \quad k \rightarrow \begin{bmatrix} -\,\text{grave} \\ +\,\text{diffuse} \end{bmatrix}$$

Suppose now that we were to establish Princ. 6, as follows:

Principle 6: Two successive lines of a derivation can differ by at most one feature specification.

Princ. 6 would require us to interpret rule (32) as comprising two steps: the first of these converts /k/ to the corresponding [−grave] segment [k,]; and the second step introduces the feature [+diffuse]. But now observe that rule (31) will apply when /k/ becomes [k,] in the first step of this process, converting it to [č]. Introduction of the feature [+diffuse] by the second step of the rule will now convert [č] to [c], as required. Such examples as this seem to offer support for Princ. 6, as a principle of interpretation of a system of phonological rules.

Notice that we have begged a certain question in interpreting Princ. 6 as we did. Alternatively, it might have been interpreted, in the case of rule (32), as first introducing the feature [+diffuse] and then the feature [−grave]. Under this interpretation, rule (31) would not have applied, and velar softening

would, incorrectly, give [t] as the phonetic reflex of /k/. The choice, then, is between process (33) and process (34) as an interpretation of (32):

(33) k → k, → č → c.
(34) k → p → t.

There is no doubt that (33) can be selected over (34) on quite general grounds of an entirely different sort than those considered in this paper. Thus each of the steps of (33) represents a "favored rule," while neither of the steps of (34) represents a favored or plausible rule. A general theory of rule plausibility is clearly needed as a supplement to the theory of generative phonology, for such cases as this and many others. This matter leads us into an entirely new and relatively unexplored domain—namely, into consideration of the system of substantive (not formal) constraints on phonological rules, and into the interaction of substantive constraints with the processes described by phonological rules. Some steps toward a theory of this sort are suggested in *Sound Pattern,* but many questions of principle and of detail are left quite unanswered.

To establish general principles of organization for grammar, we must show that these principles are consistent with the facts in a variety of languages and that, on the basis of these principles, one can explain phenomena that must otherwise be regarded as accidental. It is fairly clear that only a deep study of particular languages will provide the kinds of evidence that bear on the correctness of the principles suggested here, or others of equal abstractness. The evidence for the principles discussed in this paper is, needless to say, far from conclusive. Nevertheless, it seems to me that the evidence is not negligible, and that it is quite proper to propose them as tentative principles of phonological organization and structure, to be tested against whatever new material emerges from studies of greater scope and depth than have yet been undertaken.

The question why such principles hold is not one that can be easily dismissed. There is certainly nothing necessary about them; in each case, it is possible to formulate consistent alternatives. Nor are they the "simplest possible" principles in any absolute sense (so far as such notions are intelligible). There is, of course, a danger, inherent to the study of phonological structure, that what one discovers

---

[23]This is actually not a rule of English grammar, but rather is related to a certain principle of universal phonetics which, in a manner that I will not describe here, interweaves with certain rules of English phonology (for details, see *Sound Pattern*).

may be an artifact. Phonology, as distinct from syntax, is a system that is essentially finite in scope.[24] It would be possible, in principle, for the mapping from surface structure to phonetic representation to be simply memorized, case by case (in particular, each formative or word could be learned as an unstructured set of variants, each associated with its determining context). Any such assumption, however, would leave unexplained the existence of significant generalizations concerning the relationship of surface structure to phonetic representation. If principles of the sort discussed here can be firmly established, it would hardly be rational to suppose that phonology is a memorized system without internal structure. Similarly, there is no force to the claim that the internal "coherence" of a phonological system results from some analogic force or some striving for symmetry unless one can, on this basis, derive the general principles of phonological organization.

Conceivably, one might argue that such principles are in part a historical accident. Thus, if Princ. 1 held without qualification, and if the linearly ordered rules corresponded strictly to a sequence of historical sound changes, one might argue that the grammatical rules have no synchronic meaning but merely recapitulate history. But since neither of these assumptions is correct, this line of reasoning is ruled out.[25] It is difficult to conceive of any other argument that would explain, in terms of linguistic evolution, the validity of general

principles of the sort discussed here. It seems reasonable to assume, therefore, that the explanation for such principles must be sought in the pre-linguistic schematism that determines, for the language learner, what counts as linguistic data and how this material is to be structured and organized.

It is of course a matter of judgment at what point a theory of learning, or a general theory of mental processes and cognition, must be regarded as seriously defective if it fails to account for general properties of language or of other complex systems that humans construct on the basis of the fragmentary data available to them. The evidence in support of such properties and principles must be compared with the evidence in favor of psychological theories that cannot accommodate them. This is an intricate matter; conclusions must be drawn carefully, with attention to the nature and scope of several sorts of evidence. To me it seems that, even in the present early state of investigation of these questions, there is sufficient evidence to suggest that all existing approaches to the study of human intelligence and human behavior and learning are seriously defective. It can hardly be seriously proposed that abstract principles of phonological organization of the nature of those discussed here are learned by any inductive process; furthermore, they resist intelligible formulation in terms of any notion of "habit" or "behavioral repertoire," or, in fact, in terms of any moderately clear concept of psychological theory with which I am familiar. It seems to me quite reasonable to suppose that these are a priori principles, part of the basis for language acquisition rather than a result of some process of learning or generalization. No doubt they result in part from organism-environment interaction (as does, no doubt, the fact that a human has two legs), but there is little reason to expect that any theory of learning can provide a useful framework for studying their emergence and application to linguistic material. There is, then, a larger context within which questions of the sort discussed here are immediately relevant, and it also seems clear how one can proceed to study these questions in detail. The study of general principles governing the form, organization, and application of phonological rules is a relatively new, but quite promising, field. If principles of depth and generality can be firmly established, this will be a result of

[24]This follows from the fact that there is a maximal domain of phonetic processes—the phonological phrase—beyond which the principle of the transformational cycle does not operate.

[25]An attempt to explain linear ordering of rules as a historical artifact, in this way, would also be refuted by the fact that items introduced into the language after the sound change has occurred characteristically are assimilated into the rule system (or into one of several separate but interwoven systems, in many languages). That is, their phonetic shape and variants can ordinarily be accounted for by assigning them an underlying phonological representation, of the type permitted in the synchronic grammar, which then undergoes all linearly ordered rules. It seems, in fact, that a coherent account of sound change can itself only be developed within a framework of assumptions about the form of grammar of the sort discussed here, and that, therefore, the attempt to derive such principles as a historical artifact is misguided in the first place. For further discussion of this matter, see Postal, *Aspects of Phonological Theory.*

considerable importance not only for general linguistics, but for psychology as well.

REFERENCES

BOLINGER, D. L., and L. J. GERSTMAN. 1957. "Disjuncture as a Cue to Constructs," *Word* 13. 246–255.

CHOMSKY, NOAM. 1951. *Morphophonemics of Modern Hebrew.* Cambridge, Mass. (mimeographed).

———. 1964. *Current Issues in Linguistic Theory.* The Hague, Mouton. (A slightly earlier version appears in Fodor and Katz 1964: 50–118.) [39]

———. 1965. *Aspects of the Theory of Syntax.* Cambridge, Mass., MIT Press.

———. 1966. "Topics in the Theory of Generative Grammar," *Current Trends in Linguistics,* III, ed. by T. Sebeok, pp. 1–60. The Hague, Mouton.

CHOMSKY, NOAM, and MORRIS HALLE. 1965. "Some Controversial Questions in Phonological Theory," *Journal of Linguistics* 1.97–138. [42]

———. In press. *The Sound Pattern of English.* New York, Harper & Row. [Now 1968—VBM.]

CHOMSKY, NOAM, MORRIS HALLE, and FRED LUKOFF. 1956. "On Accent and Juncture in English," *For Roman Jakobson,* ed. by M. Halle et al., pp. 65–80. The Hague, Mouton.

FODOR, J., and J. KATZ (eds.) 1964. *The Structure of Language.* Englewood Cliffs, N.J., Prentice-Hall.

HALLE, MORRIS. 1962. "Phonology in Generative Grammar," *Word* 18.54–72. (Reprinted in Fodor and Katz 1964: 334–352.) [37]

———. 1964. "On the Bases of Phonology," in Fodor and Katz 1964: 324–333. [38]

HOUSEHOLDER, FRED. 1966. "Phonological Theory: A Brief Comment," *Journal of Linguistics* 2.99–100. [43]

LAKOFF, G. 1965. *On the Nature of Syntactic Irregularity.* (Harvard Computation Laboratory, Report No. NSF-16.) Cambridge, Mass.

LAMB, SYDNEY M. 1966. "Prolegomena to a Theory of Phonology," *Language* 42.536–573. [53]

POSTAL, PAUL. 1964. *Constituent Structure.* (Indiana University Research Center in Anthropology, Folklore, and Linguistics, Publication 30.) Bloomington, Ind.

———. 1966. Review Article: *Elements of General Linguistics,* by André Martinet. *Foundations of Language* 2.151–186.

———. In press. *Aspects of Phonological Theory.* New York, Harper & Row. [Now 1968—VBM.]

SEUREN, P. A. M. 1966. Review of *Grammar Discovery Procedures,* by R. E. Longacre. *Foundations of Language* 2.200–212.

WINTER, WERNER. 1965. "Transforms without Kernels?" *Language* 41.484–489.

49

PHONEMICS AND
GENERATIVE PHONOLOGY*
DAVID A. JOHNS

For ten years now generative phonologists have been presenting arguments designed to show that a phonemic level is not only useless in the description of language, but is actually logically impossible.

The purpose of this paper will be to go through the main arguments leveled against phonemics by Halle, Chomsky, and Postal, and to show why I find them unconvincing. I will also indicate the usefulness of phonemics and show how a phonemic level could be incorporated into a generative grammar.

Many of the arguments which appear in the literature deal with particular formalizations of phonemic theory; with phonemic discovery procedures (e.g., many of the arguments in Chomsky (1964) [39]); or against particular claims about the power of phonemics as a tool (e.g., Postal's discussions of the description of historical change (Postal 1968)). Most of these are really irrelevant to the question of whether a phonemic level is actually possible. I agree with most of these arguments, and will therefore not consider them here, although I will cover each type of relevant argument I am aware of.

The first argument to be directed against the phonemic level, and the one I have seen most widely quoted, was presented in Halle, 1959.

To recapitulate the argument, Russian has both voiced and voiceless obstruents, and voicing alternations in obstruents, expressed partially by a rule assimilating the voicing of any obstruent to that of the following obstruent. Since most obstruents come in voiced-voiceless pairs, the alternations in question are for the most part what would be called morphophonemic. But there are several which are not paired, so that when the alternation involves these segments it is phonetic.

Halle's examples, as shown below, demonstrate this dilemma clearly.

A	B	C
dát, l,i	dát, l,i	dát, l,i
dát, bi	dád, bi	dád, bi
žéč l,i	žéč l,i	žéč l,i
žéč bi	žéč bi	žéj bi

The forms in column A are underlying, those in B phonemic, and those in C phonetic. On the phonemic level, /t,/ and /d,/ must be distinguished, since they contrast in other positions. But [č] and [ǰ] must both be written /č/, since there is no independent, contrastive /ǰ/ in Russian.

Thus what seems to be one rule has to be expressed twice; or to state it another way, if the rule is expressed only once, there will be no level one could call phonemic.

Given the arrangement of grammar Halle is working with, his conclusion is obviously right: that the inclusion of a phonemic level complicates the grammar in a counterintuitive way.

But looking at the Russian data again, I think it is clear what is going on. The fact is that the voicing assimilation rule is always phonetic, since voicing is never distinctive in obstruents in the position before another obstruent. In other words, if we have a way of representing the concept of neutralization, which is surely not incompatible with the notion of a phonemic level, Halle's problem becomes totally spurious. The correct phonemic representation for the examples mentioned, in

*Reprinted from *Papers from the Fifth Regional Meeting of the Chicago Linguistic Society* (Chicago, 1969), pp. 374–381, by permission.

feature notation, of course, will simply not have a specification for voicing in the obstruents in question.

In Chomsky, 1964 [39] another problem relevant to the existence of a phonemic level is discussed, involving what Chomsky termed the linearity condition. The best illustration for this argument is the *writer/rider* distinction in English.

Here it is clear that these two words are distinguished by their first vowel, rather than by their medial consonant: thus, [ráyDr] and [rá:yDr] respectively. It would clearly be ridiculous to set up an extra vowel phoneme which would be distinctive only before the alveolar flap; yet any attempt to retain the underlying *t/d* opposition violates linearity.

Chomsky's conclusion is that the phonemic level cannot handle this type of example and therefore does not exist.

Now it is obvious that a feature of length is phonemic in these examples. But although this length occurs all over the place, it distinguishes words only where a flap follows. Elsewhere it is in complementary distribution with voicing in the following segment.

The feature of voicing, on the other hand, is in complementary distribution with preceding length except where no vowel precedes.

In other words, what we have is two features which seem to act as a unit and never occur independently together. Yet there are cases where one of the features is not present and the other carries the entire load alone.

My conclusion from this data is not that phonemes do not exist, but that our conception of phonology must be enriched to express the facts. And the facts seem to be that features can join together in bundles of some sort, a superfeature, perhaps, with the actual manifestation of the feature conditioned by the environment.

This, of course, contradicts the principle that a contrast which exists anywhere in the system has to be represented wherever it occurs: the once-a-phoneme-always-a-phoneme and once-a-feature-always-a-feature principles. But given the same device which would produce the neutralization discussed above, and, of course, a feature notation rather than a segment notation, it would be very simple to incorporate into the grammar. The superfeature

of voicing and preceding length would simply manifest itself as both wherever possible; where the consonant is initial only voicing would be present, and where a neutralization rule applies, as in *writer/rider,* only length would remain. In a word such as *ride,* there would be no need to decide whether length or voicing is distinctive, since they cannot exist independently.

Unlike Chomsky and Halle, who deal mainly with the difficulty of integrating a phonemic level into their conception of a generative grammar, Postal attacks the phoneme directly. Many of his arguments concerning the usefulness of a phonemic level I find conclusive; e.g., it seems clear to me that historical change cannot be explained wholly at the phonemic level. I find his arguments relating to the possible existence of the phonemic level as such unconvincing, however.

There are a couple of minor arguments which I would like to comment on before discussing Postal's major attacks.

Postal claims (16–18) that it would be absurd to have a level the sole purpose of which would be to indicate ambiguity and contrast. He draws an analogy from syntax to strengthen his point. Using the sentence *the troops stopped stealing,* he points out that there are two readings possible, with either *the troops* or an unspecified noun as the subject of *steal.*

I think this example is particularly infelicitous. The argument is that even though the sentence is ambiguous—i.e., it corresponds to two distinct deep structures, we do not need a level of representation designed specifically to capture that ambiguity. And by analogy, it would be equally absurd to have a level in phonology designed especially to capture ambiguity.

I agree completely. But I don't think anyone has ever claimed that a phonemic level should indicate when a form is ambiguous and when it is not. In fact, as I understand it, it is supposed to do the exact opposite; when two distinct underlying forms are pronounced identically or with the same range of variations they must be represented identically at the phonemic level.

Furthermore, this is exactly what the surface syntactic representation does for the two readings of the sentence Postal is discussing. It indicates that the two deep structures associated with it are realized identically.

Another comment that Postal makes is that if *rider* and *writer* are distinguished by phonemic vowel length, an English speaker should have no difficulty distinguishing between a pair such as [láyzər] and [lá:yzər] (25). This conclusion does not follow, of course, under the interpretation of this type of length I have already proposed, since the length is inextricably bound up with the voicing of the following obstruent.

But besides these minor arguments, Postal offers two "new types of arguments against autonomous phonemics."

The first of these is that stating restrictions on the phonemic level is redundant, since all restrictions on sequences of segments can be expressed in the underlying representation and the rules. To substantiate his point Postal goes through the underlying and superficial consonant clusters in Mohawk. He shows that the restrictions which show up in the surface forms are a result either of the restrictions on underlying clusters, or of those plus the phonological rules.

I agree with Postal in this example, but there do seem to be cases where surface restrictions are necessary.

Take, for instance, English words such as *rabies, series, species,* etc., and names such as *Aries, Ulysses, Hades,* etc. In my speech, the last syllable of these words is completely unstressed, even though it contains the tense vowel [ī]. Normally a tense vowel can occur in unstressed final open syllables (e.g., *monkey, pillow,* etc.), but in closed syllables only if the consonant is the marker of the plural, possessive, past tense, etc. A word such as *series,* then, is anomalous.

But note that all these words have the consonant [z] following the vowel in question. Substituting any other consonant (except [d]) would make the resultant form unpronounceable. The obvious conclusion is that these words have the surface forms of plurals. Notice also that none of these words has a plural, since the resultant forms, with a tense vowel in a medial unstressed syllable, would also be impossible at the surface level.

I think that the conclusion is inevitable

that such words, even though they violate underlying restrictions, are admissible—that is, pronounceable—because they fit surface patterns formed by combinations of morphemes which themselves are acceptable.

Other examples of the same sort are not hard to find. In fact it would seem that a language's ability to borrow words is at least largely determined by the shapes permissible at the surface level, especially in the realm of proper names, where little combinability is required.

In Russian, for instance, a morpheme such as *kengurú* 'kangaroo' is totally anomalous; yet it is perfectly pronounceable. Morphemes in general, and especially noun stems, do not end in a stressed *u,* but words containing various inflectional endings do (e.g., *idú* 'I go', *stolú* 'to the table', etc.).

The word *kengurú,* of course, is marked as a borrowing in Russian, because it cannot participate in declension, is hard to assign gender to, etc. The fact remains that it can be pronounced, while borrowing the name *Pittsburgh,* for instance, would be impossible without extensive modifications, since it does not conform to Russian surface restrictions.

Postal's second major argument against phonemics is his claim that free variation is not transitive. As I understand it, what Postal is saying is that for a phonemic level to make sense, two phonemes distinct from each other cannot be in free variation with the same segment in the same environment.

One of the examples Postal gives to illustrate this problem is the English pair *affect* and *effect.* He claims that in his dialect he can pronounce the first syllable either with a full vowel or with a reduced vowel. In other words, either [æ] or [e] can be replaced by [ə], but neither can replace the other.

The first thing I think Postal is missing in this argument is that there are two very different types of "free variation." I will call them, for want of anything catchier, potentially meaningful and insignificant.

The clearest type of example of potentially meaningful free variation occurs in words such as *rather,* pronounced either with [a] or with [æ], *economics* with [e] or [ī], etc. I think every native speaker would agree that there is a substantial difference between this type of free variation and the insignificant variation between a glottal stop and [t] at the end of a word, for instance. The pronunciations [ráɗr] and [rǽɗr] could have different meanings, while [rəyʔ] and [rəytʰ], for instance, never could.

If in Postal's dialect one really is able to pronounce words such as *affect* and *effect* with unreduced vowels, I think that this would have to be analyzed simply as a special case of potentially meaningful free variation.

What seems more likely, however, is that the full vowel pronunciation is fairly rare, occurring only when there is a possibility of confusion. In other words, it is a conscious distortion of speech calculated to have a particular effect.

But the question then arises whether this type of distortion is a legitimate part of language or not. In particular, is this variation part of our linguistic competence, or is it rather a learned, cultural device produced by our spelling?

In most cases this is very difficult to determine, since orthographic variation which is slight enough to be incorporated into reasonably rapid speech is usually in the direction of what we would set up as underlying forms anyway.

I have found one case in English, however, which suggests to me that at least a great deal of precise, well enunciated, contrastive pronunciation is really spelling pronunciation.

One often hears speakers pronouncing words like *writer* in an overly precise style; one I would equate with the style in which full vowels are pronounced in *affect* and *effect*. In this style the medial consonant is pronounced as an aspirated *t*.

Now the words *spider* and *cider* are always spelled with *d*'s, which never alternate with any other segments. Yet in my dialect, and in the dialect of many other American speakers, these two words rhyme not with *rider*, as we would expect, but with *writer*. Yet it would be inconceivable in the case of *spider* and *cider* to restore what must be an underlying *t* in slow pronunciation. When I overenunciate these words I get [spə́y-dr̀] and [sə́y-dr̀]; in other words, the vowel which would be predicted from an underlying *t*, but a clear [d] in pronunciation.

My conclusion is that the pronunciation

of [t] in words like *writer* must be a spelling pronunciation. I suspect that this is also the case with *affect* and *effect*.

Once we've decided that a phonemic level is logically possible, we must still ask what it might be good for.

One thing is that native speakers seem to have fairly consistent intuitions about how phones are grouped into significant sounds. I have never doubted, for instance, that the words *bowl, boat,* and *bore* all have the same vowel, even though the individual manifestations are noticeably different. And this intuition seems to operate independently of the ultimate underlying forms; thus *evasion* rhymes with *equation,* despite the fact that the former has an underlying *d* and the latter a *t;* similarly with *relation* and *Thracian,* etc. It also operates independently of the phonetics; *might* always rhymes with *right* no matter which of the many possibilities for the pronunciation of the final consonant—glottal stop, unreleased stop, aspirated stop, etc.—one chooses for either one.

A more important feature of the phonemic level seems to be that it constrains the types of historical change possible.

As I believe David Stampe pointed out for the first time, for instance (Stampe, 1968), when a rule such as the Pig Latin rule is added to English the output still conforms to the allophonic distribution restrictions in the language. Thus if *cool* is transformed into *oolcay,* the resultant form has a fronted [k̟], as we would expect before the vowel [ēy], and not the backed [k] originally present before the [ūw].

I think the general principle is that no rule which creates strings relevant to the structural description of a phonetic rule may be ordered after that rule. This is then a strengthening of Kiparsky's principle of rule simplification as it applies to feeding order (Kiparsky, 1968). Kiparsky says that any two rules tend to become ordered so that the output of one feeds the second; my claim is that this order is not only unmarked but actually mandatory if the second rule is a phonetic one.

Obviously as far as the interpretation of historical records goes there is a certain amount of circularity involved here; if the added rule followed the phonetic one, it would force a reinterpretation of the phonemics. What I am claiming, however, is that the phonemic analysis is part of the native speaker's competence. And it is, of course, perfectly possible that different speakers could have different analyses.

As a result I object to such statements made by traditional phonemicists such as "voicing became phonemic in fricatives in English when final vowels were dropped and geminate clusters simplified." I would claim that voicing must already have been phonemic, since otherwise the voiced variants would have reverted to their voicelessness.

Thus the phonemic level gives a certain amount of explanatory justification to details of rule ordering in historical change.

The last question I will take up is that of how to fit a phonemic level into a generative phonology.

The main problem is finding a way to represent neutralization. Going back to Halle's example, for instance, voicing in obstruents in Russian obviously has to be specified in the lexicon; but it must not be specified in certain environments at the phonemic level. What is needed is a feature-deletion rule. Thus in this case the rule would say that obstruents become unspecified for voice in the position immediately preceding another obstruent.

Furthermore, the grammar would obviously be simplified if the condition that a phonemic level must coincide with one specific stage of the phonological derivation were eliminated. I envision the phonemic and phonetic levels as being parallel terminal derivations. Distinctiveness would be considered not an incomplete specification of the phonetic level, but rather something that the speaker knows about his sounds. This arrangement might be diagrammed as follows:

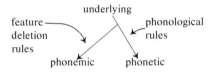

Note also that for a phonemic level to exist there is no reason why it should conform to any a priori theoretical restrictions; there is no reason why it has to be autonomous or taxonomic or conform to a pre-conceived generative phonology. It is simply a level of representation which expresses certain facts which are part of the native speaker's competence. It need not be discoverable by any rigid methodology, any more than any other part of the grammar is, nor need it be the one and only true phonological representation.

My main goal in this paper has been to show that none of the arguments allegedly disproving phonemics are valid, thereby hopefully reopening an area of inquiry within generative phonology which these arguments have held closed off for ten years. I hope that I have also been able to show that the intuitions of generations of speakers and linguists are valid, even if particular formalizations of these intuitions have not been, and that the concept of a phonemic level can play a meaningful role in the understanding of language.

BIBLIOGRAPHY

CHOMSKY, NOAM. 1964. "Current Issues in Linguistic Theory," in Fodor and Katz, *The Structure of Language,* pp. 50–118. Englewood Cliffs, N.J.: Prentice-Hall. [See here article 39—VBM.]

HALLE, MORRIS. 1959. *The Sound Pattern of Russian.* The Hague: Mouton.

KIPARSKY, PAUL. 1968. "Linguistic Universals and Linguistic Change," in Bach and Harms, *Universals in Linguistic Theory.* New York.

POSTAL, PAUL. 1968. *Aspects of Phonological Theory.* New York: Harper & Row.

STAMPE, DAVID. 1968. "Yes, Virginia . . ." Paper read at CLS 4th Regional Meetings.

IV

THE COPENHAGEN SCHOOL AND STRATIFICATIONAL PHONOLOGY

INTRODUCTION

This section is divided into two parts, the first dealing briefly with Hjelmslevian phonematics, the second with stratificational phonology.

Hjelmslev, and the Copenhagen school of linguistics in general, are poorly known in America. Only with the publication in 1949 of Volume V of *Travaux du Cercle Linguistique de Copenhague,* entitled *Recherches Structurales,* did linguists in this country become acquainted, to some extent, with what was being done there. The English translation of Hjelmslev's 1943 masterwork, *Omkring sprogteoriens grundlæggelse,* under the title *Prolegomena to a Theory of Language* (1953), served for many as an introduction to his theories. But his introduction of a whole set of new terms, numbering in the hundreds, proved to be a formidable obstacle to understanding. The fact is that in practice, although not always in theory, much of what Hjelmslev and his followers were doing in phonology was quite like Bloomfieldian analysis. As was pointed out in the preface, it has not been possible to include here any more than a representative sample of the sort of work being done by the Copenhagen school. It is hoped that these articles will serve as a brief introduction to the theory and as a stimulus to further reading on the subject. (See the bibliography below for more writings of the Copenhagen school.)

Miss Eli Fischer-Jørgensen, in the two articles included here, "On the Definition of Phoneme Categories on a Distributional Basis" (1952) [50] and "The Commutation Test and Its Application to Phonemic Analysis" (1956) [51], compares Copenhagen school phonology with Prague school and Bloomfieldian practices, explaining how phonematics is like and differs from other schools of thought. Although there are many similarities, the theoretical basis on which Hjelmslevian phonemic analysis lies is quite different from the usual Bloomfieldian theory. The important things for Hjelmslev were not the entities themselves (sound, meanings, and so on), but rather the systems of relationships which these units represent:

The real units of language are not sounds, or written characters, or meanings: the real units of language are the *relata* which these sounds, characters, and meanings represent. The main thing is not the sounds, characters, and meanings as such, but their mutual relations within the *chain of speech* and within the *paradigms of grammar* [my italics—VBM]. These relations make up the system of a language, and it is this interior system which is characteristic of one language as opposed to other languages, whereas the representation by sounds, characters, and meanings is irrelevant to the system and may be changed without affecting the system. . . . The description of a language must begin by stating relations between relevant units, and these statements cannot involve a statement about the inherent nature, essence or substance of these units themselves. . . . Linguistics describes the relational pattern of language without knowing what the relata are, and . . . phonetics and semantics do tell what those relata are but only by means of describing the relations between their parts and parts of their parts. [Louis Hjelmslev, "Structural Analysis of Language," *Studia Linguistica* 1, pp. 69 and 75 (1947).]

He goes on to say (p. 78) that "Content and expression are bound up with each other through commutation" and that "There is not a one-to-one correspondence between content and expression, but the signs are decomposable in minor components. Such sign components are, e.g., the so-called phonemes, which I should prefer to call taxemes of expression, and which in themselves have no content, but which can build up units provided with a content, e.g., words."

Stratificational linguistics, which originated with Sydney M. Lamb in the early 1960s and which has its roots in Hjelmslev's glossematics, is built on this principle that the relationships are the important part of language structure. In their *Readings in Stratificational Linguistics,* Adam Makkai and David G. Lockwood write:

The major difference between the modern version of stratificational theory and the transformational view is *not* that stratificational linguistics uses unordered rules while the transformationalists use ordered ones. Rather . . . stratificational theory does not use any rules at all, but views linguistic structure as consisting entirely of relationships, so that the notion of "rule" does not have any meaning within it.

While in transformational linguistics the ordered rules specify processes to be performed upon combinations of symbols, stratificationalists view phonology, and in fact all of linguistic structure, as consisting not of processes but of static relationships.

Stratificational linguistics, as its name implies, involves several levels within each of which items are connected to items on the next higher and next lower levels by a network of relationships. For an introduction to the theory and a collection of some of the most important writings on all aspects of stratificational linguistics, see the above anthology by Makkai and Lockwood. The articles included in the present volume are ones that deal in stratificational terms specifically with phonology.

Sydney M. Lamb's "On Alternation, Transformation, Realization, and Stratification" (1964) [52] is a comparison of the ways in which various schools of thought have dealt with the fact that, for example, a phoneme may be realized phonetically in more than one way. He proposes accounting for such phenomena in terms of stratification and realization instead of others' alternation, transformation, or classification. This article includes a much-cited comparison of process description versus realizational rules. At this stage of the theory the idea of realizational networks had not yet been formulated, and the realizations were still stated only in terms of what Lamb then called rules but which might better be termed formulas. These formulas were not rules for processes to be performed as in transformational grammar, but rather statements of static relationships.

Lamb's "Prolegomena to a Theory of Phonology" (1966) [53] is a complete statement of the stratificational position on phonology, with critical discussion of Bloomfieldian and transformational treatments. Here realizational networks appear, to express in graphic form what had heretofore been expressed only by realizational formulas.

In "Vowel Harmony in Hungarian Reexamined in the Light of Recent Developments in Phonological Theory" (1968) [54] the present author compares the way that the phenomena of Hungarian vowel harmony would be treated in Bloomfieldian, generative, and stratificational phonology, with the conclusion that the stratificational solution is to be preferred.

David Lockwood's "Markedness in Stratificational Phonology" (1969) [55] shows how the marked and unmarked features of transformationalists differ from the idea of markedness within stratificational phonology, pointing out the advantages of the stratificationalists' use of unary features in contrast to the Jakobsonian binary ones.

Lockwood's "Neutralization, Biuniqueness, and Stratificational Phonology" (1969) [56] is an analysis of the various prior treatments of these phenomena, with a discussion and demonstration of how they are dealt with in stratificational phonology. In particular he enumerates several varieties of neutralization and shows how each is treated in a stratificational framework. He argues that incorporating Praguian neutralization into stratificational phonology provides additional counterevidence to Halle's rejection of a biunique phonological level.

In "Some Types of Ordering" (1970) [57] Sydney M. Lamb argues that transformational grammar obliterates the distinction between several different types of relationships that are inherent in language by forcing everything into the same mold of ordered mutation rules. He maintains that much of the ordering necessary in transformational grammar is a feature of the system of notation being used, rather than of the language being described. He shows that in stratificational grammar the various types of inherent ordering can each be handled differently, while leaving unordered those things that are not inherently ordered.

BIBLIOGRAPHY 16
Phonematics

A. THEORETICAL DISCUSSION

BRØNDAL, V. (1936) "Sound and Phoneme"

HJELMSLEV, L. (1936) "On the Principles of Phonematics"

—— (1939) "Note sur les oppositions supprimables"

—— (1939) "The Syllable as a Structural Unit"

ULDALL, H. J. (1939) "On the Structural Interpretation of Diphthongs"

FISCHER-JØRGENSEN, E. (1941) "Phonologie, Bericht über Arbeiten in germanischen und romanischen Sprachen"

HJELMSLEV, L. (1943) *Omkring sprogteoriens grundlæggelse;* English translation: (1953) *Prolegomena to a Theory of Language,* translated by Francis J. Whitfield

Reviewed by: GARVIN, P. L. (1954)
HAUGEN, E. (1954)

HJELMSLEV, L. (1947) "Structural Analysis of Language"

FISCHER-JØRGENSEN, E. (1949) "Remarques sur les principes de l'analyse phonémique"

FOURQUET, J. (1949) "Analyse linguistique et analyse phonologique"

FISCHER-JØRGENSEN, E. (1952) "The Phonetic Basis for Identification of Phonemic Elements"

HJELMSLEV, L. (1954) "La stratification du langage"

SIERTSEMA, B. (1954) *A Study of Glossematics*

ULDALL, H. J. (1957) "Outline of Glossematics. Part I: General Theory"

B. APPLICATIONS OF THE THEORY

ULDALL, H. J. (1934) "A Note on Vowel Length in American English"

—— (1936) "The Phonematics of Danish"

BJERRUM, M. (1949) "An Outline of the Faroe Vowel System"

JENSEN, E. (1949) "The Vowel System in the Flensborg By-Laws"

TOGEBY, K. (1951) *Structure immanente de la langue française*

SIERTSEMA, B. (1958) "Problems of Phonemic Interpretation I: Nasalized Sounds in Yoruba"

—— (1959) "Problems of Phonemic Interpretation II: Long Vowels in a Tone Language"

C. BIBLIOGRAPHIES AND BIBLIOGRAPHICAL STUDIES

FISCHER-JØRGENSEN, E. (1949) "Danish Linguistic Activity 1940–48"

HAUGEN, E. (1951) "Directions in Modern Linguistics"

SEBEOK, T. A. (1963) "Selected Readings in General Phonemics (1925–1964)"

D. COLLECTIONS AND ANTHOLOGIES

Recherches Structurales, TCLC Vol. V (1949)

Reviewed by: GARVIN, P. L. (1951)
WELLS, R. S. (1951)
HOCKETT, C. F. (1952)

HJELMSLEV, L. (1959) *Essais Linguistiques, TCLC* XII

BIBLIOGRAPHY 17
Stratificational Phonology

A. THEORETICAL DISCUSSION

HOCKETT, C. F. (1961) "Linguistic Elements and Their Relations"

LAMB, S. M. (1962) *Outline of Stratificational Grammar*

―――― (1963) "On Redefining the Phoneme"

GLEASON, H. A., JR. (1964) "The Organization of Language: A Stratificational View"

LAMB, S. M. (1964) "The Sememic Approach to Structural Semantics"

―――― (1965) "Kinship Terminology and Linguistic Structure"

―――― (1966) "Epilegomena to a Theory of Language"

―――― (1966) *Outline of Stratificational Grammar*

Reviewed by: HOCKETT, C. F. (1968)

CHAFE, W. L. (1968)

PALMER, F. R. (1968)

REICH, P. A. (1968) *Symbols, Relations, and Structural Complexity*

MAKKAI, A. (1969) "The Two Idiomaticity Areas in English and Their Membership"

―――― (1969) "Why Language Is Stratified"

MAKKAI, V. B. (1969) "On the Correlation of Morphemes and Lexemes"

SAMPSON, G. (1970) *Stratificational Grammar: A Definition and an Example*

LOCKWOOD, D. G. (1971) *Introduction to Stratificational Grammars*

B. APPLICATIONS OF THE THEORY

SHIPLEY, W. F. (1964) *Maidu Grammar*

ROGERS, H. E. (1967) *The Phonology and Morphology of Sherbro*

STIMSON, H. M. (1967) "Stress in Peking Phonotactics"

BENNETT, D. C. (1968) "English Prepositions: A Stratificational Approach"

STIMSON, H. M. (1968) "Peking Tonal Hypophonotactics"

―――― (1969) "Peiping Tonal Phonotactics"

LOCKWOOD, D. G. (1969) "Russian Vowel Hypophonology"

MAKKAI, A. (1972) *Idiom Structure in English*

C. BIBLIOGRAPHIES AND BIBLIOGRAPHICAL STUDIES

FLEMING, I. (1969) "Stratificational Theory: An Annotated Bibliography"

D. COLLECTIONS AND ANTHOLOGIES

MAKKAI, A., and D. G. LOCKWOOD (eds.) (in press, 1972) *Readings in Stratificational Linguistics*

IV.a

Phonematics

ON THE DEFINITION OF PHONEME CATEGORIES ON A DISTRIBUTIONAL BASIS*

ELI FISCHER-JØRGENSEN[1]

I. PREVIOUS TREATMENTS

Sapir was probably the first to suggest that phonemes might be grouped into categories according to their possibilities of combination with other phonemes in the speech chain.[2] Bloomfield goes much farther. He maintains[3] that this is the only definition of phoneme categories which is structurally relevant, whereas the classification by distinctive features is irrelevant, because it is in reality a physiological description. This statement is probably too categorical. At any rate it may be maintained that the distinctive features are also found by commutation and can be defined by their mutual combinations, that they must accordingly be considered as linguistic units, and that it is only the next step, the analysis of these features, which is concerned with pure substance.[4] Both classifications would in that case be structurally relevant, and in a complete description of a language phonemes should be classified in both ways: (1) according to their constituent parts (their distinctive features)

and (2) according to their possibilities of combination (their distribution or relations in the speech chain). But this article is only concerned with the second problem, the establishment of phoneme categories on a distributional basis.[5]

Bloomfield did not only demand a distributional definition, he gave a complete analysis of the English phonemic system as an example of his method. But it is a striking fact that in spite of the enormous influence which Bloomfield has had on American linguistics, there have been very few to follow him on this particular point. Not that there have been objections to his method: many American linguists quote this point in Bloomfield's book with approval,[6] but they do not apply his method in their actual language descriptions. G. L. Trager is one of the few exceptions.[7] But it may nevertheless be due to Bloomfield's influence that most American linguists, even in short phonemic descriptions (such as the numerous descriptions of American Indian

---

[1]This paper was read at a meeting of the Cercle linguistique de Copenhague on the 18th of May 1951. Part of the material had been presented at the Nordisk Filologmøde, Helsingfors-Åbo, August 1950. I am grateful to Louis Hjelmslev for many discussions of the problems involved.

[2]E. Sapir, "Sound Patterns in Language" [1] (*Language* 1, 1925, pp. 37–51).

[3]L. Bloomfield, *Language* 1933, pp. 129–130.

[4]Cp. A. Martinet, "Où en est la phonologie?" (*Lingua* 1, pp. 34–58); Roman Jakobson, "On the Identification of Phonemic Entities" [30] (*TCLC* V, 1949, pp. 205–213); Roman Jakobson and J. Lotz, "Notes on the French Phonemic Pattern" (*Word* 5, 1949, pp. 151–158).

[5]Fritz Hintze ("Zum Verhältnis der sprachlichen 'Form' zur 'Substanz'" (*Studia Linguistica* 3, 1949, p. 86 ff.)) uses the terminology "internal" and "external" for these two ways of establishing categories. Knud Togeby (*Structure immanente de la langue française* (*TCLC* VI, 1951, pp. 47 and 89 ff.), which I have been able to utilize for this last version of the present paper) uses the terminology "synthetic" and "analytic."

[6]E.g., B. Bloch and G. L. Trager, *Outline of Linguistic Analysis,* 1942, p. 45; C. F. Hockett, "A System of Descriptive Phonology" [11] (*Language* 18, 1942, pp. 3–21).

[7]"La systématique des phonèmes du polonais" (*Acta Linguistica* 1, 1939, pp. 179–188).

---

*Reprinted from *Acta Linguistica, revue internationale de linguistique structurale* 7.8–39 (1952) by permission.

languages in the *International Journal of American Linguistics*), give a rather detailed statement of the syllabic structure of the language, and in this way present the material on the basis of which the phoneme categories may be established.

In contradistinction to Bloomfield, Trubetzkoy considers the internal description of phonemes as consisting of a definite number of distinctive features and their classification according to these features as the most important task. But he mentions the classification based on different possibilities of combination as a desirable supplement, and gives a classification of Greek consonants along these lines.[8] He emphasizes, however, that it is not possible in all languages to give each phoneme a unique definition in this way. This is certainly true,[9] but it should not be used as a reason for rejecting the method.[10] On the contrary, the different possibilities of establishing subcategories show interesting differences in linguistic structure.

In general the Prague phonologists do not pay much attention to this problem but like the American phonemicists they very often describe the syllabic structure of the language in question, whereas the London school of phonetics is distinguished by its almost complete disregard of syllabic structure.

But other scholars, chiefly in Scandinavian countries, have tried to find methods for a classification of phonemes in this way, partly under direct influence from Bloomfield. H. Vogt has given a detailed analysis of phoneme categories in Norwegian.[11] Hjelmslev has repeatedly called for a relational definition and suggested methods which he found appropriate for this purpose,[12] and he has applied his method to Danish[13] and French.[14] A. Bjerrum has described the categories of the Danish dialect in Fjolde,[15] Ella Jensen has mentioned some possible classifications in the dialect of Houlbjerg,[16] K. Togeby has given a complete description of French combined with a theoretical discussion of the method employed.[17] And J. Kuryłowicz has given original contributions to the methodological discussion.[18] But these various descriptions have been made according to so widely divergent principles that a comparison between the languages described is hardly possible, and it seems therefore highly desirable to take up a general discussion of this question.

II. THE PURPOSE AND METHODOLOGICAL BACKGROUND OF THE PRESENT TREATMENT

The purpose of this paper is to propose a method for establishing distributional categories of phonemes which will give a sound basis for comparisons between languages. This purpose may come into conflict with the endeavor to classify the phonemes of a particular language in the simplest possible way. There will generally be several possible ways of grouping the phonemes of a language, and most authors have chosen one of these ways as the most simple, or as that characterizing the language in the best way, or as the one which has the most evident affinity to the phonetic classification. But for these purposes it has often been necessary to choose criteria of classification which are too specific to allow of any comparison with other languages. This conflict is, however, only real when it is maintained that a language should only be described in one way. When on the other hand it is required (as in the glossematic method) that a

---

[8]*Grundzüge der Phonologie, TCLP* 7, 1939, p. 219.

[9]Although his Burmese example, *loc. cit.* p. 220, was not correct, cp., e.g., Togeby, *op. cit.* p. 15.

[10]As I have done: *Nordisk Tidsskrift for Tale og Stemme* 7, 1945, p. 92.

[11]H. Vogt, "The Structure of the Norwegian Monosyllables" (*Norsk Tidsskrift for Sprogvidenskap* 12, 1942, pp. 5–29).

[12]E.g.: "Langue et parole" (*Cahiers Ferdinand de Saussure* 2, 1942, pp. 29–44) and "La structure morphologique" (*Ve Congrès international de linguistes 1939, Rapports,* pp. 66–93); but his basic point of view is different, since he attempts a purely formal analysis.

[13]"Grundtræk af det danske udtrykssystem med særligt henblik paa stødet" (*Selskab for nordisk Filologi, Årsberetning for 1948–1949–1950,* pp. 12–23).

[14]*Bulletin du Cercle Linguistique de Copenhague* 1948–1949.

[15]A. Bjerrum, *Fjoldemålets lydsystem,* 1944, pp. 118 ff. and 228 ff.

[16]Ella Jensen, *Houlbjergmålet,* 1944, p. 46.

[17]*Structure immanente de la langue française* (*TCLC* VI, 1951), pp. 44–88, particularly pp. 79 ff.

[18]"Contribution à la théorie de la syllabe" (*Bulletin de la Société polonaise de linguistique* 1948), pp. 80–114, particularly pp. 107 ff.; and "La notion de l'isomorphisme" (*TCLC* V, 1949, pp. 48–60).

description of a language should be exhaustive in the sense that all possible classifications should be registered, the conflict is reduced to the observation that different classifications may be preferable for different purposes.

The methodological background of this paper is that of conventional phonemics. This means above all that the procedure is not purely formal, and particularly that identifications (including the identification of units belonging to different languages) are made on the basis of phonetic substance.

The terms "form" and "substance" which were introduced by F. de Saussure and have been employed by several European linguists since then, particularly by Hjelmslev, are perhaps not very happy, because they may suggest all sorts of metaphysical implications which need not interest us here, but it is mostly in these terms that the problem has been treated. Form is here taken to mean a complex of specific linguistic functions (or relations), comprising both the important relation between the two planes (content and expression), which allows the establishment of a restricted number of distinctive units in each plane (e.g., the relation between the expression [sti:m] and the content 'steam') and the relations between these distinctive units within one plane, e.g., between s and t in [sti:m]. These relations cannot be derived from the system of functions of other sciences.—But the end points of the relations may also be described in terms of other sciences, e.g., physics or physiology, and this is the "substance" point of view.

In a previous paper[19] I have discussed the possibility of establishing the inventory of distinctive elements of the expression without taking the phonetic substance into account. The result was that the linguistic analysis cannot start from pure form without taking the substance into consideration. The number of commutable elements in each position (or paradigm) is found through an analysis of the interrelations between sound and meaning (in the case of spoken languages), which presupposes the recognition of differences (as yet perhaps unspecified) in these substances. And the identification of elements in different para-

digms (e.g., p before i and before u; initial and final p) must in many cases take phonetic facts into account. If it does not, the reduction will be either impossible or completely arbitrary (e.g., initial p identified with final k), which would complicate the description of the phonetic manifestation of the elements and thus be in contradiction to the principle of simplicity. In the above mentioned article the problem was simplified by treating commutation and identification as two consecutive steps. But as a matter of fact the statement that p and t are commutable in pin and tin presupposes the identification of the in of pin with the in of tin.[20] This means that these two operations must take place simultaneously, and that the problem of dissolving the chain into phonemes consists in deciding which phonetic differences have to be considered as distinctive and which as automatic. The decision must be based on an interpretation having the purpose of describing all the facts (including the phonetic manifestation) in the simplest way.[21]

Commutation and identification form the basis for the establishment of the categories. A consonant cannot be considered as both initial and final until these two variants have been identified. But when this has been done, it must be possible to define the categories on a purely functional basis, and this whole formal structure may be transferred into another substance without any change in the definitions. It is the merit of glossematics to have emphasized this possibility.

It must also be possible to compare various languages on a purely formal basis, identifying the categories by reference to a general system of formal definitions. This is however not the generally adopted method which consists in identifying expression units in different languages on a phonetic basis.[22] It must be

[19]"Remarques sur les principes le l'analyse phonémique" (*TCLC* V), particularly p. 231.

[20]As emphasized by Buyssens (*Cahiers Ferdinand de Saussure* 8, 1949, pp. 49 ff.

[21]The point of view adopted here, i.e., that commutation and identification must involve substantial considerations if the analysis is to be of any use, is not incompatible with Hjelmslev's theory in its present form. His "purely formal analysis" is not meant as a preliminary linguistic operation, but as a final control of the results gained in this way by trial and error.

[22]Even Togeby (*Structure immanente de la langue française*), who claims to give a purely formal description, employs this traditional method.

emphasized that these two methods will yield quite different results. From a traditional phonemic point of view it is, for instance, perfectly legitimate to compare the syllabic structures of French, Russian, and Finnish, stating the differences in consonant clusters, etc. But from a purely formal point of view it may be different. Starting, for instance, from glossematic definitions, the so-called syllables in these languages are of completely different kinds, since in French their combination is free, whereas in Russian and Finnish some categories of syllables presuppose others. In glossematic terminology the latter type is called direction-syllable, the French type pseudo-syllable. The direction can be shown by further analysis to take place between smaller parts of the syllables. These parts are called accents. But these accents are stresses in Russian and vocoids[23] in Finnish. The Finnish contoids are therefore not consonants, but unspecified constituents. In other languages accents may be manifested by tones, but tones may also formally be constituents (e.g., parts of vowels) if there is no direction between them.—Consonants are defined as presupposing vowels, and vowels as presupposed by consonants. If a language has only the syllabic type cv, not v alone,[24] it can consequently not be said to have vowels and consonants in this sense. And even if two languages possess consonants both in the traditional and in the glossematic sense, their subcategories may be differently defined by the two methods. Suppose, e.g., that one language has the syllabic types V, CV, CVC (i.e., final position presupposing initial position), another V, VC, CVC (—initial position presupposing final position (this combination, by the way, has hardly ever been found)), and a third V, CV, VC, CVC (with free combination between the positions), and all have the consonants p, t, k occurring exclusively in initial position: then, when the categories of consonants are defined by their positions, p, t, k will belong to the

same category in the three languages if the positions are identified on a phonetic basis, but from a formal point of view p, t, k will belong to differently defined categories in all three languages.

This means that it is necessary to distinguish between the two methods of comparison. The purely formal method is the most consistent one, and it is an important task to attempt a description along these lines; but it requires a complete system of general definitions. Such a system is being elaborated by glossematics, but it has not yet been published in detail. The traditional procedure, which is followed here, is in a certain sense a hybrid method, since the elements and the relations are chosen, for the purpose of comparison, on the basis of phonetic similarity. This method may, however, lead to interesting observations, e.g., concerning the affinities between the phonetic qualities of a sound and its syllabic position, and concerning the frequency in actual languages of the theoretically possible categories. Finally the tendencies to free combination or to definite restrictions between different parts of the syllable seem to be more easily formulated when the parts of the syllable are identified on a phonetic basis.

The designation "phoneme," then, is also used here in a conventional sense. It has been defined in many ways, but all definitions have aimed at the same object, namely the first class of distinctive units of the expression (meaning the first class of units met with in a division of the speech chain into smaller and smaller units), of which most members (e.g., English s) are not capable of any further decomposition into successive distinctive units (some members may, however, be capable of such a decomposition; in English ph could be dissolved into the successive units p and h, but ph belongs nevertheless to the same level as s, not to the level of e.g., pr, because it cannot be dissolved into units of which both are capable of functioning in the same environments as the larger unit (ph, p, and h are not distinctive in the same environment, but $pr-, p$, and r are)).

This is not meant as a new definition but simply as a description of what is generally termed a phoneme.[25] It is usual to distinguish

---

[23]It may sometimes be convenient to use Pike's terminology "vocoids" and "contoids" for phonetic units, "consonant" and "vowel" for formal units.

[24]c and v symbolize two different classes of elements, manifested chiefly by vocoids and contoids respectively. C and V symbolize consonants and vowels in the formal sense of the words.

[25]Trubetzkoy (*Grundzüge*, p. 34) defines phonemes as "phonologische Einheiten, die sich nicht in noch kürzere aufeinanderfolgende phonologische

between segmental and suprasegmental phonemes. The latter class (comprising stress and tone) is characterized by not being able to enter into relations of sequence with members of the first class. We shall restrict our discussion to the relations between segmental phonemes.

III. THE BASIC UNIT

The first difficult problem is the choice of the unit which is to be taken as the basis within which the relations operate.

The minimal sign (the "morpheme" according to the American and the Prague terminology) may be discarded at once as not suitable for this purpose,[26] because its internal structure is much too variable: it may, for instance, contain a series of syllables (e.g., French *pantalon*) or consist of a single consonant (*s*) or a group of consonants (e.g., *-st* in German). The same is true of the "word," which, moreover, is a unit of a more dubious kind. This does not mean that the phonemic structure of words and minimal signs should not be described, but only that they should not be chosen as the general frame for the definition of the phoneme categories.

This frame must be some sort of phonemic "syllable." Most linguists who have treated this problem, simply speak of the syllable without giving any definition. K. L. Pike describes the "phonemic syllable" as "the basic structural unit which serves best as a point of reference for describing the distribution of the phonemes in the language in question,"[27] and according to Pike this may be a unit of tone-placement or a unit of stress-placement or of length, or a "morpheme" or it may simply be the phonetic syllable. This point of view is not very different from that held by Togeby, who gives different structural definitions of the syllables of different lan-

guages;[28] and there is probably no escape here: the unit serving as the best basis for describing the relations between phonemes will hardly be structurally the same in all languages. The most suitable method will probably be to choose the structural unit presenting the closest affinity to the phonetic syllable.[29] This implies the possibility of an identification between phonetic syllables in different languages, and such a possibility can in effect be maintained to a very large extent, notwithstanding the fact that the phonetic syllable has been defined in many different ways, and that its very existence has been denied. A discussion of the various definitions will not be attempted in this place. It is considered for this purpose as a unit of speech containing one relative peak of prominence. The division of the chain of speech into syllables may be due simply to the inherent loudness of the successive sounds, but the peaks may be reinforced or altered by arbitrary changes of loudness, and this means may also be used to give a clear delimitation of the units. The rhythmic impression may be reinforced by what Pike calls syllable-timing,[30] i.e., the peaks occur with equal intervals of duration as in Romance languages and in Japanese, where this seems to be a predominant feature.[31] It is in all probability particularly the role played by the inherent loudness of sounds (creating a certain similarity of internal structure) which makes the phonetic syllable a practical point of reference for describing the distribution of phonemes. But it is evident that from a phonetic point of view there will be borderline cases, perceived differently by different people, and such cases will then have to be decided on the basis of the corresponding structural unit in the particular language.

In many languages the syllable can be defined as a unit of tone- or stress-placement. But if we seek a basis for the definition of categories of segmental phonemes; it is not the syllable as a whole, but the syllable minus tones and stresses, i.e., the syllabic base,

---

Einheiten teilen lassen." The restriction "first" introduced here is necessary to exclude the distinctive features. Without this restriction the term "aufeinanderfolgend" is superfluous. If the features are not recognized as distinctive phonemic units, the phoneme will simply be the minimal distinctive unit. Trubetzkoy did not recognize the distinctive features as "phonologische Einheiten," but had taken over the term "successive" from Vachek, who did.

[26]It has been employed by Trubetzkoy, *Grundzüge*, pp. 224 ff.

[27]K. L. Pike, *Phonemics*, 1947, p. 144.

[28]*Structure immanente de la langue française*, pp. 47 and 48.

[29]This is also the common feature of all Pike's different phonemic syllables.

[30]*Phonemics*, 1947, p. 73 a.

[31]B. Bloch, "Studies in Colloquial Japanese IV, Phonemics" (*Language* 26, 1950, pp. 90 ff.).

which must be chosen as the basic unit. In most languages this syllabic base may be defined structurally as the class of the smallest units, of which each (in connection with stress, tone, and intonation, if such units are distinctive in the language in question) is capable of constituting an utterance by itself. "Utterance" is taken to mean the same as Hjelmslev's term "lexia,"[32] e.g., the first unit met with in the analysis, the parts (i.e., the immediate constituents) of which cannot all function as the whole unit.—"Capable of" does not imply that all members of this class are actually found as utterances (e.g., in French most syllables can be found as utterances, but not *pæ̃*), but it implies that the fact that some are not found must be due to accidental gaps in the inventory of signs, and cannot be explained by structural laws of the language preventing particular types from having this function. This means that if the syllabic bases can be divided into two categories with different internal structure, one capable of constituting an utterance, the other not, then the class of syllabic bases as a whole cannot be said to have this function. But this case seems to be very rare. It is often found that one type of syllables, e.g., the unaccented syllables, cannot be found alone, but the syllabic bases of the unaccented syllables will generally be the same as those found in accented syllables. Cases might be adduced where the vowel *ə* is only found in unaccented syllables, but normally this *ə* will not be a separate phoneme but will be identifiable with one or more of the vowels found in accented syllables. There are, however, some real exceptions to which we shall return below.

The fact that the syllabic base is capable of constituting an utterance base is important, because this makes it possible to decide the number of syllables in a chain and to fix the boundaries between them on the analogy of the phonemes found initially and finally in utterances. There may be cases presenting more than one possibility of division; then the choice will be of interest for the interpretation of the concrete words or phrases under consideration,[33] but it cannot have any influence on the establishment of the syllabic types or the possibilities of combination of phonemes, since this double possibility presupposes that both combinations have already been found.

But the opposite case, i.e., that some medial clusters cannot be dissolved into actually occurring final and initial clusters, is relevant to our problem. This is, e.g., the case of *vr* in Italian; and many examples may be adduced from the descriptions of American Indian languages in *IJAL*,[34] and although some may be due to restrictions in the material used, it is evident that the phenomenon is not rare. But generally these cases are exceptions, even within the system of the language in question, and if the descriptions of medial clusters were formulated not in terms of particular phonemes, but in a more general way, the exceptions would often disappear.

But there are very extreme cases of this phenomenon, which may require a different interpretation. Finnish constitutes a good example. In Finnish the only consonants admitted finally are *n, r, l. t, s,* and initially genuine Finnish words have only one consonant; but medially a great diversity of clusters is found, e.g., *ks, rst, mp,* etc. The type *kansa* may be dissolved into *kan* and *sa,* both having a structure permitted initially and finally in an utterance, but the type *maksa,* which is very common, cannot be dissolved in the same way. In Finnish, then, there is discrepancy between the syllabic base (which may be identified on a phonetic basis, and which, in Finnish, may receive a structural definition based on vowel harmony) and the minimal unit capable of constituting an utterance. And in this case it appears to be the best solution that the descrip-

[32]*Grundtræk . . . ;* cp. note 13, above. And the syllabic base corresponds roughly to Hjelmslev's "syllabeme," *ibid.* p. 15.

[33]For a discussion of methods determining the choice, see W. F. Twaddell, "A Phonological Analysis of Intervocalic Consonant Clusters in German" (*Actes du IVe Congrès international de linguistes 1936,* pp. 218–225), and J. Kuryłowicz, "Contribution à la théorie de la syllabe" (*Bulletin de la Société polonaise de linguistique,* 1948, pp. 80–114).

[34]E.g., H. P. Aschmann, "Totonaco Phonemes" (*IJAL* 12, 1946, pp. 34–43); Viola Waterhouse and May Morrison, "Chontal Phonemes" (*IJAL* 16, 1950, pp. 35–39); A. M. Halpern, "Yuma I: Phonemics; II: Morphophonemics" (*IJAL* 12, 1946, pp. 25–33 and 147–151); Paul L. Garvin, "Kutenai I: Phonemics" (*IJAL* 14, 1948, pp. 37–42).

tion of the phoneme categories on a relational basis should be founded on the syllabic base (the division of medial clusters may be undertaken on the analogy of the structure found initially, i.e., before the last consonant), but the fact that a whole class of consonants are only found finally in the syllabic base within the utterance, should not be completely neglected, but must be taken into account in the classification of the consonants.[35] A somewhat similar case would be a language like Keresan,[36] in which no utterance can end or begin with a vowel (the minimal monosyllable being cvc, but which nevertheless has words of the structure cvcvc and cvcvcvc, which, according to the author, should be decomposed into the syllables cv-cvc and cv-cv-cvc (the other theoretically possible decomposition cvc-vc would not be better). The syllabic type cv cannot form an utterance alone, but presupposes a following syllabic base. An exception of a different kind is formed by languages of the Mixteco-type. In Mixteco[37] the minimal

utterance is cvcv or cvv, containing two syllabic bases.

The difficulty, then, is this, that in languages where there is no coincidence between the syllabic base and the minimal unit capable of constituting an utterance, there is no safe means of dissolving medial clusters and delimitating the syllabic bases. A way out of this difficulty would be to choose the (phonemically) minimal utterance as the frame of reference and not the syllabic base, and classify the consonants according to their occurence and combinations initially, finally, and medially in such utterances. But this involves a definition of vowels and consonants on the basis of the utterance (e.g., vowels being capable of forming an utterance alone), which might give some more problems than the definition within the syllable (e.g., in languages where vcv is found, but not v alone). And, in practice, the procedure would not differ much from that proposed here, for it would only be advisable to describe medial clusters in minimal utterances, not dissolvable into smaller parts which in principle might occur alone, and that means that only a few languages would have medial clusters. Taking all utterance-medial clusters into account would complicate the description needlessly, since all combinations of final-initial clusters will normally be found, and restricting "medial clusters" to those found in "words," means the introduction of a rather dubious concept.

IV. THE TECHNIQUE

When the basic unit has been determined the next problem will be how to establish the categories. Two different procedures have been employed: (1) overlapping structural sets and (2) a hierarchy of categories and subcategories. Bloomfield employs the former method, Hjelmslev, Togeby, and Bjerrum the latter. The methods of Vogt and Trager present a mixture of these two procedures.

Structural sets means classes of phonemes having in some respect or other the same relations. In Bloomfield's description of English[38] the consonants form 38 different sets. Thus [ŋ] and [ʒ] form a set, because they are not found initially; [p, t, k, f, m, n] form a

[35]Hjelmslev has suggested a connection between the particular structure of Finnish syllabic bases and the fact that Finnish has vowel harmony. As already mentioned, the Finnish vocoids are, according to Hjelmslev's terminology, accents (because of their heterosyllabic relations) and the contoids are unspecified constituents (neither consonants nor vowels) and therefore not submitted to the same rules of combination as consonants in other languages. —This might also be formulated by saying that in Finnish there is a more intimate connection between the syllables within a word than in most other languages. This appears at two points: (1) vowel harmony, according to which certain categories of vocoids in the final syllable(s) presuppose the presence of certain categories in the first syllable; and (2) the fact that certain initial syllables cannot form utterances alone, but presuppose a following syllable. There is thus presupposition both ways. —A tendency to a similar cohesion is found in languages with distinctive stress (which, according to Hjelmslev, have the same type of syllables as Finnish, if there is presupposition): the weak syllable cannot be found alone as an utterance, it may have particular syllabic bases containing special phonemes (ə), and often there seem to be particular rules for the occurrence of medial consonants and clusters before such weak syllables with ə, e.g., in German.

[36]Robert F. Spencer, "The Phonemes of Keresan" (*IJAL* 12, 1946, pp. 229–236).

[37]K. L. Pike, *Tone Languages*, 1948, pp. 77–94.

[38]*Language*, p. 130 ff.

set, because they occur after [s], and for the same reason [s] forms a set of its own; [s] and [h] form a set because they never occur before [r], etc. The same phoneme may belong to different sets, so that there is mutual overlapping, but different phonemes will generally not all be members of the same sets. The sets have arbitrary numbers, and one phoneme may thus be defined by being a member of sets 1, 5, 8, and 9, another by being a member of sets 3, 5, 7, 10, and so on. In its present form this method can hardly be recommended. It is much too complicated, and it does not allow of any comparison with other languages.—The method might be used for comparisons, if only a few sets based on criteria found in various languages (e.g., four different positions) were employed, and if the numbering were undertaken according to a definite principle.

The hierarchic method may proceed by pure dichotomies (this is the form employed by Trubetzkoy), or it may be modified in such a way as to allow a class to be divided into more than two subclasses; there may be not only one subcategory having a definite relation, and another having an opposite relation, but also two other possibilities: both-and and neither-nor (this is the form employed by Hjelmslev). In both these forms the hierarchic procedure is superior to the procedure based on overlapping sets, it is simpler, and it permits of comparisons between different languages, provided that an appropriate order of the criteria is chosen. There may of course be overlapping in a certain sense, since the same criterion may be used in different branches of the hierarchy at the same level, and the members of the last subcategories must be defined by their membership of this and all the preceding classes, but the hierarchic order and the categories should be respected.

A particular problem concerning the general procedure is the use of statistical considerations. Bjerrum[39] divides the consonants into two groups having in most, but not in all, cases different relations; and Kuryłowicz[40] employs the same method, speaking of primary and secondary functions. This can hardly be recommended; it is difficult to tell just how common the relation must be.

[39]*Fjoldemålets lydsystem*, 1944, p. 230.
[40]"La notion de l'isomorphisme" (*TCLC* V), pp. 56–57.

V. THE CRITERIA AND THEIR ORDER

If we want to divide the phonemes of particular languages into as many subcategories as possible, the use of very specific criteria, different in different languages, can hardly be avoided. This, however, need not impair the possibilities of comparison, provided that these criteria are used at the last stages of the hierarchy to establish the smallest subcategories. But it is important that the criteria used for the larger categories should be such that they can be employed in a very great number of languages.

The descriptions given, e.g., by Trubetzkoy, Vogt, and Trager of Greek, Norwegian, and Polish respectively[41] do not satisfy this requirement. It is evident that they have chosen their criteria and arranged the procedure in such a way as to obtain a close affinity between the classes established on a relational basis and the phonetic classification of phonemes. It is of course interesting that this can be done, but it can only be done by choosing very specific criteria, employed in a rather unsystematic order.—On the whole, any procedure starting with relations between particular phonemes will be of a very limited application, whereas a procedure which, apart from the distinction between consonants and vowels, is mainly based on position, will be of a much more general application.

A. Vowels and Consonants   It will probably be possible in nearly all languages to divide the phonemes into two classes, in such a way that the members of each class are mutually commutable (i.e., are distinctive in a common environment), whereas members of the two different classes are not commutable (i.e., are not found in the same environment) but may be combined in the syllable.[42] If we find, for instance, the syllables *pi, ti, ki, pu, tu, ku, pa, ta, ka*, we may, on this basis, establish a class of mutually commutable members (*p, t, k*) which may be combined with another class of mutually commutable members (*i, a, u*). Theoretically there would be a possibility of identifying members of the two classes in pairs as variants of the same phoneme (e.g., *p* with *a*,

[41]Cp. footnotes 7, 8, and 11.
[42]Cp. Vogt, "The Structure of the Norwegian Monosyllables" (*Norsk Tidsskrift for Sprogvidenskap* 12, 1942, p. 11.)

t with *i*, etc.). This is not done, because there is generally no phonetic motivation for doing it in one definite way rather than in another,[43] but in some cases the phonetic relationship is evident and the identification is made (*i/j, u/w*). In this case we get a third class, whose members are commutable with members of both of the other classes.

If members of one of the two (or three) categories can constitute a syllabic base by themselves (e.g., *i, a, u*), there is an old tradition for calling members of this category vowels, and members of the other category consonants.[44] And in so far "vowels" and "consonants" are defined formally. This is a very common case. But it is not rare that no one phoneme can constitute a syllabic base by itself (i.e., cv is found, but not v). In this case we may follow the traditional procedure and call one of the categories vowels, and the other consonants, giving the name vowels to the category covering roughly the same phonetic zone as the vowels of other languages. This can be done because it has been found that the category capable of standing alone will always cover approximately the same phonetic zone, and in any case include the vocoids.—It is often said that the category forming the syllabic peak is called vowels, but this amounts to the same thing, considering that the phonetic zone normally covered by the vowels (e.g., the zone of the vocoids) has more inherent loudness than the zone covered by the consonants, and the vowels will therefore be perceived as the peak of the syllables. (This is not a formal definition, as Bloomfield[45] and others seem to believe, but it differs from the point of view taken here by considering the phonetic differences in each syllable taken separately.)

Vowels and consonants can be divided into smaller subcategories. Generally the consonants present more possibilities of categor-

izing than the vowels. They will therefore be treated first, and in more detail.

B. Subcategories of Consonants   *(1) Position as the Chief Criterion*   The most general criterion for classifying the consonants must be position. This phenomenon, position or sequence, may be considered from different aspects. Bazell[46] has emphasized that formally it need not be considered as a relation. It might be replaced, for instance, by a definite pitch combined with each phoneme without affecting the system. In this he is certainly right (and that is why the term position is preferred here to order or sequence). Position is here considered as a phonetic feature which, like other features, may be distinctive or not. It is usually said that the difference in meaning between, e.g., *tap* and *pat* is due to the permutation of the initial and final consonants, but this is only a particular consequence of two facts: (1) that in the language considered, initial and final positions are distinctive (cp. *tea∶eat*); (2) that in this language both *p* and *t* (as well as other consonants) are commutable in initial position (*pin, tin*), and also in final position (*hat, hap*). And it would not be impossible to consider position as a distinctive feature belonging to the phonemes. If initial and final position are designated I and II respectively, we would then have two commutable consonants t^I and t^{II}, and we might write *ta, at, tap, pat* as t^Ia, $t^{II}a$, $t^Ip^{II}a$, $t^{II}p^Ia$ and consider position as automatic, but this would complicate the inventory of phonemes enormously, and it is therefore preferable to consider *t* as one phoneme which may be combined with both I and II, but these two elements must somehow be considered as belonging to the phonemic system of the language. And if position is also distinctive within clusters, these positions must also belong to the system.

(2) The Hierarchic Order   The general principle should be to start with the criteria applicable to the greatest number of languages. In languages possessing only the syllabic type cv (and v) there is no possibility of subdivision of the consonants, but this is possible in languages having in addition the types cvc or ccv,

---

[43]"Remarques . . ." (*TCLC* V), pp. 227–228.

[44]Later these terms have also been employed for classes of sounds, i.e., for the sounds functioning as vowels and consonants in well-known languages, particularly Latin; according to this terminology *l* would be called a consonant, even in Czech, although functionally it belongs here to the class both-and.—It is in order to avoid this ambiguity that Pike has proposed the terms vocoids and contoids for the phonetic classes.

[45]*Language,* 1933, pp. 130 ff.

[46]"On the Neutralisation of Syntactic Oppositions" (*TCLC* V, 1949, pp. 77–86), particularly pp. 78–79.

if not all consonants occur in all positions. It may be subject to discussion whether it would be most practical to start with the difference between initial and final consonants or with the difference between their positions in clusters. The occurrence of the types cv + ccv may perhaps be more frequent than the occurrence of cv + cvc (i.e., many languages have no final consonants), but it gives a simpler procedure to start with the difference between initial and final consonants.

The first step should therefore be a classification of the consonants according to their possibility of occurring initially and finally, or, in other words, according to their possibility of combination with position I or position II. These two positions seem always to be distinctive, when both occur in a language. There will be three possibilities: only initial, only final, both initial and final.

The next step should be a division of the categories found at the preceding step according to their capacity of entering into clusters. There will be two possibilities: entering into clusters, and not entering into clusters. It may be asked why we have not proposed a similar step before the classification into initial and final consonants, i.e., a division of the consonants into those which cannot be combined with other consonants in the combination initial-final, i.e., which cannot be combined with other consonants in the same syllabic base, and those which can. The answer is that probably nothing would come out of such a division. If the language has only initial consonants, it is evident that none of these can be combined with final consonants, and if it has both initial and final consonants, it is very improbable that some of the initial consonants should not be able to combine with any final consonants. I do not know of any such language, but the possibility that such a language may be found can of course not be denied, and it would then be possible to introduce such a preliminary criterion of classification.

As the third step we propose a subdivision of the consonants entering into clusters according to their possibilities of entering into initial or final clusters. This division can only be applied to the consonants found both initially and finally, and there will be three possibilities: entering into initial clusters only, entering into final clusters only, and entering into both.

As a further criterion we may use the position of the consonants in clusters. Kuryłowicz[47] starts his classification of Greek consonants with clusters of three consonants as a basis. This may give a simple description of Greek, but it precludes comparison with the numerous languages having clusters of two consonants only. It will be better to start with position of consonants in two-consonantal clusters. Here two positions may be distinguished: the position immediately adjoining the vowel (in the following called position 1) and the position not immediately adjoining the vowel (called position 2). It is practical to start the numbering from the vowel, because then it can be continued for clusters of more than two consonants. The three possible classes at this fourth step will thus be: consonants only occurring in position 1, consonants only occurring in position 2, and consonants occurring in both positions.

The first four steps of the classification as proposed here may be represented schematically as follows (I meaning initial, II: final, cl.: entering into clusters, ÷cl.: not entering into clusters, 1: adjoining the vowel, 2: not adjoining the vowel).

Kuryłowicz maintains that the classification of consonants should always be based on the distribution of consonants in initial clusters, the distribution in final clusters serving only as a corollary.[48] This may be a good method to use for Greek or for the Slavonic languages, but there seems to be no reason for establishing it as a general procedure. But the last column in the diagram (i.e.: consonants entering into both initial and final clusters, and both adjoining the vowel and not) might be further subdivided according to position of the consonants in initial and final clusters respectively. This might be done by choosing arbitrarily the position in initial clusters as the first criterion, and the position in final clusters as the second criterion, or it would be possible to establish four overlapping sets.

In languages containing clusters of more than two consonants, these may be employed for further subdivisions. Bjerrum[49] is of the

[47]"La notion de l'isomorphisme" (*TCLC* V), p. 56.

[48]"Contribution à la théorie de la syllabe" (*Bulletin de la Société polonaise de linguistique*, 1948), pp. 107 ff.

[49]*Fjoldemålets lydsystem*, p. 218.

Consonants

(1)	I			II			I—II								
(2)	÷ cl.	cl.		÷ cl.	cl.		÷ cl.	cl.							
(3)		I cl.			II cl.			I cl.			II cl.			I—II cl.	
(4)		1	2	1—2		1	2	1—2		1	2	1—2	1	2	1—2	1	2	1—2

opinion that clusters containing two consonants will be a sufficient basis for the classification, since more comprehensive clusters are nearly always composed of clusters of two already registered. This argument is hardly tenable. In the first place the rule is not absolute, although it is valid in many languages. Hjelmslev[50] has formulated the "empirical law" that clusters of three consonants can always be dissolved into two clusters of two consonants (1 + 2 + 3 dissolved into 1 + 2 and 2 + 3) already found in the language. But there are exceptions, e.g., in Russian, where *mgl-* and *mgn-* occur initially, but *mg-* does not, and *mzd-* is found, whereas *mz-* is not. And a good many of the clusters of 3 and 4 consonants in Kutenai, as described by Garvin[51] cannot be dissolved.—But perhaps the rule is valid in a more general form, namely that consonants adjoining the vowel in clusters of more than two consonants are also found adjoining the vowel in clusters of two, and that consonant number 2 (counting from the vowel) is also found as first consonant in clusters of two, e.g., the group *sgv-* would involve that *v-* is found in groups like *kv-, sv-,* and *g-* in *gr-, gl-,* but not necessarily *gv.*[52]— But even if the rule is valid in this form, it cannot be used as an argument against undertaking further classifications on the basis of clusters of 3 consonants; on the contrary: it would mean that such a further classification would be possible, since it would not involve a complete redistribution, but respect the hier-

archy already established; and the rule cannot be reversed, so that all clusters consisting of two members may be combined into clusters of three. Generally the number of clusters consisting of more than two consonants is more restricted than the number of clusters consisting of two. It might therefore be possible to divide the given subcategories further according to the function of the consonants in clusters of more than two members.

(3) The Actual Occurrence of the Categories There are some interesting differences in the actual occurrence of corresponding categories at different steps. This concerns particularly steps 1 (initial and final consonants) and 4 (consonants adjoining and not adjoining the vowel) as compared with the first division into consonants and vowels.

In most languages the phonemes can be divided into two rather comprehensive classes: consonants and vowels, whereas the class "both-and" is usually small when it exists at all. Contrariwise with the initial and final consonants, where it will often be found that the class "both-and" comprises most of the consonants of the language, supplemented by small classes of purely initial or purely final consonants; or the class "both-and" may be the only class.—It is also frequently found that the class "only initial" comprises most or all of the consonants, supplemented by a small class of "both-and." A third possibility is this: that the two classes "only initial" and "both-and" are of equal importance.—But the class "only final" is generally small, and it seems never to be the only class found. Moreover it is very rare to find the two classes "only initial" and "only final" in the same language. The only well-known example always quoted is *h/η* in English and German and in some other languages, but even this exception may perhaps be discarded, since *η* may be considered = *n* + *g*. Yuma seems to present both cate-

[50]*Proceedings of the Second International Congress of Phonetic Sciences 1935*, p. 53.

[51]*Op. cit., IJAL* 14, 1948, pp. 37 ff.

[52]This is the case in Danish, but as *k* is not found after *s*, it would also be possible to interpret *sg-* as *sk-* and *sgv-* as *skv-*, and then there would not be any exception, since *kv-* occurs. Cf. Uldall, *Proceedings of the Second International Congress of Phonetic Sciences*, p. 57.

gories, but the facts might be interpreted differently.[53] Anyhow the phenomenon is rare. This means that normally all consonants are mutually commutable either initially or finally (and the same is true—mutatis mutandis—of the vowels), and that the further division of consonants (and vowels) into subcategories is only a further redistribution of elements which all belong to the same analytical level.

Looked at from the phonetic aspect this fact may be formulated like this: sounds found initially and finally in the marginal parts of the syllable are generally so closely related phonetically that they may be reduced two by two as variants of the same phoneme. A phonetic explanation of this may be that it is of no importance for the syllable as a phonetic unit that initial and final consonants should be phonetically of different types (excepting their particular way of pronunciation as "explosive" and "implosive"—"releasing" and "abutting" in Stetson's terminology—pronunciations which may be combined with all types of sounds), whereas it is of importance that there is a distinct peak in the syllable and therefore the classes of vowels and consonants are normally phonetically rather different. A consequence of this is that whereas it is mostly possible to identify two categories called vowels and consonants in different languages on the basis of their phonetic type, this is not possible for the subcategories of consonants.

There are, however, certain affinities between position and phonetic type: the sound *h* is often found exclusively in initial position, and it is not rare that voiced consonants, as distinguished from unvoiced, are found only initially (e.g., in some Germanic and Slavonic languages). And if the class of phonemes occurring finally (generally it will be the class of "both-and") is very small, it happens very often that it comprises exclusively dentals (e.g., Greek, Italian, Finnish) or nasals (e.g., Mandarin Chinese, Mixteco, and various African languages). It is hardly accidental that precisely these types show a particular power of resistance in sound history. They are evidently more capable than others of standing in the final part of the syllable, which, as shown by Grammont and verified by others, is weaker than the initial part and exposed to all sorts of weakenings and assimilations.[54] But these affinities are only slight and cannot form any basis of identifications of categories between different languages. Such identifications must be based on position in the syllable.

Corresponding to the three possible categories at step 1 (initial, final, both-and) we find at step 4 the three categories: only occurring in position 1 (adjoining the vowel), only occurring in position 2 (not adjoining the vowel), and occurring in both positions. But the actual occurrences of these categories are different. As stated above, it is extremely rare to find the categories "only initial" and "only final" in one and the same language; but the corresponding categories "only in position 1" and "only in position 2" are often found together. This does not, however, imply that (as in the case of vowels and consonants) some of them might be reduceable to variants of one and the same phoneme, for they may all occur separately with mutual commutation, and so cannot be reduced.—The frequency of the two extreme categories means that position in clusters is often distinctive for only a few consonants. But if it is distinctive in one case, the other distributions can be regarded as defective, and it is perfectly legitimate to define the consonants by their possibilities of combination with positions 1 and 2. If there is no case of distinction, it may nevertheless be possible to distinguish two categories on the basis of their possibilities of mutual combination (e.g., if the only clusters are *pr, tr, kr, pl, tl, kl*, there is a category *p, t, k*, and a category *r, l*), but if these categories are identified with the categories occurring in positions 1 and 2 in other languages, then a feature (position) which is only phonetic in one language has been identified with one that is phonemic in another.

The affinity between the two classes "only

---

[53]A. M. Halpern, "Yuma I, Phonemics" (*IJAL* 12, 1946, pp. 25–33). There are 6 consonants found only initially in words (but 4 are velarized or palatalized and may perhaps be considered as clusters), and 3 found only finally (ł, ł^y, t^y); but these latter are found initially in unaccented syllables within words.

[54]The specific power of resistance of dentals must be due to their place of articulation (an organ which can be moved with great precision (the tongue tip) articulating against a hard and fixed object). The nasals on the other hand may perhaps be protected by a partial fusion with the preceding vowel, and perhaps by their role as part of the tonal basis (the languages quoted are all tone languages).

in position 1" and "only in position 2" with certain types of sounds will be greater than was the case with the corresponding classes of initial and final consonants. It is not rare that the former comprises nasals and liquids, and the latter mostly stops and fricatives; thus the type *pr-* is common initially and *-rp* finally. This has the well-known phonetic explanation that the shifting between peaks and valleys of prominence (or crests and troughs in Pike's terminology) will be smoother if the consonants immediately adjoining the vowel have more inherent loudness than the consonants farther away from the peak. But it should not be forgotten that this is only essential in languages which do not use other phonetic means of delimiting the phonetic syllables (e.g., the Germanic languages). In languages with a fresh stress-onset before each syllable or with syllable-timing, the rules need not be so strict; sometimes such languages (e.g., the Romance languages) also prefer the above-mentioned type, which from a phonetic point of view may perhaps be called the optimal type of syllable; but others do not, and this "optimal" type of syllable is by no means so common as it appears from the classical textbooks of phonetics (Jespersen, Sievers, etc.). It is not at all rare to find particularly nasals entering into the category of phonemes never adjoining the vowel in clusters (position 2, type *nta*); this is the case, e.g., in Terena,[55] and Cuicateco,[56] where the affinity is therefore opposite, or there may be no affinity at all.

C. Subcategories of Vowels The vowels may be classified according to similar principles. Corresponding to the first stage in the classification of the consonants, it would be possible to start with a classification into vowels found only initially in syllables, only finally, and both initially and finally. But the type vc is often of restricted frequency, and it seems in these cases to be accidental which vowels are found in this position and which not; on the other hand, the possibility of occurring finally or not seems to yield a good basis for a classification, e.g., in German and Dutch. So it would perhaps be preferable to divide the vowels into

categories according to their possibilities of occurring: only before final consonants, only alone finally, or/and in both positions. Step 2 should be a classification according to their possibilities of entering into clusters (diphthongs and triphthongs), or not, and step 3 a classification according to their positions in these clusters.

D. Discussion of Further General Criteria It is questionable whether any further general rules can be given. This does not mean that the classification in each particular language should necessarily stop here. Further subdivisions may be made according to the particular phonemes entering into mutual combinations. But a comparison between different languages at these stages would be difficult. In languages containing not dissolvable medial clusters further subdivisions should take this fact into account.

Togeby[57] has given a complete classification of the phonemes of French according to a procedure which is intended to be general, and he makes an interesting attempt to continue the general procedure two steps further. After having divided the phonemes into consonants and vowels, he proceeds in much the same way as proposed here,[58] establishing categories of consonants on the basis of their position initially or finally in the syllable and of their adjoining the vowel or not. But there are some differences in detail. The latter division is, for instance, not restricted to the occurrence in clusters, so that all consonants are registered as adjoining the vowel.

Togeby's next stage is a subdivision on the basis of syncretisms. The class "initiale-finale vocalique" comprising ʃ, *z, m,* is thus divided into ʃ (not entering into syncretisms), *m* (entering into syncretism with *n*), and *z* (entering into syncretism with *s*).—A purely practical difficulty involved in this criterion is the general disagreement about syncretisms (neutralizations). Most American phonemicists do not distinguish between syncretisms and defective distribution. In Europe this distinction is generally made, but according to divergent principles. But apart from this prac-

[55]Margaret Harden, "Syllable Structure in Terena" (*IJAL* 12, 1946, pp. 60–63).
[56]Doris Needham and Marjorie Davis, "Cuicateco Phonology" (*IJAL* 12, 1946, pp. 139–146).

[57]*Structure immanente de la langue française* (*TCLC* VI, 1951), pp. 79–88.
[58]We have both been influenced by Hjelmslev.

tical difficulty it might be asked why syncretisms are considered as more fundamental
than defective distribution in general. Togeby
does not give any reason for his preference,
but it might be argued that syncretisms seem
to constitute a very stable part of the system
of a language, normally extended to foreign
words, even when other new combinations are
adopted. But at any rate the subdivision on the
basis of syncretisms with particular other phonemes does not allow of any comparison between different languages; it would probably
be better to divide according to the criterion:
entering into syncretisms or not. (On the whole
syncretisms may probably be described more
simply on the level of the distinctive features).

The last stage in Togeby's division is
called "extension." Here the phonemes of the
last classes are further subdivided according
to their mutual relations as "intensive" or
"extensive." These terms are used in a rather
vague sense, "extensive" meaning: capable of
entering into more combinations compared
with the other(s), depending on syncretisms
or defective distributions or, perhaps simply
on frequency. The idea of establishing this
as a general criterion is ingenious, but it might
be objected that the concept is somewhat too
vague to allow of a precise comparison, and
that it may be rather accidental whether phonemes entering into an evident opposition as
extensive and intensive will be found together
in the last subdivisions. In many cases, by the
very reason of the difference in distribution,
they will belong to different subcategories.

When a phoneme has received a unique
definition, Togeby refrains from any further
characterization on the basis of the criteria
of later stages. The possibility of continuing
in such a way that all phonemes are characterized (as far as possible) according to all criteria should however be taken into consideration.

VI. STRUCTURAL LAW OR
ACCIDENTAL GAPS[59]

A. The General Problem   Most linguists who
have established phoneme categories on a distributional basis have attempted to arrive at a
specific definition of each phoneme (in so far

as this has been possible in the particular language) by utilizing all differences of distribution. Hjelmslev seems to be the only exception.
After having divided the consonants on the
basis of the two critera 1) initial or final, 2) adjoining the vowel or not, he refrains from further subdivisions. One reason has been that
further criteria would be too particular to allow
of comparisons between languages. This is
perhaps true, but provided that the first criteria
have been such that the existing possibilities
of comparison have been utilized, this consideration should not prevent us from attempting an exhaustive categorizing of the phonemes of the particular language. Another
reason has been the fear of getting beyond the
limit between structural laws and accidences
of utilization in the given stock of words. This
indeed is a very difficult problem.[60]—Generally
one has a vague feeling that there is a difference, and there would be general agreement
in the extreme cases: anyone would probably
admit that *prust* would be a possible monosyllable in English, although it does not exist,
whereas *mlgapmt* would not. The question is
whether we can find valid arguments in the
particular language, and whether it is possible
to find general rules for all languages.

Many linguists have mentioned this problem briefly without attempting any analysis of
it;[61] other have implicitly fixed such a limit;
it is for instance evident from the examples
given by V. Mathesius[62] that he considers
combinations between consonants in clusters
as submitted to rules, whereas combinations
between vowels and consonants are considered
as accidental. Bloomfield,[63] on the other hand,
defines the English vowels by means of their
possibilities of combination with the following consonants, and consequently he must con-

[59]I am indebted to H. Spang-Hanssen for some
improvements of the formulation of this chapter.

[60]It is presupposed in this argument that the
aim of the description with which we are concerned
is not simply an enumeration of the combinations
of phonemes found in the given syllables and words,
but the formulation of general laws governing these
combinations, allowing for possible combinations
not utilized in the given vocabulary.

[61]E.g., A. Martinet, "La Phonologie du mot en
danois" (*BSL*, 1937), p. 6; A. W. de Groot, "Structural Linguistics and Phonetic Law" (*Archives néerlandaises* 17, 1941), p. 92; A. Bjerrum, *Fjoldemålets
lydsystem*, p. 117; K. L. Pike, *Phonemics*, 1947, pp.
73 ff. and 81 ff.

[62]*TCLP* 1, 1929, pp. 67–84.

[63]*Language*, 1933, p. 134.

sider these combinations as submitted to rules. Vogt[64] defines the Norwegian vowels by means of their combinations with the preceding consonant clusters, but somewhat hesitatingly, and he emphasizes that restrictions here may be accidental and that the vague feeling one has for such differences can probably be stated by linguistic means in terms of structural rules, articulatory patterns and statistical frequency.[65] These very brief remarks at the end of Vogt's article seem to include the essential aspects of the problem. In the following pages a somewhat more detailed analysis will be attempted.[66]

First it must be emphasized that it is theoretically impossible to fix a non-arbitrary borderline between law and accident. Laws may be stated as deviations from accidental distribution; and there are many degrees of deviation. But not all cases are equally dubious.

In the first place it should be kept in mind that a gap—e.g., the non-occurrence of a specific cluster—may be due to rules having a different place in the hierarchy of categories. And as this hierarchy has been established in such a way as to begin with the more general classes, it follows that the higher the rule is placed in the hierarchy the greater is the number of particular cases which it will generally cover, and the safer it is. An example may illustrate this: the fact that the cluster -sp is not found in a certain language may be due to a very general rule (covering many other gaps) that the language in question has no final consonants; it will also be due to a very general rule, if final consonants are found, but no clusters; it will be due to a somewhat more specific, but still comprehensive, rule if clusters are found but no final clusters, and to a still more specific rule if final clusters are found but none with s adjoining the vowel, and none with p not adjoining the vowel, and the rule may be somewhat more restricted, if only one

of the two consonants does not occur in this position, but this rule might still comprise the non-occurrence of, e.g., st and šk. In all these cases we may maintain with relative certainty that the lack of the cluster sp is due to structural laws of the language. But if the only explanation which can be alleged is the very fact that sp has not been found, then the chance that we are on the borderline between structural law and contingency is very great.

In these cases it is necessary to consider the relative frequency of the phonemes in the given position (not the frequency in a text, but the frequency in the material of words). In German j is not found before ɔi. This may be due to pure accident, for initial j is relatively infrequent compared with other initial consonants, and the dipththong ɔi is also relatively rare in other combinations. The probability of their occurring together is therefore not very great, and the non-occurrence need not be due to a specific law preventing this particular combination. On the other hand, there does not seem to be a similar explanation of the lack of, e.g., tl- in English. And the systematic nature of this gap seems to be corroborated by the lack of dl-. One would probably, on the whole, be more inclined to recognize a law if the occurrence or the non-occurrence can be formulated in terms of phonetically similar groups of phonemes (e.g., dentals, high vowels, etc.) and think of an accidental gap if this is not the case. Psychologically this is of course of importance. Structurally it might be motivated by the fact that in the former case the rule could be formulated in a more general way in terms of distinctive features. But this is dubious.

It is evident that if not only combinations of two, but of three, four, or more elements are considered, then the chance of finding all possible combinations realized within the (always restricted) word-stock of the language will be smaller. It is not very probable that all combinations of str- with different final clusters will be found, and consequently it cannot be proved that the non-occurring combinations are excluded by a structural law.

It is perhaps this consideration which is behind Twaddell's remark about English;[67]

---

[64]"The Structure of the Norwegian Monosyllables" (Norsk Tidsskrift for Sprogvidenskap 12, 1942), p. 25.

[65]Op. cit., p. 29.

[66]The same problems arise for the descriptions of word structure, cp. Uhlenbeck, De Structuur van het Javaanse Morpheem, 1949, pp. 5–10. He distinguishes between negative and positive structural laws. But if these positive laws include simply the possibility of combination, it is only a reversal of the negative laws.

[67]On Defining the Phoneme (Language Monograph 16, 1935), p. 50.

"We find, in American English, that all fundamental characteristics involving the absence of (presumably potential) distinctive forms can be correlated with immediately preceding or following phonetic fractions, including the omnipresent factor of stress." And he gives the example that *fet* is a possible syllable in English, because the combinations *fe-* and *-et* occur. But in this general form (i.e., if we find x + y and y + z, then x + y + z is possible) the rule is not valid, either in English or in other languages.

B. Empirical Rules Concerning the Connection Between Different Parts of the Syllable   Twaddell's assertion might be true if the syllabic base consisted simply of a series of phonemes and did not allow of any further division into parts or units. But the division into central and marginal units (comprising vowels and consonants) and into initial and final clusters proves to be significant from this point of view. —It is not a theoretical necessity, but it is an empirical fact that in most languages there are relatively strict rules for the combinations within the units, but not for the combinations at the limits, i.e., between phonemes belonging to different units. The consonantal and vocalic clusters actually found in a language will normally be of a restricted number (compared to the theoretical possibilities), and the phonemes found in the different positions in these clusters will be still more restricted, so that the clusters found can normally be said to belong to a few frequently recurring types, and thus it will not be possible to maintain that the non-occurring clusters are simply accidental gaps. —It is true that there are languages possessing a very great number of different clusters of various types (e.g., some American Indian languages) and in these languages it might be possible to assume that the non-occurrence of some of the clusters were simply due to accidental gaps. But in most languages there are laws not only for the combination of two adjoining phonemes, but also for the combinations of three and more if such occur. It is however very rare that there are any rules for the connection between initial and final consonants, or consonant clusters (that is why Twaddell's example *fet* is tenable), although a certain tendency to avoid the same consonants or the same phonetic types of consonants immediately before and after the vowel has been discovered in various languages;[68] but generally it is only a tendency.

It seems also to be very rare to find rules for the combination between the initial consonantal unit and the central unit, not only so that the combination of the first and last member in groups of three members can be said to be free (i.e., if *pr* and *ri* are found, then *pri* is a possibility), but also so that even the combination of two phonemes (a single initial consonant and a following vowel) seems to be free. Normally all theoretically possible combinations are found, and if not, the non-occurrence can often be explained by the fact that one or both of the phonemes are relatively rare in this position, so that it is statistically justified to speak of an accidental gap. In the combinations of three phonemes, for example *pri,* the probability of finding accidental gaps, and consequently the justification of considering non-occurrence as accidental, is greater, since more elements are involved, and some clusters or vowels may be rare.[69]

The connection between the central unit and the final consonantal cluster seems also to be relatively free, i.e., there are less strict rules than for combinations within the units, but often it is not so free as the connection between the initial consonant and the central unit. There may be some restrictions, which can hardly be accidental. Twaddell mentions the occurrence of vowels before *r* in English; in Danish the short vowels *i, y, u* do not occur before final nasal consonant; and before *r* there

---

[68]W. F. Twaddell, "Combinations of Consonants in Stressed Syllables in German" (*Acta Linguistica* 1, pp. 189–199 and 2, pp. 31–50); H. Vogt, *op. cit.,* p. 22 (Norwegian); E. M. Uhlenbeck, *De Structuur van het Javaanse Morpheem,* 1949, p. 10 (in Javanese the types clvl and crvr do not occur); Trnka, "Die Phonologie in čechisch und slovakisch geschriebenen Arbeiten" (*Archiv für vergleichende Phonetik* 6, 1943, pp. 65–77), mentions that repetition of the same phoneme before and after the vowel in English shows foreign origin or expressiveness.

[69]In German the gaps after clusters of two consonants concern particularly the rare vowels *ö* and *ü* (e.g., *ö:* is not found after *gl-, gn-,* and others). Among the clusters of three consonants, some are relatively rare and are consequently only found before a few vowels (ʃ*pl,* e.g., only before *i:, i, ai* (and in foreign words *e*)). These gaps are accidental.

is no distinction between *i, y, u* and *e, ø, o* (the pronunciation varies).[70] There may also be restrictions concerning the combination of groups: in German and Dutch diphthongs are not found before *r*,[71] and there are also definite restrictions to the consonantal clusters found after diphthongs; in the Germanic languages long vowels do not occur before *ŋ* (and it is possible that both long vowels and *ŋ* should be interpreted as clusters). And there are certainly languages where consonant clusters do not occur at all after long vowels (in Germanic languages a certain tendency to avoid this is obvious). This means that in many languages there is a more intimate connection between the central unit and the final one than between the central unit and the initial one. And this might serve as a further argument for the analysis of the syllabic base proposed by Kuryłowicz,[72] namely C + (V + C). (This is an analytical operation and does not prevent the establishment of vowels and consonants as the two main categories of phonemes. The establishment of categories is based upon the analysis, but does not coincide with it).

The empirical rules concerning accidence or law in the combination of different parts of the syllable mentioned on the preceding pages, seem in any case to be valid for well-known languages. This means that Vogt goes too far, when he establishes categories of vowels in Norwegian defined by their possibilities of combination with preceding consonant clusters, and that Trnka[73] goes too far when he describes English vowels in terms of their ability to combine with preceding or following consonants and consonant clusters. The same thing can be maintained of Abrahams' definition of Danish consonants,[74] particularly of

his definition of the difference between *t* and *d*, consisting in the restrictions of combination between the cluster *dj* and a following vowel. —On the other hand, it will often be possible to go farther than Hjelmslev, who does not use combinations between particular phonemes within the clusters to define smaller subcategories. And it should not be forgotten that the assumption of accidental gaps has consequences for the commutation. When the gap is accidental, the combination in question is possible, and it does not matter for the commutation that a word-pair with a minimal difference is not found, provided that it can be constructed without breaking the laws of the language. The border between law and contingency should be established for each language, and the accidental gaps should be utilized for the commutation, and all structural laws for the establishment of subcategories of phonemes.

It should be possible to verify the validity of the empirical rules concerning the relations between the different parts of the syllable, and of the hierarchy of more or less general laws, established above, by an inquiry into the treatment of loanwords containing combinations of phonemes not occurring in the receiving language. If the non-occurrence was due to an accidental gap, the introduction of the foreign word should not make any difficulties, e.g., the introduction of a word *"prust"* in English. But the more general the law forbidding this combination, the more difficult it would be to introduce the word without any change.—Thus the word *sklerose* has been introduced into Danish without too many difficulties (although the group *skl-* is not found in Danish words), since clusters of the type *spl, skr*, etc., exist, i.e., clusters with *s, k*, and *l* in the positions required, and the combinations *sk-* and *kl-* exist. The same thing is true about the group *pn-* (*pneuma*), since *pl, pr* and *kn, gn* occur. *ps-* is more difficult, since *s* is not found elsewhere as a second member of an initial group, and the *p* is therefore usually left out. A language having initial clusters but no final clusters, should then have more difficulty in introducing a final cluster than an unknown initial cluster (and still more if final single consonants were also unknown).—But only the relative difficulty of assimilation would be of interest in this connection, not the absolute

[70]In the Danish dialects described by Ella Jensen and Bjerrum (cp. notes 15 and 16), the combination between vowel and final consonant seems also to be submitted to certain rules.

[71]In the historical development this has been avoided in two different ways: in Dutch by not diphthongizing long *i:, u:, y:* before *r* (e.g., *vuur*); in German by inserting an *ə* and developing a new syllable (*Feuer*). These particular rules before *r* may be explained phonetically, cp. L. L. Hammerich, *Tysk Fonetik*, pp. 140–141.

[72]*TCLC* V, pp. 50 ff.

[73]*A Phonological Analysis of Present-Day Standard English* (*English Studies*, 1935).

[74]*Tendances évolutives des occlusives germaniques*, 1949, p. 96.

difficulty, for this depends also on social and psychological factors: many European languages are more inclined to take over foreign words without alterations nowadays than some centuries ago. In Finnish all initial clusters were simplified in older loanwords; but in recent loanwords clusters can be found. And this is not simply a question of time, but of social attitude.—There are linguistic communities where the "correct" pronunciation of foreign words is considered very important (German is a typical example), others where this pretension does not exist. These social differences must be taken into account in an evaluation of the material.

The above observations, and also the proposals concerning a fixed procedure for the classification of phonemes for comparative purposes are of a preliminary nature and do not pretend to give definitive solutions. Many questions need further discussion.—

And it should not be forgotten that for other purposes other classifications may be preferable. Position seems to be a useful basis for comparative purposes, but for the description of a single language the relations between particular phonemes might be considered equally essential, e.g., the fact that in English p, t, k adjoining the vowel are only found after s.[75]

Finally we want to emphasize that the result of such a classification depends on the way the phoneme inventory has been established. The more the inventory is reduced, the greater will be the uniformity of distribution, and the more restricted the possibilities of classification on distributional grounds. These two aims of the analysis (to get few phonemes, and many categories), seem to a certain extent to be in mutual contradiction.

[75]For an interesting description of English consonant clusters from this point of view, cp. the article by Mel Most (to appear in *Word*).

BIBLIOGRAPHY 18
Distribution

FIRTH, J. R. (1935) "The Use and Distribution of Certain English Sounds: Phonetics from a Functional Point of View"

HARRIS, Z. S. (1954) "Distributional Structure"

VOGT, H. (1954) "Phoneme Classes and Phoneme Classification"

HARRIS, Z. S. (1955) "From Phoneme to Morpheme"

SIGURD, B. (1955) "Rank Order of Consonants Established by Distributional Criteria"

HARARY, F., and H. H. PAPER (1957) "Toward a General Calculus of Phonemic Distribution"

DIDERICHSEN, P. (1958) "The Importance of Distribution versus Other Criteria in Linguistic Analysis"

SPANG-HANSSEN, H. (1958) "Typological and Statistical Aspects of Distribution as a Criterion in Linguistic Analysis"

HOUSEHOLDER, F. W., JR. (1962) "The Distributional Determination of English Phonemes"

SAPORTA, S. (1963) "Phoneme Distribution and Language Universals"

AUSTERLITZ, R. P. (1967) "The Distributional Identification of Finnish Morphophonemes"

See also the following articles in this volume:

PIKE, K. L. (1947) "Grammatical Prerequisites to Phonemic Analysis" [15]

BLOCH, B. (1948) "A Set of Postulates for Phonemic Analysis" [16]

HOCKETT, C. F. (1949) "Two Fundamental Problems in Phonemics" [17]

PIKE, K. L. (1952) "More on Grammatical Prerequisites" [18]

BLOCH, B. (1953) "Contrast" [19]

51

THE COMMUTATION TEST
AND ITS APPLICATION
TO PHONEMIC ANALYSIS*

ELI FISCHER-JØRGENSEN[1]

The practice of phonemic analysis is as old as alphabetic writing, and some of its basic operations, including the commutation test, were described as long ago as the twelfth century: "Now I shall take eight of these letters . . . and place each of them in turn between the same two consonants."[2] But it was not until around 1930 that phonemics, as an integral part of the new structural approach to language, became a branch of linguistics in its own right, with an elaborate terminology and definite operational procedures. It was, however, a multiple start. One may distinguish, roughly speaking, at least four different centers where methods for a structural analysis of the expression side of language were developed. These were Prague, London, the United States, and Copenhagen. If one goes by printed evidence, the beginning year for Prague was 1928, for London 1929, for the United States 1921 (Sapir) or perhaps 1933 (Bloomfield), and for Copenhagen 1935. The mutual influence between these centers was, up till the end of the second world war, remarkably scanty.[3] There was, however, close contact between Prague and Copenhagen. From the very start of the Linguistic Circle in Copenhagen in 1931, the works of the Prague linguists were the object of animated discussions which have left their traces in the works of several of its members. It was the reading of Trubetzkoy's and Roman Jakobson's first papers on phonemics which decided the present writer to specialize in phonemics and phonetics, and the subsequent works of Roman Jakobson have been a constant source of inspiration.[4]

The subject treated in this paper is one which is relevant for all types of structural linguistics, but it occupies a more central position in Prague phonology and in glossematics than in most Anglo-Saxon approaches, a testimony to the influence from Ferdinand de Saussure common to the former two schools. It may perhaps be said that in the London and the Yale schools almost all emphasis is laid on syntagmatic functions, whereas in the Prague school it is on paradigmatic functions (commutation is the paradigmatic function par excellence). In glossematics, equal importance is attached to both types of function.

In every structural description it is a primary task to reduce the infinite number of variants to a finite set of invariants. This is normally done by a combination of two operations: (1) finding a restricted number of distinctive (commutable) elements in each environment (paradigm), each comprising a

[1]An earlier version of this paper was presented to the Linguistic Circle of Copenhagen, April 19, 1955. The final version has profited by discussions with members of the Circle. I am particularly indebted to Jørgen O. Jørgensen and Børge Spang-Thomsen for valuable critical remarks.

[2]*First Grammatical Treatise, the Earliest Germanic Phonology, An Edition, Translation and Commentary* by Einar Haugen (= Language Monograph No. 25, 1950), p. 15.

[3]It is a good thing that this period of isolation is now over; the fact that Roman Jakobson changed his sphere of activity to America has certainly contributed largely to this end and accelerated the mutual stimulation and convergent development which may now be observed.

[4]An investigation of the relations between vowels and colors based directly on his admirable book *Kindersprache, Aphasie und allgemeine Lautgesetze* (Uppsala, 1941) could not be compressed into the space available in this volume.

*Reprinted from *For Roman Jakobson* (Mouton, 1956), pp. 140–151, by permission.

number of free variants; (2) identifying elements from different environments in order to obtain a small number of invariants, each comprising a certain number of bound variants. In actual analysis these two operations cannot be separated, since units in the same environment cannot be compared until the environments have been identified; it is, however, possible to distinguish the two operations in a theoretical discussion. The problem of identification has been treated in detail in a previous paper.[5] Here attention will be focused on the problem of commutation.

Below we shall adopt the glossematic distinction between expression plane and content plane, each comprising form and substance, the substance of expression consisting of sounds (or letters, etc.), the substance of content consisting of meanings.

The general principle of commutation can now be given the preliminary formulation that two units are commutable if the replacement of one by the other in the same paradigm (environment) is capable of entailing a change in the other plane of the language.[6]

Practically all structural linguists use the commutation test, and all would agree with the more restricted formulation that if a difference

in meaning can be caused by replacing one sound with another in the same environment, then these sounds are in "distinctive opposition" (Prague terminology), "contrast" (American terminology), or "there is commutation between them" (glossematic terminology).

It has repeatedly been pointed out (and here again there seems to be no divergence among the various schools) that the analysis of expression does not presuppose a detailed analysis of the content, it is only necessary to know whether the meaning of two utterances is the same or different (and conversely for the analysis of the content). This is true with a slight reservation. If the linguist chooses the procedure of simply taking down in phonetic transcription everything he hears in natural conversation between natives without interfering by asking questions, eliciting responses, etc., then he will have to make an equally detailed account of meaning, either in the form of situations or responses (which will be a very difficult job) or in the form of a translation given by a bilingual native. In concrete acts of speech there will always be slight variations both in sound and meaning, but given a sufficiently large text, it will be possible to find out whether there is any relation between the differences in the two planes or not. But it is true that if the linguist chooses the much quicker procedure of eliciting short utterances and presenting them to a native who has to decide whether their meaning is the same or different, then an answer of "yes" or "no" will be sufficient. The reason why this answer does suffice in the latter case is that the utterances are taken out of their natural (linguistic and non-linguistic) context. Consequently, these utterances have no contextual differences of meaning, and the native will react to them as representatives of classes of utterances and will react to their meanings as being the same (in the sense of representatives of one class of meaning) or different (in the sense of representatives of different classes of meaning). In most cases it is possible to leave this decision of being same or different to the informant, simply because the relation between sound and meaning in the linguistic sign is arbitrary and unsystematic, so that it is rare that small differences of sound (which will be the crucial ones for the investigator) correspond to small and dubious differences of meaning, whereas it will normally happen that they correspond to

[5]"Remarques sur les principes de l'analyse phonémique," *Recherches structurales 1949, TCLC* V, 214–234.

[6]The term "commutation" was introduced by Hjelmslev (first used in print in the *Proceedings of the Second International Congress of Phonetic Sciences, London, 1935,* 1936, p. 51). It has since been adopted by a great many linguists (e.g., Jakobson-Fant-Halle, *Preliminaries,* 1–4). The reasons for the success of this term are obvious. The word does not sound too odd, it already exists in English, German, and French, but it is only current in technical applications which do not interfere with its use in linguistics; it is handy, since various derivatives can easily be formed: commute, commutable, etc.; and the term "commutation test" covers an operation which has been used for several years in the analysis of expression, particularly by the Prague phonologists, but for which there did not exist an appropriate name. Most linguists use the terms "commutation" and "commutation test" as synonyms, in conformity with Hjelmslev's own use of these terms until 1942. Since 1942, however, he uses "commutation" for the function, "commutation test" for the operation by means of which this function is found (cf., e.g., *Prolegomena to a Theory of Language* (Bloomington, Ind., 1953), 47). In some connections the double use of "commutation" does not do any harm, but in some it does, and therefore in this article the two terms will be distinguished.

obvious differences of meaning, e.g., *pill, bill, till, kill,* etc. There are borderline cases where the relation is not arbitrary and where gradual differences of sound will correspond to gradual differences of meaning—e.g., this may happen for intonation and emphasis. In such cases the test will be dubious anyhow.—Of course, if the linguist himself masters the language, the problem of avoiding meaning analysis is of no practical importance.

"Distinctive opposition," "commutation," and "contrast,"[7] although denoting approximately the same facts, are, however, not completely synonymous. This may be illustrated by a few selected quotations.

"Opposition phonologique [later opposition distinctive]: différence phonique susceptible de servir dans une langue donnée à la différenciation des significations intellectuelles."[8]

"La commutation . . . est . . . une corrélation qui contracte une relation avec une corrélation du plan opposé," and applied to the expression plane: "Il y a commutation entre deux termes du signifiant dont l'échange peut entraîner l'échange de deux termes correspondants du signifié."[9]

Hjelmslev's general formula differs from the Prague version by applying equally well to content and expression. This does not mean that followers of the Prague doctrine would not use the commutation test in content analysis. They would certainly recognize different content categories, only if they had different expressions. But a complete parallelism in procedures and definitions between content and expression is a characteristic feature of glossematics. We shall, however, not enter here upon the special problems of content commutation.[10] There is further the difference that Hjelmslev

formulates the principle of commutation in terms of members of the two planes without any explicit mention of sounds or meanings. It appears from many of Hjelmslev's earlier writings[11] that linguistic analysis should start as a purely formal analysis (of which the commutation test is an inherent part), stating relations between units without involving any statement about the substance of these units. His last paper,[12] however, contains a modification of this point: "la commutation . . . et, d'une façon plus générale, les corrélations entre variantes . . . constituent le domaine propre dans lequel le concours de la substance . . . s'impose." The only problem left is then to what extent glossematic analysis can be said to be purely formal, but this problem need not occupy us here.[13]

In the following paragraphs we shall often simply refer to relations between "sounds" and "meanings" on the assumption that this is where the analysis starts, provided of course that the object is a spoken language.

Common to glossematics and Prague phonology is the recognition that both content and expression belong to language and that the relation between them, found in the linguistic sign, is the fundamental linguistic relation. The commutation (or the distinctive opposition), which is derived from this relation, is therefore also considered as something essential. The commutation test is based on minimal pairs in the sense of short utterances or words which can be considered as identical except for the distinction under consideration.

Jones apparently does not include the distinctive function in his definition of the phoneme as a family of sounds and he mentions this function as a secondary consequence, but the "speech sounds" which are combined into families are defined[14] "by the possibility of moving a section from a chain and replacing it by a section of another chain, the sections being such that the exchange is capable of changing a word into another word." This definition should not be overlooked; it means that he starts his analysis by excluding free variants by means of the commutation test.

It is more difficult to find a representative

[7]We are referring here to the general use of these terms, not to the recent proposal of distinguishing between opposition and contrast as based on commutation and permutation respectively; see Martinet, *Word* 9 (1953), 9, footnote 21, and L. Prieto, *Word* 10 (1954), 43 ff.

[8]"Projet de terminologie phonologique standardisée," *TCLP* 4 (1931), 311; cf. also N. S. Trubetzkoy, *Grundzüge der Phonologie, TCLP* 7 (1939), 30. This fundamental definition does not seem to have been changed in the further development of Prague theories by Roman Jakobson and Martinet.

[9]Hjelmslev, *Word* 10 (1954), 171, and *Cahiers Ferdinand de Saussure* 2 (1942), 32.

[10]Cf. B. Siertsema, *A Study of Glossematics* (The Hague, 1954), pp. 168 ff., and Bazell, *Word* 10 (1954), 131.

[11]E.g., *Studia Linguistica* 1 (1947), 75.

[12]*Word* 10 (1954), 171.

[13]Cf. B. Siertsema, *op. cit.,* pp. 91 ff. and 174 ff.

[14]D. Jones, *The Phoneme* (London, 1950), p. 2.

quotation demonstrating the current American use of the term "contrast." Bloomfield does not use the terms "contrast" or "opposition," and he does not consider meaning as belonging to language. Nevertheless there is no essential difference between his procedures and those of the Prague phonologists or the glossematicians on this point. Phonemes are "the smallest units which make a difference in meaning" or "a minimum of distinctive sound feature."[15]

Pike's definition of "contrast" does not include any explicit reference to meaning: "contrast: a consistent, persistent difference between two sounds in analogous environments." "Analogous environments" are of a type that "could not plausibly be considered as being responsible for the difference between the sounds," and "identical environments" are nothing but a specific case of analogous environments. "Persistent difference," however, must be a difference found between different words, in contradistinction to free fluctuation occurring within repetitions of the "same" word.[16] And the criterion for sameness is meaning. Reference to meaning is necessary to distinguish contrast from free variation. This is also said explicitly by Pike in his criticism of Bloch.[17] In practice Pike uses minimal pairs when these are available, but does not consider them necessary.

According to Harris "any two distinct segments which occur in the same environment . . . contrast in that environment"; distinct is the same as non-equivalent, and equivalent utterances or parts of utterances are such as are recognized as being repetitions of each other, by the native informant, which may be tested through substitutions. This is the point where meaning comes in. "In principle, meaning need be involved only to the extent of determining what is repetition."[18] Harris, then, also employs the commutation test as a means of distinguishing between free variation and contrast, but in phonemic analysis he does not pay much attention to minimal pairs, and his analysis of Swahili (p. 97) does not contain a single minimal pair. The same disregard of minimal pairs can be seen in Trager and Smith's *Outline of English Structure.*

Hockett in his recent book apparently avoids meaning completely, when giving this new version of the current statement about "same and different" speech events: "some speech events *sound* the same to the native speaker, regardless of any variations in actual articulatory motion which the analyst may be able to observe, while others *sound different*,"[19] and this is what concerns phonologic analysis. Now Hockett cannot simply mean that the native speaker is incapable of hearing non-distinctive differences; many examples could be cited to prove the contrary, and on the next page Hockett tells us that it is very rare to find an informant who is capable of understanding what is meant by "sounding same or different." The best thing for the linguist to do is therefore to learn the language himself. That two speech events sound the same can therefore only mean that the phonetic differences which might be heard are not such as are utilized in the given language for the distinction of meanings. Hockett's formulation is probably intended to account better for cases of synonomy and homonomy: /ruwt/ and /rut/ have the same meaning ('root') but "sound different," 'meat' and 'meet' have different meanings, but "sound the same."

In these cases it seems more appropriate to ask whether the two utterances sound the same than to ask questions about meaing. But the superiority of Hockett's formulation is not as evident as it looks at first sight.—The purpose of the commutation test is to find out whether there is a relation between a difference of sound and a difference of meaning. In all the numerous cases where such a relation is found (e.g., *bad* − *long* or (with minimal difference) *bad* − *mad*) it can safely be concluded that the two utterances are phonemically distinct. There are, however, cases where no such correspondence can be found, and these may be of three types: (1) synonymy, e.g., *meat* − *meet,* (2) homonymy, e.g., [rut − ruwt], (3) free variation, e.g., [li:f − ɫi:f] (*leaf* with clear or dark *l*). The first case need not make any difficulty in phonemic analysis. When there is no phonetic difference, there cannot be any com-

[15]Bloomfield, *Language* (New York, 1933), pp. 136 and 76–79.

[16]Pike, *Phonemics* (Ann Arbor, Mich., 1947), pp. 236 and 238.

[17]*Word* 8 (1952) [18], 112 [215] ff.

[18]Z. Harris, *Methods in Structural Linguistics* (Chicago, 1951), p. 7, pp. 29 ff., and p. 75.

[19]C. F. Hockett, *A Manual of Phonology* (Bloomington, Ind., 1955), p. 144.

mutation. If the analyst is in doubt, he may ask the informant whether the two words sound the same, or he may ask what the words mean. In both cases the result will be that they cannot be distinguished. They should of course be spoken in the same environment, e.g., in isolation, and the best method is to ask a second native informant to speak them a certain number of times in random order (as proposed by Harris, *Methods,* p. 32; cf. Hockett, p. 146; and M. Halle, *Word,* 10, 1954 [32], 200 [335]). The real difficulty lies in the distinction between (2) and (3). The commutation test will give a negative result in both examples, but whereas this will always be so for words differing only by *l-ł,* it will not be the case for all words differing by *u-uw* (cf. Hockett's example [wud – wuwd]). Cases (2) and (3) will therefore be distinguished in the final analysis, for it is only required that a replacement should be *capable* of entailing a difference in the content, not that it should *always* do so. On the other hand, if the informant is asked whether the two words "sound the same," he might give the answer "no" in case (3) as well, if the phonetic difference is sufficiently clear, and particularly if it has some social connotation. This would often be the case for example with variants of Danish /a/. Further examples would not be of any help: [li:f – łi:f, ruwt – rut, wuwd – wud] would all sound different, and would be recognized as different by the test mentioned above. A confusion can be avoided only if the informant is so sophisticated that he knows that the answer "sounds different" should not be given except when there is a difference of content or when the phonetic difference is capable of entailing a difference of content in other cases. Hockett is aware of the difficulty, but he does not say what he means by "sounding same or different."

Bernard Bloch is the only one who has tried to demonstrate that an analysis of the expression of a language is possible without any reference to content. His first formulation was criticized from various points of view, and he has therefore given more precise definitions in a later article.[20] His definition of contrast may be summarized as follows: The ranges of two sounds may be (1) mutually exclusive,

[20]*Language* 29 (1953) [19], 59–61, with references to Pike, Lotz, and the present writer; cf. Bloch's first version *Language* 24 (1948) [16], 22 [181] ff.

(2) coincident, (3) incorporating, or (4) overlapping. If the ranges are incorporating or overlapping and their common environment cannot be distinguished from the environments which are specific to each of the sounds by a general definition, but only by a complete listing of all the individual environments, then the two sounds are in contrast, otherwise they are non-contrastive. "Range" is the total set of environments, but environment (and consequently range) may be taken in a narrower or wider sense, as repeatedly pointed out by Bloch himself. Here, however, he talks of "range (however defined)," and this is too vague. It is evident that in this connection, environment cannot be taken to mean "relevant environment" (see below: e.g., "in initial position before a vowel" and the like), for this is just the sort of environment which can be described by a general definition. It may, however, be taken in the sense "environment in the minimal linguistic sign" ("morpheme" in the American terminology). Free variants will have the same environment, or there may be easily definable limitations, but there is no general rule accounting for the fact that /i/ but not /e/ is found in the environment *spl-t* in English. But this distinction between contrast and free variation will only hold in languages which do not fully utilize the structural possibilities of phoneme combinations in the formation of signs. Now there will certainly be languages (with simple syllabic structure) where this condition does not hold, i.e., where the possibilities are fully utilized, at any rate for some phonemes, and then these cannot be distinguished from free variants. In these cases it will be necessary to define environment still wider, e.g., as whole utterances, since different phonemes cannot in any language be expected to occur in exactly the same utterances; and as one never knows beforehand, whether the possibilities are utilized or not, it will always be necessary to take environment in this wider sense. But then the analysis will be an almost infinite job. In addition there will be the difficulty of finding all the examples of free variation necessary to prove the difference from contrast. Now Bloch has of course never claimed that this would be a useful method, only that it would be theoretically possible. Perhaps it could be maintained that it is possible to *define* the difference between contrast and free variation on

the basis of distribution alone (and in his last paper Bloch does not seem to maintain more than this). It cannot, however, be maintained that it is possible to *analyze* a concrete language by methods based on these definitions. The possibility of avoiding any reference to content in the definitions is of course of great theoretical interest. It does not imply, however, that this reference is simply a practical short-cut, for the difference between contrast and free variation can also, and in a simpler way, be defined by reference to content, that is, by means of a relation which is fundamental to language as a system of communication, and the commutation test, derived from this definition, can be, and indeed is, used in practice in all types of structural linguistics.

Bloch's argument has, however, helped us to a more precise conception of the difference between "commutation" and "contrast." One difference is that "contrast" almost always seems to be used at the phoneme level, whereas "commutation" denotes a function which can be found at all stages of the analysis from the largest to the smallest units. This is, in principle, also true of the distinctive opposition of the Prague school; but it has been more explicitly stated within glossematics. A second and more important difference is involved in the conception of environment. The preceding discussion has made it clear that this is a crucial point.

The commutation test should be carried out in the same environment (or within one and the same paradigm). One may first ask whether "same" should be taken to mean phonetically same or phonemically same, or in more general terms: "same" in respect of substance or of form. Trubetzkoy says "in derselben lautlichen Umgebung" (p. 42), but in the "Projet de terminologie" (*TCLP* 4) the wording was "dans les mêmes conditions phonologiques," and when Hjelmslev says "paradigm," this is also meant as a formal term. The latter interpretation must be the correct one, since all environments are slightly different phonetically. "Same environments" must mean environments which have been proved to be functionally identical, or which we, at the given stage of the analysis, consider as functionally identical, so that they cannot be made responsible for the difference of content entailed by the replacement. The safest procedure is to start with the environment zero, and then use the units found here as environments for further commutation tests. There will, however, always be cases where we cannot be sure whether it is simpler to say that the environment is the same and the units in question different, or vice versa, and where various hypotheses must be tried out.

The second question concerns the extent of the identical environment in which the commutation test is to be carried out. Two partially conflicting answers may be given to this question. (1) Since a direct relation between content and expression is only found at the sign level, the environments for the units to which the commutation test is applied cannot be of smaller extent than the minimal sign. Commutation between, e.g., *p* and *b* cannot be found by considering the two sounds in isolation or in different clusters or syllables which have no direct function to content, but only in sign units like *pill – bill*. (2) What we want to find out is whether a difference is independently distinctive or not, but for this purpose we have to take account of a different sort of environment, which may be called the relevant environment; i.e., the environment which might be responsible for the difference between the units under consideration, or, to put it differently, which can be found to have relations of determination or interdependence to these units. In the content plane this environment will often be a complete utterance, or even a unit larger than that. In the expression plane, on the other hand, it will generally be of a very restricted extent. If, e.g., in a given language *l* and *r* in initial clusters are only found in combination with certain (categories of) consonants, then the initial cluster will be part of the relevant environment; if, on the other hand, no dependencies can be found between *l* and *r* and the following vowel or the final cluster of the syllable (either because all possible combinations are found, or because the gaps cannot be explained by a simple rule and must be considered as accidental) then this environment is irrelevant; *l* and *r* must consequently be considered as being in identical relevant environment in, e.g., *plank – prop*.[21]

[21]Cf. (for relevant environment) Harris, *Methods,* pp. 60 ff.; Bloch, *Language* 24 (1948), 22 [181], and *Language* 29 (1953), 59 [224]; Haugen, *Language* 27 (1951), 217; and for the distinction between accidental gap and structural law see E. Fischer-Jørgensen, *Acta Linguistica* 7 (1952) [50], 32 [576] ff., and Vogt, *Word* 10 (1954), 28–34.

The relevant environment may be part of the sign in which the unit in question is found, or there may be overlapping with part of an adjoining sign.[22] There will be languages where both conditions are always fulfilled, and no conflict arises. This will be the case when for each pair of sounds which can be found in the same relevant environment it is possible to find at least two sign expressions where also the "irrelevant" remainder is identical, i.e., where it is possible to find "minimal pairs." It will, however, often happen that such pairs cannot be found.

The problem has always been discussed at the phoneme level. At the level of the distinctive feature the cases of conflict will be rare. Minimal pairs like *bad* : *pad* and *bad* : *dad* would be sufficient to prove the distinction between voiced – voiceless and labial – dental, even if no pairs were found for *d* : *t* and *p* : *t*. But there might be conflict even at this level, e.g., no minimal pairs found for an isolated opposition like *r* : *l;* or *b, p, d, t* found in the same relevant environment and not varying freely, but with minimal pairs only for *b* : *p* and *d* : *t* (a case which might happen in a language with very complicated syllabic structure).

Where no minimal pairs are found, the commutation test cannot be applied, since the replacement does not result in an existing sign-expression combined with a different content, and in this case Hjelmslev does not recognize any commutation. The commutation test as described in Trubetzkoy's *Grundzüge* and in the "Projet de terminologie phonologique standardisée" seems to provide for such cases by recognizing two sounds as different phonemes, if the meaning is changed or deteriorated ("est détérioré," the word becoming "unkenntlich"), but the only examples quoted are such where a change of meaning can be found in other pairs (*Fische*: [*Fasche*], *Lippe* : *Lappe*), and it is therefore not quite sure that such an application should be intended. At any rate it seems preferable not to apply the commutation test in this way; a test which produces nonexisting words is not a safe procedure. Thus, in these cases there is no commutation,[23] but there is certainly "contrast." The recognition of contrast requires only that the relevant environment be the same. It is not based upon a replacement test, but upon an analysis of possible combinations.

This difference of terminology need not influence the final result of the analysis. One simply has to admit that the commutation test is not the only means of proving two sounds to be invariants; it cannot, anyhow (according to the majority of linguists), be applied to sounds in "complementary distribution," i.e., in mutually exclusive environments definable in simple terms (or, in other words: in different relevant environments).

Togeby is one of the very few linguists who claims that there must be at least one minimal pair, if two sounds are to be recognized as different phonemes.[24] This is the more astonishing since he is also one of the few linguists who would apply the commutation test even to sounds which are in mutually exclusive environments.[25] What he means is probably that if no minimal pair is found, the sounds should be considered as occurring in mutually exclusive environments since the distinction between relevant and irrelevant environment is arbitrary. But sounds in mutually exclusive environments need not be members of the same phoneme. Togeby, therefore, cannot be supposed to mean that the same relevant environment without a minimal pair proves two sounds to be variants of the same phoneme, but only that it does not prove them to be different phonemes.

There are, however, many good reasons for assuming that the same relevant environment without a minimal pair does prove two sounds

---

[22]There might seem to be a third answer to the question: the commutation test must be performed within the same paradigm in the sense of the same functional unit, e.g., the syllable, the central or marginal part of a syllable, etc., thus there cannot be commutation between a vowel and a consonant, etc. (cf. Hjelmslev, *Prolegomena*, p. 47; Prieto, *Word* 10, 53 ff.; W. Haas, *Transactions of the Philological Society* (1954), pp. 56 ff.), but this is only a precision of (2), underlining that syllable boundaries, position in the sequence, etc., also belong to the relevant environment.

[23]"Commutation" has been used in a wider sense by the present writer in *Acta Linguistica* 7 (1952), 38 [579], covering the accidental gaps. I should now prefer to speak only of "potential commutation."

[24]Togeby, *Structure immanente de la langue française, TCLC* VI (1951), 67.

[25]Togeby, *Structure*, 72.

to be different phonemes, and each of these reasons may be sufficient: (1) The rules of phonetic manifestation would otherwise be very complicated and they would not be phonetically motivated.[26] (2) If the analysis is continued, the two units would probably be described as consisting of different phonemic features. (3) There will be a fair chance of finding a minimal pair the next day, likely to upset the whole analysis. The last argument presupposes that the linguist considers the analysed text as a sample, and that he wants to be able to make predictions about other samples belonging to the same system, and this will be the normal situation. On this assumption all linguistic truths will be statistical truths, and the limit between zero and one is no less arbitrary than the limit between one and two. Minimal pairs are important for the description of functional load; but if they are also made decisive for the distinction between invariants and bound variants, it means that not the phonemic structure of the language, but the contingencies of sign formation, or even the contingencies of the investigated material are the object of description.

One may admit this, and nevertheless choose to apply the commutation test wherever possible. Most American linguists have made a different choice: the commutation test is only used where it is necessary, i.e., for the distinction between free variants and invariants (and this is preferably done at the utterance level), whereas the distinction between bound variants and invariants is undertaken by a method which is applicable regardless of the existence of minimal pairs, e.g., the analysis of combinations.

I should be inclined to consider this as a sound and consistent method, but this does not imply agreement concerning the endeavor to neglect the relation between content and expression in linguistic analysis. This is a fundamental linguistic function, and must be recognized as such, and the fact that signs differ in expression and content is a fundamental linguistic fact. It is, however, not a fundamental linguistic fact that they should be minimally different. Most signs are not. The commutation test (preferably applied to short utterances) tells us which signs are the same and which are

[26]Cp. Pike, *Phonemics*, pp. 75–76.

different, and this is all the informant can decide. It is the linguist's job to analyse different signs into components in such a way that the difference between signs is accounted for in the most simple and adequate way.

Nevertheless, "in the process of tabulation, minimal pairs are the analyst's delight," as Hockett puts it.[27] They make the analysis so much easier, even when they are not in principle necessary. But what do we really mean, when we say that *p* and *t* are commutable in *pin* : *tin*? Should the words "replacement," "échange," "Vertauschung" be taken literally, e.g., in the sense that replacements should be made on tape, and the results played to native listeners? Some linguists have interpreted the commutation test in this way.[28]

A very brief report[29] of some experiments, most of them made for a different purpose, but by the proposed method, may throw some light on this question. The procedure was the following: a list of Danish words, spoken by the present writer, was recorded on tape (speed: 15 inches per second), spectrograms were taken, and the limits between sounds were determined by drawing the tape slowly over the reproducing head and comparing the distances with the distances measured on the spectrograms. Cuts were made at the sudden shifts of acoustic pattern. This can be done with great exactitude. Every cut was controlled by means of new spectrograms, and both the original word and the results of all successive stages of cutting and splicing were re-recorded on a second tape recorder, three copies being made of each word. The words were then played over a loudspeaker, the three examples of each word at about 1½ sec. interval, and the different words (in random order) separated by a pause of 4–5 sec., to a group of students having a certain amount of phonetic training. The listeners were asked to identify the word with an existing (or, in some rare

[27]*Manual*, p. 212.
[28]Harris, *Methods*, p. 31; Halle, *Word* 10, 202 [337]; A. Cohen, *The Phonemes of English* (The Hague, 1952), p. 20. A similar procedure must also be presupposed by Hjelmslev, *Nordisk Tidsskrift for Tale og Stemme* 2 (1938), 156, and Togeby, *Structure*, p. 72.
[29]A detailed report of most of the experiments mentioned here will be given in a forthcoming book on Danish stop consonants (*TCLC*, probably 1957).

cases, a possible) Danish word, taking it down in normal orthography and perhaps adding some indications of unusual pronunciation.

Although the signal-noise level was not in all cases completely satisfactory, the unchanged words and some words that were spliced together again were heard correctly by 90–100% of the listeners, with a few exceptions (particularly with initial *h*) which are left out in the following report.

A.   Most replacements were made in the same environments. The only test made with vowels was the interchange of /ɛ/ and /a/ in the words /mɛt/, /mat/ (41 listeners). The result was 100% positive[30] for the vowel, but in /mat/ with inserted /ɛ/ 32% of the listeners misheard the final *t* as *nˀs, lˀ, lˀt* or *lˀk* (this word was not tested unchanged.)

For consonants (21 listeners) the results may be summarized as follows: *f* : *s* + *i, a* (i.e., interchange of initial *f* and *s* before *i* and *a*) and *s(h)* + *i, a* (i.e., the replacement of *h* by *s* before *i* and *a*) gave a positive result for 90–100% of the listeners.—*b* : *f* + *i, a, u* and *d* : *s* + *i, a* was positive for 76–100%, with the exception of *f(b)a* (62%).—*ph(b), th(d), kh(g)* + *i, a, u* worked for 76–100% with the exception of *kh(g)* + *a* (52%).—*b(ph), d(th), g(kh)* + *i, a, u* was positive for 67–100% with the exception of *d(th)* + *u* (38%), *d(th)* + *a* and *g(kh)* + *a* (both 14%). The most common mistake was *ph* or *b*. The main reason for the failures is that after *ptk* most of the "vowel transition" takes place during the aspiration, and the following vowel therefore does not comprise the transition normally found after *bdg*. An exchange of explosions alone was in most cases without any effect.—For *ph* : *th* : *kh* + *i, a, u* the average was 97% positive, the lowest being *kh(th)* + *a* (86%). If, however, these sounds are analysed as stop + *h*, the result is quite different. An interchange of explosions alone does not cause any change of perception, except for *p* : *k* (62–100% positive;—for *kh* the explosion is essential), and

t(k) + *a, u* which gives *p* (100%). (It must be noted that Danish *th* has a very weak explosion and a strong affrication, here treated as part of the aspiration.)—*b* : *d* : *g* + *i, a, u* worked tolerably well for *b* : *d* + *i, d* : *g* + *i, b* : *g* + *u, b(g)* + *i* and *g(d)* + *u* (67–100%), but only partly for *g(b)* + *i* and *b(g)* + *a* (52%), most of the mistakes consisting in perception of the original consonant. But for *b* : *d* + *a, u, g(d)* + *a* and *g(b)* + *a* the normal result was: no change (57–95%), and *d(g)* + *u* gave *bu* (98%). Some smaller differences may be accidental (in most cases only one example of each type was presented, for *b* : *d* : *g* + *u* however two with very similar results), but on the whole the differences may be explained by the relative importance of the vowel transition. One case is particularly interesting: *d(g)u*, i.e., *d*-explosion + *u* with *g*-transition cannot be perceived as *du*, since the transition (formant-bending) of *u* after *g* is very different from the characteristic transition which should be found after a *d* (but very similar to that found after *b*), and it cannot be perceived as *gu*, since the explosion of *d* is very different from the characteristic low explosion of *g* before *u* (but rather similar to the explosion of *b*); therefore it must be *bu*.[31]—A supplementary test with *m* : *n* + *ɔːðə* (41 listeners) was 100% ineffective, *b(n)* + *ɔːðə* gives *dɔːðə* (94%), *d(m)* + *ɔːðə* gives /bɔːðə/ (100%).

B.   Exchange of sounds in different environments.—Hjelmslev (1938) has proposed to use a test of this type ("experimental commutation") for the identification of sounds in mutually exclusive environments. He has not insisted on this proposal in later writings, but the idea has been taken up by Togeby and A. Cohen[32] as a means of avoiding the reference to phonetic substance in the identification. The method has been criticized by Bjerrum, Martinet, and the present writer.[33] Martinet rightly pointed to the fact that the result would certainly be exactly the opposite of what the authors intended, viz., a complete

---

[30]"Positive result" is here used to designate the case where the replacement of one sound by another has the effect that the listeners hear the word as containing the latter; e.g., if *a* in /mat/ is replaced by *ɛ* from /mɛt/ and the new word is played to the listeners, then /mɛt/ will be a *positive* result, but /mat/ or /mit/ or anything else will be a *negative* result.

[31]Cf. the Haskins experiments, e.g., *JASA* 24 (1952), 597 ff. [Cooper et al.—VBM], and E. Fischer-Jørgensen, *Miscellanea phonetica* 2 (1954), 42 ff.

[32]Hjelmslev, Togeby, Cohen; cf. note 28.

[33]A. Bjerrum, *Fjoldemålets Lydsystem* (1944), p. 91; Martinet, *BSL* 42 (1946), 37, and *Lingua* 1, 42 f.; E. Fischer-Jørgensen, *TCLC* V (1949), 223, and *Le maître phonétique* (1953), 11.

dependence on phonetic similarity. Thus it would not be possible to recognize any overlapping manifestation. As a good example Bjerrum and Martinet have mentioned the short Danish vowel /ɛ/. After *r* we have [i, e, æ, a], after other consonants [i, e, ɛ, ɑ], and nobody has hitherto thought of recognizing more than four vowel phonemes on this basis. But what happens if [ɛ] is replaced by [æ]? The experiment is difficult to carry out, since the Danish *r* is a very short (voiced or voiceless) uvular fricative having its second formant at approximately 1000 cps, from where the vowel's F² starts gliding almost the whole way up to its normal position. If, in the replacement, (*r*)*æ*(*t*) → *m*(ɛ)*t*, the whole glide is transferred, the result is [mræt], when only the 5 last cs (of 9) are taken over, we get /mat/ or /maiʔ/ (54 and 24% of 41 listeners), and the last 3 cs alone give 39% /mɛt/, 15% /mat/. The opposite replacement (*m*)ɛ(*t*) → *r*(*æ*)*t* (4 cs of the glide left with *r*), gives about 17 different responses.—Anyhow, the test is clearly negative.—The Danish consonants offer a still better example. Roughly speaking, [t] and [d] are found initially, [d] and [ð] finally and before *ə*, and according to the most common interpretation, first proposed by Uldall,[34] initial *t-* and final *-d* are identified and considered as members of one phoneme, initial *d-* and final *-ð* as members of another phoneme. —*k-g-*γ behave correspondingly.—But an experiment with 16 listeners has given the following results: [(sɛ)d(ə) → (th)ɛmə] = /dɛmə/ (or /dɛnə/) (100%), [(lɛ)g(ə) → (kh)ɛmə] = /gɛmə/ (94%), [(ma:)ð(ə) → (d)amʔ] = /lamʔ/ or /laŋʔ/ (94%, a corresponding experiment with a group of 41 gave the same result), [(vɛ:)γ(ə) → (g)ɛʁnə] = /jɛrnə/ (73%), [(vɔ:)γ(ə) → (g)ɔlə] = general confusion.— Finally it may be mentioned that a replacement of *g* in [gu:lə] by *g* in [gilə] gave /bu:lə/ (81%). —Replacements in different environments have also been undertaken by Cyril Harris and Carol Schatz.[35] The responses obtained by Harris are varied and not easily explainable, whereas Carol Schatz obtained very

consistent and interesting results by placing unaspirated *k* before various vowels (without transitions).

In a way, the difficulty involved in the replacements in same and different environments is the same: exchanging *m* and *n* before the same vowel ɔ: means exchanging two variants of ɔ: in different environment.

It may be objected that it would be possible to place the cuts differently, and it is true that if the beginning of the vowel is considered as belonging to, e.g., *b, d, g* the test can be performed with excellent result for, e.g., *bilə, dilə;* the cut would then be *bi-ilə, di-ilə,* but this cut would not do for the commutation test *dilə* : *dɛlə,* and *di* would be a word which is different from *da,* so that we would either get an enormous number of consonants *dⁱ, dᵃ,* etc., or have to make a new cut. Twaddell mentions the possibility of dividing *pat* into *pᵃ-ᵃt* on the basis of spectrograms, and Householder suggests that one might come to a sort of syllabic writing on this basis.[36] But on the basis of the auditory type of test, things become still more complicated, since each combination of consonant + vowel behaves differently: *b, d* in isolation cannot be recognized, but in combination with *u* without transition they generally can, *m* and *n* can be recognized in isolation, but before ɔ: without transition, both are heard as *m,* etc.

A better objection would be that sounds cannot be separated by cuts transverse to the time axis, and this would be true both for acoustic records and (perhaps still more so) for articulation. Speech perception seems to involve a redistribution along the time axis,[37] which is confused when sound segments are mixed artificially. Phonemic analysis has to a certain extent been based upon this auditory redistribution (and perhaps on the sequence of innervations, but this we do not know), and this basis gives a simpler description. We might analyze the acoustic record from this point of view, considering the modification of the vowel (which is not the same as part of the vowel), e.g., in *du-, gu-,* as belonging to the consonant, and consequently the frequency of the *g*-explosions in *gi-, gu-* as belonging to the

[34]Uldall, *Proceedings of the Second International Congress of Phonetic Sciences* (1935), p. 54; cf. also Jakobson, Fant, Halle, *Preliminaries,* pp. 5–6.

[35]Cyril M. Harris, *JASA* 25 (1953), 962–969; Carol D. Schatz, *Language* 30 (1954), 47–56.

[36]Twaddell, *JASA* 24 (1952), 610; Householder, *IJAL* 18 (1952), 262.

[37]M. Joos, *Acoustic Phonetics* (Language Monograph No. 23), 123.

vowel, and perhaps the difference between *d-* and *-ð* in Danish as belonging to some sort of syllable juncture. This does not mean abolishing the "allophones," i.e., phonetically different bound variants (cp. Hockett, p. 156 ff.), since *g* + the particular modification of *i* would be an allophone of *g* found only with *i,* and *i* + the particular modification of *g* would be an allophone of *i* found only in connection with *g,* but it might perhaps be possible to find a common denominator for all modifications of vowels caused by a *g* explosion,[38] and for all the modifications of consonants caused by an *i,* and thus arrive at a general description covering all the allophones.

Oral replacement includes automatic changes of sound and environment at one time,

and cannot be performed by the linguist until he has learned the language. But of what use is the test then? Comparison and analysis of the recorded words would be sufficient. Similar replacements can be made by means of synthetic speech, e.g., on the Haskins pattern play-back. The experiments made with this device have been extremely interesting and instructive by demonstrating the relations between acoustic stimulus and perception, but they presuppose a phonemic analysis rather than being a means for making it. As it was pointed out by Roman Jakobson,[39] redundant features may occasionally be more important for perception than distinctive features. Just as the botanist does not classify flowers by their most obvious qualities, the linguist does not rely completely on reactions of informants. He must try to find dependencies and independencies between the linguistic elements and base his analysis on these facts as found in utterances of the given language, and not on reactions to artificial sound combinations.

At the utterance level, the commutation test can be taken literally as a replacement; at later levels, it should rather be taken to mean an analysis by means of which commutable signs are found to be minimally distinctive. This seems also to be what Roman Jakobson means when saying: "A distinction is called minimal if it cannot be resolved into further distinctions which are used to differentiate words in a given language."[40]

---

[38]This has been attempted by the assumption of a specific *b-* or *d-* or *g-* "hub" (Potter, Kopp, Green, *Visible Speech* [New York, 1947]) or "locus," now used in almost the same sense by the Haskins group (*JASA* 27 [1955], 769 f.). This is a very useful terminology, but it should be borne in mind that it is only a formula for describing the visual pattern. There is not sufficient reason for assuming either some definite acoustic resonance or a cavity capable of producing such a definite resonance at a given distance (called silent interval) from the beginning of the vowel. In sequences like *ibi, ubu* there will certainly not be any point of the closure having the same specific b-resonance. Labials do not have one specific resonance, since the position of the tongue is free, but they influence the vowel in a definite way, because the lip opening is small when the vowel starts. For dentals the conditions are different, since coarticulation is almost excluded, whereas for velars it is evident that the resonances differ.

[39]*Preliminaries,* p. 8.
[40]*Preliminaries,* p. 4.

IV.b

Stratificational Phonology

52

ON ALTERNATION, TRANSFORMATION, REALIZATION, AND STRATIFICATION*

SYDNEY M. LAMB[1]

FORMULATIONS FOR DIVERSIFICATION

Diversification is the term I use for one of the fundamental properties of linguistic stratification.[2] This condition is present wherever a linguistic unit has two or more alternate realizations on the next lower stratum. For example, phonemes have alternate phonetic realizations; morphons (i.e., morphophonemes) often have alternate phonemic realizations; the lexon ᴸ/good/ has alternate morphemic realizations in the forms *good, better, best;* the sememic combination

$$^{\mathrm{S}}\!\Big/\mathrm{FARMER}{\leftarrow}\mathrm{agt}{\rightarrow}\mathrm{KILL}{\leftarrow}\mathrm{gl}{\rightarrow}\mathrm{DUCKLING}\Big/$$
$$\uparrow$$
$$\mathrm{past}$$

is realized lexemically in a variety of ways in the expressions *the farmer killed the duckling, the duckling was killed by the farmer, did the farmer kill the duckling?, the killing of the duckling by the farmer, the farmer didn't kill the duckling, having killed the duckling, the farmer . . . ,* etc. Instead of accounting for such phenomena in terms of stratification and realization, linguists have often attempted to deal with them by means of other formulations, which can be called *alternation, transforma-*

tion, and *classification.* To characterize them briefly, let us consider an abstract example in which there are two upper-stratum units A and B such that A has the single realization a while B has alternate realizations b and c. The alternative formulations are diagrammed in Figure 1, and a brief characterization of each is given below.

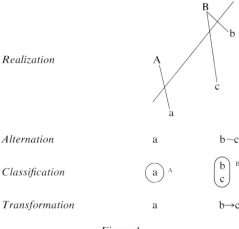

Realization		
Alternation	a	b~c
Classification	(a) ᴬ	(b c) ᴮ
Transformation	a	b→c

Figure 1

Alternation This is actually only a partial formulation and one which is clearly inadequate. Here the analyst simply says that b alternates with c. This is approximately what Bloomfield did in part in *Language* (New York, 1933) when he characterized the morpheme as a combination of phonemes and then observed that some morphemes have alter-

[1]This work is supported in part by the National Science Foundation.
[2]For an account of these properties and examples see my "The Sememic Approach to Structural Semantics," *American Anthropologist* (in press). [See now *AA* 66.57–78 (1964)—VBM.] In that paper I use the term "representation" for what is here called "realization."

*Reprinted from Georgetown University *Monograph Series on Languages and Linguistics:* Monograph 17, Report of the Fifteenth Annual Round Table Meeting, pp. 105–122. Washington, D.C.: Georgetown University Press, 1964.

nants (pp. 163–164). (In part, however, Bloomfield used the transformation formulation.) He did not really come to grips with the question of the nature of the morpheme, and he left its relation to the alternants and to the phonemes unclear. Another example would be a statement that the above-cited variations on the theme of *the farmer killed the duckling* are in some kind of alternation with each other, without carrying the analysis to the conclusion that there must be some underlying unity at a deeper level of the structure, of which the alternants are realizations. In other words this formulation falls into the category of what I'm told Kroeber used to criticize on the grounds that the analyst has cleared away the brush but hasn't cut down the tree.

Classification   Here the analyst would say that b and c are members of a class B. There are two versions of this formulation only one of which is illustrated in the figure. In the one diagrammed, the analyst also says that there is a class A, of which a is the only member, while the other version would not have an A but would put a on a par with B. Thus the former version is more nearly stratified. It recognizes that at some structural level B can be treated as a single unit and that at this level the number of members of the classes A and B is irrelevant. The other version puts a at both levels so that it must serve in one relation to B and in another to b and c. The classification formulation is the one in which we would say that a phoneme is a class of phones and a morpheme a class of morphs. It can be shown to be inadequate since the relation of realization is more complicated than the class-member relation. The membership of a class may be specified by a list of the members, but the realization of a realizate requires for its specification the identification not only of the realizations but also of the conditioning environment for each of them.

Transformation   I am using the term "transformation" here in a general sense to refer to the "process" type of formulation at any level of linguistic structure. Rules of the type which are familiarly called transformations therefore exemplify just one type of transformation formulation. In this approach one of the alternants, say b, is picked as the basic one and

it is sometimes (but not always) subjected to a transformation or process, which changes it to c, whereas when it is not so subjected it remains as b. On the other hand, a does not get subjected to any transformation and so remains. The items a and b thus serve in two functions, at two different periods in a fictional time span.[3] At the later period b alternates with c (and both are coexistent with a) whereas b also serves as the source of c and as such is in a different relation to a, which also exists at the earlier period. The process approach is more nearly adequate than the two preceding ones and is not as easily disposed of. The appropriate type of rule for this kind of formulation, like the realization rule (and unlike the class-member rule), includes specification of conditioning environments, and indeed it is undoubtedly because of this similarity as well as because modern synchronic linguistics grew out of diachronic studies that process formulations came to be used for stratificational phenomena.

In the case of the process relationship, the prior item, e.g., b, is differentiated from the resulting items, e.g., b and c, by its existence prior to the operation of the process. It must therefore be viewed as existing on the same stratum as the mutants which correspond to it; i.e., there is no need for stratificational distinctions as well. Thus, in process morphophonemics the morphophonemic processes are applied not to morphophonemes but to phonemes or, for some practitioners, to phonetic features. It is true that this practice is not universally followed, but one can easily rule out the use of both stratification and process to differentiate the "before" from the "after" as using two different entities where only one is necessary. And that, of course, is multiplying entities beyond necessity.

In other words, the essential difference between stratification and process is that the b which exists prior to the transformation is b and not a different entity B. Thus the thor-

---

[3]The more sophisticated practitioners of this approach are apparently aware that the time span which it uses is fictional and has nothing to do with either of the two aspects of real time passage which are relevant to linguistics, namely that of diachronic linguistics and that involved in the production and decoding of discourse (that which we reflect in linguistic notation by writing from left to right).

oughly consistent process approach would be one in which phonetic features were used instead of phonemic, and in which they would be present also at what would correspond to the next higher stratum, and so on up to the highest stratum. In other words, a consequence of a consistent process approach is that at the highest stratum (at which we might appropriately want our units to have some direct relation to meaning) the units will consist of phonetic features. And we find that precisely this property is present in what I understand is the current version of Chomsky's theory. The distinctive features are now introduced at his deepest structural level, even before the transformations.[4] By contrast, in the stratificational approach the phonetic distinctive features are not introduced in a generative description until the conversion from the phonemic stratum to the phonetic.

The transformation or process type of formulation and its relation to realization are examined in detail in the remainder of this paper.

APPLICATIONS OF
TRANSFORMATION FORMULATION

First we should distinguish the various ways in which transformation or process formulations have been applied in linguistics. They have apparently been used in four different functions:

1. For Conflation of Concatenation and Realization   The first involves a confusion or blending of two relations, namely realization and the one involved in tactic combination. There are two well-known ways in which this type of process formulation has been used, namely Sapir's morphological processes and Chomsky's optional transformations. Suppose that (in terms of a stratificational account) we are dealing with a lexon L/good/ which can occur with another lexon L/er/ and that there are realization rules (which define the realizations of the lexons in terms of their environments) such that the realization of L/good er/ is *better.* We would account for *better,* using a stratified approach, in terms of two separate phenom-

ena: (1) the fact that a particular lexon is combined with another, a tactic phenomenon, and (2) the fact of how this combination is realized on the next lower stratum. These two separate facts are combined into one in the morphological process approach, in which (if one is consistent and refrains from multiplying entities) there are no morphemes; instead there are two kinds of things, roots (which are phonetic or phonemic entities depending on whether a phonemic stratum is recognized) and morphological processes; and words are accounted for in terms of the application of morphological processes to roots, i.e., a process of suffixation plus suppletion in the case of *better,* in the case of *worse* just suppletion, in the case of *taller* just suffixation, and for *longer* just suffixation but of a different suffix than for *taller* (namely one which begins with g), unless the processist is willing to partially stratify and set up the root *long* in a basic form (having final g) which doesn't actually occur.

Most linguists (I hope) don't do this kind of thing any more at this level, but more recently it has been going on at a higher level, namely that of Chomsky's transformations (although Chomsky has now revised his theory so that this conflation is no longer present).[5] In a stratified account there are sememic units occurring in various combinations as specified by semotactic rules; and there are realization rules which specify how the sememic combinations are realized on the lexemic stratum. Instead of this the "lexological process" approach would have (similarly to the morphological process approach) two kinds of entities at the highest level, namely items and lexological processes (called transformations) to which these items can be subjected. For example, there would be a negative transformation which would be applied to a "sentence" to transform it from positive to negative (whereas the stratified account would have a negative semon occurring with other semons as specified by semotactic rules and, as a separate phenomenon, the realization of the combination as, say, *the farmer didn't kill the duckling*). Notice that just as morphological

---

[4]In an earlier version presented in his paper in the preprints of the Ninth International Congress of Linguists, they were introduced right after the transformations.

[5]Chomsky presented this revision in a lecture given at the University of California, Berkeley, on 25 February, 1964.

processes were applied to phonetic or phonemic entities, i.e., to things of the same kind as what emerges from the operation of the processes, so the lexological processes are applied not to semological networks, but to constituent-structure trees, i.e., entities which are like those found on the lexemic stratum.

As mentioned above, the new version of Chomsky's theory accounts for these phenomena in a more nearly correct way. All the significant elements which will be present in the sentence are now introduced during the original constituent-structure rules, so that now the transformations have the sole function of converting from what he calls the "deep structure" to the "surface structure." They do not add any new material. There are no longer, in other words, any optional transformations. (Chomsky's system is still only partially stratified, however, since his interstratal conversion is done with rules of a process type instead of realization rules.)

So it may be safe to say that this first type of process formulation is not widely used any more, except perhaps by followers of Chomsky who haven't yet heard about his new system.

2. For Concatenation and Classification   In a stratified system there is a set of tactic rules for each of the structural strata, which characterize the set of well-formed combinations of units of that stratum. Each such rule is a statement about a set. On one side of the rule is given a symbol for the set, on the other side a specification of the membership of the set, either by listing (if it is a set whose members are ultimate constituents) or in terms of other distribution classes (whose membership is in turn specified by other rules). A specification of the latter type might be

A N ,

which means the set of all strings an such that a is a member of A and n is a member of N. Without going into such rules in detail I want just to state here that the only relations involved in tactics are the class-member relation and that of concatenation (or some other type of combination, in the case of a stratum on which units occur in non-linear combinations)

and that each tactic rule is merely a statement about the membership of a set. This is a simpler type of rule than those required for realization and for mutation (i.e., the type of relation involved in linguistic change) and the tactic relations should of course be kept distinct from these more complex ones. But we find that Chomsky and his followers use replacement rules both for this function and as a substitute for realization (see 3 below), and one hears Chomsky making statements to the effect that a noun phrase, say, is "realized as" or "represented by" an article plus a noun.[6]

3. For Realization   The process type of formulation is perhaps best known and most widely used in this function, and it is this application that I will be concentrating on below. Examples are the use of ordered rewrite rules for morphophonemics, and the transformational rules of Chomsky's new semi-stratified system, which convert from his "deep structure" to his "surface structure."

4. For Mutation   If we use the term "mutation" for the relation involved in linguistic change, then it is for the mutation relation that ordered replacement rules, i.e., process statements, are properly used. Here the property that the items existing prior to the process are of the same kind as those resulting from it (e.g., both phonemic) is entirely appropriate. Of these four types of application of process, this is the one (and the only one) where it belongs. Process formulations and the study of process rules are valuable for that reason. But in synchronic linguistics they are out of place. (In the sequel I shall use the term "mutation rule" interchangeably with "process rule," "rewrite rule," and "replacement rule," and I shall focus on the differences between this type of rule and the realization rule.)

---

[6]It is true that Chomsky and the more sophisticated of his followers are aware of differences in the form of the different kinds of rules involved, and one might think they would thus be able to avoid confusion in their own minds despite the use of the same symbol (i.e., the arrow) and same set of locutions (is rewritten as, is replaced by, is represented by, is realized as) in all of the types of rule. But there is evidence that they are not entirely successful in this attempt, and it is quite certain that students and those followers who are not experts readily get confused.

MUTATION AND REALIZATION

The function of a set of realization rules is to specify how the elements of a stratum are realized on the next lower stratum. Each such set of rules may be thought of as a code relating two neighboring strata. The names *semolexemic, lexomorphemic,* and *morphophonemic* may be used for the three sets of realization rules relating the four structural strata of a system with sememic, lexemic, morphemic and phonemic strata, and there are in addition the rules defining the phonetic realization of the phonons, i.e., the elementary units of the phonemic stratum. (To keep the terminology consistent these would be called phonophonetic rules, but I am not insisting on that term.)

The realization rule, in its simple form (some modifications are described below), consists of (1) a realizate, or the name of the rule, which is an element of the upper stratum, and (2) a list of one or more subrules. Each subrule specifies (1) an environment, expressed in terms of upper-stratum elements, and (2) the realization which the realizate has when it is in that environment. In some cases (where there is free variation) a set of freely-varying alternate realizations is given in the same subrule. In the notation which I use, each subrule is introduced by "||" which may be verbalized as "when in the environment," and the realization (or set of freely-varying realizations) is introduced by "/" which may be verbalized as "is realized as." An abstract example is the rule

$$w \parallel x\text{-}y \,/\, z$$
$$\parallel t\text{-}u \,/\, v$$
$$\cdot$$
$$\cdot$$
$$\cdot$$
$$\parallel \text{---} \,/\, s.$$

Here w is the realizate; each of x, y, t, u, . . . is either (1) zero (i.e., nothing), meaning any combination of upper-stratum elements, or (2) a string of one or more symbols each of which is either an element of the upper stratum or a cover symbol;[7] "--" identifies the position of the realizate in the environment; "---" means "in any environment"; and each of z, v, . . . , s is a combination of zero or more elements

of the lower stratum or, in the case of free variation, a set of such combinations. The ordering of the subrules is significant in that a given subrule applies only if none of the preceding ones does.[8] Thus the environment symbol "---" means "everywhere" if it appears in the first (hence only) subrule and "elsewhere" (i.e., in any environment other than those specified above) if it appears in the last. For some purposes it is convenient to adopt a notational convention whereby, if it is economical to write the realizate with the same symbol as that used for the realization given in the last subrule, that subrule may be omitted. (But note that since the realizate and the realization are on different strata, use of the same symbol does not mean that they are the same unit.)

Now one might ask if this is really different from the mutation rule. Isn't it the case, one might say, that we could restate the rule in the following way, in which the arrow means "is replaced by":

$$w \parallel x\text{-}y \rightarrow z$$
$$\parallel t\text{-}u \rightarrow v$$
$$\cdot$$
$$\cdot$$
$$\cdot$$
$$\parallel \text{---} \rightarrow s,$$

or even in the form

$$xwy \rightarrow xzy$$
$$twu \rightarrow tvu$$
$$w \;\;\rightarrow\;\; s.$$

Aren't these statements formally equivalent, and aren't these alternative symbolizations and their accompanying verbalizations just different ways of stating what is really the same thing? The answer is *no*. And one lesson to be learned from this answer is that one cannot know what the structure of a system is just by looking at the form of the individual rule. One has to look at the structure of the whole system and at the way in which the parts of the rule are defined. Or, one good way to see the difference is to look at the way the rules operate. This we shall do below in order to make the difference quite clear, but first it may be helpful to look at a couple of simple examples.

---

[7]The restrictions on use of cover symbols are such that any preceding or following environment is a regular set, in terms of automata theory.

[8]Thus the list of subrules defines a partition of the set of all possible contexts in which w may occur, even though the sets of contexts as defined overtly by the individual subrules may overlap.

It is easy to see that the last formulation above leads to an entirely different result from that of the true realization rule. The realization rule above tells us only about the realizations of w, but tells us nothing about how x, y, . . . are realized. For all we know there are rules to the effect that

$$x \;||\; \text{--w/p}$$
$$y \;||\; \text{w--/q,}$$

in which case the realization of xwy is not xzy (as in the rewrite rule above) but pzq. This difference (between the correct result and the incorrect one) is a consequence of the fact that for realization the two strata are entirely distinct from each other, and the environments of the realization rules are stated in terms of the upper stratum, while the realizations are on the lower stratum. In other words, everything to the left of the "/" is on the upper stratum, while what is at the right of it is on the lower one. The set of elements of the upper stratum is disjoint from that of the elements of the lower one (except that both have the empty string as a member), and so a formulation of the type

$$xwy \rightarrow xzy$$

cannot be used since in it the x and y at the left of the arrow are the same units as those at the right. In other words this type of rule is possible only in an unstratified system.

Let us now consider a hypothetical morphophonemic example, in which the following rules apply:

$$i \;||\; \text{--} \;\#/\emptyset$$
$$t \;||\; \text{--i/c,}$$

where # is word juncture and $\emptyset$ is zero (i.e., the empty string). Then the phonemic realization of the string ^{M}/kati/ when it is followed by ^{M}/#/ (assuming that ^{M}/ka/ is realized as ^{P}/ka/) is ^{P}/kac/, since both ^{M}/t/ and ^{M}/i/ are in the specified environments. But if we restate the rules as mutation rules we have

1. $i \;||\; \text{--} \;\# \rightarrow \emptyset$
2. $t \;||\; \text{--i} \rightarrow c,$

in which I have written the rule numbers to call attention to the fact that rewrite rules are ordered. Applying these rules to the same string we get kati → kat. And there the process stops, because after rule 1 has operated, t is no longer in the proper environment for rule 2. But with

realization rules the environment is on the upper stratum and it does not get replaced. The "output" of a realization rule does not replace anything; it belongs instead on the lower stratum.

Of course, to get the right answer one can state the rewrite rules in the opposite order:

1. $t \;||\; \text{--i} \rightarrow c$
2. $i \;||\; \text{--} \;\# \rightarrow \emptyset.$

Then we get kati (when followed by #) → kaci → kac, which is correct.

Now, what if in some other dialect the phonemic realization is ^{P}/kat/? Then the ordering tried first above for the rewrite rules would be correct, and the proponent of ordered rewrite rules might wonder how we would handle this with unordered realization rules. Well, in terms of stratification, the situation is simply that the rule for ^{M}/t/ applies before non-final ^{M}/i/ but not before ^{M}/i#/. Thus the rules for this dialect would be written

$$i \;||\; \text{--} \;\#/\emptyset$$
$$t \;||\; \text{--i} \;\overline{\#}/c$$

(and they could of course have been written in either order), in which $\overline{\#}$ is a cover symbol meaning "any morphon except #." At this point we can expect that the champion of replacement rules will say, "Aha! You have had to use an extra symbol in the statement of the conditioning environment, namely $\overline{\#}$." To which my reply would be, "Aha! *You* have had to use *two* extra symbols in your rules, namely the digits 1 and 2!" Those digits cannot be ignored. They are technically an integral part of the ordered rule, since the ordered rule is ordered. In other words, the ordering is not free, when we are computing degrees of complexity by counting symbols. An ordered set is a more complex object than an unordered one and, in particular, each rule of a set of ordered rewrite rules is, formally speaking, paired with a positive integer. So every rewrite rule has an extra symbol, namely the rule number.

So here we have another difference between the two types of rule. The realization rule does not have a rule number, except in the sense that the rule number is the realizate itself. And it is instructive to think of the realization rule in these terms. I stated above that the realizate could be considered the name of the rule. It can also be considered the rule number, which is equivalent, or the location of the rule in a production system. That is, the morphon $^M/t/$ is, structurally speaking, the name or number or location of the rule which provides certain realizations that speakers of the language treat as in some way equivalent. And the occurrence of a morphon is simply a specification that a particular morphophonemic rule is to be executed. If we wanted to we could number the realization rules but if we did so these numbers would replace the alphabetic symbols now used. Such a concept is not applicable in the case of mutation rules, for which the units corresponding to morphons are "objects" which get operated upon.

These considerations will become clearer if we consider the procedures for using the two types of rule. In the stratified system the encoding from one stratum to the next lower one can be accomplished in a single left-to-right pass through each string to be encoded. For each element e_i of the string $e_1 \ldots e_n$ to be encoded we go (directly) to rule e_i and execute it. Since the subrules are ordered, the execution consists of testing the environments specified in the successive subrules one by one until the one which applies is encountered, at which time we (do not rewrite e_i but instead) put out the realization (which is in turn a specification that one or more rules of the next lower code are to be executed).

In the case of mutation rules, on the other hand, *a separate pass must be made through the string for each rule.* Here the rule numbers specify the order in which the successive passes are to be made through each string. The execution of the individual rule is also more complicated, since it involves two parts. First, each element of the string must be looked at to see whether it is one to which the rule may apply. Whenever an element e_i is encountered to which it may, then the operations of testing the successive environments are performed as in the case of the realization rule. When an applicable environment is found, then e_i *is replaced by* the symbol or symbols specified by the subrule having that environment. Note that such rewriting destroys what was previously there, namely e_i, so that the formulator of the rules must have made sure that this e_i is not a part of a conditioning environment for any following rule. In other words, each rule

must be placed into the ordered sequence in such a way that (1) no preceding rule has already altered the conditioning environment of e_i and (2) e_i will not be part of the conditioning environment in any following subrule. It is this property of rewrite rules which makes it essential that they be ordered and which evidently also accounts for various other complications in process descriptions. Thus much of the complexity seen in a transformational grammar is the result not of complexity in the language, but of an artificial restriction imposed by the type of rule being used.

There is another difference, one which at first glance might appear to favor the mutation rule. In the mutation rule it is not necessary that the subrules collectively cover all possible contexts in which the element can occur. If one of the subrules applies, then the element is not rewritten at all.[9] The corresponding situation is not possible for realization rules because the set of upper stratum elements and that of lower stratum elements are disjoint sets. Therefore there must always be a realization, even for elements which have the same realization in all environments. This consideration relates to Figure 1 above, in which we had separate units A and a even though a was the only realization of A. As I said, this difference might seem to favor the mutation rule, but only at first glance. For if the user of process rules wants to take advantage of this property of the process formulation he can do so only by having present at the earlier period in the fictional time span those elements that he has to end up with at the completion of the process. Thus in the Chomsky system the phonetic distinctive feature matrices are introduced very early in the generative heirarchy even though they are not needed (and in fact are very cumbersome) until near the end; whereas in a stratified generative system the phonons (i.e., the components of the phonemes) are not introduced until the time of the morphophonemic rules, and the components present at the top structural stratum are not phonetic but sememic.

Let us summarize the differences between mutation and realization by means of the following table.

[9]This property is quite appropriate to the proper use of these rules, which is for mutation in diachronic linguistics.

Properties of Mutation Rules
1. Ordered (i.e., each rule is paired with an integer).
   Consequence: multiple passes through string.
2. "Output" of rule replaces input (which is no longer available as environment).
3. Items can remain unchanged (but if they do their final composition must be present at beginning).

Properties of Realization Rules
1. Unordered; realizates are names of rules; single pass through string.
2. "Output" of rule is name(s) of other rule(s); input is unaffected.
3. Every item has a realization (i.e., lower-stratum elements not present at beginning).

REALIZATION FORMULATION VARIATIONS

The description of the realization rule given above characterizes what may be called the simple form of the rule. A slightly different form is needed for semolexemics, since the realizates here do not occur in strings but rather in networks. The specification of environments in subrules must therefore take a somewhat different form. In addition there are various modifications available which allow descriptions of certain phenomena sometimes encountered at lower levels to be somewhat simpler and more realistic than is possible for the simpler form of rule. These modifications buy simplicity of the rules when dealing with these phenomena, at the cost of additional meta-rules in the system which specifies the form of rules in a well-formed linguistic description. I will mention them briefly for the record although I cannot give full explanations in this brief paper.

First we may briefly consider the phenomena of portmanteau realization, empty realization, and anataxis,[10] all of which can be handled by the addition of one device which is apparently needed anyway for semolexemic rules. This device is the numerical superscript, to be attached to certain symbols appearing in the specification of environment in subrules. The function of a superscript is to specify a deviation from the usual order of execution of the rules. (Recall that the usual order is that

in which the realizates occur.) For example, to take care of a case of metathesis for which a process treatment would use the rule

$$y(p,t,k) \rightarrow (p,t,k)y^{11}$$

which actually changes the order of the units, we would use superscripts to specify that the rule for the stop of the upper stratum is to be executed before that of y, as follows:

$$y \ || \ \text{--}^2(p,t,k)^1/y.$$

Here there is no reordering of elements, since realization rules do not ever change the realizates. The rule has merely specified that instead of the usual left-to-right order of putting out the realizations, that of the stop is to be put out before that of y.

Portmanteau realization can be handled without any special devices (and for that matter so can metathesis at the cost of a little simplicity and realism), by rules like these (which are lexomorphemic):

$$er \ || \ bad \ \text{--}/\emptyset.$$

But such a formulation tends to strike the intuition of native speakers as being less than completely realistic, since *worse* would seem to be the realization of the combination ^{L}/bad er/, not just of ^{L}/bad/, which indeed is why we call it a case of portmanteau representation. A convenient notational convention for this phenomenon (which can also be used for metathesis) would allow the rule

$$bad \ er \ || \ \text{--}/wərs.$$

But it must be understood that this is merely a notational convention for what, strictly speaking, should be written

$$bad \ || \ \text{--} \ er^0/wərs,$$

where the zero superscript indicates that the rule for this ^{L}/er/ is not to be executed at all (since the realization given in this rule is that of the combination ^{L}/bad er/). The notationally convenient form of this rule violates the requirement that the realizate for any rule must be a single element, a requirement which is necessary to the manner of operation of the rules described above.

---

[10] For descriptions and examples of these phenomena, see "The Sememic Approach to Structural Semantics" (cf. footnote 2 above).

[11] The expression in parentheses is an "ad hoc cover symbol" having the values p, t, and k. This example of metathesis is presumed to be present in Zoque on the basis of problem 52 in Nida's *Morphology* (Ann Arbor, 1949).

In empty realization the realizate is zero. To handle this phenomenon without superscripts it is necessary either (1) to in effect deny it any special status and treat the empty realization as a part of the realization of the element preceding the zero realizate; or else (2) to have a rule with a zero realizate and to go to it (when encoding) after the execution of the rule for every non-zero realizate. In the formulation which allows superscripts, however, an environment expression can contain

$$\ldots -\varnothing^{1} \ldots$$

to specify that rule $\varnothing$ (i.e., the rule for the zero realizate) is to be executed next. The superscripted zero would appear only in rules for elements which can precede the empty realizate. Thus the rule for the zero realizate is executed only when, as it were, specific instructions to do so are given.

The "output" part of a realization rule is a specification that certain other rules are to be executed, except where the realization is zero. In the rule as described so far these other rules are realization rules at the next lower level of coding. The following example illustrates a type of simplification that can be achieved by modifying this feature of the rule. These rules describe a morphophonemic situation in Monachi (or Mono), a Utoaztecan language of California. (Square brackets in the specification of an environment mean that the enclosed element(s) may be present or absent in that position.)

$$w \parallel (e,a,o)h\text{--}(a,e)/q^{w}$$
$$\parallel h\text{--}/k^{w}$$
$$k^{w} \parallel (e,a,o)[h]\text{--}(e,a)/q^{w}.$$

That is, ^{M}/w/ is realized as a labialized stop when preceded by ^{M}/h/ and the stop is velar or postvelar depending on the surrounding vowels; but ^{M}/k^{w}/ is realized as ^{P}/q^{w}/ in the same vocalic environment for which ^{M}/w/ has that realization. (In some vocalic environments ^{P}/k^{w}/ and ^{P}/q^{w}/ contrast, so they are phonemically different.) The rules as stated in this simple form contain a redundancy in the specification of this vocalic environment, which can be eliminated by the adoption of a meta-rule which will allow us to state the rule for ^{M}/w/ in a slightly different form.

First, however, let us pause to make a comparison with how this phenomenon could be treated by the mutation rule. One way to write mutation rules for it is:

1. $w \parallel h\text{--} \rightarrow k^{w}$
2. $k^{w} \parallel (e,a,o)[h]\text{--}(e,a) \rightarrow q^{w}.$

Here the vocalic environment has to be stated only once, since the second rule will apply both to "original" k^{w} and to the k^{w} which is "derived" from original w. But this economy is achieved at the cost of making these rules ordered.

We should also note here an important factor which has not been made explicit in the notation so far. In the process rules above, the symbols of the notation can be taken either as (1) denoting structural elements or as (2) convenient notational abbreviations for what are really bundles of phonons or of distinctive features. If the former alternative is chosen, then all the rules of this type must be followed by another list of rules which will convert the elements of the final output string into their components. For example, there would have to be rules such as the following (if phonons are used rather than binary distinctive features, which are more complicated):

$$k^{w} \rightarrow \begin{matrix} \text{Cl} \\ \text{Vl} \\ \text{Lb} \end{matrix}$$

$$q^{w} \rightarrow \begin{matrix} \text{Cl} \\ \text{Pv} \\ \text{Lb} \end{matrix}$$

where Cl stands for "closed," Vl for "velar," Lb for "labial," Pv for "post-velar"). If the other alternative is adopted then the components are the elements which are really present at the beginning of the sequence of mophophonemic rules, and all the symbols in the two ordered mutation rules above are really abbreviations. In other words, according to this formulation the rules are actually the following:

$$1. \quad \text{Lb} \parallel \text{Gm} \text{--} \rightarrow \begin{matrix} \text{Cl} \\ \text{Vl} \\ \text{Lb} \end{matrix}$$

$$2. \quad \text{Vl} \parallel \begin{matrix} \text{Vo} \\ \text{Lo} \end{matrix} [\text{Gm}] \text{--} \begin{matrix} \text{Cl} & \text{Vo} \\ \text{Lo} \\ \text{Lb} & \overline{\text{Lb}} \end{matrix} \rightarrow \text{Pv}.$$

In measuring the complexity of a list of rules it is of course the actual structural meaning of the rules which must be measured, not the notation.

What, then, is the relation between the notation and the actual situation for the realization rules above? The answer is implicit in the description of the realization rule already given. It is that each alphabetic symbol to the left of "/" stands for a morphon, which is an indivisible structural element of the morphemic stratum, while each phonemic symbol, i.e., each symbol at the right of "/" is an abbreviation for a bundle of phonons. Thus these rules may be stated without the use of any abbreviations or notational conventions as follows:

$$w \,||\, (e,a,o)h\text{--}(a,e)/\begin{matrix} \text{Cl} \\ \text{Pv} \\ \text{Lb} \end{matrix}$$

$$||\, h\text{--}/\begin{matrix} \text{Cl} \\ \text{Vl} \\ \text{Lb} \end{matrix}$$

$$||\, \text{---}/\text{Lb}$$

$$k^w \,||\, (e,a,o)[h]\text{--}(e,a)/\begin{matrix} \text{Cl} \\ \text{Pv} \\ \text{Lb} \end{matrix}$$

$$||\, \text{---}/\begin{matrix} \text{Cl} \\ \text{Vl} \\ \text{Lb} \end{matrix}$$

$$q^w \,||\, \text{---}/\begin{matrix} \text{Cl} \\ \text{Pv} \\ \text{Lb} \end{matrix}.$$

Now we are ready to introduce the variation hinted at above, which allows us to let the "output" of a realization rule refer to another rule at the same level of coding in order to eliminate redundancy. For this type of reference we can use "|" instead of "/." Then the

above rules can be restated as follows:

$$w \,||\, h\text{--} \,|\, k^w$$

$$||\, \text{---}/\text{Lb}$$

$$k^w \,||\, (e,a,o)[h]\text{--}(e,a) \,|\, q^w$$

$$||\, \text{---}/\begin{matrix} \text{Cl} \\ \text{Vl} \\ \text{Lb} \end{matrix}$$

$$q^w \,||\, \text{---}/\begin{matrix} \text{Cl} \\ \text{Pv} \\ \text{Lb} \end{matrix}.$$

Whereas "/" is to be verbalized as "is realized as," "|" is to be verbalized as *"is realized in the same way as."* In terms of the operation of the rules, the difference between the two types of output is simply a difference of whether the specified rule(s) to be executed are at the same level of coding or the next lower one. Notice that this elimination of redundancy is achieved without resorting to ordered rules, and that the properties of the realization rule described previously are still retained in this version.

To illustrate, let us take the form M/ʔahwehci/ 'her grey hair'. Alternative treatments by the stratificational formulation and by the last process formulation above (in which the phonons are already present at the beginning of the morphophonemic rules) are shown below.

Another version of the realization rule would be that which allows for indirect specification of conditioning environment. This device involves an extension of the cover symbol

		ʔ	a	h	w	e	h	c	i
Realization	Morphemic stratum:	ʔ	a	h	w	e	h	c	i
	Phonemic stratum:	Gl	Vo Lo	Gm	Cl Pv Lb	Vo Lo Fr	Gm	Cl Gr	Vo Hi Fr
Mutation	Stage 0	Gl	Vo Lo	Gm	Lb	Vo Lo Fr	Gm	Cl Gr	Vo Hi Fr
	Stage 1	Gl	Vo Lo	Gm	Cl Vl Lb	Vo Lo Fr	Gm	Cl Gr	Vo Hi Fr
	Stage 2	Gl	Vo Lo	Gm	Cl Pv Lb	Vo Lo Fr	Gm	Cl Gr	Vo Hi Fr

(which is available for the "simple" type of realization rule, but which isn't treated above for lack of space). The usual cover symbol (such as "V" or "C" in morphophonemic rules) can be construed structurally as a reference to another rule (unless it is an ad hoc or self-defined cover symbol, such as (e,a) in the rules above), namely a tactic rule which specifies the membership of the set V or C or whatever it may be. The indirect environment is like a cover symbol but it calls for reference to another realization rule rather than to a tactic rule. To illustrate, the first subrule for $^M/k^w/$ in the last formulation above, using this device, could be stated in the following way,

where pointed brackets "< . . >" are used to enclose the indirect environment:

$$k^w \; || \; \left\langle \begin{matrix} Vo \\ Lo \end{matrix} \right\rangle [h]\text{--}(e,a) \; | \; q^w$$

The symbol $\left\langle \begin{matrix} Vo \\ Lo \end{matrix} \right\rangle$ is a cover symbol for morphons whose realization has the components Vo (vocalic) and Lo (low). Whether this symbol is simpler than the alternative (e,a,o) for the same set of morphons is open to question, but there are circumstances in which the use of this device seems to provide clearly simpler rules.

53

PROLEGOMENA TO A
THEORY OF PHONOLOGY*

SYDNEY M. LAMB

Since different writers do not in fact agree in the phonemic treatment of the same language, there arise then frequent controversies over the "correctness" or "incorrectness" in the use of phonemes.

YUEN-REN CHAO[1]

This paper discusses various types of phonological phenomena, some of the concepts that linguists have employed in dealing with them, and certain questions to which previous work in phonological theory has not provided satisfactory answers. These considerations lead to the recognition of some distinctions heretofore overlooked and to a new theory of phonology, certain features of which are outlined.

Certain fairly conspicuous features of phonological patterning have long been recognized. It is probably beyond dispute that at least the following types of phenomena (described for the present in relatively vague terms) are characteristic of all spoken languages and hence must be accounted for:

1. Units Perhaps the fundamental fact about phonology is that (in all spoken languages) the phonological entities corresponding to minimal elements of the grammatical system (i.e., morphemes in the terminology of some linguists) are in general not minimal but are divisible into smaller phonological entities. In somewhat looser phraseology it might be said that morphemes (or minimal grammatical signs) have phonological "parts" which recur as parts of other morphemes. That amounts to stating

that there exist such things as phonological units independently of grammatical units. Accordingly the term "units" may be used as a short label for this property. It has commonly also been observed that the number of such phonological units is smaller than the number of morphemes.

This fundamental property is the basis of Hjelmslev's distinction between expression and content: ". . . a description in accordance with our principles must analyze content and expression separately, with each of the two analyses eventually yielding a restricted number of entities, which are not necessarily susceptible of one-to-one matching with entities in the opposite plane."[2] Bloomfield described the property as follows in his "Postulates":[3] "Different morphemes may be alike or partly alike as to vocal features . . . A minimum same of vocal feature is a phoneme or distinctive sound. As, for instance, English [b, s, t], the English normal word-stress, the Chinese tones . . . The number of different phonemes in a language is a small sub-multiple of the number of forms."

2. Alternation The combination of phonological units corresponding to a morpheme may vary from one occurrence of the morpheme to another. It is generally agreed that the indefinitely discriminable variation in acoustic features of a unit within a fixed linguistic context is outside of linguistic structure, hence not to be counted as phonological alter-

[1]"The Non-Uniqueness of Phonemic Solutions of Phonetic Systems," *Bulletin of the Institute of History and Philology, Academia Sinica* 4:4.363–397 (1934); *Readings in Linguistics* 38–54.

[2]Louis Hjelmslev, *Prolegomena to a Theory of Language,* translated by Francis J. Whitfield, revised English edition (Madison, 1961), 46.

[3]Leonard Bloomfield, "A Set of Postulates for the Science of Language," *Language* 2.153–164 (1926); *Readings in Linguistics* 26–31.

*Reprinted from *Language* 42.536–573 (1966) by permission.

nation. Otherwise the number of phonological entities in the linguistic structure would be indefinitely large and continually growing with the occurrence of new utterances. Beyond this rather inescapable point there is very little general agreement, despite decades of work on phonological theory. According to one widespread view there are two quite distinct types of alternation and, accordingly, three clearly distinguishable types of phonological units. Although terminology varies somewhat, the terms morphophoneme, phoneme, and allophone are often used for the three types of units, and the two types of alternation are sometimes referred to as morphophonemic (i.e., alternation among phonemes corresponding to a single morphophoneme) and phonemic (alternation among allophones corresponding to a single phoneme). A conflicting view has been proposed by Halle and Chomsky.[4] It has a lower level bearing some resemblance to that of the allophones of conventional practice and an upper level somewhat higher than that of the conventional morphophonemes; but between these two no structural level is recognized. There is in any specific linguistic structure a sequence of rewrite rules, but no intervening level exists except in the sense that a level may be said to exist between each pair of ordered rewrite rules. The number of such levels is of course rather large and varies from one language to another, even from one dialect of the same language to another. The phonological units of this view differ from those of the other also in that they are binary distinctive features. Various additional ways of treating phonological alternation have been proposed, but they need not be described here, since this introductory statement is not intended as a historical survey.

3. Tactics   Phonological units occur in definite patterns of arrangement which are independent of the grammatical patterns and meanings of the morphemes which they represent.

That is, there is in every language a set of relationships concerned with the composition of syllables and other combinations of phonological units.[5] The term phonotactics has often been used in this connection.

4. Components   There exist in any language a small number of phonological features which are components of phonological segments. The term phonological unit used above is intentionally quite vague, since different theories recognize different phonological units, and there may be different kinds of phonological units recognized within a single theory. It is to be noted, however, that phonological units of two different size levels have generally been recognized. That is, it has been common to distinguish phonological segments and components of such segments. One is concerned here with a different type of level from that which relates to alternation. The morphophonemes, phonemes, and allophones mentioned above are all phonological segments, and any of them may have components according to one type of phonological theory, while another type would assert that phonemes and allophones have components but morphophonemes do not. Much of the literature dealing with components is not explicit about such matters, however. The Chomsky-Halle approach follows Jakobson in recognizing phonological components of a special two-valued type, i.e., binary distinctive features.[6] This school is also unusual in not granting any structural status to phonological units of a higher size level than these distinctive features, i.e., in not recognizing phonological segments as ele-

[4]See, for example, Morris Halle, *The Sound Pattern of Russian* (The Hague, 1959); Noam Chomsky, *Current Issues in Linguistic Theory* [39] (The Hague, 1964); Morris Halle, "Phonology in Generative Grammar" [37], *Word* 18.54–72 (1962); Noam Chomsky and Morris Halle, "Some Controversial Questions in Phonological Theory" [42], *Journal of Linguistics* 1.97–138 (1965).

[5]There may be some doubt as to whether this point is universally accepted, since one school of phonological thought, that of Chomsky and Halle (cf. footnote 4), has provided no direct means of accounting for such patterns of arrangement. An indirect account of some phonotactic features is to be provided by "redundancy rules," which add features to individual segments, but it has not been shown how or whether the facts of the phonotactics of a language in general (e.g., the structure of the English syllable) could be described by such means. Nevertheless it is clear from various remarks in their discussions of redundancy rules that they would like to be able to account for such facts.

[6]Cf. Roman Jakobson, Gunnar Fant, and Morris Halle, *Preliminaries to Speech Analysis,* M.I.T. Acoustics Laboratory Technical Report No. 13 (Cambridge, Mass., 1952).

ments in a linguistic structure.[7] The phonological side of this school's morpheme is a distinctive feature matrix rather than a chain of phonological segments.[8] (This matter is discussed below.)

Although these four types of phonological phenomena are quite generally recognized in one way or another, very little explicit detail concerning them is well established. A particularly noteworthy gap, often overlooked, is the absence of an acceptable specification of how these various types of phenomena are related to one another within a linguistic structure. For example, the following questions have not received fully satisfactory answers: (1) What are the ultimate constituents[9] of the phonotactics—phonemes, morphophonemes, components of phonemes? (2) Do morphophonemes (as well as phonemes) have components; and if so what is their relationship to components of phonemes? (3) How (in detail) do we relate to each other the two ways of specifying arrangements of phonologic units, i.e., (a) by the phonotactics, (b) by morphology plus the specification of composition of morphemes? (4) What is the proper role of phonological components in the description of alternation among phonological segments? (5) If the phoneme is not elementary but has components, then what is its structural status, if any? (This question seems particularly pertinent if the components are taken as the ultimate constituents of the tactics.)

In connection with phonological alternation there may be raised several additional questions, some of which have met with widely varying answers during the past several years. Conventional phonemics, the best known approach to phonological phenomena, provides a

good orientation for further investigation into some of these questions, even though it is a bit vague on certain points and variable on others. It may be designated C-phonemics for short; if the reader prefers he may take the C as standing for "Classical."

THE PHONEMIC PRINCIPLE

The outstanding characteristic of C-phonemics is its insistence that there is such a thing as a phonemic level. That is, it holds that some features of speech sound or of articulation are distinctive while others are not. The former are phonemic, the latter subphonemic. Another version of the principle is that contrastive phonetic differences must be distinguished from those differences which are noncontrastive. In this connection the well known concept of complementary distribution[10] and Hjelmslev's commutation[11] are important concepts. This same phonemic level is specified by the very closely related distinction, mentioned above, between alternation among allophones of a phoneme on the one hand and alternation among phonemes on the other.

Since the term phonemics has usually been used for an area which excludes treatment of morphophonemic alternation, various quite different ways of treating morphophonemic alternation have accompanied C-phonemics at different times and places. C-phonemics itself says nothing about how morphophonemic alternation is to be handled, except that it is to be sharply distinguished from alternation among allophones.

C-phonemic treatment of phonemic components has often been haphazard, indirect, or incidental, but explicit recognition to components as structural elements has been granted by, for example, Harris,[12] Bloch,[13]

---

[7]Chomsky and Halle, *Journal of Linguistics* 1.119 [472] (1965): "We conclude . . . that only feature notation has linguistic significance, and that segments are simply to be regarded as conventional abbreviations, utilized to cope with the exigencies of printing but having no linguistic significance in themselves."

[8]Noam Chomsky, *Aspects of the Theory of Syntax* (Cambridge, Mass., 1965), 84: ". . . the lexicon is a set of lexical entries, each lexical entry being a pair (D, C), where D is a phonological distinctive feature matrix 'spelling' a certain lexical formative and C is a collection of specified syntactic features . . ."

[9]I.e., the items which are treated by the tactics as atomic, items whose combinations are accounted for by it but whose composition, if any, is not.

[10]Cf. Morris Swadesh, "The Phonemic Principle" [3], *Language* 10.117–129 (1934), *Readings in Linguistics* 32–37; and numerous other articles. This principle, which follows from the distinctiveness principle discussed below, has been criticized by Chomsky and Halle (e.g., *Journal of Linguistics* 1.128–130 [477–479]) on the grounds that if it is applied as the sole criterion in phonemic analysis, absurd solutions will result. It should be obvious that the principle was not intended to be applied in isolation from all others.

[11]Cf. footnote 2.

[12]Zellig S. Harris, "Simultaneous Components in Phonology" [12], *Language* 20.181–205 (1944); *Readings in Linguistics* 124–138.

[13]Bernard Bloch, "A Set of Postulates for Phonemic Analysis" [16], *Language* 24.3–46 (1948);

Martin,[14] and Hockett.[15] Implicit recognition has quite generally been given to components by C-phonemicists when they have displayed phonemic inventories in charts organized according to manners and positions of articulation. Perhaps it did not occur to some of them, however, to ponder the structural significance of such arrangement.

With regard to phonotactics C-phonemics has had no explicit or consistent policy. Some treatments have taken phonemes to be the ultimate constituents,[16] but Hockett, in his *Manual of Phonology*,[17] took the position that the ultimate constituents are the phonemic components and that the phoneme is no more than a constitute at a particular size level of the phonotactics. He thus proposed to answer one of the long-standing problems of C-phonemics by relegating it to the status of pseudoproblem, to which there is not and should not be a single fixed answer. This is the problem involved in such questions as: Unit phoneme or cluster?, one phoneme or two?, tš or č?

C-phonemics should not be confused with the fictitious framework which Chomsky calls taxonomic phonemics (T-phonemics), a system apparently created by him to serve as the helpless victim of a dramatic onslaught.[18] Chomsky characterizes T-phonemics in terms of four conditions which he calls linearity, invariance, biuniqueness, and local determinacy. The biuniqueness condition, of which the local determinacy condition is a part, is the basic requirement stated above which distinguishes alternation among phonemes from alternation among allophones. The invariance condition, which would require that all components of a phoneme have a phonetic realization in every occurrence of the phoneme, is present for some versions of C-phonemics but not for others;[19] and C-phonemics has no linearity requirement. Chomsky's fictitious linearity condition "requires that each occurrence of a phoneme in the phonemic representation of an utterance be associated with a particular succession of (one or more) consecutive phones . . . as its 'member' or 'realization'; and, furthermore, that if A precedes B in the phonemic representation, then the phone sequence associated with A precedes . . . that associated with B . . ."[20]

That such a requirement is not a part of C-phonemics is clear from the theoretical writings as well as from the phonological descriptions of C-phonemicists. For example, no C-phonemicist ever proposed analyzing a tone language as having a separate set of vowel phonemes for each tone. As an example on the theoretical side, Bloch's "Postulates for Phonemic Analysis," a standard theoretical work on C-phonemics, contains several statements explicitly indicating that he accepted no such requirement.[21]

"Studies in Colloquial Japanese IV: Phonemics," *Language* 26.86–125 (1950); *Readings in Linguistics* 329–348.

[14]Samuel E. Martin, "Korean Phonemics," *Language* 27.519–533 (1951); *Readings in Linguistics* 364–371.

[15]Charles F. Hockett, "Peiping Phonology," *JAOS* 67.253–267 (1947); *Readings in Linguistics* 217–228; "Componential Analysis of Sierra Popoluca," *IJAL* 13.258–267 (1947).

[16]Cf., for example, the treatments of English by Leonard Bloomfield, *Language* (New York, 1933), 130–135, and Benjamin Lee Whorf, *Language, Thought, and Reality* (New York, 1956), 223–230.

[17]Charles F. Hockett, *A Manual of Phonology, IJAL* Memoir 11 (1955).

[18]Cf. *Current Issues in Linguistic Theory* (see footnote 4), 75 [406] ff.

[19]Chomsky makes the surprising assertion, for which he offers no support, that "the invariance condition has no clear meaning unless the linearity condition is also met," *Current Issues in Linguistic Theory,* 79 [408].

[20]*Current Issues in Linguistic Theory,* 78 [407]. Evidently it is also to be understood that, according to this condition, phonemes and phones may occur only in linear sequences. Chomsky incorrectly asserts that the linearity condition follows from definitions of the phoneme as a bundle of distinctive features. It would follow only if there were requirements that (1) features occurring simultaneously may not belong to different bundles, and (2) no bundle can be discontinuous.

[21]See the following sections (cf. footnote 13): 48.2, 52.4, 53.2, 53.6, 56.1, 56.2, 57.2. Note also the following statements from "Studies in Colloquial Japanese IV: Phonemics": "The order of phones in a phrase is successive, simultaneous, or overlapping: segments occur only in succession; but spans, which are coextensive with qualities common to a train of several segments, occur simultaneously with the segments that compose the train, and may overlap with other spans." "Each phoneme is defined by the quality or combination of qualities present in all its members and absent from all other phones of the dialect; and every phone that contains such a quality or combination belongs to the phoneme which is defined by it. A phone that contains two or more such qualities or combinations accordingly belongs to two or more phonemes at once."

An important part of Chomsky's attack on T-phonemics is directed against what he calls the biuniqueness condition. Since that condition, in one form or another, is shared by C-phonemics, and is in fact one of its most cherished principles, it is appropriate to consider it in some detail before going on to other matters.

THE BIUNIQUENESS OF
PHONEMIC SOLUTIONS OF
PHONETIC SYSTEMS

As Chomsky states it, "the biuniqueness condition . . . asserts that each sequence of phones is represented by a unique sequence of phonemes and that each sequence of phonemes represents a unique sequence of phones."[22] He clarifies in a footnote that "In this form, the condition is of course rarely met. What is intended, rather, is that each sequence of phonemes represents a sequence of phones that is unique up to free variation." The use of the term biuniqueness in this connection stems from a statement made by Hockett in 1951.[23]

Several points of clarification are needed if this principle is to be properly understood. First, it is important to distinguish it from the ways in which it has been used. Chomsky and Halle are correct in their criticism of the attempts of C-phonemicists to define rigorous procedures of analysis by means of principles such as that of biuniqueness and that of complementary distribution. That is to say, the C-phonemicists were surely mistaken in their supposition that it was necessary and feasible to specify such procedures.[24] But the type of use to which the principles were put must be distinguished from the principles themselves. This criticism is concerned only with basic methodology, not with the criteria which were used to implement it. The same criteria may be applicable in a different methodological orientation. Thus the so-called biuniqueness condition should be considered as one of the properties of an acceptable C-phonemic solution, not as a procedural device. Note that this statement makes no commitment as to whether the property is an independent criterion of acceptability or an automatic consequence of one or more other properties. In either case it remains interesting and useful (for reasons indicated below).

By the same token, the statement of the biuniqueness requirement should refer to linguistic structure or to the phonemic description, rather than to the raw or partially analyzed linguistic data.

A good example of the considerations involved is provided by Monachi, a Uto-Aztecan language of California. In the dialect of Bishop, California, [m] alternates with [w̃] (nasalized [w]); the latter occurs after vowels, while the former never occurs after vowels (both segments are always followed by a vowel). In the dialect of North Fork, the corresponding alternation is between [m] and [w] (non-nasalized). To the C-phonemicist this description fails to give a clear picture of the situation, since it lacks certain essential information (whose absence would not disturb Chomsky or Halle). The relevant further fact is that there is also (in both dialects) a [w] (non-nasalized) which does not participate in the alternation and which contrasts with [m]. Now the structural relationships are clear to the C-phonemicist. In North Fork there is neutralization, and [w] after vowels is phonologically ambiguous, but in Bishop [w̃] and [w] are in contrast. According to C-phonemics the alternation in Bishop is subphonemic, i.e., [m] and [w̃] are allophones of one phoneme; but in North Fork it is a morphophonemic alternation, even though the conditioning environments are the same in the two dialects. Thus the C-phonemic transcription of the forms 'will go' and 'our future going' is /miyawai/, /tawiyawai'na/ in North Fork, /miyawai/, /tamiyawai'na/ in Bishop. And the transcription /wiya/ 'acorns', /tawiya/ 'our acorns' applies for both dialects.

Consider further a hypothetical dialect just like that of North Fork except that it lacks a [w] contrasting with [m], i.e., it has no forms like /wiya/ 'acorns'. In this case [m] and [w] would be considered allophones of the same phoneme. Note that the well trained C-

[22] *Current Issues in Linguistic Theory,* 80 [408].

[23] *Language* 27.340 [316]. The example chosen by Hockett in his discussion is a hypothetical one which is perhaps unrealistic in that it assumes no phonetic difference between prejunctural and postjunctural [t].

[24] This statement in no way denies the value of working out and teaching practical procedures of analysis. The point is that such procedures should be distinguished from expositions of linguistic theory and from criteria for evaluating proposed descriptions. Linguistic theory and practical linguistic analysis both benefit from such separation.

phonemicist would analyze the components of this phoneme differently from those of the Bishop /m/. In the hypothetical dialect, the feature labial is distinctive for this phoneme but nasality is non-distinctive. In Bishop, on the other hand, the components labial and nasal are both distinctive; i.e., nasality is distinctive because of the contrast between [w̃] and [w]. Closure is not distinctive in either phoneme; when present (i.e., in environments other than intervocalic) it is determined.

What is the motivation for this principle that requires the C-phonemicist to write /tawiyawai'na/? A preliminary answer may be found by considering the concept of distinctiveness.

Any communication system must have a way to express meaning, i.e., an expression system. In general, whatever physical medium is used for expression (speech, writing, DNA, etc.) must have diversity, i.e., divergence from uniformity. Otherwise information could not be expressed. In natural spoken language, this diversity is in the speech. But speech, even of a single language, exhibits innumerably many different sound features, and only some of these differences are distinctive, i.e., are able to distinguish different meanings. It is of fundamental importance to identify these distinctive features of difference and to distinguish them from those which are not distinctive. This is the reason for separating the C-phonemic level from the phonetic in describing spoken languages. It allows the description to distinguish those features of the diversity in the medium of expression which have communicative significance from those which do not.

Perhaps an illustration from outside of language will provide perspective to help make the principle more obvious. Consider a familiar communicative device used by certain unprincipled gamblers: marked cards. Those who have seen a deck of marked cards or have heard them described by experts are familiar with the fact that the distinctive markings, which serve to distinguish kings from tens, etc., are extremely difficult to detect, since they are embedded in the design on the backs of the cards, a medium which has a great deal of nondistinctive diversity. A "phonetic" description of the backs of these cards would describe all of the diversity of the design in detail; and it would be useless to anyone wanting to know what the system was. In considering the backs of these cards from the point of view of their communicative function it is precisely the distinctive markings which are relevant. Only these are of interest to one concerned with the system. The difference between distinctive and nondistinctive, between contrastive and noncontrastive, between "emic" and "etic," is crucial.

To those who have the experience of hearing an unfamiliar language for the first time, or who see a page of unfamiliar phonetic transcription, there is a comparable situation. The speech is a bewildering variety of sound, a patterned but unfathomable diversity. Yet to one who knows the phonemic system of the language, as to the gambler who knows the "emic" system of the marked cards, recognition of the meaning encoded in the medium is immediate and effortless. Like the gambler with his cards, the linguist who is given a description of a language to read will find it relatively useless if it does not separate the distinctive from the nondistinctive. Without such separation the basis of expression—that which makes the communication system communicative—is left hidden.

The principle of differentiating the distinctive from the nondistinctive by means of phonemic as opposed to phonetic transcription means that although the phonetic transcription should show all the detail that is practically feasible, the phonemic transcription should show all those features which are distinctive, and no others. In other words, the phonemic transcription should differentiate units which have a distinctive difference, but it should not differentiate where there are nondistinctive or nonexistent differences. More precisely, the distinctiveness principle is that a correct C-phonemic solution treats two units (i.e., segments, syllables, or the like) as phonemically different if and only if there is a distinctive phonetic difference between them. By distinctive phonetic difference I mean a difference in at least one distinctive phonetic feature; a phonetic feature is distinctive if its presence is not determined by its immediate environment. (A more precise specification is given below.)

Thus (1) Bishop [m] and [w̃] are not phonemically different because the difference between them is not distinctive; (2) North Fork [w]₁ which alternates with [m] and [w]₂ which does not (corresponding to Bishop [w̃] and [w] respectively) are not phonemically different, since there is no distinctive phonetic difference between them, since there is no phonetic difference at all between them; (3) the North Fork alternants [m] and [w]₁ are phonemically different, since [w]₁ and [w]₂ are phonemically alike and [m] and [w]₂ are distinctively different (since [m] has the feature of nasality, which is not determined since it may be either present or absent in the environment in question).

The biuniqueness condition is a corollary of the distinctiveness principle. It follows from the distinctiveness principle; the reverse is not true, since the distinctiveness principle is more stringent: it allows only those features which are distinctive to be considered phonemic. The biuniqueness principle by itself would accept uneconomical solutions that failed to make use of complementary distribution, e.g., a description of the Bishop dialect in which [m] and [w̃] were treated as "phonemically" different.

The question of whether the distinctiveness principle is an independent criterion for acceptability of a phonemic solution or is merely a consequence of some other more basic principle is considered below. At this point it need be observed only that a description is relatively uninformative to the extent that it violates this principle.

On the other hand, the biuniqueness condition has been criticized on the grounds that it requires uneconomical descriptions in certain situations. The argument has been presented by Halle, using as an example the Russian obstruents:[25]

In Russian, voicing is distinctive for all obstruents except /c/, /č/ and /x/, which do not possess voiced cognates. These three obstruents are voiceless unless followed by a voiced obstruent, in which case they are voiced. At the end of the word, however, this is true of all Russian obstruents: they are voiceless, unless the following word begins with a voiced obstruent, in which case they are voiced. E.g., [m'ok l̦i] 'was (he) getting wet?', but [m'og bɨ]

[25]Morris Halle, *The Sound Pattern of Russian* (The Hague, 1959), 22–23.

'were (he) getting wet'; [ž'eč l̦i] 'should one burn?', but [ž'ež bɨ] 'were one to burn'.

In a phonological representation which satisfies [the biuniqueness condition] the quoted utterances would be symbolized as follows: /m'ok l̦i/, /m'og bi/, /ž'eč l̦i/, /ž'eč bi/. Moreover, a rule would be required stating that obstruents lacking voiced cognates—i.e., /c/, /č/ and /x/—are voiced in position before voiced obstruents. Since this, however, is true of all obstruents, the net effect of [the biuniqueness condition] would be a splitting up of the obstruents into two classes and the addition of a special rule. If [the biuniqueness condition] is dropped, the four utterances would be symbolized as follows: {m'ok l̦i} {m'ok bi} {ž'eč l̦i} {ž'eč bɨ}, and the above rule could be generalized to cover all obstruents, instead of only {č}, {c} and {x}. It is evident that [the biuniqueness condition] involves a significant increase in the complexity of the representation.

The phonemic analysis which Halle criticizes is the traditional one. He claims that it is a consequence of the biuniqueness condition. If so it would also be a consequence of the distinctiveness principle. The question that must be considered here is whether it really does follow from that principle or whether this is merely an instance of the argument post hoc ergo propter hoc.[26]

If one looks closely at the Russian obstruent clusters from the point of view of the distinctiveness principle, one finds that voicing or lack of it is not a distinctive property of the individual segments. Voicing is present or absent for the whole cluster, except that /v/ can be preceded by a voiceless obstruent, as in *svjet* 'light'. Therefore, to assign voicing or unvoicing to individual segments in a cluster is to violate the principle of distinctiveness. That is, it is uneconomical from the standpoint of C-phonemics. It is assigning phonemic status to phonetic features which in fact are not distinctive. The traditional phonemicization results not from the distinctiveness principle (or from its biuniqueness corollary) but,

[26]For a more transparent example of this argument than Halle's Russian one, see Chomsky's discussion of the analysis of the centering offglide of English, *Current Issues in Linguistic Theory*, 104–105 [420–421].

on the contrary, from a failure fully to apply that principle.

This situation may be compared with one in which, for some language, there are vowel clusters and contrastive pitch. Any vowel cluster, let us say, has either high pitch or low pitch, for the whole cluster. How does the C-phonemicist analyze this situation? He does not set up two sets of vowel phonemes, i.e., one set of high-pitched vowels and one of low-pitched vowels. Instead he sets up just one set of vowels and separates pitch from them. In the typical situation of this type (if not in all of them) one of the pitch levels will be in some sense neutral or unmarked by comparison with the other. Suppose, for example, that the high pitch is accompanied by stress and occurs only once per word while low pitched vowels occur in all other syllables. The analyst would set up one accent phoneme, represented phonetically by high pitch plus stress on the entire vowel cluster with which it occurs. Low pitch, in other words, is taken as the neutral condition. Notice what he does not do: (1) he does not set up two sets of vowels, one with high pitch, the other with low; (2) he does not have two accent phonemes, since only one is necessary; (3) he does not say that the accent phoneme occurs separately with each vowel phoneme in a vowel cluster, but only once per cluster.

Similarly, in the case of the Russian obstruents, we observe that: (1) voicing is not distinctive for the individual segments in an obstruent cluster;[27] (2) (as indicated by morphophonemic alternations) the voicing of the whole cluster is determined by its last member, or by the next to last if the last is [v]; (3) the voiced state appears to be neutral or unmarked, as evidenced by the fact that for all non-obstruents, for which there is no contrast of voicing, the normal condition is voiced.[28] Therefore, the solution is to set up a phoneme of "devoicing," whose phonetic applicability extends from the beginning of an obstruent cluster to the point of its occurrence; that is,

the devoicing phoneme is to be written at the end of the sequence which its phonetic realization accompanies. It may be symbolized as /h/.

Neither voice nor lack of it is to be assigned to individual segments. The voiced condition is the normal one, a determined feature automatically present when the speech mechanism is in operation, unless it is turned off by the devoicing phoneme, which has effect for a whole cluster rather than a single segment.

In the example concerning vowels, the corresponding statement would be that neither low pitch nor high pitch is to be assigned to individual segments, but rather that low pitch is the normal condition automatically present where vowels and other resonants occur, unless the high pitch phoneme is present, and this phoneme applies to a whole vowel cluster.

The general principle involved here relates quite closely to the statements above concerning the expression side of a communication system. An expression system must have a physical medium in which information can be encoded, in terms of consistent divergences from uniformity. It is helpful to distinguish not just two but three aspects of the physical or "etic" side of the expression system: (1) the distinctive differences, (2) the nondistinctive differences which accompany them, and (3) the background features or automatically present features of the physical medium. Naturally, just as the C-phonemicist does not set up structural elements on the "emic" level for the nondistinctive differences, so also he should refrain from setting up elements to account for the features of the medium. Instead, these features may be accounted for by the very fact that the medium is there. The medium, since it is the medium, cannot express meaning and is therefore nondistinctive; rather, meaning is expressed by things done to the medium. In the case of the marked cards, if the information is expressed by divergences in the spokes of wheels in the design, then the wheels and their normal spokes do not require structural elements on the "emic" stratum. In the case of printing on paper, one does not have to set up any graphemes for the paper. If one describes the realization of the grapheme ^G/o/ as a closed circle (where the closure is distinctive because of the contrast with ^G/c/)

---

[27]In other words, if a provisional solution had an element of voicing or unvoicing with each segment, we would find it possible to eliminate it on all but one of them.

[28]Also, it would be more difficult to handle the fact that *v* may follow voiceless obstruents if the voiceless condition were taken as neutral.

then one does not also need an element to account for the white disc inside the circle.

Similarly, some of the sound features present in speech are to be accounted for as features of the medium, automatically present by virtue of the fact that the speech-producing mechanism is in operation; and the structural elements of the phonemic level represent various types of diversity put into this medium. Since Russian has a contrast of voicing only in the obstruents, one may look to the non-obstruents for the normal, background condition; and one finds that presence of voice is the normal condition there. To say that voicing is the positive structural feature because it is louder, i.e., physically more positive, is no more cogent than to say that the disc inside the printed ^{G}/o/ is positive rather than the enclosing circle, on the grounds that the disc is brighter. For printed expression in general the white brightness is there automatically unless it is masked out by ink; and similarly, for Russian speech, voice is automatically there unless it is counteracted by the devoicing phoneme or by final position.

Thus phonemic analysis may be viewed as part of a process of accounting for articulation. Some of the articulatory features are to be accounted for as normally present when the speech production mechanism is in operation. These can, by the way, be divided into two types: (1) those which are universal for human spoken language; and (2) those which are automatically present when a specific language is being spoken but are not accounted for by (1). Of the remaining articulatory features, some are distinctive, others nondistinctive. Those which are nondistinctive are to be described as automatic accompaniments of distinctive features in various environments. For all those features which cannot be accounted for as any of the above it is necessary to set up phonemic elements. Thus one way to loosely define the set of elements of the phonemic level is to say that they are the entities set up to account, as economically as possible, for the features of the phonetic substance that cannot otherwise be accounted for.

Voicing in Russian is to be accounted for by a general rule (either for Russian or perhaps for human spoken language in general), and it is a condition that can be counteracted by the phonemic devoicing element. More-over, lack of voicing for an obstruent cluster is accounted for by a single occurrence of the devoicing element. This analysis is consistent with the principles of C-phonemics (in particular, with the biuniqueness condition) but it is more economical than the traditional phonemic analysis of Russian obstruents. In fact it is more economical simply because the distinctiveness principle has been more thoroughly applied than in the case of the former analysis.

But with this more efficient C-phonemicization, motivated independently of morphophonemic considerations, Halle's argument no longer applies. The "assimilation" in voicing can be accounted for by a single rule stating that the devoicing morphophoneme is realized phonemically as zero (i.e., has no phonemic realization) whenever it is followed by an obstruent other than /v/. This one rule accounts for the "assimilation" of voiceless obstruents to following voiced ones, while the "assimilation" of voiced obstruents to following voiceless ones requires no morphophonemic rule because it is taken care of automatically by the revised phonemicization. Halle's examples would be written according to this analysis as follows (first in morphophonemic transcription, then in phonemic): ^{M}/m'ogh l,i/, ^{M}/m'ogh bi/, ^{M}/ž'ežh l,i/, ^{M}/ž'ežh bi/; and ^{P}/m'ogh l,i/, ^{P}/m'og bi/, ^{P}/ž'ežh l,i/, ^{P}/ž'ež bi/. What is unusual about the three obstruents in question, according to the new analysis, is that they have a limited distribution. They occur only followed by /h/ or by obstruents; other obstruents occur also before resonants.

Thus the inefficiency which Halle correctly finds in the traditional phonemic analysis of Russian has nothing to do with biuniqueness. It is the result not of a basic defect in the C-phonemic principles, but of an incomplete and therefore inadequate separation of the nondistinctive features from the distinctive ones. It is therefore hard to understand why Chomsky responded to this argument[29] by asserting that my position agrees with Halle's![30] Evidently it is necessary to point out that there is a difference between (1) rejecting

[29]Previously presented in my paper "On Redefining the Phoneme," delivered at the 1963 annual meeting of the Linguistic Society of America.

[30]*Current Trends in Linguistics III* (The Hague, 1966), 119–120.

a specific analysis for a particular language and (2) rejecting a general principle of phonological analysis.

Although the foregoing pages defend the distinctiveness principle of C-phonemics, they are not to be taken as asserting that C-phonemics is altogether acceptable, for it is not. While the biuniqueness principle is not one of them, there do exist weaknesses in C-phonemics, and the system does not prove adequate to handle the problems posed below.

SOUND PATTERNS IN LANGUAGE

As indicated above, C-phonemics is vague on some points and variable on others. To certain questions about phonological relationships it has provided no clear answers. The next step is to look at some of these relationships more closely. The orientation at the outset of this examination is provided by C-phonemics, but it will be necessary to go beyond that formulation, to replace its vaguenesses with precision, and to introduce new distinctions where they are needed to provide more economical accounts of phonological phenomena.

It is appropriate to begin with the four generally recognized types of phonological patterning listed at the beginning of this paper. My aim is to identify and describe the relationships involved (rather than the objects which are manifestations of them or rewrite rules which generate such manifestations) as accurately and simply as possible. In doing so it is helpful, if not essential, to employ some system of precise notation. A graphic notation is used here.

1. Units The morphemes of a language are not altogether different from one another with regard to their expression (or phonological realization), but have recurrent partial similarities. In other words, they are, in general, phonologically complex. Moreover, the number of phonological units which occur as their components is in every language smaller than the number of morphemes. This configuration of relationships may be called a sign pattern. The example involving the morphemes *end, Ned, den, and, Dan, d, n, Ed, Nan,* and *Dad* is diagrammed in Figure 1.

Diagrams of this type are made up of lines and nodes. The sole function of the lines is to show connections between nodes (except in the special cases at the boundaries of linguistic structure, where a line connects a node to something outside the structure). Thus the length or curvature of a line is of no significance. The diagrams have two directions: upward (toward meaning) and downward (toward expression). In Figure 1 there are two types of nodes. The triangular ones show a left

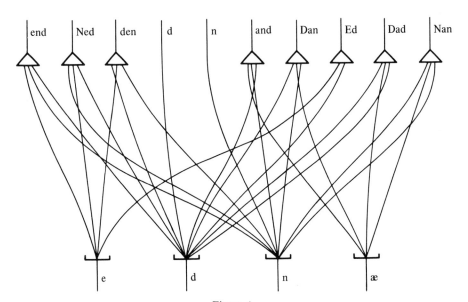

Figure 1

to right ordering of the lines connecting at the lower side, depicting the ordering of phonological elements within (the representation of) a morpheme. The lines going downward from *end* go to the same three lower nodes as those from *Ned,* but the order is different. On the upper side of each triangular node is a single line, corresponding to the morpheme viewed as an elementary unit. The lower side corresponds to the morpheme viewed as a combination of phonological units. Whether one considers the morpheme to be simple or complex is just a matter of terminology; that is, it depends upon what part of the diagram one chooses to apply the label "morpheme" to. For example, one might choose to apply it to the upper line, to the combination of lower lines, or to the node itself (still further possibilities exist if the diagram is extended upward). Those who consider the morpheme to be a combination of phonological units must nevertheless accept the single line extending upward from the node, since the morpheme is universally recognized as minimal in one sense or another (for example, as a minimal meaningful element or a minimal grammatical element). The labels "end," "Ned," etc., in the diagram are merely aids to the reader and are in no way part of the structure. It is, naturally, of no significance whatever that a combination of three letters is used as a label for a single line. What matters is that it is a single line.

Two simple morphemes are shown, *d* and *n* (as in *showed* and *shown*), and since they are treated as phonologically simple, they require no triangular node.

The nodes at the lower part of the diagram are of a different type. Any single occurrence of *e,* as part of the representation of one of the morphemes shown, "belongs" to only one of them; i.e., to *end,* OR to *Ned,* OR to *den,* etc. Accordingly, this type of node may be called an "or" node. The triangular ones may be called "and" nodes, since, for example, when *end* occurs, then *e* AND *n* AND *d* occur (together, in that order).

The fact that morphemes tend to be phonologically complex is of course depicted by the multiple lines going downward from the "and" nodes; and the fact that phonological components are recurrent, as components of multiple morphemes, is shown by the multiple lines leading upward from the "or" nodes.

Note also that the diagram distinguishes *e* as a component of *end* from the general *e* as abstracted from the various forms of which it is a component.

2. Alternation   Phonological units may alternate with other phonological units in representations of morphemes. Figure 2 shows an abstract example of some but not all of the relationships to be identified in this type of phenomenon. It is consistent with C-phonemics in distinguishing alternation involving neutralization from that among units not distinctively different; the latter are below the former.

This diagram introduces a partly new type of node, namely an "or" node of opposite direction from those in Figure 1. This type may be called a "downward or," and the other an "upward or." The morphophoneme *A* leads DOWNWARD either to phoneme *p* OR to phoneme *q.* The neutralized phoneme *q* leads UPWARD either to morphophoneme *A* OR to *B.*[31] Also present in Figure 2 are lines connecting to small circles, signifying zero. The morphophoneme *C* leads downward either to phoneme *r* or to nothing (i.e., is realized as zero). The phoneme *s* leads upward either to morphophoneme *D* or to nothing (i.e., no morphopho-

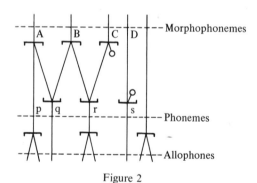

Figure 2

[31]The graphic notation and associated terminology used in my article "The Sememic Approach to Structural Semantics," *AA* 66:3:2.57–78 (1964) are related to the present version as follows: "vertical" there corresponds to "or" here, "horizontal" to "and"; since these two types of relationship were distinguished by the two dimensions in the earlier notation, diagonally upward was used for what is here simply upward. Figure 1 illustrates composite realization; Figure 2 shows diversification, neutralization, zero realization, and empty realization.

neme); in the latter case it is empty, like the second vowel in *boxes*. The diagram is incomplete in that it fails to show conditioning environments for the alternations and in that it ignores phonotactics and phonemic components. These matters are taken up below.

The formulation depicted in Figure 2 is one in which morphophonemes are granted structural status. It thus disagrees with the view which rejects morphophonemes and instead treats all morphophonemic alternation as alternation among allomorphs of morphemes, each allomorph being a combination of phonemes. The graphic notation shows the difference between these two formulations very clearly. The view which treats all morphophonemic alternation as alternation among allomorphs requires a much more complicated diagram than that for the formulation using morphophonemes. Consider, for example, the alternation in Monachi between the phonemes ^{P}/m/ and ^{P}/w/, described above. The two formulations are diagrammed in Figures 3 and 4 for the morphemes meaning "go" and "hand." With morphophonemes as structural elements there is a single downward "or" for the alternation; but for the view that denies structural status to morphophonemes there is a separate downward "or" as well as an additional "and" node for every morpheme exhibiting this alternation. Moreover, the diagram does not show the further complication that would be required in specifying the conditioning environment. The difference between the two diagrams would of course be greatly magnified if additional morphemes exhibiting the alternation were included.

The objection to morphophonemes seems to have been the erroneous notion that they require process description. This mistake has been made quite commonly by both opponents and supporters of morphophonemic rules. The process or rewriting formulation, which crept into morphophonemic description from diachronic linguistics, would recognize only two elements for the alternation shown in Figure 4, namely ^{P}/m/ and ^{P}/w/, instead of three (^{M}/m/, ^{P}/m/, and ^{P}/w/) and would use a rewrite rule which would replace ^{P}/m/ by ^{P}/w/ in intervocalic position. But Figure 4 portrays a quite different conception of morphophonemic alternation, since the line labeled ^{M}/m/ is a different line from either of those labeled ^{P}/m/ and ^{P}/w/. One must not be misled by the fact that the same letter m is used in the label for both ^{M}/m/ and ^{P}/m/. Labels are chosen for mnemonic convenience and are not part of the structure. There is no replacement of ^{P}/m/ by ^{P}/w/. Rather, either ^{P}/m/ or ^{P}/w/ occurs as realization of ^{M}/m/.[32] Many of those who have supposed that morphophonemic rules are necessarily process or rewrite rules have at the same time described allophones of phonemes and allomorphs of morphemes without supposing that process is involved in these relationships. But as Figures 2 and 3 show,

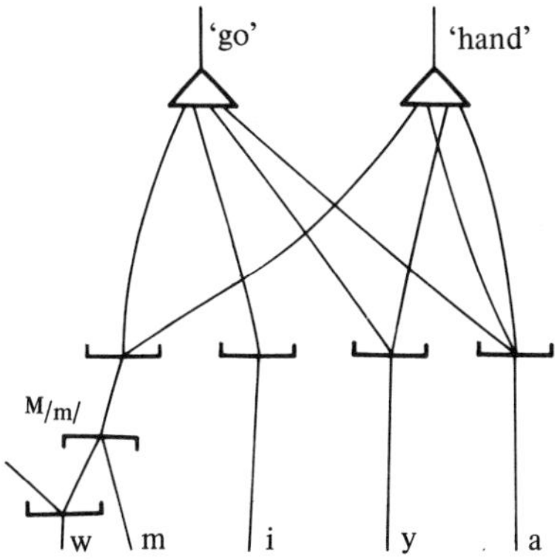

[32]For a fuller discussion of the differences between process and realization, see my "On Alternation, Transformation, Realization, and Stratification" [52], *Georgetown University Monograph Series on Languages and Linguistics* 17.105–122 (1964).

Figure 4

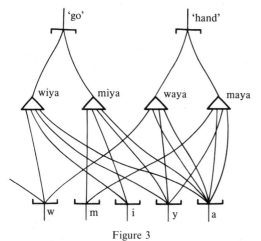

Figure 3

there is no structural basis for supposing that the situations differ in this way. All involve downward "or" relationships, in which the line above the "or" node is a different element from each of those below. (Although the analysis shown in Figure 3 is clearly inefficient for the alternation shown, this type of treatment, i.e., with the downward "or" above the downward "and" of the sign pattern, is clearly indicated in some situations, e.g., the alternation of *good* and *bett-*.) That synchronic morphophonemic alternation is quite different from diachronic phonological change (which really is a process) may be seen by comparing Figures 14 and 15 below. Since the structure shown for the Bishop dialect coincides with that of an earlier stage of North Fork, the change from Figure 15 to Figure 14, which involves moving certain lines and nodes, represents the diachronic phonological change in which pre-North Fork *P/m/ *[w̃] between vowels became modern North Fork P/w/. But the synchronic morphophonemic alternation, and likewise the processes of normal produc-

tion and decoding of speech, involve no changes of lines or nodes.

3. Tactics Combinations of phonological units conform to definite patterns of arrangement. Figure 5 shows part of the phonotactic pattern of the North Fork dialect of Monachi. The "and" labeled *S* is the syllable construction. It leads downward first to a consonant (p, t, . . .), then to a vowel (e, a, . . .), then to either /i/ or /·/ (vowel length) or nothing, then to /h/ or /ʔ/ or /'/ or nothing. (/'/ is realized as length and fortis articulation of the following consonant.) Examples of syllables generated by this tactics are: *pa, teʔ, pu', ta·, ʔai, pe·ʔ, ʔui.*

4. Components Phonemes have recurrent components, which are fewer. in number than they. This pattern is of the same basic type as that shown in Figure 1 and described above. It differs (other than quantitatively) only in that here the components tend to be simultaneous instead of successive. Thus the lines

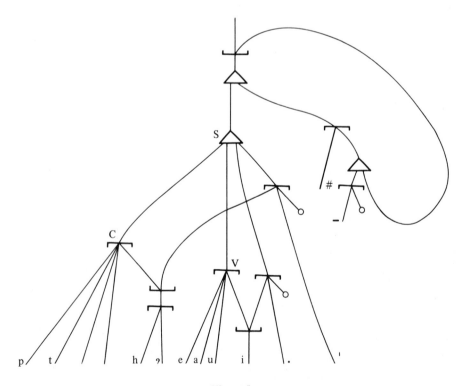

Figure 5

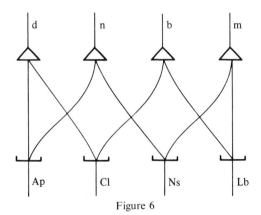

Figure 6

come down from the same point of each triangular node in Figure 6 rather than in left to right order. The example diagrammed in Figure 6 may be taken as applying to English or to Monachi or to various other languages. The labels for components stand for "apical," "closed," "nasal," and "labial."

These phonemic components, or *phonons* for short, are singular, not binary. Binary features have two values, plus and minus. To specify the presence of a binary feature would require not only identification of the feature but also indication of whether its value is plus or minus. Thus the use of binary features would require the addition of some new ad hoc device to the system of graphic notation, representing an additional type of conceptual equipment needed in a linguistic theory which would use them. Note also that the phonemes in Figure 6 have only two phonons each (some phonemes have three phonons, some only one), whereas with binary features of the type advocated by Chomsky and Halle each segment has some eleven features after the redundancy rules and about half a dozen before them.

Another question concerning distinctive features is: Why recognize two sign patterns (Figure 1 and Figure 6)? Why not "divide" morphemes directly into distinctive features, bypassing the phonemes? This is, roughly, the recommendation of Chomsky and Halle, except that they would go even further: not morphemes but lexical items (many of which, in any language, are morphemically complex) are to be represented in the dictionary by binary distinctive feature matrices.[33]

[33]Cf. footnote 8.

As in the alternative treatment for morphophonemic alternation discussed above with reference to Figures 3 and 4, it is the criterion of simplicity (or, equivalently, of economy, parsimony, or generalization) which provides the answer to this question. This criterion, in its proper use, is based upon considerations which are not specific to linguistics but are generally applicable (and are continually applied subconsciously) to scientific work.

Suppose that there are two descriptions or parts of descriptions (of anything at all) which are equivalent in effective information, i.e., in the data (real or abstract) which they account for, and which differ only in that the first states a certain relationship repeatedly, i.e., two or more times for separate entities exhibiting it, while the second, by abstracting the relationship, states it only once. Then the second is to be preferred. It describes the same effective information with less surface information, since it states the relationship only once instead of repeatedly. At the same time the statement of that relationship is more general in that it accounts once for information stated repeatedly in the first description. That is, the second description is simpler because it contains a generalization absent from the first. Generalization and simplicity are two aspects of the same property. One might almost say that the second description is closer to the truth than the first, since the first describes the relationship as if it were several different relationships rather than one, i.e., in a way that would be appropriate if they were different.

For the sake of precision the simplicity principle may be implemented concretely for any of various systems of notation. Its implementation for an algebraic notation has been discussed in a preliminary way elsewhere.[34]

[34]In my *Outline of Stratificational Grammar* (Berkeley, 1962); "Stratificational Linguistics as a Basis for Machine Translation," in Bulcsu Laszlo, ed., *Approaches to Language Data Processing* (The Hague, in press) [also to appear in Adam Makkai and David Lockwood (eds.), *Readings in Stratificational Linguistics* (University of Alabama Press, in press, 1971)—VBM]; and "Kinship Terminology and Linguistic Structure," *AA 67:5:2.37–64* (1965). See also the discussion of simplicity and related concepts in my "Epilegomena to a Theory of Language," *Romance Philology* 19:4.531–573 (1966).

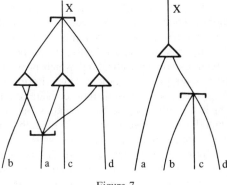

Figure 7

to *ab* or *ac* or *ad*." The second says "*X* leads down to *a* and (*b* or *c* or *d*)." The description at right states this effective information with less surface information: It uses only six lines, while the one at left uses eleven.[36] The description at right includes a generalization absent from the first, namely that every combination has the same first member, *a*. The description at the right has stated the occurrence of *a* only once, while that at the left has stated it three separate times. The one line for *a* at the right is doing the work of four lines at the left, and the "and" node at right

Here the implementation for graphic notation may be considered.[35] The two graphs shown in Figure 7 are identical in effective information. The set of all possible combinations of entities to which *X* leads at the bottom is the same for both: *ab, ac, ad*. The first says "*X* leads down

---

[35]Graphic and algebraic notations may be designed to be mechanically interconvertible (cf. graphs of conic sections and the associated quadratic equations), so that they differ only as alternative notational implementations of the same underlying set of descriptive concepts. The implementation of the simplicity principle, which must yield compar-

able results for the alternative notations, is easier for the graphic notation than for the algebraic, since with algebraic notation it is necessary to provide for ignoring nonsignificant differences that result from mechanical limitations of algebraic notation, such as its essentially linear character. In fact the easiest way to implement the simplicity principle for the algebraic notation of stratificational theory is to specify the implementation for the graphic notation plus the rules for converting from the algebraic to the graphic.

[36]It might be supposed that nodes should be counted rather than (or in addition to) lines, but nodes are not mutually comparable in a simple way since they can differ from one another in complexity: a node with six lines leading out of one side is more complex than one with only two.

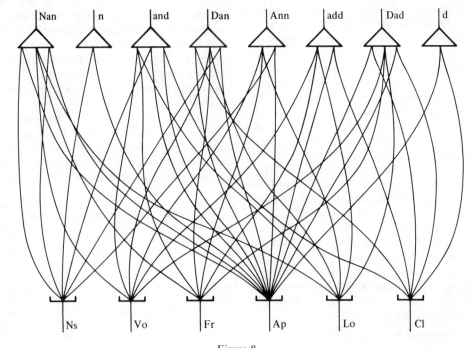

Figure 8

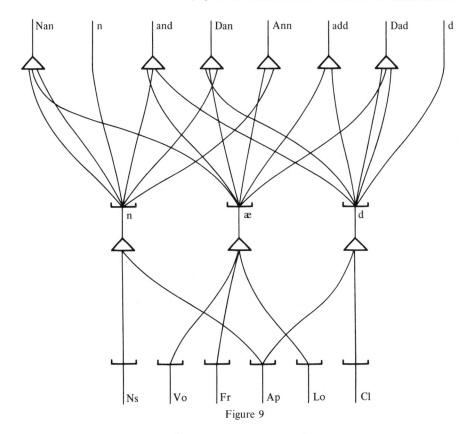

Figure 9

is doing the work of three "ands" at left. In the left hand description, the occurrence of *a* in the three combinations is stated in a way that would be appropriate if it were three separate entities. Thus this description is perhaps to be regarded as not actually revealing the whole truth about the situation. These considerations are of course quite independent of the kind of phenomena which the diagram may be describing. A configuration of the type shown could appear in a tactic pattern at any stratum of a language, but it could also appear in systems other than natural languages. The implementation of the simplicity principle for this notation is applicable to the description of any phenomena to which notation of this type is appropriate.

Figures 3 and 4 are equal in effective information but Figure 3 has twenty-eight lines while Figure 4 has only eighteen. This difference is easily correlated with generalizations in Figure 4 which Figure 3 lacks; that is, with repetitions in Figure 3 of information stated once in Figure 4. Thus for the morpheme "go"

Figure 3 says two separate times that the last three segments are *iya*.

Figure 8 illustrates the proposal that morphemes be described as leading directly to phonons in a single sign pattern. It uses 56 lines. Figure 9, using two sign patterns, has the same effective information, but only 40 lines. The difference between 40 and 56 may not seem great, but the eight lines at the top and the six at bottom correspond exactly in the two descriptions. Subtracting this constant gives a comparison for the different part: 42 lines as opposed to 26. As with Figures 3 and 4, the difference grows greater as more morphemes are added to the description. The difference in surface information is of course directly related to generalizations in Figure 9 which are absent from Figure 8. In fact each upward "or" represents a generalization, since it brings together several lines from above and allows their downward componency to be stated once instead of repeatedly. That is, the value of the phoneme-sized unit is precisely that it represents a generalization missing from the description which fails to recognize it. In the formulation of Figure 8, the componency of a given segment is stated separately for each morpheme of which it is a part, instead of once. (Needless to say, if binary distinctive features were used instead of phonons the amount of excess surface information would be even greater.)

Actually, the proposal of Chomsky and Halle is even more extravagant than the foregoing comparison reveals, for they recommend that lexical items (rather than morphemes) be given in the dictionary as distinctive feature matrices. That is, they propose to use a single sign pattern in place of three (phonemic, morphemic, and lexemic), not just two. Lexemes like *woodpecker, tightwad, crawfish, understand, New York,* etc., are to be directly provided with distinctive feature matrices. Thus if *pro-* is a component of 100 lexemes

(e.g., *propose, produce, proclaim, profess*) then the column of distinctive features for *p* is to be given 100 separate times solely for *p* as a component of *pro-,* i.e., apart from *p* as component of *pre-, per-, -pose,* etc.

A SYSTEM OF DESCRIPTIVE PHONOLOGY

Three types of phonological pattern have been identified above: the sign pattern, the alternation pattern, and the tactic pattern. The next problem is to determine how these patterns are related to one another, how they fit together to form a phonological system as a whole. In terms of the graphic notation, this is a question of how the diagrams of the patterns are to be connected to one another.

Two of the above figures show connections of one pattern directly to another of the same type without any intermediate relationships. In Figure 2 the morphophonemic alter-

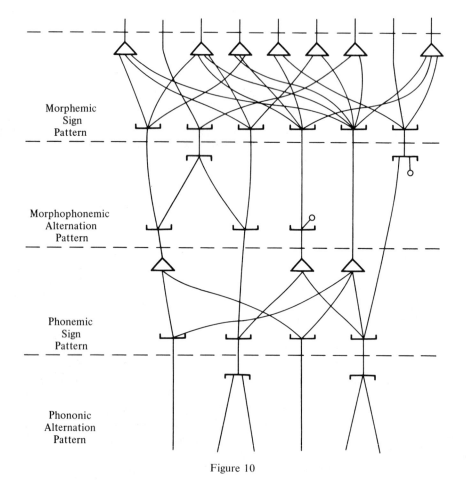

Figure 10

nation pattern leads directly to an allophonic alternation pattern, and Figure 9 shows the morphemic sign pattern connecting directly to the phonemic sign pattern. It thus omits the distinction between morphophonemes and phonemes. It is evident that the proper position of the morphophonemic alternation pattern is between the morphemic sign pattern and the phonemic sign pattern, as suggested by Figure 4. (The specific example depicted in Figure 4, however, requires refinement in another way, as indicated below.)

The integration of patterns arrived at so far, then, is the one depicted in Figure 10. A new type of node is introduced in this figure, namely the downward ordered "or " Ordering in an "or" node means that the left branch takes precedence over the right one when it is possible to take either. This type of ordering in the graphic notation corresponds to ordering of subrules of realization rules in algebraic notation.[37]

A problem left unsolved by the scheme of Figure 10 is that it appears not to take account of the fact that some (but by no means all) cases of morphophonemic alternation are more simply describable in terms of components than segments. The figure also fails to show (1) how conditioning environments relate to the alternations and (2) tactics.

It has commonly been assumed that phonemes are the ultimate constituents of phonotactics. For this conception, the lines at the bottom of a tactic pattern (cf. Figure 5) would be phonemes. But the lines at the top of the phonemic sign pattern and the bottom of the morphophonemic alternation pattern are also phonemes. There is, however, no conflict here: a phoneme has both a tactic function

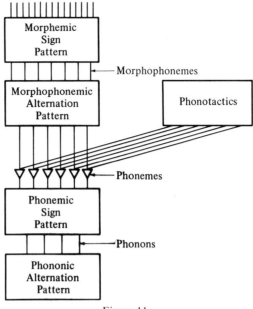

Figure 11

(according to the common assumption) *and* a connection upward to one or more morphophonemes. Thus for each phoneme there must be an upward "and" node, as shown in Figure 11.

On the other hand, it has been suggested, e.g., by Hockett in his *Manual of Phonology,*[38] that the ultimate constituents of the phonotactics are the phonemic components. For this view the row of upward "ands" would fit in below the phonemic sign pattern. Perhaps also to be considered is the possibility that the connections to tactics belong at the top of the morphophonemic alternation pattern, i.e., that morphophonemes are the ultimate constituents.

The way to answer such a question is not to speculate but to refer to linguistic data and to determine which conception reveals the tactic patterning most elegantly.

Figure 5 above shows a very neat picture of syllable structure. It has one drawback, however, if it is taken to be a tactics of C-phonemes; although it is tantalizingly close, it does not accurately fit the data. Moreover, there is no simple way to adjust it so that it will agree with the data. There are certain clearly specifiable, hence regular and structurally relevant, discrepancies from what the

---

[37]Cf. my "On Alternation, Transformation, Realization, and Stratification" [52] (see footnote 32). Ordering of subrules of a realization rule often makes it possible to state conditioning environments more simply than if they were unordered, but not always. Nevertheless, as a matter of purely practical convenience, I have used the convention of always writing the subrules of a rule in some order (i.e., even when simplification does not result). In the graphic notation, however, ordering in an "or" is specified only where relevant.

Realization rules as described in that paper have been simplified considerably as a result of work done since it was written, particularly that reported here.

[38]Cf. footnote 17.

tactic pattern generates; yet it cannot readily be adjusted to take account of them, since they involve restrictions on what can occur at or across syllable boundaries. For example, a syllable with initial P/m/ never occurs after a syllable with a final vowel. But this fact correlates with the alternation discussed above, between P/m/ and P/w/. The realization rule for this alternation states that the alternant P/w/ occurs after vowel, P/m/ elsewhere. Now it happens that there is also a morphophonemic alternation corresponding to each of the other cooccurrence restrictions. For each of the sequences which does not occur, there is something else which occurs instead. In the (incomplete) list below, the nonoccurring sequences are at left, and at the right of each is shown the sequence which occurs where the one at the left would be expected. (V stands for vowel, B for obstruent.)

(1) Vm   Vw
(2) ʔB, hB   'B
(3) hm, hn   'm, 'n
(4) '#   #[39]
(5) Vs, Vx   V's, V'x
(6) hh, ʔh, 'h   h
(7) hʔ, ʔʔ, 'ʔ   ʔ
(8) 'y   't
(9) 'w   'kʷ

Two closely related facts are crucial here: (1) the description of the tactic pattern would be greatly complicated by including specification of these restrictions; (2) such specification would be redundant anyway, since it is already given by the description of the morphophonemic alternations.

Thus it appears that the phonotactics is really the tactics of the morphophonemes and that the simplest way to account for the occurring combinations of phonemes is to describe the tactics of the morphophonemes and the morphophonemic alternations.

In English there is evidence pointing in the same direction. Syllable-initial consonant clusters ending in P/y/ occur only when P/uw/ follows, e.g., *Cupid, punitive, music.* This circumstance presents a problem in phonotactics as applied to phonemes, since it involves a co-occurrence restriction across a tactic boundary (i.e., the boundary between consonant cluster and vocalic nucleus). But the problem disappears if the phonotactics is taken as applying to morphophonemes, since P/yuw/ is the realization of morphophonemic M/u:/, a vocalic entity (cf. the morphophonemic alternation in *punitive, punish*).

It turns out, however, that an attempt to apply a simple tactics of syllable structure to combinations of morphophonemes encounters complications just as serious as those described above, if by morphophoneme is meant an element at the bottom of the morphemic sign pattern, i.e., a downward component of a morpheme. The term morphophoneme has not always been used for just these entities,[40] however, so it will enhance precision if we use from here on a term defined to have specifically that meaning. Just as the downward component of a phoneme may be called a phonon, so the downward component of a morpheme may be called a *morphon*.[41] Then we can say that the simply statable tactic pattern fails to fit morphon combinations (just as it fails to fit phoneme combinations). In this case also, however, the discrepancies between the actual combinations of Monachi morphons and the simple tactics of Figure 5 are all related to morphophonemic alternation. Some examples are presented below. At the left are shown some sequences of morphons (with spaces at morpheme boundaries) and at the right the phonemic combinations which occur as their realizations. (C stands for consonant, V for vowel, B for obstruent, R for resonant.)[42]

---

[39]The listing omits various additional alternations related to juncture.

[40]For example, in my dissertation on North Fork Monachi, the anataxis of (10) and (11) was described as having effect between morpheme combinations and morphophoneme combinations. Thus the term morphophonemic was applied to the sequences VʔBV (10), VʔRV (11). Then the morphophonemic realization rule corresponding to (2) was applicable to (10). That treatment thus anticipates in part the formulation arrived at here.

[41]On the suffix *-on*, see my "The Sememic Approach to Structural Semantics," *AA* 66:3:2.57–78 (1964). Downward components must be distinguished from upward components. For example, the morpheme M/worse/ has morphons (M/w/ etc.) as downward components, but has the lexons L/bad/ and L/er/ as upward components.

[42]The morphophoneme M/</ is realized as a specification that the realization of the following morphon occur in the immediately preceding syllable

(10) VBV <ʔ, VʹBV <ʔ   VʹBV
(11) VRV <ʔ, VʹRV <ʔ   VʔRV
(12) Ca <i   Ci
(13) #ʹC   #C
(14) ʹ ʹC   ʹC

There are also various morphophonemes of the type conventionally called "special morphophonemes" and written with capital letters. Thus ᴹ/N/ is realized as ᴾ/n/ is some environments, as zero in others; it contrasts (at this level) with ᴹ/n/, which is realized as ᴾ/n/ in all environments.

This situation differs from the preceding one in one significant respect: here it is the sequences in the right hand column, i.e., the realizations, which fit the syllable structure tactics, whereas in examples (1) to (9) it is those at the left, i.e., the realizates.[43]

Similarly in English the morphonic representations of words like *boxes* and *waited* do not fit the syllable structure tactics, since they lack the (empty) vowel of the second syllable. Note also that the presence of the vowel in the phonemic representation seems to be somehow determined by the tactics.

It appears, then, that the tactic pattern of syllable structure, if it is to be economically describable, applies neither to phonemes nor to morphons as the ultimate constituents, but to elements intermediate between them; i.e., to elements which are realizations of morphons and realizates of phonemes. In other words, there seem to be two separate alternation patterns between morphons and phonemes, and the syllable structure tactics fits between them. These intermediate units to which the tactics applies may be called *basic phonemes* for the time being.

Moreover it turns out that this separation of morphophonemic alternations into two types corresponds remarkably well to a differently motivated separation hinted at above:

some morphophonemic alternations are more easily described in terms of components than segments, while others are more easily described in terms of segments. In particular, the alternations involved in (1) through (9) are economically describable in terms of components and those of (10) through (14) are not. Thus it is apparent that a sign pattern intervenes between the two alternation patterns.

It must also be observed that there are definite tactic patterns involving phonological components as ultimate constituents. Conventional displays of phonemic inventories in charts are not only implicit analyses of C-phonemes into components, as mentioned above; they are also implicit descriptions of some features of the tactic patterning of such components. Thus in various languages the different positions of articulation recognized in such charts are mutually exclusive, hence members of the same distribution class. On the other hand, in some African languages, the features labial, velar, and closed are permitted to cooccur. That is, such a combination is well formed according to the feature tactics of some languages, ill formed according to that of others. Consider also the ᴾ/y/ of English consonant clusters, discussed above. At the level of the syllable structure tactics it is not present, since ᴮᴾ/u:/ is present instead; yet it fits neatly into the tactic pattern of English initial consonant clusters, along with ᴾ/w/, ᴾ/r/, and ᴾ/l/. The tactics of phonemic components, then, seems to be concerned primarily with the structure of clusters, including simple clusters, i.e., segments.

In Monachi the feature tactics imposes strict limitations upon what consonant clusters can occur; the permissible clusters are ᴾ/ʹ/ plus obstruent or nasal, ᴾ/ʔ/ plus resonant, ᴾ/h/ plus semivowel, and ᴾ/nt/ in a few Spanish loan words. These clusters are fewer than the clusters of basic phonemes, and the differences are accounted for by alternations (2), (3), and (5) to (9) of the lower morphophonemic alternation pattern. That is, there is a simpler cluster structure at the C-phonemic level than at the level of the basic phonemes. Moreover, in each of the clusters the two members belong to separate syllables; i.e., the tactic boundaries of the cluster structure do not correspond to those of the syllable structure. This type of discrepancy between differ-

---

(in the position specified for it by the syllable structure tactics). Examples are: (10) ᴹ/yaka <ʔʹki/ ᴮᴾ/yaʔkaʹki/ ᶜᴾ/yaʹkaʹki/ 'to cry intermittently', (11) ᴹ/miya <ʔʹki/ ᴮᴾ/miʔyaʹki/ ᶜᴾ/miʔyaʹki/ 'to go little by little', ᴹ/kiʹma <ʔʹki/ ᴮᴾ/kiʔmaʹki/ ᶜᴾ/kiʔmaʹki/ 'to come little by little'; (12) ᴹ/yaka <i/ ᴮᴾ/yaki/ ᶜᴾ/yaki/ 'to cry at'.

[43]A realizate is that which is realized—that which a realization is a realization of. Cf. my "On Alternation, Transformation, Realization, and Stratification" [52] (see footnote 32).

ent tactic patterns of the same language is also observed at higher strata.

In Russian the tactic pattern at this level specifies that an obstruent cluster may optionally have a single occurrence of the devoicing element.

Thus the picture which emerges is one of two alternation patterns and, quite closely related to them, two separate tactic patterns, as shown in Figure 12. The row of upward "ands" at the bottom of the lower alternation pattern corresponds to the C-phonemic level. But the C-phoneme is not present as a structural element. Rather, it is a combination of elements. The structural elements of this stratum are phonon-sized, not phoneme-sized. This refined view of the C-phonemic stratum was in part anticipated by the version of C-phonemics presented in Hockett's *Manual of Phonology,* discussed above.

A question left in abeyance above is the relationship of alternations to conditioning environments. What must be added to the diagrams as developed so far to make them

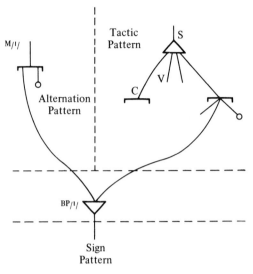

Figure 13

include the specification of conditioning environments? The answer is: nothing! The conditioning environments are already specified in the tactic pattern associated with each alternation pattern. As noted above, the realizations of the upper alternation pattern fit the upper tactics, while the realizates do not; and the same is true for the lower tactics. In other words, it is conditions within the tactic structure which control the alternation (except in the case of free variation). Of a given pair of alternants, the one which occurs in a given combination is that which fits the tactic pattern. If both fit the tactic pattern, then the occurrence of one of them is specified by ordering in the downward "or" from which they lead; if this "or" is unordered, there is free variation.[44]

An example for the upper morphophonemic alternation pattern and upper phonotactics of North Fork Monachi is shown in Figure 13. This is the alternation, noted above as (13) and (14), between ᴮᴾ/'/ and zero as realizations of ᴹ/'/. The alternant ᴮᴾ/'/ appears after vowels, i.e., in syllable final position, but initially in words ᴹ/'/ has no realization, and

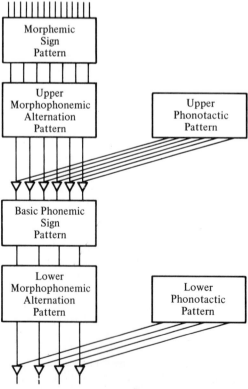

Figure 12

[44]Thus the statement of conditioning environment in a realization rule is actually only a repetition of part of the information already present in the associated tactic pattern; it is, however, a nonsignificant repetition of information stated only once in the graphic description.

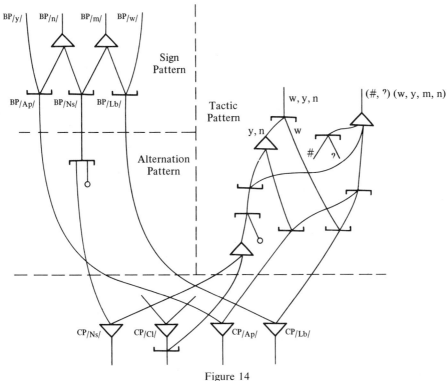

Figure 14
The alternation of [m] and [w] in North Fork.

when there are two successive occurrences of $^{M}/'/$ only one token of $^{BP}/'/$ occurs. Thus ^{M}/nohi 'muuʔa'ci/ ^{BP}/nohi'mu:ʔa'ci/ 'a very long time ago'; but ^{M}/#'muuʔa'ci/ ^{BP}/#mu:ʔa'ci/ 'a long time ago'. Figure 13 shows part of the same tactic pattern illustrated in Figure 5. This pattern allows $^{BP}/'/$ to occur only in syllable final position, and there only once (per syllable). If there is an occurrence of $^{M}/'/$ when the tactics is at that position, $^{BP}/'/$ will occur, since the path from the left side of the ordered "or" takes precedence. Under any other circumstance this path is blocked by the upward "and," and the path at right, leading to nothing, must be taken.

An example for the lower alternation pattern is shown in Figure 14. This is the alternation of C-phonemic ^{CP}/m/ (labial and nasal) and ^{CP}/w/ (labial) as realizations of ^{BP}/m/. More precisely (since this alternation is below the basic phonemic sign pattern) it is an alternation of ^{CP}/Ns/ (nasal) with zero as realizations of ^{BP}/Ns/. The portion of the tactic pattern shown in the figure accounts for all resonants and resonant clusters except ^{CP}/hw/, ^{CP}/hy/, ^{CP}/'m/, and ^{CP}/'n/, which are not essential to the example. It accommodates ^{CP}/Ns/ in the combinations ^{CP}/#m/, ^{CP}/#n/, ^{CP}/ʔm/, ^{CP}/ʔn/, and ^{CP}/n/ (intervocalic); but it does not provide for the occurrence of ^{CP}/Ns/ together with ^{CP}/Lb/ except when ^{CP}/#/ or ^{CP}/ʔ/ precedes. When ^{BP}/m/ occurs after a vowel, ^{CP}/Ns/ cannot be accommodated; in this environment the tactic pattern allows ^{CP}/Ns/ only in combination with ^{CP}/Ap/. It allows ^{CP}/Lb/, but for ^{BP}/Ns/ the path leading to nothing must be taken since the preferred path is blocked by the upward "and." Thus ^{CP}/w/ appears as the realization of ^{BP}/m/.

Figure 14 also provides an illustration of the next point to be considered. The tactic pattern at this level can account very simply for nondistinctive features. The component Cl (closed) is determined when Ns occurs (in North Fork, but not in Bishop), as shown by the downward "and" at the lower left corner of the tactic pattern. The line for this Cl goes down to an upward "or" below the row of upward "ands"; i.e., it does not lead down to an upward "and" like the other lines going down from the tactic pattern. The others have upward "ands" simply because for each of them there is a connection to the next higher stratum. In other words, they are capable of distinguishing meaning, i.e., distinctive. But the occurrence of Cl with Ns is determined and therefore cannot carry any information. In this connection it is important to observe that the analysis shown is motivated purely by considerations of economy, not by the distinctiveness principle as an independent criterion. If this feature were treated like the others, i.e., if a line were to lead up through the alternation pattern for Cl as a partner of Ns, then it would be necessary to add two additional lines to the sign pattern, since BP/m/ and BP/n/ would each now have BP/Cl/ as an additional component.

As noted above, the Bishop dialect of Monachi has an alternation which is quite similar in some ways. In both dialects there is absence of closure for the intervocalic alternant, and the conditioning environment is the same. But the intervocalic alternant in Bishop contrasts with [w] because it is nasalized, while in North Fork there is neutralization with [w]. This difference, unimportant to Chomsky and Halle, is crucial to the C-phonemicist, who insists that the alternation in North Fork must be distinguished as morphophonemic, while that in Bishop is subphonemic. Why? The structural difference may be seen by comparing Figure 14 with Figure 15, which shows the situation in Bishop. Since Ns is present in both [m] and [w̃] there is no "or" in the Bishop alternation pattern corresponding to that for North Fork. Instead, Bishop has, for Ns, an upward "or" within the tactics. Bishop's tactic pattern allows Ns to occur without Cl in one construction; in the other it is accompanied by the nondistinctive Cl. At the C-phonemic level, i.e., at the level of the upward "ands," BP/m/ always has the same realization, unlike the cognate in North Fork.

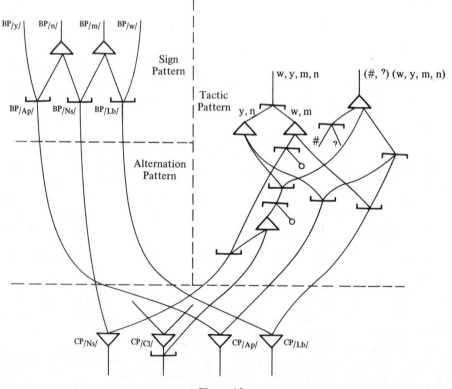

Figure 15
The alternation of [m] and [w̃] in Bishop.

Another comparison may be made with the hypothetical dialect in which the intervocalic alternant is phonetically identical to that of North Fork but in which there is no neutralization, since there is no [w] contrasting with [m]. In all other respects the hypothetical dialect may be taken as identical to North Fork, so that the only difference is whether or not the alternation involves neutralization, a difference which is either important or inconsequential depending upon one's point of view with regard to biuniqueness. The hypothetical dialect is described by three alternative graphs in Figure 16. In the first, the tactic pattern differs from that of North Fork only in accordance with the different facts of the situation; to wit, occurrence of w after # or ? is ruled out. But the sign and alternation patterns are the same as for North Fork. This graph, however, has excess surface information. Unlike the North Fork graph, it can be simplified. The two circled nodes of the first graph may be replaced by a single upward "or," circled in the second graph, and the sign pattern is thus simplified by the removal of two lines. This step is possible without loss of effective information precisely because there is no neutralization; Lb of this dialect, unlike that of North Fork, occurs alone only as realization of ^{BP}/m/. Therefore the additional component ^{BP}/Ns/ is not needed for distinguishing ^{BP}/m/ from other basic phonemes, so the line from ^{BP}/m/ to ^{BP}/Ns/ may be eliminated, and with it the downward "and." The label ^{BP}/m/ for this dialect can appropriately be changed to ^{BP}/w/, but this is of course only a change of label. In the second graph the two upward "ors" above the upward "and" for Ns can be replaced by a single "or" below the "and," resulting in the third graph. This graph shows Ns (along with Cl) as a determined feature when in combination with Lb after # or ?. This manipulation of lines and nodes amounts to an explication and justification of the well-trained C-phonemicist's observation upon encountering such an alternation, which he regards as obvious and inescapable: that nasality is nondistinctive in this segment, and hence the situation is structurally different from that of North Fork.

The foregoing demonstration indicates that a phonological description (as long as it is accurate) automatically adheres to the distinctiveness principle (hence to the biuniqueness principle) if it is free from excess surface information. The distinctiveness principle, then, is not needed as an independent criterion of acceptability of phonological solutions. The value which it imparts to a description is automatically provided by the simplicity principle. The status of the distinctiveness principle is therefore that of a practical device, a tool which can aid the linguist in arriving at the simplest possible description of a phonological system.

I remarked above in the discussion of distinctiveness that information can be expressed only by things done to a medium which allows diversity and that, generally, some of the diversity in expression is nondistinctive, i.e., determined by the medium, while the rest is of communicative significance, i.e., distinctive. It is only by allowing nondetermined divergence that a medium of expression can be communicative. Any tactic pattern is such a medium, in particular the lower phonotactic pattern, with which the classical problem of phonemic analysis was centrally concerned. Whenever a tactic pattern has a downward "or" it is providing for nondetermined diversity. A downward "or" allows a choice: any of the possibilities is permitted, but none is determined, and so the choice of one as opposed to another can be of communicative significance. In a properly constructed diagram, the paths coming down from an "or" lead, either directly or indirectly, to the upward "ands" below the tactic pattern. The path chosen at the "or" depends upon which upward "and" is not blocked, and that depends upon which of the lines leading down from the alternation pattern is "active." Occurrence of a linguistic element corresponds to "activation" of the line or node representing that element in a graph. That is, each line and node represents a type, and any instance of activation of it represents a token (i.e., occurrence) of that type. An upward "and" node (since it is an "and," not an "or") can be activated from above only if both (or all three, etc.) lines leading down to it are active. Hence one of the distinctive elements of the C-phonemic level can occur only when it is "called for" by both the tactics and the line leading down from the higher stratum. Thus choices, when allowed by the tactics, are made

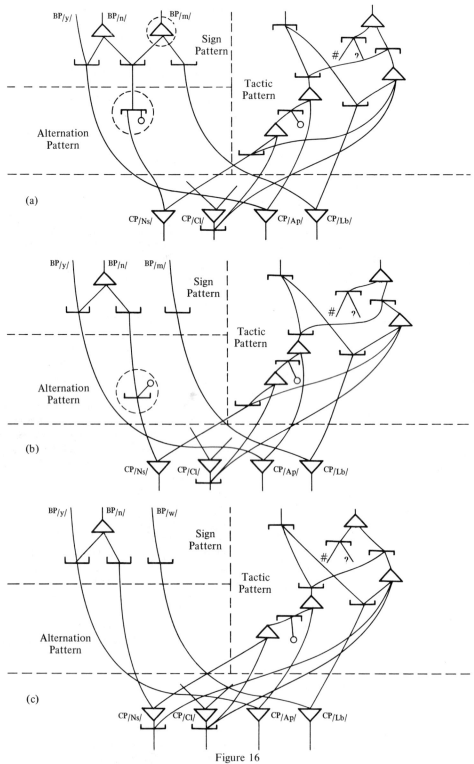

Figure 16
The alternation of [m] and [w] in the hypothetical dialect.

by the higher stratum. In Bishop (Figure 15) when Lb occurs in the tactics (in either tactic environment) it may optionally be accompanied by Ns (note the downward "or" with one line leading to nothing, the other to ^{CP}/Ns/). It will be accompanied by Ns if (and only if) ^{BP}/Ns/ is present.

The lines leading upward into the alternation pattern from the upward "ands" represent the possibilities of "doing things to the medium"; each one can determine a choice at one or more points at which the tactics has a downward "or"; hence each represents the possibility of having some communicative significance. Some features, on the other hand, are determined by the tactics. They are properties of the medium and cannot have communicative significance; they do not lead down to upward "ands," but go on past them.

Just as lines coming down from the alternation pattern control the selection of alternatives in the tactics, so the lines coming down from the tactic pattern control the selection of alternatives in the alternation pattern. This is how environmental conditioning operates.

These considerations apply at every stratum. Choices in the lower tactics are controlled by (lines coming down from) the basic phonemic system. But that system's operation is controlled by the morphemic system, which also has a tactics, one which allows choices to be made by the lexemic system; and so forth.

ON REDEFINING THE PHONEME

The foregoing considerations lead to a conception of phonological structure somewhat different from earlier ones. C-phonemics recognized a phonemic level. Chomsky and Halle put forth the alternative view that there is no structural level between their types of morphophonemic and phonetic levels.[45] But the present investigation finds not only that the C-phonemic level has a sound structural basis

[45] Chomsky, *Current Issues in Linguistic Theory* 68–69 [402–403]: "So far as I can see, there is no other significant level that can be isolated in the phonological component. . . . the existence of an additional level is highly dubious . . ."

There is no simple definition possible of just where "their type of morphophonemic level" is, since it is characterized by them in several different and mutually contradictory ways. In one sense it is a conflation of everything from basic phononic to lexemic.

after all, but also that there is another level not previously distinguished as a separate entity— that referred to above as the basic phonemic. In one sense the present recognition of the basic phonemic level is not new, since various of its properties have long been recognized. Its "eme" is the same size as the C-phoneme, its tactics is that of syllable structure; some of its properties have been ascribed to previously recognized morphophonemic levels, which in other respects are higher than it. In short, it has been conflated both with lower levels (primarily by C-phonemicists) and with higher levels (by Chomsky, Halle, myself, and many others). What is new in this study is the separation of this level from the others.

In particular, the present findings split the C-phonemic level into two distinct phonemic levels. What happens to the C-phoneme in this process? It corresponds in size to the basic phoneme, i.e., the "eme" of the upper phonemic level. But its realizational level is that of the lower one. The C-phoneme turns out not to be a structural element, but a sort of compromise which, as it were, helped to hide the distinction between these two levels from the eyes of phonological theorists; it is a unit on the lower phonemic stratum whose size is that of the basic phoneme. It is a combination of elements of the lower stratum and a realization of the "eme" of the upper one.

These findings present a terminological problem. What names shall be applied to the entities resulting from the distinctions that have been drawn? In such a situation one may either use an old term in a new meaning or invent a new term. Either choice inevitably draws criticism. Indeed there are those who would like to do away with terminology altogether; unfortunately they have not yet discovered a means of enabling people to communicate without it. Perhaps it is particularly foolhardy to tamper with a term so fraught with emotion as "phoneme." One who dares to do such a thing is sure to have his sanity questioned, perhaps even his morals. But the alternative is even worse: to leave the term phoneme in its no longer important C-phonemic meaning and thus to be forced to invent a set of new terms for the two phonological strata.

If one is to redefine the phoneme one may either retain its size and move it up one stratum or retain its realizational level and apply it to those elements which used to be called its components. The former alternative is perhaps the less unsettling, and it leaves fewer problems of finding terms for the other entities to be named. I therefore offer the suggestion that the basic phoneme be called simply the *phoneme*. Then the basic phonon, its downward component, may be called the *phonon*. A simple means is thus provided for naming the lower phonemic stratum, for it can be called the *hypophonemic*. Its "eme" (the phonemic component of C-phonemics) is thus the *hypophoneme*.

It is convenient to identify the "emes" of a stratal system as the upward "ands" which lead upward to the tactic and alternation patterns and downward to the sign pattern. The "ons" are the upward "ors" at the bottom of the sign pattern or, equivalently, the lines leading down from these "ors" to the next lower alternation pattern. The alternation pattern between the morphons and the (basic) phonemes (i.e., the upper morphophonemic alternation pattern of Figure 12) may be called the *morphonic alternation pattern;* and the "lower morphophonemic alternation pattern," i.e., that between the (basic) phonons and the hypophonemes, may be called the *phononic alternation pattern*.

Figure 12 fails to show an important relationship that is found above sign patterns. The "emes" of a stratal system are not generally in a one to one correspondence with the lines at the top of the sign pattern, since upward "ors" often intervene; i.e., lines from the upward "ands" often go down to upward "ors," as does the line going down from hypophonemic ᴴ/Cl/ in Figure 15. In that instance the other line going into the "or" is a nondistinctive feature, and this type of relationship is evidently to be found at all strata. There are also instances in which two or more "emes" (i.e., upward "ands") lead downward to an upward "or," hence to the same line of the sign pattern. For example, the English morphemes ᴹ/well₁/ as in *well, I guess so* and ᴹ/well₂/ as in *they dug a deep well* are separate morphemes since they lead upward to different lexemes and to different morphotactic categories; but they lead downward to the same combination of morphons. Thus they meet in an upward "or" just above the sign pattern.

The lines at the top of the morphemic sign pattern may be distinguished from the morphemes by being called *morphemic signs*. Thus ᴹ/well₁/ and ᴹ/well₂/ are different morphemes, but they correspond to the same morphemic sign ᴹ/wel/.

Below the hypophonemes there appears not to be a sign pattern, at least not one of the same simple type as those found at higher strata. There is, however, a need to distinguish hypophonemes from the lines below the upward "ors" into which they lead (e.g., Cl in Figure 15); and it is easy to do so by calling the latter *hypophonemic signs*. This is of course the distinction which the C-phonemicist prizes most highly, the boundary between C-phonemic and C-phonetic. The hypophonemic sign Cl leads upward either to the hypophoneme ᴴ/Cl/ or directly to the hypophonotactics. In the latter case (i.e., when it is occurring with Ns) it is nondistinctive.

The subphonemic or allophonic alternation of C-phonemics covers two separate areas: (1) the difference between hypophonemes and hypophonemic signs (e.g., [m] and [w̃] as C-allophones of ᶜᴾ/m/ in Bishop), (2) variation below the level of the hypophonemic signs. Both types of information are of course important in a phonological description, but as the two areas are structurally different, their descriptions should be separated.

Below the hypophonemic signs it is likely, but not certain, that the type of structure to be dealt with differs from that above; i.e., it appears that the regular succession of pattern types found from hypophonemic signs upward does not continue below them into a hypophonemic sign pattern, etc. If so, this level marks a boundary between one type of structure and another. Below this level one may speak of phonetic manifestation of the hypophonemic material. The primary manifestation is articulatory; it consists of articulatory features. For example, Cl is manifested as oral closure. The position of closure, when Cl occurs, is determined by another hypophonemic sign, e.g., Ap (apical). An occurrence of a hypophonemic sign is a specification to a part of the articulatory apparatus to perform its function. The labels used in this paper for hypophonemes are of course chosen in accordance with these primary manifestations. At the next lower level is the secondary manifestation, which consists of acoustic features, and below this is the tertiary manifestation, consisting of auditory features. Various displaced manifestations are also possible, such as symbols on paper or operations in an artificial speech production machine.

To specify what a phonemic or morphemic sign leads down to requires only the identification of the components and their ordering; but there is at present no simple way to specify how much and what kind of description of the manifestation of a hypophonemic sign is desirable. A minimal specification for *Ap* would be "with the apex." Beyond that, varying kinds and degrees of detail are possible. For *Ap* in combination with *Cl* a more detailed specification, applicable to many languages, would be "close with that part of the apex which is closest to the alveolar ridge at the time." It will be different parts of the apex depending on the language and the environment. Thus North Fork Monachi has five positions of closure in five different environments (after front vowel, initial, after non-front vowel before front vowel, etc.). Such variation is not a property of *Ap* or *Cl* but is mainly the incidental result of where the tongue happens to be at the time the closure takes place. Therefore, the primary value of the description of such positions of closure is that it gives infor-

mation about the articulation of the vowels, the neutral tongue position, and the timing of the movements from one vowel position to another. Thus in North Fork the position of apical closure is influenced more by the preceding environment than the following. The variation in position differs markedly from that in English, in that the distance from the farthest forward to the farthest back is much greater. The same is true for velar closure. But it is also of interest that the pattern of vocalic environments which determines position of apical closure differs from that for velar. After more detailed information of this and other kinds has been obtained and analyzed for a variety of languages it should be possible to determine what properties of articulation are assignable to human speech in general and what properties are to be accounted for by a specific articulatory system (of a given language or dialect or geographic area) as a whole. The remaining articulatory properties of speech produced in the system—those not accounted for by these two means—are the manifestations of the hypophonemic signs. It is these which are capable of distinguishing meaning, of having communicative significance, within that medium . . . Could it be another stratum?

54

VOWEL HARMONY IN HUNGARIAN REEXAMINED IN THE LIGHT OF RECENT DEVELOPMENTS IN PHONOLOGICAL THEORY*

VALERIE BECKER MAKKAI

In recent years proponents of various of the newer phonological theories have made the claim that their theories may prove to be particularly valuable and interesting in the way that they are able to deal with the phenomenon of vowel harmony.[1] However, not much has been done to substantiate these claims by applying them to a large body of data, to see if, in fact, they can handle vowel harmony better than traditional methods. In this paper I shall present several different analyses of the vowel harmony system of Hungarian in an attempt to evaluate the merits of these newer systems in relation to each other and to more traditional treatments.

First a brief statement of the facts of Hungarian vowel harmony. Most traditional analyses begin with the general statement that, in principle at least, all the vowels in a given Hungarian word must be either front vowels or back vowels. The front and back vowels are listed, usually with the proviso that although /i/ and /e/ are front vowels, they may occur in the same word with back vowels. This brief statement is usually followed by a list, longer or shorter depending on the thoroughness of the treatment, of the numerous exceptions to the rule—front vowel words which take

back vowel suffixes, so-called "mixed-vowel" words which within their stems have both back and front vowels, and so on.

Table 1 presents the Hungarian vowels in traditional orthography, together with phonetic symbols to indicate their pronunciation.

TABLE 1
Hungarian Vowels

í [iː]	ű [yː]		ú [uː]
i [ɪ]	ü [y]		u [ʊ]
é [eː]	ő [øː]		ó [oː]
e [ɛ]	ö [œ]	o [ɔ]	
	á [aː]	a [ɑ]	

As Sebeok has pointed out,[2] these can be grouped into seven vowel phonemes plus one phoneme of length, by pairing each long vowel with its shorter and laxer counterpart. However, for ease of presentation here I have chosen to retain the traditional orthography throughout. There is considerable fluctuation in the use of the long high vowels, and some speakers contend that the length has been completely lost in their pronunciation of these vowels. However, since there are those who retain the length distinction, I shall mark it here.

Table 2 lists those vowels which pattern as back vowels in harmonizing, and those

---

[1]See especially Jakobson, Fant, and Halle 1951; Lightner 1965; Lees 1961; and Lyons 1962 [25].

[2]Sebeok 1943a.

*This is a revised and expanded version of a paper by the same title delivered before the Linguistic Society of America summer meeting in July 1968.

TABLE 2

Front		Back
í	ű	ú
i	ü	u
é	ő	ó
e	ö	o
		á a

which pattern as front vowels. As has already been noted above, *í* and *i,* and occasionally also *é* and *e,* sometimes occur in back vowel words, but these occurrences are in the minority—primarily they function as front vowels.

Most root morphemes in Hungarian contain consistently all front vowels or all back vowels. The vowels of the roots are fixed and do not participate further in vowel harmony except to specify which type of vowels suffixed morphemes may contain. Thus in Table 3a are examples of back vowel words; in 3b, front vowel words; in 3c, so-called "mixed-vowel" words, most of which are occurrences of front unrounded vowels in words which otherwise pattern like back vowel words; and in 3d, compound words, where each of the roots retains its voweling and does not harmonize with the other. The hyphens throughout separate the morphemes under discussion.[3]

TABLE 3a
Back Vowel Words

tanár	'teacher'
komoly	'serious'
ujj	'finger'
ház	'house'

TABLE 3b
Front Vowel Words

levél	'letter, leaf'
híd	'bridge'
tűz	'fire'
szín	'color'
közép	'middle'
kert	'garden'
derék	'waist'
cél	'goal'

[3] I have used nouns for most of my examples simply because they present the clearest picture of the situation without getting into problems of morpheme division. However the generalizations given about vowel harmony apply to the entire language.

TABLE 3c
Mixed Vowel Words

fazék	'pot'
vékony	'thin'
igaz	'true'
játék	'game'

TABLE 3d
Compound Words

hegy-oldal	'hillside'
nyereg-gyártó	'saddle-maker'
nagy-szivű	'great-hearted, generous'

Hungarian, being an agglutinative language, abounds in affixes. These can be subdivided into two types—those which harmonize with the roots to which they are affixed, and those which do not. In the latter group belong all the verb-derivational prefixes, as in Table 4a; affixes, as in 4b, containing *í* or *i,* which retain this vowel no matter what the voweling of the root is; some affixes containing *é* or *e,* as in 4c; and finally, as in 4d, a few forms with other vowels, which have traditionally been thought of as suffixes, but which it might be possible to regard as postpositions or compounds.

All other affixes, both derivational and inflectional, are suffixes which harmonize with the roots to which they are affixed. Thus, vowel harmony can be regarded as progressing forward through the word from the root on,

TABLE 4a

be-látni	'to be convinced'
ki-szabadulni	'to get free'
hozzá-kezdeni	'to set about'
el-adni	'to sell'
le-adni	'to broadcast'
agyon-ütni	'to strike dead'

TABLE 4b

ad-ni	'to give'
lád-ikó	'little box'
tág-ít-ani	'to make wide, widen'

TABLE 4c

Magyarok-ért	'for Hungarians'
Kovács-né	'Mrs. Kovacs'
tanár-né	'the teacher's wife'
orvos-é	'(is) the doctor's'

TABLE 4d

öt-kor	'at five, five o'clock'
pünkösd-kor	'at Pentecost'

TABLE 5

Vowel Alternations

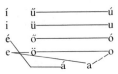

but not backward to the prefix. One can distinguish, then, three types of forms in Hungarian depending on how they are affected by vowel harmony: first, those invariable forms which do not participate, either actively or passively in harmonization; second, roots, which are invariable in form but which exhibit for the most part what might be termed "internal harmony," and which themselves call for the harmonization of suffixed morphemes; and third, variable forms which have anywhere from two to four alternating vowels, depending on the morpheme itself, and which harmonize according to the type of harmony called for by the root.

Table 5 illustrates which vowels alternate within these variable affixes. There are five pairs of front and back vowels (*ű~ú, ü~u,*

ő~ó, e~a, and *é~á*). In addition, there is a three-way alternation between *o, e,* and *ö,* and a four-way alternation between these three and *a.* As will be seen, it is this last alternation pattern which gives the most difficulty in the analysis of vowel harmony. The occurrence of the paired vowels is completely automatic: front vowel with front vowel roots, back with back. Each of the pairs is illustrated in Table 6a. (It should be remembered that most mixed vowel words as in Table 3c take back vowel suffixes.)

In Table 6b the three-way alternation pattern, which I will call V3, is illustrated. The distribution of alternants of this pattern is: back vowel with back vowel words, front unrounded with front unrounded, and front rounded with front rounded. Roots such as the last example, containing both rounded and unrounded vowels, harmonize according to the final vowel of the root.

In Table 6c the four-way alternation pattern, which I will refer to as V4, is illustrated. Here again front vowel words take one of the front vowel alternants, and back vowel words take one of the back, but the question is which one? The distribution of *e* and *ö* is more or less the same as that of V3, but not exactly. In

TABLE 6a

-ú ~ -ű	'having the quality of':	hang-ú 'voiced', szín-ű 'colored'
-ul ~ -ül	'manner adverbial':	kutyá-ul 'as a dog', vitéz-ül 'as a hero, heroically'
-ból ~ -ből	'from inside':	ház-ból 'from (inside) the house', kert-ből 'from (inside) the garden'
-ban ~ -ben	'in':	ház-ban 'in the house', kert-ben 'in the garden'
-nál ~ -nél	'at':	ház-nál 'at the house', kert-nél 'at the garden'

TABLE 6b

-hoz ~ -hez ~ -höz	'(up) to':	ház-hoz 'to the house', kert-hez 'to the garden', tök-höz 'to the squash', hölgy-höz 'to the lady', tűz-höz 'to the fire', közép-hez 'to the middle'

TABLE 6c

-ok ~ -ak ~ -ek ~ -ök	'plural of nouns':	kert-ek 'gardens', tök-ök 'squashes', közep-ek 'middles'
		hölgy-ek 'ladies', tüz-ek 'fires'
		láb-ak 'legs', báb-ok 'puppets', nyaláb-ok 'armfuls'
		fog-ak 'teeth', tok-ok 'sheaths'
		vonal-ak 'lines', vonat-ok 'trains'
		vad-ak 'wild animals', rab-ok 'prisoners'
		rút-ak 'ugly (plural)', Rúth-ok 'Ruths'

TABLE 7

tök-ök	'squashes'	tök-öt	'squash (acc.)'	tök-ök-et	(acc. pl.)
hölgy-ek	'ladies'	hölgy-et	'lady (acc.)'	hölgy-ek-et	(acc. pl.)
barát-ok	'friends'	barát-ot	'friend (acc.)'	barát-ok-at	(acc. pl.)
láb-ak	'legs'	láb-at	'leg (acc.)'	láb-ak-at	(acc. pl.)

contrast to *kert-ek, tök-ök,* and *közep-ek,*[4] we find on the other hand *hölgy-ek* and *tüz-ek.* There are a number of roots (mostly monosyllabic) which, like these last two, contain only front rounded vowels and yet take the *e* alternant. These roots must be handled in a list which specifies that they take the front rounded vowel in affixes with V3, but the front unrounded vowel in affixes with V4.

The distribution of *a* and *o* is more of a problem. There seem to be very few generalizations that one can make, as can be seen from the examples in Table 6c. For the most part, the occurrence of one vowel or the other is completely unpredictable. Thus this problem, too, must be handled by a list. Since roots which take *a* are probably in the minority, these are the ones which would be listed, with the understanding that all other roots take *o.*

Also, when two V4 suffixes succeed each other, the second one will always take either *a* or *e,* but never *o* or *ö.* Thus in Table 7 we have *tök-ök* and *tök-öt,* but *tök-ök-et,* and so on.

One further problem is that a number of roots containing only front unrounded vowels (that is, roots of the type that were listed in Table 3b) nevertheless require back vowel forms of all suffixes. Some examples are given in Table 8. These roots, too, then, must be listed.

TABLE 8

derék 'waist'—derek-ak
cél 'goal'—cél-ok—cél-ban
híd 'bridge'—híd-hoz

Now it remains to be seen how various phonological theories are able to handle these facts.

In a structural description one can categorize the vowels into front and back, rounded and unrounded, stating that in general from the root onward through the word, all the

---

[4]The morphophonemic alternation of the root need not concern us here.

vowels are either back or front, and, when there is a choice, either rounded or unrounded, based on the voweling of the root. Exceptions, namely roots which contain all front vowels but take back vowel suffixes, and roots which are unpredictable in their choice of V4 vowels, must be noted in lists, and in a dictionary, where the entry for each irregular root would specify whether it takes front or back vowel affixes, and, for V4, which of the two front or two back vowels it takes.

As Lyons has pointed out,[5] in a structural approach, one must either make use of morphophonemes in representing the harmonizing suffixes, or else list the allomorphs of each suffix with a statement of the rules governing the conditioning of each. Since many suffixes follow exactly the same conditioning rules, there is bound to be a great deal of repetition if one chooses to list allomorphs. Morphophonemes on the other hand would work fairly well. There would be seven morphophonemes —five to represent the five two-way alternations, one for V3 and one for V4. The distribution of the first six could be specified according to phonological criteria, while that of V4 could be specified partially phonologically (that is, the front-back criterion), with the additional specification that between the two front and two back alternants the choice will be made on the basis of what the preceding morpheme is. This method would neatly dispose of the problem of sequences of two suffixes which both contain V4 (as in Table 7), since phonological criteria could be brought to bear—that is, if the preceding vowel is the morphophoneme V4, then only *a* or *e* may occur but not *o* or *ö.*

There has been some disagreement among linguists in their handling of suffixes which involve the use of this V4, namely, the plural, the accusative, some of the possessives, and one or two other suffixes. (See, for example, *láb* 'leg' : *báb* 'puppet', *láb-ak* 'legs' : *báb-ok*

---

[5]Lyons 1962 [25].

'puppets', *láb-at* 'leg (acc.)' : *báb-ot* 'puppet (acc.)', *láb-am* 'my leg' : *báb-om* 'my puppet', etc.) Some (1) regard the vowel as part of the root morpheme, each root having then at least two alternants (for example, in the case of {láb}, /la:b/ and /la:bɑ/), while the suffixes have one allomorph each (that is, /-k/, /-t/, /-m/, and so on). Others (2) regard the vowel as part of the suffixed morpheme, whereupon the suffixes acquire several allomorphs each (for {pl.}, for example, the allomorphs would include at least /-ɔk/, /-ɑk/, /-ɛk/, and /-œk/). A great economy is thus effected in the root morphemes, since it involves a saving of one allomorph each for most noun roots in the language. On the other hand, describing the distributions of the allomorphs of the suffixes would involve long listings of the root morphemes with which each may occur. (3) Still a third solution (the one chosen in Hall 1944, for example) is to regard the vowel as merely a connecting vowel (an "auxiliary vowel" as Hall calls it), belonging neither to the root nor to the suffix.

This latter solution seems the least desirable of all, since one ends up with an "empty morph" which belongs neither here nor there; virtually no economy over the solution which regards the vowels as part of the suffixes, since the empty morph itself will have several allomorphs; and one still has to list the root morphemes which occur with each vowel just as in solution (2).

The choice between (1) and (2) is a little less easy to make. In a structural description, where economy is measured, at least in part, by the total number of allomorphs required, solution (2) might seem preferable. On the other hand, solution (1), while requiring many more allomorphs, would seem to need much simpler statements of distribution. But this is not quite the case. Consider the forms illustrated in Table 9. In the first place there are a number of nouns, like *határ*, which take no vowel at all with the accusative suffix, but do take a vowel with all the other V4 suffixes. This occurrence of /-t/ alone is almost always strictly phonologically conditioned and thus entirely predictable. Yet for solution (1) the allomorphs of each of the nouns taking this allomorph of the accusative must be marked individually as to their peculiar distribution. On the other hand solution (2) allows us to state only once the specific phonological conditioning of the /-t/, without having to list the morphemes with which it occurs. In addition, since in solution (1) most nouns would have more than one allomorph, statements of the distribution of each are inevitable, whereas in solution (2), since most nouns would have only one allomorph, the only major listing of distributions would be for the suffix allomorphs. Thirdly, solution (1) *requires* that each noun have a separate allomorph for each "auxiliary vowel" with which it occurs, whether or not this vowel is automatically predictable on the basis of vowel harmony. In fact, in the great majority of nouns it is completely automatic (as in examples 1, 3, and 5), and thus solution (1) involves a great waste. Solution (2), on the other hand, involves listing only the irregularities. Thus, for example, /-ɛk/ could be specified as occurring after syllables containing a front unrounded vowel and also after the morphemes {tűz}, {hölgy}, etc. For V2 and V3 suffixes beginning with a vowel (such as *-on* ~ *-en* ~ *-ön* 'on') the statement of distribution would be entirely in terms of phonological environment and no listing at all of morphemes would be necessary. Still a fourth argument in

TABLE 9

	Plural	Accusative	Acc. Plural	1st sg. poss.
1. kert 'garden'	kertek	kertet	kerteket	kertem
2. határ 'border'	határok	határt	határokat	határom
3. tök 'squash'	tökök	tököt	tököket	tököm
4. hölgy 'lady'	hölgyek	hölgyet	hölgyeket	hölgyem
5. bőröndös 'suitcase maker' (bőrönd 'suitcase')	bőröndösök	bőröndöst	bőröndösöket	bőröndösöm
6. bolondos 'giddy' (bolond 'crazy')	bolondosok	bolondost	bolondosokat	bolondosom

favor of solution (2) is that, even if the vowels were assigned to the roots, the V4 suffixes would still have to have several allomorphs each to take care of cases where the suffix is separated from the root by another affix—see, for example, all of the accusative plurals, and also forms such as *börönd* and *bolond* where the V4 suffix *-os* ~ *-as* ~ *-es* ~ *-ös* 'he who does; having the quality of' is followed by *-ök, -öket, -öm,* etc. (Note that this suffix, in certain of its uses, is an exception to the rule that two V4s may not follow each other.) Surely no one would suggest that this V4 suffix should have the allomorphs *-s, -so-, -sa-, -se-,* and *-sö-,* nor that the plural should have the allomorphs *-k, -ka-,* and *-ke-,* and so on. Thus the only sensible answer is to analyze *bolondosokat,* for example, as *bolond-os-ok-at, határokat* as *határ-ok-at,* and *lábat* as *láb-at.* Thus it appears that solution (1), while seeming appealing at first glance, must be rejected, at least for a structural description of Hungarian. The implications of these arguments for a transformational treatment are discussed below.

In any event, the only real problem, from the point of view of a structural description, is the necessity of listing roots which behave peculiarly in their specification of what the suffixed vowels may be. Any phonological theory ·which is able to improve on this situation, either by reducing the number of irregularities, or by handling them more efficiently, or by describing all harmonization patterns more cogently, is to be preferred.

TABLE 10

Distinctive Feature Matrix

	í	i	é	e	á	a	ú	u	ó	o	ű	ü	ő	ö
1. Diffuse	+	+	−	−	−	−	+	+	−	−	+	+	−	−
2. Tense	+	−	+	−	+	−	+	−	+	−	+	−	+	−
3. Flat	−	−	−	−	(−)	+	+	+	+	+	+	+	+	+
4. Grave	−	−	(+)	+	+	+	+	+	−	−	−	−	−	−

If we make a distinctive feature matrix, as in Table 10, we are able to bring into relief those qualities which serve to separate the harmonizing vowels. The two circled features represent qualities which could be disputed on articulatory grounds,[6] but which reflect the way that these vowels act in the patterning of the language. The two blank spaces represent redundancies which do not need to be marked. It is interesting to note that it is specifically these vowels (namely, *í* and *i*) which do not participate in vowel alternations, and which also often occur in roots which otherwise consist entirely of grave, that is back, vowels.

If we make a tree diagram to represent this matrix, as in Figure 1, the harmony oppositions are even more clearly brought into focus. The circles enclose those vowels which alternate with each other. The numbers at each

[6]*a* is usually pronounced with some degree of lip rounding, although not in all dialects; and *á* is pronounced much farther front than any of the other grave vowels, although not as far front as the minus grave ones. In this regard see Fudge 1967 [46], especially pp. 8–16 [505–508].

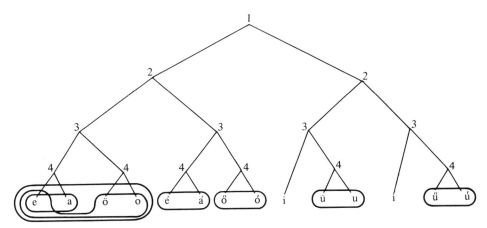

Figure 1

TABLE 11

With V2 suffix:	kert-ben	barát-ban	hölgy-ben	örmény-ben
With V3 suffix:	kert-hez	barát-hoz	hölgy-höz	örmény-hez
With V4 suffix:	kert-ek	barát-ok	hölgy-ek	örmény-ek

TABLE 12

With V2 suffix:	kert-ben	barát-ban	hölgy-ben	örmény-ben
With V3 suffix:	*kert-hez~höz	barát-hoz	*hölgy-hez~höz	*örmény-hez~höz
With V4 suffix:	*kert-ek~ök	*barát-ok~ak	*hölgy-ek~ök	*örmény-ek~ök

TABLE 13

With V2 suffix:	kert-ben	barát-ban	*hölgy-bön	*örmöny-bön
With V3 suffix:	kert-hez	*barát-haz	hölgy-höz	*örmöny-höz
With V4 suffix:	kert-ek	*barát-ak	*hölgy-ök	*örmöny-ök

TABLE 14

With V2 suffix:	kert-ben	barát-ban	*hölgy-bön	örmény-ben
With V3 suffix:	kert-hez	*barát-haz	hölgy-höz	örmény-hez
With V4 suffix:	kert-ek	*barát-ak	*hölgy-ök	örmény-ek

node refer to the features of the matrix. The left branches represent minus values and the right branches plus values.

Generative phonologists have made great use of distinctive feature matrices, but there is no reason why they should be their sole prerogative. Even within a structural description, such diagrams as that in Figure 1 should prove useful in revealing the exact relationships among the sounds of a language.

Generative phonology could handle many of the regularities of Hungarian vowel harmony as progressive assimilation, in terms of so-called alpha rules, where only the first vowel of the root is marked as to gravity (i.e., backness), and all succeeding vowels are assimilated to it. One problem with this sort of rule is that *i* and *i* will thereby sometimes be marked as grave (that is, back) when they should not be, so a second rule must be introduced to subtract this marker. Also, rules of this sort could not deal with V3 and V4 where flatness (i.e., lip rounding) is involved in addition. If we use alpha rules to specify only the gravity of the vowels, then we have no criteria on which to base our choice of suffixes which may involve lip-rounding. Thus, taking the

words *kert, barát, hölgy,* and *közép* as examples we get the results shown in Table 12. (Table 11 lists the correct forms for each word.) On the other hand, marking both gravity and flatness in the first vowel of the word, with alpha rules to supply these features for the rest of the word, we get the results shown in Table 13. Since there is no restriction on co-occurrence within words of both rounded and unrounded vowels, and since it is the quality of the final vowel of the root which determines whether the suffix should be rounded or not, a progressive assimilation rule, taking the first vowel of the root as its base, would not work. Even taking the final vowel of the root as the base would not help, since only suffixes with V3 and V4 assimilate in flatness, and even then not everywhere, so the rule would end up generating rounded and unrounded vowels where they should not be. And it would be impossible to set up a rule, based on distinctive feature criteria alone, which could subtract the unwanted features. Thus, we would get the results shown in Table 14. Also if we took the last vowel of the root as the marked vowel and used regressive assimilation to mark the earlier vowels in the word we would encounter further

TABLE 15

Ú (ú ~ ű) +diffuse
            +flat
            +tense

U (u ~ ü) +diffuse
            +flat
            −tense

Ó (ó ~ ő) −diffuse
            +flat
            +tense

Á (á ~ é) −diffuse
            −flat
            +tense

A (a ~ e) −diffuse
            −flat
            −tense

O (o ~ ö ~ e) −diffuse
                −tense

E (a ~ o ~ ö ~ e) −diffuse
                    −tense

difficulties, especially in view of the forms given in Tables 3c, 3d, and 4a, where not all the vowels of the word harmonize.

If one were to set up (à la Lightner[7]) vowel archiphonemes for the seven alternation patterns as in Table 15, where gravity and, in the case of the last two, flatness are unmarked, then all the vowels of a word except the first would contain the feature combinations shown. Assimilation rules, then, would fill in the missing features on the basis of what those features are in the first vowel of the root. The above examples, written with the archiphonemes, appear in Table 16, followed by the forms generated by the application of the assimilation rules. Note that nonexisting forms are still generated, even for words whose vowel harmony patterns are quite regular and predictable (i.e., those circled in the table).

[7]See Lightner 1965.

The problem is that both O and E are minus diffuse (that is nonhigh) and minus tense, hence no matter what vowel the assimilation rules generate, there is nothing in the distinctive features themselves on which to base a subtraction rule. Thus a grave, minus flat vowel, that is, *a,* can be generated for O, and nothing can be done about it. Also there is no way that assimilation rules could handle the problem of the successive occurrence of two E's where, as mentioned before, the second one may not contain the feature plus flat.

These are all problems which could be handled quite regularly in a structural description. When we come to the irregularities, assimilation rules fall down completely. An alternative approach to such problems has been suggested by Victoria Fromkin, who proposes the use of Firthian prosodies, and by Theodore Lightner.[8] Although he does not call them prosodies, Lightner proposes an element which works much the same way. In his approach, a root is associated with an abstract marker (say plus *grave*), and all the vowels of the word take on that feature. But this handles irregularities no better than assimilation does, because the irregularities involve specifically the problem that the vowels of the word do *not* all have the same value for the particular feature in question. He suggests the use of a subtraction rule, but again this fails for exactly the same reason that the assimilation rules did.

Prosodies are a little more successful in their handling of the situation because of the fact that they are not *abstract markers* but rather *extractions* of certain features, or as Lyons puts it,[9] "long components" which extend over more than one sound segment. The crucial difference here is that prosodies extend only as far as they need to go—that is, until some other prosody is introduced or until some marked cut-off point is reached. Abstract markers, at least as they are now formulated,

[8]Fromkin 1965 [26] and Lightner 1965.
[9]Lyons 1962 [25].

TABLE 16

	kert	barÁt	hölgy	örmÁny
bAn	kert-ben	barát-ban	hölgy-ben	örmény-ben
hOz	kert-hez	*barát-haz	hölgy-höz	*örmény-höz
Ek	kert-ek	*barát-ak	*hölgy-ök	*örmény-ök

must apply to the whole word. Also, whereas abstract markers cannot change polarity in mid-stream, prosodies can be made up of whatever features, or *sequences* of features, are appropriate to the particular word. Thus the prosodic approach, whether used in connection with phonematic units in a Firthian type of analysis, or incorporated into a generative phonology as Mrs. Fromkin suggests, has definite advantages over a strictly generative approach, since it is able to handle most of the irregularities.

It seems ironic that it is again some of the regularities of Hungarian vowel harmony which even prosodies are not able to handle. This is again the problem of suffixes with V3 and V4. The conditioning of V3 is completely regular, but prosodies cannot deal with it because of the existence of V4 where the conditioning is different and often irregular. There is no prosody which can be assigned to a word such as *hölgy*, for example, which will call for a suffix with a front rounded vowel in the one case but front unrounded in the other. Nor can prosodies handle the successive occurrence of two V4's. So generative phonology, even with the use of prosodies, apparently cannot do as well as a structural description, since in either approach irregularities must be noted in a dictionary, and a structural approach can at least handle all the regularities, which generative phonology apparently *cannot* do.

It has been suggested that generative phonology can best deal with these V4 suffixes by considering the vowel to be part of the root rather than part of the suffix. Since all V4 suffixes in fact begin with that vowel, this could theoretically solve the problem. I have already presented above my objections to attaching the V4 to the root rather than to the suffix. Most of the same arguments apply just as forcefully to transformational grammar as they did to a structural analysis—some even more so. In a structural description one of the prime concerns is economy of statement, and it was seen that it is far more economical to consider the vowel as part of the suffix. Economy is important in transformational grammar, too, but above and beyond that is the goal of achieving descriptive and explanatory adequacy. In this regard the reasons for attaching the V4 to the suffix are even more impelling.

If the generative phonologist considers the "connecting" vowel to be part of the root he could theoretically specify fully the distinctive features of all root vowels. This would solve all the problems, but it would not achieve descriptive or explanatory adequacy because it would fail to reflect the native speaker's intuition with regard to harmonization of vowels within the root. Even if one attempts to generate the vowels of the root, as well as those of the suffixes, either by the use of assimilation rules or with abstract markers, considering V4 part of the root still fails to reflect adequately the native speaker's intuition.

It is obvious that a native speaker of a language which employs vowel harmony has certain intuitions about what vowels may succeed one another in a word. When a Hungarian hears the word *kert* for the first time he fully expects the plural to be *kertek,* which in fact it is. On the other hand, he knows that it is conceivable, although not likely, that the plural might be **kertak* or **kertok*—that is, that it could take a back vowel suffix as do the forms in Table 8. But he knows that the plural *could not* be **kertök,* even though *ök* is one form of the plural suffix, because there are no nouns in the language containing only front unrounded vowels which take a front rounded vowel in the plural. Likewise upon hearing the word *tűz* he would expect the plural to be **tüzök,* but he knows that it may be *tüzek,* as in fact it is. He also knows that the plural *could not* be either **tüzak* or **tüzok,* again because there are no words in the language which pattern in this way. Even once he learns that the plural is *tüzek,* he still knows that with a V3 suffix like *-on~-en~-ön* 'on' the only possible form would be *tüzön.* In addition, and most importantly, he knows that the plural suffixes of *kert* and *tűz* could not possibly contain any other vowel than *e, a, o,* or *ö.* He knows that there could never be such a word as **kertik* or **tüzük,* for example, where the *-ik* or *-ük* signified plural. Since the native speaker's intuition tells him that for the plural of *kert* (or for that matter for *kert* plus any V4 suffix) the only possible vowels are *e, a,* or *o,* an adequate grammar should reflect this fact by limiting the choices to these three vowels, that is by automatically ruling out all other choices, including *ö.* But this could be done only if the vowels are considered part of the suffix rather than of the root. If they are attached to the root there is no way to *generate automatically* these and only these vowels, since roots can and do end with a variety of vowels, often followed directly by /-k/ in the plural, /-t/ for the accusative, and so on. (Compare for example: *kutya* 'dog'—pl. *kutyák; nő* 'woman'—pl. *nők; só* 'salt, acid'—pl. *sók* 'salts', but *savak* 'acids'; *mese* 'story'—pl. *mesék*.) Thus even if one specifies in the root only those features of the vowels which are unpredictable from the environment (that is, which could not be handled by assimilation rules) it turns out that the V4 must be fully specified except for gravity in almost every case—something which certainly does not reflect the native speaker's intuition. In other words, it fails to make all the linguistically significant generalizations that an adequate grammar should make.

Kučera's discussion of English (1967 [45], p. 1116 [493], fn. 3) states clearly the generative view of the matter:

I am assuming in this paper that a grammar must state, in one form or another, the general phonological constraints operative in the language (in the present case, the restrictions on initial clusters of consonant plus liquid). Naturally, if we reduced the requirements on grammars and defined the aim of a grammar solely as the generation of correct output, we would not need to be at all concerned with the specification of the first segment as to stridency; the dictionary would simply contain no morphemes beginning with $\begin{bmatrix} -\text{continuant} \\ +\text{strident} \end{bmatrix}$ plus [+consonantal] segments. The same is true about the specification as to nasality. This latter kind of grammar, however, would make it possible to reach the conclusion that there are no initial clusters of affricates plus liquids in English only if we inspected every relevant morpheme in the dictionary. Such a grammar thus does not make significant generalizations about the language and does not, in my opinion, meet the level of descriptive adequacy, although it may be correct at the level of observation and, moreover, contain simpler rules than a more adequate grammar.

It is clear, then, that the V4 vowels must, from a transformational point of view also, be considered to belong to the suffixes, not to the roots, if one is to achieve descriptive adequacy. And yet, as is pointed out above, although some descriptively adequate generalizations can thus be made, this solution cannot adequately handle all the facts. The failure to generate the correct V3 vowels, as in Tables 12, 13, 14, and 16, is particularly disturbing, since the occurrence of these is quite regular and predictable. In the V3 pattern there is only one back vowel, the +flat vowel *o*, while the V4 pattern has two back vowels, the +flat *o* and the −flat *a*. The generative rules must incorporate flatness assimilation to generate the correct front vowels, and yet this also allows them to generate V3 forms with *a*, an impossibility in Hungarian. The difficulty lies in the fact that generative phonologists insist on using distinctive features rather than phonemes, i.e., *bundles* of distinctive features. If one states the choice in terms of bundles of distinctive features there is no problem. The choice, for a V3 suffix, is then between:

e	ö	o
−diffuse	−diffuse	−diffuse
−tense	−tense	−tense
−flat	+flat	+flat
−grave	−grave	+grave

If one needs a +grave vowel then *o* is automatically selected. If one needs a −grave vowel then a further selection is made between −flat and +flat. Since generative phonology, in its usual form, totally rejects the phoneme, this obvious solution to the problem cannot be employed. Chomsky and Halle themselves have said (1965 [42], p. 123 [474]) that in order to refute distinctive feature theory "it is . . . necessary to show that certain generalizations that are linguistically significant cannot be extracted if we restrict ourselves to the categories provided by distinctive feature theory." One might even expand upon this claim and say that in order to refute a generative theory of phonology in general it is necessary to show that certain generalizations that are linguistically significant cannot be extracted if we restrict ourselves to the framework provided by that theory. It appears that such is the case for Hungarian vowel harmony.

Of course, the generative phonologist could argue, as in fact Mrs. Fromkin does, that some syntactic information may have to be brought down into the phonological rules. That is, if one could specify which morphemes or morpheme classes a particular phonological rule applies to, then perhaps the situation could be handled. But it appears that in allowing prosodies and syntactic information to sneak into the phonological rules, generative phonologists are getting dangerously close to giving up the basis of their entire system in favor of a different one which is better able to deal with the facts of language.

The real problem with the V4 pattern is that the occurrence of the various vowels is conditioned neither strictly phonologically nor syntactically, nor even morphemically. Several syntactic markers with widely differing functions are involved in these suffixes, and the syntactic or morphemic function has nothing to do with the vowel harmony problem. On the other hand, as we have seen, the conditioning cannot be based entirely on the distinctive features, or even the phonemes, of the preceding root. It appears that the only way to handle the situation properly is at the level where the conditioning actually occurs, that is, in terms of morphophonemes. It should be noted that although Lightner suggests using what he calls "archiphonemes" these do not function in the way that archiphonemes or morphophonemes have usually been used. Lightner's archiphonemes are simply convenient abbreviations for incomplete distinctive feature matrices, where the remaining features are to be filled in by assimilation rules. On the other hand, traditional morphophonemes, in at least one sense in which they have been used, are cover symbols for two or more phonemes (each completely specified as to its features). It is in this latter sense that morphophonemes must be used to treat vowel harmony. Since generative phonology does not even recognize phonemes, let alone morphophonemes in this sense, it cannot really expect to be able to deal with problems occurring on this level.

Even in structural linguistics, where morphophonemes have sometimes been accepted, this is not recognized as a separate level of operations, to be distinguished from phonemics on the one hand and from morphemics on the other. The only current linguistic method which recognizes a level which could be termed morphophonemic is stratificational theory.

The morphons of stratificational grammar are roughly equivalent to morphophonemes.

The difference is that they also incorporate some characteristics of traditional phonemes. But the essential thing is that the phonetic nature of each is fully specified on a lower level —not left partially unspecified as in transformational grammar. And an intermediate level may, if necessary, specify the "phonemic membership" of the morphon. That is, if the facts are such that the most economical statement of distribution is in terms of features, there need be no subdivision of the morphon on the phonemic level; but if the most economical statement of distribution is in terms of whole segments the morphon will be split up on the phonemic level into two or more segments, each of which, again, will be fully specified on the lower (or hypophonemic) level.

To illustrate how this works with Hungarian vowel harmony, let us first consider the V2 suffixes. The distribution of these is quite predictable—back vowel with back vowel words, front with front. Thus a morphonic representation of, say, the suffix *ban~ben* would be something like *bAn* where each symbol represents a morphon. The morphon *A* does not need to subdivide into the phonemes *a* and *e*, but rather is still represented as a single unit on the phonemic level. Only on the hypophonemic level does the subdivision occur. At that level, where the units are phonetic features, the segment *A* is broken down into such features as *vocalic, low,* and either *front* or *back*.[10] The choice between *front* and *back* is determined by the environment of other *front* or *back* features in the word. Thus we get *kert-ben* and *hölgy-ben,* but *láb-ban.* The conditions for determining the choice are given in the tactics (i.e., the "syntax") of *that level* —what is called the hypophonotactics. Thus the distribution of the vowels of the V2 suffixes is determined on the level on which the conditioning actually occurs—namely the feature level. The same is true for the V3 suffixes, whose distribution is also determined completely in terms of features—in this case front-back, and, for the front, rounded-unrounded. Taking the suffix *-on~-en~-ön,* the morphonic

---

[10]Note that it does not need to be specified as unrounded or as non-tense. Since in stratificational grammar, features are not binary, but unary, only the presence of a feature need be marked, but not its absence.

representation would be something like *On*. Again no subdivision is necessary on the phonemic level, and on the hypophonemic level the *O* is specified as *vocalic* and *low*. It also subdivides into *front* and *back*, just as did the *A*, with the criteria for the choice being specified by the hypophonotactics. But now there is a further subdivision if the path to *front* is taken—namely, to *rounded* or to nothing (i.e., unrounded). Again the criteria for the choice are given by the hypophonotactics: the path to *rounded* may be taken only if the preceding *vocalic* segment also contains the feature *rounded*. This takes care of words like *közép* where it is the final vowel of the root which determines the rounding of the suffix. There would be no problem, as in transformational phonology, of producing an unrounded back vowel *a* in these V3 suffixes. If the path to *back* is taken in a suffix like *On*, then the path to *rounded must also* simultaneously be taken. There is no option, with the morphon *O*, of going to *back* without also going to *rounded*. With the morphon involved in the V4 suffixes, however, as we shall see, this option is open.

The V4 suffixes of Hungarian are the only ones whose occurrence is conditioned other than strictly by phonetic features. Let us take the plural suffix *-ok∼-ak∼-ek∼-ök* as an example. It will be remembered that all roots with a front unrounded vowel as the last root vowel take *-ek* in the plural. Also, front vowel words take a front vowel in the V4 suffixes and back vowel words take a back vowel. So far the conditioning is still strictly phonetically conditioned. The problems are with words with front rounded vowels, a few of which, like *hölgy*, take *-ek;* and with back vowel words, where the choice of *-ak* or *-ok* is quite arbitrary. Since the conditioning here is, for the most part, not in terms of phonetic features, the most economical place, in fact the only possible place to specify the conditioning accurately is on the next higher level. Thus the plural suffix will be represented morphonically as *Ek*, the *E* representing the V4 vowel. But instead of this passing intact through the phonemic level as did the V2 and V3 morphons, this *E* subdivides on the phonemic level into *e*, *a*, *o*, and *ö*. It must be understood that these are not the traditional phonemes /ɛ/, /ɑ/, /ɔ/, and /œ/. Rather they represent these vowels only as they occur in V4 suffixes. Thus the choice between them can be specified strictly according to their distribution in these suffixes, and the conditioning can be specified in terms of whole segments—a necessity in dealing with the V4 suffixes. Any word which behaves peculiarly in its vowel harmonization patterns will be marked as such by containing a different morphon than those words which behave regularly. Thus, although *hölgy* and *tök* both contain the vowel [œ], they would be represented differently morphonically—perhaps as *tök* and *hÖlgy*. The realization of both *ö* and *Ö* will be the same on lower levels, but the difference lies in their combinational properties. The phonotactics will specify that while *ö* may be followed by the *ö* realization of *E*, *Ö* must be followed by the *e* realization. Actually, the phonotactics need only specifically note the exceptions to the rule. Thus they will specify that, after *Ö*, *E* must be realized as *e*, and that otherwise the usual hypophonemic conditioning (rounded-unrounded) applies. In terms of the back vowels, as was noted earlier the *o* realization of V4 is by far the more common, so only those words which require *a* need be marked. Thus *láb* and *báb* would be represented morphonically, for example, as *lÁb* and *báb*, and the *a* realization of *E* would be required after *Á*. For back vowel words not containing a morphon requiring the *a* realization of *E*, the *o* alternant would automatically be chosen. Words, such as *cél*, which contain front vowels but take back vowel forms of all suffixes, would contain a morphon whose combinational properties are such that it must always be followed by a back vowel. Also it will be specified on the phonemic level that, of two successive *E*'s, the latter would be realized as either *e* or *a* depending on whether the preceding *E* was realized as a back or a front vowel. The beauty of this system rests in the fact that all regular patterning, including that of V3, could be handled on the phonemic and phononic levels (where in the latter, features are already specified). Since the conditioning of *these* forms really does occur in terms of features—back-front, and rounded-unrounded, in a stratificational approach one is able to separate the two types of patterning in the language into the levels where each type of conditioning actually occurs.

Thus, of the theories examined, the only ones able to handle all of the regularly predictable harmonizations are the structural and the stratificational, and they are also both able to handle all the irregularities.

To return to the challenge issued earlier in this paper, none of the approaches has been able to *dispose* of any of the irregularities of Hungarian vowel harmony, and, in fact, the generative approach added a few new ones of its own. Since generative phonology is not able to deal adequately even with some of the regularities, let alone the irregularities, without bringing in features of other phonological systems, it seems that, at least in its present state of development, it must be ruled out of the running.

In terms of describing the process of vowel harmony in general, it was observed that an improvement could be made by *illustrating* it in terms of distinctive feature matrices, whatever phonological theory one chooses to use.

This leaves us with the final question—which of the remaining theories (structural or stratificational) handles the irregularities of Hungarian vowel harmony most efficiently? Both approaches must deal with the same data, but the significant difference is in the *way* that they deal with it. A structuralist must list irregularities in a dictionary, in which all different types of information (phonological, morphological, syntactic, and semantic) are jumbled together. The stratificationalist, on the other hand, can neatly sort out each of these areas from all the rest and deal with it on its own level. The great virtue in being able to do this is that the facts of the language are thereby presented in a much more orderly and systematic way, and, most important, in a way which reflects much more clearly the patterning forces which are at work, *on different levels,* within the language.

Proponents of generative grammar have claimed superiority for their theory on the basis that it displays greater explanatory adequacy. Even assuming that this is true, I think this is a measure to be employed only when all other things are equal. But it appears that in the present case all other things are *not* equal, and that the balance has swung in favor of stratificational analysis. To reach for explanatory adequacy at the expense of descriptive or even observational adequacy is to destroy the very groundwork on which explanatory adequacy must stand.

BIBLIOGRAPHY

A Mai Magyar Nyelv Rendszere: Leíró nyelvtan. Vol. 1. Bevezetés, hangtan, szótan. 1961. Budapest: Akadémiai Kiadó.

AOKI, HARUO. 1966. "Nez Perce Vowel Harmony and Proto-Sahaptian Vowels," *Language* 42.759–767.

——— 1968. "Toward a Typology of Vowel Harmony," *IJAL* 34.142–145.

AUSTERLITZ, ROBERT. 1967. "The Distributional Identification of Finnish Morphophonemes," *Language* 43.20–33.

BALASSA, JOZSEF. 1943. *A Magyar Nyelv Könyve.* Budapest: Dante Press.

BERRY, J. 1957. "Vowel Harmony in Twi," *BSOAS* 19.124–130.

BLOCH, BERNARD. 1948. "A Set of Postulates for Phonemic Analysis," *Language* 24.3–46. [16]

BOLINGER, DWIGHT L., and LOUIS J. GERSTMAN. 1957. "Disjuncture as a Cue to Constructs," *Word* 13.246–255.

CARMONY, MARVIN D. 1966. "Surface and Deep Phonology," *Journal of Linguistics* 2.208.

CARNOCHAN, J. 1960. "Vowel Harmony in Igbo," *African Language Studies* 1.155–163.

CHOMSKY, NOAM. 1957. Review of *Fundamentals of Language,* by R. Jakobson and M. Halle (The Hague: Mouton, 1956.) *IJAL* 23.234–242. [33]

——— 1964. *Current Issues in Linguistic Theory.* (Janua Linguarum, Series Minor, 38.) The Hague: Mouton. [39]

——— 1965. *Aspects of the Theory of Syntax.* Cambridge, Mass.: M.I.T. Press.

——— 1966. "Topics in the Theory of Generative Grammar," *Current Trends in Linguistics III,* ed. by Thomas A. Sebeok, 1–60. The Hague: Mouton.

——— 1967. "Some General Properties of Phonological Rules," *Language* 43.102–128. [48]

CHOMSKY, NOAM, and MORRIS HALLE. 1965. "Some Controversial Questions in Phonological Theory," *Journal of Linguistics* 1.97–138. [42]

——— 1968. *The Sound Pattern of English.* New York: Harper & Row.

COURT, C. 1967. "A Distinctive Feature Analysis of the Phonemes of Měntu Land Dayak," *Phonetica* 17.202–207.

FROMKIN, VICTORIA. 1965. "On System-Structure Phonology," *Language* 41.601–609. [26]

FUDGE, E. C. 1967. "The Nature of Phonological Primes," *Journal of Linguistics* 3.1–36. [46]

GREENBERG, J. H. 1966. "Synchronic and Diachronic

Universals in Phonology," *Language* 42.508–517.

HALL, ROBERT A., JR. 1944. *Hungarian Grammar.* (Language Monograph, 21.) Baltimore: Waverly Press.

HALLE, MORRIS. 1959. *The Sound Pattern of Russian.* The Hague: Mouton.

——— 1962. "Phonology in Generative Grammar," *Word* 18.54–72. [37]

———. 1964. "On the Bases of Phonology." *The Structure of Language,* ed. by. J. A. Fodor and J. J. Katz, 324–333. Englewood Cliffs, N.J.: Prentice-Hall. [38]

HILL, ARCHIBALD A., 1967. "The Current Relevance of Bloch's 'Postulates,'" *Language* 43.203–207. [22]

HOCKETT, CHARLES F. 1955. *A Manual of Phonology.* (*IJAL* Memoir 11.) Baltimore: Waverly Press.

——— 1968. Review of *Outline of Stratificational Grammar,* by S. M. Lamb. *IJAL* 34.145–153.

HOUSEHOLDER, F. W., JR. 1959. "On Linguistic Primes," *Word* 15.231–239.

——— 1965. "On Some Recent Claims in Phonological Theory," *Journal of Linguistics* 1.13–34. [41]

——— 1966. "Phonological Theory: A Brief Comment," *Journal of Linguistics* 2.99–100. [43]

JAKOBSON, ROMAN, C. G. M. FANT, and MORRIS HALLE. 1951. *Preliminaries to Speech Analysis.* Cambridge, Mass.: M.I.T. Press.

JAKOBSON, ROMAN, and MORRIS HALLE. 1956. *Fundamentals of Language.* The Hague: Mouton.

——— 1962. "Tenseness and Laxness," in *Roman Jakobson: Selected Writings I,* 550–555. The Hague: Mouton.

JONES, DANIEL. 1962. *The Phoneme: Its Nature and Use.* 2d ed. Cambridge: Heffer & Sons.

KATZ, JERROLD J., and PAUL M. POSTAL. 1964. *An Integrated Theory of Linguistic Descriptions.* Cambridge, Mass.: M.I.T. Press.

KUČERA, HENRY. 1967. "Distinctive Features, Simplicity, and Descriptive Adequacy," *To Honor Roman Jakobson,* 1114–1126. The Hague: Mouton. [45]

LAMB, SYDNEY M. 1964a. "On Alternation, Transformation, Realization, and Stratification," *Monograph Series on Languages and Linguistics,* 17. 105–122. Washington, D.C.: Georgetown University Press. [52]

——— 1964b. "The Sememic Approach to Structural Semantics," *American Anthropologist* 66:3:2.57–78.

——— 1966a. "Epilegomena to a Theory of Language," *Romance Philology* 19.531–573.

——— 1966b. "Prolegomena to a Theory of Phonology," *Language* 42.536–573. [53]

LEES, ROBERT B. 1961. *The Phonology of Modern Standard Turkish* (Uralic and Altaic Series, 6). Bloomington: Indiana University.

LIGHTNER, T. M. 1965. "On the Description of Vowel and Consonant Harmony," *Word* 21.244–250.

LYONS, JOHN. 1962. "Phonemic and Non-Phonemic Phonology: Some Typological Reflections," *IJAL* 28.127–134. [25]

MARTINET, ANDRÉ. 1936. "Neutralisation et archiphonème," *TCLP* 6.46–57.

MILLER, ROY A. 1966. "Early Evidence for Vowel Harmony in Tibetan," *Language* 42.252–277.

PIKE, KENNETH L. 1943. *Phonetics.* Ann Arbor: University of Michigan.

POSTAL, PAUL M. 1966. Review of *Elements of General Linguistics,* by André Martinet (Chicago: University of Chicago, 1964). *Foundations of Language* 2.151–186.

——— 1968. *Aspects of Phonological Theory.* New York: Harper & Row.

SEBEOK, THOMAS A. 1943a. "Notes on Hungarian Vowel Phonemes," *Language* 19.162–164.

——— 1943b. "Vowel Morphophonemics of Hungarian Suffixes," *SIL* 2.47–50.

SEUREN, PETER. 1966. Review of *Grammar Discovery Procedures,* by Robert E. Longacre (The Hague: Mouton, 1964). *Foundations of Language* 2.200–212.

SMITH, HENRY LEE, JR. 1967. "The Concept of the Morphophone," *Language* 43.306–341.

SZÉPE, GYÖRGY. 1967. "A Magyar Generatív Fonológia Néhány Kérdése," *A Nyelvtudományi Értekezések* 58.305–310.

WATERSON, NATALIE. 1956. "Some Aspects of the Phonology of the Nominal Forms of the Turkish Word," *BSOAS* 18.578–591.

WILSON, ROBERT D. 1966. "A Criticism of Distinctive Features," *Journal of Linguistics* 2.195–206. [34]

WINTER, WERNER. 1965. "Transforms without Kernels?" *Language* 41.484–489.

ZIMMER, KARL E. 1967. "A Note on Vowel Harmony," *IJAL* 33.166–171.

BIBLIOGRAPHY 19
Vowel Harmony

BERRY, J. (1957) "Vowel Harmony in Twi"

CARNOCHAN, J. (1960) "Vowel Harmony in Igbo"

SPRIGG, R. K. (1961) "Vowel Harmony in Lhasa Tibetan: Prosodic Analysis Applied to Interrelated Vocalic Features of Successive Syllables"

BOADI, L. A. (1963) "Palatality as a Factor in Twi Vowel Harmony"

LIGHTNER, T. M. (1965) "On the Description of Vowel and Consonant Harmony"

AOKI, H. (1966) "Nez Perce Vowel Harmony and Proto-Sahaptian Vowels"

MILLER, R. A. (1966) "Early Evidence for Vowel Harmony in Tibetan"

STEWART, J. M. (1967) "Tongue Root Position in Akan Vowel Harmony"

ZIMMER, K. E. (1967) "A Note on Vowel Harmony"

AOKI, H. (1968) "Toward a Typology of Vowel Harmony"

MARKEDNESS IN
STRATIFICATIONAL PHONOLOGY*
DAVID G. LOCKWOOD

The use of phonons in stratificational phonology is compared with the use of marked vs. unmarked features by transformationalists. In
connection with a Bulgarian vowel alternation,
the simplicity of the total description is taken
as a basis for preferring one possible assignment of markedness over another within the
stratificational view. The assignment of markedness preferred here runs counter to that
taken as universal in recent transformational
discussion. At the same time, it allows an
analysis which agrees with some basic intuitions of classical phonemics. Markedness, it
is concluded, is not necessarily universal; and
its implications for simplicity must also be
considered.

The distinction between marked and unmarked entities in linguistic structure has been
receiving increased attention in recent years
from linguists of various points of view. Most
prominently, we see transformational phonology taking up the distinction in the form of a
universal marking convention supposed to
hold for all languages and to serve to explain
certain allegedly universal tendencies in phonology (Postal 1968, ch. 8; Chomsky and
Halle 1968, ch. 9).

Perhaps not so well-known is the fact that
stratificational theory also makes use of marking, and has done so in phonology for a number of years. This fact becomes clear when one
realizes that the phonons of stratificational
phonology, unlike the roughly equivalent
Jakobsonian distinctive features, are single-
valued rather than binary. (Lamb has variously
used the terms *unary,* 1965:44, and *singulary*
1966a [53]: 553 [619].) This means that while
a binary distinctive feature has to be indicated
both as present in the first place, and as having
a plus or a minus value in the given case, a
phonon is either present or absent. The recent
development in transformational phonology,
using the distinction marked vs. unmarked

with only the marked having a "cost" (Postal,
166), can be seen to a certain extent as the
adoption of the phonon concept by the transformationalists.

On the other hand, there are basic differences between the recent use of a marked vs.
unmarked distinction in certain portions of a
transformational phonology and the use of
singulary phonons in a stratificational phonology. Among the most important of these is
that in stratificational theory no assumption
is made of the universality of markedness;
rather, the marked vs. unmarked nature of a
given phonetic feature, as reflected in the assignment of phonons, may differ from language
to language, according to the system which
most efficiently accounts for the various phenomena of the language under consideration.

This paper is intended to illustrate the
point by indicating the stratificational treatment of a particular vowel alternation in one
variety of standard Bulgarian. At the same
time, it will illustrate the treatment of certain
kinds of phonological alternation within the
model of phonological structure set forth in
Lamb 1966a.

1. The Bulgarian Vowel System Contemporary Standard Bulgarian has a system of six
vowel phonemes (in the traditional sense):
/i e ə a u o/.[1] Figure 1 is a phonetic chart indicating their usual articulation.

[1]In this paper the following bracketing conventions will be used to distinguish different types of
units: double slant lines for morphons (traditional
morphophonemes); single upright lines for phonemes and phonons in the sense of Lamb 1966a;
and single slant lines for classical phonemes and
Lamb's hypophonemes. Phonons and hypophonemes will be indicated in all cases by two-letter
abbreviations, the first letter of each being a capital,
while both classical and Lambian phonemes will be
in lower case letters only (e.g., /a/ = classical pho-
neme; |a| = Lambian phoneme).

*Reprinted from *Language* 45.300–308 (1969) by permission.

```
    i               u
        e   ə   o
            a
```
Figure 1

Figure 2 indicates a reasonable analysis in terms of articulatorily defined components, recognizing two dimensions of contrast: *height,* with contrasting relative positions *high* and *low;* and *advancement,* with contrasting tongue positions *front, central,* and *back.*

	FRONT	CENTRAL	BACK
HIGH	i	ə	u
LOW	e	a	o

Figure 2

Figure 3 indicates an analysis in terms of Jakobsonian distinctive features, somewhat more abstract than that in Klagstad (1958: 162).

	i	e	ə	a	u	o
VOCALIC	+	+	+	+	+	+
CONSONANTAL	−	−	−	−	−	−
GRAVE	−	−	+	+	+	+
FLAT	0	0	−	−	+	+
DIFFUSE	+	−	+	−	+	−

Figure 3

Finally, Figures 4a and 4b indicate two alternate analyses in terms of phonons. Both of these alternate analyses assume that the front vowels will be marked with the phonon |Fr| "frontal," which will also be a component of palatal consonants; that the back vowels will be marked with the phonon |Lb| "labial," also a component of labial consonants; and that central vowels are unmarked. The two analyses differ in their treatment of the height contrast, in that one recognizes the phonon |Hi| "high tongue position," while the other uses |Lo| "low tongue position" (considered unmarked in the analysis of Figure 4a) and considers high vowels unmarked. In other words, these analyses differ as to whether

```
        Fr      −       Lb
Vo  {   i       ə       u       Hi
        e       a       o       −
```
Figure 4a

```
        Fr      −       Lb
Vo  {   i       ə       u       −
        e       a       o       Lo
```
Figure 4b

they mark the vowels /i ə u/ and leave /e a o/ unmarked, or mark the low vowels, leaving the high ones unmarked.

At first glance it appears that the choice between these two analyses, although either seems simpler than a third alternative which would recognize both |Hi| and |Lo| with no unmarked height, is completely arbitrary. But in stratificational theory we have to consider the consequences of each analysis for the total description. Before we can say that the choice is truly arbitrary, we must examine the consequences of each of the alternatives for the simplicity of the total description of the language (cf. Lamb 1966b).

2. A Vowel Alternation   It so happens that in some varieties of colloquial Bulgarian (Bidwell 1963:21, n. 2) there is an alternation that involves high and low vowels. This alternation occurs in such examples as /glás/ : /gləsə́/ 'voice' : 'the voice';[2] /mét/ : /midə́/ 'honey' : 'the honey';[3] /móst/ : /mustə́/ 'bridge' : 'the bridge'. These indefinite and definite forms of Bulgarian nouns show an alternation involving a low vowel when stressed and the corresponding high vowel when unstressed. The stems in these examples are members of a stress class in which the stress always falls on the final syllable (at least for the forms considered here). These contrast with members of another stress class which maintains the stress on the same syllable of both forms, with the same stressed vowels, as in the following examples: /znák/ : /znákə/ 'sign' : 'the sign'; /léf/ : /lévə/ 'lev' : 'the lev' (Bulgarian currency unit); /gróst/ : /grózdə/ 'bunch (of grapes)' : 'the bunch'. The "basic" nature of the stressed rather than the unstressed vowel in the forms showing alternation may be established by comparison with the following forms, illustrating stems of both stress classes which always show a high vowel, regardless of which stress pattern they follow: /də́p/ : /dəbə́/ 'oak' : 'the oak'; /də́x/ : /də́xə/ 'spirit' : 'the spirit'; /mík/ : /migə́/ 'moment' : 'the moment';

[2] In addition to the pronunciation /-ə/ for the definite suffix, there is a more formal variant suggested by the writing system: /-ət/. Further variants also exist for stems of different classes.

[3] Some of these examples also illustrate a consonant alternation whose treatment is beyond the scope of this paper. This is the alternation between a voiced obstruent in prevocalic position and the corresponding voiceless obstruent in final position.

/líst/ : /lístə/ 'page' : 'the page'; /lúk/ : /lukə́/ 'onion' : 'the onion'; /zvúk/ : /zvúkə/ 'sound' : 'the sound'.

3. The Stratificational Treatment In the model presented in Lamb 1964a and other articles of the same period (Lamb 1964b, Gleason 1964), the only way to treat the alternations exhibited in the above examples is to view them as alternations between morphons, the minimal components of morphemes (analogous to traditional morphophonemes), and phonemes of the traditional type. The morphonic forms of the alternating stems for such a system would be, respectively //glas// 'voice', //med// 'honey', //most// 'bridge'. Each of these would be allowed by the morphotactics to combine with the definite suffix //ə//, which for these examples would carry the stress. Morphophonemic realization rules would then recode the morphons //a e o// into the phonic combinations (phonemes)

$$\left/ \begin{array}{ccc} \text{Vo} & \text{Vo} & \text{Vo} \\ \text{Lo} & \text{Lo} & \text{Lo} \\ & \text{Fr} & \text{Lb} \end{array} \right/$$

when stressed, but

$$\left/ \begin{array}{ccc} \text{Vo} & \text{Vo} & \text{Vo} \\ \text{Hi} & \text{Hi} & \text{Hi} \\ & \text{Fr} & \text{Lb} \end{array} \right/$$

when unstressed.[4] This could be given as a single realization rule with such cover symbols as V_L and V_H for low and high vowels, respectively; but in a completely explicit account there would be no alternative to providing separate, though parallel, realization rules of the form

$$
\begin{array}{ccccc}
\text{a} & \| & \underline{\quad\prime\quad} & / & \text{a} \\
 & \| & \underline{\quad\quad} & / & \text{ə} \\
\\
\text{e} & \| & \underline{\quad\prime\quad} & / & \text{e} \\
 & \| & \underline{\quad\quad} & / & \text{i} \\
\\
\text{o} & \| & \underline{\quad\prime\quad} & / & \text{o} \\
 & \| & \underline{\quad\quad} & / & \text{u}
\end{array}
$$

However, in the model presented in "Prole-

[4]Both /Hi/ and /Lo/ will be considered marked for the present purposes, but this is not to imply that markedness could not have been used at this point of development of the theory.

gomena to a Theory of Phonology" [53], provision is made for two separate alternation patterns to account for what are traditionally called morphophonemic alternations. One of these treats alternations which are better characterized in terms of whole segments, while the other handles alternations which are better characterized in terms of components.

It seems clear that in this newer model the vowel alternations concerned would be among those better treated in terms of components, which would be handled by the lower of these two alternation patterns. The situation would be as follows, in terms of the segments of the upper of the two phonological strata, termed phonemes by Lamb (though they are partially morphophonemic in nature, a compromise between traditional morphophonemes and traditional phonemes): |glas| with phonemic |a|, |med| with phonemic |e|, and |most| with phonemic |o| (in all environments).

The phonemic sign pattern then specifies each vowel phoneme in terms of phonons, i.e., morphophonemic components. Let us assume there are two possible analyses of these according to the two possible views of markedness for vowel height illustrated by Figures 4a and 4b. These patterns would be exactly the same in complexity for either analysis; but below this pattern would be an alternation pattern, which would have to take care of the alternation in question, as well as others. Such alternations would be treated as alternate realizations of these phonons in terms of the units of the lower phonological stratum, the hypophonemes. The environments for these alternations would have to be specified in terms of the tactics of this lower stratum, which would specify well-formed arrangements of the hypophonemes into segments and clusters. It is on this stratum that bi-unique representations, analogous to those of classical phonemics, would be found. They would be stated in terms of component-sized entities — hypophonemes), however, not in terms of segment-sized entities (classical phonemes).

There is also a tactic fact, which would have to be accounted for on this stratum in any case, which is related to this morphophonemic alternation. This tactic fact is that (for this variety of Bulgarian) the low vowels /e a o/ can occur only if accompanied by stress; therefore the only unstressed vowels are /i ə u/. Let us see how this can be accounted for under each of the alternate analyses of the vowel phonemes (now in the sense of Lamb 1966a [53]) under consideration.

First let us try analysis in Figure 4a, which considers |Hi| marked, leaving the low series unmarked. The relevant portions of the phonemic sign pattern, phononic alternation pattern, and hypophonotactics are shown in Figure 5.[5] This pattern shows no alternations at

[5]In place of the upward *ands* in a "knot pattern" (as in Lamb 1966a [53], b), a different node, the diamond, is currently being used (cf. Bennett 1968). Difficulties in definition for purposes of encoding and decoding have required the change to a different type of node.

all in the alternation pattern, since each of the phonons it postulates is always realized by a single hypophoneme, a different one for each. The hypophonotactics for this solution, however, specifies several things. The relevant portion, of course, is that which generates vowel segments. All of these have in common the hypophoneme /Vo/, shown from the leftmost branch from the unordered *and* at the top of this partial diagram. The second branch of this *and* states that simultaneously with /Vo/ one also selects /Fr/, thus specifying a front vowel; or /Lb/, specifying a back rounded vowel; or zero, meaning that the vowel will be central—all under the control of choices already made on the upper stratum, as shown by

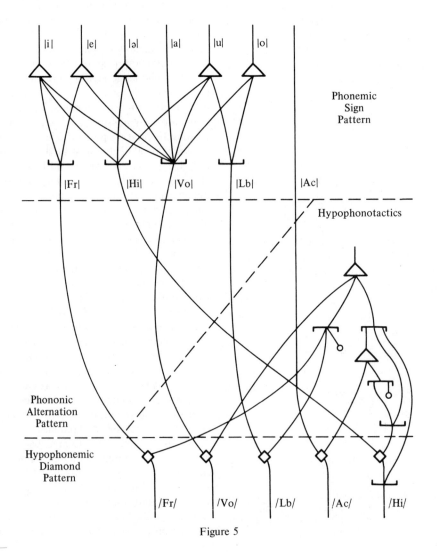

Figure 5

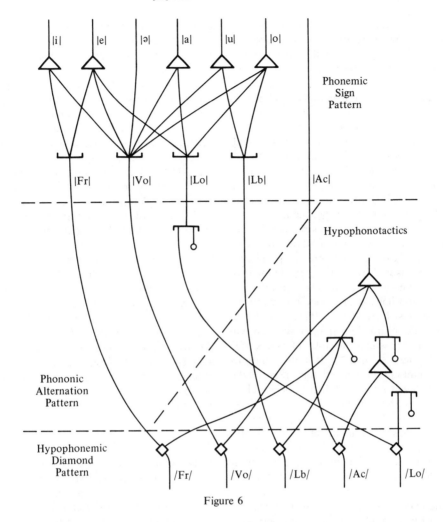

Figure 6

the diamonds. The third branch has to do with stress and its relation to the occurrence or non-occurrence of /Hi/, which this solution takes to be the marked height. If stress (symbolized /Ac/, for "accent") is selected, as will be specified through the diamonds by selections already made on some higher stratum (whose detailed treatment is beyond the scope of this paper), one may select /Hi/ or not, according to whether or not it is specified. This fact is shown by the leftmost branch of the downward-ordered *or*. The second branch from this *or* allows /Hi/ to be specified quite apart from /Ac/, i.e., if the specifications from above indicate an unstressed high vowel. Finally, the third branch of this *or* is needed to specify that an unstressed vowel must be high even if this is not specified from above. It in-

serts /Hi/ without control from the upper stratum in cases where neither |Ac| nor |Hi| accompanies |Vo|, thus providing for the alternation for which we are accounting.

Now let us examine Figure 6, which indicates the alternate analysis, that which considers |Lo| to be marked, and high vowels therefore unmarked. The sign pattern differs in this detail from that of Figure 5, but in its complexity it is identical. For this diagram, the alternation pattern indicates something, for the phonon |Lo| is shown to have alternate realizations /Lo/ and zero by the downward ordered *or* attached to its line. As for the hypophonotactics, it shows /Vo/ accompanied by simultaneous /Fr/, /Lb/, or zero in exactly the same way as Figure 5. The third branch from its initial downward *and*, however, differs from that of Figure 5 in several respects. It leads to a downward ordered *or* whose first branch leads to /Ac/ if specified from above, in which case /Lo/ may be chosen or not, according to whether it is specified; but if /Ac/ is not specified from above, this branch allows no further selection, for the second branch of the *or* goes to zero. Thus a phonon |Lo| which is not accompanied by |Ac| could not be realized, for it would have to take the second branch of the ordered *or* in the alternation pattern. So this diagram, also, provides for the alternation between the two sets of vowels and the related tactic fact that unaccented vowels must be high, in this case unmarked for height.

How can these two solutions be compared? They can be compared for simplicity, which is measured by counting the number of nodes in a solution, and adding to this the number of excess lines at any node (above three, since we must have at least three in order to have a node at all). The simpler solution will be the one for which this total of nodes plus "extra" lines is smaller. If both solutions should count out the same by this measure, the one with fewer nodes is taken to be simpler.[6] Let us apply this simplicity measure to these two solutions. The sign-pattern portions, as noted previously, are identical in complexity, though different in detail. The number of diamonds (5) is also identical in these two solutions; therefore these two portions will not be considered. We have only to consider the remaining nodes. These additional portions contain, for Figure 5, seven nodes and three extra lines, and for Figure 6, six nodes and two extra lines. Therefore, by our measure of economy, Figure 6 is the simpler and is the preferred analysis. This consideration gives us a reason to prefer one of the solutions differing only in the assignment of markedness over the other, despite their superficial appearance of being equal in complexity.

Let us now consider some of the further implications of this comparison. According to Lamb (1966a:571 [632]), the hypophonemic stratum is the level at which phonological representations have a biunique relation to phonetic representations, and at which distinctive

phonological properties are distinguished from non-distictive ones. The latter is indicated by the difference between hypophonemes, those minimal units of this stratum which are specified from above through the diamond pattern (then treated as a knot pattern with upward *ands*), as opposed to determined *hypophonemic signs,* which are automatically inserted by the tactics as determined elements, bypassing the diamonds. The analysis of Figure 5 makes the assertion that the highness of such vowels as the first /ə/ in /gləsə́/ 'the voice' is just a determined element; and in fact it says that the /ə/ in this word is not the same on this stratum as the /ə/ in /dəbə́/ 'the oak', which is a |ə| on the higher stratum as well, while the former is an |a|. The classical phonemicist, however, would surely want to insist that they *are the same.* His intuition would be confirmed by the fact that the analysis of Figure 6, which treats them as the same, is simpler than that of Figure 5, which considers them different: in Figure 6 the first vowels of /gləsə́/ and /dəbə́/ would be treated as the same, as /Vo/ hypophonemically; but in Figure 5 the first /ə/ of /gləsə́/ would be /Vo/, while that of /dəbə́/ would be

$$/ \begin{array}{c} \text{Vo} \\ \text{Hi} \end{array} /$$

They would be the same only when viewed as hypophonemic signs, which include non-distinctive as well as phonemic elements: here both would be /Vo/ and /Hi/.

Another fact that the analysis of Figure 6 treats better is that there is indeed a phononic alternation in these examples, as indicated by the downward *or* for |Lo| in the alternation pattern; the analysis of Figure 5 would assert that there is no alternation, only a determined element /Hi/ in the absence of stress.

4. Implications The considerations brought forward in this paper tend to suggest that the marked vs. unmarked distinction is not a matter of universal treatment, but rather a matter which is to be decided individually for each language, depending on which decision will result in the simplest overall treatment of the given language in accordance with a simplicity measure of the type used here. The treatment of alternations such as that considered here is an area which one should take

---

[6]This refinement in the measure for surface information outlined in Lamb 1966b, chap. 3, is derived from Reich 1968.

into account when deciding such matters of simplicity. Another consideration is the simplification of the lower tactics (that of segments and clusters) for other areas in the language, and the relation of the vowel system to the consonant system. So if one has a choice of one solution with an element which can serve for both vowels and consonants, versus another solution which requires separate elements in each subsystem, one would obviously opt, all other things being equal, for the former.

Similar considerations, it should be noted, allow the use of marked and unmarked distinctions for various morphological, syntactic, and semantic categories, each on its own stratum of a stratificational description.

It is not to be assumed a priori, of course, that the marked vs. unmarked nature of a given contrast *cannot* be universal; but, on the other hand, it seems dogmatic to assume that any particular one, or all, of such contrasts are *necessarily* universally marked or unmarked without sufficient empirical evidence.

It has recently been asserted by transformationalists (for example, Chomsky and Halle, 409) that /a/ is the universally unmarked vowel. The solution of Figure 5 for Bulgarian takes /a/ to be the unmarked vowel, and it results in a more complex stratificational solution for one of the phenomena to be accounted for than does Figure 6, which takes /ə/ to be the unmarked vowel for this language. In still other languages, it seems altogether possible that we may want to consider some other vowel to be maximally unmarked. Therefore it seems, at least from the point of view adopted here, that we should not be too hasty in concluding that marked vs. unmarked is a universal property, since in doing so we may wind up complicating rather than simplifying our linguistic descriptions.[7]

---

[7]One could, of course, claim that the requirement of differing uses of marked and unmarked according to the language is a defect of stratificational theory vis-à-vis transformational, seeing it as a

REFERENCES

BENNETT, DAVID C. 1968. "English Prepositions: A Stratificational Approach," *Journal of Linguistics* 4.153–172.

BIDWELL, CHARLES E. 1963. *Slavic Historical Phonology in Tabular Form*. The Hague: Mouton.

CHOMSKY, NOAM, and MORRIS HALLE. 1968. *The Sound Pattern of English*. New York: Harper & Row.

GLEASON, H. A., JR. 1964. "The Organization of Language: A Stratificational View," *Monograph Series on Languages and Linguistics* 17.75–95, ed. by C. I. J. M. Stuart. Washington, D.C.: Georgetown University Press.

KLAGSTAD, HAROLD L., JR. 1958. "A Phonemic Analysis of Some Bulgarian Dialects," *American Contributions to the Fourth International Congress of Slavicists,* 157–168. (Slavistic printings and reprintings, 21). The Hague: Mouton.

LAMB, SYDNEY M. 1964a. "On Alternation, Transformation, Realization, and Stratification," *Monograph Series on Languages and Linguistics* 17.105–122, ed. by C. I. J. M. Stuart. Washington, D.C.: Georgetown University Press. [52]

———. 1964b. "The Sememic Approach to Structural Semantics," *American Anthropologist* 66:3, part 2, 57–78.

———. 1965. "Kinship Terminology and Linguistic Structure," *American Anthropologist* 67:5, part 2, 37–64.

———. 1966a. "Prolegomena to a Theory of Phonology," *Language* 42.536–573. [53]

———. 1966b. *Outline of Stratificational Grammar*. Washington, D.C.: Georgetown University Press.

POSTAL, PAUL M. 1968. *Aspects of Phonological Theory*. New York: Harper & Row.

REICH, PETER A. 1968. *Symbols, Relations, and Structural Complexity*. New Haven: Linguistic Automation Project, Yale University (mimeographed).

---

failure to take account of such putative universals. This difference is related to the general attitudes toward language universals taken by proponents of the respective theories.

I am indebted to Sydney M. Lamb, Ilah Fleming, and Helen Ullrich for a number of useful suggestions which led to improvements in earlier versions of this paper.

56

NEUTRALIZATION, BIUNIQUENESS, AND STRATIFICATIONAL PHONOLOGY*

DAVID G. LOCKWOOD

1. NEUTRALIZATION

The term "neutralization" has been used by linguists in two distinct but related senses.[1] In the usage of the Prague School, it refers to the situation in which a phonological contrast (in Praguian terms, "opposition") implemented in one set of environments within a particular language is not applicable in another set of environments (cf. Trubetzkoy 1936, Martinet 1936, Bazell 1956). To cite a well-known example, Russian /t/ and /d/ contrast prevocalically, as in /tám/ 'there' and /dám/ 'of the ladies', but in final position they do not contrast, as only /t/ can occur, as in /vót/ 'here is' (*vot*) or 'of the waters' (*vod*). This concept has been applied primarily in phonology, but its extension to other portions of linguistic structure has also been suggested by some linguists (e.g., Bazell 1949, Saporta 1956).

A different sense of "neutralization" has been proposed by Lamb (1964: 63–64). In stratificational theory, the term refers to the situation in which two or more entities of one realizational level have an identical realization on a lower realizational level (the levels involved may be either between or within stratal systems). It might be objected that these situations are not really distinct, since the classical situations in which Praguian neutralization has been said to occur—such as the Russian example cited above and an analogous situation in German—involve both phenomena. But there are, in fact, cases in which the Praguian definition of "neutralization" would be satisfied without the occurrence of Lambian neutralization, and vice versa.

To take first an example of the latter situation, it appears that Praguian neutralization is always a *conditioned* phenomenon. It involves a particular set of environments in which a contrast is inapplicable. In stratificational terms, however, the adverb *well* and the noun *well* (as in the sentences *They work well together* and *It's a deep well,* respectively) may be said to neutralize unconditionally into the single morphemic sign //w e l//. As I understand the doctrine of the Prague School, however, not even those who have extended the concept of neutralization from phonological to grammatical structure would claim that a neutralization occurs in such an example.

As an example of the opposite case, consider a language which, like German and Russian, has contrasting voiced and voiceless obstruents in initial and medial positions, but has only voiceless ones finally. Suppose further that unlike German and Russian, this language has no suffixes before which the distinction between voiced and voiceless obstruents would be maintained (e.g., suffixes beginning with a vowel). This would mean that there would be no means of resolving the neutralization, and no basis for establishing even a morphophonemic distinction between voiced and voiceless obstruents in morpheme-final position. All such obstruents could therefore

[1] In revising an earlier version of this paper, I have profited from the comments of Ilah Fleming, Sydney M. Lamb, Adam Makkai, and William Sullivan. Slant lines enclose symbols for entities on the hypophonemic stratum, including classical phonemes. Upright lines indicate entities on the stratificational phonemic stratum, and double slant lines (// //) entities on the morphemic stratum.

*This paper, written in 1969, appears in print for the first time here.

be treated without reference to any distinction on all realizational levels on which individual segments are provided for. In such a language, we would find an example of neutralization according to the Praguian definition, but there would be no neutralization in the sense discussed by Lamb, since there would be no case in which a contrast establishable on higher realizational levels would be lost on a lower level.

In this paper, I will be discussing primarily neutralization in the sense of the Prague School, in reference to its application to stratificational theory. To avoid terminological conflict, I will henceforth refer to neutralization in the Praguian sense as P-*neutralization,* and neutralization as the term is usually used in stratificational theory as S-*neutralization.*

2. BIUNIQUENESS

The biuniqueness of phonological representations has been the subject of widespread debate among linguistic theorists during the past decade. This discussion originated with Halle's assertion of 1959 that phonological theories which attempt to define an abstracted level of representation which has a biunique relation to the phonetic, such as classical phonemics in its variant forms, inevitably misses generalizations when there exist in the given language phonological asymmetries of a certain fairly common type. Halle gave an example based on the Russian obstruent system. This example has been quoted and further discussed by other transformational writers such as Chomsky (1964 [39]; 88–90 [413]; 1962: 133–134; 1966: 78–82) and Postal (1968: 39–40). Among those who have questioned the validity of Halle's reasoning on this point are Lamb (1966 [53], 1967) and Johns (1969 [49]).

Lamb has claimed that while there are defects in the traditional phonemic analysis of Russian which Halle criticized, these shortcomings have nothing to do with the principle of biuniqueness. He has further argued that these difficulties can be overcome within the confines of the usual neo-Bloomfieldian theoretical framework by an analysis which extracts voicelessness as a separate phoneme.[2]

In the same article (Lamb 1966 [53]) he further offered a demonstration that, within the stratificational framework, biuniqueness can be said to follow ultimately from a far more general principle of simplicity, which applies not only to linguistics, but to all science.

Johns also attacks Halle, Chomsky, and Postal quite directly. He claims in particular that their arguments are vitiated by an analysis which, while adhering strictly to the principle of biuniqueness, allows the recognition of P-neutralization.[3]

Let us now examine a concrete example in order to go over these arguments in more detail. Halle's original Russian example has been discussed numerous times, by opponents as well as advocates of his view. Rather than using it once more, I will take the following hypothetical example, which incorporates two separate instances of the phenomenon Halle was talking about.

Suppose that in some language the following obstruents occur phonetically:

INITIALLY: [p t k b d g f s x]
MEDIALLY: [b d g v z ɣ]
FINALLY: [p t k f s x]

Assuming no cases of free variation in the data cited, it seems clear that the Neo-Bloomfieldian phonemicist would set up 9 phonemes, all of which would occur initially: /p t k b d g f s x/. Medially he would state that only /b d g f s x/ occur (and the voiced allophones of the three spirants, namely, [v z ɣ] occur). In final position, he would say that only

devoicing element /h/ applying to an entire obstruent cluster, does not represent the stratificational analysis within the system developed in that paper. Although Lamb did believe at an earlier date that this analysis was correct, the actual stratificational treatment of 1966 is presented later in the article, where he says (p. 562 [626]) "In Russian the tactic pattern at this [i.e., the hypophonemic—D.G.L.] level specifies that an obstruent cluster may optionally have a single occurrence of the devoicing element."

[3]Johns' otherwise excellent paper is weakened in the final portion, where he proposes a model which attempts to fit a phonemic level into a generative grammar in such a way that the derivation originating with a morphophonemic ("systematic phonemic") representation branches off in two directions, one to the phonetic level, another to the phonemic. He does not give full enough consideration to the alternative of allowing the derivation of the phonetic from the phonemic.

[2]The analysis of Russian obstruents presented by Lamb (1966: 544–547 [612–614]), involving a

/p t k f s x/ occur, the latter in the form of their voiceless allophones [f s x]. If alternations among voiced and voiceless stops happened to be produced as a result of these distributional restrictions, they would be regarded by the neo-Bloomfieldian linguist as morphophonemic. So there might be justification for a morphophoneme //p// with alternate realizations /p/ (initial, final) and /b/ (medial), and a contrasting //b// with alternate realizations /b/ (initial, medial) and /p/ (final). Alternations between voiced and voiceless spirants, however, would be strictly allophonic, so there would be a phoneme /f/ with the allophones [f] (initial, final) and [v] (medial).

The Praguian phonologist, however, would view the situation differently. He would recognize the same total of obstruent phonemes, but in the medial and final positions he would consider the voicing contrast to be neutralized, since it is predictable from the phonological environment whether a stop or spirant will be voiced or voiceless in these positions, making this phonetic detail nondistinctive there. The Praguian treatment would therefore recognize the archiphonemes /P T K/, representing the P-neutralization of the phoneme pairs /p-b, t-d, k-g/, respectively. In this treatment, therefore, the voicing of medial obstruents and the voicelessness of final obstruents could be handled in statements applying to the obstruents in general, whether stop or spirant, but in the case of the stops the archiphonemes /P T K/ would be involved.

The usual neo-Bloomfieldian objection to this approach, of course, is that it is uneconomical because of the need to recognize additional units, namely the archiphonemes. But if one counts not the number of different segmental units in the inventory but rather the phonological components or features needed to specify an utterance containing an instance of the neutralization in question, the Praguian approach will turn out to be more economical than that of the neo-Bloomfieldians, since the archiphonemes involve fewer feature specifications than the corresponding fully specified phonemes.[4]

Which of these approaches is more economical, however, is entirely a matter of how one looks at the measurement of economy. If one counts the number of distinct phonemic segments in the inventory, as was the practice of the neo-Bloomfieldians, the approach which does not allow P-neutralization turns out to be simpler. But if one counts specifications of features or components instead, the approach allowing P-neutralization will be simpler. Little can be said beyond this, short of providing a means of evaluating the competing methods of measuring relative simplicity.

The follower of Hallean phonology would establish the same inventory of distinct segments—his "systematic phonemes"—as the other analysts for this data, but he would use them as a means of assigning a shape to each morpheme on the basis of its morphophonemic behavior. The phonetic shapes of these morphemes would then be obtained by the application of rules to the effect that (1) medial obstruents will be voiced, and (2) final obstruents will be voiceless.

He would point out the inefficiency of the neo-Bloomfieldian treatment requiring one morphophonemic rule to deal with the alternation among the stops and a separate allophonic rule to deal with the alternation among the spirants, for each of the two cases of P-neutralization (i.e., medial and final). The same could not be said of the Praguian analysis, however, because, in view of the P-neutralization of voicing, it will not be distinctive in these positions for either stops or spirants. Thus the rules requiring medial voicing and final voicelessness can be made applicable to stops and spirants alike. Still, the Praguian analysis retains its biunique character, since a given phone will have a unique phonemic representation in a given environment. What is different from the neo-Bloomfieldian treatment, of course, is that the specification of voicing or voicelessness in neutralized position can apply to both stops and spirants, so it will be an allophonic rather than a morphophonemic rule in both cases. The treatment of the stops is still distinguished from that of the spirants under this analysis. For the stops, assum-

---

[4]The neo-Bloomfieldian analysis could be modified, however, along the lines suggested for the Russian data by Lamb (cf. fn. 2). A phoneme of stop voicing, occurring only initially with one of the stops, could be set up. Such an analysis would be consistent with the neo-Bloomfieldian avoidance of P-neutralization. Cf. fn. 5 for the use of marked voicing instead of the marked voicelessness postulated earlier.

ing occurrences of morphophonemically resolvable S-neutralization, it will be necessary
to account for an alternation involving the
specification of voicing or its absence (in environments where there is no neutralization)
vs. the irrelevance of this specification (in positions of neutralization). Morphophonemically
voicing or its absence will be specified for the
stops, but in positions of neutralization this
specification will not be realized phonemically.
For the spirants, on the other hand, there will
be no specification of voicing either phonemically or morphophonemically.

This evidence seems to show conclusively
that it is *not* the property of biuniqueness
which renders the traditional analysis unable
to capture the generalization which Halle
wants to show. Yet Halle and his followers
have inexplicably attributed the deficiency to
this property, and have insisted that this shortcoming can be overcome only by eliminating
the phonemic level with its property of biuniqueness. It seems inconceivable that Halle
himself could be unfamiliar with Praguian
forms of analysis. He was, after all, long associated with Roman Jakobson, who had been
one of the leading figures of the Prague School.
Also Halle compares a feature of his own
theory, the notion of the "incompletely specified morphoneme" to the archiphonemes of
the Prague School in a later section of his
book (1959: 39).

Yet for some reason Halle failed to note
that the offending property of the traditional
analysis was not the maintenance of biuniqueness but rather the refusal of the neo-Bloomfieldians to admit P-neutralization. This feature of neo-Bloomfieldian phonological theory
may be termed *non-suspendability*. Such a
principle has often been summarized by the
dictum "Once a phoneme, always a phoneme."
Quite clearly also, the justification of non-
suspendability is closely connected with the
notion that the phonemic segment is to be
granted primacy over its components or distinctive features, which was also maintained
by most neo-Bloomfieldians, whether or not
they granted components any status at all.

3. P-NEUTRALIZATION IN STRATIFICATIONAL THEORY

One of the major points of this paper is
that P-neutralization is not only compatible

with stratificational theory but also that it is
required in at least some instances if a maximally simple account of the linguistic facts is
to be provided. In order to show this, let us
consider the stratificational treatment of the
hypothetical data introduced above. I am assuming that these facts will be dealt with primarily in the hypophonotactic portion of a
stratificational description. The *hypophonotactics* is that tactic pattern which determines
the distributional potentialities of phonological components called *hypophonemes*. A transcription in terms of hypophonemes will bear
a biunique relation to the phonetic transcription.

The obstruents of the language under consideration may be broken down componen-
tially as in Table I. Here the components are
/Cl/ "closed," /Sp/ "spirant," /Lb/ "labial,"
/Ap/ "apical," /Do/ "dorsal," /Vd/ "voiced."

Table I

/p	t	k	b	d	g	f	s	x /
/Cl	Cl	Cl	Cl	Cl	Cl	Sp	Sp	Sp /
/ Lb	Ap	Do	Lb	Ap	Do	Lb	Ap	Do /
/			Vd	Vd	Vd			/

I assume on several grounds that voicing
will be the marked situation for obstruents, so
that the voicelessness of obstruents will be
treated as equivalent to the absence of a specification of voicing. These grounds include the
fact that languages are often found which lack
voiced obstruents, but seldom if ever do we
find a language which lacks voiceless ones.
Furthermore, it appears that if a voicing contrast is lacking for some major subpart of the
obstruent system (e.g., the stops, the spirants,
the affricates), voiceless sounds usually occur
as the realizations of the phonemes involved
in those positions where a contrast is possible
for the other obstruents. This situation is illustrated by the data under consideration, in
which spirants lack a voicing contrast, but in
initial position, where voiced and voiceless
stops can contrast, voiceless spirants occur.
The situation reflected by this hypothetical
language has been purposely set up to reflect
this typical situation for languages in general,
of course, rather than the relatively bizarre

situations which would be presented if the occurrence of voicing and voicelessness were reversed.[5]

Figure 1 shows an attempt to graph the situation under consideration in the notation introduced in Lamb 1966 [53], under the assumption of non-suspendability and using the componential analysis of Table I. The lines at the top of the diagram, marked I, M, and F, indicate the points which would connect in a larger diagram to the respective positions of initial, medial, and final obstruents. An initial obstruent is shown to be either labial, apical, or dorsal, and either closed or spirant in articulation, and if closed, either voiced or not. A final obstruent is shown to be either labial, apical, or dorsal again, and either closed or spirant, but in no case voiced. A medial obstruent is shown to have the same choices for articulator and manner of articulation as elsewhere, but a stop is obligatorily voiced. No voicing

is shown for the spirants, because this is considered subphonemic.[6]

If we wish to fit such a tactics into a stratificational grammar of the language in question, however, we must also consider the matter of how the tactics will be connected to the stratum above. Each hypophoneme will have an upward connection to one or more of the phonons (morphophonemic components) of which it is the realization. Such connections are made with a *diamond node* with connections leading upward to the higher stratum and to the tactics, and downward to the ultimate realization. There is no problem for the articulators and manners of articulation—the diamonds for them can clearly be put at the bottom of each corresponding line in Figure 1. The question comes when we deal with /Vd/, since it will not always be the realization of a phonon. We are assuming, that is, that there will be an S-neutralization in medial position such that /Vd/ will be realized for a stop whether or not the corresponding phonon |Vd| is signaled. We might assume that there is a diamond at the bottom of the branch marked /Vd/ which leads upward to either the phonon |Vd| or to zero, as shown in Figure 2. This possibility would clearly allow the voicing to be supplied to

[5]See Lockwood 1969 [55] for a fuller discussion of the use of markedness in stratificational phonology. The position with regard to the marked nature of voicing for obstruents is in conflict with that expressed in Lamb 1966 [53], where it was maintained that voicing is unmarked for language in general, or at least for most languages. Lamb has since indicated (personal communication) that he now feels that his earlier position is valid only for nonobstruents, and that the position expressed here is correct with reference to obstruents.

[6]See the discussion of the analyses presented in Figures 4 and 5 for the treatment of the nondistinctive voicing.

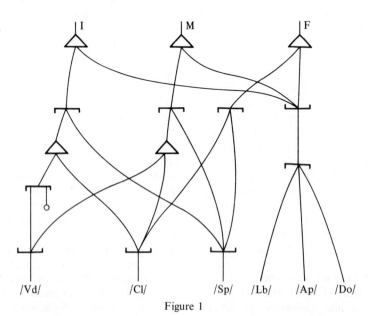

/Vd/ /Cl/ /Sp/ /Lb/ /Ap/ /Do/

Figure 1

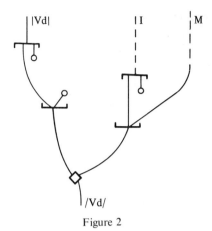

Figure 2

stops in medial position, even if not signaled from above. But for the broader situation, this solution would prove unworkable. An upward *or* with one branch to zero in this case would mean that the component down to which it leads, namely, /Vd/, will be realized wherever the tactics permits it to occur, regardless of the specifications of the upper stratum. This is descriptive of the situation in medial position, but not that of initial position, where we want /Vd/ to be selected only when the corresponding phonon |Vd| has been signaled. So the addition of what is shown in Figure 2 to the tactics of Figure 1 would render the choice

which we need to have in initial position between /Vd/ and its absence completely vacuous, and in so doing it would not correctly represent the facts of the language.

It might be possible to save the situation by distinguishing two voicing hypophonemes, one the realization of the phonon |Vd| in initial position and the other the realization of either |Vd| or zero in medial position, but such a recourse seems unattractive for obvious reasons. An alternative which seems somewhat more attractive would involve giving up the notion of markedness for voicing, so that there would be both a hypophoneme /Vd/ "voiced" and a contrasting /Uv/ "unvoiced." The effects of this interpretation are graphed in Figure 3. This abandonment of markedness inevitably results in additional complications, but this is perhaps the best interpretation of the intentions of the neo-Bloomfieldian analysis, translated into hypophonemic terms.[7]

[7]Of course not all neo-Bloomfieldians accepted the relevance of the notion of phonological components or features on which hypophonemic treatments are based. All neo-Bloomfieldians, however, accepted an implicit componential analysis in their recognition of suprasegmental phonemes in the treatment of vowels. Those who rejected componential analyses of other aspects of the vowel system, and the whole consonant system, failed to apply the same logic throughout the phonological system. (Cf. Lamb's discussion 1966: 545–546 [612–614].)

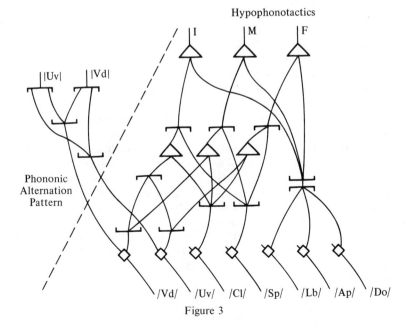

Figure 3

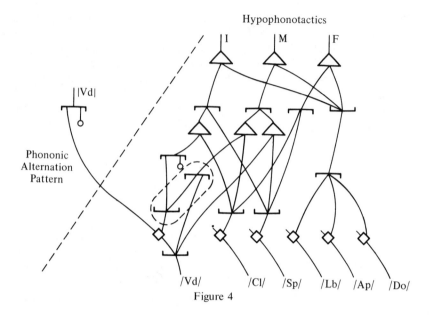

Figure 4

Figure 4 shows an analysis which attempts to preserve the markedness principle while still accounting for all voicing. It differs from that presented in Figure 1 only in the treatment of medial obstruents. It shows that stops in this position will take voicing whether or not it is signaled from the upper stratum, but by a means different from that which we found to be unworkable in Figure 1. The diamond for /Vd/ leads upward only to |Vd|, but even when |Vd| is not signaled, a line leads down to /Vd/, bypassing the diamond. This analysis will correctly account for the facts. It should be noted that this analysis also accounts for the fact that medial spirants will be voiced, though this fact is never signaled from the upper stratum.

This brings us to the distinction between hypophonemes and *hypophonemic signs*. According to Lamb (1966: 571 [632]), the hypophonemic transcription is defined by the diamonds (then upward *ands*) which are activated. Those phonetic features signaled from the upper stratum by the activation of a diamond are termed hypophonemes, and are distinctive. Those which are not directly signaled from the upper stratum but are determined by the tactics of the hypophonemic stratum are nondistinctive hypophonemic signs. Hypophonemic signs are therefore either the realizations of hypophonemes or automatically determined features inserted by the tactics.

Analogous considerations define emes and emic signs on the other strata as well.

Now for a voiced stop such as /b/ in medial position—in terms of hypophonemic signs $\Big/{}^{Cl}_{Lb}{}_{Vd}\Big/$—there are two hypophonemic realizates by this analysis: $\Big/{}^{Cl}_{Lb}{}_{Vd}\Big/$ in which the /Vd/ would be considered distinctive, and $\Big/{}^{Cl}_{Lb}\Big/$ in which the hypophonemic sign /Vd/ is only a determined element. So given the hypophonemic sign /Vd/ in this position, there would be no direct way of determining whether it realizes a hypophoneme or not. For this reason the analysis of Figure 4 fails the biuniqueness condition, for it does not assign a biunique hypophonemic transcription.

But it should further be noted that the diagram of Figure 4 can be simplified. The same effective information can be obtained if we eliminate the ordered *or* leading either to distinctive /Vd/ or to the determined hypophonemic sign /Vd/, and allow only the latter specification. An occurrence of the phonon |Vd| will fail to be realized in medial position just as in final position, and its signal will take the alternate path to zero in the phononic alternation pattern. But in medial position, unlike final position, voicing will be determined anyway in the form of an occurrence of the hypophonemic sign /Vd/ regardless of what is specified from above. This simplified account, obtained by eliminating the nodes encircled in Figure 4, can then be subjected to further mechanical simplifications of the type discussed in Reich 1968. The result of this will be the analysis shown in Figure 5.

This account is not only the simplest shown so far, but it also represents the type of analysis favored by the Prague School, since it incorporates P-neutralization in the same places as the Prague phonologist would. It states that /Vd/ is distinctive for initial obstruents in this language, but nondistinctive for medial and final obstruents. The hypophonemic sign /Vd/ is, however, determined for all obstruents in medial position, while it is obligatorily absent for final obstruents and all nonmedial spirants. It therefore appears that, in this and similar cases, phonological analyses incorporating P-neutralization are preferable under stratificational assumptions to the competing neo-Bloomfieldian treatments of the same data. Furthermore, this solution, the simplest of those considered, still meets the biuniqueness condition, like the Praguian analysis of which it is a formalization.

4. MARKEDNESS AND P-NEUTRALIZATION

In this section the various subtypes of P-neutralization which can be recognized at the current stage of research will be examined

with reference to their treatment in stratificational phonology. Particular attention will be devoted to the relation of P-neutralization to markedness.

In general, P-neutralization may be defined in stratificational terms as that situation in which a choice allowed by the hypophonotactics in some environments is disallowed in others for segments of essentially the same type.

Perhaps the most common situation in which P-neutralization is represented in stratificational phonology is that in which a component may contrast with its absence in some positions, but only the segment without this particular component may occur in the positions of P-neutralization. Two instances of this phenomenon have already been treated in some detail in the rather limited literature on stratificational phonology. One of these is the situation of /m/ and /w/ in North Fork Monachi, as discussed in Lamb 1966 [53]. In this language /m/ and /w/ both occur initially and after /ʔ/, but after a vowel only /w/ (of this pair) may occur. Lamb analyzes /m/ as $\begin{pmatrix} Ns \\ Lb \end{pmatrix}$ (where /Ns/ = "nasal") and /w/ as simply /Lb/ and sets up the hypophonotactics so that /Ns/ is disallowed in the same segment with /Lb/ after a vowel. S-neutralization also occurs in this example, since a zero accompanying /Lb/ in the position of P-neutralization is the realization of either the phonon |Ns| as in |m|, or of zero, as in |w|. The assignment

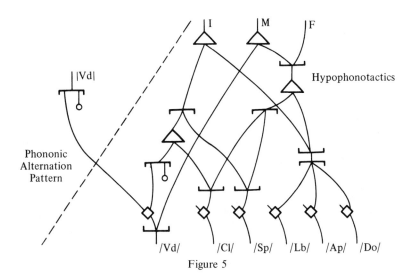

Figure 5

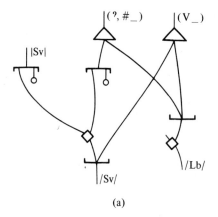

(a)

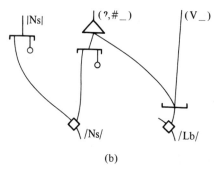

(b)

Figure 6

of the additional marked component to /m/ in this case is justified by the principle of simplicity. If an extra component were assigned to /w/ instead of to /m/, the resulting treatment would be more complex on the hypophonemic stratum. This fact may be seen if one compares Figures 6a and 6b. The former, showing the alternate analysis which views /w/ as $\left/ \begin{array}{l} Lb \\ Sv \end{array} \right/$ (/Sv/ = "semivowel"), is more complex than that shown in 6b, which represents Lamb's analysis.

The situation in a variety of colloquial Bulgarian treated in Lockwood 1969 [55] is the same. Here again the less marked situation is the one which occurs in the position of P-neutralization, as shown by a comparison of the alternate analyses represented in that article by Figures 5 and 6.[8] Also note that

[8]Actually the situation represented in Figure 5 in that paper is not the simplest way to represent the analysis involving /Hi/ as marked in Bulgarian. There is a simpler way, analogous to that of Figure 4 here. But this alternative would still result in a

again an instance of S-neutralization occurs in the Bulgarian example, since zero in unstressed position will correspond either to phononic |Lo| (in the realization of |e a o|) or zero.

From these two examples it seems safe to generalize as follows:

In the case that only one member of a contrast occurs in the total range of positions for a given P-neutralization, it will be the unmarked member, and the one which never occurs there will be the marked member.

This principle corresponds, of course, to an important analytical principle set forth by Trubetzkoy.[9] Stratificational theory provides a formal justification for this principle by showing it to be the simplest alternative according to its simplicity measure.

There are, however, some cases of P-neutralization which are somewhat more complex. One of these is the situation in which one member of the contrast subjected to P-neutralization is realized in one set of neutralized environments while another is realized in the remaining ones. This is, for example, the case in the hypothetical language which we have been considering. The contrast between voice and voicelessness is neutralized in medial and final positions alike. But in the former voicing is demanded, while in the latter voicelessness prevails.

Another such situation is found in the P-neutralization of voicing in Russian obstruents, one aspect of which is represented by Halle's example. Voicing is subject to P-neutralization in a number of positions. In some of these, voicing is realized (e.g., before voiced obstruents other than /v/) and in other positions voicelessness occurs (e.g., in absolute final position).

Still a further possibility is the occurrence of free variation in all or part of the positions

more complex treatment than the analysis presented in Figure 6 of the earlier paper. At the same time, it will be the case that the simpler alternative involving marked /Hi/ will be in conformity with the principle of biuniqueness, while the more complex solution originally presented is not.

[9]I am grateful to Charles E. Bidwell for pointing out this correspondence to me. It is enunciated, for example, in Trubetzkoy 1931: 98, 1935: 27, 1949: 84.

where a given P-neutralization is applicable. Suppose, for example, that in the medial positions of our hypothetical example either voiced or voiceless obstruents can occur in free variation. Such a situation can be represented by a downward unordered *or* with one branch to zero and the other to a determined occurrence of the hypophonemic sign /Vd/, i.e., an indication that the determined voicing of Figure 5 is optional.[10]

If the free variation does not occur in all of the positions in which the P-neutralization is applicable, there are various possibilities for its combination with other situations, including either one of the otherwise contrasting phonetic properties, or one of them in one subset of environments and another in another subset, and so on.

There is also the possibility that the sound realized in all or part of the positions of neutralization will be phonetically distinct from both or all of the sounds which contrast in those positions where the neutralization does not apply. For example, the position before final /r/ may be considered a position of P-neutralization for the distinction illustrated by the vowels of the words *bet* and *bait* in many varieties of American English. Rather than either of these phonetic qualities, we get the intermediate sound found in *bear*.

In such instances as these, the assignment of markedness is not as easily resolved as it is in the simpler examples in which the unmarked situation occurs in all positions of P-neutralization. As always, this assignment will be determined according to the simplicity principle, but the results of the application of this principle will not be obvious without experimentation. In any case the sound realized in positions of P-neutralization will be identified *phonologically* with the less marked situation, whatever this turns out to be in the given case. Its phonetic specification will, of course, be determined by its actual phonetic quality.[11]

A considerable number of the cases ·in which P-neutralization occurs involve phe-

nomena which have commonly been described as "assimilation." As an example, let us imagine a language with the three independent nasals /m n ŋ/ and three corresponding independent stops /p t k/. We may further suppose that among clusters consisting of a nasal followed by a stop we get only those in which both members agree in point of articulation, namely, /mp, nt, ŋk/. How is such a situation to be handled? There are two hypophonotactic configurations which adequately account for the clusters involved, namely, those shown in Figure 7 (a and b).

At first glance these two diagrams seem to provide us with an embarrassment of riches. We seem to have two alternatives of equal structural complexity to account for the same set of facts. The only difference between the t.vo is that the diagram of Figure 7a asserts that the points of articulation for the nasal are independent, while those for the stop are determined by a repetitive reduplication element (symbolized by a wedge lying alongside of a line). The analysis of Figure 7b, on the other hand, asserts that it is for the stop that points of articulation are independent, while they are determined for the nasal by an anticipatory reduplication element.

It is in general true, we must observe, that in determining the relative simplicity of competing solutions, we have to consider not only the internal relations of the particular set of data being accounted for but also the relation of these facts to other facts in the language for which we are accounting. This is all the more true when the internal relations can be accounted for by two equally complex treat-

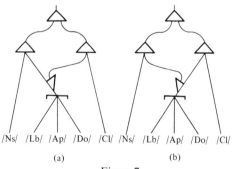

/Ns/ /Lb/ /Ap/ /Do/   /Cl/   /Ns/ /Lb/ /Ap/ /Do/   /Cl/

(a)   (b)

Figure 7

ments, as in the present case. An appropriate bit of related data to consider in this case will be any morphophonemic alternations in the language, for which the hypophonotactics, interacting with the phononic alternation pattern, will be called upon to account.

In this hypothetical language, it might be the case that we find single morphemes with alternate shapes ending in /m n ŋ/, conditioned by following /p t k/, respectively. On the other hand, it might be the case that we find single morphemes with alternate shapes beginning in /p t k/, depending on a preceding nasal. In the former case, the diagram of Figure 7b would be appropriate, since it would allow the inherent point of articulation of the stop, as specified from the upper stratum, to prevail, while in the latter the diagram of Figure 7a will be more appropriate, in that it allows the inherent point of articulation of the nasal to dominate.[12]

A third alternative is suggested by some of the treatments mentioned in Lamb 1966 [53]. This analysis is graphed in Figure 8. It simply states that the point of articulation will pertain to both members of the cluster. In situations for which either of the treatments of Figure 7 will be appropriate, however, Figure 8 will not provide sufficient information to indicate which specification from the upper

[12]Structurally trained linguists may object to such a consideration, on the ground that a mixing of levels is involved. In this case, however, we are merely considering how the system connects together and how this connection can be made in such a way as to assure that it will account for the pertinent data in the maximally simple way. In short, there is no objection to the mixing of levels in the process of *analysis* in stratificational theory. Mixing of levels is to be avoided in *description,* however.

stratum—that for the nasal or that for the stop—is to predominate.

There are at least two conceivable situations, however, for which the analysis of Figure 8 might be deemed appropriate. One of these is the case in which no S-neutralization is involved, because all such clusters occur within the bounds of single morphemes. In such a case, it would be arbitrary from any point of view to specify a "direction" for the determination of point of articulation. Another case for which it might be deemed appropriate to use the solution of Figure 8 is the case in which the "assimilation" operates both ways, but it will always be the case that only one of the morphophonemically specified segments will carry a point of articulation. In other words, in the case that when a point of articulation is specified for the nasal, it will be absent in the adjacent stop, and vice versa. I do not know of any situation of this kind in an actual language, but it seems at least conceivable.

In such a case as the latter, there would be some segments specified as only /Ns/, others as only /Cl/, while the rest would carry /Ns/ or /Cl/ as the case may be, plus the specification of a point of articulation. It would be useful if we could avoid postulating a distinct segment for the unmarked stop and nasal in such instances by considering one of the points of articulation inherently unmarked. Lamb has suggested (personal communication) that it is at least widespread for dorsal to be unmarked in this regard.[13] If we accept this as at least a typical case, we could redefine /k/ as equal to simply /Cl/, and its point of articulation will be dorso-velar unless otherwise specified. We can analogously specify /ŋ/ as /Ns/.

5. ON THE ARCHIPHONEME

I have outlined a view of P-neutralization which has many points of contact with the classical views of the Prague School. It lacks one important ingredient of many versions of

[13]As evidence for this position, we may cite the variability of its realization, ranging from palato-velar to uvular. Also in many languages consonants patterning with the velars with regard to distribution and morphophonemic behavior may be pharyngeal or glottal in articulation (e.g., Czech /h/ is realized as a voiced glottal fricative.) Also the rarity of non-nasal resonants in this position (with the exception of uvular *r*) would be expected, since these resonants are usually considered the unmarked manner.

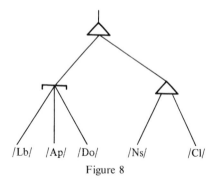

/Lb/   /Ap/   /Do/   /Ns/   /Cl/

Figure 8

the Praguian theory, however, namely, the concept of the *archiphoneme*. I would like to argue that this concept is appropriate only to a theory which regards all the terms which occur in positions of contrast as in fact marked, i.e., carrying a specification, which may be either positive or negative. In such a theory, one of the specifications may be termed "unmarked" while the other(s) are "marked," but a distinction is made between the occurrence of the unmarked pole of the contrast and the irrelevance of the contrast.

For example, if a contrast between voiced and voiceless is conceived of as involving the mutually contrastive components /Vd/ "voiced" and /Uv/ "unvoiced," we might symbolize /p/ and /b/ as follows: $\Big/ \begin{matrix} Cl \\ Lb \\ Uv \end{matrix} \Big/$ and $\Big/ \begin{matrix} Cl \\ Lb \\ Vd \end{matrix} \Big/$. Then the archiphoneme for this contrast would be equal to the combination of components shared by the two, namely, $\Big/ \begin{matrix} Cl \\ Lb \end{matrix} \Big/$. If the principle of markedness as understood in stratificational theory is applied, however, only one of the two mutually exclusive components /Uv/ and /Vd/ of this example needs to be considered an actual component, specifically /Vd/, and voicelessness will be indicated in its absence (for those segment-types for which the contrast is ever relevant). In a position of P-neutralization, however, the absence of a distinctive occurrence of /Vd/ may be countervened by a determined occurrence of /Vd/ as a hypophonemic sign. In terms of hypophonemes, however, this segment remains equivalent to a voiceless consonant, since the voicing present is not distinctive.

The view I express here, in other words, is very close to that expressed by Trubetzkoy when he wrote:

In those positions where the correlative property of a phoneme loses its phonological significance, this phoneme is identified with the unmarked member of the correlation, even though it is objectively identical to the marked member of the correlation (Trubetzkoy 1931: 98).[14]

Such a position, Vachek records, was the subject of considerable dispute within the Prague Circle and "a majority of the Prague people never endorsed Trubetzkoy's views on this issue" (Vachek 1966: 62). Also Trubetzkoy does not express the same view in many of his other writings, at least not as forcefully and explicitly as he does here.

Nevertheless, as I have tried to show in this paper, given a system involving a tactics of components, such a position follows from the principle of simplicity. At the same time, the incorporation of neutralizations of this sort allows a theory of phonology to escape Halle's charges concerning the inefficiency of some classical phonemic interpretations, and to offer further demonstration that the inefficiency of these interpretations comes not from the incorporation of a level having a biunique relation to the phonetic but rather from the failure to carry the principle of distinctiveness to its ultimate conclusion. As Lamb has already pointed out, the principle of biuniqueness is only a special case of the distinctiveness principle, which is in turn a consequence of the simplicity principle.

The best-known of the views of componential analysis in phonology which does not incorporate markedness in the way that is done here, and is therefore compatible with the notion of the archiphoneme, is the binary theory of "distinctive features" associated with the name of Roman Jakobson. The notion of "distinctive feature" found in this theory is not to be equated with the phonon or hypophoneme in stratificational theory but rather with the notion of *opposition* as found in Trubetzkoy—in American structuralist terms a minimal phonemic contrast. The phonon or hypophoneme will correspond rather to one of the "terms" of the feature. A particular characteristic of Jakobson's approach is that, while for Trubetzkoy and many of his followers an opposition could have as many terms as were necessary, for Jakobson and his followers, each distinctive feature has been thought of as having two and only two terms, symbolized as + and −. Of these two, the one with the (+) value has often been thought of as

---

[14]In the original: "In den Stellungen, wo die korrelative Eigenschaft eines Phonems seine phonologische Gültigkeit verliert, wird dieses Phonem mit dem merkmallosen Korrelationsglied identifi-

ziert, selbst wenn es objektiv mit dem merkmalhaltigen Korrelationsglied identisch ist."

"marked," but there is a difference between the "unmarked" but distinctive (−) value of the feature and what may be called its zero (0) value, which represents the complete irrelevance of the feature in question. In keeping with this view, we might choose to symbolize /Uv/ and /Vd/ as /−Vd/ and /+Vd/, respectively, where /−Vd/ is still distinct from the lack of any specification of the feature ±Vd at all. For this reason, it may be said that a binary theory requires both a specification of the relevance of a contrast for a particular segment and also a specification of whether it will have a plus or a minus value.

In the stratificational view, on the other hand, only the presence of a component (phonon or hypophoneme depending on the stratum being dealt with), and not its absence, will count in the evaluation of alternate solutions identical in their effective information, regardless of whether this absence corresponds to the unmarked term of the contrast, or to its complete irrelevance. As I have already pointed out elsewhere, the view of markedness recently adopted in transformational phonology corresponds in this respect to the stratificational view, although there are also many points of difference (cf. Lockwood 1969 [55]). The stratificational view is particularly flexible, in that it may recognize contrasts with as many terms as necessary to handle the facts economically. It may further allow one of any number of such terms to be unmarked, and may allow P-neutralization, i.e., the case in which the unmarked state occurs phonologically due to the irrelevance of the contrast. In allowing unmarked terms and P-neutralization for contrast of more than two terms, this view contrasts with that of Trubetzkoy for whom (at least at one period of his career) only privative binary oppositions were subject to neutralization. The contrast (equivalent to Trubetzkoy's opposition and Jakobson's distinctive feature) is represented in a stratificational account, incidentally, by a downward *or* (or sequence of same) in the hypophonotactics, leading down to its various terms, one of which may be zero, equivalent to the unmarked term.

One apparent advantage of the binary Jakobsonian approach is that it allows an easy reference to classes of segments when all members of such a class share a set of feature values not also characteristic of any non-members of the class. The class of stops (for English and presumably many other languages) could be characterized in terms of the features set forth in Jakobson, Fant, and Halle 1952, for example, as:

$$\begin{bmatrix} -\text{Vocalic} \\ +\text{Consonantal} \\ -\text{Nasal} \\ -\text{Continuant} \end{bmatrix}$$

In a system employing strictly a marked/unmarked distinction, such as stratificational phonology, on the other hand, an analogous approach is not possible, since a reference to the single hypophoneme common to all stops, namely, /Cl/ (at least for many languages), would be identical to the specification of the maximally unmarked stop, which under the assumptions mentioned above would be /k/. This situation would create a problem for an approach based on a rule formulation, such as current transformational phonology, in which the Jakobsonian approach has been used extensively (and until recently, exclusively).[15] No problem is presented for the stratificational approach, however, since stratificational theory recognizes a tactics of each of its strata in which the classes appropriate to this stratum may be recognized. In the case of phonology, these classes will be recognized either in the phonotactics or the hypophonotactics, whichever turns out to be most appropriate for the economical handling of the phenomena to be accounted for.

So a stratificational hypophonology will provide the basis for a transcription which has the following properties: (1) It is componential; (2) it is biunique with respect to a phonetic representation, so that identical utterances may be identically represented; (3) it accounts for P-neutralization; (4) it is based on a marked/unmarked distinction, such that one member of a contrast may be interpreted structurally as the absence of the other member(s). It is the contention of stratificational theory that the simplicity principle requires the postu-

---

[15]This is undoubtedly one of the reasons why the marked/unmarked specifications now used (following Postal 1968, Chomsky and Halle 1968) in transformational work in phonology have to be converted into full +/− specifications before the application of any phonological rules takes place.

lation of such a level to account for the facts of human language.

REFERENCES

BAZELL, C. E. 1949. "On the Neutralisation of Syntactic Oppositions," *Travaux du cercle linguistique de Copenhague* 5.77–86.

———. 1956. "Three Conceptions of Phonological Neutralisation," in *For Roman Jakobson* (Morris Halle, ed.), 25–30. The Hague: Mouton.

CHOMSKY, NOAM. 1964. *Current Issues in Linguistic Theory*. The Hague: Mouton. [39]

———. 1966. *Topics in the Theory of Generative Grammar*. The Hague: Mouton.

——— and HALLE, MORRIS. 1968. *The Sound Pattern of English*. New York: Harper & Row.

HALLE, MORRIS. 1959. *The Sound Pattern of Russian*. The Hague: Mouton.

JAKOBSON, ROMAN, FANT, C. GUNNAR, and HALLE, MORRIS. 1952. *Preliminaries to Speech Analysis*. Cambridge, Mass.: M.I.T. Press.

JOHNS, DAVID A. 1969. "Phonemics and Generative Phonology," *Papers from the Fifth Regional Meeting, Chicago Linguistic Society* (Binnick, Davison, Green, and Morgan, eds.), 374–381. Chicago: Department of Linguistics, University of Chicago. [49]

LAMB, SYDNEY M. 1964. "The Sememic Approach to Structural Semantics," *American Anthropologist* 66: 3, pt. 2.57–78.

———. 1966. "Prolegomena to a Theory of Phonology," *Language* 42.536–573. [53]

———. 1967. Review of Chomsky 1964 and *Aspects of the Theory of Syntax* (Cambridge, Mass.: M.I.T. Press, 1965), *American Anthropologist* 69.411–415.

LOCKWOOD, DAVID G. 1969. "Markedness in Stratificational Phonology," *Language* 45.300–308. [55]

MARTINET, ANDRÉ. 1936. "Neutralisation et archiphonème," *Travaux du cercle linguistique de Prague* 6.46–57.

POSTAL, PAUL M. 1968. *Aspects of Phonological Theory*. New York: Harper & Row.

REICH, PETER A. 1968. *Symbols, Relations, and Structural Complexity*, Linguistic Automation Project Report. New Haven: Yale University.

SAPORTA, SOL. 1956. "Morph, Morpheme, Archimorpheme," *Word* 12.9–14.

TRUBETZKOY, N. S. 1931. "Die phonologischen Systeme," *Travaux du cercle linguistique de Prague* 4.96–116.

———. 1936. "Die Aufhebung der phonologischen Gegensätze," *Travaux du cercle linguistique de Prague* 6.29–45.

———. 1949. *Principes de phonologie* (Tr. by J. Cantineau of *Grundzüge der Phonologie* = *TCLP* 7).

VACHEK, JOSEPH. 1966. *The Linguistic School of Prague*. Bloomington: Indiana University Press.

57

SOME TYPES OF ORDERING*

SYDNEY M. LAMB

The purpose of this paper is to clarify certain features of stratificational theory and to make some comparisons with generative-transformational theory. The specific topic concerns certain phenomena which in transformational theory come under a single heading, namely, ordering of rules. From the viewpoint of stratificational theory these phenomena are seen to be of quite different kinds; there is no structural reason for bringing them together at all, but I nevertheless treat them as a group in this paper simply for the sake of making comparisons with transformational theory, in which they do have something in common—that is, the property that they require ordering of rules. I choose this topic only because of the current popularity of process description and of the concept of rule-ordering.

The first and most important point to be understood is that, according to stratificational theory, a linguistic structure is not a system of mutation rules, that is, rules which operate with symbolic representations and change them into other representations. In fact, according to stratificational theory, a linguistic structure does not consist of rules of any kind. Rather, it consists entirely of relationships. If one can speak of rules at all in a stratificational context, then these rules would belong only in a particular type of description of a linguistic structure rather than in the structure itself; that is, they would be one notation for indirectly describing the structural relationships. But actually, the type of algebraic statement that is most appropriate for describing structural relationships is so different from the process rule of transformational grammar that it is probably misleading to call it a rule, since this designation tends to lead one to think that

there is some resemblance between these two quite different types of statement. To avoid such confusion we may adopt the alternative term *formula* to designate the type of algebraic statement that is appropriate for the description of structural relationships according to stratificational theory. Thus what I used to call a realization rule ought rather to be called a realization formula, because it is entirely different from the rewrite rule to which it bears a superficial resemblance.

The only processes in stratificational theory are those involving change in the linguistic structure (so that it becomes a different system) and those which involve the movement of impulses through networks of structural relationships during encoding and decoding. The latter processes may be specified by rules stated for the types of nodes in relational networks. These rules are few in number, are language universals, and apply for all levels of a linguistic structure. (In fact, they are universals for some nonlinguistic cognitive systems as well.) Below are some simple versions of these for some of the nodes; the nodes to which these rules apply are shown in Figure 1.

Unordered *and*:	a → b and c (simultaneously)
	b and c (not necessarily simultaneous) → a
Ordered *and*: (Type 1)	a → b
	b → c
	c → a
Unordered *or*:	a → b and c (simultaneously)
	b → a
	c → a
Ordered *or*:	a → b if possible, otherwise c
	b → a
	c → a

*This is a revised and expanded version of a paper originally presented at the Summer 1966 meeting of the Linguistic Society of America at Los Angeles.

Diamond: a and b (not necessarily simulta-
(Type 1)   neous) → c
                b and c (not necessarily simulta-
                neous) → a and b

At the left of the arrow in each rule are identified the connections at which incoming impulses lead to outgoing impulses from the connections identified at the right of the arrow.

How do the structural relationships of stratificational theory differ from the mutation rules of generative-transformational theory? In the first place, process or mutation rules operate with symbolic representations, that is, strings of symbols; a process rule replaces a certain symbol in the string by one or more others, or sometimes it deletes or permutes symbols. In other words, a process description is an *item-and-process* description—the items are the symbols of which representations are formed, and these are an essential part of the system. The rules have significance only in that they perform operations upon these items.

Second, when alternation is present between two entities at any level of a linguistic system, the process approach is to "derive" one of the alternants from the other. In stratificational thinking, on the other hand, the two alternants are considered alternative realizations of a higher-level, or more abstract, entity. As such, it cannot be identical with one of the

Unordered   Ordered
AND   AND

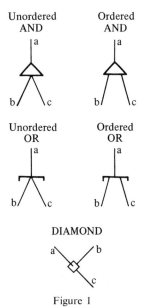

DIAMOND

Figure 1

alternants. The essential difference is that three separate entities are distinguished, not just two; the third is the higher-level entity (Figure 2).

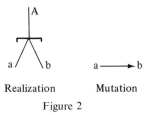

Realization   Mutation

Figure 2

The failure of process description to recognize the underlying entity as different from the alternants is of great importance for the linguist's conception of how a linguistic structure is organized. The underlying entity, since it is equated with one of the alternants, must be on their level rather than at a higher or more abstract level. Therefore, a mutation system, if it is consistent in using the process approach, really has only one level. Thus, for example, the difference between deep structure and surface structure is not really a stratal distinction as formulated by the transformationalists, since process rules—that is, transformations—are used to relate them. The so-called deep structure is largely a selection of surface items and it thus fails to live up to its name.

Speaking only somewhat loosely, one may say that the best one can do using a mutation framework is to talk about manifestations of linguistic structure rather than about linguistic structure itself. The process description tends to derive manifestations of linguistic structure from other manifestations of linguistic structure, while the stratificational description shows how manifestations of linguistic structure are derived *from linguistic structure*. The difference is something like that between prescribing medicine to alleviate the symptoms of a disease and prescribing medicine intended to treat the disease itself. A better nonlinguistic example is the strike in baseball. A structural element in the system of the game, the strike is manifested as a swing and miss or as a called strike or as a foul ball; but the foul is ambiguous in that it has no function if there are already two strikes. This description is consistent with the stratificational way of thinking (Figure 3). A process description, on the other hand, would select one of these mani-

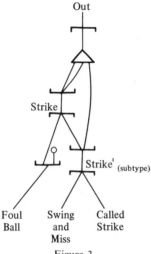

Figure 3

festations, perhaps the swing and miss, as basic and would derive the other two from it: "Optionally replace swing and miss by called strike; optionally replace swing and miss by foul ball in the environment of zero or one strike." Lacking, in this description, is the element "strike" as abstracted from its three manifestations.

We now come to the central topic of this paper. Of the various phenomena which in a process or mutation description require ordering of rules, some reflect significant features of the linguistic structure while others do not. Ordering of the latter type may be called artificial ordering. It is present in the description as a consequence of the structure of the notation system being used rather than because of some property of the structure of the language being described.

An example of artificial ordering is provided by the following rules for Russian discussed by Chomsky (1964: 84 [410]):

(i)   o → ǫ in the context: — l
(ii)   l → Ø in the context: Vowel ——— Nasal + Consonant

For example, phonemic /sólncǎ/ 'sun' is phonetic [sǫ́ncə]. According to Chomsky, "the rules must be ordered as given." But this is true only if it is required that (1) there be only one symbolic representation present at a time (a fixed requirement of mutational systems), and (2) only one rule can operate at a time. Both of these requirements appear to be

features of the system of notation being used, rather than properties of the linguistic structure. Notice that the rules need not be ordered if they are allowed to operate simultaneously; and also, what may not be so obvious, they can operate *in either order* (for example, ii may be applied before i) if the phonemic and phonetic levels are separated from each other on a realizational basis, so that the rules are interpreted as realizational formulas instead of mutation rules; in this case the conditioning environment is stated in terms of the higher level and is not altered by the operation of any rules. In short, as far as the linguistic structure is concerned, there is no ordering involved in this example.

Speaking more generally, a process description requires needlessly intricate ordering of rules because (1) it allows only a single symbolic representation to be present at one time, whereas in reality the speaker has available at a single time the entire linguistic structure; and (2) mutation rules replace symbols by other symbols, and the symbols thus replaced are no longer available to serve as conditioning environments for other rules. Consequently, (3) each rewrite rule must be ordered relative to the others so that

(a)   its conditioning environment has not yet been replaced *and*
(b)   it comes after all rules for which the symbol to be replaced serves as a conditioning environment.

Let us now turn to real or structural ordering; that is, that ordering of mutation rules which corresponds to actual features of linguistic structure. We may distinguish three major types, (1) stratificational ordering, (2) precedence ordering, and (3) tactical ordering.

The name stratificational is, of course, intended to suggest that a language has several layers of structure. These may be thought of as existing on top of one another, as it were. In a stratificational framework one views the entire structure as present at one time, and the different structural layers or levels take the place of different derivational periods in a fictional time span. We speak of these various levels as differing from one another in height. Higher levels are closer to meaning, lower levels are closer to expression. As seen from the stratificational standpoint, a process description characteristically (and unrealistically, by the way) moves through the layers sequentially in one direction or the other. For phonology it has become traditional to move from the higher layers to the lower ones, although there is no structural (as opposed to notational) reason for going in this direction rather than upwards. Thus, *some* of the ordering of mutation rules in a process phonology reflects differences in the relative height of relationships in linguistic structure; when this correspondence does exist, the "earlier" mutation rules correspond to higher layers of structure, the later rules to lower layers. In other words, if we translate a process description into structural relationships, then, as the name stratificational implies, ordering—that is, stratification—is an inherent, integral part of linguistic structure according to the stratificational view. I must emphasize this point, since some critics have expressed the view that statificational grammar (despite its name) does *not* provide for ordering! To give some impression of the extent of stratificational ordering in linguistic structure, it is necessary to say a little bit about the configurations into which the elementary relationships enter.

It is not the case that the elementary relationships can freely occur in any combination. Rather, there are strict limitations upon what configurations of these relationships are allowable in a language. Such limitations are defining properties of linguistic structure, and as such presumably reflect built-in features of the human brain. There is not time here to fully characterize these constraints, nor have they been fully identified as yet, but some hint of them can be given by the following rough specifications:

1. A major portion of the linguistic network consists of roughly vertical lines and interconnecting nodes, extending from expression at the bottom to content at the top; this may be called the realizational portion.

2. Intersecting the realizational portion at various levels are several horizontal patterns of lines and nodes; these may be called tactic patterns; each of them has the function of specifying allowable sequences of line activations of vertical lines intersecting it. Tactic patterns may further be distinguished on the basis that, unlike the realizational portion, they operate in roughly the same way for encoding and decoding.

3. The number of such tactic planes, while it may vary from one language to another, is quite small in all languages.

4. The number of nodes encountered along a continuous vertical path from one tactic plane to the next, while variable, is also quite small.

5. Recursion, represented in the network by looping, is found only in tactic patterns.

6. In general, the number of vertical lines at any level of the network is larger than that at a lower level.

In accordance with properties (3) and (4) one may identify an ordering of lines from top to bottom (or from bottom to top) in a linguistic network. This is what I call stratificational ordering.

The actual extent of the limitations of stratificational ordering is an empirical question which still requires further research. The hypothesis of 1966 (Lamb 1966b), identified by Fleming (1969) as Stage IV, provided for six tactic patterns, hence six strata, for at least some languages. Some critics, comparing this hypothesis with the extent of ordering found in mutational grammars, have supposed that it provides insufficient stratification. But such comparisons are carelessly supposing that all mutational ordering would require stratificational ordering if translated into relational network notation, whereas stratificational ordering is actually only one of the four types of situation which correspond to ordering of rules in a process grammar. In fact, work done since 1966 on the over-all organization of linguistic structure suggests that the hypothesis of 1966 was too liberal in this regard; it now appears possible to account for the data of at least most languages with no more than four or five strata. In the new version—perhaps it could be called Stage V in continuation of Fleming's numbering scheme—tactic patterns make greater use of upward *and* nodes than previously, so that conflicting tactical configurations can be accommodated within single tactic patterns. (This new version comes closer to Halliday's systemic grammar.) For example, in the phonology of some languages there is a conflict between syllable constructions and consonant cluster constructions, which can cross syllable boundaries. This type of conflict was previously thought to constitute evidence favoring the recognition of two separate tactic patterns in phonology, hence two separate strata, and the terms phonemic and hypophonemic were proposed for these (Lamb 1966a [53]). But through the use of upward *and* nodes it is possible to take care of both types of construction in a single tactic pattern. The upward *and* in a tactic pattern indicates two separate functions for an element or class of elements, so that a given consonant or class of consonants, for example, can simultaneously have one function in a syllable construction and another function as member of a consonant cluster.

Although there are fewer stratal systems in the new framework, each of them has two alternation patterns (cf. Bennett 1968) in accordance with the hypothesis of Stage III (Lamb 1965); this feature of Stage III was mistakenly abandoned in Stage IV. (In the hypothesis of Stage IV the only alternations allowed below the tactic pattern were those involving portmanteau realization; these made up what was then called the upper portion of the sign pattern.) Within each alternation pattern the limitation of the 1966 hypothesis (Stage IV) still applies, that only one layer of alternation exists. This means that a continuous vertical path through a single alternation pattern can pass through at most one downward *or* node.

For alternations below the tactic pattern, conditioning environments are at the level of the realizates—that is, the higher level. It was for this situation that the realization formula (Lamb 1964 [52]) was devised. Conditioning environments for alternations above the tactic pattern are provided by the tactics (as in Stage IV); these environments are thus at the level of the realizations. For this type of alternation a second type of realization formula is required (see below).

In the hypothesis of Stage II there was only one level of alternation between morphophonemes and phonemes. There was likewise one level from lexons to morphemes, so that two levels of alternation were provided between the morpheme and phoneme levels of neo-Bloomfieldian frameworks; this was one

more level of alternation than those frameworks usually provided (Hockett 1961). In late Stage II (Lamb 1964) provision was made for the application of two successive realization formulas at a single level, for cases of what is here called stratificational ordering. This provision was later changed, so that in Stage IV there were two phonological alternation patterns, one in each of the two stratal systems then recognized in phonology, and only one level of alternation was allowed in each alternation pattern. This constraint remains in the new hypothesis, but the two phonological alternation patterns are now seen as the upper and lower alternation patterns of the single stratal system in phonology. Since there are likewise two alternation patterns in morphology according to the new hypothesis, four levels of alternation are present between the levels of the morpheme and the phoneme of neo-Bloomfieldian linguistics. The availability of these levels, by the way, presents no lack of economy for elements without alternate realizations; they are simply lines which go through the alternation pattern without a downward *or*, as if the alternation pattern did not exist.

It is important to realize that the two phonological alternation patterns are present not merely to provide for stratificational ordering of alternations but because of the basic difference in the relationship of the alternations to their conditioning environments. This difference will be apparent in the examples below.

Let us now consider the same example of stratificational ordering that has been described previously according to the late Stage II treatment (Lamb 1964). In mutation rules, the alternations would be described as follows:

R1 $w \rightarrow k^w$ / ' ——
R2 $k^w \rightarrow q^w$ / (a,e,o) [']——(a,e)

(Square brackets enclose elements which may or may not be present; comma means "or" and parentheses are used as in ordinary algebraic notation; to keep the discussion simple I refrain from going into phonological components throughout this paper and identify all phonological elements in terms of segments; the element /'/, described in Lamb 1966a [53], was written as /h/ in Lamb 1964 [52].)

In this example, rule 2 must follow R1; that is, this ordering of the process rules is real, not artificial—it reflects actual ordering in the linguistic structure.

The elements involved in these alternations, and their levels, are:

In realization formulas (which identify relationships in the linguistic network rather than operations upon symbols), these alternations may be described as follows:

F1   w / '] k^w
F2 k^w ‖ (e,a,o)[']——(e,a) / q^w

Formula 2 describes relationships in the lower phonological alternation pattern, according to the notation previously described (Lamb 1964): the double vertical line separates the element to which the formula applies from its environment, which is at the same level as this element; the diagonal separates the upper level, at left, from the realization, on the lower level, at the right. Formula 1 is written in a different format, in keeping with the fact that in the upper phonological alternation pattern the conditioning environments are at the level of the realizations, that is, at the phonotactic level. The diagonal here has the same function: it separates the higher level at left—in this case just the realizate—from the lower level at the right, which has the realization and the significant part of the tactic environment in which it appears, separated from the realization by a square bracket. (The use of the square bracket for identifying and separating the conditioning environment is taken from the classroom notation used by M. B. Emeneau during the early 1950s.) Formula 1 may be read "morphonic w is realized as k^w after '." Formula 2 may be read, "basic phonemic k^w, when preceded by . . . and followed by . . . , is realized as q^w."

Precedence ordering of mutation rules corresponds to the ordering in a downward ordered *or* node (see Figure 1). In the mutational framework the ordering is used to allow the conditioning environment of the earlier rule to take precedence over that of the sec-

ond. There is no sequential application of rules here. The second rule does not operate on some item *after* the first but *instead* of it. In other words, the second rule is allowed to operate only if the conditioning environment of the first does not apply.

Precedence ordering always involves rules with the same symbol at the left of the arrow, and these rules are alternatives; that is, they are in an either-or relationship to one another. The single symbol at the left of the arrow corresponds to the single line above the *or* node in the relational network notation. In representing this situation formulaically, we use a single formula for each realizate, with a separate subformula (on a separate line) for each environment and realization. The subformulas are listed in the order of precedence (Lamb 1964 [52]); and since this is a precedence ordering of alternatives, they all occupy the same realizational level.

The term *tactical ordering* is a handy one that is not very revealing; but no term that is both simple and revealing is readily available. This is another type of ordering of mutation rules that does not correspond to difference in levels of the linguistic structure. In this situation there is sequential application of realizational formulas, for the sake of providing the proper conditioning environment for the one which applies second; but this sequential application is entirely accounted for by the tactically determined "left-to-right" temporal ordering of the elements being activated, hence does not involve any difference in levels.

The following data, also from Monachi, illustrate the situation:

Gloss:	to haul water	bucket
Morphonic:	pa noo	ʔa' na pa noo 'nu hE
Basic Phonemic:	panoo	ʔa'napanoo'noho

Morpheme boundaries are indicated by spaces in the morphonic transcription. The lexeme for bucket is morphologically a deverbative noun meaning 'instrument for hauling water'; the instrument suffix ^{M}/'nu/ is followed by the empty morpheme ^{M}/hE/ in certain morphologically defined environments. In the mutational format the rules which apply are:

R3   E → V_1 / V_1K——
R4   u → o / oK——

Here the cover symbol K stands for any consonant or consonant cluster. Thus /u/ is replaced by /o/ if the vowel of the preceding syllable is /o/ (R4); and /E/ (a "chameleon vowel") is rewritten as the same as the vowel of the preceding syllable (R3). It may appear that for the data cited above, R4 must operate before R3 or else the final vowel will be /u/ rather than /o/. On the other hand, the given order will work if R4 is applied twice after R3 operates, so that the final vowel in our example is first rewritten as /u/, then as /o/ after R3 has operated on the preceding vowel. This sequence of three operations instead of two may appear to constitute an unnecessarily clumsy formulation, but that formulation rapidly gains in attractiveness if the following data are added to our corpus:

Gloss:	gold	specifically gold
Morphonic:	ʔoono ʔE	ʔoono ʔE 'su
Basic Phonemic:	ʔoonoʔo	ʔoonoʔo'so

Here rule 3 must operate first; and therefore, according to the requirements of mutational notation, R3 must precede R4 in the system. Thus the less efficient procedure must be used for the previous example. On the other hand, if variable ordering were possible, so that both examples could be treated efficiently, then the sequence of rule applications would correspond to the left-to-right ordering of the morphons involved. Now it is in just this manner that the situation may be accounted for by means of the realizational framework. The two realizational formulas are at the same level of the structure:

F3 $E / V_1 K] V_1$
F4 $u / o K] o$

Not just in this type of example but in all cases, realization formulas at the same structural level are applied in the order in which the elements involved are occurring (Lamb 1964 [52]), so that their order of application is variable and does not depend on any ordering within the linguistic structure.

This example also provides a good illustration of the conditioning environment at the level of the realization, a characteristic feature of alternations in the upper phonological alternation pattern.

The independence of order of application from order within the structure is a direct consequence of one of the fundamental properties of stratificational grammar: the linguistic system in itself is static—it contains no processes—and it is thus independent from the processes which use it, such as that for converting from a semantic representation to speech. This type of independence is essential for a realistic model of such processes. When encoding is in progress, the activation of the network is proceeding at lower levels for the beginning of a sentence while it is still at higher levels for the end. Indeed, the first few words of a sentence may be completely produced from the bottom of the phonology while the remainder is still incompletely formulated at the lexemic stratum. The order of operations in encoding a given linguistic form is not the same as the order of levels (top to bottom) in the network; in other words, it is not the case that one performs all of the necessary operations for a sentence at one level before proceeding to the next (as one must do in a mutational system). For any single item it is true that the order of "operation" (that is, of line activations) is from higher to lower in the network; but the "operations" for two separate elements may occur at different times—in general, the phonological "operations" for the beginning of a word precede those for the end, and so forth.

From these considerations we see that one of the reasons for the excessive ordering of rules found in mutational descriptions is the failure of that framework to separate the linguistic information from the operations for using the information. The result is that when a particular sequence of operations is required, this same sequence must be built into the information structure, in this case as ordering of rules.

I conclude with a conjecture that I will not attempt to validate here. The difference between the realizational framework and the mutational one is perhaps of greater consequence than just that the former accounts for the data with fewer layers of ordering. One might suppose that a mutational description of a given linguistic system would have all the levels of a realizational description plus many additional intermediate layers; but this is likely not to be so. It may be that the mutational description would not have the realizational strata at all. The larger number of layers of representation which it does provide are largely artificial products of the system of notation, which may have the effect not only of proliferating order but also of jumbling it out of the actual layering of the corresponding relationships in the linguistic structure. Thus the finding that if one uses mutation rules in phonology there will not be a level of representation corresponding to that of the classical phoneme (Chomsky 1964 [39]) is insufficient evidence for doubting the existence of such a level. This finding is perhaps rather to be interpreted as a further indication of the inappropriateness of mutational notation for describing linguistic structure.

This work was supported in part by the National Science Foundation.

REFERENCES

BENNETT, DAVID C. 1968. "English Prepositions: A Stratificational Approach," *Journal of Linguistics* 4.153–172.

CHOMSKY, NOAM. 1964. *Current Issues in Linguistic Theory*. The Hague: Mouton. [39]

FLEMING, ILAH. 1969. "Stratificational Theory: An Annotated Bibliography," *Journal of English Linguistics* 3.37–65.

HOCKETT, CHARLES F. 1961. "Linguistic Elements and Their Relations," *Language* 37.29–53.

LAMB, SYDNEY M. 1964. "On Alternation, Transformation, Realization, and Stratification," *Monograph Series on Languages and Linguistics,* No. 17, Report of the 15th Annual Round Table Meeting on Linguistics and Language Studies, 105–122. Washington, D.C.: Georgetown University Press. [52]

————. 1965. "Kinship Terminology and Linguistic Structure," *American Anthropologist* 67, no. 5, part 2, 37–64.

————. 1966a. "Prolegomena to a Theory of Phonology," *Language* 42.536–573. [53]

————. 1966b. *Outline of Stratificational Grammar.* Washington, D.C.: Georgetown University Press.

ABBREVIATIONS

AA   *American Anthropologist*

AcL   *Acta Linguistica, Revue Internationale de Linguistique Structurale (Copenhagen)*

ACLS   American Council of Learned Societies

AJP   *American Journal of Philology*

AL   *Archivum Linguisticum*

AS   *American Speech: A Quarterly of Linguistic Usage*

BSL   *Bulletin de la Société de Linguistique de Paris*

BSOAS   *Bulletin of the School of Oriental and African Studies* (London University)

BSOS   *Bulletin of the School of Oriental Studies* (London University)

FofL   *Foundations of Language*

FRJ   *For Roman Jakobson,* ed. by M. Halle, H. G. Lunt, H. MacLean, and C. H. Van Schooneveld. The Hague: Mouton, 1956.

HAIL   *Handbook of American Indian Languages,* ed. by Franz Boas. Washington, D.C. Part I (1911) and Part II (1922)=Bulletin 40, Smithsonian Institution, Bureau of American Ethnology.

IJAL   *International Journal of American Linguistics*

IMJRF   *In Memory of J. R. Firth,* ed. by C. E. Bazell, J. C. Catford, M. A. K. Halliday, and R. H. Robins. London: Longmans, 1966.

IPA   International Phonetic Association

JAL   *Journal of African Languages*

JAOS   *Journal of the American Oriental Society*

JASA   *Journal of the Acoustical Society of America*

JCLA   *Journal of the Canadian Linguistic Association*

JofL   *Journal of Linguistics*

JPs   *Journal de Psychologie Normale et Pathologique*

LCP   *Language, Culture, and Personality: Essays in Memory of Edward Sapir,* ed. by L. Spier, A. I. Hallowell, and S. S. Newman. Menasha, Wisconsin: Sapir Memorial Publication Fund, 1941.

Lg.   *Language, Journal of the Linguistic Society of America*

LSA   Linguistic Society of America

LSNA   *Linguistic Structures of Native America,* Viking Fund Publications in Anthropology, 6. New York: Wenner-Gren Foundation for Anthropological Research, 1946.

MDU   *Monatshefte für Deutschen Unterricht*

MLN   *Modern Language Notes*

MLQ   *Modern Language Quarterly*

MPh   *Le Maître Phonétique*

PICL__   *Proceedings of the __ International Congress of Linguists.* For bibliographical data on each volume of the Proceedings look up alphabetically under P.

PICPS__   *Proceedings of the __ International Congress of Phonetic Sciences.* For bibliographical data on each volume of the Proceedings look up alphabetically under P.

PMLA   *Publications of the Modern Language Association*

RIL   *Readings in Linguistics,* ed. by Martin Joos. Washington, D.C.: American Council of Learned Societies, 1957. Reissued as *Readings in Linguistics I.* Chicago: University of Chicago Press, 1966.

RJ:SWI   *Roman Jakobson, Selected Writings I: Phonological Studies.* The Hague: Mouton, 1962.

RLE-QPR   *Quarterly Progress Reports,* Research Laboratory of Electronics, Massachusetts Institute of Technology, Cambridge, Mass.

RP   *Romance Philology*

SaS   *Slovo a Slovesnost*

SIL   *Studies in Linguistics*

SILA   *Studies in Linguistic Analysis,* Special Volume of the Philological Society, with introduction by J. R. Firth. Oxford: Basil Blackwell, 1957.

SLMA   *Structure of Language and Its*

Mathematical Aspects: Proceedings of the Twelfth Symposium in Applied Mathematics, ed. by Roman Jakobson. Providence: American Mathematical Society, 1961.

SofL — *The Structure of Language: Readings in the Philosophy of Language,* ed. by J. A. Fodor and J. J. Katz, Englewood Cliffs, N.J.: Prentice-Hall, 1964.

STL-QPSR — *Quarterly Progress and Status Reports,* Speech Transmission Laboratory, Royal Institute of Technology, Stockholm.

SWES — *Selected Writings of Edward Sapir in Language, Culture, and Personality,* ed. by D. G. Mandelbaum. Berkeley and Los Angeles: University of California Press, 1949.

TCLC — *Travaux du Cercle Linguistique de Copenhague*

TCLP — *Travaux du Cercle Linguistique de Prague*

TLP — *Travaux Linguistiques de Prague*

TPS__ — *Transactions of the Philological Society for the Year __*

THRJ — *To Honor Roman Jakobson: Essays on the Occasion of his Seventieth Birthday* (3 vols.). (Janua Linguarum, series maior, 31, 32, 33.) The Hague: Mouton, 1967.

GENERAL BIBLIOGRAPHY

Following the bibliographical information for each item is a list, in square brackets, of the reference numbers of each article in this volume in which that item is referred to. Also in this list are the reference numbers, preceded by B-, of each topical bibliography (see the Index of Topical Bibliographies) in which the item is listed. Thus [12] indicates that the item is referred to in article 12, while [B-12] indicates that the item is listed in bibliography 12. The listing for an article which is included in this volume is followed by its own reference number in boldface type. Asterisks denote those items listed in the general bibliography which are not referred to anywhere else in this volume.

A Mai Magyar Nyelv Rendszere: Leíró Nyelvtan. Vol. 1. 1961. Budapest: Akadémiai Kiadó. [54]

ABERCROMBIE, DAVID. 1949. "Forgotten Phoneticians," *TPS* 1948. 1–34. [B-2]

ABERCROMBIE, DAVID, D. B. FRY, P. A. D. MACCARTHY, N. C. SCOTT, and JOHN L. M. TRIM (eds.). 1964. *In Honour of Daniel Jones.* London: Longmans, Green. [40, B-11]

ABRAHAMS, H. 1949. *Études phonétiques sur les tendances évolutives des occlusives germaniques.* Aarhus: Universitets-forlaget. [50]

*ALBRIGHT, ROBERT WILLIAM. 1958. *The International Phonetic Alphabet: Its Backgrounds and Development.* (Indiana University Research Center in Anthropology, Folklore, and Linguistics, Publication 7.) Bloomington: Indiana University.

ALLEN, W. S. 1950. "Notes on the Phonetics of an Eastern Armenian Speaker," *TPS* 1950.180–206. [24, 25, B-12]

———. 1951a. "Phonetics and Comparative Linguistics," *AL* 3.126–136. [24, 25]

———. 1951b. "Some Prosodic Aspects of Retroflexion and Aspiration in Sanskrit," *BSOAS* 13.939–946. [24, 25, B-12]

———. 1953. *Phonetics in Ancient India.* (London Oriental Series, 1.) London: Oxford University Press. [24, 25]

———. 1954. "Retroflexion in Sanskrit: Prosodic Technique and Its Relevance to Comparative Statement," *BSOAS* 16.

556–565. [24, 25, B-12]

———. 1956. "Structure and System in the Abaza Verbal Complex," *TPS* 1956.127–176. [25, 46]

———. 1957. "Aspiration in the Hāṛautī Nominal," *SILA* 68–86. [25, B-12]

*ANDERSON, JAMES M. 1961. "The Morphophonemics of Gender in Spanish Nouns," *Lingua* 10.285–296.

*ANDERSON, JOHN. 1969. "Syllabic or Non-Syllabic Phonology?" *JofL* 5.136–142.

ANDRADE, MANUEL JOSÉ. 1936. "Some Questions of Fact and Policy Concerning Phonemes," *Lg.* 12.1–14. [B-1]

ANDREYEV, N. D. 1962. "Models as a Tool in the Development of Linguistic Theory," *Word* 18.186–197. [40]

ANIS, IBRAHIM. 1941. *The Grammatical Characteristics of the Spoken Arabic of Egypt.* Unpublished Ph.D. dissertation, University of London Library. [23]

AOKI, HARUO. 1966. "Nez Perce Vowel Harmony and Proto-Sahaptian Vowels," *Lg.* 42.759–767. [54, B-19]

———. 1968. "Toward a Typology of Vowel Harmony," *IJAL* 34.142–145. [54, B-13, B-19]

AQUILINA, JOSEPH. 1940. *The Structure of Maltese: A Study in Mixed Grammar and Vocabulary.* Unpublished Ph.D. dissertation, University of London Library. [23]

AREND, M. Z. 1934. "Baudouin de Courtenay and the Phoneme Idea," *MPh.* III. 12.2–3. [B-2]

ASCHMANN, HERMAN P. 1946. "Totonaco Phonemes," *IJAL* 12.34–43. [14, 50, B-1]

AUSTERLITZ, ROBERT P. 1967. "The Distributional Identification of Finnish Morphophonemes," *Lg.* 43.20–33. [54, B-4, B-18]

*AUSTIN, WILLIAM M. 1957. "Criteria for Phonetic Similarity," *Lg.* 33.538–544.

*BACH, EMMON W. 1962. "The Order of Elements in a Transformational Grammar of German," *Lg.* 38.263–269.

*———. 1964. *An Introduction to Transformational Grammars.* New York: Holt, Rinehart and Winston.

*———. 1968. "Two Proposals Concerning the Simplicity Metric in Phonology," *Glossa* 2.128–149.

BALASSA, JOZSEF. 1943. *A Magyar Nyelv Könyve,* Budapest: Dante Press. [54]

BAR-HILLEL, YEHOSHUA. 1957. "Three Methodological Remarks on *Fundamentals of Language,*" *Word* 13.323–335. [B-14]

BAUDOUIN DE COURTENAY, JAN. 1894. *Próba teorji alternacyj fonetycznych* (Essay on a Theory of Phonetic Alternations). Cracow. German translation: 1895. *Versuch einer Theorie phonetischer Alternationen.* Strassburg. [B-2]

BAZELL, CHARLES E. 1949. "On the Neutralisation of Syntactic Oppositions," *TCLC* 5.77–86. [50, 56, B-4]

*———. 1952. "Phonemic and Morphemic Analysis," *Word* 8.33–38.

———. 1953. *Linguistic Form.* (Istanbul Üniversitesi, Edebiyat Fakültesi, Yayinlarindan, No. 574.) Istanbul: Istanbul Press. [25]

———. 1954. "The Choice of Criteria in Structural Linguistics," *Word* 10.126–135. [51]

———. 1956. "Three Conceptions of Phonological Neutralisation," *FRJ* 25–30. [56, B-4]

———. 1958. *Linguistic Typology.* London: School of Oriental and African Studies, University of London [25, B-13]

BAZELL, CHARLES E., J. C. CATFORD, MICHAEL A. K. HALLIDAY, and R. H. ROBINS (eds.). 1966. *In Memory of J. R. Firth.* London: Longmans. [B-12]

BENDOR-SAMUEL, JOHN T. 1960. "Some Problems of Segmentation in the Phonological Analysis of Tereno," *Word* 16.348–355. [B-12]

———. 1966. "Some Prosodic Features in Terena," *IMJRF* 30–39. [B-12]

BENNETT, DAVID C. 1968. "English Prepositions: A Stratificational Approach," *JofL* 4.153–172. [55, 57, B-17]

BERGER, MARSHALL D. 1949. "Neutralization in American English Vowels," *Word* 5. 255–257. [B-4, B-6]

BERRY, J. 1957. "Vowel Harmony in Twi," *BSOAS* 19.124–130. [26, 54, B-12, B-19]

BEVER, T. G. 1963. "Theoretical Implications of Bloomfield's 'Menomini Morphophonemics,'" *RLE-QPR* 68. 197–203. [39, B-1, B-4]

———. 1967. *Leonard Bloomfield and the Phonology of the Menomini Language.* Unpublished Ph.D. dissertation, M.I.T. [B-4]

BIDWELL, CHARLES E. 1963. *Slavic Historical Phonology in Tabular Form.* The Hague: Mouton. [55]

BJERRUM, ANDERS. 1944. *Fjoldemålets Lydsystem.* Copenhagen. *Acta Philologica Scandinavica* 18. [50, 51]

BJERRUM, MARIE. 1949. "An Outline of the Faroe Vowel System," *TCLC* 5.235–243. [B-16]

BJÖRKHAGEN, I. 1947. *Modern Swedish Grammar.* 6th ed. Stockholm: Svenska Bokförlaget. [6]

BLACK, JOHN W. 1948. Review of *Tone Languages,* by K. L. Pike. *Quarterly Journal of Speech* 34.519–520. [B-8]

BLOCH, BERNARD. 1935. "Broad Transcription of General American," *MPh.* III. 13.7–10. [9, B-1]

———. 1941. "Phonemic Overlapping," *AS* 16.278–284. Reprinted in *RIL* 93–96. [**8**, 9, 11, 12, 13, 16, 39, 40, B-4]

*———. 1946a. "Studies in Colloquial Japanese I: Inflection," *JAOS* 66.97–109.

———. 1946b. "Studies in Colloquial Japanese II: Syntax," *Lg.* 22.200–248. Reprinted in *RIL* 154–185. [15, 18, 29]

———. 1948. "A Set of Postulates for Phonemic Analysis," *Lg.* 24.3–46. [**16**, 17, 18, 19, 22, 24, 33, 36, 51, 53, 54, B-10, B-18]

———. 1950. "Studies in Colloquial Japanese IV: Phonemics," *Lg.* 26.86–125. Reprinted in *RIL* 329–348. [18, 19, 29, 33, 39, 50, 53, B-1]

———. 1952. "A Bibliography of Descriptive Linguistics: American Writings to 1952." Mimeographed. [B-1]

———. 1953. "Contrast," *Lg.* 29.59–61. [**19**, 33, 39, 51, B-10, B-18]

BLOCH, BERNARD, and GEORGE LEONARD TRAGER. 1940. *Tables for a System of Phonetic Description* (preliminary edition). New Haven: Chinese Printing Office. [9]

———. 1942. *Outline of Linguistic Analysis.* (Special Publication of the LSA.) Baltimore: Waverly Press. [13, 15, 16, 18, 20, 50, B-1, B-6, B-8]

BLOOMFIELD, LEONARD. 1926. "A Set of Postulates for the Science of Language," *Lg.* 2.153–164. Reprinted in *IJAL* 15.195–

202 (1949) and in *RIL* 26–31. [9, 16, 22, 31, 39, 53, B-1]

———. 1927. "On Recent Work in General Linguistics," *Modern Philology* 25.211–230. [31, 42]

———. 1930a. "German ç and x," *MPh*. III. 8.27–28. [B-1]

*———. 1930b. "Linguistics as a Science," *Studies in Philology* 27.553–557.

———. 1933a. *Language*. New York: Henry Holt. [3, 8, 9, 11, 13, 16, 20, 24, 27, 29, 30, 31, 37, 39, 46, 50, 51, 52, 53, B-1]

———. 1933b. "The Structure of Learned Words," *A Commemorative Volume Issued by the Institute for Research in English Teaching* on the Occasion of the Tenth Annual Conference of English Teachers, 17–23. Tokyo: Institute for Research in English Teaching. [12]

———. 1935. "The Stressed Vowels of American English," *Lg*. 11.97–116. [8, 9, 15, 20, B-1, B-6]

———. 1939a. *Linguistic Aspects of Science*, in *International Encyclopedia of Unified Science* 1.4. Chicago: University of Chicago Press. Reprinted in *Foundations of the Unity of Science: Toward an International Encyclopedia of Unified Science*, Vol. I, ed. by Otto Neurath, Rudolf Carnap, and Charles Morris. Chicago: University of Chicago Press, 1971. [20]

———. 1939b. "Menomini Morphophonemics," *TCLP* 8.105–115. [7, 37, 39]

———. 1943. "Meaning," *MDU* 35.101–106. [18]

BOADI, L. A. 1963. "Palatality as a Factor in Twi Vowel Harmony," *Journal of African Languages* 2.133–139. [26, B-12, B-19]

BOAS, FRANZ (ed.). 1911 and 1922. *Handbook of American Indian Languages*, Vols. I and II. Washington, D.C. Bulletin 40, Smithsonian Institution, Bureau of American Ethnology. [11]

BOLINGER, DWIGHT LEMERTON. 1947. "Comments on Pike's American English Intonation," *SIL* 5.69–78. [B-8]

———. 1951. "Intonation: Levels Versus Configurations," *Word* 7.199–210. [B-8]

———. 1955. "Intersections of Stress and Intonation," *Word* 11.195–203. [B-8]

———. 1958. "A Theory of Pitch Accent in English," *Word* 14.109–149. [B-8]

———. 1961. "Contrastive Accent and Contrastive Stress," *Lg*. 37.83–96. [B-8]

———. 1963. "Length, Vowel, Juncture," *Linguistics* 1.5–29. [B-3, B-6, B-8]

BOLINGER, DWIGHT L., and LOUIS J. GERSTMAN. 1957. "Disjuncture as a Cue to Constructs," *Word* 13.246–255. [48, 54, B-8]

BOLLING, GEORGE MELVILLE. 1934. Review of *Language*, by Leonard Bloomfield. *Lg*. 10.48–52. [16, 39, B-1]

BOWEN, J. DONALD, and ROBERT P. STOCKWELL. 1955. "The Phonemic Interpretation of Semivowels in Spanish," *Lg*. 31. 236–240. Reprinted in *RIL* 400–402. [B-6]

———. 1956. "A Further Note on Spanish Semivowels," *Lg*. 32.290–292. Reprinted in *RIL* 405. [B-6]

BOYD, JULIAN C., and HAROLD V. KING. 1962. "Annotated Bibliography of Generative Grammar," *Language Learning* 12.307–312. [B-15]

BRØNDAL, VIGGO. 1936. "Sound and Phoneme," *PICPS*-2.40–45. [B-16]

BROZOVIĆ, DALIBOR. 1967. "Some Remarks on Distinctive Features Especially in Standard Serbocroatian," *THRJ* 412–426. [B-14]

BÜHLER, KARL. 1936. "Das Strukturmodell der Sprache," *TCLP* 6.3–12. [24]

BURSILL-HALL, G. L. 1960–1961. "Levels Analysis: J. R. Firth's Theories of Linguistic Analysis," *JCLA* 6.124–135 and 164–191. [B-12]

BUYSSENS, ERIC. 1949. "Mise au point de quelques notions fondamentales de la phonologie," *Cahiers Ferdinand de Saussure* 8.37–60. [50]

CAIRNS, CHARLES E. 1969. "Markedness, Neutralization, and Universal Redundancy Rules," *Lg*. 45.863–885. [B-4, B-13, B-15]

CARMONY, MARVIN D. 1966. "Surface and Deep Phonology," *JofL* 2.208. [54, B-15]

CARNAP, RUDOLF. 1942. *Introduction to Semantics*. Cambridge, Mass.: Harvard University Press. [31]

———. 1949. "Truth and Confirmation," *Readings in Philosophical Analysis*, ed. by H. Feigl and W. Sellars. New York: Appleton-Century-Crofts. [32]

CARNOCHAN, J. 1948. "A Study in the Phonology of an Igbo Speaker," *BSOAS* 12.417–426. [23, B-12]

———. 1951. "A Study of Quantity in Hausa," *BSOAS* 13.1032–1044. [24, 25, B-3, B-12]

———. 1952. "Glottalization in Hausa," *TPS* 1952.78–109. [24, 25, B-12]

———. 1957. "Gemination in Hausa," *SILA* 149–181. [25, B-3, B-12]

———. 1960. "Vowel Harmony in Igbo," *African Language Studies* 1.155–163. [26, 54, B-12, B-19]

CARROLL, JOHN B. (ed.). 1956. *Language, Thought and Reality: Selected Writings of Benjamin Lee Whorf.* Cambridge, Mass.: Technology Press of M.I.T. and New York: John Wiley. [42, 53]

CASSIRER, ERNST A. 1945. "Structuralism in Modern Linguistics," *Word* 1.99–120. [24]

CHAFE, WALLACE L. 1968a. Review of *Outline of Stratificational Grammar,* by Sydney M. Lamb. *Lg.* 44.593–603. [B-17]

———. 1968b. "The Ordering of Phonological Rules," *IJAL* 34.115–136. [B-15]

CHAO, YUEN REN. 1934. "The Non-Uniqueness of Phonemic Solutions of Phonetic Systems," *Bulletin of the Institute of History and Philology, Academia Sinica.* 4.363–397. Reprinted in *RIL* 38–54. [5, 6, 10, 12, 13, 16, 26, 33, 53, B-1]

———. 1956. "Tone, Intonation, Singsong, Chanting, Recitative, Tonal Composition and Atonal Composition in Chinese," *FRJ* 52–59. [B-8]

CHERRY, E. COLIN. 1956. "Roman Jakobson's 'Distinctive Features' as the Normal Co-ordinates of Language," *FRJ* 60–64. [B-14]

———. 1957. *On Human Communication.* Cambridge, Mass.: Technology Press and New York: John Wiley. [34]

CHERRY, E. COLIN, MORRIS HALLE, and ROMAN JAKOBSON. 1953. "Toward the Logical Description of Languages in Their Phonemic Aspect," *Lg.* 29.34–46. Reprinted in *RJ:SWI* 449–463. [31, 32, 33, 34]

CHEW, G. F., M. GELL-MANN, and A. H. ROSEN-FELD. 1964. "Strongly Interacting Particles," *Scientific American* Feb. 1964. 74–93. [41]

CHISTOVICH, LIUDMILA A. *et al.* 1966. "Mimicking of Synthetic Vowels," *STL-QPSR* 2/1966. 1–18. [35]

———. 1966. "Mimicking and Perception of Synthetic Vowels, Part II," *STL-QPSR* 3/1966. 1–3. [35]

CHOMSKY, NOAM. 1951. *Morphophonemics of Modern Hebrew.* Unpublished master's thesis. University of Pennsylvania. Also mimeographed. [39, 48, B-4]

———. 1953. "Systems of Syntactic Analysis," *Journal of Symbolic Logic* 18.242–256. [42]

———. 1955. "The Logical Structure of Linguistic Theory." Mimeographed. Also on microfilm, Cambridge, Mass.: M.I.T. Library. [34]

———. 1957a. Review of *A Manual of Phonology,* by C. F. Hockett. *IJAL* 23.223–234. [B-1]

———. 1957b. Review of *Fundamentals of Language,* by R. Jakobson and M. Halle. *IJAL* 23.234–242. [**33**, 34, 39, 54]

———. 1957c. *Syntactic Structures.* (Janua Linguarum, series minor, 4.) The Hague: Mouton. [36, 37, 39, 40, 41, 42, B-15]

———. 1959. "The Transformational Basis of Syntax," paper presented at the Fourth Texas Conference on Problems of Linguistic Analysis in English. Unpublished. [39]

*———. 1961a. "On the Notion 'Rule of Grammar,'" *SLMA* 6–24. Reprinted in *SofL* 119–136.

*———. 1961b. "Some Methodological Remarks on Generative Grammar," *Word* 17.219–239. Reprinted as "Degrees of Grammaticalness," in *SofL* 384–389.

———. 1962a. "A Transformational Approach to Syntax," *Proceedings of the Third Texas Conference on Problems of Linguistic Analysis in English, May 9–12, 1958,* ed. by A. A. Hill, 124–158. Austin: University of Texas Press. Reprinted in *SofL* 211–245. [21, 56]

———. 1962b. "Explanatory Models in Linguistics," *Logic, Methodology, and Philosophy of Science,* ed. by E. Nagel, P. Suppes, and A. Tarski, 528–550. Stanford: Stanford University Press. [21]

———. 1962c. "The Logical Basis of Linguistic Theory," *Preprints of Papers for the Ninth International Congress of Linguists,* ed. by M. Halle, 509–574. Cambridge, Mass. Reprinted in slightly revised form as Chomsky 1964a. For bibliographical cross-references see Chomsky 1964c.

———. 1964a. "The Logical Basis of Linguistic Theory," *PICL*-9. 914–978. Comments pp. 978–1008. Reprinted in revised and expanded form as 1964b. For bibliographical cross-references see Chomsky 1964c.

———. 1964b. "Current Issues in Linguistic Theory," *SofL* 50–118. Reprinted in slightly revised form as Chomsky 1964c. For bibliographical cross-references see Chomsky 1964c.

———. 1964c. *Current Issues in Linguistic Theory.* (Janua Linguarum, series minor, 38.) The Hague: Mouton. [34, **39**, 40, 41, 42, 45, 46, 48, 49, 52, 53, 54, 56, 57, B-15]

———. 1965. *Aspects of the Theory of Syntax.* Cambridge, Mass.: M.I.T. Press. [42, 48, 53, 54, B-15]

———. 1966a. *Cartesian Linguistics: A Chapter in the History of Rationalist Thought.* New York: Harper & Row. [22]

———. 1966b. "Topics in the Theory of Generative Grammar," *Current Trends in Linguistics,* Vol. III, ed. by T. A. Sebeok, 1–60. The Hague: Mouton. Also published as a separate monograph with the same title (Janua Linguarum, series minor, 56). The Hague: Mouton. [48, 53, 54, 56, B-15]

———. 1967. "Some General Properties of Phonological Rules," *Lg.* 43.102–128. [**48**, 54]

CHOMSKY, NOAM, and MORRIS HALLE. 1965. "Some Controversial Questions in Phonological Theory," *JofL* 1.97–138. [**42**, 43, 44, 45, 46, 48, 53, 54]

———. 1968. *The Sound Pattern of English.* New York: Harper & Row. [37, 38, 39, 42, 47, 48, 54, 55, 56, B-15]

CHOMSKY, NOAM, MORRIS HALLE, and FRED LUKOFF. 1956. "On Accent and Juncture in English," *FRJ* 65–80. [39, 48, B-8]

CHOMSKY, NOAM, and GEORGE A. MILLER. 1963. "Introduction to the Formal Analysis of Natural Languages," *Handbook of Mathematical Psychology,* ed. by R. D. Luce, R. R. Bush, and E. Galanter, Vol. II. 269–322. New York: John Wiley. [39, 40]

COHEN, A. 1952. *The Phonemes of English.* The Hague: Uleman. [51]

COLE, DESMOND T. 1955. *An Introduction to Tswana Grammar.* London: Longmans, Green. [46]

CONTRERAS, HELES. 1969. "Simplicity, Descriptive Adequacy, and Binary Features," *Lg.* 45.1–8. [B-14]

CONTRERAS, HELES, and SOL SAPORTA. 1960. "The Validation of a Phonological Grammar," *Lingua* 9.1–15. [37, 42, B-15]

COOPER, FRANKLIN S., PIERRE C. DELATTRE, ALVIN LIBERMAN, JOHN M. BORST, and LOUIS J. GERSTMAN. 1952. "Some Experiments on the Perception of Synthetic Speech Sounds," *JASA* 24.597–606. [51]

COURT, CHRISTOPHER. 1967. "A Distinctive Feature Analysis of the Phonemes of Měntu Land Dayak," *Phonetica* 17.202–207. [54, B-14]

COWAN, J. MILTON, and BERNARD BLOCH. 1948. "An Experimental Study of Pause in English Grammar," *AS* 23.89–99. [B-8]

CRYSTAL, DAVID, and RANDOLPH QUIRK. 1964. *Systems of Prosodic and Paralinguistic Features in English.* (Janua Linguarum, series minor, 39.) The Hague: Mouton. [B-12]

*DELATTRE, PIERRE. 1951. "The Physiological Interpretation of Sound Spectrograms," *PMLA* 66.864–875.

DELATTRE, PIERRE C., ALVIN LIBERMAN, and FRANKLIN S. COOPER. 1955. "Acoustic Loci and Transitional Cues for Consonants," *JASA* 27.769–773. [51]

DIDERICHSEN, PAUL. 1949. "Morpheme Categories in Modern Danish," *TCLC* 5.134–153. [39]

———. 1958. "The Importance of Distribution versus Other Criteria in Linguistic Analysis," *PICL*-8. 156–182. [39, B-18]

DIEBOLD, A. RICHARD, JR. 1961. "Incipient Bilingualism," *Lg.* 37.97–112. [B-5]

DIETRICH, G. 1932. "Das Wort als phonetische Einheit," *MPh* 38.31–33. [9]

DUDLEY, H., and T. TARNOCZY. 1950. "The Speaking Machine of Wolfgang von Kempelen," *JASA* 22.151–167. [32]

DUNN, H. K., and S. D. WHITE. 1939. "Statistical Measurements on Conversational Speech," *JASA* 11.278–288. [32]

ECHOLS, JOHN M. 1949. Review of *Phonemics,* by K. L. Pike. *Journal of English and Germanic Philology* 48.377–379. [B-1]

EDGERTON, WILLIAM F. 1947. "Stress, Vowel Quantity, and Syllable Division in Egyptian," *Journal of Near Eastern Studies* 6.1–17. [B-3, B-9]

EINARSSON, STEFÁN. 1932. "Parallels to the Stops in Hittite," *Lg.* 8.177–182. [6]

ELIASON, NORMAN ELLSWORTH. 1942. "On Syllable Division in Phonemics," *Lg.* 18. 144–147. [B-9]

EMENEAU, MURRAY BARNSON. 1943. Review of *Outline of Linguistic Analysis*, by B. Bloch and G. L. Trager, and of *Outline Guide for the Practical Study of Foreign Languages*, by L. Bloomfield. *JAOS* 63. 208–209. [16, B-1]

EVANS, EILEEN M. 1950. Review of *Phonemics*, by K. L. Pike. *BSOAS* 13.531–534. [B-1]

FANT, C. GUNNAR M. 1954. "Phonetic and Phonemic Basis for the Transcription of Swedish Word Material," *Acta Oto-Laryngologica, Supplement* (Stockholm) 116.24–29. [35]

——. 1958. "Modern Instruments and Methods for Acoustic Studies of Speech," *Acta Polytechnica Scandinavica* (Stockholm) 246. Also *PICL*-8. 282–358. [35]

——. 1959a. "Acoustic Analysis and Synthesis of Speech with Applications to Swedish," *Ericsson Technics* 15.1–106. [35]

*——. 1959b. "The Acoustics of Speech," *Proceedings of the Third International Congress of Acoustics, Stuttgart*, ed. by L. Cremer, 188–201. Amsterdam: Elsevier Press.

——. 1960. *Acoustic Theory of Speech Production*. (Description and Analysis of Contemporary Standard Russian, 2.) The Hague: Mouton. [46]

——. 1962. "Descriptive Analysis of the Acoustic Aspects of Speech," *Logos* 5. 3–17. [35]

——. 1965. "Structural Classification of Swedish Phonemes," *STL-QPSR* 2/1965. 10–15. [35]

——. 1967a. "Auditory Patterns of Speech," *Proceedings of the Symposium on Models for the Perception of Speech and Visual Form, Boston, Nov. 11–14, 1964*, ed. by W. Walthen-Dunn, 111–125, Cambridge, Mass.: M.I.T. [35]

——. 1967b. "The Nature of Distinctive Features," *THRJ* 634–642. [**35**]

FANT, C. GUNNAR M., and B. LINDBLOM. 1961. "Studies of Minimal Speech Sound Units," *STL-QPSR* 2/1961. 1–11. [35]

FEIGL, HERBERT, and WILFRED SELLARS (eds.). 1949. *Readings in Philosophical Analysis*. New York: Appleton-Century-Crofts. [32]

FERGUSON, CHARLES ALBERT. 1957. "A Manual of Phonological Description," *Word* 13.335–345. [B-1]

——. 1959. "Diglossia," *Word* 15.325–340. [B-5]

——. 1962. Review of *The Sound Pattern of Russian*, by M. Halle. *Lg.* 38.284–298. [**36**, 39, 42]

——. 1963. "Assumptions About Nasals: A Sample Study in Phonological Universals," *Universals of Language*, ed. by J. H. Greenberg, 42–47. Cambridge, Mass.: M.I.T. Press. (2d ed. (1966) pp. 53–60.) [B-13]

FIRTH, JOHN RUPERT. 1934. "The Word 'Phoneme,'" *MPh.* III.12.44–46. Reprinted in Firth 1957b. 1–2. [B-2, B-11]

——. 1935a. "The Technique of Semantics," *TPS* 1935.36–72. Reprinted in Firth 1957b. 7–33. [24]

——. 1935b. "The Use and Distribution of Certain English Sounds: Phonetics from a Functional Point of View," *English Studies* 17.8–18. Reprinted in Firth 1957b. 34–46. [B-11, B-18]

——. 1947. "The English School of Phonetics," *TPS* 1946.92–132. Reprinted in Firth 1957b. 92–120. [23, B-11]

——. 1948a. "Sounds and Prosodies," *TPS* 1948.127–152. Reprinted in Firth 1957b. 121–138. [**23**, 24, 25]

——. 1948b. "The Semantics of Linguistic Science," *Lingua* 1.393–404. Reprinted in Firth 1957b.139–147. [24, 25]

——. 1950. "Personality and Language in Society," *Sociological Review* 42.37–52. Reprinted in Firth 1957b.177–189. [24]

——. 1951. "General Linguistics and Descriptive Grammar," *TPS* 1951.69–87. Reprinted in Firth 1957b.216–228. [24, 25, B-12]

——. 1957a. "A Synopsis of Linguistic Theory 1930–1955," *SILA* 1–32. [25, 26, B-12]

——. 1957b. *Papers in Linguistics 1934–1951*. London: Oxford University Press. [B-12]

FIRTH, JOHN RUPERT, and B. B. ROGERS. 1937. "The Structure of the Chinese Monosyllable in a Hunanese Dialect (Changsha)," *BSOAS* 8.1055–1074. [23, B-9, B-11]

FISCHER-JØRGENSEN, ELI. 1941. "Phonologie, Bericht über Arbeiten in germanischen und romanischen Sprachen," *Archiv für vergleichende phonetik* 5.170–200. [B-16]

———. 1949a. "Danish Linguistic Activity 1940–48," *Lingua* 2.95–109. [B-16]

———. 1949b. "Remarques sur les principes de l'analyse phonémique," *TCLC* 5.214–234. [18, 19, 50, 51, B-1, B-16]

———. 1949c. Review of *Phonemics,* by K. L. Pike. *AcL* 5.104–109. [B-1]

———. 1952a. "On the Definition of Phoneme Categories on a Distributional Basis," *AcL* 7.8–39. [**50**, 51]

———. 1952b. "The Phonetic Basis for Identification of Phonemic Elements," *JASA* 24.611–617. [32, B-16]

———. 1954. "Acoustic Analysis of Stop Consonants," *Miscellanea Phonetica* 2.42–59. Reprinted in Lehiste 1967.137–154. [51]

———. 1956. "The Commutation Test and Its Application to Phonemic Analysis," *FRJ* 140–151. [**51**]

———. 1958. "What Can the New Techniques of Acoustic Phonetics Contribute to Linguistics?" *PICL*-8. 433–478, discussion 478–499. [34]

*———. 1967. "Perceptual Dimensions of Vowels," *THRJ* 667–671.

FLEMING, ILAH. 1969. "Stratificational Theory: An Annotated Bibliography," *Journal of English Linguistics* 3.37–65. [57, B-17]

FODOR, JERRY A., and JERROLD J. KATZ (eds.). 1964. *The Structure of Language: Readings in the Philosophy of Language.* Englewood Cliffs, N.J.: Prentice-Hall. [34, 42, 46, 48, B-15]

For Roman Jakobson. See M. Halle *et al.* 1956.

FOURQUET, J. 1949. "Analyse linguistique et analyse phonologique," *TCLC* 5.38–47. [B-16]

FOWLER, MURRAY. 1952. Review of *Methods in Structural Linguistics,* by Z. S. Harris. *Lg.* 28.504–509. [B-1]

FRANCESCATO, GIUSEPPE. 1959. "A Case of Coexistence of Phonemic Systems," *Lingua* 8.78–86. [B-1, B-5]

FRANCIS, W. NELSON. 1958. *The Structure of American English.* New York: Ronald Press. [B-1]

FREI, HENRI. 1936. "Monosyllabisme et polysyllabisme dans les emprunts linguistiques," *Bulletin de la Maison Franco-Japonaise* (Tokyo) 8:1. 76–164. [30]

FRIES, CHARLES CARPENTER, and KENNETH LEE PIKE. 1949. "Coexistent Phonemic Systems," *Lg.* 25.29–50. [25, 46, B-1, B-5]

FROMKIN, VICTORIA. 1965. "On System-Structure Phonology," *Lg.* 41.601–609. [**26**, 54, B-10]

FUDGE, ERIK C. 1967. "The Nature of Phonological Primes," *JofL* 3.1–36. [**46**, 54]

GARCIA, ERICA C. 1963. Review of *A Phonological Grammar of Spanish,* by S. Saporta and H. Contreras. *Word* 19.258–265. [B-15]

GARVIN, PAUL LUCIAN. 1948. "Kutenai I: Phonemics," *IJAL* 14.37–42. [50]

———. 1951. Review of *TCLC* V, *Recherches Structurales. IJAL* 17.252–255. [B-16]

———. 1953. Review of *Preliminaries to Speech Analysis,* by R. Jakobson, C. G. M. Fant, and M. Halle. *Lg.* 29.472–481. [B-14]

———. 1954. Review of *Prolegomena to a Theory of Language,* by L. Hjelmslev. *Lg.* 30.69–96. [56, B-16]

GARVIN, PAUL LUCIEN, and MADELEINE MATHIOT. 1958. "Fused Units in Prosodic Analysis," *Word* 14.178–186. [B-7, B-8]

GAUTHIER, MICHEL. 1956. Review of *Language in Relation to a Unified Theory of the Structure of Human Behavior, Part I,* by K. L. Pike. *JPs* 53.205–206. [B-1]

GLEASON, HENRY A., JR. 1961. *An Introduction to Descriptive Linguistics.* 2d ed. New York: Holt, Rinehart and Winston. [39, B-1]

———. 1964. "The Organization of Language: A Stratificational View," *Monograph Series on Languages and Linguistics* 17. 75–95. Washington, D.C.: Georgetown University Press. [55, B-17]

GODEL, ROBERT. 1957. *Les sources manuscrites du Cours de linguistique générale.* Geneva and Paris: Librairie E. Droz and Librairie Minard. [39]

GRAFF, WILLEM LAURENS. 1932. *Language and Languages.* New York and London: Appleton. [11]

———. 1935. "Remarks on the Phoneme," *AS* 10.83–87. [B-1]

GRANDGENT, C. H., and E. H. WILKENS. 1915. *Italian Grammar*. 6th ed. Boston: Heath. [6]

GRAY, G. W., and C. M. WISE. 1959. *The Bases of Speech*. 3d ed. New York: Harper & Row. [46]

GREENBERG, JOSEPH HAROLD. 1962. "Is the Vowel-Consonant Dichotomy Universal?" *Word* 18.73–81. [B-13]

———. (ed.). 1963. *Universals of Language. (Report of a Conference Held at Dobbs Ferry, New York, April 13–15, 1961.)* Cambridge, Mass.: M.I.T. Press. 2d ed. 1966. [40, B-13]

———. 1966. "Synchronic and Diachronic Universals in Phonology," *Lg.* 42.508–517. [54, B-13]

GREENBERG, JOSEPH HAROLD, CHARLES OS-GOOD, and JAMES JENKINS. 1961. "Memorandum Concerning Universals," *Preprint for the Social Science Research Council Conference on Language Universals* held at Dobbs Ferry, April 1961. Reprinted in Greenberg 1963. [25]

GRIMES, JOSEPH E. 1955. "Style in Huichol Structure," *Lg.* 31.31–35. [B-5]

———. 1959. "Huichol Tone and Intonation," *IJAL* 25.221–232. [B-8]

DE GROOT, A. W. 1941. "Structural Linguistics and Phonetic Law," *Archives Néerlandaises* 17.71–106. [50]

GUDSCHINSKY, SARAH. 1964. "Phonetic Similarity and the Phonemes of Maxakalí," paper read at LSA meeting Aug. 1, 1964. [47, B-1]

HAAS, WILLIAM. 1955. "On Defining Linguistic Units," *TPS* 1954.54–84. [51]

*———. 1957. "Zero in Linguistic Description," *SILA* 33–53.

*———. 1958. "The Identification and Description of Phonetic Elements," *TPS* 1957.118–159.

*———. 1959. "Relevance in Phonetic Analysis," *Word* 15.1–18.

*———. 1960. Review of *Introduction to Linguistic Structures*, by A. A. Hill. *Word* 16.251–276.

HALDANE, J. B. S. 1945. "A New Theory of the Past," *American Scientist* 33.129–145. [17]

HALL, ROBERT ANDERSON, JR. 1944a. *Hungarian Grammar*. (Language Monograph,

21.) Baltimore: Waverly Press. [54]

———. 1944b. "Italian Phonemes and Orthography," *Italica* 21.72–82. [B-1]

———. 1946. "Colloquial French Phonology," *SIL* 4.70–90. [B-1]

———. 1951. "American Linguistics, 1925–1950," *AL* 3.101–125. [B-1]

———. 1960. "Italian [z] and the Converse of the Archiphoneme," *Lingua* 9.194–197. [B-4]

HALLE, MORRIS. 1954. "The Strategy of Phonemics," *Word* 10.197–209. [**32**, 33, 34, 51]

———. 1957. "In Defense of the Number Two," *Studies Presented to Joshua Whatmough*, ed. by E. Pulgram, 65–72. The Hague: Mouton. [34, 47]

———. 1958. "Questions of Linguistics," *Il Nuovo Cimento* 13.494–517. Reprinted in revised form as Halle 1964. [42]

———. 1959. *The Sound Pattern of Russian: A Linguistic and Acoustical Investigation.* With an Excursus on the Contextual Variants of the Russian Vowels by Lawrence G. Jones. The Hague: Mouton. [26, 32, 33, 34, 36, 37, 39, 42, 45, 47, 49, 53, 54, 56, B-15]

*———. 1960. Review of *Fonetika sovremennogo russkogo literaturnogo jazyka*, by R. I. Avanesov. (Moscow, 1956.) *Word* 16.140–152.

———. 1961. "On the Role of Simplicity in Linguistic Descriptions," *SLMA* 89–94. [26, 34, 37, 39]

———. 1962. "Phonology in Generative Grammar," *Word* 18.54–72. Reprinted in *SofL* 334–352. [34, 35, **37**, 38, 39, 41, 42, 45, 48, 53, 54]

*———. 1963. "Phonemics," *Current Trends in Linguistics, Vol. I*, ed. by T. A. Sebeok, 5–21. The Hague: Mouton.

———. 1964. "On the Bases of Phonology," *SofL* 324–333. Revision of Halle 1958. [34, **38**, 42, 45, 46, 47, 48, 54]

HALLE, MORRIS, and NOAM CHOMSKY. 1960. "The Morphophonemics of English," *RLE-QPR* 58.275–281. [B-4]

HALLE, MORRIS, G. W. HUGHES, and J.-P. A. RADLEY. 1957. "Acoustic Properties of Stop Consonants," *JASA* 29.107–116. Reprinted in Lehiste 1967.170–179. [33]

HALLE, MORRIS, HORACE G. LUNT, HUGH MAC-LEAN, and CORNELIUS H. VAN SCHOONE-VELD (eds.). 1956. *For Roman Jakobson.*

The Hague: Mouton. [B-14]

HALLE, MORRIS, and KENNETH N. STEVENS. 1964. "Speech Recognition: A Model and a Program for Research," *SofL* 604–612. [38, 39]

HALLIDAY, MICHAEL A. K. 1961. "Categories of the Theory of Grammar," *Word* 17. 241–292. [26]

HALPERN, ABRAHAM M. 1946a. "Yuma I: Phonemics," *IJAL* 12.25–33. [50]

———. 1946b. "Yuma II: Morphophonemics," *IJAL* 12.147–151. [50, B-4]

HAMMERICH, LOUIS L. 1934. *Tysk Fonetik.* Copenhagen: G.E.C. Gad. [50]

———. 1954. "Die germanische und die hochdeutsche Lautverschiebung," *Beiträge zur Geschichte der deutschen Sprache und Literatur* 77.1–29. [37]

HAMP, ERIC P. 1954. "Componential Restatement of Syllable Structure in Trique," *IJAL* 20.206–209. [B-7, B-9]

*———. 1957a. *A Glossary of American Technical Linguistic Usage 1925–1950.* Utrecht and Antwerp: Spectrum.

———. 1957b. "Stylistically Modified Allophones in Huichol," *Lg.* 33.139–142. [B-5]

*HAMP, ERIC P., FRED WALTER HOUSEHOLDER, JR., and ROBERT P. AUSTERLITZ (eds.). 1966. *Readings in Linguistics II.* Chicago: University of Chicago Press.

Handbook of American Indian Languages. See F. Boas 1911 and 1922.

HARARY, FRANK, and HERBERT H. PAPER. 1957. "Toward a General Calculus of Phonemic Distribution," *Lg.* 33.143–169. [B-18]

HARDEN, MARGARET. 1946. "Syllable Structure in Terena," *IJAL* 12.60–63. [50, B-9]

*HARMS, ROBERT T. 1968. *Introduction to Phonological Theory.* Englewood Cliffs, N.J.: Prentice-Hall.

HARRIS, CYRIL M. 1953. "A Study of the Building Blocks in Speech," *JASA* 25.962–969. [51]

HARRIS, ZELLIG SABBETTAI. 1941. Review of *Grundzüge der Phonologie,* by N. S. Trubetzkoy. *Lg.* 17.345–349. [16, **27**]

———. 1942. "The Phonemes of Moroccan Arabic," *JAOS* 62.309–318. [12, 15, B-1, B-7]

———. 1944. "Simultaneous Components in Phonology," *Lg.* 20.181–205. Reprinted in *RIL* 124–138. [**12**, 13, 16, 25, 46, 53]

———. 1948. "Componential Analysis of a Hebrew Paradigm," *Lg.* 24.87–91. Reprinted in *RIL* 272–274. [B-7]

———. 1951a. *Methods in Structural Linguistics.* Chicago: University of Chicago Press. Later editions entitled simply *Structural Linguistics.* [17, 24, 32, 33, 39, 40, 42, 51, B-1]

———. 1951b. Review of *Selected Writings of Edward Sapir,* ed. by D. G. Mandelbaum. *Lg.* 27.288–333. [39, B-1]

———. 1954. "Distributional Structure," *Word* 10.146–162. Reprinted in *SofL* 33–49. [B-18]

———. 1955. "From Phoneme to Morpheme," *Lg.* 31.190–222. [B-1, B-18]

HARRIS, ZELLIG SABBETTAI, and FRED LUKOFF. 1942. "The Phonemes of Kingwana-Swahili," *JAOS* 62.333–338. [15]

HAUGEN, EINAR. 1949a. "Phoneme or Prosodeme?" *Lg.* 25.278–282. [B-7, B-12]

———. 1949b. Review of *Phonemics* by K. L. Pike. *AS* 24.54–57. [B-1]

———. 1950a. *First Grammatical Treatise, The Earliest Germanic Phonology: An Edition, Translation and Commentary.* (Language Monograph, 25.) Baltimore: Waverly Press. [51]

———. 1950b. "Problems of Bilingualism," *Lingua* 2.271–290. [B-1, B-5]

———. 1951. "Directions in Modern Linguistics," *Lg.* 27.211–222. Reprinted in *RIL* 357–363. [39, 51, B-1, B-16]

———. 1954a. "Bilingualism and Mixed Languages: Problems of Bilingual Description," *Monograph Series on Languages and Linguistics* 7.9–19. Washington, D.C.: Georgetown University Press. [B-5]

———. 1954b. Review of *Prolegomena to a Theory of Language,* by L. Hjelmslev. *IJAL* 20.247–251. [B-16]

———. 1955. "Problems of Bilingual Description," *General Linguistics* 1.1–19. [B-5]

———. 1956. "The Syllable in Linguistic Description," *FRJ* 213–221. [B-9]

———. 1956–1957. "The Phoneme in Bilingual Description," *Language Learning* 7:3–4.17–23. [B-5]

———. 1958. Review of *Papers in Linguistics 1934–1951,* by J. R. Firth. *Lg.* 34.498–502. [B-12]

——. 1962. "On Diagramming Vowel Systems," *PICPS*-4. 648–654. [B-6]

——. 1963. "Pitch Accent and Tonemic Juncture in Scandinavian," *MDU* 55. 157–161. [B-8]

HAUGEN, EINAR, and WILLIAM FREEMAN TWADDELL. 1942. "Facts and Phonemics," *Lg.* 18.228–237. [**10**, 20, B-6]

HEFFNER, ROE-MERRILL S. 1934. "Concerning Transcription," *Lg.* 10.286–290. [B-1]

——. 1937. "Notes on the Length of Vowels," *AS* 12.128–134. [10, 20, B-3, B-6]

——. 1941. "Notes on the Length of Vowels," *AS* 16.204–207. [10, B-3, B-6]

*——. 1949. *General Phonetics*. Madison: University of Wisconsin Press.

HEIDBREDER, EDNA. 1933. *Seven Psychologies*. New York and London: Century. [16]

HENDERSON, EUGÉNIE J. A. 1949. "Prosodies in Siamese: A Study in Synthesis," *Asia Major,* New Series, 1.189–215. [23, 24, 25, B-12]

——. 1951. "The Phonology of Loanwords in Some South-East Asian Languages," *TPS* 1951.131–158. [24, 25, B-12]

——. 1952. "The Main Features of Cambodian Pronunciation," *BSOAS* 14.149–174. [24, 25, B-12]

——. 1966. "Towards a Prosodic Statement of Vietnamese Syllable Structure," *IMJRF 163–197.* [B-12]

HENDON, RUFUS S. 1966. *The Phonology and Morphology of Ulu Muar Malay.* (Yale University Publications in Anthropology, 70.) New Haven: Yale University Press. [B-1]

HERZOG, GEORGE. 1949. Review of *Tone Languages,* by K. L. Pike. *IJAL* 15.236–244. [B-8]

HILL, ARCHIBALD ANDERSON. 1958. *Introduction to Linguistic Structures: From Sound to Sentence in English.* New York: Harcourt, Brace. [B-1]

——. 1959. "The Audibility of /+/," *JCLA* 5.81–82. [21]

——. 1961. "Suprasegmentals, Prosodies, Prosodemes: Comparison and Discussion," *Lg.* 37.457–468. [B-8, B-12]

——. 1962. "Various Kinds of Phonemes," *SIL* 16.3–10. [**21**]

——. 1967. "The Current Relevance of Bloch's 'Postulates,'" *Lg.* 43.203–207. [**22**, 54]

HILL, T. 1948. *The Phonetics of a Nyanja Speaker, with Particular Reference to the Phonological Structure of the Word.* Unpublished master's thesis, University of London Library. [23]

——. 1966. "The Technique of Prosodic Analysis," *IMJRF* 198–226. [B-12]

HINTZE, FRITZ. 1949. "Zum Verhältnis der sprachlichen 'Form' zur 'Substanz,'" *Studia Linguistica* 3.86–105. [50]

HIORTH, FINNGEIR. 1963. "Hypostasis," *Lingua* 12.211–216. [41]

HJELMSLEV, LOUIS. 1936. "On the Principles of Phonematics," *PICPS*-2.49–54. [30, 50, 51, B-16]

——. 1938a. "Essai d'une théorie des morphèmes," *PICL*-4.140–151. [24]

——. 1938b. "Neue Wege der Experimentalphonetik," *Nordisk Tidsskrift for Tale og Stemme* 2.153–194. [51]

——. 1939a. "La structure morphologique (types de système)," *PICL*-5.66–93. Reprinted in Hjelmslev 1959. 113–138. [50]

——. 1939b. "Note sur les oppositions supprimables," *TCLP* 8.51–57. Reprinted in Hjelmslev 1959.82–88. [B-16]

——. 1939c. "The Syllable as a Structural Unit," *PICPS*-3.266–272. [46, B-9, B-16]

——. 1942. "Langue et parole," *Cahiers Ferdinand de Saussure* 2.29–44. Reprinted in Hjelmslev 1959.69–81. [50, 51]

——. 1943. *Omkring sprogteoriens grundlæggelse.* Copenhagen: Ejnar Munksgaard. Translated in 1953 as *Prolegomena to a Theory of Language* by Francis J. Whitfield. (Indiana University Publications in Anthropology and Linguistics, Memoir 7 of *IJAL*.) Revised English edition 1961. Madison: University of Wisconsin Press. [24, 46, 51, 53, B-16]

——. 1947. "Structural Analysis of Language," *Studia Linguistica* 1.69–78. Reprinted in Hjelmslev 1959.27–35. [24, 51, B-16]

——. 1951. "Grundtræk af det danske udtrykssystem med særligt henblik paa stødet," *Selskab for nordisk filologi, Årsberetning for 1948–1949–1950.* 12–23. [50]

——. 1954. "La stratification du langage," *Word* 10.163–188. Reprinted in Hjelmslev 1959.36–68. [51, B-16]

——. 1959. *Essais linguistiques.* TCLC 12. 1–272. [B-16]

HOCKETT, CHARLES FRANCIS. 1942. "A System of Descriptive Phonology," *Lg.* 18. 3–21. Reprinted in *RIL* 97–108. [10, **11**, 13, 15, 16, 29, 44, 50]

———. 1947a. "Componential Analysis of Sierra Popoluca," *IJAL* 13.258–267. [16, 53, B-1, B-7]

———. 1947b. "Peiping Phonology," *JAOS* 67.253–267. Reprinted in *RIL* 217–228. [53, B-1]

———. 1947c. "Problems of Morphemic Analysis," *Lg.* 23.321–343. Reprinted in *RIL* 229–242. [16, 18]

———. 1947d. Review of *Morphology*, by E. A. Nida. *Lg.* 23.273–285. [17]

———. 1948a. "A Note on 'Structure,'" *IJAL* 14.269–271. Reprinted in *RIL* 279–280. [18, 39]

———. 1948b. "Implications of Bloomfield's Algonquian Studies," *Lg.* 24.117–131. Reprinted in *RIL* 281–289. [29, 37, B-1]

———. 1948c. "Potawatomi I: Phonemics, Morphophonemics, and Morphological Survey," *IJAL* 14.1–10. [18]

———. 1949. "Two Fundamental Problems in Phonemics," *SIL* 7.29–51. [**17**, 18, 25, 29, B-10]

———. 1950a. "Peiping Morphophonemics," *Lg.* 26.63–85. Reprinted in *RIL* 315–328. [18, 29, B-1, B-4]

———. 1950b. "Which Approach in Linguistics Is 'Scientific'?" *SIL* 8.53–57. [18, 29]

———. 1951. Review of *Phonology as Functional Phonetics*, by A. Martinet. *Lg.* 27. 333–342. [**29**, 39, 53]

———. 1952a. Review of *Methods in Structural Linguistics*, by Z. S. Harris. *AS* 28. 117–121. [B-1]

———. 1952b. Review of *TCLC* V, *Recherches Structurales. IJAL* 18.86–99. [B-16]

———. 1953. "Short and Long Syllable Nuclei," *IJAL* 19.165–171. [B-3, B-6]

———. 1954. "Two Models of Grammatical Description," *Word* 10.210–234. Reprinted in *RIL* 386–399. [24, 37]

———. 1955. *A Manual of Phonology.* (Indiana University Publications in Anthropology and Linguistics, Memoir 11 of *IJAL=IJAL* Vol. 21, No. 4, Part I.) Baltimore: Waverly Press. [20, 24, 25, 39, 51, 53, 54, B-1]

———. 1958. *A Course in Modern Linguistics.* New York: Macmillan. [B-1]

———. 1961. "Linguistic Elements and Their Relations," *Lg.* 37.29–53. [57, B-17]

*———. 1966. "Language, Mathematics and Linguistics," *Current Trends in Linguistics* Vol. III, ed. by Thomas A. Sebeok, 155–304. The Hague: Mouton. Also published as a separate monograph by the same title (Janua Linguarum, series minor, 60). The Hague: Mouton.

———. 1968. Review of *Outline of Stratificational Grammar,* by S. M. Lamb. *IJAL* 34.145–153. [54, B-17]

HOCKETT, CHARLES FRANCIS, and ROBERT ASCHER. 1964. "The Human Revolution," *Current Anthropology* 5.135–147. [22]

HODGE, CARLETON TAYLOR. 1946. "Serbo-Croatian Phonemes," *Lg.* 22.112–120. [15, B-1]

HOENIGSWALD, HENRY MAX. 1944a. "Internal Reconstruction," *SIL* 2.78–87. [12]

———. 1944b. Review of *Phonetics,* by K. L. Pike. *JAOS* 64.151–155. [16, B-1]

———. 1945. *Spoken Hindustani.* U.S. Armed Forces Institute, Education Manual, 544. [16]

———. 1952. "The Phonology of Dialect Borrowings," *SIL* 10.1–5. [B-1, B-5]

HORÁLEK, KAREL. 1965. "Zur Theorie der unterscheidenden Eigenschaften," *PICPS-5.* 365–366. [46]

HOUSEHOLDER, FRED WALTER, JR. 1947. "Descriptive Analysis of Latin Declension," *Word* 3.48–58. [41]

———. 1952. Review of *Methods in Structural Linguistics,* by Z. S. Harris. *IJAL* 18.260–268. [24, 41, 42, 46, 51, B-1]

———. 1959. "On Linguistic Primes," *Word* 15.231–239. [37, 41, 54, B-1]

———. 1961. "On Linguistic Terms" (expanded version of Householder 1959), *Psycholinguistics, A Book of Readings,* ed. by S. Saporta, 15–25. New York: Holt, Rinehart and Winston. [41]

———. 1962a. "On the Uniqueness of Semantic Mapping," *Word* 18.173–185. [41]

———. 1962b. "The Distributional Determination of English Phonemes," *Lingua* 11.186–191. [46, B-18]

———. 1965. "On Some Recent Claims in Phonological Theory," *JofL* 1.13–34. [34, **41**, 42, 43, 45, 46, 47, 54]

———. 1966. "Phonological Theory: A Brief Comment," *JofL* 2.99–100. [**43**, 48, 54]

———. 1967. "Distinctive Features and Phonetic Features," *THRJ* 941-944. [**44**]

HUFFMAN, DAVID A. 1952. "A Method for the Construction of Minimum Redundancy Codes," *Proceedings of the IRE* 40: 9. 1098-1101. [31]

HUGHES, GEORGE W., and MORRIS HALLE. 1956. "Spectral Properties of Fricative Consonants," *JASA* 28.303-310. [33]

*HULTZÉN, LEE S. 1957. "Free Allophones," *Lg.* 33.36-41.

*———. 1962. "Voiceless Lenis Stops in Prevocalic Clusters," *Word* 18.307-312.

In Honour of Daniel Jones. See D. Abercrombie *et al.* 1964.

ISAČENKO, A. V. 1947. *Fonetika spisovnej ruštiny*. Bratislava: Slovenská akadémia vied a umení. [31]

IVIĆ, PAVLE. 1965. "Roman Jakobson and the Growth of Phonology," *Linguistics* 18. 35-78. [B-14]

JACOBS, MELVILLE. 1931. "A Sketch of Northern Sahaptin Grammar," *University of Washington Publications in Anthropology* 4. 85-292. [3]

JACOBS, RODERICK A., and PETER S. ROSENBAUM. 1968. *English Transformational Grammar*. Waltham, Mass.: Blaisdell. [B-15]

——— (eds.). 1970. *Readings in English Transformational Grammar*. Waltham, Mass.: Ginn. [B-15]

JAKOBSON, ROMAN. 1921. *Novejšaja russkaja poèzija*. Prague. [B-14]

———. 1927. "The Concept of the Sound Law and the Teleological Criterion," *RJ:SWI.* 1-2. (A brief extract from a paper delivered at the Prague Linguistic Circle on Jan. 13, 1927. The full text of the speech was not published and no longer exists.) [B-14]

———. 1928. "Proposition au Premier Congrès International de Linguistes: Quelles sont les méthodes les mieux appropriées à un exposé complet et pratique de la grammaire d'une langue quelconque?" *Actes du 1er Congrès International de Linguistes*, 33-36. Reprinted in *RJ:SWI.* 3-6. [B-14]

———. 1929. *Remarques sur l'évolution phonologique du russe comparée à celle des autres langues slaves*. *TCLP* 2. Reprinted in *RJ:SWI.* 7-116. [37, 40, B-14]

———. 1931a. "Phonemic Notes on Standard Slovak," in Czech ("Z Fonologie Spisov-

né Slovenštiny") in *Slovenská Miscellanea* presented to Albert Pražák, 155-163. Bratislava. Reprinted in English in *RJ:SWI.* 221-230. [39, 42]

———. 1931b. "Prinzipien der historischen Phonologie," *TCLP* 4.247-267. Reprinted in a revised version in French ("Principes de phonologie historique") as an appendix to the French translation of Trubetzkoy's *Grundzüge der Phonologie*, and in *RJ:SWI.* 202-220. [40]

———. 1939. "Observations sur le classement phonologique des consonnes," *PICPS*-3. 34-41. Reprinted in *RJ:SWI.* 272-279. [**28**, 32]

———. 1941. *Kindersprache, Aphasie und allgemeine Lautgesetze*. Uppsala: Språkvetenskapliga Sällskapets i Uppsala Förhandligar. Reprinted in *RJ:SWI.* 328-401. [32, 51]

———. 1949a. "On the Identification of Phonemic Entities," *TCLC* 5.205-213. Reprinted in *RJ:SWI.* 418-425. [**30**, 32, 50]

———. 1949b. "The Phonemic and Grammatical Aspects of Language and Their Interrelation," *PICL*-6. 5-18. [18, B-10]

———. 1958. "Typological Studies and Their Contribution to Historical Comparative Linguistics," *PICL*-8. 17-25. Reprinted in *RJ:SWI.* 523-532. [34, B-13]

———. 1960. "Kazańska skoła polskiej lingwistyki i jej miejsce w światowym rozwoju fonologii" (The Kazan School of Polish Linguistics and Its Place in the World Development of Phonology), *Bulletin de la Société Polonaise de Linguistique* 19.3-34.

———. 1962a. *Selected Writings I: Phonological Studies*. The Hague: Mouton. [28, 34, 35, B-14]

———. 1962b. "The Phonemic Concept of Distinctive Features," *PICPS*-4. 440-454. [B-14]

———. 1966. "Henry Sweet's Paths Toward Phonemics," *IMJRF* 242-254. [B-2]

JAKOBSON, ROMAN, C. GUNNAR M. FANT, and MORRIS HALLE. 1952. *Preliminaries to Speech Analysis: The Distinctive Features and Their Correlates*. (M.I.T. Acoustics Laboratory Technical Report, 13.) 2d edition. Cambridge, Mass.: M.I.T. Press. [31, 32, 33, 34, 35, 38, 39, 40, 45, 46, 47, 51, 53, 54, 56, B-14]

JAKOBSON, ROMAN, and MORRIS HALLE. 1956.

Fundamentals of Language (Janua Linguarum, 1.) The Hague: Mouton. [25, 33, 34, 35, 40, 54, B-14]

———. 1962. "Tenseness and Laxness," *RJ:SWI*. 550–555. Also in *In Honor of Daniel Jones*, ed. by D. Abercrombie et al., 96–101. [35, 54, B-14]

JAKOBSON, ROMAN, and JOHN LOTZ. 1949. "Notes on the French Phonemic Pattern," *Word* 5.151–158. Reprinted in *RJ:SWI*. 426–434. [30, 50, B-14]

JENSEN, ELLA. 1944. *Houlbjergmålet: Bidrag til Beskrivelse af en østjysk Dialekt.* Copenhagen: Schultz. [50]

———. 1949. "The Vowel System in the Flensborg By-Laws," *TCLC* 5.244–255. [B-16]

JENSEN, MARTIN KLOSTER. 1958. "Recognition of Word Tones in Whispered Speech," *Word* 14.187–196. [B-8]

JESPERSEN, OTTO. 1913. *Lehrbuch der Phonetik.* 2d ed. Leipzig and Berlin. [12, 50, B-2]

JOHNS, DAVID A. 1969. "Phonemics and Generative Phonology," *Papers from the Fifth Regional Meeting of the Chicago Linguistic Society*, 374–381. Chicago: Department of Linguistics, University of Chicago. [**49**, 56]

JONES, DANIEL. 1931a. "On Phonemes," *TCLP* 4.74–79. [3, B-11]

———. 1931b. "The 'Word' as a Phonetic Entity," *MPh*.III.9.60–65. [9, B-11]

———. 1932. *An Outline of English Phonetics.* 3d ed. Cambridge: Heffer. [8, 9, 16, 24, 36, B-11]

———. 1939. "Concrete and Abstract Sounds," *PICPS*-3. 1–7. [24, 46, B-11]

———. 1944a. "Chronemes and Tonemes," *AcL* 4.1–10. [B-11]

———. 1944b. "Some Thoughts on the Phoneme," *TPS* 1944. 119–135. [24, B-11]

———. 1950. *The Phoneme: Its Nature and Use.* Cambridge: Heffer. [24, 46, 51, 54, B-11]

———. 1957. *The History and Meaning of the Term "Phoneme."* Supplement to *MPh*. July–December 1957. [B-2]

JOOS, MARTIN. 1934a. "Regional and Personal Variations in General American," *MPh*. 12.3–6. [9, B-1]

———. 1934b. "Stressed Vowels Plus *r* in General American," *MPh*. 12.93–97. [9, B-1, B-6]

———. 1942. "A Phonological Dilemma in Canadian English," *Lg*. 18.141–144. [37]

———. 1947. *Basic Notions for Acoustic Phonetics.* Mimeographed. [16]

———. 1948. *Acoustic Phonetics.* (Language Monograph, 23.) Baltimore: Waverly Press. [16, 23, 51]

——— (ed.). 1957. *Readings in Linguistics.* Washington: ACLS. Reissued as *Readings in Linguistics I.* Chicago: University of Chicago Press. [25, 39, 46, B-1]

———. 1962. "The Definition of Juncture and Terminals," *Second Texas Conference on Problems of Linguistic Analysis in English, 1957*, ed. by A. A. Hill, 4–38. Austin: University of Texas Press. [B-8]

*JUILLAND, A. G. 1953. "A Bibliography of Diachronic Phonemics," *Word* 9.198–208.

KATZ, JERROLD J., and PAUL M. POSTAL. 1964. *An Integrated Theory of Linguistic Descriptions.* (M.I.T. Press Research Monograph, 26.) Cambridge, Mass.: M.I.T. Press. [46, 54, B-15]

KENT, ROLAND G. 1934. Review of *Language*, by L. Bloomfield. *Lg*. 10.40–48. [16, 39, B-1]

KENYON, JOHN SAMUEL. 1935. *American Pronunciation: A Textbook of Phonetics for Students of English.* 6th ed. Ann Arbor: George Wahr. [8, 9, 14, 40, B-1]

KINGDON, ROGER. 1958. *The Groundwork of English Intonation.* London, New York, Toronto: Longmans. [B-8]

KIPARSKY, PAUL. 1968. "Linguistic Universals and Linguistic Change," *Universals in Linguistic Theory*, ed. by E. Bach and R. T. Harms, 170–202. New York: Holt, Rinehart and Winston. [49, B-13]

KLAGSTAD, HAROLD L., JR. 1958. "A Phonemic Analysis of Some Bulgarian Dialects," *American Contributions to the 4th International Congress of Slavicists*, 157–168. The Hague: Mouton. [55]

KOPP, GEORGE A., and HARRIET C. GREEN. 1946. "Basic Phonetic Principles of Visible Speech," *JASA* 18.74–89. [14]

*KOŘINEK, J. M. 1939. "Zur Definition des Phonems," *AcL* 1.90–94.

KOZHEVNIKOV, V. A., and LIUDMILA A. CHISTOVICH. 1962. *Speech: Articulation and Perception.* English translation: U.S. Department of Commerce, JPRS: 30, 543. [35]

KRAFT, L. G. 1950. "Correlation Function Analysis," *JASA* 22.762–764. [32]

*KRÁMSKÝ, JIŘÍ. 1967. "Some Remarks on the Problem of the Phoneme," *THRJ* 1084–1093.

KRUSZEWSKY, MIKOŁAJ. 1881. *Über die Lautabwechslung*. Kazan. [B-2]

KUČERA, HENRY. 1967. "Distinctive Features, Simplicity, and Descriptive Adequacy," *THRJ* 1114–1126. [**45**, 54]

KURATH, HANS. 1940. "*Mourning* and *Morning*." *Studies for William A. Read*, ed. by N. M. Caffee and T. A. Kirby, 166–173. Baton Rouge: Louisiana State University Press. [9]

———. 1945. Review of *Outline of Linguistic Analysis*, by B. Bloch and G. L. Trager. *AJP* 66.206–210. [20, B-1]

———. 1956. "The Loss of Long Consonants and the Rise of Voiced Fricatives in Middle English," *Lg.* 32.435–445. [20]

———. 1957. "The Binary Interpretation of English Vowels," *Lg.* 33.111–122. [**20**, B-6]

———. 1958. "Some Questions of English Phonology: A Reply," *Lg.* 34.259–260. [B-1, B-6]

KURATH, HANS, BERNARD BLOCH, JULIA BLOCH, and M. L. HANSEN. 1939. *Handbook of the Linguistic Geography of New England*. Providence: Brown University Press. [9]

KURATH, HANS, and RAVEN IOOR MCDAVID, JR. 1961. *The Pronunciation of English in the Atlantic States*. Ann Arbor: University of Michigan Press. [42, B-1]

KURYŁOWICZ, JERZY. 1948. "Contributions à la théorie de la syllabe," *Bulletin de la Société Polonaise de Linguistique* 8.80–114. [50, B-9]

———. 1949. "La notion de l'isomorphisme," *TCLC* 5.48–60. [50]

LACKOWSKI, PETER. 1963. "Words as Grammatical Primes," *Lg.* 39.211–215. [41]

LADEFOGED, PETER N. 1959. "The Perception of Speech," *The Mechanisation of Thought Processes: National Physical Laboratory, Symposium 10, Teddington*, 397–409, discussion 411–417. London: Stationery Office. [38]

———. 1960. "The Value of Phonetic Statements," *Lg.* 36.387–396. [B-1, B-11]

*———. 1962. *Elements of Acoustic Phonetics*. Chicago: University of Chicago Press.

LAKOFF, GEORGE P. 1965. *On the Nature of Syntactic Irregularity*. (Harvard Computation Laboratory. Report NSF-16.) Cambridge, Mass.=*Irregularity in Syntax*. 1970. New York: Holt, Rinehart and Winston. [48]

LAMB, SYDNEY M. 1962. *Outline of Stratificational Grammar*. Berkeley: University of California Press. [53, B-17]

———. 1963. "On Redefining the Phoneme," paper delivered at the 1963 Annual Meeting of the LSA. [53, B-17]

———. 1964a. "On Alternation, Transformation, Realization, and Stratification," *Monograph Series on Languages and Linguistics* 17.105–122. Washington, D.C.: Georgetown University Press. [42, 46, **52**, 53, 54, 55, 57]

———. 1964b. "The Sememic Approach to Structural Semantics," *AA* 66:3:2.57–78. [52, 53, 54, 55, 56, B-17]

———. 1965. "Kinship Terminology and Linguistic Structure," *AA* 67:5:2.37–64. [53, 55, 57, B-17]

———. 1966a. "Epilegomena to a Theory of Language," *RP* 19.531–573. [53, 54, B-17]

———. 1966b. *Outline of Stratificational Grammar*. Washington, D.C.: Georgetown University Press. [55, 57, B-17]

———. 1966c. "Prolegomena to a Theory of Phonology," *Lg.* 42.536–573. [48, **53**, 54, 55, 56, 57]

———. 1967. Review of *Current Issues in Linguistic Theory* and *Aspects of the Theory of Syntax*, by N. Chomsky. *AA* 69.411–415. [56, B-15]

———. 1970. "Some Types of Ordering," paper originally delivered at the summer 1966 meeting of the LSA. Published in a revised and expanded version in the present volume. [57]

———. In press. "Stratificational Linguistics as a Basis for Machine Translation," *Approaches to Language Data Processing*, ed. by Bulcsu Laszlo. The Hague: Mouton. Also to appear in A. Makkai and D. Lockwood, 1971, in press. [53]

LANGENDOEN, D. TERENCE. 1964a. *Modern British Linguistics: A Study of Its Theoretical and Substantive Contributions*.

Unpublished M.I.T. Ph.D. dissertation. [39, B-11, B-12]

———. 1964b. Review of *SILA. Lg.* 40.305–321. [B-12]

———. 1968. *The London School of Linguistics: A Study of the Linguistic Theories of B. Malinowski and J. R. Firth.* (Research Monograph, 46.) Cambridge, Mass.: M.I.T. Press. [B-11, B-12]

———. 1969. Review of *IMJRF. FofL.* 5.391–408. [B-12]

LAWRENSON, A. C. 1935. "On the Broad Transcription of Southern English," *MPh.* 50. 22–24. [9]

*LAZICZIUS, GYULA. 1932. *Bevezetés a fonológiába* (Introduction to Phonology). Budapest.

LEES, ROBERT B. 1957. Review of *Syntactic Structures,* by N. Chomsky. *Lg.* 33.375–408. [36, 42, B-15]

———. 1960. *A Grammar of English Nominalizations.* (Indiana University Research Center in Anthropology, Folklore and Linguistics, Publication 12.) Bloomington: Indiana University Press. [37]

———. 1961. *The Phonology of Modern Standard Turkish.* (Uralic and Altaic Series, 6.) Bloomington: Indiana University Press and The Hague: Mouton. [36, 39, 54, B-15]

LEHISTE, ILSE. 1960. *An Acoustic-Phonetic Study of Internal Open Juncture. Phonetica* Vol. 5, supplement. Basel: S. Karger. [22, B-8]

———. 1965. "Juncture," *PICPS-5.* 172–200. [B-8]

*———. (ed.). 1967. *Readings in Acoustic Phonetics.* Cambridge, Mass.: M.I.T. Press.

———. 1970. *Suprasegmentals.* Cambridge, Mass.: M.I.T. Press. [B-8]

LEHISTE, ILSE, and GORDON E. PETERSON. 1959. "Vowel Amplitude and Phonemic Stress in American English," *JASA* 31. 428–435. Reprinted in Lehiste 1967. 183–190. [B-8]

LEOPOLD, WERNER F. 1948. "German ch," *Lg.* 24.179–180. Reprinted in *RIL* 215–216. [39, B-1]

LI, FANG-KUEI. 1950. Review of *Tone Languages,* by K. L. Pike. *Lg.* 26.401–403. [B-8]

LIEBER, LILLIAN, and HUGH GRAY LIEBER.

1944. *The Education of T. C. Mits.* New York: Norton. [17]

*LIEBERMAN, PHILIP. 1965. "On the Acoustic Basis of the Perception of Intonation by Linguists," *Word* 21.40–54.

LIGHTNER, THEODORE M. 1963. "A Note on the Formulation of Phonological Rules," *RLE-QPR* 68.187–189. [B-15]

———. 1965. "On the Description of Vowel and Consonant Harmony," *Word* 21. 244–250. [54, B-19]

Linguistic Structures of Native America. 1946. Viking Fund Publications in Anthropology, 6. New York: Wenner-Gren Foundation for Anthropological Research. [15]

*LISKER, LEIGH. 1963. "On Hultzén's 'Voiceless Lenis Stops in Prevocalic Clusters,'" *Word* 19.376–387.

LISKER, LEIGH, and ARTHUR S. ABRAMSON. 1964. "A Cross-Language Study of Voicing in Initial Stops: Acoustical Measurements," *Word* 20.384–422. [35]

LOCKWOOD, DAVID G. 1969a. "Markedness in Stratificational Phonology," *Lg.* 45.300–308. [55, 56]

———. 1969b. "Neutralization, Biuniqueness, and Stratificational Phonology." First published in the present volume. [56, B-4]

———. 1969c. "Russian Vowel Hypophonology." To appear in *Readings in Stratificational Linguistics,* ed. by A. Makkai and D. G. Lockwood, 1971, in press. [B-17]

———. 1971. *Introduction to Stratificational Grammars.* New York: Harcourt, Brace. [B-17]

LONGACRE, ROBERT E. 1955. "Rejoinder to Hamp's 'Componential Restatement of Syllable Structure in Trique,'" *IJAL* 21. 189–194. [B-7, B-9]

———. 1964. *Grammar Discovery Procedures: A Field Manual.* The Hague: Mouton. [48, 54]

LOTZ, JOHN. 1950. "Speech and Language," *JASA* 22.712–717. [19]

LOWMAN, GUY SUMNER, JR. 1933. "Regional Differences in Virginian Speech," paper read at the tenth annual meeting of the LSA. [3]

———. 1935. "The Diphthong *au* in Virginia," paper read before the Practical Phonetics

Group of the MLA at the 52nd annual meeting. [9]

LYONS, JOHN. 1962. "Phonemic and Non-Phonemic Phonology: Some Typological Reflections," *IJAL* 28.127–134. [**25**, 46, 54]

MACDONELL, A. A. 1911. *Sanskrit Grammar.* 2d ed. London: Oxford University Press. [24]

MACKAY, D. 1959. "Mindlike Behaviours of Artefacts," *British Journal for the Philosophy of Science* 2.105–121. [38]

MACKAY, D. M. 1952a. "In Search of Basic Symbols," *Cybernetics: Transactions of the Eighth Conference.* New York. [31]

———. 1952b. "The Nomenclature of Information Theory," *Cybernetics: Transactions of the Eighth Conference.* New York. [31]

MAKKAI, ADAM. 1968. Review of *The Phonology and Morphology of Ulu Muar Malay,* by Rufus S. Hendon. *AA* 70.431. [B-1]

———. 1969a. "On the Validity and Limitations of Generative Morphophonemics," *Linguistics* 49.11–17. [B-4, B-15]

———. 1969b. "The Two Idiomaticity Areas in English and their Membership," *Linguistics* 50.44–58. [B-17]

———. 1969c. "Why Language is Stratified," *Kivung* 2:3.16–51. [B-17]

———. 1972. *Idiom Structure in English.* (Janua Linguarum, series maior, 48.) The Hague: Mouton. [B-17]

MAKKAI, ADAM, and DAVID G. LOCKWOOD (eds.). 1972, in press. *Readings in Stratificational Linguistics.* University, Alabama: University of Alabama Press. [B-17]

*MAKKAI, VALERIE BECKER. 1966. Review of *L'élaboration du français fondamental (ler degré); étude sur l'établissement d'un vocabulaire et d'une grammaire de base,* by G. Gougenheim, P. Rivenc, R. Michéa, and A. Sauvageot. *RP* 20.98–101.

———. 1968. "Vowel Harmony in Hungarian Reexamined in the Light of Recent Developments in Phonological Theory," paper presented to the LSA summer meetings, July 1968. Published in a revised and expanded version in the present volume. [**54**]

———. 1969. "On the Correlation of Morphemes and Lexemes," *Papers from the Fifth Regional Meeting, Chicago Linguistic Society,* 159–166. Chicago: Lin-

guistics Department, University of Chicago. Reprinted in revised form in A. Makkai and D. G. Lockwood, 1971, in press. [B-1, B-17]

MALÉCOT, ANDRÉ. 1960. "Vowel Nasality as a Distinctive Feature in American English," *Lg.* 36.222–229. [39, 40, B-14]

———. 1966. "Mechanical Pressure as an Index of 'Force of Articulation,'" *Phonetica* 14.169–180. [35]

MALMBERG, BERTIL. 1955. "The Phonetic Basis for Syllable Division," *Studia Linguistica* 9.80–87. Reprinted in Lehiste 1967.293–300. [B-9]

*MALONE, JOSEPH L. 1970. "In Defense of Non-Uniqueness of Phonological Representations," *Lg.* 46.328–335.

MALONE, KEMP. 1936. "The Phonemic Structure of English Monosyllables," *AS* 11.205–218. [B-1]

———. 1940. "The Phonemes of Current English," *Studies for William A. Read,* ed. by N. M. Caffee and T. A. Kirby, 133–165. Baton Rouge: Louisiana State University Press. [9, B-1]

*———. 1942. "Syllabic Consonants in English," *MLQ* 3.5–8.

———. 1962. "On Symmetry in Phonemic Analysis," *Lg.* 38.142–146. [B-1]

MANDELBAUM, DAVID G. (ed.). 1949. *Selected Writings of Edward Sapir in Language, Culture, and Personality.* Berkeley and Los Angeles: University of California Press. [B-1]

MANDELBROT, BENOIT. 1954. "Structure formelle des langues et communication," *Word* 10.1–27. [32]

MARCKWARDT, ALBERT. 1962. "'On Accent and Juncture in English'—A Critique," *Second Texas Conference on Problems of Linguistic Analysis in English, 1957,* ed. by A. A. Hill, 87–93. Austin: University of Texas Press. [B-8]

MARKOV, A. A. 1913. "Essai d'une recherche statistique sur le texte du roman *Eugène Onĕgin,* illustrant la liaison des épreuves en chaine." *Bulletin de l'Académie Impériale des Sciences de St. Pétersbourg* 7. 153–162. [31]

MARTENS, PETER. 1955. "Einige Fälle von sprachlich relevanter Konsonantendauer im Neuhochdeutschen," *MPh.* 103.5–7. [33]

MARTIN, SAMUEL ELMO. 1951. "Korean Phonemics," *Lg.* 27.519–533. Reprinted in *RIL* 364–371. [53, B-1, B-14]

——. 1956. Review of *A Manual of Phonology*, by C. F. Hockett. *Lg.* 32.675–705. [B-1]

MARTINET, ANDRÉ. 1936. "Neutralisation et archiphonème," *TCLP* 6.46–57. [54, 56, B-4]

——. 1937. "La phonologie du mot en danois," *BSL* 1937. [50]

*——. 1939. "Un ou deux phonèmes?" *AcL* 1.94–103.

——. 1945. *La prononciation du français contemporain.* Paris: Droz. [29]

——. 1946. "Au sujet des fondements de la théorie linguistique de L. Hjelmslev," *BSL* 1942–1945.19–42. [51]

——. 1948. "Où en est la phonologie?" *Lingua* 1.34–58. [29, 50, 51, B-14]

——. 1949a. *Phonology as Functional Phonetics: Three Lectures Delivered Before the University of London in 1946.* (Publications of the Philological Society.) London: Oxford University Press. [29, B-14]

——. 1949b. Review of *Phonemics*, by K. L. Pike. *Word* 5.282–286. [B-1]

——. 1953. "Concerning the Preservation of Useful Sound Features," *Word* 9.1–11. [51]

——. 1955. *Économie des changements phonétiques.* Berne: Francke. [40]

——. 1964. *Elements of General Linguistics.* Chicago: University of Chicago Press. Translation of *Éléments de linguistique générale* (Paris: Librairie Armand Colin, 1960). [48, 54]

MÁRTONY, JÁNOS. 1964. "The Role of Formant Amplitudes in Synthesis of Nasal Consonants," *STL-QPSR* 3/1964. 28–31. [35]

MATHESIUS, VILÉM. 1929. "La structure phonologique du lexique de tchèque moderne," *TCLP* 1.67–84. Reprinted in Vachek 1964a. 156–176. [50]

——. 1932. "O požadavku stability v spisovném jazyce" (On the Postulate of Stability in the Standard Language), *Spisovná čeština a jazyková kultura* (Standard Czech and Culture of Language), 14–31. Prague. [40]

——. 1935. "Zur synchronistischen Analyse fremden Sprachguts," *Englische Studien* 71.21–35. Reprinted in Vachek 1964a. 398–412. [40]

MATTHEWS, G. H. 1961. "Analysis by Synthesis of Sentences of Natural Languages," *First International Conference on Machine Translation of Languages and Applied Language Analysis (Teddington, 1961)*, 531–542. (National Physical Laboratory, Symposium 13.) London: Stationery Office. [39]

*MATTHEWS, W. K. 1958. "Phonetics and Phonology in Retrospect," *Lingua* 7.254–268.

MAZON, ANDRÉ. 1921. *Grammaire de la langue tchèque.* Paris: Institut d'études slaves. [11]

MCCAWLEY, JAMES D. 1965. *The Accentual System of Modern Standard Japanese.* M.I.T. Ph.D. dissertation. Revised and published as 1968. [B-8]

——. 1967a. "Le rôle d'un système de traits phonologiques dans une théorie du langage," *Langages* 8.112–123. Appears in this volume for the first time in print in English translation under the title "The Role of a Phonological Feature System in a Theory of Language." [47]

——. 1967b. "Sapir's Phonologic Representation," *IJAL* 33.106–111. [B-1, B-15]

——. 1968. *The Phonological Component of a Grammar of Japanese.* (Monographs on Linguistic Analysis, 2.) The Hague: Mouton. [B-15]

MCDAVID, RAVEN IOOR, JR. 1952. Review of *The Phoneme*, by D. Jones. *Lg.* 28.377–386. [B-11]

*MCQUOWN, NORMAN ANTHONY. 1951. Review of *General Phonetics*, by R.-M. S. Heffner. *Lg.* 27.344–362.

——. 1952. Review of *Methods in Structural Linguistics*, by Z. S. Harris. *Lg.* 28.495–504. [B-1]

——. 1957. Review of *Language in Relation to a Unified Theory of the Structure of Human Behavior*, Parts I and II, by K. L. Pike. *AA* 59.189–192. [B-1]

MEILLET, ANTOINE. 1925. *La méthode comparative en linguistique historique.* Oslo: H. Aschehoug. Later editions: Paris: Librairie Honoré Champion. [37]

——. 1929. *Linguistique historique et linguistique générale.* Paris: Champion. [37]

MEINHOF, CARL. 1912. *Die Sprachen der Hamiten.* Hamburg: L. Friederichsen. [6]

MEL'ČUK, IGOR ALEXANDER. 1963. "On the Standard Form and Quantitative Characteristics of Several Linguistic Descriptions," *Foreign Developments in Machine Translation and Information Processing*, No. 120. Washington, D.C.: Superintendent of Documents. (Translated from *Voprosy Jazykoznanija* 1.113–123 (1963).) [41]

MENZERATH, PAUL. 1937. "Neue Untersuchungen zur Lautabgrenzung und Wortsynthese mit Hilfe von Tonfilmaufnahmen," *Mélanges de linguistique et de philologie offerts à Jacques van Ginneken*, 35–41. Paris: Librairie C. Klincksieck. [32[

———. 1938. "Neue Untersuchungen zur Wortartikulation," *PICL*-4. 67–75. [16, 38]

MENZERATH, PAUL, and ARMANDO DE LACERDA. 1933. *Koartikulation, Steuerung und Lautabgrenzung.* (Phonetische Studien, 1.) Berlin and Bonn: F. Dümmler. [8, 16, 32]

MICHAELIS, HERMANN, and DANIEL JONES. 1913. *A Phonetic Dictionary of the English Language.* Hannover and Berlin: Carl Meyer. [9]

MILLER, GEORGE A. 1956. "The Perception of Speech," *FRJ* 353–360. [41]

MILLER, GEORGE A., and NOAM CHOMSKY. 1963. "Finitary Models of Language Users," *Handbook of Mathematical Psychology*, ed. by R. D. Luce, R. R. Bush, and E. Galanter, Vol. II.419–492. New York: John Wiley. [39]

MILLER, ROY ANDREW. 1966. "Early Evidence for Vowel Harmony in Tibetan," *Lg.* 42. 252–277. [54, B-19]

MITCHELL, TERENCE F. 1953. "Particle-Noun Complexes in a Berber Dialect (Zuara)," *BSOAS* 15.375–390. [24, 25]

———. 1957a. "Long Consonants in Phonology and Phonetics," *SILA* 182–205. [25, B-3]

———. 1957b. "Some Properties of Zerara Nouns with Special Reference to Those with Consonant Initial," *Mémorial André Basset (1895–1956)*, 83–96. Paris: A. Maisonneuve. [24]

*MOHRMANN, CHRISTINE, F. NORMAN, and ALF SOMMERFELT (eds.). 1963. *Trends in Modern Linguistics.* Utrecht and Antwerp: Spectrum.

*MOHRMANN, CHRISTINE, ALF SOMMERFELT, and JOSHUA WHATMOUGH (eds.). 1961. *Trends in European and American Linguistics, 1930–1960.* Utrecht and Antwerp: Spectrum.

*MOL, H. 1962. "On the Phonetic Description of the Phoneme," *Lingua* 11.289–293.

*———. 1963 and 1964. "The Relation Between Phonetics and Phonemics," *Linguistics* 1.60–74 and 7.55–62.

*———. 1965. "Are Phonemes Really Realized?" *PICPS*-5.426–430.

MOL, H., and E. M. UHLENBECK. 1954. "The Analysis of the Phoneme in Distinctive Features and the Process of Hearing," *Lingua* 4.167–193. [B-14]

*———. 1959. "Hearing and the Concept of the Phoneme," *Lingua* 8.161–185.

MOULTON, WILLIAM GAMWELL. 1947. "Juncture in Modern Standard German," *Lg.* 23.212–226. Reprinted in *RIL* 208–214. [15, 16, 18, B-8]

———. 1954. "The Stops and Spirants of Early Germanic," *Lg.* 30.1–42. [37]

*MULDER, J. W. F. 1968. *Sets and Relations in Phonology.* Oxford: Clarendon Press.

MURRAY, LINDLEY. 1795. *English Grammar.* [23]

NAVARRO-TOMÁS, TOMÁS. 1932. *Manual de Pronunciación Española.* 4th ed. Madrid: Revista de Filología Española. [11]

NEEDHAM, DORIS, and MARJORIE DAVIS. 1946. "Cuicateco Phonology," *IJAL* 12.139–146. [50]

NEWMAN, STANLEY STEWART. 1946. "On the Stress System of English," *Word* 2.171–187. [B-8]

———. 1947. "Bella Coola I: Phonology," *IJAL* 13.129–134. [B-1]

NIDA, EUGENE ALBERT. 1947. Review of *Bases of Phonology*, by R. H. Stetson. *Word* 3. 132–136. [B-1]

———. 1949. *Morphology.* Ann Arbor: University of Michigan Press. [46, 52]

O'CONNOR, J. D. 1951. Review of *An Outline of English Structure*, by G. L. Trager and H. L. Smith. *MPh.* 96.42–44. [B-1]

———. 1957. "Recent Work in English Phonetics," *Phonetica* 1.96–117. [B-1, B-11, B-12]

O'CONNOR, J. D., and JOHN L. M. TRIM. 1953. "Vowel, Consonant, and Syllable—A Phonological Definition," *Word* 9.103–122. [B-6, B-9]

OKUDA, KUNIO. 1970. Review of *The Phonological Component of a Grammar of Japanese*, by J. D. McCawley. *Lg.* 46. 736–753. [B-15]

ORLOVA, V. G. 1959. *Istorija affrikat v russkom jazyke*. Moscow: Izdatelstvo Akademii Nauk SSSR. [37]

*OSWALD, VICTOR A., JR. 1943. "'Voiced *t*'—A Misnomer," *AS* 18.18–25.

OŽEGOV, S. (ed.). 1949. *Slovar' russkogo jazyka*. Moscow. [31]

PALEK, BOHUMIL. 1963. "Informace o transformační gramatice" (Information on Transformational Grammar), *SaS* 24. 140–151. [40]

PALMER, FRANK ROBERT. 1955. "The 'Broken Plurals' of Tigrinya," *BSOAS* 17.548–566. [24, 25]

——. 1956. "'Openness' in Tigre: A Problem in Prosodic Statement," *BSOAS* 18. 561–577. [24, 25, B-12]

——. 1957a. "Gemination in Tigrinya," *SILA* 139–148. [25, B-3, B-12]

——. 1957b. "The Verb in Bilin," *BSOAS* 19.131–159. [24, 25]

——. 1958. "Linguistic Hierarchy," *Lingua* 7.225–241. [39]

——. 1968. Review of *Outline of Stratificational Grammar*, by S. M. Lamb. *JofL* 4. 287–295. [B-17]

PALMER, HAROLD E. 1922. *English Intonation*. Cambridge: Heffer. [13]

PALMER, HAROLD E., and F. G. BLANDFORD. 1939. *A Grammar of Spoken English*. 2d ed. Cambridge: Heffer. [13]

PARMENTER, CLARENCE EDWARD, and SALMÓN NARCISO TREVIÑO. 1935. "The Length of the Sounds of a Middle Westerner," *AS* 10.129–133. [14, B-3]

PASSY, PAUL. 1912. *Petite phonétique comparée*. Leipzig: Teubner. [B-2]

PEIRCE, CHARLES SANDERS. 1932. *Collected Papers of Charles Peirce*, ed. by Charles Hartshorne and Paul Weiss. Cambridge, Mass.: Harvard University Press. [31]

PERCIVAL, W. KEITH. 1960. "A Problem in ˙ Competing Phonemic Solutions, *Lg.* 36. 383–386. [B-1]

PEŠKOVSKIJ, A. 1952. "Desjat' tysjač zvukov russkogo jazyka," *Sbornik statej* 167–191. Leningrad. [31]

*PETERSON, GORDON E. 1951. "The Phonetic Value of Vowels," *Lg.* 27.541–553.

*PETERSON, GORDON E., and CHARLES J. FILLMORE. 1962. "The Theory of Phonemic Analysis," *PICPS*-4.476–489.

PIKE, EUNICE VICTORIA. 1951. "Tonemic-Intonemic Correlation in Mazahua (Otomí)," *IJAL* 17.37–41. [B-8]

PIKE, KENNETH LEE. 1941. *A Reconstruction of Phonetic Theory*, University of Michigan Ph.D. dissertation. [11]

——. 1943a. *Phonetics: A Critical Analysis of Phonetic Theory and a Technique for the Practical Description of Sounds*. (University of Michigan Publications in Language and Literature, 21.) Ann Arbor: University of Michigan Press. [16, 32, 54, B-1]

——. 1943b. "Taxemes and Immediate Constituents," *Lg.* 19.65–82. [15]

——. 1944. "Analysis of a Mixteco Text," *IJAL* 10.113–138. [15, B-10]

——. 1945a. *The Intonation of American English*. (University of Michigan Publications in Linguistics, 1.) Ann Arbor: University of Michigan Press. [14, 15, 16, B-8]

——. 1945b. "Tone Puns in Mixteco," *IJAL* 11.129–139. [15]

——. 1946. "Another Mixteco Tone Pun," *IJAL* 12.22–24. [15]

——. 1947a. "Grammatical Prerequisites to Phonemic Analysis," *Word* 3.155–172. [**15**, 17, 18, 24, 25, 39, B-18]

——. 1947b. "On the Phonemic Status of English Diphthongs," *Lg.* 23.151–159. [**14**, B-6, B-10]

——. 1947c. *Phonemics: A Technique for Reducing Languages to Writing*. (University of Michigan Publications in Linguistics, 3.) Ann Arbor: University of Michigan Press. (Preliminary editions: Glendale, California: Summer Institute of Linguistics, 1943, 1945, and 1946.) [15, 16, 17, 24, 36, 50, 51, B-1]

——. 1948. *Tone Languages: A Technique for Determining the Number and Type of Pitch Contrasts in a Language, with Studies in Tonemic Substitution and Fusion*. (University of Michigan Publications in Linguistics, 4.) Ann Arbor: University of Michigan Press. (Preliminary edition: Glendale, California: Summer Institute of Linguistics, 1945.) [15, 17, 24, 46, 50, B-1, B-8]

————. 1950. "A Problem in Morphology-Syntax Division," *AcL* 5.125–138. [18]

————. 1952. "More on Grammatical Prerequisites," *Word* 8.106–121. [**18**, 19, 24, 25, 39, 51, B-10, B-18]

*————. 1957. "Abdominal Pulse Types in Some Peruvian Languages," *Lg.* 33.30–35.

————. 1958. "Interpenetration of Phonology, Morphology, and Syntax," *PICL*-8. 363–371; discussion 371–387. [40, B-10]

————. 1960. "Toward a Theory of Change and Bilingualism," *SIL*. 15.1–7. [B-5]

————. 1967a. *Language in Relation to a Unified Theory of the Structure of Human Behavior.* 2d rev. ed. The Hague: Mouton. (First edition appeared in three parts 1954, 1955, and 1960. Santa Ana, California: Summer Institute of Linguistics.) [B-1, B-12, B-14, B-15]

————. 1967b. "Suprasegmentals in Reference to Phonemes of Item, of Process, and of Relation," *THRJ* 1545–1554. [B-8]

PIKE, KENNETH LEE, and EUNICE VICTORIA PIKE. 1947. "Immediate Constituents of Mazateco Syllables," *IJAL* 13.78–91. [14, B-9, B-10]

————. 1960. *Live Issues in Descriptive Linguistics.* 2d ed. Santa Ana, Calif.: Summer Institute of Linguistics. [B-1]

PILCH, HERBERT. 1965. "Zentrale und periphere Lautsysteme," *PICPS*-5. 467–473. [46]

*PITTMAN, RICHARD SAUNDERS. 1948. "Nuclear Structures in Linguistics," *Lg.* 24. 287–292. Reprinted in *RIL* 275–278.

POLDAUF, IVAN. 1962. "Strukturalismus a americký deskriptivismus" (Structuralism and American Descriptivism), *Problémy marxistické jazykovědy* (Problems of Marxist Linguistics), ed. by J. Bělič, L. Doležel, and S. Peciar, 79–110. Prague: Naklad. [40]

POLLACK, IRWIN. 1953. "The Information of Elementary Auditory Displays. II," *JASA* 25. 765–769. [32]

POLLACK, I., and H. FICKS. 1954. "The Information of Elementary Multidimensional Auditory Displays," *JASA* 26.155–158. [32]

POS, H. J. 1938. "La notion d'opposition en linguistique," *Onzième Congrès International de Psychologie.* Paris. [30, B-14]

POSTAL, PAUL M. 1964a. "Boas and the Development of Phonology: Comments Based on Iroquoian," *IJAL* 30.269–280. [42, 46]

————. 1964b. *Constituent Structure: A Study of Contemporary Models of Syntactic Description.* (Indiana University Research Center in Anthropology, Folklore, and Linguistics, Publication 30.) Bloomington: Indiana University Press. [48, 54]

————. 1966. Review of *Elements of General Linguistics,* by A. Martinet. *FofL* 2. 151–186. [48, 54]

————. 1968. *Aspects of Phonological Theory.* New York: Harper & Row. [46, 48, 49, 54, 55, 56, B-15]

POTTER, RALPH K. 1945. "Visible Patterns of Sound," *Science* 102.463–470. (Also Bell Telephone System Technical Publications, Monograph B-1368.) [16]

POTTER, RALPH K., et al. 1946. "Technical Aspects of Visible Speech," *JASA* 17.1–89. (Also Bell Telephone System Technical Publications, Monograph B-1415.) [16]

POTTER, RALPH K., GEORGE A. KOPP, and HARRIET C. GREEN. 1947. *Visible Speech.* New York: Van Nostrand. [16, 46, 51]

POTTER, RALPH K., and J. C. STEINBERG. 1950. "Toward the Specification of Speech," *JASA* 22.807–820. [32]

POTTER, SIMEON. 1962. "Syllabic Juncture," *PICPS*-4.728–730. [B-8]

PRIETO, LUIS J. 1954. "Traits oppositionnels et traits contrastifs," *Word* 10.43–59. [51, B-14]

Proceedings of the 1st International Congress of Linguists, The Hague, April 10–15, 1928. 1930. Leiden: A. W. Sijthoff.

Proceedings of the 2d International Congress of Linguists, Geneva, August 25–29, 1931. 1933. Paris: Maisonneuve.

Proceedings of the 3d International Congress of Linguists, Rome, September 19–26, 1933. 1935. Ed. by Bruno Migliorini and Vittore Pisani. Florence: F. LeMonnier.

Proceedings of the 4th International Congress of Linguists, Copenhagen, August 27–September 1, 1936. 1938. Copenhagen: E. Munksgaard.

Proceedings of the 5th International Congress of Linguists, Brussels, August 28–September 2, 1939. 1940. Bruges: Imprimerie Sainte Catherine.

Proceedings of the 6th International Congress

of Linguists, Paris, July 19–24, 1948.
1949. Ed. by Michel Lejeune. Paris:
Klincksieck.

*Proceedings of the 7th International Congress
of Linguists, London, September 1–6,
1952.* 1956. Ed. by F. Norman and P. F.
Ganz. London: International Booksellers.

*Proceedings of the 8th International Congress
of Linguists, Oslo, August 5–9, 1957.*
1958. Ed. by Eva Sivertsen. Oslo: Oslo
University Press.

*Proceedings of the 9th International Congress
of Linguists, Cambridge, Mass., August
27–31, 1962.* 1964. Ed. by H. Lunt. The
Hague: Mouton.

*Proceedings of the 1st International Congress
of Phonetic Sciences, Amsterdam, July
3–8, 1932.* 1933. *=Archives Néerlandaises
de Phonétique Experimentale,*
Vols. 7–9.

*Proceedings of the 2d International Congress
of Phonetic Sciences, London, 1935.*
1936. Ed. by D. Jones and D. B. Fry.
Cambridge: Cambridge University Press.

*Proceedings of the 3d International Congress
of Phonetic Sciences, Ghent, 1938.* 1939.
Ed. by E. Blancquaert and W. Pee. Ghent,
Belgium: Laboratory of Phonetics of the
University.

*Proceedings of the 4th International Congress
of Phonetic Sciences, Helsinki, September
4–9, 1961.* 1962. Ed. by Antti Sovijärvi
and Pentti Aalto. The Hague: Mouton.

*Proceedings of the 5th International Congress
of Phonetic Sciences, Münster, August
16–22, 1964.* 1965. Ed. by Eberhard
Zwirner and Wolfgang Bethge. Basel: S.
Karger.

"Projet de terminologie phonologique standardisée."
1931. *TCLP* 4.309–322.

*PULGRAM, ERNST. 1951. "Phoneme or Grapheme:
A Parallel," *Word* 7.15–20.

QUINE, WILLARD VAN ORMAN. 1953. *From a
Logical Point of View.* Cambridge, Mass.:
Harvard University Press. [41]

RAY, PUNYA ŚLOKA. 1961. "The Logic of Linguistics,"
Methodos: Language and Cybernetics
13.239–254. [40]

*Recherches structurales 1949: Interventions
dans le débat glossématique.* Vol. 5 of
TCLC (1949). [B-16]

REIBEL, DAVID A., and SANFORD A. SCHANE
(eds.). 1969. *Modern Studies in English:
Readings in Transformational Grammar.*

Englewood Cliffs, N.J.: Prentice-Hall.
[B-15]

REICH, PETER A. 1968. *Symbols, Relations,
and Structural Complexity.* New Haven:
Linguistic Automation Project, Yale University.
[55, 56, B-17]

REICHLING, ANTON. 1956. "Feature Analysis
and Linguistic Interpretation," *FRJ* 418–
422. [B-14]

———. 1961. "Principles and Methods of Syntax:
Cryptanalytical Formalism," *Lingua*
10.1–17. [40]

REVZIN, I. I. 1962. *Modeli jazyka.* Moscow:
Izdatelstvo Akademii Nauk SSSR. [40]

ROBINS, R. H. 1953a. "Formal Divisions in
Sundanese," *TPS* 1953.109–142. [24, 25]

———. 1953b. "The Phonology of the Nasalized
Verbal Forms in Sundanese,"
BSOAS 15.138–145. [24, 25, B-12]

———. 1955 and 1956. Review of *Language
in Relation to a Unified Theory of the
Structure of Human Behavior,* Parts I and
II, by K. L. Pike. *MPh.* 104.34–36 and
106.38–40. [B-1]

———. 1957a. "Aspects of Prosodic Analysis,"
*Proceedings of the University of
Durham Philosophical Society,* Series B,
1.1–12. [**24,** 25, 26 B-10]

———. 1957b. "Vowel Nasality in Sundanese:
A Phonological and Grammatical Study,"
SILA 87–103. [25, B-12]

ROBINS, R. H., and NATALIE WATERSON. 1952.
"Notes on the Phonetics of the Georgian
Word," *BSOAS* 14.55–72. [24, 25, B-12]

ROGERS, HENRY E. 1967. *The Phonology and
Morphology of Sherbro.* Yale University
Ph.D. dissertation. [B-17]

ROSSI, MARIO. 1965. "Analyse spectrographique
et interprétation fonctionnelle de la
nasalité dans un parler de l'Italie du nord,"
*PICPS-*5. 512–516. [46]

SAMPSON, GEOFFREY. 1970a. "On the Need
for a Phonological Base," *Lg.* 46.586–
626. [B-15]

———. 1970b. *Stratificational Grammar: A
Definition and an Example.* (Janua Linguarum,
series minor, 88.) The Hague:
Mouton. [B-17]

SAPIR, EDWARD. 1921. *Language: An Introduction
to the Study of Speech.* New
York: Harcourt, Brace. [B-1]

———. 1922. "The Takelma Language of
Southwestern Oregon," *HAIL,* Vol. 2.
1–296. [11]

———. 1925. "Sound Patterns in Language," *Lg*. 1.37–51. Reprinted in *RIL* 19–25. [1, 3, 9, 39, 46, 50]

———. 1928. "The Unconscious Patterning of Behavior in Society," *The Unconscious*, 114–142. New York. [30]

———. 1930. *The Southern Paiute Language. Proceedings of the American Academy of Arts and Sciences*, 65. 1–730. [2]

———. 1933. "La réalité psychologique des phonèmes," *JPs* 30.247–265. Reprinted in English in *SWES 46*–60 under the title "The Psychological Reality of Phonemes." [2, 3, 4, 5, 16, 39, 42]

———. 1949. *Selected Writings of Edward Sapir in Language, Culture, and Personality*, ed. by D. G. Mandelbaum. Berkeley and Los Angeles: University of California Press. [B-1]

SAPIR, EDWARD, and MORRIS SWADESH. 1939. *Nootka Texts, Tales and Ethnological Narratives with Grammatical Notes and Lexical Materials*. Iowa City: LSA. [27]

SAPORTA, SOL. 1956a. "A Note on Spanish Semivowels," *Lg*. 32.287–290. Reprinted in *RIL* 403–404. [B-6]

———. 1956b. "Morph, Morpheme, Archimorpheme," *Word* 12.9–14. [56]

———. 1963. "Phoneme Distribution and Language Universals," *Universals of Language*, ed. by J. H. Greenberg, 61–72. Cambridge, Mass.: M.I.T. Press. [B-13, B-18]

SAPORTA, SOL, and HELES CONTRERAS. 1962. *A Phonological Grammar of Spanish*. Seattle: University of Washington Press. [42, B-15]

*ŠAUMJAN, SEBASTIAN K. 1962. "Two-Level Theory of Phonology," *PICPS*-4.757–761.

DE SAUSSURE, FERDINAND. 1916. *Cours de linguistique générale*. Paris: C. Bally and A. Sechahaye. [23, 24, 32, 39]

ŠČERBA, LEV V. 1911. *Court exposé de la prononciation russe*. IPA. [B-2]

———. 1912. *Russkie glasnye v kačestvennom i količestvennom otnošenii. St. Petersburg*. [B-2]

SCHANE, SANFORD A. 1967. "Bibliographie de la phonologie générative," *Langages* 8. 124–131. [B-15]

———. 1968a. *French Phonology and Morphology*. (Research Monograph, 45.) Cambridge, Mass.: M.I.T. Press. [B-15]

*———. 1968b. "On the Non-Uniqueness of Phonological Representations," *Lg*. 44. 709–716.

SCHATZ, CAROL D. 1954. "The Role of Context in the Perception of Stops," *Lg*. 30. 47–56. [39, 51]

SCHIRMUNSKI, V. M. 1962. *Deutsche Mundartkunde*. Berlin: Akademie Verlag. [47]

SCOTT, N. C. 1948. "A Study in the Phonetics of Fijian," *BSOAS* 12.737–752. [23, B-12]

———. 1956. "A Phonological Analysis of the Szechuanese Monosyllable," *BSOAS* 18.556–560. [24, 25, B-12]

SEBEOK, THOMAS ALBERT. 1943a. "Notes on Hungarian Vowel Phonemes," *Lg*. 19. 162–164. [46, 54]

———. 1943b. "Vowel Morphophonemics of Hungarian Suffixes," *SIL* 2.47–50. [54, B-4]

———. 1963. "Selected Readings in General Phonemics (1925–1964)," *SIL* 17.3–9. [B-1, B-12, B-14, B-15, B-16]

*——— (ed.). 1966. *Current Trends in Linguistics, Vol. III: Theoretical Foundations*. The Hague: Mouton.

SEUREN, PETER A. M. 1966. Review of *Grammar Discovery Procedures*, by R. E. Longacre. *FofL* 2.200–212. [48, 54]

SHANNON, CLAUDE E., and WARREN WEAVER. 1949. *The Mathematical Theory of Communication*. Urbana: University of Illinois Press. [29, 31, 32]

SHARP, ALAN E. 1954. "A Tonal Analysis of the Disyllabic Noun in the Machame Dialect of Chaga," *BSOAS* 16.157–169. [24, 25, B-8, B-12]

———. 1958. "Falling-Rising Intonation Patterns in English," *Phonetica* 2.127–152. [B-8]

———. 1961. "The Analysis of Stress and Juncture in English," *TPS* 1960.104–135. [B-8]

SHEWMAKE, EDWIN F. 1925. "Laws of Pronunciation in Eastern Virginia," *MLN* 40. '489–492. [9]

———. No date. *English Pronunciation in Virginia*. No publisher. [9]

SHIPLEY, WILLIAM F. 1964. *Maidu Grammar*. (University of California Publications in Linguistics, 41.) Berkeley and Los Angeles: University of California Press. [B-17]

SIERTSEMA, BERTHA. 1954. *A Study of Glosse-*

matics: Critical Survey of its Fundamental Concepts. The Hague: Nijhoff. [51, B-16]

———. 1958. "Problems of Phonemic Interpretation I: Nasalized Sounds in Yoruba," *Lingua* 7.356–366. [B-16]

———. 1959. "Problems of Phonemic Interpretation II: Long Vowels in a Tone Language," *Lingua* 8.42–64. [B-3, B-16]

SIEVERS, E. 1876. *Grundzüge der Phonetik.* Leipzig: Breitkopf and Härtel Press. [38, 50, B-2]

SIGURD, BENGT. 1955. "Rank Order of Consonants Established by Distributional Criteria," *Studia Linguistica* 9.8–20. [B-18]

SJOBERG, ANDRÉE F. 1962. "Coexistent Phonemic Systems in Telugu: A Socio-Cultural Perspective, *Word* 18.269–279. [B-5]

SKALIČKA, VLADIMÍR. 1948. "The Need for a Linguistics of la Parole," *Recueil linguistique de Bratislava* 1.21–36. [40]

SLEDD, JAMES H. 1955. Review of *An Outline of English Structure* by G. L. Trager and H. L. Smith, and of *The Structure of English,* by C. C. Fries. *Lg.* 31.312–345. [20, 39, B-1]

———. 1958. "Some Questions of English Phonology," *Lg.* 34.252–258. [39, B-1, B-6]

———. 1959. *A Short Introduction to English Grammar.* Chicago: Scott, Foresman. [39]

SMALLEY, WILLIAM ALLEN. 1955. "A Problem in Phoneme Identification Without Differential Meaning," *General Linguistics* 1.62–69. [B-10]

SMITH, HENRY LEE, JR. 1967. "The Concept of the Morphophone," *Lg.* 43.306–341. [54, B-4]

SMITH, NEILSON V. 1969. Review of *French Phonology and Morphology,* by S. A. Schane. *Lg.* 45.398–407. [B-15]

SOMMERFELT, ALF. 1931. "Sur l'importance générale de la syllabe," *TCLP* 4.156–160. [B-9]

———. 1936. "Can Syllable Divisions Have Phonological Importance?" *PICPS*-2.30–33. [B-9]

SPANG-HANSSEN, HENNING. 1949. "On Simplicity of Descriptions," *TCLC* 5.61–70. [46]

———. 1958. "Typological and Statistical Aspects of Distribution as a Criterion in Linguistic Analysis," *PICL*-8. 182–194. [B-13, B-18]

*SPEISER, EPHRAIM AVIGDOR. 1938. "The Pitfalls of Polarity," *Lg.* 14.187–202.

SPENCER, ROBERT FRANCIS. 1946. "The Phonemes of Keresan," *IJAL* 12.229–236. [50]

SPIER, LESLIE, A. IRVING HALLOWELL, and STANLEY S. NEWMAN. 1941. *Language, Culture, and Personality: Essays in Memory of Edward Sapir.* Menasha, Wisc.: Sapir Memorial Publication Fund. [B-1]

SPRIGG, R. K. 1954. "Verbal Phrases in Lhasa Tibetan," *BSOAS* 16.134–156, 320–350, and 566–591. [24, 25]

———. 1955. "The Tonal System of Tibetan (Lhasa Dialect) and the Nominal Phrase," *BSOAS* 17.134–153. [24, 25, B-8]

———. 1957. "Junction in Spoken Burmese," *SILA* 104–138. [25, B-8, B-12]

———. 1961. "Vowel Harmony in Lhasa Tibetan: Prosodic Analysis Applied to Interrelated Vocalic Features of Successive Syllables," *BSOAS* 24.116–138. [B-12, B-19]

STAMPE, DAVID. 1968. "Yes, Virginia . . . ," unpublished paper presented at the Fourth Regional Meeting of the Chicago Linguistic Society. [49]

STANKIEWICZ, EDWARD. 1967. "Opposition and Hierarchy in Morphophonemic Alternations," *THRJ* 1895–1905. [B-4]

STANLEY, RICHARD. 1967. "Redundancy Rules in Phonology," *Lg.* 43.393–436. [B-15]

STETSON, RAYMOND HERBERT. 1936. "The Relation of the Phoneme and the Syllable," *PICPS*-2.245–252. [B-9]

———. 1945. *Bases of Phonology.* Oberlin, Ohio: Oberlin College. [15, B-1]

*———. 1948. "Traits of Articulate Language," *Quarterly Journal of Speech* 34. 191–193.

———. 1951. *Motor Phonetics: A Study of Speech Movements in Action.* 2d ed. Amsterdam: North-Holland Publishing Co. [B-8, B-9]

STEWART, J. M. 1967. "Tongue Root Position in Akan Vowel Harmony," *Phonetica* 16.185–204. [54, B-19]

STIMSON, HUGH M. 1967. "Stress in Peking Phonotactics." *Monumenta Serica* 26.202–212. [B-17]

———. 1968. "Peking Tonal Hypophonotactics," *Papers of the CIC Far Eastern Language Institute,* 29–38. Ann Arbor: Panel on Far Eastern Language Institutes of the Committee on Institutional Co-operation. [B-17]

——. 1969. "Peiping Tonal Phonotactics," *Bulletin of the Institute of History and Philology* 39.197–201. [B-17]

STOCKWELL, ROBERT P. 1959. Review of *SILA*. *IJAL* 25.254–259. [B-12]

——. 1960. "The Place of Intonation in a Generative Grammar of English," *Lg.* 36. 360–367. [B-8, B-15]

STOCKWELL, ROBERT P., J. DONALD BOWEN, and ISMAEL SILVA-FUENZALIDA. 1956. "Spanish Juncture and Intonation," *Lg.* 32.641–665. Reprinted in *RIL* 406–418. [B-8]

STOCKWELL, ROBERT P., PAUL SCHACHTER, and BARBARA PARTEE. 1968. *Integration of Transformational Theories on English Syntax.* Los Angeles: University of California at Los Angeles. Mimeographed. [B-15]

Studies in Linguistic Analysis. Special volume of the Philological Society, with introduction by J. R. Firth. Oxford: Basil Blackwell. 1957. [B-12]

STURTEVANT, EDGAR HOWARD. 1940. *The Pronunciation of Greek and Latin.* 2d ed. Philadelphia: LSA. [11]

——. 1943. Review of *Outline of Linguistic Analysis,* by B. Bloch and G. L. Trager, and of *Outline Guide for the Practical Study of Foreign Languages,* by L. Bloomfield. *Lg.* 19.42–44. [16, B-1]

SWADESH, MORRIS. 1934a. "The Phonemic Principle," *Lg.* 10.117–129. Reprinted in *RIL* 32–37. [**3**, 4, 5, 8, 9, 15, 16, 53]

——. 1934b. "The Phonetics of Chitimacha," *Lg.* 10.345–362. [6, B-1]

——. 1935a. "The Vowels of Chicago English," *Lg.* 11.148–151. [9, 14, B-1, B-6]

——. 1935b. "Twaddell on Defining the Phoneme," *Lg.* 11.244–250. [**4**, 5, 9]

——. 1937a. "A Method for Phonetic Accuracy and Speed," *AA* 39.728–732. [15]

——. 1937b. "The Phonemic Interpretation of Long Consonants," *Lg.* 13.1–10. [**6**, 8, 9, 13, 16]

——. 1939. "Nootka Internal Syntax," *IJAL* 9.77–102. [15]

——. 1941. "Observations of Pattern Impact on the Phonetics of Bilinguals," *LCP* 59–65. [B-5]

——. 1947. "On the Analysis of English Syllabics," *Lg.* 23.137–150. [14, B-1, B-6]

SWADESH, MORRIS, and CHARLES FREDERICK VOEGELIN. 1939. "A Problem in Phonological Alternation," *Lg.* 15.1–10. Reprinted in *RIL* 88–92. [B-4]

SWEET, HENRY. 1877. *A Handbook of Phonetics.* Oxford: Henry Frowde Press. [24, B-2, B-11]

——. 1900. *The Practical Study of Languages: A Guide for Teachers and Learners.* New York: Henry Holt. [B-2]

——. 1913a. *Collected Papers of Henry Sweet,* arranged by H. C. Wyld. Oxford: Clarendon Press. [23, B-11]

——. 1913b. "On Danish Pronunciation," *Collected Papers of Henry Sweet,* 344–361. (Originally in *TPS* 1873–1874. 94–112.) [23]

——. 1923. *The Sounds of English.* 2d ed. Oxford: Clarendon. [9, B-11]

——. 1932. *A Primer of Spoken English.* 4th ed. Oxford: Oxford University Press. [9, B-11]

SZÉPE, GYÖRGY. 1967. "A Magyar Generatív Fonológia Néhány Kérdése" (Some Questions of Hungarian Generative Phonology). *A Nyelvtudományi Értekezések* 58. 305–310. [54]

THOMAS, CHARLES KENNETH. 1948. Review of *Phonemics,* by K. L. Pike. *Quarterly Journal of Speech* 34.384. [B-1]

To Honor Roman Jakobson. 1967. The Hague: Mouton. [35, 44, 45, B-14]

TOGEBY, KNUD. 1951. *Structure immanente de la langue française.* TCLC 6.7–282. [50, 51, B-16]

TORÍO DE LA RIVA, TORQUATO. 1802. *Arte de Escribir.* Madrid. [23]

TRAGER, GEORGE LEONARD. 1930. "The Pronunciation of 'Short *a*' in American English," *AS* 5.396–400. [9, B-1]

——. 1934. "The Phonemes of Russian," *Lg.* 10.334–344. [B-1]

——. 1935. "The Transcription of English," *MPh* 49.10–13. [9, B-1]

——. 1939a. "La systématique des phonèmes du polonais," *AcL* 1.179–188. [11, 50]

——. 1939b. "The Phonemes of Castillian Spanish," *TCLP* 8.217–222. [11, B-1]

——. 1940a. "One Phonemic Entity Becomes Two: The Case of 'Short *a*,'" *AS* 15.255–258. [9, B-1]

————. 1940b. Review of *Phonologie,* by N. Van Wijk. *Lg.* 16.247–251. [16]

————. 1941. "The Theory of Accentual Systems," *LCP* 131–145. [13, 24, B-8]

————. 1942a. "The Phoneme 'T': A Study in Theory and Method," *AS* 17.144–148. [B-1]

————. 1942b. "The Phonemic Treatment of Semivowels," *Lg.* 18.220–223. [B-6]

————. 1943. Review of *Phonetics,* by K. L. Pike. *SIL* 2.16–20. [B-1]

————. 1946, "An Outline of Taos Grammar," *LSNA* 184–221. [15, 18]

————. 1948. "Taos I: A Language Revisited," *IJAL* 14.155–160. [18]

————. 1949a. Review of *Tone Languages,* by K. L. Pike. *Journal of English and Germanic Philology* 48.285–286. [B-8]

————. 1949b. *The Field of Linguistics.* (SIL Occasional Papers, 1.) Norman, Oklahoma: Battenburg Press. [18]

————. 1950. Review of *Phonemics,* by K. L. Pike. *Lg.* 26.152–158. [B-1]

TRAGER, GEORGE LEONARD, and BERNARD BLOCH. 1941. "The Syllabic Phonemes of English," *Lg.* 17.223–246. [8, **9**, 10, 11, 13, 14, 15, 16, 20]

TRAGER, GEORGE LEONARD, and HENRY LEE SMITH, JR. 1951. *An Outline of English Structure.* (SIL Occasional Papers, 3.) Norman, Oklahoma: Battenburg Press. Several reprintings by ACLS, Washington, D.C. [9, 18, 20, 51, B-1, B-6]

TRESIDDER, ARGUS. 1941. "Notes on Virginia Speech," *AS* 16.113–116. [9]

TREVIÑO, SALMÓN NARCISO. 1946. Review of *Bases of Phonology,* by R. H. Stetson. *AS* 21.127–129. [B-1]

*TRIM, JOHN L. M. 1962. "The Identification of Phonological Units," *PICPS*-4.773–778.

TRNKA, BOHUMIL. 1935. *A Phonological Analysis of Present-Day Standard English.* Prague: Nákladem Filosofické Fakulty University Karlovy. [45, 50, B-14]

————. 1939. "On the Combinatory Variants and Neutralization of Phonemes," *PICPS* -3.23–30. [B-4]

————. 1943. "Die Phonologie in čechisch und slovakisch geschriebenen Arbeiten," *Archiv für vergleichende Phonetik* 6.65–77. [50]

TRNKA, B. *et al.* 1964. "Prague Structural Linguistics," *A Prague School Reader in Linguistics,* ed. by J. Vachek, 468–480.

Bloomington: Indiana University Press. [B-14]

TRUBETZKOY, NIKOLAJ SERGEJEVIČ. 1929a. "Sur la 'morphonologie,'" *TCLP* 1.85–88. Reprinted in Vachek 1964a. 183–186. [B-4]

————. 1929b. "Zur allgemeinen Theorie der phonologischen Vokalsysteme," *TCLP* 1.39–67. Reprinted in Vachek 1964a. 108–142. [3, 24, B-14]

————. 1931a. "Die Konsonantensysteme der ostkaukasischen Sprachen," *Caucasica* 8.1–52. [6]

————. 1931b. "Die phonologischen Systeme," *TCLP* 4.96–116. [3, 56, B-14]

————. 1933. "La phonologie actuelle," *JPs* 30.227–246. [24, B-14]

————. 1935. *Anleitung zu phonologischen Beschreibungen.* Brno: Edition du Cercle Linguistique de Prague. [24, 27, 39, 40, B-14]

————. 1936a. "Die Aufhebung der phonologischen Gegensätze," *TCLP* 6.29–45. Reprinted in Vachek 1964a. 187–205. [56, B-14]

————. 1936b. "Die phonologischen Grundlagen der sogenannten 'Quantität' in den verschiedenen Sprachen," *Scritti in onore di Alfredo Trombetti,* 155–174. Milan: Ulrico Heopli. [6, B-3]

————. 1936c. "Essai d'une théorie des oppositions phonologiques," *JPs* 33.5–18. [B-14]

————. 1939. *Grundzüge der Phonologie.* *TCLP* 7. Reprinted in 1958 by Vandenhoeck and Ruprecht, Göttingen. Translated into French as *Principes de phonologie,* by J. Cantineau. Paris: Librairie C. Klincksieck, 1949. [8, 9, 11, 12, 16, 24, 27, 36, 38, 39, 40, 50, 51, 56, B-14]

TWADDELL, WILLIAM FREEMAN. 1935. *On Defining the Phoneme.* (Language Monograph, 16.) Baltimore: LSA. Reprinted in *RIL* 55–80. [4, 5, 8, 9, 11, 16, 22, 24, 30, 32, 39, 50, B-1]

————. 1936a. "Answers to Andrade's Questions," *Lg.* 12.294–297. [B-1]

————. 1936b. "On Various Phonemes," *Lg.* 12.53–59. [**5**, 6, 9, 11]

————. 1938a. "A Note on Old High German Umlaut," *MDU* 30.177–181. Reprinted in *RIL* 85–87. [16]

————. 1938b. "A Phonological Analysis of

Intervocalic Consonant Clusters in German," *PICL*-4.218–225. [50]

——. 1939 and 1940–1941. "Combinations of Consonants in Stressed Syllables in German," *AcL* 1.189–199 and 2.31–50. [50]

——. 1942. "Phonemics," *MDU* 34.262–268. [B-1]

——. 1946. Review of *Bases of Phonology*, by R. H. Stetson. *IJAL* 12.102–108. [B-1]

——. 1952. "Phonemes and Allophones in Speech Analysis," *JASA* 24.607–611. [51, B-1]

——. 1953. "Stetson's Model and the 'Supra-Segmental Phonemes,'" *Lg.* 29. 415–453. [B-8, B-9]

UHLENBECK, EUGENIUS M. 1949. *De Structuur van het Javaanse Morpheem*. Bandoeng: A. C. Nix. [50]

——. 1950. "The Structure of the Javanese Morpheme," *Lingua* 2.239–270. [18]

——. 1963. "An Appraisal of Transformation Theory," *Lingua* 12.1–18. [40, B-15]

UŁASZYN, H. 1931. "Laut, Phonema, Morphonema," *TCLP* 4.53–61. [3, B-4]

ULDALL, H. J. 1934. "A Note on Vowel Length in American English," *MPh.* III. 12.97–98. [B-3, B-16]

——. 1936. "The Phonematics of Danish," *PICPS*-2. 54–57. [50, 51, B-16]

——. 1939. "On the Structural Interpretation of Diphthongs," *PICPS*-3.272–276. [B-6, B-16]

——. 1957. "Outline of Glossematics, Part I: General Theory," *TCLC* 10.1–89. [B-16]

UŠAKOV, D. (ed.). 1935–1940. *Tolkovyj slovar' russkogo jazyka*. Moscow. [31]

VACHEK, JOSEF. 1932. "Professor Daniel Jones and the Phoneme," *Charisteria Guilelmo Mathesio Quinquagenario a Discipulis et Circuli Linguistici Pragensis Sodalibus Oblata*, 25–33. Prague: Cercle Linguistique de Prague. [B-11]

*——. 1936a. "One Aspect of the Phoneme Theory," *PICPS*-2. 33–40.

*——. 1936b. "Phonemes and Phonological Units," *TCLP* 6.235–239. Reprinted in Vachek 1964a. 143–149.

——. 1949. "Yaleská škola a strukturalistická fonologie" (The Yale School and Structuralist Phonology), *SaS* 11.36–44. [40, B-1]

——. 1954. "Notes on the Phonological Development of the Modern English Pronoun *she*," *Sborník Prací Filosofické Fakulty Brnénské University (Brno)* 2. 67–80. [40]

——. 1958. "Dvě vyznamné fonologické publikace zehraniční" (Two Important Foreign Books on Phonology), *SaS* 19. 52–60. [40]

——. 1962. "On the Interplay of External and Internal Factors in the Development of Language," *Lingua* 11.433–448. [40]

——. 1963. "The Phonematic Status of Modern English Long Vowels and Diphthongs," *Philologica Pragensia* 6.59–71. [40, B-6]

—— (ed.). 1964a. *A Prague School Reader in Linguistics*. Bloomington: Indiana University Press. [B-14]

——. 1964b. "Notes on the Phonematic Value of the Modern English [ŋ]—Sound," *In Honour of Daniel Jones*, ed. by D. Abercrombie *et al.*, 191–205. Also in *Brno Studies in English* 4.46–54 (1964). [40]

——. 1964c. "On Some Basic Principles of Classical' Phonology," *Zeitschrift für Phonetik, Sprachwissenschaft und Kommunikationsforschung* 17.409–431. [**40,** 42]

——. 1964d. "Prague Phonological Studies Today," *TLP* 1.7–20. [40, B-14]

——. 1966. *The Linguistic School of Prague: An Introduction to Its Theory and Practice*. Bloomington: Indiana University Press. [56, B-14]

VACHEK, JOSEF. and JOSEF DUBSKÝ. 1960. *Dictionnaire de linguistique de l'école de Prague*. Utrecht and Anvers: Spectrum. [40]

VAN WIJK, N. 1939. *Phonologie: een hoofdstuk uit de structurele taalwetenschap*. The Hague: Martinus Nijhoff. [16]

VOEGELIN, CHARLES FREDERICK. 1935. "Shawnee Phonemes," *Lg.* 11.23–37. [6, B-1]

——. 1948. "Distinctive Features and Meaning Equivalence," *Lg.* 24.132–135. [B-10, B-14]

——. 1949. Review of *Phonemics*, by K. L. Pike. *IJAL* 15.75–85. [17, B-1]

——. 1956. "Linear Phonemes and Additive Components," *Word* 12.429–443. [B-7]

VOEGELIN, CHARLES FREDERICK, and M. E. ELLINGHAUSEN. 1943. "Turkish Structure," *JAOS* 63.34–65. [25]

VOEGELIN, CHARLES FREDERICK, and JOHN YEGERLEHNER. 1956. The Scope of Whole System ('Distinctive Feature') and Subsystem Typologies," *Word* 12.444–453. [B-13]

VOGT, HANS. 1942. "The Structure of the Norwegian Monosyllables," *Norsk Tidsskrift for Sprogvidenskap* 12.5–29. [50, B-9]

———. 1954. "Phoneme Classes and Phoneme Classification," *Word* 10.28–34. [51, B-18]

WALLIS, ETHEL. 1956. "Simulfixation in Aspect Markers of Mezquital Otomi," *Lg.* 32.453–459. [B-12]

WANG, WILLIAM S.-Y. 1967. "Phonological Features of Tone," *IJAL* 33.93–105. [B-8]

*———. 1968. "Vowel Features, Paired Variables, and the English Vowel Shift," *Lg.* 44.695–708.

WARD, IDA C. 1931. *The Phonetics of English.* Cambridge: Heffer. [8, 40]

WATERHOUSE, VIOLA, and MAY MORRISON. 1950. "Chontal Phonemes," *IJAL* 16.35–39. [50]

WATERSON, NATALIE. 1956. "Some Aspects of the Phonology of the Nominal Forms of the Turkish Word," *BSOAS* 18.578–591. [25, 46, 54, B-12]

WEATHERS, NADINE. 1947. "Tsotsil Phonemes with Special Reference to Allophones of b," *IJAL* 13.108–111. [15]

WEINREICH, URIEL. 1953. *Languages in Contact.* New York: Linguistic Circle of New York. [B-1, B-5]

———. 1957. "On the Description of Phonic Interference," *Word* 13.1–11. [B-1, B-5]

WEISS, ALBERT PAUL. 1929. *A Theoretical Basis of Human Behavior.* 2d ed. Columbus, Ohio. [11]

WELLS, RULON SEYMOUR, III. 1945. "The Pitch Phonemes of English," *Lg.* 21.27–39. [13, 16, 18]

———. 1947a. "Immediate Constituents," *Lg.* 23.81–117. Reprinted in *RIL* 186–207. [15, 16]

———. 1947b. Review of *The Intonation of American English,* by K. L. Pike. *Lg.* 23. 255–273. [15, 16, 18, B-8]

———. 1947c. "De Saussure's System of Linguistics," *Word* 3.1–31. Reprinted in *RIL* 1–18. [39]

———. 1949. "Automatic Alternation," *Lg.* 25.99–116. [19, B-4]

———. 1951. Review of *Recherches Structurales,* *TCLC* Vol. 5. *Lg.* 27.554–570. [B-16]

WELMERS, WILLIAM EVERETT. 1946. *A Descriptive Grammar of Fanti.* (Language Dissertation, 39.) Baltimore: LSA. [15]

———. 1947. "Hints from Morphology for Phonemic Analysis," *SIL* 5.91–100. [18, B-10]

———. 1959. "Tonemics, Morphotonemics, and Tonal Morphemes," *General Linguistics* 4.1–9. [B-8]

WELMERS, WILLIAM EVERETT, and ZELLIG SABBETTAI HARRIS. 1942. "The Phonemes of Fanti," *JAOS* 62.318–333. [12, 15]

WHITNEY, WILLIAM DWIGHT. 1889. *Sanskrit Grammar.* 2d ed. Oxford: Oxford University Press and Cambridge, Mass.: Harvard University Press. [11, 37]

WHORF, BENJAMIN LEE. 1940. "Linguistics as an Exact Science," *Technology Review* 43:61–63 and 80–83. Reprinted in Whorf 1956. 220–232. [42]

———. 1956. *Language, Thought, and Reality: Selected Writings of Benjamin Lee Whorf,* ed. by John B. Carroll. Cambridge, Mass.: Technology Press of M.I.T. and New York: John Wiley. [42, 53]

WIENER, NORBERT. 1948. *Cybernetics, or Control and Communication in the Animal and the Machine.* New York: John Wiley. [17]

WILSON, ROBERT D. 1966. "A Criticism of Distinctive Features," *JofL* 2.195–206. [34, 46, 54]

WINTER, WERNER. 1965. "Transforms without Kernels?" *Lg.* 41.484–489. [48, 54, B-15]

WONDERLY, WILLIAM LOWER. 1946. "Phonemic Acculturation in Zoque," *IJAL* 12. 92–95. [B-5]

WRIGHT, JOSEPH. 1905. *The English Dialect Grammar.* Oxford: H. Frowde. [9]

ZAXAROVA, K. F. 1959. "Arxaičeskie tipy dissimiljativnogo jakan'ja v govorax Belgorodskoj i Voronežskoj oblastjax," *Materialy i issledovanija po russkoj dialektologii,* 6–55. Moscow. [37]

ZIMMER, KARL E. 1967. "A Note on Vowel Harmony," *IJAL* 33.166–171. [54, B-19]

ZWIRNER, EBERHARD. 1939. "Phonologische und phonometrische Probleme der Quantität," *PICPS*-3. 57–66. [32, B-3]

INDEX OF
TOPICAL BIBLIOGRAPHIES

LANGUAGE INDEX